# CUSTOM MAID REVOLUTION
## For New World Disorder

## *Made to Order From Scratch*

*A Manifesto on How We the People Can Sweep
Washington and Beijing Clean of Career Politicians,
Retake and Remake America, China and the World*

*The Founding Fathers Constitution*

*The Original Interlocal Political Social Network*

*Peter G. de Krassel*

CAL Books
*The Moving Political Party Line*
Hong Kong, Los Angeles

*Revolution*

– Beatles

Copyright © 2012 by Peter G. de Krassel
All rights reserved

Published in Hong Kong by CAL Books

Library of Congress Cataloguing-in-Publication Data is available
ISBN 978-988-97666-0-3

*TO MY CHILDREN, GRANDCHILDREN AND ALL
CHILDREN OF THE NEW WORLD ORDER–PLEASE
DO NOT BECOME ALIENATED - GET TO KNOW AND
UNDERSTAND EACH OTHER, LEARN THE TRUTH,
FEED THE HUNGRY, EDUCATE THE IGNORANT.
THEN WE SHALL HAVE PEACE.*

*DO NOT BE BLINDED BY YOUR PARENTS'
CIVILIZATIONAL AND RELIGIOUS PREJUDICES –
LEARN FROM THEIR MISTAKES.*

*DO NOT BE AFRAID TO GAMBLE FOR CHANGE.*

Peter G. de Krassel – Hong Kong,
January 1, 2013

Also by Peter G. de Krassel:


Custom Maid Spin for New World Disorder (2004)

Custom Maid War for New World Disorder (2005)

Custom Maid Knowledge for New World Disorder (2007)

Feasting Dragon, Starving Eagle (2009)

*It is what you read when you don't have to that
determines what you will be when you can't help it.*
– Oscar Wilde

*All revolutions are created by crazy men, not by wise men.*

– Khalid Khoja, Syrian Opposition leadership

**Revolutionary Ingredients
Made to Order From Scratch**
*Exodus*
– Bob Marley

*I Still Haven't Found What I'm Looking For.*
– U2

# POSTSCRIPT AS PROLOGUE – NEW WORLD ORDER
*In the Meantime*
– Dolly Parton


### *Frustrated Postscript Patience*

This book was finished in September 2012, and the flash drive on which it was imbedded was dropped off at the printer in Hong Kong. I then headed back to the U.S. I wanted to observe first hand the nail biting "too close to call" presidential election, looming "fiscal cliff" and the stories and comments of those doomsday prophets who predicted the world would end on December 21$^{st}$ – when in fact it didn't. All that happened was what I have been writing about in my last four books and this one: *We the Apathetic Maids* have been sleep-walking witnesses to the dawn of the New World Order, something I want to re-emphasize. Hence this postscript as a prologue.

I concluded this book by discussing the Mayan-Sumarian predictions of a New World Order dawning in December 2012 and rolling itself out majestically in 2013 – led by America and China – that included the launch of a new interlocal political movement in both countries and globally. The Interlocal Citizens Action League Movement. More information on the party can be found at i-calm.org.

I did a couple of my usual China to U.S. quick-turnaround trips that fall, before and after Barack Obama's re-election, and wanted to observe and experience first hand some of the ridiculous doomsday predictions and fiscal cliff nonstarter gridlocked negotiations and political pundit comments – and outcome.

I gladly accepted an invitation from Julie Chapin, a Pets Central Media board member and trail-blazing actress, who was performing in *End of the World Etiquette*, episode 12 of the live television series *Zombie Etiquette*, to go to Princeton to attend the 4th Annual Winter Solstice celebration hostedby Princeton Community Television and to be a guest with Julie on Adam Bierman's *Breezin' with Bierman* TV show on Dec. 21st 2012 – doomsday!

I woke up that Friday at Julie's house in Pennington, New Jersey. It was no different than any other day. I rolled out of bed, showered, shaved, grabbed a cup of coffee, read the newspaper, went to a meeting, had lunch and then went to watch Julie's rehearsal before the show.

We introduced Pets Central Media, the New World Order pet care concept and I discussed the fact that 12/21/12 was only the end of the Old World Order and the beginning of the New World Order – and watched Julie and the zombies perform.

Watching America closely and intensely from the inside at this critical crossroad and change-over of global world orders, I came to the realization that there were many transformational changes taking place, so many in fact, that I had to actually capture and share my end-of-the-year observations in this prologue because they were heralding the New World Order and the fast-paced revolution shaping it, especially after the senseless slaughter of 20 innocent children and their heroic teachers in Newtown, Connecticut.

The Mayan doomsday prophesy fell onto the pool of blood and tears of the innocent children slaughtered at schools and focused a spotlight on violence at schools, with particular focus on school shootings or bomb threats, not only because of the increase in guns sales and ammunition in America after the Newtown slaughter, but the NRA's insane call for more guns in schools.

Many schools closed because their students were heard saying things like "Let's go out with a bang on Friday."

In China, the man who slashed 22 primary school students with a knife – none of whom died – in Henan the same month America was mourning Newtown's innocents told investigators that his rampage had been prompted by the end-of-world jitters. Additionally, the Christian sect the Church of Almighty God, followers of the Mayan end-of-the-world prophesy, saw thousands of its members arrested. It was branded an "evil cult" by the Communist Party and maligned by mainstream Christian groups for claiming that God has returned to earth as a Chinese woman hiding in China and latched on to the Mayan end-of-days legend for non-believers soon after the Hollywood blockbuster disaster flick *2012* took Chinese theaters by storm.

NASA, the Vatican, Mexico's archaeological institute, the Smithsonian Institution, and governments in places like China, Russia and France where hysteria took deep root, all declared it to be a misunderstanding that would make this, as several debunkers put it, the Y2K of doomsdays.

The date, aside from the winter solstice, merely marked the end of a 5,125-year cycle – the 13th *baktun* – and the beginning of the New World Order.

There are many fast-moving signature developments in our over rapidly expanding socially networked wired worlds of order and disorder, on both the domestic and foreign fronts and frontiers. Not only those leading up to the 2012 presidential election in the U.S. and the leadership change in China, but those that followed, which I discuss in this postscript.

Since my main premise for a revolution is that career politicians are corrupt, self-serving and the main political parties in America and China are morally bankrupt and must be replaced by the new party I propose in this book, I thought it best to stop this book from going to press ahead of the U.S. 2012 presidential election and change in China's leadership, to see if there would be any change in the destructive and acrimonious bickering that repeatedly results in *We the Maids* having to clean up the mess career politicians make of our economy – and then also pay for the privilege of cleaning up their mess. Taxes and fiscal cliffs being only the latest in the long list of messy predicaments *We the Apathetic Maids* are saddled with.

That is why I decided to hold off sending this book to the printer to add this prologue, and where appropriate throughout the book, add any relevant updates or changes, even though it meant a publication delay of at least six months. I felt it was important to make sure I included some of the rapid-fire post-election events, including legalizing of the recreational use of marijuana in Colorado and Washington states, but especially the murder of innocent children and adults that tragically testifies as to how out of control gun control and mental health care are in America, in order to make this book – in the tradition of its forerunners – timely, timeless and relevant.

The vocal congressional chorus questioning the Sept. 11 terrorist attack on the U.S. Consulate in Benghazi that killed Ambassador Chris Stevens and three other Americans, the resulting damning report and sophomoric acrimony between Democrats and Republicans over U.S. Ambassador to the U.N. Susan Rice's talking points at the time, which had been edited and cleared by the government's intelligence leadership, only reinforced the already desperate public outcry for drastic change in Washington and American politics as usual.

Confronted with the fiscal cliff, Republicans needed to score political points before appearing to compromise. Rice, nominated by President Obama to replace Hillary Clinton as secretary of state, was an easy target confirmation sideshow that America doesn't need. It gave Republicans the wiggle room they needed, especially after Sen. John McCain's political punches landed where he wanted them to – on Obama's designated brawler on foreign policy issues during their 2008 presidential campaign – which had irreparably bruised McCain.

The rational Republican congressmen and senators who put country before party and defected from their Grover Norquist "no tax increase" pledge took center stage in the contentious bipartisan fiscal cliff slippery slope arguments, drummed out momentarily by the dramatic resignation of General David Petraeus ("Betrayus," some said), because of his inappropriate sexual relationship, only to be drowned out by the louder meteoric rise of Mohamed Morsi, an Egyptian statesman and regional Middle East peace broker, who engineered the ceasefire between Israel and Hamas on November 22, 2012 – and the next day became a presidential pharaoh-role-model exemplifying how difficult it is to plant and grow democracy in the Arab world – because Arabs have never before experienced any form of democracy or democratic freedoms. Imagine birds that have been caged for generations, over centuries, all of a sudden told they are now free and can fly away. They wouldn't know where to go or how to get there. That is the case in the free Arab world today in the ongoing Arab Cleansing.

On a much quieter, less vocal front, the year ended for online activists the way it started when they helped defeat in January 2012 the Hollywood-sponsored anti-piracy legislation in Congress – with the defeat of a proposed new global treaty on Internet governance that would have given governments pernicious powers to meddle with and censor the web.

These dramatic developments were the primary contributing post-election political events that inspired this postscript prologue, to again emphasize why America and China must lead the New World Order together as partners if *We the Apathetic Maids* are to avoid Armageddon, which will make the fiscal cliff look like a picnic in the Grand Canyon.

The very predictable presidential *Moneyball* election outcome, especially after Superstorm Sandy, predictable that is, to those who follow "quants" – people I describe in mathematical detail in my upcoming Forethoughts – such as Nate Silver of *The New York Times* who called all 50 states correctly and prophesied the popular vote to within a half a percentage point. Not one traditional pundit had come close.

The pundits were so wrong again. Some pundits, commentators and writers even went so far as to raise the question of "What happens if Obama and Romney tie in the Electoral College?" Some of the possible outcomes were hilarious. My favorite was a Romney-Biden outcome. Because the house is controlled by Republicans, who decide the president when the Electoral College vote is tied, it was clear who they would vote for. Likewise, the Senate would decide the vice presidential winner in case of an electoral tie. Being controlled by Democrats, it would vote for Biden. "To close to call?" Nonsense.

The Obama campaign made an "unparalleled" $100 million investment in technology, demanded "data on everything," "measured everything" and ran 66,000 computer simulations every day. So why was anyone surprised? The only people who should have been surprised were Romney and his bankers team – and they were – again.

That was followed by the immediate post-election dire predictions of the fiscal cliff as the party gridlock in Washington thankfully started reluctantly easing-up as Republican senators and congressmen began breaking their 20-year-plus Norquist pledge of no tax increases, and took to heart the message *We the People* sent career politician with the thunderous re-election of Obama with 332 electoral votes.

The political poker game President Obama played with Speaker John Boehner to avert the cliff was one that was played out in public with both their hands on full display and clear to see why each hand was out of reach of the other and that neither would fold – and both would lose.

Those political developments made the dawning of the Age of Aquarius a very beautiful and uplifting bright one to watch from my vantage point on the California coast as America and the world spun toward the cliff.

Hanging out on the waterfront at night at the entrance to the marina in Los Angeles' Marina del Rey, looking across the channel at the dark foreboding rain clouds, lighting up periodically and reflecting their silver lining, as the blinking lights of planes departing Los Angeles International Airport passed by, reminded me of past and upcoming New World Order travels – and the rare bright moments in Washington and Beijing.

"Good morning," the security guard responded to my "Good evening," as he walked by. He was right. Not only with his salutation because of the late hour, but the dawning of the New World Order in America and China – and the world they must lead.

### Future Ripples of Political, Musical and Poetic Hope
America and China's leadership for the next four years, and probably longer, was decided in November 2012. Both countries' respective tough political campaign rhetoric maligning each other – especially the China-bashing that took place in America's most expensive presidential campaign in history – changed overnight once the leadership of the two superpowers settled into their post-election political skins and offices, determined to work together

to bring about constructive change and leadership in the New World Order.

Long sighs of relief were heard in China's Great Hall of the People when Obama was re-elected. And not only in China, but staterooms across Asia.

Romney promised to launch a trade war with China, and to declare it a currency manipulator on day one – a promise that gave him little wiggle room. At the same time, he promised to expand the military, spending more on weapons that do not work against enemies that don't exist, namely China.

A teary-eyed President Obama thanked his staff and volunteers on his re-election night in Chicago. "What Bobby Kennedy called the ripples of hope that come out when you throw a stone in a lake, that is going to be you," he told them as he regained his composure.

Obama is only the 16th U.S. president to be elected to a second term. Quite an achievement actually, but one overlooked by most mainstream media. The other sad fact is that all second-term presidents went through political hell, Bill Clinton's impeachment being the most recent example, something Obama is already being threatened with because of his gun control executive orders and proposals to Congress. The Republican threat to derail Ambassador Rice's nomination as secretary of state and former Senator Chuck Nagel as secretary of defense, made it clear that nothing will be easy for the president in his second term.

The vocal opposition to Nagel's nomination is not really surprising considering his enthusiasm for defense cuts. There are few people better qualified to know where the cuts should fall. The U.S. spends more on its military than the next 10 countries combined – fully 40 percent of global defense spending. The Pentagon budget doubled in real terms between 1998 and 2010 and has fallen only 5 percent in real terms since then.

Capitol Hill's dirty secret is that there is rare bipartisan consensus on maintaining the Pentagon as the chief conduit for pork-barrel spending. "Our Defense Department is not a jobs program," Hagel told the Council on Foreign Relations in 2012. "It is not a development program for my state or any district."

Hagel has widely advocated paring the bloated defense budget. His biggest challenge will be to streamline the Pentagon. The largest obstacle to a more efficient Pentagon sits across the Potomac – Congress and its indentured career politicians. No wonder Adm. Mike Mullen, former chief-of-staff, called the national debt the country's biggest security threat.

Hagel was nominated to supervise the beginning of the long process of defense cutbacks. A Democratic president trying to slash defense spending needs a Republican at the Pentagon to give him political cover, and it helps if he is a decorated war hero to boot.

Hopefully, Obama will fare better than Clinton in his second term and won't be subjected to an impeachment proceeding. That will allow him to lead America back to the global pinnacle of leadership – alongside China.

Obama and the America he leads can define America's future leadership role for decades – if not the rest of the 21$^{st}$ century – and beyond. Just like President Abraham Lincoln did when the country was wretchedly divided. Lincoln cut all kinds of deals, as the movie *Lincoln* accurately portrays. America's true political leaders fought for what they thought was right for the country, not the party, and made their case to the people along the way. Obama, like Lincoln whom he has studied and admired, did what was right for America when it came to the fiscal cliff.

In the meantime, America and the world enjoyed some good old '60s and contemporary American rock 'n' roll, rap and hip hop as the New World Order unfolded and rolled in.

The 12.12.12 Madison Square Garden benefit concert for those affected by Superstorm Sandy, which ravaged New York City and surrounding areas in October 2012, featured British rockers Paul McCartney, Roger Waters, The Who, the Rolling Stones, Eric Clapton and America's Bruce Springsteen, Billy Joel, Pearl Jam's Eddie Vedder, Coldplay's Chris Martin and rapper Kanye West, and was just the latest of the British-U.S. kindred spirits that make the two ideal transatlantic partners in the New World Order, a topic

I discussed at length in *Custom Maid Knowledge*, thanks to their activist ethos dating back to the American Revolution through the '60s – and today.

I often go to Penn Station, in the bowels of Madison Square Garden, to catch trains to Newark International Airport, Washington, D.C. and Philadelphia. Whenever I am there I can't help flashing back to the 1976 Democratic Convention I attended in the Garden, not to mention the Knicks games, rodeos and concerts. To me, like most immigrants, rock 'n' rollers, loafers, homeless and high rollers – all of whom can be found at the station and Garden – New York and Madison Square Garden, like the Statue of Liberty, symbolize America at its finest – and its worst. Doing both very well.

At 12:12 pm on 12.12.12 I had lunch with New Yorker Mary Catherine McBride, the president of Pets Central Media Inc., and Rudy Cohen, one of its directors. We were celebrating Mary Catherine's birthday, planning the launch of Pets Central Media in America and China and brainstorming how to best serve children and animals to ensure a better world as we toasted the dawning of the New World Order.

The innocence and lack of concern or fear of America's youth about their future – notwithstanding the recent killing of school children and the fiscal cliff – really registered with me on Sunday, December 23, 2012, after the last Newtown victim was buried. I was staying with friends in Old Greenwich, Connecticut, one of whom is a teacher and who like all Americans was mourning the senseless killing of children in schools. My pessimistic downbeat mood about America after my visit changed when I caught the train, make that trains, to leave the country.

I had to take a train from Old Greenwich to Grand Central Station, the shuttle to Times Square, another train to Penn Station to catch another train to go to Newark International Airport to catch my flight to Scotland where I would spend Christmas and ring in the New Year. There are quicker ways of getting to the airport. But I enjoy taking trains and meeting and conversing with fellow travelers and have written about several of my train experiences.

This particular train ride was no exception because of the cheerful multicultural excited teenagers I met and saw coming and going to New York to do their Christmas shopping, see the sights or catch a show on the trains and at three of New York's main train stations. Bubbly, exuberant, full of life, laughter and optimism about their future and the New World Order. They are the true embodiment of the Founding Fathers' optimistic idealism that is America and the American dream.

Watching the New York Knicks play the Brooklyn Nets, a team owned by a Russian oligarch catering to the former communist Russian community now living the capitalist life in New York – in a Big Apple bar in November 2012, the day after watching the lighting of the Christmas tree in Rockefeller Center – while discussing the demise of Europe and the rise of China with a German psychiatrist visiting New York, is so American – and so promising.

Listening to and watching the street musicians in New York, whether they are playing on 5th Avenue, in the train stations, or even aboard the trains, be it African bongos, Latino wind instruments, Chinese strings, or classical violins, are contemporary reminders of America's creative capitalistic entrepreneurship.

New York is not alone as America's goodwill ambassador to the world. There are many. My personal favorite after New York is Los Angeles – especially now that the city has named Eloise Klein Healy, an "immigrant from Iowa," as its first poet laureate, tasked with writing for big occasions and with making poetry a public matter. In other words, make L.A. a literary city.

L.A. is becoming a literary city, thanks to its libraries literacy programs. The program dedicates computers, work space and trained assistants specifically assigned to families looking for jobs, those taking English as a second language courses or working on homework.

The success of the program is due in large part to its implementation across all the city's libraries as well as the expanding variety of services it provides.

At the Central Resource Library in Overland Park, Kansas, blacksmithing, bowling and butchering trade exhibitions are regular fare. In an age where people use search engines instead of reference books and download novels on Kindles, Nooks and iPads, some public libraries are taking extreme measures to stay relevant.

The Berkeley Public Library in California, which has long offered tools like saws and demolition hammers for checkout, is expanding its selection in response to growing demand.

Public libraries have long served as gathering places and offered a range of nonliterary programs.

Trade schools and the need to reintroduce them in the New World Order is a topic I address and recommend in *Custom Maid Knowledge*.

Why can't libraries in Los Angeles and across America provide returning veterans GI Bill equivalent educational services with qualified teachers, where they can actually get academic credit for time spent learning in the library, or learn a trade – a budget the Pentagon could contribute to? Computer companies should be encouraged to donate hardware and software, in exchange for tax credits, so that everyone can have access to and be trained on state-of-the-art computers with the latest software programs – which could be funded by the Defense Department.

If that happens, there is near-term hope for America and its public education system.

L.A. is the birthplace and home of Hollywood, great musicians, artists, athletes, writers, politicians, economists and ideas – and will continue to be so in the New World Order – and has already taken the first giant steps in that direction with Silicon Beach – a three mile stretch running from Venice to Santa Monica.

### *America's Future – Silicon Beachfronts*

America, like Los Angeles, despite all its economic problems, is an increasingly dominant home to the next generation of technology companies that will drive the digital revolution in the 21st century.

Silicon Beach is a slice of territory in L.A. which initially referred to Venice and Santa Monica and now includes the rest of L.A. County, where Apple, Facebook and Google have opened major campus-size operations and where more than 500 newcomer ventures have taken root. Silicon Beach culture, unlike Silicon Valley's, is more consumer-oriented, drawing on art, entertainment and commerce to explore the intersections between technology and gaming, fashion, advertising and video.

Tax breaks and incentives, not to mention all the other creative attributes Hollywood and America have, are continuing growth drivers and stabilizers.

America, like L.A., has extraordinary resources to sustain and build its tech boom. Starting with its strong technology pool, be it MIT, Harvard, Princeton, Penn's Wharton, like UCLA, USC and Caltech, collectively graduate more talent than any other country.

Americans also, particularly tech staffers, especially in L.A., tend to possess more interdisciplinary skills than their foreign counterparts, having developed expertise in cinema, communications, music, design and enterpreneurialism while pursuing engineering degrees.

The death in a plane crash in December 2012, of Los Angeles born and raised resident Jenni Rivera, the daughter of Mexican immigrants and one of the most successful female *banda* singers in a male-dominated music style, was another tragic reminder of the evolving New World Order. By busting into the boys' club and delivering experiences, rebuttals and celebrations from a woman's perspective, she drew the attention of a whole gender of listeners no doubt tired of their husbands' favorite *banda* singers crooning out uncontested boasts.

Jenni reminds me of China's glass-cracking soprano diva first lady Peng Liyuan, a pop-folk icon who, unlike her predecessors, is a cosmopolitan first lady embodying a more modern and open China.

### *Political Brotherhood*
China's Communist Party brotherhood of comrades has brought about the greatest economic expansion in world history. It lifted hundreds of millions

of people out of poverty. In the decade since Hu Jintao became secretary-general of the Communist Party, China's economy has gone from a size of $1.5 trillion, the world's sixth-largest, to $7.3 trillion, second only to the U.S. Since 2002 per capita income has more than tripled from $1,135 to $5,445, transforming China from a low-income country to a middle-income one.

Back then, 38 percent of people lived in cities as opposed to 50 percent today. China had no high-speed rail. Now it has the longest network in the world. When Hu came to power, just 45 million Chinese used the Internet. As he approached the end of his term, almost 600 million were hooked up.

China survived the global financial crisis with the biggest stimulus package in history.

Only in 2002, with the withdrawal of Jiang Zemin and the ascendance of Hu, has China institutionalized a generational transfer of authority. These are huge achievements. Nevertheless, the Communist comrades faced more than 300,000 protest-related incidents in 2012, mostly against government corruption. The most common complaints include land grabs by property developers in cahoots with corrupt local officials.

Xi Jinping, China's new president, had his own Communist-style primary battles with his opponents, including the disgraced Bo Xilai – whose political downfall many attribute to Xi.

Obama is not alone in his post re-election challenges with a Congress that is supposed to represent the people. China's Xi was challenged directly by the people and had to deal and balance them with those of his fellow princelings in the hierarchy of the Communist Party.

Striking Chinese journalists from the *Southern Weekend*, a popular weekly reform-minded newspaper, in a stand-off with government censors in the southern city of Guagzhou, presented Xi and his fellow new leaders with their first full-blown political crisis.

It is the first case of open revolt against press censorship since January 2006, when the magazine *Bing Dian* (Freezing Point) was closed.

The protest by the journalists was triggered by the reworking of a New Year's editorial that originally called on authorities to respect the constitution, which guarantees the right of free speech and assembly, but ended up as a celebration of the government's achievements.

The striking journalists drew high profile support in the media and blogosphere, with fellow journalists from other media outlets, prominent academics, bloggers and even movie stars joining in.

The protestors encountered push-back from the Communist Party-run media with editorials and counter demonstrations in support of the government denouncing the striking journalists and their supporters.

Under reasonable assumptions, China's economy should double in size during Xi's tenure. That would make it bigger than the U.S. in purchasing power parity terms.

China and its leadership, like America's, must fundamentally change and transform itself or face the kind of social upheaval that swept away the imperial dynasties and ancient warring kingdoms, or political parties in the case of America.

Obama's Asia pivot and China offensive should be given the time necessary for Obama and Xi to embrace each others' country and lead their people to embrace each other and together lead the world away from Armageddon.

The re-emergence of China as a world power has created a high degree of discomfort in Washington because America is used to being the dominant power in the Asia-Pacific region. The fact is that America has to accept and accommodate China, and China must do the same. China became a world power in part thanks to the U.S. nuclear umbrella in the region that brought about stability and allowed and encouraged strong tiger economies to emerge in several countries, China reaping the lion's share of the benefits.

It is not in China's interest, nor is it its intention, to remove America's presence from the region, assuming of course it could, which it can't. Both countries' economies can grow by working together.

In our interlocal world, a concept I explained in *Custom Maid Knowledge* and the upcoming Forethought, America's ability to lead has become more constrained, according to the U.S. National Intelligence Council. Hence the need for America to team up with the right partners to maintain its leadership position, even if that means sharing the role with China.

How else can America fix its multilateral trade deficit with China and more than 80 other countries since 2010? Washington has to come to grips with the fact that the country is facing an unprecedented shortfall in national savings. Lacking saving and still wanting to grow, the U.S. must import surplus savings from abroad – as it is now doing from China.

China is America's third largest and most rapidly growing export market. U.S. focus needs to shift "towards market access – ensuring its companies engage Chinese markets as the nation ushers in what could be the greatest consumption story of the modern era," wrote Stephen Roach, former chairman of Morgan Stanley Asia and a member of the faculty at Yale.

The outlook for sustainable world growth depends on how the U.S. and China address rebalancing imperatives. A role reversal is in order. America has to start saving more as China starts consuming more.

### Transformational America

Listening to Hank Williams *Low Down Blues* album on one of my fall 2012 flights from Tokyo to L.A., *Wearin' Out Your Walkin Shoes* brought a smile to my face as I reflected on what a metaphor the song is for both the U.S.-Japan and Sino-American relationships.

America has been a transformational country since its inception. Adapting to changing times is in the nation's founding DNA and a constitutional cornerstone.

American music and movies move the world – and change it. I was reminded of this reality watching *Lincoln* and *Argo*. Legislative wheeling and dealing are what made America great. Legislative gridlock has been the cause of its rapid demise. *Lincoln* demonstrates the way history, refracted through the imaginations of artists, can clarify our values, reminding us of what we stand for, why we stand for it and how much we have sacrificed to achieve and safeguard these ideals.

In shaping a narrative around watershed moments of the past, writers, filmmakers and songwriters – all artists actually – naturally reflect the worries of their own time. But they also have the opportunity to inspire us to higher ground. *Lincoln* was in the works long before the term "fiscal cliff" ever passed the lips of a career politician or news reporter, but a drama about a rancorous partisan stalemate can't help resonating in today's divided partisan America.

Charles McNulty, *Los Angeles Times* theater critic, summed it up best: "'Lincoln' arrives at an unusual blend of austerity and sentimentality to unite an audience in a collective appreciation of something that has been lost in America – a shared sense of the common good."

L.A.'s NBA champion Lakers basketball team had a hard time winning any games early in the 2012-2013 season and became a local embarassment, while their cross-town rival Clippers were trouncing their opponents in a very hot 17-game streak of wins to rise from the division basement to become the division leader – and a New World Order reminder of how American determination, patience and persistence does pay off – and how easy it is for winners and champions to become losers – not only in sports but business. Sears vs. Walmart, Kodak vs. Japan, GM & Chrysler vs. Japan, AT&T vs. Verizon, Apple vs. IBM, Comcast vs. Universal/NBC, Microsoft vs. Macrohard and of course U.S.A. vs. China.

NBC's L.A. studio produced *Revolution*, "thematic gold" in the words of Mary McNamara, senior culture critic for the *Los Angeles Times*, mining the vein running through our collective unconsciousness: Where once we feared corruption, we now fear collapse, a technological, social or political cataclysm that will change everything.

Like good Spenglerians, we anticipate the inevitable fall – of technology, of government, of social structure, of human ascendancy. How long, really, before the grand experiment of democracy fails, before a super flu emerges or an alien race, before the melting polar ice does us in?

America is searching for its idealized self, best portrayed in the films *The Master* and *Holy Motors*, with their explorations of the substance of identity and self-definition. In both films, characters grapple with who they are and who they might yet be, striving for some idealized self they may never become. A metaphor for America?

Mark Olsen summarized who we are best in a piece he wrote for the *Los Angeles Times*. "The answer from this year's films seems to be a clear declaration that we are whoever we want to be, becoming whoever we must."

The emergence of two Angelinos near the top of many 2012's best albums lists confirms that observation. Kendrick Lamar and Frank Ocean, who create a remarkable "yin-yang of the California dream," in the words of Randall Roberts, *Los Angeles Times* pop music critic, restores my faith that the American dream is alive and well – in my old hood and in its Sunset Strip and West Hollywood haunts as well.

The year 2012 crystallized the New World Order, a time of rapid change, so much so that the Democratic and Republican parties now represent a "Coalition of Transformation and a Coalition of Restoration" in the words of columnist Ronald Brownstein. The Democrats having the Coalition of Transformation because of its coalition of African-Americans, Latinos, Asians, women and gays, the largest big cultural and demographic forces in America today. The Republicans on the other hand are the Coalition of Restoration, overwhelmingly dependent on the votes of whites unsettled by these transformational changes.

Americans and their political leaders, regardless of what party they belong to, have to respond to the New World Order America, the new transformational America. Especially when it comes to the fiscal cliff.

### Self-Imposed Fiscal Cliff
The fiscal cliff deadline of January 1, 2013 was self-imposed, make that self-inflicted, by the career politicians in Washington. They knew there would be automatic cuts to defense and social programs of more than $1 trillion – yet again they kicked the can down the road and avoided making them.

With the 2012 election ad wars barely over, the fiscal cliff ad wars began. Targeting members of Congress and the White House with ads to preserve and fight for the preservation of their respective budget entitlements of the past. Some groups were pushing to overhaul entitlement programs such as Social Security and Medicare. Others were trying to prevent just that. Some wanted budget talks to include corporate-tax changes; others want to ensure protection for sector-specific tax incentives.

Meanwhile, neither the White House nor Congress would "back down," to paraphrase, Tom Petty & the Heartbreakers.

And guess what? The career politicians in Washington don't really know what they are talking about because their respective arguments are based on projections that are 20, or even 70 years away. If they can't work with yesterday and today's numbers, which is what got America into the mess it is in in the first place, why does anyone think they can or will with projected guesses?

We're talking about projections of the cost of "entitlements" – a noxious way of referring to Medicare and Social Security, excellent programs that most workers have paid for during their working careers and that have kept millions of Americans healthy and out of poverty.

No one – no business, no government agency – makes plans today based on a vision of the world 20 years ahead. IBM doesn't do it. Google doesn't do it. The Department of Defense doesn't do it. "Not even life insurance companies, which might be said to live in the future, do it," wrote Michael Hiltzik, a *Los Angeles Times* columnist.

Forecasting healthcare costs is a mug's game, make that a shmuck's game. In a 2008 paper, economists Glenn Follette and Louise Sheiner of the Federal Reserve observed that the nonpartisan Congressional Budget Office unwisely projected healthcare costs into the future by assuming that the trends of the past would continue.

There is something fundamentally wrong when people who have worked and paid their share into Social Security are being asked to delay their retirement and receive less when they do.

It is also fundamentally wrong to make today's and tomorrow's workers and taxpayers bear the burden of career politicians' mistakes – while their capitalist cronies continue to benefit from tax breaks and federal corporate entitlements.

The first part of the fiscal cliff is the end of the tax cuts enacted under President George W. Bush. In order to bypass a rule forbidding laws that would significantly increase the federal deficit over a 10-year period, Congress mandated that the tax cuts would lapse after 10 years. Congress passed a two-year extension in 2010. If Congress did nothing by Dec. 31, tax rates would return to 2000 levels.

In case you don't remember the 2000 tax code: The maximum tax rate was 39.6 percent vs. 35 percent. Dividends were taxed at your maximum income tax rate, vs. 15 percent. Long term capital gains were taxed at 20 percent vs. 15 percent. Congress also has to fix the alternative minimum tax levels which will kick in at 2000 levels if no action is taken. About 30 million more people would have to pay AMT for the 2012 tax year than for 2011 if the fix isn't made.

Also scheduled to end is the holiday on the payroll tax. As part of the federal stimulus efforts, the payroll tax temporarily dropped from 6.2 percent to 4.2 percent. Because that was not extended, the typical worker has to pay an additional $1,000 a year in taxes.

Then there is sequestration, which would mean $110 billion in mandatory cuts in defense and other government spending, excluding Medicare and Social Security. The effects of the cuts and the tax increases would cut the 2013 deficit in half, which is good if you hate the deficit. But the cost is high. Taxes will increase by at least $2,200 for the average family and rise to $3,700 for many taxpayers. The CBO estimates it will push the nation into recession and send the unemployment rate up to at least 9 percent.

Is that really that bad? Isn't it time *We the Maids* stopped career politicians from kicking the can down the road and start tackling and cleaning up the deficit mess before it is too late and America faces the unemployment and desperate times Greece, Spain, Portugal and many other European and African countries are confronted with today? After all, as House Speaker John Boehner said during the fiscal cliff negotiations, "Washington has a spending problem. Let's be honest – we're broke."

It is time *We the Apathetic Maids* sweep in the tax reforms needed to recharge and restart the economy – a subject I discuss with tax reform proposals in Chapter 3.

America took in $2.45 trillion in 2011 and spent $3.54 trillion, leaving us with a deficit of about $1.1 trillion. America can do that from time to time, but 2011 marked the fourth year in a row *We the Apathetic Maids* spent over $1 trillion more than we took in. Just in that time, we've borrowed more than $17,000 for each man, woman and child in America.

The interest payments on all that debt is a massive $258 billion a year. That is more than we spend on the departments of Commerce, Education, Interior, Energy, State, Homeland Security and Justice combined!

The Congressional Budget Office projects that if we don't tackle some of this debt, our interest payments will soar to $1 trillion a year by 2023.

I agree with Sheila Bair, former chair of the FDIC and a *Fortune* magazine contributor, who wants to institute pay for performance for elected officials.

Pay for performance has improved management in the private sector. So why not try it with the folks in D.C.?

For instance, one-half of compensation for corporate directors is frequently paid in stock, which must be held for several years. The idea is to align their economic incentives with the long-term profitability of the company. There is no stock ownership in the federal government, obviously, but we do issue a lot of debt in the form of Treasury bonds. So why not start paying members of Congress and the president half of their compensation in 10-year Treasury debt, which they must hold until maturity. Members of Congress make roughly $180,000, so under this proposal, they would get $90,000 in cash and $90,000 in 10-year Treasuries. For the president, it would be $200,000 cash and $200,000 in T-bonds.

Most career politicians have never run a business or had to meet a payroll. Yet they are charged with running our nation's economy and business. This point was brought home to me in a discussion I had with Craig Kisciras, president of Rx Vitamins for Pets at the Central Veterinary Convention in San Diego in early December 2012. "None of them have ever done anything, not even run a lemonade stand," Craig said in exasperation as we discussed the approaching fiscal cliff. "Yet they have the power to regulate business and run our lives," he added.

"You mean *ruin* our economy and lives," I said in response.

If the economy does well and if they get our fiscal house in order and institute pro-growth tax and spending policies, those 10-year bonds should hold their value. If not, those bonds become worthless. Aligning pay with long-term performance can be a good way to change politicians' behavior for the better. Not only in America, but in China and the rest of the world.

### Short-Term Gain is Long-Term Pain
The temporary short-term partial fix by only increasing taxes on those earning $400,000 or more, 1 percent of the population, while kicking the necessary agreed to sequestration cuts can down the road, actually increased the deficit, gave money to Puerto Rican rum companies and increased taxes for all U.S. taxpayers.

The fix allowed a two-percentage point payroll-tax cut to expire. That will reduce the annual purchasing power of workers by $115 billion, or roughly $1,000 per working household.

As if that is not a bad enough way to start 2013, central banks are pumping up the money supply in order to restore a semblance of growth. This, together with keeping interest rates at rock bottom, is forcing down the value of currencies in an attempt to promote exports.

The Japanese are leading the herd with the new prime minister, Shinzo Abe, strong-arming Japan's central bank into printing oodles of new yen in a bid to deflate the currency and out-export China.

The U.S. Federal Reserve is not far behind and has promised to print as many dollars as needed to bring down unemployment below 6.5 percent.

China has countered by turning on its own monetary taps, flooding China's inefficient state firms with endless subsidy.

In the short term, this monetary policy is going to send stock markets soaring in early 2013, much to the bankers delight as they lobby Congress to continue to avoid addressing the fiscal cliff calamity by continuing to kick the can whenever and wherever they can.

While trying to protect and develop new factory jobs, while devaluing their currencies in the vain hope of selling more overseas and jacking up the prices of stock markets, what is the end result? A flood of under-priced goods on the world market – which is precisely what happened at the beginning of 2013. The long-term result being a major slump which has already started to unfold in Europe because of its political and economic impotence.

America did nothing to arrest the escalating national debt in either the short or long term. It did not raise the legal debt ceiling, without which the Treasury will have to suspend new bond issues and stop paying some bills.

The temporary fix cuts $737 billion from deficits over the coming decade, primarily through $618 billion of higher taxes on the rich and the resulting interest savings. But that barely dents the $10 trillion in deficits America was on track to accumulate in that time, roughly 5 percent of GDP on current policies, according to the Congressional Budget Office. The Committee for a Responsible Federal Budget, an independent watchdog, reckons it will take tax increases and spending cuts totaling $2.65 trillion-3.9 trillion to stabilize the debt near its 2012 ratio, 74 percent of GDP, by 2022.

The deal, in the words of Ronald Brownstein, a senior writer at the *National Journal*, was the fiscal deal of doom that "simultaneously set back the goals of the left, right and center." The entire country and many others.

The deal was a political nonstarter. A slow-burning fuse to disaster. It does not even qualify as a stop-gap measure. It did not address spending, nor raise the debt limit. Democratic Sen. Joe Manchin from West Virginia summed it up best. "Something has gone terribly wrong when the biggest threat to our American economy is the American Congress."

The dysfunctionality of Congress is caused by one primary fact: Too many career politicians in Congress who no longer worry about general elections, and therefore the national good. They are only concerned that they are not confronted by well-funded primary opponents who will challenge them for not being ideologically pure. Especially now that they can raise unlimited funds without having to disclose where the money is coming from.

Only *We the Apathetic Maids* can change that at the ballot box.

We have to acknowledge and recognize that President Obama, in the words of Gideon Rachman of the *Financial Times*, "is a prisoner of circumstances." He is a helpless prisoner of a broken system and cannot pass any law or get a budget through without the consent of a House of Representatives that is controlled by his bitter ideological and political enemies. And for good reason. They are beholden to their financial masters who fund their elections.

According to a study by the nonprofit groups Demos and the U.S. Public Interest Research Group, contributions to super PACs by just 61 large donors averaged $4.7 million each, matching the combined donations of 1.4 million donors of $250 or less to the Romney and Obama campaigns.

Whose voices were the most likely to have resonated more loudly in the halls of the White House and Congress – the 61 donors or the 1.4 million?

### Sandy & Friends

It took the devastation of Superstorm Sandy to get President Obama to mention climate change. He acknowledged that global warming is "a threat to our children's future, and we owe it to them to do something about it."

Visiting New York and New Jersey a couple of months after Sandy's devastating impact and listening to friends' stories of their tragic loss, or that of their friends and relatives loss of homes, was heart-wrenching.

What was even more shocking was that the career politicians in Washington had done nothing to provide the $60 billion needed to pay for the emergency relief so desperately needed because they were preoccupied with the fiscal cliff nonstarter political storm as temperatures dropped and winter storms approached to inflict even more misery on the battered East Coast.

When the politicians did finally get around to voting for the long overdue relief package, they also approved a measure that authorize the Federal Emergency Management Agency to make direct grants to churches, mosques, synagogues and other houses of worship "without regard to religious character of the facility or the primary religious use of the facility."

The House dispensed with holding even a single hearing before passing the bill, which abandons decades of Supreme Court precedent and longstanding administrative rules barring direct taxpayer financing of religious activities.

The First Amendment does not allow a Hurricane Sandy exception to pay for the rebuilding of damaged houses of worship.

What puzzled me was the lesson lost after the Katrina storm surge took 1,800 lives and cost taxpayers more than $100 billion to rebuild New Orleans. To encircle it with a state-of-the-art steel-based wall with enough powerful pumping stations to drain the bowl-city of New Orleans. So why wasn't America prepared for Sandy and the damage its storm surge would do? Especially when Congress vowed after Katrina that never again would America be unprepared.

Much of the damage caused by Sandy could have been avoided if America had been better prepared. That is where infrastructure dollars should be spent by the Defense Department and outsourced to the private sector. That would also bring down unemployment.

So what is America going to do to prepare for Katrina and Sandy's successors? They will only be more intense with greater storm surges because of the melting polar icebergs and icecaps in Greenland.

I left the devastation of America's East Coast for Scotland to spend Christmas and New Year, only to be greeted there by a flooded United Kingdom. The worst floods England had ever experienced and the second worst the U.K. as a whole had experienced – the floods I wrote about and warned were on their way in *Feasting Dragon, Starving Eagle*.

Scotland's dramatic countryside was featured in the Bond film *Skyfall*. Its great scenic hiking trails and whisky trails are a sight to behold and a great way to celebrate Hogmany – New Year's Eve and the New World Order.

Waking up to the smell of fresh brewed coffee, a light drizzle and the sight of grazing sheep across lush pastures of different hews of green on undulating hills capped with trees at Hawknest farm, a friends' farm off the road from Galashiels to Lauder near the Scotland-England border, after sharing good conversation, listening to local country rocker George Inglis sing *Barstool Cowboy* and the rest of his CD *Rockin Horse*, to the sound of 80 mph winds howling through the night, while sipping single malts, is one of the many reasons Scotland was named the world's top travel destination in 2013 by CNN – and in September 2014, was the first to question by popular vote union, secession, devolution, independence and interlocalism!

Sandy and other storms across America, including the downpour that flooded Las Vegas, and contemporary China super storm Vincent, severe tropical storm Saola, typhoon Danry and their flooding downpours in Beijing, Tianjin, Fujian and across the rest of China and Asia, which all caused severe damage across China as Sandy did to America, ended the silence about climate change. Sandy and friends, including 2012's historic heat waves – 2012 was the hottest year on record for the Lower 48 contiguous U.S. states, according to the National Oceanic and Atmospheric Administration – droughts in the U.S. and China – and wildfires and deadly blizzards that battered the Plains and Midwest in the U.S. – not to mention an unprecedented ice melt in the Arctic and flooding in the United Kingdom and Europe, has brought global warming back into political focus. Let's make sure we keep it in focus in the New World Order.

### Egypt's Unfinished Revolution

Egypt's Mohamed Morsi was not only a peacemaker but a naive saboteur of his country's unfinished revolution. Morsi's successful brokering of a cease-fire between Israel and Hamas had given him widening international and domestic support, a feat unmatched by any other Arab leader in the modern era, and offered the prospect that Egypt might again lead the region in the New World Order, as it did under Gamal Abdel Nasser in the 1950s.

Egypt is the first Islamic government to negotiate with Israel, even though as only an intermediary between Israel and Hamas, while leaning toward Hamas' point of view – and securing for itself other economic, military and political benefits that only further empower Egypt.

But then he overreached. Instead of consolidating the power he had amassed in service of his country's emerging democracy, he grabbed for more by issuing an emergency decree on November 22, 2012, appropriating sweeping new powers, including immunity for his decisions from judicial challenge, thus doing the impossible – uniting the opposition.

On assuming the presidency, he displayed a previously hidden talent for deft public stagecraft: During his inaugural speech in Tahrir Square, he opened his jacket to reveal that he, unlike Mubarak, didn't need a bullet-proof vest, suggesting he was a man of the people. Then, less than two months after his swearing-in, he astonished both his allies and critics by replacing several top generals and making himself the military's commander-in-chief, modeled after America.

His first few foreign trips to China and Iran were quickly interpreted by the punditocracy as an effort to pull Egypt out of the American orbit.

The facts are that although Morsi declined to adopt the harshest interpretation of Shari'a law, did not imposed dress codes on women and tourists, and whatever his rhetoric, did not tear up Egypt's peace treaty with Israel nor flung open Egypt's border with Gaza to take pressure off Hamas, he was a repressive pharaoh.

Morsi believes that Islam and the Muslim Brotherhood are democratic, a subject I addressed in *Custom Maid Spin*.

"This stems from Islamic belief – freedom for everyone, freedom of belief, freedom of expressing their opinions, equality, stability, human rights. This is coming from our belief: democracy. But also responsibility. We cannot get stable unless we have freedom, democracy, rights for everyone, equal rights, equal rights for men and women, for Muslims Christians, for whoever is carrying an opinion. The common thing is the nationality, the citizenship – Egyptian, that's all," Morsi told *Time Magazine* in an article published in its December 10, 2012 issue.

Unfortunately, Morsi did not practice what he preached and was deposed in July 2013 by military chief Abdel Fattah el-Sisi after popular protests demanded an end to his rule. Sisi gave up his posts as field marshal and defense minister to run for president. It was a foregone conclusion he would win.

President Sisi is more repressive than the Brotherhood and dictatorships that preceded them. In the first case under his presidency, a criminal court handed down in June 2014 a 15-year prison sentence against one of the leading figures of the 2011 uprising against Hosni Mubarak. The heavy sentence for Alaa Abdel Fattah and his 23 codefendants bodes ill for any easing of the crackdown on dissent in Egypt in the near future.

Many Egyptians were disillusioned by Morsi's incompetence and high-handedness, but the Arab Spring released a desire for political reform that can't be permanently stifled. Only by allowing democracy and rule of law to flourish can there be a hope of Egypt's troubles being reversed.

Egypt is the cradle of the Old World Order civilization represented by the pyramids, its rich history of centuries past and now the cradle of the New World Order in the Arab world. Its past is prologue to the New World Order in the Arab world and the Middle East.

### Yin, Yang and Hope
China is America's banker, its largest creditor. The more than $1.3 trillion in American debt held by China could threaten the U.S. financial system even more than a fleet of submarines or aircraft carriers. It therefore makes imminent sense for both countries to work together to restructure their own respective economies – and the global economy. Given the political, military and economic complexity of the U.S.-Sino relationship, it is imperative that the leaders of the two countries get to understand each other better, not only their people's security, but the political and economic security needed to restore a peaceful and stable global economic environment.

The leaders of both countries have much to learn about each other. Both possess the tools necessary to forge a constructive all-inclusive coalition. All it takes is patience, time and constructively digesting history.

Great powers of the past, starting with Portugal in the 15th century, with an empire from the Western Pacific in Macau, through the Indian Ocean with its outpost in Goa, to both West and East Africa and stretching across the Atlantic to Brazil. Portugal was followed by Spain, the Netherlands, Britain, France Germany, Russia, Japan and America.

Every one of these nine powers built their empires by conquest, destruction, enslavement, executions, rape and pillage.

America was built by slaves, the genocide of native Americans, wars and territorial acquisitions from Mexico, France and Russia, the control of neighboring countries in the Caribbean through the expulsion of other powers, the unilateral imposition of the Monroe Doctrine declaring Latin America a U.S. sphere of influence, culminating in the Spanish-American war that expelled Spain from Puerto Rico, Cuba, Guam and the Philippines.

China is trying to break its nine predecessors pattern and great-power rising paradigm by resorting to historical legal arguments that merit America's support.

Ties between America and China will grow stronger as long as the two focus on their common interests instead of their differences. The U.S. has to come to terms with the new multipolar world order and embrace it. The seeds of the now all-important U.S.-China relationship were sown in 1784 when America had been an independent nation for only a few months.

The Empress of China set sail from New York to Canton and established the first direct contact between the two countries.

China and America have to build on the bilateral foundation stone laid by Barack Obama and Xi Jinping at their informal summit at Sunnylands in southern California in June 2013. Only then can both countries live their dreams.

There is no doubt that America and China are global powers. But in the more complex world of cooperation and competition today, what counts most is cooperative leadership. It is time for America and China to accept each others' superpower status, notwithstanding their different forms and style, because they are complimentary – yin and yang. That is the only way to prevent Armageddon.

## REASONS FOR AMERICA'S THIRD REVOLUTION
*It is words, not weapons, which change the world.*
– Sebastien Condemine, Teacher, Nairobi

### Words and Their Actions

The pen has always been mightier than the sword. Words, like those of the Founding Fathers, can change the world, but they take time to study, learn, rehearse, practice and lots of patience and perserverence. Much has changed on the geopolitical landscape since 2004 and 2007, when *Custom Maid Spin* and *Custom Maid Knowledge,* Volumes I and II of the Custom Maid trilogy, were published. Long overdue dramatic political changes are taking place in America and the world it once led and aspires to lead again. More changes are needed, not only in America, but in China and all freedom-loving countries, where change is taking place at a much faster pace than in America.

A cursory review of the global disorder discussed in the first two volumes of the trilogy is in order to set the backdrop for this book – the final installment.

The introduction to *Custom Maid Spin* spelled out my definition of America and Americans. "America is a borderless and seamless ideal created by the Founding Fathers. Many throughout the world dream and aspire to become 'Americans'. The term American in the book therefore refers to all Americans. Citizens, residents, dreamers and wannabees. The true believers, atheists, Buddhists, Christians, Hindus, Jews and Muslims who worship the ideal that is America."

The first two volumes of the trilogy shared my observations on the dysfunctional state of domestic and foreign affairs in America, questioned our acceptance of political and religious hypocrisy, its violent mismanaged distortion of the truth by the media and career politicians, misperception of what is false, and our inability and reluctance to acquire the knowledge needed to wisely and deliberately bring about constructive political change – back to the fundamental principles of the Constitution.

*Custom Maid War* (2005) and *Feasting Dragon, Starving Eagle* (2009) were respectively penned and published after each of the first two volumes of the trilogy to point out and emphasize the political and economic devastation that Washington and Beijing career politicians and their Wall Street bankers have brought about with unnecessary wars that have allowed China to grow and prosper at the expense of America's economically and politically starving citizens.

Among the many resulting devastating legacies our children in America inherited as a result were a President George W. Bush and his top aides who lied thousands of times on hundreds of occasions, to justify the March 2003 invasion of Iraq – without being punished for their malfeasance; and the global financial meltdown that followed the subprime and corporate credit rating lies that will haunt our children and grandchildren in the future – while the bankers and career politicians, Democrats and Republicans alike, who created the mess *We the Apathetic Maids* have to clean up – and are now paying for the privilege of doing so – are handsomely rewarded.

Likewise, among the many resulting devastating legacies children in China inherited are the massacre of innocent students in Tiananmen Square in 1989 that the Communist Party refuses to acknowledge to this day, and a political dictatorship that supports like-minded brutal dictatorships in Africa, Asia and Syria that oppress and slaughter their own people – without being punished for their malfeasance, and a global flood of refugees – which *We the Apathetic Maids* have to pay for – while the corrupt dictators bank their ill-gotten spoils.

*We the People* just accept these conditions as irreversible. But imagine the possibilities if the interlocal *United States of Apathy* again becomes an active harmonious and UNITED community that acts on words – true and false – with the spirit and determination of the Founding Fathers.

## Apathy to Revolution

When I first sat down to write the Custom Maid trilogy in the 1980s, this volume was to be titled *Custom Maid Apathy* because of the lethargy of citizens worldwide, but especially in America, where people who have the power to bring about revolutionary change through the ballot box refuse to exercise their hard-fought basic human and personal rights for which so many patriotic Americans have sacrificed their lives to preserve.

My book *Custom Maid Spin* lamented the political apathy of America's young adults because it enabled the political establishment to focus its campaign budgets on the vegged-out seniors whose paid excursions to the ballot boxes ensured the perpetual residence in Washington of Wall Street's political puppets.

Much has changed in America and the countries it leads – tries to contain and is in conflict with – since the late 1990s and the early years of the $21^{st}$ century. Youth has been awakened because of the Internet and their growing awareness of their surrounding corrupt political and religious injustices. In the process, they also woke up their employed and unemployed wage-slave parents and grandparents – and together elected and re-elected President Barack Obama – and germinated and recharged in 2012 the Jasmine Revolution and Tea Party and Occupy Wall Street movements. Starting with the heirs of the Founding Fathers' Boston Tea Party that spilled over and was lapped up by the Arab and Iranian lovers of Jasmine flowers and tea, along with the coffee drinking Greeks and Europeans.

The election of Obama in 2008 and 2012 was the result of America's reawakening to the ideals of the Founding Fathers, the U.S. Constitution and Bill of Rights – to the chagrin of many career politicians and their extremist political hijackers – that *We the People* regret having lost and were determined to retake – and did.

Young Americans voted in their largest numbers in 2008 and 2012 since the Vietnam War. Not surprising really when, for 25-to-54-year-olds – the bulk of the work force in 2012 – the unemployment rate was 7.1 percent. But for 18-to-24-year-olds, the rate was more than twice that at 15.7 percent.

"These numbers could mean real problems for all Americans, but particularly for the next generation. Maybe tomorrow's young married couples will decide they don't have enough money to have a child, or to raise a second or third one. Maybe, day-care costs them so much, they decide it makes more sense for a spouse to stay home and care for the kids than to work. One-income families would have lower incomes, longer commutes and lower standards of living," wrote Keith Hall, a senior research fellow at the Mercatus Center at George Mason University, chief economist for the White House Council of Economic Advisors from 2005 to 2008 and commissioner of the Bureau of Labor Statistics from 2008 until 2012.

Many Americans were under-employed, or were unemployed and no longer actively looking for jobs. They did not show up on the jobs reports radar screens. At the same time, many baby boomers watched their retirement savings tank in their last years before retirement and today are still working longer or have gone back to work to make up the difference.

Youth and their elders, of all colors, races, sexes and sexual persuasions, turned out in more than respective numbers to keep Obama in the White House and allow the Republicans to retain their chokehold on the House of Representatives. Latinos and Asian-Americans turned out in great numbers and voted overwhelmingly for Obama.

Latino and Asian-American voters made the difference in the swing states of Virginia, Nevada, Pennsylvania and Florida.

The time is right for another American Revolution. Actually, it is imperative for America and China to get back to their constitutional foundations as envisioned by the Founding Fathers of both countries – Washington, Adams, Jefferson, Madison and the rest of the boys, together with   Chen Duxio (1921-1927), Qu Qiubai (1927-1928), Xiang Zhongfa (1928-1931), Qin Bangxian (1931-1935), Zhang Wentian (1935-1945) and Mao Zedong (1945-1976) and his Long March followers and modern-day gang of self-serving adherents – and away from the precipice of another self-inflicted Armaggedon cliff like the Great Leap Forward.

America is unraveling domestically at the federal, state, county, and city levels and geopolitically in the Arab and Muslim world – and far beyond in Asia, Europe and Latin America – as *We the Maids* kick back and bear witness to the historic economic disintegration of U.S. power. Notwithstanding its economic decline, America remains overwhelmingly the most powerful country in the world, or in history. Its military might overshadows most of its allies and enemies combined – to no economic avail to *We the People* – only to the military-industrial complex and the plutocrats.

Why does America repeatedly continue to get its foreign policy wrong and back totalitarian regimes that can be its puppets and oppose those democratically elected by the people, who refuse to have America be their puppeteer? The result is that America continues to become more isolated and rejected in the world it once dominated.

This book looks at the political and economic injustices that an oversized, bloated and dysfunctional federal government has created to support itself and its financial backers – including China – and recommends the steps and actions we must take to minimize – and hopefully end – political apathy in the New World Disorder. It is time for *We the Maids* to sweep in the revolutionary changes needed to fix America – to reduce the size of the federal government, restore state rights and the constitutional cornerstones designed by the Founding Fathers that created the great democratic republic.

### Change in the Air

In 2003, I wrote in the preface to Volume I of this trilogy that "America has undergone a tremendous transformation since the pilgrims landed. America has changed from vanilla WASP to Cherry Garcia white-patched butterfly, with butterfly ballots. Or is it a multicultural scoop of Ooey Gooey cake? Apple pie America is a racial blender of carmelized apple. Rich, heavy and lite."

Racial identity in America today is more culture than color. The 2010 census confirmed that American reality – especially for Asian-Americans and Latinos of all shades of Americana.

The good news from the 2008 and 2012 presidential elections was Barack Obama, who fits the carmelized bill to a tee. What's more, he got *We the Apathetic Maids* to register to vote – and to actually turn out. His slogans "Yes We Can" and "Forward" messages of change resonated throughout America and the world across all color and religious lines.

From my perspective at the time during both elections in Hong Kong, the level of interest and enthusiasm voiced by locals, foreigners and American expatriates about the Obama candidacy was unprecedented. Obama polled 65.6 percent of the Democrats Abroad primary votes. He took 72.6 percent in the Asia-Pacific region and 75.3 percent of the Hong Kong votes. The Hong Kong vote for Obama was among the highest proportion in 164 countries and territories where Democrats Abroad voted. The complexity of the carmelized blending of his makeup and personality has universal appeal and has re-ignited the American Dream. *We the Apathetic Maids* are starting to wake up and speak up and demand change for a forward thinking better government.

In the 2008 election, 60 million Americans eligible to vote didn't because the registration rules were too complicated to follow. Voter registration is governed by state law, which varies from county to county in most states and city by city. So there are at least 50 different registration rules for federal elections. Not much had changed by the 2012 election and in fact some states made it harder to register and are being challenged in the federal courts.

The Obama administration wants voter registration to be simpler. It should be. Why not automatically register people of voting age as a birthday present from America?

While watching the 2012 U.S. presidential, congressional and state election returns with several fellow American expatriates at the Main Bar of the Foreign Correspondents Club in Hong Kong, the list of electoral reforms needed to fix democracy in America kept growing longer after each round of celebratory drinks consumed when the electoral vote tallies were announced after a state's votes were completed, or close enough to project.

Walter Kent, a retired banker and long time FCC member, got everyone's silent attention as he presented his case on why American expatriates should have their own representatives in Congress. "We expats are the 18th or 19th largest state of the union with more than 7.5 million, maybe eight. And yet we don't have a single representative in Congress because we vote from our last registered districts in the U.S. where we voted. We should have a representative in Congress representing expatriate Americans," Walter declared to a round of applause and toasts of "right on" and another round ordered.

"How many representatives should we and D.C. that has non get?" I asked.

"The fairest way is to give us and D.C. the same as each of the states have," Walter answered. "But I recognize that it would distort too many factors such as population. Why not do what was done in 1960 with Washington, D.C.," Walter continued. "It was given three electoral votes based on the number given to the smallest state, either Hawaii or Alaska. So why shouldn't we expats and D.C. get the same number?"

American expatriates and D.C. citizens should have their own voting representatives in Congress. They cannot be non-voting members like the current six members representing the Virgin Islands, Guam, North Manana, Samoa and Washington, D.C.

By giving U.S. expats three electoral votes, the issue of a potential tie in the electoral college would become a moot point.

It took President George W. Bush just eight years to reincarnate and reinforce the ugly-American Islamaphobic prejudice and greedy war-mongering oil-thirsty underbelly to trigger the demand for change.

For a multiracial black American to receive so many votes from WASPs, barely 43 years after the 1965 Voting Rights Act gave African-Americans full participation in U.S. elections for the first time is the most dramatic evidence of how America has become a carmelized apple. The kind of apple the world wants – but many Americans hate.

That hate surfaced in the November 2010 midterm election when the young carmelized voters dropped out again and allowed the old, rich, white Republicans, who turned out by the millions, to catapult the Republicans into Congress, governors mansions and statehouses. The newborn Tea Party movement became a high-octane caffeinated "get out the vote" jolt. That jolt continued to rock the country during the 2012 presidential election until racism took another ugly turn.

### The Retreat

I was visiting the U.S. that tragic February 2012 when 17-year-old Trayvon Martin was killed in the gated community of the Retreat at Twin Lakes in Sanford, Florida. I was there through March and early April as the protests and counter-protests overshadowed an even uglier Republican primary campaign season. A killing that mirrored how divided America is was reflected in the Republican primary and the unfair and unjustified criticism of the nation's president.

Instant racist polarization. A single shot that exposed how raw and divided vigilante America still is over the issue of race and racism, not to mention gun control. The ensuing supercharged national debate highlighted how explosive the subject of race is in America. The partisan news cycles, fueled by social media, instead of trying to bring the country together, further polarized and poisoned the nation. It was ugly. What happened to looking at the facts and having an honest exchange of views instead of pre-calibrated destructive arguments that bear no relevance to the facts?

An unarmed African-American teenager killed by an Anglo-Latino Neighborhood Watch coordinator under questionable and conflicting circumstances.

For Sanford to be elevated and be mentioned and compared with Selma and Birmingham is an insult to the civil rights activists of the 1960s. All one has to do is look at the racial divide that once defined racially integrated Sanford. U.S. Highway17-92 served as the inviolable line that separated black and white communities.

The Retreat, and the tragic death of its guest Trayvon, is a reflection of how broken and dysfunctional America is. Homes that sold there for $250,000 at the height of the real estate market before the 2008 subprime crash now sell at half that price. George Zimmerman, the Neighborhood Watch coordinator, used to make $10,000 a month as a mortgage banker before he became unemployed; vacant storefronts; and Trayvon's single father visiting his girlfriend and her teenage son Chad at the Retreat – for whom Trayvon bought the Skittles. Both Trayvon and Zimmerman had their run-ins with the laws they couldn't live with. Don't we all?

They got into a fight. An innocent African-American boy died because his Anglo-Latino opponent had a gun and was justified in using it under Florida's Stand Your Ground law. Is this the kind of ground America wants to stand on? Trayvon is America's child, and like all our children, had the right to live.

America shouldn't be about color. It doesn't matter if one is black, brown, yellow or white. Let's just do what is right. It's about life. The lives of our children and grandchildren. How do we stop their pointless premature deaths? That is our responsibility as parents. Life is too precious. Especially the lives of our children.

The blame game – especially when it is debatable and not clear-cut black-and-white, only inflames the nascent injustices in society that we should be consciously working to heal. Periodically picking at a healing scab only brings back the pain and reopens wounds that *We the Apathetic Maids* should be tending to ensure they heal and we grow.

### Time to Reconcile

The expensive slick packaged politically acrimonious and vindictive mud-slinging ads that marked the November 2010 midterm election and 2012 presidential campaigns showcased the country's deep divisions and were un-American and not something I believe the Founding Fathers would look kindly upon.

Reconciling America again with itself and the rest of the world, especially China, is a priority *We the Maids* must adopt if America is to again become the powerful bright beacon on the hill that it once was.

America was built by come-back-kids who dared challenge establishment pundits whose poor judgment was proven wrong. So why is there no room in America today for the public to discuss or debate self-serving establishment laws and regulations that the career politicians serving financial and corporate interests push through? America today has none of the democratic philosophical or political debates of Jerusalem in the talmudic Moses-Jesus tradition, Athens during the time of Aristotle-Plato, or of the Founding Fathers in Philadelphia and today in Washington and every state capitol as envisioned by the Constitution and Bill of Rights. Why?

Judeo-Greco-Euro-English Enlightenment democracy, the best of which was adopted by America's Founding Fathers, is like American baseball, football and basketball, full of surprises. You don't have to be a league champion to win the championship. Underdogs win it as well. That's true in democracy too.

The Packers and Jets, two No. 6 NFL seeds, made it to the conference championship games and the Packers went on to win Super Bowl XLV in 2011. Talk about wild cards! Superbowls have featured non-division winners. How the trash-talking Jets beat the Patriots in the Super Bowl shocked a lot of people, but not Rex Ryan, the Jets boastful coach. He is the epitomy of American brashness with attitude, that is so American – that changes expectations – game plans and results.

Better yet, how about the San Francisco 49ers shootout win over the favored New Orleans Saints in January 2012, on their road to the Super Bowl that was side-tracked by New York's Giants, who went on to win it against the favored New England Patriots? Especially now that we know the Saints secretly doled out cash rewards to players who intentionally injured opponents to get them off the field and out of the game.

The same happened in basketball in 2011 when the defending champion Los Angeles Lakers got eliminated by the Dallas Mavericks who then went on to the finals against Miami – and won!

What about the Cardinals winning the 2011 World Series? A team that erased a 10½-game deficit to squeeze into the playoffs? A team given no chance against the mighty Milwaukee Brewers and Texas Rangers. They trailed the Brewers in the NL Championship Series before winning four of the next five games to get to the World Series. And once there they had to overcome deficits five times in Game 6 alone to stay alive, forcing a decisive Game 7.

For Texas in the World Series, twice in Game 6, they were ahead by two runs and just a pitch away from a championship. Yet each time St. Louis came back, and that persistence eventually wore the Rangers down. And how about the L.A. Kings in the Stanley Cup playoffs in 2014?

If the NFL, NBA and NHL could only have trash-talked themselves out of the players lockouts. Unfortunately, labor relations in corporate America are exemplified and reflected by the NFL, NBA and NHL lockouts. Basketball players making $2.17 billion in salaries and benefits at the end of the 2011 season are not happy with any cut in pay during a recession. No different than America's bankers and corporate CEOs who paid themselves extravagant multibillion dollar salaries and bonuses. The NBA had offered players a minimum of $2 billion a year in salaries over the course of a 10-year labor deal that was rejected by the players because it represented an immediate $170 million reduction. Let's get real. Athletes are grossly overpaid and they, like bankers, CEOs and career politicians, have to have their salaries re-calibrated. I raised the same complaint in *Custom Maid Spin* during the baseball strike.

The Founding Fathers wrote the original American game plan for all fields from politics, economics, religion and sports. If Americans were half as devoted to politics as they are to sports – both as participants and spectators – America would again become the ideal and beacon that the Founding Fathers envisioned for the Republic.

### Political COPS
Change Obama-Palin Style – COPS – is exactly the kind of political change America needs, or is it? The operative political consensus from both Senators John McCain and Obama during their 2008 presidential campaign was that "change" is coming to Washington and the Beltway insiders were in for an unpleasant shakeup-wakeup call no matter who won. They

were both right. Obama won and a few months after he took the oath of office, he became the manure that spawned the Tea Party movement and its nominal head, Sarah Palin.

I'm sure the change that swept across America since Obama's first inauguration is not the change that either Obama, McCain or Mitt envisioned or want. America is going to have to come to grips with a change that is going to not only shake up D.C., but the world it leads. First term senator-African-American president, or small state governor-vice president vying for the top political offices of the land, regardless of their experience and credentials, was unquestionably the first volley of the 21$^{st}$-century revolutionary change being swept by *We the Maids* into U.S. and global politics.

### Dying Dream

I started off the *Custom Maid* trilogy by saying in the preface to *Custom Maid Spin* that "The America Dream, however, is for many just that. They keep waking up. For others it has become a nightmare that has to be confronted at the dawn of the new millennium."

The American Dream has not only turned into a nightmare but is dying. People the world over dream of coming to America to better themselves the way millions of immigrants, myself included, did. America was a place where if one worked hard, one got ahead and created a better world for their children, who in turn did the same for theirs. It was a dream all Americans believed in. Today less than half believe so, according to a poll by ABC News/Yahoo News in September 2010.

This point was brought home to me wherever I went in America in 2010, 2011 and 2012. Homeless people shuffling and pushing shopping carts with all their worldly possessions. As a lawyer who represented mobile home and trailer park developers when I practiced law in California in the '70s, I couldn't help think – my, my – mobile home living sure has changed in America these days. Not surprising then, considering that more than 17 percent of Americans were unemployed, no longer looking for work, or employed only part time. I'm sure the number is much higher today.

The seeds of today's global economic disaster were sown in the 1980s. From 1980 to 2005, the U.S. economy, adjusted for inflation, more than doubled. But the average income for most American families actually declined. The standard of living for the average family improved not because income grew but because women entered the workplace by the millions. As hard as it may be to believe, the peak income year for the bottom 90 percent of Americans was way back in 1973, when the average income per taxpayer, adjusted for inflation, was $33,000. That was nearly $4,000 higher than in 2005!

The American Dream was alive and well and evidently unassailable. Yet somehow, following the oil shocks, the hyper inflation and other traumas of the 1970s that triggered my protest horseback ride to my Beverly Hills office in 1979, *We the Apathetic Maids* allowed the energy companies and their extremist career politicians in the military-industrial Congress to smother the Founding Fathers' dreams and environment.

America can and must restore the American Dream. The dream can be revived. It will take time, courage and sacrifice. The American experiment is alive, and although dying, can and must be resuscitated and restored by reaching back to the founding principles of the great republic envisioned by the Founding Fathers and enshrined in the Constitution.

## *Middle-Class Crisis*

The underlying anxiety gripping America today runs deeper than the latest economic slowdown or business cycle. The fact is, middle-class America has been devastated by Washington career politicians, just as the Chinese middle class is exploding in its growth and imploding the Communist Party.

America's middle-class has run out of options – the coping mechanisms used for more than three decades – political and pharmaceutical – to get by on median wages that are barely higher than they were in 1970, adjusted for inflation, is a great fertilizer for today's revolutionary frustration and anger.

Male wages today, despite all the political rhetoric, are in fact lower than they were in the '70s. Not only in America. The income of a young man in his 30s is now 12 percent below that of a man his age in the '70s. Yet for years, America's middle class has lived beyond its paycheck. I know first hand, because I was one of them. Middle-class lifestyles flourished even though median wages got stuck in the times. And now Americans, Chinese and workers around the world are paying the price with money they don't have.

The first coping mechanism was getting more women into paid work. The percentage of American working mothers with school-age children has more than doubled since 1970 – from 38 percent to more than 70 percent. Some parents are even doing 24-hour shifts, one on child duty at home while the other works. These families are known as Dins: double income, no sex.

When the limit of working mothers was reached, what was the next coping mechanism? Longer working hours. The typical American works at least two weeks more each year than in the 1970s. Compared with any other advanced developed nation, Americans are addicted workaholics putting in 350 more hours a year than the average European, more even than the industrious Japanese.

But then again, there are only 24 hours in a day, so that mechanism had its built-in daylight savings time limitations. The next coping mechanism? Borrowing big time. Homes became dirt-cheap equity-loan ATMs to buy plasma televisions, cars and vacations, financed by China and the rest of the world. But when that credit bubble burst, America took a nose-dive, economically, financially, politically and globally.

With consumer car, credit card and student loans not far behind, it should be no surprise that personal bankruptcies rose to record highs. Meanwhile, China and other foreign governments started investing less in dollars and more in other currencies, especially the Chinese yuan. The losers? American, Chinese and global wage-slave-workers and immigrants.

### *Poor America*
Class warfare was a common theme during the 2012 presidential and congressional races among America's underclass. A majority of Americans are in the underclass. Not just African-Americans and Latinos for whom the

word was a euphemism in the '60s, but for Anglos as well.

The number of people living in poverty in America in 2010 was the most in at least a half a century – 46.2 million, according to the U.S. Census Bureau. Squeezed by rising living costs, a record number of Americans, almost 1 in 6, have fallen into poverty or are scraping by on earnings that classify them as low income. Unemployment insurance, food stamps and tax credits for the working poor lifted the income of 3 million to 5 million U.S. households above the poverty line in 2010.

The proportion of men of prime working age with only a high school education who say they are "out of the labor force" has quadrupled since 1968 to 12 percent. Working-class unskilled laborers are competing with immigrants, legal and illegal.

The reality is that in major U.S. cities, the youth unemployment rate exceeds 50 percent. At least 10 percent of U.S. households have lost homes to foreclosures since 2008; 28 percent of homeowners with mortgages have negative equity; more than 25 million people who want to work are unemployed; and the real median household income has fallen 10 percent since 2007.

It should therefore come as no surprise that as more men become unemployed and the woman becomes the main bread winner, it results in more women wanting to remain single moms and married women questioning their relationship. This as their children and grandchildren have to move back home to join dad on the unemployment couch.

Better than giving their children away, as so many families are doing in Asia and Europe.

Meanwhile, the rich get richer. In 2010, as America continued to recover from the recession, a mind-boggling 93 percent of the additional income created in the country that year, compared to 2009 – $288 billion – went to the top 1 percent of taxpayers, those with at least $352,000 in income. That delivered an average single-year pay increase of 11.6 percent for each of these households.

More amazing was the extent to which the super rich got rich faster than the merely rich. In 2010, 37 percent of these additional earnings went to just 0.01 percent, a thimble-size collection of about 15,000 households with average incomes of $23.8 million. These fortunate few saw their incomes rise by 21.5 percent.

The bottom 99 percent received a microscopic $80 increase in pay per person in 2010, after adjusting for inflation. The top 1 percent, whose average income is $1,019,089, had an 11.6 percent increase in income.

One out of five families owes more on credit cards, medical bills, student loans and other unsecured debt than they have in savings, according to a University of Michigan report released in May 2012.

The disparity gap between the worlds of the rich and poor – the haves and have-nots – is so wide that it is unsustainable. All one has to do is look at the rich enclaves of former wealthy merchants in Europe, China and even America to see that they are now housing the poor whose labor allowed them to prosper. This is graphically on display in Xidi, in the Huizhou region of Anhui Province, the city that was home to China's prosperous merchants from the 13th to early 20th centuries. It ended with the demise of the Qing Dynasty in 1911.

Meanwhile, those in the private sector are being shortchanged on their retirement benefits because corporate America has systematically plundered their pension plans, while retirees who worked in the public sector are confronted by employers going bankrupt and wanting to renegotiate the benefits.

Any wonder people young and old want to occupy Wall Street? At least they can get shelter in a park and a warm meal and dream of *Hunger Games*.

### *Hunger Games*
The young-adult trilogy and movie was not only a best seller and a hit on the screen, it got people thinking about revolution and survival skills with alternatives to guns in a totalitarian state, one not that different from America, according to some of the media pundits, which has risen from the

postwar ashes of where America once stood – archery.

The Hunger Games, a brutal kill-or-be-killed annual event between boys and girls between the ages of 12 and 18 – known as tributes – marked the anniversary of a peace treaty that ended a bloody revolution.

"This is how we remember our past," intones the official propaganda for the 74th annual games set in a sizable wooded area that functions as an outdoor arena. "This is how we safeguard our future."

*We the Apathetic Maids* have already become tributes to our career politicians and their corporate financial backers for whom we are repeatedly asked to sacrifice. But, just as Katniss, the heroine of the story, repeatedly rescues herself with resourcefulness, guts, goals and true aim to a new world order – so can we.

### Gold

Is it any wonder then that so many people are demanding a return to a gold-backed dollar? South Carolina, like more than a dozen other states, introduced a bill in April 2011 that would make gold and silver coins legal tender in the state. These states are looking ahead to the possibility of economic catastrophe that would leave the dollar worthless.

"The impulse for moving to some kind of metallic money comes from the strong sense right now of distrust and anxiety about the financial and the government's stability," said Perry Mehrling, an economics professor and historian of monetary policy at Barnard College in New York.

Walter Samaszko, the Carson City, Nevada, loner who only had $200 in his bank account, but enough gold bars and coins to fill two wheelbarrows worth $7 million in his home where he died, like many Americans, was distrustful about the government's financial stability.

In New England, another loner-hoarder American known simply as Radkin, from Alburgh, Vermont, who was crushed to death by his tractor-pulled horse trailer on his property, left more than $200,000 in gold coins stashed in his dilapidated house. How about the millions of dollars of the 1,427 gold coin find in rusted cans in California Gold Country in 2014?

In Utah gold became legal tender and is exempt from sales tax and creates a tax credit to partially reimburse state residents who must pay federal capital gains tax on profits from holding gold. Maybe those Mormons have got it figured right when it comes to Mammon – the God of Money – that the Chinese believe is the highest power – and that's why other Christian denominations in America have it in for them, because they missed the Mormon revolutionary religious boat when it ventured out West into the sea of sand and the land of milk and honey.

"The centerpiece of U.S. monetary policy for the last 100 years has been the constant depreciating dollar," said Larry Hilton, a businessman credited with first proposing the law enacted in Utah. "Sometimes, just as a citizen, you have to stand up and say this is a problem."

The U.S. and most of the rest of the world operated on a full gold standard until the Great Depression, the U.S. until the 1970s. Economists generally agree that the policy helped cause the Depression and earlier and later severe downturns by limiting the amount of money the government could create, constraining its ability to stimulate the economy because of its incompetence and self-serving economists and bankers – the same people who gave us deregulation, subprime loans and today's unabated corporate greed.

I can see why paying for groceries or liquor with gold or silver is going to be a problem. How do you deal with change? Using it as collateral for what one spends on a credit card makes more sense, as long as it is priced to market, the way gold, silver and commodity dealers do around the world by the minute.

Article I, Section 10 of the Constitution says that no state shall coin money. However, it goes on to add that no state shall "make anything but gold and silver coin a tender in payment of debts," which can be read as a license for any state to mint its own currency, something the federal government should reconsider.

The reality is, every U.S. dollar cannot be backed by gold and silver alone. Other metals and commodities, including food and energy, definitely merit consideration as collateral and can be priced to market daily.

## Country Roads

Traveling in America in the spring of 2010 as unemployment hit 10 percent and schools were being closed across the country as the nation was imploding over the destructive and divisive debate over the Obama health care bill, watching the euphoric Democrats and dismayed Republicans march to their political extremes as they prepared to mount their war machines for political battles determined to destroy each other at the upcoming midterm congressional elections over Obamacare – I couldn't help wonder what went wrong and why the Founding Fathers' brilliant ideals that created the beacon of hope on the hill that all peoples around the world aspired to reach – was slowly being extinguished – but still dimly lit and ready to shine brightly again if only the country could come together.

My cross-country trip started in San Francisco in early March 2010, during street protests by students and their parents and supporters in the Bay Area opposed to tuition hikes at San Francisco State, California State University, community colleges and K-12 campuses. The protests spread to 33 states and reminded me of my law school day protests in San Francisco in 1969-71 against the Vietnam War and the Kent State student killings. Tuition was relatively inexpensive and affordable in those good ol' days.

The American high school and college student protests that spring were a forerunner to similar protests a few months later in China and England, over tuition hikes and canteen food price increases, and in France over legislation to raise the retirement age from 60 to 62. The students anger against the rising tuition fees was highlighted in an attack on a car carrying Prince Charles and Camilla Parker-Bowles, Duchess of Cornwall, in London's worst day of protest violence for years. The rioters chanted "off with their heads," broke a window of the royal Rolls-Royce and splattered the car with paint. These protesting students in the cradles of contemporary Western democracies and China sowed the seeds of the Third American Revolution – the Arab Jasmine Revolutions were the saplings.

The violent protests in Greece, the cradle of Western democracy, and across Europe in the closing months of 2012 against austerity measures necessary to balance their budgets reflect the anger people have toward their elected career politicians and their financial backers – the bankers.

They have a right to be angry. Bankers, whom we allowed to bankrupt the global economy leading up to the Great Recession of 2007-2011, were bailed out by these students' parents and grandparents' hard-earned taxes that these students will have to repay with their hard-to-find future taxable earnings. Besides stiffer tuition, they also have to pay higher food prices in their cafeterias because of the resulting inflation caused by government printing presses pumping out stimulus dollars. Why is anyone surprised that bright students who know they are being triple-gang-banged take to the streets in protest?

Driving south to Los Angeles on Interstate 5, I was surprised by the number of signs posted on farmland adjoining the highway reading "Congress Created Dust Bowl." One sign near the Coalinga turnoff was in the middle of a flock of sheep and lambs. A new cycle of life, new hope, I thought to myself, as I drove on.

Once I arrived in Southern California, it seemed like every freeway ramp from Ventura through Los Angeles and on into Orange County had opponents to the Obama health care bill protesting with placards and signs. One large and boisterous group of at least 100 people of all ages dressed in red, white and blue colonial garb that got my attention was dispersed at all four corners at the intersection of Carlota and El Toro in Orange County as I got off Interstate 5. Their colorful outfits, Pilgrim costumes, cowboy dress and "Kill the Bill" chants represented American democracy at work as the Founding Fathers intended – not the destructive, misleading un-American mud-slinging many of their Tea Party supporters were resorting to.

### *Demography Is Destiny*
I was back in America in May-June 2011. My travels across California, New York and New England, in the ongoing Arab Cleansing and post-Osama bin Laden era, was a refreshing reminder of why America's multicultural euphoric, creative and revolutionary youth will always be in the forefront of the cultural and political state of mind instilled by the Founding Fathers and emulated by all free-thinking people, no matter how repressive their career

political leaders and masters of the Washington money and lobbyist games are.

"How do you like Berkeley?" I asked Molly McBride, the daughter of good friends Kevin and Mary Catherine McBride, when I stopped to visit with them in Newbury Park. Molly had just finished her first semester there after two years at Moorpark College and had gotten straight A's. "I love it," was her quick reply.

"Any interesting protests like the 1960s these days?" I asked.

"Yeah, there sure are. Students taking over buildings. Cops on campus all the time to make sure some protest doesn't get out of control. But nothing like the '60s, I understand. Very civilized," Molly said, impersonating a proper British lady. "The other day I was walking down the street munching on a croissant and I came across all these cops watching a handful of protesters at Sproul Plaza. "What are they protesting?" I asked a cop.

"Hunger in Africa" he replied.

"Oh, I said as I looked at my croissant and decided to keep munching and walking."

America, like the rest of the world, is in the grip of three profound transformations: First, a far greater proportion of children are reaching adulthood; second, women have far fewer children, if any; and third, adults live far longer. These are happy developments: People are freed from fear of premature death; parents are freed from watching their children die young; and women are freed from endless childbirth. Such great changes inevitably will result in revolutionary upheavals and political changes. For example, in 2011, half of Egypt's population was under 25, while 36 percent were aged between 15 and 35. A lot of angry young idealistic and frustrated adults looking for work in order to support a family. The same, to varying degrees, holds true in most developing and developed countries, including America.

That 2011 trip came amid fast-rising gasoline prices – in some cases exceeding $5 a gallon, stalled cars on the roads with their drivers holding "Out of Gas" signs, the five biggest oil companies announcing record multibillion-dollar profits, as their CEOs testified before a Senate committee to justify the $4 billion in subsidies they receive. The fact is they don't deserve anything. Why is it that America cannot accept the truth and repeatedly spins it into glimmers of false hope that *We the Apathetic Maids* meekly accept? The only answer I could come up with is in Saul Bellow's words: "A great deal of intelligence can be invested in ignorance when the need for illusion is deep."

American and Chinese authors have continuously lamented people's ignorance.

"Whether past or present, a writer must focus on people's ignorance," wrote Xiao Hong, one of seven outstanding Chinese women chosen by the International Astronomical Union to name craters on Venus in 1991.

### What Change?

From pre-Shakespearean biblical times to modern Americana, writers have repeatedly tried to wake up *We the Apathetic Maids*. Author Samuel Langhorne Clemens is an American national treasure, wordsmith and archetypypal writer. Better known by his pseudonym Mark Twain, a name derived from the call for safe water from river boat pilots, he was born in 1835 and spent his childhood in the backwater of Hannibal, Missouri, in the decades before the American Civil War. After apprenticing as a printer, he worked briefly as a journalist before training as a steamboat pilot, a career interrupted by the outbreak of war in 1861. He served fleetingly in the Confederate army before deserting.

As did his Huck Finn character, the young Clemens "lit out for the territory" of the West, where Confederate forces were unlikely to pursue him, and sought his fortune in silver mining. When that failed, he returned to journalism.

Twain had a knack for registering contemporary social pressures in sharp-eyed aphorisms that weren't merely quotable but often well ahead of their time. His indictments of imperialism in *Following the Equator,* for example, read like post-colonialist mottos *avant la lettre:* "The very ink with which history is written is merely fluid prejudice;" "There are many humorous things in the world, among them the white man's notion that he is less savage than the other savages;" "Man is the only animal that blushes. Or needs to;" "Man is the only [creature] that kills for fun; he is the only one that kills in malice; the only one that kills for revenge ... He is the only creature that has a nasty mind."

Twain's social and political outrage, including startlingly contemporary denunciations of American military intervention abroad and condemnation of a society increasingly dominated by corrupt corporations, greedy capitalists and vested interests, are just as relevant today as when he penned them. Writing of gilded-edge monopolists and robber barons, Twain's prescience is remarkable: He denounces Jay Gould, the financier and speculator, for example, as "the mightiest disaster which has ever befallen this country." His description of bankers still holds true.

He was equally critical of American foreign policy, condemning its imperialist ventures in Cuba and the Philippines and calling its soldiers "uniformed assassins." He was proud of his affiliation with the "Mugwumps," a faction of Republicans who voted Democratic in the 1884 election in protest against the corruption of the Republican candidate. Derided as traitors in an age when party loyalty was at a premium, the Mugwumps were reform-minded independent voters. In this respect, they might be held to anticipate the Tea Party movement. Although Twain would have sympathized with the Tea Partiers' anti-tax, small-government agenda, he would have loathed their historical ignorance and susceptibility to manipulation by the same kind of corrupt corporate interests he was railing against.

One of the lessons he left America – which I take to heart and endorse – is that "travel is fatal to prejudice, bigotry, and narrow-mindedness." Twain himself had been an admitted bigot before becoming enlightened through travel.

### Jobless and Voiceless
The lack of jobs and the repeated sharp downturns in America's housing and stock markets were all anyone talked about during my May-June

2011 travels. The hockey and basketball championship finals were secondary. The economic recovery was faltering, Republican presidential aspirants were declaring their non-candidacies quicker and faster than the contenders, as the economy skidded back into a recession. The slowdown in manufacturing and consumer spending, as well as the nagging weakness in the depressed housing market, were exacting a toll Americans could ill afford.

More than 14 million Americans were unemployed. For every job opening, four people were still looking while many others had simply given up trying to find work. Those who did find a job got smaller paychecks, meaning they had less to spend, which made companies reluctant to hire more employees or give pay raises to those they have. It was a clear sign that quantitative easing had only a marginal effect in creating jobs.

In the meantime, during the same period, bank chiefs and other financiers got pay raises of at least 36 percent!

Those employed in the public sector as teachers, health professionals and social workers, mostly women, were being axed left and right by state and local government cutbacks. Public schools alone accounted for nearly 40 percent of the nation's public sector job losses in 2010.

From March 2010 to March 2011, women lost 214,000 public sector jobs, compared with a loss of 115,000 public jobs by men. Women also tend to be real estate agents, appraisers and home decorators and took a hit on those fronts as well as home sales continued to slump. Women working in the retail and hospitality sectors also took a hit as consumers cut back on discretionary spending. According to a report by the California Budget Project in the spring of 2011, the recession erased more than half the jobs that single mothers in California had gained from 1992 to 2002.

In California, like the rest of the country, blacks continued to be hard hit. Black unemployment hit 20 percent in March 2011, up 5 percent from the year before. They were among the last hired before the recession and the first to be let go in the downturn. The ranks of the unemployed include many young high school and college graduates unable to land their first job. Employers who have their pick of applicants see no reason to hire someone without a track record, especially those without much education. Unemployment among high school dropouts was hovering around 30 percent. Older workers losing their jobs faced the most dismal prospects.

What do the jobless have in common? Robert Reich, the former U.S. Secretary of Labor and professor of public policy at UC Berkeley, summed it up best. "They lack the political connections and organizations that would otherwise demand policies to spur job growth. There's no National Assn. of Unemployed People with a platoon of Washington lobbyists and a war chest of potential campaign contributions to get the attention of politicians."

Putting Americans back to work should be career politicians' top priority. They make it seem like it is with all their political sound bites and expensive campaign ads.

"A consensus has emerged among movers and shakers that nothing can or should be done about jobs. Instead of a determination to do something about the ongoing suffering and economic waste, one sees a proliferation of excuses for inaction, garbed in the language of wisdom and responsibility," columnist Paul Krugman astutely observed. "So someone needs to say the obvious: Inventing reasons not to put the unemployed back to work is neither wise nor responsible. It is, instead, a grotesque abdication of responsibility," Krugman adds. I agree wholeheartedly.

"As I see it, policy makers are sinking into a condition of learned helplessness on the job issue: The more they fail to do anything about the problem, the more they convince themselves that there's nothing they could do. And those of us who know better should be doing all we can to break that vicious cycle," Krugman concludes in a column aptly titled "Against Learned Helplessness."

Is it any wonder there are so many angry citizens ready to revolt? Used to be a person could trade a high school diploma for a job on the assembly line and provide his family a comfortable life. With those opportunities gone, many Americans, especially Anglos, blame illegal immigrants as the most compelling reason for "what went wrong."

What is wrong with the proposal Obama made in 2010 to give a $5,000 tax credit for every net new worker that a business hired? The credit was aimed at the economy's main problem – jobs – and its annual cost was to be a mere $35 billion, easily offset by longer term cuts to military programs. The proposal got killed in the Republican Congress.

*Stagflation*

Traveling across America in the late spring-early summer of 2011, there was no doubt in my mind that stagflation was blanketing America with a vengeance every time I pulled into a gas station and had to pay close to $5 a gallon. Stagflation is an ugly situation that fuses persistent high inflation combined with high unemployment and stagnant demand in the economy. Living in America today is nearly twice as expensive as when Obama took office in January 2009. America has not experienced stagflation since the bad old days of the 1970s.

Although many forces buffet the U.S. economy, the near-zero interest rate policy of the Federal Reserve was the prime contributor to the latest bout of stagflation. Most of the world has been on a dollar standard. It is used for invoicing both imports and exports, especially in emerging markets. It is also the intermediary currency used by banks for clearing international payments, and the intervention currency used by governments. To avoid conflict in targeting exchange rates, the rule of the game is that the U.S. remains passive without an exchange-rate objective of its own.

Not having an exchange-rate constraint, the Fed can conduct a more independent monetary policy than other central banks. How it chooses to exercise this independence is crucial to the stability of the international monetary system as a whole. For more than two years since the crash of 2008, the Fed had chosen to keep short-term interest rates on dollar assets close to zero and in 2010-2011 applied downward pressure on long-term rates through the so-called quantitative easing measures to increase purchases of Treasury bonds. The result has been a flood of hot money to emerging markets, particularly in Asia and Latin America, where interest rates are much higher.

Wanting to avoid sharp appreciations of their currencies and the resultant losses in international competitiveness, many Asian and Latin American central banks intervened to buy dollars with domestic base monies and lost monetary control. This caused a surge in consumer price index inflation of more than 5 percent in major emerging markets such as China, Brazil and Indonesia, with the dollar prices of primary commodities rising more than 40 percent worldwide during 2010-2011. So the proximate cause of the rise in U.S. prices is inflation in emerging markets, but its true origin is in Washington.

"The stagflation of the 1970s was brought on by unduly easy U.S. monetary policy in conjunction with attempts to 'talk' the dollar down, leading to massive outflows of hot money that destabilized the monetary systems of America's trading partners. Although today's stagflation is not identical, the similarities are striking," wrote Professor Ronald McKinnon, a senior fellow at the Stanford Institution for Economic Policy Research, in a column in *The Wall Street Journal*.

### *Creative and Broke*

America, the country the Founding Fathers created in the 18th century, was the most creative, innovative, entrepreneurial commercial and political nation on earth through the 1960s. Its political and economic decline began in the 1970s when the country's Vietnam War and reliance on imported Middle East oil became addictions the U.S. dollar could no longer support or back with gold.

Today, many Americans are no better off than their brothers and sisters in China and the Third World. That is because of the economic, military and political quagmire that its undemocratic two-party system has wrought. Partisan Washington totalitarian leaderships' preoccupation with retaining power and their political careers and party at any cost – and *We the Apathetic Maids* be damned. An expense and strategy that Wall Street bankers, capitalists and the military-industrial Congress are willing to continue bankrolling to ensure their entrenched career-minded team players perpetuate the gravy train they are riding – with a total disregard and disrespect for the Founding Fathers' ideals and principles.

It is up to *We the Maids* – the People – to sweep out the career politicians and their bankers – and again sweep in the Founding Fathers' lofty ideals to restore the constitutional cornerstones and pillars that made America great.

America's bloated Banana Republic scale and scope of government deficits, deadlocks, bureaucracy, failed public service and institutions, broken infrastructure, and nonexistent education dictated by career politicians and mandated by their financial backers instead of citizen taxpayers – We the People, the multicultural people – will be reclaimed because of Americans' humourous, upbeat, positive and constructive attitude. I was reminded of this during a rush-hour commuter train ride from New York's Grand Central station to Old Greenwich where I was staying. I was standing at the end of a crowded car leaning against the wall minding my own business and observing people when I was approached by a group of seven rather tough-looking African-Americans in their 20s, who got on at Larchmont and were making their way through the cars to the back. "Hey man, how many stops to Stamford?" one asked me.

"About a half dozen," I responded to their hilarious laughter. "What's so funny?" I asked. "You dude, that's a good answer," said their apparent leader to an outburt of more laughter and high-fiving from the group and nearby passengers. "Nice rap" it was. The mix of New England, New York, Asian and Latino accents and laughter from the passengers, young and old, on the jam-packed train was a refreshing reminder of what America is: a multicultural, interracial and interlocal country of people interacting as we all laugh at and with each other as we try to understand each other as we build a better life, country, world and future.

### Riding the Rails
Riding Amtrak's Vermonter to and from New York's Penn Station to Brattleboro, Vermont, in 2010, through Connecticut, Massachusetts and Vermont, the states America's Founding Fathers traveled through on horseback, cobbling together the ideals of the American Republic, in the wake of the passage of Obama's health care bill in the spring of 2010, I couldn't help wonder what they would think of the bitter partisan divide in America today. A country where not one congressional member of the Republican Party voted for the bill in the House of Representatives or the Senate. A partisan divide that makes the Grand Canyon look like a pothole on the Washington Beltway.

Riding the train alongside and over the meandering Connecticut River from Connecticut to Vermont, passing vacant and graffiti-littered buildings, junked cars, looking at the loving couples and broods of ducks and other waterfowl cruise by and enjoy themselves, people fishing and just enjoying the day in the calmer sections of the river, as children played happily in backyards and their fathers chopped wood, my faith in what made America great was restored and I had no doubt that its constitutional foundation and ideals are still in place and can be revitalized.

The train stopped at Palmer, Massachusetts – the state where the Democrats lost Ted Kennedy's safe Democratic seat to Republican Scott Brown – to re-orient itself from going west to east and change tracks so that it could continue north again. I couldn't help but chuckle to myself when I overheard the server in the café car where I was eating a late lunch tell the conductor that he was applying for a position on another route because he needed an "attitude adjustment." Just what America, China and the world need, I thought to myself as the train was steered onto the right track heading north.

Brattleboro is the closest train station to Winchester, New Hampshire, where I went to visit longtime friends Mark Tigan and his wife Laurie. Meeting some of their friends in New Hampshire, the state where the starter's gun is fired to launch the primary election season for the U.S. presidency, I found myself wondering why the Founding Fathers' New England states can't take the initiative to get America fired up again – back to the country's founding constitutional principles. Maybe they will.

### Coffee, Tea or Revolt?

What fascinated and absolutely captivated me during my fall 2010 visit to America during the primary season was the emergence of the anti-establishment tea and coffee party movements and their vocal disgust and active revolt at the political process, system, expanding government, rising taxes and the career politicians and bureaucrats for their lack of adherence to the Constitution, who were enriching themselves and their Wall Street sponsors at the expense of America's founding principles and taxpayers. Career politicians are not what the Founding Fathers had in mind for America.

The volatile 2010 midterm election brought out angry voters willing to punish career politicians, Democrats and Republicans alike. The anti-incumbent wave went beyond anger at the Democrats, Republicans, left, right, conservative or liberal. Voters were angry at every Washington career politician and their Wall Street corporate influence peddlers who have hijacked the system and created a corporate welfare state at the expense of hard-working taxpayers.

The Tea Party is the new phenom on the U.S. political landscape. It concluded the primary season with eight "citizen" Senate nominations and 33 candidates running in congressional districts, shocking not only the Democratic and Republican establishments, but the political pundits, who again got it wrong, misreading the anger and revolt brewing in America leading up to the country's Third Revolution.

### *"Man-up" Politics*

On September 15, the morning after the primary season elections and the "stunning" upset in the Delaware Republican primary by Tea Party candidate Christine O'Donnell against former Delaware governor and congressman Mike Castle – a direct descendant of one of America's Founding Fathers, the great-great-great-great-great grandson of Benjamin Franklin – I was driving to Las Vegas to attend the Super Zoo pet care convention.

I was traveling with Arnie Costell, inventor of Watson's Bottoms Up Leash for senior dogs. Arnie had been a pitcher for the New York Yankees from 1973 to 1983. Arnie is a 6 foot 3 giant teddy bear of a man who has a fear of flying. He is very animated, passionate and expressive, especially when it comes to animals, women, politics and the Tea Party movement that he supports. It made for an amusing political debate during our drive. He is a devoted fan of all Fox network talk show hosts and calls CNN the "Communist News Network."

"Watch it buddy, you are in Tea Party country here in Nevada, where we are going to kick that Harry Reid's ass out of Washington, and you don't want me to do the same to you out here in the desert," Arnie said in response to my comment that the Tea Party Express tactics in winning elections were no different than those of the Democrats and Republicans.

"The Tea Party is not winning these elections only because of its grass roots people-powered support, although granted it is a contributing factor. It's winning the same old-fashioned way the Democrats and Republicans do," I said of the string of Republican primary surprises that Arnie was attributing to people-power. "It's lots of money from billionaire and millionaire backers who continuously hijack the system by stoking fear, political attack ads and dirty politics that are not only divisive for the Republicans but for the country," I continued as we argued about the capabilities and qualifications of Tea Partiers Sharron Angle and Christine O'Donnell to serve in the Senate.

The Silver State senatorial race between Reid and Angle was a nail-biting "man-up" showdown, the nastiest and highest-profile Senate race that epitomized two of the strongest political trends of the 2010 election year: anger against incumbents and the vulnerabilities of the Tea Party candidates.

"Hey, remember, I'm the guy who rode his horse in 2005 on the streets of L.A. dressed as Paul Revere protesting against big government, big oil and excessive taxes," I said as Arnie continued to attack my "liberal" leanings. "I've been writing, saying and protesting against career politicians and big government since you've been playing ball," I continued as I shored up my barricades in the face of Arnie's southpaw onslaught and challenged his notions and definitions of liberal and conservative. "We are all Americans with overlapping and cross-pollinated 'liberal' and 'conservative' beliefs, not two Americas made of liberals and conservatives," I continued as Arnie cut me off.

"I may be left-handed but I'm always right," he said, a common response from Arnie when he disagrees. His license plate is 1STHPAW. After a while it sounded like a broken record.

"What do you have in common with people who advocate abstinence, are opposed to same-sex marriage, oppose abortion, and oppose the exclusion of religion from the public square – a cornerstone of the Constitution that the Founding Fathers insisted upon – and in fact don't have a clue what the Founding Fathers represented or the fact that some of them did not believe in Christ or the Trinity?" I asked him. "Witches, Nazis, American history and religious ignoramuses, homophobes and here in Nevada, Sharron Angle has raised the prospect of '2nd Amendment remedies' and talked about young rape victims making 'a lemon situation into lemonade' in support of her argument in opposition to abortion under any circumstances, even incest."

I proceeded to give Arnie my abbreviated U.S. History 101. Thomas Jefferson made Senator John Edwards look like a choir boy. I elaborated on his sexual escapades in *Custom Maid Spin*. Jefferson denied that Jesus was the son of God. While he was at it, Jefferson also rejected as self-evidently absurd the Trinity, the Virgin Birth and the Resurrection.

Jefferson was not an atheist, as his enemies in the election of 1800 claimed. He believed in the Creator whom he invoked in the Declaration of Independence and whom he thought had brought the natural universe into being. By his own lights he thought himself a true Christian, an admirer of the moral teachings of the Nazarene. It had been, he argued, generations of the clergy who had perverted the simple humanity of Jesus the reformer, turned him in to a messiah, and invented the myth that he had died to redeem mankind's sins. Hence Jefferson's absolute determination never to admit religion into the institutions of the public realm.

So the philosopher-president whose aversion to overbearing government makes him a Tea Party patriarch was also a man who thought the Immaculate Conception a fable. "But then real history is like that – full of knotty contradictions, its cast list of heroes, especially American heroes, majestic in their complicated imperfections," says Simon Schama, a professor of history at Columbia University.

As one of Jefferson's favorite books, Gibbon's *Decline and Fall of the Roman Empire*, so luminously argued, there is no surer sign of a country's cultural and political decay than an obtuse blindness to its unmistakable beginnings.

Facts, as John Adams insisted when defending British redcoats after the Boston Massacre, "are stubborn things."

Taken aback, and after thinking about it for a moment, much to my surprise. Arnie agreed.

"You know, Peter," he began slowly, uncharacteristically. His answer was thoughtful, quiet and polite. "I guess you have a point and I have to hand it to you. I don't agree with their positions on many personal values and really only agree with their positions on big government and the Euro-socialization of America."

What really got him was when I told him that the Tea Party doesn't even own the domain name teaparty.com. It is owned by a Canadian rock band whose last hit was in the 1990s. In anticipation of traffic from supporters of the political movement, the band's website proclaims: "No Politics ... Just Rock and Roll."

Arnie and I concluded that we actually could agree on many, if not most issues, liberal and conservative, once we dropped the political polemic bombast and listened to what the other had to say. Not much choice on a six-hour drive – and not much different than it is for most Americans.

We share an artistic bent, Arnie not only on the field of dreams, but on canvas as well, myself as a writer, and both of us as lovers of music and water who live on the ocean's edge, fellow Aquarians. Arnie's seascapes, dark and foreboding with their angry clouds, solitary boats, fishermen and menacing waves in the blue ocean wilderness, with its once-vast resources being depleted, metaphorically capture the state of America.

"The oceans are fished out," he is fond of saying. And after a recent salmon-fishing trip, I couldn't agree more. It underscored the dark clouds in his paintings.

Arnie goes to the beach every day, where he would always swim in the salty waters. That is, until July 25, 2006, when he had a near-death experience as a 40-foot rogue wave – a mini tsunami – hit the Los Angeles coastline, kicked up by an earthquake that had hit far-away New Zealand. It's not an uncommon occurrence. The wave carried him 200 feet out, stripped him of his swimsuit and the crystal he had worn for 20 years, before dumping him naked on the beach.

"Hey," he says, "at least I'm still alive."

He still gets to the beach every day. I can relate because I too love to be near the ocean. Both of us have enjoyed fishing since boyhood. Arnie's grandparents were in the fishing boat rental business in New York's Hamptons on the far eastern end of Long Island. Arnie spent his young summers there, fishing and working. For me it was Cyprus, where I grew up and was schooled by the local Greek and Turk fishermen.

Learning that Arnie, the macho pitcher, was also a sensitive artist was a surprise that also had a practical benefit: It gave a bigger left hook.

I learned that Arnie also is devoutly religious. Maybe his near-death experience in that rogue wave had something to do with it, I thought to myself. Religion and prayer are dear to him, and he practices it daily. He is a solitary religious person who practices Judaism and reads daily from the same Bible he was given at his bar mitzvah in 1965. It is autographed by members of his temple's Women's Club.

Arnie, along with some of the former politicians he plays ball with, are a dying breed of Americans. People from different and competing parties, gang bangers from competing gangs, African-American, Asian and Latino. Their passion is America's pastime – baseball. "I just checked out on the radar at 95," he said referring to miles per hour in response to my query as to how he felt after a recent hip operation.

His teammates and league mates include former Chicago Seven defendant and California State Senator Tom Hayden; Mel Levine, former Assemblyman and Congressman; Rick Garcia, a former sportscaster who is now an anchorman; Charlie Sheen, the actor, and one of J. Lo's husbands. One of his favorite team names that got us both laughing again was the Compton Tar Babies. For those who don't get it, Compton is in predominantly black South-Central L.A.

"They were bad ballplayers, as in terrible and not baaad as in good," said Arnie when we stopped laughing. "Not of the caliber of a Darryl Strawberry, Eddie Murray or Tony Guinn that came from the same hood," he added.

"Let's not talk about the vatos, the Latinos in East L.A. who were tougher and always ready for a fight."

"The beauty of baseball is that it ties everyone up, binds people of all political and religious beliefs in a common objective – to win together," Arnie says.

Just as he wants people to respect the game, he wants them to adhere to the letter and spirit of the Founding Fathers' Constitution and the powers it has vested in the people of America, not their self-serving career politicians and bureaucratic enforcers.

### *Money Talks, Not People*
The Tea Party movement's primary concern, like all political alliances, is winning and retaining power and it will do so at any cost and use any proven political tools. The only difference is that the Tea Party openly declares it wants to restore America's founding principles and rejects the Washington Beltway establishment and its authority. The Tea Party movement is the advance team – avant political guard – on the front lines of the Third American Revolution.

The Tea Party Express began as a PAC called Our Country Deserves Better that political operative Sal Russo, a long-time conservative Republican adman, and former California Assemblyman Howard Kaloogian formed in 2008. They were frustrated that Senator John McCain wasn't drawing enough contrast with Obama during the 2008 presidential campaign. They rebranded the PAC after CNBC's Rick Santelli made his famous "tea party" remarks on the air in February 2009 that spurred the conservative protest movement.

Christine O'Donnell, notwithstanding her refreshing frank wackiness and "checkered background," is on the Tea Party frontline carrying the banner of big business, like her sister Sarah, who told Karl Rove to "buck up" after he referred to O'Donnell's "checkered background." It doesn't matter to the party movers and shakers if O'Donnell loses, as long as she sweeps some like-minded people into office elsewhere in the country on her tea leaves.

Frank Rich, a columnist for *The New York Times,* wrote, "Whatever her other talents, she's more than willing to play the role of the useful idiot for her party and give populist cover to the billionaires and corporate interests that have been steadily annexing the Tea Party movement and busily plotting to cash in their chips if the GOP prevails."

Rich adds that by latching on to O'Donnell's growing presence, the establishment can claim it represents struggling middle-class Tea Partiers rather than Wall Street potentates and corporate titans. The more she is villified, the bigger star she becomes and can reinforce the Tea Party's narrative as a "spontaneous and quite anarchic movement" populated by everyday folk upset by big government and the massive federal deficit. This airbrushed take has had a surprisingly long life, even in some of the nonpartisan press. In September 2010, the influential *National Journal* delivered a breathless report on how the Tea Party functions as a "headless" movement where "no one gives orders." To prove the point, a leader of the headless Tea Party Patriots declared that "75 percent of the group's fundraising comes from small donations, $20 or less."

In fact, local chapters of Tea Party Patriots routinely received early training and support from FreedomWorks, the moneyed outfit run by former Republican House majority leader and corporate lobbyist Dick Armey. FreedomWorks is itself a spinoff from Citizens for a Sound Economy, a pseudo-grassroots group whose links to the billionaire Koch brothers are well known. The same headless person who bragged to the *National Journal* about all those small donations a week later announced a $1 million gift from a man she would identify only as an entrepreneur. The donor's hidden identity speaks even louder than the size of the check. As long as we don't know who he is, we won't know what orders he's giving either.

Big money rains down on the "bottom up" Tea Party insurgency through phantom front organizations such as Americans for Prosperity and Americans for Job Security that exploit legal loopholes to keep their sugar daddies' names secret. Reporters at *The New York Times* and *Washington Post* have made strides in explaining how the game works – $300 million worth of stealth funding in support of GOP candidates and $100 million for Democratic candidates – but we still don't know the identities of most of those anonymous donors.

What we do know is that billionaire brothers David and Charles Koch and their political network meet twice a year to plan and expand their efforts "to review strategies for combating the multitude of public policies that threaten to destroy America as we know it."

The invitation to their January 2011 get-together in the Palm Springs area at the Rancho Las Palmas Resort and Spa opened with a grand call to action: "If not us, who? If not now, when?"

The Koch brothers have a fortune of $35 billion, and run the second-largest private company in America, Koch Industries, with an annual turnover of $100 billion. They throw money at conservative think tanks and campaigns that have spread doubts about climate change, while the Koch oil and coal interests have been named among the top 10 air polluters in America.

The Kochs seek to cultivate Americans' growing concern about the growth of government and its regulatory assault on the energy and health care sectors and make donations to higher education and philanthropic organizations to advance the Koch agenda. At a June 2010 gathering at the St. Regis Resort in Aspen, Colorado, that agenda was expressed as "a vision of how we can retain the moral high ground and make the new case for liberty and smaller government that appeals to all Americans, rich and poor."

The audience of corporate titans listened to a presentation on "microtargeting" to identify like-minded voters, as well as a discussion about voter mobilization featuring Tim Phillips of Americans for Prosperity, the political action committee founded by the Kochs in 2004, which campaigned against the Obamacare legislation and is helping Tea Party groups set up get-out-the-vote operations.

Impressed by the Koch efforts for the midterms, the invitation cover letter to the January 2011 soire extolled the Aspen participants "committed to an unprecedented level of support." They dined under the stars at the top of the gondola run on Aspen Mountain and listened to Glenn Beck. The attendees included some of America's wealthiest families and biggest names in finance, private equity and hedge funds, media, entertainment, multi-level marketing, energy and construction executives. The group also included longtime Republican donors and officials. Previous guests included Supreme Court judges, governors, senators and congressmen, all conservative Republicans, of course.

The January 2011 soire was the first one to encounter opposition. The anti-Koch gathering was staged down the road from Rancho Mirage. Its panel discussions and rally highlighted the pernicious impact of the Kochs on democracy. Among the panelists was Robert Reich, labor secretary under Bill Clinton. He said the Kochs represented a perfect storm that was battering American democracy.

"This is the worst I've seen it in my lifetime. In the late 19th century, robber barons would deposit bags of silver and gold on the desks of legislators. We have progressed significantly since then, but once again, big business is engaging in politics," Reich said.

The reach of corporate political activists personified by the Kochs was extended by Citizens United in a landmark ruling by the Supreme Court in January 2010 that again opened the door to unlimited corporate spending on political campaigns for the first time since 1947. The Koch brothers have made good use of the ruling. Americans for Prosperity, the Tea Party-aligned group founded and funded by the Kochs, has put its own spending at $45 million.

Common Cause, a lobby group in the forefront of the opposition to the Kochs' political activities, called on the U.S. attorney general to investigate a possible conflict of interest. It pointed out that two Supreme Court judges

– Clarence Thomas and Antonin Scalia – had taken part in strategy sessions at a previous Koch gathering. Both voted in favor of lifting the ban on corporate political spending. They should have recused themselves.

From what we do know, it's clear some Tea Party groups and candidates are financed directly and indirectly not just by the Kochs but by a coterie of fellow billionaires like Robert Rowling and Trevor Rees-Jones. Even their largess may be dwarfed by Rupert Murdoch and his News Corp., whose known multi-million cash contributions are dwarfed by the avalanche of free promotion they provide Tea Party candidates and personalities daily at corporate-owned Fox and *The Wall Street Journal*.

Granted these corporate contributors may share the Tea Party minions' antipathy toward President Obama; however, their economic interests hardly overlap. The rank and file Tea Partiers say they oppose government spending and deficits. The billionaires have no problem with federal spending as long as the pork is corporate pork. They also don't mind deficits as long as they get their outsize cut of the red ink – $3.8 trillion worth if all the Bush tax cuts are made permanent. But while these billionaires' selfish interests are in conflict with the Tea Party agenda, they are in complete sync with the Republican leadership and their new "Pledge to America" that promises the $3.8 trillion addition to the deficit and says nothing about serious budget cuts or governmental reforms.

A conservative civil war started, the first shots of which were fired as soon as President Obama had taken his oath of office. What a concept. Conservatives who have had enough of "RINOs" – Republicans in Name Only." The "Limbaugh Laws" replaced the "Buckley Rule" that held conservatives should vote for the most rightward electable candidate. "Limbaugh Laws" hold that when the country is in open revolt against liberalism and Republicans are riding an election wave, you should vote conservative. Is it any wonder the Republicans have reluctantly embraced the Tea Party movement, even though they disagree on many issues?

Corporate America and wealthy individuals with a mercenary economic interest in influencing the outcome of the midterm election dished out gargantuan amounts of money not seen in generations.

This process was facilitated by the Supreme Court and Congress. The high court's 5-4 decision in *Citizens United v. Federal Election Commission*, which overturned provisions of the bipartisan McCain-Feingold campaign finance act that prohibited corporations and unions from making supposedly independent, third-party expenditures to influence the outcome of election contests.

The Supreme Court effectively crippled American democracy by making politics and the elections that determine the winners a game limited to those with money, lots of it, and not *We the Apathetic Maids*. What really amazed me was how corrupt, unchecked and imbalanced the country's checks and balance referee – the Supreme Court – had become. This was best evidenced by the active role Justice Clarence Thomas's wife played in conservative causes and legislation her husband had to pass judgment on without anyone blinking an eye. Virginia Thomas was not only a conservative activist, but just as nutty as some of the Tea Party candidates – especially with her call to Anita Hall asking her to apologize for the testimony she gave against Clarence Thomas at his confirmation hearings in October 1991.

Congress expedited and greased the corporate money machine wheels by amending the Tax Code to allow the creation of 501(c) (4) political action committees to which donors can contribute anonymously. Such organizations are supposed to make less than half of their expenditures for political purposes. But, because the definition of "educational" activity is debatable, organizations are able to lump a lot of political ads under that moniker.

As if these legal financial plumbings weren't enough, a federal judge in Virginia ruled in May 2011 that a century-old law banning contributions by corporations was unconstitutional and a violation of corporations' right to freedom of speech.

The opportunity to spend limitlessly and secretly has created many groups flush with millions of dollars from unknown sources spending at an unprecedented rate, mostly on behalf of Republicans. One of the most active of these new groups is Crossroads GPS, a political action committee operated by GOP strategist Karl Rove and funded mainly from secret sources.

The architect of political fund raising in America was 19th-century Ohio financier Mark Hanna. He pulled together big money contributions to create the truly modern national campaign on behalf of William McKinley's successful presidential campaign in 1896. Hanna once remarked: "There are two things that are important in politics. The first is money and I can't remember what the second is."

"Money and more money by political operatives milking the system and enriching themselves in the process from the billionaire and corporate powers that be, it's business as usual that is bringing about political surprises but no real change," I said, countering Arnie's blistering tirade as I turned up the volume on the radio to drown him out and listen to the lyrics of Josh Thompson's *Way Out Here*. Looking at the stark desert landscape dotted with cacti and the occasional trailer and empty horse corrals in the middle of nowhere, my mind drifted to America's cowboy culture, code and ethics that opened up the West. I pondered how the nation had gotten so far off track from the cowboy ethic and the constitutional principles of the Founding Fathers.

The blended cowboy-Constitution seed was sown a couple of weeks later when Robert Burck, known as the Naked Cowboy, announced his intention in Times Square "to lead the Tea Party to the office of the presidency" in 2012. The Naked Cowboy's manger, iconic Times Square, where an estimated 1.7 million people pass through every day, happened also to be serving as China's media blitz center with a 50-meter outdoor video display called "China Experience" to showcase a taste of real China to boost its image in the U.S.

The looped 1-minute promotional videos featuring some of China's most famous faces as well as ordinary citizens, shown 15 times an hour to coincide with President Hu Jintao's visit to the U.S. in January 2011, was just another media savvy campaign by China to ingratiate itself to Americans.

The "new era" image of China's campaign is to represent the optimistic, upwardly mobile spirit of contemporary China in an effort to undo some of the damage inflicted by the "China bashing" ads run roughly two months earlier during the midterm U.S. elections. The featured celebrities were meant to present an image of the Chinese as "wise, beautiful, courageous, talented and wealthy," *Xinhua* reported.

The extreme conservative constituency of the Tea Party is no different than that of the extreme right of Republican Party, formerly known as the John Birch Society. There were always, and always will be, extreme conservatives who not only sip hot brews but actually go out and take to the political barricades and ballot box – as opposed to their "liberal" café lattistas – who spout criticism of the way things are and then stay home on Election Day.

That is exactly what Tea Party revolutionaries did when their candidate Dave Brat defeated Rep. Eric Cantor, the second-ranking Republican in the House of Representatives in the June 2014 Virginia primary.

### *What Are the Solutions?*

"Besides complaining and attacking the career politicians, what solutions are your fellow tea brewmeisters offering?" I asked Arnie as we continued our political repartee. "Nada, nothing! All they do is bitch and attack. What is their plan to restore America's constitutional ideals? I haven't heard one credible solution, have you?"

"They quietly put up with the Bush-Cheney Republican deficit spending spree and wars in Iraq and Afghanistan, but now attack the Obama-Pelosi-Reid Democratic stimulus, healthcare program, but have not made one credible suggestion as to how they will grow the economy and restore America to its competitive global status," I said, refusing to let Arnie respond until I finished.

"Who and where is the chief brewmeister with real strong brews that are solutions for what ails America and will make it great again. Sarah Palin? She has no substance. She's just a flash in the political pan. A slow-playing one-hit-wonder creation of the 'lamestream media' as she herself says," I concluded as Arnie spurted out the words that had been swelling impatiently in his lungs.

"Screw you!" he blurted. "You're so smart with all your questions and answers – what is your solution? You? Maybe you should run for office."

"Not a bad idea. Maybe…," I said, pondering the thought.

"You know you are not the first person who has made that suggestion," I continued. "My longtime friend Sara Kinder, married to Mel Kinder, a prominent psychologist, has brought the idea up several times and constantly encourages me to run for office. In fact the last time she brought it up we were sharing a lovely dinner with our mutual friends Perla and Ami Karney, who endorsed the idea. Perla is the artistic director at Hillel at UCLA and Ami is a retired investment banker. Not a bad base to start with, is it?"

At the time, I was actually thinking about starting a new political movement that would truly embrace the Founding Fathers' principles. A centrist party that would not pander to any emotional extreme. The movement I now propose to launch is discussed at length in Chapter 5. "But on second thought, nah, it's not my cup of tea," I told Arnie.

"Cute. Funny. Hey, since you're so smart with all the answers, what do you have to say about Obama's proposal to tax aspirin?" Arnie asked as he turned down the radio and jolted me back into the moment.

"What are you talking about?" I asked.

"Figures you haven't heard, living in China. It's just another Obama tax, because aspirin is white and it works!"

### *Original Tea and Horse Trail*
When there was a break in our political banter, Arnie would often regale me with baseball stories and I reciprocated with China historical snippets or personal antidotes. One that received his undivided and uninterrupted attention was the historical tea trail in China that dates back more than 1,300 years. This trip, through Nevada, past trails once traveled by cowboys, brought the tea trail to mind.

The 5,000-kilometer tea trail started in Yunnan province and ended in the

Tibetan capital of Lhasa. The Yunnan stretch runs from Xishuangbanna, where people were drinking tea more than 3,000 years ago, to Zhongdian, which is surrounded by breathtaking snowcapped mountains. The trail runs down into India and Nepal before ending in Tibet.

The tea-horse trail was part of the Silk Road that spanned the tea heartland of China, through the Himalayas to Tibet, India, Nepal and on to the Middle East. The diverse exchange of political, economic and religious ideas and beliefs between the Han, Tibetan, Thai, Indian, Bai, African and Arab traders played a major historical role in the development of today's multi-cultural civilizations and tea-flowered-party revolutions around the world.

Horse trails in America and China all seem to head west – much like the cowboys, ranchers, miners, entrepreneurs, adventurers and outlaws in both countries have done for centuries. Whether it is U.S. bankers packaging subprime loans in California, Arizona and Nevada, selling Lehman mini-bonds in Hong Kong, or dodgy Chinese firms wanting to head west by going public in America, the pattern continues to blend the best and the worst that America and China have had on offer for each other over the years.

### Country in Hock

One of the things I like to do whenever I am in a gambling mecca such as Las Vegas is visit pawn shops. As a young lawyer, a new admittee to the California Bar, the law firm I went to work for represented auctioneers and pawnbrokers, two professions that taught me the fundamentals of the economy and gauging how it is really doing. If you really want to know how a community or country is doing, go talk to your local pawnbroker, something I do periodically to this day. They are the best source of information.

"Want to go check out some pawnshops for good deals if we have time?" I asked Arnie.

"Are you kidding me? Why would I go to a pawnshop?" Arnie responded, somewhat perturbed.

"You'll be amazed what great deals you can find there," I said. "Think about it, shmuck. Where else are you going to get a good deal on gold or silver watches, rings, coats. I have bought some phenomenal items in pawnshops at unbelievable prices."

"Makes sense now that I think about it," Arnie said sheepishly.

Pawnbrokers see and feel the erosion of the economy before the economists, bankers and politicians do. But who listens to pawnbrokers? I do, which is why I like to frequent them whenever I can. They are the loan brokers of last resort. That is the actual business they are in. They are personal property loan brokers who take all the items people hock as collateral for their loans. The loans can run for a few weeks or months. They are not cheap either. Their annual interest rate works out to anywhere from 50 percent to 250 percent, depending on the state. Maybe the career politicians in Washington should be talking to the National Pawnbroker Association at the next Pawn Expo for their next bailout and hock whatever assets they haven't already squandered.

Middle and upper-class Americans are using pawnshops to get by these days as well. Hocking items to get through to the next payday, much like the country as a whole.

### Occupy Wall Street
I caught up with Arnie again in Las Vegas in early 2012, at the height of the Republican presidential primary. We were both attending the Western Veterinary Conference, he as an exhibitor and I as an attendee. We naturally picked up where we left off on our political discussion about the Republican Party, its candidates for president, and how they were influenced by the Tea Party faction. But our conversation was dominated by the Occupy Wall Street movement that had emerged since we last met.

"Scumbags. Losers. Parasites on society. Socialists who want everything for nothing. Get a shower and a job is all I have to say to them," Arnie said in response to my question of what he thought about the new national and international movement.

"C'mon, Arnie. You can't be serious," I said, knowing he was. "You don't think they have a legitimate beef about politicians and bankers ripping the public off and you and I being part of the 99 percent? I even read an editorial opinion that your goddess of the Tea Party, Sarah Palin, wrote a couple of months ago in *The Wall Street Journal* lamenting how career politicians and their Wall Street cohorts were enriching themselves at the taxpayers' expense."

Mark Twain famously wrote, "There is no distinctly native American criminal class except Congress."

Much to my surprise, I agreed with most of what Palin wrote in her op-ed piece. She questioned how politicians who arrive in Washington, D.C. as men and women of modest means leave as millionaires. The answer is simple. By accepting sweetheart gifts of IPO stock from companies seeking to influence legislation, practicing insider trading with privileged government information, earmarking projects that benefit personal real estate holdings, and even subtly extorting campaign donations through the threat of legislation unfavorable to an industry. The list goes on and on and certainly gives legitimacy to the Occupy movement – not only in America but globally.

One of my favorite protests was in Tokyo's Roppongi nightclub district. It could have begun in Nihonbashi, home of the Tokyo Stock Exchange; or Nagatacho, Japan's Capitol Hill. Instead, activists chose the city's hedonistic Vegas-style melting pot of hipsters, strippers, gamblers, gangsters, expatriates and bankers. Not just any bankers – Goldman Sachs types who work in the swanky Roppongi Hills complex. Some of the signs carried by the hundreds of protestors read "No Greed," "Taxiderm the Rich" and "Stop Vampire Squids," a reference to Goldman Sachs, which was labeled a "great vampire squid wrapped around the face of humanity" in a 2009 article in *Rolling Stone* magazine. When this sentiment reaches egalitarian Japan, you know it has legs.

"Besides, Mr. Yankee New Yorker," I continued, "are you aware that this is not the first such protest of its kind in New York?" knowing full well he didn't. "There was a similar protest in 1874. The occupation of Tompkins

Square Park, after a national financial crisis. Then, like today, protestors were injured by the police trying to clear them out."

"They should be cleared out and hosed down, "Arnie said" they need a shower. Their campsite is a filthy health hazard and if they resist, what do you think will happen? Of course they'll get hurt."

A few weeks later, I was back in New York where I watched the opening scenes of the fifth season of *Mad Men*, set in 1966. It depicted the sort of knucklehead-racism at work at the time, when young men from the advertising firm dropped bags filled with water on protestors on the Madison Avenue sidewalk below. Wet and angry, several protestors came upstairs to demand to know who had dropped the water bombs. One protestor said in disgust, "And they call us savages."

Everything in the scene really happened, written almost verbatim from an article on page 1 of The Times on May 28, 1966. The article described more than 300 people picketing the Office of Economic Opportunity chanting "O-E-O, we've got the poverty, where's the dough?" Executives upstairs at Young & Rubicam, half a block from the building, shouted at the protestors, pitched water bombs that splashed demonstrators and hung signs saying, "If you want money, get yourself a job."

Funny and sad how little has changed in America today.

### Funny and Sad

Arnie is a frustrated comic who goes out of his way to get people to laugh, even if the audience is one person. On our way out of Vegas on our 2010 trip, we saw a big Hooters billboard which got Arnie going again.

"Hey, Peter, we all know that good-looking girls with big tits can get a job at Hooters. In your politically correct world, where does a well-endowed lady with one leg go to work?" he asked as I tried to get into the right lane to get onto the freeway back to L.A.

"I have no idea," I answered.

"IHOP you idiot," Arnie cried as we both burst out laughing.

"Contract From America," the Tea Party's pledge to America, and the Republican manifesto "Pledge to America" are pathetically funny because of their lack of substance. Empty words that contain no hint of solutions.

What was even funnier was the official Washington announcement in June 2009 that the recession was over. The National Bureau of Economic Research, a private panel of academic economists, said the recession lasted 18 months, from December 2007 to June 2009. Yeah right! What planet are they living on? The NBER is notably deliberate in its ridiculously funny pronouncements – it didn't call the start of the 2007-2009 recession until it had been under way for a year or the end of the 2001 recession until it had been over for 20 months.

No wonder middle America is upset. It is being ignored by the extremists on the right sipping tea and those on the left sipping lattes while government think tanks, like the government they serve, get everything wrong.

On our way back to Los Angeles from Vegas we decided to stop off in Yermo, California, for coffee and a meal at Peggy Sue's '50s-style diner, where Arnie took a picture of himself with a statute of Elvis that was next to our table – and sent it off to his friends on Facebook.

"This will blow their mind," he said as he chuckled and continued to devour the tuna melt we had both ordered along with the Susie-Q fries.

"Yeah, tell them you're drinking coffee," I said as he looked up ready to cuss me out, which he did. "What happened to your tea?"

The meal and coffee hit the spot, as did the music and pictures on the wall – mostly of celebrities who had eaten there on their way to or from Las Vegas.

Peggy Sue's opened in 1954 in the Calico Mountains of the Mojave Desert, about the time air-conditioning was helping turn politicians in Washington into the career office-holders that plague the country today. Air-conditioning meant that politicians weren't so eager to flee the heat and humidity of the capitol for their home states and instead could stay in town to cook up new taxes and be wined and dined on the lobbyists' dime.

Maybe it's time to pull the plug on those air-conditioners and return to the term limits envisioned by the Founding Fathers.

### The Postman and the Nutcracker

Returning to the relative cool of Los Angeles, I attended the opening event of the L.A. Opera season on September 23, the world premiere of *Il Postino (The Postman)*, starring 69-year-old Placido Domingo in the title role. I had been invited by Jacqui Brandwynne to join her, Stanley and Joyce Black, and Jacqueline Rosenberg at the premiere.

Talk about karma, coincidence and synchronicity, subjects I address at length in *Custom Maid Spin*. It was another September 23rd – in 1973 – when the great Chilean poet and Nobel laureate Pablo Neruda, portrayed by Domingo in *Il Postino*, died in Santiago at the age of 69.

Neruda died just 12 days after the fall of Chile's first democratically elected Marxist president, Salvador Allende, in a bloody coup led by General Augusto Pinochet on, of all days, September 11th. Suspicions have lingered that Neruda was killed by lethal injection before he could flee Pinochet's coup and be a powerful voice in exile. Pressure has been building to exhume his body to examine the cause of death. Allende reportedly killed himself that same day as the coup unfolded. Avowed Communist Neruda's exile in the years before Allende was elected was the inspiration for the award-winning romantically tinged 1944 Italian film *Il Postino*, as well as the opera.

What I loved in the movie and the opera was how Neruda explains to Mario, the postman, the concept of metaphors, the most versatile of rhetorical devices. As figures of speech, metaphor and simile express the unfamiliar in familiar terms; the difference is that simile uses *like* or *as* to get the comparison across. The metaphor offers more subtle opportunities for expression than the simile, whose code words alert us to its presence. Metaphors, which I use extensively in my writing, are a tool that helps us acquire self-knowledge.

The heavy-handed political campaigns and broken promises of the right-wing politician portrayed in *Il Postino* to bring water to the fishing village, to the dismay of the people, was a reminder of how little things have changed in America and China today.

Watching *The Nutcracker* ballet a couple of months later in Hong Kong, a few days before Christmas with my partner Pauline Taylor, I couldn't help flashing back to Nerudo's explanation of metaphors. *The Nutcracker* with Chinese characteristics – Chinese and Anglo dancers – with King Rat and his mice fighting the toy soldiers over the Nutcracker Prince as America and China wrangled over how to crack the North Korean nut and his prince who had lobbed shells into the South a few weeks earlier was surreal. The dream scene in *The Nutcracker* was a reality not only on the Korean Penninsula but in many countries around the world where America and China are in geopolitical mortal combat over the control of princes – and resources.

"So who is the King Rat in the ongoing conflict between America and China?" Pauline asked as we left the Cultural Center for a walk along the Kowloon waterfront to enjoy the visual feast of colorful Christmas lights adorning the skyscrapers across Victoria Harbor on Hong Kong Island on a rare crispy clear night as we tried to decide where to go for supper.

"Hmm, good question," I replied as I tried to figure out the answer when we stopped at an open spot along the crowded waterfront rail to take in the sights and sounds of barges and boats chugging along the busy waterway with the city's skyline as a backdrop. "They are both ratty and both can be felled as the Nutcracker Prince was, or killed politically and economically as King Rat was," I said with some hesitation. "Both are vulnerable to each other and both the American Dream and the Communist Dream are dead like King Rat.

"The political parties in America, Democrats and Republicans, and the Communist Party in China are the dead King Rats, killed by the people because of their broken promises. The problem is, the citizens of both countries haven't realized that they can enjoy an enchanted political adventure like Clara and the Nutcracker Prince did when Herr Drosselmeyer magically saved the day by bringing them to the Ice Palace where they were entertained by the dancers from exotic lands. Like Lucille Ball said in the movie *Auntie Mame*, 'Life is a banquet and most poor sons of bitches are starving,' and so am I right now," I said as we decided to head for the coffee shop at the Intercontinental Hotel and get a waterfront table to continue enjoying the view and conversation.

### Quitting Time
Jacqui Brandwynne had served on the board of directors of the L.A. Opera for more than 20 years and recently resigned; Joyce served on the board as well but had taken a leave of absence. "A polite way to resign," she said. Her remark surprised me, as Joyce is not known for her political politeness or correctness. Jacqueline was still on the board but thinking of resigning. Apparently, many board members were either resigning or thinking of doing so.

"Why so many resignations?" I asked Joyce as we milled around in the Founders Room during intermission as they socialized with other founders.

"They don't do anything. You go to one gala dinner a year, get good seats for the season and for this I have to pay $50,000?" Joyce said. "There are better charitable causes for our money."

In fact, Joyce and Stanley Black are very charitable.

"They could and should be doing several events a year at members' homes," Jacqui added.

"Look around you –the average age of these alta kackers (old farts) is over 100," Joyce said. "They're lucky to make it out of bed in the morning to one event a year and you think they'll make it to more? But you're right, they should be doing more."

The resignations of the L.A. Opera board members brought to mind the resignation from politics of the many U.S. congressmen and senators who decided not to seek re-election in 2010. The nasty political environment and culture of Washington had permeated and destroyed not only the political fabric of the Beltway, but the economic, cultural and charitable fabric of society in America. The L.A. Opera is just one example. Discussing the metaphor with Joyce, I was taken aback by her direct attack and description of America's political system.

"We live in a constipated country," she said. Before I could ask her to elaborate, "They are all full of shit," she declared as we both laughed and headed back to our seats.

The early 2010 decisions of several entrenched career U.S. senators to retire and not seek re-election were a dramatic reminder of how radically the political landscape in America had changed in the 12 months since President Obama took office. The politics of hope had given way to the politics of unmanageable vitriolic anger.

The news that Senators Chris Dodd, Byron Dorgan and Evan Bayh were dropping out was not only a confirmation of how polarized American democracy has become, but how powerful the anti-establishment movement, best represented by the Tea Party, has become. No wonder everyone is quitting on all American fronts.

Indiana Senator Bayh's retirement announcement caught my attention more than most that year. That was because I had met his father, Senator Birch Bayh, on more than one occasion in the 1970s during my stint on the Finance Council of the Democratic National Committee. One particular event that comes to mind is an afternoon cocktail fundraiser in Beverly Hills. I was taken aback at the time by the senator's frankness in discussing what it would take to change the party and the system. As a newcomer, he was giving me sound fatherly advice that clearly still echoed with his son Evan.

Short-listed for the vice presidential slot on the 2008 Obama ticket, Evan Bayh said the Senate had become too divided.

"I value my independence," he said. "I'm not motivated by strident partisanship or ideology."

He referred to the way the Senate did business as "brain-dead." This was at the height of the Obama health care legislation debates when Democrats and Republicans voted straight-up-and-down along party lines. Since 75 percent of Americans disapprove of the job Congress is doing, Bayh became an editorial page and evening news hero.

The upcoming 2014 U.S. Senate election is going to take place with several Senate dropouts not seeking re-election because of the oppressive partisanship. Democrats Tom Harkin of Iowa, Frank R. Lautenberg of New Jersey and John D. Rockefeller IV of West Virginia are heading for the exits along with Republicans Saxby Chamblis of Georgia and first-termer Mike Johanns from Nebraska.

I can understand long-serving old-timer D.C. career politicians quitting because of the partisan gridlock, but I was surprised to see a first-term newly elected conservative Republican join the exodus. Johanns, a soft-spoken former Nebraska governor and agricultural secretary in the George W. Bush administration, was not on any Democratic target list. But it wouldn't surprise me if he was on a Republican primary challenge hit list because in 2012 he angrily criticized conservative groups that tried to step in and influence the Senate election in Nebraska. He was also a member of the "Gang of Eight" who tried to broker a bipartisan accord on deficit spending that failed.

I am glad to see former Senators Olympia Snowe, R-Maine, and former Representative Dan Glickman, D-Kan., co-chair the new Commission on Political Reform, whose members include former Senators Tom Daschle, Trent Lott and Dirk Kempthorne. The commission held a "National Conversation on America Unity" around the country that started in March 2013 at the Ronald Reagan Presidential Foundation and Library in California, and invited *We the Apathetic Maids* across the nation to join the dialogue online. They want to start a long overdue national exercise that hopefully will unite the country, delightful if they do, but doubtful. I believe it is a needed but futile exercise that will fail because the partisan divide, not only in America and China, but across the globe, is too wide.

Their effort is to be applauded because, as George Washington warned in his farewell address, "The alternate domination of one faction over another, sharpened by the spirit of revenge ... is itself a frightful despotism."

Our Founding Fathers knew what we in our hearts still know today – that our political system must allow us to strongly advocate our different views, but still agree on solutions to the problems that we face together.

The L.A. Opera, like many cultural, charitable and political entities across America, had to deal with cutbacks and a multi-million dollar deficit. The staging of *Il Postino* was made possible by a generous gift from Milena Kitic-Panic and Milan Panic. Panic is the founder of major pharmaceutical and biomedical companies he built shortly after immigrating to the U.S. from Yugoslavia in the late 1950s. An American citizen since 1963, he received special permission from President George W. Bush to serve as prime minister of Yugoslavia from 1992 to 1993.

"I am blown away by what a metaphor and double, make that triple entendre, The Postman is of the political and economic times we are living through in America today," I said when Jacqui asked what I thought of the opera, a sentiment I echoed to Gerry Lee Frye the following year when we saw with the Blacks Placido Domingo conduct *La Boheme*.

### Fishing and Hot Fire
During that fall 2010 visit to the States, I was invited by my daughter's father-in-law in August to Isleton, California, to go fishing for salmon in the Sacramento River on Labor Day weekend. It was the first time in two years that salmon fishing was being permitted and hopes were high. I was excited and looking forward to the weekend; it had been decades since I had been fishing. Driving my rented Chevy on the Sacramento Delta levees to get to Isleton, channel surfing satellite radio stations as I overtook cars carrying families and towing boats heading to the delta to enjoy the holiday weekend, I couldn't help wonder if my fellow travelers would be as disappointed with their weekend excursion as they are with America's political system and career politicians.

We all were disappointed in the fishing. Only two fish were caught in the entire delta on Sunday and one on Labor Day, according to the game wardens who approached us periodically to ask if we had caught anything, which we hadn't. The absence of salmon that were once so plentiful in America's rivers, like the lack of so many other American basics, including the lack of adherence to the Founding Fathers' constitutional principles, have been slowly fertilizing the seeds of the Third American Revolution.

I left for New York on a business trip after that disappointing Delta weekend hoping to catch some bigger fish with the investment bankers I was meeting with there for my Pets Central Media venture – which I did – with plans to return to Isleton on 9/11 for more salmon fishing.

Watching the late news in New York a couple days before my return to California, a breaking news story about a raging fire in San Bruno near San Francisco International Airport, first thought to be the result of a plane crash, but later confirmed to be a deadly gas pipeline explosion, caught my attention. That's the exit I would take to drop off my rental car at the San Francisco airport – the same one I had used three days earlier.

San Bruno was the first of many such pipeline explosions, followed by blasts in Fairport, Ohio; Philadelphia; Wayne, Michigan; Mont Belvieu, Texas; Allentown, Pa., East Harlem, N.Y., and many more.

There are thousands of aged pipes nationwide, not only under the earth, but offshore, as the deadly explosion of the BP Deepwater Horizon drilling platform off the coast of Louisiana in 2010 that spewed millions of barrels of oil into America's pristine fishing waters and onto its shores reminded us. What metaphors and double entendres for outraged Americans expressing their explosive emotions and feelings at the country's broken political system and constitutional cornerstones, I thought to myself. As if that wasn't bad enough, a couple of weeks later I was in Los Angeles on the hottest day ever recorded there. The National Weather Service's thermometer downtown reached 113 degrees fahrenheit and then stopped working. It was the first time since records began being kept in 1877 that had happened. Talk about a country and its political system overheating to the breaking point. What great metaphors.

Landing in San Francisco on 9/11/2010 after having just watched *Karate Kid II*, there was no doubt in my mind that America, although down and blown out and overheated, can and will continue to lead the New World Order if it can return to the basics of the Founding Fathers' spirit and determination in their revolutionary zeal to create a new order – a government of the people, for the people, by the people. Not only in America, but in China and the world that both countries can and must lead.

It is important to keep in mind the words of Machiavelli, the brilliant political philosopher and tactician: "It must be considered that there is nothing more difficult to carry out, nor more doubtful of success, nor more dangerous to handle, than to initiate a new order of things."

*Karate Chop Japan*

The first Karate Kid movie involved Japanese actors and took place in Japan. *Karate Kid II* took place in China with Chinese actors and Jackie Chan. Isn't it time Washington dumped a broken and broke Japan as its major ally in Asia and replaced it with a prosperous China, like Hollywood did? This is a theme I have raised in my earlier books. I am at a loss as to why America is still so closely allied with Japan, the country that attacked and brutalized Americans during World War II, and continues to do so with its economic policies today, while Washington shuns China, America's World War II ally that fought side-by-side with America to defeat Japan, and still wants to partner with the U.S.

Moody's Investors Service said in December 2011 that Japan must make progress in containing the world's largest public debt burden after the government compiled a budget that showed a record level of reliance on debt sales. Japan's continuing economic and geopolitical decline over the last three decades – amid China's ascent – was highlighted when China surpassed Japan in the summer of 2010 to become the world's second-largest economy after the U.S. Some economists predict that China's economy will overtake that of the U.S. by 2030. China's growth rate for 2010 was 10 percent, compared to America's anemic 2.4 percent.

China's expanding economic might is buying up small and mid-size Japanese companies and real estate, taking advantage of depressed asset prices – the same as it is doing in the U.S. China is also now Japan's biggest trading partner and a bulk purchaser of Japanese government bonds. The bond purchases are helping drive up the value of the yen, making Japan's exports less competitive with China's.

China's dominant shadow over Japan was further highlighted in September 2010, after a Chinese trawler collided with a Japanese coast guard vessel off the islands known as Diaoyu to the Chinese and Senkaku to the Japanese. The uninhabited islands northeast of Taiwan are claimed by both countries and are administered by Japan.

Japan arrested the trawler's captain for illegal fishing but released him after anti-Japanese protestors rallied outside the Japanese Embassy in Beijing and across China and Hong Kong. China also canceled high-level political and cultural exchanges, instructed travel agencies to cancel tours to Japan and withheld the shipment of rare earth metals used in electronics, posing a significant threat to the Japanese economy. China controls more than 95 percent of the world's rare earth minerals. It's no wonder Japan went looking for alternative sources – and found them in the middle of the Pacific.

Anti-Japanese protests continued in China for weeks after the trawler captain was released.

So why is a U.S. president bowing to the emperor of Japan, the way he did to the king of Saudi Arabia? More importantly, why is the U.S. supporting Japan in the dispute? The U.S. government's continued support of Japan in regional disputes between China and Japan is a shortsighted, outdated foreign policy – again – especially now that Japan has impaled itself yet again with another nuclear disaster!

The fact that the captain's arrest coincided with the September 18 anniversary of an incident that led to Japan setting up a puppet government in Manchuria in the early 1930s, a date that stirs bitter memories in China of the brutal Japanese occupation, stirred China's nationalistic outburst and effective economic reaction to the arrest. It's a point U.S. foreign policy experts at the State Department overlooked, or chose to ignore when Secretary Hillary Clinton announced American support for Japan in the dispute – a view China harshly criticized.

The unresolved issue of compensation and an apology to comfort women – war-time sex slaves – not only nags at China after all these years, but South Korea and the Philippines, two close U.S. allies, as well.

The bureaucratic incompetence of Japan was highlighted on New Year's Eve 2011, when the police turned away the nation's most wanted fugitive when he tried to surrender at Tokyo police headquarters after nearly 17 years on the run. Makoto Hirata is a former member of the Aum Supreme Truth doomsday cult, responsible for the 1995 nerve-gas attack on the Tokyo subway system. According to media reports, he approached a police officer and said: "I am Makoto Hirata. I am turning myself in."

But the officer dismissed him as a fake, even though posters with his picture were posted in the police station, and urged Hirata to go to a police station about 700 meters away, where he was then arrested.

Japan's response to the Fukushima Nuclear power plant crisis that followed the March 11, 2011 earthquake and tsunami was confused and riddled with problems, including an erroneous assumption that an emergency cooling system was working and a delay in disclosing dangerous radiation leaks, according to the government's independent report.

A self-nuked Japan blinked and China smiled. Japan lost face big time and got into deeper debt because of the earthquake-tsunami-nuclear disaster, while China gained big face as its government's piggy banks overflowed. Which face makes more sense for America to include in its 21st-century geopolitical picture?

### *China-Bashing*

I never cease to be amazed at how prevalent China-bashing becomes during election season in the U.S. The midterm 2010 and 2014 elections and 2012 presidential and congressional elections were no exception. China was again blamed for the low value of its currency, high unemployment in the U.S. caused by outsourcing to China and the bilateral trade deficit – the all-time high trade imbalance with China marked in August 2010 only added heat to the already boiling teakettle. A typical campaign ad: "You're 53, you've given them 26 years of hard work, and now you find out they're sending your job to China."

China is the common enemy of both Democrats and Republicans during an election. "Is Baron Hill running for Congress in Indiana – or China?" asked a television ad by the National Republican Congressional Committee in 2010 that featured revolutionary-style images of a Chinese flag and clenched fists in the air.

A spot by MoveOn.org aimed to tar Republican candidates for having the backing of the U.S. Chamber of Commerce – part of a broader Democratic attack against the organization for the funding it gets from outside the U.S. "Where has the chamber been getting some of their money lately? From foreign corporations in countries like China...," the ad said.

My personal favorite, because what it portrays can happen if *We the Apathetic Maids* continue to snooze, was filmed in Chinese with English subtitles. It purported to show a Chinese professor in 2030 teaching "Why do great nations fail," from ancient Greece to America. His lesson was that they failed because of reckless spending and large deficits. In the case of the U.S., the professor concludes triumphantly: "We owned most of their debt and now they work for us."

The volume of China-bashing during the 2010 midterm elections was aimed at deluding voters into believing that America's problems – created by career politicians of both parties in Washington and their financial backers – were all China's fault.

As a result, the House of Representatives voted overwhelmingly to impose stiff tariffs on virtually all Chinese imports to the U.S. Such a threat is not only highly unusual, but of dubious legality under international trade law – as is the case on China's currency manipulation, which the World Trade Organization does not define as illegal.

The decibel level of China-bashing increased dramatically during the 2012 Republican primary. Donald Trump was screaming on TV every night for a time, accusing China of ripping off the United States.

Mitt Romney and Rick Santorum launched aggressive blame games aimed at China. "If I am fortunate enough to be elected president, I will work to fundamentally alter our economic relationship with … I will begin on Day One by designating China as the currency manipulator it is," wrote Romney in an op-ed piece in the *Washington Post*, using words like "cheat" and "steal" to describe China.

"I will not stand by while China pursues an economic development policy that relies on the unfair treatment of U.S. companies and the theft of their intellectual property," he declared, promising "targeted unilateral and multilateral sanctions" to protect American businesses. Meanwhile, during the campaign, in December 2011, Bain Capital, the private equity firm founded by Romney, bought the Chinese manufacturer of "infrared anti-riot" video surveillance cameras and software that enable the Chinese government's security apparatus to blanket the country under its Safe Cities scheme and share information over the Internet in real time. The cameras are installed in university campuses, hospitals, mosques and Tibetan monasteries.

Is China a currency manipulator? Of course it is – as are all countries that maintain a fixed or a close-to-fixed ratio of their currency relative to the dollar, euro or gold. But the reality is that the value of China's yuan in terms of dollars is not the major reason why China exports three times as much to America as we do to them. Its exchange rate is a minor source of weak U.S. job growth.

"Export growth is determined primarily by factors other than exchange rates," said Edward P. Lazear, chairman of the President's Council of Economic Advisers from 2006-2009, and a professor at Stanford University's Graduate School of Business and a fellow at the Hoover Institution in an editorial opinion he wrote for *The Wall Street Journal*.

Disappointing job and wage growth in the U.S. has much more to do with America's economic policy than with the value of China's currency.

Santorum was even more ferocious. "I want to go to war with China," he declared, without specifying what type of war.

My favorite comment by an elected official that accurately sums up America's dysfunctional policy toward China was made by New York City

Mayor Michael Bloomberg, who criticized the decision by the U.S. Trade Representative's office to probe China's clean energy industry at the height of China-bashing in 2010.

"Let me get this straight," he said. "There's a country on the other side of the world that is taking their taxpayers' dollars, and trying to sell subsidized things so we can buy them cheaper and have better products, and we're going to criticize that?" But then again, Bloomberg is not a typical career politician. He is a smart businessman – more of which are needed in politics in America.

The U.S. posted deficits in 2010, as it has for many years, with almost every major trading partner, including Canada, Mexico, Japan and Germany. Yet China alone is continuously singled out.

"Fixing" China's currency won't solve America's problems. A revaluation of the *yuan* addresses only one of the many pressures shaping the imbalances in the Sino-U.S. relationship, a subject I discuss at length in *Feasting Dragon, Starving Eagle* – a book readers can enjoy as they sip California wine from vineyards owned by Chinese investment cartels.

### China's Growth – Economic and Taste
Napa Valley winery Silenus Vitners was the first major Chinese purchase in 2010 and started the trend. This is not surprising, considering how Chinese consumption of California wine has grown over the past few years. It has quadrupled in the last five years as prosperous Chinese develop a taste for the finer things in life.

China's growing domestic wine industry imports wine in bulk from U.S. The domestic wine industry also got a boost when the government encouraged Chinese to drink alcohol made from grapes rather than grain so that more grain could be devoted to food production.

What better place to enjoy good California wine than in a bargain-basement home in California. Bargain-hunting Hong Kong and mainland Chinese buyers are flocking to California to capitalize on the deflated home prices.

Nearly half of China's super-rich are considering emigrating, according to a joint report released in November 2011 by the Bank of China and Hurun Report, which also publishes an annual list of the richest Chinese. The average respondent was 42 and worth more than 60 million *yuan*. Forty-six percent said they planned to emigrate, citing the better quality of education available for their children overseas, concerns about the security of their assets on the mainland amid political and economic uncertainty, and hopes for a better life in retirement as the main reasons.

Hong Kong and California are the destinations of choice.

California today has the largest ethnic Chinese population in the U.S. In terms of business ties, Hong Kong is California's sixth-largest trading partner.

Is it any wonder then that China keeps pushing America for a more level playing field for Chinese investments in the U.S. before it opens up to corporate America? The U.S. mantra of "national security concerns" in denying Chinese investments in corporate America just doesn't cut it anymore. The reality is that both countries have to open up a lot more to each other – and will.

Now that Chinese companies are not only allowed, but encouraged, to invest their surplus *yuan* overseas, especially in America, the inflow of Chinese investment will be mind-boggling. Since January 2011, domestic Chinese companies have been allowed to start new businesses overseas and to pursue mergers and acquisitions. Interestingly, the top recipients of Chinese investments were Hong Kong, the Cayman Islands and Australia. As a lawyer who has handled international transactions, I can understand why.

According to a report published by the Asia Society, China is likely to spend more than $1 trillion in foreign direct investments between 2011 and 2020. According to *The Economist,* China's stock of direct investments in Asia reached $185 billion in 2009. Its investment in Latin America hit $30 billion and reached $9 billion in Europe. In contrast, its stock of investments in the whole of North America came to a relatively meager $5 billion. Because of "public attacks by wealthy lobby groups and frothing congressmen," the magazine argued, the U.S. is losing out. I agree! Big time.

Chinese telecom giant Huawei has made two attempts to buy into U.S. companies and was rejected. Its attempt to buy into 3Com in 2009 and its 2011 attempt to buy assets and patents from California-based 3Leaf were respectfully declined. The same happened to Haier, a major Chinese appliance manufacturer. It tried to buy the iconic American company Maytag in 2005, but dropped its bid after objections were raised in Congress.

But that setback hasn't stopped Haier from becoming a major player in the U.S. Today the company operates a manufacturing plant in South Carolina and boasts U.S. sales of more than $1 billion. It makes a handsome 20 percent profit on its operations. It employs locals in senior positions and is a good U.S. corporate citizen.

China invested a record amount in the U.S. in 2012. The biggest Chinese takeover of an American company was the $4.2 billion acquisition of Los Angeles-based International Lease Finance Corp., one of the world's largest aircraft leasing firms.

Another Chinese company bought three U.S. factories and other assets of electric-car battery maker A123 Systems Inc.

Chinese companies in 2012 also picked up AMC Entertainment, one of the largest movie theater chains in America, as well as stakes in energy, real estate and other companies in service industries.

Excluding the ILFC deal, which was expected to close in the spring of 2013, direct investments by Chinese companies in the U.S. reached $6.5 billion, breaking the previous record of $5.2 billion in 2010.

2013 started with the world's most famous movie theater finally living up to its name. Chinese TV maker TCL paid more than $5 million for the naming rights to the venerable Hollywood Boulevard landmark Grauman's Chinese

Theatre.

Shouldn't America be trying to attract more of the $1 trillion China plans to invest overseas? That would not only bring down unemployment in America, but help bring an end to stagflation. What is wrong with Chinese companies buying in America and creating jobs while cutting down the number of jobs being outsourced to China?

It will be interesting to see if China's top offshore oil producer, CNOOC, will have its $1.1 billion stake in Chesapeake Energy Corp. approved by Congress. The bid represents the Chinese government's latest testing of the U.S. political climate and attitude, the first major test since CNOOC's failed bid for Unocal in 2005.

A bigger and real concern is the fact that China is on track to produce enough crude oil outside its borders to rival OPEC members such as Kuwait and the United Arab Emirates, after its state-owned oil companies spent a record $35 billion buying foreign rivals in 2012.

Chinese national oil companies have been on a buying spree, spending $92 billion since the start of 2009 on oil and gas assets in countries from the U.S. to Angola.

Acquiring key technologies is another goal of the acquisitions, particularly for deep water drilling and extraction of shale gas and oil sands deposits.

While China is encouraging investment in the U.S., it is also urging the world's largest economy to improve its investment environment and reduce barriers.

The fact is that China's economic modernization and growth are surpassing in mere decades what took developed nations centuries to achieve. China saves and invests 35 percent of its GDP, while Americans consume more than they produce or save.

The U.S. has unsustainable trade deficits globally, besides its huge deficit with China. It has transformed itself from the largest creditor into the largest debtor nation in just 20 years. China's success and savings enable it to invest massively in its future. For example, it has invested $1 trillion in green technology from 2010 to 2013 – much more than America.

While the U.S. and China duke it out over deficits and exchange rates, Europe has quietly overtaken America as China's No. 1 trading partner. China has also become far more dependent on Europe for importing the technology and infrastructure that underpin its breakneck development – at the expense of an America that refuses to sell China high-tech products.

The Chinese feel that America is trying to curb China's growth, and thus its power. So why are Americans surprised that China refuses to assist America in its efforts to isolate Iran and North Korea?

China, as America's largest creditor, has become more confident in its dealings with the U.S. and on the world stage. Why should China make economic concessions to a country many blame for plunging the world into financial crisis? Why should China make its exports and imports more expensive? Why should China bail America out of its financial abyss at the cost of its exports becoming more expensive and Chinese factories being shut down and millions of workers becoming unemployed? Would America do so if the roles were reversed? I don't think so. The U.S. should be thankful that China is helping finance America's unjustified deficit spending spree and stop blaming China for the mistakes of Washington's career politicians. The alternative is an American default on its financial obligations, or worse, bankruptcy – both of which are overdue.

Is it China that is financing the expensive and vigorous U.S. Navy activities in the Western Pacific and eavesdropping on China? How much longer can a government that is going broke engage in these activities and wonder why China will not accommodate its wishes to revalue the *yuan* to make America more competitive? After all, it was China that came to America's economic rescue and it does not appreciate the "gratitude" the U.S. has shown in return – regional containment and tariff barriers.

China, like America, is going to do what its career politicians think is best for the people and country, and of course the politicians themselves.

So what does China do? Instead of revaluing the *yuan* as America has pushed it to do, it thought a surprise interest-rate hike was in order, a move that battered stock and commodity prices around the world and raised fresh uncertainties over continued recovery in the U.S. and other developed nations.

The primary objective of the quarter-point interest hike was to cool China's overheated real estate market and rising inflation. Chinese consumers get bigger returns on their savings. Higher interest rates also attract more capital inflows that could eventually boost the value of the *yuan*. In the meantime, America and its career politicians and unemployed workers be damned. That's Washington's problem – and indeed it is. Having said that, China's economic boom may well be followed by an American super-sized bust. The ramifications of a Chinese economic slowdown would be profound, ranging from the risk of domestic social instability to the collapse of several commodity markets. Commodity prices started falling in May 2011, led by a huge fall in silver futures that extended their biggest decline since March 1983. Oil prices dropped, U.S. unemployment claims rose, as did the dollar with QE2's cheap minted dollars that flowed into the commodity markets coming to an end.

A trade war with China, the world's leading tea-drinking country, does not help U.S. exports or employment in America, as members of the Tea Party movement advocate. China can buy elsewhere, hurting U.S. export industries while American consumers pay higher prices for essential consumer goods and also have higher tariffs imposed on U.S. products, which China defiantly imposed on U.S. poultry before the House vote. On the day of the vote, China warned of dire consequences and further economic disruptions and let the value of the *yuan* fall.

### Clash of the Currencies

The "shellacking" that Obama and his Democratic Congress received in November 2010 was not limited to the midterm elections. They also took a beating for their monetary policy at the G20 in Seoul that same month.

While the U.S. demanded – make that ordered – China to revalue the *yuan* under threat of sanctions, America decided to print $600 billion to stimulate its economy with the second round of quantitative easing, commonly spun as QE2. The result, a weaker devalued dollar – 15-year lows against the yen and an all-time low against the Swiss franc – with China taking the biggest hit because of its multi-trillion U.S. debt dollar holdings. The result, instead of China being criticized for its currency policy at the G20 in Seoul in November 2010, it was America that was roundly criticized by world leaders, including China, for its destabilizing currency policy that is causing trade imbalances and disparities not only at home but globally. The U.S criticism of China's *yuan* policy and its push to revalue the *yuan* was soundly rejected by world leaders.

The biggest force undermining the dollar is the U.S. Federal Reserve's penchant for printing more and more of the stuff – not China. It is time this is acknowledged and that the U.S. reconsider its exchange rate policy in rebalancing the U.S. economy. With interest rates in the U.S. at nearly zero, the country is printing more money and pumping it into the American markets from where it flows to the rest of the world. As a result, the dollar has tumbled; inflation expectations have increased; asset and commodity prices have hit new highs. Even worse, the dollar's slide has negatively impacted other economies and currencies, forcing them to act, either by imposing capital controls or intervening in their own exchange rates.

Banks take the U.S. dollars the Fed prints and instead of investing and circulating them in the U.S. economy as they promised, look for better returns in emerging countries and fan inflation, asset and housing bubbles with their hot dollars which they withdraw when they have maximized their returns, leaving the local economies in shambles – a repeat of the 1997-98 financial crisis in Asia that nearly killed a number of economies. The only difference this time around is that Asia has learned from its near-death experience, one it does not want to repeat as it sits back and watches Europe, from Ireland to Iberia, do so. It should therefore come as no surprise that countries as diverse as Brazil, Indonesia, South Korea, Vietnam and China have imposed restrictions on investment inflows to defuse the danger of hot money from abroad.

America asking China and other emerging markets to revalue their currencies is a self-serving nonstarter. The sheer amount of hot money that headed their way was a financial tsunami. The Institute of International Finance estimated in October 2010 that net private capital flows to emerging markets rose to more than $825 billion that year, up sharply from $581 billion in 2009. In 2010, net private capital flows into emerging Asia topped $248 billion, of which $93 billion was in equity portfolio flows and $95 billion was in flows. In other words, hot foreign money was chasing both equities and fixed income debt.

For China and other emerging markets to allow their currencies or exchange rates to appreciate would hurt exports, destroy jobs and, worse for those countries like China with a net foreign exchange surplus, induce a stock loss from the revaluation. That is because dollar holdings depreciate when a currency appreciates against the greenback. The worst aspect of currency appreciation is that it attracts even more hot money inflows, because the speculators rush into the action.

As long as America and other developed nations have deficits, they will try to depreciate to get out of their liquidity traps. The tragedy of this strategy is that global capital flows are highly leveraged. This means that the carry traders borrow heavily to speculate in emerging markets. No single emerging market can easily defend itself against such large inflows, as Asia found out in 1997-1998. In the short run, it feels good, but when the foreign money leaves, the locals are left to pick up the pieces. In other words, global bankers gain, leaving local pain in their wake.

During the 2008-2009 crisis, the U.S. nationalized a lot of private debt, but in the post-crisis period, it tried to internationalize its public debt. The policy is shortsighted, benefiting neither U.S. economic growth nor global recovery and stability. Shifting America's accumulated debt burden across the world by softening the dollar only forces other countries to take action to protect their own currencies. That ultimately isolates the dollar and its users. Historical experience shows that policymakers must be cautious about aggressively shifting exchange rates.

In the 1970s, the U.S. pursued a devaluation policy for the same purpose and using the same justifications. It led to chaos around the world and plunged the U.S. economy into a prolonged period of stagflation. Maybe the world can stop the U.S. from repeating the mistake, through currency interventions. That isn't a currency war, it is good medicine, not only for the countries protecting themselves, but for America as well.

America's weak-dollar policy backfired big time, leading straight to inflation without growth along the way. There is no mileage in politicizing currency management. There are no winners in a clash of currencies, except for the *yuan*.

While the value of the dollar plummets, offshore trading in the *yuan* is taking off. Daily trading in the *yuan* offshore has grown from zero to $55 billion, 7 percent of the total by the first quarter of 2011 as the Chinese currency increases its role in global markets. *Yuan* deposits in Hong Kong alone at the end of April 2011 rose to an estimated 511 billion, a massive ninefold increase from July 2009 when the settlement program was launched as the city became the epicenter of the increasingly international currency – a factor that contributed to Hong Kong becoming the No. 1 financial center in the world. The city-state leapfrogged the U.S. and Britain in 2011, according to the World Economic Forum rankings.

Asset managers have launched *yuan*-denominated funds in Hong Kong, including bonds for American corporate icons the likes of McDonalds and Caterpillar – and the World Bank.

As if to confirm the point, the *yuan* hit a 17-year high against the dollar, just as President Hu Jintao was getting ready to head to his summit with President Obama in Washington in January 2011. To really hammer the point home to the career politicians in Washington who still didn't get it on the eve of Hu's visit, the Bank Of China began offering *yuan*-denominated accounts in its New York branch on Madison Avenue.

To further emphasize the point, China announced in late 2011 that it planned to set up a new $300 billion sovereign wealth fund to acquire real assets instead of U.S. Treasuries, Euro bonds or the depreciating dollar.

"China has decided that real assets are better than broken debt fix promises and low interest rates," says Paul Markowski, president of MES Advisers and a long-time external adviser to China's monetary policy-makers on global financial markets.

Beijing has watched for two years as Europe's crisis has choked growth and demand in China's biggest export market and stoked default risks on the near $800 billion of euro-zone government bonds it is estimated to own. It has been a painful lesson. China had actively bought euro assets to guard its $3.2 trillion reserve pile against overexposure to U.S. dollars, which have lost about a third of their value in the past 10 years as U.S. Treasury yields have sunk to record lows.

"China has intervened massively in the foreign exchange markets for at least five years, buying at least $1 billion every day to keep the dollar strong and its own reminbi weak," Fred Bergsten, director of the Peterson Institute for International Economics, said in August 2011. Bergsten estimated the *yuan* at the time was undervalued by at least 20 percent against the U.S. dollar as a result of Beijing's currency intervention.

Blaming the *yuan* and the Chinese government policies for the U.S. woes holds no currency, if you'll pardon the pun. A report released by the San Francisco Federal Reserve Bank in October 2011 said that "Made in China" isn't taking over U.S. consumption as much as believed. Of every dollar U.S. consumers spend on a Chinese-made product, about 55 cents pays for services in the U.S. Think about it. When you spend $90 on a pair of Nike sneakers, only a fraction of it flows to China. The U.S. economic woes are not *yuan* or China related. They are American made.

The spat between the U.S. and China over the *yuan's* value exposes just how dysfunctional the global financial system is and why there is no forum for rational discussion.

The *yuan* appreciated by as much as 5 percent in 2011, and is expected to gradually become freely convertible by 2015, at the latest. Once it does become freely convertible, the *yuan* will proceed to become a leading foreign reserve currency. The *yuan* replaced the British pound sterling as the third most-popular currency for trade settlements in 2011 and is now the third most-used currency for trade settlements after the dollar and euro.

The *yuan* will make up 5 percent of the global currency reserve by 2020, predicts Xia Bin, a former adviser to the People's Bank of China's monetary policy committee. The instability that has come to be associated with major currencies such as the dollar and euro propelled China to speed up the internationalization of its currency. "Had there been a stable international currency system, China wouldn't need to internationalize the *yuan*," Professor Xia said at an investment conference in Hong Kong in March 2012.

March was also the month that mainland imports outpaced exports by the largest margin in two decades, a sign of an end to the *yuan's* rise.

Many Chinese economists, in addition to U.S. politicians, have also urged the Chinese government to let the *yuan* float freely as a way to reduce the country's immense foreign-exchange reserves and to ease inflationary pressure. They are also pushing China to stop piling up dollar assets to avoid losses as the U.S. currency weakens.

Interestingly, a report from the United Nations Conference on Trade and Development in December 2010 said that the *yuan* was not undervalued, as its real effective exchange rate has nearly doubled since 1995, factoring in the unit of labor cost. The fact is that the Chinese currency is approaching fair value. Jim O'Neill, chairman of Goldman Sachs Asset Management, said his firm's investment model no longer suggests that the *yuan* is undervalued at all.

"There is quite a lot of evidence [that] most adults in Washington and the rest of the U.S. choose to ignore," says O'Neill. "The Chinese trade surplus and current-account surplus have declined sharply, so I would say the ongoing evidence is quite supportive for those who don't believe the *yuan* is that undervalued anymore."

In terms of trade clearing, the *yuan* has become a regional "hard" currency, and has a large and growing influence with neighboring trade partners. Additionally, a number of Asian, African and Latin American countries already regard *yuan* products as reserve assets. And, in addition to accelerating innovation in Hong Kong's offshore *yuan* products,

New York, London and other traditional financial centers are now conducting an impressive volume of *yuan*-denominated investment business.

Nevertheless, the dollar's status as the world's reserve currency will likely remain unchallenged in the foreseeable future. Why? The other major global currencies, namely the euro and yen, are in even bigger trouble than the dollar and the *yuan* is suspect in many financial quarters because of China's corrupt management of its financial reporting and banking systems. China admits as much. It will likely take 15 to 20 years for the *yuan* to pass through the three stages needed to become a global currency, said Dai Xianglong, chairman of the National Council for Social Security Fund and former head of China's central bank. The first step being massive global trades in the *yuan*, which it is well on its way to achieving, followed by free convertibility and then the third and final step – it becomes an accepted reserve currency.

*Planes, Trains ....*
It is not only on the dollar financial front that the U.S. is getting shellacked by China. It is taking a beating from the depths of the ocean to the moon. On the plane, train, supercomputer, drone and GPS fronts, China is catching up and overtaking America. China has produced the world's darkest dark-matter detector, the longest long-range quantum teleporter, the deepest deep-sea exploration submarine and a supercomputer that leaves its foreign competitors in its dust.

China's seizing the lead in pioneering cutting-edge frontiers once dominated by the U.S. is a rude shock. Supercomputer technology has been hijacked by China with its new fastest supercomputer in the world – the Tianhe-1A which can perform a mind-numbing 2.57 quadrillion calculations per second.

The supercomputer is a key research tool in such fields as climate change, product design and weapons development. It is an expensive and serious national security issue for both countries. China is rapidly catching up with the U.S. in the supercomputer installation business. So why not work together on joint projects that are not security threats in the interest of building mutual trust, and stop wasting taxpayer money?

China's ability to build drones, commercial jets and get a satellite to Mars, launch GPS satellites that can show people how easy it is to get around on earth, without getting lost and not using GPS, ends America's role as the sole provider of global GPS services. China is now challenging America on earth and in the skies.

Unmanned aerial vehicles, or drones, are considered the future of military aviation and could one day replace the fighter jet. China has developed more than 25 different models of drones – a fact that is causing anxiety in the Pentagon because "when deployed, [they] will expand the PLA Air Force's options for long-range reconnaissance and strike" capability.

Drones will dominate future air wars because they are cheaper to build and operate than conventional aircraft. So much so that America is now training its first drone test pilots to develop more effective fighting machines. Like climbers who blaze a path up a mountain peak, test pilots help those that follow them avoid costly mistakes.

China has flight-tested a hypersonic glide vehicle that can outfox U.S. defenses and deliver a nuclear warhead at a speed above Mach 10.

China has more than a dozen satellites capable of covering the Asia-Pacific region and by 2020 it will have complete global coverage with 35 satellites that will give it strategic independence and another commercial gold mine. The GPS was a navigation revolution comparable to the invention of the compass, except that it was controlled by one power. America is no longer the world's sole traffic cop in the sky at the dawn of the new space age.

By 2014 China's new C919 commercial passenger jet is set to take wing – and take on industry giants Boeing and Airbus. The two Western aircraft manufacturers currently dominate a Chinese market estimated by Boeing to be worth $480 billion over the next two decades.

As someone who prefers train travel over other modes of transportation, I was delighted to hear that China has cemented itself in the No. 1 position in the world's high-speed rail sector and that it has partnered with GE in its bid to build high-speed train lines in California. The mainland had built 13,000 kilometers of high-speed tracks by 2012 and plans to have 16,000 kilometers by 2020, including a link to Hong Kong.

The Chinese-built CRH380A train hit a record speed of 486 kilometers an hour during a test run in December 2010. When the train goes into actual service, it will travel at an average speed of 350km/h.

China is considering merging its two dominant state-owned railway equipment producers to lead a high-speed rail export drive and become the global leader in that realm. The merger would create the world's largest company of its kind in terms of operating revenue.

The ocean is another frontier where China has made breakthroughs. In August 2010, the manned deep-sea submarine Jiaolong, or Sea Dragon, planted a Chinese flag on the floor of the South China Sea. Its mission is to explore for minerals that will be shipped through the canal China is building in Nicaragua that will dwarf the 100-year-old Panama Canal.

Giving America a run for its money on earth and in the skies and in the sea is not enough for China. It is also reaching for the moon. China's lunar probe Chang'e-2, launched October 1, 2010, sent dramatic photos of the lunar surface and areas for China's Chang'e-3 mission that successfully landed a rover on the moon in December 2013. The telescope has attracted international attention because it will be the only lunar-based telescope and could lead to exciting new astronomical discoveries.

To make sure it can get there and not rely on America, Chinese authorities announced in November 2011 that they will begin construction of their own space station as soon as 2013 and it is expected to be up and running by 2016. China received a boost to its space program in November 2011, when it added a tracking station in western Australia to its network in Namibia, Kenya, Pakistan and Chile. It got an additional boost in June 2012, when a Chinese spacecraft with three astronauts on board docked manually with an orbiting module, an important step toward China's goal of building a space station.

Is it any wonder China fumes every time the U.S. announces it will continue to maintain its curbs on the high-tech toys China wants to buy to reverse-engineer in order to speed up its development even faster? Kind of ironic actually. America won't sell China high-tech equipment even at a premium price that China is prepared to pay to offset the balance of trade deficit. Instead, America would rather have China buy it as "surplus scrap" at bargain basement prices a few years later – as it does. More on that later.

### Destructive Deficit Spending

The global financial crisis is eventually going to blow over. The only question is when, not how. The how is certain. With ugly stratospheric budget deficits. Investors will need to be persuaded to hold Himalayan high mountains of debt for decades. The history of financial crisis shows that public debt typically doubles, even adjusting for inflation, in the three years following a crisis. America and many rich and poor nations are well on their way to meeting those projections.

Throwing money at the problem and propping up the greedy banks that created the speculation is, as Jim Walker of *Asianomics* says, like trying to put out a fire by pouring gasoline on it. The result will be an even bigger, more searing conflagration.

Deficit spending is "a symbol of the government's inability to manage its own affairs," former U.S. Treasury Secretary Robert Rubin says in his memoir. I couldn't agree more! It does not make sense for America to continue excessive consumption financed by excessive leverage, and simply increase public debt to make up and cover Wall Street losses.

In January 1981, when Ronald Reagan took the oath of office, the national debt was just under $1 trillion. By the time he left office, that figure had nearly tripled and today, more than three decades later, it has soared beyond $14 trillion.

The massive U.S. deficit financing is crowding many emerging economies and their companies out of the international capital markets, which only creates more resentment toward America.

The last-ditch extension in December 2010 of the Bush-era tax cuts and unemployment benefits added $858 billion to long-term deficits without any commitment to reductions in the future, even though supporters argue that if such measures boost growth, America's budgetary position will improve too.

If the U.S. does not get its financial house in order, "we will have a European situation on our hands, and possibly worse," claimed Paul Ryan, the new Republican chairman of the House budget committee and Mitt Romney's vice presidential running mate in the 2012 election. "We will have the riots in the streets, we will have the defaults, we will have all those ugliness problems," he said, referring to the French kids lobbing Molotov cocktails at cars and burning down schools because of the change in the retirement age from 60 to 62.

The U.S. debt hit its congressionally mandated limit of nearly $14.300 trillion in mid-2011. If the Obama administration and Capitol Hill hadn't agreed on a deal to raise that threshold, the U.S. would have had to shut down the government and default on its international debt obligations.

Staying on the path America is on, the federal debt could hit 344 percent of GDP by 2050. Interest payments alone would absorb nearly all federal tax revenue. I echo Winston Churchill who said, "The United States will always do the right thing – when all other possibilities have been exhausted." As the son of an American mother, he was entitled to say such things.

The reality is that in order to rebuild America and restore it to its former glory, the current financing models have to be torn up and replaced with fiscal prudence. A depression will undoubtedly follow with mass unemployment and wealth destruction. But it can be short and sweet as opposed to the prolonged agony America and the world have gone through the last five years – and also lay the foundation for a new era of healthy, sustained growth.

### *Devaluation of the Almighty Dollar*
Trashing the U.S. dollar appears to be the only road that career politicians are prepared to seriously explore. Sacrificing the dollar's value against other currencies, especially China's *yuan*. That is the message I repeatedly encountered during the 2010 midterm elections – and again leading up to the 2012 presidential election.

Devaluing the greenback carries risks. High on any Wall Street list of calamities is always the idea of a sudden collapse of the dollar. That seems remote, though less so than in the past. Fed policymakers appear to be gung ho to keep their money presses rolling to flood the financial system with more dollars to keep long-term interest rates low.

A cheaper dollar helps U.S. manufacturers compete at home and abroad with foreign rivals. But if the global economy weakens further, a key risk is that governments could engage in a race to the bottom with their currencies via repeated devaluations, reminiscent of the 1930s. The U.S. could lose that race, meaning the dollar could rise instead of falling against its major rivals, confounding the export push.

A drive to devalue the dollar also could spin out of control by eroding confidence in the currency, leading global investors to cash out of dollar assets to cut their losses. The potential for a mass dumping of the dollar, especially by the Chinese, is a very realistic scenario.

No nation has ever devalued its way to prosperity. The Japanese tried and failed in the late 1990s. A weaker dollar, or the mirror image of a stronger Chinese *yuan,* would be no exception to that time-tested premise.

### *"The Moment of Truth" – A Political Nonstarter*
The Bowles-Simpson bipartisan National Commission on Fiscal Responsibility and Reform, appointed by President Obama to recommend solutions to America's dire economic problems and deficit spending – did just that. It made very constructive observations and sweeping recommendations on how America spends money and collects taxes and proposed solutions to tackle the U.S. debt by harshly trimming federal spending, especially defense outlays, that even the commission recognized were political nonstarters – even though imperative for America to get back on a sound financial footing.

"We'll … be in a witness-protection program when this is all over," said former Republican Senator Alan Simpson, co-chair of Obama's deficit-reduction committee when he and his Democratic colleague Erskine Bowles, former President Bill Clinton's chief economic advisor, released a draft of their 59-page report in December 2010.

The report proposed cutting 200,000 federal jobs by 2020, roughly 10% of the government work force. The proposal would achieve nearly $4 trillion in deficit reduction by 2020, reduce the deficit to 2.3% of gross domestic product by 2015, overhaul the tax code, trim defense spending, cap government revenue at 21% of GDP and reduce debt to 40% of GDP by 2035.

"Throughout our nation's history, Americans have found the courage to do right by our children's future. Deep down, every American knows we face a moment of truth once again," the report said.

The 18-member commission could not get the 14 votes needed to issue a formal recommendation to Congress and the White House. Is this any way to run the prudent Founding Fathers' Republic?

America needs some major structural solutions and changes to get back on a sustained growth path. The necessary structural fixes can happen only with bipartisan consensus and sacrifice, two ingredients that have been sorely lacking in politically hog-tied Washington.

America milked the stock market in the 1990s to have a good life. When the bottom fell out in 2000, the country switched to the property market for another decade of the good life. When that crashed, the government decided to print money and suck on the treasury market in a desperate effort to defend America's lifestyle through government spending. That has not and will not work either. The federal government is laden with more than $14 trillion in debt. If the Fed were to buy it all up, it would lead to a collapse of the dollar and hyperinflation.

The Washington gridlock and bipartisan stalemate has frozen career politicians' ability to realistically and meaningfully address the country's economic problems. America cannot continue its debt-fueled growth model on borrowed money from China for unjustified tax cuts and entitlements without long-term structural changes and investments in new growth enterprises.

Bowles and Simpson, the fiscal reform committee co-chairs, acknowledged that the reality of the Washington Beltway – both of them are Beltway insiders – is that their recommendations will never see the light of day because of the built-in self-serving interests of plutocratic America that will be adversely affected by their recommendations and command their lobbyists and supporters in Congress to ensure their recommendations never get to first base. They were right. Congressional leaders from both parties severely criticized the committee's report and recommendations even though what it recommended is exactly what the Tea Party movement and citizen taxpayers want.

How sad. It was another missed opportunity for real economic and political reform. An opportunity to get back to the basics of the Founding Fathers' Constitution.

### Government Shutdown

As if that wasn't bad enough, what do the politicians do? Talk government shutdown unless the U.S. debt ceiling is raised, which they do, all under the guise of trying to cut the deficit and balance the budget. It's easy to cut the deficit and restore a balanced budget. Just do what the Bowles-Simpson report says, for starters. Start listening to the taxpayers who paid for the report and stop ignoring *We the Maids* who must repeatedly clean up your mess while you choose to ignore us and just take care of yourselves and your financial family and enterprises, usually both.

Raising the U.S. debt ceiling devolved into a game of political brinkmanship ahead of the 2012 presidential election, with Republicans demanding huge spending cuts as their price of support. Democrats on the other hand refused to sign off on any spending cuts without at least some tax increase on America's wealthiest individuals and closing corporate tax loopholes. What is wrong with the country's wealthiest citizens and giant corporations shouldering a little more of the burden? Why shouldn't they? What am I missing?

Why should career politicians in Washington care if their headstrong extreme political stubborness shuts down the government. They still get their $174,000 a year paychecks. They made sure of that first. It's the hundreds of thousands of federal workers who won't get theirs, or the suppliers and vendors that provide what the government needs to function to serve the people. The taxpayers and Social Security recipients, who already paid their fair share of taxes to support and receive basic benefits, will be denied their basic services, including enrolling sick people into life-saving medical trials, answering medical hot lines, cleaning up toxic waste or processing passport applications.

As the satirist Andy Borowitz wrote in a Twitter message: "That's like eliminating the fire department and sending checks to arsonists."

For the U.S. government to even utter those thoughts, when it knows the consequences of the 1995 shutdown and what that did to America and its image, is a disgrace. It is a disrespectful act that the Founding Fathers would consider tantamount to treason. After all, isn't that what King George and the British traders did that caused the Founding Fathers to rebel?

A great e-mail "Employee Notice" I received from a few friends in America, the Philippines and China summed up best how the public feels about career politicians:

> *Due to the current financial situation caused by the*
> *slowdown in the economy, Congress has decided*
> *to implement a scheme to put workers of 50 years*
> *of age and above on early, mandatory retirement,*
> *thus creating jobs and reducing unemployment.*

> *This scheme will be known as RAPE (Retired Aged*
> *People Early).*

> *Persons selected to be RAPED can apply to Congress*
> *to be considered for the SHAFT program (Special Help*
> *After Forced Termination).*

> *Persons who have been RAPED and SHAFTED*
> *will be reviewed under the SCREW program (System*
> *Covering Retired-Early Workers).*

*A person may be RAPED once, SHAFTED*
*twice and SCREWED as many times as Congress*
*deems appropriate.*

*Persons who have been RAPED could get AIDS*
*(Additional Income for Dependents & Spouse)*
*or HERPES (Half Earnings for Retired*
*Personnel Early Severance).*

*Obviously persons who have AIDS or HERPES will*
*not be SHAFTED or SCREWED any further by Congress.*

*Persons who are not RAPED and are staying on*
*will receive as much SHIT (Special High Intensity Training)*
*as possible. Congress has always prided themselves*
*on the amount of SHIT they give our citizens.*

*Should you feel that you do not receive enough SHIT, please*
*bring this to the attention of your Congressman, who has*
*been trained to give you all the SHIT you can handle.*

*Sincerely,*
*The Committee for Economic Value of Individual Lives*
*(E.V.I.L.)*

*P.S. Due to recent budget cuts and the rising cost of electricity,*
*gas and oil, as well as current market conditions, the light*
*at the end of the tunnel has been turned off.*

The game of chicken played by Democrats and Republicans over raising the $14.3 trillion debt ceiling, with talk about credit rating agencies downgrading U.S. debt, not only threw America's credibility as a borrower into doubt, but darkened its credibility as a global leader and whether it can be trusted anymore. The U.S. merely hastened its decline and the further decline of the dollar. (On August 2, 2011, President Obama signed a compromise bill lifting the debt limit after weeks of bipartisan political silliness in Congress. But the discussion here remains valid.)

## Default

We are not just talking about a government shutdown. America was debating how to avoid a first-ever federal default and the resulting domestic and global financial mayhem – especially in China, America's largest foreign creditor.

The reason the debt ceiling was routinely raised before the 2011 impass is because the status of the dollar as the world's reserve currency and the universal understanding that U.S. Treasury bills are the safest investment on earth are key attributes of American power – as important, if not more so to the U.S. role in the world as military power.

For the Tea Party and the Republicans to hold America's "full faith and credit" hostage to the partisan gridlock in Washington is inexcusable, destructive ignorance and un-American.

This fiscal irresponsibility was not limited to Washington and Beijing, but was evident in many individual states as well.

This was most graphically displayed in Minnesota and California.

In Minnesota, Republicans shut down government rather than raise taxes on the 7,700 Minnesotans who make more than $1 million a year. Democratic Governor Mark Dayton could not get Republicans to budge. As a result, more than 40 state agencies had to close, as did essential services for the poor. What's the logic of this as most of the laid-off workers will receive unemployment and health benefits, while the treasury is unable to collect on tax audits, lottery tickets and park fees? The extremist Republican ideology is senseless.

In California, the so-called cutting-edge political pioneering state, state voters were assured in the 2010 midterm elections, when they passed Proposition 25, that lawmakers would be punished by having their pay docked if the state budget is not finished on time. But leave it to creative career politicians and their lawyers to find a personally beneficial loophole. All they have to do is pass a budget – the law says nothing about a balanced budget. All they have to do is pass any budget, no matter how unbalanced it may be, and their paychecks keep rolling into their bank accounts.

"This was a sham," said Jon Coupal, president of the Howard Jarvis Taxpayers Assn., who campaigned against the measure. "Voters who approved this thing will feel cheated."

The proposition is just another example of a bait-and-switch tactic by effective lobbyists who wanted to shift away from Republicans the power they had to block state budgets. Before the proposition passed, a budget bill could be approved only with a two-thirds vote of the Legislature, which required some GOP support. Polls consistently showed that Californians wanted lawmakers to pass budgets on time or be punished.

"For every day the budget is late, legislators are docked a day's pay plus expenses," the ballot pamphlet stated. "Importantly, they can't pay themselves back when the budget is finally passed."

So what is the point of legislators passing an unbalanced budget just so they can collect their paychecks even if the budget is unbalanced and sends the state into a faster economic tailspin – which is what happened? Another example of *We the Apathetic Maids* cleaning up still another political mess.

The bankruptcy filing by American Airlines in November 2011 as it sought to shed debt, cut labor costs and find a way back to profitability was a timely metaphor for American government at all levels. Jefferson County in Alabama has been teetering on the verge of filing the biggest U.S. municipal bankruptcy in history. The filing could add to heightened concerns of more problems in the $3.7 trillion U.S. municipal bond market, which has been hit by the high-profile debt crisis in Pennsylvania's capital of Harrisburg. The city of Stockton in California teetering on the verge of bankruptcy only added to the anxiety.

Even Republican budget-cutting darling Rep. Paul Ryan's hometown of Janesville, Wisconsin, feels the pinch. The U.S. Department of Housing clawed back $344,000 from the city's affordable-housing fund, so the city voted to drain its reserves to keep 525 families in the program.

What some cities are doing to meet their pension obligations and avoid filing for bankruptcy protection is to borrow from the pension funds to which they already owe money to pay for them. Talk about double dipping. Across New York, state and local governments borrowed $750 million in 2012 to finance their contributions to the state pension system, were likely to borrow at least $1 billion more in 2013. The number of municipalities and public institutions using this new borrowing mechanism to pay off their annual pension bills has tripled in a year.

A growing number of states are sharply limiting hospital stays under Medicaid to as few as 10 days a year to control rising costs of the health insurance program for the poor and disabled.

As if that is not enough, it was revealed that career politicians in Los Angeles and New York City had special clout to get parking tickets dismissed – many without justification. The "Gold Card Desk" in Los Angeles noted that the city card holder may have an "urgent need to resolve any parking citation matter which requires special attention."

Auditors concluded that in "90 percent of those cases there was no paper trail showing where those original requests came from or justification for that dismissal."

To make matters worse, the city pays the ticket-handling contractor hundreds of thousands of dollars to process citations, even if they have been voided, and the city collects nothing from the well-connected offender. Ticket fixing is routine for those who have an "in" with government, including police officers. No wonder governments at all levels across the U.S. are on the verge of financial and moral political default.

As bad as it is in America, it's even worse in China, where the corruption involves a lot of bank financing as opposed to just fixing parking tickets. Provinces in China, like California, are struggling to repay debt. The Yunnan government had difficulty paying its debt on a highway project, sparking fears of a "debt domino" crisis. Lax budget controls by local government are a chronic problem, and officials are accustomed to borrowing heavily to solve their financial problems. "Borrow first, ask questions later" is how many local governments in China operate.

Projects in China are approved by central government departments before the funds are given out. But in an effort to balance local interests, the amount given out often ends up being only a portion of what is needed. Thus, local governments are expected to contribute a share, with other sources contributing the rest. In some underdeveloped regions of central and western China, funds for projects are usually raised through loans, mainly from banks, that will not be repaid because of the indemic corruption that permeates the public and financial sectors.

### Super Failure

The failure of the U.S. Congress' 12-member bipartisan deficit-cutting "supercommittee" in November 2011 to propose even one dollar in deficit reduction reflects how wide the divide is in Washington, and has left Capitol Hill without a strategy for tackling the nation's spiraling debt. The committee could not come up with the minimum $1.2 trillion of deficit reduction required under its mandate, much less the $4 trillion that deficit hawks said was necessary to help stabilize the finances of the U.S. government, whose debt at the time topped $15 trillion.

The committees' failure further rattled the financial markets and set the stage for mandatory cuts to defense and domestic programs that began in 2013. There are many skeptics, myself included, who believe that such cuts cannot ever take place because of the intense lobbying by defense contractors and the health care industry.

What is shocking, but not surprising, is that hours after convening the first panel working meeting of the committee, members of both parties on the panel excused themselves to go to fundraisers they planned for themselves, giving lobbyists and influence peddlers an opportunity to "express" their First Amendment right of free speech.

Despite the growing calls for the committee members to stop raising money until they concluded their task of cutting $1.2 trillion from the federal budget, most adhered to the time-honored tradition of mixing their politics with plenty of cash.

The threat of mandatory cuts was intended to spur agreement, but lobbyists for the firms affected by such cuts wasted no time going to work on members of Congress to overturn the automatic steep cuts in the defense budget. It will be interesting to see if the mandatory cuts take place.

### United We Stand

America was united like never before after 9/11. It was never more divided than on 9/11/10. These United States of America can only survive united. Divided we fall.

The election of Barack Obama, stimulus package, health care plan, building of a mosque near Ground Zero, Koran-burning threat by a hate-mongering preacher from Florida blown out of all proportion by a duped and misguided media, broad-net surveillance of law-abiding Muslims, unemployment at over 10 percent in many parts of the country all added fuel to the teakettles boiling across America.

Not only is America's political fabric in tatters, but so is the family fabric. The U.S. crossed an important marital threshold in 2009. The number of young adults who have never been married surpassed, for the first time in more than a century, the number who were married. The result, declining birthrates that are reshaping suburban communities around the country. Children, the mainstay of suburbia and residential neighborhoods across America for more than a half-century, are fewer and increasingly sparse in many places. Maybe that is a good thing, since a third of Americans have been arrested by the age of 23 for an offense other than a minor traffic violation. That figure is significantly higher than the 22 percent found in a 1965 study. Add to that the sustained physical and emotional abuse of bullying that damages the lives of young people whose only sin is appearing weak or weird to their peers and *We the Apathetic Maids* have to wake up to the fact that teenage crime and bullying are problems linked to the broader issues of violence in American life – and the disappearing family.

According to the 2010 census, the share of the population under age 18 dropped in 95 percent of U.S. counties since 2000. There are exceptions, of course. The Sperminator Arnold Schwarzenegger and Senator John Edwards are the poster fathers for having secret extramarital children, a subject I first discussed *in Custom Maid Spin*. There are now more households in America with dogs than children. The main reasons are job insecurity and concerns about the country's economic future.

The ailing U.S. economy, jobs, taxes and big government were the key issues of the 2008 and 2012 presidential elections and the 2010 congressional elections. Foreign affairs, national security and the conflicts in the Middle East and the Caucuses – and, of course, the wars in Iraq and Afghanistan – played second fiddle. Most American voters know little about U.S. foreign policy and care even less. Their top concern is domestic policy, which includes a job, an affordable home, health care, education for their children – and sports.

Unemployment hit its highest monthly rate in five years as Sarah Palin accepted the GOP's vice presidential nomination in 2008. U.S. joblessness shot up to 6.1 percent in August during the American political convention season while China basked in the glory of its outstanding opening and closing ceremony showmanship and gold medal performance at the Beijing 2008 Olympics. America, notwithstanding the brilliant performance of the Redeem Team, came in a distant second in the gold medal count.

While the Chinese were drinking tea by the gallons as their economy grew by more than 11 percent in 2010, Americans were flocking by the millions to the Tea Party movement as unemployment reached 10 percent or more in many parts of the country.

America is in desperate need of change, something both 2008 U.S. presidential contenders and their vice presidential nominees recognized and thankfully addressed. The reality is that both the Democratic and Republican senators who vied for the presidency are maverick Beltway politicos. Neither one has accepted or played by party convention or rules. Add to that a vice presidential nominee who was not a traditional Beltway insider – notwithstanding her Alaskan moose-hunting values – and one has to acknowledge change is on its way to D.C.

But is the change brought about by the 2008 presidential election and 2010 congressional elections good for America? I for one don't think so. It is very destructive.

The criticism of both Obama and Palin was aimed at their lack of experience. What experience? The Washington Beltway "Good Ol' Boy Network" failed domestic and foreign policies experience? Where does one start? Education, health care, housing, employment, Social Security, Medicare, federal deficit, default, failed foreign policies in the Middle East, the Americas, Iraq, Afghanistan, Russia, China…?

The experience of career politicians has brought about gridlock in the Beltway. It is long past time to get rid of the career politicians and adopt term limits so that real change can take place. Term limits that bring new young blood to Washington will be a refreshing change that America so desperately needs.

### *Conspiratorial Rebirth and Hope*
I attended a talk about conspiracies in America and a book signing by former Minnesota Governor Jessie Ventura in Santa Monica, California. He reminded his listeners that America belongs to *We the People,* but we have allowed the CIA and corporate-congressional powers to repeatedly conspire on ways and means to assassinate progressive leaders from Lincoln to Kennedy, character-assassinate leaders they disagree with like Clinton and Obama and conspire to start wars by creating false attacks on U.S. assets like the Gulf of Tonkin incident that got America into the Vietnam War and 9/11 that got America into Afghanistan and Iraq, as they continue to hijack our government and political system.

"This is a former Navy Seal and governor saying these things," I thought to myself as many others who listened to the talk voiced similar opinions as we stood in line to get our books signed. "Yeah, scary stuff, huh?" was the collective response. "Why can't someone like Ventura, who tells it like it is, run for the presidency? What is wrong with democracy in America?" were common questions discussed by several conspiracy theorists who expanded on Jessie's thoughts.

The truther, birther, nativist and 9-12 Patriot movements born and spawned virally by the Internet in the wake of the election of Barack Hussein Obama,

America's first multiracial president, was a reminder of how paranoid, divisive, conspiratorial and gridlocked the American constitutional process of checks and balances has been checked and choked without any balance.

The "birther" movement exemplifies just how off-track the country is from its founding ideals. For the president of the United States to have to repeatedly defend his American birthright after being in office for a couple of years and proof positive that he was born in Hawaii is a pathetic farce. For Republican presidential wannabes to repeatedly bring it up as some kind of conspiracy issue during America's Great Recession, as the country is on the verge of economic collapse, confirms how baseless and irrelevant issues become political issues while the real problems are debased and ignored by career politicians and their mainstream parties.

The outrage and backlash of many Christian white Americans at the election of a Christian president of color whose father was a Muslim must have created one hell of a breakdancing spin in the Founding Fathers' heaven as they tried to understand how their revolutionary political cornerstone – the Constitution – and Republican system of government, could be hijacked by a technologically savvy group of Christian fundamentalist extremists.

The Founding Fathers were predominantly religious Puritan Protestants – protest being the operative verb in their religious belief and rebellion against Catholicism – yet they made sure that a Catholic, Jew and Baptist were signatories to America's founding cornerstone. Had Muslims or Mormons been around, I have no doubt they too would have been invited to be signatories.

The absurdity of the Muslim paranoia sweeping America was highlighted during President Obama's visit to India and Indonesia after the midterm elections in November 2010. Sikhs were angry that he didn't visit their most sacred shrine – Amritsar's Golden Temple. But the White House feared that even more Americans would mistakenly believe Obama is a Muslim if they saw news images of him with a covering over his head – as temple rules require – accompanied by turbaned, bearded men.

Yet in Indonesia, Obama had no qualms about visiting Indonesia's largest mosque. Michael Chugani, a Hong Kong political commentator, summed up America's Islamophobia best. "Let's get this straight. White House officials worry Obama will look like a Muslim if he visits a Sikh temple but not if he visits a mosque. Is that because they think Sikhs look more like Muslims than actual Muslims? Or do they think Americans believe Sikhs are Muslims but that Muslims are not? We give up. The Muslims probably think it's all a Sikh joke."

There is no doubt in my mind that the Founding Fathers would support the building of the mosque and community center near Ground Zero – especially since a mosque has stood nearby for years before 9/11.

### Religious Tolerance
God, contrary to the Founding Fathers' wishes, appears to have seeped into all things American – in a very divisive and destructive way. Politics, family, education and domestic and foreign policy.

A trip I took in 2007 to Dubai confirmed another major subject I addressed in *Custom Maid Knowledge* – religious tolerance and co-existence. There in the heart of the city, across the street from the Emirate's main mosque, was a Hindu temple with barefoot worshipers leaving like their Muslim brothers and sisters across the street to find the shoes they had left outside to wash their feet before entering their houses of worship to pray for peace and prosperity. The Muslim and Hindu owned shops on the street outside the temple were selling Christmas decorations. What a refreshing reminder of how people of different religious stripes can co-exist.

Jews, Christians and Muslims share common roots in Abraham, patriarch of all three religions and founder of monotheism. According to the book of Genesis, God had sent Abraham on a mission to heal the divisions between men. His message was that regardless of language, culture or belief, all of mankind was to be part of one human family, before one God who sustains the whole of Creation.

I was reminded of this religious ideal – one America's Founding Fathers inscribed in the nation's founding cornerstones – during a conversation I had with my accountant Bob Dworkin while we were celebrating his 70th birthday in L.A. in January 2013. We were discussing religious differences, tolerance and the role of religion in America.

"You know, I have an Egyptian Muslim client who is married to a Christian woman and has a Jewish partner. 'Only in America,' he proudly proclaims, can he maintain this lifestyle without fear of religious recrimination."

In March 2008, Qatar opened its first church in an isolated compound outside Doha designed to cater to the spiritual needs of several Christian denominations. The first – and long overdue – church to be built in Arabia.

With Muhammad, and all 14 variant spellings of the name becoming the most popular name in the world, it is time Muslims, Christians, Hindus, Buddhists and Jews in America and elsewhere started taking Abraham's message to heart.

In Malaysia, a Muslim family donated their dead son's heart to a dying non-Muslim Chinese girl in 2007 during the holy month of Ramadan. It is another reminder of how much *We the Maids* can achieve if we sweep race and religion aside and see ourselves as one human race and stand up and fight together for our fundamental rights.

I went to Israel in May 2010 to attend a high school reunion. There I took my partner Pauline Taylor, a Scottish Presbyterian lass, to Jerusalem to visit the religious heartland of all monotheistic religions. I had taken Pauline to several Passover seders in the States, including one in 2009 at my high school classmate Rudy Cohen and his wife Smadar's home to share the Passover festivities with their family and friends. Passover celebrants always chant a prayer that hopes to celebrate the festival of freedom "next year in Jerusalem."

That prayer came true for Pauline, even though we weren't there for Passover, the dinner Jesus was at when he was nabbed and nailed. We were there for Purim and Succoth, the Israeli equivalent of American Halloween and the Chinese Full Moon Festival.

Everyone should visit the Holy Land and Jerusalem, no matter what their religion or personal beliefs. In fact, Israel should think of launching an annual multi-denominational religious celebration of all global religions to pray for peace and harmony if it doesn't already do so. People should go to the old city of Jerusalem and drink some revolutionary Jasmine tea or Arab coffee. It tastes different somehow, sipping it on the ancient cobblestones where Jesus and other prophets and saints of all faiths have walked. All political and religious extremes have managed to co-exist over the centuries despite many battles. Some bloodier than others, especially between Muslims and Christians rather than Muslims and Jews. Never mind the facts, the Jews still got blamed by everyone for everything – including Jesus' death. Hopefully that will change after Pope Benedict XVI exonerated the Jews for Jesus' death.

Jerusalem, home to the Israeli parliament, is the host city of the longest-serving democratically elected Arabs. Arabs living in Israel have the most individual human rights of any of their cousins living in nearby countries. They, like all Israelis, Jews and non-Jews alike, applaud at the sight of fellow semites throwing off the chains and shackles of oppression in the pursuit of the very freedoms enshrined by America's Founding Fathers and practiced in Israel.

Religious intolerance is also alive and well in Europe's enlightened Christian countries. Religious pluralism is becoming an endangered cultural cornerstone. Forbidding the building of new minarets in Switzerland and wearing of burqas in France – while Christian religious processions that require face-covering hoods are still allowed. The Grand Chamber of the European Court of Human Rights ruled in March 2011 that the presence of crucifixes in Italian primary schools does not violate the right of freedom of conscience of non-Christians. It was a success for the Italian government and 19 other governments that had urged the court to respect the national identities and dominant religious traditions of each of the 47 member states party to the convention. Minority religions have yet to win a case involving freedom of religious expression before that court.

Hopefully, the newly elected "progressive" Pope Francis will change the church's dismal record in the New World Order.

The American-led crusades in Iraq, Afghanistan, Pashtunistan and Libya have promoted everything but religious tolerance and co-existence. Assassinations, suicide bombings, protests, demonstrations and marshal law have spread beyond Afghanistan, Iraq and the Pashtun tribal areas in Pakistan to the entire country, Europe and America.

## Blind Faith

American religious followers of most major faiths do not know as much about their religions as atheists and agnostics, according to a survey released in September 2010 by the Pew Forum on Religion & Public Life. Atheists and agnostics are better informed than Catholics, Protestants, Baptists, Jews and Mormons about religions. In other words, Americans know almost nothing about their own religion and even less about the religions of other people. They follow their faith blindly, much the way they do their politics, even though they may be active participants in both. They are no different than the Muslim extremists that Americans are so quick to criticize.

This was highlighted by NPR's decision to fire news analyst Juan Williams for saying on Fox News' *The O'Reilly Factor* that he worries when he sees Muslims in traditional garb on airplanes. His firing was an example of how emotional the topic of Islam was in the 2010 midterm election. Naturally, he got hired by Fox News.

Park 51, the controversial mosque and community center near Ground Zero, opened with minimal fanfare in the wake of the 9/11 10th anniversary. The mosque portion of Park 51 had been open for religious worship for a year. It was the community center that opened its doors to the public. Sharif El-Gamal, the developer of the community center and the mosque, spoke at the event and said he hoped the center would be "a place that will bring a wounded community together."

"We had been shut out from this tragedy for almost 10 years. And then when we tried to do something that was a center of healing and a center of openess to all, people said, 'No, this is not your tragedy. You're not going to do this here. This is not your country.' And that hurt for the first time, because I had never experienced discrimination first hand," said Daisy Khan, executive director of the American Society for Muslim Advancement.

There is no room for religion in politics. That was the fundamental cornerstone the Founding Fathers built into the U.S. Constitution. Theocracies have repeatedly proven that over the centuries and today it is repeatedly reaffirmed in Islamic states. There is no place for a theocracy in the modern world. Religion has a role in society and the public discourse. But not in a modern world of representative governments that have replaced religion as a source of authority, regulation and security. Islamic Afghanistan, Somalia, Iran and Saudi Arabia believe only faith can amend the deficits and alleviate the pain caused by modern life.

The prism of the Muslim Middle East shows how the public role of religion has varied over time. In the late 19th-century Middle East, several religious movements emerged in response to Islam's encounter with the European colonial conquest and modernity. Traditionalists like Saudi Arabia's Wahhabis sought to preserve their culturally specific Islamic heritage. The modernist trend advocated an evolving Islam that would co-exist and flourish within this emerging modernity. And some people demanded separating Islam from the state entirely.

The 1970s brought revived and aggressive religious engagement in society and politics. Iran's Islamic Revolution of 1979 bolstered a new global era of religious politics in the Middle East and beyond by offering a tangible model of Islamic rule. That same year, Islamic militants seized the Grand Mosque of Mecca in a failed attempt to dislodge the Saudi rulers. The shocking assault spurred radicalization and accelerated rivalry between Wahhabi and Salafi trends. By the mid-1990s, the public space in the Middle East was dominated by Islamic movements, institutions and sensibilities. Religious groups in Sudan, Saudi Arabia, Afghanistan and Iran ruled through Islamic states.

"But the realization of an Islamic state carries within it contradictory seeds of its own decline. History has shown that religious states of any faith inevitably lead to the secularization of theology, for leaders, religious or not, must respond to day-to-day exigencies of governance. Sacred injunctions are bent, revised or cast aside to accommodate the requisites of governance or merely to justify power. Religion thus descends from the height of devotion and spirituality to be a pliable instrument to serve secular objectives," said Asef Bayat, a professor of sociology and Middle East studies at the University of Illinois. He has written a series *Religion, Politics & the Public Space*. I agree and highly recommend his articles.

"Cynical secularization of the sacred by the 'Islamic' states is alienating many Muslims. Secular faithful and even many members of the *ulema* – Muslim spiritual leaders – have pleaded for the separation of religion from the state, to restore both the sanctity of religion and the rationality of the state," Bayat added.

It's no different than what America's Founding Fathers believed. Most Muslims are seeking a post-Islamic trajectory where faith is merged with freedom and Islam with democracy, in which a civil democratic state can work within a pious society.

"For Muslim societies, not modernizing is no longer an option. Only a secular democratic state respecting basic human rights for all can provide good governance for the faithful and secular alike," Bayat concluded.

The divisive nature of the blind faith Americans have in their hypocritical preachers, many of whom are sexual predators, opposed to same-sex marriage while they have same-sex orgies, and support extremist politicians on the radio and TV talk shows they host and worship, were the thoughts going through my mind on September 11, 2010, as I boarded an 8 a.m. flight from New York to San Francisco.

Amazingly, but not to my surprise, nothing had changed by March 2012, when the February Koran burning "incident" by American servicemen near the detention center in Parwan, Afghanistan, brought relations between the U.S. and Afghanistan to a new low – and the unnecessary loss of more American lives.

It highlighted religious ignorance and intolerance, not only by the American Koran burners, but by the Taliban. Masked Taliban gunmen who shot 14-year-old Malala Yousafzai in the head on a school bus filled with terrified children because she spoke up about her passion for education and became a symbol of defiance against Taliban subjugation. Thankfully, she survived.

That Malala's voice could be deemed a threat to the Taliban – that they could see a schoolgirl's death as desirable and justifiable – is evidence of both the militants' brutal intolerance and her courage.

In Somalia, Abdi Jeylani Marshale, a comedian who ridiculed Islamic militants, was assassinated in August 2012, for his courage.

Religion also took center stage in the ugly and divisive Republican presidential primary that year. Front runner Mitt Romney's Mormon religion became an obstacle and was denounced as a "cult." Many prospective primary voters told pollsters that they did not regard Mormons as Christians. Two controversial aspects of the Mormon religion were pervasive. Mormon posthumous proxy baptism of Jews – especially Holocaust victims – and the church's historical ban on black men in the Mormon priesthood until the ban was lifted in 1978.

Jews do not believe that baptism has any religious significance – it's just water – but the Mormon practice leaves many Jews offended and feeling disrespected. "It smacks," said Rabbi Moshe Waldoks of Temple Beth Zion, in Brookline, Mass., "of a certain sense of proselytism: If you can't get them while they're alive, you'll get them while they're dead."

Rick Santorum said that John F. Kennedy's speech in which he declared that "I believe in an America where the separation of church and state is absolute," made him want to throw up because it was "an absolute doctrine that was abhorrent at the time of 1960."

Santorum campaigned on the notion that religion must take center stage in public life and the public sphere. "I don't believe in an America where the separation of church and state is absolute," he said.

Some big historical names beg to differ. James Madison, "Father of the Constitution" and the fourth president of the United, wrote in 1822 that: "Every new and successful example therefore, of a perfect separation between the ecclesiastical and civil matters, is of importance; and I have no doubt that every new example will succeed, as every past one has done, in showing that religion and government will both exist in greater purity the less they are mixed together."

Adding to the religious frenzy of the 2012 presidential primaries was the Denver Bronco's evangelical scrambling quarterback Tim Tebow, the most popular Christian in sports, honored with the viral phenomenon verb Tebowing – his kneeling on one knee and praying after every game. He has more followers than most preachers and evokes more passion than most politicians. Not because he is a quarterback, but rather because his conduct – kind, charitable, chaste, guileless – seems to actually vindicate his claim to be in possession of a life-altering truth.

His six outrageous comebacks took the Broncos to the playoffs against the New England Patriots, in New England, where his riveting ride to the Super Bowl was cut short, two steps short of paydirt. Denver lost to New England 45-10. I watched the game on TV and couldn't help wondering. What did he expect would happen? The Founding Fathers have home court advantage. Many people, especially in New England, find his on-field religious displays offensive.

That should have been a warning to Gisele Bundchen, the supermodel wife of New England Patriot quarterback Tom Brady, who sent an e-mail to friends and family encouraging them to pray for her husband's success in the Super Bowl against the New York Giants. The Giants upset the favored Patriots. Another message from the Founding Fathers, I wonder? God abandoned the Patriots, just like he did religious Republican primary contenders Governor Rick Perry, Congresswoman Michele Bachman, former Senator Rick Santorum and Newt Gingrich.

Faith may be a virtue, but there are times when it has to bend. Clashes over religion in the public square are as old as the Republic. Jon Meacham reminds us of this historical reality in an op-ed piece he wrote for *Time* where he said: "Believers should remember that when he was on trial before Pontius Pilate, Jesus said his kingdom was not of this world. It still isn't."

Religion cannot be the answer to what ails *We the Maids*. It is merely a moral guide. That is the sole role of religion in politics. That was the Founding Fathers' clear and unequivocal message. Something even China's Communist leaders are coming to terms with by reintroducing Taoism as a guide to healing moral lapses in a modern society.

Unlike political and religious leaders in America, China is reintroducing religion to heal children and ensure they are given the moral tools to tackle a revolutionary future.

This moral lapse was horrifically exemplified by the cold-blooded response of passers-by who looked the other way and ignored an injured two-year-old struck three times by two cars and left on the street for dead in October 2011 in the southern city of Guangzhou. A street cleaner finally came to her aid. Wang Yue was critically injured and in a coma and eventually died in a hospital.

Some scholars attribute China's moral collapse to the "Little Emperor" traits of the generations of only-children born under the government's rigid 1979 "one child" policy. Generations of spoiled, selfish and lazy citizens.

China's moral collapse was magnified by an American woman who a week earlier saved a Chinese woman from drowning in West Lake, a famous scenic spot in the eastern city of Hangzou. Commentators noted that only a foreigner would dare such a rescue. Just another metaphor for how America can contribute to China's political salvation.

Taoism was first articulated thousands of years ago. My book *Custom Maid Spin* discusses the religion at length. Unlike Buddhism and Christianity, Taoism is China's only indigenous religion. It flourished and gained official status during the Tang and Song dynasties, but gradually lost influence. Like other religions, it was eventually banned, and Taoists were persecuted during the Cultural Revolution. It has seen a recent revival as a relative degree of religious tolerance and freedom has been restored as moral compasses for people who no longer believe in communism.

To accuse President Barack Obama of "dismantling religious liberty" in the 2012 presidential campaign feud over health insurance coverage of birth control, accusing him of a systematic assault on religion, convinced me that religion should take election years off. What is it about religion that, when it enters the political arena, we are suddenly arguing over vomit, contraception, sluts and prostitutes?

Back to my 9/11 10th anniversary visit, the controversy of the Westboro Baptist Church protests at military funerals because of its view that the deaths are God's punishment for the nation's tolerance of homosexuality; the fight over building a mosque at Ground Zero; calls for Koran burning on the eve of the 9/11 anniversary and the looming November 2010 midterm elections, with enriched Wall Street bankers and long unemployment lines and ever-growing lists of foreclosed homes were overshadowed by what I had experienced the preceding two days in the Big Apple.

## *A New Start*

All religions and major cultures have New Years Day festivities to celebrate a new start with family and friends. Mine started out on September 9, 2010, the first day of the Jewish New Year 5771, in a restaurant on Seventh Avenue for lunch with the Bermans – Jake, my classmate from high school, his wife Kris, their children Lielle, Alex and his wife Brennan, and Kent, their cousin. The conversation and mood of the luncheon, much like America's, was downright depressing. Kris' brother Scott had just become a single father at the age of 57 after his partner and mother of his daughter died a few days earlier in a pregnancy complication, leaving him with a daughter born 20 days prematurely. The conversation at lunch was all-American and focused on the role each family member would play to support Scott in raising his daughter.

When you stop and think of how many New Year celebrations there are a year, and the numbers of years apart they are, Jewish 5771, Chinese 4708, and Christian 2011, and that's not counting the Hindu, Mayan and Muslim, to name just a few, it's a wonder anyone knows when to start anew. As if that isn't bad enough, an astrophysicist has pointed out that at the dawning of the Age of Aquarius, a naturally occurring wobble in the earth's rotation – technically known as a "precession" – had altered the alignment of stars' overhead from their traditional positions in Western astrology.

Accordingly, Capricorn, which astrologers say begins its month-long term in December, starts on January 20, based on the actual position of the stars. Aquarius moves from January 21 through February 19 to February 16 to March 11 and I am no longer an Aquarian, but have become a Capricorn – and there is a new hitherto little-heard-of 13th astrological sign – Ophiuchus. Babylonians had it in their daily horoscopes but it got dropped somewhere along the line.

Imagine what would happen if there were no leap years. Absolute chaos. Why? The Earth doesn't circle the sun in exactly 365 days. Rather it takes 365.2425 days instead of a nice round number. Those extra digits add up to almost a full day, but not quite, every four years. Since the Roman ruler Julius Caesar first added a leap year to the calendar every four years around 46 B.C., roughly 500 leap days have come and gone. That wasn't perfect because the Julian calendar was adding too many days. By the 1500s, Easter was slipping back into winter about 10 days off. So the modern calendar used today dates to 1582, when Pope Gregory XIII instituted the Gregorian calendar with its first leap year in 1584.

2010 turned out to be a good year for the Jews. The German-born Pope Benedict, who was a member of the Hitler Youth in Nazi Germany, made a sweeping exoneration of the Jewish people for the death of Christ. The Pope deconstructs one particular account which has the crowd saying, "His blood be on us and on our children" – a phrase frequently cited as evidence of the collective guilt Jews bore and the curse that they carried and the resulting anti-semitism over the centuries that culminated in Hitler's

Holocaust. It was a landmark statement that would help fight anti-semitism. It was not a good year for Coptic Christians in pre-or-post-Mubarak Egypt. The deadly fighting between Christians and Muslims was re-ignited in post-Jasmine Revolution Egypt by Muslim extremists. Not a good year for two Muslim politicians in Pakistan who stood up for Aasia Bibi, an embattled Christian mother of four sentenced to death for allegedly insulting the prophet Muhammad. They were opposed to the blasphemy law under which she had been tried and were gunned down by Muslim extremists for their convictions.

After lunch, I decided to continue the start of my New Year by checking out three New York scenes, Ground Zero, Wall Street and Union Square, to reflect on the New World Disorder.

Construction at Ground Zero was well underway with one of the original columns returned. Mourners who lost family members and friends, and others, like myself, honoring the memory of those who perished there that fateful day, reflecting on the domestic policy changes in America and the geopolitical events triggered in the aftermath of 9/11, were everywhere under the watchful eyes of the construction crane operators – and the NYPD. Tears, flowers, prayers, American flags, memories, fears and thoughts of the future of America were blowing in the afternoon breeze.

Wall Street, a few blocks from Ground Zero, where George Washington was sworn in as America's first president and where the financial titans and stock market that collapsed global financial markets and brought America and the world to its knees with the Great Depression of the 1930s and the Great Recession of 2008 are based, was another depressing stroll down a depressing memory lane. The fact that nothing had really changed only made me more depressed and angry, convinced of the reality and need for a Third American Revolution.

America's mood was reflected in a snippet of conversation I overheard on the street as I dodged the herds of panhandlers. An unemployed construction worker was complaining to his female companion how hard it was for him to find work, and "God knows" when he would.

Disgust washed over me as I thought about the flip side of the coin – the return to extravagance and free-spending by the Wall Street crowd, now that their pay and bonuses are flying high again despite the financial misery they helped create and the massive handouts they pocketed. Goldman Sachs, Morgan Stanley, Citigroup, Bank of America and JPMorgan Chase alone set aside nearly $90 billion for bonuses in 2010. Even worse, how about the 50 Lehman Bros. employees who were awarded nearly $700 million in the year before that investment bank collapsed?

A Citigroup whistle blower accused the troubled bank of "knowingly" vouching for the quality of a large number of "deficient" loans sold to

Fannie Mae and Freddie Mac. Sherry Hunt, a Citigroup quality-assurance vice president, cited an "overall systematic failure that threatens the thin ice the entire market is treading on."

These are the institutions that *We the Apathetic Maids* bailed out. Not one banker or wheeler-dealer at these financial giants that brought the world to its knees has gone to jail. None of them were subjected to a criminal trial. They got slapped on the wrist. Pay some fines and continue doing business as usual while *We the Apathetic Maids* continue being wage slaves – assuming we can find work.

In two of the biggest civil settlements since the financial crisis, the major banks agreed in January 2013 to cough up nearly $19 billion to resolve federal allegations of mortgage misdeeds and foreclosure abuses. Under the settlement, cash relief will go to borrowers who went through questionable foreclosures in 2009 and 2010, and mortgage assistance to homeowners in danger of losing their homes to help them reduce the principal owed or monthly payments.

The civil settlement was agreed to after prosecutors dropped criminal investigations against the bankers responsible for the financial meltdown. Why? Since when can Americans buy their innocence and avoid criminal prosecution by making a civil settlement – and with taxpayer dollars to boot?

JPMorgan Chase and Credit Suisse agreed in November 2012 to pay the SEC $417 million over their deceptive packaging and sale of troubled mortgage securities to investors.

Goldman Sachs and JPMorgan agreed to settle with the U.S. Securities and Exchange Commission and pay hundreds of millions of dollars in fines for the subprime games they played. JPMorgan agreed to pay $153.6 million to end an SEC suit. The SEC alleged that the bank failed to tell investors in 2007 that a hedge fund helped pick, and bet against, underlying securities in the collateralized debt obligation that JPMorgan purchased, which later became worthless.

Just as worthless and meaningless as the Libor interest rate, which has little basis in reality. An open secret to the banking world that was unmasked for *We the Apathetic Maids* to see how dirty the banking world really is. Banks will collude with one another solely for their own selfish gains.

The credit-default swap market deals in insurance-like derivatives, or side bets, that protect investors from bad events, like a company going bankrupt or a country failing to pay its debts. It operates under a similar principle as Libor and is just as vulnerable to manipulation.

How about the sneak previews that hedge funds get from research analysts at investment banks about a change in a company that allows the funds to trade on the information – and make a lot of money – before other investors find out?

The financial scandal scoreboard seems to be adding new shenanigans every few weeks. What is really scandalous is how the enforcement agencies meant to oversee and regulate banks actually allow them to perpetuate their scandalous behavior because the enforcers are reined in by their superiors and the career politicians financed into office by these very banks.

The bank settlements and their multibillion-dollar chump-change penalties have short-changed *We the Apathetic Maids* by allowing bankers, bank regulators and career politicians to again get away with murder – financial assassinations of *We the People*.

HSBC laundered money for drug cartels and terrorists as the Office of the Comptroller of the Currency, which is the nation's primary bank overseer, "had failed to take a single enforcement action against the bank, formal or informal, over the previous six years, despite ample evidence" of money laundering, read the 2012 report prepared by investigators for the U.S. Senate.

HSBC agreed to pay $1.9 billion to settle the case. Again, no bank executives were charged as part of the investigation, leading some analysts, myself included, to question the government's willingness to hold powerful Wall Street firms accountable.

?rite HSBC story is that of American businessman Craig Briggs who withdrew cash from an HSBC ATM machine in Shanghai, only to find out that the 100-yuan notes were counterfeit when a taxi driver and a McDonald's restaurant refused to accept them. When he informed his Hong Kong branch of the problem, the bank refused to reimburse him or to even investigate. The bank assured him that he would get genuine yuan notes in Hong Kong and did not reply when asked how to get genuine notes in China.

Briggs expected the incident to spark concern at HSBC regarding the problem of fake notes. "I want to be able to go to China and travel with confidence that the currency I am getting from their machines is genuine. Now I have doubts about that," Briggs said.

During the decade leading up to the 2008 financial meltdown, Standard Chartered knowingly laundered money for Iran, while every other major U.S. bank was blindly financing the building of unsalable subdivisions across the country, as the New York Federal Reserve stood idly by and marveled at the desperate antics of home builders seeking to lure buyers, just as they did with Libor when they first heard about the rate rigging – instead of getting off their lazy bureaucratic comfort zones and making sure the laws governing these financial institutions were enforced.

The Fed regulators gave little credence to the possibility that the faltering housing market would weigh on the economy, according to transcripts that the Fed released in January 2012. Instead, they continued to tell one another throughout 2006 that the greatest danger was inflation – the possibility that the economy would grow too slow. Talk about incompetent bank regulators – at America's central bank, no less – and bankrolled by *We the Apathetic Maids*.

What is even more stunning, under-reported by the media and its pundits, is the fact that the Federal Deposit Insurance Corporation, since 2007, has depleted the FDIC deposit-insurance fund with $92.5 billion in losses to bail out 471 failed U.S. banks – yet it has settled with the guilty culprits for their failures for a mere $787 million – a fraction of its total losses. The FDIC has refused to pursue any civil or criminal actions to severely penalize or jail bankers, in order to scare others into behaving – and to make matters worse – has agreed to a "no press release" clause that requires the FDIC, with certain exceptions, never to mention the deal.

The FDIC excuse? It benefits by collecting money without the hassle and expense of litigation. Easy for them to say at *We the Apathetic Maids* expense.

While career politicians in Washington and other financial centers worry about funding their reelection campaigns, central bankers kill time by printing money and denying or delaying the inevitable – until it's too late – just so they can maximize their pension benefits.

Goldman Sachs paid a record $550 million fine for failing to inform clients in 2007 that it allowed a hedge fund that also bet against housing to help formulate the CDOs. In other words, the banks that make billions each year admit they messed up, usually pay a relatively small fine, announce a public mea culpa and have no more liability. They continue doing business as usual. No surprise really, considering that one or more of their partners have been running the U.S. Treasury Department under every president I can think of. Sounds like a grand slam to me, not just for Goldman Sachs, but for all the banks. It's no wonder bankers are continuing to celebrate and earning and spending money like drunken sailors. And for good reason.

Notwithstanding the hefty fines the big banks have been hit with, they still managed to increase their earnings dramatically. JPMorgan Chase & Co., the country's largest bank by assets, posted $5.7 billion in earnings in the fourth quarter of 2012, a 53 percent increase over the same period a year earlier.

The results surprised analysts who had totally underestimated bank earnings and profitability, giving *We the Apathetic Maids* a view into Wall Street's profitability as the U.S. and global economy struggles to recover and as the industry struggles as it grapples with new banking regulations they are actively trying to repeal.

Bankers' arrogant swagger and extravagant spending on parties, dinners and bidding more than $400,000 for a summer rental in the Hamptons was just the tip of the iceberg. A Morgan Stanley trader tried to hire a dwarf for a bachelor party in Miami, and asked the dwarf to meet him at the airport in a "Men in Black" style suit because he wanted to handcuff the dwarf to the bachelor.

The scene was even more extravagant a few months later in Hong Kong at the 50th birthday party for Brian Brille, head of Bank of America Asia Pacific, who is well known on the New York social scene. He wore a grey Hugh Hefner-esque jacket. Women dressed like Playmates, with feather boas and satin ears, and danced behind a pink silk screen. All this as the unemployment line back home snakes around the block. And bankers want to know why Americans are angry and demand change?

I echo the harsh sentiments of Charles Munger, vice chairman of Berkshire Hathaway, who squarely blamed the bankers for the financial crisis. He said: "The cause was a combination of megalomania, stupidity, insanity, and I would say evil on the part of bankers and mortgage brokers.

"Wall Street was a gambling house, and the house's odds were better than a Vegas casino... . It was hog heaven for them. But it created vast damage with terrible consequences to civilization.

"In the 1920s they called it bucket shops – just the name tells you it's bad – and they eventually made it illegal, and rightly so. They should do the same this time," Munger says.

The big banks that dominate derivatives and other financial instruments with fancy names are aggressively fighting any regulatory tightening, especially increases in the leverage ratio, which measures the amount of capital the bank holds against its assets, even though they know these instruments are prone to catastrophic failure.

The bankruptcy of MF Global Holdings in late 2011 sent shock waves through financial markets, but nothing else. This "mini Lehman" crash became another financial yawn and banks continued business as usual. Again, no criminal charges were filed, even though hundreds of millions of clients' funds had disappeared.

The catastrophic losses that can be suffered by banks' speculative investments in financial instruments that most people can't even pronounce was again demonstrated in the spring of 2012 by none other than Wall Street powerhouse JPMorgan Chase. It announced it had suffered more than a $5 billion trading loss. The bank wasn't so apologetic about its loss, but the episode surely undercuts the financial industry's complaints about too much regulation.

It was JPMorgan lobbyists who led the charge to weaken the tougher regulations so desperately needed to prevent bankers from sticking *We the Apathetic Maids* with the cleanup bill for their risky trades that boost their bonuses when things go right, but wreak havoc and blow up the financial system and broader economy when they are wrong.

This is not what Paul Volcker had in mind with the Volcker rule, a crucial provision of the Dodd-Frank financial reform law. It was supposed to stop banks from doing the sort of risky trading that was one of the big causes of the financial meltdown. The banks hate the rule because less speculation means less profit and lower bonuses for traders and bank executives. The banks and their lobbyists just watered down the regulations and dumbed down the regulators. Banks must be regulated by *We the Maids*. We must sweep in the reforms advocated by Volcker. Especially when under today's rules even as a trader of JPMorgan in London was selling piles of insurance on corporate debt, figuring that the U.S. economy was on the upswing, a mutual fund elsewhere in the bank was taking the other side of the bet. A repeat of what Goldman Sachs did in 2007, when it sold subprime mortgage securities while betting against them.

No surprise really. With insider trading by members of Congress, no different than their financial backers, why should they stop it? Hopefully, now that a bill banning insider trading by members of Congress has been approved, things will change, not only in Washington, but on Wall Street. But I have my doubts about the Security and Exchange Commission's ability to enforce the law as long as the current duopoly game of Republicans and Democrats financed by bankers' lobbyists continues.

Governments have much to do with regulating bankers, capital requirements and their bonuses – or at least they should have.

"Big bonuses in banking these days are to a significant extent the result of government interventions in banking. These bonuses would be nowhere near as big if governments in developed economies did not routinely change the fundamental risk/reward balance of the business by guaranteeing public deposits," wrote Hong Kong columnist Jake van der Kamp in a January 2012 column. I complemented Jake on his colum when I caught up with him at the Main Bar of the Foreign Correspondents Club in Hong Kong.

"I sympathize with the opposing view," Jake said. "I myself would not like to wake up one morning and find that I am to be paid only 50 cents on the dollar for my deposits because the bank in which I put those deposits had run into trouble. I also accept that most people these days have no easy way of knowing which bank might be a safe one and which not," he added as we ordered another round of drinks.

"There is no escaping the corollary of government guarantees," Jake continued. "When you protect the liabilities side of a bank balance sheet while letting the same old rogues run the asset side, you inevitably encourage them to take greater risks with money entrusted to them by others and to keep the rewards themselves."

The time is long overdue for these selfish bankers to pay the price for their reckless behavior. They must face justice. They, not *We the Apathetic Maids*, must bear the cost of their mistakes. If necessary, they must go to jail for their crimes. Banking can no longer continue with a business as usual attitude. Enough of bailouts and tax breaks for criminal banking behavior.

Judges and career politicians must start following the example of New York Federal Judge Jed Rakoff. He rejected a proposed $285-million settlement between the Securities and Exchange Commission and Citigroup Inc. that would have allowed the bank to avoid admitting it defrauded investors over toxic mortgage securities. He said that other similar settlements had not stopped banks from breaking the law, and added that the fines are "pocket change to any entity as large as Citigroup."

Rakoff's order, based on the jury's message to him and Wall Street, echo public outrage that Wall Street and the banks have been let off too easy for their role in causing the Great Recession of 2008 – which, along with the resulting fallout, is still with us today. Surely there is a better way than bankruptcies, bailouts, bail bonds and billion-dollar settlements.

## Glass-Steagall Act

There was and still is an option that can again kick-start the New World Order in banking. The Glass-Steagall Act, the 1933 law passed after the Great Depression that separated commercial banks from investment banks, to prevent another financial disaster by limiting the size and power of American banks. The law prompted the breakup of J.P. Morgan & Company, which spun off its brokerage arm to create Morgan Stanley.

With the Depression-era fading from memory, the increasingly powerful banking industry started to chip away at the provisions. One of its foremost critics and leader in the successful effort to repeal the act in the 1990s, Sanford I. Weill, founder of Citigroup, confesses that the repeal was a mistake and in July 2012 called for its reinstatement.

Bottom line: Wall Streets behemoths are too big to regulate and must be cut back down to size. The alternative? Nationalize.

Economists in and around the University of Chicago, who founded the modern conservative tradition, believed that the only way to preserve competition was to nationalize. One of the most important Chicago School leaders, Henry C. Simons, declared in 1934 that "the corporation is simply running away with our economic and political system."

Simons, a hero of libertarian idol Milton Friedman, was skeptical of enormity. "Few of our gigantic corporations," he wrote, "can be defended on the ground that their present size is necessary to reasonably full exploitation of production economies."

Gar Alperovitz, a professor of political economy at the University of Maryland, summed it up best in an Op-Ed column he wrote for *The New York Times* on July 23, 2012.

"The central problem, then as now, was that very large corporations could easily undermine regulatory and antitrust strategies. The Nobel laureate George J. Stigler demonstrated how regulation was commonly 'designed and operated primarily for' the benefit of the industries involved. And numerous conservatives, including Simons, concluded that large corporate players could thwart antitrust 'break-them-up' efforts – a view Friedman came to share.

"Simons did not shrink from the obvious conclusion: 'Every industry should be either effectively competitive or socialized.' If other remedies were unworkable, 'The state should face the necessity of actually taking over, owning, managing directly' all 'industries in which it is impossible to maintain effectively competitive conditions.'

"Think about it. In the mid-20th century, banks were far less concentrated than they are today, when the five biggest – JPMorgan Chase, Bank of America, Citigroup, Wells Fargo and Goldman Sachs – dominate the industry, with combined assets amounting to more than half of America's economy.

"With high-paid lobbyists contesting every proposed regulation, it is increasingly clear that big banks can never be effectively controlled as private businesses. If an enterprise or five is so large and concentrated that competition and regulation are impossible, the most market-friendly step is to nationalize its functions."

Hmmm, money-for-honey thought. Especially today, when banks' credibility is so low and their clout clobbered.

### *Political Stink Hole*

I love New York City, a fact I discuss at length in *Custom Maid Knowledge*. I love it because of its energy, creativity and history. It is, after all, the cradle of America, where the Federal Republic and American capitalism was founded. George Washington was sworn in as America's first president there, and it is home to many other historical moments, including 9/11. It is a city that represents America's finest and worst. It is the city that gave us Michael Bloomberg and mud-slinging Rudy Guiliani and Hillary Clinton in the 2008 presidential election.

I periodically drive through Hunts Point when I'm in New York. The stink in the air reminds me of how rotten to the core American politics has become since Washington became the Republic's founding president. The fact that three of the four top contenders for the White House in 2008 came from New York brought to mind Tammany Hall politics and Hunts Point, which has the largest food market on the East Coast, several waste transfer stations, a city-operated waste-water treatment plant and a private company that turns sewage sludge into fertilizer pellets.

Washington, D.C. needs a similar fertilizer plant to turn its political sludge into public benefits for We the Apathetic Maids and get the career politicians out of town.

Hillary and Rudy G. were both embroiled in political scandals, accepted donations from criminals and tried to buy their party's nominations by raising more money from corporate America than any of their fellow contenders. Bloomberg self-financed his campaign with money he made the good old-fashioned American way – from corporate America, primarily New York banks.

Bloomberg, whom I had the pleasure of meeting to discuss business in Hong Kong in 2000, had flown over in his new jet. He did it again in November 2010 to attend an environmental summit, where he was crowned chairman of the global climate change network C40. Only this time he got himself into a typical political-business hypocrital environmental mess by not walking the talk. He was the only delegate among the 1,679 international guests who insisted on flying to town in his private jet. The 16-hour flight accounted for 106,366kg of carbon dioxide – or 8.17 percent of the total carbon output represented at the 2010 C40 Climate Dialogue.

To put that into perspective, that's more carbon than was used to run the entire four-day international conference – including all the electricity, water and gas used at the convention center in over 219 conference hours, and all the energy consumed at the hotels that some 450 international delegates stayed at. It also includes all the food served, waste produced and transport used to shuttle delegates around town.

New Yorkers have had a stinking run of politicians going back to the founding of the Republic. More recently, former Governor Eliot Spitzer was forced to resign in 2008 over a call girl scandal. His successor, David A. Paterson, has been mired in a series of scandals and ethical questions. At least five of Paterson's staff members have resigned under a cloud of misconduct. Fraud and kickbacks in New York state pension funds, highway construction and the building industry in general are accepted as norms of doing business with the state.

When I was visiting New York in the fall of 2010, in the midst of the gubernatorial race, I was astounded by how much more mud-slinging was taking place than during the 2008 campaign.

The state was broke. It was facing a $5.5 billion deficit, an extraordinary exodus of residents that could drain an additional $4 billion in tax revenue and result in the loss of two congressional seats, yet neither the Democratic candidate, Attorney General Andrew Cuomo, nor the Tea Party-backed Republican businessman Carl Paladino, addressed any of these issues. Instead, the campaigns continued the New York tradition of dirty politics with such weighty issues as manliness, pornography, sexual infidelity and hypocracy. Paladino spoke openly about his mistress and love child as he trashed Cuomo for his alleged infidelity and that of his former wife, Kerry Kennedy, daughter of Robert F. Kennedy.

Leaving JFK airport in a bus heading to New York City after a "red eye" flight from the West Coast or Asia is something I painstakingly enjoy after a large cup of coffee and a shave, because of the changing faces of the drivers and ticket collectors that have been a pretty revealing barometer over the years of America's latest immigration waves.

One thing that sticks in my craw on my visits over the last few years are the tip jars at coffee shops that solicit gratuities regardless of the quality of service. As if that isn't bad enough, once on the bus, still blurry-eyed at 7.30 a.m., there are two signs staring me in the face: "Tips Not Included in Fare," and "Tips Welcome."

The bus drivers, many of them Chinese, also make sure they remind you at least once during the journey into the city that tips are not included but welcome. They remind me of the mainland Chinese beggars that seem to have taken over the streets of Hong Kong. Many of the beggars are disabled, terribly deformed, limbless or burnt. Are they legal or illegal and who are the traffickers benefiting from their misfortune? Just another daily reminder of the futility of immigration laws.

There were seven candidates in the New York gubernatorial race grovelling like the Chinese beggars in Hong Kong and the Chinese bus drivers delivering travelers to and from the New York City airports. The candidate who made the most sense to me was Kristin Davis, a former madam who said during a debate: "The career politicians in Albany are the biggest whores in New York state. I might be the only person sitting on this stage with the right experience to deal with them."

The public has not only lost faith in its career politicians, but law enforcement as well. That is the saddest commentary of our times. This was exemplified by stories of "ticket fixing" during my 2011 visit, and the acquittal of two New York police officers accused in the rape of a woman they had been called to help get home from a club after she got drunk with friends celebrating a job promotion.

"It's scary because I feel there are less and less people you can trust," said Erin Walsh, 31, a school teacher in New York. "It's hard to wrap my brain around the situation. People in positions of power should do the right thing."

Reactions to the officers' acquittal revealed the simple terror elicited by the case – that the very people sworn to protect you can take advantage of you – even rape you.

New York City, where the Republic was founded, is representative of how dirty and corrupt America is – politically and economically. Its "Tammany Hall" politics stinks to high heaven. It is up to *We the People*, the *Maids,* to sweep in the reforms needed to clean up America.

*Financial Spin*

An example of how bad the political stinkhole is in New York and America was summed up by New York State Comptroller Thomas DiNapoli in April 2010. He issued a damning report on the Empire State's financial practices. Albany's budgets, he observed, increasingly employ "fiscal manipulations" to present a "distorted view of the state's finances."

Money shuffled among accounts to hide deficits, loans made to the state to itself, and other maneuvers DiNapoli called a "fiscal shell game" are meant to "mask the true magnitude of the state's structural budget deficit."

DiNapoli's report describes in refreshingly candid language a growing lack of transparency, which hides the state's true fiscal condition in a "deficit shuffle."

In neighboring New Jersey, the Securities and Exchange Commission filed fraud charges against the state for misrepresenting its financial situation, particularly its pension obligations, and misleading investors in its bonds.

Taxpayers in New Jersey, like those in many other states, are still paying off bonds for stadiums and arenas that have been abandoned by the teams they were built for. An example is the old Giants Stadium, demolished to make way for the new Meadowlands Stadium. It still carries about $110 million in debt, or nearly $13 for every New Jersey resident, even though it is now a parking lot.

Stadiums, convention centers, aquariums, trash incinerators and other things such as schools and courthouses, are another source of potential defaults in the massive municipal bond market. That's because cities and counties guaranteed the financing of these projects when times were good but today cannot afford to make the payments. Bonds backed by so-called "non-core" services make up 10 to 15 percent of this collapsing municipal bond market.

New York and New Jersey are not alone in their budget shell game. The Citizens Budget Commission of New York that measured states' obligations against their economic resources concluded that California, Illinois and Rhode Island, among others, also employ questionable accounting practices.

Any wonder these states and most others in the union are broke?

The fact that California, the Golden State, my home state, is broke is not only depressing but infuriating. Cities and Orange County filing for bankruptcy, state employees, taxpayers and vendors paid with IOUs and state and city employees facing retirement with uncollectable medical benefits and pensions. The state, like many, is technically bankrupt and is papering over the deficits with clever accounting, such as assuming billions in federal aid that will never materialize. But unlike cities and counties, the state is not allowed to seek protection under the Federal Bankrupcy Code.

No different than what happened on May 22 back in 1850, I thought to myself. What happened on that date? California became a state. The state had no electricity. The state had no money. Almost everyone spoke Spanish. There were gunfights in the streets. Pretty much like California today.

What a great metaphor, I thought to myself when I heard the U.S. Supreme Court decision in May 2011 that the overcrowding of California prisons is cruel and unusual punishment and 30,000 inmates should be freed.

Californians are all prisoners of a bankrupt political system and themselves need to be set free. California is not just facing a prison crisis but a financial, economic and political crisis of frightening proportions – and it is not alone.

State governments have unfunded obligations totaling more than $445 billion to subsidize health insurance for teachers, judges and other civil servants after they retire. Nationally, unfunded state pension liabilities stand at well over $1 trillion. The arresting details of these arrangements, only now receiving close attention, have justifiably become political issues in their own right.

When Wisconsin Republican Governor Scott Walker tried to curb the collective bargaining rights of public-sector unions in an effort to cut deficits and public spending, Democratic legislators fled to Illinois in an attempt to thwart his efforts and union supporters took over the state Capitol building in Madison in protest. The same thing happened in

Indiana. Its Democratic legislators also fled to Illinois. Why couldn't they reach an amicable compromise like the Founding Fathers' states of Massachussets and Vermont? The union that represents 7,000 Vermont state employees agreed to a voluntary furlough program that lets some workers take at least 40 hours of unpaid time off a year as a way for the state to save money. If the Founding Fathers' stomping grounds states can come up with compromises that are acceptable to unions and the state governments, why can't the rest of the country?

For years, governments complied with balanced budget rules and other supposed constraints by creating quasi-government agencies that could borrow by selling and leasing back buildings and other assets, by bundling future years' lottery proceeds, and other creative maneuvers. But now the squeeze is upon them. It's payback time. The federal stimulus is gone and the gimmicks are all used up. For state finances, it's the day of reckoning.

Cities that should have filed bankruptcy were saved by state distressed cities programs – another taxpayer waste-management program. Michigan has more than 37 cities in its program, Pennsylvania has more than 20, New Jersey has more than seven, and Illinois, Rhode Island and California each have at least one. This is on top of the troubled housing, utility and hospital agencies.

Cities America are spending more on Wall Street fees than on basic public services.

If states let cities and towns keep borrowing, without acknowledging the magnitude of existing debts – like the pensions they owe retired public servants – they might never solve their problems. They could wind up like miniature versions of Fannie Mae and Freddie Mac – broke and stuck in conservatorships under government oversight with no clear way out.

This can only lead to sudden state collapses, as happened to Arkansas during the Great Depression, causing the only default by a state on general-obligation bonds in American history.

State payrolls are being met with money earmarked for bondholders and the bondholders are being paid with funds earmarked for pensions that in turn are bailed by the state – and the shell games continue to grow.

State and local governments nationwide have set aside virtually no money to pay $1 trillion or more in medical benefits for retired civil servants. No wonder so many career politicians – Republicans mostly – want to end Medicare benefits for seniors and crack open the Social Security program.

Cities, school systems, park districts, water authorities and other local governments entities have even bigger obligations, in excess of $500 billion. These crippling obligations are only part of what America's aging population is facing. The federal government has more than $1 trillion in unfunded obligations to pay medical costs for retired federal workers and military personnel. Medicare and Social Security push the nation's unfunded promises above an astounding $50 trillion.

During the 2002 recession, a report by the National Association of State Budget Officers admitted that states were employing "creative, innovative … adjustments" to budgets. They include financing current operations with debt, moving money from trust funds dedicated to specific tasks (like highway maintenance) into general funds, and pushing payments to vendors into future fiscal years.

The federal government has served as enabler. Not only to the states and local municipalities, but to their investment bankers.

As you might guess, America's biggest banks are lining up to profit from worries about the declining finances of U.S. cities and states. Banks, starting in 2010, began making markets in derivatives tied to municipal bonds and other securities. The credit-default swaps (CDS) obligate swap sellers to compensate buyers if a municipal issuer misses an interest payment or restructures its debt. The five largest derivatives dealers, Bank of America Corp.'s Bank of America Merrill Lynch, Citi-group Inc., Goldman Sachs Group Inc., JPMorgan Chase & Co., and Morgan Stanley, met in November 2010 in New York to discuss standardizing the paperwork for "muni CDS" in their effort to attract more buyers and sellers. Hedge funds are always looking for the next subprime. One would think these funds and the banks would have learned from their subprime experience. But then again, why should they? After all, the government will probably bail them out again at taxpayer expense.

"There is no evidence that CDS trading has provided any benefits to the municipal-bond market, and further, we have seen little evidence that it serves much purpose beyond allowing speculators to get rich," said Tom Dresslar, spokesman for the California State Treasurer's Office.

Although the special tax-free status it bestows on municipal bonds amounts to a subsidy, Washington does little to enforce responsible budgeting or curtail banking shenanigans – even after the subprime crisis. In its fiscal stimulus packages of 2009 and 2010, for example, the federal government funneled hundreds of billions of dollars to the states without regard for their fiscal practices, treating irresponsibility in New York, California and New Jersey the same as prudence in Texas, where they still live by and honor the cowboy code.

Now multiply this local and national financial nightmare globally, starting with Greece, Cyprus, Iceland, Ireland, Portugal, Spain, Hungary and the countless financial dominoes that just keep cascading across Europe, and one can understand why the euro, like the European Union, is bankrupt too.

### State Rights

The federal governments of many countries – definitely in America – have hijacked many state rights over the centuries as national governments have continued to grow with states' tax revenues that feed its ferocious federal appetite to continuously grow the central government at the states' expense. States have to reclaim their basic rights and bring government back to the people at the local level. Not only in politics, but the basic cost of living by cutting out runaway federal government waste.

Family farming is a good example. Agribusiness, facilitated by federal legislation, has decimated family farming, and allowed captains of industry to dominate agriculture. The price we pay for food today is quite detached from the actual cost of producing it. Where the natural pressures of a legitimately free state market would push prices down to reflect a product's true value, the federal government's capitalist restrictions on competition allow big business to suck up monopoly profits.

In still another departure from real market state discipline, federal taxpayer-subsidized transport means that most people get their food from hundreds of miles away, rather than hundreds of meters. When the price of oil rises, so does the price of the food that has to make the journey. Is it any wonder city dwellers in America and China are seeing food prices rise?

High energy and transportation costs abroad are starting to bring manufacturing jobs back to America. U.S efficiency also has helped make manufacturing back home more competitive. All that is needed is a few more tax breaks or credits and unemployment will go down.

"I can manufacture combination locks in Milwaukee for less than I can in China," said Bob Rice, a senior vice president at the largest U.S. padlock manufacturer, Master Lock, at its 90-year old factory.

Efficiency is the key. The machines in Milwaukee are about 30 times faster than those used at the Chinese factories the company had been buying from, requiring only one-sixth of the workers, more than making up the difference in wages. Systems costs, rather than traditional unit cost analysis, is getting many American firms to boost production at their U.S. factories. A variety of factors are driving the shift, including rising wages in Asia, surging fuel prices and the greater expense and complexity of shipping goods across the Pacific.

The one direction the conservative U.S. Supreme Court is taking that is encouraging is its support of state rights and their right to challenge "the supreme Law of the Land" – federal laws.

### Real Change – Time to Reorganize

The failure of governments and banks to honestly tackle the financial crisis – the Great Recession of 2008 – leaves *We the Apathetic Maids* with the only remaining option: bankruptcy reorganization. We have to get rid of the old debt and ongoing deficit financing needed to support it, which are unsustainable and saddling future generations with a financial burden that should be borne by the parties that created it – the career politicians, corporate America and bankers! Not only in America, but in China and many other countries around the world that need to reorganize and restructure their economies.

Regulations governing Wall Street investment banks, hedge funds, savings and loans and commercial banks were adopted after the Great Depression that Wall Street triggered. Repealing those regulations – deregulation – brought about the Great Recession and should give *We the Apathetic Maids* pause for concern. Since Wall Street and its financed career politicians and self-serving cabinet appointees triggered both the Great Depression and the Great Recession, why should these same bankers and career politicians be allowed to continue dictating what needs to be done to restore a sound and strong America, politically and economically, when the sole beneficiaries are these same bankers at *We the People's* expense?

It is time for America to learn from its financial history and mistakes and rebuild the country by sweeping the slate clean of the unsustainable debt we are piling up for future generations. Wall Street has the most to lose and they deserve it. They are not too big to fail. A big bust and cleansing with new financial regulations is long overdue.

The defaults and reorganization of the economies of Argentina, Greece, Iceland, Indonesia, Ireland, Mexico, South Korea and Thailand, to name a few countries, not to mention the counties and cities in the U.S. that have already done so, only confirms the need for tough, new financial regulations. As a lawyer who started my legal career with a firm that specialized in bankruptcy reorganizations, "The graveyard of bad business deals" as my mentor Martin Gendel would say, I am a firm believer that those who have enriched themselves unfairly at the expense of the lenders, in this case taxpayers as opposed to the usual suspect bankers, should be called to account and pay back their unfair gains. That includes government pensions being paid out or due to undeserving long-serving career politicians and their undeserving and under serving bureaucrats.

Granted the consequent tremors for the world's financial markets will be earth shattering, but necessary. Career politicians and their bankers in America, China and the rest of the world can no longer live on borrowed time by a money-laundered Ponzi scheme of global proportions financed by worthless bonds that will be paid for by *We the Apathetic Maids* and future generations. The public sector can no longer be asked to pay for the mistakes of the private sector and their career politicians and bureaucratic enablers.

"Most Americans did not share in the Mother of All Bubbles. So should those who gained nothing from fake prosperity be made to pay even more?" asks Joseph Stiglitz, a Nobel laureate in economics. I for one don't think so.

America is running an annual budget deficit of more than $1 trillion – and it is growing by the minute.

Things will only get worse for America before they get better as China and its neighbors in Asia become the biggest consumers in the world, creating more economic hiccups and unemployment in America – unless the U.S. gets its act together – which it can.

We've heard enough preaching about pain and suffering. It is time to act. The pain must be borne, at least the brunt of it, by those responsible for the crisis, and those who benefited most from the bubble that preceded it. Debt restructuring of governments is the key to future prosperity. It will eventually happen. The delay is costly and unnecessary. There is life after debt restructuring.

The Democratic, Republican and Communist parties talk a good game as their rich financial supporters gain and taxpayers feel the pain. This is not the political system the Founding Fathers had in mind. They wanted a government built on social justice for all – and no wars or foreign engagements.

Watching all eyes turn to the U.S. from New Zealand in September 2011, after the Labor Day weekend, as European stock markets tumbled on fears that bailouts for some euro zone countries were less than certain, dragging U.S. and China stock markets down the fast moving recession escalator, together with the U.S. dollar and job prospects – as the price of gold continued to rise – only confirmed that it is time for America to restructure.

### Destructive War Economy
The economic theory and belief in Congress and the Pentagon that it was World War II that got America out of the Great Depression – and not FDR's

New Deal – continues to erroneously permeate American foreign and economic policy today, especially during hard economic times.

War and the military have been glamorized by Hollywood movies and TV shows since World War II. Many of these films and TV series are indirectly financed and supported by the Pentagon, through its Hollywood office, by furnishing and allowing the use of expensive military equipment for combat scenes whose subliminal propaganda message to the unsuspecting viewing public is that war and the military-industrial complex are good for the country – and that fighting for America and "freedom" is patriotic.

Films that the Pentagon doesn't like because the story line, plot or message is anti-war or anti-military and portray the damaging effects of war on America or its soldiers are denied any Pentagon support because of their "unpatriotic" message. Never mind the First Amendment and the taxpayer dollars that buy the military equipment.

Granted, World War II did help the economy, but it is no reason to start a war whenever the economy tanks or the military-industrial Congress feels like starting one. It is a major reason America finds itself at war in every decade since the end of World War II. Korea, Vietnam, Lebanon, Somalia, Kosovo and the Gulf wars, not to mention all the local and regional skirmishes in Africa, Asia, Latin America and the Middle East. The Afghanistan and Iraq wars and Libya bombing missions are 21st-century reminders of this dated justification for war and purported economic benefits for a recovery, with the unfinished Korean War waiting in the wings with its new companions Libya, Syria, Yemen and Somalia.

Rep. Howard "Buck" McKeon, chairman of the House Armed Services Committee who represents a district north of Los Angeles that is home to 20,000 people employed by defense industry contractors such as Boeing and Lockheed-Martin, is always gunning for higher defense spending and is a prime example of how *We the Apathetic Maids* get lulled into believing that higher defense spending is good for jobs and the economy. He and his cohorts fail to mention that it is deficit spending that finances defense and that it is destructive to America and jobs.

"As Chinese naval, air and nuclear power rapidly grows – ours diminishes by comparison," McKeon said about the Pentagon's August 2010 annual report on Chinese military power.

The report "validates the need to modernize and increase our Navy's force structure," he said. China's military might is an issue McKeon has returned to again and again during his tenure on the Armed Services Committee as a leading proponent of military spending and a "war economy" to keep America economically strong.

During my May 2011 visit to Los Angeles, a front-page headline in the *Los Angeles Times* proclaimed that "New bomber could bring a jobs payload." High unemployment in the bankrupt Golden State encouraged the Southland aerospace industry to go public about its secret work on designs for a fleet of 80 to 100 nuclear-capable stealth bombers that could operate with or without a pilot in the cockpit taking shape at Air Force Plant 42 in the Mojave Desert. The estimated $55-billion contract is expected to provide jobs and decades of work for Southern California's aerospace industry.

There was $197 million set aside for developing the bomber in the 2012 fiscal budget and $3.7 billion was allocated for the program over the next five years because of the strong support of McKeon – all in the cause of employment and building a strong economy.

Meanwhile, some of the nation's top guns, at the risk of significant reprimand – or even discharge from the Air Force – are refusing to fly the radar-evading F-22 Raptor, the world's most expensive fighter jet plagued by ongoing problems with its oxygen systems.

It is time for America to stop wasting billions of dollars on weapons that America's finest refuse to use.

A week later when I was in New England, the front page headline in *The Boston Globe* proclaimed "GE jet engine survives House ... Jobs at stake at Lynn facility." The engine in question is the proposed engine GE will build as a backup for the F-35 joint strike fighter that nobody but GE and the

Pentagon want. The White House and Department of Defense, going back to 2007, opposed the building of the engine. Presidents George W. Bush in 2007 and Barack Obama starting in 2009 urged Congress to kill the engine, yet lawmakers resisted and continued to pump money into it. As of May 2011, the engine program had received about $3 billion from the Pentagon.

These efforts are pursued by the Pentagon as it continues to illegally waste billions of dollars on sole-source fuel contracts for U.S. military aircraft and naval fleets to companies controlled by ruling dictators who mow down their own people just because they clamored for democracy, Bahrain being the prime example. This Pentagon welfare program for brutal dictators being enriched with American taxpayer dollars has to cease-and-desist if America's credibility in the region is to be restored. A *Newsweek* investigation of Pentagon contracting practices in Abu Dhabi, Kuwait and Bahrain in 2011 uncovered more than $14 billion paid mostly to sole-source despotic potentates.

The U.S. wars in Iraq and Afghanistan had passed the $1 trillion mark in June 2011, according to the Defense Department. The figure covered the period from when the "war on terror" began in 2001 through the end of April 2011. The cost did not include about $95 billion paid to personnel for operational costs, replacement of weapons systems and construction. It also did not include about $100 billion the Pentagon excluded as not "war related," such as intelligence, or any of the long-term costs for Veterans Administration care, disability costs for wounded Iraq and Afghan veterans, or all of the reconstruction funding for the war-damaged countries. Many economists place the actual cost of the Iraq and Afghan wars at more than $5 trillion. Surely that astounding amount is money that America could better use putting Americans to work at home fixing and building the nation's crumbling infrastructure instead of putting America's unemployed in harm's way.

Obama's promise to end the war in Afghanistan and fight poverty and unemployment in America is in sight. Unfortunately, to get there he made Afghanistan his own war. It is now the longest war in U.S. history. Thankfully, he has heeded Richard Holbrooke, the late special envoy for Afghanistan and Pakistan, whose dying words to his Pakistani doctor as he went into surgery were, "You've got to stop this war in Afghanistan."

More importantly, Obama has listened to the voice of the American people who elected him and who repeatedly say the Afghanistan war is not worth fighting. Sixty percent of Americans surveyed in an ABC News/Washington Post poll in December 2010 said they do not support the war in Afghanistan.

"Negative views of the war for the first time are at the level of those recorded for the war in Iraq, whose unpopularity dragged George W. Bush to historic lows in approval across his second term," ABC News said.

A White House report released at the same time said the U.S.-led forces were making headway against the Taliban and al-Qaeda, but warned the gains were "fragile and reversible." This is nothing but political spin. Of course they are reversible with a continued unnecessary waste of lives and taxpayers dollars.

In the early 1990s, in the wake of the Tiananmen Square massacre and the collapse of Soviet-style communism, then paramount leader Deng Xiaoping touted the idea of *tao-guang yanghui* as the guiding principle in China's foreign and security affairs. The phrase – expressing Deng's "lie low" policy, which recommends refraining from being too proactive in international affairs and focusing on building economic strength – is still China's official diplomatic policy. However, the phrase has been misinterpreted by the Pentagon in its annual reports on China's military power to mean "hide our capacities and bide our time." The idea that China's official military tactic to keep its ability deliberately hidden while waiting for a chance to strike is part of the Pentagon's "China threat" theory that perceives China as an aggressive global military player.

The Pentagon's AirSea Battle concept for the Western Pacific, first mentioned in 2010 and actively promoted in the *Quadrennial Defense Review* in early 2011, is a dangerously provocative piece of cold war-era strategy that irrationally justifies increased military spending. The concept envisions the full integration of U.S. Air Force and Navy forces, weapons and systems to be able to defeat "adversaries equipped with sophisticated anti-access and area denial capabilities" to counter "growing challenges to U.S. freedom of action." In other words, it is aimed at China.

Senior PLA Colonel Fan Gaoyue, a resident fellow at the Pacific Forum of the Center for Strategic and International Studies, warned that such a concept only forces China to develop its own counter-systems in return. In other words, just what the Pentagon wants. A new arms race and faster-paced war economy.

"This cycle is not beneficial to China or the U.S.," Fan said in a Pacific Forum exchange in March 2011. "In fact, the PLA will never target the U.S. military except if it intervenes in a Taiwan conflict or launches pre-emptive strikes against China.

"If AirSea Battle aims to stop a growing tilt in the balance of power, it means that the U.S. intends to obtain even greater advantage over regional militaries. The U.S. already enjoys the balance of power in the Asia-Pacific; the U.S. has the strongest military and has no counterpart in the world."

Dusting off a cold war plan that may have been applicable to Western Europe and introducing it into the Asia Pacific region is the "wrong decision at a wrong time and a wrong place," said Fan. The U.S. "is not realistically threatened by a nation or groups and the Asia-Pacific region is a relatively stable area."

U.S. officials at the time highlighted the use of submarines to support air strikes in the ongoing Libyan campaign as a sign of the doctrine at work.

As if the AirSea Battle plan is not enough to alarm China over U.S. military intentions in the region, the Pentagon is renewing plans for regional shields against ballistic missiles in Asia. The U.S. push for new anti-missile bulwarks includes two sets of trilateral dialogues – one with Japan and Australia and the other with Japan and South Korea.

"The anti-missile shield in Asia will definitely cause a negative impact to China's national security," Professor Shi Yinhong, a Sino-U.S. expert at Renmin University, said. "It will increase the mistrust element between Beijing and Washington."

The mistrust has been growing since then Defense Secretary Leon Panetta visited Asia in October 2011 and announced that the U.S. was at "a turning point" that would allow a strategic rebalancing toward Asia. Matters only got worse when during Panetta's June 2012 visit to Vietnam, he announced that 60 percent of America's warships would be based in the Asia-Pacific region by 2020.

In the midst of all this came a report that more than a million Chinese counterfeit electronic parts are estimated to be in use in U.S. military aircraft?

I laughed when I read the 112-page report listing 1,800 cases of bogus parts, including on the Air Force's largest cargo plane, special operations helicopters and Navy surveillance planes – and Washington laying the blame on Beijing, and that U.S. authorities and contract companies merely contributed to the vulnerabilities. Let's put the blame where it belongs.

A sad and infuriating report is that of Afghan contractors responsible for preventing culverts from being used to hide roadside bombs on a major highway falsely claiming to have completed the work, putting American troops at risk.

"We've heard this tune again and again for the last 10 years," said Peter Singer, director of the 21st Century Defense Initiative at the Brookings Institution. "Another sad illustration of how corruption in the realm of contracting not only led to lost taxpayer money but also potential lost lives."

All the AirSea Battle and defense shield concept does is raise, rather than diminish, the level of mistrust. Continuously jockeying for strategic advantage is a waste of time and taxpayer money. Why not just start a new transparent bona-fide military relationship, a true partnership? Explaining military developments and why they are necessary will ease concerns and fears. To keep secrets and press a provocative military strategy only exacerbate tensions and mistrust.

China has every right to upgrade and improve its military capabilities. The U.S. is not going to downgrade its military capabilities or presence in the region. Better understanding of intentions and enhanced cooperation is not only mutually beneficial, politically and militarily, but cost effective. U.S.-China military ties must be based on mutual respect, trust, honest communications and exchanges. Healthy and stable military ties are an important part of U.S.-China relations.

The joint concert held at the John F. Kennedy Center for the Performing Arts in Washington in May 2011 by the Military Band of the People's Liberation Army and the United States Army Band "Pershing's Own" was the first such concert in the history of the two militaries. Entitled "Friendship and Cooperation Through Music," the performance was "symbolic of what we share in common and what the better relationship between the U.S. and China means for our people," said U.S. Army Chief of Staff General Martin E. Dempsey. This kind of harmony has to be extended to the military front in the Pacific.

It was in October 2012 when the United States Army Band "Pershing's Own," became the first U.S. military band to stage a joint performance with a Chinese military band at the National Center for the Performing Arts in Beijing. The performance was just the start of a flurry of military exchanges between the two countries as 2012 drew to a close.

Hopefully, Admiral Michael Mullen, chairman of the Joint Chiefs of Staff, and the 39-member delegation he led to China in July 2011, were satisfied after visiting every type of Chinese military unit including the army, navy, air force and the PLA's 2$^{nd}$ Artillery Force, the strategic missile force that controls the country's nuclear weapons, about which China is as transparent as one could expect it to be under the current courting arrangement between the two countries.

The PLA Air Force will be able to challenge the air superiority of the U.S. and its allies by 2015, according to a Rand Corp. report released in 2011. The report claims that the U.S. Air Force's Western Pacific bases would not remain safe from PLA attack in the event of conflict in the Taiwan Strait. It adds that the U.S. should continue to invest in supersonic B-1 and B-2 bombers, revive some cancelled next-generation bomber programs and enhance its longer-range cruise missile capabilities to maintain its advantage in the face of rapid Chinese improvements in those areas.

Mainland military experts said the Rand study was an attempt to exaggerate the capabilities of the PLA Air Force to justify boosting the U.S. military budget in the middle of what President Barack Obama has called "extreme fiscal duress."

I agree with Antony Wong Dong, president of the International Military Association in Macau, who echoed many military analysts when he said the study was aimed at saving the declining U.S. military industry amid the financial crisis. The military-industrial complex and its war theory continues to be one of America's key economic pillars in the 21st-century.

U.S. Rep. Ileana Ros-Lehtinen, chairwoman of the House Foreign Affairs Committee, is another advocate of defense spending as a means to revive the depressed economy. She advocates continuation of the U.S. policy of arms sales to Taiwan to contain the "China threat." The U.S. continues to unnecessarily fan the flames of fear about China's rise, its military might and potential threat.

The $10 billion worth of business deals with India announced by President Obama during his visit to that country in November 2010 was highly touted for the 50,000 jobs that would be created. It's another example of the war economy mentality that permeates U.S. government policy. Most of the jobs created will be in the defense industry. These are jobs building weapons that only escalates the arms race. Given the lobbying of the U.S. defense industry, which employs an estimated 3 million people, it is not surprising that U.S. presidents and congressmen serve as brokers for military contractors. But like many other U.S. foreign policy-relations brokers, they failed in their mission in India and cost U.S. taxpayers for their economic and foreign policy blunders.

President Obama led the charge for America to replace Russia as the biggest arms supplier to India, the world's largest arms importer in 2009. That didn't stop Russia from following up after Obama's visit to sell even more arms to India. Russia, like America, peddles arms and supports wars and conflicts that can fuel its own military-industrial complex.

Then President Dmitry Medvedev arrived in India to promote military equipment in December 2010, hot on the heels of Obama's visit. One of the agreements he signed is for India and Russia to jointly design and develop a fifth-generation fighter aircraft, which could be ready for production by 2020 and is valued at $35 billion. Russia has been emphasizing its long-term role in co-developing military equipment with India – rather than just selling arms to New Delhi – as the U.S. has done in Pakistan.

Russia even trumped the U.S. It secured agreements to provide missiles to the Indian Army, develop advanced stealth fighters and build four new nuclear reactors.

India has doubled spending on its military since 2004, to $32 billion in 2010. In 2011, it picked the winner of an $11 billion tender to supply 126 fourth-generation fighter jets to the Indian Air Force, one of its largest-ever military contracts. America's Boeing Co. and Lockheed Martin Corp. were right there doing their best to win the bidding war – and lost. No surprise there.

Asia has become the promised land for the U.S. defense industry – and China the villain justifying the military buildups. According to the Stockholm International Peace Research Institute, the amount spent on weapons purchases in Asia doubled between 2005 and 2009, the most recent figures available. Asian nations are spending heavily on weapons in part because older arms are becoming obsolete. A more disturbing reason for the arms race is that the region's historically most unstable and aggressive states are remilitarizing, and as a result, the region's peaceful democratic states feel forced to do the same because of the fear-mongering the Pentagon and its defense contractors spew about China.

A consistent theme in Pentagon reports about how the pace and scope of China's military modernization have increased emphasizes that this buildup will "increase China's options for using military force to gain diplomatic advantage or resolve disputes in its favor." A good reason for Asia's military generals to arm themselves to the teeth. No doubt the new arms race in Asia will help America economically, but is this really a sustainable economic or viable political model in a world of nuclear-armed extreme religious fundamentalist camps that further polarize in the 21$^{st}$ century? I think it is America's kiss of death, best demonstrated in the deadly nibbles in Vietnam, Lebanon, Somalia, Afghanistan and Iraq.

The U.S. Navy has 70 ships and aircraft operating on any given day in Asia, including one or more aircraft carrier strike groups and an amphibious ready group. The nuclear-powered submarine force has been realigned so that 60 percent of it is now in the Pacific, with enhanced maintenance facilities in Guam and Diego Garcia in the Indian Ocean. U.S. mine warfare capabilities doubled in 2010 with the addition of two mine countermeasures ships deployed to Japan and a detachment of MH-53 mine-hunting helicopters on duty in South Korea.

The U.S. has ruled the waters of the Western Pacific since 1945, thanks to its fleet of 97,000-ton carriers – each one "4.5 acres of mobile sovereign U.S. territory," as the Navy puts it. Until recently, China had little choice but to watch American vessels ply the waters off its coast with impunity.

The U.S. is building the USS Gerald R. Ford, a supercarrier that will have a formidable arsenal of aircraft and weapons and be delivered in 2015, which is supposed to help secure another half-century of American naval supremacy. The Navy is developing pilotless, long-range drone aircraft that could take off from aircraft carriers far out at sea and remain aloft longer than a human pilot could do safely. In addition, the Air Force wants a fleet of pilotless bombers capable of cruising over vast stretches of the Pacific.

Throughout history, control of the seas has been a prerequisite for any country that wants to be considered a world power.

U.S. joint naval exercises in the region have increased dramatically as well. In 2010, the U.S. Navy had its first naval exercise with Cambodia since 1970. The U.S. Navy's Cooperation Afloat Readiness and Training, or Carat, exercise series invites countries in the region, like Cambodia, Bangladesh and Vietnam, to join.

"The U.S. Navy has maintained a continuous presence in the region since 1852. Our interests in this region – in its stability, prosperity and security – is enduring. Our commitment is not waning. On the contrary, our growth in capabilities and maritime partnerships reflects a clear focus on security and our steadfast commitment to our friends and allies. The U.S. 7th Fleet is here to stay," said Vice Admiral Scott Van Buskirk, commander of the 7th Fleet, in a speech to the Asia Society in Hong Kong in February 2011.

The admiral added that China must not be viewed as a "direct threat" and "Indeed, to look at China through the lens of an adversary would be counterproductive."

So why is America so upset that China is finally able to launch an aircraft carrier and launch and land domestically produced J-15 Fighter Shark jets? Keep in mind we are not talking about a carrier built from scratch, but a retrofitted Soviet carrier. Because its deployment will significantly change the "perception" of the balance of power in the region. In other words, it is merely symbolic but the U.S. defense establishment and its lobbyists are trying to create a mountain out of a molehill to justify increases in the Pentagon's spending. The U.S. already has 12 carriers, including the world's most sophisticated nuclear vessels.

America must accept China's growing naval presence in the Pacific and beyond. As China grows economically and globally, it is only natural that its naval capability will grow as well to serve and support its economic interests. The evacuation of more than 35,000 Chinese workers from war-torn Libya is an example. The Libyan evacuation was the Chinese government's largest-ever overseas evacuation operation, with the PLA sending Arabic-speaking foreign liaison officers, a missile frigate, and four Russian-built Ilyushin Il-76 transport aircraft.

America must make room for China in the Pacific rather than trying to maintain its dominance and creating a bipolar world starting in the Pacific. We know medically and scientifically that being bipolar is not healthy. It is mentally and physically debilitating. The same holds true economically, politically and militarily.

Is it any wonder China distrusts America and its wild military spending to maintain its presence in Asia? Why is America fighting wars in Afghanistan, Iraq and Libya instead of poverty, decay and unemployment at home?

The People's Liberation Army is no threat to the U.S. and has no intention of challenging it. The PLA is one of the world's largest bureaucracies and rotten to the core. Corruption is pervasive. Senior positions are sold to the highest bidder.

"The world has no need to worry about, let alone fear, China's growth," said General Chen Bingde, chief of the PLA general staff, in a rare address to a packed room of U.S. military officers and faculty at the National Defense University in May 2011.

The general said there was still "a 20-year gap" between China's military and Western powers. He went on to add at a joint news conference at the Pentagon with Admiral Mike Mullen, chairman of the Joint Chiefs of Staff: "I can tell you that China does not have the capability to challenge the United States."

I agree with what Mullen said at his last news conference to foreign media in July 2011. "I'm not naïve. I understand the concerns of those who feel that any cooperation benefits China more than the United States. I just don't agree. This relationship is too important to manage through blind suspicion and mistrust. We've tried that. It doesn't work."

The naivete with which *We the Maids* buy the Pentagon's patriotic propaganda, hook, line and sinker was brought home to me when I read about the Manhattan Project veterans gathered at Los Alamos in New Mexico to commemorate their work on developing the atom bomb. Operating under the U.S. Army Corps of Engineers – the same people managing the Mississippi, Missouri and other major flood plains in America – the project officially began in 1942 out of fear the Nazis were developing an atomic bomb. About 125,000 people were involved in the effort around the U.S., including many young scientists and engineers from elite universities.

Some 5,000 worked at the V site in Los Alamos where scientists detonated the Trinity device tested in 1945 over Alamogordo in the first nuclear explosion.

"We felt like if we could perfect that bomb and stop that war, then we were doing a good thing," said Daniel Gillespie, who worked on Trinity and other "Fat Man" bombs. "We were saving lives."

Jay Coghlan, an executive with the watchdog group Nuclear Watch New Mexico, said nuclear weapons continue to be produced in a far murkier geopolitical landscape. "The Manhattan Project gentlemen have their reunion, their memories. But meanwhile, Los Alamos is getting ready to fight the next war, in which the use of nuclear weapons is entirely possible," he said.

That point was not lost on Robert Gates – not the former Defense Secretary – but an 80-something engineer who worked on the Manhattan Project. Although nostalgic about Los Alamos, he also remains haunted by the power that he helped unleash. "I wish I could tell young people today how naïve they are," Gates said. "We were like that, too, young and naïve. We truly believed that by building that bomb, there'd never be another war."

So why not accept and practice what the other Robert Gates, the former U.S. Defense secretary, said before he left office: "We are not trying to hold China down. China has been a great power for thousands of years. It is a global power and will be a global power."

The melancholy reflections aired publicly as he was retiring are quite telling. The U.S. is in danger of losing its global supremacy!

"I've spent my entire adult life with the United States as a superpower, and one that had no compunction about spending what it took to sustain that position," Gates said. "It didn't have to look over its shoulder because our economy was so strong. This is a different time."

After a pause, he added: "To tell you the truth, that's one of the many reasons it's time for me to retire, because frankly I can't imagine being part of a nation, part of a government ... that's being forced to dramatically scale back our engagement with the rest of the world."

*Spat Over the Spratlys*

Think about it for a minute. Vietnam, the country America went to war with in the '60s, based on a bogus Tonkin incident, is now a U.S. ally in an alliance to contain China in the Spratly Islands spat in the South China Sea, arguably the world's most politically sensitive waters, with six governments contesting ownership of all or part. Joint naval exercises in July 2011, officially classed as an "enhanced naval engagement," less than a month after its live-fire exercise off Vietnam's central coast that enraged China. But of course the U.S. retort is that it is merely a search-and-rescue exercise as part of a pattern of annual drills with regional allies and partners in recent months that have included Thailand, Indonesia and Malaysia. U.S. destroyers and salvage vessels drilling with the Philippine navy off Palawan, the closest Philippine island to the disputed Spratly archipelago, are part of the effort.

The April 2012 Philippine-American joint military exercise involved 4,500 U.S. troops and 2,500 from the Philippines. America's denial that the exercise was aimed at China rang hollow when China and the Philippines were both taking harder lines on the disputed waters known to be rich in fishing and petroleum resources.

This as Manila says that U.S. forces would be obliged to help defend Philippine troops under a 1951 treaty if they came under attack in the Spratly dispute – and as if that isn't provocative enough, decides to rename the South China Sea the "West Philippines Sea," something Philippine President Benigno Acquino restated to President Obama during his visit to the White House in June 2012, because Vietnam calls it the East Sea, which only unnecessarily fuels tensions and encourages China to build up its maritime presence and bases as Beijing reiterates it will not use force to resolve the dispute.

That is a separate issue from that fast-accelerating dispute involving what the Chinese call Huangyan Island, but which Filipinos, and world atlases, call Scarborough Shoal, which is another unfolding drama in the South China Sea that could end up in a military confrontation, but preferably a peaceful diplomatic resolution.

Columnist Philip Bowring, a former Foreign Correspondents Club

Hong Kong president and regular FCC Main Bar fly, is adamant about China ignoring history and rewriting it to suit its own political agenda. "China's case as expounded by the Foreign Ministry is one where the only history that matters is Han Chinese who claim to have discovered Huangyan and drew it into China's map during the Yuan dynasty (1271-1368 AD). This is like Europeans claiming that they got to Australia before the Aboriginals or the Americans before Native Americans. The Chinese were actually latecomers to navigation beyond coastal waters," Philip, a competitive sailor, added as he continued to challenge China's historical claim.

"For centuries, the masters of the oceans were the Malayo-Polynesian peoples who colonized much of the world, from Taiwan to New Zealand and Hawaii to the south and east, and Madagascar in the west. Bronze vessels were being traded with Palawan, just south of Scarborough, at the time of Confucius. China's current power may make such issues of actual history irrelevant. But if it wishes to be respected by its Southeast Asian neighbors, and in particular the 400 million Malays of the island states, it had better develop some respect for their history. The Han sense of superiority may seem justified by the role of overseas Chinese commerce – much helped by Western colonialism – in modern times. But it cannot be assumed to be permanent and is a poor basis for regional peace," Philip continued unabated as we ordered another glass of wine.

Filipino and Chinese fishermen have worked easily and peacefully side-by-side in the Scarborough Shoal sharing the rich harvest the shoal has on offer for decades, but the recent flareup is testing that friendship.

"If we wanted to ask for water, we just held up a container and made a drinking motion and they would give us water," said Filipino boat mechanic Glenn Valle. The fisherman used hand signals to communicate, recalling how they would ask Chinese crews for help.

China and the Philippines recognize the cooperative relationship – and benefits to their fishermen – so both have found an answer to the Scarborough Shoal stand-off. Coinciding and overlapping two and a half month fishing bans. More must be done to improve the bilateral relationship.

More than 1,000 oil wells have been drilled in disputed parts of the South China Sea by the Philippines, Vietnam and other countries, but none are owned by China – yet. That is because it lacked the technology. But now that Beijing has developed deep-sea technology to explore and even start drilling for oil in disputed parts of the South China Sea to reinforce its sovereignty, it probably will.

In late June 2012 Chinese oil giant China National Offshore Oil Corp. invited foreign oil companies to bid for oil and gas blocks that overlapped territory being explored by Vietnam. "China's view is that the little countries, like Vietnam and the Philippines, are increasingly stealing its resources and it must demonstrate it is serious about upholding its claims," said Ian Storey, a senior fellow at the Institute of Southeast Asian Studies in Singapore.

China is "committed to maintaining peace and stability in the South China Sea," Foreign Ministry spokesman Hong Lei said at a news conference in June 2011 as tensions heated up. It makes one wonder who is stirring up the Spratly hornet's nest and arms race. The U.S. military-industrial complex?

The U.S. argues that it wants to ensure "freedom of navigation" in the South China Sea. However, China and the U.S. have appreciable differences in interpreting what constitutes freedom of navigation for "peaceful use," especially when it comes to the U.S. Navy's intelligence-gathering within China's exclusive economic zones. The U.S. uses freedom of navigation to justify its reconnaissance operations close to China's space and water.

It is commonly suspected that, without the implicit or explicit encouragement and support of the U.S., neither Vietnam nor the Philippines would provoke Beijing, as they know they are no military match for China's military and naval might.

I chuckle when I remember that China and Vietnam followed up the U.S.-Vietnam joint naval exercise with two days of joint naval patrols of their own in the Tonkin Gulf. Vietnamese ships even made a port call in China.

"Respecting the signed agreements is one of the factors that will promote friendly and neighborly relations between (our) two countries and ensure stability and security at sea," said Colonel Nguyen Van Kiem, deputy chief of staff of Vietnam's navy.

The 2011 joint patrol was the 11th between China and Vietnam, who have clearly got the United States caught in another Asian conundrum. Yet the U.S. continues to spend dearly to strut its superpower stuff in the Pacific, an expensive exercise in futility that *We the Apathetic Maids* – and our future offspring – will be paying for dearly for many years to come.

Why do *We the Apathetic Maids* allow this scenario to play out again and again? Why is the U.S. meddling in yet another misguided foreign adventure? Does the American military machine, already spread so thin, really need another power keg? Can the crumbling American economy handle it?

China should also clarify its stand and take some initiative to resolve the Spratly dispute amicably. While China's neighbors firmly believe that all claims to rights and jurisdiction on the islands must be consistent with the 1982 United Nations Convention on the Law of the Sea, they overlook the fact that the convention only addresses activities in the oceans. It contains no provisions on how to decide competing sovereignty claims over the islands. These rules are found in decisions of international courts and tribunals – exactly where China, Vietnam and the Philippines should be looking – if they cannot reach a mutual agreement all can live with.

Since neither China nor Vietnam have accepted the jurisdiction of the U.N.'s International Court of Justice, and since the Philippines has done so with reservations on its jurisdiction over the sea, trying to get the parties together there is a nonstarter. There are precedents between the countries. On June 30, 2004, the China-Vietnam Agreement on the Demarcation of the Beibu Gulf and the Beibu Gulf Fishery Cooperation Agreement came into force. On March 14, 2005, China, Vietnam and the Philippines signed the Tripartite Agreement for Joint Marine Seismic Undertaking in the Agreement Area in the South China Sea. More importantly, all parties are talking to each other to resolve outstanding issues. If agreement cannot be reached on the Spratlys, a mutually agreed-upon institutionalized means or judicial proceeding and venue may be in order.

A set of preliminary guidelines to resolve disputes in the South China Sea was agreed on between China and the 10 ASEAN member states on implementing the 2002 Declaration of Conduct in the South China Sea at their annual meeting in July 2011. It was the first time since 2007 that senior officials from China and ASEAN have held talks solely on the South China Sea issue. The parties agreed to cooperate in marine environmental protection and safety of navigation.

The Spratlys, like North Korea, are one of the hot spots in Asia that could spark another war that is in no one's interest – other than the military-industrial complex. Former Philippine President Fidel Ramos, a general and former defense secretary himself, summed up the solution best: "The region's economic growth and progress require that we Asians contain our rivalries and avoid the arms races that, unfortunately, now seem to be under way."

I had the privilege of meeting Ramos when he was president. He was a practical politician who not only brought his country back from the brink of bankruptcy and civil war, but has a lot of good advice to offer the U.S. and China. What is needed, above all, is a covenant among the leaders of Asia-Pacific that will make peaceful dispute resolution binding on all stakeholders, big or small. Only such a pledge can provide the certainty investors will need if the Spratly resources are to be developed. Ramos has proposed to the leaders of the Association of Southeast Asian Nations that the Spratlys be demilitarized as a first step toward building trust. An idea the U.S. should support if Admiral Mike Mullen is to be taken at his word when he said during his July 2011 visit to China: "We have an enduring presence here; we have an enduring responsibility. We seek to strongly support the peaceful resolution of these differences."

China did suffer a political regional setback when the U.S. succeeded in getting the Spratly dispute tabled as an agenda item at the East Asia Summit in Bali, Indonesia, in November 2011, over China's objection that the dispute should be resolved regionally without U.S. intervention.

"Outside forces" should not be involved in the dispute for any reason, Premier Wen Jiabao told the Southeast Asian leaders.

The reality is that the Pax Americana that has "guaranteed regional stability" for decades has to be replaced by local Asian leaders with a more comprehensive Pax Asia that is built on inclusiveness and burden-sharing. It must be based on a balance of mutual benefits rather than the balance of power. Pax Asia institutions must be built – as Europe's peace was built after WWII – without an unnecessary war!

Singapore claims no part of the Spratlys and may be a suitable venue for resolving the dispute once and for all. As a neighbor in harm's way, it has asked China to clarify its position with more precision to minimize future misunderstandings – and another confrontation with Vietnam over the islands. China has had several confrontations with Vietnam, the most recent in 1979. Another conflict between the two is not out of the question.

By 2020, a total of 15,000 personnel, compared with 9,000 in 2011, will serve in the China Maritime Surveillance force. The CMS air arm will be increased to 16 planes and the patrol fleet will have 350 vessels during the period of the 12$^{th}$ Five-Year Plan (2011-2015) and more than 520 vessels by 2020.

China has also been invited to build a naval base by Pakistan at its highly strategic Gwadar port on the Arabian Sea and is already building port facilities in Kyaukpyu, in western Myanmar on the Indian Ocean. Unlike the Pacific, the Indian Ocean is dominated by powers not resident there, aside, of course, from India. The U.S., France, Russia and Britain have long been active in the region and have access to a wide network of friendly ports, particularly in the Red Sea and the highly strategic Persian Gulf, where the U.S. bases its 5th Fleet in Bahrain. The U.S. also maintains a vast naval facility at Diego Garcia – smack in the middle of the Indian Ocean.

It sure looks like a collision course between China and its neighbors. I just hope the U.S. doesn't make another one of its short-sighted decisions that places it and China on opposite sides as adversaries. America has no reason to get involved militarily in the Spratly dispute. As an honest broker, yes, but not under the guise of being the guardian of freedom of navigation on the high seas.

That is not as far-fetched as it sounds. When President Obama tried to push the U.S. to finally ratify the U.N.'s Law of the Sea in July 2012, his effort was thwarted by Republican senators who said such a move would jeopordize U.S. sovereignty – a move that certainly provides China with fresh ammunition in its bid to limit U.S. involvement in the disputed South China Sea.

The development was a blow to the Obama administration, military leaders and the business community led by the U.S. Chamber of Commerce, who had argued that the treaty would improve national security and enhance U.S. standing in the world. They had pressed for ratification of the treaty, which was concluded in 1982 and has been in force since 1994. The U.S. is the only major nation that has refused to sign the pact.

For those readers who still find it hard to believe that America would make up an incident like the Tonkin II affair as it did to justify the Vietnam War, think about what the new Secretary of Defense Leon Panetta said to U.S. troops in Iraq in July 2011. He said the reason troops are in Iraq is because of 9/11, an outright lie repeated over and over by the Bush administration, when in fact everyone knows Saddam Hussein and Iraq had nothing to do with 9/11. Panetta apologized for his gaffe. Michael Kinsley, jokingly but accurately, defines a Washington gaffe as a politician caught telling the truth.

No wonder China tells the U.S. to back out of its backyard. Why not have the Spratly matter resolved by the International Court of Justice or a special tribunal set up to settle the dispute? The matter must be resolved amicably to avoid another unnecessary war.

## *Cyprus Gas*

The naval dispute in the Spratlys is not the only argument over vast energy deposits, potentially so vast that the economic map of the region is being redrawn. Israel, in addition to its land-based military disputes with its neighbors, also has the potential for a naval confrontation because of the natural resources beneath the eastern Mediterranean. The Levant Basin, which encompasses Israeli, Lebanese, Syrian and Cypriot waters, could contain 122,000bn cubic feet of undiscovered gas reserves.

Israel and Cyprus struck an agreement on their maritime borders in 2010, a move that facilitated exploration for both sides. Soon after news of the Cypriot drilling emerged, Turkey reached an agreement with Northern Cyprus – which only Ankara recognizes – and dispatched a research ship to the area. With such high stakes – and high tensions – the eastern Mediterranean has become as volatile as the Spratlys.

### Greek Drama & Drachma

Greece and Cyprus are bankrupt and are not sustainable as members of the eurozone. The drachma, the former Greek currency, is already back in circulation in certain parts of the country. The cost of Greece's or Cyprus's exit from the eurozone could be as high as $1 trillion and the reverberations would be felt around the world, from Spain to China. The old world order, starting with the cradle of democracy, is dying a slow painful economic and political death. Greece's economic and political sickness is spreading and world leaders are at a loss to find a cure as political quacks fight each other over unworkable solutions.

A eurozone breakup could have frightening implications. The European economy accounts for 30 percent of global GDP. Euro sovereign debt outstanding in June 2012 stood at about $11 trillion, of which at least $4 trillion is a near-term risk of restructuring.

What will happen to the $185 trillion in euro-denominated derivatives? Who has got a plan to handle capital fright on that scale?

### Taiwan

For Beijing, Tokyo and Washington – and of course Taipei – Taiwan is a key military issue. It is the biggest, most sensitive sticking point in China's core interest of sovereignty and territorial integrity, as well as the political foundation of Sino-U.S. relations.

It is the biggest bump on what otherwise might be a smooth train ride for Sino-U.S. relations. That is why Defense Minister Liang Guanglie refused to guarantee that Beijing would refrain from suspending military ties with the U.S. in the future, especially if there were arms sales to Taiwan.

Steve Chicorel, my Hollywood producer friend whose wife Taiyun is Taiwanese and lives in Taiwan, was in Beijing during Gates' visit and stopped off in Hong Kong on his way back to Taiwan. U.S. sales of arms to Taiwan and the motives behind China's suprising transparency dominated our discussion during his one-night stayover.

"What is the point of trying to be the biggest swinging dick in the Pacific over Taiwan? Why can't America and China just be two nice little pricks and Taiwan can be both their balls?" I asked Steve as we continued our discussion about the merits of an arms race between America and China over security issues in the South and Yellow seas. "China will outspend the U.S., just the way the U.S. did to the USSR," I continued as Steve waived me off with his right middle finger as he got up to get a refill of a smooth single-malt scotch.

Closer cross-strait relations between China and Taiwan and the opening of official representative offices between Hong Kong and Taiwan are the initial stepping stones to a totally integrated China. The reality is that a democratic Taiwan, like Hong Kong and Macau, will become an integral part of a democratic China – and in fact play an important role in getting China there and become an even more peaceful co-democratic partner with America.

### *Japan Jets Junket*
What's the first thing Defense Secretary Robert Gates does when he arrives in Japan after his goodwill tour to China in January 2011 to improve Sino-U.S. military relations? He encourages the Japanese to buy American fighter jets. In a meeting in Tokyo with Defense Minister Toshimi Kitazawa, Gates "suggested Japan consider three U.S. planes to upgrade their fleet," the F-35 Joint Strike Fighter, the F/A-18 Hornet and the F-15 Eagle, a senior U.S. defense official said.

Japan is being told to take stock of its defensive hardware in the face of China's growing military might and assertive stance in the Pacific and "if they bought the right airplane – to have a fifth-generation capability ...

I might have a few suggestions for them," Gates told reporters.

Fifth-generation fighters are equipped with stealth radar-evading equipment. The F-35, which is still under development, meets those requirements.

Gates also suggested that the sinking of a South Korean warship and the shelling of an island in 2010 by the North was raising pressure on South Korea to shift from a policy of restraint toward one of military response, were Pyongyang to strike again – with the support of American troops on the ground in South Korea and the U.S. military machine backing them.

China's surprise test flight of its J-20 stealth fighter jet, which came sooner than the Pentagon expected, was the ideal excuse for Gates to raise military alarm bells in Tokyo. The message was clear. China is transparent and has deterrence capability – and a high-performance jet engine made of several families of top-secret, heat-resistant alloys. Secrets China got from America.

An American F-117 Nighthawk stealth warplane was shot down over Serbia on March 27, 1999, during NATO's aerial bombing during the Kosovo war. The pilot ejected and was rescued. Makes you wonder how stealthy it really was. The Pentagon believes a combination of clever tactics and sheer luck had allowed the Soviet-built SA-3 missile used by the Serbs to bring down the jet.

The F-117 began service in 1983. While not completely invisible to radar, its shape and radar-absorbent coating made detection difficult. Insight into this critical technology, and particularly the plane's secret radiation-absorbent exterior coating, would have significantly enhanced China's stealth know-how.

Western diplomats have said China maintained an intelligence post in its Belgrade embassy during the Kosovo war. The building was allegedly mistakenly struck by U.S. bombers in May 1999, killing three people inside. Was that intelligence post reason enough for America to bomb China's embassy and then wonder why the Chinese got upset, or were there other reasons as well?

It takes decades of testing to prove the air worthiness and consistent performance of a jet engine. Now that China can produce high-performance jet engines, it won't be long before cheaper Chinese engines will begin to replace foreign-made engines in both the military and civilian sectors, not just in China, but around the world.

Xu Guangyu, a retired People's Liberation Army general, said it would be at least five years before an operational stealth fighter can be incorporated into the Chinese air force. "There is some question about just how stealthy it is," Defense Secretary Gates said of the J-20.

I wonder what Gates and his successor Leon Panetta had to say in November 2012 when China launched its second stealth fighter, the J-31. Judging from the landing gear and its comparatively superior mobility compared with the J-20, it is possible that the J-31 is designed to be launched from an aircraft carrier. The J-31 can, according to aviation experts, match the U.S. military's F-35 Lightning II in future performance and may boast better avionics.

The J-31 appears to have borrowed features from the U.S. Air Force's twin-engine F-22 and U.S. Navy's single-engine F-35C. China is only the second country after the U.S. to test successfully two fifth-generation, advanced, multirole fighters.

The Chinese scoured a wide area of Serbian farmlands where the F-117 wreckage was strewn and collected and bought as many parts as they could get their hands on – some the size of cars.

"We believe the Chinese used those materials to gain an insight into secret stealth technologies … and to reverse-engineer them," said Admiral Davor Domazet-Loso, Croatia's military chief of staff during the Kosovo war. A Serbian military official confirmed that pieces of the wreckage were removed by souvenir collectors and some ended up "in the hands of foreign attaches."

The government of former Serbian President Slobodan Milosevic routinely shared captured Western equipment with his Chinese and Russian allies.

The Pakistanis will probably do the same thing with the remains of the stealth helicopter that crashed and burned in the U.S. raid that killed Osama bin Laden in his Abbottobad compound.

The Chinese spy network doesn't have to be secretive or stealthy to get its hands on secret U.S. high-tech military technology the way it has in Serbia, Pakistan or Libya. They can just come to America and buy it legally from an incompetent Pentagon.

China's "carrier killer," the Dong Fong 21D anti-ship ballistic missile, had a unique origin. Guess where? From where else but America? Buying military trash legally that was dumped by incompetent Pentagon and military bureaucrats. A key part of the rocket system was obtained from Martin Marietta in the 1990s. From the tons of military scrap China bought from military contractors and the military itself, there was enough intelligence to develop the radar guidance system that is now being used in the Dong Feng 21C and enabled the development of the DF-21D medium range "carrier killer."

Incorrect coding on sensitive items and lack of oversight meant that $20 billion worth of U.S. military equipment was being moved from American bases each year, an unmitigated disaster that persisted despite repeated warnings from inside whistle-blowers.

It didn't take the Chinese long, being that they are the primary buyers of all scrap metals, to figure out they had hit the military espionage Mother Lode. One Chinese buyer in Georgia referred to a military surplus depot as "the candy store." The military base, he wrote in a note to his boss, "will fill our needs into the next century."

The U.S. seized one container bound for Hong Kong after investigators found "fully operational encryption devices, submarine propulsion parts, radar systems, electron tubes for Patriot guided missiles, even F-117A stealth fighter parts. Many of these parts sold as "surplus," were brand new, according to *U.S. News and World Report*. The vast quantities of sensitive military equipment China has spirited out of the U.S. is mind boggling. And the Pentagon wants to spend more so it can discard more new equipment?

To fully appreciate and understand what an oxymoron "U.S. military intelligence" is, one has to appreciate that when the U.S. began dismantling its Pershing-II medium range ballistic missiles as part of the 1987 U.S.-Soviet Intermediate Nuclear Forces Agreement, it discarded the parts from these missiles into the unregulated military trashpile.

China is close to deploying sub-launched nuclear weapons, according to a report released by the U.S.-China Economic and Security Review Commission released in November 2012. "[Beijing is] on the cusp of attaining a credible nuclear triad of land-based intercontinental ballistic missiles, submarine-launched ballistic missiles, and air-dropped nuclear bombs," the report says.

"China's garbage espionage may have contributed to their being able to develop a terminally guided ballistic missile," said Richard Fisher, who has kept close tabs on the transfer of military technology to China.

As if the stealth fighter wasn't enough ammunition for Defense Secretary Gates to go with on his military sales mission to Japan and South Korea, he came up with his "disconnect" theory between the civilian and military leadership in China. He said that President Hu Jintao and the civilian leadership may not have been aware of the test flight of the J-20 because the military didn't tell them.

"I believe we've seen some instances where specific events took place and the Chinese civilian leadership might not have known about them in advance," Gates said.

Clearly, telling the Japanese that the Chinese leadership does not control the military would make Japan nervous and insecure enough to buy more U.S. armaments and keep the American bases in Japan longer.

The fact is that the "party controls the gun" principle dominates the civilian-military hierarchy in China. Just like the U.S. president is commander in chief of America's armed forces, the president of China is chairman of the Central Military Commission. It's a command structure shared by both countries, but one that neither practices perfectly.

## The Mission

Gates' mission was to improve Sino-U.S. military ties after almost a year's suspension because of U.S. arm sales to Taiwan. The see-saw military relationship between the two countries as they jostle for military dominance in the Asia-Pacific region has been disconcerting. Washington has become less confident and more insecure and suspicious about China's growing military by adopting a policy of returning and re-engaging in Asia. It was up to Gates to mend the damaged ties between the two militaries a week ahead of a crucial state visit by President Hu to Washington.

"I think the discussions were very productive and set the stage for taking the military-to-military relationship to the next level," Gates said.

Policymakers in Washington and the Pentagon believe that their strategic military architecture has been unsettled by China's growing influence and ability to project power. China didn't play by the rules laid down by Pentagon planners, or meet their erroneous expectations or provocations. China plays by its own rule book. Why can't policymakers from both countries meet each other halfway and work together to fuse the best each has to offer?

That is what I thought the Gates mission was trying to achieve. To develop sustained and reliable military-to-military contacts, improve trust, avoid misunderstanding and miscalculation. Hopefully it did after Gates visited the 2nd Artillery Corps of the People's Liberation Army headquarters for a rare glimpse of China's nuclear and missile arsenal. Gates was the second U.S. defense secretary to visit the command center, following in the footsteps of his predecessor Donald Rumsfeld, who came in 2005.

America wanted a glimpse at China's military objectives and got it. China insists that its nuclear policy and strategy is defensive and it will not use nuclear weapons preemptively.

"We hope Gates can recognize that China's missiles are defensive, with restrained scale, and are meanwhile effective in defense and counterattacks," said Peng Guangqian, a Beijing-based military strategist. America got it.

During President Hu's visit to the U.S. in January 2011, Obama announced that America and China had agreed to establish a jointly financed nuclear security center in China. The agreement is an opening to expand security cooperation between Washington and Beijing. The pact was signed by China Atomic Energy Authority Chairman Chen Qiufa and U.S Energy Secretary Steven Chu. The venture is aimed at training to improve security at nuclear facilities and accounting of nuclear materials. Officials also hope to hold joint exercises on responding to nuclear disasters and terrorism and to share nuclear detection technology. Beijing would pay most of the center's cost, but Washington would provide technology and expertise. The idea for the center was first proposed by Hu at Obama's nuclear security summit in April 2010.

Thankfully the Sino-U.S. relationship got stronger with the "candid and constructive" discussion Defense Secretary Chuck Hagel had with his counterpart Chang Wanquan and President Xi Jinping in Beijing in April 2014, when President Xi told Secretary Hagel that co-operation is crucial to conflict resolution.

### Back to Basics – The Cowboy Code

Texas had one of the largest and fastest growing economies in the U.S. during the Great Recession, which merits a closer look for what other states can learn from the Lone Star State. Its infrastructure is excellent. Labor is cheap. It is the only state among the 20 largest in the nation to have maintained a net gain of jobs from 2007 through 2010. Its population increased by more than 480,000, according to the latest census figures. There are no state personal income or capital gains taxes. Housing costs are low. The regulatory environment is business-friendly, which explains why Texas is home to the corporate headquarters of 57 Fortune 500 companies, more than any other state because it has the strongest free-enterprise economy of any state; it is the top state in export revenues, with more than $200 billion a year generated by high energy prices and tort law reforms that have accorded corporations better protection against massive lawsuits – and business development is a priority across party lines – something the career politicians in Washington and all other states should take note of. Bipartisanship is alive and well in Texas!

"Texas has all the advantages of being a lean and mean red state," says Christopher Lockwood, *The Economist's* U.S. editor, "with all the cool of a blue state in the cities."

"That is why I love America," says Lockwood, who happens to be an Englishman. "There is always a new model, a new way to expand, and it seems to me that right now Texas has that in spades."

Texas also has shale oil in spades and another economic boom looming on the horizon. Catarina, Texas, an impoverished area near the Mexican border, is the hottest new oil play in America. More than a dozen oil companies are planning to drill thousands of wells there over the next few years. The shale oil fields hold two or three times as much oil as Prudhoe Bay, the Alaskan field that was the last great onshore discovery, more than doubling real estate prices and filling restaurants and hotels.

It is estimated that fields that produced about half a million barrels daily in 2011 will produce up to 3 million barrels daily by 2020. Oil companies invested an estimated $25 billion in 2011 alone.

"This is like adding another Venezuela or Kuwait by 2020, except these tight oil fields are in the United States," said Daniel Yergin, chairman of HIS CERA, an energy research firm.

The new drilling makes economic sense as long as oil prices remain above $60 a barrel. With oil prices hovering at about $100 a barrel, shale wells can typically turn a profit within eight months – three times faster than many traditional wells.

The 2010 U.S. census confirmed that Texas is the state of opportunity and the runaway winner in congressional seats and political clout. It gained four new congressional seats because of its population gains. Texas is the 21st-century California – showing the way for the others.

That is because Texans think big and honor the Cowboy Code. No one can say with authority exactly what the Code of the West was. Because there was no framework of law in the Wild West, for the cowboy the code was the one civilizing influence that could be relied on. It was not carved in stone; in fact, it was not even written down on paper. Yet, while not every cowboy abided by the code, every cowboy knew what it was. The code is best summarized by James P. Owen in his book *Cowboy Ethics, What Wall*

*Street Can Learn From the Code of the West*. The 10 commandments of the code are:

1. Live Each Day With Courage.
2. Take Pride in Your Work.
3. Always Finish What You Start.
4. Do What Has to Be Done.
5. Be Tough, But Fair.
6. When You Make a Promise, Keep It.
7. Ride for the Brand.
8. Talk Less and Say More.
9. Remember That Some Things Aren't for Sale.
10. Know Where to Draw the Line.

It is time for America to get back to its cowboy ethics, not the myths in Hollywood films, but the traditional social and ethical mores. Something Wells Fargo bank, with its western-cowboy image, has done and as a result become the most valuable bank in the Western world. Although Wells Fargo still has fewer bank deposits than its closest competitor, its total stock market value in early 2012 was about $178 billion – that's about $70 billion more than Citigroup and about $9 billion more than JPMorgan. It has even overtaken the largest bank in Europe, London's HSBC.

Wells Fargo focuses on the more straightforward business of taking in deposits and doling out loans. It is the only one of the four major U.S. banks with more than a trillion dollars in assets that does not have a major Wall Street operation. What does that tell us?

### Dust Bowl Judgment Day

The Day of Judgment – The Rapture – was supposed to take place during my May 2011 visit to the States. Of course it didn't, but the movie *The Tree of Life* opened. A religiously themed allegory set in Waco, Texas, in the 1950s, its aesthetic glories are tethered to a humble and exalted purpose, which is to shine the light of the sacred on secular reality.

That secular reality, the one the Founding Fathers preached, is that the Constitution and the Bill of Rights enable us to make our heaven or hell here on earth – starting in America – as Texas, with all its conflicted fundamentalist religions, has proven.

The predictions of the world coming to an end in 2012 are true in a way. The political and economic world as we know it is coming to an end – not the world itself. The Third American Revolution has stopped the world from continuing on its destructive path to Armaggedon. *We the Maids* have to sweep America and the world it must co-lead with China back to the well-grounded American foundation stones laid by America's Founding Fathers – the Constitution and the Bill of Rights – which are also the foundation stones laid in China by Mao and China's founding fathers.

Cowboys, farmers, oilmen, and let's not forget the politicians and bankers, whose fast talking and moving mouths they feed and grease. Texas is a metaphor for America's heaven or hell that all religions preach. The sad reality is, very few acknowledge that *We the Maids* have the power to make our heaven here and now. For us, our children and grandchildren. It is time we did. Sweep in our heaven and sweep out our hell. Why continue to believe and tolerate more unfulfilled political promises?

With all the glowing statistics coming out of Texas, part of the secular reality is that many farmers in Texas have been struggling for years to survive the worst drought since the Dust Bowl of the 1930s. While most Americans focused on the flooding Mississippi River, the Oklahoma panhandle, like the rest of the nation, endured its longest drought on record. Texas has been especially hard-hit. More than 82 percent of the state experienced extreme or exceptional drought. Texas ranchers, the nation's top cattle producers, had no natural grass to feed their animals. The Cowboy Code helped them survive.

If only today's career politicians would follow in the footsteps of the Founding Fathers and adhere to the letter and spirit of the Declaration of Independence and Constitution, and the Code of the Cowboys who settled the great plains, prairies, mountains and deserts, from the Atlantic, Hudson River and Cheasapeake Bay, to the Pacific, Columbia River and Sacramento Delta, America could again become the great nation it once was.

The Dallas Mavericks reminded America of what living the Cowboy Code can do to team spirit, winning the NBA title in 2011.

### False Hopes and Profits

The global meltdown of 2008 triggered a $145 billion U.S. government stimulus package dubbed Project Lifeline. Project False Hope is more appropriate – and a clear breach of the Cowboy Code. The stimulus was created and advocated by the banks that service half of the U.S. mortgage market – Bank of America, Citigroup, Countrywide Financial, JPMorgan Chase, Washington Mutual and Wells Fargo – all members of the so-called Hope Now Alliance. Banks are always hoping to be given a lifeline by taxpayers whenever they mess up. And guess who cleans up? *We the Apathetic Maids.* Why should the government repeatedly come to the banks' rescue whenever enough of them are in trouble at the same time – while homeowners and the unemployed, who are in the majority, are not only ignored, but taxed to pay the banks' heavy-handed interest clobbering and foreclosure club?

The Treasury Department expects to lose $75 billion on the federal bailouts, with most of the losses in its housing finance program and the auto industry rescue plan. The government expects to lose $17 billion from its investments in GM, Chrysler and the auto finance companies, as well as $46 billion from housing programs like the Home Affordable Modification Program. That does not include losses from the federal bailout of Fannie Mae and Freddie Mac, the government-backed housing finance companies. A government report said Fannie and Freddie were expected to cause "substantial losses," but noted that they were financed using other funds, not the troubled asset funds – another government shell game – wasting even more hard-earned taxpayer dollars.

A prime example of how stimulus money was wasted is the case of the bankrupt solar company Solyndra. The start-up had received a well-publicized $535 million federal loan guarantee, offered in part to reassert American dominance in solar technology while generating thousands of jobs. President Obama visited the company factory in Fremont, California, as part of his campaign to promote government efforts to create jobs in the green energy sector.

The subprime story is a bad rerun. Nothing new here. It happens repeatedly. New financial instruments and an enthusiasm for risk-taking create dramatic increases in credit, which drives up asset prices thereby justifying still more credit expansion and still higher asset prices. Then comes a top to asset prices and they have to be marked to market. Panic selling followed by a credit freeze that results in mass insolvencies and a recession – or worse.

All that the millions of struggling homeowners receive is false hope.

Borrowers who have outstanding student or automobile loans and consumer credit will face the same false hope unless real political will to tackle the credit crisis is asserted.

"I was gradually coming to believe that the U.S. economy's greatest strength was its resiliency – its ability to absorb disruptions and recover, often in ways and at a pace you'd never be able to predict, much less dictate," former Federal Reserve Chairman Alan Greenspan wrote in his book *The Age of Turbulence*. Wishful thinking by the man who helped create the mess. Was he ever wrong. How could he not see the crisis coming? Is that any way to manage monetary policy? Is it any wonder the financial system is broken and broke?

What happened at the beginning of 2008 was the meltdown of the biggest pyramid game in human history. Since the burst of the Nasdaq tech bubble in March 2000, hedge funds, private equity funds and proprietary trading at banks have come to dominate money making. The new business model depended on asset prices constantly rising. Because so many wanted the same assets at the same time, demand pushed up asset prices and the model became a self-fulfilling prophesy. "Higher return" came to mean "faster appreciating" instead of "higher yielding." Once banks started making margin calls and hedge funds and private equity had to liquidate and assets had to be marked-to-market, the house of cards collapsed.

The Bank for International Settlements said credit default swaps totaling $43 trillion, half the entire asset base of the global banking system, were outstanding at the end of 2007. That's the reality.

To make matters worse and further undermine a fragile economy, just when everyone thought the housing market was recovering and the recession was over, banks decided to halt foreclosures nationwide – three weeks before the November 2010 midterm elections. The reason? "This is not a silver bullet to keep millions of Americans in their homes. This is a chance to... get the process right," said Tom Miller, the Iowa attorney general, who is spearheading an investigation by the attorney generals of all 50 states and the District of Columbia. Under his leadership, coalitions of states have won lending-abuse settlements of $484 million from Household International Inc. and $325 million from Ameriquest Mortgage Co.

Audits of foreclosures revealed that most involved either legal violations or suspicious robo-signed documentation. The improprieties ranged from the basic – a failure to warn borrowers that they were in default on their loans as required by law to the arcane. Transfers of many loans in the foreclosure files were made by entities that had no right to assign them and institutions took back properties in auctions even though they had not proved ownership.

Almost 2 million struggling homeowners nationwide, including about half a million in California, received some relief from the $26 billion settlement reached by the attorney generals and the banks.

The legal settlements to date, whether against bankers for their fraudulent behavior in packaging and selling subprime securitized loans, to improper foreclosure procedures, highlight the fact that the bankers responsible for these disastrous mishaps get off with a slap on the wrist and a fine that is a fraction of the wealth they amassed during the subprime bubble while *We the Apathetic Maids* suffer.

A case in point is the story of Angelo Mozilo, the chief executive of Countrywide. From 2000 to 2008, he received total compensation estimated at $521.5 million; in 2010, without admitting or denying any wrongdoing, he paid $67.5 million to settle civil fraud charges brought by the SEC. The Justice Department decided not to pursue a possible criminal case against Mozilo.

In the meantime, the victims of the fraud living in foreclosed homes because of their inability to pay are left in limbo and uncertainty – that is better than living on the street – because lenders, forced by the harsh realities of the real estate market, were increasingly allowing defaulting owners to remain in their homes, a strategy that preserves the value of the properties by helping buoy some neighborhoods while slowing down the foreclosure process.

Change of prosecutable approach is needed. The kind of change that brought the New York attorney general and the inspector general supervising Fannie and Freddie and the Federal Housing Finance Agency to work together. They agreed in December 2011 to share documents and findings and pool their resources. A much more efficient way to spend taxpayers' money to properly prepare their cases against the banks and bankers.

The fact is, banks screwed up again and acknowledged that employees who were supposed to verify the foreclosure documents under oath hadn't actually read them. In other words, the paperwork was botched. The root cause of the botched paperwork is simple. Originating mortgages, bundling them and reselling the packages as securities was immensely profitable. Servicing the loans – basically keeping track of all that paper – was not. So it was left to low-paid, poorly trained and inexperienced workers.

There are 23 judicial foreclosure states – states in which foreclosures are handled by the courts that require affidavits be made under oath by people who have read the paperwork filed with the court to proceed with the foreclosure. Bank of America, JPMorgan Chase and Ally Financial decided to stop foreclosures nationwide because attorney generals in non-judicial foreclosure states decided to launch an investigation to see if their foreclosure laws had also been violated.

Since the start of the recession in December 2007, more than 2.5 million homes have been foreclosed and their owners evicted. The banks seized 816,000 homes through the first nine months of 2010 and were on track to foreclose on 1.2 million by the end of 2011. In September 2010, the month before the foreclosure moratorium, banks seized 102,134 homes, a record for any month, with California in the lead. Not something any career politician or their financial backers want to see continue to spike before a critical presidential election.

That's not all that complicated the foreclosures. The corporate greed gets worse. The Mortgage Electronic Registration Systems Inc., known in the industry as MERS, whose shareholders include Bank of America, CitiMortgage, Fannie Mae, Freddie Mac and Wells Fargo, was used as a shortcut and listed on about 20 million home loans as the mortgage owner, standing in for the lenders – to avoid paying filing fees for recording documents nationwide. MERS was created in 1995 to speed up record keeping of mortgages. It keeps track of repeated sales of mortgages as they go through the process of being turned into packages of loans and the basis for securities sold on Wall Street. MERS allowed banks to avoid the trouble – and the recording fees – of filing deeds and other documents at county registrars' offices every time ownership of a mortgage changed hands during the subprime feeding frenzy. MERS has 65 million loans registered in its database.

The high courts in Arkansas, Kansas and Maine ruled that MERS is not the true owner of the mortgages because it only maintains the database and called into question MERS right to foreclose on homes in its name. The company's murky legal status as owner of the mortgages also led to class-action lawsuits in California, Nevada, Arizona and Kentucky challenging its right to foreclose on delinquent loans and accused MERS of costing counties more than $100 billion in property recording fees since it began operations.

The government's distressed homeowner program was aimed at helping out those who took out subprime loans or other risky mortgages during the heady days of the housing boom. That was short-sighted because the primary cause of foreclosures is unemployment. The focus should be on creating jobs, not helping speculators, be they corporate or individuals.

There were more than 872,000 homes in foreclosure during my May 2011 visit to the U.S., almost twice as many as when the financial crisis began in 2007, with several million more on the sidelines ready to go into foreclosure in the years to come, which only further depresses the real estate market.

Prices in some markets had fallen back to the levels of 2003.

The equity Americans had in their homes in 2011 plummeted to nearly the lowest percentage since World War II. Average home equity fell from more than 81 percent at the start of 2001 to 38 percent between January to March 2011. Debt accounted for 119 percent of disposable income – down from a peak of 135 percent in late 2007. Many Americans were subtracted from total home mortgage debt because they were going into default on their payments and losing their homes.

In the good ol' days, when people paid down their mortgages, their home equity rose. But since the housing bubble burst in 2006, prices have fallen more than they did during the Great Depression of the 1930s. In many cases, people are paying on mortgages and losing equity at the same time.

There were during my May-June 2011 visit 74.5 million homeowners in the U.S. Nearly 25 percent of those were "under water," which means they had negative equity in their homes, according to the private real estate research firm CoreLogic. Another 25 percent were nearing that point with water up to their chins.

Meanwhile, back home in Hong Kong, real estate prices have been climbing by 40 percent a year since 2009. Basically, Hong Kong property prices increased by 45 percent while the U.S. decreased by 30 percent over the same period. Any wonder Chinese were buying up depressed California properties, as well as in most of the other 49 states, as if they were at a fire sale that would soon run out? Maybe they knew something Americans didn't? In fact, they did.

The month of July 2011, had five Fridays, five Saturdays and five Sundays. That happens once in every 823 years. The year of the money bags. That's when I decided to seriously start looking for a home base back home in California – and moved back.

False hope and austerity measures are not the way to correct domestic or global imbalances. America needs to export its way back to balancing its books domestically, state to state, and with countries like China and OPEC members increasing their imports from America. It doesn't make sense and is unsustainable for America, with only 5 percent of the world population, to consume 30 percent of global resources. Growth and prosperity in the developing world also offer America more export opportunities.

In 1997, during the Asian financial crisis, the U.S. Treasury and International Monetary Fund warned East Asian countries about the risks of bailouts or raising interest rates. Ten years later, America ignored its own past lectures and bought up billions of dollars of bad mortgages and lowered interest rates. This after America managed to pass off hundreds of billions of dollars worth of bad mortgages to banks around the world. Isn't it time *We the Apathetic Maids* get career politicians to practice what they preach – and what America stands for?

The Fed's actions cast doubt on the future of paper money. China experimented with paper money 1,000 years ago. As the government printed more and more to fund its own profligacy, people refused to hold it and paper money disappeared from history. The current monetary system – paper money with no tangible anchor to back it up – is but four decades old. As soon as the Nixon administration abandoned the dollar linkage to gold, it led to a severe bout of inflation that was contained by globalization. Inflation is back and can no longer be contained by globalization. It can only be contained by Sino-U.S. interlocalism, balanced budgets, and a well-fed, gainfully employed and educated electorate.

China was able to withstand the subprime crisis and recent global recession that created economic havoc in America because it is no longer dependent solely on America. Furthermore, it has usurped the U.S. as the driver of world growth. The U.S. subprime crisis made Hong Kong the China beachhead for foreign funds. Today China has overtaken the U.S. as the largest seller to the eurozone and is rapidly doing the same in the Middle East, Latin America, Russia and Africa. Isn't this a geopolitical partner America should be embracing so that it can cushion any future global inflationary or recessionary economic disasters?

### Corporate Milk
The first known whistle-blower lawsuit to assert that U.S. taxpayers were

defrauded when the government bailed out AIG was unsealed in May 2011, joining a number of suits seeking to settle the score on losses related to the financial crisis of 2008. The suit alleges that AIG, Goldman Sachs and Deutche Bank engaged in a variety of fraudulent and speculative transactions, running up losses well into the billions of dollars. Then the three institutions persuaded the Federal Reserve Bank of New York to bail them out by giving AIG two rescue loans, which were used to unwind hundreds of failed trades.

The loans were improper, the suit claims, because the Fed made them without getting a pledge of high-quality collateral from AIG, as required by law.

"To cover losses of those engaged in fraudulent financial transactions is an authority not yet given to the Fed board," said the plaintiffs, Derek and Nancy Casady, in their complaint.

Senior Fed officials have stated repeatedly that they had to take unusual steps in 2008 because of the global financial system was close to breaking down. Michael J. Aguirre, the Casadys' lawyer, argued that even so, the Fed was required to comply with its own governing statutes. He said that when the Fed bailed out an institution that was not a bank, it was required to secure the loan with the same liquid, high-quality collateral it required when lending to a troubled bank.

The litigation shines a critical light on the Federal Reserve's on-again-off-again power to bail out non-banking institutions like Wall Street firms and insurance companies. The Fed first got that authority during the Great Depression, but Congress revoked it in 1958. And then, as the legal walls between banking and other financial services began to fall in the 1990s, Congress once again gave the Fed the power to make emergency loans to institutions that were not banks. The relevant language is contained in a single, murky sentence inserted in a bill passed the day before Thanksgiving in 1991, as members of Congress rushed to catch flights home. Former Senator Christopher Dodd added it at the request of Goldman Sachs and other Wall Street firms, which were still burning from a major market crash in 1987 and eager to empower the Fed to step in if they created a similar problem again, which as we all know, they did. Good, timely lobbying at the expense of *We the Apathetic Maids*.

Career politicians decided to take Social Security and Medicare money, and whatever other taxpayer dollars they could find in the so-called "Lock Box," to bail out incompetent bankers at the expense of hard-working taxpayer seniors. Not something the Founding Fathers, even bankers like Alexander Hamilton, would approve.

"Congress did not show a legislative intent to convert the Federal Reserve into a bank for bailing out failed speculators," the complaint asserts. I agree. The primary beneficiaries of the financial meltdown, besides the bank executives who handsomely rewarded themselves, are lawyers. The demand for litigation and regulatory lawyers is booming as they prepare their banking clients for years of fines and lawsuits.

A prime example of the type of litigation preoccupying lawyers – and the ingratitude taxpayer bailed-out financial institutions have – is the shareholder lawsuit filed by AIG shareholders claiming the government cheated them when it rescued the company from bankruptcy.

*Mediscare*

The Republican defeat in New York's 26th Congressional District special election, the loss of their safe and "sure" seat during my visit to the state in May 2011, was a wakeup call to Republicans and Congressman Paul Ryan – that *We the Apathetic Seniors* are not going to allow career politicians to mess with Medicare. When the shocking results were announced, the political establishments of both parties were stunned.

Republicans can scream "Mediscare!" all they want. Seniors who have made their fair share contribution to America's growth and prosperity have every right to be angry and fight any draconian plan that would replace the current Medicare plan, in which the government pays major health costs, with a voucher system in which seniors would, in effect, be handed a coupon and told to go find private coverage. Especially if the cost estimates of the Congressional Budget Office are correct and the vouchers – which by 2030 would cover only about a third of seniors' health costs – would leave many, if not most, older Americans unable to afford essential care. Why shouldn't citizens get, at the very least, the same coverage career politicians enjoy and which Congressman Ryan falsely asserted is contained in his proposals?

The career politicians have no right to mess with Medicare, Medicaid or Social Security in their efforts to balance the budget. Why not take a closer look at federal expenditures that are truly wasteful, like the Department of Defense budget for unnecessary wars that no one can explain or justify, subsidies to oil companies and entitlement programs?

An educated and healthy citizenry is the best defense America can have against any adversary. A dumbed-down unhealthy nation, no matter how sophisticated and advanced its weapons are, will lose any military conflict – especially against a smart and determined adversary. So why waste precious resources on useless weapons systems instead of investing in the health and welfare of our citizens?

What is of graver concern is how Congress was also trying simultaneously to delegate its "war powers" to the president. While on the one hand the Republican Congress was trying to do away with Medicare, it was also trying to hand over to the president Congress' constitutional authority to declare war, substantially altering the delicate balance of powers that the Founding Fathers so carefully crafted.

The Fiscal Year 2012 National Authorization Act of the Department of Defense contained unprecedented and dangerous language that gives the president virtually unchecked power to take the country to war and keep it there.

"The language in the bill significantly undermines the Constitution, the institution of Congress and sets the United States on a path of permanent war," said former Ohio Democratic Congressman Dennis J. Kucinich. "It's as if the Constitution, which requires Congress to have a say in when and where we go to war and which guarantees U.S. citizens the right to a fair and speedy trial, was never written. Congress must protect the American people from the overreach of any chief executive who is enamored with unilateralism, pre-emption, first strike and the power to prosecute war without constitutional or statutory proscriptions.

"Permanent, global war is not the answer. It will not increase our national security. Far from ridding the world of terrorism, it will become a terrorist recruitment program," Kucinich said.

Defense spending is the biggest U.S. budget item, although interest payments on the federal debt could exceed military spending in less than a decade – two budget items that must be reduced drastically for the Republic to survive as an economic and military power.

That's not all. While *We the Apathetic Maids* were being distracted by the budget deficit debate and Mediscare, Congress managed to quickly and quietly vote to renew the Patriot Act and its draconian, undue overreach surveillance and invasion of privacy of American citizens for another four years.

How can America realistically believe it can continue to be a relevant world power when it is imploding at home because of career politicians' selfish and short-sighted stupidity?

"Whatever America hopes to bring to pass in the world must first come to pass in the heart of America," President Dwight D. Eisenhower reminded us. Something we must keep in mind today.

"Starving the beast" of government, cutting taxes, worthwhile regulations and social services – slashing everything but the military – not only violates and breaches the most fundamental ideals of the Founding Fathers, but is also the foundation of a military dictatorship.

Over the years, during my travels through Asia, Africa, Latin America and the Middle East, I have seen plenty of modern tanks and fighter aircraft – but schools and hospitals that have trouble paying teachers and doctors. Sound familiar?

"Maybe that's why the growing inequality in America pains me so,"

Nicholas D. Kristof said in his column in *The New York Times*. "The wealthiest 1 percent of Americans already have a greater net worth than the bottom 90 percent, based on the Federal Reserve data. Yet two-thirds of the proposed Republican budget cuts would harm low-and moderate-income families, according to the Center on Budget and Policy Priorities."

The country must recall John Quincy Adams's cautionary advice: America "does not go abroad in search of monsters to destroy. She is the well-wisher to the freedom and independence of all. She is the champion and vindicator only of her own."

### *Corporate Spin*

During the 2010 midterm elections and 2012 presidential election, a recurrent theme spun by corporate America and the Republicans was that they blamed the lack of hiring on a lack of clarity – the uncertainty – in the Democrats' federal policy. What nonsense, I thought to myself every time I heard a career politician or aspirant make that statement. The fact is that unemployment and underemployment have become chronic even as the overall economic indicators have stabilized and companies – especially big ones – are raking in phenomenal profits.

Corporate America is not hiring because it is highly profitable even with fewer workers. Companies have spent billions on technologies that have made them more efficient and productive. And they are adding jobs abroad – where the growth is. Corporate America knows it can service a still highly affluent U.S. market with fewer workers. In fact, the companies of the S&P 500 – the epitome of corporate America – have been reporting strong earnings for the past three years. They have reaped billions in profit even as the employment rolls have shrunk.

The fact is that America's CEOs, once they pocketed the stimulus loot, prefer to scoot because they have become risk-averse and prefer to repay debt, buy back stock, or build reserves against the next crisis rather than hire people.

Corporate America usually invests 100 percent or more of cash flow (profits plus depreciation) in new buildings, equipment and software. The ratio dips during recession, but as former Fed chief Alan Greenspan points out, from 2010 onward it's been below 80 percent – the lowest since at least 1952.

The point is not to demonize business leaders. Their reasons for not hiring make some sense, given the reality of the marketplace and the imperative to remain competitive. But the uncertainty mantra is yet another example of the blame game that has become endemic in American political life. It's always someone else's fault, and government makes an easy and familiar target.

Corporate America has no incentive to hire domestically unless there is a robust U.S. economy that justifies more bodies. Government can help or hinder such robustness, but it cannot create it. The fault, as Shakespeare reminds us, is in ourselves – *We the Apathetic Maids* – no matter how much easier it is to point the finger.

### Hedge Fund Republic – Income Inequality

America has become a corporate hedge fund republic where the richest 1 percent possess more net worth than the bottom 90 percent. The top 1 percent of Americans own 34 percent of America's private net worth, according to figures compiled by the Economic Policy Institute in Washington. The bottom 90 percent owns just 29 percent. That also means that the top 10 percent control more than 70 percent of Americans' total net worth. Huge concentrations of wealth corrode the soul of any nation. All one has to do is look at Africa and Latin America. The same is now happening to America – and to China as well.

Just like America, there is a yawning income gap in China that is getting wider. People who work in Shanghai's highest-paid industries earn an average of 6.4 times more than those who toil in blue-collar sectors with meager salaries. A majority of the city's residents, about 68 percent of its working population, are employed in the lowest-paying sectors, including manufacturing, construction, catering and retail.

The minimum monthly salary in 2010 was 1,120 *yuan*, or $170. About 30 percent of city dwellers live on that income, a drop from 44.6 percent in 1993. It falls further when compared to the internationally accepted level, according to which people who receive a minimum monthly salary earn no less than 50 percent of a city's average income. The income gap is also widening within Chinese companies as corporate executives earn an average of five times that of their employees. In some cases, more than 10 times.

"The government and state-owned enterprises have the biggest share in the distribution of national income, but more should be directed to residents to narrow China's income gap," said Hu Yijian, a professor of tax studies at Shanghai University of Finance and Economics.

Emmanuel Saez, an economist at the University of California at Berkeley and one of the world's leading experts on inequality, notes that for most of American history, income distribution was significantly more equal than it is today. And other capitalist countries do not suffer disparities as great as ours. "There has been an increase in inequality in most industrialized countries, but not as extreme as in the U.S.," Professor Saez said.

Yet career politicians insist on granting $370,000 tax breaks to the richest Americans as a way to stimulate the economy during a recession? I don't get it. How is that going to stimulate the economy? Do politicians really think these rich taxpayers are going to stimulate the economy by buying fancy cars and yachts and hiring more groundskeepers and chauffers? Of course not. But they are the people who fund the politicians' re-election campaigns.

The unemployed poor are given no breaks because they don't have money to spare to donate to career politician's re-election campaigns. A study commissioned by the Labor Department during the George W. Bush administration makes clear the job-creation power of unemployment benefits because that money is spent immediately. It is pumped back into the economy rather than into a savings account or politicians' re-election coffers.

Andy Xie, an independent economist, summed up best how America's financial model crash-landed. The two decades following the fall of the Berlin Wall will be remembered as a gilded age, he wrote. After the ideological struggle of the Cold War, the world embraced globalization and making money in any way possible. The pursuit of profit became the most powerful force shaping the world. Factories were moved to wherever wages and environmental standards were lowest. Main Street shops were put out of business by mega-box-stores in the suburbs. Wherever regulation stood in the way, deregulation took its place in the name of efficiency.

This relentless cost-cutting has meant a rising share of income for capital and a declining one for labor. Left unchecked, deflation followed and destroyed the returns for capital as working consumers have less income to buy the abundant products that capital produces.

Financial capitalism extended the profit dream by shifting capital into paper assets. It shot two birds with one stone. Workers could support their consumption by borrowing against asset appreciation, supporting the returns on productive assets. Capitalists could deploy their surpluses into paper assets, indirectly lending to consumers, rather than physical assets that would hamper returns. This happy combination continued to shift income from labor to capital. The boom planted the seeds for its inevitable destruction. The capitalists, blinded by their greed, were unknowingly paying for their profit dream by lending to consumers with overvalued paper assets as collateral.

The two decades of income shifting to capital and asset inflation came to an abrupt halt in 2008 when the house of cards came apart, as derivatives were exposed as frauds rather than ingenious designs that reduced risk to capitalists with no cost.

The lower level of consumption in the future will significantly cut into capital's returns. And without asset appreciation to supplement lower wages, workers will naturally demand higher wages. Contrary to the misguided popular belief of Wall Street that a weak economy means low inflation, the opposite happened. The cutting-edge financial models forgot to consider or factor in the most important human ingredient: greed. Their greed helped wipe out $50 trillion in global wealth, causing untold human suffering and misery.

Why did the global financial crisis happen and what can be done to prevent a repeat? That was the topic of 2003 Nobel Laureate in Economic Sciences Professor Robert Engle's engrossing lecture at the Hong Kong University of Science and Technology in July 2011. He identified two principle causes. The first was the clear failure of risk management by banks, investors and regulatory agencies. The second was the fact that so many institutions and individuals ended up being paid very well to, in effect, ignore the risks that exist – and are doing so again.

Disproportionate compensation set the stage for increased risk taking. And, as multiple examples made plain, this put governments and taxpayers in a compromised position when institutions went to the brink.

Bankers' greed and bonuses were highlighted as the financial crisis made a temporary recovery in late 2010 and 2011, and bankers went back to their good old self-rewarding ways.

"How can investment banks have the gall to pay huge bonuses to already high-paid staff so soon after a financial crisis that they themselves were instrumental in causing?" asked columnist Jake van der Kamp, a fellow barfly at the Main Bar of the Foreign Correspondent's Club in Hong Kong, in response to my compliment of his March 8, 2011 column, which was critical of bank bonuses and mountain-bikers on hiking trails.

"It is an insult to the rest of society when a few people are paid huge amounts of money generated by activities that, in fact, have undermined the stability of the financial system on which the rest of society depends," Jake continued.

It used to be that investment banks underwrote every share offering they introduced to the market. No longer. They now negotiate the price with their clients, and only when they are satisfied that an offering will be fully taken up do they finalize the price, sign the deal and publish the prospectus. They no longer take any risk. But they still collect the full underwriting fee.

Disciplined and effective lobbying by the financial services industry. I know first hand. I saw it coming as a lawyer-lobbyist who represented financial institutions in the 1970s and '80s. I was also the founder of Mercantile National Bank in Los Angeles in 1980, the largest initially capitalized national bank at the time.

Investment banks have also managed to virtually abolish the rights issue, a highly efficient and equitable way for listed companies to raise more money. That's because rights issues are not big fee generators. And what bankers can't get from issuances, they increasingly pick up by flogging complicated derivatives to retail investors. This is in line with Jake's No. 4 Rule of Investment – "For every adjective you add to the instrument you add 2 percent to the fee." That's just the stated fee. "It takes no account of how much you get ripped off in determination of the price," Jake added as we segued into the stupidity of *We the Maids,* the investors.

Jake and I agreed that the biggest reason investment banks get away with it is that *We the Maids,* the intended victims, too often tell ourselves that we don't understand anything about investment and must leave it up to the experts.

"The expertise of these experts, however, lies in parting you and your money. The real skill required in investment banking does not amount to much. It mostly consists of a sales job of convincing companies seeking to list their securities that you can get them a better price than your competitors can," Jake said. He should know. He was an investment bank analyst before he became a writer.

"To do it you use big investment words, present these companies with mounds of paperwork they have no hope of understanding and otherwise call on all your resources of bafflegab," Jake said as we left the bar, him to go hiking and me to go writing.

### *Family Banking Parallels*

Establishment families run banks, business and politics in general in both America and China. They don't really care about what is good for the people or country. Their only blinded preoccupation is their family business and how they can continue to enrich themselves. Plutocracy – a governing wealthy elite – has been exposed as the real face of capitalism in America and China. Capitalism in both countries is essentially an economic theory that disguises and hides, charades that mask a mutually beneficial, self-serving plutocracy.

There is the "family business" argument put forth by Carl Walter and Fraser Howie, authors of *Red Capitalism: The Fragile Financial Foundation of China's Extraordinary Rise,* and there is the "banana republic" argument about the U.S. put forward by Yves Smith, an economics blogger, and Simon Johnson, a former IMF chief economist. Johnson caused an uproar among top bankers and politicians with his May 2009 article in the *Atlantic Monthly* in which he compared the stranglehold of the financial oligarchy on Wall Street and Washington with that of politically-connected business elites in emerging countries.

"In its depth and suddenness, the U.S. economic and financial crisis is shockingly remincent of moments we have recently seen in emerging markets," Johnson wrote.

"There's a deeper and more disturbing similarity: elite business interests … played a central role in creating the crisis, making ever-larger gambles, with the implicit backing of the government, until the inevitable collapse," he said.

Johnson elaborated further on his theme in *13 Bankers: The Wall Street Takeover and the Next Financial Meltdown,* co-authored with James Kwak: "The fact that our American oligarch operates not by bribery or blackmail, but by the soft power of access and ideology, makes it no less powerful.

"We may have the most advanced political system in the world, but we also have its most advanced oligarchy," he wrote.

"The idea that a sophisticated, unrestrained financial sector was good for America became part of the conventional wisdom of the political and intellectual class. A casual observer would be forgiven for thinking Washington has behaved like an emerging market government – using public resources to protect a handful of large banks with strong political connections. Wall Street became stronger as a result of the financial crisis.

"Never before has so much taxpayer money been dedicated to save an industry from the consequences of its own mistakes. In the ultimate irony, it went to an industry that had insisted for decades that it had no use for the government and would be better off regulating itself – and it was overseen by a group of policymakers who agreed that government should play little role in the financial sector," Johnson wrote.

Who needs "money-under-the-table" corruption when a company like Goldman Sachs could legally earmark $11.4 billion in bonuses in the first half of 2009, when the financial crisis was still boiling?

The era of Western-dominated globalization and the so-called Great Moderation was an illusion perpetuated by an unholy alliance of finance, hands-off government and academia, especially in the U.S.

China is no different. The financial reforms introduced by Jiang Zemin and Zhu Rongji to make the People's Bank of China more professional, reform the financial system and turn the big four state-owned banks into more professional outfits were reversed by Hu Jintao and Wen Jiabao, not because of different beliefs in how the institutions should be run, but as Howie and Walter argue in their book, at the heart of the struggle is "family" control.

"China is a family-run business," they write. "When the ruling groups change, there will be an inevitable change in the balance of interests; but these families have one shared interest above all others – the stability of the system. Social stability allows their pursuit of special interests. This is what is meant by calls for a 'harmonious society'." Zhu's financial reform helped to roll back the families' influence, Howie believes, and Hu and Wen essentially launched a counter-reformation.

"What moves this structure is not market economy and its laws of supply and demand, but a carefully balanced social mechanism built around the particular interests of the revolutionary families who constitute the political elite," they write.

I concur with the authors who argue that these families control the national champions in key industries, and most other state-run enterprises.

China is essentially a "family business," a ruling elite dominated by families with deep roots dating back to the revolutionary era. The heart of the problem is that Beijing's top priority is not market efficiency or world domination, but domestic control and the necessary domestic stability to ensure continued family domination.

### *Why We Don't Understand*
Since the 1980s, armies of highly trained mathematicians, engineers, physicists and computer scientists have joined the financial industry. These "quants," as they are known, have come up with impenetrable mathematical models and software systems that financial traders use to make decisions in buying and selling securities. The increasing complexity of the financial markets has led to a symbiosis between the quants and traders that make both a lot of money but create the illusion that numbers and equations are reality. That illusion has been blamed for triggering the global financial crisis.

It not only allows the quants to exercise their mathematical prowess but also suits their psyche: the challenge of mining massive amounts of information to create highly complex mathematical models that explain how the financial world works.

"The mindset is no different to the way Isaac Newton explained planetary movements by using the astrological data collected by those such as Kepler and Copernicus," said Tom Yam, a Hong Kong-based electrical engineer and an MBA from the Wharton School of the University of Pennsylvania.

The world is awash in financial data. No industry creates, stores and distributes more data than the financial industry. A report in 2010 from the World Federation of Exchanges identified a total of 45,503 companies listed in 52 regulated stock exchanges around the world. Historical and real-time information on those companies is reported at ever-increasing speeds approaching hundredths of a second. Add the macroeconomic data – interest rates, money supply, unemployment rates, housing prices, cross-border trades, currency exchange rates – and you have a number-crunchers' nirvana.

With the colossal amounts of financial data available and their deep training in advanced mathematics, the quants try to formulate a "law of financial physics" and become masters of the universe while making millions and sneering at Luddites like me who want to do business the good old-fashioned way: Build a business, make money. Get known and established in the community. Come on, what's wrong with extending an overdraft credit line. What's wrong with the equity side of the bank participating? Conflicts of interest and inside information take interesting turns when the quants and bankers get together and try to figure out how to make a buck before they even consider helping finance the business the way they used to. Got to be enough vigorice for them to participate.

I experienced that first hand when dealing with bankers and quants when I put Pets Central together. These quants didn't know what real animals were like, how pet shops and puppy farms smell or what the real animal world is all about. They relate to Avatars and financial models that don't compute or work in the real pet care world – and conversely, the real pet care world can't handle or deal with the MBAs regardless of whether they are quants or not, and certainly not with bankers.

In their paper on the complexity of jobs in the financial industry, Thomas Philippon and Ariell Reshef report that since the 1980s increasing competence in mathematics and statistical methods is expected of its practitioners. Until the 1980s, no degree program in the U.S. focused on the quantitative aspect of finance; now there are more than 70 graduate programs in financial engineering that emphasize quantative methods. That's all America and the world needs. More quants to join the army of MBAs that has grown even faster since the 1980s and who together led America and the world over the precipice of financial disaster.

I for one don't believe the advent of the quants has led to better understanding of the financial markets. I think they have complicated it beyond comprehension for most people and have limited its understanding even to the "insiders." They have not contributed anything to the welfare of society. On the contrary, they are the welfare recipients in a society that continues paying them for their behavior, mistakes, past, present and future. Their false sense of security created at the altar of advanced mathematics has led to risky behavior, resulting in chaos and systematic failure.

There are many examples. Portofolio insurance theory developed by quants was a critical factor in "Black Monday" on October 19, 1987, the single biggest one-day crash in the history of the U.S. stock market. The Nobel laureates in economics Robert Merton and Myron Scholes behind the hedge fund Long Term Capital Management could not prevent its meltdown in 1998, threatening to destabilize global markets. And in the days before the collapse of Lehman Brothers in 2008, traders witnessed a crashing of their positions that their mathematical models deemed impossible.

The reality is, quants are engrossed in the mathematics and detached from reality; finance as practiced in the real world is not all about solving scholastic differential equations and numerical analysis. It is about survival and dealing with the real world, one that doesn't always come across the computer screen in a mathematical formula that makes any sense to a quant. How can any methodology or model consider or predict the unpredictability of human behavior? Integrating human behavior in the mathematics of quants remains elusive and always will as long as the human animal, with the Founding Fathers' spirit, walks this earth.

Why not take the rocket science out of modern banking and get back to basics? Amar Bhide, a professor at Tufts University's Fletcher School of Law and Diplomacy, raises a valid parallel. "Imagine that the arguments triggered by the Hindenberg disaster were about the fire extinguishers that airships should carry, rather than about the design flaws that might cause them to ignite. Unfortunately, today's debates about banking reform have just this character."

Reversing the cold robotic gigantism of banking ought to be the top priority for reform. Bankers were once supposed to know every borrower, and to make case-by-case lending decisions. Now, however, banks use models conjured up by faraway quants to mass-produce credit and a range of derivative products. These behemoths' defective models have been disastrous. The financial statements of megabanks are impenetrable works of fiction or wishful thinking.

Radical proposals that would help restore a more resilient system have been smothered by noisy discussion of measures that do nothing to address modern banking's fundamental defects. Bank regulation, like lending, was once decentralized and judgment-based. Regulations relied mainly on examining individual loans, not capital-to-asset-ratios.

Lending and regulation cannot be governed by one super-model dictated in Basel that fits all banks and banking activities. Lending must again incorporate local knowledge and characteristics in a dynamic, unregimented entrepreneurial economy, where each borrower and loan are judged individually. However, with huge profits and bonuses at stake, the mega-banks won't easily ditch their model-based business.

Let's not forget it was quants and their metric-driven campaign that propelled Obama back into the White House in 2012. The Obama re-election campaign's analytics department was five times as large as that of the 2008 operation, with an official "chief scientist" who in a previous life crunched huge data sets, to among other things maximize the efficiency of supermarket sales promotions. In politics, the era of quants and their data banks are here to stay.

### Anti-MBA

I am delighted to hear universities today are questioning and challenging the merits of MBA holders – versus creative strategic types – running a successful business. Most graduate business degrees "are destructive" and the case-study method, the hallowed approach adopted by Harvard and many of the world's other leading business schools, is actually "demeaning."

I agree wholeheartedly with Dr. Henry Mintzberg, a professor of management studies at McGill University in Montreal and author of the 2004 book *Managers Not MBAs,* who has acquired a hard-earned reputation as the scourge of conventional management education because he says the rise of business-school-trained MBAs is "a menace to society." Mintzberg holds two graduate degrees in management from MIT.

"The philosophy of the case study method is that you simulate management practice on the basis of reading a 20-page study: George W. Bush went to Harvard Business School and I don't think he even read 20 pages. But he is a good example of how disastrous that approach can be," said Dr. Mintzberg.

"Any CEO who allows himself to be paid 400 or 500 times more than the workers is not a leader but an exploiter," he said, adding, "Of course, you can make a lot of money being an exploiter."

### Corporate Lobbyists

The ultimate exploiters? Bankers and their lobbyists. Is it any wonder the banks and bankers are working tirelessly to repeal the Dodd-Frank financial reform law that required banks to sell their proprietary trading desks, overhaul their derivative business and established the Consumer Financial Protection Bureau to protect citizen-consumers? Even though the financial regulatory overhaul has become law, it is not being enforced because banks are critical of its requirements, saying it will cost them billions of dollars. Well, that's the whole idea. Why should consumers have to pay billions for the bankers mistakes? Roughly two dozen bills are pending in Congress to delay, dismantle or repeal the law altogether.

Under pressure from Republican lawmakers and lobbyists, the Commodity Futures Trading Commission decided to delay some new derivatives rules. The agency, like other regulators, missed key deadlines under the law. As if that isn't bad enough, the banking industry and its lobbyists and congressional supporters fought for a year to successfully block Elizabeth Warren, the consumer-friendly Harvard professor who was President Obama's first choice to head the agency.

With top corporate lobbyists repeatedly filling key administration posts in successive administrations since Ronald Reagan became president – in the good ol' American capitalist tradition – regardless of whether the president is a Democrat or a Republican, why are *We the Apathetic Maids* surprised that banks get what they want and that *We the Maids* have to pay for the privilege and their bonuses? President Obama's former White House chief of staff William Daley being the latest D.C. uber installment.

Before leading the president's White House team, Daley was a top executive at JPMorgan Chase, where he supervised Washington lobbying efforts for the nation's second-largest bank. He also served on the board of directors at Boeing, the giant defense contractor, and Abbott Laboratories, the global drug company, which has billions of dollars at stake in the overhaul of the health care system.

Daley played a key role in influencing the terms of the TARP bailout, pushing for easier terms on repaying bailout funds in 2008. Why does one forfeit as much as $5 million a year from JPMorgan, $230,000 from Boeing in compensation and stock and $220,867 from Abbott Laboratories, which is what he earned in 2009, for a government job that pays $170,000 a year? Public service? Maybe. More likely it's access, power and future earnings.

Daley comes from one of America's most royal political families. His father, Richard J. Daley, was the kingpin of Chicago and Democratic Party politics in the second half of the 20th-century. His brother, Richard M. Daley was mayor of Chicago for six terms from 1986 to 2011. Bill Daley worked as a lawyer, a bank president, a telecommunications executive, a political strategist, fund-raiser and campaign chief, lobbyist for foreign corporations, including a Canadian oil company, and commerce secretary in the Clinton administration. In other words, he had all the right stuff – access to power and money.

The right response to this financial abuse would have been to nationalize financial institutions, restrict speculation with implicit or explicit government guaranteed funding, subsidize employment, and expand unemployment benefits. Capital mispricing has been the root cause of the serial bubble phenomenon. Reforms that insured the right pricing of capital would have triggered real economic restructuring and laid the foundation for a new growth cycle. However, the "bubble establishment" on Wall Street had the clout to obtain government bailouts that saved their asses but cost taxpayers trillions in dollars and assets.

Taking advantage of the public panic amid the crisis, they had their lobbyists convince stupid career politicians that only reviving the financial sector could stem the economic slide. It was a self-serving lie! Directly supporting the unemployed would have cost a fraction as much while stabilizing the economy. The remaining fiscal capacity could have been used to support economic restructuring.

Jobs, jobs and more jobs for the unemployed working masses is what America needs, and is what Washington should have created instead of refinancing banks and bonus-drunk bankers.

America's infrastructure is dated and irrelevant to the 21st century. Its roads, highways, air traffic control systems, ports, power grids and communications infrastructure lag behind China's and many other developing countries and desperately need upgrading. The government, with private sector investment capital can do the job in a much more efficient way by removing many of the costly regulatory obstacles. Cutting corporate taxes would attract foreign investment.

The government should also have invested more of the stimulus money in America's broadband infrastructure, which would have not only created hundreds of thousands of jobs, but would make America more competitive and relevant in the 21st-century knowledge-based economy. The government squandered a once-in-a-generation opportunity to modernize its digital footprint. Only $7 billion of President Obama's $787 billion economic stimulus went toward broadband, mainly grants to help municipal, non-profit, and private entities connect rural backwaters.

The near-death experience of America in 2008 has merely delayed the economic funeral of the flawed self-serving economic policies of Washington career politicians and Wall Street bankers. America and the world it leads will not be so lucky next time when all the inflated IOUs come due – and neither will China.

### Capitalism Run Amok
America has become the global headquarters for dirty unabashed corporate greed. Corporate capitalism has run amok at the expense of *We the Apathetic Maids*. This is evident from the minute one arrives at many U.S. airports and has to fork out U.S. dollars for a luggage cart. Luggage carts are free most everywhere around the world. But not in America.

To make matters worse, if an incoming passenger does not have dollars, fuhgetaboutit. Schlepp the luggage. Is this any way for the world's beacon of democracy and free enterprise to behave?

Simplifying regulatory requirements for businesses would help boost employment and confidence. Giving tax breaks to companies that bring jobs back home is another mandatory tax credit that would help revitalize capitalism in America. Minimizing regulatory hurdles and fees for start ups would give a boost to the entrepreneurial spark sorely lacking in America today. Bureaucratic regulatory red tape over the last few decades has gradually smothered the vitality and spirit of American capitalism. America is slowly heading down the road Greece is on.

In Greece it can take 10 months to get the necessary permits and approvals to start a business. Fotis Antonopoulos, a successful Internet designer, is an example. His efforts to start an e-commerce business selling olive oil took that long criss-crossing the city to collect dozens of forms and stamps, including X-rays and stool samples, since this was a food company. His story grabbed headlines in Greece in early 2012 as a glaring reminder of how far Greece has to go to become a country that encourages new business ventures. America is not far behind. That is because on the global stage, the U.S. is to China what Greece and Italy are to Germany – a debtor nation on the brink.

The Greek tragedy highlights what happens when career politicians fail to come to terms with economic reality and refuse to adopt the austerity measures necessary to balance their budgets.

The fact is that American capitalism has changed dramatically over the last few decades, giving rise to unstable levels of inequality and a mistaken belief in the self-correcting power of free markets.

From education to health care to politics, America has become the very country the Founding Fathers tried to avoid. It has become a pay-as-you-go for everything – including elected career politicians – in order to cover up and pay for their mistakes that *We the Apathetic Maids* have to not only clean up– but also pay for the clean-up job – and then have our votes miscounted for the privilege.

Isn't it time our voice and vote were counted? The political system in America is not only broken but shattered to pieces. *We the Maids* have to clean up the mess and sweep in the necessary changes and reforms needed to make America functional again.

The quality of life in America is dominated by WASP cultural brainwashing which is enforced by religious leaders, bureaucrats, career politicians, spin doctors and their lawyers and the military-industrial complex – made up of all religions and cultures. If we keep going on the path they have us on, we could well wind up as a mere historical footnote. Actually, *We the Apathetic Maids* will make the dinosaurs look good if we don't get involved and bring about the Third American Revolution.

America and its crony capitalist democratic institutions, and China and its crony communist state enterprises, are being challenged by those wallowing in disappointment and disillusionment. No different than the Arabs and Muslims rising up in Africa and the Middle East.

The American people, just like those under the iron rule of totalitarian regimes, have lost hope. They don't vote. They are too busy trying to make a buck – wage slaves. Yet ironically, a fusion of the best both systems have to offer is a 21st-century ideal. Nothing else seems to have worked.

Meanwhile in Zambia, opposition leader Michael Sata, who once swept floors in London's Victoria Station – and a harsh China critic – was sworn in as president in September 2011 after a political upset that ushered in a smooth handover of power in Africa's biggest copper producer.

The world needs robust long-term mechanisms to foster proper government, corporate, financial and economic governance. The short-term crisis policies have been a dismal failure. America and China must show the world they have the political courage to form a consensus and make tough decisions that are revolutionary, but essential, for the world to survive and thrive.

Democracies, most notably the U.S., have adopted laws and governmental institutions that represent the very institutions their Founding Fathers rebelled against. The laws and their adopters and enforcers have consumed and taken over these unique systems like a virus. *We the Maids* have given them our brooms and allowed them to clean up. It is time we *Maids* reclaim our brooms again and sweep them out! If an ex-floor sweeper can be swept into the office of the president in Zambia, why can't *We the Maids* do the same in Beijing and Washington?

Democracy must be recaptured by *We the People* – the maids who it represents and is supposed to benefit. Too many people, and the numbers are growing, are joining the Bush-Cheney conservative extreme because they are being outflanked by the Tea Party movement, while the Obama-Clinton centrist-to-left extreme are going AWOL. Do *We the People* want to capitulate to committed extremists who have allowed America to become their sole domain? A tool of the wealthy religious extremists and corporate military establishment who manipulate us at our own expense – with their welfare associates, corporate, government and individuals continuing to suck the taxpayers dry as *We the Apathetic Maids* keep complaining but not acting.

Career politicians and their moneyed financial backers in Washington and Beijing are ignoring the will of *We the People*. The governments just don't listen or respond to America's or China's critical needs. *We the People* do have a voice as to what happens in our nation's affairs and it is up to us to use that voice for the positive changes needed to replace and repair what is wrong in our world– at home and abroad. If we don't, what happened to the Mississippi Delta and the local communities that were deliberately allowed to be washed away will happen to the country as a whole.

### Mississippi Wipeout

Watching the horrific scenes of the Mississippi breaching levees across the Delta and the Army Corps of Engineers deliberately flooding communities to save major cities like New Orleans during my 2011 travels across America was heart-wrenching. Surely there is a better way.

"Right now there's a historic flood carrying record amounts of sediment, and we have no way to capture any of it," David Muth of the National

Wildlife Federation said at a conference during the flooding in New Orleans that brought together scientists, politicians and lobbyists to discuss ways of reversing land loss. "It is ridiculous that we're sitting here and all that sediment is going past, and most of it is going to be lost."

"Saving this coastline has economic ramifications that are just astonishing for the rest of the country," he said, warning of the potential damage to industries that survive off the delta's land and water, including seafood, oil and natural gas.

The problem of sediment deprivation is no surprise. In the late 1880s, engineers seeking ways to prevent the river from swallowing communities were debating whether to adopt the levee-only system, as opposed to one that would combine levees with outlets to allow the river to run free in spots and disperse sediment. But devastating floods in 1927, which killed nearly 250 people and displaced 700,000, ramped up the urgency to tame nature, leading to the levee-dominant system. Another hasty short-sighted decision by career politicians. The Mississippi and other major waterways in America must be better managed. In populated areas, levees were a necessary response to the cataclysmic floods of the 1920s. But some were built solely to attract more development, while others closed off flood plains that once acted as natural safety valves.

Meanwhile, over the years, the upper Mississippi watershed has lost millions of acres of wetlands that served as a natural sponge for floodwaters. Some experts also believe that dikes, jetties and other structures designed to channel the river and speed navigation have also helped raise water levels to dangerous levels. Career politicians forgot that "haste makes waste." They did what was politically expedient at the time for themselves and their financial backers, just as it is today.

Climatic catastrophes like Hurricane Katrina in 2005, Superstorm Sandy in 2012 and the floods of 2011 and 2012 have helped drive efforts to address the loss of land from lack of river sediment. My contribution to the discussion is: How come it's the Army Corps of Engineers doing the job? The Army has outsourced everything from cooking to fighting, so why not engineering? Why should the feds be involved at all? Surely the local communities and states can do a better, faster job. Fargo and the state of North Dakota proved that during the devastating flood that hit there in 2009. Let the locals deal with issues close to home and keep the feds and the Army out.

The reports that some people who fled the ravaged Gulf Coast in the wake of Hurricane Katrina were spending taxpayer disaster relief money on tattoos and topless bars instead of food and shelter highlighted America's "moral hazard." The term sounds like the name of a video game set in a bordello – much like many operas are. Actually, it is an obscure insurance term that has taken on a whole new currency in America's troubled economy. In economic terms, it refers to the undue risks that people are apt to take if they don't have to bear the consequences. In other words, if the money is free, why not spend it at a topless bar? If you know that you'll be bailed out, why not roll the dice on some tricky mortgage investments – or splurge on a home you can't really afford?

Moral hazard became part of the national conversation in the financial crisis of 2008, when ordinary Americans wondered why they should rescue banks that helped drive the economy off a cliff or, as Rick Santelli put it in a famous rant on CNBC, "subsidize the losers' mortgages."

The cherished American ideal of self-reliance has a flip side: discomfort with the idea of bailouts and safety nets. The specter of moral hazard haunts a basic tension in American life and is a primary percolating force underlying the Tea Party and Occupy Wall Street movements – and America's Third Revolution.

To what extent are people responsible for their own problems? The more trouble you're in, moral hazard suggests, the less we should help.

What happened with the penalty funds put up by BP for its Deepwater Horizon oil stream that spilled into the Gulf of Mexico in 2010? Getting access to those funds has turned into a turf war between Louisiana and the feds. The feds are determined to get the funds into the U.S. Treasury, while Louisiana senators sponsored a bill to have 80 percent of the penalty fund paid directly to the affected Gulf states for restoration. This is a different fund than the $20-billion fund established to compensate individuals and businesses hurt by the spill. Why shouldn't the money go to the people who need it the most?

Another example of moral hazard is how federal offshore drilling plans are understating the risks and ignoring Deepwater.

ConocoPhillips, the U.S. oil and gas company that was involved with two oil spills in June 2011 off the coast of Shandong, China, had to pay significant fines to the central government that was used to pay the province for the economic damage to the local fishing industry and some endangered species.

The feds have it bass ackwards. They give the oil companies making hundreds of billions of dollars in profits a $4-billion a year tax and subsidy break while they tax the states and then refuse to give them the funds needed to restore a state disaster caused by licenses issued by the feds to BP to drill and licensed federal inspectors who did nothing to ensure that safety laws were enforced.

Why is it that the federal government is the first with its hand out, not only for taxes and penalties, but any other license fees and admission fees to national parks and other resources it can get, which would be better managed and operated at the state level? Yet they are so reluctant to pay states in need any of the funds received from the states because the money is spent on unnecessary wars.

These repeated federal-state inequalities are the best reason for citizens and states to retake and restore the state rights the Founding Fathers envisioned instead of continuing down the river of federal destruction that *We the Apathetic Maids* have allowed. How many more Katrinas, Mississippi, Missouri and other rivers do we need to flood before we clean up our act?

Cleaning up the engineering mess in America's flood zones is a great job enabler and would put Americans back to work. A modern-day Tennessee Valley Authority like the one that put America back to work during the Great Depression. Why not take the billions spent annually on wars no one can justify and use them to fight a war on the home front to protect America's citizens, current and future? The cost of maintaining a single American soldier in Afghanistan for a year is $1 million. That's because of the stupefying cost of transporting supplies and the continuing construction of bases there. Wouldn't *We the Maids* be better off constructing a better and safer America?

Reading and watching the news about the Mississippi flood and Joplin, Missouri, killer twister is one thing. What surprised me even more was that when I was on the train headed for Vermont in May 2011, the conductor announced that the same tornado that devastated Joplin in the midst of the flooding deltas and bayous, had touched down in Vermont and caused flash floods and several communities had been cut off and that we should call ahead to make sure those meeting us could make it to the stations. Local thunderstorms dropped more than 4.25 inches of rain in an hour.

"Look how high the Connecticut River is," Mark Tigan, a friend whom I was visiting in New Hampshire exclaimed as we drove around to look at properties for sale and criss-crossed the river. "They must have opened the dams or there was one hell of a rainfall that came down," he said as we marveled at how much higher the water was than the day before. Little did we know at the time that what we were looking at was a sneak preview of the flooding havoc and devastation that Hurricane Irene had in mind a few months later.

As if that wasn't enough uncharacteristic East Coast weather caused by climate change that brought down the buckets full of water and blocks of ice in late-May early-June, there was plenty more where that came from pelting in the Northern Rockies and Northern Plains. Torrential rainfall and record snowmelt contributed to a slow-motion flood disaster along the Missouri River and its tributaries. The residents of Montana, the Dakotas, Nebraska and Iowa endured the worst of it.

"This is the worst flooding I've seen, and I've been working here for 20 years," said Tom Gurss, a hydrologist with the Missouri River Forecast Center in Pleasant Hill. Some people couldn't return to their homes for months.

Watching another devastating tornado hit Springfield, Massachusetts, a few days later, after I had stopped there for a couple hours on my way back from my Vermont visit, was simply too much. That is, until I got back to California and decided to take 101 north, from Los Angeles to the San Francisco Bay Area – instead of the quicker Interstate 5 that runs through Merle Haggard's Bakersfield country where I enjoy listening to his *Rambling Fever* on satellite radio or CD.

Driving the Purple Heart Trail between Santa Maria and Los Alamos, after leaving Santa Barbara, listening to Brad Paisley's *Welcome to the Future,* what I saw shocked me as I cruised mellowly up the coast. Undulating hills, introduced and fronted by beautiful California spring yellow-colored trees along the highway and bright yellow rapeseed blooming on the meridian and the vineyards beyond. The grapes were too wet to harvest and growing moldy because of the heavy rains. Millions of dollars of beautiful grapes wasting away and adding additional horrific financial difficulties for their pickers, legal and illegal – and, of course, the taxpayers subsidizing their corporate growers. No different than the flooded rice fields in China except those are still mostly family owned.

The news was peppered with reports on the Arizona wildfire that was heading toward New Mexico, scorching hundreds of thousands of acres and forcing thousands to flee their homes as it raged out of control, while residents in the drought-hit states of the South and Southwest prayed for rain together with their drought-stricken brothers and sisters in China's parched farmlands – a prelude to the devastating wildfires that swept across drought-stricken Texas – and the political wildfires spreading across America that were led by Texas Governor Rick Perry.

Climate change is a global security threat we must address before it is to late. Global conflict fueled by climate change goes back more than 3000 years. Civilizations have collapsed at the hands of Mother Nature.

The rare early snowstorm and icy rain that hit the U.S. East Coast in October 2011 killed at least three people. It wreaked havoc on air, rail and road traffic from Washington to Boston – and was the Grinch that stole Halloween from trick-or-treaters from New Jersey to Massachusetts – raising concerns about the horrific winter all would face, which turned out to be a false alarm. It was the only snowstorm New Englanders experienced that winter.

The unexpected snowstorm following so closely on the heels of August's tropical storm Irene, which shut down New York City, killed at least 14 people on the East Coast, flooded much of the region and caused more than 9,000 flights to be canceled, brought a smile to my face because I was glad not to be in the U.S. trying to make one of those flights. I wondered what it would take to convince *We the Apathetic Maids* that climate change is a reality. Especially when Irene was followed by tropical storm Lee less than a month later.

"In 2005 we had the 100-year flood, and in 2006 we had the 500-year flood," said Stacey Gould as she and her son watched at their charming two-story home on the banks of the rolling Susquehanna River in southern New York state be engulfed in water and washed away. "What year flood is this?" Stacey asked. Isn't that a question we should all be asking?

Estimates of financial loss rank the 2011 floods among the most devastating natural disasters in the world.

Superstorm Sandy killed almost 200 people in the U.S. and the Caribbean, where it had hurricane status. Sandy displaced thousands of Americans, more than 8 million people lost power during the storm and tens of thousands lacked basic utilities for weeks and months. More than 414,000 people registered for FEMA assistance and the overall cost of the storm is estimated to have exceeded $60 billion. And what did the career politicians in Washington do about it? Nothing. The storm made landfall October 29, just before the 2012 presidential election and the fiscal cliff negotiations, matters that politicians consider more important than *We the People*. They are so preoccupied with party that they have forgotten the people.

The floods that drowned America in 2011 and 2012 are the same unrestrained hell and high water that killed people and crops in China, Thailand, Laos and Vietnam. The global weather patterns in 2011, especially in the U.S., were unseasonably extreme and deadly. From continued drought to unexpected killer storms. The U.S. was hit by 12 weather-related events that cost at least $1 billion each. Talk about weird weather or "weather weirding," as it is known in the scientific community – lurching from one weather extreme to the other.

Interestingly, climate change has been linked to social unrest. Researchers at Hong Kong University found that Europe's cooler conditions from 1560 to 1660 resulted in shorter plant-growing seasons and reductions in arable land. Because of that, grain prices soared by 300 percent, wars got longer and bloodier, and individuals became shorter and hungrier. "Many disturbances eventually developed into armed conflicts," the researchers said. Any wonder the Third Revolution has been percolating the last couple of years?

"What is it going to take for *We the Apathetic Maids* to wake up to climate change and realize we all depend on farmers and food?" I asked myself. Not only in America, but in China and the rest of the world. Better yet, I wondered, why is it that the starting-gun primaries are in New Hampshire and Iowa – which represent only 1% of the U.S. population – that then ensure the path and set the tone and image of the eventual party nominees? Doesn't sound fair to me. Sounds like China's Communist Party where less than 1% of the population decides who will run their country.

China, like America, was experiencing devastating floods in June 2011. China's deadly Zhejiang floods were the worst the country had experienced in more than six decades. The same happened in Sichuan a few weeks later, with more than 10,000 homes destroyed. Millions of people had to be evacuated as they, like their brothers and sisters in the Mississippi Delta and Great Plains, watched billions of dollars of property and family farms damaged, destroyed or washed away.

### The American Spirit

The flooding of the Mississippi Delta was the opening scene of my May-June 2011 visit to America. More than 100 tornadoes hit Missouri, Oklahoma, Indiana and Illinois in May and killed more than 500 people and injured thousands more – the most devastating one hitting hard-luck Joplin,

Missouri. But the heart-wrenching scenes of devastation had a silver lining. It restored my faith in the American spirit.

People picking up the pieces. People coming together. Neighbor helping neighbor, regardless of ethnic or religious background. Tattered Old Glory proudly fluttering in the wind in the devastated neighborhoods, just as it did during the first and second Revolutionary Wars and the aftermath of 9/11 and Katrina. A vivid reminder that America can not only survive and overcome any hardships, but become a better and stronger country in the process. A country built by Puritan-inflected rugged individuals who subscribed to ideals of generosity, compassion, hard work and individual responsibility. That is America's spirit, its soul, which must be rediscovered and restored during the Third American Revolution so that America can not only survive, but continue to thrive and guide the world through the budding 21$^{st}$ century.

America and the world were reminded of this repressed potential in December 2011, when 15-year-old U.S. teenager Jordan Romero became the youngest person to successfully climb to the summit of the seven tallest mountains on the Earth's seven continents.

"The American dream was really created here in Hollywood," Israeli President Shimon Peres told a group of film executives in March 2012. "I don't know what influenced the world more – the American Constitution or the American dream."

No wonder America is still the No. 1 destination for global investors and immigrants!

### Constitutional Foundation
Hong Kong's colonial experience, like that of America's, is fertile political soil to build strong, resilient and creative legal and political foundations for a living constitutional government that reflects the will of the Founding Fathers and the people in China and not any one political establishment or party.

Hong Kong's defacto constitution, the Basic Law, is taking root, much like the U.S. Constitution. It is a growing political organism that is flourishing in the shadow of the Chinese motherland. It is a living constitution. Not a dead constitution like the one adopted by the People's Republic of China that embodies all the right ideals, principles and rights, but does not practice what it preaches. China embodies "People" in both its constitution and name; however, the people don't have much say about how either should be for the benefit of the people and not the privileged few.

If the *Maids of China* sweep out the people who do not live by or uphold the constitution created by the people and peasants of Mao's Communist Revolution, China will build upon Hong Kong's constitutional Basic Law and eventually become a lot more like Taiwan and America.

Fictional governments of the people, for the people, by the people should be replaced regardless of what political philosophy or party they represent or which hat they wear. That applies to all political parties worldwide – including America. Just look at the number of political parties the U.S. has had since the American Revolution.

Hong Kong's fledgling Special Administrative Region of China, created after the British Handover in 1997, has already developed 12 political parties. Beijing's one-party rule cannot dampen the ingrained rule of law and Magna Carta constitutional democratic heritage that Hong Kong inherited from its colonial master – the same constitutional heritage that Britain gave America.

### China's Unconstitutional Governance

China's constitution, like that of many one-party regimes, enshrines the basic rights of the U.S. Constitution, but they are not respected or adhered to by the Communist Party – not that they are in America either. The denial of people's fundamental political rights, in America, China, India, Iran, Africa, Asia, Europe, Latin America and the Middle East, leaves citizens no choice but to unite and demand political change that will give them their fair share of liberty, knowledge, financial and food security, freedom and control of their political destiny.

China's Communist Party appears to have tuned out both its domestic and foreign critics and is intent on ignoring the truth about itself, its history, and on jailing its critics. Beijing doesn't care what America, or anyone else, for that matter, thinks about its political system or the way it props up renegade regimes like North Korea, Myanmar, Zimbabwe and others.

When President Hu Jintao said in a pomp-filled ceremony in the Great Hall of the People on July 1 that "The Communist Party of China was founded 90 years ago today," he was wrong.

The Chinese Communist Party was founded on July 23, 1921, according to official records. The strange story of the wrong founding date of the world's biggest political party is the result of Mao Zedong's mistaken memory and the party's disregard for the truth. Mao wanted to commemorate the party's 20th anniversary in 1941 but had forgotten the exact date in July, so he decided to make it July 1st. The fact the date has never been changed to reflect the true historical date is because, well, the decision was made by Mao.

But how long can China ignore the truth and its homegrown critics and continue jailing them in the interest of a "harmonious society"?

As a Foreign Correspondent's Club regular, columnist Frank Ching points out: "A harmonious society is a worthy goal. But the government should realize that no society is without conflict. From a practical standpoint, China should provide more resources for the resolution of conflicts rather than artificially bringing about 'harmony' by throwing in jail everyone with a grievance, on the grounds that they are troublemakers ... ."

Chinese intellectual thinkers have a centuries-old tradition of criticizing their government. Free speech is protected by China's Constitution and erupts periodically, as it did in Tiananmen in 1989– and has continuously since in countless villages, cities and provinces across the country where people express anger at the unrestrained government corruption at every level and demand the most basic individual rights. It will continue.

China targets people who dare question the Communist Party's rule and acts decisively against any potential challenge, jailing those questioning its authority or actions. Most dissidents arrested aren't calling for revolution. They are merely asking the government to allow them the freedom to express themselves as granted by the Constitution.

China's ongoing repression of free speech and its toxic distaste for criticism was highlighted when imprisoned pro-democracy activist Liu Xiaobo won the 2010 Nobel Peace Prize. The award was a mark of validation from the rest of the world for Chinese writers and thinkers who have taken risks and paid the personal sacrificial price. It will have a profound impact on the development of China's democratization.

The award came despite threats from Chinese officials who sought to dissuade the Nobel judges from honoring Liu. The threats continued even after the award ceremony. Norway used to be China's top supplier of fresh salmon. That all changed after the Nobel ceremony. Norwegian salmon is held up for days and sometimes weeks by Chinese food safety inspectors well past its sell-by date. Meanwhile, Scotland stepped in in January 2011 with an agreement to ship fresh salmon to fill the vacuum.

As a writer, I am upset that Liu's writings have brought him lengthy stints in prison, labor camp and house arrest, and have stripped him of his right to publish or teach in China. Liu's most recent sentence came in 2009 after he helped write and publish the Charter 08 manifesto that demanded democratic political reform, infuriating the Communist Party. The banned manifesto was signed by hundreds of critics across China. Liu was convicted of inciting subversion against the state and trying to overthrow the government. He was sentenced to 11 years in prison.

Charter 08 was modeled partly on Charter 77, the document that called for political change in communist Czechoslovakia.

"The government was using a fist to fight against the tongue," said Li Datong, a journalist who was among those who signed Charter 08.

The smooth-talking Vaclav Havel, former head of the Czech Republic, and Desmond Tutu, archbishop emeritus of Cape Town, South Africa, summed up China's paranoia best in an editorial they co-wrote a few days before the Nobel award ceremony. China's "extreme sensitivity to criticism demonstrates its lack of confidence domestically. This lack of confidence ultimately only serves to further undermine the credibility of the government with its people," they wrote.

When Liu heard the news of his Nobel Peace Prize award in prison, he dedicated it to the "lost souls" of Tiananmen Square.

The delicate and controversial Nobel dance between China and the Nobel Committee continued into 2012 when Chinese writer Mo Yan won the 2012 Nobel Prize in Literature for works of "hallucinatory realism" that merge "folk tales, history and the contemporary."

Celebrated for his gritty tales of peasant life, Mo is described as a "mixture between Faulkner, Rabelais and Dickens."

In contrast to previous Chinese recipients of Nobel prizes, such as the dissident Liu Xiaobo, Mo's award was widely celebrated across China. Mo is a Communist Party member and former soldier of the People's Liberation Army. As vice chairman of the government's China Writers' Association, he holds a semi-official role. But many consider Mo a party stooge because of his refusal to speak up for writers and dissidents jailed in China.

Mo's detractors are vocal. "For him to win this award, it's not a victory for literature, it is a victory for the Communist Party," raged Yu Jui, a writer and democracy activist, in a blog post.

Mo Yan means "don't speak" in Chinese and is the pseudonym of Guan Moye. Mo said he picked his pen name during the Cultural Revolution, when his father feared he might say something that would get the family in trouble. "So he told me not to speak and to appear to be a mute."

Another demonstratively active Chinese democracy advocate is performance artist Ai Weiwei. He has become one of the most persistent and recognisable critics of China's Communist Party.

In April 2011, at the height of government fears that turmoil in the

Arab world might spread to China, Ai was seized by police at Beijing's international airport just before boarding a flight to Hong Kong. He was released after 81 days of isolated detention and "mental torture," his hefty figure noticeably reduced and his voice uncharacteristically stilled.

As part of the agreement that led to his release on bail, Ai reportedly agreed to stay off Twitter and to reject interviews with the news media. It did not take long, however, for Ai's pledge to fade. He published a caustic essay in *Newsweek* in August 2011, and his Twitter postings became increasingly frequent and incendiary.

"In the battle between creating evil laws and creating good laws, speaking out is golden and silence is death," read one item that he forwarded to his more than 100,000 followers.

His defiance resulted in him being charged with tax evasion. He was coerced into depositing an 8.45 million *yuan* guarantee with the tax authorities to avoid being jailed over a large tax bill that he disputes and says is retaliation for his criticism of the central government.

The money was raised by nearly 30,000 supporters into a Beijing tax bureau account set up to hold funds as collateral during his legal challenges and appeals. Some people tied cash to pears and threw it into the yard of his house. Some made paper planes out of the yuan notes and "flew" them into the yard. The overwhelming support of people to help Ai pay his tax bill reveals what they think of the Chinese government's charge of evading payment – and the damage done to Beijing's legitimacy.

Many of Ai's supporters said it was a way to show their defiance to the authorities. "If you are not wealthy, you can at least spare five or 10 *yuan* because each postal remittance receipt says 'No' to the authorities," said one Internet user.

Artist Liu Qiming said on his Sina microblog account that Ai had transformed the incident into a piece of artwork, with thousands of people participating from around the world, even though Ai possibly did not need the money.

Ai loves taking nude photographs of himself, friends and fans. To be photographed naked or half-naked is part of Ai's character, and a trait of his artistic career. He began to take nude photographs of himself and others in the mid-1980s, in his basement apartment and on the streets of New York's East Village. It was a kind of catharsis, and developed into a deliberate show of scorn, a physical confrontation with state power.

Not surprisingly, Ai was also investigated for pornography after he started challenging the Chinese government on the tax charges lodged against him. The result, Ai's fans staged a mass nude protest by posting photos of themselves naked on a website called "Ai Wei Fans' Nudity – Listen, Chinese Government: Nudity is not Pornographic" – a rare form of protest in a country where public nudity is still taboo.

The fact is that the Communist Party and government are unscrupulous, with officials and the rich conspiring together in limitless greed and corruption, plundering China's citizens and perpetuating injustices – no different than the Washington career politicians and their Wall Street bankers.

The limitless greed of corrupt Chinese officials and their rich cronies was highlighted by the downfall of Chongqing City party chief Bo Xilai, one of China's most famous "princelings," the son of Bo Yibo, one of the Communist Party's founders. He rose through party ranks because of his public arrests of party officials and their business cronies on corruption charges.

According to Wang Lijun, the city's police chief and Bo henchman, who sought political asylum in the U.S. consulate because he feared for his life, Bo's wife, Gu Kailai is alleged to have poisoned British businessman Neil Heywood over a dispute on how much of a cut he should get for helping her move bribe money overseas. A Chinese court agreed and found her guilty of murder.

The real-life Hollywood-style political-murder thriller transfixed China, because Bo's sacking added a new twist to the leadership reshuffle at the Communist Party's 18th Congress. It signaled a schism in the mainland's top leadership – rarely exposed in public.

Czech communist reformist Alexander Dubcek, one of the authors of Charter 77, said it best: "You can destroy the flowers but you cannot stop the spring."

It's time for China to constructively engage and embrace its critics, both domestic and global, if its economic and political spring are to survive. Under its 12th five-year plan, 2011 to 2015, there is a drive to increase innovation, develop the service sector and diversify investments and business activities abroad. How is it going to do that if it arrests its most creative outspoken critics?

How can the party survive if it doesn't acknowledge and embrace its own constitutional basic human rights, including freedom of speech and expression, rule of law that allows lawyers, artists, teachers, bloggers and political activists to express their concerns and anger to a free press? It's going to happen with or without the Communist Party's approval.

### Balanced Global Leadership

America's economic and financial crisis offers China a unique opportunity to become the new global leader. China could replace the U.S. as the world's new superpower. But will it? China has little debt, enormous savings with huge growth potential. Its current per capita income of $3,300 could be raised to $10,000 within two decades through a combination of growth and currency appreciation. At the same time, gross domestic product could rise from today's more than $4 trillion to $13 trillion. Such an increase could offer plenty to investors willing to bet on China's future. Many countries are retreating from some free market rules that have guided international trade in recent decades and have started playing by Chinese rules.

But to surpass America, China must become the greatest country in the world. To do that it needs to establish a continental coalition with Russia and India or reorganize the G20 into an organization led by the BRICs – Brazil, Russia, India and China – an issue I address at length in *Feasting Dragon, Starving Eagle*. But that alone will not suffice.

For China to engineer a new capital and political world order, it must end the rampant corruption, fraud, intellectual and political misrepresentation, allow its currency to float freely, open its capital markets, have a truly independent judiciary that follows the rule of law, a free press and a more democratic political system – all of which are achievable – and a good reason why America should embrace China as its partner and lead the world together to a peaceful and harmonious future. It's a theme I have repeatedly advocated in my earlier books. Hong Kong and Macau, like the Hong Kong, Macau, Zhuhai bridge linking the region economically, are the democratic political interlocal bridge that will carry China to democracy. Taiwan is just another democratic stepping stone that Sun Yat Sen rebelled for that both Beijing and Taipei respect and honor because of his quest for freedom.

Fading superpower America has lost its way and needs a helping hand to get back on to the Founding Fathers' constitutional track. The point was driven home by the WikiLeaks public disclosure of U.S. diplomatic cables. America not only lost the confidentiality and secrecy of its diplomatic communications, but, as the documents reveal, its moral purpose and global role as well.

As a 9-year-old kid living in Cyprus, I remember all the British and French military vehicles and personnel that one day in 1956 showed up and were parked in the fields near my home not far from two British military bases. The Suez Canal crisis was not something I understood at the time. All I knew was that the Egyptians had taken over the canal and the British and French, the pre-eminent European powers in the region and co-owners of the canal, were going to retake it. I later found out, as a political science student, that America told them to back off and leave the canal in Egyptian hands. That was the beginning of the end of the British and French empires.

Will the same happen to America in the Asia-Pacific region? I think the answer is an unequivocal yes!

No single country is able to bear the cost of world hegemony and leadership. America and China are no exceptions. America has found out the hard way. Furthermore, there is an increasing global tendency to spurn and reject single-country hegemony today.

"Countries like China, India and Brazil are growing by leaps and bounds," President Obama said in a keynote speech to Britain's parliament in May 2011. "Perhaps, the argument goes, these nations represent the future, and the time for our leadership has passed.

"That argument is wrong. The time for our leadership is now."

I couldn't agree more and I said so at length in *Custom Maid Knowledge* – but the leadership must be together with – not alone.

"As two of the most powerful nations in history, we must always remember the true source of our influence hasn't just been the size of our economy, the reach of our military, or the land we've claimed," Obama said. "It has been the values we must never waiver in defending around the world – the idea that all human beings are endowed with certain rights that cannot be denied."

So what happened to those freedom-loving human beings in Syria and Iran who fought and died for those rights while America ignored their plight as they were mowed down by snipers while Iran, Syria's sponsor, worked on triggering technology for nuclear weapons?

The reality is that the world is not anxious to embrace China as the world's new superpower. The world still looks to America for leadership because of its constitutional ideals and humanity. But America cannot do so alone anymore. America has to shift some of the global financial burdens it has unilaterally taken up to China. America needs a partner. That partner is not Russia, Japan or the EU. It is China. The alternative? China, Europe and Russia hook up while the U.S. and Japan continue to hold hands and watch from the sidelines amid global political tsunamis.

### Mutual Trust and Benefit

Before America and China embrace each other, there has to be true mutual respect, as distinguished from politically expedient respect – and China becomes more democratic. This is one critical relationship that cannot flourish by being limited to words alone, as much as words do change the world. It is one that must be based and developed on geopolitical and economic facts. The domestic political reality of each – verbal and factual – are just the special national nuances that each has to get used to, and learn to trust.

Much like California and New York did. In California, more than a dozen giant steel bridge deck modules for the new San Francisco-Oakland Bridge, one that I love to traverse thinking about the scene in the movie and the song *Mrs. Robinson*, were built in China and assembled in the Bay Area by Americans, who also poured the concrete surface and did most of the site work. The state saved more than $400 million by turning to China.

New York followed suit and hired Chinese companies to renovate the city's subway system, refurbish the Alexander Hamilton Bridge over the Harlem River and build a new Metro-North train platform near Yankee Stadium. Why is anyone surprised? After all, it was Chinese who built America's "Gold Mountain" railroads, levees and mines. Why can't other states and Washington do the same?

China's growing technological capabilities are not limited to basic engineering and construction, but cyberspace – highlighted when it rerouted massive volumes of Internet traffic from both the U.S. government and military networks, including the Senate, Army, Navy, Air Force, Marines, secretary of defense's office, NASA, the Department of Commerce, National Oceanic and Atmospheric Administration and many U.S. companies like Microsoft to China in March and April of 2010. Such actions are anything but confidence builders. The incidents highlight the security vulnerabilities of the public Internet, which uses a trust-based system to route data from one server to another. Information follows the most efficient path, not necessarily the shortest, and servers advertise their ability to handle traffic. There are more than 100,000 routers in the world. Any one of them can be "spooked" to reroute traffic. The majority of Internet traffic in the world is routed through the U.S.

China Telecom sent erroneous messages that led servers around the world to route traffic through China in 2010. The tactic could be used to spy on specific users, disrupt communications or conceal a separate attack.

Wikileaks' release of all those highly classified confidential U.S. State

Department cables didn't do much to restore the already eroding trust. Accusing China's Politburo of directing the 2010 and 2011 cyber intrusions into Google's computer systems as part of a "coordinated campaign of computer sabotage carried out by government operatives, private security experts and Internet outlaws," something I had warned would happen in *Custom Maid War* and *Feasting Dragon, Starving Eagle,* is again shifting blame and responsibility from where it belongs – Washington and the Pentagon for not being adequately prepared. China only did what America is trying to do.

After all, it is Washington and the Pentagon that launched the "Internet in a suitcase" program – sponsoring projects such as the creation of secretive cell phone networks inside foreign countries that allow users to connect to independent wireless networks. The suitcase project relies on a version of "mesh network" technology, which can use devices like cell phones or personal computers to create an invisible wireless web without a centralized hub. These new networks allow opposition forces to circumvent government control of electronic communications. As usual, freedom of speech and democracy are the high-sounding rhetoric the U.S. uses when selling its suitcase project or "shadow Internet." The U.S. State Department has carefully framed its support of such projects as promoting free speech and human rights, but it is clear that the policy is aimed at destabilizing national governments.

The U.S. government admitted spending $19 million in 2011 to launch a series of cyber attacks against the "Great Firewall of China." It needs to spend significantly more dollars to upgrade its servers and create more bandwith if it is serious about attacking China's firewall. Is it any wonder China has lashed out at the Pentagon's first formal cyber strategy, saying it would open the door for the U.S. to use military force against perceived cyber attacks? The Pentagon concluded that computer sabotage coming from another country could be considered an act of war, to which the U.S. could respond with traditional military force. Come on now, is this the new justification for the next war?

The U.S. strategy to treat destructive state-sponsored cyber attacks as an act of war while it treats its own U.S. cyber destruction as a normal covert action equivalent to espionage just won't fly.

The U.S. and Israel are widely believed to be responsible for creating and unleashing the Stuxnet computer worm that wreaked havoc with Iran's nuclear program – probably more damaging than could have been accomplished by an air raid, setting back Iran's nuclear ambitions by several years. By the logic of Obama's own strategy, this was an act of war against Iran.

The U.S. "cannot on the one hand treat cyberdestruction by others as an act of war but then say the U.S. cyberdestruction is a routine covert action. It must demonstrate that its use of cyberweapons will be extremely rare and subject to the same rules and standards as the conventional use of force. Stuxnet must be the exception, not the norm," said Thomas Wright, executive director of studies at the Chicago Council on Global Affairs.

America, according to Wright, "can then put international pressure on China to follow. The longer the wait, the more severe the threat will become."

When Secretary of State Hillary Clinton launched the battle cry to protect Exxon-Mobil's "huge energy find" in Papua New Guinea in March 2011, she said China was jockeying for influence in the region and seeing how it could "come in behind us and come in under us." Now, how diplomatic is that?

As if that wasn't bad enough, former U.S. Commerce Secretary Gary Locke, now ambassador to China, accused Beijing of "serious backtracking" on promises to make its economy more friendly to foreign companies and improving human rights in May 2011, a week before the high-level bilateral Strategic Dialogue in Washington.

Mutual suspicion continues to hamstring China-U.S. relations, preventing the two from drawing closer. It's not surprising, considering their inherently different political systems – one openly authoritarian, the other also authoritarian but posing as democratic. There is bound to be mistrust. But that conflict doesn't serve the purpose of either country. It behooves both to find a way forward, to meet each other halfway for the good of the planet.

Each country has a lot to teach the other.

Positive reinforcement and cooperative actions are a lot more constructive and productive. Certainly more so than the political duplicity that has marked the relationship and finds one side cheating and the other responding in kind – tit for tat.

America's insistence on selling arms to Taiwan is no motivation for China to restrain North Korea. If America doesn't listen to reason, why should China? The fact that Obama has met with his Chinese counterpart Hu more than any other foreign leader is meaningless unless a foundation of trust can be established. China doesn't like to be lectured, especially by an America that doesn't listen.

Obama's 2010 visit to the four largest Asian democracies – India, Indonesia, South Korea and Japan – skipping China along the way, only served to underscore the question of trust.

America refuses to sell its high-tech technology to China. So why then is America surprised when China refuses to sell its precious rare earths to Japan? And let's not forget about the Dalai Lama. China asks American presidents not to meet the Tibetan Buddhist spiritual leader, but they do, and then wonder, as do many political leaders who receive the Dalai Lama, why China reciprocates with the "Dalai Lama effect."

A research paper published by the University of Gottingen in Germany in 2010 outlined the "Dalai Lama effect" on trading nations who dare meet with the Dalai Lama. Analyzing data from 159 countries, it found that if a king, head of state, or government met with the Dalai Lama at any time between 2002 and 2008, that nation's exports to China decreased by an average of 8.1 percent a year for the subsequent two years. And this during a period when Chinese trade was booming. It will be interesting to see the results of the post-2008 study of the impact of Dalai Lama visits on trade, especially Obama's July 2011 meeting with His Holiness as the spiritual leader of Tibet.

Now that Harvard legal scholar Lobsang Sangay has taken over political leadership from the Dalai Lama and is the new prime minister of the Tibetan government-in-exile, it will be interesting to see if negotiations with Beijing will be less complicated. It is the first time in centuries that the top Tibetan monk is not also the political leader. Dominance of politics by religious figures has historically always failed. Theocracies, like feudalism, are historical political relics.

The 18th-century philosopher Immanuel Kant argued that constitutional republics were a condition for peace.

"His ideas have been built upon in the modern period by empirical evidence showing that democracies rarely, if ever, fight each other," said Steve Vines, a Hong Kong columnist, as we debated the subject at the FCC Main Bar because of his columns repeatedly attacking the Hong Kong and mainland Chinese bureaucratic government approach to politics.

Politics, to be effective and peaceful, must be controlled by the people, not bureaucrats or career politicians, regardless of whether they are democratically elected or totalitarian. Once people lose control and career politicians and their bureaucrats or extremist enforcers take control, *We the Apathetic Maids* are doomed.

We were reminded of this stark brutal reality in the spring of 2011 by the assassination of artist Juliano Mer-Khamis, a cross-border dreamer during the revolutionary Arab Spring that put the Arab world where it belongs on the crossroads to peace by becoming more democratic.

"If words don't help, we will have to speak in bullets," said an ultimatum circulated in the Palestinaian territories before Juliano's murder on the doorstep of his Freedom Theatre in a Jenin refugee camp. "Jul," as he was known to his young thespians, took the exact opposite stance: Bullets cannot resolve the Palestinian-Israeli quandry, so let's try words. The last show he staged was *Alice in Wonderland*.

I can relate to Jul because, like me, he was a Middle Eastern dreamer. We were both born to Jewish Israeli mothers and Christian fathers. His Arab, mine Anglo. He was a political artist living on the faultline of creativity and doom – where *We the Apathetic Maids* all live but don't realize it. Fania Oz-Salzberger summed it up best in an article she wrote for *Newsweek*. "A double lesson should be learned from the life and death of Jul: romanticize nothing, yet keep working on the side of hope.

"His life was marred by hate from both parent-nations. He was an Arab to Jewish extremists, who loathed him, and a Jew to Palestinian fanatics, who likely killed him."

Knowledge and hope are bulletproof. So are the Founding Fathers' Constitution and Bill of Rights.

### The D.C. Summit
Watching the picture-perfect pomp and ceremony surrounding President Hu Jintao's state visit to Washington on January 18, 2011, was a dream come true. After writing four books that each, in its own way, advocates a Sino-U.S. partnership to lead the world through the 21st century, and having given a talk that same day at the Foreign Correspondent's Club in Hong Kong advocating a Sino-U.S. partnership that is long overdue, I came to the realization that America and China are finally coming to terms with each other. Both Presidents Obama and Hu understand that a crisis in one country will adversely impact on the other. What happens to one affects the other, and why shouldn't the results be positive?

"The China-U.S. relationship is not one in which one side's gain means the other side's loss," said Hu.

"What Deng Xiaoping said long ago remains true today. There are still great possibilities for cooperation between our countries," Obama said.

On the day Hu arrived in Washington, my luncheon talk at the Foreign Correspondents Club in Hong Kong focused on my last book, *Feasting Dragon, Starving Eagle*. I expressed my hope that Hu's trip would be historic like "Nixon in China" and become "Obama-Hu Washington Communique I."

As my partner Pauline and I watched Hu's arrival on TV, I said, "Time to head back to California and focus on domestic issues now that the U.S.-China trains are on the right track heading in the same direction. Not that there won't be bumps and detours along the way. There will be and already are."

"I want to be in America at the start of the Third American Revolution, now that it has already started in Tunisia and is on a slow burn across the Middle East, Asia and in its infancy in America," I said as I started California dreaming.

Hu's flawless formal red-carpet, black-tie arrival, with welcomes from President Obama and Vice President Joe Biden and their wives, and a long line of Cabinet members and Chinese dignitaries, was a sign of the long overdue respect that protocol-conscious China and Hu craved and deserve. China needed to see Hu being treated as the respected leader of a nation taking its place at the head of the global table.

Obama and Hu stood at attention as a military band played both national anthems. The ceremonial pomp-filled 21-gun salute, with full honors and color guard welcoming ceremony on the South Lawn of the White House, including a rope line where both presidents shook hands and greeted a group of children and young people holding Chinese and U.S. flags, ushered in a new era of Sino-U.S. relations.

The mutual feel-good factor by Americans and Chinese toward each other seemed to overnight replace the mutual mistrust and is on a harmonious trajectory for the smooth growth of bilateral ties. Both countries have recalibrated their tone and the direction of their ties. Most Americans and Chinese regard Sino-U.S. ties as "very important." With the changing of the global political and economic landscape, Sino-U.S. relations now go well beyond the boundaries of bilateral ties and have global ramifications. China and the U.S. share many common interests and both sides must "work together to open a new chapter of cooperation as partners," Hu said. The repeated calls for broader cooperation as partners by both presidents was music to my ears.

In fact, the last 30 years of Sino-U.S. relations have been marked by continued exchanges and increased mutual understanding, Obama said, adding that Hu's visit serves to lay the foundation for deeper prosperity between the two nations in the next 30 years. Obama concluded his speech by saying in Chinese: *huanying* (welcome).

A joint statement released after the summit also unveiled $45 billion in deals that would support an estimated 235,000 American jobs. China is the only major market to meet President Obama's goal of doubling U.S. exports over the next five years. No surprise there. China wants to buy even more from America.

China's National Energy Administration and the U.S. Department of Energy signed 18 deals worth $13 billion. The clean energy trade deals coincided with the Second China-U.S. Strategic Forum on Clean Energy Cooperation. The agreements include biofuels and clean coal technology. Cleaner-burning coal would slow the output of greenhouse gas emissions by the world's top two emitters of gases linked to global warming.

Chicago trumped the West Coast cities as "China's Gateway to America." About 300 Chicago area companies, such as Motorola, Wrigley and Boeing, are operating in China, while 7,000 businesses owned by ethnic Chinese operate in Chicago. Mayor Richard Daley characterized Hu's visit as a "big, big, big, big, big deal." It was. Chicago boasts America's biggest Putonghua-teaching program.

"We hope the U.S. side will provide a level playing field for Chinese companies pushing to invest in the United States so that they will have more opportunities to contribute to the development of the U.S. economy," said Hu. Chinese built the American railroads and levees, so why not today's technological superhighway?

As a Californian, I can't believe that Los Angeles, San Francisco and the Silicon Valley let Hu be hijacked by Chicago. Watching Hu's supporters and protestors face off from the grounds of two Chicago landmarks, the Old Water Tower and the Pumping Station, despite the bitter cold, brought back memories of the 1968 Democratic Convention and my first year of law school in the Windy City, where icicles formed on my mustache as I waited for buses or trudged through the snow.

Hearing China for the first time join the U.S. in publicly voicing concerns about North Korea's uranium enrichment program and agree on the importance of a denuclearized Korean Peninsula brought a smile to my face. Hu said China hopes Pyongyang and Seoul can achieve reconciliation and eventually realize reunification peacefully and independently. It seems like the two superpowers have finally recognized that their bilateral relationship is the most important one in the world.

The Hu-Obama get-together featured a private dinner in the Old Family Dining Room in the White House residence. It illustrated Obama's careful mix of warmth and firmness for the leader of a nation that is at once the largest U.S. competitor and its most important potential partner. It is a complicated relationship between two affectionately competing super-powered partners.

Breaking bread together over a glass of wine or two, formally and informally, breaks down barriers, allows people to get to know each other, establish a solid foundation on which a partnership can build and brings them closer together. Especially when eating a down home all-American meal that included apple pie, ice cream and jazz. Important ingredients for effective diplomacy that are much needed to address the many sensitive issues, including human rights, intellectual property and currency between the two countries.

A genuine heart-warming reassuring dialogue that enables them to develop a much-needed personal chemistry and connection to enhance trust and clear up doubts. Shoot some hoops, play ping pong. Come up with a mutually designed game plan and a framework for global governance.

Underscoring the desire for candor, the White House said there were no official note-takers at the dinner and offered no readout of the discussions. Very important to set the right tone for the future, considering it was to be the last major summit between the two presidents, with Hu stepping down in 2012 and Obama up for re-election. Hu declared that China is committed to the development of socialist democracy. "Without democracy, there can be no socialist modernization," he said.

"We will continue to expand people's democracy and build a socialist country under the rule of law in keeping with China's national conditions."

"We also know this: History shows that societies are more harmonious, nations are more successful and the world is more just when the rights and responsibilities of all nations and all peoples are upheld– including the universal rights of every human being," Obama said.

The fundamental principles of the Marxist party are to "put the people first" and "govern for the people." Sounds a lot like the U.S. Constitution declaration of "Government of the people, for the people, by the people." America's Founding Fathers' words had a far greater global influence than most people realize. They even influenced Karl Marx. Sometimes I wish they would influence today's leaders of the Communist, Democratic and Republican parties in America and China. It is in the interest of all three parties to recognize, safeguard and develop the fundamental interests of the majority of the people – *We the Maids* who have the power to sweep them out.

Cross-cultural literary and political pollination never ceases to amaze me. In China, the Bard, Shakespeare, better known in China as Old Man Sha, despite being purged during the Cultural Revolution, underwent reconstruction and is known to the mainland's many English students as a working-class hero who mocked the elite and wrote for the people. From China's perspective, Shakespeare was a communist. Marx and Engels were fond of quoting him and both refer to *The Life of Timon of Athens*, not one of his better-known plays, in their writings on class struggle, which conferred – at least initially – a degree of acceptability on the Bard after 1949.

What a contrast to the snubs President Hu received during his 2005 and 2006 visits to the U.S. The 2006 arrival ceremony was marred by protocol blunders and an outburst from a Falun Gong protester.

China, unlike America, is not a proselytising power. America was founded on ideas and documents. That, along with its Christian roots, produces a strong evangelical streak. Whether in regard to its constitution or the merits of its liberal democracy and free-market ideology, much of the U.S. discourse assumes it has fashioned a superior system. America has often led by example and through the attractiveness of its model. And it has not shied away from using force – through coups in Latin America or Iran or war in Vietnam and Iraq and Afghanistan – in an effort to impose its vision on the world. Something China is not into. China doesn't want to be converted, politically or religiously. All the Communist Party is preoccupied with these days is its own self preservation and how its cadres can continue to enrich themselves.

China went through a generational change in leadership in 2012 and government officials have repeatedly voiced their commitment to "peaceful development," and acknowledged that the U.S. will enjoy global leadership for decades to come. When President Hu reiterated this policy during his Washington summit, it was welcomed as helpful in reducing mutual mistrust.

"While it is easy to focus on our differences, in cultures and perspective, let us never forget the values that our people share," Obama said in a toast to Hu, pointing to mutual traditions of hard work, sacrifice and love of family – personal, national and global.

### Rise and Shine

If the citizens of the cradle of human creation in the Middle East – the Garden of Eden – are prepared to again stand up and revolt against corrupt career politicians, why aren't American and Chinese citizens who have just as proud a revolutionary history – actually much better at revolutions – George Washington and Mao Zedong being the revolutionary leaders and founders of their respective country's political model, I asked myself before my May 2011 trip to America. The answer actually crystalized in my head after a discussion with Bruce Grill, a fellow American – and a New Yorker at that – who had just returned to Hong Kong after spending a few weeks back home with family and friends.

Bruce is a businessman married to Marinoel, a French lady, and has lived in Greater China for more than 30 years. It was Friday the 13th at the Foreign Correspondents Club Main Bar.

"You know," Bruce began hesitatingly after we greeted each other and I asked him how things were back home, "I always thought there were two kinds of people in America – stupid and evil. This trip I concluded that Americans are stupid people led by evil people," he added, much to my surprise.

Thank God it was still early in the evening and we were only into our second glass of wine.

"People are angry, depressed and can't understand why things are so bad. How can they not?" Bruce continued. "Everyone is cutting back. Politicians talk nonsense and lie through their teeth and people buy it, although I must admit, the Tea Party is challenging conventional wisdom and making people ask questions. But Sarah Palin, come on, how stupid and low can we go before it's too late?"

Carolyn Gary, an American stockbroker and wealth manager whom I have known since the early '90s, joined in the conversation.

"C'mon y'all, ain't that why we all is here?" she asked in a mocking Minnesota high plains accent that she quickly switched mid-sentence to a Southern drawl. Carolyn is from Minnesota and has been a worthy sparring partner over the years on the subject of U.S. politics.

A few days after my return from the U.S. in June 2011, I received the following e-mail from Carolyn: "The 26th Amendment (granting the right to vote for 18-year-olds) took only 3 months & 8 days to be ratified? Why? Simple! The people demanded it. That was in 1971 ... before computers, before e-mail, before cell phones, etc.

"Of the 27 amendments to the Constitution, seven (7) took 1 year or less to become the law of the land ... all because of public pressure.

"I'm asking each addressee to forward this e-mail to a minimum of twenty people on their address list; in turn, ask each of those to do likewise.

"In three days, most people in the United States of America will have the message. This is one idea that really should be passed around.

### Congressional Reform Act of 2011

1. Term Limits.
   12 years only, one of the possible options below.

   A. Two six-year Senate terms
   B. Six two-year House terms
   C. One six-year Senate term and three two-year House terms

2. No Tenure/No Pension.

   A Congressman collects a salary while in office and receives no pay when they are out of office.

3. Congress (past, present & future) participates in Social Security.

   All funds in the Congressional retirement fund move to the Social Security system immediately. All future funds flow into the Social Security system and Congress participates with the American people.

4. Congress can purchase their own retirement plan, just as all Americans do.

5. Congress will no longer vote themselves a pay rise. Congressional pay will rise by the lower of CPI or 3%.

6.  Congress loses their current health care system and participates in the same health care system as the American people.

7.  Congress must equally abide by all laws they impose on the American people.

8.  All contracts with past and present Congressmen are void effective 1/1/12.

The American people did not make this contract with Congressmen. Congressmen made all these contracts for themselves.

Serving in Congress is an honor, not a career.
The Founding Fathers envisioned citizen legislators, so ours should serve their term(s), then go home and back to work.

If each person contacts a minimum of twenty people, then it will only take three days for most people (in the U.S.) to receive the message. Maybe it is time.

**LET'S FIX CONGRESS!!!!! If you agree, pass it on.**

If not, just delete."

I thanked Carolyn for the e-mail and told her she was "Right on, sister!"

"You won't believe it," she said. "I sent it to 30 Americans in the States and here and you are the only one who responded. What is the matter with Americans? Do they just not get it, or are they that apathetic?"

"Both," I responded.

### *Real Hope and Change*
To get out of my funk on September 9, 2010, after my visit to Ground Zero

and Wall Street, I caught a train to Union Square to check out the street scene. I started going to Union Square regularly again in early 2000 to visit Mark Caparosa, the graphic designer of my book covers. His office overlooks the square and going out for a bite to eat, a beer or a game of darts was always a hoot.

I enjoy to this day meeting friends for lunch or dinner at one of the many fine dining establishments around Union Square. Its name celebrates neither the Federal union of the United States nor labor unions, but the union of New York City's two main thoroughfares – Broadway and the former Bowery Road, now 4th Avenue. Union Square is known for its impressive equestrian statue of George Washington, unveiled in 1856, the first public sculpture erected in New York after the equestrian statue of George III in 1770 and the first equestrian statue cast in bronze. Other statues in the square commemorate Marquis de Lafayette, Abraham Lincoln and Mahatma Gandhi.

Historically, the square has been the starting or ending point for many political demonstrations. It has also been a frequent gathering point for radicals of all stripes to make speeches and demonstrate. In April 1861, after the fall of Fort Sumter, it was the site of a patriotic rally of approximately a quarter of a million people that is thought to have been the largest public gathering in North America up to that time. It was named a National Historical Landmark in 1997, primarily to honor it as the site of the first Labor Day parade. A very appropriate place to unite America and start the Third American Revolution.

The Greenmarket days are my favorite time to visit. The smells and fresh tastes of fruits, vegetables and cheeses, not to mention home brews, were a millennium reminder that America is still an agrarian society that can sustain itself. Americans are still the most creative people in the world.

The buzz and pure raw creative energy of New York City streets always lifts my spirits and gives me hope. Walking across the square from the train station, I was drawn to a crowd listening to the uplifting quintessential American sound of bluegrass country rock.

The Hogslop String Band from Nashville, Tennessee, had people clapping and children dancing to their music. Their finale *Blackeyed Susie* got people to walk over to their fiddle case to add to the growing pile of cash in response to their plea saying they needed to get home because their "mothers missed" them – classic American capitalist enterpreneurship.

I thought about that day as I read Holly Eliot's letter to the editor of *Newsweek* before my return visit to New York in May 2011.

"As a 56-year old woman who will never lack for a job, I have to tell these unemployed men: Get over it and get to work. Be willing to hoist some boxes and pour some coffee. Realize that those you once looked down on are just as smart as you; they just haven't had the breaks you did. Learn to respect work for its own sake and not for the status it bestows. Get creative and get humble, and you will survive," she wrote.

Right on, sister, I thought to myself. The ranks of sidewalk merchants and garage sales households are swelling with unemployed 9-to-5ers.

New York and Hong Kong are my two favorite uplifting creative cities in the new world disorder, and they are similar in so many ways. Concrete canyons abuzz with creative multi-ethnic, cultural and religious people. Substitute New York's yellow cabs, MTA, African Americans, Asians and Latinos in casual dress for Hong Kong's red cabs, MTR, Cantonese and South Asians in their straight-laced street clothes and you have the perfect recipe for the New World Order.

Heartland Brewery, on Union Square across the street from where the Hogslops were playing, is just as creative with its menu as the band is with its music. Fried pickles and a tuna sashimi burger washed down with the house brews – lagers, ales, beers and stouts – is an uplifting refreshing experience and a reminder of how creative America is and how it survives. The knowledgeable wait staff are a reminder of what America was and can be again.

As I left the brewery, I remembered the words of Vaclav Havel: "Isn't it the moment of most profound doubt that gives birth to new certainties? Perhaps hopelessness is the very soil that nourishes human hope; perhaps one could never find sense in life without first experiencing its absurdity ... . "

The absurdity really came into focus with Obama's uplifting speech at the memorial services in Tucson Arizona, for the victims of the failed Rep. Gabby Giffords assassination attempt, as well as his 2011 State of the Union address.

The pundits were unanimous, an all time-high of political accord, on Obama's Tucson memorial speech that temporarily healed a nation torn between love of the gun and mourning innocent victims.

That didn't last long. A couple of weeks later, the nation got back to its vitriolic partisan divisiveness the moment the president finished delivering his State of the Union address that called on Americans to unite in "our generation's Sputnik moment" to counter the "devastation that remains" even though the "worst of the storm has passed."

Really, what did he know that we didn't? Nothing, obviously, because he, like all establishment career politicians, got it wrong again. I don't know who his weathermen are, but he and America better get new ones – fast.

Obama's political weathermen not only got it wrong domestically, but like his predecessors, got it wrong geopolitically. Why is the U.S. continuing to spend hundreds of billions of dollars in foreign aid to countries that refuse to honor the political chit they owe? Israel and Egypt are two prime examples that have highlighted the point recently. The two countries are the largest recipients of U.S. foreign aid in the Middle East, billions that could be much more wisely spent rebuilding America's cities and farms instead of benefiting political leaders who ignore America's wishes as they continue to extend their hand of ingratitude begging for more greenbacks.

When Israel's Prime Minister Benjamin Netanyahu was asked to desist from building any new settlements for a short period to encourage a renewed peace process and help the Palestinian leadership in what could have been a peace treaty, he basically gave America the finger. Understandable after the way he was treated like a delivery boy the last time he visited the White House and was asked to enter via the kitchen. He and Obama behaved like naughty boys.

Things didn't get any better with Egypt when President Obama implored President Hosni Mubarak to leave right away and enable an orderly transition of power. Again, Obama and America were rebuffed. America should have been publicly more supportive of the protesters – like its Founding Fathers would have been.

The U.S. has been a longtime supporter of repressive regimes in Arab countries, lusting for their oil. Supporting the protesters could undermine those long-standing oil ties. On the other hand, the U.S. cannot sit idly by and watch regimes like the one in Syria kill and put down their people. Supporting the status quo will be disastrous for America's long-term foreign policy once revolutionary movements succeed and come to power. Iran is a classic historical lesson that the U.S. has chosen to ignore.

The same will eventually happen in Bahrain and Saudi Arabia. Their repressive monarchies are unsustainable. The sooner America comes to grips with this realization, the sooner its credibility as a freedom-loving nation will be restored.

When will America learn from history, including its own? When will it learn that other countries do what is best for them today and not what the White House, the State Department or the Pentagon think they should do anymore. The Jasmine-Nile revolutions highlight what a colossal failure American foreign policy has become.

The U.S. cannot continue backing the wrong autocratic horses and then be surprised that the African, Arab, Asian, Caspian and Latino streets hate America and its military-industrial political machine. How many more foreign policy failures does America need before it changes course – back to the revolutionary principles of the Founding Fathers?

"I have always given it as my decided opinion that no nation had a right to inter-meddle in the internal concerns of another … and that, if this country could, consistent with its engagements, maintain a strict neutrality and thereby preserve peace, it was bound to do so by motives of policy, interest, and every other consideration," George Washington wrote in a letter to James Monroe on August 25, 1796.

In his farewell address September 17, 1796 Washington went on to add, "Observe good faith and justice toward all nations. Cultivate peace and harmony with all....The nation which indulges toward another an habitual hatred or an habitual fondness is in some degree a slave. It is a slave to its animosity or to its affection, either of which is sufficient to lead it astray from its duty and its interest."

It got better. "The great rule of conduct for us in regard to foreign nations is, in extending our commercial relations to have with them as little political connection as possible....Why, by interweaving our destiny with that of any part of Europe, entangles our peace and prosperity in the toils of European ambition, rivalship, interest, humor, or caprice? It is our true policy to steer clear of permanent alliances with any portion of the foreign world....We may safely trust to temporary alliances for extraordinary emergencies.... There can be no greater error than to expect or calculate upon real favors from nation to nation. It is an illusion which experience must cure, which a just pride ought to discard," Washington said.

It reminded me of President Dwight Eisenhower's warning to America and the world nearly two centuries later about "America's military-industrial complex."

When will Americans stop being afraid to launch the Third American Revolution to get back to the country's founding principles – which the Arab revolutionaries from ancient and proud civilizations did in the spirit of the Boston Tea Party? The only difference is the blend of tea. What will it take for *We the Apathetic Maids* to re-enact the original tea party with all its new flavors – alcoholic and non-alcoholic – again in America, China and beyond?

*We the Apathetic Maids* must become the reluctant citizen-soldiers, like our forefathers, who won the First Revolutionary War and are celebrated as the original American patriots.

### Reborn Pride

I wish I could have been in New York City, Ground Zero specifically, when the news of Osama bin Laden's death was announced. Party with all the proud Americans. Not sure I would be climbing a lightpost to wave the flag and sing *America the Beautiful* and *The Star Spangled Banner*. I can do that on the ground and enjoy the bottles of champagne being passed around as New York's finest ignored the city ban on drinking and dancing in the streets. I love street parties. They're the best. People enjoying themselves and taking pride in their neighborhood – as the skeletal frame of the new One World Trade Center – the Freedom Tower – reached some 60 stories.

I couldn't help thinking about and asking friends if they had heard the story of what happened to bin Laden on his way to the Pearly Gates. There he is greeted by George Washington. "How dare you attack the nation I helped conceive!" yells Washington, slapping Osama in the face.

Patrick Henry comes up from behind. "You wanted to end the Americans' liberty, so they gave you death!" Henry punches Osama in the nose.

James Madison comes up next, and says, "This is why I allowed the federal government to provide for the common defense!" He drops a heavy weight on Osama's knee.

Osama is subjected to similar beatings from John Randolph, James Monroe, Thomas Jefferson and dozens of others.

Osama finally screams, "This is not what I was promised!"

An angel replies: "I told you there would be 72 Virginians waiting for you. What did you think I said?"

But I was happy to be there three weeks later. We are all part of the 9/11 generation, regardless of age, country of origin or religious belief. 9/11 and the wars in Afghanistan, Iraq, Libya and countless other countries like Pakistan, Syria, Somalia and Yemen, not to mention open seas while political and economic earth-shattering seismic events almost achieved what bin Laden couldn't. Destroy the Western World as we know it. That is until America's Founding Fathers' ideals and principles kicked in again in America and the Arab world with a vengeance. The Arab cleansing and the death of bin Laden are the dawn of a New World Order being swept in by *We the Maids,* interlocally and globally.

Standing at Ground Zero looking up at the rising Freedom Tower, I shuddered at the realization that as the 10th anniversary of the 9/11 terrorist attacks neared, one of the main recommendations of the 9/11 Commission remains unfulfilled: the creation of a common communications system that lets emergency responders talk to one another across jurisdictions. The problem had been laid bare in the tragic cacophony at the World Trade Center, on that fateful day, when scores of firefighters unnecessarily died because police and fire officials couldn't communicate with each other. The same thing happened four years later during Hurricane Katrina. In New Orleans, they had to resort to running handwritten notes around to warn of shifting conditions.

Career politicians in Washington should be haunted by the threat of new disasters finding rescue workers still incommunicado. But they are not. They and their overpaid bureaucrats and financial supporters are vying for a piece of the lucrative communications pie while Americans die unnecessarily. The faulty emergency communication on 9/11 was "probably the greatest killer other than the planes themselves," said Senator John Rockefeller IV, chairman of the science and transportation committee. Yet nothing has been done about it.

Young crowds rejoicing, chanting "U-S-A!" at Ground Zero and the White House. An exhilarating sense of victory, closure and jubilation. Satisfaction at accomplishing a mission to be truly proud of. A reminder of what the U.S. is capable of. That brings a lot of newfound respect, something America has been lacking for a long time. A feeling of a new beginning. The good ol' "can-do spirit." Why can't that feeling of unity we all felt then and after 9/11 be maintained daily, especially in Washington and Beijing? Wasn't it – and isn't it – worth fighting for? America still has what it takes to be a superpower the world envies and respects, done so smartly with China.

"So what did you think of Osama bin Laden's death?" I asked Abassi

Iftikhar Hussain, a devout Muslim Pakistani veterinary assistant whom I work with who drives the Pets Central mobile medical unit.

"Great news, no?" Abassi responded. "He killed too many innocent people, not just Christians like you, but Muslims as well. The Koran does not allow what he did," he said.

### Real Change

Did the election of Barack Obama really change anything in America? The honest answer is an emphatic "no!" That thought shocked me as I mulled over the question one drizzly morning in my rooftop garden in Hong Kong, listening to the beautiful sounds of spring 2011. Chirping crickets, a chorus of birds, watching my dog Spud chill out at my feet as Tyra the hunter cat stalked a nearby tweeter. Reflecting on the question, I could reach only one conclusion.

Alabama Governor George Wallace was right when he said of America's two-party system when he decided to run for president under the banner of a third independent party in the '70s: "There ain't a dime's worth of difference between the Democratic and Republican parties." I agreed with him then and still do today.

Obama ran as the Democratic alternative to the Republican Bush policies espoused by rival John McCain. Obama was going to be the global team player, not a Republican cowboy. He was going to bring about real change you could believe in, which he did in many ways – but not to fundamental U.S. domestic or foreign policies.

Look at government debt and deficit spending. As a senator, Obama was highly critical of President Bush when he tried to raise the U.S. debt ceiling, but Obama does so repeatedly.

Obama criticized Bush for sending suspected terrorists to Guantanamo Bay, Cuba, but he is doing the same. The same holds true for policies dealing with the U.N., Iraq, Afghanistan, North Korea, Saudi Arabia and newcomers Libya and Syria.

On taxes, Obama called the Bush-era cuts for the wealthy wrong and demanded their end. But in December 2010, he signed a deal with the Republicans who took over the House in the midterm election to extend them for two years, and yet had the audacity to say the entire tax-cut package was good for the country.

And Obama was not going to have any lobbyist or any person related to one in his administration, remember? Right.

Even with Obamacare, his stand wasn't so much a reversal of Bush's approach as an escalation. Bush also pushed through a massive expansion of Medicare by adding a costly prescription drug benefit – at the time, the biggest expansion of a federal entitlement program since Lyndon Johnson's Great Society. What happened to that America? Hopefully, it will re-discover itself in the wake of the enthusiasm and pride that swelled every American heart and made them feel proud to be an American when they heard that bin Laden, the man behind 9/11, had been killed.

### *"Live Free or Die"*
New Hampshire license plates sum up how the Founding Fathers felt: "Live Free or Die." It's a refreshing reminder every time I spot one, especially when visiting the Granite State and being surrounded by the sentiment. It's the best reason I can think of to start the presidential primary season there.

How do *We the Apathetic Maids* want to live? Freedom is not limited to the right to vote, but free to live the American Dream, which includes basic human rights such as a home, job, health care and freedom from the burden of undue taxation imposed to pay for the bailouts of banks caused by their greed.

The rallying cry of the Founding Fathers was "No Taxation Without Representation." How are *We the Apathetic Maids* represented in Washington when we are repeatedly asked to clean up the mess that career politicians and their bankers create and then asked to have our children and grandchildren pay for the privilege as our bonus? Isn't it time we honor the words and actions of the Founding Fathers?

"One person with a belief is equal to the force of 100,000 who have only interests," English philosopher John Stuart Mill encapsulated so well that it can easily be a modern-day bullet point that not only motivate Tea Party members, but many Americans from across the entire interlocal political landscape that is Americana.

### Gateway to the Revolution

Massachusetts was the gateway to the first American Revolution and, not as well known, the Civil War – America's Second Revolution. Its abolitionist and Civil War heritage is well known to historians. Massachusetts abolitionists like William Lloyd Garrison helped organize resistance to slavery; a Boston publisher released *Uncle Tom's Cabin;* Bay State politicians like Charles Sumner spearheaded the Union cause in Congress. Once the war began, volunteers like Clara Barton answered the call for volunteers, staffing the nursing corps. The armory in Springfield produced millions of the weapons carried by Union soldiers. A fort in Boston Harbor guarded high-profile Confederate prisoners. Julia Ward Howe wrote The *Battle Hymn of the Republic.*

Flying from New York to Los Angeles on Memorial Day 2011, it occurred to me that most Americans only know that the holiday honors the country's war dead, but have no clue when and why it started or its true meaning. I decided to check out my theory on glassmates at the airport lounge and, sure enough, no one had a clue. I decided to share an article I had just read in *The New York Times,* written by David W. Blight, a professor of history and director of the Gilder Lehrman Center for the Study of Slavery, Resistance and Abolition at Yale.

At the end of the Civil War, Americans faced a formidable challenge: how to memorialize the 625,000 dead soldiers on both sides. As Walt Whitman mused, it was "the dead, the dead, the dead – our dead – or South or North, ours all" that preoccupied the country. After all, if the same number per capita had died in Vietnam as died in the Civil War, 4 million names would be chiseled into the Vietnam Veterans Memorial instead of 58,000.

Officially, in the North, Memorial Day emerged in 1868 when the Grand Army of the Republic, the Union veterans' organization, called on communities to conduct grave-decorating ceremonies. On May 30, memorial events attracted thousands of people at hundreds of cemeteries in countless towns, cities and mere crossroads. By the 1870s, one could not live in an American town, North or South, and be unaware of the spring ritual.

Memorial days were initially occasions of sacred bereavement, and from the war's end to the early 20th century they helped forge national reconciliation around soldierly sacrifice, regardless of cause, something America has to start doing again if it is to reunite and survive.

To put things in perspective, we must return to that earliest and most remarkable Memorial Day. By the spring of 1865, after a long siege and prolonged bombardment, the beautiful port city of Charleston, S.C., lay in ruin and occupied by Union troops. Among the first soldiers to enter and march up Meeting Street singing liberation songs was the 21st United States Colored Infantry. Their commander accepted the city's official surrender.

Whites had largely abandoned the city, but thousands of blacks, mostly former slaves, had remained, and they conducted a series of commemorations to declare their sense of the meaning of the war. The largest of these events took place on May 1, 1865. During the final year of the war, the Confederates had converted the city's Washington Race Course and Jockey Club into an outdoor prison. Union captives were kept in horrible conditions in the interior of the track; at least 257 died of disease and were buried in a mass grave behind the grandstand.

After the Confederate evacuation of Charleston, black workmen went to the site, reburied the Union dead properly and built a high fence around the cemetery. They whitewashed the fence and built an archway over an entrance on which they inscribed the words, "Martyrs of the Race Course."

The symbolic power of this was not lost on the freed people, who then in cooperation with white missionaries and teachers staged a parade of 10,000 people on the track. The procession was led by 3,000 black schoolchildren carrying armloads of roses and singing the Union marching song *John Brown's Body*. Several hundred black women followed with baskets of flowers, wreaths and crosses. Then came black men marching in cadence, followed by contingents of Union infantrymen. Within the cemetery enclosure, a black children's choir sang *We'll Rally Around the Flag,* the *Star Spangled Banner* and spirituals before a series of black ministers read from the Bible.

After the dedication the crowd dispersed into the fields and did what many of us do on Memorial Day: enjoyed picnics, listened to speeches and watched soldiers drill. Among the full brigade of Union infantrymen participating were the famous 54th Massachusetts and the 34th and 104th United States Colored Troops, who performed a special double-columned march around the gravesite. The war was over, and Memorial Day had been founded by African-Americans in a ritual of remembrance and consecration.

Despite its size and some newspaper coverage, the memory of the event was suppressed by white Charlestonians in favor of their own version of the day. From 1876 on, after white Democrats took back control of South Carolina politics and the Lost Cause defined public memory and race relations, the day's racecourse origin vanished.

The old racecourse is gone now, but an oval roadway survives on the site in Hampton Park, named for Wade Hampton, former Confederate general and the governor of South Carolina after the end of Reconstruction. The old gravesite of the Martyrs of the Race Course is gone too; they were reinterred in the 1880s at a national cemetery in Beaufort, S.C.

Memorial Day, in other words, is the Second Revolution equivalent of Independence Day of the First American Revolution. The home of the Founding Fathers can and must again lead the charge for America's Third Revolution. Except this time, North and South should join hands and fight the revolution as One Nation. Americans should join hands and sing Lynyrd Skynyrd's *Sweet Home Alabama* – because it is not just the South that will rise again – but a stronger, united America.

### Party Time

America and China are both ready to party – for a new political party that represents the interests of the people, the citizens, and not the career politicians and the outdated irrelevant parties they represent. That became crystal clear to me in the late spring 2011 during my visit to the U.S. and on my return to Hong Kong. What struck me as either coincidence or synchronicity, a subject I discuss at length in *Custom Maid Spin,* is how the political parties in America and China were behaving the same.

The career politicians for the Republican nomination to run for president against Barack Obama were a pathetic joke as they tried to figure out how to renounce their past policies to appease the party's fired-up conservative base. There was Mitt Romney distancing himself from his own health care plan he passed into law in Massachusetts which mirrors Obamacare, and Tim Pawlenty, who passed a cap-and-trade law in Minnesota as governor saying that Obama's cap-and-trade to limit greenhouse gases is bad for the nation, while Sarah Palin, the former governor of pristine Alaska, rides Harleys and buses in New England that burn more fuel and emit more emissions than Mayor Bloomberg's private jet.

Republican ideals were being trashed. Bush and the Republican-controlled Congress in 2003 created an entitlement by establishing the Medicare prescription drug benefit that they now want to trash. In 2006, with Bush's support, 23 GOP senators voted with 39 Democrats to provide a pathway to citizenship for illegal immigrants that the 2012 crop of Republican presidential hopefuls all rejected outright.

The 2012 GOP presidential contenders abandoned and apologized for positions they took earlier, all in the interest of appeasing what is left of the conservative right wing of the party after the Tea Party movement hijacked the party script.

Disenchanted Democrats who are unhappy with the lack of promised change resigned themselves to the fact that Obama would be the party's nominee in 2012 and, no matter what, he's still better than any of the Republican choices.

Meanwhile, back in China, the widening chasm in the Communist Party split over Mao's legacy, role and relevance to the party today resembles Arizona's Grand Canyon.

In late 2012, at about the same time as Americans went to the polls, the Communist Party, during its 18th national congress, installed its new leadership that will run the country for the next 10 years in the Great Hall of the People in Tiananmen Square.

Americans have come to believe that China is a well-oiled dictatorship with smooth transitions. That is a false perception. Only one transition – that from Jiang Zemin to Hu Jintao in 2002 – has been smooth. The Communist Party has its extremist idealogues who, like Sarah Palin, have appropriated powerful national insignia, "red" television programs and Mao's "red songs."

China, like America, is ready for its Third Revolution. The Communist and Cultural Revolutions being the first two.

American and Chinese citizens – the people of the most powerful economic and military countries – have a lot more in common than they realize. Both have been exploited by their career politicians and plutocracies that have enriched themselves at the expense of their citizens' sweat and labor. Both have the same motivations to sweep out their abusive self-serving leaders and their financial backers.

The citizens of America and China, like their counterparts in most countries, want the same things: jobs, an affordable quality education for their children, a level playing field, rule of law, justice, equality and religious, political and sexual freedom.

### *America Reunite & Fight*
The Magna Carta established the rights of the English people and curbed the power of the king. Rebellious barons forced the oppressive King John to sign the charter in 1215. It was enacted as law in 1297 by the British parliament when it was reissued by King Edward I. The 1297 document was the basis for both the U.S. Constitution and the Declaration of Independence.

People have the right to separate themselves from each other and oppressive leaders – Arabs shedding despots being the 21$^{st}$-century messengers reminding us of this inalienable right – in order to reassert their lives and the form of government to their liking to conform to the words and spirit of America's founding principles. America the political rock band has the right to break up and reunite. Why is the greatest political union any different than many of the great American musical unions like Aerosmith, the Back Street Boys, Bruce Springsteen and the E Street Band, the Dave Mathews Band, the Eagles, Crosby Stills, Nash and Young, Fish and Buffalo Springfield.

"We're Buffalo Springfield, and we're from the past," said Neil Young as he smirked into the microphone as he summarized the vibe for the packed Fox Theatre crowd in Oakland at their reunion concert in June 2011. Many politicians, like musicians, are not only from the past – but stuck in it. Stuck in a political world that is irrelevant to America today. What is the point of being stuck in the past? It reminds me of many of Bob Dylan's fans.

I went to a Dylan concert in Hong Kong when he performed there in April 2011, the 23$^{rd}$ year of his Never Ending Tour. He played guitar, keyboards and harmonica during the 18-song set. Wearing his trademark snow-white Stetson, and playing the keyboards, he jammed a 10-verse version of *Desolation Row*. A boogie-woogie rendition of *Highway 61 Revisited* followed. His gravely voice was at times incomprehensible.

"I paid to listen to this shit? Boo, boo," yelled out a contemporary balding man sitting next to me.

"C'mon man, enjoy Dylan for what he is. What he has evolved into at 69 in 2011, not the counter-culture Dylan of the '60s, which is what I suppose you came to hear," I said to my upset seat mate.

"This is absolute crap and I can't bear to listen to it anymore," he said as he got up and left.

The times they are a-changin', not just for musicians and their fans, but for politics and politicians.

Remember the past, yes. Live it continuously without change – absolutely not! Even the Founding Fathers ideas cannot be practiced today as they were when the nation was founded. They are fluid and adjustable in a changing America – and Americans. America's political rhythm, like its music, evolves with the times – and the political and musical beat in America and China today is – Revolution!

America the arrogant, selfish, impotent, loud-mouth white cowboy has to be replaced by America's strong, gentle, compassionate and all-embracing complex universal carmelized cowboy identity and code imbedded in the Founding Fathers' ideals. America's inherent Native American and European Puritan roots are the beacon of interlocal hope and opportunity, starting with China and followed by other forward-thinking people everywhere.

America with all its present troubles remains the indispensable beacon for global harmony. America must rediscover and reactivate its creative pioneer spirit, adventurism and entrepreneurship, to its own enduring political beat if it is to again become the Shining Beacon on the Hill. It's up to *We the Apathetic Maids* to wake up and sweep in the political reforms needed to restore America to its former glory.

More desperately needed changes – from immigration reform to electoral college reform – are proposed in this book, adding to solutions proposed in Volumes I and II. By no means do I suggest that they are the only solutions.

Volume III of this trilogy explores and outlines changes and solutions on how *We the Maids* can improve personal, business, charitable, legal, political and institutional relationships in 21$^{st}$-century America and the forward-thinking world with *Custom Made Orders From Scratch* – from the Founding Fathers' recipe book – the Constitution and the Bill of Rights.

## Sex, Drugs and Cultural Revolution
*Just Another American Saturday Night*
– Brad Paisley

### Sixties Spirit

Dr. Timothy Leary, the Harvard professor and LSD guru, would occasionally dine in the mid-'80s with his wife and my racquetball partner, Dr. Warren Bennis, a professor at the University of Southern California, and a well-known author and authority on business management and leadership, at Scratch – my first wife Gail's restaurant. My son Jonas attended the same school as Zachary, Timothy Leary's son.

Meeting Leary was a treat. Of all the celebrities who dined at Scratch, he was one of the few who really influenced a generation. I had the pleasure of having in-depth conversations with Leary during cocktail receptions Bennis hosted at his nearby Santa Monica beachfront home.

The issues facing us as we confront the 21st century are not that different from the issues of the '60s. Youth today are just as disenchanted and frustrated with the "system" and the "establishment" as we were back then. They still question authority. Nothing has really changed. Youth around the world have always had more in common with each other than they do with their parents, their government or their system of government. While Bob Dylan was singing *The Times They Are a-Changing,* and *Blowing in the Wind,* America was getting deeper into Vietnam, free love, sex, drugs and rock 'n' roll and China was in the throes of the Cultural Revolution.

What Leary and Chairman Mao had in common was that they were both proposing radically different solutions to what each perceived to be the ills of their societies. Neither solution could work in isolation and both proved to be failures. Hallucinogenic drugs and the extermination of intellectuals both deprive society of the creative brain power it needs to move forward. Nevertheless, Mao and Leary succeeded in uniting a generation and community at the expense of many innocent victims. Their actions, however, paled in comparison to Pol Pot's killing fields in Cambodia.

### *Drugs*

The spirit of the '60s still haunts the current world disorder. LSD and opium are making the biggest comeback at the dawn of the 21$^{st}$ century in both America and China. China was clean for 40 years, until the demise of Maoism. Now it is again one of the biggest consumers of opium with more than a million addicts. It is also one of the world's most important opium growers. Raves and the spirit of the '60s are being blamed for the comeback of not only opium, but cocaine and LSD.

In Hong Kong, a former village leader was jailed for 22 years in March 2011 for storing the largest amount of cocaine ever seized in the city – 232 kg with a street value of HK$330 million.

LSD is so popular that Hong Kong even has an LSD political party –the League of Social Democrats. Its elected officials throw jasmine flowers and bananas at Hong Kong's chief executive and his ministers whenever they address the Legislative Council.

Its members attack and try to injure the chief executive at public functions. Kind of like the '60s Weathermen in America, without the firearms and explosives. Political protests and democracy run amok.

I was first introduced to LSD in Los Angeles when I arrived there in 1966. Discussing its hallucinogenic benefits 20 years later to escape reality with Leary, who openly advocated its use and benefits, was a real trip. Ergot, the poisonous fungus that grows on rye, had been used for centuries as a folk remedy to induce childbirth and ease headaches. The father of LSD, Albert Hoffman, believed ergot could be a storehouse of new medicines and he started synthesizing chemicals from it. In 1938, Hoffman synthesized the 25$^{th}$ chemical: lysergic acid diethyla – LSD, or simply acid, as it came to be known in the '60s.

"Through the late '40s and most of the '50s, LSD caused a revolution in psychiatry. Therapists and doctors like myself used it to treat forms of mental illness, including neurosis, psychosis and depression," Leary told me. "More than 40,000 people underwent psychedelic therapy. Respected doctors, myself included, consider it a wonder drug. More than 2,000 papers had been published on LSD by 1965, many reporting extremely positive outcomes in treating anxiety, obsessive-compulsive behavior and alcoholism," Leary added as I continued listening to his private tutorial on LSD. A nice escape from the ugly political reality of the '60s. A drug that allowed people to be "reborn" and escape a society facing growing industrialization and urbanization, alienation, boredom and an ever-growing unrepresentative political establishment.

LSD and magic mushrooms were adopted as the sacraments of the counterculture movement that opposed the wealth-driven homogeneity of capitalist America. In the age of moon landings and space exploration, both became the tools that allowed a metaphorical journey of equal significance – a shortcut to enlightenment.

### Mother's Little Helper
One of the Rolling Stones hits in the '60s was *Mother's Little Helper*. It was about America's all-time favorite pill, not for birth control, but anxiety. It is the potent tranquilizer called Miltown, named after the New Jersey village where it was born in 1955. It became the fastest selling drug in U.S. history, inspiring cocktails, jewelry – even an Oscar-night shout-out in 1956, when host Jerry Lewis cracked that nominees who didn't win an award could enjoy a buttered Miltown in the lobby.

Popping pills was something our parents did while we smoked weed and dropped acid. Today, pills are the norm in America and everyone seems to be a homegrown Internet pharmacist. America's youth and middle-aged – and many seniors – are deciding on their own what drugs to take. Self prescription of stimulants, anti-depressants and other psychiatric medications is commonplace. Many who can't find the drugs they want on the Internet just lie to their doctors because they have researched the symptoms to obtain the medications they think they need. The untimely death of Oscar-winning actor Philip Seymour Hoffman underscored the epidemic surge in heroin use by pain-pill addicts seeking a less-expensive high.

The big difference in culture from the '60s is that the goal for many young adults today is not to get high but to feel better. Less depressed, less stressed out, more focused, better rested. The easiest route to that end often seems to be medication for which one needs a prescription, or a source that does not require one on the Internet, or a friendly barter transaction.

Better living through chemistry purveyed by amateur pharmacists has become a cultural compulsion. Not only in America, but in China, where herbal medications are thrown into the mix, as well as most of the rest of the world where people have access to the Internet and trade notes on "head meds."

Under pressure at school, U.S. students rely on addictive prescription medications they get from friends, student dealers, or fake symptoms to their parents and doctors to get prescriptions to help them focus on their homework.

"This view of psychology as a series of problems that can be solved with pills is relatively brand new," said Andrea Tone, a professor of the social history of medicine at McGill University. "It's more elastic, and more subjective, so it lends itself more to taking matters into our own hands."

As a result, the number of babies born in America addicted to prescription painkillers has nearly tripled in the first decade of the 21$^{st}$ century. About 3.4 in every 1,000 infants born in a hospital in 2009 suffered from a type of drug withdrawal commonly seen in the babies of pregnant women who abuse narcotic pain medication, according to a study published in May 2012 in *The Journal of the American Medical Association*.

Not surprising really when one considers the billions of dollars pharmaceutical companies spend on marketing drugs – both legal and illegal – as the $3 billion GlaxoSmithKline settlement with the federal government in July 2012 for illegally marketing and promoting well-known drugs that were not approved by federal regulators underscores.

Glaxo was fined $492 million by the Chinese government in September

2014, the largest penalty ever in China, for bribing doctors and hospitals to use its products."

Pfizer Inc. pleaded guilty in 2009 to similar U.S. criminal charges and agreed to pay $2.3 billion. Eli Lilly & Co also pleaded guilty the same year and paid $1.42 billion for unapproved use of its schizophrenia drug Zynprexa. Takeda, Japan's biggest drug maker and Eli Lilly were ordered in 2014 to pay $9 billion in punitive damages over a best-selling diabetes drug that causes bladder cancer.

In Hong Kong today the most popular drug among youth is "K-Jai." It's the horse tranquilizer ketamine. It comes as a powder and can be added to drinks, injected or popped as a pill. It is valued by users because of its ability to knock them sideways and send them into the "K-hole", a state of dissociation from the body. Its popularity in Hong Kong is unmatched in the rest of the developed world, where cannabis and cocaine are the two most prevalent recreational drugs. That is because the non-users of ketamine in developed countries are resentful at people taking the drug in a club and requiring non-users to take care of them while they trip out on their K-ride. Hong Kong people are more tolerant and supportive of their unconscious trippers.

## Sex
The sexual revolution was led by pinup queen Bettie Page, who helped usher it in with her saucy photos. A cult figure, Page was most famous for the estimated 20,000 4-by-5-inch black-and-white glossy photographs in sexually provocative poses wearing high heels and bikinis or negligees, bondage apparel or nothing at all – from 1949 to 1957. Hugh Hefner, who came from a puritanical upbringing, reinvented himself to become the godfather of the sexual revolution with *Playboy* magazine and its centerfolds and bunnies. Bettie was a *Playboy* centerfold herself in 1955.

Once shocking revealing photos are now passed in America. Even squeaky-clean Disney now allows its stars to escape unscathed after their nude photos surface on the Web. Nude photos of Vanessa Hudgens, star of Disney's *High School Musical 2*, brought only a mild rebuke.

University classes on sexuality are today being suspended because of '60s orgies being practiced and tested. Ma Yaohai, a college professor in Nanjing, got 31/2 years in jail in 2010 for organizing swinger parties. Wang Yu, a deputy secretary of Anhui's Hefei University's Communist Youth

League committee, and his wife confessed to having photos taken at an orgy. Unsafe sex is rife among college students in China, who get their sex education from porn on the Internet as mandatory sex education in primary schools was only made mandatory in 2009. The same holds true for unmarried boomers in America today who are reliving the '60s, according to a survey published in the *Journal of Sexual Medicine* on October 4, 2010.

Marriage and two-parent families are on the decline in America, courtesy of the sexual revolution. About a third of adults ages 46 through 64 were divorced, separated or had never been married in 2010, compared to 13 percent in 1970, according to an analysis of census data released in 2012 by demographers at Bowling Green State University in Ohio. The same holds true in China. This decline is on the rise, as is intimacy between couples, because of the stresses of modern work, especially when economic downturns take hold and wives or significant others nag – but porn sales and hits on the Internet are way up.

The sale of sex toys at sex fairs and online in China, like America, is a booming business as more adults explore new sexual pleasures and erotica.

In America Pure Romance sells what it bills as "relationship enhancers" – oils, creams, lingerie and a variety of mostly pink sex toys with winky names like the Cabana Boy.

The company operates on the Tupperware sales model success story founded in 1993, in the Cincinnati suburb of (no joke) Loveland by Patty Brisben, a former pediatrician's assistant and mother looking to make money on her own schedule. Consultants – or sisters, as they are sometimes called – sell products at women-only parties in their homes, recruiting others into the pink sisterhood.

In China, it has become a $15 billion-plus annual business. Online sex today, buying, selling, viewing and sharing on indiscreet media, Facebook and Twitter, not to mention micro-blogging – has warped many male brains, especially those of powerful politicians, affecting their judgment about sex and causing them to have more difficulty controlling their impulses.

Gone are the days of powerful men's sexual discretion and judgment that left no uncovered tracks, because today's hackers access confidential communications illegally.

Why are moral conservatives shocked and horrified at this trend? The fossilized remains of two 380-million-year pregnant fish indicate that sex as we know it – fertilization of eggs inside a female – took place as long as 30 million years earlier than previously thought. Sex has always been the ultimate expression of personal freedom.

The Internet has spawned cybersex dens in which women perform acts for online clients. These dens have replaced the 900 numbers for phone sex of the last millennium. Online clients pay for private shows and anything goes

Internet users can also find casual sex partners online. For $20 a month, one can join the Adult FriendFinder community, where the usual rules of courtship are turned on their head, and no one makes any pretense about their intentions – just their preferred sex acts and partners. FriendFinder networks is a U.S.-based company that owns *Penthouse Magazine* and claims more than 484 million members worldwide.

A political knee-slapper was when the pro-adultery website that bills itself as "the most recognized name in infidelity" endorsed Newt Gingrich for president because of his wife-cheating ways. It had Gingrich with a finger over his lips and labeled him "Faithful Republican … Unfaithful Husband.

Sitting in a Burger King in Hong Kong in November 2011, munching on a burger, reading about the latest political sex scandal in the U.S. Republican primary – Herb Cain – I almost choked. I couldn't help reflect on all other preceding sex scandals of politicians. Ah, what am I missing? Hollywood-Broadway plays that are a real pleasure, like *It's Just Sex!* that I caught at the Two Roads Theatre in North Hollywood in April 2012, are real theater. Real sex. Real America. Real China. Real world.

Republican voters supported Herb Cain and pushed him to the top of the potential Republican ticket to challenge his African-American brother on the Democratic ticket. But he was brought down by sex – American style. What is more important? What is best for America or what Old World political party stalwarts dictate?

What about the New World Order that *We the Apathetic Maids* are going to address? Is *Nymphomaniac: Volume II* and its protagonists dissatisfaction and self-loathing an accurate summation?

Sex is part of Americans DNA. The Founding Founders' practical, extramarital relations only created creative juices that helped build the Republic. Their sexual dalliances had a constructive impact on their lives and the the foundation stones they laid. Why are *We the Maids* surprised that these sexually creative men forged the greatest political enterprise and democratic Republic in the world that everyone wants to emulate?

Were they good leaders? Was FDR, JFK, Nixon or Clinton? Consider the alternatives that have occupied the White House and what they have done for – or to – America and the world.

Sex scandals are the talk of the Internet – especially when it comes to politicians in America and China. Shanghai's "femme fatale" brought down the government there in the city's 2007 pension fund scandal. She supplied government officials and business executives with sexual favors and kept videos of the liaisons as evidence. The highest level official to fall was former Shanghai party secretary Chen Liangyu. Sex tapes have become the new political weapon to smear foes. Just ask former Senator John Edwards.

What about America's femme fatale, Amanda Knox, who was convicted in Italy of sexually assaulting and murdering British student Meredith Kercher? An ultimate interlocal tale of '60' style sex, drugs and murder that evoked memories of the Manson family's bloody orgy of death. Her conviction was later overturned.

Sex scandals have become so commonplace in China that the Communist Party in 2009 banned party members from having concubines and mistresses, labelling such activities as decadent. Those found having such extramarital affairs will find their careers at a sudden end, the regulation warned.

China's Shenzhen, bordering Hong Kong, has infamously been dubbed the "love nest" of wealthy, pleasure seeking businessmen, bureaucrats and politicians who travel regularly across the border from Hong Kong – and other parts of China – to rendevouz with their mistresses or *er nais*. I devoted a good part of a chapter to the subject in *Custom Maid Spin*.

Former President Bill Clinton got impeached for his sexual dalliance; former Speaker of the House Newt Gingrich admitted having sexual affairs while impeaching the president; former New York Governor Eliot Spitzer got busted for soliciting high-priced prostitutes; ex-New York Mayor Rudy Giuliani got busted for having an affair with a staffer, as did New York Governor David Paterson who succeeded Spitzer; former South Carolina Governor Mark Sanford had an affair with a woman in Argentina; presidential candidates Gary Hart and John Edwards had affairs while running for president; Nevada Senator John Ensign, chairman of the Republican Policy Committee, had to resign for having an affair with a volunteer married to a staffer; Senator Larry Craig from Idaho was forced to resign after being caught in a gay sting operation; New York Congressman Eric Massa resigned in 2010 after male staffers accused him of groping and propositioning them; Congressman Christopher Lee of New York had to resign in 2011 after he sent a shirtless photo of himself to a woman he met online; Congressman David Wu of Oregon resigned in 2011 over an "unwanted sexual encounter" with an 18-year-old woman; and former Vice President Al Gore's 2006 "masseuse grope" investigation was reopened in 2010. And, oh yeah, let's not forget New York's Congressman Andrew Weiner and his explicit Twitter photos of his underwear and Kosher salami. Am I forgetting anyone? Oh yeah, Vladimir Putin and his alleged illegitimate children in Germany and fondness for boys.

Sexting is a 21st century online fad, not only with politicians and athletes – but teenagers sending them to fellow teens – often not their girlfriend or boyfriend. But as experts warn, there are seriously disturbing aspects to sexting. The images children are taking of themselves are rarely simple nude shots. They are often crude imitations of the graphic images seen in hardcore pornography. Combine technology and pornography with teen hormones and it becomes a dangerous "digital footprint" not withstanding Snapchat pictures that self destruct.

I was in the U.S. that June 2011 when Weiner's matzo balls were bouncing all over the Internet. As a matter of fact, the weekend before, I had a couple of hours to kill in Springfield, the state capitol of Massachusetts, after the bus from Brattelboro dropped us off to catch Amtrak's Vermonter back to New York.

"Any good restaurants or bars around here?" I asked the driver as we got off the bus in front of the train station. It was early afternoon and I hadn't eaten lunch.

"Yeah, sure, go straight ahead to the square," he said in his thick New England accent. "There's a few there."

"Thanks," I said, heading down the deserted street. Sure enough, there was a square with a few restaurants and bars, but they were closed because it was Sunday Memorial Day weekend. As I turned a corner, I heard loud rock music coming from about a block away. I headed in its direction and found myself at the door of the Mardi Gras, a "gentleman's club" – a strip joint for the uninitiated – the kind that got Tiger Woods' golf balls splattered across his SUV.

Beer, popcorn and beautiful well-endowed ladies willing to share their God-given gifts. "Popcorn, or I can pop your corn" was the answer when I asked if there was any food being served as one of them leaned over, shaking her attributes in my face.

Dessert before the main course? I asked myself, or is it the main course? After a second beer, I decided I needed some real food and asked the Sunday afternoon delight if she could recommend a place. She did.

A half-block away, just past the Commonwealth of Massachusetts State Capital Legislative Offices, near the train station, was a nice saloon that not only served alcohol and food, but also had slot machines. The hot dogs were delicious. Seems like every state capitol I have been to – and Washington – have similar gentlemen's clubs. Is it any wonder politicians are tempted and eventually act out their fantasies? Are they representative of *We the Apathetic Maids?*

Sex seems to be the only common political ground in America these days.

The mother of all American political sex scandals was that of holier-than-thou Florida Congressman Mark Foley. He called child sex offenders "America's most depraved."

The six-term Republican Foley was co-chairman of the Congressional Missing and Exploited Children's Caucus. He authored legislation to block child pornography, repeatedly warned parents that the Internet had become "a new medium for pedophiles," and became a vocal proponent for the overhaul of sexual predator laws.

"For too long, our nation has tracked library books better than it has pedophiles," he declared on the *America's Most Wanted* TV show in 2005, vowing to root out child sex offenders.

"If I was one of those sickos, I'd be nervous," he added. As it turned out, he was one of those sickos. A gay, alcoholic sicko who had been abused as a child by a clergyman.

Too many children have been abused worldwide by "celebrities," as the report by Scotland Yard on the BBC's Jimmy Savile scandal in Britain revealed, especially during the heyday of the '60s, when free love was in and groupie culture was starting to make a name for itself.

Foley preyed on the young male volunteer pages who go to Washington to work in Congress for a year. Many then go into politics themselves. Two former pages said that they had sex with Foley after they had left the program.

Foley was the fourth Republican congressman to resign in 2006. Tom

DeLay of Texas, the former majority leader, stepped down over campaign finance irregularities; Bob Ney of Ohio admitted to federal bribery charges, and Randy Cunningham of California was imprisoned for bribery. These cases highlighted the hypocritical immorality and arrogance of those trying to legislate sexual morality.

Chinese Communist Party officials' juicy sexual trysts attract the most hits on Internet forums as a result of vigilante-type data searches, commonly known as "human flesh searches."

In Hong Kong, politicians are sexually scandalized even without sex having taken place. An example is legislator Kam Nai-wai's alleged sexual scandal, which became headline news without even a hint of bodily contact.

One of the most bizarre and extreme political sex scandals is that of South Korean lawmaker Kang Yong-seok. He was given a six-month suspended sentence in 2011 for saying that the country's female broadcasters should be willing to offer sex to advance their careers.

How about the sexual dalliances of the security personnel who protect the political leaders of their country? The U.S. Secret Service agents assigned to President Obama's April 2012 visit to Cartagena, Colombia, were "idiots," according to Dania Londono Suarez, one of the 20 prostitutes the 12 agents spent the night with. Her john allowed her to walk away with his wallet and all his papers when he tried to short-change her.

*We the Maids* have also been short-changed by the secret service. Omar Gonzalez, a war veteran who served three tours of duty in Iraq, breached five layers of White House security with a knife and made it to the East Room in September 2014, 10 minutes after the president left for Camp David. That after a shooting attack on the White House in 2011 that took the secret service several days to realize. A *Maid* brought it to their attention.

The U.S. Secret Service has a history of protecting the secret sexual affairs of presidents as well as their own dalliances from *We the Apathetic Maids*.

A Secret Service agent stood guard while President Warren G. Harding and his mistress slipped into a coat closet in the White House; Secret Service agents escorted FDR to wartime meetings with his former mistress Lucy

Mercer Rutherfurd (her Secret Service code name was "Mrs. Johnson") when they began regularly seeing each other 20 years after their affair had ended; and, according to Ronald Kessler's *In the President's Secret Service,* agents kept one eye out for Jackie Kennedy while her husband dallied with his fling of the moment. Not for nothing was the Secret Service code name for Kennedy "Lancer."

The Secret Service, according to agents' grand jury testimony, also bent the rules for frequent Oval Office visitor Monica Lewinsky.

Bill Clinton was only doing what the president he admired most did to perfection – JFK. The tell-all memoir of White House intern Mimi Alford, a tall, slender, 19-year-old college sophomore, describes giving her virginity to the president in the White House residence and an 18-month long affair that was cut short by Kennedy's assassination.

It appears that there are no pantheons in America, from the White House to every other sacred institution idolized by *We the Apathetic Maids,* that is not mired in sex and sex scandals.

With Mitt Romney, a Mormon running for president, the first prophet of Mormonism, Joseph Smith, who had 87 wives, of whom the youngest was 14, and Brigham Young, the second Prophet, who had 70 wives, Mormonism was highlighted in many mainstream media.

College football at Yale and Penn State are two well-outed and publicized examples. The case of Yale quarterback Patrick Witt, who allegedly turned down the prestigious Rhodes scholarship competition because he preferred to play in the football game against Harvard on the same day. The fact is the Rhodes committee heard he had been accused of sexual assault.

Then there is the sex scandal that killed college football coach Joe Paterno, an icon at Penn State.

The Boy Scouts of America, one of America's oldest youth organizations, disclosed more than 1,200 files on suspected sexual molesters in October 2012. Suspected abusers from all over the country are named in the files – many of them never reported to police or charged with a crime. Doctors, lawyers, politicians and policemen are among those named.

The one sex scandal that really surprised me as to how naïve *We the Apathetic Maids* are is the yoga sex scandals. Living in Asia for as long as I have, when yoga again became the rage in America in the 21st century, friends and people I would meet at various social functions would ask me if I was "into yoga?"

"Which aspect, the sex or the stretching exercises?" I provocatively ask. "I'm into the sex, but not the stretching and breathing exercises," is a common response, especially to an attractive lady.

Why are Americans so surprised that the wholesome image of yoga, like that of the Catholic Church, periodically takes a sex-scandal hit? The latest being John Friend, the guru of Anusara yoga, based in the U.S. and one of the world's fastest-growing styles. Arousal, sweating and heavy breathing with someone who turns one on leads to very predictable results. Sex.

In fact, yoga started as a sex cult, something yoga teachers don't tell *We the Apathetic Maids,* and we don't bother to find out. Hatha yoga – the parent of the styles now practiced around the globe – began as a branch of Tantra. In medieval India, Tantra devotees sought to fuse male and female aspects of the cosmos into a blissful state of consciousness.

The rites of Tantric cults, while often steeped in symbolism, could also include group and individual sex. One text advised devotees to revere the female sex organ and enjoy vigorous intercourse. Candidates for worship included actresses and prostitutes, as well as the sisters of practitioners.

As a writer who regularly checks out the best-seller lists, I was delighted but not surprised to see *Fifty Shades of Grey* go like the new non-NASA government funded rocket to the space station at the top of the list. It's a saucy, sexy, erotic sex book that tells it like it is. Shouldn't *We the Maids* demand that our politicians do the same?

Just like E.L. James' book is reinvigorating sexual relations, marriages and relationships, isn't it time *We the Apathetic Maids* did the same on the political front?

The word "sex" alone in any headline sells, and always has. Political sex scandals are not limited to America and China. They are a global sexual-political phenomenon. Italy's Prime Minister Silvio Berlusconi paid for sexual favors with prostitutes and underage girls; Israel's President Moshe Katsav was sentenced by an Arab Israeli judge to seven years in jail for sexual aggression without consent against women who worked for him; South Africa's polygamous President Jacob Zuma's second wife became pregnant by her bodyguard, who reportedly committed suicide in 2010; a butt-naked aroused former Czech Prime Minister Mirek Topolanek was caught standing next to a reclining woman in a red swimsuit at Berlusconi's villa, and Frances serial philandering leaders, President Francois Hollande being the latest.

Nothing really new in Berlusconi's behavior. All one has to do is look at Italian operas. Most seem to be set in whorehouses.

*The Beltway*
Members of Congress, movers and shakers, lobbyists, congressional staffers and sex-starved power lovers of all sexual persuasions mingle comfortably at the Capital Grille bar on Pennsylvania Avenue exchanging stories of the political and personal conquests they have amassed.

The news that Speaker-designate Bob Livingstone had several affairs while in office while pontificating about Clinton's collectible Lewinski cracked everyone up into hysterics at the bar during one of my Washington visits in 1999. "Can you believe this crap is happening?" Joshua Simons asked as we waited to be seated. "What did they think was going to happen once Larry Flynt offered a million dollars to anyone coming forward and proving a relationship with a politician?" Joshua continued. "Right on brother! Power to the People! I hope they bring out all the dirt on all those lying sons of bitches in Congress with their poked trophies," a slightly tipsy bar patron volunteered. "I can't wait to hear who some of those fat ugly morons been poking," he continued before he was asked to tone it down by a nearby congressman.

The Reverend Jessie Jackson was warmly greeted and congratulated by friends, associates and plain ol' strangers for counseling President Clinton during the impeachment hearings and his role in the release of prisoners from Syria, Cuba, Kuwait, Iraq and Yugoslavia. In 2001, Jackson admitted to an affair of his own with a staffer that produced a daughter.

I ran into some congressional staffers I hadn't seen in a few years at the Capital Grille bar. "How about getting together after dinner at one of the peeler bars on M street?" one of them volunteered. "Great idea," I responded. "I'll see you guys over at either the Gentlemens Club or Camelot around midnight," I said as Joshua and I were shown to our table.

"You know certain things never change in Washington," I pronounced as we sat down. "Here we are in D.C., home of the impeachment debate over whether the President lied about his sexual affair, a Speaker designate who resigned and acknowledged he's had several affairs, where the conservative religious right run the country and their Congressional staffers want to get together at some of the best strip joints in the world where you can drink and look at gorgeous naked beauties while debating the merits of the stupidity on the hill. I love this town," I said, as I hoisted my glass to toast the hypocrisy of D.C.

Sitting at the gentleman's club bar admiring a nude blonde, the thought occurred to me that here is an establishment full of guys, very few of whom have come with dates, while sex-starved women all over D.C. were bar hopping all over town searching in vain. "You know," I said to Joshua, "The best pickup joints in D.C. where women should be going in this politically incorrect town are strip joints like this. Hell, everyone gets turned on and is looking for action!"

"You know, you have a point. But what do you expect? This town doesn't seem to be doing anything right lately," Joshua replied as we both laughed and downed our drinks.

Joe DiMaggio hung out at bars and lounges. He was a lonely, persistent hero who changed the game of baseball. How many more lonely known and unknown heroes like DiMaggio are there out there in bars and strip joints that can change the New World Disorder I wonder?

### Wanker Bankers

And let's not forget the sex scandals of the bankers who, while they were screwing up the world's financial system, also screwed their brains out with elicit affairs. Fred Goodwin, former head of the Royal Bank of Scotland, had an affair while he led his bank to financial collapse during the 2008 Great Recession and had to be bailed out by British taxpayers. He was not alone.

The mother of all serial sexual predators and rapist of *We the Maids* – and chamber maids – is Dominique Strauss-Kahn, former managing director of the IMF and front-runner in the 2012 French presidential election. He not only screwed every woman he could, but the world financial system and France's tolerance of the sexual adventures of its political elite, as I have repeatedly pointed out in earlier books. Not unusual really. Many fellow business travelers I have been with over the years expect sex along with their room service – a fact that a *Newsweek* poll confirmed in the wake of the DSK scandal.

What was even more mind-boggling, not to mention sexually frustrating, was the fact that DSK could not only order hookers to join him and his friends for an orgy anywhere in the world, but that he may have had a piece of the action outside the bedroom. Hearing him ask in his defense how one call tell if naked girls are prostitutes or not, I thought, no wonder the world is in the dire financial mess it's in. If a guy can't tell the difference in the women he's with, how the hell is he going to manage all those global currencies – not to mention economies – and their interlocal consequences.

DSK's successor at the IMF, Christine Lagarde, France's former finance minister, was subjected to "a judicial inquiry" into charges of embezzlement of public funds and complicity in falsifying documents within weeks of her appointment, a case punishable by up to 10 years in prison and a fine of 150,000 euros. Lagarde was accused of exceeding her authority after sending a legal battle between a French tycoon and a state-owned bank to private arbitration that resulted in the tycoon, a supporter of Lagarde's then boss, President Nicolas Sarkozy, being awarded about 400 million euros. And this person who allegedly embezzled France's public money was put in charge of the IMF?

Speaking of maids, let's not forget "The Inseminator," Arnold Schwarzenegger and his love child with his housekeeper – like Karl Marx -- and John Edwards knocking up a campaign volunteer while campaigning for president.

Then there are the nude maids of the Fantasy Maid Service of Lubbock, West Texas, were denied a permit because they didn't meet the city requirements of being an entertainment establishment. What happened to good old American capitalist, free market entrepreneurialism that allows *We the Maids* to make a buck sweeping out and cleaning up America and sweeping in what America needs most?

A federal grand jury indicted Edwards on six counts of violating campaign finance laws, lying to the government and conspiring to protect his candidacy by breaking the law. At trial, the jury could not agree, so a mistrial was declared.

I've met both of these out-of-wedlock dads and frankly was not surprised when I heard about their dalliances. I met Schwarzenegger on several occasions in the mid-1980s when he used to dine at Scratch, my first wife's restaurant, which was across the street from his office in Venice, California. He was always flirtatious, not only with the wait staff, but with any attractive nearby female diners.

I met Edwards briefly in New York in 2004 while he was being screened by the Gore team for the vice presidential spot on the Democratic ticket. I had just returned from dinner with an old friend, Democratic Party activist and fundraiser Cindy Strom. I had met Cindy during the 1976 presidential campaign when we both worked on Senator "Scoop" Jackson's campaign. Cindy was staying at the Regency Hotel where we went after dinner for a nightcap. Edwards was staying there as well. He and Cindy knew each other from Democratic circles. Cindy introduced us and we spent some time chatting about the unfolding campaign and issues. I decided to excuse myself as I found him to be a total phony and offensive.

"He's a sleazeball," I whispered in Cindy's ear as I kissed her goodnight and bid the senator farewell.

Reminiscing about that evening after we caught up again in January 2013, Cynthia, as Cindy now likes to be called, let out a sigh of disgust as she told me Edwards took her to the booth where his videographer and mother of his future child was sitting.

Cynthia was an Obama volunteer in his 2008 presidential run, and was appointed U.S. ambassador to Luxemburg.

My kind of guy – and I'm sure most guys and probably many women will agree – is German playboy Rolf Eden, the more than 80-year-old self-anointed playboy in swinging, cold war West Berlin. He pressed age-discrimination charges against a 19-year-old woman who refused to have sex with him when he was 77 years old.

"She said, 'You're too old for me.' "

"I did it for equal rights," said Eden, who later dropped the charges. He has seven children by seven different women, as well as five grandchildren and one great-grandchild.

Career politicians think, because of *We the Maids'* apathy, that they can just help themselves to the help – and that includes all of us – *We the People*.

The Muslims have a solution to keep men from having extramarital affairs – The Obedient Wives Club. It has branches in Malaysia and Jordan and is expanding into other Muslim countries. It teaches brides how to keep their husbands happy in bed by claiming that women are to blame for domestic violence and spousal infidelity. The key to becoming a good wife, according to the club, is simple: obey your husband. Have dinner waiting for him when he gets home; make sure the children are tucked in bed; dress in sexy clothes; smell nice, and be ready to meet his every sexual need.

"The wife should entertain the husband more than the first-class prostitute," says Fauziah Ariffin, president of the club.

The club claims that if wives would only be more sexually obliging, the world would be free of "social ills." Now, considering that a Muslim can legally marry up to four women, it sounds like the club has one-up on all the university classes teaching the benefits of orgies. I know a lot of guys who would say "Right on!" I'm not one of them, however, as I believe this is a primitive approach that is offensive not only to women, but to most men.

We now know that porn delivers rewards to the male brain in the form of a short-term dopamine boost, which, for an hour or two afterwards, lifts men's mood and makes them feel good in general. The neural circuitry is identical to that for other addictive triggers, such as gambling or cocaine.

Every country I can think of has politicians and religious leaders who enjoy sex regardless of what laws they wrote or are on the books that dictate morality. They break them because of their addiction to power and the sex that comes with it. *We the Maids* want, and are entitled to, law and order, good education, government services, including health care, and an enjoyable job – or not. What business or right do political and religious leaders have to legislate and dictate sexual behavior between two consenting adults? None, especially when the violators of the law are those very leaders who preach the morality they themselves do not practice.

The career politicians, Catholic priests, Evangelical preachers who can't resist sexual temptations, even at the risk of losing everything – families, constituents and followers – are living examples and the best reasons for barring both politicians and religious leaders from making any laws governing morality.

I found ridiculously amusing a $1.8 million study commissioned by Roman Catholic bishops that concluded by blaming Woodstock and the sexual freedoms of the flower children of the '60s for the inexcusable sexual abuses and pedophile behavior of its priests. God forbid it should be the celibate culture of the church or the fact that many of its priests are gay.

What was even more surprising was the blistering criticism the Vatican's orthodoxy office hurled at Sister Margaret Farley, a member of the Sisters of Mercy religious order and emeritus professor of Christian ethics at Yale Divinity School because of her book *Just Love: A Framework for Christian Sexual Ethics,* because it contradicts church teachings on such issues as masturbation, homosexuality and marriage as "defective understanding of Catholic theology."

Farley has received 11 honorary degrees over her lifetime, is a past president of the Society of Christian Ethics and the Catholic Theological Society of America, and won an award in 2008 for *Just Love.*

The '60s live in other ways too. The new establishment 21$^{st}$-century Rolls-Royce is inspired in design by the Silver Cloud and Silver Shadow models of the '60s. The term "globalization" is also an invention of the '60s. It first appeared in 1962. My personal favorite is a tiny '60s symbol making a comeback – the mini, not the car – the miniskirt. I don't want to sound sexist, because I don't believe I am – I'm just a guy who enjoys looking at beautiful women.

I am very conscious and aware of the women's movement of 1968, and the 100 women who protested at the 1968 Miss America Pageant on the boardwalk in Atlantic City that year.

I actually laughed at the fact that some of them were arrested for spraying a pageant sponsor's "noxious liquid," Toni hair spray. They dumped symbols of female oppression – girdles, bras, stilettos and steno pads – into a "freedom trash can" that ignited the women's liberation movement. It was the kind of protest the Founding Fathers would endorse and support.

The lily-white Miss America who spent her time hustling sponsors' products and entertaining troops in Vietnam made her the perfect symbol of racism, capitalism and militarism, according to Robin Morgan, an activist and fellow writer, who gets credit for taking the women's liberation movement mainstream as a result of that boardwalk protest, in which she played a leading role.

The rival Miss USA pageant, which started in Long Beach, California in 1952, took a profound multicultural turn in 2010 when 24-year-old Rima Fakih, an Arab-American immigrant from Lebanon, won the crown, the first Arab-American Muslim to do so. She attended Catholic school and celebrates both Muslim and Christian faiths at home in Dearborn, Michigan. She strutted her stuff in an orange-and-gold bikini and a strapless white gown that looked like a wedding dress. She said she thought health insurance should cover birth-control pills.

First runner-up Morgan Woolard of Oklahoma declared that she's "a huge believer in states' rights. I think that's what so wonderful about America."

Olivia Culpo, who arrived in Las Vegas as Miss Rhode Island and left as Miss USA, by saying it would be fair if a transgendered contestant won the pageant over a natural-born woman, is the latest installment of not only how far the pageant has come – but America's.

These beauties represent the new liberated American woman – an outgrowth of the '60s revolution. I'm sure there are still people who would like to see these pageants banned, but is it not a way that smart young women like Fakih and Woolard can get the Founding Fathers' message out to the ignorant, apathetic males enjoying all of the eye candy?

Helen Gurley Brown's *Sex and the Single Girl,* an advice book published in 1962, became a bestseller that shocked America with its candid encouragement to take pleasure in orgasms, affairs with married men and financial independence.

Taking over as editor of *Cosmopolitan* in 1965, she turned it into the women's sex bible, splashing voluptuous models on the cover along with tantalizing lines written by her husband.

Meantime, an estimated 100,000 to 300,000 American-born children are sold into sex each year, with Asian-American girls the most valuable. Their abusers are often the pimps – sometimes even relatives – who recruit or kidnap the girls from the streets and market them over the Internet where they are featured in pulsating ads for massage parlors, escort services, strip clubs, even acupuncturists.

The Polaris Project, a national advocacy group, says a stable of four girls can bring in $60,000 a year – tax free! Now drug dealers are moving in on the exploding sex trade, lured by the profits and fewer risks. Besides, there is a finite supply of drugs, whereas a girl is reusable.

Dr. Kimberly Chang at Asian Health Services in Oakland, California, is in the vanguard of a new public health effort to treat girls lured into the sex trade as victims of abuse, and not criminals. The emphasis is on intervention and counseling. The effort is based on the idea that doctors, as first responders, can intervene and possibly prevent years of exploitation and abuse from taking an even heavier toll.

Of course, the sex trade is not limited to America. In China, officials often seize babies born in violation of the one-child policy and send them to welfare centers, where they are often sold.

India probably has more modern slaves than any country in the world. It has millions of women and girls in its brothels, often held captive for the first few years until they grow resigned to their fate.

UNICEF estimated in 2011 that 1.8 million children enter the worldwide sex trade each year.

Sex sells and always has. I can't imagine what Google's sex app that lets lovers switch views and replay sessions will do. The sexual revolution of the '60s is making a comeback because it mirrors our times. Is it any wonder that recent television dramas *The Playboy Club, Pan Am* and *Mad Men* that glamorize the sexy '60s have made it into mainstream?

### Today's 1968 Protests

The ghosts and spirit of the protests of the '60s are definitely smoldering in America again. If anyone doubts it, look at the news footage of what happened in Cincinnati, Ohio where protests turned to riots that were followed by a boycott of the city hotels, restaurants and entertainment venues in protest of the city's ongoing racist policies. The worst since the assassination of the Rev. Martin Luther King Jr. in 1968. That night, as news of King's assassination became known in the black ghettos, there were riots in 110 burning cities, causing 39 deaths and injuring 2,500. Those fires are still burning today, metaphorically.

I remember 1968 well. I was a witness and participant to the political turmoil unfolding. On June 4th of that year, the day of the California presidential primary, I was a student in Los Angeles studying for an exam on Government and Politics of the Middle East the next day. I was listening to music on the radio awaiting the results of the primary election results. Senator Robert Kennedy, who was running for the Democratic Party presidential nomination, had made a campaign speech at California State University Northridge, where I was a student, a few weeks earlier. I attended his speech and remember being a few rows from the stage on the lawn as a political science student and photographer taking pictures for my photo agency in New York. I was blown away by RFK's remarks about civil rights, poverty, injustice and opposition to the war in Vietnam and what America and its founding principles represented to the world.

I was delighted when I heard that Kennedy had won the California primary, But delight turned to shock minutes later when news came that he had been shot and mortally wounded by a Jordanian-born Palestinian.

That day – June 4, 1968 – changed the political dynamics and landscape in America, as it would in China 21 years later in Tiananmen Square. I had been in Beijing just a few days before the 1989 tragedy. Karma, coincidence, synchronicity? It's a topic I discuss in *Custom Maid Spin?*

In August 1968, I moved to Chicago to attend law school and continue to work as a freelance photographer. The Democratic Party convention in Chicago that month was another karma moment for a photographer-political science student about to start law school – and a topic I discussed ad nauseum with protesters and the police officers who clobbered them.

Many of the protesters and a couple of cops were fellow first-year law classmates at John Marshall Law School. I am still in touch with some of these students and we reminisce about those turbulent days.

I caught up with Bruce Krell, a first-year law school classmate from Chicago, in St. Helena, California, in 2008. I had lost touch with Bruce when I moved to Hong Kong in the late '80s. I knew he had a practice in San Francisco, where he lived with his wife Pam and two daughters.

"Goddamn, it's been a long time. How the hell are you?" I asked as we hugged and laughed after I made the windy drive up to his beautiful mountaintop home in the wine country. "Nice place you guys have here," I said as Pam greeted me with a hug and a kiss.

After catching up on the 20-odd years since we had last seen each other over a delightful home-cooked meal and generous pourings of local reds, we started reminiscing about law school in Chicago in 1968 and some of our more memorable classmates.

"Remember Tom the cop who clobbered heads at the Democratic Convention? He always came in a suit and tie and thought you were a long- haired hippie and called you that on more than one occasion after you would debate an issue or argue a point in contracts?" Bruce asked as we sat on his porch overlooking the Napa Valley and sharing a nice California cabernet.

"Yeah, I sure do. Whatever happened to him?" I asked. "Those were great political times of phenomenal change that we really didn't appreciate or realize at the time," I said as we swapped updates on our families and former classmates.

"Tom Hoffman now sits on the Illinois Appellate Court," Bruce replied. "Remember 'Philadelphia Cream Cheese?' You gave him that nickname and it's stuck to this day," Bruce said.

"Sure. How can anyone forget Lenny? He was so Philadelphia," I responded. Lenny Lundy was one of our study group and a great guy. He still lives in Philadelphia and runs a successful litigation firm. I caught up with Lenny a couple of months later in New Jersey – and since in Philadelphia.

"Those were amazing times" said Lenny, a Tea Party supporter, as we reminisced about our life experiences, U.S. politics and what is still wrong with America. Always good to catch up with old friends and fellow students with whom one has shared such vivid experiences.

Jack McGrath is another one. Jack was a fellow student at Cal State Northridge and organized the Robert Kennedy primary speech there. I caught up with Jack a few years later when we worked together on different political campaigns in California.

These former fellow baby boomer students who today are lawyers, judges, politicians and corporate citizens can and should reunite with all our fellow boomers to re-create the spirit of 1968 in America and the world and bring about the long overdue revolutionary change that we promised ourselves we would.

We were accidental rebels in 1968 who got caught up in the university and street protests of the time because we believed in civil rights and opposed the Vietnam War– but believed more in our education for future job security.

The protesters of 1968 were branded by many as a bunch of liberal hippies run amok. The word "liberal" carried a special meaning. Discussions and debates began and revolved around John Stuart Mill's still controversial 1859 essay *On Liberty*. It states that "the sole end for which mankind are warranted, individually or collectively, in interfering with the liberty of action of any of their number, is self-protection," that is to "prevent harm to others. His own good, either physical or moral, is not a sufficient warrant."

We didn't accept our parents' generational selfishness or justification for doing things without giving thought to the consequences of their acts on others or the environment. Their apathetic response to our calls for change were infuriating and the anger swelled until it exploded in 1970 when

President Nixon announced the invasion of Cambodia. The campuses exploded. When National Guardsmen shot and killed four unarmed students at Kent State in Ohio, virtually the entire system of higher education shuddered and stopped. Students who had never picked up a rock in their lives took over classrooms, colleges and universities across America and went on strike. The UC Hastings Law School I was attending in San Franciso, like most UC campuses across California, was strikebound.

Students took to the streets of San Francisco to protest the invasion and the continuing Vietnam War. Talk about a generation gap. A Gallup Poll at the time asked if there was a generation gap and 74 percent of the young respondents of the era thought there definitely was. Interestingly enough, today's millennials don't feel the same. They respect their elders, those same rebels of the '60s, because our moral values were generally superior to their own. As a result they are not as rebellious – at least yet.

Today's Americans are better educated, more diverse, more optimistic and less likely to have a job than previous generations. Let's see how long they have to be unemployed or underemployed before they take to the streets like their parents did.

1968 was not only a year that changed America, it was also a year that changed politics in Europe. France was, and continues to be, in the forefront of those troubled times. In May 1968, French students demanding a better future ripped up the cobblestones in the Left Bank of Paris to build barricades and, in the process, exposed the sand foundation that lay underneath – another metaphor for how soft and fragile the rock-solid political facade is. Their slogans of the day, "It is forbidden to forbid" and "Beneath the cobblestones, the beach!" are as relevant today as they were then. The reigning sentiment then, like today, was simple: strip away the edifices of established disorder. Get to a better – and above all, a fairer – future. Thousands were arrested and injured, but not a single person was killed. The ideal model of peaceful, vocal dissent advocated by America's Founding Fathers.

In Czechoslovakia, now broken into two countries, the "Prague Spring" that began in March 1968, tried to rip down the Iron Curtain – until Moscow sent troops and tanks to brutally crush the uprising, much like the Chinese government did in Tianamen in June 1989. Just like the USSR collapsed in the wake of its brutal response, so will the Chinese Communist Party and China as we know it today.

Today's demonstrations at meetings of global leaders in Prague, Gothenburg, Genoa and Quebec at the summit of American leaders discussing the American Free Trade Zone Agreement, not to mention the World Economic Forum in Davos, harken back to the protests of the '60s – protests that objected to injustice.

### Rule of Law & Injustice
Starting law school in Chicago in the wake of the chaos at the Democratic national convention, in the shadow of the Federal Building housing the court that was trying the "Chicago Seven" charged with inciting the protests and rioting, was a unique way to be introduced to the American system of jurisprudence and its many injustices. The parallels and comparisons to what happened in Chicago with the Boston Tea Party, the War of Independence, the Bill of Rights, freedom of expression, with the debates and protests about the Vietnam War, civil rights and women's rights dominating class discussions with every point of view being vocally shared by fellow students was a valuable and revealing first-hand introduction and experience in American democracy, the rule of law and its many faults.

Continuing my studies in San Francisco during the Berkeley free speech era and anti-Vietnam War protests was another extracurricular course on democracy in action, freedom of speech and the rule of law in real time.

The schism between the law as written and practiced, with all the accusations and arguments of racism, corporate dominance by the male "establishment"– cspccially when the subject of who can legally declare war came up – were openly debated and in many cases encouraged by some professors, who were also questioning the meaning and definitions of the law they were teaching and its effect on justice. These are subjects I still debate and question today.

I've experienced first-hand as a lawyer how money and politics can influence and corrupt the judicial process. Getting elected officials and judges to change a law is in many cases just a question of "effective" political persuasion – money for their next re-election campaign – or in the case of judges who do not need to run for re-election, the promise of an appointment to a higher court.

This is true not only in America, but everywhere there are elected officials and judges who seek career advancement. That includes Hong Kong where, like America, the rule of law is one of the three pillars of checks and balances that are supposed to be sacrosanct. Many today argue that was true until the British handover in 1997, when corrupt mainland practices started permeating the judicial process. This was laid bare for the public to see when the niece of a High Court judge had her wrist slapped and was fined after her third arrest for drunk driving and smacking a police officer when asked to take a breathalyzer test.

Other mortals would have been sent to jail for a good long time and heavily fined. People were outraged and took to the streets in protest.

Justice Kemal Bokhary, a retiring judge of the top court in Hong Kong and uncle of the slapper, warned in October 2012 that "a storm of unprecedented ferocity is gathering against the rule of law in Hong Kong."

An ongoing wave of retirements gives Beijing a chance to influence the top courts.

I have personally experienced the abusive long arm of the law in America and the corrupting influence on a judge in Hong Kong. In California, Santa Monica to be exact, where my former wife Gail ran a very hip restaurant and bar, police were called out periodically because of complaints from neighbors that the bar was open after 2 a.m., the mandatory closing time. The fact is that on occasion, after closing time, some of the restaurant investors, staff and regular patrons would stick around until dawn, and sometimes get rowdy. The fact is that during those times the restaurant was closed to the public, cash registers had been emptied and we were just

293

hanging out debating the issues of the day in the mid-1980s.

On one of those occasions, as I walked a friend out to the restaurant parking lot, I was approached by a policeman who wanted to see my driver's license and wanted me to submit to a breathalizer test after I volunteered that I owned the grey Mercedes in the lot he had inquired about. I was accused of driving my car at excessive speed and erratically a few minutes earlier on Main Street and running into the restaurant to avoid the officer. The fact that I had been in the restaurant all night and asked the officer to touch the hood of the car to see that it was stone-cold and witnesses supported my story meant nothing. I was charged with driving under the influence of alcohol and hauled off to jail where I spent the rest of the pre-dawn.

In Hong Kong, where I got a divorce from my mainland Chinese wife who stole my money, business and child and fled to China with the help of an American lawyer – it was a grand slam fuck. Bases loaded. Mother of my child, wife and partner. How do I make sure I don't strike out?

The facts were simple. Julia, my ex, on the advice of her American lawyer, Oliver Silsby, who at the time was not licensed to practice anywhere in the world, including Hong Kong, had conspired and helped my ex take the corporate records from our legal firm, rewrote the minutes and resolutions, allowing her to clean out our bank accounts while I was away on a business trip.

I was a duly licensed lawyer. I had bankers and lawyers as witnesses testify under oath that I was a principal in the company and that I had been ripped off by Silsby and the ex.

The judge in our divorce case even wrote an opinion saying that the letters drafted by Silsby "taken in sequence are a clear indication that the plan was to have the [plaintiff] distanced and then removed entirely from [the Company].... I mention as an aside this demonstrates appalling professional misconduct on [Silsby's] part."

The judge hearing my conspiracy case against my ex and her lawyer, notwithstanding this overwhelming evidence in my favor, ruled against me on the grounds that I was "dishonest, evasive, untruthful and unreliable" and Silsby, who broke the law by practicing without a license, was an "honest, credible and reliable witness whose evidence I believe and accept."

Not only did Silsby lie under oath in Hong Kong, but in Shanghai, where he filed a suit against my ex-partner-wife and me for unpaid legal fees owed by the company that in the conspiracy case he claimed I had no interest in. Not only did he lie about that, but said he didn't know where to serve me, even though we were in litigation in Hong Kong where he declared me bankrupt, so I didn't know about the Shanghai case until the appeal time lapsed and someone mailed me an anonymous package with the entire case and judgment.

Many members of the Hong Kong legal fraternity, in addition to my solicitor and barrister, were shocked at the ruling and shared their dismay with me at the Main Bar of the Foreign Correspondents Club. "He's a lazy bugger" was a common comment and "He probably didn't bother to really understand the facts" was another.

"Hey, remember, it was Fok's last case before going onto the bench, so maybe the judge didn't want to upset an incoming judge," said one prominent barrister. Joseph Fok was the barrister for Silsby and was arguing his last case before joining the bench.

"Maybe your ex and her lawyer got to him? The rule of law is not what it used to be pre-Handover," was the most credible comment.

Great, I thought to myself, "I'm a man with a past with a woman with a future," as I trudged out of the FCC bar with Pauline, my current partner. The rule of law, indeed, is not what it used to be in Hong Kong.

Bribing judges on the Mainland is the way justice is routinely meted out. It's "more profitable than drug dealing," wrote Mimi Law in one of her Pearl Briefing columns.

To make matters worse on the business front, my fellow shareholders and directors in Pets Central Asia Inc., got into a dispute with a former director and shareholder, who was denying he was a shareholder, even though he signed the corporate resolution issuing him his 11 percent shares in the company, was registered as such in the corporate register of members and the appropriate regulatory body in the British Virgin Islands, where the company was registered, signed various e-mails insisting he was "definitely" a shareholder, was invited to shareholder meetings and even signed a notice approving a shareholder meeting on short notice, but then decided to sue us for not being a shareholder. Why? Loss of face, a very Chinese concept that judges have not come to grips with.

He received his shareholding in the company in exchange for rent on a mutually agreed barter basis, with the understanding that we would merge our companies if the company financial statements he represented were accurate to enable both of us to take our merged company public sooner. The proposed merger agreement was subject to a financial due diligence that proved his representations were not only exaggerated, but false. Meanwhile, he had advised the world that he was going to merge with Pets Central, so when that did not materialize, he lost face and decided to sue and engage in a lot of other illegal intimidation and harassment activities.

Once the case was ready for trial, because of the shortage of judges in Hong Kong and the delay in appointing judges in the British pre-handover tradition to ensure a continued smooth running of the rule of law in Hong Kong, retired ex-judges who had been sent out to pasture in Britain were brought back to fill in the gaping judicial holes.

My judicial streak of bad Hong Kong luck with an incompetent judge just kept on rolling down the hall of injustice. Retired judge Conrad Seagrott, a known personal injury lawyer, and judge who traditionally rules pro-plaintiff and in whose best known white collar crime case was asked to be removed by the defendants because of his prejudicial comments – and refused – is the clueless business-corporate law, senile, dogmatic, prejudiced anti-American lawyer judge we got assigned to our case.

His mind was clearly made up before he even got to the bench on the opening day of the trial, before he had heard one witness or saw one bit of evidence. His rude and nonjudicial behavior prompted me to ask our barrister and solicitor to request that he be removed and replaced.

"If this was a case in the U.S., I would demand the mofo be recused for obviously and clearly being biased before hearing one iota of evidence," I told my instructing solicitor.

That is not something they did in Hong Kong under the former British colonial system. The judges and barristers still wear horsetail wigs – and some of the judges act like the horses' asses. Nevertheless, judges are referred to as "My Lord" and the barristers refer to each other as "My learned friend."

While they are all chummy and civil, justice is sidelined by a judge who has clearly made up his mind but no one dares offend because they are all so civilized. Give me American uncivilized justice any day where lawyers can object to each other's leading or inappropriate questions instead of being so polite and non-adversarial.

The judge vocally expressed his opinion and judgment at the beginning of the trial, even before the opening argument of the plaintiff – and throughout the trial. His rude questioning of our barrister, my partner and myself contrasted with the kind leading questions he directed at the opposition was "appalling," to quote a few of the other company shareholders and friends who attended the trial.

"I can't believe his rude attitude and challenging follow-up questions to Peter," Julie Wicks a former director and shareholder of the company, said to Pauline Taylor, the company group managing director after witnessing one of the morning sessions of the 14-day trial.

"He is an arrogant pompous pom who has definitely made up his mind," said Graeme Scott, another shareholder, an Air New Zealand pilot who happened to be in town when I was being examined in the witness box.

"How can he be allowed to get away with his obvious prejudicial predetermined opinion?" Graeme asked me after I finished testifying and joined him for lunch before he had to go fly his jumbo jet back to New Zealand. "He really doesn't like you and sounds like he has made up his mind. That is pretty obvious."

"Welcome to the new Hong Kong rule of law where sclerotic, incompetent retired morons who know nothing about business or corporate law are asked to pass judgment in a business dispute in one of the most capitalistic societies on earth," I said in a very deliberate restrained way without resorting to the "F" word.

To make matters worse, when the judge asked my barrister for legal arguments as to why the plaintiff was a shareholder on the final day of trial, he was surprised they were submitted in writing and clearly stated all the precedent case law that confirmed the plaintiff was a shareholder in the eyes of the law because he had been registered as such and had no business suing us. The judge disregarded the fact that the plaintiff always was – and still was during trial – a registered shareholder and stuck to his original opinion on the opening day of the trial.

So here I was in Hong Kong, forced into personal and a business bankruptcy because of judges who play God and disregard the rule of law. I have observed this as a lawyer, party and witness to numerous legal proceedings, not only in Hong Kong, but in America. As a result, I have told clients going to trial over the years, "I have seen sure winners lose and sure losers win."

I had already made contingency plans as I prepared for the worst while hoping for the best. Judges are human and some do bring their personal biases and prejudices to the bench. Such judges must be removed by *We the Maids* – they have no right dispensing objective justice.

Personally, I am doing fine, as is our business. Bankruptcy today is not what it used to be. It was a way of doing business in the old world order.

The judicial extremes in China and Hong Kong – and what has happened in Hong Kong since the Handover – are no different than the political extremes between the two parts of China and the political extremes between the developed and undeveloped world and their respective annual gatherings.

*Political Extremes*

The first World Social Forum held in Porto Alegre Brazil at the dawning of the 21st century to offer an alternative global social model to the Anglo-Saxon model of globalization, which was simultaneously being fine-tuned by the World Economic Forum in Davos, was a logical extension of the earlier protests challenging the establishment economic models. The global political agenda can no longer be dictated by capitalists alone. They have proven themselves to be short sighted, self-serving incompetents.

The World Economic Forum was founded in 1971 by Klaus Schwab, a professor of business policy at the University of Geneva, in the little-known town of Davos, to discuss the international marketplace. Like the G-8, it has gotten to be an expensive relic of the old world order.

The 2003 World Economic Forum in Davos opened with dire forecasts about the economic impact of a war on Iraq. A warning that was ignored by America. Listening to Brazil's leftist President Luiz Inacio Lula da Silva, who would have been more at home at the World Social Forum held in his country's Porto Alegre, address the capitalists was heartwarming and an encouraging first step of the new millennium.

While Davos drew the chief executives of the corporate world who sleep in four-star hotels and take turns on the Swiss ski slopes, the participants in the World Social Forum are happy to camp on the sides of roads or sleep in the homes of locals in order to take part in the yearly anti-capitalist gathering. Instead of suits, many arrive wearing tie-dyed shirts and cotton pants.

Today the conference draws some 30,000 participants from 123 countries. In the early years, the forum held teleconferences with members of the Davos conference in an attempt to exchange ideas.

Globalization has hit the developing world the hardest – and Africa, the poorest continent, worst of all. Africa, home to 10 percent of the world's population, accounts for less than 1.5 percent of global trade and has been completely bypassed by globalization. In the 1950s, Africa's share of world trade was around 7 percent. Granted, endemic corruption, political instability and bad governance are major contributing factors.

As a result, the sixth World Social Forum, a gathering of non-government organizations, fair trade advocates and critics of the world trade system, was held in Africa in 2006. The African talk-fest, like all World Social Forum gatherings, was modest by comparison to the well-heeled Davos gab-fests; it addressed the solutions needed to change the inequalities in the global trading system, but failed to come up with any solutions acceptable to the government leaders and their capitalist backers in Davos.

The solution is that socialists have to take matters into their own hands through revolutionary means, as they have in Latin America. Fidel Castro and Hugo Chavez were in the forefront of the socialist revolution that is also now taking root in Africa. The socialist movement went into high gear with the election of Chavez in Venezuela in 1998. It spread to Ecuador, Bolivia, Paraguay, Argentina and Brazil. The "Bolivarian Revolution," named for Simon Bolivar, who liberated a large part of Latin America from Spanish colonial rule in the 19th century, is now directed against America and its corporate capitalists that have exploited the continent for more than a century.

Eliminating farm subsidies, which total billions of dollars a year, is a major demand of developing nations. Their primary objective is to get an agreement signed between developed nations, namely the U.S., Japan and European countries, to eliminate trade-distorting export subsidies to farmers. This would give developing nations more flexibility in opening their markets to foreign competition and give exporters in the world's poorest countries duty-free access to wealthy markets that would raise their standard of living dramatically.

The people's trust in governments, companies, and above all banks, has broken down and is being challenged, a political reality that was acknowledged by the humbled politicians and fat cats who gathered in Davos in 2010 – and every year since.

Davos congregants are asking "Is 20th-century capitalism failing 21st-century society?" in its panel discussions. Of course it is! Capitalism, like any great machine, has to be periodically fine-tuned and recalibrated.

The capitalist and socialist extremes seem to have called a temporary truce and merged after 9/11. The relatively peaceful World Economic Forum held in New York City instead of Davos after September 11 was a reminder that people with different points of view, no matter how extreme, can live in peace with honest, timely, constructive dialogue. Capitalists, their financiers and labor can constructively and respectfully communicate their concerns and ideas while uniting collectively in the war on terror and fighting unemployment and poverty.

War, unemployment and poverty, like capitalism, socialism, communism and globalization, are man-made political, economic human disasters with different points of view, political factions and sides. Nevertheless, mutually acceptable compromises can be found because globalization and information technology have made it easier for people of all points of view to transcend traditional ill-conceived differences that are totally irrelevant today.

A close examination of one of the bedrocks of U.S. foreign policy casts some light on two of the main causes of the millennium protests – wars and subsidized trade barriers. The policy rationale behind trade barriers was articulated with brutal candor more than half a century ago by U.S. State Department official George Kennan: "We have 50 percent of the world's wealth but only 6.3 percent of its population. In this situation, our real job in the coming period ... is to maintain this position of disparity. To do so, we have to dispense with all sentimentality ... we should cease thinking about human rights, the raising of living standards and democratization."

This policy was subtly reaffirmed in the '60s. "World peace ... does not require that each man love his neighbor – it requires only that they live together with mutual tolerance," President John F. Kennedy reminded America after the 1963 Cuban missile crisis.

Slavoj Zizek, philosopher and psychoanalyst at the University of Ljubljan in Slovenia, reminds us that "On September 11, the U.S. was given a unique opportunity to realize what kind of world it was part of. It might have used this opportunity, but it did not. Instead, it opted to reassert its traditional ideological commitments. Out with the responsibility and guilt feelings towards the impoverished Third World; we are the victims now!"

*Missed Opportunity*

The peaceful New York soire of the World Economic Forum was a missed opportunity to bring the political extremes together. The post 9/11 get together was the beginning of the end of Wall Street's global capitalist binge. The handwriting was on the rubble of the remains of the World Trade Center towers at Ground Zero. The beginning of the end of the modern capitalist gilded age that would implode like the towers as America embarked on a self-destructive war economy on two fronts, in Afghanistan and Iraq, financed by an even more explosive double-edged mechanism – hedge funds and securitized subprime loans.

The follow-up capitalist gab-fests at the World Economic Forum, World Trade Organization, G-8, G-20, APEC and numerous other boring alphabet soup kitchens, in exotic locations and settings, were just more empty-suit capitalist malarky at taxpayer expense, repeating their earlier unfulfilled promises to eliminate trade barriers and farm subsidies, reduce deficits, impose stricter regulatory controls on banks and their regulators. Taxpayers not only picked up the tab for the events themselves, but the multi-million dollar security arrangements for a bunch of fat cats in denial that they had anything to do with the Great Recession – who wanted to be compensated for their miscalculated multi-trillion dollar losses – and they were – by *We the Apathetic Maids*. Is it any wonder they are repeatedly greeted by protests and "EAT THE BANKERS" placards whenever they get together anywhere in the world? That really hurts! Why aren't they asked to pay for their misdeeds instead of us?

The monied bullies believe they are invincible and can continue to bulldoze their failures onto the tax rolls of the undereducated, ignorant wage-earning masses, not realizing their mantra of trade has been replaced with the mantra of revolution. The door on the era of unbridled capitalism has ended. It has morphed toward stronger government oversight of economics, albeit not strong enough, violent protests and revolution, with workers justifiably demanding their fair share and students objecting to being saddled with the payments.

"For too long, rich countries saw us as peripheral, problematic, even dangerous," said Lula, Brazil's former first working-class president and an icon of the downtrodden, at the 2011 World Social Forum in Dakar, Senegal. "Today we are an essential undeniable part of the solution to the biggest crisis of the last decade – a crisis that was not created by us, but that emerged from the great centers of world capitalism."

The explosive high food prices, unemployment, inflation and cheap information that fueled the Jasmine-Nile revolutions in Tunisia and Egypt had clearly not registered as a sign of the times and things to come among the capitalist delegates at Davos in January 2011. That is because the global economy is managed by people who believe in the magic of monetary stimulus that inflates assets and boosts demand temporarily. The people who manipulate this money game have become fabulously rich and get together in Davos every year to celebrate the success of their brand of capitalism, disregarding and disrespecting the fact that most people in the world live hand to mouth.

Financial institutions played the wrong hand in 2008, but the crisis that ensued didn't convince this ruling class of the error of their ways.

"They poured money into bailing out the institutions, and the bailed-out billionaires gathered again this year in Davos to celebrate the survival of the system," wrote Andy Xie, an independent economist.

The gathering was inconvenienced by Cairo's revolution. The capitalists in Davos were annoyed by the limelight being diverted elsewhere, not realizing that the glitz in Davos and the revolution in Cairo are linked. It didn't register with them that they were the cause of the explosion – inflation. Every inflationary bubble eventually bursts, some worse than others.

Career politicians and their policymakers know this, but their hope is to defer the resulting economic explosion to a future date, after they are dead or no longer in office, and *We the Apathetic Maids,* our children and grandchildren, who are being handed the tab, be damned. The Bush-Obama handover was the mother of all handovers.

While the fat cats in Davos were feasting and skiing, 40 percent of Egyptians lived on just $2 a day. Is it any wonder that people who can't afford to feed their families want to change the status quo? When the food tipping price is reached, people revolt. It's always been that way.

More than 14 percent of Americans lived in poverty in 2009, according to the U.S. Census Bureau. Including those who have given up looking for a job, one-sixth of American workers are unemployed or underemployed. A huge number of Americans have no cushion against massive increases in the cost of food and energy. In addition, the prices of imported consumer goods from China and elsewhere that low-income Americans depend on are rising and are likely to continue upward. With some 50 million or more Americans suffering the same economic plight as Egyptians, how long will it be before the streets of Washington burn like Cairo's?

I was hopeful that now when China agreed to host the Summer Davos-style annual World Economic Forums, starting in June 2007, the capitalist and socialist extremes might reach some accommodation. That was not to be. China's Communist Party leadership has clearly not taken to heart the lessons of Tiananmen 1989, and Tahrir-Liberation Square 2011, because it became a victim of its own invincible socialist-market-capitalist propaganda. China is the new capitalist on the world stage.

## May Day

Why are people surprised that students and workers flock to these annual capitalist gab-fests no matter where they are held and vent their anger violently? From Seattle in 1999, to Toronto in 2010, and Edinburgh, Hong Kong, London, Genoa, Sydney, Pittsburgh and every other city, no matter where.

May Day marches the last few years have become mass global labor demonstrations, and in many cases riots, as millions of workers across Asia, Europe and the Americas, angered by the worst global recession, take to the streets and clash with police. These mass protests are not limited to May Day.

With global unemployment reaching record levels – more than 27 million in the 27-nation EU as a whole, including non-euro giants Britain and Poland in 2010 – workers have taken to the streets by the millions and gone on strike, violently protesting the austerity measures adopted in America, China, Algeria, Bangladesh, Belgium, Britain, Egypt, Greece, Hungary, Indonesia, France, Spain, Kashmir, Romania and Turkey, just to name a few.

Sipping on coffee served to me by a Chinese waitress in a Greek Cypriot restaurant in Cyprus on May 20, 2010 as I read the *Cyprus Mail,* my attention was drawn to a headline reading *Romanians protest austerity measures; Police say some 30,000 people in protest; Union leaders call for general strike.* It was one of the largest mass protests since the fall of communism in 1989. Two other headlines on the page announced that *Spanish union says to challenge pay cuts in court,* and *Italy convicts police for G8 Genoa violence.*

That's when it became crystal clear to me that the social fabric everywhere is fraying and the message to governments across the globe is clear: reform or revolution.

The Social Security system in America, like its counterparts in many countries, is in trouble because of the increase in people collecting benefits as more baby boomers retire – and live longer – to the dismay of career politicians. In fact, most social security systems, including America's, are forecast to go into the deep red in the years ahead.

That means even more government borrowing until budgets can be balanced. I never could figure that one out.

Unemployment and poverty can only be reduced further by the extremes of capitalism and labor working together. Let's not forget that in the last 20 years global poverty rates have declined substantially. China and Asia as a whole are a great success story after 1980. Latin America reduced poverty dramatically in the 1970s but progress stopped in the 1980s and 1990s. Africa is another story. There poverty rates have increased, thanks to corrupt political leaders and their foreign and corporate enablers.

The economic predicament of the unemployed and poor across the world cannot be reversed by withholding from them the great advantages of contemporary technology, the benefits of international trade and exchange, and the social as well as economic merits of living in open rather than closed societies. The main issue is how to make good use of the remarkable benefits of economic intercourse and technological progress in a way that addresses the interests of the deprived, Amartya Sen, 1998 Nobel Laureate in Economics, reminds us.

"It is not adequate to understand that the poor of the world need globalization as much as the rich do; it is also important to make sure that they actually get what they need. This may require extensive institutional reform, and that task has to be faced as globalization is defended," he says.

It is hard to prosper in the modern world – especially in a world of globalized trade – if one is uneducated, or if one is hungry or sick, or if artificial barriers such as discrimination related to race or gender or social background exclude fair participation. Many advocates of the market economy do not seem to take the market sufficiently seriously. If they did, they would pay more attention to spreading the virtues of market-based opportunities.

"The market economy may be highly productive, but it cannot substitute for other important institutions. Development of appropriate non-market institutions is important also for tackling inequalities between nations. The need for a global commitment to democracy and to participatory governance can hardly be overstressed," Sen said at a seminar on globalization.

### Occupy Movement

Participatory governance is one of the major underlying themes of the Occupy movement. The fact that so many Occupiers wear masks of Guy Fawkes, the Catholic radical who plotted to blow up British Parliament in 1605, should have been an obvious clue to the detractors of the movement. Fawkes is a household name in Britain for plotting with 12 others to blow up Parliament with explosives, assassinate King James I and install a Catholic in the botched "Gunpowder Plot."

Britain celebrates every November 5th with fireworks and the burning of effigies known as "guys" around the country. I first heard of Fawkes in the British Army Childrens School in Cyprus where we had to recite, "Remember, remember the 5th of November...."

Watching Occupiers and "hackivists" Anonymous wearing the masks, with the numbers growing, one can't help but conclude that the mask is a way of reminding government authorities that they can be challenged by the masses. Hopefully, it is not a nod to violent radicalism.

It is a bold challenge to what is perceived as a violent "guns and gold" driven movement known as American Legislative Exchange Council that is corporate backed and lobbyist driven. It is a low profile organization that exerts vast influence on legislation in Washington and every one of the 50 states. It claims to be nonpartisan, but it is very much a conservative-movement funded by the usual suspects: the Koch brothers, Exxon Mobil....

Unlike other organizations, it doesn't just influence laws, it literally writes them, supplying fully drafted bills to legislators. Florida's now-infamous Stand Your Ground law is one example. Union-busting, undermining environmental protection, tax breaks for corporations and wealthy individuals and privatization are their primary objectives and the beneficiaries of their crafty lobbying and laws are its members and financial backers.

ALEC's claim that it stands for limited government and free markets is deeply misleading. To a large extent the organization seeks not limited government but privatized government, in which corporations get their profits from taxpayer dollars, dollars steered their way by friendly politicians. In other words, ALEC isn't so much about promoting free markets as it is about expanding crony capitalism – the 1%.

I first heard about ALEC in New York City on February 29, 2012. I was walking down 5th Avenue from Rockefeller Center to my hotel on 45th Street after lunch on a chill, drizzly day. I ran into a boisterous crowd of protesters on the sidewalk going up 46th Street toward 6th Avenue. Noticing a long line of NYPD men in blue walking along side of them, accompanied by a convoy of motorcycles on the road, I decided to follow and see what the protest was all about. As I caught up with the protesters, I ran into a woman handing out leaflets.

"We're objecting to corporate greed and control of our lives and legislation," she said as she handed me a leaflet and pirouetted to the left to hand out leaflets to the growing number of storekeepers and their patrons crowded in the doorways, who like me were wondering what the loud shouts, whistles and clanging tambourines were all about.

As I peeled away from the protesters on 45th Street to go to my hotel, I started reading the flyer. "WHAT IS ALEC: Why are corporations writing our state legislation?" was the title.

**WHAT IS ALEC?** Was the first subtitle. **"ALEC** is a corporate-funded, right-wing **501(c) (3) NON-PROFIT organization.** Through ALEC, corporations hand state legislators **"copy and paste"** or **"model bills"** behind closed doors. These bills change the states' laws so that they directly **benefit the corporations' bottom line.** Corporations sit on all nine ALEC task forces and vote with legislators to approve these "model bills."

The two-sided flyer went on to describe ALEC's backers. Oil industry, drug companies, low-wage employers, telephone companies, insurance companies and of course the Koch brothers, who pledged to raise $100 million for the 2012 election cycle.

As I walked into the hotel, I flashed back to my first encounter with the Occupiers on September 18, 2011, in Zucotti Park, previously known as Liberty Park, before it was renamed after the developer of the nearby skyscraper – but still called Liberty Park by the protesters. A formless and leaderless movement that passed the test of authenticity – the first requirement for a citizenry that no longer has faith in the institutions of the 1 percenters. People with the gumption to do what they think needs to be said and demonstrated. Where will the movement go, I wondered? At the time I was concerned that if nothing positive was achieved, people would just get tired, pack up their tents and leave. Instead, the movement spread across America and the world – more than 1,300 cities worldwide, according to OccupyTogether.org – and had even morphed into other anti-crony capitalist movements like the one I had just encountered.

The continuing dialogue and growing number of the have-nots – the 99 percenters – joining the Occupier movement confirms that *We the Maids* are no longer cynically apathetic or satisfied with just grumbling to each other about the corporate financed political injustices we are faced with today. We no longer accept that doing everything we are told will necessarily lead to a better life. On the contrary, it leads to more debt and misery and only enriches the corporate elite.

The movement now features in presidential news conferences and congressional debates. The violent break-up of some of the Occupier encampments by police only served to further galvanize the movement and made it grow from a handful of placard holders with catchy phrases to a global revolutionary movement.

Arrests, beatings, tear gassing, macing and shooting of peaceful protesters only adds fuel to the movement by enhancing its media exposure that rallies new supporters and disciples to the movement, including politicians and celebrities, and in some cities igniting the burning fuel into unnecessary violent confrontations.

Time is definitely on the side of the movement. It has grown from complaints about corporate greed and bank bailouts to everything from nuclear power plants, the environment, employment, student loans, housing, education, over-consumption and war.

The movement has survived its first winter and many activists have turned their temporary campsites into permanent homes. The movement started in the basement of an old house in Vancouver, Canada, at the world headquarters of *Adbusters,* a counterculture magazine. In July 2011, the magazine known for campaigns like "buy nothing day," printed a poster calling on activists to occupy Wall Street in New York on September 17. Thousands responded and many stayed.

People, especially youth, have been pushed to the edge by the brass knuckles of the hidden hand of capitalism. Educated college graduates saddled with debt cannot find jobs, mid-life workers whose careers are cut short, seniors suddenly too pinched to retire, immigrants scapegoated as job thieves, and the impoverished underclass trapped more than ever have been left with no alternative but to join the revolutionary movement.

The protesters are on firm ground because they are demanding fairness in a corporate plutocracy that has become indefensible because it is so one-sided. Heads the bankers win, tails the taxpayers lose. For these oligarchs to try and suppress any criticism of the sources of their wealth and the fact that it has been gifted to them by their crony politicians at the expense of *We the Apathetic Maids* is short-sighted and self-defeating.

The Founding Fathers' First Amendment ideals cannot be suppressed by any lobbyist, politician or law enforcement official.

The Occupy protesters are right-on-the-money and cannot be marginalized by political pundits or career politicians, because they represent 99 percent of America and the world. Their movement, unlike the Tea Party movement that was financed by corporate America, is spontaneous and has grown without corporate support – and will continue to do so. It is as significant a movement of the 21st century as the civil rights and anti-war movements of the '60s were in the 20th century.

"If at first the idea is not absurd, then there is no hope for it," said Albert Einstein. That is why the Occupy movement will grow and flourish into America's Third Revolution.

### The Solution
Trying to marginalize, or worse, ignore legitimate citizen complaints has never worked and never will. America's Founding Fathers are an eternal reminder of that fundamental truth. The solution is to address complaints directly, honestly and objectively. That is what Israel did after more than 400,000 of its citizens took to the streets protesting social inequality and demanding economic reforms in 2011. The government did not try to marginalize them, but did the right thing. It appointed 14 members to the Trajtenberg Committee for Socioeconomic Change to look into the grievances raised. The panel was chaired by Prof. Manuel Trajtenberg and delivered a report within 50 days. The 267-page report concluded that "the shout of the protesters is legitimate."

Trajtenberg set out what the panel believed should be the overriding principles governing all socioeconomic policy.

"We were assigned the task of translating the protest into a language that could yield solutions," Trajtenberg wrote. "So here is what the dictionary that we developed has to say: "Social justice means that there is congruence between the normative behavior contribution and effort of the individual, and how he is compensated. Social justice means equal opportunities at the start, fair hiring and competitive practices down the line, and a basically secure and honorable retirement. Social justice means that if fate deals a blow to an individual, for whatever reason, society will help assure his basic survival, accessibility and respect."

Trajtenberg noted that "economic growth is the key to having the ability to provide the growing needs of Israeli society over time," but stressed that economic growth statistics cannot be the sole gauge of economic success, because "many quality-of-life aspects are not included in it, such as measures of inequality, health, the environment and the like."

"The new breed of Israelis of summer 2011 presented to us on a silver plate that rare and wonderful opportunity to instigate change and to establish a fairer and more just society," said Trajtenberg.

The committee recommended actions to lower the cost of living and housing, halt tax reform and raise taxes on the rich. It recommended the government spend 60 billion new Israeli shekels on the reforms and that the money come from cuts in defense spending.

The committee recommended a long-term increase in housing supply with temporary solutions for affordable housing for struggling families, including more aid for those eligible for public housing, structural changes to the laws regulating the Antitrust Authority, removal of import duties and lowering of sales taxes, expansion of institutional involvement in education for ages 0-3, compulsory education for ages 3-4 and deployment of after-hours school care for ages 3-9, increase in public transport accessibility, removal of labor force barriers to Arab women and religious Jewish men, cancellation of direct tax reductions, creation of a new top tax bracket of 48%, increase capital-gains tax to 25%, increase company taxes to 25% and cancellation of a gasoline excise hike.

Not bad, I thought when I read the report. I was in Israel when it was released and taken aback by the criticism it received from different political parties and the protest leaders. They all gave dismissive responses to the findings, saying that the recommended changes were not far reaching enough to meet the demands of their social issues movement.

At it founding, Israel's leaders, headed by David Ben Gurion, believed and hoped that they were creating a social democracy, with all the requisite egalitarian accoutrements, including socialized national health care, progressive income tax, child benefits and subsidized cheap housing. Ben

Gurion, who owned almost nothing and retired to a primitive hut in the Negev Desert, typified the austere lifestyle, and greatness, of the nation's founders.

Today, many moderate Israelis fear the country is heading for ruin. Indeed, the country's ruling class, including Benjamin Netanyahu and his predecessor Ehud Olmert, who was on trial for corruption during my brief visit, and Ehud Barak, the former head of the Labor Party and defense minister at the time, live in opulence, and the feeling is that they are out of touch with reality. A widespread chant during the summer protest movement, set to a popular children's ditty, was "Bibi has three apartments, which is why we have none."

The self-immolation of Moshe Silman, a desperately indebted man, stunned and galvanized the protest movement.

Add to that the frustration secular Israelis have at the large slice of the state's economic pie the ultra-Orthodox, who contribute almost nothing to the economy and avoid mandatory military service, receive because of their powerful political parties that can make or break a coalition government, and you have the ingredients for revolution.

Women have become the core of the debate over orthodox Judaism, the social protest movement and political parties in Israel. Daphni Leef and Stav Shaffir led the social protest movement, Shelly Yacimovich, was elected to head the Labor Party and Tzipi Livni, head of Kadima is her main rival.

It's reminiscent of the prominent role women played in America's presidential election in 2012.

Spending time with Michal Yudin, chairwoman of WePower, a nonprofit, non-Israeli NGO, promoting women's leadership, gender integration and equality at all levels of Israeli society, especially in politics and the public arena, was a sheer delight as always. I went to high school with Michal. Her mother taught my mother how to sew, and her husband Michael and I enjoy debating U.S. politics over a nice single malt until the wee hours.

"The difference with what you see here is a round table of women from A to Z, exchanging ideas on changes and how to constructively bring them about peacefully, versus what the Occupy movement in New York is advocating – storming Wall Street. How does that bring about change?" Michal said when I asked about the difference between the social movements in America and Israel.

### Street Protests

The force of viral global protests for change today partly reflects a new mood and a fresh inclination to challenge the political-corporate-military establishment. It is, to a great extent, the global equivalent of national protests associated with labor movements and the political radicalism of the '60s.

China finds itself caught up in a growing wave of unrest early in the new millennium and barely two decades after Tiananmen Square. The new anger revolves around pocketbook issues, heavy-handed and corrupt government bureaucrats, farmers being forced off their land, police brutality, environmental degradation, and ethnic clashes in Inner Mongolia, Tibet and Xinjiang.

Three days of anti-government riots in the Pearl River Delta village of Dadun in the town of Xintang, Guangdong, the "Blue Jeans Capital of the World," highlighted the plight of both migrant workers and the Communist bureaucracy. The riot started after a pregnant 20-year-old hawker, Wang Lianmei, a migrant from Sichuan, was manhandled by security staff who wanted her to stop selling her goods in front of a supermarket because she didn't have enough money to bribe them away. More than 1,000 migrant workers took to the streets and burned cars and public facilities, including a police station, despite the heavy police presence. They brazenly defied the authorities. It was one of the most violent riots in Guangdong in years.

The years of discrimination and disrespect, including brutal beatings by the authorities and locals, not to mention the hundreds of deaths from the toxic heavy-metal poisoning of the land, food and water, pushed migrants to a hot Sichuan boiling point in June 2011.

Dadun has about 7,000 permanent residents and more than 60,000 migrant workers churning out 60 foreign brands of jeans, accounting for about half of the 450 million pairs of jeans sold in the U.S. every year. Blue jeans are much dirtier to make than one would expect, according to Greenpeace researchers, who point out that "cool distressed denim wash is the result of several chemical-intensive washes," with fabric printing and dyeing involving heavy metals such as cadmium, lead and mercury.

The summer of 2011 was especially hot with riots and protests breaking out seemingly across all of China. From Guangzhou's Zengcheng, in the same province as Dadun, to Mongolia, which saw its biggest protest in about 20 years, when a man angry over land seizures set off three bombs in government offices in Fuzhou, Jiangxi, killing three people and wounding nine.

In the Hubei city of Lichuan, thousands of protesters attacked government offices after the alleged beating death of a local council member in police custody.

In restless Xinjiang, ethnic violence left 21 people dead in mainly Muslim Kashgar in August 2011, in the latest bout of unrest stemming from Uygur frustration at Beijing's rule. These clashes followed on the heels of similar deadly ethnic clashes in Hotan weeks earlier.

Public anger over the high-speed crash of two bullet trains in Wenzhou in July 2011, which left 40 people dead and hundreds injured, boiled over into protests at the site of the crash, online and across the country, demanding an investigation and that the corrupt officials who compromised the safety of passengers be brought to justice.

The almost non-stop outbreak of mass protests in 2012 in China severely tested the government's "stability maintenance" efforts. The different types of protests have succeeded in their own way and together have showed that the use of the police force to violently suppress mass protests is no longer effective. Silent protests are becoming louder slaps in the face of government power.

Anger at the Establishment is not limited to China, of course. Anger today is a worldwide phenomenon that is boiling over at every corner of the globe at gatherings of capitalists, unfair changes to labor laws, injustice and unnecessary killing of innocents that collectively are leading to the third revolution.

Think about the protesters who disrupted the first WTO confab in Seattle in 1999 – and every WTO get-together since; and the fifth annual Forbes Global CEO Conference that made "the corporate pirates" flee in Sydney in August 2005.

Also Paris in 2005, 2006 and 2010 over changes in labor and retirement laws, and 2011, when judges took to the streets in fury at Sarkozy over murdered Laetititia Perrais; lawyers taking to the streets and getting clobbered by police in Pakistan because of their fury at the military government's ousting of the chief justice of the Supreme Court in November 2007.

The APEC summit in Sydney in September 2007; violent anti-war protests at the "die in" near Capitol Hill in Washington and major cities worldwide in September 2007; left-wing supporters of congressman Satur Ocampo who was being tried for sedition in Manila in 2007; Georgian President Mikhail Saakashvili's call for a snap election after he declared a state of emergency in response to violent clashes between police and anti-government protesters in November 2007; Athens students and anarchists enraged over the police shooting of Alexandros Grigoropoulos in 2008 – and again over austerity measures in 2011.

Middle-class Indians after the Mumbai attacks in 2008; British students and anarchists trashing banks in London's financial district during the G-20 meeting in 2009 – and again over austerity measures in 2011; Thailand's red-shirts forcing cancellation of the ASEAN summit in Bangkok in 2009 after violent protesters stormed the meeting venue and forced the emergency evacuation of regional leaders, and the shutting down of the country because of street riots in May 2010 that triggered a deadly military response.

Moscow police's monthly clashes with political activists demanding the right to freedom of assembly and speech in Triumfalnaya Square in 2010; Israel's student and middle-class tent encampment along Tel Aviv's elegant Rothschild Boulevard protesting the high cost of housing and food in 2011, with an estimated 400,000 who turned out across Israel in September 2011 to demand economic reforms; and many more smaller protests by farmers, workers, students and anarchists in cities, towns and villages worldwide.

In Israel, as with many Occupy movements worldwide, peaceful protesters blame the government's shift toward privatization and capitalism for spurring a housing crisis and many want the country to move back toward social democratic policies. The fact is that America already has, with banks being nationalized and Obama's national health care becoming law. America is moving toward becoming a modern European socialist state. It was under the conservative George W. Bush administration that America enacted the largest expansion of the welfare state in 30 years: prescription drugs for the elderly.

### Bloody Brits Cleansing
The bloody violent riots, rampage and looting across England in early August 2011 highlighted the anger and frustration of economically disenfranchised, disillusioned and alienated underclass youth. The districts that took the brunt of the London rampage were upper-middle-class sections of the city represented by conservative Tory MPs.

"I'm taking my taxes back," said one woman carrying a TV out of a shop. A narrative of unfairness, of economic despair, has taken hold, and this is its expression.

"We have a generation of young people inured to cheap luxuries, especially clothes and technology, but further than ever from the sort of wealth that makes them adults. A career, a home of your own – the things that can be ruined by riots – are out of sight," said Danny Kruger, a former adviser to Prime Minister David Cameron who runs a London crime prevention charity called Only Connect. He's right.

The angry underclass that has been suffering in silence for too long reached its tipping point when Britain's economic woes forced the government to axe more desperately needed social benefits that only made matters worse for the unemployed and unemployable youths. All they needed was a spark. London police provided that spark with the questionable shooting death of Mark Duggan, a 29-year-old father of four with reputed gang ties.

The sour relationship between the police and public was highlighted by a woman who told an officer who came to attend to her stabbed friend: "We hate you." A throwback to the '60s when cops in the U.S. were called "pigs" by protesters and riots left American cities in flames.

The London riots that spread across England started on the weekend of August 5, 2011, the same day Standard & Poor downgraded the U.S. debt rating from AAA to AA+ after America failed to reduce its habitual practice of deficit spending when it raised its debt ceiling. That same weekend more than 250,000 people protested peacefully in Israel, as people across America started waking up to the realization that the U.S. and its political establishment isn't working any more.

The debt debate in Congress confirmed that the two-party system has come to a grinding halt. According to a CNN poll taken after the acrimonious debate, 77 percent of Americans said that elected officials in Washington behaved "like spoiled children" in the tug-of-war over raising the debt ceiling.

The blood on the streets of England and the Arab world was not just from the riots and protests but the stock markets as the value of holdings worldwide crashed. They chalked up more than $2.5 trillion in losses in the value of global shares, the biggest loss since the Great Recession of 2008 started. Many retirees and workers saw their retirement savings wiped out – again.

The first weeks of August 2011 saw a perfect revolutionary cleansing storm taking shape. Not only on the streets of England, Israel and the Arab world, but in Washington on the military front. A key component of the debt reduction compromise was a serious cut in defense spending if the Democrats and Republicans can't agree on future debt reductions. So what does China do? It announces that General Chen Bingde, chief of the General Staff of the PLA, will visit Israel, the first trip of a Chinese military chief to that country. The visit is significant because all of Israel's ties with China are under careful U.S. scrutiny and in most cases are approved ahead of time by the Pentagon.

The winds of change blowing across China, America, Europe and the Middle East in 2011 are not limited to politics and the economy. The dynamics of the changing military puzzle are just as revolutionary.

After the destructive riots across England, a call went out over social media for cleaning parties to help sweep up the mess, and thousands of citizens turned out. We *the Maids* should think about bringing the same zeal to sweeping out the career politicians and their corporate lobbyist cronies in Washington.

The global protests, riots and rampages by disenfranchised and economically deprived underclasses are a daily reminder that *We the Maids* have a lot more to clean up than broken homes, stores, hearts and glass.

*Global Doubt*

The violent and deadly clashes in the streets of England, France, Tunisia, Egypt, Algeria, Yemen, Bahrain, Libya and Syria in 2011 and Tehran and other Iranian cities after the disputed national election in 2008 – and again in 2011 – are all vivid reminders that revolutionary demands for change are not limited to the cradles of modern-day Western democracies, but are also on the march in Islamic autocracies and theocracies.

As a lawyer, I am encouraged to see lawyers and judges taking to the streets in Pakistan, India, France, Egypt, China and America protesting injustices.

The protests over the last few years are not restricted to failed national or global government policies. They are visible at the grassroots level by workers everywhere. People protesting policies in professions as diverse as the performing arts in Italy, when cinema workers blocked the red carpet opening night of the 2010 Rome film festival to protest the government's arts budget cuts, BBC journalists striking over pension reform in November 2010, and the ultimate protest that highlighted worker discontent – JetBlue's flight attendant Steven Slater, who cursed at passengers over the intercom, and grabbed a couple of beers before sliding down the emergency-evacuation chute and into popular worker folklore. Johnny Paycheck's 1977 anthem of alienation, *Take This Job and Shove It* has a global chorus.

The outburst of global doubts have something in common with the spirit of an old American song – a defiant verse traced to blues legend Leadbelly: "In the home of the brave, land of the free, I will not be put down by no bourgeoisie."

The protesters and the capitalists and career politicians they harangue have more in common than they realize. Neither benefits from the status quo. Change benefits both. Globalization hurts labor by relocating jobs from industrialized nations to countries that can really use them. Granted they may not be under the ideal conditions America and the developed world demand of manufacturers today. They weren't always that way in America either. In fact, working conditions in many American overseas factories and sweat shops are just as appalling today as they used to be in America. Debt bondage is standard hiring practice today for many foreign workers. What used to be indentured servants are today in debt bondage to labor brokers who demand and receive the bulk of the employees' salary because of the usurious compounded monthly interest they add on to their fees.

Let's not forget that the same used to be true in Hong Kong. Workers in Hong Kong factories worked like coolie slaves in America. However, a generation or two later these workers' children own the factories in China and other Asian countries. No different than the children of American coolies, indentured servants, slaves and laborers who now own or finance the factories in China and other developing countries as they are criticized for outsourcing. And let's not forget that the only way a developing country becomes developed is through manufacturing and the jobs that industry creates. Substandard menial labor jobs at wages that are deemed inhuman in America are better than back-breaking jobs in local factories or brothels – or worse – no jobs and no income. All the more reason sophisticated U.S. labor union organizers should reorient themselves and truly interlocalize globally.

*Parallels*

While people were protesting against the Vietnam War in America and Europe in the '60s, America was also funding a resistance movement of CIA-trained Tibetan monks and farmers to fight the Chinese, and China was in the throes of the Cultural Revolution.

The CIA's Tibet Task Force was a covert operation from 1956 to 1974 that trained Tibetan guerrillas in the U.S. and parachuted them into China. The operation yielded key intelligence on China during the Cultural Revolution, including the first official evidence of the widespread famine that resulted from the agrarian reforms of the Great Leap Forward.

Hong Kong experienced the spillover of the Cultural Revolution from China in the Hong Kong riots of 1967. Fifty-one people died, including 15 killed in bomb attacks. The riots were anti-British and involved the frustrated lower-middle classes who, like today's anti-globalization protesters, were fed up with working and social conditions. The riots prompted the British colonials to introduce sweeping social reforms. These included a reduction in working hours, more public housing and a nine-year compulsory education program.

While Americans worldwide protested against George W. Bush's war against Iraq, Hong Kongers not only joined the anti-war protests but close to 10% of the population took to the streets to object to Hong Kong's equivalent of the Patriot Act – Article 23.

The protests of the '60s and opening years of the 21st century are nothing new. History is replete with protests that either force governments to reform or collapse. The Lyndon Johnson administration in America collapsed in the face of the Vietnam War protests in the '60s, as did China's bamboo curtain in the wake of the Cultural Revolution.

The Hong Kong government backed down from its insistence on adopting Article 23 in the face of mass protests in the streets of Hong Kong. Would President Bush have backed down in his desire to go to war with Iraq if more Americans had taken to the streets? Imagine if 10% of U.S. voters had poured into the streets of American cities and Washington, D.C., to protest the Iraq War and the Patriot Act. Would Bush still have chosen to go to war and curtail basic American rights? I doubt it.

Most people in America, *We the Apathetic Maids,* accept the government's power as absolute, and therefore underestimate citizens' people power. *We the Maids* can vacuum out of Washington the career politicians who are not responsive. The same holds true for all national and state capitals. The time to sweep in the fundamental changes we demand is long overdue. Not only in America, but in China. After all, free speech and freedom of assembly are enshrined in the constitutions of both countries.

Bruce Springsteen is to be applauded for speaking in support of the Dixie Chicks' embarrassment at being from the same great state of Texas as the president who fought a war for oil. "To me, they're terrific American artists expressing American values by using their American right to free speech," The Boss wrote on his website. "For them to be banished wholesale from radio stations, and even entire radio networks, for speaking out is un-American."

### Post-'80s Political Rebels

Hong Kong has a proud history of speaking out against injustice and taking a stand against authoritarianism and any encroachment on freedoms. Today's Hong Kong political generation, commonly referred to as the Post-'80s activist-rebels, like their counterparts in America, mainland China, Britain, France, Greece, Philippines and every other country with a 20s-plus activist student community, are spontaneous and rely on social media, Google maps and Twitter to summon like-minded anti-government protesters into the streets.

They are a product of our time and the long-existing social conflicts and deep socioeconomic rifts in our changing world disorder and will only escalate because of public wrath willing to question and challenge unfair and unjust government authority. They live by Mao Zedong's saying that "A revolution is not a dinner party or writing an essay or painting a picture or doing embroidery."

Christina Chan Hau-man became the face of the movement in Hong Kong because of repeated clashes with police, which resulted in her arrest for allegedly assaulting a police officer.

Chan's generation, globally, is justifiably pessimistic about the future and angry at how big business runs governments at their expense.

The 1966 Star Ferry riots – triggered by a fare hike of five cents for the boat ride between Central Terminal and Tsim Sha Tsui – was one of the biggest protests in the city's recent history and exposed the deep discontent of youth in '60s Hong Kong.

So Sau-chung, then a 27-year-old translator, staged a hunger strike on April 4, 1966, outside the Star Ferry Terminal in Central District to protest against the fare increase. Before the cross-harbor tunnel was completed in 1972, the ferry was a vital link between the island and Kowloon. His actions drew sympathy and supporters that got him arrested the next day, prompting thousands to take to the streets in violent protests with hundreds arrested. One person was killed and 26 injured. So was charged with causing "obstruction and disturbance" and jailed for two months.

But his protest was a success: Star Ferry limited the fare hike to first-class passengers and exempted those under 16 and students.

A few months later, Hong Kong faced its worst unrest to date – the 1967 riots that claimed 51 lives – a spillover from the Cultural Revolution in China that resulted in a confrontation between the leftist workers movement and the colonial government with extremists planting bombs in the street. T.C. Wu, a friend and former director of Pets Central and one of the 800 members of the Select Committee to elect Hong Kong's chief executive, wrote an editorial opinion at the time encouraging Hong Kongers to take the guns of the British constabulary and shoot them. He was arrested for inciting sedition and jailed for three years until he was freed in a prisoner swap in which China released two British spies.

"People were angry," said T.C., describing how the riots started. "They were unhappy at how the British were treating them. We didn't think the government represented the people. Only the U.K. companies ... not the people."

The 1967 riots were "Hong Kong's watershed year and T.C. was a key player that historical year," said Gary Cheung, a *South China Morning Post* associate news editor, at T.C.'s wake, as we toasted his rebellious renaissance spirit.

In a commentary in the *Far Eastern Economic Review* in June 1967, editor Derek Davies wrote that the disturbances revealed the existence of a "groundswell of discontent" and a widespread sense of frustration among young people. After the riots, the colonial administration introduced social reforms.

Young activist protests have been a Hong Kong landmark of freedom of expression ever since. On Christmas Day 1981, young activists took part in rioting sparked by a traffic accident in Central and 18 were arrested. Youth activism was renewed after the 1989 Tiananmen massacre in Beijing and became an annual protest calling card to commemorate those killed and demand more representation in government. The youth movement refused to accept the party line. They refuse to be *Apathetic Maids*.

Hong Kong's youth have in many ways become the model of what youth worldwide should be – make that people of all ages. They have become a model for youthful disobedience challenging the status quo, not only in the Far East, but worldwide. Many of them were raised in America, Canada, Britain and Australia and not only appreciate the freedoms advocated by America's Founding Fathers, but they put words into actions.

When artist-activist Ai Weiwei was released from jail in Beijing in

2011, he thanked Hong Kongers for their support and called the special administrative region a model for Chinese society. "I was aware that many people in Hong Kong have appealed for and supported my release," he said.

The Occupy Wall Street movement in Hong Kong was one of the longest continuous Occupy movements – probably the longest. It ended in late August 2012. It had started 10 months earlier when the Hong Kong Occupiers decided to take over the public space on the street level under the HSBC bank headquarters that has a block of covered public space that rises several floors before the first floor of the building starts. As the 9 p.m. court ordered deadline approached on August 27 for the occupiers to vacate, they decided to party. They cranked up live music, sang and danced and periodically barked out chants of "We won't go."

Inspired by Occupy Wall Street in New York, protesters started Occupy Central as an anti-capitalist movement. They also advocated other local issues, such as condemning the "hegemony" of property developers and supporting residency rights for Filipino maids.

Hong Kongers' approach to protest is not mob rule, as some politicians and editorials have suggested. It is true democracy in action as advocated by America's Founding Fathers. There are no dangers in people expressing their will against self-serving governments. There are more dangers of mob rule by uncontrolled politicians and their self-serving financial backers and bureaucrats than *We the People* taking to the streets peacefully.

Hong Kong's activist energy spread to Macau in 2006, when labor unrest transformed the former Portuguese colony from a fishing village with gambling dens into the Las Vegas of Asia.

Hong Kong's annual protests to commemorate the victims of Tiananmen has morphed into anti-Beijing and Hong Kong government interpretations of the Basic Law – Hong Kong's constitution – and successfully evolved into a movement demanding early universal suffrage, one-person, one-vote that forced Beijing to make a political U-turn and accept the Democratic Party's proposal of five new Super Constituencies "to thwart radicals."

That didn't stop Democratic Party activists from splitting from the party and taking to the streets to protest their leaders' sellout to Beijing and labelling the mainstream Democrats turncoats who betrayed Hong Kong's people over political reform. Why can't *We the Apathetic Maids* do the same in America, the Founding Fathers' beacon of democracy?

## World Trade Protests

The World Trade Organization protests in Hong Kong in December 2005, during the global body's meeting there, became a continuous protest from the minute it started until days after it ended. The South Korean farmers Korean Peasants' League, Asia's most militant demonstrators against globalization, were the most vocal group in attendance, reminding the world of the sacrifice their fellow rice farmer Lee Kyeong Hae made two years earlier at the WTO meeting in Cancun, Mexico, when he sat on a high fence, drew a knife and stabbed himself in the chest. "He sacrificed his life to protect farmers around the world," was a protest mantra among the militant Koreans as they drew media attention by hurling themselves into the polluted toxic waters of Victoria Harbor wearing life jackets. The images of farmers bobbing in the water and being doused with pepper spray dominated evening news bulletins worldwide.

The Korean protesters' peaceful tactic of taking three-steps in unison and one-kowtow as they marched toward the Hong Kong Convention Center where global leaders were meeting became a model for Hong Kong's post-80 rebels when they protested against a 26-kilometer section of the Guangzhou-Shenzhen-Hong Kong Express Link. In a four-day peaceful protest, they proceeded slowly but surely along rural roads and city streets to the beat of a single drum. Their only action was to prostate themselves every 26 steps.

The Korean farmers' protests were an effective lesson in how to influence the course of trade negotiations – they were neutralized.

Koreans are in the forefront of protests against injustice. Kim Jin-suk, a 51-year-old labor activist who works for the Korean Confederation of Trade Unions, is an example. She became a prisoner-of-choice for more than 200 days, cloistered in a metal cell 15 floors above ground in a solitary protest on Crane 85, a mammoth industrial apparatus, to condemn the layoffs of 400 workers at a major South Korean shipping company.

On hot days, the temperature in the windowless control room was nearly unbearable. She used a bucket for a toilet, could not wash and was refused access to books or newspapers. Meager meals of rice porridge and sweet potatoes, cooked by fellow activists, were hoisted in a pail.

Crane 85 was used by another protester in 2003 in a three-month vigil to protest working conditions. Kim Ju-ik, a 40-year-old father of three, hanged himself in the crane's control room. His suicide note said: "This is a country where a laborer has to risk his life to live like a human."

Sound familiar?

### *Unlikely Band of Brothers*

When the last 11 of the South Koreans arrested in the wake of the WTO protests were released, on their way home they offered thanks for the warm welcome they received in Hong Kong. "We will respect the law and the courts and legal system of Hong Kong," Yang Kyung Kyu, the ringleader, told supporters at the airport.

A large group of Hong Kong supporters showed up to see the South Koreans off in a tearful farewell, singing and chanting "Down, down WTO!" one last time. Some of the South Koreans said they would miss Hong Kong; while others wore "I Love Hong Kong" T-shirts.

Not only South Koreans went to jail in Hong Kong during the WTO summit. Protesters from France, Taiwan, Thailand and the Philippines were arrested, along with Chinese mainlanders. Businessman Wen Zhiming was one of the mainlanders arrested. He was in Hong Kong on business and was drawn to the protests out of curiosity. He was arrested along with 300 others and accused of being a member of the group. Wen professed his innocence to no avail.

"I was so relieved to finally get out, but when the whole block erupted in chants of Down! Down! WTO! in support of me, even though I had to ask someone what it meant, I wanted to stay and be released with everyone else," he said.

"Their respect for one another and their fearlessness and devotion to their cause moved me," Wen said after he was released without being charged.

Back in Shunde, in Guangdong province, Wen reflected on the events of his Hong Kong experience and realized that the political battles between the protesters and the WTO, the police and the democrats, all paled in comparison to the brotherhood and dedication behind bars.

The respect policemen show protesters was highlighted when an officer died after he slipped in the rain and suffered severe head and chest injuries in June 2011, as he tried to tackle a lone chicken trader who was protesting against government officials and their policies on a footbridge. In China and America, it is highly unlikely that a police officer would risk his life to get a protester to safety. A more violent approach is the norm.

The first cross-border parallel protest took place in a Guangzhou park and in a playground in Hong Kong on August 1, 2010. The joint campaign was the first to mobilize Cantonese speakers in Hong Kong and Guangdong in defense of the dialect, which they say has been increasingly marginalized. The hundreds of protesters gathered in the park in defiance of government orders not to rally and had to be forcibly removed by police. Many shouted "We protest! We protest!"

Others screamed: "Police, go away! And:"Fuck his mother, persist against all odds!" emulating the obsene rallying cry reportedly used by Ming dynasty national hero Yuan Ghnghuan. Several protesters were "taken out for coffee" by Guangzhou police, a euphemism for soft detention. Among the protesters in Hong Kong were a handful of mainlanders who covered their faces with medical masks to avoid reprisals back home.

The protest was sparked by a government proposal to switch from

Cantonese to Putonghua in Guangdong television broadcasts, but the underlying issue has been there much longer and is more profound. Cantonese, like Shanghainese and the non-Chinese-based languages of the Uygurs and Tibetans, has been submerged by the national language. Cantonese enhances a sense of identity. This scares the officials in Beijing. Like the Communist Party in the Soviet Union that was ruthless in trying to obliterate the many languages that existed within its borders, and Fascist Spain that criminalized use of the nation's minority languages, China has demonstrated an equal determination to curb the linguistic diversity that exists in the nation in its efforts to unite the country. Just as the regimes in the Soviet Union and Fascist Spain failed, so will the Communist Party in China.

One of the saddest and most depressing national protests in China, yet most telling about the government's insecurity, is that of the parents of missing children pleading with the authorities for help. Up to 70,000 children go missing each year in China. Many families desperate for sons under the country's one-child policy try to buy abducted boys. Girls are sold to rural families as brides because of the shortage of females brought on by the preference for boys. The parents stage protest rallies across the country as they search for their children. They are periodically detained overnight and ordered to stop their rallies because they could spark unrest.

China set up task forces in 2009 to keep the lid on domestic and cross-border protests. Vice President Xi Jinping, heir apparent to take over the helm in China, was put in charge of a massive public security campaign and apparatus to respond swiftly to any possible social unrest. Beijing is trying to reconcile a tradition of rule based on virtue with an alien decision-making structure that threatens the Communist Party's very survival.

### Free Speech

Watching free speech fighting to emerge in China from the depth of Communist Party oppression reminds me of the "Free Speech" movement in America in the '60s, best exemplified in Berkeley, on and off the University of California Berkeley campus. I periodically witnessed the movement evolve whenever I would traverse the Bay Bridge from San

Francisco to Berkeley in my red MG convertible to go to the Berkeley law school library to do research.

The raging debate at the time was the limit of free speech and what its limitations were. Burning draft cards, the American flag, calling police "pigs" and protesting without permits that usually ended in tear-gassed confrontations with baton-wielding law enforcement officers were common occurrences.

Reading about how Socrates, the ancient Greek philosopher and teacher, is being acquitted today in reenacted trials over the crime for which he was sentenced to death is a refreshing reminder on how old and cherished the concept of free speech is.

Judges narrowly acquitted Socrates in a "retrial" in Athens in May 2012, billed as a lesson for modern times of revolution and crisis.

Socrates defended himself at his trial in the 4th century BC, but this time, in his absence, a panel of 10 U.S. and European judges heard pleas by top Greek and foreign lawyers at the Onassis Foundation in Athens. They then voted on whether he was guilty on the ancient charges of evil-doing, impiety and corrupting the young.

In 399 BC, Socrates was put to death by being forced to drink hemlock poison after being convicted by a jury of hundreds of Athenians. Unrepentant, he had insulted the judges and cheekily asked to be rewarded for his actions.

The modern-day judges spared him that dishonor, with a split vote – five guilty and five not guilty, meaning that under ancient Athenian law he was not guilty as charged.

Socrates questioned conventional wisdom on sensitive notions of politics, religion and morality and earned powerful enemies. He was branded an enemy of democracy, accused of treason in favor of the Spartan enemy, and influencing a violent uprising against the Athenian republic by a group of oligarchs that included some of his pupils.

Arguing in Socrates' defense, prominent French lawyer Patrick Simon said: "An opinion is not a crime. Socrates was searching for the truth." He added: "My client has one fault: he likes to poke fun and is fiercely ironic. By acquitting him, you will show how solid and reliable democracy is."

Versed in Socratic literature, the legal talent came from Britain, France, Germany, Greece, Switzerland and the U.S. At an earlier enactment of the trial in New York in 2011, Socrates was also acquitted.

Organizers of the trial said the issues of democracy and free speech raised by Socrates' trial were resonant for global politics today.

"The issues that we will be debating here are global issues and are very pertinent," said Anthony Papadimitriou, a lawyer and president of the foundation.

## Globaloney

The term "Globaloney" was apparently coined by U.S. Congresswoman Clare Boothe Luce in 1943 to trash "global thinking" Vice President Henry Wallace, then as today, argued that global commerce would bring about world peace. It hasn't. On the contrary, it has brought about more armed conflicts, hunger, unemployment, poverty and suffering.

As so many people in America are asking over tea, coffee or most likely a beer: If globalization is so great, how come I'm unemployed and all the jobs are going overseas? But 9/11 definitely put globalization on ice. Business is now interlocal.

Global trading multinationals have been around for centuries. From the British East India Company in the 18th century to today's giant multinationals. Unfortunately, many are short-sighted and self-defeating because they are driven by quarterly and annual reports to shareholders, which in the best of circumstances can create a Coca-Cola company and at worst an Enron.

The fact is, America is falling asleep at school and on the job. It used to be just blue-collar factory jobs that relocated overseas. Today it is also the higher-paying white-collar and tee-shirt jobs of accountants, engineers, designers and creative thinkers.

Foreign-educated engineers, accountants and creative people perform just as well, if not better, than their U.S. counterparts. The standard of education in America is a disgrace. It is producing people with an attitude and fancy degrees who cannot compete with their smarter, lesser paid and less demanding foreign counterparts. Public schools and universities are much easier in the U.S. than most other countries. I know first hand. I found university easier than high school, and that was in the '60s when America and its universities were considered the best. So were U.S. Steel, General Motors, AT&T and the dollar. Do we want America to continue down the road its universities, steel, auto, telephone and financial institutions are on in the 21st century? I don't think so.

A knowledge-based economy needs smart, well-trained people who can compete in cost-effective ways, understand and participate in the political process that governs their lives. Something America is no longer doing as it enters the 21st century. The outflow of jobs from America is no longer something that can be ignored by *We the Apathetic Maids*. During the eight years of George W. Bush's presidency, more than 14 million jobs in America have been lost. If America does not address this issue realistically soon, the soup kitchens of the Depression era will look like a picnic at the beach.

### Ineffective Strikes

When the International Machinists Union went on strike against Boeing, the government and the Clinton administration decided to investigate union charges that U.S. industrial competitiveness was being seriously undermined by the shift of aerospace production to China by McDonnell Douglas and Boeing in exchange for airplane orders. The union represented 34,000 production workers in Seattle; Portland, Oregon, and Wichita, Kansas. All important states in any election.

China was already a major customer for McDonnell Douglas and Boeing products and is expected to buy an additional $100 billion worth of airplanes by the year 2015. The fact that Boeing today owns McDonell Douglas is another issue.

"This type of commercial and technological blackmail has occurred for years, but is now reaching a level to which the U.S. government must respond," said George Kourpis, the Machinists Union president.

Why? Is it worth losing the orders to Airbus in Europe, which the U.S. has and is? What jobs will that create for America's overpaid union members with unfunded pension benefits? The Chinese and French are delighted and thankful. America can have its freedom fries.

The 850,000-member United Steelworkers union decided to file a trade case against China in September 2010, as the midterm congressional elections heated up. The union accused China of unfairly subsidizing its clean energy industry solar pancls and wind turbines in violation of the World Trade Organization's free-trade rules.

Chinese makers of clean energy equipment have become global leaders, while manufacturers in the U.S. and Europe have struggled financially, cut jobs and in some cases moved operations to China. How is filing the complaint going to bring jobs back to America?

The only way to bring jobs back home is to restructure companies, just like General Motors and Chrysler were involuntarily, or voluntarily the way Herman Miller, a furniture maker based in southwestern Michigan, and Caterpillar and John Deere did. Slashing labor costs by 50 percent and diversifying internationally. Competitive U.S. companies today are leaner and meaner than they were in the '90s and operate worldwide. I recall conversations I had with executives of U.S. corporations based in the Midwest in the 1980s and '90s and advising them to go global and focus on Asia and being told: "We are international. We have operations in California and have some Chinese working for us," was not an unusual response. Corporate America was, and in many cases still is, very insular and provincial.

Midwest America has restructured. New efficient technologies, cost-cutting, outsourcing and developing new foreign markets – beyond California – are key. But a disturbing report by the National Association of Manufacturers at the height of the 2009 recession found that one-third of small and medium-sized U.S. manufacturers had no sales overseas and did not purchase materials or components internationally.

U.S. manufacturers and labor have to not only accept and restructure to survive, but remember the Darwinian and Founding Fathers' principals of survival of the fittest – politically and economically. That means getting meaner and leaner on both fronts, something America not only knows how to do because its Founding Fathers wrote the book, but something *We the Apathetic Maids* must demand.

The big bonus profit-sharing checks, some $8,000 or more, UAW union workers received from Ford and General Motors in early 2013 should be incentive enough and proof that the pudding of restructuring actually not only works, but tastes and feels good as well as an extra bonus. It was the second year such bonuses have been paid.

The checks underscore the financial stability GM and Ford have achieved in the recovery of the North America auto market. Ford's approximate 44,000 hourly workers could get paid more than $8,000 each. I am delighted to have contributed to their bonuses by leasing a Ford Mustang.

American manufacturers and workers were once the world model for production and economic benefits and there is no reason that it cannot happen again. I once worked in Detroit in what used to be the heart of America's global manufacturing leadership. Why can't America lead the new environmental revolution and cutting-edge industries instead of getting bogged down in traditional irrelevant industries in today's high-tech world?

The American worker is competing for every job in a global marketplace. They are losing out to cheaper workers in foreign countries because their U.S. employers are relocating jobs to lower-cost countries. Today, skilled and unskilled labor for just about every job in America can be shipped out to a foreign country at substantial savings.

## Contemporary Unions

When an internal fight at a trade union erupts into the news, American culture has a ready frame. It's Marlon Brando versus Lee J. Cobb in *On the Waterfront* once again, perhaps updated by a recent episode of *The Wire,* set among the corrupt and gritty longshoremen of the Baltimore docks. Or it's a modern-day retelling of the Jimmy Hoffa/Teamsters story, destined to end in another mysterious gangland murder.

But there are no shiny suits or pinkie rings in the conflict at the Service Employees International Union, the big, fast-growing organization of janitors, hospital workers and public employees with more than 650,000 members in California alone. All the dramatis personae are idealists who came out of the social movements of the 1960s and '70s, and although turf battles and dues money are certainly on the agenda, the real question they are debating is the road forward for the battered American trade union movement.

American labor unions must actively start thinking and acting out of the box. Like U.S. manufacturers, they have to become innovative and reinvent themselves, much like Sara Horowitz has done with the Freelancers Union she founded to meet the needs of today's workers.

The Freelancers Union has more than 40,000 members in New York and Connecticut and is expanding nationally.

"I had an epiphany that existing labor laws and regulations didn't fit the way people were working," Horowitz said. At Harvard's Kennedy School, she set about rethinking unionism. What do modern workers need? What gives a union power? She concluded that a union is a means for workers to join together to solve problems. To be effective it needs an economic model that makes it independent of government, employers and other institutions. And the biggest problem for freelancers? The lack of health insurance, which in America is mostly provided by employers, and usually only to permanent staff.

She has rejected the traditional union model of confrontation and charging membership dues unrelated to benefits received. Instead, with an un-unionlike enthusiasm for the discipline of the marketplace, she adopted a customer-centric approach. She provides members with a menu of services that they can choose to pay for, thus generating the funds to spend on the union's advocacy of freelance-friendly labor laws. For example, freelancers in America are generally not entitled to unemployment insurance, even if a job they have done for 18 months comes to an end. She has found a way to use the bulk-purchasing power of her members to drive down the cost of health-insurance premiums.

American labor should get back to its nobler goals. People have no tolerance or sympathy for Hollywood-type strikes, be they the Writers Guild of America, Screen Actors, Producers or Directors. Dock workers and machinists earning $100,000 plus a year going on strike these days generate about as much public support and sympathy as overpaid pro athletes and entertainers.

Since the late 19th-century, the Democratic Party has stood for workers' interests, and it interpreted their interests as being served by free trade. It used to be that big American corporations favored high tariff barriers to protect themselves against cheaper foreign goods, but Democrats saw that workers were served not by insulating their employers from competition, but by food, clothing and other necessities sold in the United States at low prices. The policy has created the disparity in disposable income.

As a result, America is a country of haves and have-nots co-existing on a very vulnerable and explosive economic tether. This was brought home in 2002 when 10,500 longshoremen and warehouse union workers were locked out at the 29 West Coast ports because of a contract dispute with the Pacific Maritime Association. A global economy designed by American haves making millions of dollars in bonuses was torpedoed and brought to a standstill by a bunch of $100,000 have-nots working the docks.

The same thing happened again in September 2010 when longshoremen went on a two-day strike in New York and New Jersey.

"People's livelihood is the prime mover of all social movements," said Sun Yat Sen. Karl Marx said that it is the economic base of the societal superstructure that determines the development of peoples. U.S. labor unions should look at the societal superstructures in other countries. Trying to impose trade barriers in America or in other countries' Economic Free Trade Zones, as they did to Jordan, is short-sighted.

While Americans are adjusting to economic change, the middle class is becoming an endangered species and a new underclass of illegal immigrants is emerging.

*We the Maids* have to find a way to save ourselves from ourselves. That requires that we get back to basics. Education and a realistic honest re-assessment and new approach to the geopolitical, domestic political and economic prison we are wallowing in.

### Effective Strikes

China's labor movement was shaken by the numerous unprecedented wildcat strikes that took place in 2010 that shut down foreign-owned factories, namely Japanese and Taiwanese. The "world's factory" has 400 million workers who are itching for a stronger voice and independent union representatives. The All China Federation of Trade Unions, which is run by the Communist Party, is seen as a tool of government and management and has lost all credibility with workers. Unlike their American counterparts which are independent of management, China's labor unions get most of their funds from their companies. As a result, workers led the strikes and ignored their union leaders with successful demands for better pay and the right to elect their own union representatives in their government-sanctioned union, or independent union.

The Labor Contract Law enacted in January 2008 was part of a government effort to move Chinese manufacturers upstream to higher-value products and away from those that rely solely on inexpensive labor for their competitive edge. The law specifically targets factories with poor working conditions, sets minimum standards for key employment terms such as working hours, overtime and severance policies. These protections have raised employees' expectations and awareness of their rights. It has also raised the costs for their employers.

Police officers who handed out leaflets to striking workers saying that going on strike was illegal and offenders could be thrown in jail for three to five years were ignored. Riot police and the paramilitary People's Armed Police were put on standby and had orders to swing into action to crush prolonged strikes and the widespread formation of illegal trade unions.

China has 1.7 million grassroots labor unions that have and can continue to play a constructive role with workers complaints as long as the government makes the necessary revamp to the union structure in China to ensure efficiency and collective bargaining to assure fair pay and fair working hours and working environment.

The world's largest contract electronics manufacturer, Foxconn Technology Group from Taiwan, doubled employees' basic salary after a spate of worker suicides in Shenzhen factories. Honda and Toyota also capitulated to wildcat strikes by workers who chose to ignore their company or government appointed union representatives who bullied, clashed and beat them to force them to return to work, and eventually received 24-28 percent or more in salary increases. The strikes at Honda led to parts shortages that closed four company factories in Guangzhou and Wuhan.

The Internet and mobile phones have become powerful tools that enable striking workers to quickly communicate the results of their negotiations, threatening to set off an epidemic of strikes nationwide if not addressed swiftly and constructively. The unrest poses serious risks for the Communist Party, which wants to avoid the development of alternative centers of power. That is why China's top leadership has acknowledged the grievances in an attempt to sooth the nation's increasingly restive population of migrant workers.

The Politburo members are very conscious that unless the government makes fundamental changes to how the economic pie is shared, it risks a wholesale revolution that could tear asunder the country's already tattered fabric. After all, Marxist theory holds that workers are the most important force in communism. They are also well aware of the late patriarch Deng Xiaoping's warnings about how Poland's Solidarity Movement undermined communist parties throughout the former Eastern Bloc.

I discussed the strikes with Tom Mitchell, president of the Foreign Correspondents Club Hong Kong in June 2010. He had written a few articles on the strikes for his paper, the *Financial Times*. Mitchell had joined David O'Rear, the chief economist of the Hong Kong General Chamber of Commerce, and I who were discussing the future of industrial actions in China over a drink at the FCC Main Bar.

"Quite remarkable. It is fascinating to watch and listen to these young workers, children of the peasants who brought the Communist Party to power, protest against the party's union and demand more workers rights and money," Mitchell said as he picked up his drink and walked off to continue politicking his way around the bar.

"I never cease to be amazed at the pompous arrogance of so many presidents. It doesn't matter if they are a president of a club or country. What is it with this attitude and air they put on when they take office?" I asked David. "How many times have you introduced me to him?" I asked.

"A couple," David said as we continued our debate about politics in America and the upcoming midterm election and the role unions play in the election of Democratic Party candidates, not only in the U.S., but Hong Kong.

Rival unions are a common phenomenom in America, China and Hong Kong. This was not only highlighted by the strikes in China, but in Hong Kong during the metal workers strike in 2007. The pro-democracy Confederation of Trade Unions took over negotiations in a pay dispute from its pro-government rival the Federation of Trade Unions. The strike lasted for 36 days. The striking metal workers received support from their fellow union members in America who came to Hong Kong to join them in their protests and advise on tactics – with the support of Democratic

Party legislators – a model to be emulated and duplicated in future labour disputes in America, China and elsewhere.

## *"Si Se Puede!"*

The boisterous American representatives of the Los Angeles County Federation of Labor, chanting "Si se puede!" – "Yes we can!" – in Spanish in Beijing in July 2007 really befuddled their bewildered translator. Their presence in China was an indication that a decades-old freeze between trade unions in the two countries had begun to thaw. Some U.S. labor leaders finally saw the light and decided to try out a new policy: "If you can't beat 'em, join 'em."

"This isn't just the theory of, 'Workers of the world unite,' " said Maria Elena Durazo, head of the L.A. Federation. "This is about very real needs that workers in both countries have."

"The Cold War is over," said Dave Arian, past international president of the ILWU and one of the members of the Los Angeles delegation. "The economy that they have in this country is essentially the same as we have in the United States."

The larger point made repeatedly by members of the delegation was that what happens in China affects the United States, and the management of multinational corporations is more than a decade ahead of labor in recognizing that. "Capital sees no boundaries," Durazo said. "Why should labor see a boundary?"

"We're just really dumbfounded about how they were able to organize Wal-Mart here," said Ray Familathe, director of international affairs for the International Longshore and Warehouse Union and one of the 10 members of the L.A. delegation.

Teamsters President James Hoffa also led a delegation from the Change to Win labor coalition to Beijing in June 2007.

The L.A. Federation established a formal sister-city partnership with the

Shanghai Trade Union Council, the first of its kind between unions in the two countries. The agreement establishes formal relations between the two unions and aims to "strengthen worker rights and to improve the conditions of workers in our countries."

The agreement would, in part, allow the U.S. union to offer assistance to the mainland union in organizing workers at multinational corporations in Shanghai. Both unions can learn from Germany's Works Councils – elected bodies representing all workers in a plant, blue and white collar – one of the best innovative features of a labor relations system.

## Migrant Worker Benefits – Rice & Rights

Migrant worker strikes and protests in China are not just about pay raises They are about the basic social welfare rights they have been denied by a government that has forced them to work long hours in dangerous unsafe conditions, without bereavement leave or pensions, for derisory pay. There were more than 10,000 labor disputes in the Pearl River Delta, the manufacturing heartland of China. In 2008, a high-ranking local union official described strikes as "as natural as arguments between a husband and wife." With two ex-wives, I can relate. The reality is, it is the only way migrant workers draw attention to their plight.

Migrant workers put in 12 hours a day six days a week, 60 hours a month overtime. They make up more than 40 percent of the urban labor force. They are the "silent majority backbone" of China's impressive economic development. Yet they are excluded from education, health care and social services in the cities where they work. The existing hukou, or household registration system, is too rigid to accommodate today's realities. They are a floating population of more than 200 million people on the move, with some analysts predicting that it will reach 300 million by 2015.

The strict regulation of social benefits legally ties residents to one area of the country. Most of the migrants are unregistered and therefore unable to claim either government benefits or protection from employer exploitation. They are second-class citizens in their own homeland. The country of Mao's Communist Party that used to honor and respect the workers. Workers were the model citizens. Today, living alongside their urban cousins, migrant workers not only face unfair treatment from employers, but are held in contempt by city dwellers. They are deprived, angry people.

The minimum wage is not enough for even a basic lifestyle of food, rent and clothing. Professor Lu Huilin, from Beijing University, says the minimum wage policy, meant to protect worker's rights, actually helps employers exploit workers. "Migrant workers spend most of their income on food, which means their other basic needs such as accommodation, transport or basic social contacts can't be fulfilled."

As the need for more urban workers – the human capital fueling economic development the rest of the world envies – rises in China, government regulation of internal migration needs to be changed and evolve with the times to put these workers on an equal footing in education, medical treatment and insurance.

Things are much worse for Chinese migrants in Japan. Their plight was laid bare in a 2011 report titled "Throwaway Labour," by *China Labour Bulletin*. It documents the long hours, low pay and bad living and working conditions of Chinese in farms, textile plants and other factories. It focuses on Japan, but the same story is repeated in many countries. Most revealing is the fact that the exploitation is arranged with an acceptable name – "trainee." Since Japan severely restricts the import of unskilled labor, it had to create a "trainee system" to legalize these workers. Workers willing to do the work that no Japanese wants to do.

They are required to hand over their passports and bank books to their employers upon arrival. They are not allowed to leave the town where they work. They are forbidden from using the Internet or having a mobile phone.

The March 2011 nuclear tsunami only made matters worse, not only for the Japanese, but for migrant workers there, including the Chinese.

"China is entering into a new era of enhanced consciousness among workers," says Dong Baohua, professor of law at East China University of Politics and Law. "Workers born after the 1980s and 1990s are concerned not just about pay but about safety, rights and respect."

As a result, many migrants are moving back home to China's farming heartland where factories from the coastal regions are also relocating. Lower labor costs for workers happy to receive less but be with their families and friends and receive the benefits denied them in the cities and manufacturing centers. Today's mainland migrant workers want to build a life where they work. Company campus dorms are no longer an acceptable option for China's new generation of workers unless the working conditions and pay make it really worth their while to save enough and then move back home. Less than 44 percent of migrant workers plan to return to their hometowns today, according to a 2010 report by the China Youth Research Center. This was in sharp contrast to a 1999 study by Tsinghua University that showed 90 percent of migrant workers left their home to earn money and intended to return.

The same happened in America during the Great Migration from 1915 to 1970, when nearly 6 million African Americans migrated North out of the South because of Jim Crow's "invisible hand" that hanged or burned alive someone every four days from 1889 to 1929, according to Isabel Wilkerson in her epic story of America's Great Migration, The Warmth of Other Suns, changing the face of not just the South but the entire country – just as China's migrant workers are doing today.

The unexpected upside bonus for these returning migrants is that their home provinces are adopting minimum wage laws modelled after the industrial cities the workers left. Northwest China's Qinghai province announced that starting September 2010, its minimum wage would increase by 28.8 percent, making it the 27th province in the country to adopt a minimum wage law. Each province has different minimum wage laws. Shanghai has the highest monthly minimum standard take-home pay and Beijing has the highest minimum hourly wage. Different regions within each province have different minimum wage laws. Something America should consider. What happened to the state rights that the Founding Fathers advocated?

The U.S. Labor Department should be abolished and each state, county and city allowed to adopt their own labor laws – many already have – and minimum wage laws to get their citizens jobs with local employers, even foreign employers who are now outsourcing to America. Indian firms that are the primary beneficiaries of outsourcing from America are now outsourcing back to America. The future of outsourcing, said Ashok Vemuri, senior vice-president of Indian technology giant Infosys, is "to take the work from any part of the world and do it in any part of the world."

India's Cognizant Technology Solutions, with most of its operations in India, has opened offices in Phoenix, Arizona. Wipro, another Indian company, has opened a software development center in Atlanta. Wipro's chairman, Azim Premji, told Wall Street analysts in 2007 that he was considering establishing hubs in Idaho and Virginia, in addition to Georgia, to take advantage of "states which are less developed."

To address this return-home migration trend in China, provincial governments are adopting urban residency schemes to allow migrant workers from rural parts of a province to apply for permanent residency in small and medium-sized cities and townships and share in all the local social welfare benefits they are currently denied. Shouldn't America be doing the same?

A snapshot of China's increasingly volatile two-tier society in its major cities was a 2010 picture of a 2-year-old boy chained to a tree in Beijing. Far from being a gross act of child cruelty, the boy was restrained by his loving father to keep him safe from child snatchers who had taken his 4-year-old sister only days earlier because his hard-working dad was too poor to pay for a proper minder or a school. A cheap lock and chain were the only affordable option.

New Labor, a band known across China, was formed by Xu Guojian and Sun Heng, two former migrant laborers who are repaying their migrant fans by funding a school for their children and a migrant workers' museum. Their story is no different than a lot of America's musicians and singers who started out life working as migrants, or worse, sharecroppers like B.B. King. America's blues from the Mississippi Delta are being retuned in China's new world disorder to a hotter-redder beat.

*Slavery*

The misery that millions of migrant workers endure in China pales in comparison to the pain the millions of people trapped in Asian slavery suffer – and slaves suffer worldwide – including America.

Shocking images of men and children padlocked and brutalized in stifling brickworks, with the young girls forced into prostitution and mentally disabled workers grinding rock into powder in China, shipworkers locked in outdoor cages to prevent them from complaining about their unpaid wages in Singapore, fishermen enslaved on fishing boats in Thailand and Malaysia without pay or seeing land for three years, sweat shop workers and maids in America. When these slaves get sick, most notably on the fishing boats, their bodies are thrown overboard, just as they were when the trans-Atlantic slave trade thrived in the 15th through 19th century.

More than three-quarters of the world's 12.3 million forced laborers are in Asia and the Pacific, where 9.5 million are trapped by debt bondage, trafficking and other coercion, the International Labor Organization estimates. The organization puts the global slave work force at about 27 million, many of them children. Child slavery is rife. For China's Communist Party, the worker's liberator, this can be fatal. Especially when the slave traffickers and employers are allowed to continue operating by the workers party.

I can understand how easily one can be trapped by debt bondage. When I decided to migrate to America from Cyprus in 1964, after returning from Israel where I graduated from high school, I had no money and my single working mom didn't have money to spare for a one-way ticket. Luckily for me, I had a British passport that allowed me to immigrate legally because the quota system at the time was based on country of citizenship, so I did not have to contend with a long waiting list as one does today, or getting there illegally.

Getting to America legally was another story. Loan sharks and snakeheads, who were smuggling Greek and Turkish Cypriots to Europe, Australia and the U.S. on credit, were charging exorbitant prices. In the end, I decided to approach some of the travel agencies I had worked for as a tour guide during the summers to see if I could buy a ticket on credit from to get to the States by ship, the cheapest mode of transportation at the time. Luckily, I found one that agreed to sell me a ticket on onerous terms to get back to Israel on an overnight ship where I could catch another ship to New York, via several stops across the Mediterannean and Atlantic. The journey took two weeks.

It took me almost two years to pay off that ticket. I had to send monthly checks whenever I could and my mother contributed to the cause.

I can understand how ruthless criminal gangs lure innocent country bumpkins into debt-traps from which they find it almost impossible to escape. Interest rates are so high that, in effect, they never get out of debt.

Leading slave nations include China, India, Pakistan and Indonesia – nations where child labor remains common – as well as Burma, where the military regime oversees widespread forced labor.

America has its fair share of slaves to this day. Illegals trafficked into the U.S. from Africa, Asia, Latin America and the Caribbean. Having lived in the Philippines for a couple of years, where Filipinos pride themselves on their scams to get jobs overseas and send money back home to support their families, I am more familiar with their experience of voluntary and involuntary servitude. Filipinos even have a name for the legions of undocumented who go to America and choose to overstay their tourist visas. In Filipino slang they are TNT, *tago ng tago,* or "always in hiding," many as slaves. Not just in America, but throughout the Middle East.

Nena Ruiz, a Filipina working as a domestic servant for a vice president of legal affairs for Sony Pictures Entertainment, sued him and his wife for enslaving her. She worked 18 hours a day. Her work included microwaving chicken nuggets and cutting up bananas and pears for the couple's dog. Ruiz, meanwhile, was fed leftovers and slept in a dog bed. A jury awarded her $825,000 in back wages and punitive damages.

In another case, Elma Manlinguez was paid 6 cents an hour to work under slavelike conditions as a caregiver for the family of a Merrill Lynch executive in New Jersey. They settled with her for $175,000.

Then in 2008, a Milwaukee jury awarded close to $1 million in compensation to a Filipina who worked illegally for 20 years for a Wisconsin physician couple.

A former housekeeper for the top diplomatic official at India's consulate in New York filed a lawsuit in 2011 saying that Consul General Prabhu Dayal took her passport and intimidated her into a year of forced labor, where she was subjected to 105-hour work weeks for only a few dollars an hour in pay – along with sexual advances.

The one that really got my attention and outrage was the forced labor used by the secretive Catholic group Opus Dei. A lawsuit filed by Catherine T. in France claims she joined a hoteliers' school in northeastern France in 1985, aged 14, which she later discovered was run by associates of Opus Dei, who forced her to take vows of obedience, poverty, chastity and made her work for 12 years as a domestic servant for virtually no pay. Staff members followed her every move, even to visits to Opus Dei doctors who prescribed tranquilizers that left her "senseless."

Why does slavery still exist today? Poverty is the root cause and drives the engine of supply and demand. Supply: abundant cheap labor. Demand: First-world clamor for anyone to do disagreeable, menial tasks that no one else will do.

Why is it that Muslim and Catholics are in the forefront of slavery – even today – as Jews and Protestants duke it out in a Buddhist and Hindu world that condone it?

Human rights groups say that many of the world's estimated hundreds of millions of migrant workers are in dire predicaments and becoming slaves as economic woes in the Middle East, Gulf states and Africa lead to mass layoffs.

*Slavery Lessons*
The past is present in America, many African, Asian, Latin American, Catholic and Muslim countries. In America, illegally smuggled maids are treated like slaves at the dawn of the 21st century and pursue their civil rights claims under an 1865 statute that allows parties to sue for involuntary servitude.

In Sudan, the Islamic fundamentalist government has been using slave raids as the terror weapon of choice in its self-declared "holy war" against the Christians and Tribalists in the south in failed efforts to prevent the mineral-rich south from voting for independence, as it did in 2011.

Charles Jacobs, president of the American Anti-Slavery Group in Boston, reminds us of this ugly present-day reality.

"Theresa Nybol Deng is a slave. She was taken captive when the government-armed militia stormed her village in southern Sudan. Soldiers shot the men, looted the village and carted off as many women and children as they could. Theresa is 12 years old. She can be purchased for $50. Like all women and girls being traded, she is usually gang-raped at night while in transit.

"If her fate is anything like that of tens of thousands of black Africans who have become chattel in Sudan's civil war, Theresa has been sold and bought. She is likely serving a master somewhere in northern Sudan, Saudi Arabia, Libya or the Persian Gulf. If she was selected as a concubine, she will have been genetically mutilated – to be acceptable in her master's culture – and then she will have been bred." So what else is new? Another war for oil!

SOS Slaves is a group based in France and run by former slaves and Abdel Nasser, a former slave owner. SOS uses ex-slaves to infiltrate nomadic camps in remote parts of Africa to let current slaves know that freedom is possible.

Zurich-based Christian Solidarity International raises funds to buy slaves and their freedom. Thousands have been bought at $50 a head or two goats. Children in Benin, Togo and across West and Central Africa are also sold daily for a lot less. Desperately poor parents give up their children for as little as $15. The Abidjan market in the Ivory Coast is open for the slave business in the 21st-century world disorder we live in. Children are still sold into slavery to work on plantations or as domestics in Saudi Arabia, the Gulf States, Africa and Asia.

The same practice took place in the Pacific Islands for slaves needed in Australia to work the cane fields. From 1863 to 1903, ships from Australia scoured the South Seas, forcibly removing thousands of "kankas," the Hawaiian name for "boys." About 62,000 South Sea Islanders were enticed onto ships bound for the cane fields from Melanesia - modern day Vanuatu, New Caledonia, the Solomon Islands and Papua New Guinea. Recruiters stood on deck singing Christian hymns, inviting islanders on board to hear a sermon. Once aboard, they were promptly thrown in the ship's hold and never seen by their relatives again.

Slavery dates back to Mesopotamia in 6,000 B.C. and still flourishes today. Estimates of the numbers trafficked each year range from 700,000 to 4 million, but few reliable figures exist. The reason for the disparity is that the number includes people who agree or pay to be smuggled across borders to places where they can find work who are then trafficked, illegal adoptions, fake marriages, and cases of high-level officials who traffic in servants under cover of diplomatic immunity.

Sergei Ponomarev traveled to the village of Arshty from Tyumen in Siberia 28 years ago looking for work, but found himself drafted into slavery for nearly 30 years until he was freed by Russian soldiers in the Caucasian republic of Ingushetia. The mountainous Caucasus republics of southern Russia have a tradition of slavery.

When the Portuguese, the first Europeans to arrive in Africa, traveled down the Senegal River south of Mauritania in 1444, they reported a flourishing trade in slaves, with the Moors getting nine to 12 per horse. It was common practice for African kings to take captives from other tribes and use them as slaves or to exchange for goods and arms.

Cocoa traders from Europe on buying trips to Africa sample cocoa beans picked by kidnapped children, who are slaves.

America and China have to lead the global effort to wipe out this rampant slavery and exploitation.

For Africans to ask for compensation from Europeans or America for the slave traffic of the 19th century when they engaged in the trade for hundreds of years before that – and still do – is absurd.

It is estimated there are approximately 50,000 serfs held in virtual slavery in Pakistan. They are swapped and sold like animals and kept in chains. In India, millions of school-age children are kept in virtual slavery as household domestics. The Indian government is addressing this grave injustice and passed a law in 2003 mandating that all children up to age 14 go to school to be educated.

In China, beggar children, many of whom have been kidnapped, are being reunited with their families through an online campaign that encourages Internet users to post photographs of the children and their whereabouts to be compared with pictures of missing children.

In Thailand, Vietnamese women are enslaved in illegal baby-breeding factories to produce adoptive babies for wealthy overseas couples who place orders online. The "eugenics" surrogacy service, from egg and sperm donations to delivery of a baby, is advertised for $32,000 and is mostly aimed at Taiwanese customers.

Approximately 27 million individuals around the world today are held in some form of slavery. Why do *We the Apathetic Maids* allow this travesty to continue in the New World Disorder?

The Jewish Passover feast celebrates freedom, not only the escape from slavery; we must also be our true selves, thereby becoming truly free.

There is no reason why the tragic lessons of slavery should not be taught in every school in the world today. There is every need for a thorough and dispassionate return to the teaching of history and current affairs by honest professionals.

### Credit Culture & Revolution

Getting to America in 1964 on credit was my introductory lesson to micro-credit finance. Once here, living off credit cards that were easily obtainable, was a great part of the American dream and a way of life, especially in L.A. Easy and cheap credit allowed me to pay off my ticket to America. Credit cards were literally the "gold that paved the streets of America" – especially the gold cards. They paid for everything – gas, food and life. Using one card to pay the monthly payment of another, or better yet, switching to another card from another bank at a lower rate was the norm. Credit and sex were easy and plentiful, as was an affordable college education, jobs that helped pay for the lifestyle, with prospects for a great future is what America was all about in the '60s and '70s.

Government guaranteed student loans that ensured a good education without having to worry about how to pay for it. Money was easy and jobs were plentiful to pay off loans. Cashing checks without money in the account to cover them was the norm. After bouncing a few rubber checks, banks showered you with overdraft protection and new credit cards – or increased the limit on existing cards – or both. Supermarket check-cashing cards made bouncing checks a breeze as all one had to do was present a check to the store cashier with a check cashing card and presto! – cash in hand. It didn't matter that there was no money in the account. Not just for individuals but for corporate America. The corporate "check-kiting" schemes of the day were a wonder to behold for lawyers like myself who represented banks.

And people are surprised that the subprime crisis hit? Took down a few banks, millions of jobs and homes, neighborhoods, towns and communities?

Buying a home back then was affordable and low-interest 20-30 year mortgages were common. I bought and sold three fixer-uppers within a few years and more than doubled my money each time I sold – and that was while raising a family and building a law practice. A credible story was the only collateral required. That's when bankers were bankers and financed capitalist entrepreneurs. Then the MBAs who grew up on video games took over banking with their software programs.

And how about credit reports? The credit reporting industry is like a government unto itself. It puts together credit information it then sells to determine the credit-worthiness of consumers – many of whom have been victims of inaccurate reports with no power to do anything about it. Estimates of the error rate in credit reports vary anywhere from 3 percent to 25 percent. People who find errors are caught in a trap in which they must prove that they do not owe the debt but are ignored when they try, unless, of course, they are a politician or a celebrity.

I know first hand. I found out about the new credit system when I moved back to the U.S. and went to lease a Mustang. My credit score was zero because there was no credit history on me in America. No surprise really since I had lived in China and Asia the last 24 years. But that was it. None of the banks working with Ford would finance my lease. Ford went ahead and financed the lease. So it cost me more, but look at the bright side on the floor of the Ford plant.

Try writing a rubber check or getting a cheap long-term mortgage to buy a home today. Impossible. The only people allowed to write rubber checks are the banks. Big ones too. The bigger the bank – the bigger the bounce. So big they brought the world to its knees in 2008. But unlike the '60s and '70s when *We the People* had to cover our rubber checks, bankers don't think they should. They convince the career politicians they bankroll to bail them out and cover their multi-trillion rubber checks and make *We the Apathetic Maids* clean up their financial mess.

What happened? The '80s, inflation and payback time. Savings and loans, Chrysler, Lockheed and other icons of capitalist America went broke and guess who picked up the tab again? *We the Apathetic Maids*. Taxpayers then, like today, got stiffed. How much more before *We the Apathetic Maids* say, "Enough is enough!"

How come at a time when the average American can't get a loan or an overdraft line, the taxpayers have to clean up the banks' financial mess to cover and pay the humungous multi-trillion bounced checks of these swindlers in pinstripes?

One answer is that we have gone from being a credit-driven economy to a debit-driven one. Individuals and families, like government agencies and the state or federal government – and China and many other countries – are sitting on a fiscal cliff because of the financial and economic changes engineered by bankers and their paid-for career politicians that has now given us a deficit spending-driven economy that precludes credit instead of the prudent credit-driven economy that fuels growth and prosperity.

Sex may be the only good thing left in America today. People "hooking up" the way I remember it. But then again, so is the whole world. So sex alone no longer makes America special.

Easy credit, affordable education, jobs that paid for a middle-class lifestyle are gone the way of the Founding Fathers' dream.

### Agrarian Cities

Flying across America and the world, as I do regularly, I'm always amazed at the vast expanses of uninhabited arable land everywhere. Mountains, deserts, forests, and endless countryside surrounding the world's mega-cities and towns that could easily be utilized by the world's unemployed poor and trillions of dollars otherwise wasted by career politicians on senseless wars and ego-maniacal-mega-edifices honoring themselves.

The point was really brought home to me in May 2009, when I came across a report – "Land Grab or Development Opportunity?" prepared by the Food and Agricultural Organization and the International Fund for Agricultural Development of the U.N. and the International Institute for Environment and Development, a London-based think-tank.

The report highlighted how African countries are giving away vast tracts of land to other countries and investors in exchange for vague promises of jobs

353

and infrastructure. Rich countries like Saudi Arabia and South Korea invest in overseas land to boost their food security. The investors plan to export all, or a large share of, the crops back to feed their own people. Locals are lucky to get any jobs while the political leaders who give away the people's land to foreigners surely benefit handsomely for their benevolence.

The report studied cases in Ethiopia, Ghana, Mali, Madagascar and Sudan and discovered foreign government farmland investments totalling 2.5 million hectares – the equivalent of about half the arable land of the United Kingdom. In other words, poor local farmers see their land and water given away to foreign governments to feed those people while the locals go hungry.

The same thing is happening in Latin America and the Philippines, where China is trying to buy up as much land as it can to farm soybeans to feed chickens and hogs back home and its nearly 1.5 billion people. The Latinos are not so quick to sell, so China is providing credit to farmers resulting in the tripling of the amount of soybeans grown. China, like Saudi Arabia, is farming out its nation's fervor for agricultural self-sufficiency overseas.

Why isn't this fertile African and Latin American land – and the millions of dormant acres of fertile arable land in Africa, the Americas, Asia, Europe and the rest of the world – put to productive use by having experts from around the world work with locals to show them how to share in the profitable production of the land through farming or urban development?

With so many crowded slums in so many cities worldwide, why haven't these people who have lost their land and jobs been resettled in new agrarian towns where they can be taught to be self-sufficient?

The world reached a turning point in 2008, when for the first time most of its population lived in towns and cities. The poor, unemployed city dwellers are the advance teams for political unrest and armed conflict. We see it in Detroit, Rio de Janeiro, Tripoli, Cairo and every other major city in the world with overcrowded unemployed slum dwellers who provide unscrupulous career politicians and gangs with a ready pool of foot soldiers and slaves.

Nearly 80 percent of Americans now live in urban areas. Why not provide them with the educational opportunities to become self-sufficient farmers or small business entrepreneurs and move them back to the country?

## Free Trade

The protesters in Seattle during the first World Trade Organization meeting in 1999 reminded me of the protests of the '60s. Most of the young protesters had pagers, portable laptops and palm tops, all toys made overseas thanks to free trade and commerce. Like their predecessors, they were protesting a value system and demanding the right to know the truth. They demanded to know by what right they could be told by career politicians what they could buy and sell and where.

Free global trade benefits all. Trade barriers and trade wars hurt all of *We the People*. Look at what happened in 1930 when a new faction gained power in the U.S. Congress. President Herbert Hoover signed the Smoot-Hawley bill raising tariffs on imports. Retaliation followed in other countries, followed by counter retaliation, and as world trade declined, a severe global depression set in. The same thing had happened in China several centuries earlier.

In 1430, a new faction of mandarins gained influence at the court of the Chinese emperor. They argued that commerce was contemptible, agriculture was the true source of wealth and the great voyages to the Indian Ocean, Africa and the Americas of the previous 25 years had proved the futility of trade.

The Chinese evidently took some persuading. But by 1436 it was illegal to assign new craftsmen to shipyards, by 1500 it was a capital offense to build a three-masted ship, and by 1551 it was a crime even to go to sea on a multi-masted ship. The result was four centuries of decline for China, four centuries of prosperity for America, Europe and Hong Kong.

The Hong Kong government is opposed to subsidies and a believer in an open, fair and free international trading system. Hong Kong's former Secretary for Commerce, Industry and Technology, Henry Tang Ying-yen, said: "We firmly believe that free trade is an important foundation of economic growth."

The Permanent Normal Trading Relations bill does not open the United States to more Chinese products. Rather, it opens China to more American goods and investment and creates a mechanism that can be used by unions to challenge alleged unfair Chinese practices. Ka-ching is not the premier of China. It's the sound of American cash registers receiving payment from China.

Unions should support lowering tariffs not just for China, but for Japan, Thailand, Vietnam, Africa, the Caribbean, Iraq, Iran – anywhere there are people to unionize. Labor should capitalize on American jobs moving overseas. It should organize those workers!

American union members who lose their jobs when they are outsourced can get training for new jobs in the new global economy. One in 20 U.S. workers was employed in the high-tech sector in 1999 – nearly 6 million jobs. They earned 82 percent more than the private sector average. The implosion of the tech bubble in 2000 resulted in the loss of more than 1 million jobs over the next three years, but these workers are back in demand again and high-tech payrolls are rising in 2011. The U.S. exported $181 billion worth of high-tech goods in 1999. By 2008, it had reached $233 billion before tailing off in the Great Recession to $188 billion in '09. Now those exports are edging back up and projections are for dramatic increases.

The new global reality requires that American labor get out of its narrow old mind-set and begin to see the high-tech cyber world in a new light – at home, in Asia and throughout the developing world.

Corporations go global for a simple reason – to reduce costs and maximize profits. That's corporate capitalism's mandate. But profits in many cases are excessive and even obscene, when measured against what workers producing the goods are making. As long as workers struggle to put food on the table while their greedy corporate employers wallow in excessive profits, there will be anger and frustration and confrontation. At the dawn of the 21st century, there has to be a better way – a balance, a new middle ground. Yin and yang. That is, the capitalists make less, the workers get more. It's a balance that must be achieved between management and workers – or else.

Hong Kong demonstrated in 2010 how divisive the debate over fair wages can be, and that it can be resolved. Hong Kong, the capital of monopolistic unbridled capitalism, never had a minimum wage law, but finally adopted one that summer. The widening wealth gap forced the government, as it should all governments, to respond and adopt realistic minimum wage laws relevant to today's world to shrink the widening wealth gaps. Hong Kong's experience is a working model. America and other countries with minimum wage laws should revisit these laws every two years, as Ireland did when it had to be bailed out in November 2010, in light of today's global economic quagmire and dire unemployment – and easily employable, cheaper illegal immigrants.

The first national minimum wage law was passed in the 19th century in New Zealand. Most sustainable industrialized and industrializing capitalist economies in the world enforced a minimum wage in the 20th century. Even less developed countries like Angola and Cameroon in Africa, Bangladesh and Cambodia in Asia and Bolivia and Dominica in Latin America have minimum wage laws in place. In 2004, China passed its first minimum wage law.

These laws do not protect only the unskilled labor pool. Labor is not merely a producer or a part of the cost of production or services. It has more far-reaching implications. Labor is also a consumer. The more workers make, the more they consume. Economic growth depends on consumer demand. Minimum wage laws are often skirted by employers who force employees to become self-employed independent contractors.

Half the world's 2.8 billion workers and their families today survive on less than $2 a day; 550 million workers earn less than $1 a day, according to the

International Labor Organization.

A comprehensive graduated global minimum wage is something that must be considered in the 21st century. The current flood of illegal migrants will be stemmed in the future only when the gap between worker income in rich and poor countries is narrowed by a comprehensive global minimum wage to allow for the global free flow of people with the same ease as capital, goods and services.

Michael Ardon, a professor of chemistry at the Hebrew University in Jerusalem, astutely observes: "In the aftermath of September 11, the time has come to realize that a deluxe globalization for the rich, without globalization of the labor force, is not sustainable, and that until some equity is attained between poor and rich countries, no true globalization will be achieved. Furthermore, if the gap between the two worlds is not narrowed, the poor countries will continue to breed forces that endanger the very existence of our civilization."

Powerful words indeed. Hong Kong is very realistic about its brewing revolution. Chief Executive Donald Tsang Yam-kuen delivered a blunt message to the business community in November 2010. He quoted Bob Dylan, telling them times are changing. He told them that people are fed up with the greed and excesses of the business class. He told them the people will no longer tolerate the inequalities forced on them for so long. He told them to change with the times.

"He, in essence, told business leaders to wake up and smell the revolution," Michael Chugani, a Hong Kong political columnist, told me at Bert's Bar at the Foreign Correspondents Club in Hong Kong when I complimented a piece he had written entitled *Smell the Revolution*. Shouldn't the White House and Congress be telling America's corporate titans and their lobbyists the same thing?

Fortune 100 companies today are what empires used to be. Unelected and unaccountable to career politicians, regulators, shareholders and taxpayers, even though in theory and law they are supposed to be. Many are mismanaged, unmanageable, corrupt and disintegrate, as Bear Stearns, Lehman Brothers, Enron, Arthur Anderson, WorldCom, Global Crossing, and General Motors reminded us at the dawn of the 21st century.

The Koening sphere at the World Trade Center in New York City, which managed to survive 9/11, symbolizes a world at peace and trade. Interlocal and interactive.

"A world where some live in comfort and plenty while half of the human race lives on less than $2 a day is neither just nor stable," President George W. Bush declared at the G-8 summit of 2001.

Yet what has America done to back up that concern? Nothing. The country's aid budget stands at 0.1 percent of GDP, the lowest share of any country in the 22-member Organization for Economic Cooperation and Development, and much lower than the 0.8 percent of GDP that the United States gave in 1960.

The World Bank estimates that scrapping all rich-country tariffs on goods from sub-Saharan Africa would boost that region's income by $2.5 billion a year! A good beginning to alleviate poverty. Economic integration of rich nations and poor ones is not just a humanitarian nobel task. It is a matter of global self-preservation and security to reverse the hatred and frustration felt by the hungry and deprived that religious extremist terrorists prey upon and recruit. A level playing field without government intervention and subsidies benefits all and eliminates weak well-funded career politicians and their inept corporate financial backers.

### Genoa Salami-8 and 20 Slices Too Many

The Genoa G-8 summit of 2001 became a Genoa salami. A very expensive old world unhealthy and unsettling dining experience for the career politicians and bureaucrats of the New World Disorder.

The Genoa summit was the anti-poverty summit. Italy says it spent $110 million to host the event. Roughly $45 million more than Japan spent the previous year in Okinawa. This does not count the $20 million in property damage caused by the demonstrators. The figure spent by the Italian taxpayers does not include the cost the taxpayers of each country that attended had to pay for their delegation members. America with a delegation of 600 naturally had the biggest tab picked up by *We the Apathetic Maids*. Tabs for fat cats flying in private jets, driven around in limos and dining on fine wines, cheeses and expensive meats.

For a summit that was addressing debt reduction and world poverty, one can't help but weep at the waste of money that could be better used to alleviate poverty.

The G-8 summits began in 1975 when French President Valery Giscard d'Estaing suggested that the leaders of the industrialized nations get together for a weekend to discuss common problems and solutions. What started as the G-5 soon became the G-7 and then the G-8 and finally the G-8-plus 5 that took place in L'Aquila, Italy in 2009. Entourages of bureaucrats kept growing to the point where they self-imploded at L'Aquila, best remembered as the group's wake – because the last piece of the Genoa salami was sliced off – circumcision a-la-Berlusconi. The G-20 is the current successor wasteful overstuffed fat cats' hot dog.

The second G-20 meeting that took place in Pittsburgh in September 2009, as well as the subsequent meetings, marked by continued clashes with protesters, injuries, arrests and broken windows of America's iconic global banks and fast-food outlets, only confirmed the futility of these 20th-century salamis that are irrelevant to the 21st century, no matter whether they have 8, 20 or any other number of slices. The absurdity of G-20 is the number of actual participants, which is far greater than 20. It wasn't just China, India, Argentina, Australia, Brazil, Indonesia, Mexico, Saudi Arabia, South Africa, Turkey and the EU that were added. The heads of the U.N. agencies, ILO, IMF, Unctad, the World Bank, the WTO, plus regional heads of Africa, Asean and Latin America are also there. One has to seriously question if anyone listens or cares to the cacophony of conflicting voices. The results of these meetings, other than the multi-million-dollar taxpayer bills, are empty pronouncements that bear no fruit and only reaffirm the fact that the global system is broken.

Countries are preoccupied with their own domestic political agendas and view such get-togethers as photo-opportunities with other world leaders to prop up their domestic political standing.

America and the world it leads should try going back to G-Zero and the Interlocal Security Council I proposed in *Custom Maid Knowledge*.

### Cancun Snakepit

Cancun means snakepit in the local Mayan language. The collapse of the world trade talks at Cancun highlighted the snakepit of problems underlying subsidized world trade barriers. In Cancun, big emerging market players like Brazil, China, Nigeria, India and South Africa led a group of 22 countries that insisted on concessions in the massive subsidized agricultural sectors in America, Europe and Japan before they made any more on behalf of the developing world. Something the developed world was not used to, as it usually forced its will on the poorer nations by promising more aid. The developed worlds insistence on maintaining their agricultural welfare programs to the detriment and hunger of developing nations in Africa, Asia and Latin America is another nonstarter in the 21st century. America and Europe must exert the political will necessary to reduce and eventually remove their state subsidized agricultural welfare programs if they are to meet their Doha 2001 commitments and undertakings.

China's agricultural exports account for just over 5 per cent of its overseas trade. Nevertheless, as a newcomer to the WTO that does not benefit by the reduction of farm subsidies, it gave fellow emerging markets the moral support they needed to highlight their plight and humble America and its arrogant Euro-Japanese subsidizing alliance.

### Hong Kong Contribution

During the Cancun get-together anti-globalization protesters in Hong Kong staged peaceful protests in front of government headquarters and the U.S. Consulate. They carried "Down with U.S. Imperialism," "NO GATTS," and "No to WTO" placards in support of their fellow protesters in Cancun.

The repeated failure of WTO member states to agree on eliminating subsidies has resulted in roughly 250 bilateral and multilateral trade agreements being signed by member states, with about 50 more under negotiation. These agreements were supposed to be eliminated by the WTO adopting agreements that all members ratified. America and Europe see two-way agreements as a way to liberalize global trade. Many economists disagree. They feel bilateral agreements threaten the stability of the global system. Arvind Panagariya, a trade expert at the University of Maryland, says the proliferation of such agreements, given that the purpose of the WTO was to ensure that low tariffs available to one member were available to all, is "fragmenting the world trading system badly."

Joseph Massey, a former U.S. trade negotiator who teaches international business at Dartmouth College, doesn't believe global trade talks will achieve much until agricultural subsidies are tackled.

"If we want to get serious about trade, the U.S. and the European Union have to get serious about the removal of farm subsidies," Massey argues. "Why are we making demands on smaller countries to give up their domestic barriers, but we don't give up our own?"

Hong Kong hosted the WTO's sixth ministerial conference, which brought over 8,000 visitors – along with hordes of anti-globalization activists.

*Neutral Asia-Pacific Forum*
A Interlocal Security Council structured and headquartered in Hong Kong, as proposed in *Custom Maid Knowledge,* offers a neutral setting to discuss and explore all political, military and economic points of view. Hong Kong is not tainted by the distorted career political lenses so prevalent at Davos, New York, Quebec, Washington and Seattle. Neither is it prejudiced by the market economies of China, America or Porto Alegre.

Protests and demonstrations, like political parties, are going global in the 21st century. In Hong Kong, at least they are peaceful. Common causes are global and unite people everywhere thanks to the Internet. A blend of grass roots disorder and new age discipline. Protesters in Hong Kong demonstrate vocally, creatively, but peacefully. This was evident during the 1989 Tiananmen protests in Victoria Park when a million people rallied peacefully and again during the 2003 protest by an estimated half-million people against Article 23, the proposed anti-subversion law, China's version of the Patriot Act.

The same happened again in the fall of 2012, when Beijing tried to impose a Communist Party curriculum, courses from their point of view that the Hong Kong Education Department accepted and tried to force-feed Hong Kong schools. The Hong Kong public was outraged – and let the government and Beijing know – and the government backed down and withdrew the curriculum.

Hong Kong's youthful new rebellious mood was again on display in January 2010 when the so-called post-1980s generation rose up in anger against what they saw as a rigged system that favors the privileged class at their expense. Their siege of the Legislative Council, Hong Kong's equivalent to Congress, clashes with riot police and jeering outside Government House put the government and the business community on notice that Hong Kong had reached its breaking point.

Hong Kongers can easily welcome and embrace fellow global citizens to peacefully demand the sweeping changes that *We the Maids* must sweep in in the 21st century.

Watching Republicans orchestrate chaos and mayhem in Florida during the 2000 election recount was just another vindictive battle in the ongoing partisan war in America that reminded the world how violent demonstrations are orchestrated in America to mismanage perception. They are "Democratic" tactics from the labor movement of the 1920s and disillusioned Americans of the '60s. The retaliatory counterattack with protesters carrying "Hail to the Thief" placards at Bush's inauguration was the beginning of the 21st-century revolutionary democratic demonstrations that led to the Tea Party movement and the Third American Revolution.

Thousands of activists in colorful costumes and bearing banners with diverse messages crowded the streets of Los Angeles and Philadelphia during the last Democratic and Republican conventions of the 20th century to express their dissatisfaction with America's career politicians. Some turned to violence, like their '60s parents at the Democratic convention in Chicago in 1968. The police brutality of 1968 reverberated in Philadelphia and L.A.

The protesters included more than 200 groups supporting issues from environmental protection and animal rights to campaign finance reform and an end to police brutality. Injured protesters and policemen were a reminder that *We the People* are still frustrated. We can get active for the right cause.

"The vast majority of the hundreds of people arrested came here in the spirit of peace and brotherhood for which this city is named," said Ron McGuire, a Philadelphia civil rights lawyer who represented several of the protesters.

In Los Angeles "they were gassing and bombing us," said Laura Engleman of the police on horseback, wielding clubs and firing pepper spray and rubber bullets at the L.A. Democratic Convention protesters. The protesters pelted police with chunks of concrete and steel balls from sling shots. Nice to see the downtrodden peace lovers attempting to maintain arms parity.

Glad to see things changed in 2012, when protesters laid down at an intersection near the Bank of America Corporate Center in Charlotte, North Carolina, ahead of the Democratic National Convention there to express their views peacefully, without the need for slingshots. The big protests that were planned outside the Republican National Convention that same year in Florida never materialized because of a hurricane warning and superstorm.

While children of the '60s generation in America were violent in Philadelphia, their counterparts, children whose parents lived through Mao's Cultural Revolution seeking the right of abode in Hong Kong, after three days of peaceful protests and stand-offs with the local police, fire-bombed the immigration office's reception area after a four-hour standoff. The Chinese mainland abode seekers demanded Hong Kong ID cards from the immigration officials. An immigration officer died from burns, as did a mainlander. Many others were critically injured.

The Falun Gong movement in China is also reminiscent of the movements of the '60s. People dissatisfied with government seeking spiritual refuge and change. They set themselves on fire in Tiananmen Square and engage in almost daily acts of civil disobedience to express their frustration with Chinese government policies.

The wave of nonviolent protests that the Reverend Jesse Jackson's Rainbow/Push organized starting January 15, 2001, in honor of Martin Luther King Jr.'s Day that culminated at federal buildings across America on Bush's Inauguration Day was a replay of the '60s nonviolent civil rights protests.

America is going through a perpetual cultural revolution. The beauty of America's cultural revolutions is that violence is at a minimum when compared to other countries. The outcome of the Bush-Gore election and Americans' patience in awaiting the outcome, with a few exceptions, was a millennium reminder. Each revolution produces less fatalities and more hurt psyches in the minorities being integrated into the mainstream. The beneficiaries of America's revolutions are its new army of shrinks rather than the military. Isn't it time *We the People* became the primary beneficiaries?

Surveys of college students today show that in fact they have inherited and learned a lot from their 1960s parents' values, whether they are American or Chinese. They are into making money! That has helped drive their parents' economic locomotive on the cyber highway at a pace that has bewildered all the skeptics. They are more into making money than developing philosophy, but then, they were raised on it!

It was depressing to read about the several hundred Yalie Ghandians 2002 protest in support of workers rights that was "a cross between a voter-registration drive and an arts and crafts fair" where protesters lined up voluntarily at impromptu booths set up by the police to receive their citations for demonstrating without a permit. A police loudspeaker blared: "Please wait in line until the officer who will place you under arrest arrives" so protesters could hand in their completed ticket and be slapped with an $88 infraction notice.

It blew me away. These "protests" were nothing like the ROTC protests on campus in the '60s. I remember angry, sometimes violent demonstrations nationwide against the Vietnam War war on college campuses, which often targeted the closest symbol of the U.S. military, the Reserve Officers Training Corps – with more than 200 campus ROTC units reporting acts of vandalism during that war. The '60s outcast is now back on campus.

No doubt the Founding Fathers, Mahatma Gandhi and Martin Luther King Jr. would not have known what to make of the Yalie Ghandians – or maybe they would? Maybe their dreams are finally coming true.

### *Political Protests*
Political demonstrations, another cornerstone of democracy, are also flourishing in Hong Kong. This was highlighted by the July 1, 2003, march against the adoption of Article 23, a Hong Kong anti-subversion law. More than 500,000 people registered their opposition to the proposed legislation with their feet – that's almost 10 percent of the population! They included business leaders, professionals, the middle class, and multiple generational households. Peaceful protesters, many in costumes, carrying placards letting their career politicians know that they are no longer *Apathetic Maids* and want to sweep in change. Most of the protesters did not have any party affiliation. They came together to demand change and send the career politicians a strong message. They succeeded. The anti-subversion legislation was withdrawn and delayed indefinitely by a government that had publicly stated: "It is the duty of Hong Kong to implement Article 23… a matter relating to the national dignity and glory of the Chinese race."

Not just economic change as some political commentators had suggested – but political.

"I think the people of Hong Kong have passed another milestone after the July 1 dispute. The general perception that the public are politically apathetic is no longer valid," said Professor Shih Chi-ping, former deputy secretary-general of the Straits Exchange Foundation and currently chief editor of *BizNews Weekly* in Taiwan.

"After the July 1 incident, Hong Kong has been reborn and is nurturing a new era," added Paul Yip Kwoh-wah, an organizer of a seminar entitled "Hong Kong's Past, Hong Kong's Future: More Than an Economic City."

This was reaffirmed July 1, 2012, during the swearing-in ceremony of C.Y. Leung, Hong Kong's third chief executive since the 1997 handover, when a heckler – an invited guest – interupted Chinase President Hu Jintao's speech by yelling slogans calling for China's leaders to condemn the June 4 Tiananmen crackdown and also called for an end to one-party rule in China.

Historically, demonstrations in Hong Kong were mostly economic in nature. As the real estate market collapsed, homeowners protesting plummeting property prices took to the streets without any government interference. Greenpeace and other environmental groups repeatedly protest government actions and inactions. On active days, up to five protest rallies take place at the same time. Homeowners protest their negative equity, small business complains about the regional economic slowdown, welfare workers protest proposed new lump-sum financing for nongovernmental organizations, doctors protest revamping of the medical profession's grading structure, mainlanders protest being refused the right of abode, overseas domestic workers protest their minimum wage cuts, and students seem to always be protesting something.

The Fortune Global Forum held in Hong Kong in the opening year of the millennium saw Falun Gong members from all over the world converge to protest. They were all over town in their yellow T-shirts spelling out their demand to Jiang Zemin, who was attending the forum. The message "China: Free the Jailed Falun Gong Practitioners" was everywhere. Subways, streets, parks, shopping malls, restaurants and even some bars. That was after they dispersed from their officially sanctioned protests and needed to quench their thirst.

*Silly Old Tung* and *Silly Old Man's Wife* were runaway best-seller satirical books of cartoons and jokes about Hong Kong's chief executive and his wife. *Getting Heard: A Handbook for Hong Kong Citizens,* written by former Legco councilor Christine Loh, is a "how to" guide on influencing government.

In a mobile, highly international society like Hong Kong's, the domestic allegiance of younger people cannot be taken for granted. Indeed, 44 percent of the youth polled indicated they would leave Hong Kong if changes took place that they found unsuitable. Since so many have foreign passports and experience (better than one in five), that is not an idle threat. Hong Kong's younger people, unlike their apathetic counterparts in America, not only let their sentiments be known, but act on them. Similar active sentiments and actions in America would be a breath of revolutionary fresh air.

Falun Gong, banned in China, still flourishes openly in Hong Kong under "one country, two systems." It has been branded an "evil cult" by the chief executive and community leaders but nevertheless its members are left alone.

Many Hong Kong civil servants openly practice Falun Gong. One of the movement's spiritual leaders lives in Hong Kong. They were even allowed to use Hong Kong's City Hall for their first international gathering of the 21st century.

Thousands march in Hong Kong every year to commemorate and honor those who died on June 4th, 1989, at Tiananmen Square. Even after the 1997 handover. A million people took to the streets in 1989 to protest the massacre. The tenth anniversary brought out over 70,000 people.

Szeto Wah, who was the head of the Hong Kong Alliance in support of the Patriotic Democratic Movement in China, and a democrat, said at the 1999 anniversary: "There are no borders for human rights and democracy." He mourned the dead: "Do you hear our cries? May your heroic souls descend here – the only piece of Chinese soil where we can gather to remember you in public."

"We would like to convey the message of passing the torch of democracy from the older generation to the younger one."

Isn't it time that America's Founding Fathers' torch was picked up by their descendants in the same proud way in the 21st century?

Hong Kong is debating its political structure for the 21st century and beyond. But for all the accolades I have piled on Hong Kong and its fused functionality as a model for America and the New World Order to emulate, Hong Kong does have one critical deficiency that it is painfully coming to terms with. The lack of true democracy – universal suffrage.

When a million voters in a population of just 7 million turned out to vote in the November 23, 2003, District Council elections, people took note. The turnout was significant because the councils have very little power. They merely advise government on simple community concerns such as street cleaning and garbage collection. Their advice and recommendations can be ignored by government. Of the 81 seats where there was a direct contest between the Democratic Party and the pro-government Democratic Alliance for Betterment of Hong Kong, the democrats won 69.

"On July 1, the people voted with their feet, while this time they voted with a stamp chop. The people have made history again," said Democratic Party leader Yeung Sum.

But then Hong Kong's even younger youth upped the ante and did one better. When China tried to impose a national education curriculum in Hong Kong in September 2012, people of all ages took to the streets in peaceful protest. But it was Joshua Wong Chi-fung, the 15-year-old co-founder of Scholarism, who deserves the credit for getting the anti-national education law and its derogatory and false slant of history out to the public and rallying their widespread support. From a YouTube video showing his eloquent engagement with reporters, to mass rallies organized by a group he co-founded, he has grown in stature beyond his years, becoming an icon in the snowballing movement against the classes.

He said he believed that by gathering small efforts, it was possible to take on power, quoting Japanese author Haruki Murakami: "If there is a hard, high wall and an egg breaks against it, no matter how right the wall or how wrong the egg, I will stand on the side of the egg."

His Facebook page had attracted more than 100,000 "likes," significantly more than the 19,000 that Chief Executive Leung Chun-ying's page drew.

Cutting a skinny figure with black-rimmed glasses, Joshua prompted a big round of applause every time he took the stage during the 10-day siege of the government headquarters by the protestors.

The child of a middle-class Christian family, he said his father started taking him to visit the poor and the downtrodden when he was six or seven. Social movements first caught his eye in 2009, when activists opposed the government's plan to construct a high-speed cross-border railway link. Back then, he seldom read the newspapers, he said, but because the activists used the Internet a lot to discuss and promote their cause, his interest in social issues grew.

"The government cannot do whatever it wants. [People] will fight for their rights on their soil. Hong Kong will win. This movement will not fail," Chi-fung insisted when he – and hundreds of thousands of Hong Kong protesters – took to the streets insisting the government withdraw its plans to introduce national education – branded it a brainwashing tool to be used by Beijing to indoctrinate future generations. Protesters laid siege to government headquarters and boycotted high school and university classes as part of their successful campaign that forced the government to scrap the national education curriculum.

What the government proponents of both the national education system and the Article 23 anti-subversion laws revealed was an inability to understand how smart and protective of their freedoms Hong Kong people are.

"Both people's victories go to the very heart of Hong Kong's determination to force the mainland government to honor the pledge of 'one country, two systems.' There is something remarkable about the clarity of vision shown by the majority in their determination to preserve Hong Kong's way of life and freedoms," said Englishman Stephen Vines, former president of the Hong Kong Foreign Correspondents Club at the Main Bar as the dramatic political differences between Hong Kongers and mainlanders were compared by several Brits and Americans.

Some Hong Kongers expressed their anger by carrying and waving the British flag and the old Hong Kong flag at the protests amid what appeared to be a growing wave of nostalgia for the colonial era.

Tens of thousands took to the streets of Hong Kong in the opening days of 2013 to call for the resignation of the city's chief executive, Leung Chun-ying. Leung was caught up in a scandal related to illegal building structures added to his home, a delicate and polarizing issue in Hong Kong where property prices are sky high.

Shouldn't the citizens of the Founding Fathers' democratic beacon be doing the same? Isn't it time *We the Apathetic Maids* sweep out the career politicians in Washington and the state capitals and their dysfunctional parties and sweep back in the changes the Founding Fathers did when they founded the Republic?

### *Islamic Democracy*

Islamic democracy is a topic I devoted seven pages to in *Custom Maid Spin*. I wrote back in 2003 that "democracy and Islam are compatible if allowed to develop the Islamic way .... Democracy and Islam can co-exist in the New World Order. Not only in Ameri   eca, Bangladesh, Indonesia, Turkey and Qatar, but throughout the entire Muslim world, including the Arab Middle East....

"Even the grandson of the late Ayatollah Ruhullah Khomeini, Sayyd Hussein Khomeini, welcomes the long-awaited freedoms that democracy can bring. He even went so far as to welcome U.S. intervention in Iran to bring about democracy. He labeled Islamic theocracies as misguided....

"U.S. foreign policy was a major contributor to the quashing of democracy in the Muslim world, a result of its confused petro-dollar policy that conveniently fused it with its Cold War policy....This misguided and shortsighted foreign policy not only brought fear to America's shores, but quashed democratic movements in the Muslim world. *We the Maids* have to Hoover out this oil-colored policy in the New World Order and sweep in democracy and American values."

I criticized Saudi Arabia and its policy of funding terror groups because of its fear of democracy. I added: "The government of Hosni Mubarak in Egypt is also afraid of democracy because it will bring an end to his lucrative family business. Like other dictators in the Arab world, he is grooming his son to take over as president. The fact that America has kept him in power at the expense of U.S. taxpayers is an embarrassment. It should therefore come as no surprise that the Egyptian Mohammed Atta led the kamikaze attack on 9/11 because of his anger at America's support of Mubarak's repressive dictatorship in Egypt.

"September 11 and the harsh prison sentence handed down by an Egyptian court against American human rights activist Saad Eddin Ibrahim for his criticism of the repressive Mubarak regime are 21st-century reminders of why America has to fight for and defend democracy in the Arab world if it is to be respected there in the new millennium. Even if democracy yields some extreme Muslim governments, this is a short-term risk worth tolerating."

What I wrote back then has been proven correct. America's democratic ideals enshrined in its Constitution and Bill of Rights are aspired to by all, including Muslims.

### Global Bedouins

Americans, Chinese, Europeans, Asians and Latinos are familiar with the 24-year travels of Marco Polo in the 13th century, and Chinese Admiral Zheng He's 28 years of treasure fleet expeditions as far west as the Middle East and East Africa that started in 1405. What they are not as familiar with is Muhammad Ibn Battuta's 30-year travels from Morocco in 1325, which covered 120,000 km and took him on the Silk Road to nearly every part of the Islamic world, including India and China.

Rambling fever is not limited to cowboys, Europeans and Chinese. People have roamed the globe since time immemorial, including Arabs, a subject I address at length in *Custom Maid Knowledge*.

Battuta was a 21-year-old legal scholar when he set off from his home in Tangier, Morocco, in the summer of 1325 to traverse the entire Muslim world and beyond in his quest to "seek knowledge," as the Prophet Mohammed encouraged his followers to do.

Battuta's numerous sexual escapades with slave girls and the many wives he married along the way in the countries he visited make sex in the '60s and today seem pale by comparison.

The supremacy that medieval Islam enjoyed in science, trade, mathematics and architecture has, in many parts of the Muslim world, given way to stagnation and decline. Colonialism, Western imperialism, corruption, civil wars, extremism and terrorism have exacted their toll on the cultural and artistic dominance that marked the Islam of Battuta's time.

Young people across Muslim North Africa and the Middle East, the lands Battuta traveled centuries ago, are interconnected by today's communication technologies and have formed a new interlocal identity that is transnational. It is an identity founded on young people's shared ambition to free themselves from the grip of their corrupt and inept political, religious and economic institutions and return their culture and society to the days of glory it achieved in Hajji Abu Abdullah Muhammad Ibn Battuta's time. Shouldn't Americans be doing the same by trying to get America to return to the ideals of the Founding Fathers? A new broom to sweep out corrupted career politicians and sweep in America's founding ideals.

### Tahrir and Tiananmen Squares
The pictures of the Arab cleansing revolutions that swept Tunisia, Egypt, Bahrain, Yemen, Jordan, Syria – especially those American-made tanks all over the squares in Bahrain, Yemen and Egypt's Tahrir Square – were a

totalitarian-military-dictatorial-political reminder of the tanks sent by the same kind of regime in China in 1989 into – Tiananmen Square.

Tiananmen was the mother of all student protests that ended in the massacre of an unknown number of students and workers. Thousands of Hong Kongers hold annual candlelight vigils in Victoria Park to mark the anniversary of the crackdown. The Alliance in Support of Patriotic Democratic Movements in China organizes the event.

"Through the candle light, we see the bloody scene and the dead bodies in Tiananmen Square 18 years ago," says Szeto Wah, former alliance chairman.

"Back then, Yuan Mu was shamelessly covering up the massacre. Today Ma Lik does the same," Szeto said referring to Ma's claim that the Tiananmen deaths did not amount to a massacre. Ma was head of Hong Kong's leading pro-Beijing political party at the time.

"Let us raise our candles high and condemn these whitewashing remarks. They distort historical truth and go against one's conscience," Szeto said.

Voices from June 4, like Szeto's, echo in today's fight for basic human rights. This serves as a reminder that the June 4 Tiananmen protesters were airing genuine grievances and issues that remain valid today, such as corruption and political reform. The Beijing government has failed in its efforts to erase June 4 from the public memory. A government that deliberately has its troops open fire on its citizens is a government that has lost legitimacy, because if the only way a government can retain power is through brute force – and is in denial of what it did – it is a government that will be swept out by its citizens.

The 23rd June 4 vigil in Hong Kong in 2012 had a record turnout of close to 200,000 mourners. Their numbers were swelled by more young people and mainlanders. Waving candles and singing, the crowd chanted: "Release pro-democracy activists, build a democratic China, vindicate the June 4 movement, and end one-party dictatorship."

The crowd was so big that the organizers ran out of candles. They appealed to people to use their phones as sources of light. Young and old, families, tourists, expatriates and ethnic communities went hand-on-heart to light candles ringing the stage.

Two giant Goddesses of Democracy – one near the stage and the other at the center of the park – were bathed in light. To ease crowding, gates to the park were left open so people could circle the park and re-enter.

Mr. and Mrs. Yu, both teachers, brought along their two babies, 18 months and eight months. "My children are too young to understand but at least they have an impression in their minds," said Mrs. Yu, who was a toddler when her parents brought her to the vigil 23 years ago.

First-timers from the mainland tell of their shock when they learn about June 4 and want to learn more. Their numbers are swelling annually as the word spreads across the mainland. The spark Mao was concerned about has become a wildfire.

"It's very bad on the mainland. Those who were born in the 1990s or later know absolutely nothing about the crackdown," said Li Runzhou, 38, from Zhejiang. Li said he would tell his children, aged 3 and 6, about it when they grow up.

Most university students in Hong Kong and the mainland were born after the Tiananmen military crackdown in 1989, but for some June 4 is more than just a page in a history book – it is inspiration for a pursuit of justice and a country free of corruption. To Johnson Yeung Ching-yin, who was born in 1991, June 4 shows how powerful mass movements can be in the face of injustice.

A group of eight mainland students studying in the U.S. published an open letter to President Hu Jintao and Vice President Xi Jinping calling for a reassessment of the Tiananmen massacre and advocating reform in the run-up to the senior leadership reshuffle that autumn.

"It's rather puzzling to us why such an obvious mistake or even crime has been covered up for 23 years rather than being reflected upon and corrected," the letter states.

"We hope that the Communist Party will vindicate June 4 during the 18th National Congress of the Party, hold decision makers accountable and compensate the victims, which could be a first step towards political reform that could shift China from the rule of man to the rule of law and democracy."

The letter reflects a rising tide of opinion in society daring to call for a new look at the student-led pro-democracy movement. The June 4 crackdown will be rejudged. It is just a matter of time. Time is on the Founding Fathers, side of democracy and is getting closer each year. Society in the mainland is different now than it was 23 years ago. The mushrooming Internet has enabled everyone to access information – no matter how powerful the censors and government are.

Hong Kong is the testing ground for the ongoing Tiananmen soul-searching and the results are looking good. There is now a museum in Hong Kong commemorating the emergence and subsequent suppression of the Tianamen pro-democracy movement. It is the only institution in China commemorating the June 4 massacre. The display outlines the events leading up to the crackdown and how it unfolded, as well as artifacts such as leaflets circulated by the students and black-and-white photographs of corpses and spent cartridges.

There are also copies of Hong Kong newspapers and advertisements placed by professionals after the crackdown in 1989. One was from Hong Kong's newly elected Chief Executive Leung Chun-ying, who said he "strongly reprimands the Chinese Communist authority for their bloody massacre of Chinese civilians."

One of the star attractions at the 2012 vigil was former Tiananmen student activist Fang Zheng, whose legs were crushed by a tank during the military crackdown. He flew into Hong Kong from his home in San Francisco on a

Chinese passport.

"I have come to talk to people, especially young people, so that they can know the truth about the June 4 killings," Fang said. "The most effective weapon to fight the communist regime is to refuse to forget what the government wants us to forget, and to refuse to forget what the government has done.

"We June 4 activists overseas have always known that Hong Kong people are still very much concerned about June 4. We are very moved."

Shielded by the "one-country, two-systems" policy guaranteed by Beijing, Hong Kong is the only place on Chinese soil where large-scale activities marking the Tiananmen killings are tolerated.

"We want the truth, we want vindication, we want the perpetrators to be brought to justice," added Fang, who was a student athlete when he lost his legs.

"Fang Zheng's speech was so emotional it brought tears to people's eyes," Martin Metz, told me the next day when we caught up with each other at the Foreign Correspondents Club Main Bar. "I've been going for years, but I have never seen anything like this. The emotional power, the numbers of people were just unbelievable," Marty spluttered in his very Melbourne Australian accent as I listened in awe to a kindred political activist who has been in the shoe business in China for more than 30 years with his American partner Bruce Grill. Marty is fluent in Chinese and simplified Chinese characters and also translates books from Chinese to English and vice-versa.

"You won't believe what happened to me when I got to Victoria Park as I was getting out of the cab and trying to pay the taxi fare," Marty continued after we toasted democracy and freedom in China. "The taxi driver refused to take my money and told me to donate it to the cause of democracy! Can you believe that? A Hong Kong taxi driver refusing to take money!"

That was a shocker.

Political repression of students and workers exercising their right of freedom of expression will be repeated if history is allowed to be whitewashed.

China banned all coverage and reporting about the Egyptian unrest, except for the official written reports of Xinhua, the government mouthpiece, fearing it could remind the public of the Tiananmen Square student-worker protests of 1989. That didn't stop people from trying to reignite China's revolutionary flame with sparks from the Jasmine revolutions that swept through the Middle East and North Africa.

Protesters in Tahrir and Tiananmen squares were tea drinkers who inspired many in America's Tea Party movement. Steve Stevlic, organizer of the Tea Party Patriots Chicago, is one of them.

"In the Tea Party movement, we believe just one person can make a difference. And when we first started, one of the images that a lot of people were motivated by was the image of that one man in Tiananmen Square facing the tank. We consider ourselves freedom fighters, and he'd be at the top of the list," Stevlic said.

The Jasmine Tea revolutionary freedom fighters of Tahrir Square took on a brutal, repressive military machine that was ruthless in its defense of the Mubarak regime. The generals did apologize for their inexcusable behavior after Mubarak resigned and was put on trial for the murder of protestors. But the military ran the country and rejected demonstrators' demands for an immediate end to military rule.

President Mohamed Morsi made his political power grab after first replacing the Mubarak military command with his own younger officers – with a side deal allowing the retiring commanders and military to continue running businesses; and secondly, he was acknowledged as a regional peacemaker by America for preventing an all-out war between Israel and Hamas in November 2012.

Morsi's decision to weaken the courts and free himself from judicial oversight meant that all actions he takes in office until a constitution was adopted were not subject to legal review. He became the ultimate force – a pharaoh – in a country without a constitution or parliament. His decision deepened the political intrigue and united the opposition – which was opposed to the proposed constitution because of its Islamic leanings.

The judiciary, which had been appointed by Mubarak, had disbanded the Islamist-led democratically elected parliament earlier in the year, and was thus perceived by Morsi as disrupting the country's transition to democracy.

Morsi disrupted the country's lunge toward democracy further by adopting a pro-Islamic constitution that he put to a vote of the people in a referendum on December 15, 2012.

The lead-up to the vote became violent when pro-Morsi Islamists violently confronted the growing number of peaceful protestors, Christian and Muslim, opposed to the constitution and the referendum. The constitution was approved by a majority of voters, even though there was a low voter turnout because of an ineffective boycott by the opposition. Not a good sign for an emerging democracy.

The constitution, although leaning to transforming Egypt into an Islamist society, left much of the document open to interpretation by legislators, law enforcement officials and judges.

"When the constitution passes, the next few years are going to see policy-making and legislation happening in the parliament and on the streets," said Karim Medhat Ennarah, an expert on Egypt's security services at the Egyptian Initiative for Personal Rights, a Cairo-based advocacy group. "It's going to be very fluid and it might be violent."

The good news is how many Islamists were offended at the aggressive and brutal tactics of supporters of the Muslim Brotherhood and the constitution. Many Islamists admitted voting against it to express their anger.

The reality is, there are a huge number of steps that must be taken to transform a revolutionary movement into a functioning government delivering public services and building a robust economy – both of which are still sorely lacking in Egypt because of the ongoing turmoil. A good reason for Islamists to abandon the Brotherhood.

The protests and counter-protests after the constitution was adopted leading up to the parliamentary elections were inevitable and disruptive – especially after the Egyptian court of appeals overturned the life sentence of the polarizing deposed Egyptian president

Tahrir and Tiananmen, like the U.S. and French protests of 1968 and today, are about young people and students, a contemporary-Internet age generational rebellion starting their own tea party against corrupt nepotistic regimes stifling their channels of upward mobility based on meritocracy – the keys to the future.

A millennium wake-up call to Beijing and Washington on how unpredictable *We the Apathetic Maids* can be when it comes to sweeping out the crumbs and dirt of corrupt authoritarian parties that can so easily crumble when challenged by *We the People*. Closed political societies controlled by powerful families and their sycophant elites are what America's Founding Fathers rebelled against and wanted to make sure didn't happen in America – their Constitution is America's self-assured political manifesto – when adhered to and enforced by *We the Apathetic Maids*.

Look at what happened when Bahrain, Yemen, Syria, Tunisia, Libya and Egypt's *Apathetic Maids* woke up. They burned the Egyptian national party headquarters to the ground and in 18 days got rid of the human infrastructure of the corrupt-autocratic-self-serving party and its leadership – and rewrote their constitution to reflect the values of America's Founding Fathers – across religious lines that in the footsteps of Turkey's democratic revolution makes Iran's Islamic revolution of 1979 feel dated and ready for a long overdue overhaul.

Both the Chinese and Egyptian regimes have maintained monopolies on political power, repressive control over their people in exchange for social stability and have been plagued by rampant corruption and injustice. So why are dictators surprised that *We the Maids* are aware of our rights and no longer bow-down in submissivness and apathy? People power is the only way to bring about the necessary political change of our world disorder. The spirit of Tiananmen is alive and well in China and reawakened. It is being kindled with the Arab cleansing revolutions.

### Chinese Jasmine Revolution

That became evident when the Bauhinea-Jasmine Revolution seeded itself in Hong Kong and mainland China in February 2011 in the wake of the successful peaceful people-power revolutions in Tunisia and Egypt. Jasmine with Chinese characteristics. No slogans, no banners and no petitions. In cities across China, disgruntled youths and elderly activists have been gathering on Sunday afternoons in business, commercial or shopping districts to  *wei guan,* which literally means to "surround and stare," stroll for reform, hang out, exchange knowing looks and deliberately "not protest."

"We were raised glorifying Chairman Mao's guerrilla warfare tactics," says Flower Girl, the online pseudonym of one of the organizers, "Hit and run, hide among the people like fish in water, advance when your adversary retreats and retreat when they advance, hide and bide: hide your resources and bide your time."

As Chairman Mao said, "Revolution is not a dinner party."

An open letter posted on the U.S.-registered boxunblog.com encouraged mainlanders to go for a "walk" at 2 p.m. every Sunday in prominent locations across the country before the site was attacked and paralyzed. Organizers had to set up sites on other platforms such as Facebook and Google Blog. "You only need to walk to the allotted venue, watch from a distance, follow in silence, and go with the flow, bravely call out your slogans," the letter said. It gave the operation the code name "dual session" – a reference to the simultaneous meetings of the CPPCC and the National People's Congress in Beijing that started a couple of weeks later on March

3 and 5 respectively.

"The code of action [for March 6] is the set meal No. 3 at the McDonald's and the KFC," said the online message.

"We only need one slogan for our jasmine revolution and that is ... terminate one-party rule."

Students at major universities across China were encouraged to protest. Many did.

"We cannot keep silent in a cruel reality in which a son of a police official in Baoding, Hebei, received a light sentence after running over and killing a person and another student was beaten to death by a train administrator," said the letter to Peking, Tsinghua, Renmin, Fudan, Sun Yat Sen, Xiamen and many other universities.

The strategy was very effective because it freaked out a sclerotic and paranoid Communist Party hierarchy into mobilizing police and security forces to break up crowds, arrest political activists, human rights lawyers, foreign correspondents. Any mention of the movement's titular flower was enough to bring websites and blogs into the censorship spotlight of the security apparachniks. Foreign journalists were given a new interpretation of reporting rules. Their movement to the rallying locations was severely restricted, as was their right to question dissidents.

"Now China's government clearly shows its horror and fear of the people, as it is facing a deadly enemy," a statement released by the self-professed organizers declared. "A modest amount of people, just by walking, have demonstarated the people's power, and the government's response has revealed its weakness to the world."

The authors of the 700-word statement – the first to be circulated in English – call for a three-stage rebellion using "the sound of laughter, singing and salutations instead of the sound of guns, cannons and warplanes."

Reading and hearing some first-hand accounts of the farcical incidents of police in Shanghai not knowing how to determine who was in fact a provocateur, protester, shopper or Sunday stroller, brought a smile to my face. The protesters included pensioners, retirees with a particular gripe, Internet-savvy hipsters tasting and testing for the first time their right of freedom of expression. In one incident, when police scuffled with an elderly petitioner, possibly to detain him, the crowd reacted instantly and angrily, emitting a guttural roar and surging forward almost at once. The police quickly closed ranks, with one or two officers exchanging clearly nervous glances.

There was a certain dramatic aesthetic to the security actions, like a ballet gone horribly wrong. As soon as uniformed and plainclothes officers broke up one possible gathering, the crowds simply reformed somewhere else. It was almost the embodiment of the ancient Taoist philosophical concept of *wu wei*, "active non-action."

Disgruntled citizens were encouraged to become more open as the movement gained momentum, including "holding a jasmine flower and using mobile phones or music players to play the popular folk song *Beautiful Jasmine*.

> *"What a lovely jasmine flower*
> *What a lovely jasmine flower*
> *Branches full of buds fragrant and elegant*
> *Everyone praises you*
> *Let me gather you*
> *and offer to those I love*
> *Jasmine flower, oh jasmine flower."*

For more than a century, the song *Jasmine Flower,* or *Mo Li Hua* in Chinese, was the undisputed unofficial national anthem in China, recognized by billions of Chinese worldwide and by many Westerners following Giacomo Puccini's decision to feature it in his last opera *Turandot*.

The beguiling folk song, just seven lines long, was the first Chinese tune to make an impact on the West when *Turandot* had its first performance in the early 20th century. Despite the enormous changes that China has undergone over the past 200 years, the song has survived and grown from strength to strength, reaching a pinnacle at the 2008 Olympics where every medal ceremony was accompanied by the *Jasmine Flower* tune.

But that all changed after the song was performed at the Nobel Peace Prize ceremony for jailed Chinese dissident Liu Xiaobo. Now the song is banned in China because its fate is tied to the popular people power Jasmine Revolutions that swept through the Arab world.

The Chinese government's heavy-handed response was political evidence on how insecure and fearful the party leadership is of *We the Maids*. They know we can sweep them out and the freedoms being demanded can be swept in. The political instability and uncertainty in China has become self-evident.

The relentless arrests of activists and bloggers to silence political dissent is unprecedented since the Cultural Revolution. This was highlighted by the arrest of Ai Weiwei, the artist who painted the 100 million porcelain sunflower seeds, exhibited in early 2011 at London's Tate Modern gallery. Ai's installation seems to imply that the Chinese are like the millions of seeds spread across the Tate's gargantuan entrance hall. No one cares whether they are humiliated or crushed under foot, as the seeds were allowed to be at the exhibition's opening.

His artistic vigor and refusal to be silenced was again highlighted in November 2012, when after he was found guilty of tax evasion, he started refunding the cash donated by more than 30,000 supporters to help him fight the authorities – and did a video cover of the South Korean hip hop hit *Gangnam Style,* in which he shakes his ample belly and twirls a pair of handcuffs as though daring the Chinese authorities to arrest him again.

Intellectuals can be purged, but they cannot be silenced. Their words and art reach all freedom-loving people. Ai used to argue that the Chinese regime's despotism is boosted by shameless liars. He, like many Chinese artists and intellectuals, understands that true art and politics can never march hand in hand. They must eventually confront each other on the field of free conscience.

The Arab cleansing threw another light on those sunflower seeds at the Tate. Once the seeds come together, like *We the Apathetic Maids* must do, they show their unity and power. Power to remove the entrenched career politicians, money and their lobbyists that repeatedly subvert the public interest. If the Arabs who cowered in fear for centuries are eager to take freedom's ride, why not the cowered disgruntled Americans and Chinese?

*We the Apathetic Maids* are. We just need the right party horse. An elephant, donkey and hammer and sickle are obsolete and no longer work.

Incoming Chinese President Xi Jinping says the Communist Party must embrace reform with fresh vigor to stave off social and economic malaise. America must do the same.

In Hong Kong, activists from the China Human Rights Lawyers Concern Group, the Hong Kong Alliance in Support of Patriotic Democratic Movements in China and the Justice and Peace Commission of the Hong Kong Catholic Diocese repeatedly marched and protested to demand that Beijing release detained activists and lawyers.

### Revolutionary Spark

In his early revolutionary days, Mao famously said that a single spark could start a prairie fire. He was referring to the unstoppable nature of a revolutionary movement. Today, Chinese leaders who fear social instability quote the phrase to justify their heavy-handedness.

China is spending too much money on "maintaining stability" instead of tackling the roots of the social problems. The 2011 national budget revealed that, for the first time in its history, the publicly stated budget to "maintain stability" surpassed the defense budget. Not a good sign for a leadership that craves a harmonious society and wants to avoid challenges to its legitimacy. Leadership challenges cannot be beaten into submission forever.

The Jasmine Revolutions in the Arab world were all sparked by oppression and heavy handedness of government officials against individual citizens. Citizens' anger cannot be supressed by a repressive regime forever. Sparks and fires can be put out. But eventually, a spark comes during a perfect political storm and becomes unstoppable.

That happens when *We the Apathetic Maids* who work hard to create national wealth are ignored and bypassed politically and economically. It's a long-standing Chinese political, philosophical reality that has brought down every Chinese dynasty that ignored the will of the people – and will do the same to the Communist dynasty.

That reality goes far back as the Chinese philosopher Hsunzi (313-238 BC), who said: "Without enriching people materially, there is no way to develop them."

The book *Guanzi,* attributed to Guan Zhong, a statesman around 725-645 BC, similarly states: "When the granaries are full, people know their rights and manners; when fed and clothed, people know their sense of honor and shame." A modern translation, according to Chung-Yue Chang, who teaches philosophy in the U.S. is: "To live well is the most fundamental of human rights."

What the Chinese government did that upset a lot of people, and will be one of the many sparks, is it imposed on the average worker a 40 percent social security "tax," known as a "deduction" in the U.S., on their income. China, according to the World Bank, has the highest social security "fee" among 181 countries worldwide. In America, *We the Apathetic Maids* know what happens to that "locked lunchbox" containing our Social Security benefits. They've been "deducted" and used by career politicians to cover the expense of their misguided wars, failed economic and foreign policies – and pork barrel earmarks.

The sparks are flying everywhere and the Chinese Communist leadership doesn't know or understand what is happening, because it is out of touch with its frontline cadres in the provinces.

In Anshun, Guizhou, a one-legged fruit-vendor died in front of the gate of a market when he and other vendors were being forcibly removed by "urban management" officers. The result was a full-blown riot with police being pelted with stones and one of their vehicles being burned and others damaged.

In Chaozhou, Guangdong, a riot involving thousands of migrant workers erupted outside the government offices after a father and his 19-year-old son, migrants from Sichuan, were beaten and the son seriously wounded in a knife attack after they went to their boss demanding their unpaid wages.

"We had never called on those migrant workers for help," a relative of the father-son victims said. "They came to protest because we've all been owed back pay by local bosses for a long time and the local authorities have given us little help."

In Guangzhou's Zengcheng municipality, factory workers attacked police stations and torched vehicles over a weekend in June 2011. Tens of thousands of migrant workers took to the streets after the reported beating of a pregnant street vendor from Sichuan.

Is it any wonder the Politburo is trying to "strengthen and innovate" social management? The term "social management" – first introduced by Hu Jintao at a Politburo meeting in February 2011 – has become a buzzword used by the central government as a euphemism for social controls aimed at defusing tensions between a disenfranchised public and their political overlords. There are too many fuses being lit across China from Mongolia, Xinjiang, Tibet to Guangdong and Hong Kong that signal that Communist Party power keg is going to blow. The Party's 12th five-year plan, covering the years to 2015, contains for the first time a chapter dedicated to "social governance" – measures to reduce social problems.

The social problems in China are no different than the social problems worldwide, including America – problems that America's career politicians have chosen to ignore – as they continue to live in denial and smugly sit on the explosive powder keg about to wipe them out.

## *"The Road to Damascus Is a Road to Peace"*

That is what House Speaker Nancy Pelosi said during her 2007 visit to Syria. The pictures of Syrian protesters being brutalized by baton-swinging goons and felled by snipers as tanks brazenly fired at them for good measure, without serious criticism from the U.S. administration, the type of criticism it dished out against the leaders in Tunisia, Egypt, Yemen and Libya, was mind-boggling and unbelievable. Another blatant example of America failing to uphold the ideals of the Founding Fathers.

The excuse that Syria is different because its president is a "Westernized leader" and that "he'll react if he believes he is being lumped in with brutal dictators" as a defense of U.S. policy was confirmation of the effectiveness of Syrian lobbyists in D.C. and America and its founding ideals be damned.

The fact that Syria is Iran's closest ally in the Middle East, hosts terrorists in Damascus, champions Hezbollah in Lebanon which it sees as a part of "Greater Syria" and has funneled al Qaeda terrorists into Iraq to kill American soldiers is conveniently overlooked. The U.S. analysis of the Syrian regime's beliefs, intentions and capacity for change was flawed. Run by an Alawite minority, the regime was never going to break with its Shiite benefactors in Tehran and join the Arab Sunni orbit. A regime that builds its domestic legitimacy on hostility to Israel is also unlikely ever to make peace.

Hafez Assad turned down multiple offers from several Israeli prime ministers for the return of the Golan Heights. His son and successor, Bashar Assad, once told a Lebanese newspaper that "It is inconceivable that Israel will become a legitimate state, even if the peace process is implemented." Syria brutalized Lebanon throughout a 29-year military occupation, climaxing with the assassination in 2005 of Prime Minister Rafik Hariri and 21 others.

Syria nearly provoked a war with Turkey in the late 1990s by harboring the leader of the PKK, the Kurdish terrorist group. It continues to harbor the leadership of Hamas and other Palestinian "resistance" groups. It serves as the principal arms conduit to Hezbollah. It pursued an illicit nuclear program courtesy of North Korea. It is Iran's closest ally in the world.

Tehran and Damascus first signed a military cooperation treaty in 1998. At the time, Iran's minister of defense, Adm. Ali Shamkhani, stated publicly that the treaty would also cover "intelligence and security issues" with regard to dissident groups. I will therefore not be surprised if the rumors of Iranian snipers killing Syrians is confirmed. The Iranian regime used snipers effectively as a tactic during the protests that followed the disputed presidential election of Mahmoud Ahmadinejad in 2009. Neda Agha-Soltan, the young woman who became the symbol of the pro-democracy uprising in Iran, was killed by one such sniper.

Syria is the only country with which the Iranian armed forces and the Islamic Revolutionary Guard Corps hold joint staff meetings at least once a year. Iran is also Syria's main arms supplier and also ships arms to Hezbollah in Lebanon through Syria.

Iran started using the Assad regime as a means of dividing the Arabs in the 1970s, when the shah wanted to squeeze the Baathist regime in Iraq. To this end, he supplied Syria with cut-price oil and aid totalling $150 million in 1977. Under the mullahs, Syria retained its role in preventing the Arabs from ganging up against the then-fragile Islamic Republic. Throughout its eight-year war with Saddam Hussein, Iran benefited from Syrian support, including vital intelligence on Iraqi armed forces. As a gesture of goodwill, Tehran arranged for some mullahs to issue fatwas declaring the Alawite minority, to which the Assad family belongs, to be "part of Islam." Most Islamic scholars have long regarded the esoteric Alawi sect as heretical. So why did America defend the Syrian dictatorship when the Syrian people demanded democracy?

The Assad dynasty has favored the minority Alawite sect, causing resentment among the Sunni Muslim majority. When the protesters in Daraa pulled down a statue of Assad's late father, they not only shattered the statue, but the barrier of fear.

"The barrier of fear is broken. This is the first step on the road to toppling the regime," said Ibrahim, a lawyer in Daraa.

When the Assad regime intensified its ferocious sniper attacks, random shooting of civilians in the streets and tank shelling of protesters several months after the protests started in mid-March 2011, the U.S. started complaining through diplomatic channels and asked Assad to introduce democratic reforms. Meanwhile, the protesters whose patience for international support was running thin, in order to minimize the loss of life, started burying loved ones in their gardens for fear of being killed if they ventured out to cemeteries, and protesting at night in the expectation that security forces would be more reluctant to shoot at them and have more difficulty identifying them for arrest. The evening protests became popular because they attracted people after work and school. It is also easier for protesters to run and hide from security forces in houses, shops and alleys. Still, within a few weeks there were more than 10,000 protesters jailed and more than 1,000 killed. More than 200,000 killed when the book went to publication.

The U.S. should have immediately recalled its new ambassador to Damascus, after a six-year hiatus without one, expelled Syria's ambassador from Washington, frozen and seized the Assad's overseas assets, designated Syria's elite units responsible for human rights abuses as Specially Designated Global Terrorist entities, as it did with Iran's Revolutionary Guards, imposed sanctions on companies providing the regime's tools of repression, and provided the Syrian opposition with encrypted communication technology to dodge the regime's surveillance and actively support the Founding Fathers' Syrian disciples.

It eventually did, but only after it became abundantly clear that Assad's savagery, like Gaddaffi's, knows no boundaries and is unsustainable. The U.S. even got the sclerotic Saudi King Abdullah to come out publicly condemning the Assad regime's ruthless oppression and call for political reforms – during Ramadan. Nice call. But long overdue considering that the kingdom's arch enemy in the region, Shiite Iran, is one of Assad's strongest puppeteers and supporters in the political massacres. Much like Saudi Arabia is in Bahrain. To little 2 late. Better late than never.

## *Bahrain's Democratic Ruins*

Bahrain's minority Sunni Muslim ruling family did to the Shiites what Assad did to the Sunnis. Shoot them in the street and call in troops from neighboring Saudi Arabia and United Arab Emirates, courtesy of the fellow minority ruling Sunni monarchies governing predominantly Shiite oil fields. More than 60 percent of Bahrainians are Shiites. Most protesters have campaigned for a constitutional monarchy, but calls by hardliners for the overthrow of the monarchy spooked the Saudi royals enough to send 1,000 troops to help keep their fellow throne-sitters in power.

The Gulf troops, martial law and ferocious assault on peaceful protesters have stunned the majority Shiites and enraged Tehran. Shiites across the region have complained for decades of oppression by the Sunnis, politically dominant throughout the Arab world.

Especially the bright unemployed Shiite youth in all Gulf states, including Saudi Arabia. The Saudi royals pay protection money to their people to stay in power. In effect, bribing them. It is a welfare state. The estimated $93 billion of government handouts doesn't address the kingdom's most destabilizing problem – persistent high unemployment. Most private sector jobs are held by the kingdom's 8 million expatriate workers, while most working Saudis are employed by the state, where they can get higher pay.

"Many in my generation don't wake up before midday and now that there's an unemployment allowance I doubt they will have the incentive to go and search for jobs," said Ahmad Ghalib, a 25-year-old engineering graduate.

Is it any wonder they want regime change? It is only a matter of time before the Saudi royals are toppled like Saddam Hussein, Hafez and Bashir Assad, Hosni Mubarak and the various other unrepresentive repressive regimes, no matter what their religious beliefs. The kingdom regards the Koran as its constitution. Allah will not save them.

It is the women in Saudi Arabia who are making a difference and who are on the revolutionary front lines. Manal al-Sherif, a Saudi woman who defied the country's ban on women drivers, was arrested in May 2011, for five days while she was investigated for "violating public order." Other women protesters are demanding the release of their imprisoned relatives – husbands, sons, brothers and cousins, many of whom have been jailed without charges for years.

This year's protests are not the first. In 1990, 47 women drove through Riyadh in a formal demonstration. They were all arrested, they all lost their jobs, and they – and their husbands – were barred for a year from leaving the kingdom.

Saudi women live in virtual confinement within their own country. They need approval from a male guardian to work, leave the country, or file a police report. They can be arrested for driving or sitting in a coffee shop with an unrelated man. There is nothing in the Koran that prohibits women from driving. At least two of the Prophet Muhammad's wives are known to have ridden camels.

Allowing women to drive is about more than getting from one place to another. It's a symbol of more profound changes that could fundamentally alter Saudi society. Driving is a stepping stone to more freedoms.

Reforms in the '60s opened the way for female education; now women make up 58 percent of Saudi university population, but less than 15 percent of the work force. Many middle-class families see little incentive in letting their daughters and wives work if they end up spending their salaries on drivers.

Any wonder the Saudis are dispensing billions of dollars to prop up the "Club of Kings." The idea is to signal to Shiite Iran that the Sunni Arab monarchs will defend their interests. The Saudis worry that an empowered Muslim Brotherhood in Egypt could damage Saudi legitimacy by presenting a model of Islamic law different from the Wahhabi tradition of an absolute monarch. How much longer can such a society survive in the 21st century?

Why is the U.S. continuing to provide the oppressive kingdom protection when the Saudis are shifting their alliance from America and criticizing U.S. policies?

### Libyan Latte
The Libyan rebels just couldn't pull it off without outside help and support.

Militarily, politically and economically. That's understandable, living under the thumb of Gaddaffi's brutal regime. They are to be applauded for the fact that the fear, terror, tension and nervousness that had characterized Libyans – political or otherwise – is no longer acceptable. The aroma of freshly brewed Jasmine tea or coffee is much more preferable.

Col. Gaddaffi did not limit the terror tactics of his regime to Libya. He globalized. That included the downing of a French airliner over Chad and the Lockerbie jetliner bombing in the late 1980s. And yet, with all that innocent American and interlocal citizens' blood on his hands, what do the U.S. oil companies do? They lobby on his behalf! They succeeded in getting Libya exempted from a 2008 law giving compensation to victims of terrorism. American terror victims can seize assets of countries found to be liable for terrorist acts.

Gaddaffi had taken responsibility for the 1988 bombing of the Pan Am flight over Lockerbie, Scotland, that killed 270, including 189 Americans, and his assets anywhere in the world could be seized by the victims if not for that exemption.

According to secret disclosures from WikiLeaks, six U.S. oil companies and two U.S. units of foreign companies operating in Libya boosted lobbying expenditures 63 percent to $75.8 million in 2008, when they were pursuing the waiver. The exemption was a relief for Occidental, ConocoPhilips, ExxonMobil, Marathon Oil, Hess, Chevron and the U.S. subsidiaries of BP and Royal Dutch Shell. In return, they cemented their relationship with Gaddaffi, whose country has Africa's largest proven reserves. In 2008, U.S. oil companies accounted for 30 percent of Libya's daily 1.7 million barrels of oil, according to one cable.

On March 18, 2008, four cabinet members – Condoleezza Rice, Defense Secretary Robert Gates, Energy Secretary Samuel Bodman and Commerce Secretary Carlos Gutierrez – had written to congressional leaders proposing legislation to let President George W. Bush exempt Libya from the amendment. Attaching Gaddaffi's assets would affect "U.S. energy security," the secretaries wrote. The Libyan Claims Resolution Act passed by unanimous consent in Congress five months later.

As if that wasn't bad enough, files found in Libya's External Security agency in Tripoli by the National Transitional Council after Gaddaffi and his forces were defeated, show that the CIA and Britain's M16 cooperated with Gaddaffi. The CIA, under the administration of then-President George W. Bush, brought terror suspects to Libya and suggested questions Libyan interrogators should ask them as part of the secret CIA rendition flight program that transported dozens of terror suspects around the world to third countries to be interrogated. The files showed that in 2004 the CIA moved to set up "a permanent presence" in the country, the excuse being that at the time, Libya was breaking diplomatic ice with the U.S.

What the U.S. policy in the Middle East has done, especially its decision to bomb Libya while idly standing by as thousands get slaughtered in Syria, Bahrain and Yemen, is expose the difference between the country's real American values and its petroleum interests. It is clear the U.S. uses its moral values as a ploy to fulfill its national oil interests. In other words, the U.S. manipulates its democratic values to justify its continued embrace of repressive dictatorial allies that have no interest in American values – as long as they have oil.

*Jasmine Oil*

The Jasmine Revolutions, the Arab cleansings in the Middle East and North Africa have an adverse spillover effect on oil production and spell higher oil prices, especially the protracted Libyan revolutionary civil war. The Middle East accounts for 37 percent of the world's oil production, of which two-thirds is exported. And it still has 62 percent of the world's proven oil reserves. The political instability in the region has increased the risk factor in oil prices and could push them above their 2008 peak.

The biggest victim of the revolutionary Jasmine oil shock is China. Its net imports of crude and oil products reached 6 million barrels a day in 2011, nearly quadrupling in a decade. If the trend continues, China's imports will reach 16 million barrels a day by 2020, far higher than the 13 million barrels imported by the U.S.

Energy has become the Achilles' heel of China's modernization, much like America's was during the energy crisis in the '70s. Gas rationing in Southern California in May 1979. Fights breaking out among frustrated drivers waiting for hours in gas lines, people standing guard beside their cars at night against thieves who siphoned out fuel, a board game called Gas Crisis – and me taking to my horse and riding to my law office in Beverly Hills from the Pacific Palisades in protest.

The oil shock decreases global demand for China's exports, raises its production costs and worsens inflation. Without structural rebalancing to reduce the energy intensity of the growth model and export dependency, China could slide into persistent stagflation along with the rest of the world – with slower growth and higher inflation. Inflation decreases the value of people's savings and income.

China's more than 200 million migrant workers, along with the millions of migrants across the world, have worked hard for very little over the last few decades. They have struggled to save money for their children's education. Letting inflation erode their savings is grounds for revolution.

China is not that different from many other nations, including America, in closing an eye to professed ideals when strategic or economic interests are at stake. But now that tens of thousands of Chinese migrant workers have been forced to flee Libya and be rescued, Beijing has been given a wake-up call about its international obligations and responsibilities toward its citizens.

China is believed to have had 5.5 million overseas workers in 2011 when Libya imploded. That figure has been growing by between 9 or 10 percent each year. People's Liberation Army transport planes and chartered planes brought its citizens home from Libya. No Chinese military hardware had ever before been deployed in an overseas civilian evacuation mission.

For too long, China's policies, like America's, have focused too much on special interest groups with effective lobbying machines and too little on the plight of working men and women whose muscle actually fuels national economies. There were many great cartoons that depicted both U.S. and Chinese political hypocrisy during the Jasmine revolutions. My favorite appeared in the *International Herald Tribune* on March 4, 2011. There was U.S. Secretary of State Hillary Clinton at a podium with the seal of her office and the Stars & Stripes behind her, smirking and saying: "We support the struggle of the people ... against the regimes we supported."

Many American and Chinese citizens feel the same as their fellow Arab Jasmine revolutionaries. Not enough obviously, but their numbers are growing and the political instability they have created is percolating. It is just a matter of time. Inequality of income, wealth and opportunity is arguably greater than at any time in the past century. Corporations across the world, on every continent and country, are bulging with cash as their drive for efficiency continues to yield huge profits. But the workers' share of the pie is decreasing, thanks to high unemployment, shortened working hours and stagnant wages.

Oil's spillover effect is to grease, oil and fire up the revolutionary zeal pent up in so many Americans, Chinese and other national patriots weary of unending inflation, unemployment, corruption, crony capitalism super-sized government and career politicians. And it will grease the long overdue revolutionary changes bubbling now until there are enough citizen soldiers prepared to stop being apathetic and sweep in the necessary reforms.

### Arab Cleansing

Watching the moon-lit rising tide roll ashore, as the wind gently whistled through the trees and plants on my Hong Kong rooftop garden as it conducted the rhythmic beat of the chimes – while reading about the cleansing sweeping through the Arab world – brought to mind the many moon-lit desert sandscapes I have seen over the years. The barren deserts of the Middle East mirror the Arab world's meager freedoms, but all that is changing.

Billions of dollars have left the countries where revolutions have succeeded because rich Arabs don't trust in them. Revenues from tourism have evaporated. Stock markets are trading below their peaks of the pre-cleansing days. Before volunteering solutions, it is important to understand history.

The pre-conditions for democracy are lacking in the Arab world partly because Hosni Mubarak and other Arab dictators spent the past half-century emasculating the news media, suppressing intellectual inquiry, restricting artistic expression, banning political parties, and co-opting regional ethnic and religious organizations to silence dissenting voices – much like China does.

But the handicaps of Arab civil society also have historical roots that transcend the policies of modern despots. Until the establishment of colonial regimes in the late 19th-century, Arab societies were ruled by Shariah law, which essentially precludes autonomous and self governing private organizations. Thus, while Western Europe was making its tortuous transition from arbitrary rule by monarchs to democratic rule of law, the Middle East retained authoritarian political structures. Such a political environment prevented democratic institutions from taking root and facilitated the rise of the modern Arab dictatorships.

Most importantly, Shariah lacks the concept of the corporation, a perpetual and self-governing organization that can be used either for profit-making purposes or to provide social services.

"Islam's alternative to the nonprofit corporation was the waqf, religious endowment established in accordance with Shariah to deliver specified services forever, through trustees bound by essentially fixed instructions. Until modern times, schools, charities and places of worship, all organized as corporations in Western Europe, were set up as waqfs in the Middle East," writes Timur Kuran, a professor of economics and political science at Duke and the author of *The Long Divergence: How Islamic Law Held Back the Middle East*.

A corporation can adjust to changing conditions and participate in politics. A waqf can do neither. Hence the road to free market economic prosperity and democracy in the Middle East is going to be a rough road to hoe.

The G-8 nations pledged $20 billion in aid at their soire in Deauville, France, in May 2011. Like that means anything to anyone anymore, since they haven't delivered, or honored, many of their past pledges made while consuming millions of dollars worth of fine wines, champagnes and government food.

America and Europe are not the answer. They have too many problems of their own. The answer lies in East Asia. China, Hong Kong and Taiwan are good examples. They have five common features that can serve as inspirational models: Openess to the world, investment in education, pragmatism, defined role of government not as a captain of a team, but as a referee, and the incentives and ability to attract overseas home-grown talent to return home.

### Kent State-Tiananmen

The families of those killed at Tiananmen in 1989 have been inspired by the Spanish arrest warrant for General Augusto Pinochet. As a result, they filed a petition signed by 105 people living in China in 1999. Shouldn't the families of the four victims killed at Kent State when America was bombing Cambodia be doing the same?

The constitutions of America and China guarantee the right to assemble and the right to free speech. Kent State, Cultural Revolution, Tiananmen and Waco are examples of how both governments infringed upon those constitutional rights. Those responsible for stomping on the constitutional rights of We the People must be identified and held accountable.

The Tiananmen petitioners' strategy, worked out with lawyers in China and America, is to exhaust Chinese legal options as the first step toward a campaign for an international inquiry. Hopefully, it won't come to that. A Chinese Truth and Reconciliation Commission modeled after the South African model will be the solution that can finally exorcise not only the ghosts of Tiananmen, but the Cultural Revolution as well. Until then, the Great Helmsman's contributions to building China will always be overshadowed by the senseless killings and will, like Tiananmen, continue to haunt China domestically and internationally.

Chinese authorities for the first time are discussing financial compensation to families of known victims. The Tiananmen Mothers Support Group has documented 203 victims. Many victims' relatives are yet to be located. Beijing has never released an official count of casualties.

The Tiananmen crackdown sparked fears about the future of Hong Kong after its return to China, then only eight years away. Yet more than a million people turned out in 1989 for the first candle-lit vigil right after the crackdown. But these insecurities have long since given way to confidence, increasing integration and a growing sense of national identity and pride.

The intolerance of the Chinese authorities of any dissent, whether the students and workers in Tiananmen, or artist Ai Weiwei and pro-democracy campaigner Liu Xiaobo, who was awarded the Nobel Peace Prize, or any one of the numerous lawyers and human rights activists, only encourages Hong Kongers to continue attending the annual June 4 vigil, the only one of its kind on Chinese soil. The vigil remains relevant. So much so that many mainlanders go to Hong Kong to participate. The Chinese local and national governments don't mind mainlanders going to Hong Kong to participate in the vigil so long as they don't organize similar events back home.

The same holds true for 9/11, Kent State, Ruby Ridge and Waco. Spin doctors can no longer spin these Sino-American tragedies into oblivion.

Chinese ex-political prisoner Xu Wenli visited the gaping hole on the site of the World Trade Center where the September 11 attacks did their greatest damage as soon as he arrived in New York in 2003.

"It was a very moving experience and stirred very strong emotions," he said of his visit. "But it did bring to my mind the equally needless deaths that happened in Tiananmen Square in 1989 and how we Chinese are unable to mourn those dead, like Americans can mourn their September 11 dead."

The tragedies of Tiananmen and 9/11 both involved innocent citizen soldiers who paid with their lives for the mistakes and shortcomings of their government's career politicians – who had inadequate evacuation plans – because they themselves have no intention of leaving under any circumstances.

Truth and Reconciliation Committees, should be the legal venues for people to come to terms with their murderous genocidal past. It is there that they must decide whether any former leaders should be brought to trial like Egypt's Hosni Mubarak. Such commissions should be an integral part of overcoming and coming to terms with a repressive past in the 21st century.

### Repressive & Resilient for How Long?

The "China model" of repression that coexisting with economic growth defies the long-held link between economic development and political evolution. China's leadership has proven itself "surprisingly resilient" in the face of unprecedented political repression of human rights activists, lawyers, artists and critics of the regime and its repressive policies. The self-censorship of the mainland media only compounds the repressive atmosphere and mood of the country.

China has a proud history of revolting against repression. The Communist Party's victory in 1949 was such a success, as was the 1911 Revolution by Sun Yat-sen, considered by many to be the "Father of Modern China."

Historians today agree that the spark that finally ignited the flames of rebellion came from two events in May that year – a Qing decree that set up a cabinet comprised largely of members of the royal family, and the forced nationalization of two railway lines. First, the cabinet announcement was a slap in the face for the moderate gentry who had put their trust in a new constitution, pushing them to back the rebels. Second, the seizure of two privately owned railway lines triggered a mass movement.

In other words, it was the lack of progress on political reform that set the stage for revolution. The reform rolled out by the Qing rulers in 1901 consisted merely of non-political measures to rationalize the administration for more effective functioning, and did nothing to foster wider political participation. The government pledge in 1906 to draw up a constitution raised hopes that were dashed when the "royal cabinet" was announced. Faced with a government blinded by self-interest, society finally chose change through revolution.

Undeniably, the Western-influenced call for modernization that started in the late 19th century also played a large role in shaping people's consciousness of civil rights. At the forefront of the movement were progressive thinkers and scholars, many of whom supported a constitutional monarchy for China. Among them, reformist Liang Qichao pioneered the concept of citizenship. "Chinese people do not know the meaning of citizenship," he said. "Citizens are the people of the nation, and the nation is the sum of its people. Without citizens, there can be no nation."

His idea implied the separation of nation from government; and of loyalty to the nation from loyalty to the government. So when it became clear that the Qing reform would happen only on paper, the people sought to overthrow their rulers.

In the 1912 provisional constitution unveiled by the interim government of the Republic of China, the opening chapter made it clear that "the sovereignty of the nation belongs to the people."

The second chapter affirmed the equality of all, stating that all Chinese may enjoy the freedom of the person and property, free speech and a free press; and the freedom of assembly, association, communication and religion. All have a right to petition and litigation; take part in exams and run for elections.

Sun Yat-sen's vision of revolutionizing politics and society did not pan out because the country soon succumbed to warlord conflicts and rampant official corruption.

Hong Kong was a cradle of China's 1911 revolution. A park behind Pak Tsz Lane in the Central district was a secret rendezvous where revolutionaries, including Sun Yat-sen and Yang Quyan, gathered and plotted a series of rebellions that eventually led to the overthrow of the Qing dynasty in 1911.

Members of the social elite who had received a Western education set up the Furen Literary Society on the second floor of 1 Pak Tsz Lane in 1892.

Yang later set up the Revive China Society with Sun Yat-sen in Staunton Street in 1895 and initiated several attempts to overthrow the Qing rulers. He was shot dead by a Qing assassin in 1901.

"All Chinese from both sides of the Strait are the successors of Sun Yat-sen and the 1911 Revolution," said Zhang Haipeng, the leading researcher at the Modern History Research Institute of the Chinese Academy of Social Sciences, at a centenary celebration of the revolution in 2011.

Sun's goal was a united democratic China that could only be accomplished with "tremendous perseverance, patience and bearing of hardship without complaint." In other words, people had to be more resilient than their repressive leaders.

It's no wonder the party today is trying to perfect "a social management system with Chinese characteristics." I doubt it will succeed because the repressive tactics on the mainland only encourage more openness and political debate in Hong Kong that will inevitably spill over the border onto Tiananmen Square with the force and devastation of a democratic tsunami.

Hong Kong is still the cradle of revolution in China. Hong Kong bookstores are a favorite destination of visiting mainland readers seeking politically sensitive points of view that are banned in China. Many Chinese tourists, especially young people, buy books on the Tiananmen crackdown and the Cultural Revolution.

Cultural and political revolutions today, like the Tea Party, Jasmine and Occupy movements, are vigorous social movements that aim to effect change in the power structure or social system peacefully, not through the barrel of a gun.

The violent revolutions of the past can never again take place in today's society, no matter how unjust the social system is, how arrogant wealth and privilege becomes, nor how often government-business collusion forces people out of their homes and drives them to set themselves on fire.

I agree with Chang Ping, a current affairs commentator in China who is an astute observer of the political and social transformation taking place in China – and applies to America. Revolutionary social movements can and will continue to take place; they cannot be suppressed. Modern political social movements have and will continue to revolutionize the power structure in society in an open advocacy of rights for the individual and a nation's citizens.

Revolution today is more intellectual than ever. Today's thinkers and intellectual explorers are interlocally connected by the Internet that allows them to share knowledge that applies to contemporary society, renewing the Founding Fathers' eternal truths for the present. C.L. Max Nikias, president of the University of Southern California, foresees a fruitful alliance between scholars from America and the Pacific Rim.

"If we are to meet the challenges of the future, we will need to draw on the talent and resources from around the Pacific Rim. Together we have the chance to take part in an intellectual revolution that will resonate around the world and throughout the centuries."

### Referendum

Five Hong Kong legislators resigned in January 2010 to force a referendum on democracy and to pressure Beijing for direct elections. Flashing victory signs, the lawmakers from the League of Social Democrats and Civic Party held up their resignation letters for photographers before handing them to the secretary of Hong Kong's Legislative Council.

Their objective was to spark a special election that they wanted to use as a referendum on universal suffrage for the next election in 2012. This created some unease in Beijing and local oligarch business interests. The resignations came hard on the heels of a series of protests focused on local issues expressing dissatisfaction "over abuse of power by officials who are often in league with business interests," said columnist Philip Bowring at the FCC Main Bar as resignations became the opening hot topic of the new year.

"Growing underclass that is suffering from Hong Kong's widening income gap that believes the government is simply an accomplice of big business and stuffs its many advisory boards with bureaucrats and yes-men," Bowring shot back when challenged by David O'Rear, chief economist of the Hong Kong Chamber of Commerce, about the need for a minimum wage in Hong Kong.

Hong Kong's chief executive, its leader, is chosen by an 800-member committee and its Legislature is half elected, half chosen by interest groups. China ruled in 2007 that Hong Kong could not elect its leader until 2017 or its entire Legislature until 2020.

The five legislators who resigned represented each of the five geographical constituencies and their re-election campaigns were designed as a de facto referendum on the public's desire for genuine universal suffrage and the scrapping of the Legislative Council's functional constituencies.

Former Secretary of Justice Elsie Leung raised the concern that referendums could lead to anarchy. She was not alone. Members of the Basic Law Committee and pro-Beijing parties weighed in against the referendum idea. The pro-democracy camp was conflicted because some thought the idea would backfire. But that is what democracy is. That's what referendums are all about. Granted, the Basic Law does not address the question of referendums directly, but it does talk about democracy at length, and referendums are an essential tool and vehicle of the democratic process.

Well, Beijing didn't think so following the controversial resignations of the five Civic Party and LSD lawmakers that triggered by-elections four months later as a referendum on universal suffrage – and winning comfortably. Beijing leaders had the Hong Kong Legislative Council introduce in June 2011 a bill to scrap by-elections in geographical constituencies and the five new district council-sector functional constituency seats without public consultations. In other words, ramrod a bill through the legislature without public input.

Under the proposed law, when a lawmaker resigns, dies or is disqualified during his or her four-year term, the candidate who received the next highest number of votes would automatically fill the vacant seat.

The result? All 12 pan-democratic lawmakers resigned en masse from the Legislative Council committee examining the bill in protest of the government trying to pass the law without any public discourse. In announcing their resignations, the pan-democrats called on the public to show their disapproval of the bill by joining an upcoming July 1 protest march.

Some legislators didn't think their mere resignation from the Committee was a strong enough protest. They wanted all 23 pan-democratic legislators to resign from the legislature. "If all 23 of us left ... there would be no one checking the government and there would be more disgusting legislation," said Civic Act-Up lawmaker Cyd Ho Sau-lan of the proposal.

Public calls for withdrawal of the proposed legislation turned into a heated public debate. As pan-democrats stepped up their calls for people to take to the streets on July 1, Secretary for Justice Wong Yan-lung and Secretary for Constitutional Affairs Stephen Lam Sui-lung issued a strong legal defense of a revised proposal that would see Legislative Council seats vacated midterm filled – in most cases – by people on the same party list as the ex-incumbent.

The Hong Kong Bar Association assailed the government's proposal as a violation of Article 26 and 68 of the Basic Law and several articles of the International Convention on Civil and Political Rights, as well as the Hong Kong Bill of Rights Ordinance. For a political junkie like me, the debate was fascinating.

On July 1, while on the train from our Pets Central Mongkok hospital to visit our North Point hospital, I stopped by Victoria Park, where the protesters objecting to the proposed law – and many other perceived injustices – were assembling to start their protest march to the Legislative Council chambers. In a way, I didn't have much choice as the sardine-packed train disgorged me with the enthusiastic crowd at the Causeway Bay station. The rhythm and flow was intoxicating and I gladly joined in. Young, old, families, couples and individuals all united and happy to exercise their freedom of expression – and opposition to government.

It was the biggest show of discontent with the government in seven years. Organizers claimed the turnout was more than 200,000, while police put the number at a more modest 50,000. The march raised the pressure on the government to postpone or withdraw its controversial bill – and it did. The government made a U-turn and decided to postpone the vote on the bill to allow for two months of public consultation. The people had spoken and the government listened. People power prevailed again.

It didn't end there. The government reintroduced the bill in May 2012 that triggered a 33-hour marathon filibuster for the first time in Hong Kong. It was brought to an abrupt end after the Legislative Council president invoked for the first time powers in the rules of procedure to halt debate on the controversial bill to restrict Legco by-elections.

Protests in Legco and on the streets of Hong Kong are becoming more spontaneous and disorderly with results that were unimaginable a few years ago. No different than what happened in the Arab cleansing in the Middle East and North Africa. The old order is changing and a new world order is settling in, not only in Hong Kong, but America, China and the rest of the world. People have decided to stare down the ruling elites because they will no longer tolerate the excesses of the ruling class.

There is no democracy without a healthy and honest exchange of ideas between individuals, within a party and between parties. The essence of democracy is the exchange of ideas and utilization of all political tools available to get the people's voice heard and acted upon. After all, true democracies are governments of the people, by the people, for the people. No government of self-appointed political leaders is sustainable without the support of the people. Not Democratic, not Republican, not military, not monarchical and not Communist.

A vibrant living democracy is all about people duking it out in elections. Parties, whether in Beijing or Washington, cannot control the will of the people. They must listen to the people if they want to survive. Parties that insist on controlling the agenda and dictating to the people is a sure formula for political suicide. Whether a few decades, or even centuries, it's only a matter of time before the people wake up and oust these tone-deaf leaders.

### The '60s Retro

Call them the children of the '60s or '80s, same difference or no difference. They are people who not only want the changes that most of us do, but are willing to do something about it. Go into public service to sweep in the necessary changes as they sweep out self serving career politicians and address the hopes and needs of *We the Apathetic Maids* – people who are waking up to that fresh brew of political tea and coffee.

I take great offense when I hear so-called democracy activists like Richard Tsoi Yiu-cheong in Hong Kong say that while confrontational political protests may embarrass the government and its leadership, they also risk diverting public attention from real policy debates. Really? In one case, a young LSD member ducked security and snatched a microphone from Secretary for Transport and Housing Eva Cheng as she was speaking to protest against rising railway fares.

"Each of us was surrounded by many security guards. So we had no choice but to change our way of protest, to air our grievances," said Anson Wong Hin-wai, the LSD member who ambushed the secretary.

At another Hong Kong public event on the same day, Secretary for Food and Health Dr. York Chow Yat-ngok was besieged by protesters angry at the Hospital Authority's decision to suspend bookings of obstetrics services for mainland mothers. Isn't that what democracy is all about? Expressive, not oppressive or repressive in any manner, shape or form. That is true Judeo-Athenian-Native American democracy. All points of view are entitled to be expressed and heard. That is the basic constitutional cornerstone that the Founding Fathers embedded in the American Constitution and the Bill of Rights.

In Egypt, the brutal murder of Khaled Said, a 28-year-old businessman, by plainclothes policemen who pulled him from an Internet café because of his Facebook posting depicting the murdering cops as corrupt drug dealers, was one of the catalysts that helped cleanse Egypt of corrupt self-serving career politicians.

The defection of top military generals in Yemen and Libya to the rebel side is an expression of democracy. No different than Mari Kiviniemi, the leader of the Finnish anti-euro populist party, who refused to support any more EU loan guarantees or other forms of bailout to the likes of Greece, Ireland, Portugal, Spain and Italy.

In China, it is the leaders born in the '60s now coming to power who are forcing more democratic inroads to the sclerotic failed Mao doctrines. They are taking over center stage of the Communist Party because they are well-educated and more open-minded, having experienced both the Cultural Revolution and the country's reform and opening up.

One could see the revolutionary steps change pace and direction leading up to today's revolutionary changes worldwide with the anti-Iraq war protests of 2007.

### Promising Millennium First Step

The anti-Bush Iraq war protests that took place simultaneously worldwide in March 2007 as the war was about to enter its fifth year shattered all previous records. Fifteen million people took to the streets, the most against any individual in the history of mankind. People prostrated themselves on 5th Avenue in New York City, stopping traffic – but not the war. People dumped bottles of Coke and Pepsi, trashed McDonald's restaurants, and boycotted America's cultural icons, as Americans did the same to French wines, cheese and perfumes. Meanwhile, America's economy slumped into a double-dip recession that even a big-spending war could not rescue.

The global protests calling for an end to the war in Iraq in 2007, brought out millions of protesters to denounce the conflict. In Washington, thousands crossed the Potomac River from the Lincoln Memorial to rally loudly but peacefully near the Pentagon.

"We're here in the shadow of the war machine," said anti-war activist Cindy Sheehan, the mother of a soldier killed in Iraq. "It's like being in the shadow of the Death Star. They take their death and destruction and they export it around the world. We need to shut it down."

Hollywood movies about the Iraq war even as the conflict was raging were an pleasant surprise. It was a departure from the usual Tinsletown tradition. It was three years after the fall of Vietnam before filmmakers felt brave enough to make explicit anti-war movies about that conflict. Jerry Sherlock, director of the New York Film Academy and executive producer of movies, including *The Hunt for Red October,* welcomed the prospect of movies coming out while wars were still raging.

"I think it is great because films do influence people. I hope that the films coming out influence people. The truth sets us free, after all the bullshit that we ever get every day in Washington and the airways and Cheney... . I am surprised it has taken so long," he said in 2007.

The penultimate anti-war message was contained not in a movie, but a pair of shoes. The shoes thrown by Iraqi journalist Muntadar al-Zaidi at President Bush during a news conference in Baghdad in December 2008. Zaidi jumped up and shouted: "This is the farewell kiss, you dog!" as he hurled his shoes at Bush. Too bad he missed. Soles of shoes are considered the ultimate insult in Arab culture, as is calling someone a dog.

In China, academics, students and even expats, including Americans, took to the streets of Beijing and Hong Kong protesting the Iraq war. The anti-war songs and placards were straight out of the '60s. *Where Have all the Flowers Gone?* to *Give Peace a Chance.* The human shields from America, Asia and Europe who went to Baghdad to symbolize their opposition to the war made Hanoi Jane look like a Girl Scout.

The comparisons between "Hanoi Jane" and "Condom Leezza" took on a spirited partisan flavor at the FCC Main Bar.

"How can Condom Leezza, who came out of the oil industry, had a tanker named after her, advising an oil man with an oily VP and greasy cabinet, be considered patriotic, while Jane Fonda, who expressed her right of freedom of speech, still be considered an unpatriotic American to this day?" asked Arthur Hacker, author and graphic artist after a series of Condom Leezza jokes were offered up by those around him.

"Yeah, all her condom is good for is oil and the Arabs who supply it," said a Vietnam veteran who was a Jane Fonda fan. A valid debate that should have taken place in Congress. After all, Condoleezza Rice was a senior executive with the Chevron oil company from 1991-2000, and they did name a tanker after her. How honest and non-politically compromising can a national security adviser from the oil industry be to a president and vice president from the same industry? What about *We the People?*

Oil got America into the 1991 Gulf War, the Afghan War and the Iraq War. It is time to learn and educate, as well as demonstrate, if America is to survive the 21st century with or without oil. There are alternatives.

### *Blood For Oil*

In 1973 America imported 35 percent of the oil it used, 5 percent of it from the Persian Gulf. By 1990, when Iraq invaded Kuwait, America imported 42 percent of its needs, with 12 percent coming from the Persian Gulf. When America went to war with Iraq, it was importing 53 per cent of its oil with more than 25 percent coming from the Persian Gulf. By 2020, the Energy Information Administration estimates that imports will reach 64 percent.

"We are truly sleepwalking through history," former Senator Robert Byrd reminded his fellow senators and *We the Apathetic Maids* on the eve of the war against Iraq. "Many of the pronouncements made by this administration are outrageous. There is no other word.

"Yet this chamber is hauntingly silent. On what is possibly the eve of horrific infliction of death and destruction on the population of the nation of Iraq – a population, I might add, of which over 50 percent is under age 15 – this chamber is silent," Byrd said.

Is it any wonder that when the European edition of *Time* magazine conducted a poll on its website asking "Which country poses a greater danger to world peace in 2003?" America was the winner? With 318,000 votes cast, the responses were: North Korea, 7 percent; Iraq, 8 percent; and America, 84 percent! As John le Carre put it to *The Times of London:* "America has entered one of its periods of historic madness, but this is the worst I can remember." No wonder people, employed and unemployed, are taking to the streets in unprecedented numbers.

### Right to Protest

My faith in the American protest movement was restored when I read that more than 100,000 people had descended on Washington, D.C., to protest the war in Iraq. It was the largest antiwar demonstration since Vietnam. Over 300,000 protested nationwide joining the millions of protesters around the world, including Hong Kong. Former Hong Kong legislator, 89-year-old Elsie Tu, said she was encouraged by the active involvement of Hong Kong people. Four-year-old Hong Konger Alix Head's message was simple but clear. "[I am] here against shooting. I like peace [and] peace means no fighting."

The February 15, 2003 worldwide Iraq war protest was testament to the global appeal of the First Amendment to America's Constitution.

Former Soviet Premier Mikhail Gorbachev reminds us of how precious the fundamental American rights of free speech, assembly and protest are.

"What I like most is Americans. They are people who were born and raised in conditions of democracy. They're open. Sometimes they are carefree. I like Americans. I have a lot of confidence in Americans. My confidence and support is much less when I look at foreign policy pursued by the United States. But as far as the domestic issues are concerned, they were quite spectacular in the past 10 years. I like that Americans reaped the benefits of globalization. But the gap between the rich and poor countries is widening. What happened in Seattle is just the bell that is tolling for all of us."

That includes Russia. Gorbachev engineered the Second Russian Revolution that transformed and broke up the USSR to its constituent countries – including a democratic Russia "built on corruption and hands-on control," said Mikhail B. Khodorkovsky, former head of the Russian oil company Yukos, who has been in prison since 2003 for daring to support independent parties in Russia. He was granted clemency in 2013 on condition he abstains from politics and criticizing Vladimir Putin.

"In my youth, the leaders of the USSR had no desire whatsoever to leave power. But history obliged them to do so just the same. Today's Russian theoreticians and practitioners of 'vertically corrupt management' have no intention of going anywhere. But they will have to. I know. I've seen it before," Khodorkovsky wrote in 2010 as he was tried on new charges of corruption and tax evasion. The Third Russian Revolution is coming.

Gorbachev is also critical of Putin, whom he blames for taking the country back to the times of a one-party state, and describes Russia as an "imitation" of democracy, where parliament and courts lack independence from the government and the main pro-Kremlin party is a "bad copy" of the Soviet-era Communist Party. He said his own attempt to found a political party failed when a Kremlin aide bluntly told him that authorities would not register it.

Russian youth, like their peers in Hong Kong, America, China, the Middle East, Africa and Europe, who are fueled and powered by the Internet, agree with Gorbachev. That is why they have also taken to the streets by the thousands demanding revolutionary changes be made by Putin and his brutal kleptocracy.

Russian punk band Pussy Riot, four young women in balaclavas who performed a crude anti-Putin song called *Mother of God, Drive Putin Out,* on the altar of the Cathedral of Christ the Saviour in Moscow in February 2012, represent Russian anger and disgust at Putinocracy – for which they were accused and tried for hooliganism. Their trial became one of the most politically charged trials of the country's post-Soviet era. A Russian court found them guilty. A big mistake. Two of the women are mothers of young children. At the trial, the band apologized to Christians for any offense, saying their protest was strictly political.

The trial highlighted the cultural divide between the secular, Westernized forces that are protesting against Putin's 12-year domination of the country's politics, and the conservative Russians who, led in part by the Orthodox Church hierarchy, have supported him.

The First Amendment to the U.S. Constitution states: "Congress shall make no law respecting an establishment of religion, or prohibiting the free exercise thereof; or abridging the freedom of speech, or of the press; or the right of the people peaceably to assemble, and to petition the government for a redress of grievances."

Americans have rarely refrained from criticism and dissent when the country was heading toward war. Even during the American Revolution, a third of the colonists, according to John Adams, opposed the drive toward independence. The War of 1812 provoked serious and strident dissent. The historian Samuel Eliot Morison called it "the most unpopular war that this country has ever waged, not even excepting the Vietnam conflict." President Madison's request for a declaration of war narrowly passed the Senate by 19 to 13 votes and the House of Representatives by 70 to 49. After war was declared, Governor Caleb Strong of Massachusetts proclaimed a public fast to atone for a war "against the nation from which we are descended." Most New England governors turned down presidential requests to supply troops.

The Mexican-American War was almost as unpopular, stirring fierce opposition.

"People of the United States!" Horace Greeley cried in the *New York Tribune*. "Your rulers are precipitating you into a fathomless abyss of crime and calamity!... Awake and arrest the work of butchery ere it shall be too late to preserve your souls from the guilt of wholesale slaughter!"

The Massachusetts Legislature passed a resolution declaring that the war, "so hateful in its objects, so wanton, unjust and unconstitutional in its origin and character, must be regarded as a war against freedom, against humanity, against justice, against the Union." Henry David Thoreau wrote his famous essay on *The Duty of Civil Disobedience* in protest of the war.

In 1848 the U.S. House of Representatives itself resolved that the Mexican War had been "unnecessarily and unconstitutionally begun by the President of the United States." A few days later a young congressman attacked the presidential justification for the war as "from beginning to end, the sheerest deception." Explaining to a friend his opposition to the war, Representative Abraham Lincoln of Illinois challenged what is known today as the Bush Doctrine of anticipatory self-defense: "Allow the President to invade a neighboring nation, whenever he shall deem it necessary to repel an invasion ... and you allow him to make war at pleasure." The Founding Fathers, he continued, "resolved to so frame the Constitution that no one man should hold the power of bringing this oppression upon us."

Thirteen years later, Lincoln faced a war of his own as President. The Civil War saw acute divisions even in the North. Men like Fernando Wood, former mayor of New York City and member of the House of Representatives, denounced Lincoln as a dictator and called for a negotiated peace.

The Spanish-American War, and especially the follow-up campaign against the Filipino insurrection, provoked vigorous criticism of the White House. It wasn't until World War II that the U.S. Supreme Court handed down a decision that confirmed that going to war does not abrogate freedom of individual conscience and does not suspend the Bill of Rights. Even when the republic faces mortal dangers, the First Amendment of the Constitution is still there.

After the start of World War II, the Supreme Court in *West Virginia State Board of Education v. Barnette* held that a law compelling students in public schools to salute the flag and to recite the Pledge of Allegiance was unconstitutional.

As Justice Robert H. Jackson said for the court, "If there is any fixed star in our constitutional constellation, it is that no official, high or petty, can prescribe what shall be orthodox in politics, nationalism, religion, or other matters of opinion."

That decision was handed down on Flag Day 1943!

Americans' right to protest and the "Flower Power" of the '60s was best represented in the opening year of the 21st century, when Alina Lebedva hit Prince Charles with a carnation in Riga, Latvia. She said she was protesting the Afghan war.

### Respectful Reflection

*We the Apathetic Maids,* like Alina, have to sweep out the career politicians with brooms made of flowers in the New World Order and reclaim the America of the Founding Fathers. The post 9/11 World Economic Forum held in New York in 2002 brought into sharp focus the mellow reflective impact that the events of 9/11 had on a stunned world trying to grasp and come to terms with why and how such a tragedy could happen. While protesters gathered, a Chinese scrap metal firm bought and shipped the twisted steel remains of the World Trade Center to China. A cold reminder of how seamless globalization is.

The death of Carlo Giuliani in Genoa, Alexandros Grigoropoulos in Athens and other young protesters in Kashmir, Bahrain, Yemen, Oman, Tunisia, Egypt – China and America – were senseless. All these young people were killed by "security forces." Whose security forces? The people's or the career politicians? Youth don't expect to die when they go out onto the streets to demand their basic rights the way their parents and grandparents did. Why are their parents and grandparents in America and China no longer as brave as *We the Maids* used to be? Why are *We Maids* now afraid to take to the streets the way our brothers and sisters in the Arab world have done?

After 9/11, revolutionary change merited a collective reflection on how to effectively mobilize and constructively convey the message of the need for drastic dramatic changes in the international democracy and freedom-of-expression marketplace in the New World Order of the 21$^{st}$ century.

The colorful costumes and street theater of the '60s that made a dramatic comeback in the closing decade of the 20th century and opening years of the new millennium are in a post-9/11 reflective mode best articulated by Alexis de Tocqueville in *Democracy in America*. There is a fundamental difference between the artistic culture of an aristocracy and that of a democracy. In an aristocracy, members of the nobility form a small class with fixed interests, inspiring a uniform style among artisans and creators. Attention is paid to detailed craftsmanship, and artistry is a form of service.

In a democracy, Tocqueville said, there are no restrictions of class or guild on the artisans or their public. Styles are less firmly defined; social arrangements are more fluid; human aspirations vary widely. So artisans offer what Tocqueville called "imperfect satisfaction" for diverse audiences rather than perfection for the few. Tocqueville also accurately predicted the nature of pop culture: democracy, he wrote, shifts the preoccupation of art from the soul to the body, from the ideal to the real.

Reality today in Muslim Afghanistan, Iran and the rest of the Arab world is that youth there also want freedom and do protest like their contemporaries in America, China and Hong Kong and make their leaders listen. Afghan students protest about conditions at their university dormitories. Students in Iran protest against the unpopular conservative clergy ruling their Islamic Republic. Youth in Afghanistan, Iran and the Arab world are the majority of the population. The older generation has been killed off by wars. More than half of Arab countries' populations are under 25.

The Arab cleansing revolutions in Tunisia and Egypt should therefore not have come as the surprises they did. The departure of Tunisia's President Zine el-Abidine Ben Ali, after a month of popular rebellion against unemployment, high food costs and corruption, forced him to flee to Saudi Arabia, resulting in an Arab country for the first time empowering people to build a government from scratch.

The same happened in Egypt. Inspired by the Tunisians, Egyptians took to the streets of Cairo and other major cities and villages demanding Hosni Mubarak and his regime resign and leave office. In 18 days, millions of Egyptians of all ages and walks of life took to the streets and succeeded in overthrowing a corrupt-autocratic regime. A stark lesson not only for Arab autocrats and monarchies, but all autocratic dictatorships – including China's.

When the barriers of fear, despondency and loathing by techno-savvy 20-somethings fall, the resulting flames fanned by social networking become all-consuming of career politicians and their parties. The same can happen in America and China.

This "youth bulge" is transforming the world. Similar phenomenons occurred before the French Revolution of 1789, the 1968 political protests in the U.S., the Iranian Revolution of 1979, and today's anarchist and revolutionary movements around the world. Something to reflect on as the Third American Revolution unfolds and the youth demanding change do more than just mouth the words.

The mysterious letter bombs sent by young anarchists to foreign embassies in Athens and Rome were the follow-up messages to the worldwide student protests challenging the establishment policies they reject because of their refusal to pay for the sins of career politicians and their destructive capitalist cronies. They are the future and their message is loud and clear.

*Immigration*

Among all its other problems, America's immigration laws and enforcement policies are a mess, irrelevant and outdated for the 21$^{st}$ century. So much so that even though immigration is governed by federal law, states have decided to take matters into their own hands, with Arizona leading an unconstitutional charge in the wrong direction.

Busting illegal immigrants makes no sense. They provide a clear economic benefit, but illogical and outdated laws prohibit them from contributing their fair share of taxes to the communities they serve. The reality is

417

that America, like most countries, has outdated laws that make legal immigration very difficult and expensive, and as a result encourage illegal immigration, which is easier and cheaper than the legal route. Arbitrary piecemeal immigration laws adopted, or proposed each election cycle, are defeatist, destructive and self-serving to the career politicians who enact them. Arizona's get-tough immigration law, SB 1070, signed into law in April 2010, before the November midterm elections, is a case in point. The law authorizes law enforcement officials to stop and question any Hispanic-looking person when there is "reasonable suspicion" that they are in the country illegally.

Arizona Governor Jan Brewer was facing certain defeat in her 2010 re-election campaign. She presided over a state with a dire budget deficit, faced two dozen challengers in the Republican primary and her approval rating was well below 50 percent. That all changed when she became the country's biggest defender of a get-tough stance against illegal immigration. She got re-elected. But Arizona's economy tanked even more as legal Mexican tourists and shoppers stopped coming. Four days after Arizona's illegal-immigration law was signed, Mexico issued a warning to its citizens about travel to Arizona. Major civil rights groups, cities and towns held protest rallies across America denouncing the law as illegal and discriminatory and asked people to boycott Arizona.

As a result, the number of visitors from Mexico and America plummeted and Arizona took an even bigger financial hit. A study issued in January 2010 by the University of Arizona's Economic and Business Research Center says that more than 24 million legal visitors who visited the state in 2007-2008 spent about $2.7 billion at stores, restaurants, hotels and other businesses. "Almost 23,400 wage-and-salary jobs in Arizona are directly attributable to Mexican visitors spending," the report says. Business owners in Arizona's border shopping districts that cater to customers from Mexico complain that business is down 70 percent, the worst in 50 years! How is this law good for hard-working Americans or the tax base of Arizona? What am I missing?

Casey J. Nethercott, a former leader of the border-watching group Ranch

Rescue, is missing his ranch that he was forced to turn over to migrants he detained there illegally. Edwin Alfredo Mancia Gonzales and Fatima del Socorro Leiva Medina sold the 60-acre property for $45,000, and their lawyers at the Southern Poverty Law Center continue to seek the rest of the $850,000 judgment against Nethercott. He is not the only Arizona rancher who has been forced to pay punitive damages to illegal migrants forcibly detained on private property.

Arizona voters, outraged that illegal immigrants were winning court judgments against American citizens, approved a constitutional amendment in 2006 banning undocumented immigrants from collecting punitive damages in the state.

Arizona has felt the effects of a boycott before. The state lost about 170 conventions from 1990 to 1993 from boycotts because of the state's failure to approve a Martin Luther King Jr. holiday.

I agree with the Justice Department that the Arizona law is illegal and unconstitutional because it targets Latinos, violates their civil rights and exposes them to increased scrutiny based on ethnicity and race. Arizona has no right to "interpose" its own judgment on the rights of law-abiding citizens. It is un-American and not what the Constitution stands for. As an Anglo who travels quite a bit, I always chuckle to myself when I answer "Hong Kong" whenever I am asked where I'm from. "Hong Kong? You don't look Chinese," they say.

Many people still nurse misconceptions about where people are from based on the color of their skin. Immigration has changed the color and makeup of many countries, especially America. If Hong Kong adopted a law similar to Arizona's, I and many Anglos like me would be repeatedly stopped and questioned.

Border fences, concrete, barbed wire or virtual, designed to keep illegal immigrants out of America, are ineffective and a waste of hard-earned taxpayers' money. Immigrants determined to get to America will find a way around, under, above or through any fence the government builds.

The so-called $4.4 billion Secure Border Initiative, the invisible fence the Department of Homeland Security has been trying to build since 2006 along the U.S.-Mexican border incorporating high-tech cameras, radar and vibration sensors, is shaping up as the latest failure. It is not practical to fence a 1,933 mile border that more than 350 million people cross legally each year.

Border agents rely on obsolete ground sensors that periodically transmit false alarms, as was the case in October 2012, when a false alarm from a sensor in southern Arizona was to blame when several U.S. Border Patrol agents rushed to a remote canyon shortly after midnight and opened fire on each other. One was killed and another was wounded.

The incident has raised concerns that a deteriorating network of more than 12,800 ground sensors, as well as other outdated technology, could endanger the lives of more agents who police the long border with Mexico.

The Obama administration spent nearly $18 billion on immigration enforcement in 2012, significantly more than its spending on all other major federal law enforcement agencies combined. Obama deported 410,000 foreigners in 2012, giving him the record for the highest number of removals during his first term in office.

The number of agents assigned to patrol the border has nearly doubled since 2006, even though the number of people attempting to enter the U.S. illegally appears to be at a near 40-year low. The increased number of agents has upset many residents in Arizona border towns, who feel like they now live in a military-like occupied camp because security infrastructure has caused an unacceptable impact on property, nature and their desert way of life.

How much more do *We the Apathetic Taxpayers* have to waste in America's vast deserts before we realize that trying to keep illegal immigrants out is an act of futility that only benefits security contractors?

People will continue to cross illegally into the U.S. tucked under the dashboards of cars, tunneling under the fence, throwing bicycles over the barriers and pedaling, crawling through brush, swimming and walking,

walking and walking – sometimes dying in the desert. America is the top destination of illegal immigrants and deports the largest number of illegals each year.

If it weren't for illegal immigrants, America wouldn't be the country it is today – nor would many other countries. Human migration has been going on since man first stood up on two legs and started walking. The discovery of stone tools at an archaeological site in the Caucasus suggests there was an early flow of humans in and out of Africa as far back as 1.85 million years ago, according to a report in the June 2011 Proceedings of the National Academy of Sciences. Discovering stone tools and materials from such an early date raises the possibility that Homo erectus evolved in Eurasia and might have migrated back to Africa, though much more study is needed to confirm that idea. An alternative theory is that Homo erectus originated in Africa and migrated to the Caucasus. Either way, humans migrated from the beginning of mankind.

Sitting at the bar at Annie Moore's pub and restaurant on 43$^{rd}$ Street, a few hundred feet from Grand Central Station in New York, as I do periodically whenever I am in the city before catching a train, I couldn't help notice how relevant Annie Moore's is to today's immigration debate.

On January 1, 1892, a young Irish girl made immigration history. Just 15 years old, Annie Moore sailed from Cobh harbor in County Cork, Ireland, to America. As the ship docked and the gangplank lowered, Annie Moore stepped ashore to a cheering crowd. She was handed a $10 gold piece and became the first immigrant to be processed through the newly-opened Ellis Island immigration center.

America, and the world as we know it, emerged out of the ceaseless wandering of humans on Planet Earth. The world can only improve by regulating the movement of people constructively, rather than trying to stop it. It can't be stopped.

Not only does a fence not keep out illegal immigrants, it encroaches on private property, destroys the environment and hurts local economies. So what is the point?

Tightening border controls and immigration laws have failed to keep several hundred thousand illegals a year out of America. U.S. immigration policies have backfired. America has to find a way to ensure that illegal immigrants in America – and those on their way – don't forever remain marginalized and victimized. Why not accept them as taxpayer citizens? The point really hit home during the 2010 midterm election and California gubernatorial campaign. Immigration and the role Latino voters would play in the elections was again a hot button election issue.

Meg Whitman, the Republican candidate for governor in California, spent more than $120 million of her own money only to lose to Jerry Brown, because of the Latino vote going to Brown.

"I cannot win this election without the Latino vote," Whitman said whenever she was questioned about the undocumented worker that she fired after her campaign got underway. She didn't get the Latino vote and lost.

She lost the vote after that undocumented helper, Nicandra "Nicky" Diaz Santillan, who worked for Whitman for nine years, was thrown out "like garbage," as she told reporters.

Listening to Whitman's Republican Party mantras for opposing amnesty for illegals, who are commonly employed across America, infuriated me. "Does Whitman really think she can win after saying those stupid outdated racist remarks, no matter how much money she spends?" I asked Grover McKean, former deputy treasurer of California, at a fund raiser he was hosting for Nadia Lockyer at his home in October 2010. Nadia, a beautiful Latina married to California State Treasurer Bill Lockyer, was running for a Marin County Board of Supervisors seat – which she won–and then gave up when she self-destructed with sex and drug scandals.

Immigration, legal and illegal, amnesty and temporary-worker programs became a topic of major conversation that evening among the former and current Democratic Party office holders at Grover's after Nadia proudly mentioned her immigrant background. Latino voters' dejection and apathy in the midterm elections across America, unlike their turnout in California, did make a difference that helped Republicans win. The Arizona law rewrote not just the rules on immigration, but also the rules on how immigration is talked about on the campaign trail and gave a boost to candidates who favor tougher rules and enforcement.

I am an immigrant gypsy who spends a lot of time on the road globally and locally across America. I have spent a lot of time in John Steinbeck's *Grapes of Wrath* California, and each time I see Latino farmhands planting, pruning or harvesting California farms, I am more befuddled as to why so many fellow California and American gypsies across the U.S. forget their immigrant heritage and how dependent we are on migrant workers. Why have Americans become so parochial close-minded – and closed-border-minded?

### Birthright

Birthright citizenship, the 14th Amendment of the Constitution, was another hot button campaign issue brought to the forefront by the Tea Party movement, which wants it renounced and made it a major campaign issue during the 2010 midterm elections. In other words, U.S.-born children of illegal immigrants would no longer automatically qualify for citizenship.

The 14th Amendment declares: "All persons born or naturalized in the United States, and subject to the jurisdiction thereof, are citizens of the United States."

Congress inserted the citizenship clause in the 14th Amendment, ratified in 1868, to overrule the Dred Scott decision of 1857, in which the Supreme Court held that even free blacks were not citizens. Those who want to change the law argue that the purpose of the amendment was solely to ensure that newly freed black slaves received all the rights of other Americans.

It's not hard to see why many Americans would like to change the law. The Pew Hispanic Center issued a report in August 2010 indicating that one in every 13 babies born in the U.S. in 2008 – about 340,000 out of a total of 4.3 million – had at least one parent who was an illegal immigrant. About 85 percent of those parents were Latinos.

The center also found a huge increase in the number of children under age 18 living in the U.S. whose parents were illegal immigrants: 4 million in 2008, compared with 2.7 million in 2003. Los Angeles County paid out a record $52 million in July in welfare checks and food stamps to illegal immigrants for their U.S.-born children. That represented 23 percent of all county welfare and food stamp assistance.

America is one of only 30 countries that grants automatic citizenship to practically anyone who happens to be born there. The overwhelming majority of nations follow the Latin concept of *jus sanguinis* – right of blood – in which the citizenship of the parent governs the citizenship of their children. The concept, like Latin, has no place or relevance in the 21st century.

What does citizenship and belonging mean today? Children born, raised, educated and living in America, or any country for that matter, willing to serve in its military are citizens of America because that is their country of origin and home. They are citizens. The fact that their non-citizen parents entered America legally or illegally, to make a better life for their children, does not take that constitutional birthright away. To do so serves no constructive purpose. It is destructive and disruptive for the individuals, their families and the country.

What benefit is there to America to dispose of people it bore, bred and educated who are upstanding taxpayers – and citizens? These are the kind of people who helped make America the great nation it is. Why self-destruct by discarding one of America's greatest ingredients?

The arguments about illegals creating an undesirable Latino underclass is not a new or valid argument. When Irish, Italians, Jews and other Europeans flocked to the U.S. in the late 1800s, there was fear of an exploding underclass. An 1892 report by the U.S. superintendent of immigration referred to "an enormous influx of foreigners unacquainted with our language and customs." It noted that "the majority of these unfortunates came here without money and without skill as workmen," and warned that they were turning into a "new undesirable class."

Those groups long ago entered the American mainstream and there is no reason to believe or support the argument that Latinos won't do the same. Immigrants and their children are the building blocks that built the nation the Founding Fathers designed.

### Maternity Tourism

San Gabriel, a town I know well from my lawyer days in L.A., is a suburb just east of Los Angeles, and has grown rapidly in the decades since the '60s and today is an interlocal community of Chinese from Hong Kong, Taiwan, mainland China, Vietnam, Korea and every other country in Asia who have created the most delightful buffets of fused Asian dishes with the right balance of salt and pepper of Anglos and Latinos.

Townhouses are common among the modest apartment buildings and homes along San Gabriel's palm-lined streets. Many of these townhouses are home to "maternity tourists" from China. They give birth to children who are American citizens the minute their sore ass and loud mouth birth cries pierce the skies of freedom.

Much of the birthright debate has focused on immigrants entering the U.S. illegally from poor countries in Latin America. The Chinese maternity tourists are not only relatively wealthy, but also in the country legally, on tourist visas. Most of them, after their children's births are registered, return to China with their American babies.

Maternity tourism packages are sold not only in China, but in Mexico, South Korea and many other countries. Travel agencies there advertise tours that arrange for doctors, insurance and postpartum care. The Marmara, a Turkish-owned hotel on the Upper East Side in New York City, has advertised month-long "baby stays" that even come with a stroller.

It is not uncommon for boarding houses in many U.S. suburbs, like many countries and states, including Hong Kong, to be home to as many as 40 people. But the boarders are usually men, often working to send money to their families back home. But nowadays, it appears to be "many, many young women" going in and out of these residential maternity wards.

Many Chinese see this as a sort of insurance policy to freedom should they need to leave their homeland in a hurry for any political, legal or economic reason. The U.S.-born children, once they turn 21, are able to petition for their parents to join them in America.

Angela Maria Kelley, vice president for immigration policy and advocacy at the Center for American Progress, a liberal-leaning research group in Washington, said the existence of the businesses helping foreign women give birth in the U.S. has only just begun to enter the public consciousness and deserves further study. "But to say that you want to change the Constitution because of this feels like killing a fly with an Uzi," she said.

The U.S. State Department, which grants tourist visas, is not permitted to deny visa applications simply because a woman is pregnant.

### Illegal Gangs and Employers
Immigration quotas and restrictions benefit only criminal gangs and heartless exploitive employers who encourage illegal immigration. Many of them are based in the San Gabriel Valley catering to the needs of the Asian and Latino hordes craving to be in America and to become citizens.

Coyotes and snakeheads charging exorbitant fees to smuggle people, fake documents, identity thefts, rape and robberies because illegals carry cash, the result of not being able to open a bank account and not reporting the crimes to authorities for fear of deportation, not to mention the criminal activities engaged in by some illegals themselves in order to survive because of their inability to get a job at a fair wage, are the result of unrealistic and unenforceable immigration policies.

Illegal immigrants are not limited to poor, uneducated welfare recipients exploiting America's largesse. They include top players in America's favorite pastime–pro baseball players. More than 40 players in the big leagues were smuggled into the country illegally. Top pitchers and shortstops have surpassed dope, rum and tobacco as the commodities of choice for traffickers working the old Spanish Main.

Joe Kehoskie, a Syracuse, New York-based sports agent who has represented more than a dozen Cuban athletes, said the smuggling of baseball players "has become a cottage industry," an example of "bare knuckles capitalism."

Cuban authorities have clamped down on travel for players seen as defection risks. Since then, only one is known to have defected at an international event – while smuggling has soared.

"It's like somebody threw a switch," Kehoskie said, "They stopped defecting at tournaments and they all started taking speedboats to Miami."

Unscrupulous employers, whether owners of a baseball team, sweatshop or meatpacking factory, encourage illegal immigration by employing illegal migrants to cut costs. The periodic high-profile raids on factories employing illegals only benefit politicians who bask in the momentary media glow of the raid. They certainly don't benefit the families of the illegals or their employers. One such raid that I vividly remember was directed at Agriprocessors Inc., the nation's largest kosher meatpacking plant, in May 2008 in Postville, Iowa. Many of the 389 arrested illegals were minors, some as young as 13, who were exploited like slaves. They worked 12-hour or longer shifts, without overtime or rest, six days a week in unsafe conditions.

The cost to convict and deport the people from the Postville raid with criminal offenses was a waste of precious taxpayer dollars. The federal government spent significant sums to process the litigation, manage the complicated logistics and imprison more than 260 people, most for five months. The continuous, senseless, politically vindictive wasteful spending by the government only further benefits the criminal gangs and unscrupulous employers.

I agree with the decision by the Supreme Court in May 2011 to uphold the Arizona law making it illegal to hire illegal immigrants and placing the burden of proving their legality on the employers – and punishing them for failing to do so. Arizona mandated the use by all employers of a federal electronic program for verifying the status of new hires known as E-Verify. Mississippi and South Carolina have adopted similar laws.

### Deportation Damage & Dream

Legal help eludes many detained migrants. Many illegal immigrants are held in rural jails without ready access to legal representation. In a 2010 survey of immigration detention facilities nationwide, the Chicago-based National Immigrant Justice Center found that more than half did not offer detainees information about their rights, and 78 percent prohibited private phone calls to lawyers. More than 80 percent of detainees are in facilities that are isolated and beyond the reach of legal aid organizations.

The Immigration and Customs Enforcement agency detains about 400,000 immigrants annually at a cost of $1.7 billion in 2010. Illegal immigrants facing deportation have no guaranteed right to a lawyer, but a network of nonprofit organizations offers legal help to immigrants in detention. A 2005 Migration Policy Institute study found that 41 percent of detainees applying to become lawful permanent residents who had legal counsel won their cases, compared with just 21 percent of those without representation. In asylum cases, 18 percent of detainees with lawyers were granted asylum, compared to 3 percent for those without.

Zeituni Onyango, President Barack Obama's aunt, the half-sister of his late Kenyan father, who lives in a Boston public housing project, had been in the U.S. illegally since 2002. Republicans made an issue of candidate Obama's aunt being an illegal immigrant in the closing days of the 2008 presidential campaign. She was granted political asylum in May 2010. She had been seeking asylum since 2002. Her asylum application was rejected in 2004 and she was ordered to leave the country. This time around, she was represented by a team of lawyers.

Granting immigrants better access to counsel could save taxpayer money because detainees often would be released sooner, saving the $122-a-day cost of keeping them locked up.

The damage done to U.S - born children of illegal immigrants whose parents are deported is horrific and well documented. What is even more horrific but not as well documented is the damage done to the children of legal immigrants who are deported for "minor criminal convictions." Authorities have deported more than 88,000 legal immigrant parents of U.S. citizen children in the first decade of the 21st-century. A report by the UC Berkeley and UC Davis law schools in March 2010 found that the deported parents had lived in America an average of 10 years and more than half of them had at least one child at home.

The deportations caused their children depression, sleeplessness and behavioral problems, plummeting grades and a greater propensity to drop out of school, according to interviews with family members.

The deportations began increasing after Congress made several controversial revisions to immigration laws in 1996. The revisions broadened the types of deportable offenses considered "aggravated felonies," required mandatory deportation for those convicted of such crimes, and severely limited a judge's ability to consider the effects of deportation on children.

"It is a travesty that this is happening without any judicial discretion," said Aarti Kohli, director of immigration policy for Berkely Law School's Warren Institute. "We're not saying you can't deport people. We're saying there should be a fair judicial process that takes into account the impact on their children."

I agree. There should be such a process.

The report detailed many cases that I found repulsive and good reason to repeal the law. A case in point is a California man who had fled Cambodia's murderous Khmer Rouge regime in the mid-1970s. He resettled in the U.S. in 1981, graduated high school, served in the U.S. Army and worked as a mechanic. He was married and had five children. He was convicted of a misdemeanor domestic violence offense in 2002 but it was reclassified as a felony because he served a 365-day sentence. He was ordered deported.

What makes even less sense are the thousands of illegal immigrants who have been ordered to leave the U.S. but remain because no other nation will recognize or accept them. Without a passport or visa to travel, they remain in America. Palestinians born in refugee camps who do not belong to any country, people born in the USSR that does not exist anymore, or people born in countries that do not have diplomatic relations with the U.S., such as Cuba. The time and money wasted on cases against people who wind up staying in America anyway, regardless of what a judge rules, is absurd.

I applaud the federal appeals court judges across America who have criticized immigration judges for what they call a pattern of biased and incoherent decisions in immigration cases.

Judges must regain discretionary authority in cases involving legal permanent residents and their innocent citizen children who are being unnecessarily victimized by a capricious law. The current definition of "aggravated felonies" for immigration law purposes has to return to the pre-1996 definition.

The arbitrary laws applied to illegal immigrants must become more humane, or better yet, repealed. Another ridiculous law is called Secure Communities. It is a controversial immigration enforcement program that requires fingerprints acquired by local law enforcement agencies to be sent to the FBI so that the Immigration and Customs Enforcement agency can determine if they match those of someone known to be in the country illegally. If so, ICE orders the immigrant detained as a first step toward deportation. Tens of thousands of undocumented immigrants have been removed from the U.S. under the program. Many of the deportees committed minor offenses or no crimes at all.

Many cities and other jurisdictions refuse to participate in the program because they think it is unfair and voluntary – only to find out it isn't voluntary.

Massachusetts, New York and Illinois were the first states to refuse to go along with the program. They join a list of elected officials, Congress members and law-enforcement professionals who want nothing to do with the program for the simple reason that it does more harm than good.

One enlightened city that went to the other extreme to validate illegal immigrants is New Haven, Connecticut. Starting in November 2007, the city offers illegal immigrants municipal identification cards that allow access to city services such as libraries, parks and a chance to open bank accounts. Yale University Law School, based in New Haven, helped research the idea and volunteered legal services.

Some cities, like Farmers Branch, Texas, go to the other extreme to identify and exclude illegal immigrants. Elected officials there have spent four years and more than $4 million defending their misguided ordinance that bars landlords from renting to undocumented immigrants. Court after court has struck down the law as an unconstitutional intrusion into the federal government's sole authority to regulate immigration. Still, city officials persist, arguing that the law is merely an attempt to regulate housing, not to target immigrants who are in the country illegally.

The American dream of illegal immigrant children – children who were brought to the States by their migrant parents – is to become legal. It's a dream that U.S. Congressman Luis Gutierrez is determined to fulfill.

"I have only one loyalty," he says, "and that's to the immigrant community."

He was in the forefront of securing passage of the DREAM Act that would legalize undocumented youths who attend college or serve in the military. The act was voted down by Republican senators, putting the dreams of millions on hold.

"They believe in their heart of hearts this is home; this is the only country they have ever known. All they're asking for is a chance to serve this nation," said Democratic Senator Dick Durbin, one of the measure's sponsors.

Too many innocent American-born and raised children are being forced into the current tide of reverse migration – going back to Mexico – a country they do not know. Thousands of U.S.-born children of former illegal immigrants now live in cities and towns across Mexico. Disoriented by cultural differences and often unable to speak the language, they frequently struggle, clinging to one another in a society that views them with a mix of envy and pity.

The peaceful "coming-out" protests of illegals in America who do not want to be pitied back home are to be commended. Their "undocumented and unafraid" youthful protests are on the revolutionary forefront of America's Third Revolution.

The Deferred Action for Childhood Arrivals program, the result of Obama's policy shift in June 2012, is a small but significant step that could help more than a million immigrant students and military veterans who were brought into America illegally as children and who have lived in fear of deportation ever since.

Many of these innocent youths learn the truth about their immigration status only when they apply to college or try to get a driver's license. The DREAM Act should be made law because it acknowledges that thousands of promising young people are not to blame for the misdeeds of their parents. More importantly, its passage is clearly in the economic interest of the country. All children in the U.S. are entitled to a public K-12 education – worth roughly $113,568 per child in California – and given this significant investment, it makes no fiscal sense to foreclose further opportunity for young illegal immigrants just when they are poised to repay the society that nurtured them.

Comprehensive immigration reform is long overdue. There are alternatives to blanket deportations. Illegals can be permitted to stay as employed taxpayers without becoming citizens. That is one of many options.

With more than 60,000 Hispanics in the U.S. turning 18 every month between 2012 and 2016, I have no doubt immigration reform is on its way.

These residents should be embraced and offered services such as those at the St. Anselm's Cross-Cultural Community Center in Garden Grove, known as the "refugee club."

The club offers newcomers the basics: how to write a resume, how to find a better job and how to get a handle on America.

## Boat People

I first became aware of the "boat people" in the late '70s, when it became clear that America was going to be defeated and leave Vietnam. The victorious Communist North took over the South and reunited the country. Many Vietnamese decided to flee the country by boat rather than live under a totalitarian communist regime, especially those who had worked with or had links to the U.S. military during the war.

The Vietnam exodus was the largest mass movement of refugees in modern times. About 1.5 million people, mainly from southern Vietnam, fled in small overcrowded, wooden craft that were unsuitable for the open sea. As many as 500,000 died, mainly due to bad weather, starvation, thirst and attacks by Thai pirates.

Many of these people made it to Hong Kong. They were housed in a refugee camp until their identity and status could be determined and a new home found, usually in America.

These were desperate people, many of whom turned to cannibalism to survive the boat journeys. "They wanted to eat me and had a large pot of boiling water ready," said Dao Can Cu, a 15-year-old boy tethered to the mast of a boat that arrived in Hong Kong in 1981. His life was spared only because the boat had made it to Hong Kong.

"These poor, wretched, bewildered and totally traumatized pieces of human flotsam were provided with basic medical help and fed and watered," said Talbot Bashall, the former controller of the Refugee Control Centre, the body created in Hong Kong in 1979 to handle the developing refugee crisis. Despite the crowding of more than 12,000 men, women and children in "generally primitive conditions" in a dockyard, the boat people were happy they were not pushed back out to sea, he says.

"I believe it is to Hong Kong's eternal credit that the policy was adopted and I know that those of us who were in the front line would not have had it any other way.

"It is enormously important that the genuine values of people fleeing danger and terror in their own lands be heard and understood," says Talbot. I endorse and echo his sentiments.

The abuse and mistreatment of refugees from war-ravaged countries and repressive totalitarian regimes reached a new height of ugliness and inhumanity in late 2008 and early 2009, when stories of the plight of the Muslim Rohingya boat people came to light. Hundreds, and possibly thousands of Rohingya, people from Myanmar and Bangladesh, had perished after being towed out to sea by the Thai military and deliberately cast adrift in flimsy unpowered boats.

Thousands of Rohingya fled their homes in Myanmar's northern Rakhine state to risk crossing the Bay of Bengal and then the Andaman Sea in rickety boats in the hope of reaching Thailand, Malaysia or Indonesia. It has become an annual migration that takes advantage of winter calms and the numbers grow every year.

The horrific pictures and stories of the Rohingya boat people arrested by Thailand's military, marched ashore with their arms in the air in the pristine waters and beaches of Thailand's idyllic tourist islands, lined up in the hot sand and sun, many with their hands tied behind their backs for months, before being herded onto unpowered boats and towed out to sea and set adrift were mind-numbing. Some of the boats were rescued by the Indonesian navy off Sumatra. The starving men were picked up after being spotted by fishermen.

"Fishermen found a wooden boat without any engine drifting in the sea with 198 Myanmar migrants on board," Lieutenant Tedi Sutari told the Agence-France-Presse. "The migrants said the Thai authorities towed them out to sea and set them adrift."

The men claimed to have been drifting for 21 days.

"During the journey about 20 people among us died," said Rahmat, a 43-year-old survivor. "We performed prayers in the boat for them before we threw the bodies into the sea. ... Almost every day someone would die."

And as if the Rohingya who survive haven't suffered enough on their boat ride through hell, those who wind up in Bangladesh – across the Naf River from the land they fled – are often secretly shipped back to Myanmar, where they face almost certain persecution, even death. Now Myanmar, taking a page from the American playbook, is planning to build a 65-kilometer fence along its border with Bangladesh to keep people in as well as out.

These Muslims with nowhere to go – like their Palestinian brothers in Gaza and angry Muslims elsewhere – are suicide-bombers-in-waiting. After all, cavorting with virgins in heaven has to be better than leaky boats, cannibalism and refugee camps.

Africa has its desperate boat people, too, thousands trying to reach the "Pearl of the Mediterranean" – Italy's Lampedusa island, 22 square kilometers of limestone between Tunisia and Malta wrapped in breathtaking beaches and blue seas. It's a tourist magnet, much like the islands off Thailand, but with a dark side. It's the closest European port to Africa, and nearer Africa than it is to mainland Italy.

Tens of thousands of immigrants – many fleeing the tumult in Libya and Tunisia in early 2011, have put ashore in Lampedusa. Libya's Gaddaffi had vowed to unleash "an unprecedented wave of illegal immigration on Europe after NATO began bombing his armed forces. He kept his word. The hordes were promptly rounded up and put in detention camps that resemble the military prisons in Iraq or Afghanistan. Armed men patrol the floodlighted iron fences around the clock. The detainees sleep in large metal hangers, dark and primitive, where no outsider is allowed to go.

Stereotyped images – of out-of-work Africans engaging in a variety of criminal and anti-social activities – haunt many. Such fears have been blown out of all proportion by Europe's new crop of rightist politicians, fanning and fueling an avoidable anguish for blacks and whites alike.

People will always gravitate toward better opportunities of earning a living. That legitimate human instinct explains history's great migrations. It accounts in large part for the Anglo-Saxon populations of North America, Australia and New Zealand, and for the Chinese and Indian diaspora. The urge for self-betterment cannot be denied in a globalized age that exalts the ideal of a borderless world.

Closer to home, America is not that kind to boat people either. The U.S. is regarded as one of the prime offenders of human compassion toward refugees and asylum seekers. Take the case of the Golden Venture, a rusty old freighter that ran aground off Rockaway Beach off the Queens shoreline in June 1993, spilling 286 Chinese from Fujian Province into the glare of the world's media. Many of the immigration cases related to the Golden Venture have still not been resolved.

The Golden Venture was a golden opportunity for America to show its compassion toward refugees and asylum seekers. Instead, America dropped the ball of moral responsibility and let the national security team pick up the fumble and run with it.

These boat people had risked their lives in squalid, cramped conditions, with 10 not surviving the voyage. Many were so emaciated from the year-long trip – where the only food was two or three bowls daily of tainted rice and filthy drinking water – that emergency teams recalled ribs cracking as they attempted to resuscitate survivors. All the Chinese were promptly arrested and jailed indefinitely, except for six who fled and have never been seen again.

"When the Golden Venture passengers were detained in 1993, the government ignored human rights standards," said Stanley Mark, of the

Asian American Legal Defense and Education Fund, the first attorneys permitted to visit and represent the Golden Venture passengers in court. "Unfortunately, what the Golden Venture passengers were subjected to – indefinite incarceration in jails far from relatives and their attorneys – is no longer extraordinarily punitive. It was a dramatic policy reversal at the time that has tragically become the norm."

## *Gypsies*

France's systematic deportation of thousands of gypsies, or Roma as they are called, back to Romania and Bulgaria in 2010, and the destruction of their camps landed the French government in the European Court of Justice for violating European Union law.

Italy is no better. Gypsy camps are being burned to the ground and the people beaten and deported. In 2008, European Parliament member Viktoria Mohacsi, a gypsy of Hungarian origin, visited the nomad camps in Italy and prepared a report for Parliament.

"The situation of the Roma in Italy is horrible. It is unbelievable that in a democratic country, there are people that live without rights and without documents, even if they have been there for more than 40 years," she wrote. "There are children here belonging to third-generation immigrants that still do not have fundamental rights of citizenship. A program of integration is urgent, particularly for the people arriving from new member states of the European Union."

There is little reliable data on the gypsy population. Estimates range from 2 million to 5 million. Originally from India, gypsies were virtual slaves until the 19th century, working for aristocrats and in monasteries. When democracy took hold, they were freed. But they were landless, uneducated and dark-skinned. They are discriminated against across Europe with few prospects. Unless they are accepted, educated and integrated into society, their petty crimes to survive will continue, as they do for all migrants not accepted by the communities they live in – including America.

*Anti-Immigration Laws*

Living in Asia for more than 20 years, I have seen and experienced, personally and as an observer, both the ugly racist anti-immigration side of discrimination toward boat people, illegal immigrants and refugees, and the welcoming all-embracing arms of tolerance. I am still dismayed at how Australia, a country to which my paternal grandfather and father immigrated and are buried, continues to harshly reject migrants and refugees by isolating them in prison-like camps.

Australia has a policy of mandatory detention for asylum seekers while their claims are processed, and generally holds them on remote Christmas Island, nearly 1,600 kilometers from the mainland in the Indian Ocean. But the increasing number of boat people has seen increasing use of mainland centers where periodic riots take place. Nine buildings were torched by asylum seekers at the Villawood Detention Center in Sydney in April 2011.

These are people fleeing war-torn areas in Central Asia and the Middle East, mostly from Afghanistan, who arrive in Australian waters in rickety boats by the thousands each year. The internationally criticized "Pacific Solution" under which these people were sent to remote islands for processing was abolished in 2007.

The Australian government tried to remedy the problem by entering into a refugee-swap agreement with Malaysia whereby it would send 800 asylum seekers from Christmas Island to Malaysia in exchange for 8,000 refugees with United Nations accreditation. The Australian High Court ruled the agreement invalid, saying Australia had no power to send asylum seekers to a country without international or legal protections for their human rights.

Australia not only rejects boat people-refugees outright, but well-to-do white Anglos trying to migrate there legally.

"We have tried everything, talked to top immigration lawyers and even politicians," said Sue Hirst, a neighbor in Hong Kong who is married to Harry, a prominent maritime lawyer in Hong Kong whose firm has offices in Australia. They had rented out their house in Hong Kong and moved to Australia to be with their daughter Alexandra, who was attending high school in Brisbane while they tried to secure immigration status. They couldn't. They could only get temporary status as the parents of a student.

"The government says we're too old, if you can believe that," said Sue, who is a qualified nurse in her late 40s.

"We can't qualify as professionals or investors because we're not young enough or pensioners," she told me over a lunch in Hong Kong in December 2010, during a holiday visit.

"The only way we can qualify now is if I register as a student and get a student visa as well."

Alexandra, who had graduated from high school, had registered as a freshman university student.

"Well, at least you can have fun studying together and probably qualify for permanent residency as the parents of an Aussie after Alexandra graduates. She will certainly qualify to become a citizen by then," I said as we pondered Australia's shortsighted immigration policy. Unfortunately, Sue's student visa was denied as well.

The Hirsts' frustration echoes that of my friend Earl Klein, a retired American banker in Hong Kong. He decided to retire in Australia with his girlfriend Catherine Newman. She is also in her 40s.

"They won't let Catherine back in the country even though I am a legal resident, can secure employment for her and we have everyone under the sun prepared to sponsor her," Earl told me during one of their many visits to Hong Kong.

They would leave Australia every few months for short periods and then return because Catherine was only allowed to enter on a tourist visa. She did this for a few years until the Australian government refused to let her re-enter as a tourist anymore.

"The only way she can return legally and long-term is if we get married," Earl complained, but he had no intention of getting married again at his age and made arrangements to move to Bangkok.

Like Australia, China has strict racist immigration policies. For a country that has traditionally been a source of economic migrants to other countries – where they are welcomed as permanent residents and citizens — I find China's immigration policy offensively racist. China does not have an immigration law. But in fact, the mainland is so unwelcoming that even foreigners married to Chinese citizens face annual visa renewals after they are reminded they are in the country on sufferance. I have an Chinese ex-wife and son living in Shanghai and have spent many years travelling there both as a tourist and businessman with a temporary resident visa. I could never become a permanent resident, let alone a citizen, because I am not Chinese.

When I was a long-term temporary worker in China in the' 90s, I was just one of a handful in Shanghai. The number of long-term foreign workers remains tiny today compared to the vast local population. In Beijing there are just 110,000; in Shanghai 152,000. According to the Ministry of Public Security, fewer than 600,000 foreigners stayed to work for more than six months in 2007, the last year for which figures are available.

China not only makes it almost impossible for foreigners to migrate there, but makes it tough for returning Chinese as well. My friend and business partner Nelson Wong was born near Shanghai and migrated to Hong Kong where he became a resident. When he returned to Shanghai to buy a car and have it registered, he found out he couldn't do so because he was no longer a local but an illegal immigrant.

"I can't believe the government is telling me I'm not a citizen or resident cvcn though I was born here and lived here most of my life without any problems. It's ridiculous," he said.

For the first time, China is now mulling an immigration law because its buoyant economy has become increasingly attractive to foreigners since the onset of the global financial crisis. There is no timetable for the law nor any word on whether foreigners will be accepted as citizens long term.

Just like the U.S. and Europe, the vast majority of immigrants to the Chinese mainland, whether legal or illegal, have a function in society. They do the jobs the locals can't – or don't want to do.

In Hong Kong, even though it is a part of China, under the "One Country, Two Systems" law that governs the Special Administrative Region status of the city state, I am a permanent resident, can vote in local elections and use my permanent identification to enter and leave the territory without a passport. I can obtain a passport if I renounce other citizenship. I have decided to just be a permanent resident and keep my American and British passports the best of all worlds.

Hong Kong, like America, was built by immigrants, legal and illegal. Over a 30-year period from the 1950s to the '80s, about a million people made their way into Hong Kong from the Chinese mainland. They risked everything to find a better life and ended up providing the city with a cheap labor pool that made it the prosperous city-state what it is today.

The question today in Hong Kong is whether foreign maids who have lived and worked there for seven years or more should be entitled to permanent residency like other foreign workers. Five Filipinos in three families argue that the Immigration Ordinance and policy barring them from being permanent residents violates the Basic Law and international covenants.

Grave social undesirable underbelly scaremongering arguments were raised by the opponents of granting the maids residency. They marched on the Civic Party headquarters the Sunday before the colorful opening arguments in August 2011 in the landmark case, after 19 of the hundreds of demonstrators and supporters of the maids who tried to stop them were arrested. The two sides hurled insults at each other during the standoff until the police moved in to clear the way for the marchers. The demonstrators accused the marchers of racial discrimination and said the police should not be "helping racists."

"Like a mistress and a maid" – that was the colorful analogy given for the relationship between the basic Law and Immigration Ordinance on the first day of the landmark judicial review. The legal argument centered on the definition of "ordinary resident." The lawyer for the maids argued that an Immigration Ordinance provision that foreign domestic helpers cannot be treated as "ordinary residents" – a requirement for permanent residency – is unconstitutional as it adds an extra hurdle to the requirements under the Basic Law. The argument in favor of the maids permanent residency compared maids to mistresses and said the policy for maids can be changed depending on the times, but the bedrock of the constitution, the Basic Law, cannot.

The argument against granting the maids permanent residency compared maids to prisoners, refugees, consular officials and military personnel garrisoned in Hong Kong whose residency is limited by strict conditions and so their residency is "out of the ordinary."

I agree with Hong Kong political commentator Albert Cheng King-hon, who wrote: "Hong Kong is intrinsically a society of immigrants, who have contributed to the city's economic success. The city is regarded as a melting pot of Eastern and Western cultures. The city owes its success to this mosaic of nationalities."

When the Basic Law was being drafted, due consideration was given to foreign residents. Article 24 stipulates that anyone who has entered the Special Administrative Region with a valid travel document, and has ordinarily resided there continually for at least seven years, will be eligible to become a permanent resident. Furthermore, Article 25 states that all Hong Kong residents shall be equal before the law. The law seems pretty clear. But Beijing disagreed.

If maids can march, protest and fight for their basic human rights, why can't *We the Apatheic Maids,* who are constantly asked to clean up the mess career politicians and their financial backers make and leave us to clean up – and then pay for the privilege?

The Philippines, where I lived for a couple of years and visit regularly, is one nation that has welcomed with open arms migrants and asylum seekers looking to start afresh. I never bothered applying for temporary residency status because I had to leave the country every few weeks to travel on business and the government makes it so easy to travel there, not just for tourists and business people, but for refugees too.

When we think of refugees we may picture row upon row of white tents in a sprawling emergency camp. And that is an image the dictators and monarchs ruling the Arab world deliberately created, and perpetuated, as I spelled out in great detail in *Custom Maid Knowledge*. But the reality is that as many as half of the world's 10.5 million refugees live in towns and cities.

Cities present obvious opportunities to remain anonymous and make money, but there are also dangers; refugees are vulnerable to exploitation, arrest and detention, and they can be in competition with the poorest locals for the worst jobs. The Philippines is one of the few exceptions. Filipinos welcome foreigners and refugees with open arms and a warm smile. What Filipinos lack materially, they more than make up for in spirit.

For a country ravaged by natural disasters, poverty and corruption, it is the Filipinos' natural optimism and cheerfulness that keeps them going.

"The Philippines is supportive and hospitable despite all their own problems. It's not diplomacy, it's just how the people are," says Bernard Kerblat, who has worked with the UNHCR for nearly 29 years.

Waves of refugees have come to the Philippines over the decades. In that time Kerblat has witnessed the generosity of Filipinos first-hand.

"It's a place filled with human stories, human experiences and human life. A place that welcomes others who've had a past of fear and pain into a future of rebuilding and normalcy. It is give and take, though. The refugees that have come here don't want to just reap the benefits, they want to contribute as well. The Philippines is unique in its hospitality, so the refugees who come here want to repay this kindness to them," Kerblat said.

Many of the Christian and Muslim refugees fleeing the genocide in Sudan went to Israel and have been accepted as residents fleeing political persecution – even though Sudan does not recognize the state of Israel. That is because the people of the Jewish state, with many citizens of just about every religious denomination in the world, have experienced religious and political persecution first-hand for centuries.

Isn't it time that America, China and the rest of the world adopted the same enlightened Filipino-Israeli refugee policy in the 21st century?

*Global Issue*

Immigration is a global issue of mammoth proportions. As a perpetual immigrant and world traveler, I am constantly reminded on the road of how massive and pervasive global migration is. From a Latino pilot on a Chinese airline in China, Eastern European waitresses in Western Europe, Chinese waitresses and bartenders in the Middle East, Filipina cashiers in supermarkets in Scotland, Russian waitresses in restaurants across Europe, Brazilian housekeepers in New Zealand, Irish farmers in Australia and New Zealand, Scottish staff working the ski slopes of New Zealand, and Italian and American waiters and waitresses working the restaurants and bars of New Zealand.

I was in Queenstown, New Zealand in September 2011, and was surprised to be waited on by an American woman from Florida and having our table cleared by a bus boy from upstate New York. "No way," was how both responded when I asked if they planned to go back to the U.S.

"I'm waiting for my visa to Australia to meet up with my boyfriend and this is a quick and easy way to earn good money while waiting to get it," said Nicky, our waitress from Florida. "There is no way I would go back home. I'm a designer and my prospects of employment are zero. Finding a job there is unbelievably difficult. Many of my friends are already in Australia and more are on the way."

Her words reminded me of a conversation I had earlier in the year at a bar at Los Angeles International Airport while waiting to board a flight to New York. The young lady sitting beside me, with whom I had struck up a conversation, was also on her way to Australia to join her friends because she could not find a job in America. She had majored in art history. "I graduated Columbia last year and haven't been able to find any job other than waiting tables or bartending. I can get a teaching job in Australia."

What I found fascinating while in New Zealand was the raging debate about immigration there triggered by a Maori academic who said immigration by whites should be restricted because they pose a threat to race relations due to their "white supremacist" attitudes. The controversial comments came in response to a Department of Labour report that found Maori are more likely to express anti-immigration sentiment than whites or any other ethnic group.

Margaret Mutu, head of Auckland University's department of Maori studies, called on the government to restrict the number of white immigrants arriving from countries such as South Africa, England and the United States because they brought attitudes destructive to the Maori. "They do bring with them, as much as they deny it, an attitude of white supremacy, and that is fostered by the country," she said.

It is not the first time Maori commentators have sparked controversy by suggesting racial immigration policies trying to stop the "browning" of New Zealand through immigration.

Immigration is a hot button issue everywhere these days. On a layover in Frankfurt in 2011, while waiting for my connecting flight, I decided to have some German sausages and sauerkraut and wash the meal down with a beer. The bartender, Dora, was Polish. She had been in Germany for 12 years. We struck up a conversation about the different people from all corners of the earth passing through that she encounters, immigration and why she moved to Germany. Our conversation was periodically interrupted by other bar patrons who would volunteer their unsolicited opinions about immigration and why blacks, browns and Muslims should be banned from

Europe. Dora and I politely questioned and challenged their opinions to no avail. Dora was married to a Turk.

Flying Lufthansa back to Hong Kong from Frankfurt, admiring and talking to tall blonde stewardesses, was a mind-boggling experience after so many years of flying Asian airlines. I was jolted back in time rethinking my German heritage and my family's immigrant trail that brought them to Germany before they moved on to Russia, Palestine and Britain, especially after talking to Dora.

## *Chungking Beacon*

Hong Kong's Chungking Mansions is probably the most interlocalized building on earth. Its guest register logs 129 different nationalities. It is a place where globalization is peaceful. About 5,000 people call it home, and another 10,000 pass through its blocks every day. I've enjoyed many great curries in the building's mess halls and look forward to taking visitors there. The Pakistanis say about Indians: "I do not like them. But I am here to make money, as they are here to make money. We cannot afford to fight."

The building is a paragon of bourgeois capitalism. The people in Chungking Mansions and Hong Kong residents mirror each other in their values.

Sitting at an English pub in a Hong Kong seaside community, being served by Filipina barmaids, while I read the stack of newspapers I had picked up earlier, my eye caught the headline, "Chance meeting and an immigrant's story, tucked in a seaside bar." *Shun Li and the Poet,* is a movie based on the true story of a Chinese barmaid working in a tavern in a small Venetian lagoon town in Italy. She winds up buying the tavern and raises her family there. Her children are Italians. The movie is a contemporary snapshot of Italy; a slice-of-life reflection on the meeting of two cultures, each rooted in longstanding and at times contrasting habits, beliefs and prejudices.

These prejudices periodically erupt into ugly and violent riots as they did in Milan's Chinatown in April 2007. Riot police were called in when local merchants and residents, who first settled there in the 1920s, took part in a sit-in that brought traffic to a standstill. The "pavement revolt" started when traffic police, who want to tighten control of commercial traffic in the area full of wholesale clothing stores, fined a driver 50 euros and took away his license because he was carrying merchant goods in a private car.

In June 2011, Italian police raided 70 Chinese-owned businesses in the textile hub of Prato and seized assets worth more than 25 million euros in an anti-fraud raid. Financial police said the alleged crimes included fraudulent money transfers and the creation of shell companies, something many respected Italian business people do. Officers froze 396 bank accounts, seized 183 vehicles and 76 properties. A total of 500 officers were involved in the operation. Officers say Prato has become a Chinese gangland, but immigrants defend it as a revitalized hub of Italy's flagging textile industry.

There is a high probability that many of these police officers' parents and grandparents are being attended to by foreign caretakers – legal and illegal. Italians, like all Europeans, do not like immigrants. The European Parliament voted in June 2008 to allow illegal immigrants to be held for up to 18 months pending deportation. "Families are both perpetrators and victims" of illegal immigration, said Maurizio Ambrosini, a professor of sociology of immigration at the University of Milan. "They want tough laws on illegal immigration, but they are the reason that many immigrants come to Italy illegally."

*Shun Li and the Poet* tells a story that takes place today in every country in the world. Just different cultures, religions, races and colors. The story reminded me of my days in the early '90s as a lawyer in Palau, hanging out at the local "Mini-Mart" bar with local fishermen and divers being served by Filipina barmaids.

Italy, like many European countries, has more than its fair share of fascists to this day who are vehemently anti-immigration. One such far-right extremist, 50-year-old author Gianluca Casseri, shot dead two Senagalese men and wounded three others before killing himself in December 2011.

Immigration is a hot button issue boiling and bubbling not only under the skin of Italians, but in all white Christian European countries. Especially when it comes to dark-skinned Muslims. This is best expressed in politically progressive Holland, in elections and the end of the barrel of a gun. Far-right Dutch lawmaker Geert Wilders, whose anti-immigrant Party for Freedom believes he is on a mission to fight the Islamization of his country, is their hero. "More safety, less crime, less immigration and less Islam is what the Netherlands has chosen," is the cornerstone of Wilders' fundamentalist policy platform.

Such policies not only boil the blood of whites about darkies, but that of darkies about Asians.

During the Great Depression, Mexican authorities backed by mobs rounded up Chinese citizens, pressured them to sell their businesses and forced many to cross into the U.S. or go back to China.

Now that more Asians than Hispanics are settling in the U.S., reflecting the fact that employers are looking to recruit more highly skilled workers, illegal immigration of Hispanics is on the decline.

Perhaps no force in modern life is as omnipresent yet overlooked as global immigration, that vehicle of creative destruction that is reordering our world disorder. Even people who study migration for a living struggle to fully grasp its effects.

"Politically, socially, economically, culturally – migration bubbles up everywhere," said James F. Hollifield, a political scientist at Southern Methodist University in Dallas. "We often don't recognize it." I couldn't agree more. I have lived it and experienced it my entire life.

It is estimated there are more than 214 million migrants across the globe, an increase of about 37 percent in two decades from the 1990s. Their ranks grew by 41 percent in Europe and 80 percent in North America. "There's more mobility at this moment than at any time in world history," said Gary P. Freeman, a political scientist at the University of Texas.

Europe is experiencing a huge wave of migration from east to west that rivals the great migration – Vólkerwanderung – of Europe from the fourth to sixth centuries. Within the first year of Romania's accession to the European Union on January 1, 2007, for example, roughly 1 million Romanians migrated to Italy and Spain. More than a million East Europeans have become workers in Britain, most coming from Poland. In London, about one-third of the high-skilled workers surveyed in 2007 were foreigners and so were about one-third of the low-skilled workers.

Portugal, laid low by the Great Recession, is urging its citizens to leave and go to former colonies such as Brazil, Macau and Angola that offer better employment opportunities. About 200,000 Portugese citizens were living in Mozambique and Angola in 2012, where jobs are available in the mining and construction industries. More than 330,000 Portuguese live in Brazil.

Polish plumbers and builders abandoned their homeland to the tune of 1,000,000 since it joined the EU in 2000. Poland now has to import construction workers from neighboring Belarus and other former Soviet Union satellite states. China also sends builders, electricians, carpenters and stone masons to the former Communist states – the same crowd it sends to Africa, the Middle East, Asia and the Americas. Today, North America offers the least economic opportunities.

Western Europeans fear not only Muslim immigrants, but immigrants from Eastern Europe, especially Poland and Romania, as well. Far-right racist leaders exploit these fears to promote anti-immigrant sentiment and legislation, deliberately ignoring the benefits of immigration. European economies that have taken in many migrant workers have also benefited, not only in total output but also in terms of GDP per head. Native workers such as fruit-pickers, builders and waiters are unhappy because immigration keeps their wages down. But this has an upside because it also keeps inflation down.

Acute labor shortages in Scandinavia are prompting the Nordic nations to admit workers from their Baltic neighbors. Sweden is a good example of not only welcoming migrants, but of a tight labor market as rigid as Germany's. Sweden has one of the world's most comprehensive tax-based welfare systems. The average Swede takes 17 weeks off work each year – mostly through a combination of holidays, sickness, and parental leave.

The country manages to combine a high degree of social security with flexibility. Flexibility, in this instance, does not mean a regime in which it is easy to hire and fire workers but one characterized by welfare-to-work programs, ambitious retraining schemes, specific programs to integrate the disabled into the labor force and a world-class education system. Sweden produces one of the largest proportions of high school graduates in the world and is a champion of life-long learning. In Sweden, it is not the system that is flexible. It is the people. Makes me proud of my Swedish heritage.

Immigration in Europe, like the U.S., benefits the immigrants as well as their host country. The immigrant receives a higher wage than at home, and the host country benefits from cheap labor, which creates more value than it costs.

In reality, immigration is often not as beneficial as it could be because the host country has a rigid wage structure that prevents the creation of the additional jobs needed to employ the immigrants. For example, if a host country provides minimum wage guarantees and replacement incomes for the domestic jobless, immigrants simply force domestic residents into the care of the welfare state. This is not an immigration problem, but one of poorly designed domestic social and labor market institutions created by career politicians.

The traditional sources of U.S. immigration – England, Ireland, Italy, Greece, Spain – are now migrant destinations, with a town in Ireland electing a Nigerian-born man as its first black mayor in 2007. No different than Louisiana that elected Republican Piyush "Bobby" Jindal, son of Indian immigrants, governor in 2009 – the first ever Indian-American governor and the first man of color in the statehouse there since 1873. The last non-white governor of Louisiana was P.B.S. Pinchback, a black Republican who served for little more than a month from December 1872 to January 1873. That was during the post-Civil War reconstruction era, when many white voters were disenfranchised because of their support for the failed rebellion by secessionist Southern states.

"People want to make everything about race," Governor Jindal said before the election. "The only colors that matters here are red, white and blue."

Since the 1970s, international migration has been primarily a one-way journey from poorer countries to wealthier ones and rural areas to cities. But now, in possibly one of the most dramatic effects of the Great Recession, the human tide is slowing and is even starting to reverse itself. The global economic slowdown has clearly slammed the brakes on cross-border migration flows and in many cases reversed it as unemployed migrants return home. The era of massive global migration is slowly winding down.

The Public Policy Institute of California reported in December 2007 that 45 percent of some 300,000 Indian-born IT professionals in Silicon Valley would probably return home. More than 200,000 Chinese immigrants have returned to the mainland in recent years as China's economy continues to expand. The truth is that most migrant workers, given a choice, usually prefer to return home once jobs open up.

### Migrants Remittances – Most Effective Foreign Aid
Many countries' economies, including America's, would collapse without the armies of guest workers. The money earned by migrants, legal and illegal, not only sustains the families left behind but props up national economies.

Foreign aid has been cut dramatically by leading donor nations. America, Japan and Europe were in the forefront of donor nations but have now reduced their generosity and replaced it with migrant workers remittances.

Migrants sent home an estimated $317 billion in 2009 – three times the world's total foreign aid. In at least seven countries, remittances account for more than a quarter of the gross domestic product. *We the Maids* must acknowledge and come to grips with the fact that the world's prosperity is created and shared by all in inequitable ways that can and must be remedied by sweeping immigration reforms. There are huge potential developmental gains from migration that must be acknowledged and recognized. The interests of humanity and economic survival are common to all of us.

Millions of families in developing countries rely on relatives sending hard earned remittances from overseas jobs. Dollars, euros, any foreign currency, weak or strong, to prop up spending at home. I witnessed this first hand when I lived in the Philippines and in Hong Kong where I, like many people there, had Filipina maids. World recessions, economic downturns, the restaurants and shopping malls in the Philippines were busy with shoppers spending their overseas family members' earnings. Former First Lady Imelda Marcos used to serenade overseas Filipino workers while on visits to the Middle East in the 1980s.

In 2011 remittances accounted for 10 percent of the Philippine economic output, making it one of the most remittance-dependent countries in the world. It is a welfare state. But then again, what else should we expect of a country that was a friartocracy under Catholic Spanish rule for more than 300 years and then an American one for another century?

There are many stories of Filipinas working in slave-like conditions for high net worth individuals in banking and other high income professions like medicine, law and government. High-profile stories like these are beginning to form their own genre, a Cinderella narrative that takes the hapless victim from the pits of despair to wealth beyond his or her imaginations. One hell of a way of going about getting a visa. Surely there are more humane ways.

A tenth of the population of the Philippines lives overseas, a diaspora second only to that of Mexico. Remittances are Mexico's second-largest source of foreign income after oil. In 2008, the year the world almost collapsed and died economically, Filipino overseas workers sent back $14 billion in remittances – one-fifth of the country's GDP. Remittances are a cornerstone of the economy. One that is in quicksand unless the economy reforms.

"The underlying weakness of the Philippine economy lies in its inability to create productive employment opportunities for its fast-growing labor force," concludes economist Arsenio Balisacan in the *Philippine Daily Inquirer*. There are simply too many people for too few jobs thanks to the Catholic Church's birth control edicts that their poor adherers worship and believe. Salvation is in heaven if their suffering is worthy of a happy and prosperous afterlife. Meanwhile, suffer. The more the suffering, the bigger the heavenly insurance policy.

The practice and reliance on remittances is not limited to Filipina-white Anglo-Christains. Many of the Filipino expatriates are Muslim. In the Middle East and Arabia, Muslims are the predominant group of Filipinos.

Many Muslim countries, including Bangladesh, Indonesia, Pakistan and Senegal, rely on their diaspora's remittances to keep the countries afloat. The City of Touba in Senegal is an example of how a village of 5,000 people in a country that gained independence from France in 1960 has turned into a bustling city built on remittances.

Today, after more than three decades of expanding at 15 percent or more, it is Senegal's second-largest city, the center of a global network of street traders, merchants and wage laborers, with a population of around a million or more. Touba's evolution mirrors that of other cities in Africa that depend on remittances and where the weakening of the state and the expansion of the informal private sector has been accompanied by frantic urbanization.

Touba's origins in the remote savannah were purely spiritual. The city was the sight for a prophesied utopia chosen in 1887 by Cheikh Ahmadou Bamba, a mystic who sought to protect Senegalese society from the corrosive effects of colonial rule and return it to the straight path of Islam. He spent years in exile and prison for his nonviolent struggle against Senegal's French colonizers.

"Pray as if you will die tomorrow and work as if you will never die" inspired a puritan work ethic that lives on the Mourides, a Sufi brotherhood founded by Bamba whose members form the bulk of Senegalese hawking everything from African arts and crafts to fake glasses and name-brand watches, jewelry, DVDs, socks and underwear, not to mention all the New York traditional souvenirs on Big Apple sidewalks, working the Marseille docks or picking Spanish tomatoes. A lot like the Nigerians, but without the e-mail scams.

In the process, Touba has become a potent symbol of cultural and religious revival, the ultimate destination for the itinerant Mourides whose earnings have fueled the city's expansion and funded its infrastructure. Meanwhile, rural Senegalese supported by family members abroad have moved there in droves, taking advantage of the services the city offers. "If you depend on transfers to live, you don't need to be in an isolated village," says Serigne Mansour Tall, a professor at Dakar University and an expert on migration.

On wealthier backstreets of Touba, the BMWs, four-by-fours and Mercedes of the "golden boys" who made it big abroad are in evidence. "Before the example of success was the petty bureaucrat, with his regular salary. Now it is the émigrés. It is they who build and rent their houses to officials," says Tall.

To develop economically and be weaned off remittances, people have to be encouraged to become entrepreneurial. In a country like the Philippines where the average per capita income in 2011 was around $1,790, is it any wonder large numbers of people are still leaving in search of better prospects on the high seas and overseas? It's amazing how many long-lost relatives these overseas workers have when word gets around that they have landed a job. The culture and cycle of extended families dependent on the foreign workers' wages can have devastating effects on entire communities when those workers become unemployed and all their dependents go hungry. Many have. Not only in the Philippines, but Bangladesh, Mexico, Vietnam, Indonesia and even China. China has both overseas and in-country migrant workers.

The cheap foot soldiers who power China's export boom are dependent on export markets. The remittances of these workers in "factories without chimneys" back to their home villages sustain many communities.

"Families with at least one migrant worker are almost immediately lifted above the $1-a-day-poverty level," said Yu Xiaoqing, human development sector coordinator with the World Bank in Beijing. But it also means that in some villages, 80 percent of the working-age population is gone.

Poverty, of course is the root cause. It is the fuel that drives the engine of supply and demand. Supply: abundant cheap labor. Demand: first-world clamor for someone, anyone, to do disagreeable, menial work.

When I sponsored my friend and high school classmate Jake Berman to the U.S. in 1968, I got him a job taking care of my wife's elderly grandfather who was suffering from emphysema and could not find a local caretaker. Jake was thankful for the job that helped pay for his college tuition.

So why continue to perpetuate this myth that immigrants, legal and illegal, take jobs away from locals?

### Borderless and Unregulated Mixed Bloods

The movement of people around the world is a constant across all oceans and continents. Unlike trade and finance that are regulated by global institutions, there is no global body regulating migration. The most personal and perilous form of movement – people – is unregulated globally. Nation states make their own rules about who can come and go, rules that are usually unenforced and exploited by criminals and employers.

The demand for migrant workers will continue to rise in the foreseeable decades, according to a U.N. report released in 2009. The demand will be highest in developed countries because of lower birthrates and a fast-aging population. European birthrates have reached a historic and prolonged low. Countries from Italy and Germany to Poland and the Czech Republic, straining pension plans and depleting the workforce across the continent. The number of elderly already exceeds the number of young people in many countries, and the European Union's executive arm, alarmed by the trend, estimates there will be a shortfall of 20 million workers by 2030 if today's low birthrates persist. A double-barreled reason migrants will stop at nothing or nowhere to fulfill a dream and support a family.

The U.N. projects by 2050, the population of Europe – home to around 730 million people – will shrink by 75 million. The U.N. expects Japan, with 128 million people, to lose 16 million and South Korea, with about 48 million people, to lose more than 3 million. The U.S. is projected to grow from nearly 300 million people to about 420 million.

The reality *We the People* need to accept is that aging and shrinking populations in Europe and Asia will lead to economic crises if not tackled because there will not be enough workers or consumers to fuel economic growth and support retirees.

The rich, aging countries in Europe, as well as America and Japan, need workers. People in poor countries need jobs. China needs both. Because so many rural youths take off for the cities, they leave lonely aging parents who need to be taken care of by migrants from nearby North Korea, Myanmar, Laos, Cambodia, and even within China itself.

According to China's Ministry of Civil Affairs, there were about 167 million people over the age of 60 in the country at the end of 2009 – 12.5 percent of the entire population. Analysts say the number of people older than 60 is increasing by 3 percent a year, and will reach 450 million by 2050.

The rise of this global inequality means that migrants, legal and illegal, have more to gain than ever by seeking work abroad. Migration networks that have been in place for centuries are impossible to shut down. Migration networks are a challenge to the order set by the 1648 Peace of Westphalia Treaty that established the territorial sovereignty of nation-states.

"Judging by the wall rising along the Mexican border, nation-states do not appear to be going away. Their people increasingly do," Jason Deparle accurately summed up in a piece he wrote for *The New York Times*.

These networks are two-way streets also used by migrants to return home whenever they need to for whatever reason. People do move with the times. Migration flows reversed during the Great Recession as unemployment rose in America and other developed nations. They also reverse because of civil unrest, as they did in Libya in 2011. When the foreign workers fled the violence in Libya, the oil industry and economy came to a standstill.

There are many countries that depend on migrants to keep their economies growing. In fact, so much so in some countries that there are more migrants than locals. That is the case with Palau and is also with Dubai – and elsewhere in the Arab emirates.

When work dries up, so does illegal immigration. People stay home or return home. If there are no jobs, why take the risk?

In the past, "when you came to the United States, you came on a one-way ticket on the Mayflower or Air India," says Vivek Wadhwa, a senior research associate at Harvard who recently completed a study on migration trends. "But now, there are many lands of opportunity."

Copy that! I'll vouch and confirm – on both counts. Been there, done that, and still doing it.

Wadhwa's study found that among Chinese nationals who immigrated to the U.S. and later returned home, 72 percent said they thought professional opportunities were better in their own country. Among Indians who returned home, 56 percent said the same thing. Wadhwa estimates that as many as 200,000 skilled workers from India and China will leave America and return home by 2014, compared to roughly 100,000 over the past 20 years. America is educating, financing, banking and paying the wages of its foreign competitors as Americans stand idly unemployed in bankrupt cities and states.

Even the number of Latino immigrants in the U.S. has fallen at the end of the first decade of the $21^{st}$ century and the opening years of its second, according to a 2009 study by the Pew Hispanic Center. The population of Hispanics from South America, other than Mexicans, declined by as much as 400,000 from a peak of about 3 million in 2006, said Pew demographer Jeffrey Passel. Much of the decline was among high-skilled workers from Columbia, where the security situation has improved, and Brazil, whose economy has seen huge growth in recent years.

"What we're seeing is the normal outflow" of migrants leaving the U.S. to go back home, and "a huge drop-off in the inflow" coming into the U.S., Passel said.

In the case of Mexico, the largest supplier of migrants to the U.S., data released in 2009 by the Mexican government showed the numbers heading north dropped 13 percent in the first quarter of 2009. In the same period, more people returned to Mexico than left for the U.S. The majority of people coming to the U.S. via Mexico are the refugee women and children fleeing political, cultural and gang violence, who like those who fled the Holocaust, deserve protection.

America is no longer it once was land of opportunity. In late 2009, the number of foreign-born people in the U.S. declined for the first time since at least 1970.

Migrants are the first to be hired when times are good and the first to get fired when times get rough. That's true not only in America but in Malaysia, Spain, Japan, Libya, the Gulf States and elsewhere.

The graduating classes of top U.S. universities are packed with foreign students, and more than 27 percent of doctors practicing in the U.S. today came from abroad. America's postwar growth and dynamism owes much to skilled immigrants.

Diverse pools of immigrants add to a country's vitality, bringing with them new ideas and innovation. More than 50 percent of all Silicon Valley start-ups between 1995 and 2005 were launched by immigrants.

As heirs to an immigrant past, America has an edge in a migrants' age that it is not capitalizing on. Even worse, it is allowing it to go to waste and be exploited by career politicians and their unscrupulous financial cronies.

### *Green Cards for Greenbacks*
Immigrants who come to America with at least $500,000 in greenbacks can

get green cards. According to the State Department, the number of "investor greencards," known as EB-5 visas, issued to non-Americans in 2009 nearly tripled to 4,218. About 1,800 of those recipients were from China. South Korea was second with 903.

Chinese invest to get U.S. residency primarily for their children's education. For many wealthy Chinese, investing $500,000 is a convenient way to achieve the American dream for their children.

The migration of China's wealthy social elite to America is becoming a concern to the government in Beijing. That is because the first three decades of the People's Republic of China saw almost no exodus of social elite. Today, China's social elite are all too eager to move their money and children – and change their nationality. This means China's elite are ready to sacrifice the comforts they enjoy at home in exchange for American citizenship, or that of another country. They choose to do so mostly because of a lack of faith in China's arbitrary legal system, because its capricious uncertainties cannot guarantee them a "successful and peaceful" life. They are willing to trade the comforts they enjoy at home for the lure of a peaceful future in America.

Such a brain drain, while beneficial to America, is bound to harm China's economic construction and modernization, because the elite's knowledge, innovativeness, creativity and capital are valuable resources in building a better future. China's loss is America's gain.

Interestingly, while China's elite migrate to the U.S., Taiwanese who began flocking to America in the 1950s are now forsaking life in the U.S. to return home as mainland Chinese take their place. Today Taiwanese are staying home or heading for the mainland where prospects are much better and living standards higher. A reverse brain drain.

The returning immigrants from America are being joined by America's unemployed youth, engineers and other unemployed U.S. talent heading to China to seek work. While searching for that ideal job opportunity, they earn a living as English teachers. There is an interesting reverse knowledge migration taking place between America and China. Interlocalism on all fronts. Pedal to the metal.

The cross-border interlocalization of people has created an interesting integration of like-minded people from different countries living together in the same community and feeling more comfortable with each other than they do with their own kind back home. When such an interlocal group has a few locals in their midst, those locals feel more comfortable with their immigrant neighbors than they do with the locals who all of a sudden become real bores. Hong Kong is the best interlocal example I know of, followed by Los Angeles and New York.

### *Immigrant Unions*

Migrant workers, like their fellow migrant capitalists, pursue their dreams wherever they may be. The difference is, unlike their fellow capitalists, they cannot afford legal representation and rely on the broken promises of smugglers. What is needed to protect them is a global Migrant Workers Union.

This became abundantly clear to me when I saw how America's two big labor federations, the AFL-CIO and the Change to Win federation, did a gigantic political U-turn in April 2009 and decided to support immigration reform. After all, many Americans believe they have a hard enough time competing with cheap foreign labor. Why undercut them within America's own borders when millions of citizens are losing their jobs?

The answer is simple. Unemployed construction and assembly line workers are not lining up to pick onions, work in car washes, or as bus boys. And they won't when the economy picks up either, whereas illegal immigrants will – and their numbers will grow – no matter what barriers the career politicians put up.

Unions finally understand that immigration reform is an issue of worker empowerment. If undocumented immigrants undercut wages and job conditions for Americans, it is because they cannot stand up for their rights.

"Workers don't depress wages. Unscrupulous employers do," said Terrence

O'Sullivan, president of the Laborers' International Union of North America.

Unemployment in his industry was more than 21 percent. Nearly 2 million construction workers were out of work. The solution? Reform that allows immigrants to gain legal status.

"If we can free them so they can come out of the shadows, we can not only improve their lives, but all workers' lives," he said. I couldn't agree more! Eliseo Medina, international executive vice president of the Service Employees International Union, agreed. "First and foremost, this is an economic argument," Medina said.

Medina said union leaders are going to have to work hard to make members understand that false populism is not on their side.

"You may not want to do this," he said, "but this affects you. Your standard of living is not going to improve, and you're not going to be in a stronger position to solve your problems as long as you have all these people out there without any rights – without any ability to contribute. Things will only get worse, not better."

The need for immigration reform is more urgent than ever. The current system hurts wages and working conditions for everyone. It has created job paralysis. The job market is impotent and unable to grow. Granted that unionizing workers across borders may serve to bring down U.S. salaries. But aren't American workers better off being employed at lower pay than being unemployed at no salary – financially and emotionally?

Unions should then focus their attention on organizing workers in China and other developing nations with a manufacturing base and low-paid workers. A greater wage equilibrium must be created in the world labor pool.

The solution lies in greater mobility for migrants and a new emphasis on workers' rights. If migrants could move between jobs, they would be free to expose abusive employers. They would flow to regions with a shortage of workers, and would also be able to return to their home countries when the outlook there brightened, or if jobs dried up in their country of employment. Migrant mobility has been tried with success in the European Union. When the EU expanded in 2004 to include eight Eastern European countries, workers in Western Europe feared a flood of job seekers who would drive down wages. In Britain, for example, the volume of newcomers from countries like Poland was staggering. Instead of the prediction of roughly 50,000 migrants in four years, more than a million arrived. Yet as far as economists can tell, the influx did not take a serious toll on the native workers' wages or employment. Migrants who were not trapped in exploitive jobs flocked to areas that needed workers and shunned the intense competition in the cities. And when job opportunities grew in Poland or shrank in Britain, fully half went home again.

Workers should be able to join interlocal transnational unions. By doing so they can join the union in their home country and come to work in America legally. They could take jobs anywhere in the country where they are needed and stay as long as they liked. Such a plan would give employers access to more workers on fairer terms. It would address the inhumanity and inconsistency of policies that support free trade in goods and jobs but bar the free movement of people.

I agree wholeheartedly with Jennifer Gordon, professor of labor and immigration law at Fordham Law School, who said: "The United States needs an open and fair system, not a holding pen. The best way forward is to create an immigration system with protection for all workers at its core."

Not just unskilled workers, but skilled workers as well. Why should college-educated legal immigrants not be allowed to fulfill their full potential just because their credentials aren't recognized because of the lobbying efforts of the local professional associations that raise the bar as high as they can to prevent foreign competition? Barriers stifle the potential of college-educated immigrants. Why waste brain power?

A story in the *Los Angeles Times* caught my attention – that of Luis Garcia, who was a practicing physician in Peru. Unable to meet the requirements for a U.S. medical license, he earned a degree specializing in geriatrics at a community college, but the only work he could find was cat-sitting, dog-walking and elder care. His story is typical of highly educated and skilled immigrant professionals who could potentially, with a little aid from an interlocal transnational union, help ease growing shortages in California and nationwide in health care, computer sciences and other skilled jobs.

Nationwide, more than 1.3 million college-educated legal immigrants were unemployed or working in unskilled jobs such as dishwashers or cab drivers in 2008, according to a report by the Washington-based Migration Policy Institute – and that was before the Great Recession.

Two of the biggest barriers are a lack of English proficiency and non-recognition of foreign academic and professional criteria

### Bibles, Badges and Businesses
Religious, law enforcement, business and other conservative groups are lobbying Congress to create a path to legal status for illegals. Traditional pillars of the Republican base, such as evangelical pastors, police groups and the U.S. Chamber of Commerce, have begun to push skeptical GOP lawmakers to change federal immigration laws to allow most of the nation's 11 million illegal immigrants to apply for legal status.

The battle over immigration reform will not be between Democrats and Republicans. It will be fought inside the GOP. "Now it's conservatives versus conservatives over how much immigration reform should happen," said Alex Nowrasteh, an immigration expert at the Cato Institute, a libertarian think tank in Washington that has advanced a free-market argument for opening up the immigration system.

Obama needs Republican support to pass any significant legislation in the GOP-held House. Polling shows that a majority of Republican voters would support a plan that simultaneously tightens border security, requires employers to check the immigration status of new hires and creates a path to legal status for immigrants who have paid a fine and back taxes.

The U.S. Chamber of Commerce is trying to convince local chapters that businesses will benefit from laws that make it easier for non-Americans to obtain work visas and allow illegal immigrants to apply for permanent legal status. The chamber is working with labor unions and other groups to craft provisions for an immigration reform bill.

The campaign is supported by several major Christian groups, including Sojourners, the National Assn. of Evangelicals and the Southern Baptist Convention.

### *Kick In Immigration, Kick Out Discrimination*

Soccer figured this out long ago. Soccer embodies globalization like no other sport or profession. From advertisers, spectators and players. The market for professional soccer players is, by far, the most globalized labor market. A Nigerian or Brazilian soccer player can land a job more easily in America or Europe than a skilled surgeon or engineer.

Taking a closer look at how soccer has changed in England, and globally when England allowed foreign players to play there, is a good example of what can happen in every profession and occupation, skilled and unskilled. Modified to the field of endeavor, it is a workable solution in any arena.

Soccer played by Englishmen in England, the country that invented the game, is disappearing. When the English Premier League decided it had to raise the level of its game, it did so by allowing foreign players to play in its league because they were better and cheaper. From just 11 foreign players in the first year of the Premier League – the 1992-1993 season – in 2011 there were more than 280 spread across the 20 teams, including some 60 first-team players. They have definitely raised the playing standards of the game and the league.

Imported talent in the U.K. has made a difference not only in the game of soccer, but in politics. Listening to how African, Caribbean, or South Asian Muslims complain about the Eastern European migrants from Poland – and how they could swing the U.K. vote – made me chuckle. Talk about the pot calling the kettle black.

Speaking of soccer and black, AC Milan midfielder Kevin-Prince Boateng, who is black, is to be commended for being the first player to cause a game to be abandoned because of racist abuse after his teammates followed him off the field in protest at his treatment by opposition fans.

In the U.S., the proposed Agricultural Job Opportunities, Benefits and Security Act could plant the right seed in the quest for sensible immigration reform. It would create a pilot program to give certain immigrant farmworkers, legal and illegal, the opportunity to obtain a "blue card" – a temporary work permit – and, later, the possibility of permanent legal residency. It would also provide blue cards to the spouses and minor children of such farmworkers. It is not a cure for all that ails agriculture or national immigration policy, but it is a big first step.

Why leave desperately needed food crops to rot on the vine because of a lack of migrant pickers?

Former Secretary of State Colin L. Powell supports immigration because it is "what's keeping this country's lifeblood moving forward." He says illegal immigrants do essential work in the U.S. and he has firsthand knowledge of that – because they fix his house.

New York Mayor Michael Bloomberg told Congress that the public is tired of their talking and not doing anything. "This is all about leadership. We need immigrants. That's the future of this country. And whether the public understands that or not, it's Congress' job to lead and to explain to them why. ... We're going to become a second-rate power ... unless we fix our public-education system and fix immigration."

News Corp. Chairman Rupert Murdoch said in support of immigration reform that as an immigrant, he felt "an obligation to speak up for immigration policies that will keep America the most economically robust, creative and freedom-loving nation in the world."

So many companies that we view as American icons were started by immigrants, including Aussie-born Murdoch's Fox News. Since 2000, more than half of Silicon Valley start-ups have been founded by immigrants.

These immigrant-founded tech companies employed 450,000 workers and had sales of $52 billion in 2005.

Bloomberg and Murdoch are both members of the Partnership for a New American Economy, a coalition of mayors and business leaders working to promote immigration reform.

### Immigration Reform

Immigration reform has been a hot-button political issue for as long as I can remember. Being an immigrant myself who arrived in the U.S. in 1964, I am very conscious, sensitive and aware of the feelings of disdain expressed by many born and bred red-blooded Americans toward immigrants – legal or illegal.

The subject of immigration reform, amnesty for illegals, quotas, bracero programs, border fences and tough enforcement laws enacted by states are topics I am constantly engaged in as an "American lawyer" who has not only assisted many people to immigrate to America but discussed and debated for years with career politicians and immigration law specialists. Some of them have become friends, including Les Frank, an immigration law practitioner in Los Angeles who chaired the Immigration Law Committee of the L.A. Bar Association in the 1970s when I was head of the Customs Law Committee there. Frank had the most objective and realistic attitude toward immigration.

"Illegal immigration cannot be stopped," he told me. "The only realistic question is how do we absorb all immigrants prudently?"

The U.S. immigration framework is broken, as it is in many countries, and desperately needs repair. A universal, lasting fix – an overhaul – and not the occasional tune-up or periodic tweaks that benefit only the career politicians and exploitative employers. A comprehensive and compassionate rewriting of the law would benefit the country as well as the lives of the immigrants – legal and illegal.

## Equality for All

As I walked past a group of abode seekers from the mainland protesting their plight in Hong Kong one day a while back, a smile crossed my face as I remembered the freedom fighters of the '60s in America.

Eighteen buses carrying 900 Freedom Riders converged on Washington, D.C. in October 2003. One of their leaders, the Rev. James Lawson, was a colleague of the Rev. Martin Luther King Jr. The Freedom Ride, Lawson said, "is a great idea to make our land live up to the idea of equality for all."

With more than 12 million marginalized undocumented immigrants in the U.S. today, maybe a new Freedom Ride is in order.

Before 9/11, moves were under way to legitimize millions of undocumented immigrants. But since then, immigration controls have tightened and the issue dropped off the political agenda until the 2004 presidential election. Organizers of the Freedom Ride succeeded in resurrecting the issue. President Bush introduced a new guest worker program to offer jobs to migrants that no American will take. A job registry offers jobs to illegal immigrants already in America and to foreigners.

The 2003 recall of California Governor Gray Davis and his replacement by the Terminator, Arnold Schwarzenegger was primarily the result of undocumented workers. Californians voted by a wide margin a couple of years earlier for Proposition 187, which would have cut off school and health services to illegal immigrants. Davis effectively nullified the vote by refusing to appeal a judge's ruling that invalidated some of the law's provisions. Is it any wonder so many Democratic Hispanics turned against him? Immigration and the undocumented workers issue is not a WASP, African-American versus Latino issue. It is legal immigrants versus illegal regardless of where they are from. Furthermore, it is not just a California and Western states issue in the 21st century. California, with 12 million Hispanics, did not even make the Top 10 in terms of growth of Hispanics in the three years after the 2000 census.

The 2010 census revealed how multicultural and multiracial America's social fabric has become because of the constantly changing waves of immigrants washing ashore. By 2050, there should be no racial or ethnic lines.

This point was brought home to me during the 1984 Los Angeles Olympics and every international sports competition thereafter. The African teams all looked African. The Asian teams all looked Asian. The European teams looked European, the Middle Eastern teams looked Middle Eastern and the American team looked like all of them blended into one. The ideal political and religious team the Founding Fathers envisioned.

### *Immigrants by the Numbers*
Within three years of the 2000 census, Georgia had the fastest-growing Hispanic population in America – an increase of almost 19%. Atlanta had the fastest Hispanic growth rate of any major city in America. Six of the top 10 Hispanic growth states were in the South. North Carolina's Hispanic growth rate of 17.3% in just over two years fell a hair short of Nevada's second-place 17.4%. At those rates of growth, a population doubles every four years. And that is assuming the census counts everyone!

Oregon's Hispanic population swelled to more than 312,000 in 2002, according to the Census Bureau. However, a Mexican consular official told a local paper that the actual number was at least 500,000. The other states following Georgia, Nevada, North Carolina and Oregon to complete the top 10 were South Carolina, Kentucky, Virginia, Arizona, Alabama and – while not a state – Washington, D.C.

Nationally, Hispanic growth was almost four times that of the population as a whole and some 14 times greater than the rate for whites. A profile of the growing Hispanic population drawn by the Census Bureau in 2002 is even more revealing. It shows that the percentage of Hispanics under age 18 is more than 50% higher than that of non-Hispanic whites. Nearly 27% of Hispanic households have five or more people, compared to fewer than 11% of non-Hispanic white households. Nearly three times as many Hispanics live below the poverty level as do whites.

These statistics confirm that illegal immigrants are here to stay. Most of them are not going anywhere. There's not going to be a deportation program that sends more than 12 million people back to where they came from. *We the Maids* have to sweep in laws that deal with this reality. Nearly 3 million illegal immigrants in the late 1980s, including my gardeners, were granted amnesty. Millions more, many of them relatives of the newly documented, quickly took their place.

"Unless we're going to close our borders, the pragmatic solution is to fully integrate immigrants of all statuses into our economy, teach them English, make them productive citizens and collect their taxes," said Don Campell, a member of *USA Today's* board of contributors. I agree.

### *Immigration Is a Global Issue*

Immigration and undocumented workers are also a hot political issue in Hong Kong, Japan, Malaysia and across Europe. It is a political issue that has moved to center stage, highlighted by 32-year-old Norwegian right-winger-anti-Muslim Anders Behring Breivik, who set off a bomb in Oslo and went on a shooting massacre at a Labor Party summer camp on Utoya Island that left 77 aspiring political activists dead. He had been a member of the Progress Party, the second-largest in Norway's parliament and which literally came out of nowhere. How many other unknown anti-immigration extremists are out there among us?

Just like in America, illegal immigrants in Hong Kong, Japan and Europe do the menial work that locals turn down, as well as skilled labor in certain labor-short fields. It is estimated there are more than 5 million illegal immigrants in Western Europe.

Malaysia has a population of 28 million people and about 2 million legal foreign workers and an estimated 2 million illegal immigrants, mostly from nearby Indonesia. It is considering amnesty for them in order to increase the labor force, tax base and foreign investment. Foreign investors want a larger legal labor pool. So do Malaysian companies that have been investing abroad, partly because they could not find enough workers at home. Sound familiar?

The tighter post 9/11 border controls in America and Europe have increased the cross-border smuggling trade whose primary beneficiaries are organized criminals. It is estimated that between 100,000 and 200,000 people are smuggled annually at an average cost of $30,000 per person. You do the math. It is a very lucrative business with far less risks than smuggling drugs, weapons or money. People also have the added advantage of legs, which allows many of them to flee the long arm of the law.

"Smuggled" people are to be distinguished from the unknown millions of people who are "trafficked" each year, mostly women and children, many of whom wind up working in the sex trade.

Immigrants, like the Pilgrims and our Founding Fathers, who migrated to the unknown, are no different than the great migrations of our ancestral tribes, clans and animal herders who lived and roamed in a borderless world – and flocks of free flying birds. The free flow of people then, like now, is natural. That is why open borders, an ancient reality, make sense today.

*Open Borders to Immigration*
America, Hong Kong, Japan and Europe must stop living in denial. Legal migration quotas must not only be increased dramatically to meet the real demands of developing societies – but ended once and for all. That is how illegal immigration is stopped. People have to be allowed to move freely across borders just like capital, goods and services. Only then will we have true interlocalism.

Interlocalism, the interaction and merger of like-minded people in different locales, a topic I discuss at length in *Custom Maid Knowledge* and *Feasting Dragon, Starving Eagle,* is a primary driving force of immigration, legal and illegal. Such human interaction can be traced back to the beginning of time. The tribes and clans of Africa, Asia, Europe, Israel, Arabia all interlocalized with their fellow tribesmen or clansmen who moved on to other tribes or clans for personal, commercial, political or military reasons, usually the result of conflict, war or empire building.

Today, people immigrate to communities of their fellow tribesmen and clansmen legally and illegally. They do so to be with relatives and friends and to work and send money back home. No law or fence can stop this movement of people. In America, the Latinos head north to hook up with their compadres, and in Europe the Africans and Middle Easterners do the same.

Immigration quotas and restrictions on the flow of human resources while the flow of capital, goods and services is unrestricted creates an unrealistic destructive imbalance that is unenforceable and self contradictory. Cheap and unskilled labor from undeveloped countries should be encouraged to come to America and go to Europe and Japan to fill the jobs locals don't want or aging retirees vacate. Conversely, skilled professionals, managers and bureaucrats in America, Europe and Japan should be encouraged to go to undeveloped countries. Immigration does not have to be a one-way street. The undeveloped world needs skilled labor just as much, and probably more so, than the developed world needs unskilled labor. Global immigration quotas to meet a particular country's needs could be easily adopted and implemented by a Global Security Council, the U.N.'s successor I proposed in *Custom Maid Knowledge*.

Funds to finance development would be controlled and monitored by the donors and their skilled professionals rather than just being turned over to corrupt local officials who are used to usurping money for their own personal benefit while the intended beneficiaries continue to suffer in squalor.

The unskilled workers accepted to work in America, Europe, Japan and other developed countries would be required to return home with their savings and families after five years, or alternatively if they met certain financial qualifications, allowed to become permanent residents. This would allow them to impart their experience and learned skills and culture to their homeland upon their return, joining the skilled professionals who also may have returned.

### Free Flow of People
Forget border fences and unenforceable laws that are costly to implement

and don't do anything to stop illegal immigration. The only achievement of all these so-called politically expedient solutions with good sound bites is waste. Waste of billions of valuable taxpayer dollars; waste of career politicians' and bureaucrats' time that could be much better spent getting America back on track to the Founding Fathers' constitutional principles; and the waste of lives of innocent people whose only goal is to earn an honest dollar to support their families.

What is wrong with the idea of having people come with money in their pockets, register themselves as migrant workers and get a Social Security number entitling them to work and pay taxes? What is wrong with having these migrant workers invest some of their hard-earned money in the local economy, pay taxes and send their savings home? Isn't this how America was built, by waves of immigrant workers whose descendants are now trying to prevent others from doing what their own ancestors did?

"As a tool for spreading wealth, open borders makes foreign aid look like a child's lemonade stand," writes Robert Guest, business editor of the *Economist in Borderless Economics,* a rapid-fire case for the free movement of labor from one country to another. Central to his case is a 2005 study by Lant Pritchett, a former economist at the World Bank, titled *Let Their People Come: Breaking the Gridlock on Global Labor Mobility.* Pritchett found that if developed countries slightly liberalized their immigration laws and increased their work forces by a mere 3 percent, the gains in remittances and other benefits to developing countries would amount to more than $300 billion annually. Compare that benefit with the $70 billion spent annually on foreign aid by developed countries, much of which ends up in the Swiss bank accounts of corrupt politicians.

Guest concludes with the argument that, thanks to America's immigrants, the U.S. is likely to remain for decades the richest and most powerful nation in the world. America has the largest foreign-born population by far – an astonishing 43 million people, 10 million more than the entire population of Canada. China, by contrast, has a foreign-born population of less than a million.

## Win-Win

Today's emotional issues of unemployment and immigration, and the proposed solutions to fire up the job market in America and globally, will persist until the two issues are merged and treated as one related issue and there is a free-flow of people and workers across borders. It would be a win-win for employers, workers, governments and local communities, not only in America, but worldwide.

According to U.S. Census Bureau projections, the nation's population will climb to 420 million by 2050. Hispanic-Americans will be almost 25 percent of the total – double their share in 2000, the bureau projects. Asian-Americans will also double their share to 8 percent in 2050. Over the same period, whites will drop from 69 percent to 50 percent of the count. Blacks will stay at around 13 percent. Immigration has a profound affect on these projections.

Add an aging population to unemployment and immigration and the problem becomes even more vexing. The solutions, a radical U-turn and open borders.

## Passport Please

What is a passport? Proof of nationality, loyalty, patriotism or just a travel document? Personally, being the holder of more than one passport and entitled to more over the years, I believe it is just a convenient travel document that has no bearing on one's loyalty or patriotism. Of course, one has loyalties and a certain amount of patriotic pride in belonging to the country issuing the passport, but real loyalty and patriotism lie with the country or countries that one feels part of. Historically, family ties, business, cultural affinity or mere residence and paying taxes, or collecting social security or welfare benefits define one's nationality and patriotism more than a passport.

The reality is that people can be loyal and patriotic to more than one country. That point was brought home to me in 2008, when five of the eight deputy ministers selected by the government in Hong Kong had foreign passports and officials debated whether deputy ministers and other

473

government officials should be able to hold foreign passports.

"Whatever you may have been led to believe in the past few weeks, giving up a foreign passport does not rocket someone into the ranks of the super patriots," said Michael Chugani as he debated the subject at Bert's Bar at the Foreign Correspondent's Club in Hong Kong.

"Is the mud-soaked volunteer who pulls an earthquake survivor from the Sichuan rubble less of a patriot if he holds a foreign passport acquired from an early childhood abroad? Would surrendering the passport improve his credentials to save lives? What about the thousands of Chinese-Americans who faced down those who jeered the Olympic torch relay? Was their patriotism second-class just because many may have dual nationality?" Chugani continued in response to Willem Lau, a mainland-born Chinese who is living in Hong Kong as a local permanent resident and holds a U.S. passport. Lau insisted that local officials should give up their foreign passports.

"Strangely, no one seems to be asking the obvious question at the heart of the current furor over the foreign passports held by new ministerial appointees," said Stephen Vines, a Hong Kong journalist and former president of the club. "The question is rarely asked because the answer is rather embarrassing. But it is no mystery why there was a surge of applications for foreign nationality before the handover of power, which was accelerated by the 1989 crackdown on China's democracy movement. It was all about buying insurance. To put it bluntly, Hong Kong people understand that citizenship of a one-party state entails risk, and the risk is mitigated by having an escape route."

Hong Kong's Basic Law – its constitution of sorts – allows a fifth of legislators to have foreign citizenship, but not political appointees. The family of Tung Che Wah, Hong Kong's first chief executive, all held American citizenship. Donald Tsang, his successor, was a British Commonwealth citizen, which entitled him to receive a non-honorary knighthood.

"Many people still believe it is only prudent to have a foreign passport so that, if the worse came to worst, they could get themselves and their families out," said Frank Ching, a local columnist and club regular. "This does not mean they don't care about Hong Kong. In fact, because they have less reason to fear for their personal safety, they can do more for Hong Kong and not be anxious about what they should do or say whenever a politically sensitive issue comes up."

By law, a Chinese national automatically loses his citizenship once he takes foreign citizenship. Dual nationality is used by some corrupt cadres to make it easier to hide illicit payments.

Multiple identities in today's interlocal world are natural. Citizenship laws should catch up.

A passport is proof of nationality, not a measure of the holder's nationalism. It facilitates ease of travel; it does not confer patriotism. As a lawyer who advised many Iranians after the fall of the Shah, South Africans fleeing apartheid, and Hong Kongers anticipating the 1997 handover on how to get U.S. residency and citizenship, I have no doubt that people acquire foreign passports not only as a travel necessity but as an insurance policy with an "escape clause." Allegiance to their adopted countries was never an intention.

Looking around the bar that day, I couldn't help but chuckle and point out that all of those involved in the discussion were multiple passport holders, with multiple residences around the world, currently living in Hong Kong.

### '60s Herbal Medication
I spent the mid to late '60s in Detroit, New York, Los Angeles, Chicago and San Francisco. Living in Motown in 1964-1965, after I immigrated to America and started working in a machine shop making parts for the Ford Mustang. It was my first glimpse of racism in America.

Precision Auto Parts, where I worked, was in Pontiac and I lived in Detroit. To get to work I took a bus to a White Castle on Woodward Avenue, where I got a ride to work with Willie, an African-American. I would join Willie and some other African-Americans during the lunch break. Being called

475

a "nigger lover" by white fellow workers because of my friendship with Willie, was my first American racist eye-opener.

Living on 137th Street between Spanish and Black Harlem in New York City in 1965 and '66, 12 blocks from the Apollo Theater, while working as a photographer for a photo library in Midtown covering the music scene in the Village and elsewhere was a trip fueled by herbals. I attended CCNY, a few blocks from where I lived. Harlem in the '60s was home to the largest black community outside of Africa. They were downtrodden and angry. The anger of the race riots in many U.S. cities at the time was reflected in the music and the Apollo. Quite an introduction to America.

It was another real eye-opener, especially for an immigrant white boy visiting the Apollo with an African-American beauty. Sharing the experience a decade later in California with my law partner Timothy Tierney, an Irish New Yorker married to an African-American, I realized how unconventional inter racial dating was back then, even in New York and Los Angeles.

"People would spit at Janice and me when they walked by us," Tim said in response to my expression of surprise at how people stared at me at the Apollo. The people who spat were white.

Living in San Francisco from the fall of 1969 through the summer of 1971 was a perpetual trip! My wife Gail and I lived in an apartment on Green Street. It had a large bay window overlooking the garden of Imogen Cunningham, a founding member of the California Group f/64 in 1932 with Ansel Adams, Edward Weston and Willard Van Dyke. Her botanical photographs, usually taken among the succulents, flowers and cacti of her own garden, were fascinating. She regarded fertility as an important theme. I couldn't believe my Karma and luck. We spent hours talking about photography, Vietnam, the city, the sexual revolution and flower power, her favorite subject.

The traditionally socially conservative city began changing at the end of World War II, when naval recruits suspected of being gay were discharged and dumped in San Francisco. Hence the city's development as a gay capital. The beginnings of a youth underground led to the beat movement in the 1950s, which thanks to Jack Kerouac's *On the Road*, began to inspire young people to make the trip out West.

Electric guitars and LSD, which was legal then, did the rest. Life magazine did a cover story on the hallucinogenic effects of LSD, which led to a hasty state ban by the California Legislature. But by then it was too late. The mystique of the San Francisco scene, drugs and sex, was too well entrenched in the minds of rebellious youth.

Burning Man, one of the most creative metaphors about America, started in San Francisco in 1986. Like the Occupy movement, Burning Man is beloved for having no planned attractions or entertainment save for the ritualistic burning of a towering wooden human effigy – relying entirely on attendees to construct their own artwork, costumes and installations.

The event has grown and now draws 50,000 people over Labor Day weekend to the windswept desert outside of Reno.

San Francisco has always been a city on the cutting edge of creativity and sexuality. The proud libertine heritage. The search for personal transformation, including through sex, led to the oceanside hot tubs at the Esalen Institute in Big Sur, cradle of the human potential movement, and in the 1960s communes flourished in the city, many espousing free love. Experiencing it firsthand was a treat. Visiting the city as I do every year on trips to California, I make it a point to catch up with the latest sexual trends and direction America is taking.

The OneTaste Urban Retreat Center, a live-in coed commune dedicated to the female orgasm, got my attention. It is the latest fad in this sexual underground America, weaving together strands of radical individual freedom, Eastern spirituality and feminism.

"The notion of a San Francisco sex commune focused on female orgasm is part of a long and rich history of women being public and empowered about their sexuality," says Elizabeth Armstrong, an associate professor of sociology at Indiana University, who has studied San Francisco's sexual subcultures.

Imogen Cunningham would have applauded the way Alina Lebedva slapped Prince Charles in the face with a red carnation and the continued exploration of female sexuality – with Jasmine tea and flowers.

San Francisco does take, push and challenge conventional sexuality issues to the max. One example was the attempt to outlaw infant circumcision in the city, making it a criminal offense. Supporters of the initiative say infants should not be forced to participate in what is essentially culturally accepted genital mutilation. A Jewish religious tradition challenged on the grounds of American human rights.

The image of a bearded, black-hatted Jew with an evil grin and bloody blade, "Monster Mohel," used in a comic book as part of the campaign to ban the practice, was straight out of the annals of classic European anti-Semitism. "Foreskin Man," a buff blonde hero who battles dark evil Jewish characters, like most of the other good characters in the book, are Aryan. Anti-Semitism, like racism, is still alive and well in America and Europe.

In Germany, a Cologne court ruled that a child's circumcision constitutes "bodily harm" and thus is verboten. Unless the German Bundestag intervenes, which it has pledged to do, about 4 million Muslims and more than 100,000 Jews will have to practice a central part of their religion in the catacombs of Germany.

"The often very aggressive prejudice against religion as backward, irrational and opposed to science is increasingly defining popular opinion," said Michael Bongardt, a professor of ethics at Berlin's Free University, who added that the ruling reflected a profound lack of understanding in modern Germany for religious belief.

"If my theory of relativity is proven successful, Germany will claim me as a German and France will declare that I am a citizen of the world," Albert

Einstein quipped in 1922. "Should my theory prove untrue, France will say that I am a German and Germany will declare that I am a Jew."

Unfortunatly, anti-semitism is on the rise in America and Europe.

Anti-Semitism, in my experience, does not exist in China. Jews are respected in China, not only because of the historical Silk Road link from the Middle East to China, but for their ability, like the Chinese, to survive the ages and today play an active and constructive role in all aspects of humanity. Intellectual, financial, medical, agricultural, educational, high tech and military.

"The Chinese are the lost tribe of Israel," I would often conclude political discussions comparing Jews and Chinese.

While the circumcision debate was being played out in California, I was invited to one in Shenzhen, China, by my neighbor Ed Pinshow, a South African-Israeli. His daughter, who lived there with her husband and first grandchild, had given birth to his second.

"I didn't realize the Israeli community was so large in Shenzhen," I said to Ed as we returned to Hong Kong on the ferry, a mere 50-minute ride away as an unexpected rainstorm battered the boat. They have their own rabbi, mohel, the "whole megila," I said as we shared another toast of whisky in honor of his grandson and the " lost tribe of Israel" in China.

"Hey Ed, you can take your yarmulke off," I said as I noticed he was still wearing his skullcap from the circumcision ceremony.

"Which reminds me," I continued. "Did you hear the one about the Chinese businessman buying bras from the Jewish businessman?"

"A Chinese businessman goes to a Jewish businessman in Hong Kong to buy black bras size 38. The Jew says that black bras are rare and difficult to get from his current suppliers, especially in that size, but for $50 a bra he can get them. The Chinese buys 25 bras. He returns a few days later to place a new order. But this time the Jew tells him that they have become harder to come buy and charges him $60 a bra. The Chinese returns a month later to buy out the entire remaining stock of black bras at $75 a bra. The Jew is somewhat puzzled by the large demand for black bras and asks the Chinese, 'Please tell me, what do you do with all these black bras?' The Chinese answers, 'I cut them in half and sell the halves as skullcaps to the Jews for $200."

San Francisco's Chinatown is the oldest in the U.S. The restaurants, markets, fresh vegetable stalls, seafood counters and people drew me in. Much like the many fresh food markets throughout Hong Kong do today. My then-wife Gail, who worked as a buyer for I Magnin while I studied law, also ran a catering business on the side. Many of the people I met in Chinatown had fled the Hong Kong riots and the Cultural Revolution convulsing China. We would talk whenever they were willing to open up.

San Francisco has the largest percentage of Asian-Americans in continental America. Six Asian-Americans ran for mayor in the November 2011 election and Ed Lee, a Chinese-American, won.

To win an election in San Francisco, a candidate not only needs to garner the Asian-American vote, but that of pet parents – especially dogs. There are more dogs than children in San Francisco. There are an estimated 150,000 dogs compared with 108,000 children, according to the San Francisco Society for the Prevention of Cruelty to Animals and the 2010 U.S. census.

Dog lovers have formed a political action committee to promote the interests of their four-footed friends, namely space to run free in one of the world's largest urban national parks.

I would have loved to debate dog issues and the shark fin bill introduced in the California Legislature in 2011 to ban the sale, distribution and possession of shark fin, with some of our food suppliers. State and federal laws prohibit shark finning in U.S. waters, but do not address the importation of fins. Finning is inhumane and a threat to ocean ecosystems. More than 73 million sharks are slaughtered annually for their fins alone, which go into the soup often served at Chinese weddings and banquets –

another cherished cultural and tradition being questioned in America.

I agree with now-retired basketball star Yao Ming, who urged San Francisco residents to "Join me – say no to shark fin soup."

San Francisco is one of the most diverse cities in America. This was best exemplified by the San Francisco Giants 2012 promotional lineup. Included in the schedule were two nights each honoring the heritage of Chinese, Japanese, Irish and Filipinos, plus, among others, the Cinco de Mayo Celebration, LGBT (lesbian, gay, bisexual and transgender) Night Out and Firefighter Appreciation Night. My favorite was Sept. 4, in a nod to the Year of the Dragon, A Bruce Lee Tribute Night for the San Francisco native.

Herbal medicine shops dispensing Eastern cures for Western ailments also got my attention. These alternatives to drugs seemed to work and appeared so much healthier. When I shared these experiences with good friends who had become doctors, they laughed at me.

"There is no medical proof that these herbal medicines work," Dr. Thomas Kun told me.

He became the head of Saint Johns Hospital in Santa Monica and was my personal physician for many years. I'm delighted to see today that doctors like Andrew Weil preach the benefits of "integration of modern medicine with old low-tech practices," and John Sarno, author of *Healing Back Pain,* lecture that most pain is all in our head.

In fact, plants have been vital in the development of 25 percent of all modern prescription drugs. Aspirin, the first mass-marketed pill, was used in leaves and bark and bushes in ancient times to relieve all sorts of pains. Prescription drugs became a major election issue in the last U.S. presidential election of the millennium. People, baby boomers in particular, need their drugs. Affordable drugs. If the government is going to continue its subsidies, shouldn't it be subsidizing prescription drugs for all Americans instead of having them go to Canada and Mexico or online to buy them?

### Constructive Human Interaction

Civil rights, hip-hop, affirmative action, cultural revolution, Vietnam, flower children, cold war and drug culture have all accelerated today's constructive human interaction. Individuals can reassert their power, learn from past mistakes and stick to fundamental truths rather than self-serving political propaganda.

Activists and artists today emulate and rephrase the feelings and expressions of anger and frustration of the '60s. People are just as angry and frustrated today, but the weed and LSD has been mostly replaced by cocaine, addictive painkillers, and antipsychotic drugs dished out like candy.

Richard Nixon had a grasp of international issues that I appreciated. However, I disagreed wholeheartedly with him on his interpretation of what happened in America during the '60s. He said, "We will get America back on the path of civilization when Americans once more respect and demand civilized behavior.

"From the 1960s on, our laws and our moves have been driven by the cultural conceits that took hold during the heyday of the counterculture...," Nixon said.

Both America and China tried to force-feed their people cultural propriety. Both failed. The Vietnam War and the Cultural Revolution were failures. Forced "mass conversions" to accept career politicians self-serving political philosophy, agendas of their financial supporters and decisions have never succeeded, and never will.

It was the counterculture activists and their followers who brought about many of the changes we enjoy today. Cassius Clay, who became a Muslim and changed his name to Muhammad Ali, like many American activists in the '60s, took a stand and lost much of his career for it. He represented the 1964-1974 decade of American hope and turmoil. He is admired for his principled stand. Shouldn't *We the Apathetic Maids* be doing the same in the 21st century?

David Halberstam accurately defines the protests of the time as "not against personal hardship or tyranny but against the values inherent in a culture of affluence and bigness." I would add, hypocrisy and managed misperception!

The greatest tribute to the '60s sex, drugs and rock 'n' roll culture are the museums built to archive a culture and generational influence that will have a great influence in the New World Order. The DEA Museum in Arlington, Virginia, traces the history of drugs in America. The Rock and Roll Hall of Fame in Cleveland, Ohio, traces the history of rock music everywhere. The Museum of Sex in New York City traces the history of sexuality in America.

Having been an active participant, I can only testify to the benefits of the counterculture. As Nixon points out in *Beyond Peace:* "After Grant's victory at Vicksburg in 1863, as Lincoln was considering appointing him commander of all union forces, one of his advisors urged him not to do so because Grant was a drinker. Lincoln reportedly responded, 'Get me the name of his brand of whiskey so that I can give some to my other generals'." Easy for Nixon, a drinker himself, to say. What if Grant had smoked weed? Would Lincoln or Nixon have responded differently? I don't think so.

### Conservative Religious Backlash

The anti-war and civil rights movements of the 1960s transformed collective and individual political expression in the streets, music and sexual behavior. Television, a relatively new mass medium, beamed these changes across America and the world and instantly offended traditionalists and conservatives.

"The rise of the televised church in the 1970s was one response to the evangelicals' sense that their values had been closed out of mainstream media in the 1960s. Like so much in contemporary conservatism, the Religious Right's attack on the media betrayed a certain nostalgia for the ordered world of the 1950s." As E.J. Dionne Jr. reminds us, conservatives' search for entertainment that was morally acceptable gave us Pat Robertson's Christian Broadcasting Network that became a showcase for the revival of religious television from the 1950s.

Southern Evangelists and Baptists had deliberately refrained from political activity since the backlash and public anger they attracted after successfully lobbying for Prohibition. That all changed on January 23, 1973, when the Supreme Court handed down the *Roe v. Wade* decision that legalized abortions. In his autobiography, Jerry Falwell acknowledges that was the day he decided that preachers should again get involved in politics. Conservatives throughout America were prepared to back him. "Acid, amnesty and abortion" in various variations became the Republican battle cry. The "Moral Majority" with Falwell leading the charge helped elect Ronald Reagan and other conservative Republicans across the nation.

The Republicans did not win the evangelical vote on the basis of conservative religious themes alone.

"Most of the evangelical conservatives were white Southerners who began voting against the Democrats because of civil rights," Dionne concludes in *Why Americans Hate Politics*.

Paradoxically, leading churchmen of the organized denominations in the South in the '50s and '60s spoke out in favor of the Supreme Court rulings and civil rights, endorsing the rulings as morally correct.

President Franklin D. Roosevelt's epoch-changing New Deal coalition survived only so long as its constituent groups agreed not to discuss the one difference between them they could not reconcile – race. The Roosevelt Democratic New Deal Coalition was shattered by the racial politics of the civil rights movement of the '60s. It inadvertently created a religious cultural divide. Southern white evangelical conservatives emerged and united because of their opposition to the civil rights movement. A divisive religious cultural divide that has politically and culturally polarized and alienated America from the founding ideals of the Constitution. A religious divide that continues to be fractious and politically divisive at the dawn of the 21st century.

The relationship between the Religious Right and the '60s was thoroughly paradoxical. The Religious Right arose in reaction to "'60s permissiveness." Yet the rise of the Religious Right and more generally, the growth of evangelical Christianity, were also very much part of the revolt during the '60s against the status quo in the churches as well as in the broader society. The resurgence of old-time religion was part of the broader revolt against '60s modernism and scientific rationality.

Billy Graham was the decisive figure in the rebirth of conservative Protestantism. Even for intellectuals, Graham was reassuring.

"Graham was no bigot," historian William L. O'Neill wrote by way of explaining his respectability. "His call for Americans to rediscover their traditional beliefs did not stir up old hatreds. Graham asked only that the individual rediscover Christ. If that was a far cry from the Social Gospel, it was a far cry too from the chauvinism and provinciality of that old-time religion."

The new religiosity affected Congress, which in violation of all the principles laid down by the Founding Fathers, accorded God new forms of official recognition. It was in the 1950s that the words under God were inserted into the Pledge of Allegiance and "In God We Trust" was stamped onto coins.

### Cultural Civil War – Political Hardball
The ongoing quiet subtle nonviolent divisive cultural civil war in America reached its destructive political Gettysburg on election day 2000 when the election of America's 43rd president got tangled up in Florida's plump chads, butterfly ballots, legal eagles and Supremes. The divisive cultural civil war saw America divided into blue and red camps. Democratic urban minorities versus Republican rural whites. The imploded failure of America's political ideologies-liberalism and conservatism. With us or against us. No different than the war on terrorism. Black or white. No grey or room for any other color, shade or point of view. Two colors, two parties, two philosophies, two extremes, two limited false choices. State versus individual. *We the Apathetic Maids* are being deliberately

polarized in America's cultural civil war by the spin doctors, lobbyists, lawyers, religious zealots and the career politicians and bureaucrats they represent who perpetuate the same divisive non-issues with all-consuming debilitating sound bites that dumb us down and bog us down even though we want to move on.

The flag burners of the '60s being blamed for the resurgent flag wavers of today.

"The controversies over Vietnam and race eliminated the vital center as the dominant force in American politics, and we have not been the same since," columnist E.J. Dionne Jr. astutely observes. The turbulent extremism between liberalism and conservatism has paralyzed America and left a gaping apathetic hole between the two extremes.

The Florida quagmire was the culmination of a series of partisan battles that have raged continuously since the Civil War whenever career politicians cannot compromise. It all started with the Compromise of 1876 when the Southern Democrats allowed the Republican Rutherford B. Hayes to become president instead of the Democrat Samuel Tilden after a disputed election – similar to the Bush-Gore dispute, in return for the end of Reconstruction in the South over which the Civil War was fought. Whenever career politicians reach a political accommodation and trade-off, it is usually at the expense of *We the Apathetic Maids*. When they don't, it is also at our expense, the only difference being that the tab is much higher.

This was brought to the public's glaring attention during Bill Clinton's impeachment trial and the debate over the Obama health care plan when career politicians got over-vindictive at *We the Apathetic Maids'* expense. They take us for granted and just assume they can continue to do their business as usual because we allow them to. The latest cycle started in November of 1984 to May 1985 over the close election battle for Indiana's 8th District House seat. Democrat Frank McCloskey's election-night victory was reversed in a recount. The Democratic controlled House voted to give McCloskey the seat. The Republicans stormed out en mass and are still upset.

In October of 1987, the Senate rejected President Reagan's nomination of Robert Bork to the Supreme Court by a 58-42 vote. The Democratic-controlled Senate followed this up two years later in March of 1989 when it rejected President Bush's nomination of former Senator John Tower as defense secretary. Republicans refused to back down even though there was substantial evidence that Tower was a drunk, a womanizer and had shared arms secrets with defense contractors – as many career politicians do.

The Republicans retaliated in June 1989 when Newt Gingrich led the GOP charge to oust House Speaker Jim Wright for ethics violations. Gingrich had sold copies of his autobiography to lobbyists in bulk to avoid House limits on speaking fees. He resigned, calling the Republican campaign "mindless cannibalism." Things got worse in October 1991 when the country was subjected to one of the most brutal and public confirmation hearings of a justice for the U.S. Supreme Court the Clarence Thomas hearings with star witness Anita Hill. The Democrats were accused of orchestrating a "smear campaign" against Thomas.

Democrats retaliated in October of 1992 when Iran-contra prosecutor Lawrence Walsh indicted former Defense Secretary Casper Weinberger days before the presidential election on a charge of lying to Congress. He also released some evidence that appeared to implicate President George H.W. Bush. Bush lost the election to Bill Clinton. The Republicans counter-attacked in July and August of 1995, investigating Bill and Hillary Clinton's personal finances and reopening the suicide of Deputy White House counsel Vincent Foster. This culminated in the November and December 1995 budget battles that resulted in the shutdown of the government for three weeks.

The mother of all political battles was fought from November 1998 through February 1999: the impeachment of President Clinton. This political battle is still ongoing even though Clinton is long gone from the Oval Office. His political adversaries now want to discredit his legacy and his wife. While they're at it, why not take down President Barack Obama in the process – which they have been working diligently to do since he got elected.

The Clinton impeachment, the first of an elected president, fractured America's political process and system. But it became a hyperpartisan political tool nevertheless. It was almost used again on Obama to link him to Illinois Governor Rod Blagojevich when Blogojevich was indicted for trying to sell Obama's Senate seat to the highest bidder after Obama was elected president.

The hypocritical destructiveness of the Clinton impeachment, over sexual liaisons with a former White House aide, was highlighted after Clinton was acquitted and survived his political execution. He left office holding his head high while Newt Gingrich, Bob Livingston and Tom DeLay, the House Republican leaders during his impeachment, all eventually resigned under pressure for various sex and bribery crimes and indiscretions.

The Clinton impeachment represented the triumph of partisanship on both sides of the aisle, a divide that remains today. Democrats made a calculated decision to stick by a president of their party no matter his transgressions and to promote partisan division in the congressional proceedings so they could discredit the other side. Republicans were so intent on impeaching Clinton that they turned away from opportunities for a bipartisan solution.

The result has been a distaste for impeachment and little appetite for consensus. Liberal Democrats agitated to impeach George W. Bush in connection with the Iraq War, warrantless surveillance and torture, but party leaders had no interest in going down that road again.

"Although there are powerful arguments that President Bush has committed high crimes and misdemeanors, there are questions about whether it is prudent to [seek impeachment]," said Bruce Ackerman, a Yale Law School professor.

Says who? *We the People? We the Maids?* I don't think so.

A better case for impeaching Bush could have been made by addressing why he started two wars, wasted so many thousands of American, Iraqi and Afghan lives, and saddled the U.S. with trillions of dollars of debt that haunts us today. Taxpayers, as usual, left holding the bag and standing in the unemployment line, fallout from the failed domestic and foreign policies of a failed administration.

A few hours after the terrorist attacks of September 11, 2001, Republican Congressman Dana Rohrabacher announced his explanation for the cause.

"We had Bill Clinton backing off, letting the Taliban go, over and over again."

Conservative radio commentator Rush Limbaugh wrote an editorial in *The Wall Street Journal* saying, "Mr. Clinton can be held culpable for not doing enough when he was commander in chief to combat the terrorists who wound up attacking the World Trade Center and Pentagon."

Yet when Clinton was president and ordered missile strikes in August 1998 against terrorist training camps in Afghanistan in an attempt to kill Osama bin Laden, there was widespread Republican speculation – from such people as Senator Arlen Specter – that he was acting precipitously to draw attention away from the Monica Lewinsky scandal. Arguably, the Democrats can now try and strike back about the Justice Department's May 21, 2002 findings that there were voting irregularities in Florida by the Republicans that put Bush in the White House and the security lapses that led to 9/11 under a Republican watch.

To career politicians, politics is nothing more than a game. A game they play at the people's expense. The cost that *We the People* pay to watch professional athletes playing baseball, football or basketball pale in comparison to what we pay as we watch professional career politicians play political hardball. But public service is not a game. It is a commitment to people and country. Something the career politicians have forgotten.

The "change of tone" George W. Bush promised during the campaign, to bring back bipartisanship, evaporated during the battle over his tax cut legislation, missile defense, education, budget and just about everything else. It was back to the usual divisive political hardball until September 11.

Terrorists brought back bipartisanship. Do *We the Maids* want this messy game to continue in the 21$^{st}$ century? Of course not, but it is.

Barack Obama also promised change and bipartisanship to get things done in Washington. His campaign promise to reach across the aisle could not be fulfilled. Like his two predecessors, he has failed to bridge the widening partisan divide. In fact, his efforts to do so had the opposite effect. The hard-drawn partisan wall separating Democrats and Republicans along party lines was highlighted during the debate and vote on health care reform, increasing America's debt ceiling and just about everything else.

The Republicans have become mere obstructionists. The party of "no." They remained unified to block the White House at every turn as they successfully fired-up and rallied their conservative base leading up to the midterm November 2010 elections and followed up with their obstructionist tactics looking ahead to the 2012 presidential election.

Any possibility or promise of bipartisanship ended with the swearing in of President Obama and the launch of the Tea Party movement that exposed the deep anger of people at both major political parties' mismanagement of the economy and anxiety over the consequences of that failure.

The Obama health care debate drove home the reality that the differences between Democrats and Republicans are too profound to be bridged. The Republican warnings that Obamacare was all about "socialism" and "death panels" was pure political spin and all about protecting corporate America, companies with 50 or more employees, that will be required to pick up most of the new health care costs.

When it suited corporate America to offer health care to attract employees after World War II, they gladly did so. Corporate America offered generous health care plans because wages were fixed, international competition all but nonexistent, and corporations ruled the roost. Powerful unions added new features to their "Cadillac plans" with the same enthusiasm that Detroit added tail fins to Coupe de Villes. Now that the world has changed, corporate America wants to shrug off its health care responsibilities and leave it to the government and individuals.

Health care costs in America are out of control – absolute malpractice – and a looming disaster for business. The proportion of GDP devoted to health care grew from 5 percent in 1962 to 16 percent in 2010 before Obamacare became law. Rising health care costs appear to have suppressed wages, as firms try to make up for the expense.

America spends 53 percent more per head on health care than the next most profligate country and almost 2½ times the rich-country average for a lot less care. With health-care costs rising much faster than general inflation and 500,000 fellow baby boomers now becoming eligible for Medicare every day, health-care spending is likely to hit 20 percent of GDP by 2017 and 25 percent by 2025.

There is no doubt that Obamacare is another deficit spending entitlement at the mercy of whatever debt instruments are financing and backing the various parts of the scheme.

The Senate in December 2009 gave President Obama the 60 votes needed to pass his top domestic priority. *We the Maids* had to pay one hell of a price. A commitment to Senator Ben Nelson, a Democrat, that federal funds would not be used to pay for abortions and providing extra Medicaid funds for his home state of Nebraska got his critical 60th vote. The agreement came over a handshake, as all agreements should, except when there are side deals that are not publicly disclosed that benefit individual senators and their small sparsely populated states at the expense of the country as a whole. People and country must come first. Not senators and their pet home-state projects that *We the Maids* have to pay for.

Talk about the tail wagging the dog. Another one of many reasons to get rid of the Senate in Washington and in the state governments as well. It wasn't really meant to be there to begin with, according to the Founding Fathers. America's Senate does to America what Rome's did to the Roman Empire. Why perpetuate a political relic from the 17th century that was devised to keep these United States together when there were divergent state populations that gave populous states an unfair advantage that had to be balanced. It worked, but it has served its purpose and now is ready to be retired before it does any more damage and disunites the states it is supposed to keep together and balanced.

Another quaint arcane Senate procedural power play is "reconciliation." It was brought to light again by the way in which the Obama health care legislation was passed into law. Reconciliation in effect protects bills from filibusters and thus from the requirement for a 60-vote supermajority to end debate, and instead allows legislation with a budgetary impact to pass by a simple majority after limited debate. The idea is to reconcile spending with revenues. Minority parties – Republicans when Obamacare became law – hate it. But Democrats had little choice in the matter since no Republicans voted for the legislation. Obamacare was strictly a partisan affair. Democrats and Republicans voted strictly along party lines.

Compare this sad state of affairs to the great domestic reforms of the '60s. Most notably, the Civil Rights and Voting Rights acts. Some 80 percent of congressional Republicans, and a smaller percentage of Democrats, voted to give black Americans equality before the law. In the same decade, roughly half of Republicans joined the Democratic majority in voting to create Medicare and Medicaid. Bill Clinton's welfare reforms, which chivvied the jobless to seek work, were also solidly bipartisan. The American system of checks and balances makes it hard to pass sweeping changes without broad consensus.

Sixteen of the 22 "reconciliation bills" that have made it through Congress were passed in the Senate when Republicans had majorities, including George W. Bush's signature tax cuts, overhaul of the welfare system, Medicare Advantage insurance policies and a few other doozies that have contributed a significant portion of the budget deficit because spending was never properly reconciled with revenues.

Paul Krugman correctly points out that the way Obama's health care bill was worked over and compromised going through the Washington political grinder confirms how dysfunctional the U.S. government has become.

"The need for 60 votes to cut off Senate debate and end a filibuster – a requirement that appears nowhere in the Constitution, but is simply a self-imposed rule – turned what should have been a straightforward piece of legislation into a nail-biter. And it gave a handful of wavering senators extraordinary power to shape the bill. Now consider what lies ahead. We need financial reform," Krugman writes.

The heart of Obamacare is a restructuring of the flawed health insurance market. Insurers now face tough new regulations forbidding such practices as dropping people with "pre-existing conditions," real or trumped up, or putting lifetime caps on coverage. In return, though, the insurance industry will benefit from a big expansion of the country's private insurance sector.

After the history-making health care reform package was finally passed into law, at least 10 Democratic lawmakers received death threats and were victims of vandalism because of their votes in favor of it – including Representative Gabrielle Giffords of Arizona.

The health care fight only widened the already cavernous chasm between Republicans and Democrats. Repealing Obamacare became the new rallying cry of the GOP and its tea-baggers, steeped in obstructionist fervor, as the 2012 election battle lines were being drawn.

The anti-Obamacare cheers only got louder and angrier when a federal appeals court ruled in August 2011 that the law's requirement that all Americans buy insurance or face a penalty was unconstitutional.

The U.S. Supreme Court decision to uphold Obamacare in June 2012 reaffirmed the constitutional genius and endurance of the Founding Fathers' vision of separating political power into three branches of government. No one thought Chief Justice John G. Roberts, a conservative, would provide the fifth vote, joining the so-called liberals, to uphold a Democratic president's single most important legislative achievement.

There is a lot that career politicians can learn from the respect, integrity and honesty that Roberts and Obama, two Harvard Law graduates, have shown each other. Their legacies are intertwined, notwithstanding the rare public irritation the chief justice expressed after Obama scolded the high court during his 2010 State of the Union address for the court's decision in *Citizens United*.

"The Affordable Care Act's requirement that certain individuals pay a financial penalty for not obtaining health insurance may reasonably be characterized as a 'tax'," Chief Justice Roberts wrote in the majority opinion. "Because the Constitution permits such a tax, it is not our role to forbid it, or pass upon its wisdom or fairness."

The Republicans' vitriolic demonization and vilification of the president that hit a crescendo during the health care debate has its roots in the Bill Clinton presidency and impeachment. Jay Leno summed it up best on "The Tonight Show:" "President Obama hosted Republican leaders for lunch at the White House. The president had to do without salt, bread, pepper and butter. Not for health reasons, though. Republicans refused to pass anything."

The Republicans also opposed the $700-billion stimulus package – a "crap sandwich," House Speaker John A. Boehner called it – and made it a campaign issue, arguing that it created no jobs and did nothing to stimulate the economy, even though the nonpartisan Congressional Budget Office said it would create between 1.4 million and 3.3 million jobs. As FactCheck.org, the indispensable truth squad on the Web, put it: "It's just false to say that the stimulus created 'no jobs'."

The extension of the Bush tax cuts was another bankrupt Republican campaign issue that they successfully used to mislead the American voters. They argued that under Obama's tax cut extension excluding the rich, government would tax the rich to benefit the poor. According to the nonpartisan Tax Policy Center, the richest 0.1 percent of Americans who earn an average of $8.4 million would get an average tax cut of more than $61,000 under Obama's plan. Under the Republican proposal, they would get an average tax cut of more than $370,000, the center says. In other words, the Republican plan creates not only a wider divide between Democrats and Republicans, but a gargantuan gap between rich and poor.

As Warren Buffet put it: "There's class warfare all right. But it's my class, the rich class, that's making war, and we're winning."

But the Obamacare brinkmanship and all other partisan paranoia over issues pales in comparison to the bitter fight over raising the federal debt ceiling in mid-2011. The political grandstanding and bickering gripped the nation and cost the country a downgrade in its credit rating before it was all over, like a laid-off working stiff who can't keep up with his car payments.

What has happened to the spirit of bipartisanship for the greater good? The kind of political middle ground that ideological opposites like conservative icon William F. Buckley and the liberal Daniel Patrick Moynihan could reach for the sake of "the politics of stability" as anti-Vietnam protests tore at American social harmony in the '60s and '70s. What has become of that kind of two-part harmony, putting country above party and politics?

Questions *We the Maids* should keep in mind as we ready our brooms for the next great house-cleaning in Washington.

House Speaker Boehner talked a good compromise game during the debt debate, but he figured he could outmaneuver the Democrats again in the run-up to the 2012 presidential election, as he did in the 2010 midterm elections and after he took control of the House.

He managed to bluff Obama into extending the Bush-era tax cuts – a move many people saw as a concession to Republican hardball political blackmail. Having done it once, Boehner figured he could do it again with the debt ceiling, as the 2012 presidential campaign heats.

Iowa and New Hampshire, two states that represent less than 1 percent of the nation's citizens, get to set the pace of the country's presidential contenders and make an early preferential determination that affects the rest of the country's primaries because of how the early winners are glorified and crowned by the media and the political media-talking-heads getting it wrong as usual.

Anyway, back to the debt ceiling. The federal debt limit is a strange quirk of U.S. budget law; since debt is the consequence of decisions about taxing and spending, and Congress already makes those decisions, why require an additional vote to raise the limit? And traditionally the debt limit has been treated as a minor detail. During the administration of President George W. Bush – who piled more than $4 trillion onto the national debt – Congress, with little fanfare, voted to raise the ceiling no less than seven times.

Since 1962, Congress has enacted 75 separate measures to alter the limit on the debt, including 17 under Ronald Reagan, six under Jimmy Carter and four under Bill Clinton. Congress has raised the debt limit 10 times since 2001. It was never a partisan issue. The fierce 2011 partisan posturing and brinkmanship in the acrimonious budget face-off between Democrats and Republicans that at the last minute came up with a default-dodging deal to raise the debt ceiling and cut $2.4 trillion in expenditures over 10 years, was just another temporary fix. The U.S. stepped back from economic disaster for a few days before Standard & Poor downgraded the U.S. creditworthiness for the first time ever from AAA to AA+. It was a change that will cost plenty in the long run.

The dollar and world stock markets tanked, the country slipped back into recession as America's already tarnished image got battered even more and Washington's self-obsessed narcissistic career politicians left town to raise funds for their re-election campaigns and the 2012 presidential race.

It was a watershed moment. America admitted to the world that the two party system is broken and the country is broke. Nevertheless, as Erskine Bowles, co-chairman of the deficit reduction commission says, "We're the healthiest horse in the glue factory."

The use of the debt ceiling to extort political concessions is a new hardball pitch in American politics. And, surprise, it looks like Obama and the Democrats were blindsided again.

"So what's really going on," columnist Paul Krugman wrote in a July 2011 column, "is extortion pure and simple."

As Mike Konczal of the Roosevelt Institute puts it, the Republican Party has, in effect, come around with baseball bats and declared, "Nice economy you have here. A real shame if something happened to it."

The Republicans insisted that the more than $2-trillion in spending cuts they demanded be accomplished with no tax hikes, while Democrats insisted that taxing the wealthy must be part of the deal.

Obama caved in once over tax cuts, and the Republicans expected him to cave in again. They believed they had the upper hand, because the public would blame the president for the economic crisis they threatened to create – and did.

"Republicans believe, in short, that they've got Obama's number, that he may still live in the White House but that for practical purposes his presidency is over," Krugman concludes. "It's time – indeed, long past time – for him to prove them wrong."

The end result, another short-term fix to get both parties through the November 2012 elections – and the country and people be damned.

What happened to the promise of change we can believe in?

Parties working together in the interest of the American people, *We the Maids,* is what needs to be swept in. The ability to listen, to place oneself inside the mind of the others, is the essential requirement of democratic statesmanship. The function of conservatives is not to meet every liberal program or scheme with a denunciation or a destructive counter scheme, but rather to weigh its advantages and defects, supporting the first and challenging the latter. A declaration of ideological warfare against liberalism is by its nature profoundly unconservative. It meets perceived radicalism with a counter radicalism of its own. The result? Bipartisan gridlock and dysfunction.

True democracy needs more than two parties to truly flourish. That is why America's democracy is dysfunctional and is awaiting the Third American

Revolution to revitalize the Founding Fathers' democratic dream.

Even judicial appointments that ideally should be party-neutral and ideologically independent take on disgustingly partisan overtones with overwhelming questionable vitriol. Especially when it comes to the U.S. Supreme Court, because it periodically appears to get a firm grip on the political reins of America and runs the country. Obama appointed two great Supremes, women with great legal minds and who are as American as American pie with a touch of flan and kugel. Imagine an Asian on a high federal court, and the debate that triggers, as it did when Obama nominated Goodwin Liu to be the first Asian-American on the U.S. Court of Appeals for the 9th Circuit in San Francisco.

Liu, superbly qualified to sit on the federal bench, withdrew his nomination after Senate Republicans, drunk with partisan vitriol, banded together in a filibuster to deny the UC Berkeley law professor a confirmation vote. Liu was unfairly demonized and accused of wanting to rewrite the Constitution to achieve liberal ends, and making America more like "communist-run China." The claims were ludicrous – "shameful obstructionism," as the L.A. Times put it – but effective.

Liu's legal writing is scrupulously accurate. Even leading conservatives such as Bill Clinton inquisitor Kenneth Starr and John Yoo, author of the "torture memos" that the Bush administration used to justify its questionable interrogation techniques, supported his nomination.

But that was not enough. Liu got fed up and withdrew. Not long after, he was nominated to serve on California's high court.

A new Congresses every couple of years tests the system to the max, with a new more vehement partisan vitriol that only magnifies and intensifies the gridlock and growing distrust of career politicians and their self-serving agendas. It is a self-defeating and destructive constitutional approach to a one-party democratic path that is laden with partisan IUDs that would make any "Hurt Locker" implode, especially a freedom-loving people who relish their First Amendment rights of freedom of speech and assembly, and who reject destructive partisanship. It must be swept away, make that blown away, in the Third American Revolution!

Watching the shellackers take over the House of Representatives in January 2011 was classic political theater.

It's time John Boehner and the other career politicians stop talking about kicking cans and start kicking their own cans and elephant fannies before they get swept out by *We the Maids*. It's time to recharge with good old American Founding Fathers' creative political Puritan juice.

Surely there is a reservoir of that old Puritan ethic left in America that could be revived with the right type of political leadership. That ethic says: Live within your means, avoid debt, don't covet.

It's a good thing America's military appears to be apolitical and neutral, staying on the political sidelines during these vitriolic times – busy as they are fighting two wars and a few other firefights globally on land and sea.

GOP leaders are preparing to regain subpoena power for intensified scrutiny and investigations of Obama administration actions and the White House is adding legal staff as a result. Surely this is not what the Founding Fathers had in mind. Mindless political subpoenas for destructive political theater last witnessed during the Clinton impeachment.

"The outgoing Congress was the most polarized in history," says Bill Galston at the centrist Brookings Institution. "The next one – the 112th – is likely to be off the charts."

The ugliness of political vitriol has permeated American politics at the state level as well. In California, someone in Jerry Brown's gubernatorial campaign called his opponent Meg Whitman a "whore." In Alaska, GOP Senate nominee Joe Miller compared a third-party bid by sitting Republican Sen. Lisa Murkowski to prostitution.

The partisan political vitriol is destructive economically to the nation and states where Democrats and Republicans are at loggerheads, California being in the forefront. A state with unrivaled human and financial resources is broke. It should not be in fiscal crisis; it should not be on the verge of cutting essential public services and denying health care to almost a million children. But it is, and as Paul Krugman said, "You have to wonder if California's political paralysis foreshadows the future of the nation as a whole."

In the Deep South, the centrist and fiscally conservative white Democrat is a disappearing breed, and has been since 1964, when President Lyndon B. Johnson pushed through the Civil Rights Act giving African-Americans the rights of full citizenship. Known for their courtly manners and readiness to work with Republicans, white Democratic Southerners were often the reason legislation got enacted.

"My fear about the next Congress is that it will be dominated by Republicans who want to stop the train from derailing by blowing up the rail tracks," said Galston.

"The decline of the Southern Democrat comes with a heavy price."

Make that the South comes with a heavy price. Booming cannons ushered in the 150th anniversary of America's Second Revolution – the Civil War. The annual reenactment of the opening shots of the Civil War toward Fort Sumter on April 12, 1861 in Charleston, South Carolina, continues to underscore a racial divide that has plagued the nation since its founding.

In Montgomery, Alabama, the firing of a cannon, the raising of the Stars and Bars and the singing of "Dixie" reenact the inauguration of Jefferson Davis as president of the Confederacy in 1861. The parade to the state Capitol along Davis' 1861 route takes place in a political revolutionary landscape that has become the Jerusalem of Southern politics – sacred to both the Confederacy and the civil rights movement.

The procession starts near the spot where, in 1955, black seamstress Rosa Parks boarded a public bus and refused to give her seat to a white man, sparking the Montgomery bus boycott. It then goes up the avenue where Martin Luther King Jr. and his followers completed the Selma-to-Montgomery voting rights march in 1965. It passes the Dexter Avenue Baptist Church, where King first served as pastor, and whose parsonage was firebombed in 1965 while his wife and baby daughter were inside.

The parade comes within two blocks of the old Greyhound bus station where the Freedom Riders, trying to desegregate interstate bus travel, were attacked and bloodied by a white mob in 1961 as police stood by.

"The ironies are rich," says Mark Potok of the Southern Poverty Law Center, a civil rights group, "and particularly ugly. This is a racist event, celebrating a government that stood on the foundation of slavery."

Bernard Simelton of the Alabama NAACP likens the reenactment to "celebrating the Holocaust."

The group that stages the event, the Sons of Confederate Veterans, says it's merely honoring those who fought in what it calls "the War for Southern Independence."

"We're celebrating the only president the Confederate States of America ever had," says Tom Strain, an organizer. "It's not about slavery. It's about remembering our history."

The sesquicentennial observances of the Civil War revealed as much about America's mindset about the Civil War as they did about who did what to whom in which battle. It coincided with a revival of notions such as secession and nullification, ideas that flourished in the South in the first half of the 19th century and should have been snuffed out by the Civil War but continue to flourish today.

Jefferson Davis wrote after his inauguration that when he looked at the throngs below, "I saw trouble and thorns innumerable." Today, 50 steps up from the street, standing on the brass star that marks the spot where Davis spoke, you can still see the thorns. Not just in the South, but the entire nation.

Any wonder vitriolic paralysis has become the norm in Washington? More than 100 former members of Congress, the "Former Members of Congress for Common Ground" sent an e-mail asking for "a change in rhetoric and tone that can lead to a focus on problem solving. This needs to begin now, especially as we head into the heat of the 2010 campaign," it implored to no avail.

The one destructive vitriolic rant Congressman John Boehner repeated on the campaign trail that I agree with is: "Your government is disrespecting you, your family, your job, your children. Your government is out of control," he said. "Do you have to accept it? Do you have to take it? Hell, no, you don't. That's what elections are for!"

That's something *We the Maids* must remember. Elections are to sweep out career politicians and sweep in maids to clean house – just like the Arab cleansing. Thanks, John.

The extreme conservative political vitriol is blasted on the airwaves and blogosphere by the conservative Republican Tea Party cheerleader in chief, moose hunter Sarah Palin. She targeted for defeat 20 congressional districts with cross-hairs of a gunsight on a campaign map in the 2010 midterm election posted on her Facebook page. Democratic Arizona Representative Gabrielle Giffords was one of the targets.

Palin said journalists and pundits trying to link her to the shooting were using the attack to incite hatred and violence that amounted to "blood libel," an anti-Semitic remark that is offensive to Jews. Palin was criticized from both the left and the right.

Eric Fuller, 63, a military veteran who was wounded in the knee during the Giffords assassination attempt in Tucson, was arrested after he took a picture of a Tea Party leader at a televised town hall meeting and yelled "You're dead."

As finger-pointing erupted in Washington and beyond over whether harsh political rhetoric played a role in motivating the attack, President Obama sought to calm the waters. "The forces that divide us are not as strong as those that unite us," he said.

Arizona has become ground zero for U.S. political divisions. The state voted to make the Colt revolver its official firearm and is pushing for laws focused on arming professors and others over 21 on Arizona's campuses. It's no surprise that Palin has bought a home there.

Its statewide "Gunfight at OK Corral" mentality put a gun to Gabby Giffords' head and fired at close range during a community outreach event in a Tucson shopping center parking lot. Miraculously, she survived. Six people were killed, including 9-year-old Christina Taylor Green and Arizona's chief federal judge, John Roll, 63. Giffords was one of 14 wounded.

Giffords is a Democrat but belongs to the more conservative wing of the party. She has advocated tougher law enforcement on the porous Mexican border and, incidentally, the right to gun ownership. But she had become a top target of the Tea Party movement because of her support of Obamacare.

The toxic tone of the national debate is certain to draw greater scrutiny. House Speaker Boehner declined an invitation to travel with President Obama to Arizona on Air Force One for a memorial service for the Tucson victims. Boehner and the Republicans had been scheduled to introduce laws to repeal Obama's health care reform and the Dodd-Frank legislation regulating financial institutions before the Giffords assassination attempt put their plans on hold.

Boehner, along with Senate Majority Leader Harry Reid and Senator Mitch McConnell, the Republican leader, also declined Obama's invitation to a state dinner in honor of China's President Hu Jintao. Talk about petty political acrimony and bush league politics.

"If this tragedy prompts reflection and debate – as it should – let's make sure it's worthy of those we have lost," Obama said of the Tucson tragedy.

Christina Taylor Green was born on 9/11. Her blossoming interest in politics and American democracy brought her to the Giffords event where she was shot and killed.

"I want us to live up to her expectations," Obama told the capacity crowd at the University of Arizona basketball arena – and to millions of others watching around the country and world. "I want our democracy to be as good as she imagined it."

The Department of Homeland Security has been warning for several years that right-wing extremism is on the rise, with a growing potential for violence. As Clarence Dupnik, the sheriff responsible for dealing with the Arizona shootings, put it, it's "the vitriolic rhetoric that we hear day in and day out from people in the radio business and some people in the TV business."

The randomness in which Christina was killed made her death particularly wrenching and sparked a debate over gun control and whether toxic political rhetoric helped fuel the incident. If her death promotes some real soul-searching, it could prove a turning point. If it doesn't, the child's atrocious death will be just the beginning.

It was the first step on the bloody road to Newtown, Connecticut; where 20 first-graders were slaughtered at Sandy Hook Elementary School on December 14, 2012. President Obama proposed sweeping changes to gun laws just over one month after the tragic shooting in Newtown. He signed 23 executive orders and called on Congress to pass specific initiatives "right away."

His proposals include research on the causes and prevention of gun violence, universal background checks, restoring a ban on military-style assault weapons, and limiting magazines to 10 rounds, plus strengthening prosecution and penalties for those who sell firearms to criminals. Here again, Obama hopes to split the Republican opposition.

"If you think we've suffered too much pain to allow this to continue, put down the paper, turn off the computer, and get your members of Congress on record," Obama wrote in an opinion piece in the *Connecticut Post*. "Ask them why getting an A-grade from the gun lobby is more important than giving parents some peace of mind when they drop their child off for first grade."

Obama used his fearsome grass roots campaign infrastructure to take on the National Rifle Association – and lost.

The president's aggressive frontal assault against the NRA was preceded by action at the state level, with New York becoming the first state in the wake of Newtown to enact the toughest gun laws in the nation.

The Newtown shooting along with one on Christmas Eve in Webster, New York, that killed two firefighters spurred New York lawmakers to move quickly – too quickly, according to the NRA.

At the local level, New York City Mayor Michael Bloomberg, co-chair of the bipartisan Mayors Against Illegal Guns, whose membership grew by 100 mayors following the Newtown shooting, commended both the president and vice president for "a bold and comprehensive plan to tackle gun violence."

In Los Angeles, City Councilman Paul Krekorian proposed that the city explore the feasibility of banning possession of high-capacity gun magazines, a first step toward instituting stricter city gun and ammunition laws.

From shooting ranges to churches, gun control was the subject of vigorous debate in the aftermath of the Sandy Hook shooting. Rallies to persuade gun owners to turn in their firearms to be destroyed competed with rallies that urged people to resell their firearms rather than destroy them.

The surge in domestic political terrorism is not surprising. Ohio State University historian Randolph Roth published a groundbreaking book,

*American Homicide,* that offers a theory of why Americans kill each other at such a high rate.

After meticulously tracing trends in violence and political power in the U.S. from colonial times to the present, Roth concludes that high homicide rates "are not determined by proximate causes such as poverty, drugs, unemployment, alcohol, race or ethnicity, but by factors ... like the feelings that people have toward their government and the lack of opportunities they have to earn respect without resorting to violence."

Roth's analysis in fact puts politics at the very root of the highest homicide rate of any First World democratic country. He points to the Civil War as the genesis of unrest even in peacetime. It was not simply a case of violence begetting violence. Rather, high homicide rates were the symptom of low overall political confidence. The Civil War, Roth says, was "a catastrophic failure in nation building," when a large percentage of the population lost faith in government and eyed their countrymen with distrust.

"Our high homicide rate started when we lost faith in ourselves and in each other," he says.

Conservative pundits like to argue that distrust for government is part of our birthright as Americans. And they're right. It's built into the system and can be found in the writings of Thomas Paine and Thomas Jefferson. But there is a difference between distrust and disdain. The tradition of truly hating government began with the Civil War and a nation literally torn apart by contrasting visions and mores.

Roth essentially believes, and I tend to accept his reasoning, that antagonism plays out today when elections leave half the nation feeling empowered and the other half disenfranchised. The more people who feel empowered, the lower the homicide rate. If people feel their government shares their values and acts on their behalf, they have greater trust and confidence in their dealings with others. Conversely, those who feel out of power and mistrustful of government carry those attitudes into everyday relationships, often with murderous results.

As Roth sees it, even activists and politicians – from the right and left – who sew bitter disdain for government are indirectly encouraging the mistrust that breeds violence. Does that suggest that Barack Obama's election caused a shift in rates of violence? You betcha! According to Roth, FBI data shows that in the first six months of 2009, urban areas that Obama carried saw the steepest drop in homicide rates since the mid-1990s.

During that same period, the states with the largest percentage of counties that voted more heavily Republican in 2008 than they did in 2004 saw an 11 percent rise in homicide in cities of over 100,000 residents.

It is time for *We the Maids* to reconsider and recalibrate the political weapons used in America's legislative bodies – and our streets – before the homicide rate gets totally out of control.

Obama's prime-time addresses in Tucson and Newtown were compared to President George W. Bush's speech to the nation after the attacks of September 11, 2001, and the memorial service that President Bill Clinton led after the bombing of the federal building that killed 168 people in Oklahoma City in 1995. But unlike 9/11 and Oklahoma City, which at least temporarily united a mournful country and quieted partisan divisions, the Arizona and Connecticut incidents had the opposite effect of inflaming the divide.

"Politics has become too personal, too nasty and perhaps too dangerous," said Jonathan Cowan of the centrist Democratic group Third Way. "Perhaps out of this senseless act some sense can return to our public discourse."

Both the Democrats and Republicans have a long history of promising to make changes in Washington – but doing nothing and ruining America in the process. The self-described angry Tea Party movement voters represent about 23% of the electorate. Most of them are Republicans. But most of the electorate is angry and tired of the bipartisan gridlock that has paralyzed Washington and have become apathetic because they have given up on and lost hope in the Founding Fathers' political noble dream.

The Tea Party movement reaffirms that America is ready for a new party that will get the country back to the founding constitutional principles of the Republic. But is the Tea Party the way forward?

I don't think so unless they can come up with a leader who can articulate how these 50 polarized states can become united again. Americans still believe their nation was meant for something bigger. They still seek a roadmap to the future, fractured though the solutions may appear. Tea Party fanaticism hardly seems like the answer.

Politics in America since the founding of the American Republic have been fluid, creative and accommodating to all points of view, at least up until recent times. The political gridlock in Washington today reinforced by *We the Apathetic Maids'* disgust and resignation to the political process, have left America divided and vulnerable to the deep challenges it faces at the dawn of the 21st century. Not just at home but globally. The engine of America's growth and prosperity can be fueled in the New World Order only by recharging and raising the living standards at home and in the undeveloped and developing world.

*We the Apathetic Maids* have to sweep out America's cultural civil battles and war and start to address the real issues facing us today if we are to grow and prosper culturally in the 21st century. Creative periods of human development inspire people to conceive and pursue new ideas and ideals with enthusiasm and passion. The Renaissance, the Industrial Revolution and the '60s have been witness to such creative periods. Isn't it time *We the Maids* get creative again and explore what new ideas we should be sweeping in at the dawn of the 21st century?

### New World Order

I watched the first two 2012 presidential debates between Obama and Romney in America, and the third one in Hong Kong. I watched all three debates with a handful of Americans – Democrats, Republicans and independents. The unanimous consensus, regardless of party affiliation, was that politics in America has become ugly, destructive and the win-at-all-cost mentality – financial and factual misrepresentation – must end if America's Founding Fathers' ideals are to continue being the world's beacon of hope in the New World Order.

The Republican-led House of Representatives vote to hold Attorney General Eric H. Holder in contempt for failing to disclose internal Justice Department documents in response to a subpoena in connection with the botched Arizona-based gun-running operation known as Operation Fast and Furious was brought up as a recent example. President Obama had invoked executive privilege to block the subpoena.

It was the first time in American history that Congress had imposed the sanction on a sitting member of a president's cabinet. As if that was not bad enough, the House Republicans also passed a civil contempt citation, which allows them to hire their own attorney and legal staff to file a civil lawsuit – at taxpayer expense, of course – asking a judge to force Holder to turn over any documents related to the case. What a waste of time and money. The entire exercise in June 2012 was intended to embarrass Holder and inflict political damage on Obama during the presidential race.

The incident had been brought up by Romney during the debates.

The vitriolic 2012 presidential campaign accelerated the confrontation between the two parties and it became clear that neither Democrats nor Republicans have any intention of reconciling. Confrontation has become the political recipe of the day. A recipe Obama carried into his second term of office.

After years of courting the Republicans, the president shifted into confrontation mode and transformed his re-election machine and volunteers into a political weapon to fight the Republican political arsenal.

Obama's new tax-exempt group called Organizing for Action will fight for the president's legislative priorities. The group, largely volunteer-driven, will tackle issues such as gun control, climate change and immigration reform. One of its first projects was spreading the word to people without health insurance about how they can get coverage under Obama's healthcare overhaul. Sure-fire recipes for more confrontation.

The art of political compromise has evaporated from Washington. Career politicians today are constantly campaigning. They have forgotten how to govern. For more than two centuries, politicians with competing convictions have found a way to reach common ground and move America forward.

"The 113th Congress has an opportunity to once again embrace compromise and understand that our differences are also our strength. They are what has made us the strongest and greatest democracy in the world," wrote former congressman Elton Gallegly in an op-ed piece in the *L.A. Times*.

The deep partisan divisions in Washington and in the wider electorate promised to get wider after President Obama's inauguration speech on January 21, 2013 – Martin Luther King Day.

Obama made it clear that he, like every president, was elected to lead and do what is right for the country, not just the party, special interest groups or financial backers.

America is about leading a united people by example, at home and abroad, and I hope it does so again soon – before it is too late. Obama's challenge to Republicans to work with him to bring about the changes necessary for America to become the united strong economic global power it once was is one I hope Republicans and independents will embrace. That is what made the United States of America the superpower it is.

### Overdue JFK Inaugural Moment
Today's United States is anything but united. It is a polarized land. A far cry from the country that President John F. Kennedy summoned Americans to with his famous inaugural address and call to service – "Ask not what your country can do for you; ask what you can do for your country."

His idealistic call for a united world to "explore the stars, conquer the deserts, eradicate disease, tap the ocean depths" reverberated around the world. I remember hearing them on a transistor radio in agricultural high school in Israel.

"Unfortunately, in today's environment, speeches are more likely to say, 'Ask not what you can do for your country; ask what you can do for your party'," says Mark McKinnon, a former adviser to both Republicans and Democrats who helped establish the nonpartisan organization No Labels.

Kennedy represented a new generation of leadership that became unacceptable to the establishment, because it was so radical and different than what they were used to. The New World Order Kennedy tried to instill in America was unacceptable to the military-industrial complex that Dwight Eisenhower warned the country about, and their anger and resentment was such that they decided it was in the country's best interest to replace him with a "good ol' boy" from Texas in order to perpetuate the war in Vietnam and various other parts of the world, from Latin America to Tibet, Africa and the Middle East.

Nevertheless, the dominant ideals that Kennedy outlined, among them service and freedom, remain a focus of American citizens today. Many believe America was meant for something bigger. They still seek a roadmap to the future. The Founding Fathers' ideals still rule. That is why to this day the words of Kennedy's inaugural have remained ingrained in the American consciousness.

"He seemed to give everyone the confidence that we could do whatever we wanted as a country," said Richard Donahue, who earned a prized ticket to the inauguration of Jan. 20, 1961. He is now a retired Boston attorney and trustee of the John F. Kennedy Library and Museum.

"Kennedy was trying to write words for the ages," says Richard Tofel, author of *Sounding the Trumpet: The Making of John F. Kennedy's Inaugural Address*. "Idealism and optimism are not always in style, but they continue to stand out and they continue to have real power."

The middle spectrum that Kennedy, Johnson and Nixon occupied have been muted by the far right and left that dominate the Republican and Democratic parties today.

The voice of reason and rational discussion – even debate – without political vitriol, has long been AWOL and its return is long overdue.

### *A Tree Grows in Manhattan*

When I lived in New York, one of my favorite places to visit was President Grant's Tomb on Riverside Drive and 122nd Street. It has a sweeping view of the Hudson River. Two circular ante-chambers display the flags under which Grant served, along with maps marking key battles. A single quotation, "Let us have peace," is chiseled into the pediment high above the entranceway.

Behind the tomb, inside a little fenced-in-area, is a ginkgo tree and a Chinese cork tree planted when the monument was completed in 1897 by two Chinese dignitaries, Li Hung Chang, Grand Secretary of State, and Yang Yu, Envoy Extraordinary and Minister Plenipotentiary. The quaint effect of these trees, and the descriptive plaque in English and Chinese, are a reminder of how deep and close the cultures and people of America and China really are. A perpetual quiet contrast to the very public cherry blossom trees given by Japan to America and planted along the Potomac in Washington.

JFK, LBJ, Vietnam, civil rights, 1960s flower power, Tiananmen, Arab Spring – all share something in common. They speak to the struggles of people to bring about change and honesty, freedom, peace and equality.

Robert McNamara, defense secretary under both Kennedy and Johnson, would come to agree with the flower children of the '60s many years later when, in his memoir, he said that he had decided that the Vietnam War was "wrong, terribly wrong."

Isn't it time former President George W. Bush and former Vice President Dick Cheney say the same about the Afghanistan and Iraq wars?

The admission by many Chinese government officials that the Cultural Revolution and the bloody crackdown in Beijing's Tiananmen Square in 1989 were folly and failures carries a ring of the despair that McNamara must have felt.

The Chinese flower children who flocked to Tiananmen for that fateful showdown were "not only the voice of a few Beijing students, but expressed the concerns of all the Chinese people," says Chinese dissident Bao Tong, who spent seven years in prison and remains under house arrest even today.

Bao says the Chinese government still rules by force. Some things change and some do not, at least not quickly.

But as the '60s proved, change is possible, especially when it is grounded in dedication and honesty. And so, let's dedicate the Third Revolution to the flower children, past and present, wherever they may be.

### Leaders

Tom Hayden, one of the Chicago Seven, became a California assemblyman and state senator representing Santa Monica. My then-wife Gail and I hosted fundraisers for him at our restaurant Scratch in the mid-'80s. We would discuss *Man's Fate* by Andre Malraux and other issues of the day.

"China has to open up more," Hayden would admonish me. "People will not stand still, even in Shanghai as *Man's Fate'* so eloquently articulates."

"Give it time," I would respond. "China cannot and will not allow the kind of dramatic change you propose today. Hell, even the U.S. won't! China learned the hard way during the Cultural Revolution what happens when you try to force artificial change. It has to evolve, gradually, organically within the culture of the country and visionary leaders."

I was attempting tonal humility, telling this to a political leader with a superb political track record of understanding mass movements.

"Let me tell you a story I heard recently that says it all," I continued. "Malcolm Forbes recently led a business delegation of Fortune 100 company CEOs to China. They met with Paramount Leader Deng Xiao Peng and started lecturing him on human rights and how he has to change the system. He mulled over their comments for a few moments and then

513

responded, 'Since you are all so rich and so smart, how would you like to buy lunch for every person in China for one day. I'll give you a limit of one dollar per meal. Do you think any one of you can do it?' he said, looking around at his distinguished visitors. None responded. 'I have to do it three times a day,' he concluded."

"Wow, that does make the point," Hayden responded. "Feeding 11/2 billion people is no easy task," he said, clearly impressed by a political master when he heard one. Real political leaders who pursue their convictions against all odds are rare and refreshing. They are essential in the New World Order.

Elected officials today are so preoccupied with sex, money and reelection that they ignore the constituency that got them elected in the first place and to whom they are responsible. Leaders, as Warren Bennis would tell me, "truly lead and don't worry about reelection."

Those who deliver economically survive no matter what their private peculiarities may be. The public doesn't really care about sex, drugs or rock 'n' roll when it comes to today's political leaders. Most baby boomers experimented or tried drugs. Barack Obama, Bill Clinton, Al Gore, Susan Mollinari, George W. Bush to name a few.

We're all aging rock 'n' rollers having a good time no matter what culture or revolution we choose to pursue into the 21st century. We've all partied and will probably continue to do so. So why continue to lie to our children?

While we were screwing our brains out in America and uniting the "counterculture," the Chinese were screwing their culture and themselves intellectually with the Cultural Revolution, but uniting as a country and people.
China's one-child policy hasn't helped their sex life much either. Actually, it has hurt families and children more.

The Cultural Revolution in China, notwithstanding its horrors and destruction, was one of the most honest civilizational upheavals. Put in the context of pronouncements made at a recent gathering of the National Peoples Congress – when government ministries were abolished, bureaucrats fired, Roosevelt New Deal-type infrastructure projects approved, human rights conventions signed – one has to step back and say the evolution has been honest, expensive and has given the people what they have been asking for regardless of the short-term consequences and criticism from America. These are some of the major advantages of having effective leaders running a country who do not have to worry about reelection.

The one flaw with democracy is that its leaders are constantly preoccupied with reelection. Fundraising and running. Former President Jimmy Carter said in a PBS program that all surviving presidents he talked to after he left the White House agreed that the job should be for one six-year term. The way things are now, one election runs into another. A lot of time is "lame quack time."

### Sexual Revolution

While enjoying the great uninhibited sex that America had to offer in the '60s, I didn't realize at the time that I was a foot soldier – navy diver is probably a more accurate description – in the sexual revolution. I thought it was just flower power. In reality there was another counterrevolution going on that was being led by liberated women on the pill. It took me a few years to figure that out.

As Linda Grant points out, "Because for 20 years—between the invention of the pill and the beginning of the AIDS epidemic—there was a moment that had never occurred in history before, a time when sex was free from the threats of both pregnancy and disease. From a woman's point of view, there were two great inventions, the tampon and the pill."

James R. Peterson in his book, *The Century of Sex: Playboy's History of the Sexual Revolution, 1990-1999,* adds another dimension. "What deterred sex was the fear of detection and the fear of infection. In 1943, doctors had figured out penicillin. Conception was taken care of by condoms, the IUD and the pill. And by the '60's no one cared about detection."

Discussing the sexual revolution with Hugh Hefner at the Playboy Mansion in Holmby Hills took on two planetary extremes whenever I went there with the "Godfather of Rock 'n' Roll", Bill Gazzari and his Vegas Pals or with L.A. City Councilman Zev Yaroslavsky. With Bill and his pals it was sex, drugs and rock 'n' roll in the infamous Grotto, staircases, any one of the rooms or up on the roof. With Zev they were rather staid affairs. Zev even held a fundraiser at the mansion. It was hard to recognize some of the bunnies fully dressed.

Discussing the incomplete accomplishments of the sexual revolution, Linda Grant believes, "The year of the hard body has given rise to the belief that a second sexual revolution is imminent, one that would accomplish three things: reassert the gains made in the '60s and vanquish the New Right; abandon the sex-negative cul-de-sac along which feminism had taken female desire in the '70s; and formulate an overdue language for the clitoris ... . A clitoris-and-vagina-centered sexual and cultural revolution is an inevitable next step.

"No sexual revolution can be fully accomplished without a proper equation between male and female sexuality."

The play *Vagina Dialogues* is in the vanguard of this revolution.

Penis envy may be a thing of the past now that it has been shown that the clitoris is 10 times bigger than the average person realizes. Dr. Helen O'Connell, a urology surgeon, reached that conclusion after years of research. Whereas no man is likely to be 10 times bigger than a gal ever guessed, the clitoris extends deep into the body and is twice as large as depicted in most anatomy texts.

"There is a lot of erectile tissue down there that is not drawn in any anatomy textbooks, " O'Connell told *New Scientist* magazine.

Almost a century ago, among the various cures for women suffering from sexual "hysteria," the symptoms of which included "wandering of attention, insomnia and irritability," was manual massage of the vulva by physicians or midwives, resulting in "hysterical paroxysm." The "service" was available until the invention of a floor-mounted vibrator called the Chattanooga, which did the job much faster and was on sale by 1904 to doctors only. By 1918, women could buy their own portable vibrator, with attachments – "very useful and satisfactory for home service" – from the Sears catalog.

Sex three times a week can shave years off one's looks, concludes David Weeks, a Scottish neuro-psychologist at the Royal Edinburgh Hospital after surveying 3,500 sex-happy subjects on both sides of the Atlantic over a 10-year period who responded to his 1988 ad in *New Scientist* magazine.

"I had expected that the usual combination of good diet and exercise would do it, but it turns out it's sex," said Weeks. "I would say people who look young for their age, like Goldie Hawn or Robin Williams, have active sex lives."

With these kind of statistics, the Bush administration's push to spend millions on selling the virtues of virginity and abstinence as a government policy was bound to fail as an unsustainable fallacy. The virginity moral order only encourages mutual masturbation, oral sex and anal sex. Is that what the Christian evangelical right really want to encourage? Even family values superstar Britney Spears admitted that her avowed virginity spin was popular fiction.

### The Wave

Studying Mao and Sino-Soviet communism in the States in the '60s while the Vietnam War and Cultural Revolution were in full swing – and hanging out in Haight-Ashbury with Timothy Leary disciples, listening to Janis Joplin and Jimi Hendrix, did not fully prepare me for bringing Jan and Dean to China in 1986.

China during the Cultural Revolution, like the Bible Belt bonfires in America, was burning Elvis records and all other rock 'n' roll recordings. Imagine my surprise when I was asked to bring a rock band from America.

The idea for the concert evolved at Scratch. Julia Chu, who later became my second wife, had just brought an all-girl band to China at the insistence of her boss, whose daughter was a band member. Wham had just completed a limited tour. The bamboo curtain was parting and China was ready to expose itself to the decadence of the West in a moderate dose.

"Can you help me find and bring a typical American band that is not political, no sex, drugs or rock 'n' roll that people can enjoy and understand?" was the brief Julia gave me after we met in the summer of 1986.

Great, I thought to myself, even the Monkees don't meet that criteria. Julia along with Mary Catherine, producer of *Knotts Landing,* who was a Scratch regular and friend, and I got together at the restaurant after a meeting with Donny Osmond that afternoon. Tony Pastor had set up the meeting with Donny, who had visited China as a tourist and loved it. We could not agree on financial terms and had to come up with another act.

Dr. Don Altfeld, lyricist of the Jan and Dean hit *Little Old Lady From Pasadena* in 1964 who had overheard our discussion joined us and volunteered to deliver Jan and Dean if he could join the tour in some capacity. Talk about karma, luck and timing! The Chinese victims of the Cultural Revolution, especially Deng Fang, Deng Xiao Ping's son who was crippled after being thrown from a balcony, could relate to Jan, who had never fully recovered from *Dead Man's Curve*. That and the innocent sound of surf were all that mattered.

The cars, woodies, deuce coupes, surfboards, the surf sound and surf bunnies were perfect. Having worked as a still photographer on Dale Davis surf movies when I first arrived in Los Angeles in 1966, and with a cameo appearance in *Golden Boys,* I could relate. Besides, Jan and Dean weren't signed to any label at the time and the lack of hassle with lawyers simplified matters even more.

The tour was a smash and a movie of the tour, *Jan & Dean in China,* still makes the rounds on late-night reruns. Even Jiang Zeming, the mayor of

Shanghai at the time, attended the concert.

"The California surfboards are riding the waves of change in China," I told Jiang as we shook hands and he thanked me for bringing "an acceptable American band to China." The bamboo curtain was definitely on its way up. Granted it was not lifting fast enough for many Western governments or political activists. Nevertheless, to most average Chinese, it was unbelievable! We were riding the cutting edge wave of a new cultural revolution in China.

The first few nights of the concert, the audience was polite, in deference to the political leaders in attendance, and merely applauded after each song, no matter how much they wanted to dance in the aisles, clap and shout during the performance. Jan and Dean and the band members were embarrassed and thought they were not being appreciated or understood.

"Don't worry, wait until there are no officials in the audience and you'll see a dramatic change. Keep doing your thing and just be patient," I kept telling the band members.

Sure enough, the audience finally exploded into song, clapping, dancing and rushing the stage to be closer to the performers the minute the officials left. A few heads were bashed, including that of the student body president of Fudan University. Student demonstrations followed in the streets of Shanghai in December of 1986 as we left for Hong Kong and denied witnessing any acts of violence when repeatedly questioned by the Hong Kong press.

The Jan and Dean concert tour contributed to China's ride on the wave of democracy into the 21st century. Listening to Bill Clinton wrap up his nine-day tour of China in 1998, I couldn't help but smile when he invited the leaders in Beijing to "ride the wave of change and take China fully into the 21st century." We beat him to it.

The following year, when we had the U.S. and Canadian ice skating champions perform at the opening of the 1987 Shanghai Arts Festival, I ran into Elton John at the Jing Jiang Hotel. He was there with his soccer team from England who had just won a match against the Chinese National team. I approached him, introduced myself, and mentioned how I and Bernie Taupin, his lyricist partner, rode together because Bernie kept his horse at my ranch house in L.A. Bad idea. He was not on speaking terms with Bernie. He had been asked not to perform in China. What did he expect. They didn't even know Elvis, the Rolling Stones, Grateful Dead or the Beatles. The biggest stars were Jan and Dean. In China, he was just the owner of the Watford football club.

When we brought XCL, a California rock 'n' roll band, to play in the Midnight Express in the Shanghai Hilton in 1992, our earlier suspicions of living in the midst of a new cultural revolution were confirmed. Whenever the band would do its rendition of Cui Jian's *Nothing to My Name,* the anthem for the student protests at Tiananmen in 1989, it would bring the entire audience to their feet dancing and clapping. The Midnight Express, a fast-food joint, morphed into a nightclub at 8.30 p.m. And rocked until 2 in the morning. Ocassionally it rocked until the wee hours until we were asked to knock it off because of complaints from hotel guests who couldn't sleep. The place would be packed with people drinking and dancing. Lines would form outside and curl around the block. People would stand in the freezing, snow-swept nights of Shanghai waiting to get in. Until we brought XCL, most foreign bands visiting China were Filipino.

We kept XCL in town for six months. During their stay other foreign bands were allowed to enter China and the rock 'n' roll culture was there to stay. Visiting the different clubs in Shanghai and Beijing today, I get a knot in my stomach thinking of how much China has changed since those ground-breaking days.

Watching the movie *Mao's Last Dancer* in Los Angeles in October 2010 brought a tear to my eye. It is the true story of a ballet performer who defected to the U.S. in 1981 in an incident that sparked a politically charged standoff between China and the U.S. It was a poignant reminder of what I went through in bringing about cultural exchanges between the two countries. The film is the redemptive story of a man who, through talent and determination, is able to defy and defeat a powerful government.

## Woodstock Nation

The outdoor rock concerts in China today remind me of those big outdoor concerts in America in 1969. All were celebrating a seismic explosion in conscious rock – music put forward by the Beatles, Bob Dylan and "the movements," anti-war, civil rights, feminist, ecological, psychedelic and served up by the likes of Jefferson Airplane, Santana, Janis Joplin, The Who, Creedence Clearwater Revival, Canned Heat, Joe Cocker and The Band.

Today Beijing, Shanghai and Chengdu rock to homegrown bands and Cui Jian, the grandfather and godfather of Chinese rock, who organizes Woodstock-like festivals at Lijiang and plays in Beijing clubs. I remember when he was banned and had to be secretive about his movements. We had met in the early '90s to explore his musical options and *Beijing Bastards,* a movie he was producing. He was seeking funding. It was a memorable meeting but we never did get around to doing anything together.

Finding out that this rocker was actually a classical musician raised in a classical musical family blew me away. Cui Jian's father was a trumpet player in the People's Liberation Army, which inspired his taste for classical music. He joined the Beijing Symphony Orchestra in 1981 and played with it for seven years. Hearing the Beatles in 1985 got him into the electric guitar and a new rocking cultural revolution in China.

His dream was to fuse his musical passions – rock and classical – a dream I was delighted to see come true in his collaboration with the Beijing Symphony Orchestra in two concerts in Beijing on New Year's Eve and New Year's Day 2011.

Cui Jian is not only a revolutionary rocker, but an environmentalist and crafty concert organizer as well. He performed at a two-hour outdoor concert, Green Now, on June 5, 2010, to celebrate World Environment Day at the Shanghai World Expo.

As an explosion of free-wheeling concerts across China is demonstrating, local Communist Party cadres have come to realize that pierced rockers flailing around a mosh pit caused by periodic downpours a-la-Woodstock, are not necessarily interested in upending single-party rule. Young Chinese fans just want to enjoy the right of freedom of expression.

Vendors hawk everything from vintage Mao buttons to "grass-mud horses," a mythical creature that has become a symbol of defiance against Internet censorship.

### Reflections

Whenever I was feeling down while living in or visiting Shanghai, I'd head for the Cotton Club, which was the closest thing to Bert's Bar at the FCC in Hong Kong. Slouching back in my seat at the Cotton Club leisurely puffing a nice Cuban while listening to Mathew do an Eric Clapton blues tune and absorbing the meaning of the lyrics, I couldn't help thinking of the New Wave cultural and political revolution sweeping China.

Greg "Mathew" Smith, a self-confessed lapsed Mormon missionary in the Philippines and Taiwan, became disenchanted with the church and its ways. He decided to become a saloon keeper, and he was a blues singer extraordinaire.

"Why sing to convert people who have more soul and morals than we do?" he asked himself one day. "Besides, there's more money, fun and personal satisfaction in what I'm doing now," he told me.

American music represents freedom to the Chinese. Allen Ginsberg, Jack Kerouac and many of the other Beat writers who howled at Establishment America in the 1950s had their creative DNA encoded by the music.

"In this modern jazz, they heard something rebellious and nameless that spoke to them, and their lives knew a gospel for the first time," wrote Beat author John Clellon Holmes. "It was more than a music; it became an attitude toward life, a way of walking, a language and a costume. These introverted kids ... now felt somewhere at last."

Half a century later and half a world away, Feng Yu Cheng, an introverted 24-year-old from Chengdu, finds his voice in the jazz trumpet he plays at Shanghai's Cotton Club.

In Beijing, Sanlitun is a 260-meter-long strip with people packed into 30-odd bars, restaurants and nightclubs listening to great local bands. What remarkable changes since Jan and Dean, I kept mentally muttering to myself like an off balance-street person. The club scene in Sanlitun is mind-boggling. From underground signless holes in the wall to state of the art New York-style clubs. Listening to Brain Failure sing *Anarchy in the PRC* brought back a flood of memories. Both from my American and China rock scene experiences.

North Sanlitun used to be a nondescript Beijing commercial street selling household items near the foreign embassy area. In 1995, two young Chinese entrepreneurs invested $12,000 and opened Yungsheng, the first bar on the street. The rest followed. Now that the Communist Party has expanded membership to include entrepreneurs, Xu Jian, night shift manager of the Boys & Girls Pub, has been appointed secretary of the bar street's Chinese Communist Party sub-branch committee. It gives a whole new meaning to "party on."

"Now people know that we are not bad guys, even though we do rock 'n' roll," said *Confucius Says* vocalist Qiu Ye. *Confucius Says* established a style that critics say is the root of traditional Beijing rock 'n' roll. Its lyrics, steeped in ancient poems, archaisms and Buddhist literature, are set to the beat of American rock with a Beijing flavor all its own.

The hustlers on Bar Street, as Sanlitun is known, are West African. Tempted by easily obtained student or tourist visas in their home nations that are often swapped for bogus work and business permits on arrival, or simply left to expire, scores of young Nigerians, Sudanese, Ghanaians and Liberians have taken up residency. They aggressively peddle drugs and have sown the seeds of creeping racism among the Chinese towards Africa.

Tree Village between Beijing's university belt and the technology park Shangdi in the heart of the capital is a migrant settlement where underground musicians live not far from a landfill where ragpickers inhabit brick hovels. There are other "rock villages" in the suburbs. Dongbeiwang and Huoying. The hardcore grunge and punk scene rivals anything seen in America during the '60s cultural revolution. Sex, sex and more sex with drugs, drugs and more drugs is the norm.

The patron saint of Chinese punks is the late Kurt Cobain, front man for America's seminal grunge band Nirvana. His persona – unloved son, alienated wanderer, outcast who did drugs and shot himself to kill the pain – inspires Chinese youths trapped in boring lives. They wear Cobain T-shirts and pound out Nirvana riffs on their guitars. Cobain, too, was self-taught, and Chinese fans find meaning in his lyrics such as "come as you are."

The fact that Cobain was in the forefront of the grunge scene and not punk is missed by most Chinese because grunge was misinterpreted as punk when his music was introduced to China. Not an unusual misinterpretation and "misunderstanding" – musically and politically.

Along with its musical awakening, China is also undergoing a phenomenal sexual revolution that makes what America experienced in the '60s look tame by comparison. Young people in their 20s who've had sex with more than 100 partners are not uncommon. Many meet on the Internet where they indulge their fantasies or find partners.

China's party scene has spread from Beijing and Shanghai across China's cities like a virus. Chengdu is now China's party capital. It has more bars than Shanghai, though its population of 10.5 million is half the size. It has about 3,000 pubs and karaoke bars and some 4,000 teahouses that are often packed with people playing or betting on mahjong, playing cards and listening to professional ear pickers.

Chengdu ranked last in income in a survey of residents in 10 mainland cities. Its residents earn almost half of what Shanghai residents do. But Chengdu rated higher than Shanghai and every other city except Hangzhou in "happiness," a '60s attitude that the rest of China and America need more of.

The mellow pace of the city – its music, bar scene and laid-back culture – was spawned by its two-millennium-old irrigation system. Du Jiang Yan, as it's called, was built in 256 BC to control and channel the waters of the Min River, which had caused floods when torrential waters rushed down the mountains.

"The irrigation system solved almost all the problems in the local agricultural industry and made Chengdu free of any natural disasters for 2,000 years," says Tan Jihe, a researcher at Sichuan Provincial Academy of Social Sciences.

It is no accident that Sichuan's capital of Chengdu features heavily in the movie *Kung Fu Panda 2*. Mount Qingchong, spicy dandan noodles, mapo tofu and hot pot all appear in the movie. It's not just the pandas that are laid back and cool.

Having been there, and having advised on the advance work and filming of one of the first foreign TV series with an episode filmed in China, *Young Indiana Jones,* in the early '90s, I am thrilled by the Sino-American fusion of film, music and just about every other kind of art.

Taiwan boy-bands and beauty contests that were banned in China are now breaking the latest cultural barriers, the way Jan and Dean did, and are reluctantly and quietly being welcomed by the officials. Boy-band F4 has contributed to the cementing of cross-strait relations, much like Jan and Dean did to U.S.-Sino relations. They helped bring down the barriers between the mainland and Taiwan more rapidly, with music and commerce rather than war.

Beauty contests were banned historically because they were the means by which emperors and the powerful selected their wives and concubines. Zhou Ling won the Miss China title in 2002 in an underground competition held by a Miss Universe-sanctioned event. When she was declared the surprise 2002 second runner-up at the Miss Universe contest in Puerto Rico, beamed live around the world, it became impossible for the government to deny the existence of beauty pageants. Consequently, China went on to host the 2003 Miss Universe pageant and many others.

Needless to say, Hong Kong is still the electrical socket between China and the American current. Its music scene and drugs have been an integral part of its cultural fabric since colonial days.

### Burned Out and Sold Out

Burned-out youth who sleep all day and party all night was something I had experienced in America in the '60s and '70s. But seeing it in China today is still difficult to fully digest. Chinese youth drop ecstasy, cruise the nightclubs and have sex with teenage girls—sometimes two at a time—in $12 hotel rooms. Shenzhen, indeed, is a good place to look for pioneers of China's new blitzed-out fringe culture. The city has become known for rampant corruption, lawlessness and sleaze. To the city's youth, the future seems to be one of greed, selfishness, loveless sex and loneliness. Ideals have no value.

"That stuff is bullshit," they say. "Why do people think that life should have meaning?"

Jia Hongsheng, a mainland Chinese action-movie hero, personifiess the growing pains of modern China. He went from superstar to drugged-out dropout. A nervous breakdown or two along the way, institutionalized and then rehabilitated with a new movie *Quitting,* which sums it all up.

What happened? In 1989, the students on the streets of Beijing, calling for democracy and a cleaner government, were heartbreakingly idealistic. They were in love with America, struggling to absorb everything they could of the West, desperate to be part of the changes that were sweeping China. I know first-hand because I was there. But after the crackdown at Tiananmen, the dreams of a generation died. The government made a cynical pact with the people: You're free to get rich, but stay out of politics. Most young people accepted the bargain and now struggle to get into university and find good jobs.

The Communist Party has bought the souls of most citizens since the late 1970s, and more particularly since 1989: extraordinary economic freedom, and considerable social, cultural and even intellectual freedom, so long as they do not rattle the central political pillars of the party-state. In this regard, Nobel Laureate Liu Xiaobo is not comparable to Nelson Mandela or Ayn San Suu Kyi, leaders of oppressed mass movements.

One must acknowledge, as the Nobel committee did in its citation, that China's unprecedented hybrid version of authoritarian capitalism has lifted hundreds of millions out of poverty and is delivering benefits for many of its citizens in many ways. Unlike Myanmar or apartheid in South Africa, the Chinese state enjoys a great deal of support from its people. The true tests will come when economic growth slows and more political freedoms are demanded by the people.

Speaking of Myanmar, a brief sidebar. Hip-hop and comedy are providing an outlet for that beleagured country's youth and protest movement, much like it did in the U.S. in the '60s. Thxa Soe blends traditional Burmese songs with computer-generated beats and his fluid hip-hop lyrics wrapped in rhymes and youthful argot make it a perfect modern format for subtly spreading an anti-authoritarian message.

The Moustache Brothers, Myanmar's only political satire show and arguably the world's bravest stand-up comics, make fun of the ruling military junta. Between the two brothers, they have spent 12 years in jail for speaking out against the government. Unlike most Chinese and Americans, they are not burned out or apathetic. They are actively networking and waiting for the right economic frustrations to bubble to the surface all over the country at the same time, like the Arab cleansing revolutions sweeping North Africa and the Middle East.

Americans, like their Chinese counterparts, are burned out and have dropped out. Alienated and apathetic. *We the People* all sold out, and whatever wasn't sold was hijacked, something all citizens in America, China and worldwide want to reclaim.

Burnt out and sold out to such a degree in China that the government was comfortable enough to allow the hit musical *Les Miserables* to become the first Broadway production to debut there. The musical, adapted from Victor Hugo's tale of street urchins, students and reformed thieves plotting a new future for France, had powerful echoes with China's own turbulent history. The liberation of China by the Communist Party and the Tiananmen protests being the most obvious. During the Tiananmen protests, the popular *Les Mis* song *Do You Hear the People Sing?* was broadcast over loudspeakers throughout the square. Talk about revolution and alienation!

Street urchins, kids under 18, make up China's fastest-growing criminal group. Gangs have become surrogate families for abandoned youth, just like in America. Police routinely arrest gangs of youth aged 13 to 15 for rape, violence and vandalism. Lost and alienated in a moral vacuum, young Chinese are turning to crime.

And it's not only alienated youth that sell out to sex and drugs. For many bright attractive college students, sex is a career step and many students become escorts or mistresses to wealthy sugar daddies to enhance their career prospects. No different than the more than 250,000 co-eds in the U.S. looking for sugar daddies to fund their college educations. Many attractive college students who moonlight as mistresses or escorts can't imagine getting married – they have lost faith in male monogamy and hate the idea of playing the role of the wife, sitting at home while their husbands cavort with younger women.

Alienation, in fact, has become a growth business in China. People are alienated by corrupt party officials; unemployment as state enterprises hemorrhage jobs and families dissolve as rural populations disperse into the cities, leaving citizens rootless. Punk rock, the sound of disaffected youth, has now also become one of the hottest alternative trends in urban China. China has more James Dean wannabes than the entire populations of America and Europe combined – rebels without a clue. What about America? Isn't it a country of rebels with a cause?

*Coming of Age*

Having lived in China in the late '80s and early '90s as a resident with a green card who was bringing Hollywood and rock bands to China, I got to go to some pretty exclusive clubs in Beijing, Shanghai and many other Chinese cities. What amazed me was the arrogance and self-centeredness of the princelings and princesses of the communist revolutionaries who transformed and restored the world's most populous country to again become its wealthiest. They sure knew how to spend their wealthy parents' money in nightclubs. Having hung out in some of the coolest clubs in Beverly Hills and New York City where money flowed like the Yangze or the Nile, I was blown away by how China's *ballinghou,* the post-'80s selfish, apathetic and materialistic generation, made America's big spenders look like pikers.

China's "Me Generation" was born after the adoption of the 1979 one-child policy and were raised like the best of America's spoiled brats.

Hanging out in these nightclubs with former *zhiqing,* the intellectual youths of Mao's Cultural Revolution who were sent to be reeducated in the countryside communes, who are now government officials responsible for censorship of the Hollywood television series and movies I was selling their party and country, was the ultimate trip, especially when we were tripping out in Los Angeles, Las Vegas and New York.

At the end of 1968, Mao wrote in the *People's Daily* that young people who had already attended school for some years had to go to rural areas and be "reeducated" by poor farmers. But before that, as early as 1953, some "outstanding" students had given up their comfortable lives in cities and voluntarily thrown themselves into the villages. They were highly praised by Mao and became the models for the country's youth. It is estimated that from the 1950s to 1978, when the movement ended, about 17 million teenagers were sent to these remote villages. Since the 1980s, most of them have returned to cities.

These lost youths of Mao's Cultural Revolution are now being honored in several museums across the country, including Young Intellectuals' Square in Shanghai, with a museum and an old train, like the ones that took them to the countryside. It is a long overdue tribute to their resilience and survival, much like Deng Xiaoping, the father of China's new cultural and economic revolution.

China's Cultural Revolution was a civil war unlike any country has ever experienced. In August 1966, the year I moved from New York to Los Angeles to continue my studies in comparative government, including Sino-Soviet communism, the Cultural Revolution started. August 1966 is known as Red August – *hong bayue* – for the supporters of the great Proletarian Cultural Revolution. Red symbolizes revolution and the ardor for uncompromising and radical change. For them the slogan of the day was "rebellion is justified." Sound familiar?

"Bloody August," the opening salvo of the Cultural Revolution, consisted of verbal abuse, ransacking and murder that set the tone for the devastation that was to follow. The pent-up fury of the masses was not just against the halls of power, but the socialist state's callous rule. The party's arrogant elitism, its entrenched system of privilege and the yawning gap between its high-minded rhetoric and day-to-day reality, all fed into a frenzy that eventually saw the country awash in blood.

What blows me away today is the bright red colors of Chinese fashion. What a contrast to the drab dress code limited to baggy, military-style garb of blue, black, green and grey of the decades of Cultural Revolution. Jeans, tank tops and high fashion are now the uniform of the day.

The new China is captured in the documentary *Young and Restless in China,* which shows the waves of change since the Cultural Revolution and the angst and dissatisfaction of China's youth created by the ideological vacuum between the country's communist past and schizophrenic present. No wonder James Cameron's *Avatar* was such a hit in China.

The Chinese take on the movie centers on the fight of ordinary people against the all-engulfing greed of real estate developers. In Chinese parlance, the Na'vi would be called "nail houses," people who refuse to give up their legally owned properties. They protect their rights and houses and stick out like nails amid a field of debris. The bulldozer has become a sign of both progress and threat.

The growing confusion and conflicts created by the political spin of the proponents of traditional Chinese and Western politics, culture and music manifests itself in another sphere – medicine.

### Chinese Herbs

Traditional Chinese medicine shops in Hong Kong are now branching out to the U.S. McGraw-Hill heir Bob McGraw has invested his personal fortune to bring *luohanguo* medicines to America. Tried and tested though centipede and leech remedies may be, centuries of effectiveness cut no ice when the FDA, goaded by the pharmaceutical industry and the press, demands scientific proof that exotic remedies really work. Chinese traditional medicines have been around 10 times longer than the U.S. itself, let alone the FDA.

The FDA has been too preoccupied for years worrying about the proper labeling for condoms to worry about Chinese herbs. I'm not kidding. Condom labeling has become another battleground in America's cultural wars. Social conservatives who advocate abstinence believe condoms encourage sex so they lobbied to get labels that emphasize that proper condom use "greatly reduces, but does not eliminate" all risk of sexually transmitted diseases. Previously, the FDA warning labels on condoms warned only of allergic reactions to latex. Planned Parenthood argues that adding caveats to condom labels could discourage their use and thus increase the likelihood of unprotected sex. As if America doesn't have more pressing issues to address, like Chinese medicines that might benefit all Americans regardless of their political or sexual proclivities.

If Chinese medicine is no more than some form of Taoist quackery with no proven effectiveness, one would expect that by now that fact would have been noticed. It's tough to pull the wool over the eyes of so many Chinese for so many centuries.

The herbal practice is based on qi, the life force present in all living things that travels along 12 major meridians – energy and communication pathways – in the body. When qi flows smoothly, you're healthy. But if qi is blocked, stagnated or deficient, illness comes knocking. It's an unseen energy, the way emotions are invisible energy. These forces can contribute to health or disease – a mind-body connection finally being acknowledged in Western medicine.

Some Chinese medicine practitioners believe dreams are early signs of physical problems.

"The simplest link between dreams and the body is a similarity in shape," says Dr. Liu Jie. "For example, if you dream of an overpass, it could correspond to the colon, because they have a similar structure."

Likewise, dreaming of a pond or small lake might indicate a bladder problem. Dreaming of the sky or clouds could refer to the lungs needing air. Mountain climbing could suggest a problem with the back.

References to acupuncture can be traced to about 2700 BC. Even the word "medicine" fails to encompass the full range of meaning in traditional Chinese views on health. Chinese medicine is based on the complex philosophy of yin-yang about balance within the human body, which is the core of traditional Chinese medicine.

"An experienced traditional medicine doctor can feel a person's pulse and know what's wrong with him and cure him. It requires a very strong sensibility and the experience of feeling the pulse of thousands of people," says Liang Rong, a professor at the Beijing University of Chinese Medicine.

"In Western medicine, if a doctor examined 10 different people who had similar symptoms, or even the same disease, he might prescribe the same treatment 10 times in a row," says Dr. Albert Leung Wing-nang, associate head of the School of Chinese Medicine at Hong Kong Baptist University. "In traditional Chinese medicine, the doctor might see the same 10 people and prescribe something entirely different for each."

Herbal medicine shops in Hong Kong are also the gateway to America for these remedies, where people are embracing and using them by the millions.

Millions of Americans also undergo acupuncture treatment every year and more doctors are learning the science. "Battlefied acupuncture" is applied to the most prevalent combat injury, concussions or mild brain trauma, with results that doctors say are "off the charts." However, due to the lack of laws governing traditional Chinese medicine in the U.S., insurance companies refuse to pay for such treatments. Sounds to me like the pharmaceutical lobby is doing an effective job of protecting Western medicine, and wounded American vets be damned.

The truth is that FDA approval is not an absolute guarantee of safety. Take Viagra, for example. Hundreds of men who took the little blue pill for erectile dysfunction have died. That surely exceeds any harm caused by the use of herbal products over the years.

The FDA in July 2010 did finally approve the sale of one Chinese company's dietary supplement – one small step for mankind. It signaled hope that more of these ancient remedies might find their way into the American marketplace now dominated by Big Pharma.

Green tea from China has been readily accepted in America. Today, it is not only sold as a cornucopia of loose tea leaves, but the brew's essence has been distilled and added to health bars, supplements, diet aids, gum, candy bars, soft drinks and skin creams.

Another Chinese practice taking root in America is *zuo yuezi,* or "sitting the month" after giving birth, a regimen of food and rest to recover from the rigors of childbirth. *Yuezi* is based on ancient theories of Chinese herbal medicine dividing foods into "warm" and "cold" categories. Each food is linked to a health benefit for new mothers. Liver replenishes lost blood, green papaya stimulates milk production and kidney helps with aches and pains.

The Chinese government has decided to promote traditional medicine throughout the world. To this end the government has launched an industry alliance whose members include Peking University, Beijing University of Chinese Medicine, the Health Ministry's Development Center for Medical Science and Technology and 12 pharmaceutical companies.

China has signed more than 90 agreements related to traditional medicine cooperation with 70 countries and regions. Traditional Chinese medicine has spread and is now practiced in more than 160 countries.

The wall between mainstream and traditional Chinese medicine is finally crumbling, thanks to the work of free-thinking doctors.

"Orthopaedists can send patients to see physiotherapists. I don't see why family doctors can't work hand in hand with Chinese medicine practitioners to help the sick," says Donald Li Kwok-tung, a specialist in family medicine in Hong Kong.

I am delighted to see that Americans in the *twilight* of the Old World Order are embracing unconventional care as never before – and researchers are catching up. A study in 1997 showed that 83 million Americans sought out herbalists, chiropractors and other unconventional practitioners. Americans paid more visits to these healers, 629 million, than to primary care physicians, 386 million, and the cost of the whole endeavor topped $27 billion. Reliance on alternative practitioners grew by nearly 50 percent during the closing decade of the last millennium!

Chinese herbs, marijuana, and hemp have been shown to benefit their users. George Washington grew hemp. The first American flag was made from it, which may explain why some people enjoy burning it. The Declaration of Independence was originally drafted on it and a lot of people have gotten high and mellowed out from it. So why ban it and arrest people like Woody Harrelson for planting it and Willie Nelson for smoking it? It can be taxed, it is environmentally friendly and should be legalized and licensed along with marijuana and all the Chinese herbs the Food and Drug Administration can't figure out. The Chinese and Asians have only been testing them in the best labs known to mankind – a quarter of the world's population – for several thousand years!

The integration of Chinese and American drugs, like the two countries' political culture, is becoming common practice that will continue to blend as we learn from each other and grow in the New World Order.

### Cross-Pollination Wave
The Chinese impact on U.S. culture is apparent everywhere these days: in movies, fashion, food, nightlife, advertising, art and publishing and even McDonald's worldwide television commercials created in China. And why not? Watching first lady Michelle Obama sashay in her Jason Wu gowns on inauguration night in January 2009 and 2013 were refreshing reminders of the influence Chinese designers have in America. Seeing Chinese designers Richard Chai, Alexander Wang and Jason Wu named the best of the new breed by the Council of Fashion Designers of America during New York Fashion Week 2010 was the ultimate endorsement and confirmation.

Jimmy Choo's shoes and handbags are synonymous with elegance and style everywhere in the world, including Hollywood and the White House on Michele Obama.

Chinese sculptor Lei Yixin won the commission to create the centerpiece for the Martin Luther King National Memorial in Washington. Lei sees nothing unusual in a Chinese artist heading a major U.S. project.

"Martin Luther King belonged to the whole world," he says.

Does anyone seriously still doubt that?

Watching Shaolin monks shed their familiar robes in favor of hip gear and modern moves at a theater festival performance in the Polish city of Poznan in July 2010 was another revolutionary cultural eye-opener.

The ultimate, and one of my favorite cross-cultural pollinations, are the McRomance couples who exchange McNuptials. Weddings under the golden arches are on offer in Hong Kong, where couples who met in McDonald's or went there on their first date get married. Couples can tie the knot with Ronald McDonald in attendance. They can also McParty on their wedding anniversaries with their children.

Western cultural imperialism is so overpowering that many children in China think Christmas is the biggest Chinese holiday. Even bigger than Chinese Lunar New Year! Cheerleading is another American cultural icon taking the world and China by storm.

Style, fashion, cuisine, music, art, literature, television shows, movies, herbs and stock markets transcend national boundaries. People listen, watch, eat, wear and buy what appeals to their sense of personal aesthetics, growth and benefit. That is why no repressive police force can suppress American cultural influence. The Soviet Union failed, the Eastern European Communist block failed and China failed. So will Iran and Saudi Arabia, and any other repressive regime that establishes a constabulary to counter and suppress Western influence. And the Internet is only speeding up the inevitable.

Malls in America celebrate Chinese New Year to promote sales, Americans own Chinese stock, and even ride rickshaws at the Irvine Spectrum in Southern California, transporting people from their cars in the parking lot to the ticket booth. It's about time the West was influenced and fused by an Eastern cultural revolution. Why should the influence go only one way? The cross-pollination of both cultures and civilizations in the fields of medicine, drugs, culture and politics benefits all.

Mahjong, the Chinese board game in which players attempt to collect suits of tiles, similar to Western card games such as bridge and rummy, has gone global. I know Americans who play the game regularly.

Today there are world mahjong championships held annually in China with players from 13 countries.

Mao Zedong once said that mahjong was one of three treasures China had given the world, the others being Chinese traditional medicine and the classic novel *A Dream of Red Mansions*.

It is for these reasons that I respectfully take issue with Ronnie Chan, billionaire chairman of the Asia Society in Hong Kong and former Enron board member, who minced no words at a World Bank meeting: "What does the East need of the West? We need its technology, its military umbrella, its capital and its market. What does the West need of us? Not much."

America has a lot to learn from both the Enron collapse and from China – especially Hong Kong.

The West needs the East's capital and markets, not to mention its intellectual capital and creativity. The East has been a major contributor to the intellectual capital created in the West. Medicine, astronomy, gunpowder, paper and printing are some of the early contributions to the West. Not to mention the basics like pasta, herbs and Chinese calligraphic tattoos on sports stars! Even Ronaldo's 2002 World Cup hairdo. The shaved head with a tuft of hair above the forehead has been around in China for hundreds of years. It is known as "Ah Fu's head." Ah Fu is a healthy, cheerful boy often depicted in traditional Chinese New Year pictures and is a symbol of fortune.

## Cultural Imperialism

In the late 14th century, Marco Polo made his famous way along trade routes from Italy to China. Three decades later the treasure ships of the great Chinese Muslim Admiral Zheng He sailed to Arabia, where, according to one account, the Chinese "conversed in the tongue of the Prophet and recalled the mosques of Yunan" and on down the coast of Africa, where they captured a giraffe for the emperor. But such adventures were rare. The easy and cheap transportation of individuals and goods is strictly a late-20th-century phenomenon. It was not until 1972 that more than one in two Americans had ever boarded an aircraft. In two generations, in short, we have gone from a time when your vacation was limited by a day's train ride to one where it's determined by a night's flight – say, 5,000 miles compared to 500. Information technology has accelerated just as dramatically.

That shrinkage of distance and time are two of the great transformations of the world. Queen Victoria's cable greeting to President James Buchanan took 16 ½ hours to cross the Atlantic. A three-minute trans-Atlantic phone call today from London to New York costs 10 cents instead of the $300 in 1930.

It is far too early to assess their impact on the way we live, the things we believe. But standing next to a Chinese Muslim at Hong Kong's airport who was wearing high desert fashion under a Western jacket, laced shoes and no socks and talking on a mobile phone, really brought home our cultural integration, as well as America's cultural imperialism.

It was a reminder of why America is so despised by so many. America is the prime mover and chief beneficiary of the process. But it's a one-way street.

"No nation is more replete with patriotic imagery in word, song and symbol than America. No nation makes more use of its icons to express an idea of self that is explicitly a view of history, of society and of national mission. American rhetoric and the American narrative tradition are shaped by a mythic vision, one consciously created, diligently taught, incumbent upon new citizens who would be Americans," Ziauddin Sardar and Merryl Wyn Davies astutely summarize in *Why Do People Hate America?*

America is the defining power. It defines what constitutes freedom, democracy, human rights, terrorism and evil and enforces its definition by military force when all else fails.

"America defines all these things in singular terms – in terms of American self-identity, history, experience and culture, and, more often than not, in terms of American self-interest," Sardar and Davies conclude. There is no room for any different definition of American values.

### American Pop

For better or worse, American cultural imperialism has spread all over China and the world. Its television, from *Seinfeld* to *The Simpsons*. Its sports, especially basketball; restaurant chains like McDonald's, KFC, Starbucks and Hard Rock Café; movies; cigarettes; pop music; fashion, and fast-food junk! All I can say is "Thank you, America," for the fatty food gifts that have so endowed modern Chinese women.

America's biggest export is no longer the fruit of its fields or the output of its factories, but the mass products of its popular culture. Movies and music, television programs, books and computer software and other forms of "intellectual property" have in recent years surpassed tangible goods as America's most important and valuable global product.

Cupid and Valentine's Day have become the very avatar of American culture and symbols of its corrupting influence in India. They are replaced by "Love Day" cards. In Malaysia and Indonesia the Indonesian movie *Ada apa dengan cinta?* ("What's with love?") about teenage angst was a blockbuster that out-grossed *Titanic* and *Lord of the Rings*. American jeans, Nike sneakers, Oakley bags and Coca-Cola dominate the movie as much as the stars. The pair are in American dress, seldom without a Coke and meet at the school's Coke vending machine.

Not surprising really when one realizes that the Founding Fathers' noble America has gone off to become the world's biggest brand.

The traditional American cultural centers in many counties propagating the virtues of America are being replaced by high-tech, interactive facilities, heralded as their digital-age successors. The first @america was set up in 2011 in an upscale mall in Jakarta, Indonesia, the world's largest Muslim country. The technology on display – a giant, supercharged version of Google Earth called Liquid Galaxy, scores of iPads to play with, interactive monitors explaining Black History Month – thrills teenagers.

These centers are the best weapon in the entire U.S. arsenal. Forget the multibillion-dollar bombers and drones. Try the soft pings and pongs instead of big, bad bangs.

While intellectuals and religious extremists debate the benefits and disadvantages of this Yankee dominance, the penetration of U.S. culture in a post-Cold War world in which scores of countries have abandoned state controls for free markets is beyond dispute. Sociologist Todd Gitlin calls American popular culture "the latest in a long succession of bidders for global unification."

"It succeeds the Latin imposed by the Roman Empire and the Catholic

Church, and Marxist Leninism" imposed by communist governments, he says.

The spread of made-in-America pop culture follows several larger worldwide trends. At the most basic level, virtually every nation has grown richer over the past 10 years, despite the recent economic turbulence in much of the world. This halo of prosperity has provided two necessary ingredients for the entertainment boom: leisure time and disposable income.

Consumer wealth, in turn, has fueled a worldwide surge in the sales of television sets, VCRs, DVDs, stereos, personal computers and satellite dishes. It has also prompted increased investment in quasi-public entertainment facilities such as movie theaters and cable, broadband and wi-fi systems around the world.

Global consumerism and expanding channels of distribution may create more demand for entertainment, but neither says much about why people around the world prefer the American variety to that produced in, say, Venezuela, Japan or France.

The answer is partly linguistic, partly economic, and partly a reflection of the unique historical, racial and ideological development of the United States. U.S. products enjoy the competitive advantage of being created in English, the first or second language of choice for most of the developed world and much of the developing world.

This leads to the inevitable chicken-and-egg question: Is American pop riding on the coattails of English or is it propelling the spread of English around the world?

The desire to appear more American has prompted shop owners in Latin America to add an apostrophe to their stores' names – a seemingly trivial change, except that the possessive "s" does not exist in Spanish. The printing on a French McDonald's Happy Meal box is in English. English is the language of cyberspace and of international meetings. How long will it be before it's also Chinese instead of French? Many would argue it already is. In Hong Kong, the French Chamber of Commerce magazine is also published in English.

When the Taliban collapsed and fled, the old Afghan "Hippie Highway" of the '60s was reborn. Long-haired Muslim hippies shaved their beards to rebel against the old establishment and sex, drugs and rock 'n' roll were suddenly back in vogue.

Beyond its glitz and gloss, its sex, speed and violence, American pop culture sells abroad, observers say, because it reflects many of the appealing themes and myths of the United States itself: individuality, freedom, wealth, progress, democracy, tolerance, and optimism in the future.

The myth is perpetuated by America's spin doctors. So while the '60s baby boomer generation became culturally apathetic in America, their contemporaries, their children and grandchildren are picking up the gauntlet in China and the rest of the world.

A television director and scriptwriter, Alexander Singer, points to the proletarian roots of American storytelling, the amalgam of immigrant experiences that sympathetically portrayed the struggles of the common man.

"Many of our earlier movies said universal things about courage and sensitivity in the face of awful deprivation," he said, adding that American movies "offer the magical possibilities of transformation."

The future. The New World Order. Repressive regimes naturally resist the trend out of fear of self-preservation.

Western culture is not just about music, movies, dress, foods and soft drinks. It is about individuality, achievement, free markets, political parties, accountability, religious freedom, tolerance and the rule of law as prescribed by the Founding Fathers in the Constitution.

The repressive old world disorder cannot stop "Westoxication." It will only grow and further expand the spirit of our Founding Fathers wherever fundamentalist extremists try to suppress music, movies, political systems or natural human behavior. The natural human desires and demands of *We the People* shall be satisfied by local artists and politicians who fuse the best the West has to offer with the best local homegrown ingredients.

### American Graffiti

The ultimate American dream, besides the home with a white picket fence, is to own a car. I know it was for me. I'll never forget the thrill when I bought my first car in Los Angeles in 1966. A used 1962 white Chevy Impala convertible. Wow! Watching my children growing up and playing with their toy cars and pretending to be adult drivers always brought a smile to my face. My son Austen was just as obsessed in his *ba ba woo* in Shanghai as Jonas was with his firetrucks in Los Angeles. Austen is a living millennium reminder and confirmation of *American Graffiti*.

I remember teaching my children Alexandra and Jonas to drive and I can still see their excited faces as they passed their license exam and got their first car. It was almost as exciting as their first time in a voting booth. I used to take my children with me whenever I went to vote trying to instill in them the importance of participatory democracy. After a while they convinced me of the futility of the process and why driving is so much more gratifying.

"What's the point when the system and process is as corrupt and broken as you say it is?" I remember Alexandra asking me one day after we hosted a fundraiser at Scratch.

She was right. At least our cars worked and were much more enjoyable.

Her remark made me decide to take a ride down the Pacific Coast Highway and reflect on the wisdom of the words from the mouth of my babe.

The Pontiac GTO and low-slung Firebird are the iconic muscle cars that stood for performance, speed and sex appeal. Their demise is a metaphor for America's decline as an industrial power. Instead of pursuing the American cowboy image of individuality and excellence, GM decided to pursue a cost-saving strategy of providing the same car to different divisions. That was one of the company's many missteps and helped drive it straight into bankruptcy court.

The automobile has always been the ultimate American dream machine. It is now also the ultimate dream machine of mainland China – the world's No. 1 car market. An extension of our very identity as accessory, image, and fantasy. A car makes us feel "sexy and powerful." It is the real certificate of American citizenship. Detroit's demise begs the question of what will it take to get *We the Apathetic Maids* to reassert our power to drive home the necessary changes needed to leave not just a better car for our children – but a better world?

In the meantime, while working for such changes, I'm enjoying my Mustang.

### *Question Authority*
Baby boomers and rock 'n' rollers have become grandparents. My generation – born between 1946 and 1964 – now officially numbers more than 78 million U.S. citizens, according to the 2000 census. Because of our size, we redefined every life stage we entered. As rock 'n' roll becomes a lifelong pursuit for many, the debauched dream of sex, drugs and general abandon is giving way to a new set of ambitions. Young rockers have seen Mick Jagger become a "Strolling Bone" grandfather, Bob Dylan share the pop charts with his hit-making son Jakob, and they are starting to question the illusion that the rock life style could or should stave off adult responsibility. What are we doing about leaving a better place for our grandchildren than we inherited? Shouldn't we be questioning our political responsibility and apathy? Especially *We the Apathetic Baby Boomers* who were so active in the '60s?

The political dialogue that the Internet facilitates allows us to destroy the career politicians' firewalls between *We the People* and the intentions of our Founding Fathers that the politicians have camouflaged with meaningless self-serving political rhetoric, laws and lies spun as truths we have come to accept. Their firewalls can be brought down just like the Berlin Wall, Lenin, Milosevic, Mubarak and Nixon. They were rolled out of office in the 20th century and the dawn of the new millennium. What's to stop *We the Maids* from sweeping out what we no longer accept as we rock on into the 21$^{st}$ century?

The Democrats and Republicans think third-party candidates like Jessie Ventura and Ralph Nader are just a flash in the pan. They conveniently delude themselves and overlook the fact that the pan has been replaced by the Internet, which is here to stay. They don't realize people want to be turned on politically as well. Learn the truth and build New World Order families, not artificial values. The Internet is a people magnet that Senator John McCain recognized and President Obama embraced. It invites active participation, including financial contributions. The Internet challenges the traditional two-party approach of crafting mass sound bites appealing to each demographic common denominator. Voters are individuals, not a mass. The Tea Party movement is proof of that.

Freedom of speech and information are the most powerful cocktail and drug of the 21$^{st}$ century.

The hip-hop nation that succeeded the rockers was influenced by them. In America, the boundaries are more fluid and blurry than many people would like to believe: white people are listening to and using elements of rap because they relate to it, because the music is a legitimate part of their cultural heritage. Black and white music fans alike are driving around flipping back and forth between the local rock and rap radio stations, simply looking for the best music. No different than the movies. Shouldn't we also be channel-surfing for a better political system and process that better represents our political dreams?

"The pessimistic outlook that bands have today and the angst, this is a part of what we created for our children," Neil Young said, speaking of the counterculture of the '60s. "They're reflecting it back at us, and now we have to live with it. And they have a right to be pessimistic. It's not as easy to grow up now as it was in the '60s. The world is a much more dangerous place. There are a lot less dreams being realized."

Why? Because *We the Apathetic Maids* have allowed it. We can make a difference and sweep in the desired changes.

Remakes of movie classics being released in the 1990s and the 21$^{st}$ century reflect many of the common themes and desires for the old in the world today. *Reality Bites,* the Generation X movie, reflects the classic Hollywood rebel without a cause and has been artfully and cleverly woven into a book review of *Reconstructing America* by James Ccasar. The reviewer, Adam Wolfson, brilliantly points out how the critics of America misunderstand it.

"For two centuries, philosophers have been busy creating an image of America at odds with the country we are familiar with – the one, writes Ceaser, 'where we live, work, struggle and pray, and where we have forged a system of government that has helped to shape the destiny of the modern world.'

"In shaping public policy and in deciding political matters, we should be guided not by the images of America concocted by the philosophers but by our own political principles and practices. We should remember that buried beneath the 'symbolic America' foisted upon us by Hollywood – and indirectly supplied by such philosophers as Heidegger – there lies what Ceaser calls the 'real America'."
The apathetic America hijacked by career politicians and their moneyed constituents.

### *Question Images*
The Hong Kong Chinese are not the retooled Charlie Chan, the cherubic Chinese detective with the dainty step and a belly full of fortune cookie wisdom resurrected for the new millennium just because he is now played by a Chinese-American. They're Hong Kong's chopping Jackie Chan, and Jet Li, successors to Hong Kong's Bruce Lee. Kato in the *Green Hornet* TV series, kung fu master extraordinaire who was kept off Hollywood's silver screen because of his golden color.

Bruce Lee was born in San Francisco and moved to Hong Kong with his parents when he was 3, returning to the U.S. when he was 18. Lee put Hong Kong into Hollywood. Before the Hollywood martial arts movies *The Matrix* (1999), *Charlie's Angeles* (2000), *Daredevil* (2003), *Bulletproof Monk* (2003), and *Matrix Reloaded* (2003), there were the Hong Kong kung fu movies starting back in the 1940s.

Chairman Mao Zedong was among Lee's legions of fans. As Mao correctly observed, Lee's movies portray the fight between good and evil with Lee invariably embodying the good. What he expressed through his films and his jeet kune do fighting style were universal values of dignity, freedom, equality and justice.

"His performance style and character were not typically Chinese. He drew elements from the street culture of African-Americans into his performance," says film critic and screen writer Jason Lam. "For example, his jumpy leg movements were similar to the motions of black basketball players in the 1970s. This made his movies appear familiar to Western audiences."

In 1999, *Time* magazine named Lee one of the 100 most influential people of the 20th century, and in 2005, *Variety* crowned him one of the "Icons of the Century." Yet he is still snubbed in his hometown of Hong Kong, which cannot bring itself around to build a museum in his memory. One of these days, I'm sure it will.

In the meantime, I was delighted to see that more than 100 items of memorabilia telling his story went on display in July 2013 at the five-year Bruce Lee exhibition at the Heritage Museum in Sha Tin. Most of the items are on loan from the Bruce Lee Foundation, which aims to promote and preserve the legacy of the late star. The foundation is run by his wife and daughter.

The Marvels and Monsters: Unmasking Asian Images in U.S. Comics, 1942-1986 exhibition at New York University in the summer of 2011, which spotlighted Asian characters in American comics, offered fascinating insights into how the Asian-American identity was forged. The show was organized around common archetypes of Asians in the American eye: the Alien, the Brute, the Lotus Blossom, the Guru, the Brain, the Kamikaze, the Temptress and the Manipulator.

"The images presented in this exhibition are largely negative ones – a reality that reflects the timeframe itself," the text accompanying the exhibition said as it went on to describe the xenophobic atmosphere that produced these archetypes.

"Over the period of time covered by this exhibition, authentic three-dimensional depictions of Asian characters were few and far between."

The Asian stereotypes – Chinese in particular – still reflect the way they are depicted in the American media. The 2013 Chevrolet ad with Dr. Fu Manchu the archetypal "yellow peril" villain stereotype being a recent racist example.

"As I was working on this exhibition, I came to the fascinating and horrifying realization that I had read a lot of these comics as a kid, and had either not noticed or minimized the way in which Asian characters were portrayed," said Daniel Kim, co-curator of the show.

"That's how pop culture works. You're caught up in the entertainment and the pleasure of it. When I think back to my 8-year-old self, I retroactively worry for him. I wonder what this will do to him, what role it will play in developing my self-identity and the identity of all Asian boys who grew up reading comic books in America."

This type of pervasive negative imagery is not limited to Asian-Americans. Most Americans have been dumbed down and believe they are dumber than they really are because of the pervasive imagery of Americans as exploited by foreigners, today's favorite political targets being Chinese and immigrants. Any wonder they have become apolitical, apathetic, insecure, frightened wage slaves?

*We the Apathetic Maids*, who have been dumbed down, should look at the heroic defiant example of 40-year-old self-taught Chinese blind rights legal advocate Chen Guangcheng. He has taught us with his dramatic escape from house arrest in Shandong, then gaining refuge in the U.S. Embassy in Beijing, breaking his foot along the way by jumping over the wall built around his house, tripping and falling while running for several kilometers to meet his ride to Beijing, and finally getting political asylum in America.

His strategy, timing and challenges are a lesson for all of us to learn –

lessons he will hopefully teach his students at NYU.

The real Chinese are anything but cherubic fortune cookie monsters. In fact, fortune cookies are an American invention! The Chinese willingness to take to the streets and let their impolite feelings be expressed was witnessed by the world during Tiananmen and after the U.S. bombing of the Chinese Embassy in Yugoslavia and at Cornell University in New York protesting former Taiwan's President Lee Teng-hui's visit to his alma mater.

The anti-American protests unleashed by the bombing of the Chinese Embassy in Belgrade became the largest anti-foreign demonstrations since the Cultural Revolution of the 1960s.

One banner shrieked, "Kill the bitch Albright," and another proclaimed "Bill Clinton is a son of a bitch and Tony Blair is the grandson of that bitch." Polite cherubic retooled Charlie Chans?

The fact that the protesters are wearing Eddie Bauer shirts and Levis rather than Mao jackets doesn't change who they are. These protests are mild compared with earlier assaults on diplomatic enclaves. In 1900, the entire diplomatic neighborhood in Beijing was held under siege for months by anti-foreign insurgents known as the Boxers. A massive eight-power foreign expeditionary force fought its way into the capital and lifted the siege. In 1927, Chinese troops forced their way into the Soviet Russian legation in Beijing, rounded up Chinese communists who had taken shelter there and killed them. In 1967, during the height of the Cultural Revolution, the British Embassy in Beijing was gutted and burned. The Chinese government acquiesced to the anti-foreign violence.

The roots of these attacks lie in the broader history of anti-foreign protest in China, which is as diverse as the history of anti-Chinese feelings in the U.S. The U.S. spy plane that crash-landed in China in the opening year of the 21st century was a wake-up call to America and China that both countries have more to gain from each other through peaceful cooperation and mutual understanding. The global war on terrorism has sealed that 21st-century pact.

Now that Chinese-American Stan Lee, the co-creator of comic-book characters Spider Man, Iron Man, X-Men, and The Avengers is back on his home turf in China creating a new Chinese superhero, maybe his new character will come up with a solution.

"I have been eagerly awaiting this great opportunity, a chance to combine the best of American superhero epics with the best of Chinese and Asian classical filmmaking for a motion picture that would be excitedly received worldwide," Lee said.

### *Revolution 2.0*

The Arab cleansing revolutions, labor unrest in China, anti-Iraq War protests and People Power II in the Philippines are ongoing revolutions driven by the Internet, social networking and text messaging. Wael Ghonim, the Google geek Facebook freedom fighter, who engineered Egypt's social network revolution, is the embodiment of the world's new tech-savvy youth seeking broader freedoms.

"Freedom is a blessing that deserves fighting for," Wael tweeted as he was released from prison.

Political, economic and religious freedoms are the cornerstones of the Founding Fathers' constitutional ideals.

Text messages in the opening month of the millennium enabled people power to bring down a corrupt administration in the Philippines. Witnessing it first-hand was a real generational eye-opener for me. Aging prosperous baby boomers who usually lounge in massage parlors with their high society ladies who are more at home in beauty salons or playing mahjong in fancy mansions, took to the streets and texted their friends to join them and the students and workers who wanted a change of government. Corrupt career politicians who chose to ignore the will of the people. Those they are supposed to represent.

People texting friends on cellular phones, social networking via Facebook and Twitter are the people's political grass roots organizational tools of the 21st century. People Power II, the Arab cleansing revolutions and President Barack Obama proved it. The millions who took to the streets to oppose the Iraq War confirmed it. Texting and e-mails are the tools *We the Maids* need to sweep in reform and sweep out career politicians. They are the tools that can instantaneously mobilize like-minded people to activate a collective consciousness. Hearts and minds that can sweep in America's founding principles.

The convergence of technology, people power and disenfranchised interests can, if united, overthrow any phalanx of self-serving moneyed political oligarchy. Revolution is no longer a protracted process. Unlike past revolutions that took years, today's revolutions are measured in weeks, months and even days. Some still argue that what happened in the Philippines, Tunisia and Egypt was undemocratic mob rule. What is democracy? Isn't that why the Founding Fathers wanted to control the mob?

### Impeach the System

The Clinton impeachment debate of the '90s and the 21st-century war in Afghanistan and terrorism are no different than the Vietnam War debate and removal of President Nixon from office in the '60s and early '70s. Except that today, the underlying morality to the debate is intertwined with religion and self-serving career politicians rather than patriotism. America was created and founded on the premise that all people shall have religious freedom. Why then do so many insist on instilling Bible Belt and Beltway religious political values into the impeachment debate and the war on terrorism when the public is clearly questioning them? No different than when the public questioned and rejected the patriotic arguments during the Vietnam War.

Was the Clinton impeachment part of a cultural religious revolution? A continuation of the Nixon Vietnam-Watergate civil conflict that resulted in his resignation, or was it a cultural revolution to remove from office a sitting president who was a participant in those Vietnam protests? I believe the Clinton impeachment was a continuation of the civil war of values that started in the '60s. Here was a president pursued by conservative men who would have approved of Nixon because he was a liberal anti-'Nam baby-boomer.

*We the People* have to talk through the fact that the power of government belongs to *We the People*. Not to religious extremists. Not to the bureaucrats. Not to the judicial system and its lawyers. Not to any religious organization. And most definitely not to non-representative career politicians. If we forget that, the republic is doomed.

Radical movements today are different from those of the '60s in the numbers of people they attract and the kind of followers they have. But the message remains the same. They all oppose government hypocrisy and want the will of the people to be heard. This is echoed on the radio talk shows, in the music, songs, poetry, and literature of the '60s and today. Not only in America, but in every country, even Japan and Iraq.

The Japanese finally rocked the ruling political establishment by getting the ruling party to reluctantly get behind '60s rocker Junichiro Koizumi.

In Iraq, people tuned in to jihad rock that called for violent insurrection against America while hundreds of thousands of Shiites marched peacefully demanding direct elections.

"We are demanding democracy. And that is what America came to give us," cleric Faras al-Tatrasani said.

"The sons of the Iraqi people demand a political system based on direct elections and a constitution that realizes justice and equality for everyone," Ayatollah Ali al-Husseini al-Sistani's representative, Hashen al-Awad, pronounced during a protest by 100,000 Shiites in Baghdad.

They finally got them and formed a democratically elected government in 2010.

Isn't it time *We the Apathetic Maids* made the same demands in America? It takes rock 'n' roll rebels to bring about peaceful cultural and political revolutions.

If a government and its entrenched institutions won't listen to reason, it gives the people little choice but to resort to alternatives. Unity through social networking is a good way to start.

"In the past century, politics has always been interfering with literature.

It's difficult to go back to just literature itself. Now that we're in the new century, political interference has reached the final stage. Literature, I think, should surpass politics. It's not serving politics or moral judgment and is not restricted to any doctrines" said author Gao Xingjian, winner of the first Nobel Prize for Literature in the 21$^{st}$ century.

The beauty of the Renaissance Faires of the '60s, which have survived and become major profit centers through the years, is that they remind us that there are enough people who long for a modern-day Renaissance. The same global Renaissance the peaceful costumed protesters at the post-9/11 World Economic Forum 2002 in New York demanded. It doesn't have to be lived out only at the faires. In the '60s people took to the ballot boxes and the streets to get their message across to politicians and the silent majority who were numbed into believing the managed misperceptions of the time.

*We the People* can and should do the same in the New World Disorder. Honest political dialogue allows the world to mellow out in a constructive and enjoyable way as it rolls into the 21st century. Such an exchange can bring together a cultural, political, social and economic 21st-century millennium Renaissance integrating and blending the best of America and China – the Third American Revolution.

The alternatives are a bummer, man. A real bad trip.

**Will Rogers Confucian**
*Mama Don't Let Your Babies Grow Up to Be Cowboys*
– Willie Nelson and Waylon Jennings

*Roping Cowboy*

Galloping at full speed on the trails in California's Will Rogers State Park in Pacific Palisades to get to "Inspiration Point" in time to catch the sunset was at times downright nerve-racking. I rode bareback on Geronimo, a buckskin barrel racer. If we were racing other riders he was unstoppable. I had to literally wrap my legs around his girth and cling on for dear life. Sometimes rounding blind corners on the trail we would encounter hikers or Japanese tourists who would go scurrying over the side of the mountain to avoid being run over. Not that I cared. After several nightmarish visits to Japan trying to navigate their train and subway system in the 1980s, with no signs in English, I figured they could relate to a trail with no signs warning them of racing broncos.

"Ho, ho!" I would call out as I pulled back on the reins as hard as I could to slow him down as we approached the edge of Inspiration Point. Otherwise, I would probably join the hikers and Japanese tourists as I catapulted over Geronimo's neck if he came to too sudden a stop. We had just maneuvered around groups of hikers and one group of Japanese tourists who are probably still trying to get back on the trail. Think about the Japanese soldiers coming out of hiding decades after the end of World War II on islands in the Pacific.

That was L.A. in the 1980s. I thought about those riding days recently in Tokyo's Shinjuku District in February 2011, where my partner Pauline and I spent a couple of nights, during a ski trip to Kuweizara. Pauline skied as I chilled by the fireplace in the ski lodge, read and enjoyed the peaceful and beautiful serenity that life can be. What a difference, I thought to myself.

In Tokyo and Japan as a whole. Street and train signs are bilingual and in many cases trilingual, with Chinese added.

Watching "Superman" Christopher Reeves on TV after his horse-riding accident, I think back to those cowboy days and realize that were it not for my luck and karma, I might also be sitting in a wheelchair.

We lived in the old Will Rogers guest ranch in Rivas Canyon in Pacific Palisades. After all, it was Rogers who said, "So buy a ranch somewhere in the West. All your life every man has wanted to be a cowboy. Why play Wall Street and die young when you can play cowboy and never die."

In addition to the main house on three acres, there was a guest house in the back and a stable with another house for the stable hand. It backed into Rogers' main house and the park named in honor of the great American humorist, who lived there until his untimely death in a plane crash in 1935.

Picnicking in the park one weekend after we first moved in in the mid-'80s, my daughter Alexandra asked about Rogers. "Tell me his story, Daddy." She loved stories.

Rogers was America's chief humorist at a time the country in many ways was still forming itself. Born in Oklahoma in 1879, he was approximately one-quarter Cherokee Indian on both parents' side. His father was a successful rancher and trader in what would become Oklahoma, but which was originally part of the area known as Indian Territory. His mother died when he was 10 years old, and he was sent to live with an older sister and her husband.

As a young man Rogers was expert with rope tricks and horses, and started traveling the world to seek his fortune, first working as a cowboy and moving cattle. He managed his father's ranch for a time, then became a traveling performer of rope tricks from New York to Australia, under the sobriquet the Cherokee Kid. At 29, after a courtship of eight years, he married Betty Blake, a woman he would love all his life and with whom he had three sons and a daughter.

Rogers was always curious to meet people in different countries that were in the news. As part of his act, he would begin by making comments and telling jokes, based on what he'd read in that day's newspaper. That went over so well, it became his act. He became known to most Americans through radio broadcasts commenting on current affairs, lecture tours, film performances, then a weekly syndicated newspaper column. He was a movie star in silent and talking comedies, becoming at one point the top box office draw. He traveled, first by sea, which made him sick, then by plane. He was hugely popular in America, sought out and loved by both Democrats and Republicans, whom he seemed to snipe at equally in his commentaries.

Rogers left an extensive legacy of commentary on the world, the U.S. its people and policies, which remains timely today. Said to have never met a person he didn't like, Rogers seemed able to see both sides of many issues, perhaps because he was both cowboy and Indian himself. He died in 1935 at 55, in a plane crash with his friend Wiley Post as they explored Alaska in bad weather.

I can understand how he came up with some of his great one-liners. The view from Inspiration Point is breathtaking. Especially when you are trying to catch your breath, calm down your heartbeat and slow the adrenaline. What a rush! Enjoy the sunset and view. Relax and meditate. Will Rogers was right. "A man that don't love a horse, there is something the matter with him."

On a clear day you can look out over Santa Monica Bay and see all the way down to the Palos Verdes point and out to Catalina Island. The gliding jetliners making their circular approach to LAX. Jets taking off look like they are going to collide. Fishing boats and tankers sitting idly in the bay, and yachts returning to their berths in Marina del Rey. The view is spectacular.

Over the years, flying in and out to China, I've peered many a time through the porthole window to catch a glimpse of Inspiration Point where I used to sprawl on a horse and bask in that bright yellow ball of setting sun.

## Geronimo

My favorite horse was Geronimo. Free spirited, smart, quick and a leader. Always had to be at the head of the pack. Just like his namesake. Hearing that it was also the U.S. commandos' code name for Osama bin Laden made me shudder. While I understand the reason – the legendary Apache chief was said to be able to walk without leaving footprints, thus evading thousands of soldiers on both sides of the Mexican border – I was saddened and offended, because Geronimo was defending his homeland, not engaging in terrorism. The continuing cultural disconnect in America today between Native Americans and the rest of the citizenry is a sad commentary on the failings of America's education system, U.S. history in particular.

"Apparently, having an African-American president in the White House is not enough to overturn the more than 200-year American tradition of treating and thinking of Indians as enemies of the United States," wrote Steven Newcomb, a columnist for the weekly newspaper *Indian Country Today*. After bin Laden was killed, the military sent a message back to the White House: "Geronimo EKIA"– enemy killed in action.

Jeff Houser, chairman of Geronimo's Fort Sill Apache tribe, noted in a letter to President Obama that "to equate Geronimo, or any other Native American figure with Osama bin Laden, a mass murderer and cowardly terrorist, is painful and offensive to our tribe and to all Native Americans."

It is doubly offensive when one realizes that since 2001, more than 77 American Indians and Alaskan Natives have died fighting for the U.S. in Afghanistan and Iraq. More than 400 have been wounded.

Loretta Tuell, staff director and chief counsel for the U.S. Senate Indian Affairs Committee, said it was inappropriate to link Geronimo, whom she called "one of the greatest Native American heroes," with one of the most hated enemies of America.

A White House spokesman referred questions about the code name to the Pentagon. A Defense Department spokeswoman declined to comment.

"The name Geronimo is arguably the most recognized Native American name in the world, and this comparison only serves to perpetuate negative stereotypes about our peoples," the Onondaga Nation Council of Chiefs said. I agree.

Why not *Bonanza,* after the preferred small-screen fare of Osama bin Laden as a boy? A code name that is also a relevant double entendre! Why not a cowboy instead of an Indian?

Sitting on my rooftop garden in Hong Kong reading about the assassination of bin Laden, watching the moonlit rising tide roll in as I listened to the wind gently whistle through the rustling leaves of the trees, plants and chimes that sounded like one of those rhythmic bongo-bangers that seem to be on every waterfront, I flashed back to those days at Inspiration Point with Geronimo and Nickolai, my black Labrador-Dalmation mix. Nickolai was always on the lookout for deer. He could smell them and take off in their direction way before I saw them. I can understand why Labrador retrievers are used in Afghanistan to wander in front of patrols to ensure the safety of the route, because they have proven better than people or machines at quickly finding improvised explosives. I've read that a dog accompanied the SEAL team that killed bin Laden in Pakistan.

While reflecting about the future of al-Qaeda without bin Laden, I thought about a Chinese couplet that goes: "Japan saved the Communist Party; Islam rescued China."

Japan "saved" the Communist Party because, by invading China in the 1930s, it badly weakened the Nationalist government of President Chiang Kai-shek. The second part of the couplet refers to the al-Qaeda brand of Islam, which "saved" China by launching the 9/11 attacks on the U.S.

When George W. Bush assumed office as president in 2001, he called China a strategic competitor and the new administration viewed it as America's next enemy. However, 9/11 drastically changed the American focus, directing its attention to Afghanistan and Iraq instead. It is not too far-fetched to say that bin Laden saved China from American containment and isolation.

While Bush and his cowboys rode into Afghanistan and Iraq, wasting more than $5 trillion dollars and thousands of American lives, China was focusing on building its global economic growth and political influence.

### The Cowboys

One of my '80s riding buddies was Michael Lippman. Michael was the president of the West Coast office of Arista Records. He was an agent at one of the leading talent agencies when we first met as young bucks out of law school. Michael kept his horse at my stable along with "The Brown Dirt Cowboy" Bernie Taupin, the lyricist for many of Elton John's hits, Leo Sayer and other music buddies he represented. They liked to escape the concrete of L.A. the same way I did – by riding into the mountains. The trails went all the way to Santa Barbara along the Santa Monica mountain range – not far from where Michael lives today.

On one of my trips to L.A. from Hong Kong, I went into the Barnes and Noble bookstore on the Santa Monica Promenade to buy some books on Will Rogers. It was a couple of days after April 8, 1998, the day George Michael got busted for lewd conduct in the Beverly Hills Will Rogers park toilet.

"Are you doing research or a story on the George Michael incident?" the salesman asked as he walked me to the shelf where the books were.

"Oh no, no!" I said as I laughed at the coincidence. "I'm just interested in the man."

I had stables for 12 horses. We had three horses and a pony of our own, and let friends and partners use up the rest of the stable space to enjoy Will Rogers' creative haven. Heather Locklear kept her horse there and also kept our attention on the trails.

Riding or hiking through the park over the years, I would sometimes stop by Rogers' home, which is now a museum. I was always touched.

The architecture and décor of his house and stables, the natural and lush landscaping and the eucalyptus trees shading the trails, like his humor and philosophy, were simple, tasteful and to the point.

### Horse Dance

Rogers' roping and humor, like Psy's *Gangnam Style* music video, reflect the tastes of the time, the performers and their lines.

Watching and joining in the Gangnam horse dance as I did in Gangnam, South Korea, in early November 2012, was a thrill. Being a lover of horses and riding, hanging out in Gangnam brought back memories of those great horse galloping days in Will Rogers State Park. I can understand why Gangnam Style took off like greased lightning globally and Psy's monster hit reached double-platinum status – and his infectious music video became the most-watched YouTube video of all time with more than a billion hits.

The video has inspired many copy cat offshoots, especially on the political satire front with artists like Ai Weiwei, who performed the dance with a pair of dangling handcuffs.

Seoul's Gangnam district, like the rest of Korea in early November, is very cold. I stayed at the Grand Intercontinental Hotel that had adjoining underground walkways to all the bars and restaurants in underground Gangnam, and to many above ground, where warm sake was more than welcome after the chilly streets. The only way to stay warm on the streets is to gallop.

There is a Gangnam city tour that includes a visit to the 1,200-year-old Bongeunsa Buddhist Temple, surrounded by modern skyscrapers, Seolleung royal tombs, Eunma traditional market, and the trendy boutique and cafe district of Garuso-gil, as well as all the Korean products and services being marketed at the COEX Mall (Korean Exhibition Hall) and Aquarium.

The commercial battles raging in Gangnam, between not only the name-brand stores, but between buildings owned by iconic Korean corporations, are not only a metaphor for pure American capitalism in the poshest commercial and residential district in Korea, but reflect the galloping beat of the horse dance that became a hit in capitalist America. Tech titans Samsung and LG square off on opposite corners at the Hakdong intersection in Gangnam with products, services and free parking.

Psy, who grew up in Gangnam and studied in America, captured the essence of the best and worst of capitalism and the free spirit of cowboy America.

It's no surprise then that Psy started the New World Order as the star of a charity concert in Washington, where he met President Obama, also as the star of a pistachio Super Bowl commercial, and with a purchase in January 2013 of a condominium in West Los Angeles, not far from Will Rogers State Park.

### Bikers

On some occasions, it was cyclists that I raced to overtake, or make room for on the mountain trails. Some of the cyclists were training for competitive events. We would periodically compare our "wheels" whenever we caught up with each other at Inspiration Point.

Watching Lance Armstrong admit that he used performance-enhancing drugs throughout his storied cycling career, I couldn't help wonder how many of the bikers I came across on those trails were doped-up.

Armstrong was sponsored by the U.S. Postal Service when he won his seven world titles. Why was the Postal Service, a taxpayer-funded government service, spending hard-earned tax dollars supporting a cycling fraud? What happened to government due diligence on behalf of citizen taxpayers?

Even if he wasn't a fraud, what was the government thinking in the first place? Why wasn't the post office putting the millions in sponsorship money and resources into strategically competitive postal services that would allow it to compete with all the courier services and online mail services and take a global postal lead instead of supporting a drug user promoting the best undetectable super steroids – a pharmaceutical conspiracy?

The fact is people using enhancement drugs in sports, as well as their pharmaceutical partners and government sponsors, are corrupt cheaters, something neither Will Rogers nor Confucius would accept or condone.

### Parallel Lessons

There are similarities in the lives of Confucius the "philosopher king" and Rogers the "cowboy philosopher," who lived so many centuries apart. They were sons of men of substance and reputation, although Confucius' father was gone from his life early. Rogers also lost a parent early, but had the benefit of a stable home life with an extended family, who by all appearances cared very much for him. Both Confucius and Rogers had one marriage; both outlived sons. Confucius shepherded animals but seems to have looked down on actual manual labor; Rogers worked as a cowboy and also managed a ranch. Both spent much time traveling, interacting with many different kinds of people. Confucius and Rogers each had strong codes of conduct, though with Confucius that code was the message; he was first and foremost a teacher. Rogers was primarily a humorist, a self-depreciating entertainer whose commentary nevertheless contained many lessons.

Confucius was one of the most original and deepest thinkers of all time. He had the utmost respect for the mannered, feudal system in place in China during his lifetime. D. Howard Smith in his book *Confucius* says: "Confucius accepted that civilized life is governed by an elaborate system of rights and privileges." The following quote makes the Confucian attitude to the power structure of his day clear: "When good government prevails in the Empire, the initiative and final decision in matters of religion, education, and the declaration of war form the supreme prerogative of the Emperor."

It is interesting to note that he qualifies this power by attaching the word "good" to government. Confucius was also known to say that the greatest human institution was the political: "Government is rectification," meaning government is the greatest institution because it has the power to make things right and to regulate life in the proper way. Confucius believed in the traditional respect for authority of his time – son to father, junior officer to superior officer, minister to noble. Liu Wu-chi says in his book, *Confucius,*

*His Life and Time,* "…Nothing could be more distasteful to [Confucius] than to see ministers treading on the toes of the reigning prince, thereby violating the code of *li* that made strict distinction between the lord and his subjects."

Confucius was brought to the attention of the West during the 16th century by Italian Jesuit priests, among them Matteo Ricco, Michael Ruggeri, and Prospero Intorecetta, who translated his works.

"Confucius had a big influence on the liberal evolution of European governments of the time. He played a strong role in the democratization of France, England and Austria simply because many philosophers saw in his works the seeds of liberty and humanity," Angelo Paratico, a Chinese-Italian translator who lives in Hong Kong, reminds his readers and listeners at the Foreign Correspondents Club Main Bar.

Will Rogers honored God, family and country and had a great deal of respect for leaders in politics, even though he poked fun at them.

"I do joke about our prominent men, but at heart I believe in 'em. I do think there is times when traces of dumbness crop up in official life, but not out of crookedness," he said. I wonder what he'd say about Dubya?

One theme runs strongly through the sayings of both Confucius and Rogers. Both felt that people have a right to good, ethical government, and that if they did not get it, a leader – whether a senator in the 1920's America or a prince in 6th-century China – could not expect the cooperation of the citizens. In some ways, this is an early democratic view by Confucius.

"When good men are in office, government is efficient… . Therefore, good government depends upon good men. Such men should be chosen on the basis of character. When those who are governed do not have confidence in their governors, they cannot be controlled," Confucius said.

Rogers said things in a very similar way to.

"I have often said that with all our kidding or cussing about our public officials that they are as good or better than we who elect them. We are a nation that runs in spite, and not on account, of our government," Rogers said.

This lampooning tone is a main difference between Rogers' and Confucius' approaches to government and leaders.

"We are going on the assumption that nothing in public life (or out of it for that matter) is any good. Now what we have set out to do is find the worst. It's no trouble to pick out the bad, but I tell you, when you sit down to pick out the worst, you have set yourself some task," Rogers said.

A classic Rogers dialog comes from a subject close to his heart in one of his weekly newspaper articles: "... At first we were out there on Indian land dedicating a dam to get water for white people to come and use and gradually take more Indian land away ... So you see, history repeats itself, the same as it has in wars. It would be wonderful if people would quit fighting; it would be wonderful if people would leave the Indians alone and let 'em do what they wanted too. But what a chance? ... You can't blame anybody. It's just the way we are bred, that's all. If we see anything we want, we take it. The more so-called civilized we get, the more we kill and take."

And yet, even though he could sound almost bitter, Rogers was still capable of echoing Confucius' respectful and patriotic attitude.

"If there is one thing that we want to inculcate into the minds of the youth of this country, it is that honesty and fair dealing with our own government is the foundation of this nation. Our history honors many names whose morals would not stand the acid test, but our history honors no man who betrayed, or attempted to betray, a government trust."

But Rogers also never stopped joking about America and its leaders.

"America is just like an insane asylum; there is not a soul in it will admit

563

they are crazy. The president, being the warden, us inmates know he's the one that's cuckoo."

Confucius spoke extensively on corruption in its many forms. He knew the corrupting influence that money and power could exert.

"Under heaven the cases are few in which the poor have enjoyment, the rich love the rules of propriety, and families that are powerful remain quiet and orderly."

Confucius believed that certain people had the right to depose a corrupt, abusive ruler: "One in the position of a minister and inferior might remonstrate with his ruler, but not speak ill of him; might withdraw but not remain and hate; might praise but not flatter; might remonstrate but not give himself haughty airs when his advice is followed. If the ruler was idle and indifferent, he might arouse and assist him; if the government was going to wreck, he might sweep it away and institute a new one."

Confucius also spoke with weary scorn about ambition and lack of principles: "Men of old had three failings, which have, perhaps, died out today. Ambitious men of old were not nice; ambitious men today are unprincipled. Masterful men of old were rough; masterful men today are quarrelsome. Simple men of old were straight; simple men today are false. That is all."

When he found power corrupted in the state he served, he walked away not only from the Duke of Lu, but from the state itself. He sternly punished those who committed crimes against others when he had the power to do so. At one point in his career, he deftly avoided taking office in a corrupt administration. Liu Wu-chi explains why: "Confucius was yearning for a chance to make use of his immense knowledge of history and government, rituals and ethics, in the administration of the state and the uplifting of his fellow men. But herein was the rub. The man who offered to employ him was an unprincipled upstart who had tyrannized over the people and officials of Lu, and who was exactly the kind of man Master K'ung would like to dispose of, if he had his way in the government."

Confucius had core rottenness in a ruler pinned down precisely: "The conduct of a princely man is guided by the rule of propriety. One who is governed by insatiable greed even though he imposes a tax on the lands today, will still find himself in need of money tomorrow."

Will Rogers made many joking references to "graft" in government. But by joking about it, even in a philosophical way, he drew attention to it as well. When it came to politicians in America, Rogers was fairly even-handed with his barbs: "The Democrats are investigating the Republican slush fund. And if they find out where it's coming from, they want theirs."

Rogers could become particularly sarcastic about how the U.S. government can abuse its power abroad: "It had just become almost impossible for some little country to have a nice home-talent revolution …without us butting in. Everywhere an American went to invest some money in the hope of making 100 percent, why here would be a gunboat to see he had all the comforts to which he had been accustomed."

But his favorite target was how U.S. leaders treat their own citizens: "Just been reading of a fund the government has, called the Conscience Fund. If you feel that you have cheated the government, you send them the money. Say, how about the government having a Conscience Fund? They have skinned us many a time!"

Rogers ultimately seemed resigned to the foibles of people, though he was talking about the corrupting power of money in American politics 70 years before recent attempts to enact campaign finance reform. He was also openly fatalistic.

"Corruption and golf is two things we might as well just as well make up our minds to take up, for they are both going to be with us."

Being a leading espouser of civility and proper conduct, Confucius also stated the importance of honoring parents, son towards father especially. He believed that the core unit of a healthy state was a healthy family: "When good will prevails in one family, it influences the whole country, and when courtesy prevails in one family, the whole country becomes courteous. On the other hand, the selfishness and rudeness of one man can cause turmoil throughout the whole country. This is the way things work."

While Rogers was not above making jokes at the expense of women, he also revered them, and was said to be shy around the ones with whom he worked. He apparently told an actress he had to kiss during a love scene that he felt like he was cheating on his wife. This highly acclaimed performer gave a characteristically simple, but very public compliment to his wife: "On November 5, 1928, I was married to Betty Blake of Rogers, Arkansas. When I roped her, that was the star performance of my life."

Rogers joked about the lack of voting rights for women at the time of his birth, claiming he was born on election day because his mother wanted something to do.

According to Bryan B. Sterling, "Will's regard for women was not based on the fact that they were women, but on what they did and what they knew."

Rogers is quoted as having said that, though he liked President Calvin Coolidge, his wife Grace could have run things better. He also claimed that Teddy Roosevelt's daughter, Alice Roosevelt Longworth, was the most politically sharp person in Washington. He dedicated one of his books, *Letters of a Self-Made Diplomat to His President,* to two women, Lady Nancy Astor, and his wife Betty.

Rogers had profound affection for his three sisters, who helped raise him after his mother died. He loved his wife and children – and was devastated when his young son died. He provided a very comfortable lifestyle for his family, and was known to book himself into a hard round of lectures to keep that lifestyle up.

There is a delicious slyness to the humor of Will Rogers, a powerful notion inside the plain folks language and "I only know what I read in the papers" wisecracks. Two of his remarks on the status of Indians in America illustrate this point. "Did you read where my hometown of Claremore, Oklahoma, just opened an Indian hospital? Just think, Columbus discovered America a little over 400 years ago, and here they are building us a hospital. Just imagine what us Indians got to look forward to in the next 400 years. Why, they might even build us a cemetery."

Rogers was even bolder, and identified even more strongly with the Indian minority with his crack: "Let's don't get down in intolerance as far down as the Indians. Because if you monkey around, I'm Cherokee too, and a few of us will get together and run you all out of the country, that's all, and take it back over again."

Americans must not forget that this great land at one time belonged solely to the Native Americans. The Vikings and Chinese who arrived before the Europeans never made a conscious decision to conquer the land and slaughter the indigenous people in order to develop and build a new country based on a different civilization. Americans also must not forget that the Native Americans helped the White European settlers build their homes and towns. Still do, especially the skyscrapers in New York City, including the World Trade Center Twin Towers brought down on 9/11.

Native Americans, like Will Rogers, helped shape American music and culture. The punk Mohawk hairdos are a perennial reminder. The Mohawk ironworkers from the Kahnawake and Akwesasne tribes near the New York-Canada border have been helping to construct some of the most distinctive architectural landmarks in America. The Empire State Building, George Washington Bridge, the United Nations and the iconic World Trade Center. Mohawks have been working iron since the 1880s when they helped build a bridge over the Saint Lawrence River from Montreal on to Kahnawake land. Legend has it that a supervisor noticed they did not seem to be afraid of heights.

Liu Wu-chi claims that Confucius had a keen sense of humor and used humor sometimes as a tool in his teachings. For Will Rogers, humor was the tool. He even applied it in a compliment he gave to Confucius himself. This statement came out of a reply Rogers made to philosopher Will Durant's request for a piece from Rogers for Durant's book on great men of the day. Here is Rogers in one of his typically self-deprecating passages: "What all of us know put together don't mean anything. We are just here for a while and pass on. Any man that thinks civilization has advanced is an egotist... . Confucius perspired out more knowledge than the U.S. Senate has vocalized out in the last 50 years."

It's interesting to imagine what, had he known of him, Confucius would have had to say about Will Rogers.

Rogers also made a joke about China that involved Confucius directly, asserting something one suspects Confucius might have agreed with: "Always dodge the expert, you know, the one who lived in China, and knows China. The last man that knew China was Confucius, and he died feeling that he was becoming a little confused about 'em."

Rogers would really be confused seeing the polo fields and ponies China's 1% - ers have.

It is a point many wafflers round the Hong Kongs Foreign Correspondents Club Main Bar and Washington, D.C., have not yet taken.

What is confusing today is China's Communist Party embrace – or non-embrace – of Confucius. In January 2011, a large bronze statue of Confucius was erected overnight without any fanfare in Tiananmen Square, facing Mao Zedong's giant portrait. It was seen as the ultimate symbol of China returning to its roots because of the significant influence Confucianism still has in China and Chinese communities across the world. Yet a few months later, just as abruptly, the statue was removed overnight with no explanation.

Most political analysts agree that the incident is symptomatic of the deeper party dilemma of "to be or not to be." The lack of a cohesive ideology of nation-building, which needs to be in place to improve morality and fill the ideological vacuum left by the Cultural Revolution. China feels the pressure to produce a philosophical ideology that is its own. Communism after all is a Western political ideology. So since the 1990s, there has been talk about reviving Chinese traditions. That includes not just Confucianism, but Buddhism, Taoism and other "Chinese" beliefs as well.

Despite its economic resurgence, China is still fraught with internal contradictions, disparities and instabilities. Corruption is widespread and there seems to be a loss of fundamental values in the nation's transition from dogmatic communism. China is in desperate need of a cultural renaissance, all the more so because of its economic expansion.

China's Republican and Communist revolutions of the 20th century had served to demonstrate its determination to break away from the feudal past and embrace modern foreign systems and ideologies. The May Fourth movement of 1919, which groomed many of the early leaders of the party, saw Confucianism as responsible for a closed conservative dynastic order. "Down with Confucius" became a catchy slogan to free China.

Now, almost a century later, history seems to be coming full circle. Confucianism is being revisited and reinterpreted – not only in China – but in the West.

As China struggles to give its people a moral compass and ethical education fast enough to keep pace with its economic growth, Confucianism has come to the forefront as a useful philosophy. Fed up with the education system, some mainland parents are sending their children to traditional boarding schools known as *sishu,* where the sole subject is the Confucian canon. Students memorize each of the *Four Books* and *Five Classics* in their entirety. When one work is finished, the teacher moves on to the next or simply begins the same one again. One book may be read as many as 600 times. Students do not fear exams because there are none.

Such methods have naturally aroused controversy in a country where many reform advocates feel the education system lacks a respect for students' individualism and fails to foster enough free-thinking people. Some party leaders and scholars are skeptical as to whether Confucian ideals can meaningfully address modern China's ethical problems, which they say need more than mere ideology to resolve. China's lack of moral scruples is legion. It includes sales of poisonous milk powder, infected blood for transfusions, lead poisoning of waterways and agricultural land, high-speed train crashes, knock-off everything from red wines to Jeeps, and an incident in which a 20-year-old car driver who ran over and injured a woman stabbed her to death to avoid "complications."

Corruption is pervasive in China and the only universal belief is in Mammon – the God of Wealth. Not many believe in communism any more. In other words, there is no value system in China today and the country is desperately trying to come up with one that all factions of the ruling Communist Party can accept. Hence the flip-flop on the Confucius statue. Some see Confucianism as an answer to declining moral standards. It teaches wisdom, respect and benevolence – core values for a harmonious society – and the pursuit and adherence to the truth, a dilemma for party officials who want to perpetuate anything but the truth.

China is dealing with institutional decay fueled by corruption and corruption committed by former and current "tigers" at the highest political and military echelons of the party, as well as lowly "flies".

"Ritual and morality are in tatters. The system is defunct. We need to rebuild the system," said Cheng Chung-yi, a professor at the Chinese University of Hong Kong.

The reality is that Confucianism, like the U.S. Constitution – and the Chinese Constitution – is fluid and can be reinterpreted and contextualized to be relevant and meaningful in modern times, especially in a democratic China with Chinese characteristics.

Confucius said more than 2,000 years ago that "Harmony matters most." China-U.S. relations are one of the most important harmonious bilateral relationships in the world today. China is the largest developing country and the U.S. the largest developed country. They will inevitably clash on geopolitical economic issues such as the devaluation of the *yuan*, North Korea and the South China Sea. Such issues must be resolved harmoniously. History and reality have taught us that cooperation between China and the U.S. serves the interests of both countries and the New World Order they must lead in the 21st century.

### *Political and Bureaucratic Corruption*

The perception in America is that everyone in China and Hong Kong is corrupt. There is some truth to that, but it's not the whole truth, certainly not in Hong Kong.

In the face of outrageous police graft, Governor Lord MacLehose in 1973 created the Independent Commission Against Corruption, which led to the graft-free administration that would make Hong Kong into a beacon in Asia.

Lord MacLehose staffed the ICAC with clean cops from Hong Kong and overseas. It was so independent and so ruthless that it came to a turbulent head during the brief but tense police mutiny in 1977 when thousands of angry officers gathered on the parade ground at police headquarters. Later, 2,000 marched on the ICAC to protest the way in which the anti-graft body targeted police officers for sins which, until then, had been widely accepted. "Back Handers" had become a way of life, factored into the family budget. This explosive volcano of police rage only subsided when Lord MacLehose extended an amnesty for the practices of the past.

The ICAC in Hong Kong is still a powerful institution with unusual extrajudicial powers. Powers that greatly benefit Hong Kong taxpayers. Powers that should be seriously considered for all Americans in the 21st century.

Mr. X and other current and former ICAC officers are not allowed to discuss anything related to their job, hence the anonymity. X is British and has spent most of his life in the disciplined services. First as a policeman, then for several years as an inspector at the ICAC. He was involved in several of their high-profile busts before he retired. X is a good friend with whom I enjoy periodically getting together to savor a good cigar and brewsky as we mull over the world's problems. The world being limited to our significant others, children and the choices we made in life.

"The commission has become so powerful that the power in and of itself is in fact corrupting," X volunteered to my proposition that power in Hong Kong is corrupting the territory as we puffed Cuban cigars on the balcony of the Royal Yacht Club in Causeway Bay, watching the harbor traffic glide along in both directions.

"Racism is so pervasive you can't believe," X said as he drew my attention back to our conversation.

"Now that I am no longer with the commission, I feel compelled to share this with you. My supervisor, who is Chinese, would come over to my office, stand over me while I'm writing a report and try to intimidate me and get me into a fight by literally screaming, 'Hey *gweilo,* what you doing?' and continue using abusive language as I just politely answered his questions, as I had to control myself from just getting up and killing him.

"I called my wife. She calmed me down and convinced me to just bite my tongue and killing instinct and just start looking for a job in the private sector before it's too late," X reminisced. He now works in the private sector for one of Asia's tycoon family conglomerates.

"You mean before you got to be too old for anyone to hire you?" I said as we both burst out laughing and took another swig of our beers.

Policemen and politicians in Hong Kong are repeatedly arrested for accepting bribes, vote-rigging, offering inducements to vote, and intimidating voters. Thirteen policemen were arrested in September 2003 for accepting bribes in exchange for giving protection to brothels and gambling dens. They included senior inspectors, sergeants and constables.

That same month 40 people were arrested for vote-rigging in connection with the 2003 Rural Committee Election for Shap Pat Heung. The arrests included candidates, their supporters and enforcers. They were arrested for offering cash inducements, wining and dining voters and threatening the lives and property of the opposition.

Hong Kong elections are among the cleanest in the world. Nevertheless, matters went from bad to worse in the 2011 district council elections and 2012 chief executive election. The ICAC arrested more than 50 people in 2011, charged them – and the court convicted them – with vote-rigging in the district council election of November 6th. The accused had registered in districts other than the one they actually lived in and helped swing the election. The victor won by two votes.

The 2012 chief executive race resulted in Beijing's favored candidate, former chief secretary Henry Tang Ying-yen, losing after it was disclosed he had at least one affair and built an illegal 2,250 square foot palatial basement that resulted in an ICAC probe.

The ICAC was very busy in 2012 with its biggest anti-corruption probe and highest profile arrests and investigations in its history. In addition to investigating Beijing's losing choice for chief executive, it arrested Tang's predecessor, former chief secretary Rafael Hui, and three of Hong Kong's richest tycoons – the Kwok brothers at the helm of real estate giant Sun Hung Kai properties – for bribery and misconduct.

Hui had masterminded Donald Tsang Yam-kuen's successful bid to become chief executive. Tsang was also being investigated by the ICAC for bribery in the waning months of his tenure as chief executive for accepting favors from Hong Kong's tycoons. Tsang was found to have traveled on private yachts and jets and was planning to retire in a Shenzhen penthouse owned by a mainland property magnate with business interests in Hong Kong.

I can relate to Tsang wanting to kick back on a luxury yacht, having done so myself on more than one occasion.

The ICAC investigation resulted in a motion in the Legislative Council to impeach Tsang a month before his term in office expired because, according to polls, three-quarters of Hongkongers did not want to see the chief executive complete his term. The motion failed because it fell short of the two-thirds majority of legislators required.

The ICAC inquiry was expanded to include Tsang's wife, two sons and brother, former police commissioner Tsang Yam-pui, who was an executive director of NWS, the infrastructure and service flagship of New World Development.

The political intrigue reached fever pitch when it was announced that the head of the ICAC – who was appointed by Tsang and is accountable to him – would not be involved in the investigation because of his own conflict of interest. He had close links with the developer of Tsang's retirement penthouse.

That raised questions about how independent the ICAC is, even though it has acted to enforce the law against the Hong Kong political and business establishment.

To make matters worse for Tsang, the Hong Kong audit watchdog released a report just before his term of office expired at the end of June 2012, claiming he wasted millions of Hong Kong taxpayers dollars on unnecessary stays in presidential suites on his overseas trips.

According to Transparency International's annual corruption ratings, Hong Kong ranks 12th-cleanest on a list of 183 countries. The reality is that there is a growing perception – locally and globally – that the corrupt practices of the mainland are infiltrating the political and business fabric of Hong Kong because of the weak system of checks and balances of the corrupt political masters in Beijing. This was highlighted in May 2014 when the ICAC arrested Fang Fang, former CEO of JP Morgan's China investment bank, in connection with an investigation into whether he hired princelings to steer China IPOs to the firm.

Collusion between politicians – regardless of political system or party – and business tycoons, driven by greed that leaves *We the Apathetic People* on the street, results in an ungovernable society and simmering revolution.

### *Corrupt Parallels*
There are city police forces and administrations, certainly in California, New Orleans and New York, which could do with coming under an ICAC style oversight agency. The crimes committed by these men and women in uniform, especially in jurisdictions where the pay is low, is mind numbing, New Orleans is a prime example. The cops there are intent on supplementing their income. It is not just about corruption and bribery, it is also about the abuse of power within the force, where superior officers pull rank as they break the law.

Not just for their own self-enrichment, but avoidance of prosecution for something as simple as drunk driving. A classic case in California is that of Riverside Police Chief Russ Leach, who crashed his city-owned car after a night of drinking, but instead of being given a field sobriety test and arrested, was driven home by the officers who arrived at the scene.

Leach eventually stepped down after an internal investigation. He pleaded guilty to DUI and was sentenced to 30 days' house arrest, three years' probation, $1,700 in fines and alcohol education programs.

And there's the story of Denver ex-Sheriff Patrick Sullivan, who was arrested for providing methamphetamine for sex and held in a jail named for him. Sullivan was the kind of lawman Coloradoans loved: a straight-shooting Republican who once crashed a Jeep through a fence to rescue two deputies from a gunman and pleaded with legislators to keep assault weapons off the street lest any more citizens get shot.

A political corruption story most Americans are familiar with is that of former Illinois governor Rod Blagojevich, who was jailed for 14 years for corruption for trying to sell Barack Obama's Senate seat. Blagojevich's predecessor, George Ryan, a Republican, was also convicted of federal corruption charges and is serving 61/2 years.

As shocking as these crimes may be, they are nonetheless part of a long tradition of malfeasance in a state once famous for the political "machine" of the late Chicago Mayor Richard Daley. Daley's "vote early, vote often," strategy played a key role in delivering the state for John F. Kennedy – and the presidency – in his razor-thin victory over Richard Nixon in the 1960 election.

Corruption in American politics is not limited to law enforcement officers or Chicago. Former Virginia governor Bob McDonnell and his wife Maureen being a 2014 reminder. It is a national epidemic.

The mother lode of political corruption scandals, what the Los Angeles district attorney called "corruption on steroids," was that of the small working-class city of Bell in Los Angeles County. Eight city leaders were arrested in 2010 on charges of misappropriating more than $5.5 million. Former City Manager Robert Rizzo was the highest-paid government official in America. He had an annual salary and benefits package of more than $1.5 million. Those arrested included Rizzo, council members and the former assistant city manager.

Rizzo and political cohorts gave themselves pay raises without city council approval and loaned money to themselves from city coffers to repay loans they borrowed from their pension funds. Bell council members got paid for board meetings that never took place, loaned city funds to friends who never repaid them, imposed illegal sewer charge and business license increases, and the topper, declared their new incoming Police Chief Randy Adams disabled for the job the day he was hired, an arrangement that would pay him millions in tax-free pension money. Adams received a salary of $457,000 annually, double his pay at the much larger city of Glendale.

The same happened on a much smaller scale in the nearby city of Vernon. There, Donald O'Callaghan, a city administrator, in addition to his more than $380,000 annual salary, also received $243,898 in consulting fees.

El Monte Police Chief Thomas Armstrong oversaw a modestly sized department, with 120 officers patrolling a city of 113,000 residents. When he retired in 2011, he was paid nearly $430,000 – significantly more than the Los Angeles police chief or Los Angeles County sheriff.

The big payday was possible because Chief Armstrong was allowed to accrue unlimited sick days and vacation hours and sell them back to the city and the end of his career.

And he's not alone. Similar payouts have been made in city governments across California. A database published by the state controller shows 23 city employees who made more than $400,000 in 2009 or 2010.

Those employees include police chiefs in many cities across the state who earned more than $500,000.

The $200 billion California Public Employees' Retirement System, the country's biggest public pension fund, sued its former director Alfred J.R. Villalobos for $95 million in restitution and penalties for an alleged influence-peddling scandal. Villalobos stayed the proceedings by declaring bankruptcy in Nevada.

In New York, Alan G. Hevesi, the former state comptroller, pleaded guilty to a felony corruption charge after a lengthy investigation into his office's rewarding of pension investment business to firms that provided financial benefits to Hevesi and his aides.

In Washington, D.C., politicians and operatives keep passing through the doors of the federal courts and prisons, pleading guilty to felonies, as if it is the norm and to be expected.

In Chicago, Jesse Jackson Jr. resigned under a cloud of corruption stemming from his ties to imprisoned former governor Blagojevich.

In New Orleans, former Mayor Ray Nagin was indicted for corruption, as was Trenton Mayor Tony Mack in New Jersey and many more.

In fact, political corruption is rampant in most of the 50 states. From Alabama, where 11 lawmakers, lobbyists and businessmen were indicted in 2010 for corruption and influence peddling in connection with legislation that will allow gambling in the state, to New York state and city, where City Controller John Liu was accused of soliciting and receiving illegal campaign contributions to Governor David Patterson, who illegally accepted World Series tickets.

Dining in the Sky Club atop the Met Life building, the former Pan Am building, in New York City, whenever the opportunity presented itself when I was in the city, but especially early evening as the sun sets on a clear blue sky and the city lights take over, looking at the Statute of Liberty, Hudson River and the space where the World Trade Center Towers once stood, following the moving traffic snake its way across town, flashing back to my days as a member of the Finance Council of the Democratic National

Committee and the various fund raisers we put on in the city, especially during the 1976 Democratic Convention, I couldn't help ponder what needs to be done to clean up the corrupting influence money has on politics, not only in New York and America, but China and the world.

No one is above the law in a true democracy. That includes politicians and their advisers no matter how high the office they hold, including the president of the United States and the premier of China.

It is time for the states to wrestle certain oversight powers back from the federal government and impose some oversight on the feds. To oversee corrupt career politicians, public servants, bureaucrats and their corrupting influencers. What Enron officers and directors did to U.S. taxpayers, pensioners and investors in the 20th century comes to mind. And let's not forget the ultimate 21st-century rip-off by banks, insurance companies and the high-paid fliers that crash-landed them and then got handsomely rewarded for their dumb-ass decisions – at the expense of the taxpayers – *We the Apathetic Maids.*

Fellow FCC barflies Kevin Egan and Andrew Lam, two Hong Kong lawyers who have been busted by the ICAC, shared their anger and frustration with fellow glassmates after their arrest, during their trial, sentencing, sojourn in jail, suspension to practice, appeal and final vindication six years later. Listening to and participating in some of the exchanges, accusations and challenges to the different aspects and issues of their case, both in law and fact, from both their points of view, the ICAC's and the various members of the bar that frequent the FCC Main Bar, and the implications of their case on the so-called rule of law in Hong Kong and mainland China, was not only a legal eye opener, but a political ear popper.

Kevin was born and raised in Brisbane, Australia, graduated from the University of Queensland law school in 1971, worked as a prosecutor in Papau New Guinea from 1972-1979, where he became the director of public prosecutions from 1976, to his departure for Hong Kong in 1979. He is admitted to practice law in Australia, Papua New Guinea, Fiji, the U.K. and Hong Kong. In Hong Kong he was a crown prosecutor for 10 years before going into private practice. He is a barrister whose clients include criminals, including some of those busted by the ICAC, who he got off, upsetting the top brass at the ICAC.

"Revenge and payback time," was Kevin's unwavering answer to my question of why he and Andrew were busted by the ICAC if they were innocent.

"If that is the case, what is wrong with the ICAC in your opinion, and what changes, if any, would you make to improve it if you were in a position to do so?" I asked Kevin as we shared a bottle of nice Australian wine with fellow barflies and shared our frustrations about complaints we had filed with the ICAC and CAPO, complaints against police officers – the local police oversight committee – that were not pursued or are still pending.

"Let me answer the second part of your question first," Kevin said as he mulled over the double-barreled question as we sipped our wine. "No doubt the ICAC operates as an independent agency. It only reports to the chief executive and a bunch of his flunkies four times a year as a mere formality. So effectively, it doesn't answer to anyone and is truly independent. That is the root cause of the problem. Because when unshackled, they are a prime example of Voltaire's quote that 'power corrupts and absolute power corrupts absolutely.'

"The problem is you have to rely on the integrity of the deputy commissioner, head of operations, who actually runs the commission, and not the commissioner, who is a political appointee who does fuck-all except kiss babies and make the political rounds. The integrity of the commission depends on the integrity of the individuals, something that is unfortunately lacking. Today, the directors of the commission are principally Chinese, who, shall we say, feel they are on a mission from God. The ICAC doesn't have an official motto, but if it did, it would be 'The End Justifies the Means.' That's what's been driving the organization the last few years. Forcing young recruits to go to court and lie.

"The ICAC, any such organization, can only be fair and unbiased if they play by the rules of law, which they don't. That's why Andrew and I got charged."

Andrew is a Hong Kong-born and raised solicitor who started his career in 1977 as a senior ICAC investigator, where he worked for three years. He then went to the United Kingdom to study law and qualified as a solicitor in 1985. Today he is considered one of the top criminal defense lawyers in Hong Kong because of his impressive track record of keeping his clients out of jail. Many of his clients were also busted by the ICAC and their "escape from justice" also upsets the ICAC.

Kevin and Andrew are a close working barrister-solicitor team with many mutual clients. Some of their clients and witnesses in their cases can be pretty mean if they have a grudge to bear, as Andrew found out when he investigated a witness implicated against him in an ICAC case and received a death threat, followed by a knife slashing of his face. Their legal careers and cases are almost as colorful as their women, many of whom join them periodically and their fellow members of the bar at the FCC.

"Happy to, yes," both Andrew and Kevin responded to my invitation to discuss first-hand their ICAC experiences, government and criminal corruption, and the best way forward for the ICAC and the kind of reforms needed to improve the commission, not just for Hong Kong, but globally.

Andrew and Kevin were both unceremoniously arrested in the early morning hours in their homes and forced to leave their ladies of the night to ponder what they had done wrong. It is the traditional practice of the ICAC to arrest suspects in their homes in the pre-dawn hours, knowing they are at home asleep. Neither Kevin nor Andrew was asleep because of their preferred nocturnal activities in preparation for their upcoming busy trial schedule that day.

The sleepy-eyed lawyers were charged with perverting the course of justice and witness tampering in a bribery case against a chairman of a public company, his secretary and girlfriend, who were charged with bribing placement agents of the company shares to manipulate the stock price.

The chairman and the two women were arrested, but the chairman and his girlfriend were released after 48 hours because, under Hong Kong law, people can only be held for 48 hours without being charged. His secretary was detained and charged, but while in custody used her cell phone from a toilet to call the chairman's girlfriend to protest her detention.

Andrew had been contacted by the girlfriend to represent the secretary but declined the representation and referred the case to another solicitor who hired Kevin. They filed a writ of habeas corpus, a legal procedure to get the secretary released from her alleged protective custody, and for Kevin's efforts to release her and discussing the case with the media, Kevin and Andrew were accused of trying to free the secretary to convince her to change her mind and testimony and not to cooperate with the ICAC. Andrew was accused of being the "back seat driver" steering the case even though he was not representing any of the parties and had referred the case out.

"The ICAC is not answerable or accountable to anyone but the chief executive. They themselves can become a political tool of abuse of process," Andrew said in response to my question of what is wrong with the ICAC. "They should be accountable to a legislative body or commission that represents the legislature and people, not just the CE," Andrew continued, echoing Kevin's suggestions that any constructive change must include an independent body headed up by a respected truly independent judge.

The lack of accountability of its budget and how it spends its money, in many cases in effect bribing witnesses themselves by paying them to "cooperate" or provide evidence, makes certain witness testimony suspect from the outset. "Being a beneficiary of such ICAC largesse is bound to make witnesses suspect," Andrew said.

The justification for this lack of accountability is the issue of "confidentiality," much like the CIA's argument of "national security" to justify its lack of accountability and transparency on how it spends taxpayer dollars. These secretive government bodies funded by *We the*

*Apathetic Maids* in effect operate in a dark room that can't be checked, yet alone balanced by the taxpayers who support their existence. There has to be better oversight by the public. A web of accountability that is truly independent. It cannot just be limited to one individual within the ICAC who is only accountable to the chief executive.

There has to be more of a balance between the public interest and individual rights, something that is sorely lacking in its current operational makeup. There has to be more impartiality. A real firewall between the ICAC and all other departments it deals with to enforce the law and investigate corruption.

An example of this lack of impartiality is the 2006 case of ICAC Assistant Director Rebecca Li Bo-lan. She was having an affair with Department of Justice prosecutor Ian McWalters. They would have their trysts in a motel where neither registered for a room. Turns out the ICAC had a safe house room there that Li used for her personal pleasure when it was not being used by the ICAC to protect a witness. McWalters then became a judge and heard cases involving the ICAC.

"Where is the impartiality? A judge is supposed to be impartial. It is not only a breach of confidence but a breach of the so-called firewall that is supposed to exist between the ICAC, DOJ and the bench," Andrew implored when I asked him what he thought of the Li affair.

"When the ICAC was founded it was given enormous power. More than the police, the ultimate power at the time, in order to properly investigate corrupt police practices. That extra power, which they still have today, violates the Basic Law and basic civil rights, even though it was necessary at the time to tackle police corruption," Andrew said as we continued our discussion over lunch at the FCC Main Bar.

"Today they use that power to tackle a lot more than just corruption. They have unilaterally expanded their powers to investigate cases that have nothing to do with corruption. For example, fraud cases, money laundering, political crimes should be investigated by the police, not the ICAC,"

Andrew said in exasperation as he mulled over my question of how they abuse their power.

"Take the U.K. false expense claims by politicians in Parliament scandal of a couple of years ago," Andrew added. "It was the U.K. police that investigated it. Here in Hong Kong, any political scandal is investigated by the ICAC. Why not the police?"

"Same with the eavesdropping e-mail hacking scandal today in the U.K. with Rupert Murdock's news gathering operations. It is the police investigating," Andrew continued.

"And bribed policemen helped perpetrate the crime itself that they were then required to investigate," I interjected. "Any wonder everyone was exonerated in the first investigation years ago? How is that right, and why shouldn't an ICAC- type body be doing the investigation?"

We sat in momentary silence as we pondered the question and then agreed that a truly independent ICAC was needed, one that is accountable to an independent public body that polices it, not only in Hong Kong, but in Britain and probably the U.S.

The arrests of Egan and Lam in the early morning hours in July 2004 were followed by raids on newspaper offices a few hours later, to determine whether an offense had been committed under Section 17(1) of the Witness Protection Ordinance, because a story appeared in local papers that a woman detained by the ICAC in the program was being held against her will. A writ of habeas corpus was filed by Egan and Lam, but the High Court later cleared the ICAC of unlawfully detaining the woman. However, the High Court ruled against the graft busters' raid of the newspaper offices, finding that their arrest was "wrong in fact and law" when it raided the newsrooms.

"The L Group, the ICAC loves the alphabet and every one of their groups is designated by a letter in the alphabet," Kevin continued, "and is supposed to enforce the ICAC policies and procedures, but unfortunately don't, because they are an in-house department that has no power or independence.

"The solution to true independent oversight and enforcement is to make sure the operational oversight group is not made up of law-and-order fanatics who support the ICAC, no matter what, and just whitewash everything," Kevin said in exasperation as I interrupted with a question about enforcement.

"You can't solve any problem by just setting up another committee or passing another law. No point in passing another toothless law. It is all about enforcement – plus a proper review process that is genuine and has clout – and truly independent. There must be a mechanism, capability and will to enforce," Kevin said and added: "Passing a law without a proper independent review and enforcement mechanism is a pointless exercise."

As if to confirm Egan's hypothesis about a possible ICAC motto, three top anti-graft investigators were convicted of perverting the course of justice and misconduct in April 2012 for coaching a key witness to provide false evidence in a derivatives warrant fraud and money-laundering case.

Recent polls have found that fewer Hong Kongers today see the ICAC as impartial and many believe it has abused its power. Those polls were taken before the arrests and investigations of the former chief secretaries and the chief executive. Nevertheless, today the ICAC is recognized as one of the world's top four anti-corruption agencies. So much so that when the world took notice of the anti-corruption revolutionary movement in India, little did they realize that its inspiration came from Hong Kong's ICAC.

### Global Corruption

The Indian anti-corruption movement, spearheaded by 74-year-old Kisan Baburao Hazare, more commonly known as Anna Hazare, was receiving strong support and advice from the Hong Kong chapter of India Against Corruption at the India Club, a group that had been galvanizing the expatriate Indian community in Hong Kong for months before it became a global headline.

Hazare, a long-time advocate of laws for government accountability, was arrested in August 2011 after his request to carry out a 15-day fast in a public place was rejected by police. He refused to leave jail until his request was granted. After a groundswell of public support, the authorities were forced to grant Hazare's request. His fasting was part of a nonviolent protest in support of legislation that would create an independent body to investigate corruption with powers to punish those found guilty, not something Indian's infamously corrupt politicians and bureaucrats at all levels of government want.

Hazare vowed a "revolution" in India as he began his public fast. "The whole world will see you as an example of how to bring about revolution with nonviolence," the diminutive, bespectacled Hazare told the mass audience.

His campaign tapped into a deep reservoir of discontent – especially among India's burgeoning middle class – over a culture that requires bribes to secure everything from business permits to birth certificates.

"The youth of this country have woken up," Hazare said. "To the traitors who have looted this country, I say we will bear it no longer."

Hazare and his advisers studied the formation of the ICAC in Hong Kong and incorporated many of its goals into the proposed anti-corruption bill submitted to the Indian parliament.

The citizens of India, like those in many countries – developed and developing – have reached the point where corruption is no longer tolerable. The existing cycle of corruption has been broken in the Philippines, where two presidents, several senators and a Supreme Court chief justice have been arrested and jailed for corruption; Israel, where two prime ministers, cabinet members and members of its parliament have been under investigation for corruption; South Africa, where President Jacob Zuma is being investigated for corruption; Britain, where members of all parties were accused of corruption in 2009 for illegal and improper expenses they charged taxpayers; Ireland, where after 15 years of hearings, a tribunal concluded that "corruption affected every level of Irish political life" and that a former prime minister and other politicians were corrupt; Spain, where politicians and members of the royal family are charged with being corrupt; Iran, where Mahmoud Ahmadinejad and his Rasputin, Esfandiar Rahim Mashael, are accused of embezzling billions of dollars; and Japan and South Korea, where politicians resign regularly over corrupt cash payments.

In Brazil, Jose Dirceu, the ex-chief of staff under then-President Luiz Inacio Lula da Silva, was sentenced to 11 years in jail for corruption and vote-buying.

In Greece, former Finance Minister George Papaconstantinou was charged with hiding a list of Greek offshore tax cheats given to him by the French authorities and also removing the names of his relatives from the list.

In Nigeria, Farouk Lawan, a supposed graft-busting legislator, was filmed stuffing bribe money under his hat because he had already filled his pockets.

In Russia, like China, corruption is the country's biggest problem. More than 200 years ago, the reknowned Russian historian Nikolai Karamzin summed up the situation in his country in two words: "They steal."

Cases against Russian ministries, including agriculture and defense, officials at all levels of government, including the office of the president and prime minister, languish because the prosecutors charged with prosecuting the cases are also corrupt.

Corruption is not limited to politicians. It is also rampant in the Vatican and the Catholic Church as the 2012 "Vatileaks" scandal exposed. The Institute for Religious Works, otherwise known as the Vatican's bank, had its secret internals memos to the pope on the Vatican's response to the global financial crisis and how to handle the church's tax exempt status amid Italian government efforts to crack down on tax evasion divulged to the world when they were published in 2012.

In July 2012, the Vatican bank was investigated by Italian prosecutors for possible money-laundering but the probe appeared to evaporate until

January 2013, when Italy's central bank suspended credit card payments in the Vatican because it had not fully implemented anti-laundering legislation.

The legal compromise makes me wonder if Benito Mussolini's millions of dollars donated to the Vatican had anything to do with the evaporated investigation. The fact is that behind a disguised offshore company structure, the church's multi-million dollar international real estate portfolio has grown dramatically over the years using cash originally handed over by Mussolini in return for papal recognition of the Italian fascist regime of 1929. The Vatican and Italian government have gone to great lengths to preserve the secrecy of the Mussolini millions, but the story came to light after a probe by *The Guardian* in 2012.

Did Pope Benedict resign in February 2013 for health reasons or because of the unfolding and never-ending Vatican scandals?

The Vatican bank has been trying for several years to clean up its reputation as a shady tax haven beset by scandals, which include the collapse of Italy's Banco Ambrosiano and the death of its head, Roberto Calvi, who also helped manage Vatican investments and was found hanging from London's Blackfriars Bridge in 1982.

The Hong Kong ICAC was established to deal first and foremost with corrupt cops and civil servants and expanded to include politicians, business and individuals – the entire private sector as well. The key to its Confucian success was an absolute moratorium and clemency on all former corrupt activities and those involved. No different than the clemency offered illegal immigrants or tax and traffic ticket scofflaws in the U.S. Why can't this concept be extended to police departments, politicians and business people in America and China before being adopted globally?

### The Teacher
To really get to understand Confucius, one has to go to Qufu, Shandong province, the cradle of Confucianism. K'ung Ch'iu or K'ung Fu-Tsze, "the philosopher king" whose name was Latinized to Confucius, was born in Qufu in 551 or 552 BC. His father was a famous officer in the State of Lu

who, at age 70, took by force, or parental agreement, a teenage bride to give him the healthy son his other wife had not. His father died three years after Confucius was born, probably leaving Confucius to an impoverished childhood with his mother. His father was from the shih class in China, which was then a very hierarchical and feudal society. The shih were not nobles, but could claim noble ancestry nevertheless.

Confucius married at age 19 and this union produced a son. Little seems to be known of Confucius' family life, other than that there probably was not much of it, especially during the years he traveled constantly. At a still-young age, he took public office as a keeper of stores in Lu, later looking after parks and herds. But at 23 he began the work that would bring him professional fulfillment and lasting fame – he became a teacher. He taught the classics, government and conduct, being a lifelong proponent of and expert in a self-denying, highly ethical existence of correct conduct – a very important aspect of Chinese life called *li*. He gathered many students who were to follow him through his various positions and journeys. Confucius was a contemporary of Lao-Tse, or Lao Tzu, the founder of Taoism which, unlike Confucianism, actually is a religion.

At 52 Confucius was made chief magistrate of Chung-tu in Lu, and the community thrived so much that the Duke of Lu appointed him minister of crime for Lu. Wrongdoing was dramatically reduced with Confucius in power, but when the Duke accepted and spent days focusing solely on a gift of females sent to entertain him, a disillusioned Confucius left Lu. Confucius was said to be 56 at the time. Already this is seriously pushing the expected life span of that era. Legends abound about plots against the nobles that Confucius foiled, including one about a plan to disrupt a conference between the states that he salvaged. After leaving Lu, he spent the next 13 years wandering among China's states, teaching at times, consulting with leaders at others, and accumulating thousands of students. His son died while he was traveling. When he was 69 he returned to Lu an esteemed and renowned teacher. He died at the age of 72 or 73, and was buried in the K'ung cemetery, outside of K'iuh-fow, where his descendants are said to still live. His tomb has been visited by countless followers over the years. He is credited with writing or editing various parts of several

Chinese classics, including the 10 appendices of the *I Ching,* or *Book of Changes.* The book S*pring and Autumn* is said to have been written solely by Confucius, epitomizing his teachings in his 72nd year. Another important reference for Confucian wisdom is *The Analects,* a compilation of conversations between Confucius and his disciples.

Confucianism was consolidated as a mainstream social-political philosophy during the Han dynasty (200 BC). Since then, until the mid-Qing Dynasty, China remained the world's leading civilization economically and politically. The Confucian core ideals rest on morality, trust, order, stability and education. Confucianism is flexible and adaptive to change, existing in harmony with Buddhism, Taoism, Judaism, Islam and Christianity.

Tong Yun-kai, president of the Confucius Academy, said, "It has been said by a Nobel Prize winner that if mankind wants a smooth transition into the next century, then he must reflect on and study well Confucius' thoughts of 2,500 years ago.

"To make profits in proper ways with persistence and integrity is Confucius position and when we all abide by his doctrines, an atmosphere of integrity will be formed gradually," Tong continued.

Confucius declared that "The ultimate purpose of government is the welfare of the common people." It's something *We the Apathetic People* repeatedly forget.

Both Confucius and Will Rogers believed in chivalry. Confucius said: "The gentleman understands *yi*. The small man understands *li*." By *yi* he meant right conduct, morality, duty to one's neighbor, righteousness, altruism and virtue. By *li* he meant egocentricity, profit, gain, advantag– not the proper motives for actions affecting others.

Philosophers of the East and West often sound more alike than most people realize – Confucius and Will Rogers being just one case in point. Great schools of thought should talk. This idea is best articulated by 84-year-old Leonard J. Swidler, professor of Catholic thought and interreligious dialogue at Temple University in Philadelphia, who lectures and writes on Confucianism and its dialogue with Western tradition.

Swidler founded the Dialogue Institute in 1978 with the aim of fostering interreligious and intercultural scholarship, understanding and cooperation. He believes that dialogue among the different traditions is vital because "no tradition can cover the whole truth; they need each other."

The various philosophical beliefs and traditions are moral guides. Confucianism shares much in common with Western traditions because, like them, it is the pursuit of goodness that defines all the world's great systems of thought. Their differences are complimentary rather than contradictory, as they do not contradict one another when it comes to certain basic values like love, liberty and the pursuit of happiness.

Many of the ills of society can be cured by adopting the Will Rogers-Confucian philosophy that stresses a fundamental belief in family, community, respect for elders and distrust for politicians and taxes, thereby necessitating a true government of the people, by the people. We are reminded by Rogers that "This country is not where it is today on account of any man. It is here on account of the big normal majority."

Governments that do not listen to Confucius, Will Rogers or *We the People* in the New World Order will do so at their peril.

### *People Power*

People do have the ultimate power, whether they live in a democracy or under a dictatorship. People have repeatedly brought down monarchies, dictatorships, and democratically elected governments that did not listen to the will of the people or live up to their promises.

The people brought down Presidents Lyndon Johnson and Richard Nixon. The people brought down the Romanov Czars – and Communism. The same with Romania's Ceausescu, the Philippines' Marcos and Estrada. People brought down Chiang Kai-shek and his Kuomintang Party and Indonesia's Suharto and Wahid. The people brought down Yugoslavia's

Slobodan Milosevic and endless successive presidents in Argentina, Bolivia, Ecuador and Venezuela. People brought down Ben Ali, Mubarak, Morsi and Qaddafi in Tunisia, Egypt and Libya.

President George H.W. Bush borrowed the phrase new world order to describe the globe after the first Gulf War. People brought him down because his administration was out of touch with his constituency. He should have listened to Senator Barry Goldwater, who was a man of conscience and was opposed to the Christian Right controlling the Republican platform.

Bill Clinton, notwithstanding his sexual dalliances, stayed in office because the people supported him. He gave them what he promised. A better economy and more dollars. The same holds true for Jiang Zemin. Notwithstanding Tiananmen, Jiang and the Chinese hierarchy put the country on the road to improved standards of living overall, even though there was suffering brought on by the breaking of the "iron rice bowls."

People, regardless of what system they live under, have always decided the fate of that system. The Bourbons in France found it out to the delight of early Americans. Batista in Cuba found it out to the horror of later Americans.

The military has historically always played an active role in politics. Today, organized armed forces are still in the picture but out of focus. Globally – but with noticeable exceptions – they seem to be accepting a diminished role because they know that people ultimately rule when they are united in their frustration and anger at the lack of basic necessities to live decently.

Whether leaders are democratically elected, as Will Rogers kidded, or authoritarian, as Confucius understood, they had better deliver. Leaders cannot be swayed by every constituency. Leaders must lead and at the same time give the people what they need and were promised if they want to survive. It is forever a balancing yin-and-yang act.

## China's Balancing Act

China is the second most corrupt country after Russia, with its infrastructure sector among the most poorly rated of the 19 industries surveyed by Transparency International. The survey examined how much companies must bribe in a country to get business. The growing importance of China and Russia in international trade and investment makes the need for them to address bribery and corruption globally an urgent one.

The corruption-murder scandal surrounding the downfall of political rising star Bo Xilai and his wife Gu Kailai exposed to the world just how corrupt politics and business is in China. The scandal brought down the wall of secrecy that shielded China's growing elite from public scrutiny of its wealth. Although Beijing's censors have tried to control the story, China's 500 million Internet users have turned the party's crisis into its most public scandal ever. And it is exposing an uncomfortable truth for China's Communist Party rulers: the growing desire among China's elite to send their money and children to the West and the seat of capitalism and democracy – America.

Strikingly, the Bo affair is prompting some to suggest that the root cause of the scandal might be China's own system. Independent business magazine *Caixin* railed in April 2012 against "unchecked power" in China, saying the Communist Party's "authoritarian regime" may be part of the problem.

"The lesson from Bo's case is that only institutionalized oversight can prevent the abuse of power, and that only a democratic mechanism can prevent officials from becoming corrupt," *Caixin* reported.

Bo's meteoric rise, based on his Chongqing model that I discussed at length in *Feasting Dragon, Starving Eagle,* employed songs and slogans from Mao's Cultural Revolution. Political pundits speculated whether behind the scenes the Communist Party was trying to stop Bo's political rise, especially when Premier Wen Jiabao, the day before Bo's ouster, said the mainland risked a return to the Cultural Revolution unless the country continued to pursue political change.

Bo's rapid rise and fall is a metaphor for what is wrong with China, the world's fastest-growing major economy. China is high-tech central, with state-of-the-art factories, modern office towers, six-lane highways, high-speed rail, state wealth and reserves that are the envy of the world. Its nouveau riche, the Middle Blingdom, is vital to the world's luxury brands, yet the political system is stuck in Mao's communist '50s.

In 2011, the richest 70 members of China's legislature were worth more than the annual gross domestic product of Slovakia. The $90 billion concentrated among them is both emblematic of how the nation's model is failing the masses, the 99 percent, and why the Communist Party leadership stonewalls any change that threatens their income.

Those who have made it financially often squirrel away their ill-gotten gains overseas, usually in North America. When they sense their luck is running out, they follow their money. That is why China has a border watch for corrupt politicians and runaway bosses – private entrepreneurs – who have fled abroad after defaulting on billions of *yuan* owed to state banks and loan sharks.

More than 10,000 Communist Party and government officials fled to the U.S. or Europe with 650 billion *yuan* in bribes and embezzled state funds between 1999 and 2009, according to a Peking University study.

The arrest in May 2012 of Yang Kun, an executive vice president of the Agricultural Bank of China, one of China's Big Four state-controlled banks, and his associate He Juxin, a brand manager at second-tier lender Minsheng, sent tremors through the real estate industry for questionable loans made in exchange for bribes.

Corruption is so endemic in China that even charities, including the Red Cross Society of China, are corrupt and scandal-plagued. The Red Cross was accused of misappropriating millions of yuan donated to victims of the Sichuan earthquake and more recently it has been accused of misappropriating the bulk of the funds earmarked for Chinese forced to work in Japanese internment camps during World War II.

More than 40,000 Chinese were ferried to Japan to toil in internment camps during the war. Kajima Construction and Nishimatsu Construction that had employed 986 and 183 Chinese war laborers, respectively, agreed to pay 250 million *yuan* and 128 million *yuan* in an out-of-court settlement with the victims and their families through the Red Cross. The victims have not received any money and the Red Cross has not revealed what it did with the funds.

The Chinese government must allow more public scrutiny of charitable foundations and pass laws that make it mandatory for all charities to be transparent with their fund-raising activities and operations.

It is also time for mainland leaders to disclose their own personal assets as a safeguard against conflicts of interest and corruption as first called for by former President Jiang Zemin at the National People's Congress in 1994.

The downfall of Bo Xilai has exposed the degree of corruption that the unholy alliance of politics, business and wealth creates and the urgency for reform.

Premier Wen Jiabao's family is reported to control a $2.7 billion empire that includes finance, insurance, diamonds, energy and waste treatment. A *New York Times* report in October 2012 claimed his mother, wife and children controlled the Wen family empire of "hidden riches." The premier asked for a top-level inquiry into the report by the party and issued an unprecedented rebuttal to the *Times* explosive expose – the first time a top Chinese leader issued a rebuttal to a foreign media report. General Secretary Xi Jinping and family were subjected to a similar expose by *Bloomberg*.

While Communist Party regulations call for top officials to disclose their wealth and that of their immediate family members, no law or regulation prohibits relatives of even the most senior officials from becoming deal makers or investors – a loophole that effectively allows them to trade on their family name. Some Chinese argue that permitting the families of party leaders to profit from the country's economic boom has been important to ensure elite support for market-oriented reforms.

The net worth of the 70 richest delegates to the 2012 National People's

Congress was $90 billion, having risen by $1.5 billion in one year. That is more than the $7.5 billion total wealth of all 660 top officials in the three branches of the U.S. government. Such concentration of wealth, political influence and institutional power in China has worrying implications for society and is a threat to the party's political legitimacy.

In addition to Premier Wen Jiabao calling for transparency, Ren Xiaobin and Cui Wunian, former heads of the Central Organization Department, and Ma Xiaoli, a former United Front Department official who is the daughter of a revolutionary under Mao Zedong, called in an open letter in 2012 for top communist leaders to disclose their finances.

"The new party leadership must show their determined stance to the broader party and their countrymen by adopting zero-tolerance for corruption by party officials," the retirees wrote. "Without such an attitude, we believe the new party leadership will not be trusted by ordinary party members and citizens."

Party leaders heeded the call at the Communist Party's 18th Party Congress. Outgoing General Secretary Hu Jintao said that all those who violated party discipline and state laws "must be brought to justice without mercy," regardless of their place in the hierarchy.

"Combating corruption and promoting political integrity, which is a major political issue of great concern to the people, is a clear-cut and long-term political commitment of the party," Hu said. "If we fail to handle this issue well, it could prove fatal to the party, and even cause the collapse of the party and the fall of the state."

Incoming General Secretary Xi Jinping criticized cadres for their pursuit of personal gain into an "abyss of corruption," and for putting the pursuit of personal power and individual gain ahead of their duties. He warned that such extravagances could weaken the Communist Party's six-decade hold on power.

"Numerous experiences in history have taught us that a country or family can either succeed for its austerity or fail for its luxury," Xi said. "We communists should heed this warning."

Taiwan's "sunshine" laws, which compel government officials, including the president and their spouses and dependents, to publicly declare all their assets at home and abroad annually is a model for the mainland – especially if it wants Taiwan back in the national fold. The Communist Party must submit to people's scrutiny and sound rules of oversight if it wants to survive. There is zero tolerance for corruption in the New World Order and it is only a matter of time before corrupt officials will be brought to account – everywhere.

Corruption has become the primary cause of social instability and lurks behind every case of mass unrest in recent years – not only in China – but everywhere from Tunisia to India, Greece to Iran, South Africa to South America and America itself. It is the seedling that has sprouted the Third Revolution.

### Hong Kong Political Innovation
Instant democratization is not necessary for economic success. This is confirmed by many politicians and economists. As former World Bank chief in China Yukon Huang points out, "There is no direct correlation between economic progress and the nature of the government, whether it's an authoritarian or a democratic system."

Huang sees the ingredients for economic success elsewhere. "Four or five years ago, everyone thought the Japanese were going to wipe out the Americans economically, but now the U.S. seems to be strong in everything," he said.

The secret? "Innovation, responsiveness and speed became the key ingredients and the strength of the U.S. system. It is decentralized and flexible," said Huang. He believes China is in the enviable position of being able to learn not only from the Russian example but also from the Japanese and Korean conglomerate models, where high costs and inefficiencies contributed to their economic woes.

"In a sense what happened in Asia had similarities with the collapse of the Soviet Union, which was reporting glowing growth figures in the decades up to its end. But that growth was so inefficient and expensive that it basically bankrupted itself," Huang says.

Even former Hong Kong Governor Christopher Patten, who was condemned by Chinese officials as "a prostitute for a thousand generations," is now preaching that the Hong Kong government and business models should be adopted by the West.

"Do countries sustain economic growth by limiting the size of government, or do they limit the size of government by sustaining growth," Patten asks.

Five years as governor of Hong Kong have left Patten believing in the first proposition. In his view, lean government helped East Asia grow rich, and it could do the same for the lethargic economies of Western Europe, if only the region's overburdened political systems would allow it. And it would definitely work in America!

Ironically, the most relevant lesson for America from Hong Kong's growth miracle may be the need for more rather than less state involvement in the functioning of certain parts of the economy. Confucian philosophies and teachings can help. He is an old sage for the New World Order.

"The East is red, the West is blue, Elvis is dead, Confucius too," writes poet Damien Sin. That does not mean either are forgotten or irrelevant in today's globalized red, white, yellow and blue world.

Adopting a Hong Kong approach to ensuring that baby-boomers save for their old age would not, in itself, free America from the trap of low savings and growth rates. But it might stop the country from moving ever further in the wrong direction.

The political system in Hong Kong is rather simple to understand.

"Can you give me a brief summary on how the Hong Kong political system will work once the Chinese take over?" Kevin McBride asked during one of our horseback rides to Inspiration Point. "Most people don't have a clue – me included."

"For a place so small, Hong Kong's government is complicated. The British will leave and the place will be connected by long reins to the Chinese," I explained.

"At the stroke of handover in 1997, the constitutional foundation immediately becomes the Special Administrative Region's Basic Law. It was put together by Chinese government agencies and their appointed Hong Kong drafters and dutifully passed by the National People's Congress, China's parliament. It works alongside existing statute and English common law practice, guaranteed under the 'two systems' solution. Those judges will have to have stamina.

"The administration will be headed by a chief executive who will have powers similar to the old governors – except that he is directly appointed by Beijing instead of London. The Hong Kong Civil Service remains the same – except that new secretaries of bureaus have to be approved by Beijing – something London did not require since its hand was there already. At that level they actually would have all looked the same to London.

"The most noticeable handover drama will be on the legislative front – The Legislative Council. At the same stroke of handover, the colonial Legislative Council Chris Patten put together was abolished until elections more digestible to China are held," I said.

"With Patten, the British had been accelerating the pace of direct elections to the point where the council is very close to representing a one-man, one-vote franchise. This has infuriated the Chinese and conservative Hong Kong businessmen who feel the British are trying to leave a mini and defiant Westminster behind them. They'll probably tear it up."

The Basic Law provides a 10-year timeline for the gradual increase of geographical constituency seats to comprise up to half of the legislature by 2007, with the other half set aside for functional representatives. But a switch to direct elections is possible under a set of conditions including two-thirds majority support from the legislature and the consent of the chief executive.

Today the Legislative Council of Hong Kong has 60 members, only 20 of whom are directly elected by geographical constituency. Thirty are elected by "functional constituencies," which are loosely the professions and trade unions. Ten more are put in by an Electoral College. This odd constitutional cart contains 1,200 "electors" themselves elected by a complex process of proportional representation across the territory for the sole purpose of electing the other 10 members. The 1,200 are not in any way bound to the general electorate and the successful 10 have no direct connection to the electorate at all.

"Part of this determination not to have a directly elected chamber is fear of the development of parties," I continued. "It's not just that the motherland likes one party and does not want little ones appearing at her hems. In Hong Kong itself, political parties have long been thought of as disruptive, something that would get in the way of business. To use a regular phrase, they would be 'bad for Hong Kong' as are U.S. import quotas, too much social security and No. 10 typhoons. Nevertheless, there are over eight vibrant political parties in Hong Kong today. All have popularly elected representatives in the legislature.

"The Legislative Council, commonly referred to as Legco, continues to legislate, approve taxation and expenditures and monitor the government. All legislation has to be notified to the Standing Committee of the National People's Congress, which, if it believes something is not in conformity with the Basic Law as it affects relations with the central authorities, is simply invalidated then and there.

"Additionally and rather colorfully, Legco can now impeach the chief executive, dismiss the chief justice and force the chief executive to accept legislation he does not like if it persistently passes it with two-thirds majorities. Men of vivid imagination are sought to tell under what circumstances these events could realistically come to pass.

"The other constitutional branch, the law, was touched as little as possible. Ultimate appeals to the Privy Council in London had to be replaced by a Court of Final Appeal which seats some overseas judges. There is the thorny problem of Final Appeal decisions not thought to conform to the Basic Law relating to the affairs of the Central People's Government, in other words decisions that trespass on the 'one-country' policy or, more bluntly, meddle in the mainland's affairs."

That has already happened regarding court decisions on the Hong Kong right of abode for certain mainland residents and Filipino maids. The government, disliking it, referred it to the NPC Standing Committee and the parliament reversed it. This had the chief executive making referrals of law to Beijing and a Standing Committee there acting as Hong Kong's de facto very final court. No different than the Privy Council.

I know first hand. I have been personally subjected to this judicial partiality as I pointed out in the previous chapter. One of the tools used by the government is to retire judges whose decisions it disagrees with and either leave their seat vacant or replace them with a judge who is believed to be friendly toward the government, usually former prosecutors. A blatant case in point is that of Justice Kemal Bokhary. He was a judge for 23 years and hailed as the liberal voice and conscience of the Court of Final Appeal by his colleagues in the legal profession. Bokhary was born in Hong Kong to a Pakistani family and is revered for contributing to the development of the city's legal system. He was a strong advocate of the rule of law and judicial independence, shown by his repeated objections to seeking interpretations of the Basic Law from Beijing.

Bokhary was asked to retire in October 2012 when he reached the mandatory retirement age of 65, unlike other judges who are beyond 65 but are perceived to be friendly to Beijing and whose term of office is extended. Bokhary's job was handed over to a man nine months his senior. High Court judges – including those of the Court of Appeal and Court of First Instance

– can stay on for up to five years on a discretionary basis after the age of 65.

As of the writing of this chapter in the summer of 2012, Hong Kong is facing a judicial crisis as more than a quarter of its judicial positions are vacant, causing delays in bringing cases to court, or as in my cases, by bringing one of the non-permanent retired judges whose judicial pre-disposition is well known. To make matters worse, half of the 38 judges working in the Court of Final Appeal, Court of Appeal and Court of First Instance – the top three tiers of the court system – are aged over 60.

The rule of law in Hong Kong is not what it used to be – it is being corrupted.

"Injustice anywhere," said Martin Luther King Jr., "is a threat to justice everywhere."

In Hong Kong, prosecutions are not controlled by an independent director of prosecutions, as in many major common law jurisdictions, but by the secretary for justice – the equivalent of the U.S. attorney general in America – a government minister appointed by the central government in Beijing on the recommendation of the chief executive. A good reason to despair

### America's Despair

The desert roads that Oklahoma City bombing suspect Timothy McVeigh traveled are littered with drifters, dropouts, boozers, gamblers and speed freaks who take refuge in cheap motels. If some piece of the puzzle of the Oklahoma tragedy was cut from the bleak patch of the Southwest, it seems fitting. But it is a piece that speaks to despair more than to anger, to the nihilism and the anonymity of America's growing underbelly. No different than angry Brits expressed during the 2011 London riots, Greeks in the cradle of democracy, Egyptians in Tahrir Square and Chinese in thousands of villages and cities across China.

The failure of our so-called leaders to "drain the swamp" of corruption in Congress is best exemplified today by former House Speaker Nancy Pelosi, who vowed to do just that when she became speaker. She censured Rep.

Charles Rangel (D-Harlem) for 11 ethics violations in 2010 – and then endorsed his re-election in June 2012.

"He's been a person who has been here for the working people of our country," Pelosi said. "He has always, always been their champion, most recently on the health care bill," she added, calling Rangel "my friend." Must be a new way to drain a swamp that I haven't figured out yet.

You know the swamp is deep when six members of the House Ethics Committee recused themselves in February 2012 from considering ethics violations against California's Rep. Maxine Waters, who was accused of intervening on behalf of a bank where her husband owned stock and served on the board. It was the second time the investigation was sidetracked.

The way that America's career politicians continue to play in their swamp and squander trillions of hard-earned taxpayer dollars in Iraq and Afghanistan is incomprehensible to me. Why do *We the Apathetic Maids* allow this legacy of self-destructive waste and corruption to continue unabated?

Whether fueled by U.S. Army majors, lieutenant colonels, sergeants and privates sentenced to jail for accepting kickbacks in multimillion dollar defense-contracting scandals in Iraq and Afghanistan; U.S. corporate icons and their executives pleading guilty to squandering hundreds of millions of dollars to bribe foreign government officials in violation of the Foreign Corrupt Practices Act; U.S. bankers and corporate executives making billions of dollars from insider information; or the billions of dollars of U.S. political campaign contributions, legal and illegal, wasted on misleading and false political mud-slinging ads instead of education and developing America's human capital, is nothing short of national suicide.

"Listen to this," I announced to Bob Alter on a train from Hastings on Hudson to Manhattan for another day of meetings. We were both reading papers like all dutiful commuters do on their way into the city. Will Rogers would not expect anything else. "Angry that 'democracy in this country has been in decline,' Adrienne Rich, the award-winning poet, has decided to turn down the 1997 National Medal for the Arts. Rich informed the Clinton administration of her decision in a letter to Jane Alexander, chairwoman of the National Endowment for the Arts, which administers the awards.

"I am not against government in general, but I am against a government where so much power is concentrated in so few hands,' Rich said in a telephone interview from her home ."

Bob put down his paper and said, "You know, people are becoming rather cynical about government and voting. Even in our little town of Hastings, people are now apathetic and disgusted. Politicians fight about the dumbest things with a total disregard for people's needs and concerns."

Guess why?

Rich's comments reminded me of the old Confucian societies, which ranked scholar, farmer, artisan and merchant in that order. It's no wonder, since artisans make more sense than business people and their lobbyists. Artisans don't try to buy career politicians. They try to change them while they work to stay alive.

### Confucian Democracy
Former Premier Lien Chan of Taiwan claims that Confucianism has played a role in Taiwan's modernization. "Confucianism's definitive aspect involves the Golden Mean — applying moderation in human relations and avoiding prejudice. It is a recipe for social harmony as well as the cultural hallmark of a mature democracy. If a politician lacks understanding of the electorate and respect for his opponents, he cannot avoid bias, and democracy easily becomes a crass power game. If people engage in social activities with the correct Confucian attitude toward interpersonal relations, democracy will readily succeed," Lien said.

"Confucian concepts remind us that when doing anything, we must establish with whom we are dealing, and conform our behavior to norms and rules. Confucianism demands a clear distinction between right and wrong and eschews smug ignorance. Confucian discussions are excellent sources for training a modern citizenry. Taiwan did produce the first Chinese-speaking democratically elected president. The island state evolved in just over a decade, from a repressive one-party state under martial law to a full-fledged democracy. Like South Korea, Indonesia and the Philippines, it merely forecasts what will happen in mainland China, which will embrace and consume its people and institutions and welcome it back as the 'prodigal child,' " the former premier said.

While politicians in America wave the flag of family values when railing against moral decay, Asian leaders enact the values of family over all else. For the most part, members of this group support democracy in principle, but not necessarily the American application.

Meanwhile, back on the Confucian mainland, residents of Huajia, a tiny rice-growing community in Zhejiang Province, elected a village committee to manage their hamlet, population 718. The vote was very limited: Citizens selected from among four candidates – all Communist Party members – for three open positions on the committee. But it was part of an ambitious rural democratization program launched by the government that in the long term could be more significant than Taiwan's achievement. Both cases debunk myths that Chinese culture, built on the foundation of Confucian ideals, is incompatible with true democracy. Promoted by one of China's party elders, the village democracy program began in 1987 as the party struggled to find a way to make local leaders more accountable. Elected local leaders replaced the appointed chiefs of the farm collective, dismantled during the economic reforms under senior leader Deng Xiaoping. Many farmers and villagers are challenging the corrupt practices and unfair oppressive taxes imposed by their elected leaders. Isn't it time Americans did the same?

Kim Dae Jung, a leading champion of democracy and human rights in South Korea, argues that democratic ideas are fundamental to Asian culture. "Almost two millennia before Locke, Chinese philosopher Meng-tzu preached similar ideas," Kim says. If a king did not "govern righteously, the people had the right to rise up and overthrow his government in the name of heaven.... The ancient Chinese philosophy of *minben zhengchi,* or 'people-based politics,' teaches that 'the will of the people is the will of heaven' and that one should 'respect the people as heaven' itself.... There are no ideas more fundamental to democracy than the teachings of Confucianism.... Clearly, Asia has democratic philosophies as profound as those of the West.... Confucian scholars were taught that remonstration against an erring monarch was a paramount duty."

Professor Tu Wei-ming, world authority on Confucianism who teaches at Harvard University, explains what Confucius has contributed to the Asian economic miracle. Confucianism embraces two mainstreams of philosophy, politics and personal ethics. "Political Confucianism," he says "legitimates a hierarchical political system culminating in the emperor... [while the] 'Confucian personal ethic' ... regulates day- to-day life."

Some Asian governments are employing political Confucianism as an umbrella to legitimize their mode of governance, whereas Professor Tu argues that "the more important legacy of traditional Confucianism is not its political teaching, but rather the personal ethic that regulates attitudes toward family, work, education and other elements of daily life that are valued in Chinese society."

He'd have made a great Log Cabin Republican.

Many Americans do not understand that in the Hong Kong concept of hierarchy, responsibility flows in two directions: Confucianism is not just "Listen to thy father." The father must also be accountable to the son.

"Confucianism is not simply the advocacy of obedience to government, but also the accountability of government," explains Professor Tu.

He adds that student activists and radicals who protest the policies of the governments in Beijing, Hong Kong, Shanghai, Taiwan and South Korea are responding to Confucian teachings. That may explain why the statue of Confucius was removed from Tiananmen Square.

Sociologist Ambrose King has observed that modern Chinese have begun to change some of their traditional belief systems. In the crucible of the new Chinese cities, observes King, Confucianism has evolved into something he describes as "the culture of rationalistic traditionalism," a combination of traditional filial and group virtues with a pragmatism shaped by the conditions of a new competitive environment. Shouldn't America be doing the same?

### Old Sages for New Age
It is difficult to expand on the thoughts of Will Rogers and Confucius, two sages who expressed themselves so eloquently. One can generalize about the basic precepts they both believed in and shared with others: to be kind, honest, upright, honoring family and country. In Confucius' case, nature, as one's true and best nature, was an important theme, probably as significant as "the Lord" was to Rogers. Both men were strongly against crime, with Rogers having a particular disdain for kidnappers – but neither were complex political scientists. Rogers knew that.

But Confucius lived in a very decadent time, and much of his teaching was intended to lead people out of self-indulgence into striving for a higher and greater good. Confucius' concept of *datong,* or Great Harmony, was a utopian society in which there is no hatred and everyone shows concern for each other. Rogers was usually more accepting of the bad he found along with the good in people in the 20th century, and put a lot more emphasis on laughter and sheer fun, a seemingly perfectly balanced philosophy for a decadent New World Disorder. Why can't we laugh at ourselves while we harmonize the 21$^{st}$ century for ourselves and our children?

Rogers had no sympathy with government when it mistreated its own or others' citizens, and said so. He lived in a country, system and time that allowed him to do so. Though an advocate of reform, Confucius did not live in a world that allowed him access to a very large public, or perhaps the freedom to be openly critical, that Will Rogers had. Confucius was known to be a snob, and seemed a prime advocate of the feudal power structure, though there are those exceptions involving corruption and incompetence. Though Rogers consorted with the high and mighty, loving to be out on the fields playing polo or relaxing at his Pacific Palisades ranch, he remained at heart an outspoken country boy who had great empathy for the underdog and the working man. Confucius wanted to show people the way to live right. Rogers wanted to see everywhere and know everyone, letting you know them through him too – and he wanted to make you laugh, at the world and yourself.

These two sages had a lot of sense and imagination to share. Rogers as to how one could, and Confucius as to how one should, live life. But the 20th-century Rogers is the one who resonates more with people today, because he saw a world very like the one that still exists and made accepting and living in it a little easier for those who share the ride with him and want to gallop their horse home.

In the final analysis, Confucius teaches us wise and proper ways to survive and exist, but Rogers actually imparts the pleasure in being alive. Riding in his hoof steps at Will Rogers State Park, one loves the feeling of being alive. Riding bareback takes one back to Confucius' days before horses, when "flying" for all students was impossible. Things have definitely changed in China, especially Hong Kong. How about America?

Stephen Rosenfeld of the *Washington Post* reminds us that "Democracy was supposed to be the great American gift to the post-Cold War world. The difficulties and failure democracy has experienced in the former Soviet Union, Africa, Asia and Latin America ... have led many to question its suitability and adaptability in their new world order."

Many Americans are doing the same. America's final election of the last millennium resulted in a divided country. A president and Congress hopelessly engaged in mortal partisan combat. Only the Afghan war and the war on terrorism changed that temporarily.

In many places, democracy is less the solution than the problem: it has created populist illiberalism – people choosing bad things like racism and selfish power. Will Rogers pointed out the downside of democracy: "One of the evils of democracy is you have to put up with the man you elect whether you want him or not. That's why we call it democracy."

Democratic values through representative government are Anglo-Saxon practices that were ideal for America and its former colonies when adopted and genuinely practiced by *We the People*. However, they are no longer honestly practiced or ideal. America does not practice what it preaches. It's time for America to start preaching what we practice and practice what we preach. Otherwise, America's political theories will only be "Will Rogers one-liners" on the late-night talk show circuit in the 21$^{st}$ century. As Jay Leno said of Bush versus Gore: "It's good to know that America's a place where any preppy can grow up to be president of the United States."

After that election got mired in the Florida political and legal swamp, David Letterman said: "George W. Bush is not our president. Al Gore is not our president. Let's just leave it that way." Is this what *We the Apathetic People* want fellow Americans saying about America in the New World Order?

The Bush-Gore election exposed the problems with America's multi party system and lay bare that elections have become a tool for small groups fighting for power and their own interests. Once a political party comes to power, it becomes indifferent to the real needs of the people.

China is much worse. China a country with a population of 1.36 billion people is run by just over 2,500-fewer than the population of most villages in Europe, Professor Kerry Brown astutely observes in his book *The New Emperors*. Brown points out China is run by an increasingly hereditary class. "The [Communist Party] is like a partly family-run business... almost like a board member represents key shareholders in a family business that has gone public."

Both countries should probably compromise on their political systems and settle for "managed democracy" to ensure a harmonious relationship. Confucius said more than 2,000 years ago that "Harmony matters most."

Sound familiar? "Harmony" is the political buzzword, sound bite and spin of China's Communist Party. China-U.S. relations are one of the most important bilateral relationships in the world today. China is the largest developing country and the U.S. the largest developed country. They will inevitably clash on geopolitical economic issues such as the devaluation of the *yuan* and the South and East China seas. Such issues must be resolved harmoniously. History and reality have taught us that cooperation between China and the U.S. serves the interests of both countries and the New World Order they must lead in the 21$^{st}$ century.

**Flat Tax the Right Stuff**
*Taxman*
– Beatles

### The Rich Get Richer

Living in Rivas Canyon provided a country lifestyle in the middle of bustling Los Angeles that was ideal for raising children. No one had a key to the front door. It was always unlocked. Nikolai, our black Labrador-Dalmation, would bark away any unwelcome strangers. Alexandra and Jonas would take their friends and disappear for hours exploring the canyon with its streams, waterfalls and tadpoles after the heavy rains of late winter and early spring. Each had their own horse and loved riding up and down the canyon with their city-slicker friends.

Another great thing about living in Will Rogers' old guest house was that it and the horses were a tax write-off. The pleasures we were enjoying were courtesy of Uncle Sam and his subsidizing taxpayers. The horses, ranch and house were tax deductible. Taxpayers were subsidizing our lifestyle!

What we were doing was legal and in compliance with the tax law. It is a stupid, irrational law. We didn't write it or support it. But we'd have been foolish not to take advantage of it. Rogers was right on when he said, "Well, we cuss the lawmakers. But I notice we're always perfectly willin' to share in any of the sums of money that they might distribute."

Mark Zepezauer and Arthur Naiman, the authors of *Take the Rich Off Welfare,* discuss in great detail government waste and the deep-rooted subsidy culture towards wealthy individuals, corporations and industries. They estimate that $448 billion greatly understates the amount of money American taxpayers shell out every year on welfare for the rich. They say "it's not fair for people to get rich – and stay rich — by defrauding people *who are poorer than they are.* As you'll soon see, stealing from the poor

–actually, from anybody who isn't rich – has become standard operating procedure in America. In fact the U.S. government today functions mostly as a huge Robin Hood-in-reverse," they write.

That fact is at the core of the Occupy Wall Street protests spreading across the country and the world in late 2011 and through 2012.

The original idea behind the tax deduction for keeping a horse was that horses were essential to the functioning of a farm, like pigs and cattle. Although that is no longer true for most of the horses in this country, this deduction has been expanded into a major tax shelter.

If you own a horse, you can deduct the costs of food, housing, vet bills, stud fees, transportation, insurance, interest charges, depreciation, attendance at horse shows, visits to horse farms, and state and local taxes.

Wilhelmina du Pont Ross, a member of one of the wealthiest families in the world, hired her husband to run their stables and wrote off his salary on their joint tax return. Her relative, William du Pont, Jr., whose vast estate in Maryland contained a grandstand that could seat 12,500 people, deducted the cost of keeping professional fox hunters on staff.

You can trade an older horse for a younger and more valuable one without paying taxes on the exchange. And when you sell a horse, any profit is taxed at the lower capital gains rate, rather than as ordinary income. If you don't want the bother of actually owning a horse, leasing programs allow you to cash in on the tax advantages without any unpleasant odors on the estate.

All of this is kept in place by the vigorous lobbying of the American Horse Council, whose representatives virtually write the laws in this area. There isn't much opposition to these loopholes because most people don't know about them and, well, everybody loves horses.

Welfare for the rich fosters corruption, in business and in government. If anyone doubts that, just look at the Enron congressional investigations. This is a tradition that goes back to the railroad subsidies of 1870s when America became the continental power it did by subsidizing the railroad barons of the time at the expense of the public taxpayers. And it's not uncommon for two "wealthfare" programs to conflict – as when the Interior Department subsidizes irrigation water for agribusiness and the Agriculture Department pays those same companies not to grow crops with that water. What do the companies do? Why, they sell the water back to local governments at a profit, of course. Mark Twain said that "America has no indigenous criminal class – other than Congress."

Will Rogers State Park and Yosemite and Grand Canyon national parks all belong to We the People. Why do we then have to pay entrance fees to enjoy our parks? Isn't that another form of taxation? A tax rip-off? National parks and trails should be free for Americans – they are public lands. The government should be subsidizing people's access to their public lands! Not the corporations right to mine them at taxpayer expense. We the Apathetic Maids have again ceded our right to access public land to the government and its rich corporate constituent financial contributors.

## Bumper Taxes

Cruising on Pacific Coast Highway from Pacific Palisades to Santa Monica at sunset in the mid-1980s, listening to Jimmy Buffett sing Margaritaville, heading to Scratch, the restaurant in Santa Monica owned by my former wife Gail and I, in traffic-free lanes, watching commuters in bumper-to-bumper rush hour going the opposite direction home to Malibu, the West Valley or Ventura was a metaphoric daily reminder of how our tax system is all choked up, backed up and going the wrong way. It can be as simple and pleasant as driving on PCH without traffic if people are taxed right. Why not tax all individuals at a flat rate of 15 percent, the same as dividends and capital gains? I constantly asked myself that question at the time – and still do today. Especially after I received an audit notification from Uncle Sam challenging my agricultural deductions. And better yet, why not also reduce corporate income taxes as well to a flat 15 percent?

I usually arrived at the restaurant around 7 p.m. I'd work my way through the place, saying hello to those I knew at the bar or tables on my way to the back office. The first diners were usually already seated.

The best was yet to come. "I have a problem with where to seat Michael

Ovitz, who insists on his regular table, which is also Jesse Big Daddy Unruh's and Sidney Poitier's. All three parties are coming tonight," the hostess whined as she and the manager joined me with the reservation book to figure out the arrangements for the evening. Another "Scratch Cat Fever" night. All the cool cats with Scratch fever. That was a problem!

"Give the table to the Poitier party and seat Ovitz at table seven and the Unruh party at my table. Give Ovitz a bottle of wine on the house and explain to him that Poitier pre-booked for the same table with a larger party. Tell Unruh I'm joining him and the drinks are on me!" I said.

Between the politicians, agents and stars, like the tax code, it was a nightmare. Personally, I favored the politicians and stars who were not prima donnas. Having "Big Daddy" Unruh, the California state treasurer, in the house was always a treat because we would debate the issues of the day – taxes, politics, women and life – until well after closing time.

Jessie was one of the few non-lawyer politicians with whom I could discuss the scourge of lawyer politicians. He was the son of sharecroppers and had made it the hard way. He was next to Bobby Kennedy on the night of his California primary victory and assassination in 1968.

Jessie would have enjoyed being at the fundraiser I hosted for Bobby's son Joe when he first ran for Congress. The Art of Politics and Politics in Art theme of the event that exhibited well-known California artists' works raised over $40,000 for Joe, who not only got elected, but was very appreciative of not only the fact that it was his largest "net take" of any fundraiser, but for the great time he and his brother Michael had that evening.

Unfortunately, Jessie and Michael, like Bobby, left this world prematurely.

Jessie was a country music fan. Chris, his well-endowed bleach-blonde wife, was the epitome of a country music singer. When the place mellowed down in the early morning hours, she would occasionally get up and sing.

Jessie would entertain other state treasurers, governors, and local party activists at events organized by his Chief Deputy Grover McKean. It was always a pleasure to be invited to join his table to share a glass of wine and discuss the issues of the day. Reagan and Reaganomics were Jessie's favorite whipping boys. He had a lot of respect for Reagan. In fact, they were friends. But he hated the Gipper's economics!

"His supply-side economics is a disaster. He is making Carter and his administration look like choir boys and his deficit look like chump change. He is going to bankrupt the damned country," Jesse said. "Does he really think the Treasury can print money forever without accountability?" I was looking around the room as usual. Steve Martin and his party were being seated at an outdoor table.

Gregory Hines had just walked in with a friend and was immediately seated at his regular corner table. "Now there is a man who can dance," Chris Unruh giggled as everyone looked up from their plates.

"Nice place you got here, de Krassel. You pull in a good crowd. How come you let bums like us in?" Jessie joked, earning himself another bottle.

The bar was usually packed with local entertainment and advertising bar flies or customers waiting for tables.

"Yeah, I was here the other week for lunch and saw Arnold Schwarzenegger, Diana Ross, Dennis Hopper and Cher with her new young boyfriend," Chris said.

Jessie and I discussed the inequality and unfairness of the taxation system and Reaganomics on more than one occasion. I'd quote Will Rogers: "Taxation is about all there is to government ... People want just taxes, more than they want lower taxes."

Adam Smith, the great economist who had many views that are still applicable, was another favorite of mine. Smith held what are nowadays considered "liberal" positions. Unlike modern conservatives, who favor a regressive flat tax that affects the poor much more than the rich, Smith favored progressive taxes on individuals "in proportion" to their ability to pay. He thought that the "luxuries" of the rich should be taxed while the "necessities" of the poor should be exempt from taxation. He even favored what might be called a "progressive user fee," arguing that highway tolls on "carriages of luxury" should be higher than on "carriages of necessary use."

Both Smith and Jessie Unruh would echo and endorse a remark by Robert Reischauer, former U.S. Congressional Budget Office director, on George W. Bush's $674 billion tax-cut plans: "This is a pig that even a Republican python might not be able to swallow."

Ten winners of the Nobel Prize were among 358 economists who attacked Dubya's 10-year tax plan to revitalize the U.S. economy. Passing the tax cuts would worsen the long-term budget outlook, adding to projected chronic deficits, the economists said.

"To be effective, a stimulus plan should rely on immediate but temporary spending and tax measures to expand demand and it should also rely on immediate but temporary incentives for investment," one said.

Not only the Congressional Budget Office cautioned the Bush administration that the deficit would increase dramatically by the three Bush tax cuts and other debt-fattening indulgencies, but THE IMF! They even voiced concern that the Bush administration had no credible plan to balance the budget. America was getting the same warnings from the IMF that Indonesia, Thailand, Korea, Brazil, Argentina and every other bankrupt banana republic received, yet *We the Apathetic Maids* are still doing nothing about sweeping in the needed tax changes. The IMF was justifiably worried that America's red ink would have global nightmarish ramifications. They were right for a change.

The true heirs of Adam Smith today are not really free-market libertarian radicals, much less the politically influential business elites that he despised, but rather those who support government interference in the economy to support high wages, reforms that break up the guild-like professions and monopolies in the interest of consumer savings and inexpensive, universal, quality public education – with the costs of these programs paid for not only by progressive income taxes, but by progressive user fees and sales taxes on the affluent. In the 2000 presidential election, Smith would have looked left of Nader.

"I'd take it a step further," I said during one of our many ongoing tax debates. I think we must have embarked on the Stolichnayas by now. "Why tax any necessities? All sales taxes on the basics like food should be eliminated and be placed only on luxury goods, and what are commonly referred to as 'sin taxes'. Prostitution, recreational drugs, tobacco and alcohol should be taxed to the max," I said, a rather stunning stand for me to take, considering the commercial operation I was involved in.

Well, actually not. Hong Kong has proven that by not charging any duty on imported wines and becoming a world leader in wine auctions. By becoming a premier wine-trading and distribution center in Asia, retail establishments mark up the wines at will but it is still cheaper to drink quality winos at a reasonable price, with no sales tax or value-added tax, which gets business people and tourists to spend more and get a bigger bang for their buck while keeping the economy churning and people employed. Add a minimum sales tax domestically to the wine and it will still be competitive and add to the government's already overflowing coffers with surplus tax dollars.

Jessie Unruh kind of nodded in agreement as he continued to blast Reaganomics. "Well, you may have a point, but it's going to take a lot of hookers, booze and drugs to finance Star Wars."

Listening to Jack Valenti of the Motion Picture Association of America and Michael Eisner of Disney plead for more tax breaks for the studios at the State Economic Summit organized by California Governor Gray Davis in 2001, I couldn't help chuckling to myself and visualizing Jessie exclaiming, "What bullshit!"

Adam Smith was a capitalist with a soul. He gave the better part of his own fortune to charity, yet he never doubted that every man is far more interested with "whatever immediately concerns himself than in what concerns any other man." He believed that human beings, in addition to possessing self-interest, were blessed with an instinctive concern – "sympathy" – for the welfare of others. We take pleasure in seeing our neighbors prosper and feel awkward in the presence of their pain or misfortune. Even more importantly, we care deeply about what our neighbors think of us. In business as in life, Smith avowed, "honesty is the best policy."

### Founding Fathers' Tipple

Gray Davis was not a drinker and was also not one of Jessie Unruh's favorite politicians. In fact Jessie disliked him immensely. I was in Quincy, Massachusetts, the day after the 2003 California referendum that recalled Davis and replaced him with Arnold Schwarzenegger, and for some reason wondered how Jessie would have reacted.

Here I was visiting the birthplaces of Presidents John Adams and John Quincy Adams that was built in 1681, and bought by John Adams' father, Deacon John Adams in 1720, with an adjoining six-acre farm. Deacon Adams instilled in his oldest son John a strong interest in municipal affairs, farming and respect for God.

Standing in the humble law office where John Adams drafted the Massachusetts Constitution in 1779, off the Old Coast Road from Boston to Plymouth, listening to the National Park ranger make an emphatic point that notwithstanding John Adam's strict religious upbringing, he was determined to keep God and religion out of the Constitution as he sipped his whiskey, I couldn't help smile as I thought of America's religious dry drunk President Bush congratulating California's new Governor Schwarzenegger, who spent $21.5 million to get elected.

Having shared a few glasses of wine with Gray Davis over the years and seen Arnie have a few at Scratch, I was bemused at the irony of the moment. California's new governor was married at the time to Maria Shriver, whose grandfather Joseph Kennedy was a bootlegger during Prohibition, right here in Massachusetts – in the tradition of America's Founding Fathers – who went to war with England to defend their right to smuggle and trade rum. One of the causes that led to the 13 British North American colonies fighting for independence was Britain's determination to stop the smuggling of rum from Jamaica and the other British North American colonies in the Caribbean.

Kennedy family friend Frank Sinatra summed up our relationship with alcohol. "Alcohol may be man's worst enemy, but the Bible says to love your enemy."

## *Can't Legislate Morality*

Lady Godiva rode her white horse naked centuries ago to protest taxes. Religious and moral convulsions over alcohol and drugs go back to time immemorial. Prohibition tried to outlaw alcohol and failed. Trying to prohibit drug use also seems doomed to failure. Talking about drugs, Jack Osbourne, Ozzy's 17-year-old son who was in rehab, summed it up best: "If you test 100 17-year-olds, I guarantee 80 per cent will come up positive. People think I should be this perfect role model. And I am, because this is what kids do. It's not like I'm slamming heroin."

Let's not forget that many of the icons of the '60s did slam heroin. Bob Dylan, Keith Richards, Jimmy Hendrix, Jim Morrison, Janis Joplin to name a few of the enduring musical influences.

We might as well legalize mild recreational drugs like marijuana, which like alcohol would generate billions of dollars in tax revenue, I concluded one late Sunday afternoon on a drive from Sebastopol, after debating the merits of how to generate tax revenue from America's hijacked political system in the last three weeks of the 2008 presidential election with political activists at Suyin and Jim Stein's home. Driving through Napa and Sonoma wine country surfing great '60s classics on San Francisco radio stations is always a treat.

It was another one of those magical moments on the road that brought back wonderful memories of when I drove these same roads going the other way from San Francisco to Humboldt in 1969 in my red MG convertible. With my long hair blowing in the wind, I enjoyed a sample doobie from the seeds to be planted on the property of law school classmates I advised on how best to grow grass. We usually took leisurely drives heading north because of the great watering holes along the way to skinny dip with all the lovely free-loving flower children. We took the freeways back to the city to make it to school by Monday mornings.

Magical because an unexpected rain had cleared the 2008 air and highlighted the undulating green hills and blue skies with the occasional scattered white puffy clouds. The smell of ripening grapes, olives and cow manure, emanating from the seasoned vineyards, interspersed with young newly planted vines of different hues of green in the dark red and brown soil cascading through the valleys and climbing the hills, while trying to avoid the swerving drivers who spent the day wine tasting, was a definite trip down memory lane.

These days, the view includes any number of cars and trucks up on blocks in front yards and driveways, stark reminders that America, like the automobile industry it created, is up on blocks and living the redneck jokes the world has been laughing at for years.

"Anybody on the far right – or anybody else for that matter – who thinks that we can legislate our way to a more moral America is misunderstanding something about the nature of legislation. Legislation can't create morality," says former Minnesota Governor Jesse Ventura. "Morals are about character and core beliefs. No amount of lawmaking can affect them. The law might be able to deter you from certain behavior, but it can't make you believe that the behavior is immoral. That seems self-evident to me. But apparently there are still those in our society who can't seem to understand this, and who insist on imposing their beliefs on others," Ventura says, echoing Jesse Unruh.

Human beings are not designed or engineered to cope with the day-to-day stress of family and workplace naturally – unless of course they are living in a jungle, desert or other isolated community and don't have modern conveniences and communication devices that bring us the stress of 21st-century civilizational cultural conflicts and information overload. That being the case, people need their meds to cope. Religion is not a med and therefore does not fit the bill. The subject and role of religion in society, historically and today, is something I devoted an entire chapter to in *Custom Maid Spin* and also will discuss in greater detail in *Custom Maid Religion*, which I am now writing.

The point I am trying to make as I address tax breaks, alcohol, wine and religion during a country drive is simple. The Founding Fathers wanted religion and morality kept out of politics in America. Something *We the Maids* have to sweep back into the nation's fabric. Politicians should focus on keeping citizens smart, the economy strong, taxes at a minimum and stay out of the morality business. Likewise, religious leaders should stick to religion and also stay out of the morality business. That is a philosophical discussion each family and community must address without government or religious institutional interference.

The Mormons in Utah are a good example. Religious beliefs and state legislation forbid the sale and use of alcohol. As a result, Utah leads the nation in antidepressant use, at a rate nearly twice the national average! Utah also leads the nation in the use of narcotic painkillers such as codeine and morphine-based drugs.

The use of pain pills is epidemic, not only in Utah – but across America – a country with only 5 percent of the world's population but which consumes 80 percent of world opiates.

The number of overdose deaths from prescription painkillers has more than tripled in the opening decade of the 21st century. Prescription painkillers such as Oxycontin, Vicodin and methadone led to the deaths of almost 15,000 people in 2008, including actor Heath Ledger, more than three times the 4,000 deaths from narcotics in 1999. The overdose deaths reflected the spike in the number of narcotic painkillers prescribed every year – enough to give every American a one-month supply.

Doctors have become "pill mills" for the pharmaceutical companies. Why aren't doctors looking for alternative treatments for chronic pain? Narcotics should be a last resort after traditional Chinese medicine, acupuncture and holistic medications, including marijuana.

Alcohol and drugs are inherent in all religions. There were basically two very separate traditions in regard to alcohol and religion in ancient Europe. Those of the Mediterranean and those of the North, and also religious America. In the 1820s, corn whiskey in America was so cheap that the typical male drank a half a pint a day. That works out to more than five gallons a year.

W.J. Rorabaugh in *The Alcoholic Republic* says Americans drank whiskey for breakfast, lunch and dinner, before work and after and very often during. Employers were expected to supply spirits over the course of the workday:

in fact, the modern coffee break began as a late-morning whiskey break called "the elevenses." Just trying to say it makes one sound drunk. Except for a brief respite Sunday mornings in church, Americans simply did not gather – whether for a barn raising or quilting bee, corn husking or political campaign – without passing the jug. Michael Pollan reminds us that "visitors from Europe – hardly models of sobriety themselves – marveled at the free flow of American spirits."

Several of the Founding Fathers – including George Washington, Thomas Jefferson and John Adams – denounced the excesses of the "alcoholic republic," inaugurating the American quarrel over drinking. The Massachusetts Society for the Suppression of Intemperance began in 1813; the American Society for the Promotion of Temperance followed in 1826 and the American Temperance Union in 1836 that culminated a century later in Prohibition. In those early years, freeing the slaves drew less attention than locking up the alcohol.

Sir James Frazer wrote in his classic *The Golden Bough:* "The god Dionysus or Bacchus is best known as a personification of the vine and of the exhilaration proceeded by the juice of the grape. His ecstatic worship, characterized by wild dances, thrilling music, and tipsy excess, appears to have originated among the rude tribes of Thrace, who were notoriously addicted to drunkenness."

Bacchus was the son of Jupiter. He was the god of the fertility, of nature and of wine, who inspired music and poetry. In fact most men find that wine can be a severe hindrance to fertilizing or writing good music. Today Bacchus might tack on the title of "God of Viagra." As a baby, Bacchus had been torn apart by the Titians and resurrected and made a god by Jupiter. There is a connection between blood and wine in his myth which is to be found in many major religions. During the last decadent years of the Roman Empire, the vine cult deteriorated into a plethora of bacchanalian orgies with which it is associated today.

America's great general and first president, George Washington, wrote: "Since our imports of spirit have become so precarious ... I would beg leave to suggest the propriety of erecting public distilleries in different states. The benefits arising from moderate use of liquor have been experienced in all armies and are not to be disputed: ... There should always be a sufficient quantity of spirits with the army, to furnish moderate supplies to the troops. In many instances, such as when they are marching in hot or cold weather, in camp in wet, on fatigue or in working parties, it is so essential that it is not to be dispensed with ... ."

Washington became a leading commercial distiller himself in the 1790s. His farm manager, James Anderson, had operated stills in Scotland and Virginia before setting up the president's distillery. Let's not forget that the *Star Spangled Banner* was put to the melody of a 1700 paean to drinking and sex.

So why are people surprised that Barack Obama worked the crowds in sports bars and college bars – something Mitt Romney couldn't do? He even bought a round for folks at the Iowa State Fair, where the standard cry of political rallies – "Four More Years!" – morphed into the memorable "Four More Beers!" and now even brews his own in the White House.

Historians say that Obama is the first president to brew or distill alcohol in the White House. Who will be the first to smoke a joint? Or have they already? We know who it is in Canada. Political poster boy Toronto Mayor Rob Ford.

Steve Saltzman was one of my Los Angeles racquetball partners. He was, and still is, a political activist. At the time he worked as a deputy for California U.S. Senator John Tunney and then for Los Angeles Mayor Tom Bradley. Steve, like many in L.A., moonlighted as an actor or model. He made a commercial for EJ Brandy that seemed to be on every billboard in the country at the time. In honor of his Hollywood break and spreading the message of the benefits of imbibing in moderation, I hosted a party for him at Scratch. Today Steve and his third wife, Marie, have their own lovely restaurant Chez Marie in West Los Angeles, fighting landlords and government bureaucracy for a liquor license.

"You can't believe the crap I have to go through and legal expenses I have to incur to even just serve wine or even be open for dinner," Steve said.

After listening to his war stories and comparing them to what I had to go through to get the necessary licensing for Scratch, all I could say was,

"California has gone to the dogs. No wonder I left town and have come back with an animal-care business."

"Funny, but you're right. The place has gone to the dogs," Steve chuckled as he got ready to lock the place up for the night.

We have to always remember that a lone drunk built the biblical ark. A large group of sober professionals built the Titanic.

The federal National Survey on Drug Use and Health released in 2008 reported that 15 percent of adult drivers nationally admit driving under the influence of alcohol. The Upper Midwest has the worst drunk-driving rates in the country, with Wisconsin leading the way. Rounding out the worst five states are North Dakota, Minnesota, Nebraska and South Dakota. Utah had the lowest incidence of drunk driving.

The report also concluded that black people drink at substantially lower and less hazardous rates than whites. The populations in those Midwestern states are predominantly white.

The report also contains estimates of driving under the influence of illicit drugs. The rates were highest in the District of Columbia, followed by Rhode Island and Massachusetts.

Grover McKean and Steve Saltzman, who have remained friends to this day, and I would cheer up Jessie Unruh's table to no end by emphasizing that, in spite of the conversion to Christianity, alcohol in the tribes of Northern Europe will not go away. The Scandinavians, Russians, Germans and British are socially among the hardest-drinking people on earth. While the Viking berserkers went into battle blind drunk, so sometimes did their descendants. Rum was the stimulant that fortified the Royal Navy at the Battle of Trafalgar, while Wellington's troops at Waterloo had to make do with gin. There is nothing better than a half pint of gin, taken fast, to propel you against your own best interests into the teeth of the enemy. While great acts of bravery were fueled by alcohol, the non-drinking nations had to make do with drugs.

*Heavy Tokes*

At the Siege of Malta in 1565, the Turkish general Mustapha used the Iayalars as shock troops. Maddened by hashish, the Iayalars were a fervid set of Muslims, deriving their blind courage from a blend of religion and hemp. Like the berserkers of the North, the Iayalars induced a deliberate frenzy which made them oblivious to everything but the lust to kill.

It should therefore come as no surprise that the 9/11 Arab terrorists who hijacked and crashed the planes into the WTC towers and Pentagon, like their forefathers who invented alcohol and bongs, had partied hard with hookers, booze and weed in the days before their ghastly mission.

The words hashish and assassin are said to be derived from Hasan Ben al-Sabbah, known to the Crusaders as "The Old Man of the Mountain." Hasan had a nasty habit of sending out drug crazed killers to eliminate the opposition. He has to be distinguished from Osama bin Laden and today's terrorists. An assassin is not a terrorist. The assassin committed individual acts of political murder. The targets were kings and career politicians with whom they had legitimate political differences. Terrorism, on the other hand, is directed at a whole class of people of a nation, including innocent women and children, something Old Man of the Mountain Hasan would never condone.

The fanatical Hasan did not even approve of the drinking of his school fellow, the astronomer and poet Omar Khayyam, who wrote:

> "And much as Wine has play'd the Infidel,
> And robb'd me of my Robe of Honour – well,
> I often wonder what the Vintners buy
> One half so precious as the Goods they sell."

The classic *Tales of a Thousand and One Nights,* which reflects the social life of medieval Islam, is littered with hard-drinking characters, including the Caliph of Baghdad Haroun-al-Raschid (763-809). We can assume that the cult of the vine took some centuries to die out in the Middle East.

Some argue that the source of William Shakespeare's genius was smoking cannabis. Clay pipes found in his home at Stratford-upon-Avon are being tested for traces of the drug. Dr. Francis Thackeray said, "There are very few literary scholars who have recognized the potential link between Shakespeare and hallucinogenic stimuli. A close reading of his sonnets and some other lines suggests that he was aware of them and may have experienced the effects himself."

The connection between poetry and alcohol is not confined to European bards. Dylan Thomas consumed 18 whiskeys on the night he died. Oliver Reed, the hard-drinking, tough-guy British actor, died after falling ill at a bar in Malta. He had downed 10 ales, 12 rums and a couple of whiskeys. He was filming *Gladiator* at the time.

One morning during the filming, Reed was staggering home after a night on the town when he spotted co-star Russell Crowe doing pushups at dawn. Reed called out to Crowe: "Dear boy, I think you'll find she's already gone home."

In Washington, D.C., the tax-exempt status of a townhouse known as the C Street Center, where conservative right-wing alcoholic politicians go for spiritual counseling when they have sinned, is being challenged by a group of ministers who say it is not a church and should not be granted the tax-exempt status afforded a house of worship. The C Street Center received a jolt of notoriety in 2009 when Gov. Mark Sanford of South Carolina said he sought spiritual counseling there in connection with his affair with a woman in Argentina.

The residence has also been home to two other legislators who espoused conservative family values but were tarnished with sexual liaisons while under the influence. Senator John Ensign, Republican of Nevada, who admitted to an affair with an aide, and former Representative Charles "Chip" Pickering Jr., Republican of Mississippi, who faced accusations of an extramarital affair.

The multi-million dollar townhouse is an affiliate of a secretive international Christian network known as the Fellowship, or the Family. The group also sponsors the National Prayer Breakfast held in Washington and many state capitals each February.

J. Walter Hunter, a member of the Fellowship who defended the center's tax-exempt status, said, "There are religious services all the time in that building," but they are not open to the public.

He said the purpose of the residence was to encourage people to model their lives on Jesus, and added that although it might sound ironic, "One of the purposes is to give a safe place where politicians who are tempted by lust would hold each other accountable."

Accountable to what? Certainly not the taxpayers. I don't know about you, but I agree with the ministers who want to revoke the center's tax-exempt status. I have a problem with the concept of career politicians who screw the public and cheat on their wives while drunk hanging out together in fellowship and supposedly praying their sins away at taxpayer expense.

Isn't it time that the career politicians who screw us and impose excessive taxation and morality laws they themselves can't comply with be sent packing – maybe with a six-pack – in the 21st century?

While we are at it, let's send packing these religious leaders who abuse their church's tax-exempt status by amassing wealth and do not care for the poor and the needy in their flock and community, a topic I discuss at length in *Custom Maid Spin*.

### Sino-Japanese Buddhist Toasts
In China for thousands of years, the literati used to gather in riverside gardens under the full moon to drink wine and write verse. Li Po, China's legendary drunken poet, drowned when he fell into the Yangzi in an attempt to "fondle" the reflection of the moon. In spite of Chinese literature being peopled with famous drunks from Tsao Tsao, the founder of the Wei Dynasty, to Wu Sung, who killed tigers with his bare hands, China is not, and never has been, a hard-drinking country compared with the likes of Scotland or Japan. Although once China opened up after Richard Nixon's historic trip there in 1972, one would be hard pressed to tell with all the whiskey consumed at any banquet. In an essay attempting to explain why drunks are not a common sight on the streets of Chinese cities as they are in the West, the scholar James Zee-Min Lee enigmatically explained: "The

Chinese mentality on wine drinking is aptly expressed in the following ancient saying: 'The feeling of half drunkenness is the best, while flowers in half bloom are far the sweetest.' "

While the ancient Chinese imbibed gently, they seldom became enraged through drink, unlike their neighbors the Japanese. Nineteenth-century Edo was a very dangerous city. In 1868 two Ronin swordsman attacked the British Minister Sir Harry Parkes, who was on his way to attend an audience with the Emperor of Japan. Sir Harry had an escort of 70 British and 1,500 Japanese troops at the time. The two Ronin had been sitting in a wine shop drinking when the procession passed them. One of them, Ishikawa Saburo, confessed after his capture: "I did not know to what nation they belonged. It was the first time I had seen foreigners."

One more reason to drink red wine in Japan: A compound in red wine helps prevent death from radiation, according to a study by researchers at the University of Pittsburgh. Resveratrol, already celebrated as an antioxidant, has been shown to prevent death in irradiated mice.

Stories that the kamikaze suicide pilots in World War II were besotted with sake and the Chinese infantrymen during the Korean War were crazed with drugs have turned out to be largely Allied propaganda. Modern warfare is incompatible with berserkness.

The fact is that the Japanese preferred dying in hopeless circumstances rather than surrendering – because of the power of shame. Loss of face. In Japan today depression is widespread, undiagnosed and untreated because of shame. Japan has more suicides than America, yet less than half the population.

In Tibet, however, alcohol plays a part in quasi-religious events like the Ongkor Horse Festival, where large quantities of *chang* are consumed and, far from being vegetarians, yak meat is a staple food of Tibetan Buddhists. The sixth Dalai Lama, or living Buddha, was a notorious drunk and womanizer. In a poem, he explained that he was actually two different people:

"I dwell apart in Potala,
A God on earth am I,
But in the town the chief of rogues,
And boisterous revelry."

In spite of his unorthodox behavior, he was a popular religious leader, which could not be said for Pope Alexander VI, who consistently broke every one of the 10 commandments and was notorious for fathering a number of illegitimate children, including the murderous Cesare Borgia and his incestuous sister Lucrezia.

## Tradition

The "Fire Ball" at Oxford University includes food, music, entertainment and unlimited alcohol. The alcohol fueled merriment at Oxford dates at least to the 12th century, when a group of divinity students composed a drinking song *Gaudeamus igitur,* which is still sung in the wee hours of the morning at the Fire Ball.

Britons manage to combine Scandinavian binging with liver-pickling Mediterranean levels of consumption. After a three-decade-long surge in drinking, over 60 percent of British adults drink alcohol in any given week and one in six gets drunk at least once.

Drinking and drug use is a university tradition, even in Britain's colonial descendant America. *We the Apathetic Maids* are periodically reminded of this when a president's daughter or prime minister's son are arrested for being under the influence. Binge drinking on campuses in America has become a major concern. A task force of the National Institute of Alcohol Abuse and Alcoholism released a report in 2002 concluding that on an average day four students die in accidents involving alcohol. An Associated Press survey found that 157 college-age Americans drank themselves to death between 1999-2005.

In November 2012, David Bogenberger, one of 19 freshman pledges seeking entry into the Pi Kappa Alpha fraternity at Northern Illinois University, drank enough to put him nearly four times over the legal alcohol limit. Bogenberger died in his sleep.

Authorities in Illinois are holding the fraternity members who orchestrated the November initiation event accountable, and issued arrest warrants for 22 students charged with felony and misdemeanor hazing. The arrests amount to one of the largest number of people to be criminally charged in a single college hazing episode.

According to the National Institute on Alcohol Abuse and Alcoholism, more than 1,800 students ages 18 to 24 die each year from alcohol-related events.

Yet a coalition of more than 100 presidents and chancellors of universities across the U.S. have pressed Congress to lower the drinking age from 21 to 18. This would reverse a policy under which young adults find themselves old enough to go to war and vote but too young to legally down a beer. It's called the Amethyst Initiative, after the gem that in Greek mythology warded off drunkenness. Needless to say, it drew the ire of groups such as Mothers Against Drunk Driving.

At Scotland's St. Andrews University, it's Raisin Monday, which dates back to the 1400s. New students gave seniors a pound of raisins in exchange for a receipt in Latin. Lack of a receipt meant a dousing in the fountain. Today, raisins are replaced with a bottle of wine and the dousing is in foam.

Students in Britain spend three times as much on alcohol as they do on books.

Alcoholism and binge-drinking in Scotland has become a political concern. Scottish ministers have taken a tough line on alcohol abuse by fixing the minimum price of cheap booze. And guess where else it has become both a political and social problem? Iran of all places.

After years of being in denial over the amount of illegal drinking in the country, officials in Iran are for the first time publicly addressing the issue of alcoholism and the health problems drinking can cause, exacerbated by deadly home brews.

In June 2012, at a ceremony marking the International Day Against Drug Abuse and Illicit Trafficking, Iranian Health Minister Marzieh Vahid Dastjerdi announced, "We have prepared a road map to treat alcoholism and reduce the consumption of alcoholic beverages in society."

But even as the government acknowledges the problem, it continues to treat drinking as a sin and a crime. Two men in early 2012 were given rare death sentences for drinking as part of the country's three-strikes-you're-dead law.

More than 200,000 people in Iran are estimated to be involved in bootlegging and about $800 million is spent annually on smuggled booze.

Iran also has a serious problem with opium and heroin. In Iran, alcohol is commonly used as a method of breaking drug addiction. Go figure, Islam.

Drinking has long been a part of Persian society, from the upper-class elite to the blue-collar workers who drink the sometimes toxic home brews. The Islamic Revolution of 1979 attempted to squelch the custom, as part of an effort to erase the Persian culture in favor of a strictly Islamic one – and failed.

Today young people, feeling they are boxed in politically, socially and economically, are increasingly turning to alcohol as an escape.

My favorite alcohol-desperate-drinker story is one I heard from my editor Jim Houston when we were discussing the editorial time line for this chapter and comparing alcohol-fueled experiences.

"When the *L.A. Times* launched its San Diego edition, I went to San Diego to work as a copy editor," Jim said by way of introduction in a tone to what sounded was going to be a great story. "When I finished work I'd go to this nearby bar to relax and play pool. April, a drop-dead gorgeous Eurasian beauty with an hourglass body – a stunner – was the bartender. One night as I'm there playing pool and watching April and the bar, this customer walks up to the bar holding up a greenback in his hand, clearly desperate for a drink. April was busy serving customers at the other end. So what did the desperate customer with the greenback do? He took the bar towel that wipes the spilled drinks from the bar, squeezed it into a glass, downed the drink and walked out," Jim said. "Another satisfied customer," Jim shouted out to a smiling April.

Alcohol is a killer. It is a contributor to thousands of teenagers worldwide dying in car accidents, accidental drownings and assaults.

In 2013, more than three million deaths were caused by alcohol worldwide, more than Aids, tuberculosis and violence combined according to the World Health Organization. Alcohol causes one in 20 deaths globally every year.

Alcohol consumption is not limited to humans. In Germany, police called out in July 2009 to clear a road of a dead badger found the animal was blind "drunk as a skunk" and had staggered into the middle of the road after gorging itself on overripe fermented cherries.

In Palmerston, a northern Australian town, drunk parrots fall out of trees regularly, with as many as eight a day being rescued from lawns and roadsides. The birds are given sweetened porridge and fresh fruit, which is the avian version of hangover food.

A study posted online in the journal *Science* in March 2012 suggests that elements of the brain's reward system have changed little during evolution and these include some of the mechanisms that support addiction. The study involved fruit flies and showed that rejected young males do what so many men do after being repeatedly rejected by an attractive female: they get drunk, using alcohol as a balm for unfulfilled desire.

Scientists have long known that other species have their methods of stress reduction. In lab studies, mice, rats and monkeys drink more after periods of isolation, studies suggest. The same is true of mice that are bullied or are victims of aggression.

A favorite sex and alcohol story of mine is about the small boy who got lost in a shopping mall. He approached a uniformed security guard and said, "I've lost my grandpa."

The guard asked, "What's his name?"

"Grandpa."

The guard smiled, then asked, "What's he like?"

The little tyke hesitated for a moment and then replied "Big tits and whiskey." Must be related to Mark Twain who said, "Too much of anything is bad, but too much of good whisky is barely enough."

Not so funny is reading about federal agents hired to transport nuclear weapons and components across the U.S. getting drunk while on convoy missions.

In China, like America, there is zero tolerance for drunk drivers following an increase in traffic fatalities in recent years. Starting in May 2011, the Criminal Law stipulates that "those who drive when drunk should be sentenced to jail terms between one and six months and also fined."

Alcoholism is becoming a problem in China, a subject I address at length in *Feasting Dragon, Starving Eagle,* but nowhere near as bad as it is in Russia, where it has become a major blight on society.

The heaviest drinkers are said to be media professionals in England. After the *News of the World* phone hacking scandals, I can understand why. "When you stop drinking you have to deal with this marvelous personality that starts you drinking in the first place," quipped U.S. journalist Jimmy Breslin.

The fact is that booze is more dangerous than heroin and crack cocaine, according to a 2010 study paid for by Britain's Centre for Crime and Justice Studies that was published in the medical journal *The Lancet.* Alcohol outranked all drugs as the deadliest to individuals and society, followed by heroin and crack cocaine. Marijuana, ecstasy and LSD scored far lower.

Alcohol and drugs play a part in thousands of quasi-religious festivals throughout the world. It would have been unthinkable for Shaka Zulu to celebrate his great victory at the Umhlatuze River without a great deal of beer being consumed. But festivals devoted entirely to the consumption of alcohol, like the Munich Oktoberfest, are rare, or the Snow Devils Festival in Japan, where the indigenous dress up as masked straw-coated demons and wander from house to house demanding sake, in the way Western children demand treats at Halloween.

In Peru, Spanish missionaries were appalled by the ritual intoxication of the Incas, where at drinking ceremonies etiquette demanded dozens of toasts, speeches and the consumption of vast quantities of chicha beer. The Incas were not destroyed by the introduction of European liquor into their country, possibly because they already had their own alcohol culture, unlike the aborigines in Australia, or the Eskimos and the Indians or Native Americans in North America, whose cultures have been decimated by booze.

In the Himalayas, birthplace of Hindu cosmology and Buddhist mysticism, Hindu holy men, or *babas* as they are known colloquially, can be seen walking from shrine to shrine, begging for alms and smoking their *chillums* – hashish pipes.

Probably the largest religion today where a narcotic is the vital ingredient is Peyotism. The peyote cactus or *Lophophora Williamsii* grows in Mexico and parts of Texas. Its primary active medium is mescaline, a hallucinogen similar to LSD. Anthropologists claim that it has been used as a sacrament for 10,000 years, similar to the way wine is used in the Christian religion. The Aztecs believed that peyote was a deity or spirit force that helped them communicate with their gods. In 1571 the Spanish Inquisition declared the drug an instrument of Satan. This didn't prevent the religion from spreading northward from the Huichol, Cora and Tarahumara tribes into the United States through the Apaches to the Sioux, where it surfaced in the form of the Ghost Dancers cult that was wiped out at the Battle of Wounded Knee in 1890.

In the 1920s it re-emerged in the more passive form of the Native-American Church. Today Peyotism has a quarter of a million believers spread over 70 separate Indian tribes in the U.S. and Canada. There is conflict between those who see peyote as a religious sacrament that is protected by the First Amendment and those who see it as an evil narcotic. However, the Native-American Church seems to be winning the struggle. The soporific use of peyote in the rituals of the Native-American Church seems incredibly benign when compared to the terrible violence of the Viking berserkers and their bloodthirsty religion.

Whenever religious discussions started heating up, I would bring out the "How Drunk?" coasters and quiz the participants on their state of drunkenness. I would hand each participant a coaster that described a stage of inebriation and they had to ask the person to their left to define the meaning of state of drunkenness of the word on their coaster. The six coasters were held and read like cards and then put to practical use after everyone had a chance to ask for the definition of the word on their coaster.

"Sober," Adj. Possessed of iron will, but often lacking a sense of humor. Helpful with doing dishes, finding CD's and lifts home. Probably in need of several stiff drinks!

"Tipsy," Adj. The usual signs are a flushed face, stupid grin, loud voice and a profound love for mankind. The sufferer is incredibly deep, intelligent and insightful but prone to giggle.

"Plastered," Adj. Extremely generous, loud and confident. Suffering from verbal diarrhea and a belief that he/she can drink anyone under the table.

"Drunk," Adj. Suffering from vision, hearing and speech impairment, with an insatiable appetite for pizza. Will do anything that moves. Possessing an illogical belief that he/she is gorgeous despite dribbling and slobbering.

"Shit faced," Adj. Invincible but incapable. Suffering from extreme loss of balance, coordination and sex appeal. Liable to sleep anywhere. Babbling incoherently with loss of most bodily functions.

"Hung-over," Adj. suffering from near-death-like state, often catatonic and always with a pounding headache. Unbalanced with no sense of humor. Needs total silence and another drink."

### American History

"Let's get back to American history" was Jessie Unruh's suggestion. "It's not as complicated, long or confusing." Given that Jessie was a history buff, that was extraordinarily inaccurate.

He loved the revolutionary wars and the Founding Fathers, who were very complicated indeed. Alexander Hamilton was one of our favorite Founding Fathers because he was one of the most ardent opponents of slavery and racism. Jessie authored the California Civil Rights Act named in his honor.

I first got interested in Hamilton in 1966 after meeting my first wife Gail, who had attended Hamilton High, named after Alexander Hamilton. He fascinated me because he was an immigrant, adulterer, genius, journalist, lawyer, politician and begetter of America's prosperity, who was killed in a duel with Vice President Aaron Burr. Hamilton was a statesman for all seasons. Hamilton thought that blacks were probably as talented as whites and that only greed prevented whites from acknowledging it. Ron Chernow's *Alexander Hamilton* is a well-written examination of America's capitalist seed planter.

Hamilton supported a luxury tax on the rich. Though often maligned as a champion of plutocracy, Hamilton favored taxes on the rich as a way of "taxing their superior wealth," praised inheritance laws that would "soon melt down those great estates which, if they continued, might favor the power of the few," and denounced poll taxes — a version of the regressive flat tax favored by Jeffersonian conservatives – in order "to guard the least wealthy part of the community from oppression."

Though Hamilton was not alarmed by a moderate deficit, he would have been shocked by the deficits produced, like Ronald Reagan's, by an unwillingness to levy taxes to match spending. In his Second Report on the Public Credit (1795), he wrote that runaway debt is "the natural disease of all government" and that it is difficult "to conceive anything more likely than this to lead to great and convulsive revolutions of empire."

I can only imagine what he would say about George W. Bush's tax cuts for the wealthy.

Unruh loved football and would have enjoyed meeting Jerry Jones, owner of the Dallas Cowboys. They had a lot in common. He would have cracked up at some of Jerry's notions on how government should pay off the deficit.

"First, we wouldn't have a national debt. I don't know exactly how I'd solve that one, but balancing the national budget can't be any more difficult than squeezing Troy Aikman, Emmit Smith, Michael Irvin and Deion Sanders under the NFL's salary cap. In fact, I'll bet I could handle the national debt and figure out a way to make the country profitable. All government employees would wear Nikes and drink Pepsi and Dr. Pepper. The Army,

Navy and Marine Corps would be known as America's Team. Think about it. The American Express Washington Monument. The Pizza Hut Capital Building. The prospects are endless."

What a concept. Is this what America has to succumb to in order to survive in the 21st century?

Apparently so. Cities across America are selling rolling billboard rights on firetrucks, police cars and trains and buses to meet budget deficits. KFC became a pioneer in this kind of unconventional ad placement when it temporarily plastered its logo on manhole covers and fire hydrants in several cities in Indiana, Kentucky and Tennessee after paying to fill potholes and replace hydrants.

Pizza chains now advertise on some school buses, and a growing number of states are considering allowing school districts to sell ads.

Transit systems across the nation have been particularly aggressive in recent years in trying to sell naming rights of stations. They are struggling with an estimated $77.7 billion shortfall just to get to a state of good repair, at a time of growing ridership, shrinking state support and budgetary shortfalls.

Unruh hated government interference in the free marketplace and prided himself on being an astute businessman. He would have agreed with Colin Powell's assertion that "Government should not interfere with the demonstrated success of the free marketplace. ... I am concerned, however, that the present tax burden on Americans is so high that it seriously risks dampening our entrepreneurial vitality. Every tax dollar taken away from a consumer or a business is a dollar that will be spent less efficiently than if left in private hands."

That includes inheritance taxes. They are wrong taxes, especially today when so many families, middle-income families, are paying them. Why bother trying to build an estate if the government is going to take it away?

In the Charles Dickens classic *Bleak House,* a dispute over a will drags on for decades, leaving a legacy of wasted lives. One character shoots himself;

another explodes. When the estate is finally settled, the entire fortune has been gobbled up by lawyers and their fees.

The novel was written almost 150 years ago. But to many baby boomers in America, the story is alarmingly contemporary, minus the powdered wigs and spontaneous combustion.

Many of America's richest oppose abolition of the estate tax because they believe it will have a negative impact on charities and charitable contributions, while only benefiting the super-rich millionaires and billionaires. I disagree. The super-rich minimize their estate taxes by establishing trusts, foundations, gifts and finding the right tax shelters. The estate tax should be abolished on all estates below a fixed reasonable amount that encourages Americans to build estates for their families. Whether that number is one, 10, 20 or 30 million dollars has to be further explored.

Congress created the federal estate tax in 1916 to reduce the concentration of wealth among powerful family dynasties, such as the Rockefellers and du Ponts. By building in a generous exemption, Congress sought to target only the wealthiest Americans. The tax has generally hit the target. The tax was also imposed before income tax came into effect. Now, with all the other taxes adopted by the government, the tax burden is too heavy for everyone to bear. So much so that Dewer Byar, a farmer in Des Moines, Iowa, who hated taxes and died at the dawn of the 21st century, stipulated in his will that his farm and farming equipment be sold and the proceeds put in a trust with the annual income to be used to reduce his neighbors' property taxes. Isn't it time the effect of all taxes on middle to lower-income families was also revisited in the New World Order?

### Unconstitutional Taxes
Ralph Herman and I would debate the issue of taxes at Scratch. It seems Ralph was always in trouble with the IRS.

"Why the hell should we be paying taxes in the first place?" Ralph asked whenever the subject came up. He had spent the day with his accountants and IRS auditors and was furious.

"You should join Irwin Schiff and his movement. He doesn't believe taxes are legal," I suggested.

"Who the hell is this Irwin Shit?" Ralph asked.

"Schiff," I corrected. "He's written a book called *How Anyone Can Stop Paying Income Taxes* and believes individual income taxes are voluntary, and that the only reason anyone pays is because politicians have tricked the public into believing they have to with their tricky laws. Schiff preaches that 'a compulsory income tax would violate the Constitution, despite the 16th Amendment, and so the Internal Revenue Code was written to make paying income taxes appear mandatory. The government succeeded in doing this, he contends, 'by tricking the public into believing that those enforcement provisions of the code that apply to other, nonvoluntary taxes –like alcohol and tobacco taxes –also apply to income taxes, when in fact they do not.' "

When Schiff first preached his ideas, he was labeled a communist and told to leave America. Today he is a regular on the talk show circuit and he doesn't get many negative calls. People are listening and acting. His supporters are growing.

Russ Barnard, who was at the next table one night and periodically contributed to our discussion, leaned over and chimed in.

"It goes much deeper than that. David Halberstam makes the argument that we were so rich that a certain standard of living was built into our expectations. It became the responsibility of the politicians rather than ourselves as citizens to produce that standard of living.

"For some 15 or 20 years we should have picked up signs that we were going down the wrong track. The failure of the government to do honest budgeting during the Vietnam War was the first sign. The failure to deal with world energy prices in both 1973 and 1979 by not taxing citizens heavily at the pump was another. If there was an early example of a paralysis of political will, it was here: We were afraid to tax our own people honestly, so in effect we allowed the Arabs to tax us.

"We stand virtually alone in the Western world in our failure to tax gasoline. Despite all the warnings that this is not merely an economic issue, but one of national security, we remain unwilling to impose any discipline upon ourselves that demands a change in our lifestyles."

"Hold it a moment!" I interrupted. "That was part of what I protested when I rode my horse to work during the height of the May 1979 energy crisis. Remember?"

Ralph and Russ both nodded as they laughed.

"Furthermore, if we didn't have all these other taxes such as income, capital gains, inheritance and sales, we could tax gasoline at the pump. But with all these taxes, why tax more at the pump?" I demanded.

Why aren't more tax incentives used to develop alternative sources of energy? More importantly, we have to come up with alternative energy solutions from our many natural resources. Solar, hydro, wind and other environmentally friendly possibilities so that we no longer jeopardize our national security or are at the mercy of the oiligarchs or anyone else.

## Flat Tax

The flat tax rate of 17 percent works wonders in Hong Kong and the government has billions in surpluses every year. They don't have many IRS- type auditors because they rely on an honor system. They make their money off real estate sales, capital gains on stock sales and duties on luxury goods, alcohol and tobacco. Shouldn't the U.S. be doing the same?

The whole U.S. tax system must be overhauled. It's debilitating! Americans trying to beat the IRS set up offshore companies and open bank accounts in Hong Kong and other tax havens, as the Enron collapse reminded us again at the dawn of the 21$^{st}$ century. The IRS estimates that between 1 million and 2 million Americans have overseas bank accounts – the sole purpose being to evade U.S. taxes.

Steve Forbes' proposal for a flat tax of 17 percent on families earning more than $36,000 a year merits serious consideration by *We the Apathetic*

*People* here in the 21$^{st}$ century. I especially favor his idea of a tax return on a mere postcard instead of all those crazy, unintelligible forms we now must wade through.

Speaking with Forbes after he gave a talk at the FCC in Hong Kong before the 2002 midterm elections, I asked why he had dropped his flat-tax proposal to become a mainstream Republican candidate.

"Because that was the only way I could get the party establishment to consider supporting me," he said.

Is this any way to be running America in this new millennium?

In the New World Order there should be a low flat tax rate, of which two-thirds stays with the state and the other one-third goes to the federal government to finance the nation's defense, foreign and financial affairs. That is the only issue Congress should debate and pass laws on. All other laws should be made by local political governing bodies, as the Founding Fathers intended.

This further obviates the need for career federal politicians and their bureaucrats and lawyers and lobbyists. This would restore the part-time congressmen and require them to spend most of their time back in their home districts rather than goofing off in Washington. Lobbyists and lawyers would fall away too and bureaucracy would be drastically reduced. Wishful thinking, but doable.

"Do you agree with Forbes?" Ralph Herman asked on one of my visits during the last presidential primary of the last millennium.

"Well, Ralph, I would reduce it further. If America doesn't change its tax policies and endless subsidies, it will self-destruct. Overall, I do agree with Steve Forbes. Hong Kong is something of a model for Mr. Forbes, who has studied the SAR's flat-tax system when putting together his own version."

We called it a night. Forbes' moon was full in the sky.

Forbes is also right in suggesting that both major parties are in such crying need of renewal that they could fade away "like the Federalists or Whigs did in the last century."

### Tax Heavens

Tax havens are heaven to many tax dodgers. I know first-hand. As an American lawyer in Hong Kong, it was a subject I would periodically be asked about. The American sport of figuring out how to beat Uncle Sam at the tax game was highlighted in January 2009, when it was revealed that Treasury Secretary Timothy Geithner had "overlooked" paying $34,000-plus in personal taxes.

The periodic arrest and jailing of colorful high-profile tax cheats like Al Capone, Wesley Snipes, Martha Stewart and Leona Helmsley remind us that there is a legal difference between tax-cheating versus avoidance. The difference is the slammer.

Tax evasion is not only an American national sport. It is global – and one that the Chinese have mastered. The U.S. and Chinese tax authorities do have a common goal when it comes to tracking down tax dodgers. They exchange information on high-profile net worth individuals and companies.

In 2009. the U.S. sued UBS, Switzerland's largest bank, to try to force disclosure of the identities of as many as 52,000 American tax cheats who allegedly stashed billions there in secret accounts. UBS agreed to pay the U.S. $750 million to settle the case, but the bank disclosed the names of only 285 tax dodgers, merely whetting the IRS's appetite.

The Swiss government was not happy about the disclosure because it effectively ended Swiss bank secrecy laws – laws that allowed Adolf Hitler and many other world leaders, including Egypt's Hosni Mubarak and Libya's Moammar Gaddafi, to hide their ill-gotten gains. The UBS case put tax havens on notice that the U.S. Justice Department and Internal Revenue Service are on an international campaign to flush out hideaways for illicit or undisclosed money. Their searchlight hit Hong Kong when UBS disclosed that its bankers and lawyers were recommending to their U.S. clients to set up Hong Kong corporations.

Hong Kong's flagship bank HSBC was targeted for "secret" accounts in India, Singapore and Hong Kong that came on the back of two U.S.

government initiatives aimed at tightening the noose on banks involved in illegal financial activities in Hong Kong. One deals with the Foreign Account Tax Compliance Act and the other the amnesty program.

The panic that gripped the 60,000-plus American citizens living in Hong Kong, along with the thousands back home who have Hong Kong companies and bank accounts, became self-evident when it became the dominant topic of editorials, headlines and conversation at the FCC Main Bar in 2010 and 2011. "What should I do?" was a common question. "Should I voluntarily disclose what I have under the amnesty program?"

"Maybe I should give up my U.S. citizenship. Why should we be subjected to 60 plus percent taxes? It's insane," was and continues to be a common question, not only in Hong Kong but in America. Andrew Isbester, a banker in Hong Kong did. "I am celebrating the renounciation of my American citizenship today," he told me as I joined him and his friends for a celebratory toast that May day in 2014. "I am no longer an American."

Seminars and luncheon talks on how to deal with the aggressive new tactics of the IRS were the flavor of the year. Voluntary disclosures picked up sharply in the wake of the UBS agreement and disclosures.

The case of Brazilian-born Facebook co-founder Eduardo Saverin's tax plan, which included giving up his U.S. citizenship and moving to Singapore, highlighted America's onerous tax system. Singapore has no tax on capital gains and Saverin's move saved him between $67 million and $100 million, and a lot more as Facebook stock rises beyond its $38 offering price.

The Bank for International Settlements, which collects voluntary reports from banks in 44 countries, offers the best single source of data. It counts around $31 trillion of foreign-owned assets in the world's banks and estimates that about $4 trillion is in offshore financial centers. An estimated $1.5 trillion is in the Cayman Islands alone. The country of 52,000, which is about the size of Blaine, Minn., has more foreign-owned deposits than Japan or the Netherlands. Tax havens are one of the biggest hidden obstacles in the fight against global poverty according to Action Aid.

The Tax Justice Network, a global research firm that is opposed to tax havens, suggests that the amount hidden offshore is between $21 trillion and $32 trillion. If properly taxed, that could yield more than $200 billion in revenue around the world. A 2010 Mckinsey & Company report estimated the world's financial assets at around $200 trillion, which means that around 10 percent or more is effectively invisible in offshore accounts. Most probably in the hands of people and institutions that most actively influence major government investment decisions and laws protecting the rich.

Even Russia has a flat income tax of 13 percent, a fact that attracted French actor Gerard Depardieu to give up his French citizenship and the privilege of paying 75 percent tax on income of more than 1 million euros a year in January 2013, and become a Russian citizen.

In Italy, former Prime Minister Silvio Berlusconi was found guilty of fraud for his tax-avoidance schemes.

Tax breaks for the rich, such as low taxes on investment income, is one of the drivers of Grover Norquist's public pledge not to raise taxes, which thankfully has lost some ground and is opening people's minds to sensible changes to American tax laws – not only tax increases – but significant reductions. Why not shift taxes from individuals and corporations to pollution and consumption of items that are not necessities. America is taxing the wrong things at ridiculous tax rates.

The halcyon days of hiding money from tax authorities offshore are effectively over. Still, the best way to minimize tax evasion is to institute fairer tax laws that actually encourage companies and individuals to pay their fair share to support government services.

Better yet, why doesn't America become the world's tax haven? America can and should be the world's tax haven. It offers political stability, safety and rule of law. All it needs is a new tax system that would not only encourage tax payers to pay their fair share, but become the world's tax haven for those avoiding punitive tax authorities elsewhere around the globe.

### Abolish IRS and Tax Code
The taxpayer abuse hearings that Senate Republicans held in early 1998

were designed to show that the IRS is out of control. They buttressed their case with tales of tax agents in flak jackets storming houses and forcing teenage girls to strip at gunpoint.

The Republicans want nothing less than "to pull the current income tax code out by its roots and throw it away so it can never grow back," Representative Bill Archer regularly tells audiences. Archer is chairman of the Ways and Means Committee, where tax bills originate. Enough spin-doctoring. Just do it.

In March 1998, Senator Tim Hutchison, Republican of Arkansas, introduced a bill, which quickly found many co-sponsors, that would have repealed the Internal Revenue Code beginning in 2002. Well, guess what? It didn't happen. More spin. The Republicans want to eliminate taxes on capital gains, dividends, rents, royalties and interest. Doing so, they say, would bolster savings and investment and help the economy.

This all sounds wonderful. But the reality is, it's been going on for years. Once the political pressure and cameras are gone, congressmen get back to increasing taxes rather than reducing them. Political spin at its finest.

"When a party can't think of anything else, they always fall back on lower taxes. It has a magic sound to a voter, just like Fairyland is spoken of and dreamed of by all children. But no child has ever seen it; neither has any voter ever lived to see the day when his taxes were lowered," Will Rogers lamented in 1924!

Minnesota's former Governor Jesse Ventura is more direct. "The IRS has become corrupt, greedy, and way too powerful. Our tax system as it currently exists is a nightmare. It's stuffed with loopholes and unfair advantages. With the income tax system we have now, the IRS has almost unlimited power. They can take as much of your money as they want, and unless you're self-employed, they take it before you even get your check.

"Our forefathers would be appalled to hear that today the government gets your money before you do. The IRS is even allowed to act in direct contradiction to the Constitution. Do you know what an audit does? It assumes you're guilty. You have to prove yourself innocent. That's the exact opposite of the way our justice system works."

Excessive taxes discourage the production of income and capital growth. Taxes should be capped at a flat rate of 17 percent or less. Most government programs can be administered and controlled at the local level. The role of a national government should be limited to defense, foreign affairs, treasury, transportation, and post and telecommunications. Governments should legalize now-illegal activities that are consistent, proven growth industries. Prostitution, recreational and medical marijuana use are such activities that should be taxed, just like alcohol, tobacco and gambling.

Ventura proposes even more radical reform. "I'd like to see us do away with income tax entirely and go for a national sales tax. The federal government could collect the money it needs by placing a tax on the goods and services we buy. Then the states could add their own taxes on top of that. A fair national sales tax wouldn't touch the necessities of life, like food and clothing. It would make sure that people were able to provide themselves with the basics before it collected any tax from them."

### *Tax Reform*
Tax reform for individuals – rich and poor – and corporations is long overdue, not only in America, but in China and the rest of the world. The last significant tax reform took place in America in 1986. It was a top-to-bottom rewrite by President Reagan, who slashed taxes and closed some loopholes.

Since it is unlikely that any meaningful tax reform will take place before this book is published, it is imperative that a comprehensive tax reform take place as soon as possible in the New World Order, especially when it comes to taxing the rich more equitably. The "Buffet rule," although long overdue because of the ever-widening gap between rich and poor, has no chance of being passed by Congress in 2012. Robbing the poor and middle class so that the rich don't have to pay their fair share is no longer an acceptable tax policy.

The new tax code should be made simpler and fairer. It should encourage saving and reward companies for bringing jobs back to America, including online companies, and decide what is a fair e-commerce tax. Meanwhile, China is testing the merits of implementing a national property tax scheme with pilot projects in several cities.

What is wrong with just having a flat rate basic tax and a transaction tax? A tax on every personal or business transaction, whether it is a purchase at a store, speculation on a hedge fund bet, anything but what is gifted.

A smart revised tax code is a big part of the solution to today's myriad of economic problems. It is up to *We the Apathetic Maids* to sweep in the necessary reforms.

People don't mind paying a fair tax as long as they feel they are getting their money's worth in public services. No meaningful reform will come about as long as partisan battle lines are drawn on Bush-era cuts, defense spending cuts, medicare cuts and educational cuts.

Certain public services, such as first responders – police, firefighters, life guards or the military – must remain a public service and not be contracted out to the private sector. Why should private sector mercenaries get four times as much money than America's men and women in uniform fighting for their country out of passion and not pay? Why just not give half of what is paid mercenaries to those who deserve it and cut the growing deficit significantly in the process?

A key part of any tax code is enforcement, something not being done by overpaid bureaucrats in most states and the federal government. In California, last I checked in late 2010, more than $1.4 billion was owed the state by auto dealers alone. Up 25 percent since 2009 and almost double since 2007.

A story that caught my attention while watching the *ABC Nightly News* on February 16, 2004, was a story that the federal government was cheated out of at least $3 billion by private contractors. These are not just the high-powered well-connected government contractors. But 27,000 tax cheats who were doing business with the government. Some of the contractors hadn't paid taxes for 10 years. Others witheld payroll taxes, but instead of turning the money over to the government, bought yachts and fancy second homes. Surely the IRS and the Pentagon can do a better enforcement job.

With taxpaying wage-earners forced to pay up on the spot, it is appalling that billions in unpaid corporate taxes are not being collected by overpaid bureaucrats. And taxpayers were being asked in 2012 to approve still more taxes. How about collecting existing taxes, closing loopholes and cutting costs instead? How about ending class warfare?

How many more tax revolts, protests, riots or kamikaze air attacks on IRS offices, such as the one in Texas in February 2010, have to take place by angry citizens, whether in America, China, Italy, France or Britain, before tax reform becomes a reality and a fairer, more equitable system adopted to benefit all?

### Whore Tax

The first 21$^{st}$-century Nobel literature laureate V.S. Naipul admitted in a radio interview that he was "grateful" for the prostitutes who helped him through hard times during his former marriage. "They offer comfort," he said.

Prostitution in Hong Kong has thrived for as long as anyone who cares to discuss the subject can remember. Going back to the 1850s when the city had a population of only 33,000, prostitution thrived because men outnumbered women three to one. Brothels were required to register with the government in 1857 because of the high rate of sexually transmitted diseases. Licenses were issued to prostitutes.

Today, prostitutes come to the city from all over the world.

"What kind would you like?" is a question I have asked many a visiting business associate or client from the U.S. as we finish dinner and plan the rest of the evening.

"Chinese, Thai, Vietnamese, Latina, Russian, Indian, Filipina … ?"

I rattle off nationalities as we decide where to go once the preference is disclosed. Always Asian for the Westerners and always Western for the Asians. I usually know the answer before they do.

Today it is estimated there are more than 200,000 prostitutes in Hong Kong who cater to a population of 7 million – as well as millions of visitors.

The Hong Kong of 1850 was, much like today, a fast-growing immigrant city, with a crime rate to match. Police corruption was rife and, in the two decades after the island was ceded to Britain, more than three-quarters of the population was involved in triad activities. Prostitution and opium were legal and highly popular and gambling was big business. They still are.

The earliest recorded wills in Hong Kong show that a group of highly-successful women had one thing in common – they all worked in the sex trade. They owned property and bonds in public companies and took charge of their families' future – and Hong Kong's. Most of the properties mentioned in the wills were in areas with the most brothels of the day – around The Peak, Admiralty and parts of Wan Chai. High-class and working-class neighborhoods. Wan Chai's sex industry got the Hollywood treatment in 1960 with the release of the classic *The World of Suzie Wong*, starring William Holden and Nancy Kwan.

Legalized prostitution, like drugs, gambling and human trafficking, played a key role in the early development of Hong Kong.

"Perhaps this is a blend of Western thought and Eastern tradition. Hong Kong is very different from the mainland – we can see this 100 years ago in the rationale of Hong Kong's earliest people, and the way they do things," said Victor Zheng Wan-tai, a Hong Kong University professor and co-author of *Women's Wills, Property and the Early Hong Kong Society*.

"This city may have been built on things less than respectable, but it was for survival. It was done with tenacity and a hope for a better future."
Isn't that how America was built?

Hong Kong held its first international conference of sex workers, trade unions, activists and academics and lawmakers in May 2004. Guest speakers included representatives from the London branch of the International Union of Sex Workers and representatives of sex workers rights groups from Australia, the U.S., Italy and Cambodia.

"A lack of sexual outlets is hazardous to your health," Hong Kong sexologist Ng Man-lun has declared. I couldn't agree more.

"Ten out of 10 men would like to have an affair – it's just that not all of them have the courage to cheat," says Mak Ling-ling, a Hong Kong fortune teller.

Prostitution has been a part of human society since time immemorial. The Bible talks of "harlots" and every honest history and art book depicts sexual acts, houses of prostitution and prostitutes.

"Prostitution dates back to 700 BC in China," says Liu Dalin, curator of Shanghai's private sex museum. "There were palace prostitutes, military prostitutes, private prostitutes and market prostitutes."

Prostitution was outlawed in China when the Communist Party took power in 1949. The party won a short-term victory over vice in the 1950s and '60s. But when China opened up to the world again in 1978, prostitution resurfaced, giving poor and unskilled women a way to support themselves in times of economic upheaval, unemployment and rural migration.

"Working girls" in early Hong Kong were often veterans of the Barbary Coast in San Francisco or the rougher areas of Honolulu who found themselves in Hong Kong after making their way across the Pacific. Somerset Maugham's fictional Sadie Thompson immortalized the breed, so much so that for many years the term "American woman" on the China coast was synonymous with prostitute.

Today prostitution is legal in Hong Kong but with severe restrictions. Prostitutes are allowed to work solo from their homes. Many work out of licensed drinking establishments as "dancers" where one can pay the *mamasan* to take them home. Prostitutes are asking the government to consider designated red-light districts.

Hookers in Hong Kong pay a tax on their income. Isn't it time they did so again in America and China in the 21$^{st}$ century?

Even though prostitution is legal in Hong Kong, locals, including politicians who periodically get busted for doing so, prefer hiring hookers in China, because they are away from prying eyes – and cheaper. No different than congressmen in Washington who get caught up in prostitution scandals.

Prostitution is widespread in America and is not limited to the big cities hosting career politicians, but in small towns U.S.A., where many of the prostitutes are in fact sex slaves and illegal immigrants.

"Modern-day slavery is the fastest-growing criminal industry in the world," said Derek Ellerman, co-executive director of the Washington-based Polaris Project, an anti-trafficking organization.

America's history is endowed with a rich history of prostitution. America's pioneers spent their leisure time in licensed "houses of ill fame" with boarders, cribs and streetwalkers. Soiled doves. Birds in gilded cages. Drinking, drugs, gambling and prostitution are as American as apple pie and the flag. They are an integral part of America's "Wild West" heritage.

*You'll Never Make Love in This Town Again* is an honest account of America's legacy of prostitution. In the book, four Hollywood hookers to the stars tell it like it is. It is a graphic report of prostitutes servicing celebrities and business tycoons who are willing to pay exorbitant fees. Imagine the windfall to government coffers if those fees were subject to tax!

The tax-evasion bust of the Gold Club strip joint in Atlanta, where Dennis Rodman, Terrill Davis and Patrick Ewing were frequent patrons, was just another millennium reminder of the hypocrisy of trying to legislate morality.

Legalizing prostitution and drugs would not only generate significant taxes, but also save the millions of dollars now spent investigating and prosecuting corrupt police officers who accept bribes from brothels and drug dealers to tip them off before a raid.

*Salon,* the online magazine, has added a columnist described as an upscale Manhattan prostitute. Tracy Quan, whom the magazine calls "a writer and working girl living in New York," wrote a fictional book titled *Diary of a Manhattan Call Girl: A Nancy Chan Novel.*

The book chronicles the struggles of a $600-a-date call girl to balance a career with the needs of her unsuspecting fiance, a Wall Street banker eager to tie the knot. The book also segues into the prostitutes rights movement in New York, in which Quan is heavily involved.

"I was not driven by lust when I was younger," Quan says. "Instead, I was motivated by curiosity, by a desire to have sex with interesting guys, by a feeling of accomplishment when I had sex. Those are the attitudes that any professional should bring to the table. Or the bed, in my case."

That's New York honesty at its finest.

Prostitution was legal in California near the state capitol Sacramento until the 1950s, when Governor Edmund Brown, father of the current Governor Jerry Brown, decided to bring it to an end. Of course, its primary beneficiaries were the career politicians and their lawyers and lobbyists getting laid while they screwed *We the Apathetic Maids.*

In Germany, the Teutschenthal woman's soccer team is sponsored by a whorehouse. Team members sport jerseys recommending that their fans visit a local brothel. "X-Carree: Always Worth a Visit" is emblazoned across the women's chests.

"The women have no problem with it,' said coach Andreas Dittman.

In Prague, in what used to be the capital of Czechoslovakia, a country that no longer exists, a brothel offers free sex to customers who agree to let the action be streamed on the Internet.

In New Zealand, secondary school students have listed prostitution and drug dealing on a list of desirable careers in their yearbook.

Italy's former Prime Minister Silvio Berlusconi never did convince anyone that he didn't pay prostitutes to entertain him and his friends. "I have never paid a woman," Berlusconi said. "I never understood what the satisfaction is when you are missing the pleasure of conquest."

Sure. How about price?

My favorite example, if I can call it that, of how ingrained prostitution is in our human DNA and the need to come to grips and terms with this reality, is the story of Puja Mukherjee, one of the stars of *Slumlord Millionaire,* who took the stage at the Academy Awards in 2005. Today she is a prostitute.

She is a prostitute because it is a family tradition. Her mother prostituted her, just like Puja's grandmother did to her. After a fun-filled week in L.A., which included an "absolutely unforgettable" day at Disneyland, Puja returned to Calcutta. Seven months later, soon after her 17th birthday, her mother forced her into prostitution.

"I lost my virginity and self-esteem in one go. I was physically and psychologically battered. My initiation into what is known as the world's oldest profession was too humiliating for words."

It took her a long time to come to terms with her predicament. "But ultimately I accepted prostitution as my fate. Now I think I was destined to be a *randi* – prostitute. It's pointless blaming others. I have no regrets or qualms anymore about selling my body. In fact, I go to great lengths to keep it slim, trim and sexy.

"Some people might say I'm a fallen woman. But they forget that *puja* in Hindi means 'worship.' And many rich and handsome men do worship me in bed. I am living up to my name, thank you."

In Melbourne, Australia, The Daily Planet became the world's first listed brothel. The company hired "Hollywood Madam" Heidi Fleiss to spice up its stock listing. The five-star hotel has a bar lounge and 18 themed rooms and spas and touts itself as recession proof. The shares doubled on their first day of trading.

"Obviously the price is going to go up. It's sex … and everyone knows sex is a smart investment," Fleiss told reporters.

During the 2004 Olympics in Greece, the government licensed more brothels to handle the extra demand. Prostitution is legal in Greece, though only three prostitutes can work in a single brothel, which must not be near a church or school.

In Catholic Spain, where prostitution is neither prohibited nor regulated, there are some 300,000 women engaged in the sex trade, generating annual revenues of more than $22 billion. These prostitutes march in the streets with picket signs demanding labor rights, and sue club and brothel owners demanding they make pension payments – and get favorable judgments.

Even in Iran, an official has acknowledged that prostitution and drug abuse are now widespread among the predominantly young population. This in a country where such vices are punishable by death. Even hard-line mullahs can't stop it. Do Americans really think that laws can stop the practice?

Prostitution is legal in Muslim Indonesia. Prostitutes there even have their own mosque in the red-light district to pray after they service American sailors at the Tanjung Perak dockyards. The docks and their nearby brothels have been in existence since the Dutch colonial period.

In China, the economy is swelling the ranks of *san pei,* semi-legal hostesses and prostitutes. The Chinese authorities are taxing them. Shouldn't America be doing the same?

Shenyang began taxing *san pei* in 1997. Cities in Liaoning, Fujian, Shanxi, Hunan and Heilongjiang provinces have followed suit. As many as 10 million people are in the flesh trade in China, according to an estimate in the 2001 U.S. State Department human rights report. Prostitutes are taxed up to 30 percent of their earnings. Shouldn't New York, Los Angeles and the rest of America catch up with this enlightened view?

Whorehouses in China even offer student discounts. That is one way to keep students from spending all their time hanging out in bars.

Millions of people across Southeast Asia depend for their livelihoods on the sex industry, which in some countries makes up 14 percent of gross domestic product, a ground breaking study by the International Labor Organization concludes.

Prostitution also supports secondary industries – bars, clubs, hotels, taxis, courts and police. It has kept food vendors, janitors, cashiers and security guards working. It is and always has been an economic driver.

High-profile arrests of madams and the disclosure of their celebrated and wealthy johns only confirm the demand. The arrests of Daryl Strawberry in Florida, Hugh Grant in Hollywood, the tearful confession of televangelist Jimmy Swaggart and the disclosure that political adviser Dick Morris regularly used prostitutes only highlighted the reality. The nameless johns who are arrested daily for soliciting prostitutes is voluminous testimony to the failure of attempts to legislate sexual behavior.

The issue of how much could be gained by a regulated prostitution sector in the form of taxation and licensing fees is almost always pushed aside by prudency and denial. Legalizing prostitution in America is a Herculean Olympic challenge. If Greece, the cradle of democracy, can do it for the 2004 Olympics, why can't *We the Maids* sweep similar reforms into America? Billions of revenue dollars are lost while bribery and corruption thrives. Career politicians, lawyers and lobbyists benefit at the expense of *We the Apathetic People*.

Prostitution is a multi-billion dollar business in America according to a 340-page study released in March 2014 by the Urban Institute. Why not tax it?

With today's compensated dating, the Internet, varied choices of ladies of the day or night, I'm happy to keep trying to pick up chicks the good old-fashioned way, even if ocassionally, to quote Kenny Chesney, a 10 turns out to be a two.

### Grass Tax

With even more controversy than legalizing prostitution, this pragmatism should be applied to marijuana in the 21st century. The millennium's closing year poster boy Khalid El Amin, who led the University of Connecticut to its first college basketball title in 1999, was arrested for possession of marijuana

Legalizing marijuana would put the brakes on the violence and crime that is associated with its illegal trade. The tax benefits would far outweigh the problem of hard drug addiction in the U.S., which has not been notably curbed under current drug laws or the much-vaunted "war on drugs."

In fact, in early 2014, Colorado and Washington state legalize the recreational use of pot, with several other states considering doing so.

The abundance of marijuana in southwest China is well known to travelers to the region. It grows wild along country roads and even in front of new business plazas. Regrettably, the Chinese government is following America's lead in criminalizing the stuff.

Barry McCaffrey, U.S. drug czar under Bill Clinton, said that drugs are illegal because they're dangerous. Well, alcohol is also dangerous. So are cars. So are cigarettes. So is sky-diving. So are hundreds of other things. The government can't make all dangerous things illegal. It doesn't work.

"You'd think we would have learned our lesson with Prohibition, but apparently we didn't," Jesse Ventura reminds us. "I see no reason for marijuana to be illegal, and especially not for it to carry the bizarre stigma that the government has placed on it. Besides, we're wasting a huge amount of time, money and resources on trying to control marijuana, and so far what we've been doing is ridiculously ineffective. You may have heard it said that alcohol and tobacco buy their freedom. They generate revenue for the government with the taxes we pay when we purchase them. Marijuana is the opposite: The government spends a huge amount of our money trying to fight it, for no gain. It would make a lot more sense for us to legalize it and tax it."

I couldn't agree more.

In fact, marijuana is America's largest cash crop. The annual domestic marijuana harvest is worth something like $20 billion a year! Wouldn't we all be better of if this annual cash crop were taxed?

America's depressing history of working with dictators in the war on drugs, similar to its depressing history of working with dictators for their oil, "demonstrates the futility of building a foreign policy on a domestic obsession," columnist Robert Scheer reminds us.

This was exemplified in the opening year of the century by the George W. Bush administration's grant of $43 million to the Taliban in Afghanistan. It did so because the Taliban declared "in very religious terms" that opium growing is against the will of God. The fact that most human activities the Taliban support, including Osama bin Laden, were more deadly for humans than heroin, as we were reminded by the kamikaze bombers of 9/11, was ignored by the religious Bush administration. America's U.N.-supported embargo against Afghanistan, while giving them millions of hard-earned American taxpayer dollars, is also played down by the media thanks to spin doctors.

When Peter Gatien, known as the New York "King of Clubs," was acquitted of drug pushing in his clubs, he refused to promise that the establishments would be drug free.

"I can't be an oasis in New York City that's drug free. New York is not drug free," he said.

Neither is any other place in America, Hong Kong or on this planet where people get together to have a good time. Smoking is illegal in most such clubs and no smokers are seen, but there are countless snorters and pill poppers.

The extradition of Marc Emery, the "Prince of Pot," from Canada to the U.S. in June 2010, because he seeded so many marijuana legalization campaigns in America, further highlighted the absurdity of the U.S. government's misdirected anti-drug campaigns and continuing waste of tax dollars.

The arrest of film director Oliver Stone for possession of marijuana highlighted the draconian laws in some states for possession. The estimated cost of prosecuting people for mere possession was estimated to be $7 billion a year in the closing years of the millennium in the U.S. alone! Surely there are better uses for this money in the 21st century.

Robert Scheer points out that "Alcohol kills 100,000 a year, tobacco 400,000 and if there is hard evidence of the deadliness of marijuana, particularly if eaten in a brownie rather than smoked, the federal government has yet to come up with it."

More than half a million Americans are arrested for marijuana possession each year.

The Compassion Flower Inn in downtown Santa Cruz, California, is a sanctuary for medical pot users and is a mellow way to start the new millennium. Defying federal authorities, Santa Cruz is one of several California communities that have jump-started efforts to put the state's controversial medical marijuana law into practice.

Oregon's voter-approved medical marijuana law is another forerunner of what will eventually become the law of the land.

California's Mendocino County became the first in America to legalize the growing of marijuana for personal use in the closing year of the millennium. While state and federal drug laws supercede the local measure, rendering it moot, proponents say it is an important first step in challenging the thinking that makes using marijuana a criminal offense but drinking alcohol socially acceptable, even desirable. Spin doctoring at full speed.

"What this initiative does is cap a 20-plus-year war on marijuana," said Dan Hamburg, a former Democratic congressman and now one of the local Green Party members who drafted the measure. "Measure G says this war has wasted lots of money, wasted lots of lives, and the whole logic behind pot being illegal is ridiculous and false ... ."

Alaska voters put the issue of legalizing marijuana on the state ballot in the last election of the last millennium. Not only legalization but granting amnesty to those already convicted on marijuana charges. Nine Western states, 18 overall, have passed laws that give people the right to use marijuana to relieve pain or nausea so long as they have a doctor's approval. The U.S. Supreme Court refused to accept an appeal of a lower court decision that held that doctors may recommend the use of marijuana, thus making it legal for doctors to do so. Isn't it time for all 48 states to follow Colorado and Washington in the 21st century?

California's Proposition 19 that was defeated in the 2010 election Colorado and Washington would have legalized the use of marijuana in the state. If it had passed, it would have revolutionized the state's drug laws and fired up the legalization movement nationwide. Proposition 19 would have allowed people 21 and older to grow up to 25 square feet of marijuana and possess up to an ounce, and authorized cities and counties to approve cultivation, retail sales and taxation. The estimated tax revenue, had the initiative passed, would have been more than $1.5 billion a year.

The drug war has other casualties, none more obvious in major cities than the gang violence that is often a fight over the spoils of the marijuana trade. Former California state Senator Tom Hayden noted the dramatic decline of violence after the end of Prohibition and added, "We have to re-examine the whole war on drugs with respect to its social cost in increased gang violence."

Britain's Prince Harry sounds like a chip off the royal block. He admits to drinking and smoking marijuana like many healthy normal teenagers do. How else can one understand their subjects? According to the Schools Health Education Unit in Britain, which conducted a survey of 22,000 teenagers in 1997, a third admitted to smoking cannabis by the age of 15.

*The Lancet,* England's leading medical journal, published a thorough analysis of marijuana's harmful effects. On the basis of the available medical evidence, *The Lancet* concluded that "moderate indulgence in cannabis has little ill effect on health."

Unfortunately, scientists and politicians do make uneasy bedfellows and, as a result, the information and political spin that career politicians put out is not necessarily what even their own loyal scientific advisers tell them. It is the spin that generates the most votes, regardless of the truth.

This kind of conflict has a well-established history going back to Galileo in 1632. He advised the highest temporal authority of his day, the Catholic Church. He told them the Earth went round the sun and was promptly prosecuted by the Inquisition. Famously, he was proven right.

It has always been dangerous and politically suicidal for political advisers, especially scientific ones, to tell popes, princes and career politicians something they don't want to hear. Their scientific advice is suppressed until after the next election, not only by the candidates, but by their financial backers, purely for political and corporate gain.

John P. Walters, the George W. Bush White House drug czar, tried to link marijuana to teen depression and was soundly criticized for doing so and accused of trying to scare parents and teens by exaggerating the dangers.

Career politicians, regardless of their party persuasion or beliefs, want things said unequivocally, while scientists know that their advice is provisional and sometimes open to dispute. The number of government studies that are suppressed because the results are unpalatable to career politicians and their cronies is mind-numbing. It is estimated that more than 166 million people worldwide have either tried cannabis or are currently using the drug. The figure, taken from the U.N. Office on Drugs and Crime, means one in every 25 people between the ages of 15 and 64 in 2006 had some experience with marijuana, according to a research report published in *The Lancet*.

A book I highly recommend is John McCabe's *Marijuana & Hemp, History Uses, Laws and Controversy* that reminds readers that colonization of the U.S. was made possible and motivated by hemp cultivation. The book also highlights the positive environmental impact of growing hemp – a plant that has thrived for more than 10,000 years on this planet – and how not being able to do so is putting U.S. industries behind those around the world, yet again.

Hemp, for the uninitiated, actually encompasses all those plants that produce non-psychoactive flowers, meaning that not only will it not get the user high, but leaves a nasty headache. It is the female cannabis flowers that are referred to as marijuana that get people high. Leave it to the women again.

Cannabis use is highest in the U.S., Australia and New Zealand, followed by Europe. No surprises there.

Britain, like Jamaica, the Netherlands, Italy, Spain, Portugal and other enlightened countries, has loosened harsh criminal penalties for using cannabis at the dawn of the 21st century. Even Roman Catholic Italy is growing its own grass because weed from Eastern Europe is contaminated and controlled by Eastern European criminal gangs and not the local mafia boys. Isn't it time America did the same? The reality is that the war on drugs has failed.

The sooner America comes to grips with this reality, the better off Americans will be. Financially, from the savings of billions wasted every year on enforcement and locking up minor offenders, and health savings because of all the medical benefits marijuana offers. For *We the Apathetic Maids* to fully appreciate these benefits, I highly recommend reading *The Los Angeles Journal for Education on Medical Marijuana*. Articles include topics such as "The Future of Cannabis as Medicine," "The Need for Medical Marijuana Is Real & Immediate," and includes many full-page ads for co-ops and pharmacies dispensing medical marijuana.

Pot conventions, known as hempfests, such as those held annually in Los Angeles, Oakland, San Francisco, and starting in 2011, Sacramento, are great educational venues for people who want to better understand the medical and fiscal benefits of legalizing marijuana. These conventions attract thousands of visitors and raise the awareness level of people to the benefits of marijuana.

### Wasted Resources
In 1997, the year of the Hong Kong handover, roughly 695,000 people were arrested for pot in America, by far the largest number in U.S. history. In 1992, the year Bill Clinton took office, 342,000 were arrested. Eighty-

seven percent of the 1997 arrests were for possession of marijuana, a crime that usually involves less than an ounce of pot. The cost of those marijuana arrests – not including the cost of any imprisonment after a conviction – may approach $3 billion! Under the leadership of the first U.S. president who has admitted to smoking pot, but not inhaling, more Americans have been imprisoned for marijuana crimes than at any time in history. Twice as many people were arrested for marijuana during the Clinton presidency as were during the entire presidency of Richard Nixon! During the first year of George W. Bush's administration, more than 734,000 Americans were arrested for marijuana violations – more than for murder, rape, armed robbery and assault combined!

The American Medical Association, the American Bar Association and the National Council of Churches endorsed decriminalization of marijuana, as did President Jimmy Carter. Willy Nelson smoked pot on the White House roof. Someone is even growing it in Buckingham Palace! Prince Harry, like most of his peers, has already tried it. They are our future reality in the 21st century. Wouldn't we all benefit from taxing their smoke?

I have debated the legalization of marijuana while sharing a joint with congressmen, senators, assemblymen, assistant district attorneys, deputy city attorneys, police commissioners and police officers who, incidentally, always have some of the best grass. Talk about political hypocrisy!

The only outspoken honest politician to admit he used marijuana and cocaine and advocate their legalization was former Governor Gary E. Johnson of New Mexico. He advocates their legalization so they can be sold for profit. Drugs, he says, should be regulated like alcohol and people could be held accountable for what they did under their influence.

"We are spending incredible amounts of our resources on incarceration, law enforcement and courts," he said. "As an extension of everything I've done in office, I made a cost-benefit analysis, and this one really stinks.

"I would like to see a discussion on this, A to Z," he said. "The reality of what might evolve is that we get our feet wet, so that we could learn how to legalize or decriminalize. Politically, I can't ascertain if there has been a positive or negative reaction. But publicly, I've found that people overwhelmingly want to talk about it."

Reading about collectives in Los Angeles getting busted for dispensing medical pot is as absurd and ridiculous as "coffee shops" in the Netherlands being busted for having too much inventory on hand. If it is legal to sell pot, whether for medical or other reasons, what is the point of creating bureaucratic restrictions that not only defeat the purpose of the law, but deprive government coffers of much-needed tax revenue?

I am always amazed at how quickly lawyers surface in any controversial political issue, marijuana being no exception. The U.S. attorney's office filing hundreds of suits in California and other states to shut down the co-ops and pharmacies that sell medical marijuana, suits against U.S. Atty. Gen. Eric Holder to stop the raids and suits that accuse police officers in New York of ignoring guidelines not to arrest for possession of small amounts of marijuana discovered when suspects are stopped.

In early January 2013, the city of San Diego, on the order of newly elected Mayor Bob Filner, dropped all legal efforts aimed at forcing marijuana dispensaries out of business. Filner restated his support for making marijuana accessible to people "who legitimately need it for relief of pain."

Washington was the first state to legalize the recreational use of marijuana and Colorado followed in hot pursuit.

The Washington law calls for the state to impose a 25 percent excise tax on growers when they sell to processors, another 25 percent excise tax when processors sell to retailers; and another 25 percent excise tax when customers buy from a store, plus the sales tax. This is in addition to the state business and occupancy tax the state imposes on retailers. Not a bad source of significant revenue.

Legalizing marijuana, the most commonly used illegal drug in the U.S., continues to raise health concern issues, especially over the long term effects on habitual teenage smokers, and justifiably so. Lost in the fray is the fact that marijuana is medicine – and a much needed one for many ailments.

There are hundreds of strains of cannabis, with varying clinical properties – anxiety relief, sleep promotion, analgesia, anti-nausea and many more. Cannabis experts in licensed dispensaries focus on the medicinal properties of the marijuana they sell.

Legalizing cannabis would ease more than anxiety and pain. It also would ease states' money troubles. On the one hand, it would generate tax revenue on the now-illicit multi-billion-dollar industry and, on the other, it would save precious tax dollars from being wasted on law enforcement that could be better put to use protecting the public from real crimes.

Reading about Arizona's Home DePot, what local wags are calling the "Wal-Mart of Weed," brought a smile to my face.

"Maybe that is why Sarah Palin moved to Arizona," one political wag at the FCC Main Bar volunteered as the question of legalizing weed in America came up in June 2011, after the conservative Republican state became the 16th in the nation, plus the District of Columbia, to decriminalize marijuana for medical purposes.

A group of prominent former world leaders points out that the so-called war on drugs has failed and that decriminalizing marijuana could help curtail drug-related violence and social ills. "The global war on drugs has failed, with devastating consequences for individuals and societies around the world," members of the Global Commission on Drug Policy said in their report.

"Fifty years after the initiation of the U.N. Single Convention on Narcotic Drugs, and 40 years after President Nixon launched the U.S. government's war on drugs, fundamental reforms in national and global drug control policies are urgently needed," the report said.

Saying that restrictions on marijuana should be loosened, the report urges governments to "end the criminalization, marginalization and stigmatization of people who use drugs but who do no harm to others."

The group of prominent statesmen – including former Brazilian President Fernando Cardoso, former Colombian President Cesar Gaviria, Mexico's former President Ernesto Zedillo and former U.N. Secretary General Kofi Annan – said that purely punitive measures had in fact led to a situation where "the global scale of illegal drug markets – largely controlled by organized crime – has grown dramatically."

"Decriminalization initiatives do not result in significant increases in drug use," the report said, citing policies in Australia, Holland and Portugal.

In the United Kingdom, a cannabis-derived drug was launched in June 2010. Sativex is the first prescription drug made from cannabis to officially go on sale anywhere in the world. It offers a legal way for thousands of multiple-sclerosis sufferers to relieve their pain. A bigger potential market exists in the U.S., where Sativex is being developed as a painkiller for cancer patients.

The Cannabis sativa genome is being mapped and will give breeders a huge advantage in the drive to create new strains.

The benefits of legalization are many, including the establishment of labs that weed out bad and harmful batches of cannabis. The Steep Hill Lab in Oakland, California, is one such example. They assure marijuana businesses that their product isn't tainted by dangerous toxic molds or pesticides. Since there is no Food and Drug Administration oversight of marijuana, private labs are not only a necessity, but another tax-generating revenue source.

Is it any wonder the Obama administration is shifting away from the paranoid, political drug policies of its predecessors? The federal government announced in 2009 that it would end raids on groups that supply medical marijuana to patients.

A U.S. government study conducted by a panel of 11 independent experts at the Institute of Medicine, a branch of the National Academy of Sciences, concluded that there is no evidence that giving marijuana to sick people increases illicit use in the general population. Nor is marijuana a "gateway drug" that leads patients to use harder drugs like cocaine and heroin, the study said.

While the study's authors said they were surprised to discover "an explosion of new scientific knowledge about how the active components of marijuana affect the body," they added pointedly that the future of marijuana as a medicine did not lie in smoking it. Marijuana smoke, they said, is even more toxic than tobacco smoke, and can cause cancer, lung damage and complications during pregnancy.

The true benefits of marijuana, the experts said, would be realized only when alternative methods, like capsules, patches and bronchial inhalers, were developed to deliver its active components, called cannabinoids, to the body without the harmful effects of smoke. In the meantime, salad dressings and brownies will work just fine!

The battle over marijuana is a critical one, centered on the conflict between liberal and conservative philosophies that hamstrings almost everything in the U.S. these days.

In January 2013, a U.S. appeals court refused to order a change in the government's 40-year-old drug classification schedule in the Controlled Substances Act passed into law by Congress – a law Congress must repeal.

In December 2012, President Obama and Sen. Patrick J. Leahy, chairman of the Senate Judiciary Committee, said they were prepared to reconsider federal law that makes possession of small amounts of marijuana a crime.

"So what we're going to need to have is a conversation about how do you reconcile a federal law that still says marijuana is a federal offense and state laws that it's legal?" Obama told ABC News in an interview with Barbara Walters. The solution is simple. The feds get out of the marijuana control business and leave it to the states to decide.

The Supreme Court has done its damnedest in the new millennium to slam the brakes on marijuana, ruling that the Feds can prosecute violators of U.S. drug laws, even when they are following state law allowing those with a doctor's recommendation to smoke and grow marijuana, or to have it grown for them. Eighteen states have passed laws allowing the medical use of pot. The high court's rulings smack of the same partisanship that banned the Florida recount in the 2000 presidential election, handing the presidency to George W. Bush over Al Gore, the winner of the popular vote nationwide.

As this book was going to press, federal prosecutors were threatening to shut down medical marijuana dispensaries in California, warning landlords to stop sales of the drug and threatening them with property seizure and prison. Medical pot's proponents are angry, saying that the administration is breaking a promise Barack Obama made during his presidential campaign that his administration would not go after medical marijuana users and caregivers.

The liberal position on marijuana is not just driven by woolly principle. It is a highly practical, utilitarian argument. A practical example is a decision handed down by a judge in Italy where selling marijuana is a crime, but possession for personal use is not. A court in Rome ruled that a student aged 17, taking 40 joints on a school outing for himself and to share with friends and a teacher, was not guilty of any crime. The Appeals Court said they could have easily consumed the weed during the trip. And what a trip it must have been.

The drug-related violence plaguing the U.S.-Mexico border is a daily reminder and desperate cry to not only legalize the sale of marijuana, but its production. So far, no modern country, not even the Netherlands, has ever legalized marijuana production. America should take the lead and legalize weed in order to break the power of the drug cartels.

Marijuana carries the least amount of overhead cost for many of the cartels and provides a good chunk of their cash flow for buying guns and influence. Estimates vary, but analysts say pot accounts for somewhere in the range of 20 to 50 percent of the cartels' profits. A 2010 analysis by the RAND Corp. concluded that if California had passed its initiative to legalize the domestic production and sale of weed, California could become a major supplier of the product to the rest of the U.S. That, according to George W. Grayson, a professor of government at William & Mary, "would hurt the cartels badly." RAND estimates that it would have reduced the drug's pretax price by more than 80 percent.

Organized crime syndicates are estimated to gross more than $1.5 trillion a year. The value of the illegal drug trade was estimated at $400 billion in 1995, about 8 percent of world trade, more than the shares of iron and steel and motor vehicles, and roughly equivalent to textiles and gas and oil. Isn't it time it was taxed in the 21st century for all our benefit?

Coke, not the cola, is used rampantly in the halls of power. The restrooms in Congress, Parliament and the Bundestag are laced and lined. The same holds true for Wall Street, K Street and every major law firm, bank and lobbying firm that affects the lives of *We the People* – even the restrooms of the Foreign Correspondents Club in Hong Kong. "I love going to the bathroom after some of these bankers and lawyers do their lines and scrape their generous remnants," is a remark I have heard more than once from cash-strapped journalists.

The Great Recession, credit crunch and volatile financial markets do drive up the number of bankers that use and abuse hard drugs. Seabrook House, a 24-bed luxury rehab facility in Pennsylvania, has been crammed with Wall Street refugees since 2009.

Legalize grass and it would probably reduce the use of other more-dangerous illegal alternatives. If you have to get it illegally, you might as well get the one with the extra kick. Jolt! Legalize grass and the desire or will to get the jolt is reduced. At least it would allow taxpayer dollars and enforcement agencies to focus on hard drugs rather than soft ones. Soft money, not drugs, is what career politicians should be addressing while representing *We the People*.

What is the point of staying with a failed system?

### *The Right Stuff*
Progressive leaders in the U.S. are increasingly pressing for the legalization of marijuana and prostitution. They argue that adults should be permitted to engage in activities that do not harm others and that the prohibitions on cannabis and prostitution have failed. The Dutch descendants of the founders of New York City, stock exchanges and one of the European empires that left a lasting influence on the 21st century also pioneered

marijuana and prostitution taxes that should also be adopted in America.

And while we're at it, sales tax should be abolished on necessities. Government income can no longer be deficit financed by overtaxation on the wrong commodities or services in the New World Order.

"Experience should teach us to be most on guard to protect liberty when government's purposes are benevolent," said the late U.S. Supreme Court Justice Louis D. Brandeis.

Brandeis' quote came to mind when I was visiting Mark and Laurie Tigan at their mountaintop residence in New Hampshire in the spring of 2011. I had asked Mark why he wasn't trimming his trees to really enjoy the beautiful view in the seemingly endless valley below. "We get taxed according to the view we have," he responded.

"What? You must be kidding," is all I could say.

When he got through explaining the complicated New Hampshire view tax, I understood why he had not trimmed his trees. Ridiculous, actually.

I can understand why people are angry at the government and its tax policies. The kamikaze air attack on a Texas IRS office and the anti-government suicide screed posted on the Internet beforehand by wannabe country-music star Joseph Stack in February 2010, although a surprise to his friends, did not surprise me. How many more angry Americans are out there feeling they are being pummeled by unfair taxes?

U.S. tax laws are long overdue for a complete overhaul. People being penalized while corporate America is subsidized at the people's expense is inflicting unfair hardships on *We the Apathetic Maids*.

The time to rise again and protest the ever-increasing injustice in the tax system is long overdue. Why continue unfair taxation without representation? Who lobbies for the people?

The federal government, most states, counties and cities are broke. They are all looking for ways to generate taxes, including the Internet and online retailers like Amazon. It is estimated that more than $20.5 billion in global online sales is untaxed that could, if taxed, generate millions in state and local revenue – at a higher cost to the consumers – *We the Apathetic Maids*. Online sales companies should be taxed only in the state where they are based, not where their products are ultimately delivered. Taxes should be paid when it costs government to provide services. No more and no less.

We pay taxes in exchange for public services. The government in effect sells us public services, while we the taxpayers in effect buy them. The negotiated price has to be mutually agreed, not imposed on *We the Apathetic Maids* by corporate lobbyists and their paid career politicians, not only in America and China, but across the world.

I agree wholeheartedly with Winston Churchill who said: "I contend that for a nation to try to tax itself into prosperity is like a man standing in a bucket and trying to lift himself up by the handle."

Tax breaks should be given to employers who create new jobs for the unemployed. Not just for hiring them, but for keeping them. Tax uncertainty is bad for business. However, unreasonable tax certainty on employed individuals is bad for the country.

We have to tax luxury items and high-yield goods and services such as marijuana and prostitution. Combine the revenues saved from prosecution and incarceration with the revenues generated from taxation and millions of people could be educated and have their medical needs funded!

Taxation with misrepresentation hasn't worked in the New World Disorder. If we continue down the tax road we are on, our grandchildren will bear the cost of deficit spending our children will have to finance. *We the Maids* have to start sweeping in tax reforms to tax the right stuff – and quick – if our children and grandchildren are to survive in the 21st-century New World Order!

### Subsidies

The absurdity of subsidies was really brought home after 9/11. Corporate America wrapped itself in the flag as their lawyers, lobbyists and spin doctors convinced our elected career politicians to vote billions in aid and loan guarantees to airlines whose security failures contributed to the kamikazi bombers getting on board in the first place, but not a dime for laid-off airline employees who suffered because of the airlines and government incompetence and shortcomings on security. A "stimulus" package that includes $25 billion of retroactive corporate tax cuts funded by *We the Apathetic Maids* while not one dime is provided for our laid-off family members or friends.

George F. Will in his book *Restoration* points to the absurdity of subsidies. He cites the mohair subsidy as a typical example. Australia and New Zealand are the major players in the world wool market. They account for at least 85 percent of the world's wool exports. Their subsidies account for a piddling 4 percent of their producers' receipts. U.S. subsidies account for a whopping 42 percent of U.S. producers' receipts. Also, Australian and New Zealand sheep are more productive than American sheep, producing twice as much wool per head.

Now let's go to the goat side of this subsidy saga. Mohair is a negligible part of the U.S. clothing market, amounting to no more than 1/100,000th of the fiber used. In fact, most U.S. mohair is exported. That means the mohair subsidy is subsidizing European sweater-makers. They send some of their sweaters to America, where Americans pay the tariffs that fund the mohair subsidy. Not to worry, say the subsidy's supporters, U.S. mohair exports contribute to a "positive balance of trade." But Americans are paying a subsidy of 387.3 percent to produce the mohair, probably the highest subsidy rate for any agricultural product. In 1990, the average market price for mohair was 93 cents a pound; the federal mohair support price was $4.53 per pound.

Actually, the subsidy is just another welfare program for the wealthy – the more than $3 billion a year subsidies to oil companies raking in the profits being one more example that *We the Apathetic Maids* cluelessly accept. Since 1954, 80 percent of the money has flowed to fewer than 6,000 mohair producers, most of them doing quite nicely, thank you. By 1990, some producers were getting $200,000 checks for their subsidies. Jonathan Rauch quotes an industry source as saying, "We're not proud of getting these checks. It's embarrassing." To the point of returning them? Oh, no.

As Rauch says, the mohair subsidy has the "classic camouflage of a small, boring farm program."

Almost no one knows about it. No one, that is other than its beneficiaries and the politicians who benefit from the votes and financial contributions of their grateful constituents.

Meanwhile, the price of mohair fell "disastrously." Which is to say, mohair supplies exceeded demand. That is hardly a disaster for mohair consumers, but again, we are now talking politics, not economics. The program was reborn as a "rural development program" to sustain a "treasured American way of life." But not the rural life that Jeffersonians celebrate. Put plainly, the mohair subsidy is one of innumerable programs that sustain an urban way of life – the life of career politicians, toiling, they hope for as long as they like, smack in the center of the District of Columbia, Will writes.

Agriculture, which is supposed to be the repository of the virtues Jefferson associated with sturdy independence, is shot through with dependency. Consider the busy bees. During World War II, the government got into the honey business. It decided to encourage – only temporarily, of course – the production of honey as a sugar substitute, and of beewax for waterproofing combat equipment. The war ended in 1945. But the honey subsidy was going strong in the last decade of the 20th century, to the annual tune of an estimated $20 million.

In the early summer of 1992, Bill Clinton tried to use bees to balance his image, if not the budget. He said he would cut the budget, and he singled out one wee $20 million from the more than $14 billion in agricultural subsidies, the price support for honey. The beekeepers, all 2,000 of them, were as mad as hornets, but not madder than Chairman Kika de la Garza, who, according to his staff, dislikes anyone targeting individual agricultural industries for cuts. The policy is to cut all or none. Guess which it will be? Will asks.

It gets even better. The Department of Agriculture decided to spend $6 million to buy surplus ground bison meat in 1999. The industry's biggest producer, and likely biggest beneficiary of government's largesse, was Ted Turner, who raises 17,000 bison on ranches in Montana, Nebraska and New Mexico. North Dakota cattle rancher Randy Mosser has a beef with the concept. "People who get into buffalo are basically the rich, who get into it for the novelty. Why do they need a bailout?" Same reason they do for owning horses, bees, sheep, goats, water – and destroying banks and the global financial system.

The big corporations represent only 10 percent of American farming but they have expensive effective lobbyists. Corporate farmers, who put America's family farms out of business, destroy the health of rural communities at the expense of *We the Apathetic Taxpayers*. The $118 billion farm subsidy signed into law by George W. Bush in 2002 was funded by taxpayers through 2012. Like the steel tariff, it was passed in an election year to garner votes in critical farm states.

"A wasteful corporate welfare measure that penalizes taxpayers and the world's poorest people in order to bribe a few voters," a *Washington Post* editorial lamented.

Bush said he was pleased to sign the bill, and delivered a brief statement suggesting he is either dishonest or utterly ignorant of what he did, the editorial correctly pointed out. It concluded with the reminder, "When the administration says there is no new money for welfare mothers or health care or low-income housing, remember Bush's farm bill."

The demand for locally grown fruits and vegetables has increased and so has the number of urban farmers markets sprouting up across the nation everywhere I go, from California, the country's top agricultural producing state with 827 such markets, to New York and every state in between. Proof that corporate food factories, like the rest of corporate America, can't stop or change what *We the People* think is best for us and our families.

Australia's Minister of Trade, Mark Vaile, wrote a poignant opinion in *The Asia Wall Street Journal*. "The current global agricultural subsidy regime in developed countries involves a massive annual taxpayer transfer of well over $300 billion. This is six times the amount of all the aid sent to developing countries. It is neither economically sensible nor morally defensible, particularly when typically 80 percent of those transfers go to 20 percent of the richest producers and only a small fraction of the subsidy trickles down to the farmer on the land," Vaile pointed out. That is why rural poverty is a grim reality, thanks to *We the Apathetic Maids*.

Listening to lame American career politicians argue that the farm subsidy was necessary for the war effort to fight terrorism would be laughable if it weren't so pathetic.

"I'm tired of everyone saying an army marches on its stomach to imply that we need a farm bill to feed our troops," former Senator Richard Lugar said. "We've got food coming out of our ears."

"These legislative high-jinks are bad enough in peacetime," Senator John McCain told the Senate after noting that on September 13, while the Pentagon and World Trade Center "still smoldered," the Senate approved $2 million for the Oregon Groundfish Outreach Program. "America is at war," McCain said. "Congress should grow up and stop treating the domestic budget as a political Toys 'R' Us," he bellowed on behalf of *We the Apathetic Maids*. Isn't it time *We the Maids* listened up and swept out the manure pile that career politicians have buried our hard-earned tax dollars in? And we might as well sweep the career politicians out while we're at it.

Mohair. Honey. Buffalo. Peanuts. Grains and dairy products and beef and sugar and on and on. If you can buy it at a supermarket, the chances are it is a politicized product, involved in some government program. And let's not forget subsidized water for irrigation benefiting and buying the votes of America's farms.

"There was more money spent on hogs' sickness by state and federal government than there is on children, when one child's life is worth all the hogs and cows that ever had a disease. If you want the government to help you, don't tell them it is any human sickness. Tell them it is boll weevil or chinch bugs, and they will come a-running, because they have big appropriations and men paid for that," Will Rogers said in 1924.

Has anything really changed since then? No wonder the U.S. has never ranked better than 37th in health care, according to the World Health Organization.

"Lord, the money we do spend on government. And it's not a bit better government than we got for one-third the money 20 years ago," Rogers said.

Rep. Kika de la Garza, former chairman of the House Agricultural Committee, and his predecessors and successors – are living proof. What are *We the Apathetic Maids* waiting for to bring about change? What basic constitutional liberty guarantees all these questionable subsidies? None.

### Subsidized Birthright

Corporate America looks at subsidies as a federal business birthright. California native-born novelist and descendant of early Golden State pioneers Joan Didion dispels this myth in her novel *Where I Was From*. The myth of California, Didion contends, is based on a self-deception so intense that it edges into willful falsehood. The overland pioneers of the 1840s, she asserts, did not behave as well on the trail as they claimed to have done. They rushed rather pell-mell across the continent for the California land grants, leaving behind to die those to weak to keep up.

This cold-hearted dispassionate greed became magnified in the 1860s, Didion contends, when the big four – Leland Stanford, Collis P. Huntington, Mark Hopkins and Charles Crocker – leveraged untold federal dollars and land grants to create the trans-Sierran portions of the transcontinental railroad. By the 1880s, the Southern Pacific and a dozen or so corporate-style land owners owned a significant portion of California. This habit of leveraging federal dollars and deriding taxes and government would persist throughout the 19th century and the 20th century.

Californians, in the tradition of the big four, parlayed hundreds of millions of federal dollars to create an irrigation-based economy that relied on a continuing dole of federally sponsored water. Subsidized water, in turn, ballooned agribusiness through products – cotton and rice especially – that depend entirely upon irrigation paid for by taxpayers. In the 20th century, empowered by federally subsidized water and hydro-electricity from Hoover Dam, California – Southern California especially – became a garrison state dependent upon the fiscal steroids of World War II and Cold War spending.

Today, Didion concludes, California is an economic colony owned by non-Californians.

Corporations try to write everything off or in the alternative have it subsidized. Corporate America's love affair with debt is driven by a heavy subsidy, courtesy of the federal tax code. That's because the interest that corporations pay on their debt is deductible on their federal taxes.

Imagine if *We the Apathetic Maids* could do the same with our debt – credit cards, student loans, every kind of debt.

### History of Farm Subsidies
Abundant productivity and a program to discourage overproduction and encourage orderly production by America's farmers became another taxpayer-supported program for wealthy corporate farms, thanks to their lawyers and lobbyists. The Roosevelt administration established America's first program of farm support during the Great Depression. It was not created to feed the nation's hungry. It was created to manage the overproduction of food. During the Depression, America's farmers were overproducing.

The New Deal farm policy established a system of price supports, backed by grain reserves, that worked to keep surplus grain off the market, thereby breaking the vicious cycle in which farmers have to produce every year to stay even. The federal government set and supported a target price based on the actual cost of production for storable commodities like corn. When the market price dropped below that target, a farmer was given the opportunity to take out a "nonrecourse loan" using his grain as collateral instead of selling it at a low price. The farmer then stored his grain until the market improved, at which point he sold and used the proceeds to repay the loan. If the market failed to improve that year, the farmer could discharge his debt simply by handing his grain over to the government, which would add it to what was called the "ever-normal granary." This grain reserve was managed by the Department of Agriculture, which would sell from it whenever prices got high, usually during a bad harvest, thereby keeping the cost of food more or less even and predictable.

The New Deal farm policy wasn't a perfect system, but it managed to keep cheap grain from flooding the market and by doing so supported the prices farmers received. It did so at a very low cost to the government, because most loans were repaid. Even when they weren't, the government was able to unload the grain it received for the unpaid loans, often at a profit. The program actually made money in good years. Quite different than the farm subsidy programs of today that cost American taxpayers about $19 billion a year and do virtually nothing to control production.

Why was this sane and rational subsidy program abolished? Politics and the successful efforts of lawyers and lobbyists. The shift from an agricultural-support system designed to discourage overproduction to one that encouraged it dates back to the Richard Nixon administration of the early 1970s. Nixon's 1972 grain deal with the Soviet Union coincided with a spell of bad weather in the Farm Belt. As a result, commodity prices soared, and so did supermarket prices for meat, milk, bread and other staple foods tied to the cost of grain. Angry consumers took to the streets to protest food prices and staged a nationwide meat boycott to protest the high cost of hamburger.

Recognizing the political consequences, Nixon ordered his Secretary of Agriculture, Earl (Rusty) Butz, to do whatever was necessary to drive down the price of food. He shuttered the ever-normal granary, dropped the target price for grain and inaugurated a new subsidy system, which eventually replaced nonrecourse loans with direct payment to farmers.

"The distinction may sound technical," says Michael Pollan, who teaches at the Graduate School of Journalism at the University of California at Berkeley. "But in effect, it was revolutionary. For instead of lending farmers money so they could keep their grain off the market, the government offered to simply cut them a check, freeing them to dump their harvests on the market no matter what the price," Pollan concludes in a well-written piece for *The New York Times* magazine. The new system worked and food prices never became a political problem again for any president since Nixon. Is it any wonder subsidies for agribusiness have remained at an annual cost of at least $19 billion to U.S. taxpayers – and the misery subsidies create in the family farm communities in America and the developing world are a hot potato?

Things are not much better in Europe, where a European cow earns $2 a day in government subsidies, while more than 250 million poor people live on less than $2 a month.

### Subsidized Obesity

Taxpayer-funded subsidies not only hurt people in the developing world, but in America. They are the underlying cause of the obesity epidemic in America.

"Most researchers date the beginning of the epidemic to the mid '70s, just when we switched to a farm policy consecrated to the overproduction of grain. Since that time, farmers in the U.S. have managed to produce 500 additional calories per person every day; each of us is, heroically, managing to pack away about 200 of those extra calories per day. Presumably the other 300 – most of them in the form of surplus corn – get dumped on overseas markets or turned into ethanol," says Pollan.

Cheap corn, the dubious legacy of Earl Butz, is truly the building block of the "fast-food nation." Cheap corn, transformed into high-fructose corn syrup, is what allowed Coca-Cola to move from the svelte 8-ounce bottle of soda ubiquitous in the 1970s, to the chubby 20-ounce bottle of today. Cheap corn transformed into cheap beef allowed McDonald's to supersize its offerings and still sell many of them for no more than a dollar. Cheap corn gave us a whole raft of new highly processed foods, including the world-beating chicken nugget, which if one studies its ingredients, reveals itself to be really a most ingenious transsubstatiation of corn, from the corn-fed chicken it contains to the bulking and binding agents that hold it all together, Pollan points out.

Greg Critser points out in his book *Fat Land* that the bigger the portion, the more food people will eat. So McDonald's tempts us by taking a 600-calorie meal and jacking it up to 1,550 calories. Compared with marketing, packaging and labor, the cost of the added ingredients is trivial. Such cheap raw materials also argue for devising more highly processed food, because the real money will never be in selling cheap corn, soybeans or rice, but in "adding value" to those commodities. That is one reason that in the years since America moved to a cheap-food farm policy, the number and variety of new snack foods in the supermarket have ballooned

"The game is in figuring out how to transform a penny's worth of corn and additives into a $3 bag of ginko-biloba-fortified brain-function-enhancing puffs, or a dime's worth of milk and sweeteners into Swerve, a sugary milk-based soft drink to be sold in schools. It's no coincidence that Big Food has suddenly 'discovered' how to turn milk into junk food: the government made deep cuts in the dairy-farm program, and as a result, milk is nearly as cheap a raw material as water," Pollan's article astutely observes.

As public concern over obesity mounts, the focus of political pressure has settled on the food industry and its marketing strategies – supersizing portions, selling junk food to children, lacing products with trans-fats and sugars.

America's national eating disorder is the result of taxpayer subsidies to farmers, courtesy of the laws written and promoted by lawyers and lobbyists. The political challenge now is to rewrite those rules, to develop a new set of agricultural policies that don't subsidize overproduction – and overeating. The alternative is to introduce a "fat tax" like Denmark did in 2011 and decided to scrap in 2012.

### Subsidized Poverty
While Americans are overeating and complaining about their subsidized fast food obesity, Africans and others in developing countries are dying of starvation because of U.S., European and Japanese farm subsidies. Subsidies and overproduction depress world prices and close the U.S., European and Japanese markets to farmers from developing countries. In 2001, U.S. agribusiness exported wheat for $3.50 a bushel, which cost

American farmers $5.31 to produce. Cotton, which cost U.S. growers 83 cents a bushel to produce, was sold abroad for $5.30.

"How can my farmers move beyond subsistence, how can my farm-based economy free itself of aid, when the largest economies – the EU is a worse offender – dump commodities at a fraction of what they cost to grow? And how, at the day's end, can this be good for your farmers or broader economy?" asked President Yoweri K. Museveni of Uganda.

A study by the Center for Agricultural and Rural Development at Iowa State University – in the heart of America's Farm Belt – points out an absurdity. The agricultural support policies of high-income countries are crushing output and incomes of poor-world farming households. But here's the irony: Under current policies, rich country taxpayers "are paying twice for development assistance: once to reduce the incomes of poor farmers and again to alleviate the same poverty," the study concluded. According to the Iowa State study, rich-country reforms could, by 2015, increase the value of farm output in sub-Saharan Africa, excluding South Africa, by $3.4 billion a year. And American farmers would benefit too, to the tune of $5.5 billion a year. The value of agriculture in low and middle-income countries would be $63 billion greater than today – dwarfing development assistance.

### Abolition of Subsidies

Polls repeatedly show the American public does not trust Congess. If that's so, where is People Power? If Congress doesn't change its ways and people do, dramatic changes to the makeup of government and its institutions can be achieved, starting with the abolition of subsidies that only benefit the rich and tax everyone else to pay.

"We will never get anywhere with our finances till we pass a law saying that every time we appropriate something we got to pass another bill along with it stating where the money is coming from," Will Rogers famously said.

Shouldn't *We the Maids* clean up the excess subsidies mess and recapture our natural rights?

"At a time when our major competitors are slimming down their governments so that their economies can run faster, we should not be fattening up our own government, which will slow down our economy." Great advice from someone who knew – Richard Nixon.

And how much government do Americans want in their lives? Government's role should be confined to providing basic infrastructure to nurture an environment that encourages enterprise.

The Hong Kong government adopts private initiatives; makes major investment in education; keeps tariff barriers and inflation low; has a flat tax of 15 percent; and maintains a stable legal framework that attracts private private investment from abroad. Just as important, the nations that enjoy economic progress reject a major economic role for government. They recognize the fundamental truth that private rather than government enterprise produces progress. That is why there is little or no room for subsidies.

The result is there is a reverse brain drain of Asians returning to China and Hong Kong from the U.S., Canada and Europe. Ronald Skeldon of Hong Kong University describes the attraction to the reverse flow: "In Hong Kong you have high-salary, low-tax economies; in North America, you have low- salary, high-tax economies."

The 2003 budget proposed by the Bush White House marked a return to federal deficits for the first time since 1997. The tax cuts enacted by Bush when he came into office with the massive positive media spin and fanfare put out by his spin doctors managed to camouflage and hide the fact that his tax cuts were in fact a "reckless gamble with the nation's financial future." A gamble *We the Apathetic Maids* are still paying for – and will for a long time.

Even the most deft political shell game cannot hide much longer the fact that the recurring deficits in America are largely the result of decades of unchecked spending on military and domestic programs and entitlements. Each program is tied by a titanium umbiblical cord to a particular interest group or lobby, which in turn is fused at the hip to the powerful members of Congress who hold the purse strings. As Nixon found out when he tried to abolish the Office of Economic Opportunity early in his administration,

"Any president who attempts to terminate a program or department, no matter how redundant or unnecessary, is accused of insensitivity to poor people, young people, sick people, or small animals. It becomes impossible to imagine how the nation survived before the threatened program existed."

Will Rogers was right. "There's nothing will upset a state economic condition like a legislature. It's better to have termites in your house than the legislature."

The articles and books pointing to the idiocy of subsidies are a subsection of a major library. Former Senator Robert Byrd, chairman of the powerful Senate Appropriations Committee, and his fellow senators who consistently went along with his highway robbery epitomize Mark Twain's criminal senators.

"They all rob the Treasury by voting for iniquitous pension bills in order to keep on good terms with the Grand Army of the Republic, and with the Grand Army of the Republic Jr., and with the Grand Army of the Republic Jr., Jr., and with other great-grandchildren of the war – and these bills distinctly represent crime and violated senatorial oaths," Twain wrote.

Edward Crane of the Cato Institute rightly argues that in a town where the tone of life is set by a ruling class of career legislators, the prevailing mentality makes people – strictly speaking, weird. "Out of the ordinary, strange, odd, fantastic." Most of the people legislators associate with are involved in regulating other people's lives and spending other people's money.

If people served in legislatures only briefly, they would have less incentive to shovel out pork. The primary function of pork is to buy gratitude and dependency among clients, qualities that the career legislator can translate into votes, and hence into longevity. And if legislators were not too separated, for too long, from normal citizens and normal life in normal communities, they might retain the ability to discriminate between appropriate and inappropriate functions of the federal government.

Aristotle defined a corrupt regime as one that rules for its private good rather than the public good. Jefferson similarly defined corruption as "a legislature legislating for its own interests."

Contrary to the claims of doctrinaire supply-siders, deficits do matter. They distort our economy over the long run by siphoning off for short-term consumption funds that could have gone toward long-term capital investment. They confer benefits on the present generation and burdens on future ones. While sustainable in the short term, and even justifiable in recession and war, deficits act like water, lapping at and eroding the foundations of a strong economy.

### Grazing at the Public Trough

The grazing bill like many others deserves to be repealed. The mining industry also still locks in outmoded rights to extract valuable metals from federal lands for next to nothing. California agribusiness is trying to insulate against challenges to its historical access to low-cost federal water. The timber industry is still busy hacking down federal forests as it has for centuries.

Heaven for the dairy industry is a plan that does three seemingly contradictory things at once. It allows full production but, despite the abundance of dairy products, keeps prices high, and it does so without buying up the surplus and showing up as a cost in the budget. How do they do it?

They increase exports with taxpayer subsidies from the producers themselves off-budget. Enough milk products would be sold, not to say dumped, abroad to keep the domestic market taut and prices high at the checkout counter. Some of the proceeds from those high prices would be pooled and redistributed, again off-budget, to buy off or placate those milk-producing regions that have felt disadvantaged by the traditional system of supports. Although in some years federal support payments have been high, the essence of that system has been to keep prices high at the grocery store. That is where the industry has made its main money – subsidies.

A Congress true to its principles would back off dairy price supports, just as it would tighten grazing and mining laws and greatly reduce the subsidization of those two industries. The congressional attitude toward these various industries is a test of true intentions. So far it is a test that Congress has pretty consistently failed. Why? Because *We the Apathetic Maids* allow our lawmakers to consistently fail.

Since *We the Maids* and our career politicians have failed the test, let's look at the light side. Are they career politicians or comedians? Will Rogers thinks they are the latter.

"With every public man we have elected doing comedy, I tell you I don't see much of a chance for a comedian to make a living. I am just on the verge of going to work. They can do more funny things naturally than I can think of purposely."

I can see why he thought so back in 1924. This has got to be the longest-running comedy show in America.

### Mad Cow Politics

A debate over the merits of the "one country, two systems" at the FCC Main Bar in Hong Kong after mad cow disease was discovered in America from a cow born in Canada, took a cynical U-turn after I circulated an e-mail I received from Ralph Herman, a friend, client, partner in Scratch and rancher in Paso Robles, California. The title of the e-mail was: Cows-Redux (again).

DEMOCRAT – You have two cows. Your neighbor has none. You feel guilty for being successful. Barbra Streisand sings for you.

REPUBLICAN – You have two cows. Your neighbor has none. So?

SOCIALIST – You have two cows. The government takes one and gives it to your neighbor. You form a cooperative to tell him how to manage his cow.

COMMUNIST – You have two cows. The government seizes both and provides you with milk. You wait in line for hours to get it. It is expensive and sour.

CAPITALISM, AMERICAN STYLE – You have two cows. You sell one, buy a bull, and build a herd of cows.

DEMOCRACY, AMERICA STYLE – You have two cows. The government taxes you to the point you have to sell both to support a man in a foreign country who has only one cow, which was a gift from your government.

BUREACRACY, AMERICAN STYLE – You have two cows. The government takes them both, shoots one, milks the other, pays you for the milk, and then pours the milk down the drain.

AMERICAN CORPORATION – You have two cows. You sell one, lease it back to yourself and do an IPO on the second one. You force the two cows to produce the milk of four cows. You are surprised when one cow drops dead. You spin an announcement to the analysts stating you have downsized and are reducing expenses. Your stock goes up.

FRENCH CORPORATION – You have two cows. You go on strike because you want three cows. You go to lunch and drink wine. Life is good.

JAPANESE CORPORATION – You have two cows. You redesign them so they are now one-tenth the size of an ordinary cow and produce 20 times the milk. They learn to travel on unbelievably crowded trains. Most are at the top of their class at cow school.

GERMAN CORPORATION – You have two cows. You engineer them so they are blonde, drink lots of beer, give excellent quality milk, and run a hundred miles an hour. Unfortunately, they also demand 13 weeks vacation per year.

ITALIAN CORPORATION – You have two cows but you don't know where they are. While ambling around, you see a beautiful woman. You break for lunch. Life is good.

RUSSIAN CORPORATION – You have two cows. You have some vodka. You count them and learn you have five cows. You have some more vodka. You count them again and learn you have 42 cows. The mafia shows up and takes over however many cows you really have.

**TALIBAN CORPORATION** – You have all the cows in Afghanistan, which are two. You don't milk them because you cannot touch any creature's private parts. Then you kill them and claim a U.S. bomb blew them up while they were in the hospital.

**IRAQI CORPORATION** – You have two cows. They go into hiding. They send radio messages of their mooing.

**POLISH CORPORATION** – You have two bulls. Employees are regularly maimed and killed attempting to milk them.

**FLORIDA CORPORATION** – You have a black cow and a brown cow. Everyone votes for the best-looking one. Some of the people who like the brown one best, vote for the black one. Some people vote for both. Some people vote for neither. Some people can't figure out how to vote at all. Finally, a bunch of guys from out-of-state tell you which is the best-looking cow.

**NEW YORK CORPORATION** – You have 15 million cows. You have to choose which one will be the leader of the herd. So you pick some fat cow from Arkansas.

**CALIFORNIA CORPORATION** – You have a cow and a bull The bull is depressed. It has spent its life living a lie. It goes away for two weeks. It comes back after a taxpayer-paid sex-change operation. You now have two cows. One makes milk; the other doesn't. You try to sell the transgender cow. Its lawyer sues you for discrimination. You lose in court. You sell the milk-generating cow to pay the damages. You now have one rich transgender, non-milk-producing cow. You change your business to beef. PETA pickets your farm. Jesse Jackson makes a speech in your driveway. Cruz Bustamante calls for higher farm taxes to help "working cows." Hillary Clinton calls for the nationalization of one-seventh of your farm "for the children." Gray Davis signs a law giving your farm to Mexico. The L.A. Times quotes five cows claiming Arnold Schwarzenegger likes to grope cows with big teats.

The consensus at the Main Bar after all had digested that e-mail was that America is "one farm with a two-cow system."

## The Victims

People just don't get it. They don't know or understand how they are getting screwed every day by their elected representatives. *We the Victims* have ceded our power to comic robbers. Will Rogers was right. Not only are congressmen comedians. Congress is an indigenous criminal class.

We have to reign in subsidies because they are the biggest threat to a free economy.

"To argue that we cannot tamper with the spending formulas of so-called entitlement programs is to abandon any hope of bringing federal accounts into balance. Non-means tested entitlements — payments to those who have the means to take care of their own needs – currently consume almost 40 percent of the federal budget, up from 20 percent in 1970 ... . Any attempt to solve America's economic problems that does not stop the runaway growth of entitlement spending cannot succeed." Those are the words of reviled former President Richard Nixon.

Congress is very good at selling the misperception that it is doing a good and job and cutting back the federal payroll. However, the dollar value of federal service contracts with private companies has risen more than 3.5 percent a year since 1993, to an average of $114 billion per year. Another example of exquisite spin doctoring.

Senator David H. Pryor, Democrat of Arkansas, who has long been a critic of federal contracting policies, said, "The whole philosophy of beating our chest and saying how fewer employees we have but never in the same breath saying, look at how much larger we are getting in the use of private contractors, is not an honest portrayal of what is going on with tax dollars."

Michael Kinsley's experience as a D.C. Washingtonian who left for Washington state sums up our national political capitol. "It took only a few moments of residency elsewhere to realize that our capitol city is a blight and a leech on the rest of the country. The politicians there – as well as the bureaucrats, the lobbyists and, of course, the media – live in a smug and isolated cocoon of privilege and perks, oblivious to the needs and common-sense wisdom of those of us who do the real work of this great nation: meeting payrolls, raising families, giving to charity and shooting the occasional spotted owl – all activities that were completely unknown to me and my neighbors back in the suburbs of Washington. I'm newly empowered to whine and complain about high taxes and about wasteful government spending of my hard-earned dollars though. In fact, what with federally subsidized public works, utilities and national parks, I'm getting far more for my federal tax dollars living in the West than I did back East. You too can be a New You. All it takes is a change of costume, some prepackaged instant microwavable prejudices and a fresh ZIP code... ."

What a concept. Why don't we start repackaging career politicians? We can then move on to clean out the bureaucrats. It can be done. It's up to *We the Maids* to exercise our rights and reclaim the broom and power that belongs to the people.

### Who to Blame?
Stop complaining and looking for who to blame. Look in the mirror. *We* are to blame. All of us. If middle-class and even rich Americans want to find someone to blame for the burden the entitlement mentality puts on the federal budget, they should take a good hard look in the mirror at least once a day and tell themselves it's their fault and ask, "What am I going to do about it?"

Wealthy farmers say they cannot survive without price supports. Steel makers and their unions demand protection from foreign competitors. Bankers expect the federal government to cover their bad loans. Well-off retirees whose Social Security payments far exceed their contributions oppose any politician who suggests their benefits be limited. College students believe they are entitled to low-interest loans secured by taxpayers who could not afford to go to college themselves. Lawyers, farmers, doctors and business people all want their place at the federal trough.

To be a functional government for *We the People,* we have to abolish subsidies and taxes as we know them today. They benefit only the rich and corporate America. We have to start subsidizing ourselves – all of us. The managed misperception of subsidies has to be pierced and subsidies have to be exposed for what they are.

How do we abolish these wasteful subsidies, padded payrolls and an excessive, unfair tax system? A tax revolt. The Founding Fathers did it at the Boston Tea Party. Howard Jarvis did it in California with Proposition 13. Why not *We the Maids* in the New World Order? As Will Rogers said: "Discontent comes in proportion to knowledge."

Why should we continue to subsidize the rich and pay excess taxes in the New World Order?

Shout it from the rooftops: No taxation with subsidization and no continued excess taxation without real representation for *We the People* in the 21st century.

*Crawling Up a Hill*
– John Mayall

## Kiss Bureaucratic Gates to Perodise

*Bureaucracy is the death of any achievement.*
– Albert Einstein

### Bureaucracy

Standing on the Great Wall of China preparing the production crew for the filming of an episode of *The Young Indiana Jones Peking 1911*, I couldn't help but think of the historical similarities between the Chinese mandarins and their bureaucratic counterparts in the West and the incredible empires they created and ran.

Former Hong Kong Governor Chris Patten's dire warnings before the Handover of the territory back to China in 1997, that petty mainland bureaucrats would ruin Hong Kong's civil service and renowned efficiency, were unfounded. He cautioned Beijing not to "examine the engine, tinker with the tires, rather than just turn on the ignition and drive the Rolls-Royce." He forgot to mention that sometimes Rollers don't start when the ignition is turned. America, the Rolls-Royce of democracy and capitalism, isn't running properly even though the engine is on.  I know first hand. I used to own two of the cars and represented Hollywood's foremost Rolls-Royce dealer and garage in the '70s, Garthwaite Rolls-Royce, across the street from my office on Santa Monica Boulevard in West Hollywood.

The Hong Kong civil service has repeatedly been downsized dating back to colonial days when many "permanent and pensionable" posts were eliminated.

The Hong Kong government decided to freeze the wages of all of its 190,000 civil servants for the 1999-2000 financial year and then again for the 2000-2001 fiscal year.  It went further in fiscal year 2002-2003 by cutting civil service salaries and questioning perks. The government then announced that it also planned to reduce the pay for civil servants in two stages by January 1, 2005 to levels prevailing in July 1997, when Britain handed the territory back to China.

But then again, like any political bureaucracy in China and America, it didn't take long before their salaries were not only restored, but surpassed incomes in the private sector.

*The Asian Intelligence Report* published in 2003 by the Political and Economic Risk Consultancy ranked Hong Kong as the least bureaucratic among 14 economies – including those of America and Japan. That is the way to enter the New World Order and lead by example. Shouldn't America and mainland China be doing what Hong Kong is doing – albeit technologically – and try and become number one?

China and Hong Kong are cutting the size of their bureaucracies as we accelerate into the 21st century. China says that over half of its ministries will be eliminated. Isn't it time America did the same?

The Hong Kong colonial government, under Chief Secretary Anson Chan and Governor Patten, started to flush out inefficiencies, freeze bureaucrats' wages and eliminate phantom departments before the 1997 handover. This continued under the new regime.

"It is really difficult for outsiders to understand why we (still) have it," said assistant department head Kelvin Chan Kut-fai in trying to explain the continued existence of the Technical Education and Training Department that for years has had no operational function. "... It's a department leftover. It's a technical issue."

Come on. Is there room for this kind of waste and inefficiency in the New World Order? Of course not. But Hong Kong makes it public, and does something about it. What is Washington – or Beijing, for that matter – doing about useless agencies and empty staff positions that are kept on the books as a way of protecting their budgets? Isn't it time for a "wired" America, soccer moms and *We the Apathetic Maids* to kick-start the New World Order by kicking out the unwired bureaucrats and their protective career political cronies?

"The 20th century saw a massive, worldwide shift toward gigantic government. That's bad news for everybody, because historically, the bigger and more complex a government grows, the more wasteful and inefficient it becomes. It's especially bad for us. Gigantic, overgrown bureaucracies are particularly hazardous in a free society like ours," Chan says.

Big government inevitably begins to control aspects of our lives that it has no business controlling. It loses touch with its citizens and becomes insular. "They stop representing us," former Minnesota Governor Jesse Ventura cautions. Why do *We the Apathetic People* allow such warnings to continuously fall on deaf ears?

Ventura's warning hit home in March 2012, when Hong Kong's Chief Executive-elect, Leung Chun-ying, kow towed to the city's 160,000 civil servants – because they had supported his opponent and publicly expressed their concern about working with Leung. Leung held separate one-hour meetings with representatives of the eight civil servants' unions and the administrative officers association to assure them he was with them "in the same boat."

Getting into a boat with bureaucrats who are preoccupied with their petty bureaucratic rivalries while they try to reach a decision by committee is a recipe for disaster that can only sink the boat.

Institutional biases seriously affect analysis, a point well documented by Sarah Chayes, the former special assistant to the chairman of the Joint Chiefs of Staff and a resident associate at the Carnegie Endowment.

"In 2011, I saw an egregious example of institutional bias and how it can affect analysis during a debate over one aspect of the insurgency in Afghanistan. A team of Defense Intelligence Agency analysts briefing a senior official on Taliban motivations had reversed the order of the motivations listed in a document of interviews with Taliban members, so as to downplay one that was not in vogue with the intelligence community. I had read the original document and could correct the analysis, but had I not been present, the official would never have known better."

One lesson to be drawn from the Benghazi consulate tragedy in Libya is that powerful bureaucratic filters prevent crucial information from reaching senior U.S. government leaders. Whether the client at the top of the list is the U.N. ambassador, the director of Central Intelligence or the president, bureaucracies consistently massage and filter information before passing it on up the chain.

Benghazi was a timely reminder of how powerful civil servants have become and why *We the Apathetic Maids* have to wake up to the fact that bureaucrats have become the tail that wags the dog. The time is long overdue for civil servants to be reminded that they are supposed to be politically neutral and who they work for – *We the People*. Bureaucrats have to be shaken out of their cloistered world and brought back to earth and the realities of the real world – political and economic.

It is incumbent on us to change things for the better in the New World Order. Keep the ball rolling. That means bureaucratic heads have to roll, especially as there are simpler wired more efficient ways of administering government with cyber technology.

## Wired World

If ISIS, extremists, gamblers and gamers are wired worldwide, why aren't bureaucrats? "Webmistresses" have seized control of the sex industry and now control more than 50 percent of pornographic sites in cyberspace. These women are respectable, taxpaying citizens in their late 20s and 30s. Many have chosen to have children and are leading otherwise normal suburban lives, hidden by the anonymity of the Internet.

Dr. Kimberlianne Podlas, a former criminal lawyer and now a psychologist at the Bryant Institute in New Jersey, conducted the study and contacted the women through her previous links with the police and vice squads. Podlas said: "I have come to the conclusion that it is true liberation for women in the sex industry. Far from being complicit in the oppression and exploitation of women, webmistresses may reflect a degree of emancipation from male-dominated female imagery and economic control."

The fact is that the porn industry is the locomotive that drives cutting-edge technological innovation. Streaming videos, zipped file delivery and secure online payment are just some of the innovations in the past two decades that the porn industry, if it didn't invent them, surely helped popularize.

Amazon may have pioneered one-button shopping, but it was the porn industry that perfected continuous payment until you – good luck on that – cancelled. Like it or not, porn is mainstream and a public health crisis. Porn is so widespread that porn sites get more visitors per month than Netflix, Amazon and Twitter combined. The Internet hosts 4.2 million porn sites.

The Internet even uses naked people to sell clothes. Porn stars are used by clothing companies to peddle their latest styles. On the Internet, celebrities have been replaced by porn stars who frolic on beds, clothed initially. The interactive porn film is an extreme example of advertisers adapting their messages to the Internet, by making spots more compelling because the Internet can bypass traditional gatekeepers such as censors with material that would be taboo in the mainstream media. This technology of layering commerce onto Web video is known as hotspotting

There are cyber sex problems that come along with emancipation. Thousands of sex offenders not only prowl the Internet, but then move on to other social networks that have become a "virtual playground" for predators. As if that is not bad enough, how about the teenagers who are so influenced by porn sites that they adopt some of the deviant behavior they see on screen.

In Hong Kong, a case that caught my attention was that of a "shy and introverted" 16-year-old boy who developed a foot fetish and fondled girls' legs and snatched their shoes after visiting porn sites for a couple of years. He fondled girls' legs for satisfaction and stashed their shoes in his bedroom.

Sexual perverts, especially pedophiles, can easily prowl Internet "hotspots" to solicit sexual favors from children, as can criminals who engage in identity theft and other nefarious criminal acts. Known as the "deep web" and "darknet" where anything and everything takes place deep beneath the web.

The good news is that America and China are successfully cooperating in an effort to smash child porn sites. Especially Chinese language sites targeting Chinese communities in America.

The more than $100 billion wagered annually online worldwide on gambling – and the billions more on games – are daily testimonials as to why government bureaucracies should get wired.

The pictures of the revamped wired White House situation room with laptops and secure flat-screen TVs that replaced picture tubes aired in the wake of the killing of Osama bin Laden reminded the world that America's crisis room has finally gone high-tech.

The 9/11 commission found that on the day of the 2001 attacks, communications frayed, making it hard for President Bush, flying around on Air Force One, to get a picture of what was going on.

Isn't it time *We the Apathetic Maids* use cyberspace more – employ its capabilities to the max – to get liberated and emancipated from the oppression and exploitation of entrenched career politicians and their pension-pending bureaucrats?

### Expensive Bureaucrats

The high cost of bureaucracy is the reason government is always raising its fees for services. Freeze or reduce bureaucracies and the fees and taxes that *We the Apathetic People* now pay will drop proportionately in the New World Order.

I concur wholeheartedly with former Governor Ventura when he says: "I'm an advocate of minimal government for much the same reasons as the Founding Fathers: First, because I agree that it's government's nature to become corrupt. The bigger the government, the bigger the corruption. And second, I have a great deal of faith in people. I think that, left to our own, we can take care of ourselves pretty well. We don't need the government to take care of us. I believe that government's job should be to assist us when we need assistance, but at all other times, to stay out of our way."

Even so, why can't all bureaucracies KISS! For those unfamiliar with this American slang, it stands for "Keep It Simple, Stupid!" For some reason, when I deal with bureaucracies, especially in the States, it seems to take frustrating, aggravating, endless hours to get even the simplest thing done.

Getting a passport, driver's license, even mailing a letter at a post office is a hassle, notwithstanding the availability of the same services online – but not to its threatened bureaucratic underbelly. Is it any wonder the U.S. Postal Service is on the verge of bankruptcy? Its structural reorganization is long overdue. God forbid if it's the IRS, Social Security Administration, Unemployment, Welfare, or Building Departments of any municipality. We all of us huff and puff about it being our tax dollars that pays them and how they are working for us. Try that on a DMV window clerk with the attitude of a rattlesnake and when she's bitten you, go complain to her supervisor and see what doesn't happen. Better yet, try it with an IRS auditor who is not only wrong, but rude. Why aren't *We the Apathetic Maids* waking up and sweeping them out? Why do we keep taking their abuse and cleaning up their bureaucratic droppings?

Bureaucracies were fundamental in the development and formation of civilizations, especially in far-flung empires before the invention of modern communication technologies. They were the glue that held society together, the channels of communication between rulers and subjects. They have become unstuck. Except when they stick it to us.

Consulates are a case in point and, not just American, but consulates of all countries. In this world of phones, faxes, e-mail, SMS, satellites and post offices, the role of the foreign consul appears a massive waste of taxpayer money. Consuls and consulates made sense centuries ago before the advent of modern communications. Back then, when governments wanted to talk to each other, they did so through their local consuls.

"The world has outgrown 16th-century ideas of diplomacy. Most of what these consuls now do is endless networking within their own foreign services to make sure they stay on the promotion machine, mixed with backbiting to establish their relative self-importance," said Jake van der Kamp after I complimented him on a column he had written in November 2012 about the obsolescence of consulates.

There are signs of real bureaucratic change where there were none before, thanks to the Internet and social networks – Facebook and Twitter in particular.

695

## Bureaucratic Roots

To better understand bureaucracy, we have to understand its roots and attempt to determine whether bureaucracy is a benefit or a hindrance to society. Bureaucracy can be defined as a manner of organizing people for the attainment of a specific goal; a means to an end to getting things accomplished. Unfortunately, sometimes the effect of a bureaucracy upon those it is meant to serve has had rather the opposite effect, and the system, instead of functioning smoothly, becomes bogged down in endless labyrinths of paperwork and legal volumes of procedure. Most "victims" of bureaucracy tend to see the latter unfortunate outcome rather than a positive consequence.

According to Henry Jacoby in his book *The Bureaucratization of the World,* man's existence is so directed and controlled by central agencies that not only is he unable to escape from their regulation and manipulation, he seems to depend on it. The over-powerful anonymity of the control and the impenetrability of large powerful administrative machines produce fear and discontent. In spite of universal education and increasing use of the printed word and electronic media, the individual finds it increasingly difficult to understand the machinery. He has less influence on what happens in society now than before, because he lacks the means of making his will known. "Man's alienation from his own world is expressed in his dissatisfaction with bureaucracy," Jacoby writes.

However, is effective government possible without bureaucracy? Social theorist Max Weber stated that "contemporary politics was being shaped, first, by the emergence of modern bureaucracy – most especially the growing state apparatus, increasingly led by technically trained, professional career administrators ... [and] ... the rise of a new class of professional politicians, their influence based not on inherited social status, but rather on small political parties claiming the membership and suffrage of millions of ordinary citizens."

Weber was convinced that inexorable historical tendencies would make "this the century of the professional party politician and of the professional state bureaucrat." He was right!

The EU bureaucracy in Brussels is the most tangled government in the world and costs businesses that have to comply with the endless layers of rules and regulations more than 600 billion euros a year. Is it any wonder the EU is doomed to fail?

### Bureaucracy Kills

When will we start heeding Weber's warning: "Bureaucracy appears as a primary cause of the enslavement of modern man. Each man becomes a little cog in the machine, and aware of this, his one preoccupation is whether he can become a bigger cog. The question is, what can we do to oppose this machinery in order to keep a portion of mankind free from this parceling out of the soul from the supreme mastery of the bureaucratic way of life."

Jerry Jones, owner of the Dallas Cowboys, put it another way in an interview in *George* magazine, addressing what he would do if he were president of the United States.

"Finally, I'd also make sure every bureaucrat would be compassionate and caring toward those who are less fortunate and in need of our help. The government would think of citizens as customers, to whom it has an obligation to provide good service at a fair price. Besides, government workers can learn something about courtesy from the employees of a well-run company. Or from the Dallas Cowboy cheerleaders for that matter."

Maybe Jones should be recruiting those DMV clerks.

In a speech to Harvard's Kennedy School of Government in 1996, Richard Holbrooke, the late veteran diplomat who waded through U.S. government bureaucracy, as well as those of other countries and international organizations, summed it up best. He said: "If you want to make a difference, you have to care about the outcome. And caring about the outcome means taking some risks, because the bureaucracy rewards those who go along with the flow, but in the end they make no difference.

"I don't believe people ought to enter public service for the money. You don't make that much money and the bureaucracy is deadening."

Joseph S. Nye Jr., dean of the Kennedy School of Government, says that today only one-third of graduates from America's top educational Institutions go to work for government because the government's structure and pay discourages them.

"Information technology holds the promise of making government more open and the delivery of public services more accessible – but not if the government can't attract and retain good information managers and systems engineers," Nye concludes.

### Chinese Gates

The Great Wall was one of the largest construction projects in history, snaking the length of one-twentieth of the earth's circumference, according to one estimate, from the Yellow Sea to Central Asia. Yet no one even knows for certain how much it cost or exactly when it was started.

"Do you realize this wall is the only man-made object visible from space and so noted by the astronauts that went to the moon?" Rick McCullun, George Lucas' producer for *The Young Indiana Jones* series, asked during our film shoot.

"When you think about what these gates in the wall have seen come through to the Middle Kingdom over the centuries, it is mind- boggling," Rick continued as we leaned over a broken parapet looking at a gate. "If we could only get all that history into this shoot."

Never mind the past. "Imagine what the future holds and what these gates will experience," I said as I swept my eyes across the distant mountain range on which the Great Wall snaked like a dragon as I tried to count the number of gates it contained. "Can you imagine if China didn't have a cultural revolution that wiped out a couple of generations of scientists? It just struck me they probably would have a few hundred if not thousands of Bill Gates by now."

Gates visited China in 1997 to encourage development of the Chinese version of Windows and push the Chinese government to crack down on piracy and the illegal manufacture of Microsoft's highly popular software.

Like all prominent visitors to China, he was taken to the Great Wall to understand and appreciate Chinese history and culture.

Standing on the Great Wall, you can't help but pick up on any strand of history that enters your head. Into my head came the first information revolution, the invention of the printing press in 1450. For the first 50 to 100 years, printers were showered with money and honors – as developers of leading computer and software firms are today. Printer Christophe Plantin of Antwerp was the Bill Gates of his day, the richest man in town, with a magnificent palace to show for it.

But the printers' place of honor was soon taken by "what we now call publishers," Peter Drucker writes, and what was printed shifted from church texts to secular books on navigation, science, political ideas and novels. Universities arose, monasteries closed. The Protestant Reformation, Portugal's voyages to India and Columbus' voyages to the Americas followed the invention of printing.

In today's second information revolution, the few consequences we can foresee are impressive. Education will change, Drucker writes. "Long-distance learning may well make obsolete the free-standing undergraduate college. The center of gravity will shift to the continuing education of adults and move off campus to homes and cars and workplaces."

Just as the invention of printing brought about dramatic changes, it is up to *We the Maids* to sweep in all the benefits of the tools of the second information revolution at our disposal in the 21st century – in education, government and bureaucracy.

The Internet revolution is already underway. Most people forget what the world was like pre-Internet. I don't. I am reminded daily when I want a break from all the electronic gadgets around me for some "thinking time."

It was in August 1995 that Netscape made its sensational debut on the New York Stock Exchange and triggered the dot-com boom. The Web browser firm opened up access to the Internet for the masses and changed the world forever.

Developing countries can look forward to the technological revolution rather than the industrial revolution. The Web has shown itself to be an empowering force for communities and individuals – as well as for governments and corporations.

### Resulting Changes

People are no longer themselves out of fear that they will be videotaped, accused or blamed in a world where everyone is a publisher, blogger paparazzo or filmmaker and everyone else is a public figure. How unwillingly transparent we have all become in a blogosphere where most charges or allegations are taken as the gospel truth without verification.

There is so much free and easily accessible software, information and educational tools available on the Internet that anyone can get or learn just about anything. That is why I made Volume One of this trilogy, *Custom Maid Spin,* available for free on Google books in 2004.

The rise of the blog posters, myself included, has created a new class of reporters who must be given credit for their fast-paced reporting and fact-checking that have made them part of the political scene, from party conventions to street protests, much to the chagrin of conventional reporters like Dan Rather, who was forced to step down after a blogger discovered that his report on *60 Minutes* about President George W. Bush's National Guard service was based on forged documents.

Electronic human genetics, family trees, book readers, mp3 music players, iPhones, texting that is producing civilizational illiterates – Americans between the ages of 13 and 17 send and receive an average of 3,339 texts per month – of C u later NOT's. Teenagers don't read books unless they are forced to. The art of conversation is being lost. Is it any wonder America is becoming uncompetitive?

Teenagers have become Net addicts and many of them commit suicide because of their inability to cope or live in the non-virtual world. They encounter virtual liars that offer virtual alibis, lovers, business opportunities, adventure and the ultimate gaming thrill – legal drugs that can be shipped from anywhere to anywhere. The legal loopholes in e-commerce are so big that meth, cocaine and crack can fly through just as easily as the banned

Cuban cigars that the parents of these Net-savvy kids order.

What about the horrific story of the two 12-year old Wisconsin girls who, inspired by Slender Man, one of the Internet's best known fake paranormal legends, tried to stab to death their best friend in June 2014?

It is understandable why. Kids today are raised on iPads and e-books in a virtual world. Bringing up cyber children in a world where people share their most intimate secrets on Facebook and YouTube is a challenge for every parent. Calling oneself a Luddite, as I do, is no longer an option for parents. Parental cluelessness only empowers children to grow up in an online world that has no resemblance to the real world.

*We the Apathetic Maids* have to step up to develop a New World Order that is grounded in local values and culture for online life in the virtual world. We all have to learn computer code and become Internet fluent as part of our investment in the future.

There is no room in the New World Order for what North Carolinian Tommy Jordan did to his daughter's computer in February 2012, to teach her a lesson. Shooting his teenage daughter's laptop with a pistol and then posting the video clip online. It quickly went viral, attracting more than 26 million views in just a few days.

Jordan's drastic action was in response to a Facebook message his daughter posted complaining about having to do chores and that she should be paid for doing them. Feeling underappreciated, Jordan took her computer outside, set up a camcorder and filmed the shooting. His actions were not only childish, but scary. More disturbing is that so many online posts applauded him.

Dialing up does interfere with growing up. Kids getting upset and OMGing about mom and dad joining their social network because they don't want to share their exploratory sexual identity with their parents is natural. It is also natural for parents to have a right to fret about raising children in the digital age. The best example, in my humble opinion, are the virtual Valentines that I can't believe are so popular, and people would rather have virtual sex than the real deal. How could it feel as good if one doesn't know and hasn't experienced the real thing?

I'll take the real thing any day, anywhere. I have to see, touch, feel, kiss – come on, is there a better way? Social networks have taken away some of the controls we have over our feelings and lives because we can't undo or wire away a memory by merely pressing the delete button.

I couldn't believe my ears when the story broke about Notre Dame linebacker Manti Teo's fictitious dead virtual girlfriend. How could he fall for a hoax like that? Easy, I suppose today, because technology can provide the illusion of companionship without the demands of relationship. New technologies have turned being alone into a problem that can be solved.

Meanwhile, Malaysian Muslim senators who have experienced physical sex divorce by SMS because, under Islamic law in Malaysia, a man can divorce his wife with verbal pronouncements. Nevertheless, they get fined by the Sharia court that takes offense to such modern communications.

The Internet and social networking have become powerful tools in the Muslim world as the Arab cleansing has constructively demonstrated. The Internet has been a great unifier of people worldwide.

Because the Internet is such a great unifier of people, companies and online networks – after all it is a network of networks – governments and companies threatened by it are threatening to balkanize it. The sovereignty of cyberspace is now threatened by governments reasserting their sovereignty demanding that their law-enforcement agencies have access to e-mails sent from computers, smart-phones and tablets. In addition, big IT companies are building their own digital territories, where they set the rules and control or limit connections to other parts of the Internet. Meanwhile, network owners would like to treat different types of traffic differently, in effect creating faster and slower lanes on the Internet.

There is a real danger the Internet may splinter along geographical and commercial boundaries. *We the Maids* have to fight government and companies trying to increase restrictions on the Internet.

"More and more countries are trying now to regulate and control the Internet," said Uri Rosenthal, the foreign minister of the Netherlands in

December 2011. "And it is unacceptable that websites are blocked, Internet queues are filtered, content manipulated and bloggers are attacked and imprisoned."

I agree. The U.S. Congress's consideration of the onerous Stop Online Piracy Act was justifiably derailed.

I can get into traditional ways of doing things, because I just do so naturally, or force myself to. After all, I'm a Luddite who never even used a conventional land-line until I was 13. Cell phones, computers and today's modern communications technology and devices are a marvel. However, they do affect and distract *We the Apathetic Maids* from a critical human development and survival tool. Thinking time.

The human brain of today's netizens is so overloaded with data, much of it useless, that the brain freezes and becomes paralyzed when *We the Maids* have to actually think and make a decision. Decisions that are important to us individually and collectively. The result is that we are so overwhelmed with information that we have become victims of info-paralysis and either do nothing or listen and follow the political and economic Internet hucksters – modern snake oil salesmen.

The good news is that as the Net Generation, children who grew up with the Internet, comes of age, they are changing the way we live and operate, especially in the Silicon valleys, alleys, beaches and cities around the world – in a positive, more efficient and productive way.

China surpassed the U.S. in terms of Internet users in early 2008. The statistics on quantitative expansion of media in China as of 2012 are mind-boggling: more than 500 million Internet users, 320 million blogs, a billion mobile phone subscribers, more than 2,000 newspapers and 9,000 magazines, some 2,200 TV stations and more on the radio front. Netizens in China far outnumber Communist Party members – and their numbers are growing daily. It is only a matter of time before this vast number of media-savvy netizens and the Internet diminishes, if not replaces, the Communist Party – revolution with Chinese characteristics.

## Internet Security

Standing on the Great Wall, I couldn't help reflect about the managed misperception Americans have of their government and China when it comes to the Internet and the right to privacy.

China's decision to impose the State Secrecy Law on the Internet was greeted by cries of alarm and whispers of fear in America. Judging from the American media response, a reader could easily conclude that a Chinese "Big Brother" is imposing a "draconian law" that could turn China's websites into mouthpieces of the government. The fact is that America and its European allies have done the same – if not more.

The freedoms of the Internet in America and Europe have been curbed dramatically since the attacks of 9/11. The Paris-based Reporters Without Borders said that Western countries used the attacks as a pretext to adopt security measures that have curbed pre-9/11 freedoms. New laws extending the time data is held by Internet service providers and making data available to intelligence services has turned telecommunications firms into a potential arm of the police. Among the laws the group criticized as curbing Internet rights were the United Nations Security Council Resolution 1373 on fighting terrorism, the USA Patriot Act and amendments that tighten European Union rules on protecting electronic data.

America and most other G-20 governments either have passed or are pushing Internet regulation much more widespread than China's security rules. All G-20 countries have strict security rules for government employees. The National Security Agency can jail its employees for simply disclosing the name of their employer, which gives rise to the nickname "No Such Agency." What should really alarm Internet users is that the American media have not reported on the "cyber laws" in their own backyard.

A law in the U.S. titled Electronic Rights for the 21st Century gives the FBI the power to force any ISP to disclose information about any subscriber or customer. This law was cleverly attached to environmental protection legislation and was sold to the Congress as "privacy protection."

With e-commerce sales in the billions of dollars each year, it is understandable that there will be numerous consumer complaints. Fraud involving fast-moving e-commerce companies is inevitable. Does that justify courts issuing nationwide trap-and-trace orders? Louis J. Freeh, former director of the FBI, supported such legislation to fight crime. Freeh mentioned several computer crimes, including the theft of funds from an American bank coordinated from St. Petersburg, Russia, the shutting down of a 911 system in the United States directed from Sweden, and the "Phonemaster's scheme" that invaded a host of large corporate and government systems. Such threats come from a wide variety of sources, according to Freeh, including disgruntled insiders, hackers, virus writers, criminal groups, terrorists, foreign intelligence services, information warfare by hostile governments.

When President Bill Clinton signed an executive order to create a working group of experts to devise a comprehensive system of Internet law enforcement in 1997, a pro-Internet privacy article was published by a U.S. Republican senator from Missouri entitled "Keep Big Brother's Hands Off the Internet." The senator denounced efforts to give the FBI "access to decode, digest and discuss financial transactions, personal e-mail and proprietary information sent abroad – all in the name of national security." After September 11, broad legislation, including Internet wiretaps, was passed under the guise of combatting terrorism. The campaign was headed by that same former Missouri senator, John Ashcroft, who later served as attorney general.

Various U.S. lawmakers and others have pushed for more than a decade for legislation on Internet freedom at home and abroad, and Washington has tried to make it a theme of its foreign policy. The effort is aimed at China and its Internet censors, as well as countries like Vietnam, Laos, Burma and North Korea. Why Saudi Arabia and other oil-rich states are not mentioned as targets should be obvious.

Yoichi Shimatsu, former editor of *The Japan Times Weekly* in Tokyo, and editor-in-residence at the Journalism and Media Studies Centre of The University of Hong Kong, points out that "the U.S., not China, has been the world leader in monitoring and prosecuting Net violations. The number of arrests and convictions has steadily increased. Here are a few examples:

"In 1995, the FBI put the first legal wiretap on a computer at Harvard University to catch an Argentine man who broke into the computers at NASA, Los Alamos laboratory and Navy Research laboratory. In the same year, an Internal Revenue Service employee, a member of the Ku Klux Klan, was convicted of accessing information on taxpayers.

"In 1998, the Defense Infrastructure Intrusion Investigation Team arrested a Pentagon computer programmer for sending harassing messages to his former superior. In 1999, a high school student in Virginia was jailed for breaking into NASA computers; another hacker was jailed for shutting down the United States Information Agency site for eight days," Shimatsu says.

"While China's new rules are mainly defensive attempts to put up legal and practical 'firewalls,' the U.S. National Security Agency has been the world leader in proactive interception of electronic communications of other governments and foreign corporations under a now-notorious program called Echelon. The NSA is such a glutton for secretly recorded Internet communications that it took only 11 months to fill the agency's planned computer capacity for three years, according to the *New Yorker* magazine. On January 24, 2000, the overloaded NSA computer system crashed for 72 hours."

On the other hand, America's housekeeping of its own highly classified information on computers has been comic. Edward Snowden being the latest reminder. Like the former director of the CIA, staff regularly download top secret information and take it home. A laptop computer full of State Department "stuff" was lost or stolen from a meeting room. Two hard drive disks with America's nuclear secrets disappeared at the Los Alamos facility and then mysteriously showed up behind a copy machine. The surprising thing is that the Chinese and Chinese-Americans haven't been blamed for these mishaps.

McAfee, a technology security firm, claimed in August 2011 that China has a spying operation that has penetrated 72 government and other organizations, including defense contractors, most of them in the U.S., and has copied everything from military secrets to industrial designs.

Britain's security service MI5 warned chief executives and security chiefs at banks, accounting firms and law firms in 2007 that they were under attack from "Chinese state organizations" via the Internet. No surprise really. The PLA has planned for decades to cope with the Internet challenges of the future. It has more than 10,000 officers with doctorates or master's degrees building an internationalized high-tech armed forces capable of handling the most complicated modern weaponry.

Do the events of 9/11 and these security breaches justify the government's desire to monitor Americans' personal computers? Should the Justice Department have easier access to secretly enter a suspect's home or office and disable security on personal computers as a prelude to a wiretap or further search? These are valid questions. *We the Apathetic Maids* must address these issues in the 21st century before all personal freedoms and liberties enshrined in the Constitution are swept away by career politicians and their lackeys under the guise of security. After all, software programs do encrypt, or scramble, computer files, making them inaccessible to anyone who does not have a special code or "key." Do we want the government accessing and changing the "keys" to *We the People's* computer files?

### *Cybercrime*

Justice officials worry that such software is increasingly used as a means to facilitate criminal activity, such as drug trafficking, terrorism, white-collar crime and the distribution of child pornography. This is an issue that has to be deliberated on, but then every medium that has come along has been accused of this since the invention of print and pictures. The Founding Fathers in their wisdom were cognizant of these issues and correctly adopted a Constitution that enshrines *We the People's* liberties and freedoms – forever.

Granted these freedoms contain loopholes that allow cybercriminals to enrich themselves by committing online fraud and theft.

That includes the government itself. Off-the-shelf surveillance tools, include hacking software, allow governments to break into PCs and cellphones. Critics say the market represents a new sort of arms trade supplying Western governments and repressive nations alike.

"The Arab Spring countries all had more sophisticated surveillance capabilities than I would have guessed," said Andrew McLaughlin, former deputy chief technology officer in the Obama White House, referring to the Middle Eastern and African nations racked by violent crackdowns on dissent.

To make matters worse, in 2009, the Department of Homeland Security paid a contractor to monitor blogs and social networking sites like Facebook.

Computer hackers – Chinese and Americans – are breaking into banks, oil companies, IT security firms, government agencies, law firms, studio scripts and any other type of business that can yield high-value information such as the identities of high net worth individuals – more than 50 million registered accounts and codes – topographical maps worth "millions of dollars" that show the locations of potential oil reserves, military targets for terrorists, and state secrets such as those disclosed by WikiLeaks.

Hacktivists such as the members of Anonymous and LulzSec have created havoc with their raids on banks, MasterCard, Visa and PayPal that refused to process donations to WikiLeaks. Is it any wonder the Feds roam hacker conferences in search of talent they can recruit?

While the career politicians in America have their spin doctors portray China as a police state interfering with the free flow of Internet traffic, as a state that is fighting the Web and Internet technology and trying to keep it out of the hands of the Chinese public, *We the Apathetic People* are unconscious of our own liberties being curtailed. Diversionary managed misperception. In fact, the Chinese Communist Party's official newspaper, *The People's Daily,* lets citizens speak their minds in one of China's liveliest online chat rooms. It averages over 70,000 page views a day, primarily by people aged 19 to 35. Messages like "There is only one way to deal with corruption – Democracy! Democratic elections!" are not unusual. The really interesting part is that the government fully supports the site!

Meanwhile, back home in America, "Stingray" phone tracker technology used by law enforcement officials to zero in on people's locations without a search warrant has fueled a constitutional clash on whether the Fourth Amendment, which prohibits unreasonable searches and seizures, but was written before the digital age, is keeping up with the times.

Under a section of the Patriot Act, U.S. federal investigators have obtained billions of Internet search requests made by users of websites sites run by Yahoo, Microsoft and America Online, raising concerns about how the massive data trove will be used.

As if that is not bad enough, most of *We the Apathetic Maids* have no idea that our cars have a "black box" data recorder that monitors our driving. We also don't know who is seeing the data. No different than the GPS system in people's iPhones that tracks their every move and whereabouts. No wonder people are resorting to "crowd sourcing" radar detector devices that transmit radar sightings to the user's GPS-enabled smartphone that in turn transmits the information to all others nearby in the network.

### Highway to Nirvana
Former Chinese President Jiang Zemin identified Internet technology as the next major struggle and urged provincial leaders to stay competitive.

"Internet technology is going to change the international situation, military combat, production, culture, economical aspects and our daily lives significantly," Jiang said. "The Communist Party has stayed in power since 1949 through stages of revolution, construction and reform because it is a 'vanguard production force'," he added. "To continue to be a 'vanguard production force', senior cadres should equip themselves better, for example, by learning Internet technology."

Jiang and the Communist Party leadership in fact do not see any problems in developing an Internet economy. They are encouraging it. As a result, many Mainland Chinese and Chinese-American IT professionals are bound for the land of opportunity their forefathers left – China.

In China at the close of the last millennium, despite Asia's economic crisis, Internet and e-commerce growth rates were among the highest in the world, often twice as high as that in America. China overtook Japan in 2002 to become the world's second most active Internet audience. In 2001 China outpaced America and became the world's biggest mobile phone market.

By this measure, Asia is not as far behind the West as is often thought. At the close of the millennium, it had nearly two-thirds as many e-commerce servers as the European Union. Australia, New Zealand, Singapore and Hong Kong are all above the EU average of e-commerce servers per person. And China, which a few years ago had no such servers at all, is catching up at a phenomenal pace, racking up annual growth rates of more than 1,000%!

Fixed telephony grew faster than at any time in the last two decades of the 20th century, due in part to strong growth in China and the rest of the Asia Pacific. About 38 million new fixed subscribers came online, and there was enormous unfulfilled demand left at the end of the millennium.

China's former Premier Zhu Rongji aggressively pushed China to catch up to the U.S. and surpass it. Zhu cited the high-technology achievement of the U.S. as a major reason for the "world dominance of the U.S. economy." He wanted China to catch up with the U.S. in the 2020s. It will, partly because so many chipmakers from Japan and Taiwan are relocating their factories to China.

China has the world's largest at-home Internet population. As a result, it wants to spend the next few decades moving from "Made in China" to "Invented in China." More than 300 foreign companies now have R&D centers in China. Chinese scientists have invented and flourished in America and the West. They are now doing so back home in China.

Is it any wonder America's Internet giants Google, Yahoo, Microsoft and eBay are flocking to China and compromising their American ideals for the Yankee dollar and protecting free speech online be damned?

Google, Yahoo and Cisco Systems were accused by Congress in 2006 of self-censorship and aiding and abetting the Chinese government in arresting and jailing government critics. Court papers revealed Yahoo had a hand in the imprisonment of cyber-dissident Li Zhi, in addition to Shi Tao. Google has joined Yahoo and self-censors terms associated with democracy, Tibet and dissent, while Cisco has long been accused of selling network equipment used by the Chinese government for its Policenet, an elaborate system that gives the police direct access to citizens' Internet history and e-mail.

Meanwhile, Facebook and Twitter are banned in China, while their knockoff versions flourish because the government can monitor them for dissent to ensure that the Arab Spring does not see the light of day in China.

"For centuries it was a matter of national pride to ignore and belittle Western science. Now it is equally a matter of national pride to excel in it," says Chu Shing-pok, historian and former linguistics researcher at the Chinese University of Hong Kong's Institute of Chinese Studies. "There is a complex cultural sense of inferiority and superiority about scientific mastery that has characterized Chinese-Western relationships since the time of the Opium War."

Three weeks before former President Bill Clinton's visit to China, Jiang Zemin spelled out his vision for the 21$^{st}$ century at a Chinese Academy of Sciences conference.

He told an audience of more than 1,000 senior scientists and engineers that it was their duty to turn China into a world power in science in the 21st century. Jiang had earlier announced ambitious development blueprints for China running to 2020, including putting a man on the moon and achieving parity with the West in aeronautics and space technology.

The blueprints are an extension of the late paramount leader Deng Xiaoping's modernization program but now take into account projections that China's economy is likely to surpass that of the U.S. before the middle of the 21st century.

The Chinese have looked to the skies ever since Wan Hu, a 14th- century carpenter, lashed 47 gunpowder rockets to a chair affixed with kites, ignited them and vanished in a plume of smoke. America helped accelerate the modern Chinese space program in the 1950s when the U.S. deported Qian Xuesen, one of America's foremost rocket scientists at the Jet Propulsion

Lab in Pasadena, California, for being a suspected communist. When China's first astronaut, Lieutenant Colonel Yang Liwei, returned to earth safely on October 16, 2003, after a 21-hour space flight that took him around the earth 14 times, China became the third member of the exclusive space club.

Chinese-American physicist and Nobel Prize winner Professor Yang Chen-nin expressed optimism that Jiang's targets can be met within the specified time frame.

"Looking back on the very fast development of modern science in China, I would conclude that we will attain the very highest standards in the world in all areas by the middle of the century," he said. Yang argues that China's satellite launch capability is already on a par with those of most Western countries and Japan, an assessment echoed by U.S. defense analyst Shirley Kan in congressional testimony.

Yang blames anti-Western prejudices for the fact that China was left behind after being ahead technologically for millennia. The "Ah Q mentality" (after a Chinese fictional character who ridicules anything he is ignorant of) stopped Chinese from taking advantage of new scientific knowledge brought by Western missionaries.

Historian Chu concurs, adding that there was an unbroken current of Chinese intellectuals and officials bent on preserving the tradition by refusing to consult Western works, from the first arrival of the Jesuits in the 16th century to Mao Zedong in our time.

"People are always asking how come China fell behind the West when it was the first to invent printing, explosives, the compass. I think it's quasi-totalitarian political control explains a lot. If they want to make China a high-tech nation, will Beijing's leaders have the wisdom and courage to be different from the traditional emperors?"

Their words and actions certainly seem to indicate that they have every intention of not only being different, but also aggressively going 180 degrees in the opposite direction.

America and China are proceeding on parallel tracks down the cyber highway. America is far ahead and winning the race to date. However, if America is to stay competitive in the New World Order its overburdened and overstaffed bureaucratic government must take the lead.

The software created by Bill Gates and his Chinese clones along with the management systems created by Ross Perot and his clones give us the tools and means to create the Gates to Perodise in the new millennium. By doing so, we must take full advantage and use of the cyber tools at our disposal to our advantage. Technology today should give people more efficient structures and methods of administration. Theoretically, they have more time to spend with family, friends and the community, to take time out to relax and enjoy their favorite hobbies and sports. Even sex. In fact, the problem with the PC in the home is that it can be insidious. E-mails are instant and round the clock so they must constantly be answered. Games are so much fun and compulsive that kids don't go outside to play anymore. Porn and chat room sex is less stressful than the real thing, and in many cases more interesting than a live partner.

The microprocessor is one of the most staggering accomplishments of the 20th century. No invention in history has so quickly spread throughout the world or so deeply touched so many aspects of human existence.

Once man rubbed two sticks together to start a fire. Now we turn up the thermostat, and just as easily an electric light, to read a book printed by a digitized printing press. We do not yet fully understand the behavior of electrons, and yet receive images of Jupiter's moons from the Galileo space probe, log on to the Internet and access data and information previously unavailable in any form and speak to someone in Hong Kong as easily as to your neighbor over the garden fence.

"We don't know what the Web is for but we've adopted it faster than any technology since fire," David Weinberger observes.

The options are so vast as to defy the most fertile imagination. Technology is used to manage billions of people, coordinate huge proprietary corporate databases, and to simplify the task of organizing dinner recipes and the family budget.

The use of computers and modern technology is such a pervasive and fundamental mainstay of our culture that what was once a prescient attempt at science fiction is now reality. With computer-enhanced technology we are now able to look inside the living human brain and take pictures of the electrochemical processes of thought itself. Surely then our highly advanced federal government has the technological capability to increase efficiency in the workplace, replace superfluous bureaucrats, trim the budget, and save the suffering taxpayer billions of dollars.

*Government Actions*
The Internet was provided to us courtesy of *We the People's* tax dollars and Uncle Sam's Department of Defense. The Internet replaced the draft.

There are a number of international organizations and websites created to address the evolving science of cybernetics and systems engineering, with entire university departments throughout the world now devoted exclusively to the subject. In private industry, the use of technology to increase efficiency has been employed on a huge scale; computerized machines and robots have replaced entire professions with automated labor. Notable improvements have been made in all facets of the workplace. Obviously the federal government has employed some computers and software to aid in its organizational and operational functions for many years. It seems, in theory anyway, that the organization most interested in using computer and related technology for the purpose of increasing efficiency and streamlining the government bureaucracy should, in fact, be the government itself. But is it? Are the bureaucrats and the career politicians using our tax dollars in the best interest of *We the People?*

What has been accomplished by our federal government toward the goal of cutting bureaucratic waste, increasing efficiency, and passing the resulting savings on to the American taxpayer?

The National Partnership for Reinventing Government has published the closest thing to actual figures and documented results aimed at bringing the U.S. government into the modern age, reducing the overall size of the bureaucracy and cutting government spending. Formerly the National Performance Review, its mission is to create a government that "works better, costs less and gets results Americans care about."

In *A Brief History of the National Partnership for Reinventing Government*, the party line is dutifully provided to all interested parties on the partnership's official website.

The review was largely staffed by about 250 civil servants. In addition, some interns, state and local government employees on loan, and a few consultants were also engaged in the work of this interagency task force. The final report, *Creating a Government That Works Better and Costs Less*, had 38 specific accompanying reports. They total nearly 2,000 pages and expanded on the 384 recommendations by detailing 1,250 specific actions intended to save $108 billion (over a period of five years) reduce the number of "overhead" positions, and improve government operations.

The partnership's Phase II made about 200 new recommendations it claimed would save of nearly $70 billion over five years.

The partnership began to shift its strategy from encouraging scattered examples of success to transforming entire agencies. It began to target its energies among those bureau-level agencies that had the most interaction with the public, business, or the operation of other federal agencies such as the IRS, Social Security Administration, and National Park Service.

Agencies have eliminated about 640,000 pages of internal rules, about 16,000 pages of federal regulations, and rewrote 31,000 pages into plain English. Agencies are sponsoring 888 labor-management partnerships. Over 570 federal organizations have committed to more than 4,000 customer service standards. Most importantly, public trust in the federal government is finally increasing after a 30-year decline.

The Reinventing Government Initiative is the longest-running reform effort in U.S. history. Here are the major accomplishments:

Savings total $137 billion.

Agencies have eliminated more than 16,000 pages of regulations.

Government has been reduced by 309,000 positions. A nice start with a long way to go. After all the federal government can and must invest and encourage more investments in sciences and government efficiency.

A saving of $137 billion over five years is an average of $27.4 billion per year. This is a government figure, subject to certain subtle mathematical aberrations, which may have caused the numbers to be tweaked in a fashion that would mystify an otherwise rational mind. Numbers such as these in the many billions of dollars are large enough to be inexplicable. There is something about the subject of inflation in government that works both ways against an overburdened middle and *We the People* are definitely betwixt and between. We are only citizens, after all, and not clothed in a blanket of administrative padding nor privy to the forces of fiscal elasticity which commonly massage and soften all hardened government numbers. But we can be certain that our personal figures and tax returns will be judged with the keenest accounting eye by the IRS.

I myself am neither clerk nor magician, and would laugh at myself were I to offer an ironclad forecast of overall government savings based upon the figures they themselves provide. I have consulted with a wide variety of sources, from foundations who embrace and apply the science of cybernetics to professors at prestigious universities, and no one has any knowledge of studies done that address these questions from a "real world" perspective, and I employ the term loosely. Reality is rarely in the equation when a government study is done.

Every one of us would like to see the government become more efficient, and surely we would like our tax burden to be reduced and the fattened bureaucrats put out to leaner pastures, where our pocketbooks are not so obviously in the food chain. However, there is a monumental difference between talking about massive change and actually implementing that same reality. There is a need, but human bureaucratic self-interest often stands in the way of common sense.

### Cybernetics
Using computer technology to increase efficiency, cut waste and save

money is a concept that makes good intellectual sense, but what would really happen if it came to be, and how would we get there? Allen Schick has addressed that very issue in *The Cybernetic State*.

"Visions of the cybernetic age always have been of two sorts. Some have foreseen a period of unparalleled freedom, with man possessing the autonomy and leisure he has sought for ages. The cybernetic state would care for many of man's needs but would not exact a loss of freedom and selfhood; freed from the bonds of necessity and collective action, man would attain new command over himself and the world. The other version sees man as inevitably enslaved by the state, surrendering to powerful and uncontrollable institutions the freedoms that mark his selfhood... . One can make a plausible case for either version or for both... .

"As a government we have undergone several critical changes in the relationship between the administrative and the political. At the start the United States was designed as a political state; the growth of industry and public regulation in the 19th century led to the emergence of an administrative state; New Deal activism opened the door to the bureaucratic state; (and) now, according to some expectations, we stand at the threshold of the cybernetic state."

Schick goes on in detail regarding the historic movement from administrative government and the Bill of Rights to the present bureaucracy, and the legal process therein. Eventually, however, as a logical thinker with a reasonable intellect, he returns to his theme.

"Interests bargain with one another at the public trough, but they also form coalitions and drive out competition when it suits their objectives. Politics and administration sometimes seem to be split again – in a divorce of convenience – as when advisory groups are comprised of functional specialists and community leaders in order to keep the program free of politics. But it all is for the sake of enhancing interest politics, and efficiency becomes the instrument of established group interests rather than a value in itself."

The moral of the story is becoming clear, for there is little change that is truly simple. Everything in truth is terribly complex. This fact may well support the need for changing the system as advocated, but does not and cannot minimize how difficult that change will be. History will repeat itself, if only because human beings are typically invested in themselves. Especially the career politicians and bureaucrats.

Of primary importance is the need to find constitutional support for the legitimacy of interest politics. Political writers rediscover Madison's Federalist No. 10. The discovery establishes competition in the political arena as the place of legal checks and balances. It provides a substitute for electoral representation. It satisfies the requirement for external control of administration. Congress doesn't do the job well any more, but the groups do. They distribute the benefits of public activity widely, at least among those within the circle of group operations.

The courts lose interest in administrative regulation and become concerned with the nationalization of civil rights and the granting of constitutional status to the rights of association, voting and the presidential election process. Vast programmatic development of the New Deal through the Great Society period escape judicial review. The courts nationalize the Bill of Rights and apply federal standards to a widening group of police and criminal actions. They nationalize racial policies in the schools and in other public programs. They nationalize representation and apply strict one-man, one-vote rules to state legislatures and municipal councils. Except when it comes to the highest office in the land. Why do *We the Apathetic Maids* allow this? Isn't it time our authentic power is unleashed?

In the postindustrial cybernetic state, government functions as a servomechanism. Government changes from a doer of public activities to a distributor of public benefits, and the kinds of programs it operates reflect this change. For example, as welfare becomes cybernetic, it shifts to some form of guaranteed income, adjusted automatically as the income of the recipient rises or falls. The U.S. Social Security payments are a good example. Government action is triggered automatically by changes in the economic condition of the individual. Government writes the "program", establishes sociostatic norms, monitors the system and activates the money-disbursing machines. This is far different from the conventional welfare bureaucracy in which eligibility and benefits are determined by corps of caseworkers in accord with legislative and administrative rules.

In the cybernetic state, the lines between public and private crumble. Government enters markets previously reserved for private entrepreneurs, but new private institutions enter arenas hitherto dominated by public bureaucracies. The government taking over airport security after 9/11 is an example of the former. What Senator John McCain and Barack Obama have done with Internet fundraising is an example of the latter.

The penetration of government into private spheres is especially revolutionary in certain service areas such as doctor-patient and lawyer-client relationships. But as the lines between public and private erode, private institutions recapture some of the functions long regarded as public. Thus, in some instances, elementary education is turned over to private contractors, usually operating with public funds and always under public control. The market is rediscovered, but it is harnessed to public purposes, and its behavior little resembles that of the traditional bureaucratic form dominated by career politicians and their self-serving bureaucrats.

In short, change will bring consequences we will never be able to predict. As public and private commingle, distinctions between them become meaningless. Private institutions acquire legal status as "public accommodations." Some recent court rulings have brought private clubs, perhaps the last bastion of privatedom, within the orbit of public control. It is no longer possible to tell where the private ends and the public begins as public and private funds and workers flow and work side by side. In the basic social accounts, the public-private distinction no longer is significant; more and more, the accounts concentrate on the aggregate social input and output, regardless of its public or private character. It is up to *We the Maids* to make sure most of the benefits go to *We the People* – The Citizens.

You have read these sorts of reports before; but much of this is relevant, and perhaps some of it is even predictable. None of the current system will go by without a bloody fight. We could fill volumes with the fallout.

At the very least, every one of these people whose jobs are cut would either receive unemployment benefits or a pension; and there is no telling the sort of toll that might be taken on the human scale. This is much more than a matter of sheer numbers, or dollars; and if the odd postal worker is liable to shoot his or her supervisor and three unfortunate co-workers in the lunchroom under the current system of personnel management, who is to say what might occur when such massive layoffs are in full swing? These are civil service and union jobs, after all; and we all have relatives or friends who would be at considerable risk.

Schick's gloomy forecast makes some very provocative points. Because of the goal-oriented and coldly calculated nature of software programs – the indifference of data entry personnel – not to mention the attitude of the supervisory bureaucrats who will remain in the system, who can predict what kind of future such a system might hold? It's up to us.

I can only imagine the lawsuits brought forth by the American Civil Liberties Union, and how eagerly the salacious lawyers will hover like buzzards over every hapless corpse.

*We the Maids* may use computers and modern technology to encourage and implement all kinds of positive social and political change, saving countless billions of dollars for the taxpayer; but in the bargain, we will ever be slow to change the bureaucratic culture.

### *Privatize Bureaucracy*
Dead 9/11 hijackers received renewed visas from the INS and notices to take physical exams and newsletters from the Federal Aviation Administration. The FBI at the dawn of the 21st century was not properly computerized. FBI agents keep their own paper files rather than deal with antique computer programs. Critical information therefore may never get loaded into the mainframe system back at headquarters so it can be seen and searched by other agents.

"In many cases, we don't know what we know," John Kerr, chief of the FBI's bank robbery squad said, because information remains in the minds and desk drawers scattered around America, rather than in computer files.

Barriers to information sharing within the FBI are undermining U.S. national security, as laid bare by the disclosure of intelligence failures preceding the 9/11 attacks.

Federal government departments routinely cannot account for billions of taxpayer dollars because of their antiquated financial accounting systems. On October 7, 2002, Mitchell Daniels Jr., director of the Office of Management and Budget, said that the federal government's accounts would "never be tolerated in the private sector," adding that "repair of a system so badly broken will not happen overnight."

Is it any wonder the U.S. Postal Service is broke?

The Department of Defense routinely makes the largest financial blunders. In the fiscal year that ended September 30, 2000, auditors found that the Pentagon entered unsubstantiated balance adjustments totaling $1.1 trillion. The previous years the figure was $2.3 trillion. The Defense Department has more than 1,100 accounting systems. Congress advised the agency's auditors not to bother even trying to audit them. Why not? Is this any way to run a Defense Department, let alone a government?

Wouldn't we be better off contracting these government functions to companies with cutting-edge technology in the private sector that don't have the built-in inefficiencies government bureaucracies have?

China has budgeted $120 billion at the dawn of the 21st century for e-government projects ranging from office automation, license applications, approvals, qualification appraisals, human resource management, construction plans and government websites to sponsoring e-commerce for local businesses. Shouldn't America be doing the same?

Government efficiency, our self-improvement, employment, career changes or recreation can be pursued in a much more efficient and cost effective manner. Software developed by Bill Gates and others can accelerate management systems created by Ross Perot. To date, with a few exceptions, including China and Britain, these *Gates to Perodise* are not effectively used by government, business or the community at large. Properly utilized, they will accelerate a more efficient administration and management of government and business with minimal government interference.

With worldwide sales in excess of $15 billion at the dawn of the 21st century and a market value in excess of $20 billion, Perot's EDS entered the new millennium as one of the world's biggest and fastest- rising computing companies.

Through its government contracts in Britain, it already touches almost every citizen in that nation. Typically, EDS will take over the information technology work of a government department, upgrade its systems and find work for its staff.

As a result, EDS and companies like it are leading a revolution within the public sector, reinventing government, transforming the economics of bureaucracy and recasting the relationships of departments with ordinary citizens.

EDS has become one of the British government's closest partners in computing. The Inland Revenue is its biggest client, paying it 1.6 billion pounds for running Britain's tax systems over 10 years. The Department of Social Security, the Department of Transport, the National Health Service and several London boroughs are also customers. The U.S. Navy's granting EDS a record $7 billion contract for a computer network in the last year of the millennium is a good beginning. If EDS can handle a London borough and the U.S. Navy, it could surely run Sierra Leone or the Los Angeles Unified School District.

Its sheer size gives EDS buying power. With an annual expenditure of nearly 4 billion pounds on computer hardware and software, it has a tech budget far bigger than the British government's. It also invests in systems and techniques that produce results. More government agencies are reluctantly and slowly going e-government. All government services should be just a click away in the New World Order. IRS tax returns, DMV records and government auctions are a good start. What about elections? There is no reason why every government agency throughout the world should not be replacing bureaucrats with cyber technology. It's more efficient, cost effective and utterly oblivious to human complaint or political affiliation.

Robots and computers are cheaper, more efficient and easier to employ than people – so long as they are run by nonpartisan politically-neutral companies – especially today now that artificial intelligence systems are taking root.

Robotics and cyber technology are here to stay, of course. Schick says the cyberstate will cause a blurring of public and private sectors. Why should there not be a blurring between all personal options, including work, education and play? If cybernetics and robotics help you enjoy what you are doing for a living, is it really work? As these systems allow us more of our time for ourselves as we move in and out of work and play modes with much greater fluidity – as do people who work from home on computers – will we still so easily demarcate play? Will we be as bored? Today a lot of active talent and brilliant minds are bored because their minds are inactive and not busy. Why not put all active bored minds to good use that benefits society and the community in the 21st century?

## *Work and Education Options*
I know few people who truly like what they are doing, especially lawyers. They all wish they were doing something else. Many are afraid to say or do anything about it because "People just wouldn't understand. I am supposed to be so happy in such a great profession making all this money that I am forced to lie to myself and keep doing what I hate just because I don't want to hurt my family. My parents, wife and kids would never understand," lamented more than one prominent lawyer I have heard over the years grumble about their boring monotonous legal career. Endless numbers of lawyers, doctors, bartenders, bankers, accountants, taxi drivers, actors – you name the occupation and someone will express the same frustration. Why continue doing things the frustrating American way? Homer Simpson was right when he said: "Lisa, if you don't like your job, you don't strike. You just go in every day and do it really half-assed. That's the American way."

Christopher Locke reminds us that "We long for more connection between what we do for a living and what we genuinely care about, for work that's more than clock-watching drudgery. We long for release from anonymity, to be seen as who we feel ourselves to be rather than as the sum of abstract metrics and parameters. We long to be part of a world that makes sense rather than accept the accidental alienation imposed by market forces too large to grasp, to even contemplate."

If there were no such thing as change, we would never need to develop our latent powers. But change is inevitable in every aspect of our lives. It is empowering to be able to accept that fact and deploy your creativity in an adult relationship to change. Jung says it well in his *Collected Works:* "All true things must change, and only that which changes remains true."

Better-managed government and bureaucracies will create better communities that will allow people to devote more time to the community and do the things they also personally enjoy. Relaxation comes in many forms. Praying, chanting, dancing, singing, reading, talking, eating, learning, gardening, farming, walking, running, hiking, volunteer work, or sport. More time can be devoted to planning and participating in such pleasurable pursuits by all age groups and not just children and seniors.

Better-managed political systems and lifestyles allow people to devote more time to doing things they enjoy. After all, most people dislike what they are doing and what they have to show for their efforts. This holds true for their personal life at home and their occupation at work. It was true in my own situation and I did something about it. It wasn't easy. I paid a tremendous price. But I don't have many regrets. I know too many people today who regret they didn't make a change. They have paid the price personally at home and professionally at work.

Many of the current frustrations we are experiencing, whether they involve our personal lives, job satisfaction, anger at government waste and mismanagement, can be eliminated if the modern cyber tools and robotics at our disposal were fully utilized to ensure our personal, communal and occupational bliss.

Most people dislike what they are doing but hang in because of the money and fear of failure. They go through life being miserably comfortable, rich and scared. Why continue this folly in the New World Order? I agree with

David Weinberger who says, "However much we long for the Web is how much we hate our job."

Americans are not only the hardest working people in the Western world, they take the fewest holidays. People are so terrified of losing their jobs that they accept this. As if fear is not bad enough, add boredom to the mix and one understands why the American worker is fast becoming redundant to corporate America.

One in three Americans are unhappy in their job, even if they are making good money. There are many reasons for this. First and foremost, we are living longer and have to do the same job for more decades than our predecessors. Life expectancy has jumped from about 47 years in 1900 to close to 80 today. Charles Darwin was just 22 when he sailed the HMS Beagle on his voyage of evolutionary discovery. William Shakespeare is believed to have been in his mid-20s when he penned *Henry VI, Part I*. Furthermore, there are a lot of new professional educational opportunities today that did not exist in the last century – website designer, blogger and DNA specialist, to name a few.

Robert Kahn, a sociologist at the University of Michigan who has studied the role of work in people's lives said: "Currently the pattern of our life course is what some sociologists call 'age graded.' We get all this education between 18 and 22, then we work, get married, start a family, and it increasingly becomes this one small sprint until suddenly, at 65, it's nothing but leisure and retirement.

"It's crazy. If we could start from scratch, we could think of our lives in terms of a mix of education, work and leisure, all of which are altered as we age. It wouldn't be this all-or-nothing notion we live now."

I couldn't agree more. That is what I have practiced. I always keep in mind a joke I heard about a person who retired and was sitting on his rocking chair on the porch staring out at the distance. His wife asked him what he was doing? "Nothing," he replied.

"But that is what you did yesterday," she responded.

"I'm not finished yet," he said.

This "age graded" life just doesn't work anymore. What we wanted to do at 18 differs vastly from what we want to do at 40 or 65. When that realization dawns, most people get bored and frustrated. Early choices do not have to be life sentences in the Internet age. Today's technology allows us – through our governments and universities – to pursue alternative careers and possibilities.

Boredom and frustrations with jobs can be addressed by programming occupational transfers with the appropriate training where necessary. People who are happy at work are happy at home and help build happy communities. Job banks can be accessed to enable people to make seamless moves from profession to profession or occupation to occupation, not to mention making transfers within a specific industry or profession. Training and education can also be accessed online. Drummers can become strummers, butchers and bakers can become candlestick makers, and career politicians can become morticians.

"Imagine. When I've banked some money I could put in and try out as a restaurateur, professor or banker when I get tired of lawyering," my former law partner Tim Tierney proclaimed as we discussed the marvels and wonders of the computer age.

"You are always lamenting the fact that you never got a chance to travel outside the States," I told him. "You've bitched that you were relegated to all the mobile home communities throughout California. Imagine, you could put in as a travel guide and lead tours to Ireland, China or Africa. That's one way for you to see the world." I know what a frustrated world traveler Tim is. Cruel of me, really.

Although with today's Mobile City Guide apps for Android smartphones and tablets, even that is debatable. Nevertheless, the reality today is that most people will jump at the chance to change jobs.

There is no reason why anyone who is willing can't study or work in their own way. Cyber high schools, universities and job banks across the nation can connect people to an education and jobs. Technology allows people to stay home and study or work, if they have the cyber skills. This turns getting out of bed in the morning from a compulsion to delightful self-discipline.

Online education is becoming a defiantly mainstream academic experience. It is helping to create a new academic environment in which entities with names like Anheuser-Busch University, Jones International University and Western Governors University are jockeying along with Stanford, Oberlin and the University of California at Los Angeles for a share of the education market.

### The Cult of Banality

Reading about the millions of bored people who spend their time Web-surfing, in many cases watching websites that are so banal, I have to stop and ponder how to get them back into a happy workforce as I pound the keys on my computer. A good example is the more than 800,000 people who log on to watch a block of cheese aging. I'm not kidding. The cult of contemporary banality has to be addressed by *We the Apathetic Maids,* as many of us are members of the cult.

The more active minds today decide to become bankers to the poor and lend as little as $25 to small businesses from Vietnam to Kenya through Kiva.org, or become "break-up" agents who are paid by one half of a couple to tell the other that the relationship is over – a business built and promoted online. It is one of the fastest growing online sectors in China. Digital verbal process servers.

With the new cyber-tools being developed at the speed of light, such as contact lenses that allow us to see words and images displayed over our regular field of vision – just like the Terminator or Robocop, social voice messaging or voice microblogging via mobile phones, tweeting with a twist – a voice – digital medicine and other rapid computer advances, are vaporizing careers faster than workers can train for new ones. Rapid technological advances have caused a structural change in the economy that many U.S. workers and institutions, like the government and universities, are not prepared for.

No one seriously expects virtual education to replace the world of ivy-edged campuses. Instead the growth will be for working people who want high school diplomas, MBAs or college degrees who cannot take off from their job and family; working mothers; courses for engineers and computer technicians whose knowledge becomes outmoded every year.

A typical story is that of Sheila Kaplan, the president of Metropolitan State College in Denver. With 17,600 students, Metropolitan State is the largest undergraduate college in the country and the third largest school in Colorado. It represents the changing educational marketplace. The average student age is 27 years old; 80 percent of them work and many find taking courses at home by way of computer, in between car pooling or after work, enormously appealing. When the college began online courses in 1996, it had 30 courses and 420 students. By 1999 enrollment was 2,100 and 87 courses were offered.

The computer is radicalizing education in the New World Order. The only thing one won't be able to do in the 21st century while taking on-line courses will be to drink beer at a sorority house, date the student sitting next to you and find a parking space. But even "dating sites" may simulate the classroom pick-up – even if it doesn't have quite the same atavistic "rush."

Online job banks, career change banks, relocation banks for every occupation and profession banks are all possible today. Properly utilized, a lot more people will be happier because they will be happy at work. As a result, productivity will increase, making more time for recreation, travel and other pursuits.

What is the problem? It isn't the lack of hardware or software. It is the shortage of programmers and a will to aggressively implement such a system. The government's reluctance to implement in practice its own reports is out of bureaucratic fear that the unemployment numbers will increase. That would threaten the popularity of career politicians and their ability to get re-elected. What is wrong with this picture? It is up to *We the Maids* to sweep them out and the new possibilities in!

### Unabomber Manifesto

Unlike Theodore Kaczynski, better known as the Unabomber, I do not believe technology is destroying society. On the contrary, I believe it holds the power to make society more productive, efficient and enjoyable to those who capitalize on its benefits.

One of the Unabomber's victims was David Gelernter, a professor at Yale. Gelernter was lucky to survive a mail bomb that tore open his chest and abdomen, mangled his right hand and eye. His blood pressure is said to have been undetectable by the time he stumbled from his office to a Yale clinic nearby.

To Gelernter, Facebook and Twitter are partial fulfillment of something he's been writing about and thinking about since the early 1990s, an evolution of the Internet into a form far less chaotic and more useful than today's. His preferred term is "lifestream." Whatever you call it, the cybersphere as it now exists is due for an overhaul.

Prophesy comes naturally to Gelernter. He is credited in some circles for having coined the term "the cloud." But what preoccupies him is the inadequacy of our conventions and practices for organizing the wildly expanding array of digital objects that populate the cybersphere.

"The current shape of the Web is the same shape as the Internet hardware," he says. "The Internet hardware is lots of computers wired together into a nothing-shaped cobweb. The Web itself is a lot of websites hyperlinked together into a nothing-shaped cobweb."

Eventually business models based on streaming will dominate the Internet, he predicts. Digital objects as streams rather than as files in a file system. The stream will become a mirror of the unfolding story of their lives. It already has started.

Since the publication of the Unabomber's manifesto, some people have found themselves quietly speaking the unspeakable: The Unabomber made some good points in his rant against technology.

While in no way endorsing Kaczynski's violence or political extremism, some people say they share the Unabomber's fear that technology is limiting freedom and individuality. The bomber's sentiments struck a chord in some, just as the Oklahoma City bombing was an extreme expression of a popular belief that government has become too powerful.

A recent Princeton survey showed that one-quarter of the public was disillusioned with high technology.

University of Maryland computer science major Kenley Davis is representative of the disillusioned and doesn't think the Unabomber sounds so crazy. "Technology is a way of concentrating power in the hands of the people who have access."

Still, Davis adds: "I don't think that's a good reason to throw out the baby with the bathwater. There are good parts of technology.... The Unbomber's rationale of 'let's blow it all up and start over' won't work."

The fact remains that the world is rapidly evolving into a cyber automated one, which is alienating many by displacing them and affecting their loved ones. There is no reason they can't be embraced and brought into the New World Order.

As we enter the new millennium and cyber technology races forward, it is only fair and reasonable to analyze and assess its impact on society. We must adopt a plan that utilizes technology for the benefit of the most people at the least cost to taxpayers. *We the People* – the citizens the government is supposed to represent – have that power.

### Wired Third World
The developing world is its own worst enemy when it comes to bureaucracy and inefficiency. In Hong Kong and most developed countries, a new business can be up and running within 24 hours. In Brazil it takes 152 days. Any wonder foreign investors are reluctant to rush in? The time it takes to set up a new business is only half the story. The other half is the cost.

In Hong Kong, and in many developed countries, the cost of setting up a new business is less than 1 percent of a person's annual income. In Ethiopia and Niger, the cost of starting a new business can be as high as four times the average income per employee. This is the bureaucratic cost separate and apart from the investment capital needed to get started! No wonder undeveloped countries stay undeveloped no matter how many citizens want to become entrepreneurs.

Regulatory regimes in the developing world would be far better off emulating Hong Kong and the developed world by minimizing ineffective costly regulation and investing in the wired technologies that would allow them to create prosperity instead of perpetuating poverty. Martin Wolf of *The Financial Times* is right when he says: "Regulation should be reduced to what is essential, efficacious and readily enforceable. Markets themselves will do much of the regulation, provided they are competitive. Governments also need to use modern technology to improve the efficiency of what they do."

The quickest and most efficient way for the developing world to catch up to the developed world is to get wired.

## Wired World

The telecommunications, computing and audiovisual industries are growing twice as fast as the rest of the world economy, according to the International Telecommunications Union. Appropriately enough, the last ITU conference of the last millennium was held in Hong Kong.

The Internet has added more than twice the number of subscribers each year in the last few years of the last century and at the dawn of the new century. But the statistics suggest there is a long way to go before the world is "wired" at even the most basic level. According to the ITU report, there were only 1,500 people on the waiting list for new phone lines in Hong Kong, but there were 1 million in Saudi Arabia. While they are waiting, rich sheiks in nearby Dubai get text-messaged divorces sent to and from mobile phones confirmed by the family court. "Why are you late? You are divorced" was the first case of a divorce by mobile phone.

Global mobile phone use passed the 3 billion mark in July 2007. More than half the people in the world today have cell phones. More than 1,000 new customers effectively sign up for mobile phones every minute around the world, according to a survey by U.K.-based telecom analysis company The Mobile World. Watching high-fliers in the sky sitting next to me using cell phones in flight to make calls, send e-mails and texts as early as 2008 was a real eye opener. My first reaction was, "She is a terrorist who's going to blow up the plane!"

Man, was I wrong. Just reconfirmed my Luddite status.

The New World Order is changing faster than most people realize. With the steady march of new technologies, the world will get wired and connected a lot faster than many think in the 21st century.

World commerce today involves not just cargo containers traversing oceans but an ever increasing number of cables and satellites buzzing with computer programming code, product designs and engineering diagrams and formulas. How American companies charge for this mode of transportation has become contentious globally. Chinese Information Minister Wu Jichuan best articulates the universal frustration. The U.S. dominance of cyberspace results in America setting the pricing, which Wu sees as "irrational."

Traditional companies hire their workers by searching the world for computer specialists willing to come to the United States. But virtual immigration, where the workers stay put, has become far more common for 21st-century cyber companies, and is much cheaper.

America is leading the charge into the wired world of the new millennium. More than 50 percent of American workers are officially classified as "knowledge" workers, although of what and whether it is worth knowing is another question.

Information flows and the products needed to carry them have become the largest single sources of U.S. foreign currency income, and 85 percent of the digital information in international trade originates in the United States.

Software exports are vastly underestimated. A program that sells for $300, for instance, may show up in the trade statistics as only a $5 or $10 export because only the values of the instruction manual and the blank diskette are recorded.

America's technological lead gives it a competitive advantage on a broad front. Software has begun to replace machines and robots as the dominant element in manufacturing, writes Francois Sicart, chairman of Tocqueville Asset Management. As a result, he says, leadership in the development and use of computers, software and communications technology is helping the United States to leapfrog its competition and seize back the global lead in manufacturing.

For the high-technology executives, the question is how to keep America No. 1 as the center of economic gravity shifts to Asia in the 21st century. While today 46 percent of the world's electronic goods are consumed in the United States, in 50 years that figure may only be 5 percent. Dominance of the American market will not be nearly enough.

Standing on the Great Wall of China, with media and telecom business executives from the States, I couldn't help but chuckle to myself at the thought that in a world where billions are being made on Internet investments, millions of people around the world have never made a telephone call.

"China will not only challenge, but I believe will catch up to the U.S. and not only get phones into the hands of every Chinese and millions of others, but build a high-tech industry that will match the size and beauty of the Great Wall," I told the executives, who were awestruck by the size and beauty of China and the Wall. It was their first trip to China and they were starting to reassess some of their earlier opinions about the Chinese. Isn't it time America as a country did as well – not just about China – but America itself?

### The Cyber Bridge
Hong Kong is the cyberbridge between America and China that will facilitate the building of the infrastructure that both need to better understand each other – cybernetically – as well as politically and

economically. When there is a breakdown on any of those fronts, man, does Hong Kong feel it. The economic and political are not as bad as the cybernetic.

Tech-savvy Hong Kong and the region were left reeling in December 2006, when a 7.1 magnitude earthquake struck southern Taiwan and damaged four undersea cables in the Luzon Strait between Hong Kong and Taiwan. It brought to a halt Internet services such as e-mail, instant messaging, online shopping, instant stock quotes and games. The region was crippled and paralyzed. People's cyber world was disrupted for several weeks. It was a real wake-up call to a Luddite like me that it does not take much for Mother Nature to remind us how dependent we are on nature and science.

Old-fashioned pen and paper backups work wonders when the Net is down. Snail mail is better than no mail.

AT&T sold China a high-speed digital transmission system linking Hong Kong and neighboring Guangdong Province that can carry "more than 30,000 voice and data calls over a single optical fiber line." It is said to be as good as, if not better than, the lines linking New York and Washington, D.C.

"This technology is as advanced as anything we have commercially available," says Christopher Padilla, AT&T's director of government affairs. "In effect, we're helping China lay down its first information super highway."

AT&T's joint ventures in China to develop the telecommunication industry are a result of China's entry into the WTO. Many other American companies followed and continue to do so.

Technological leadership, the West's domain for many years, will probably stay with it in some areas. There are no guarantees. But technological applications will depend on many highly skilled people with an understanding of ways to use science and technology to improve the quality of life. From this standpoint, India and China will dominate the 21st century by having the largest numbers of skilled technicians able to deliver new products and services to the world. In the process, the future of professional services may shift from America to Hong Kong, China and India and the prosperity associated with these services will follow. If America is to hold onto its leadership position, it must continue developing and delivering new technologies creatively – ones that are cost effective and desirable to all consumers in the global marketplace.

The best way to do that is to again allow the world's talent to easily get to America's shores to pursue the American Dream and develop their ideas – and develop America's in the process!

### *Cyber Jurisdiction*

The global computer network is blind to the terrestrial boundaries that have traditionally dictated legal jurisdiction – and there's nothing resembling consensus among the nations of the world on what can properly flow across them.

An eclectic collection of legal scholars, libertarians, crypto-anarchists and ordinary Internet users predict that cyberspace will ultimately render the nation-state as we know it irrelevant, with law rooted in physical control of geographic territory giving way to new forms of governance springing from online communities. That became evident in the 2012 U.S. presidential election campaign.

Americans Elect is an online community of politically active citizens determined to defeat the Democratic and Republican parties by embracing their members, Independents and many *Apathetic Maids*.

Cyber corporate and ethnic communities are so intertwined and interlinked in the 21$^{st}$ century that they have redefined geographic boundaries. India, which is perpetually on a war footing with Pakistan over Kashmir, is a good example. Although stronger, India refrains from going to war with Pakistan because of the real economic loss it would suffer if the foreign multi-nationals who have their call centers and contact centers there that have generated an unprecedented $60 billion in foreign reserves were to relocate their businesses elsewhere. Thomas L. Friedman is correct when he says, "Don't thank General Powell for India's cease-fire with Pakistan; thank

General Electric and all its friends in Bangalore."

"Activity in cyberspace ultimately forecasts the end of national control," said David Post, visiting associate professor of law at Georgetown University. "People will still sell shoes and send their kids to school. But there will be an enormous upheaval in the status quo."

One looks forward to the time when one can switch off and even unplug the damned government run by career politicians and their bureaucrats. However, the tribal instincts of our civilized world, including national pride, make this dire prediction doubtful.

The challenge to the age-old notion of geographically based political power springs, first of all, from the simple fact that in cyberspace, there is no distance between two points. From Los Angeles, it takes about as long to look at a picture stored on a computer in Hong Kong as it does to view one housed in Santa Barbara.

"The supranational nature of electronic payment mechanisms may be a primary factor in the nation-state becoming a fleeting footnote in social history," said Roger Clarke, a visiting fellow in computer science at Australian National University. "In the near future, not only wealthy corporations but also ordinary individuals will utilize opportunities to place monetary flows, profits and assets beyond the grasp of national taxation agencies."

Many believe the advent of digital cash systems, which in their most sophisticated form enable people to move money over computer networks with complete anonymity, will deal another big blow to traditional government by making tax evasion and money laundering far easier – unless of course they put their money with banks that have regulatory reporting requirements, as many tax-evading American citizens have found out.

David Post and David Johnson, co-directors of the Cyberspace Law Institute, propose an explicit rejection of the view – first formalized by philosopher John Locke in the 17th century – that political power in modern society derives from the state's ability to impose physical punishment.

They say cyberspace should be treated as a legal jurisdiction unto itself, subject to laws and regulations that are created and enforced by members of individual online communities. Rather than the use of physical force, banishment could become the most effective way to deal with criminals.

If, as German social theorist Max Weber put it, "The state is a human community that successfully claims the monopoly of the legitimate use of physical force within a given territory," then cyberspace is a voluntary human community where "netizens" join based on common interests and rules are imposed as a condition of membership.

This could be regarded as the political philosophy of ultimate "nerdism". To those a little less sedentary who would break into your house, pillage your possessions, rape womenfolk and, worst, smash computers, banishment from the Net does not suggest itself as an adequate deterrent. A former Clinton administration official put it this way. "Government is formed because there's a community of allegiance people have, based on language and territory. So as communities begin to form in cyberspace that are not based on territory, the question becomes 'What is government?' "

The principality of Sealand, Europe's smallest self-proclaimed independent sea fort off Suffolk England, is the first such offshore territory data haven that says it is off limits to governments. It is governed solely by the newly created Sealand laws. Located on a World War II on two hollow concrete cylinders that rise 20 meters above the North Sea, it provides clients with broadband access speeds of a gigahertz a second. It claims high security and confidentiality that no government can breach.

It is an offshore digital data hideout, no different than Switzerland and many other offshore havens of the last millennium were in the financial realm. Any wonder the computers and servers on Sealand belong to HavenCo, which leases the space to house its offshore digital data?

Individuals who do not want lawyers and government agencies having access to their sensitive computer files and e-mails can store them there.

Sealand is no different than the high-tech fortresses in America that house the country's Internet data. The Iron Mountain facility in Boyers, Pennsylvania, and the former R.R. Donnelley printing plant in Chicago being two such examples of facilities that are critical to the financial system and the overall function of the Internet. There are at least 13,000 large data centers around the world; 7,000 of them are in the U.S. Billions of dollars are spent each year building more of these centers, not just in America, but in China and every other Internet-savvy nation.

Officials in the southern Chinese city of Guangzhou are establishing a large "virtual brain" to store networking data for governmental and financial institutions. The data center is aimed at coping with "intensifying network intrusions" from viruses, hackers and natural disasters.

Where should hackers be tried in the new Cyber World Order? For example, a Chinese hacker defaced a Japanese government website over the war-crimes issue. Does this mean that under a global Internet regime the Chinese police arrest him and extradite him to Tokyo to be tried? What about the two men who hacked into Michael Bloomberg's computer system from Almaty, Kazakhstan, who were arrested in London and prosecuted in New York?

And how about WikiLeaks' Julian Assange, who was arrested in London and ordered to be extradited to Sweden for an alleged rape after he bared America's diplomatic secrets given to him by a U.S. soldier who felt it was his patriotic duty to let his fellow citizens know the truth about their government? An act the Founding Fathers would applaud.

That appears to be the conclusion many legal minds are reaching after seven days of the preliminary hearing of Army Private Bradley Manning in December 2011. After more than 300,000 pages of documents were entered into evidence, a key question remains unanswered: How exactly did his leak of hundreds of thousands of secret documents, logs and at least one video – passed on to WikiLeaks – directly harm U.S. national security? How did he aid the enemy, the most serious charge he faces?

Manning remains a polarizing figure, a hero to some and a traitor to others.

At worst, supporters argue, he embarrassed the U.S. The defense contends that the harm done to the U.S. was negligible.

By the time both sides gave closing arguments, the government had presented no evidence of a death, injury or harm done to the U.S. that was caused by the release of the information. Instead, military prosecutors argued that Manning knew that what he was doing was illegal and could help America's enemies, which they specified as terrorist organizations.

Overzealous government prosecution led to the suicide of Internet activist and Reddit co-founder Aaron Swartz. He was an activist dedicated to promoting the free flow of information online. His most recent milestone was the launch of Demand Progress, a grass-roots lobbying group that helped defeat the Hollywood-backed anti-piracy bills known by the acronyms SOPA and PIPA.

In 2011, a federal grand jury indicted Swartz for allegedly gaining unauthorized access to computers operated by the Massachusetts Institute of Technology and to JSTOR, an online repository of academic research that MIT paid to make available on campus. The indictment accused Swartz of downloading 4.8 million journal articles – a third of which carried a fee – in order to redistribute them online for free.

His death may add to his legacy by prodding Congress to pass a piece of legislation being called "Aaron's Law" to narrow the scope of the two laws that federal prosecutors were using against him: the Computer Fraud and Abuse Act of 1986 and the wire fraud provisions of the Communications Act Amendments of 1952. The government has been using these statutes to prosecute people for an expanding range of online activities.

Anonymous commandeered a Department of Justice website in late January 2013 to denounce the prosecution of Swartz. The hackers replaced the site's content with a video denouncing the government and praising the 26-year-old Swartz. Anonymous said it hacked the U.S. Sentencing Commission's website to call attention to "the federal sentencing guidelines which enable prosecutors to cheat citizens of their constitutionally-guaranteed right to a fair trial."

From Dungeons and Dragons to Everquest, the Web is attracting people around the world to illusory places that are great escapes from political reality. In the New World Order, people should spend time online contributing to and improving our real world so we can collectively find Shangri-La together. The beauty and ease with which we can do this has never been so easily available to mankind. We now have a tool, the Internet, which allows us to communicate globally because it is timeless, borderless and interactive. Americans can create global parties, policies and agendas that can be collectively implemented to make for a much better World Order.

## Virtual Borders

But the reality is that electronic fences and borders are being raised at the dawn of the $21^{st}$ century. Electronic fences to stop gambling and pornography. A French judge ordered Yahoo to stop selling Nazi paraphernalia because French law bans such practices. Zimbabwe's President Robert Mugabe prosecuted and tried the first case of a reporter whose paper put his story on the Internet in London. The story was critical of Mugabe and was downloaded in Zimbabwe by Mugabe's secret police who felt the article was defamatory. They pressed for the reporter's prosecution. This establishes a dangerous precedent because it opens a legal path whereby repressive regimes can inflict their draconian media rules on journalists, editors and publishers throughout the world by merely downloading the story in their country. Web publications can be used by the unscrupulous as an excuse to forum-shop in countries with plaintiff-friendly libel laws. Some analysts argue that the development of "geolocation" technology, which attempts to match a person's location based on a computer's Internet address, will create virtual borders.

Intelligent homes create their own virtual borders and allow people to access everyone and find anything in the virtual world without leaving home. So, in theory, we never need to go outdoors or touch anything real. We can live in virtual bubbles. We can even stay home to vote!

## Electronic Voting

The Florida presidential election debacle of 2000 brought to light the varied and antiquated voting methods throughout America. Isn't it time we created a uniform convenient electronic voting system? One akin to online banking and ATMs? Hackers and Trojan horses can be repelled. Firewalls similar to those protecting financial and other secure transactions can be installed. Why cannot electronic voting machines be made as secure as ATMs and be managed and administered with independent nonpartisan controls and procedures in place? A system that allows people to vote electronically from home, work and electronic voting booths. An electronic election day on Sunday or an entire weekend that facilitates and encourages a maximum turnout of people to vote. Non-working days rather than the traditional Tuesdays, a workday that ensures low voter turnout.

A federal judge ruled that the punch-card machines used in California had to go by 2004, and they did. But like many states that rushed to install the new electronic voting technology without proper safeguards, there were glitches. Deliberate hacking to change results as was the case investigated in Florida by the FBI in the 2004 congressional races and the 2002 Democratic primary to make sure Jeb Bush would not have to run against Janet Reno, who presented a real threat to Jeb, but instead against Bill McBride, whom Jeb beat.

In California, Diebold Election Systems agreed to pay $2.6 million to the state and Alameda County for misleading them about the security of the vote-tabulating equipment it sold them.

A story that really horrified me as to what was happening to the democratic process in America was the security block imposed by the Defense Department that prevented American citizens overseas from accessing www.fvap.gov, the Federal Voter Assistance Program website that disenfranchised millions of overseas Americans, including me.

The preferred choice is computer touch-screen voting, in which voters press selections on a machine resembling a bank ATM. The computers offer choices in different languages and permit voters to correct mistakes before submitting their electronic ballot.

Election Day is becoming Election Month because of the increasing number of voters who take advantage of a variety of early voting procedures that have swept across America and cast their votes before Election Day. Thus the Internet is maximizing voter participation by offering a variety of ways and times to vote. America should also look at online ways to get-out-to-vote campaigns such as Denmark's sexually active Voteman.

Direct recording electronic voting machines eliminate paper ballots and their vast myriad of problems highlighted by the Florida hanging chad quagmire, decrease the number ways election officials can cheat, especially with absentee ballots, and make elections easier and more convenient, boosting voter turnout.

Elections in the 21$^{st}$ century should take place strictly over the Internet. The presidents of the California Institute of Technology and the Massachusetts Institute of Technology joined forces to push for ATM-style voting computers. Companies like election.com have simple systems. All a voter needs is a PIN to access an online ballot. It ran the elections for the Pennsylvania State Employees Credit Union and the Democratic Party primary in Arizona. The convenience resulted in a 600 percent increase in voter turnout in Arizona. Is it possible that career politicians and their bureaucrats are resisting electronic voting because it minimizes election fraud and could mean the end of their careers and that of the powerful entrenched establishment?

At a time when people can see video taken by a robot on Mars, when there are cars that can drive themselves and when people can deposit checks using their smartphones without going to a bank, why do most people still have to go to a polling place to vote?

I know about the hacking and voter fraud potential. Those are technical issues that can be resolved and should not be a political one used to minimize voter turnout.

South Korea and Estonia introduced electronic voting for all elections in 2005. Hong Kong, Australia and Japan have launched pilot projects. Isn't it time America did as well on a local, state and national level?

So what if it costs more than $10 billion to modernize America's voting system. Isn't it worth it? When compared to the hundreds of billions in useless wasteful subsidies, it certainly is. Brazil introduced computerized voting in the 1990s and is currently working on the second generation. Mexico spent several billion dollars on polling machines and equipment. The result was that the Institutional Revolutionary Party found it impossible to rig presidential elections anymore and lost as a result. Could there be a real political lesson there for *We the Maids?* It is time to sweep out the Luddite voting systems of the 20th century.

According to Curtis Gans of the Committee for the Study of the American Electorate, more than 2 million votes cast in the last election of the millennium were invalidated. That is the equivalent of throwing out the ballots of every registered voter in Los Angeles and San Francisco combined. And Florida is hardly the only state whose voting system is in need of modernization. For all the talk about "never again," another close election could lead to a Florida rerun. Is this a rerun we want to see? On the contrary. It is a strong impetus for electronic electoral system reform that can only benefit *We the Apathetic People* – the citizens.

*We the People* must ensure that the Founding Fathers' 18th-century fears of a voting public unable to make informed choices doesn't come true in the cyberspace 21st century. To that end, all voters must receive ballot pamphlets. Now used in California and several other states, these informational pamphlets are sent to voters a month before Election Day. They list the arguments for and against ballot propositions and include statements from the candidates outlining their platforms. Voters can study the material at their convenience without being limited to the barrage of political ads cooked up by the spin doctors. The same pamphlets can be made available online. So why aren't they?

Future electronic elections must be run by nonpartisan commissioners. Partisan election commissioners cannot be impartial. Florida made that perfectly clear in the last presidential election of the 20th century. To ensure fairness in future elections, we need electronic impartiality. Not just for the election but all the debates leading up to an election. The YouTube format of presidential debates not only livens up the proceedings but allows citizens to participate in addition to the media talking heads. The Internet and registered voter citizens should be the focus of political electioneering for true democracy to flourish.

How about vote-swapping websites? The last election of the millennium saw such sites proliferate to exchange Nader votes for Gore votes in states where the competition between Bush and Gore was close. Gore in return would deliver the same number of votes to Nader in states where the contest wasn't close. A judge in Los Angeles ruled such websites to be illegal. The American Civil Liberties Union argued that stopping the practice violated free-speech rights. Does it?

## Cyber Power

The war on terror in the wake of 9/11 has given way to a cyber protest movement. America's first war of the Internet age is spawning a new breed of protesters who take for granted the ability to consult a vast array of international news sources with a few mouse clicks and are teaching old activists new tricks. An anti-war petition could be signed at www.9-11peace.org. The first generation of Internet activists have spread their message farther and faster than their predecessors in political protest. Websites have become mobilization points. Facebook and Twitter have only expedited the process.

And consider the critical impetus that cyber power has given oppressed people in China, Tunisia, Egypt, Syria, Yemen, Bahrain, Kuwait and countless other countries around the world, including America. The Rodney King beating by Los Angeles police being one of the U.S. forerunners. Al Qaeda computers disclosed plans to launch chemical and biological attacks. The information superhighway is also the road to freedom for some of Asia's banned opposition groups. Activists scored their first cyberspace successes against Burma's military government.

"The Internet allows them – even in exile – to put their actions on the international agenda and so pressure foreign countries to give greater weight to human rights and democracy concerns when dealing with their governments," says Peter Eng, a Bangkok-based writer.

There will come a point though when real people will have to go into the fresh air of real Burma to bring about justice, peace and prosperity. It has thankfully started with the release of Aung San Suu Kyi and the suprisingly broad political freedoms she has been granted – freedoms that *We the Apathetic Maids* take for granted.

Internet cafes are springing up every day in traditionally closed political societies such as Baghdad, Tehran and Riyadh. Even youth in closed societies can communicate with their peers globally. The same holds true for poor youth. In Rio de Janeiro's dirt-poor Rocinha neighborhood, Latin America's largest slum, a place where people don't have enough to eat yet alone buy a computer, one can find a Future Station, a shack where each computer has a small antenna and connects using wireless technology developed by the Israeli military. Future Station is open from 9 a.m. to 10 p.m.

"From exclusion to cutting edge," said Franklin Dias Coelho, an economics professor and director of community development for Viva Rio, a rights group that works in the slums.

Coelho said he lobbied for a project similar to Future Station during the 18 months he worked in the state government's planning secretariat, but ran into bureaucratic walls.

"I could only do this outside the government," he said. "It would be ironic if it weren't tragic."

How appropriate a phrase for all bureaucrats everywhere. When will *We the Maids* sweep some sense into their time-warped minds?

Another tragedy in the New Cyber World Order is the number of new Web addicts, mostly children, teenagers or young adults. Studies show that about half of the young people who became addicted to surfing the Internet suffered some sort of major physiological setback in their childhoods and as a result have trouble trusting other people and are unable to build intimate relationships. Family influence is the single most important factor in such addictions.

Many of these Internet addicts suffer from lack of sleep, which studies show can cause other problems, even early death. As someone who has done more than my fair share of all-nighters, sometimes two-nighters or more with no sleep, as a lawyer, businessman or just plain party animal, I can relate.

The New Cyber World Order must make online vending machines available to all, rich and poor. Wireless computers that one can find anywhere, insert the local currency and – voila! – instant contact with anyone, anywhere, anytime. Sure beats guzzling a soft drink with junk food.

### Cyber Revolutions

The Arab Cleansing of 2011 and the Occupy Wall Street movement that started the same year and went viral worldwide are living testimonials to the revolutionary power of free cyber information, political and economic, that the Internet offers. The Internet enables information to spread freely within countries and across borders. Trying to censor the free flow of information today is virtually impossible – even in China. The Internet does not respect national laws or conventions or borders.

This is a reality that not only politicians are coming to terms with, but media tycoons who have been used to controlling information and how it flows. Rupert Murdoch and his heir apparent son James have reluctantly been forced to deal with virtual social media campaigners determined to bring them to justice, notwithstanding their strong political connections and influence.

E-activism has shattered what little faith the public had in the pillars of establishment, be it politicians, law enforcement, bankers or the media.

In 2007, Viacom boss Sumner Redstone decided to file a $1 billion lawsuit against Google for posting clips of content from Nickelodeon, MTV and Comedy Central without permission on Google's YouTube Website. The media giant's lawsuit is being closely watched by the world to determine what rights *We the People* have to the free flow of information – which in the future may not be so free.

The courts sided with Google, citing the only law designed to address copyright infringement on the Web – the 1998 Digital Millennium Copyright Act and its safe harbor protections. Viacom is appealing.

But as counterfeiting and piracy evolves, the law looks increasingly ineffective. "The DMCA was designed for an Internet where there were only isolated cases of piracy, and they were Stateside," says Frederick Huntsberry, chief operating officer of Paramount Pictures. "Right now the guys you're fighting are overseas. The volume is so large that you can't file enough lawsuits."

Piracy is moving rapidly online as access to high-speed Internet spreads in countries such as China, Mexico, Brazil, Russia and India.

Social media networks like Avaaz, a more than 9-million-member global campaign network, work to empower people to take action on issues large and small, local and global. Members are spread across 13 countries and the website operates in 14 languages. It takes no money from government or corporations and is largely funded by public subscriptions and promises to "close the gap between the world we have and the world we want, one campaign at a time."

Bringing down the Murdochs was one such campaign. Avaaz won several other last-minute targeted campaigns on other political fronts. In April 2011, it took the lead in supporting Anna Hazare, the 73-year-old Indian man who vowed to a fast unto death until the Indian government passed a new powerful anti-corruption law, which it did.

In May of the same year, an outpouring of 1.5 million e-mails helped stop the Ugandan parliament from approving the death penalty for homosexuality.

The same is happening in China with blogs and bulletin boards that increasingly find ways to get around the government's Great Firewall.

The efficiency and legitimacy of China's complex methods of trying to control the Internet cannot overcome the sophistication of the people's popular resistance.

James Madison famously remarked that a popular government without popular information, or the means of acquiring it, is but a prologue to a farce or a tragedy.

China's Communist Party has set out to disprove that rule. Rejecting talk of farce and tragedy, its leaders claim their authority is rooted within a new and higher form of popular government, a "post-democratic" way of handling power which delivers goods and services, promotes social harmony and roots out "harmful behavior" using state-of-the-art information-control methods more complex and much craftier than Madison could ever have imagined.

Chinese authorities may pride themselves on building a regime which seems calculating, flexible and dynamic – constantly willing to change its ways in order to remain the dominant guiding power. Yet they also know well the new Chinese proverb: "Ruling used to be like hammering a nail into wood; now it is much more like balancing on a slippery egg."

Whether the authorities in Beijing can sustain their present balancing act, so proving Madison wrong, seems doubtful.

The failure of the authorities balancing act is confirmed by artist Ai Weiwei and his lawyer Liu Xiaoyuan, who met on the Internet and are now two of the mainland's foremost rights campaigners.

The two first met in 2008 when Ai sought out Liu regarding the case of Yang Jia, a young man who barged into a police station in Shanghai and killed six officers. Liu was advocating online for Yang at the time, pointing out various procedural irregularities in the case, like why Yang wasn't given a sanity test, and why Yang's mother had disappeared after being summoned by police – she was the only one who could have testified about Yang's mental history and records. Ai had his questions too, and he decided to make a documentary of the case.

Neither Ai or Liu's advocacy helped Yang. He was sentenced to death and executed within five months.

When Ai felt that he might get in trouble in 2011 – at a time when dozens of bloggers, lawyers and dissidents had already "disappeared" in relation to the Jasmine Revolution in China – he told his family and friends that he wanted Liu to represent him if need be. But before that could happen, Liu was arrested and then Ai himself was jailed.

Liu and Ai proved Madison right. What we are seeing today in China is a farce and a tragedy.

*Bloomberg News* and *Bloomberg Businessweek* websites were shut down in the summer of 2012 because Bloomberg reported on the $376 million in assets controlled by the extended family of Chinese leader Xi Jinping – a fate that also befell *The New York Times* when it published a report on the family wealth of Wen Jiabao

Jasmine revolutions and Occupy protests around the world have inspired a new genre of serious video games designed to help activists develop revolutionary civil protests. Games such as People Power (The Game of Civil Resistance) allow would-be protest leaders to build and test their plans for peacefully opposing the police or the government without actually taking to the streets.

Occupy the Game, created in November 2011, advises players: "Collect money, water and the Constitution. Dodge the teargas, beanbags and flash grenades thrown by riot police." It concludes: "Don't get arrested!"

### Online New World Country

Teenagers around the world are today charting an Online Country and Government through the auspices of the Media Lab at the Massachusetts Institute of Technology. Isao Okawa, chairman of both CSK Corp., which makes business software, and Sega Enterprises Ltd., the game maker, has agreed to contribute $27 million to build a Center for Future Children next door to the current Media Lab.

These teenagers are plotting how to change the world with technology. It was founded in 1998, when 100 youngsters from 10 to 16 years old from around the world attended a global forum at the Media Lab. The forum, called the Junior Summit, is to the quaint old mock U.N. what a personal computer is to an abacus.

Connected online for months before they arrived for the forum, equipped with pagers with e-mail functions and Power Point presentation skills, the participants did not jabber about treaties and points of order. They planned to create an online country, to be known as Nation 1, where anyone under 19 could automatically become a citizen. Adults would need a visa or special permission to enter. Actually, most of the youngsters' goals would gladden adults hearts: reducing child labor, improving the environment, helping disabled children and simplifying computing. They do this while listening to dead artists like Marilyn Monroe sing hit songs of very alive artists courtesy of an MIT team that has combined artificial intelligence and videography to make words and songs – even in foreign languages – emerge from the lips of people who could never have uttered them. Now will adults listen?

*We the Apathetic Adult Maids* want borders to keep people out because of fear. Fear – and borders, which are the national expression of fear – stands center stage at the dawn of the 21st century. America guards its frontiers with new vigor since 9/11. The borderless globalized world where goods, people and capital flow freely was vaporized by the kamikaze bombers.

Today's digital generation, whose members have been weaned on computers and the Internet, are the rapping, hip-hopping cyber cowboys who will ride and steer the New World Order beyond the frontiers and borders we repeatedly have to cross today. They will be notable for their very wide butts from sitting permanently on swivel chairs from the age of 7.

Should anyone doubt this, just flash back to how much money Senator John McCain raised on the Internet after his victory in New Hampshire. He showed America how fast the Internet is changing democracy in America – a trend that is spreading globally like a wildfire, thanks to Campaign 2000 in the United States.

McCain will go down in history as a man who played a major role in developing the Fifth Estate – an entirely new political elite formed by the electronically liberated masses. A political elite the Republican National Committee appealed to and captivated with a personalized Get Out the Vote mass e-mailing from President Bush during the 2002 midterm and 2004 presidential elections. An estate that will grow and dominate in the 21$^{st}$ century.

Barack Obama's presidential campaign perfected the new 21st-century political estate.

The website *www.NationStates.com* allows people today to create their own "country." The possibilities are unlimited. From vegetarians demanding a halt to subsidies to cattlemen, to children skipping school and overrunning casinos.

It has already also commenced in the real world. In Poland the Citizens Platform, the country's newest political party, developed from an initiative of three people into a major political force at the dawn of the 21$^{st}$ century because of mobile phone text messages and the Internet. Text messaging and the Internet removed a corrupt president in the Philippines and brought his corrupt vice president into office.

The Philippine Center for Investigative Journalists posted on its website the mansions of President Joseph Estrada's mistresses after the traditional media refused to run with the story. The information spread like wildfire and resulted in his removal from office less than a year after the information was posted. The same happened to corrupt officials in the Bureau of Internal Revenue after their extravagant homes, vehicles and lifestyles got posted on the Net. The promise of online governance is a 21$^{st}$-century reality.

South Korea's Red Devils cheered their football team into the quarterfinals by organizing and galvanizing fans over the Internet. The raving energy at the street parties they organized before each game and after each victory could become a major political force. Roh Moo-hyun won the 2002 presidential election in part because he activated and mobilized 20-and 30-year-olds with a highly effective Internet campaign in a country that is a world leader in broadband access.

Peace activists mobilize protestors through the Internet from Hong Kong to New York. The huge turnout of Hong Kongers on July 1, 2003, to protest Hong Kong's Patriot Act-Article 23, was facilitated by the Internet. Numerous anti-Article 23 websites were set up, not only in Hong Kong, but in America. The U.S.-based Global Coalition Against Article 23 Legislation pulled out all the stops in the design of its site. The coalition's pages offered downloadable flyers, e-mail and website petitions, letter outlines and phone scripts, contacts of world leaders, and regular news updates in Chinese and English.

What happened with the Arab cleansing and Occupy Wall Street movements is self-evident.

Internet "blogs" are the individual or group-related online journals and commentaries which, by being regularly updated, provide an alternative view to understanding an issue. A political spin doctor's nightmare. America's MoveOn.org has more than 2½ million members who sign online petitions, organize street demonstrations and donate dollars to worthy causes and candidates. Phonecam bloggers have become instant investigative reporters who snap pictures with their phones and post them on the Web for all to see.

Dick Morris, the political strategist who enjoys the pleasures and company of real-time prostitutes, says: "Through interactive political and news websites, people will be able to vote on any issue they wish. Internet referendums will not, in the beginning, have any legal binding effect, but they will be politically binding. As the number of people participating in these votes grows from the thousands to well into the millions, they will acquire a political force that compels our elected representatives, anxious to keep their jobs, to heed their message."

Why should *We the Apathetic People* continue to be governed by career politicians "anxious to keep their jobs" in the 21st century? This violates both the letter and spirit of the Constitution so carefully crafted by our Founding Fathers.

## New World Cyber Order

Government as we know it has to change and come to terms with the realities of the 21$^{st}$ century. That includes bureaucracy. Not only because of cyberspace, but because of government's inability to function as a cohesive, cost-effective institution that serves and benefits all the people it serves to the best of its ability. The best example – make that the worst example – of bureaucratic inefficiency, or over-efficiency, is Japan.

Dates are fixed for when public beaches and Mount Fuji open and close. The beaches open July 15 and close on the last day of August. Mount Fuji opens to climbers on July 1 and closes on August 31. There are set dates for offices to switch their air conditioners on and off; the same for winter heating. People change clothes on set days too: winter woolies on October 1 and T-shirts and shorts June 1. These dates are held to regardless of the fact that traditional weather patterns have changed With the change in global climatic conditions, beaches are closed while the weather is still hot, office workers bundle themselves in blankets because air conditioners are on when it is cold and, conversely, are sweating because the heat is on on warm days.

Cyber tools must be utilized in full to ensure government is cost- effective and gives people what they need. We look for time, money, and the freedom to choose how to best spend both; quality time, with buckaroos, to spend with family, friends and the community.

The Internet is making brainwashed, uninformed, apathetic people smarter because they can communicate with each other openly and freely. These frustrated people urge each other to get involved. They can ignore the banner ads and their spin-doctors. Now, if only *We the Apathetic People* could become as active as citizens as we are consumer netizens, spin-doctors' roles will be relegated to that of snake oil salesmen of earlier times.

The Internet sabotages blind loyalty and respect for career politicians, their lobbyists, spin-doctors and bureaucrats. Sound bites and platitudes are a hard sell, as the 2000 presidential election, the last one of the last millennium, showed us. It didn't matter how much the candidates spent, how often they changed their messages based on the latest polls or focus groups, *We the Apathetic People* decided. So we thought until the Supreme Court stepped in and decided for us.

Silicon Valley is not only a representative slice of ethnically diverse America but a model for future elections.

"It is ground zero for the socially moderate, fiscally conservative, independent minded voter," says Kevin Spillane, a Republican consultant.

Election 2000 saw California's 15th Congressional District pitch the New Economy versus Old Goverment. The race between Democrat Mike Honda and Republican Jim Cunneen, which Honda, a Japanese-American, won, echoes and has national 21st-century implications.

Cunneen said that "Elections are about the future; they're not about the past." His Democratic opponent had the traditional labor and other Democratic endorsements and support. The Democrats also enjoyed an eight-percentage point edge in voter registration. In the last four elections, the voters had crossed party lines and sent Republicans to the House.

"You really are testing out this theory for the first time – that the new economy is going to drive elections," says Amy Walter, a congressional analyst for the nonpartisan Cook Political Report.

"Should you or the government decide the most important decisions in your lives?" Cunneen asks.

The voters decided they did and confounded the political pundits by reversing the historical Republican tradition of winning by sending a Democrat to Congress.

Silicon Valley is more than just a political metaphor for change. It is a metaphor for *We the Apathetic Maids* to wake up, join forces with each other and go back to America's roots – the Wild West. Not the lawless frontier, but the one where strangers from diverse places, backgrounds, experience and talent, running away from the Old World Order come together, driven by passion to build a New World Order based on collaboration and trust. The way America was before career politicians, lobbyists, bankers, lawyers and MBAs hijacked the system.

What God-given right do career politicians and civil servants anywhere have to lifetime tenure? Who else has a lifetime job guarantee? Even the slow-moving Japanese have started giving up on this antiquated notion. Isn't it time America did as well? Career politicians and civil servants do nothing to achieve anything – namely retirement. *We the Maids* have to sweep them up and out along with their patron financial backers and lobbyists. Then we have to clean up the mess they left us. They can and should be replaced by *Gates Perodise*. Their security blanket encourages incompetence and discourteous service because they know they can't be fired. Laws and regulations entitling civil servants to lifetime job security and pension plans that are far more generous than those in the private sector have to be re-examined and rewritten in the *New World Order*. Better yet, they should be replaced with laws governing computers, robotics and the Internet.

Bureaucrats are a major contributing factor to the high taxes in many states with bloated bureaucracies that have to be streamlined and refocused on their "public service" duties and responsibilities to the tax-paying public they serve. Bureaucrats' primary concern is how they can bide their time on taxpayers dollars long enough to make it to retirement. It's up to *We the Maids* to freeze their salaries and sweep them there quicker than they planned. If Hong Kong can do it, why can't America and China? Legislatures and other government bodies have to be strong and independent enough to make sure that money spent by bureaucrats is closely monitored and spent wisely and that it is used for its earmarked purpose. Locally, nationally, regionally and globally. Only then will *We the Taxpayers* get to keep more of our hard-earned dollars. It is up to us, not the changing promises of career politicians and their tax-increasing bureaucrats, to make sure they get cleaned out and we get a fresh, clean start.

*Our greatest glory is not in never failing,*
*but in rising every time we fall.*
– Confucius

### Retake and Remake
*I Want to Break Free.*
– Queen

### *Money, Honey, Money*

We were running late. We had left later than scheduled because I had to retrieve one of the horses that had broken out of its corral before I came home to pick up my then-wife Gail to go to a Democratic Party political fund raiser. The delay got us stuck in the evening rush-hour traffic on Pacific Coast Highway heading north to Malibu.

I was channel surfing the radio and locked on Don Mclean's *American Pie* as I admired the bright orange sun that was about to kiss the Pacific when Gail's frustration at the endless fund raisers we were attending that political season interrupted my dalliance with Mother Nature.

"Another boring fund raiser we have to rush to!" Gail exclaimed in utter disgust. "Which moocher schmuck are we supporting today?"

"It's Bob Strauss for the DNC and after that it's Gray," I answered as I tried to catch the final bit of sunshine disappearing into the Pacific.

I was a member of the Executive Finance Council of the Democratic National Committee. Gray Davis, the former governor, was the California state controller at the time. It is not unusual to attend a number of fund raisers a day in an election year. "Political panhandlers" are everywhere. On the phone. In your home and office, or some other political fund raiser's home. Not just during an election year, but every year, month and week. At our restaurant Scratch, we hosted several fund raisers a month. Democratic, Republican and independent.

Fund raisers come in many forms and costs: Traditional dinners, concerts,

VIP business trips with presidents, vice presidents and Cabinet members on their foreign trips to "promote better understanding and future cooperation" between governments and business. Sometimes I wondered which was government and which was business. Especially when they created more government subsidies for political contributors.

The extreme to which career politicians will go in their fund raising efforts is highlighted in Congress – while it is in session. Congressmen vote with one hand and "dial for dollars" with the other. House Speaker John Boehner highlighted this practice back in the mid-1990s when he was minority leader. He decided to play Santa Claus by handing out checks from tobacco lobbyists to fellow congressmen right on the floor of the House. Is it any wonder the latest polls give Congress a dismal approval rating?

America is a tarnished model of democracy that has been challenged by the electoral and legal wrongdoings committed by its king makers to lodge America's presidents in the White House and their lackeys in a dysfunctional Congress. A challenge we must meet. The multi-billion dollar Enron financial scandal, not to mention the ensuing financial scandals that have in fact bankrupted America and the Western world it leads, unveiled the questionable political contributions to the embarrassment of countless career politicians, including Presidents Bush and Obama, Attorney General John Ashcroft, Treasury Secretary Tim Geithner, congressmen and governors, and highlighted the long overdue need for radical reform of America's campaign finance laws.

Political corruption disguised as campaign and charitable contributions, many anonymously, got worse during the 2012 presidential election with the emergence of super PACs in the wake of the 2010 U.S. Supreme Court's *Citizens United v. the Federal Election Commission* decision that declared corporations to be "citizens" with the right of unlimited free speech – and the right to spend unlimited amounts to buy it. The decision overturned a century of law and, notably, struck down provisions of the 2002 McCain-Feingold legislation that limited corporations and unions to spending their own money on independent political advertising.

Not since before the post-Watergate reforms of the 1970s have wealthy individuals, unions and corporations had so much freedom to affect elections with large sums of money. The rules that once prevented these outside groups from directly advocating the election or defeat of a candidate as they wished no longer exist.

Amazingly, the justices ruled at the time that "independent expenditures, including those made by corporations, do not give rise to corruption or the appearance of corruption." The court reasoned that this was the case because the candidates' independent groups were actually independent, thus alleviating "the danger that expenditures will be given as a quid pro quo for improper commitments."

Really? What were they thinking?

"The worst decision by the Supreme Court in the 21st century. Uninformed, arrogant, naïve," said Senator John McCain, arguing that *Citizens United* is tainting U.S. elections, after conservative Sheldon Adelson said he was willing to spend $100 million to beat President Obama by making multimillion political contributions to Republican-backing super PACs. Why? Because he is opposed to Obama's "socialist-style economy and redistribution of wealth." What he really fears is the president's proposal to raise taxes on corporations like his that make huge amounts of money overseas. Ninety percent of the earnings of his company, the Las Vegas Sands Corporation, come from hotel and casino operations in Singapore and Macau.

Because of the lower tax rates in those countries – zero in Macau – the company has a U.S. corporate tax rate of 9.8 percent. Obama has repeatedly proposed ending the deductions and credits that allow corporations like Las Vegas Sands to shelter billions overseas, but the effort has been blocked by Republicans.

Adelson gave more than $68 million to super PACs in the 2012 election and funneled millions more to funds whose donors remain anonymous and candidates who ran for U.S. Senate and Congress. Despite Republican losses, he told the *Wall Street Journal* he intends to increase his political spending in the future.

Adelson is not the only billionaire investing millions of publicly disclosed dollars in Republican super PACs and millions anonymously in nonprofits to preserve his favorable tax status. He is in the illustrious company of modern-day robber barons Charles and David Koch, Harold and Annette Simmons and Bob Perry, who are among the more than 26 billionaires who have donated more than $61 million to super PACs, according to the Center for Responsive Politics.

Today, super PACs run the political campaigns, not the campaigns themselves. There is a fine line between super PACs and campaigns – a line that is easily crossed by "special interest" groups. Super PACs can outspend campaigns and have become their de facto advertising arms. The people running the campaigns and super PACs change roles as often as dance partners at a country fair.

"It's a big shell game," says Rick Tyler, who runs Newt Gingrich's super PAC. He admits the super PACs are "a horrible abomination for a freedom-loving people in a constitutional republic."

As if Super PACs aren't bad enough, nonprofit groups such as Karl Rove's Crossroads GPS and the U.S. Chamber of Commerce are not required to disclose donors, which resulted in the Democrats and Republicans trading accusations of undue influence by foreign corporations in the 2012 presidential campaign over disclosure of contributors. The Democrats accused the Republicans of "stealing our democracy" and accepting money from secret foreign donors and filed a complaint with the Federal Election Commission to compel Crossroads GPS to disclosure its contributors. Rove's response: "Have these people no shame?"

The 2012 campaign ushered in a new political order with its vulgar amount of money Super PACs and tax-exempt advocacy groups spent – more than $1 billion on federal races – and are poised to expand their efforts in the future.

A record $6 billion, $1 for every person on earth, was spent on U.S. congressional and presidential candidates in the 2012 election, up 13 percent from 2008. And more than $200 million spent on the 2012 election came from unknown donors – foreign and domestic.

Most of the secretive spending in the 2012 campaigns was coordinated through a close-knit network of veteran Republican strategists in Washington who met regularly to share polling data and decide which groups should focus on what races around the country. "There's no duplication. There's no wasteful survey research done," says Scott Reed, a Republican consultant working on the U.S. Chamber of Commerce advertising effort. "They have totally changed the way you run a campaign."

"For years, coordination was the thing you couldn't do," Grover Norquist says about the shift in power from campaigns to outside groups. "Now it's the thing you are most allowed to do."

Obama didn't beat the Super PACs; he joined them on the financial front and beat them on the technological front. Obama also helped undermine one of the vestiges of the post-Watergate campaign reforms: public financing for the general election. His decision not to accept public financing and its restrictions in both 2008 and 2012 prompted Mitt Romney to do the same. As a result, the political fund-raising season – which once drew to an end when exhausted donors and fund-raisers arrived at each party's convention – continued nearly through election day.

The good news about the pursuit of the almighty political dollar is the new financial bang heard in the Latino community and its Futuro Fund that was set up to raise $6 million – but brought in more than $30 million – for the Obama coffers.

The U.S. Court of Appeals for the Fourth Circuit ruled that the government must determine the "major purpose" of groups like Crossroads. I agree with Rick Hasen, an election law expert and professor at the University of California Irvine, who said the court decision made it clearer that groups like Crossroads were violating campaign finance laws by refusing to disclose their donors.

The basic campaign reform law passed in 1907 was enacted after the robber baron scandals of the day. The reform banned corporations from wooing candidates directly with money. *We the Apathetic Maids* can do so again because the justices in *Citizens United* wanted us to be able to judge for ourselves "whether elected officials are 'in the pocket' of so called moneyed interests."

With so many nonprofits that have the right to hide the names of their contributors, is their any doubt in any of *We the Maids'* minds that it is time for revolutionary change? Where is the outrage at Big Money's undue influence?

McCain has called the *Citizens United* decision "stupid" because it has invited the large "looming scandals" that will soon come to light and hopefully trigger campaign finance reform anew. The fallout and political bloodshed, for Democrats and Republicans alike, of these looming scandals will make *Game of Thrones* – HBO's brutal political drama of survival in the mythical, medieval-like land of Westeros – look like child's play.

Campaign finance reform is an absolutely necessary precondition to the overall constitutional and political reform that America must implement in the 21st century. The Democrats and Republicans have had their chance. It's now up to *We the People*.

"I don't think that's ever going to happen without the rise of a third party. As long as just two parties are in power, it's not going to change," former Minnesota Governor Jesse Ventura reminds us. I couldn't agree more. Music to my ears.

The time to publicly finance political campaigns and launch a new third party is long overdue.

The last presidential and national election of the old millennium – election 2000 – saw George W. Bush raise more than $187 million in direct contributions and Vice President Al Gore raise $133 million. We also saw the finance, insurance, real estate and legal industries donate more than $35 million to the Democratic Party and $58 million to the Republican Party.

The 2012 presidential election makes those figures look like chump change. Peanuts compared to the more than $1 billion President Obama raised and the almost $2 billion raised by the Republican candidates. Especially on the Republican front during the bruising GOP primary – and doubly so when Gingrich became the front-runner in Iowa and needed to raise millions of dollars to catch up to the well-organized and funded Mitt Romney.

Getting elected president costs a lot of money, and so does being inaugurated. In 2009, Obama's inaugural committee spent $45 million to kick off his first term. Even with scaled-back activities, two balls instead of 10, the 2013 inauguration still cost tens of millions – dollars that have to be raised the same way campaign funds are – from friendly, known and unknown supporters, who will be wanting favors in return. Shouldn't inaugural funding be transparent as well?

How far the country has departed from the Founding Fathers' principles and ideals was highlighted in the 2012 Republican primary. The extreme Christian fundamentalists who control and run the Republican Party funded the ABR movement – Anybody But Romney – because he is a Mormon. In other words, purely on religious grounds. A religious issue that probably had the Founding Fathers not only turning in their graves, but spinning and spitting as they recite passages from the Declaration of Independence and the Constitution.

In my opinion, the two most qualified Republican candidates in the 2012 primary were Mormons. So what? They are patriotic Americans. What constitutional right does any religious group have to dictate a party's nominee, especially when their choice goes against the popular wishes of party members? What a waste of hard-earned Yankee dollars that could be put to much better constructive use benefiting a majority of citizens instead of the exclusively few rich ones.

The Center for Responsive Politics estimates that over $3 billion was spent in the last election of the millennium – much of it loaded with political debt. Tickets to events ranged from an affordable $50 to a platinum price of half a million dollars for one ticket! The Republicans raised over $21 million in one evening – breaking their previous record of $7 million for one night.

Is it any wonder major contributors and corporate America are weary of political shakedowns?

The 21st century started like the 20th ended – elected career politicians fund raising on grander scales instead of governing. Bush had amassed $132.7 million by January 1, 2004, before the voting for the Democratic primaries even started. By comparison, his opponent Senator John Kerry had raised just $25.3 in the same period. Kerry, a millionaire in his own right, married to multimillionaire Teresa Heinz Kerry whose inherited wealth from her late husband was estimated at $550 million during the campaign, highlighted how presidential politics in America has become the province of the very rich and their rich friends and supporters.

The same holds true for gubernatorial and mayoral races. Republican candidate for governor of California Meg Whitman spent $120 million of her own money on her failed 2010 campaign. Mayor Michael Bloomberg spent $109 million of his personal fortune to secure a third term as mayor of New York.

Obama's 2012 reelection campaign opened a counteroffensive against Republican-backed changes to election laws that Democrats said will suppress votes for their candidates and limit their get-out-the-vote drives. The drives were led by former White House counsel Robert Bauer. An Ohio law limiting early voting from 35 days to 16 was suspended. Educational materials were produced to counter a Wisconsin law that required voters to produce photo IDs – but disallowed those used by Wisconsin college students.

Millions of Americans don't have photo IDs and many can't easily obtain them because getting the documentation to obtain the ID takes time and money. It is no coincidence that the people least likely to have proper IDs to vote are the ones that generally vote Democratic and were strong supporters of Obama in 2008: young people, the poor and minorities. As the Brennan Center reports, more than 1 in 10 eligible voters in the U.S. do not possess the kind of IDs required by the new eligibility laws. More specifically, 1 in 4 African-Americans, 1 in 6 Latinos and 1 in 5 Americans over 65 lack the requisite ID.

At least 180 restrictive voter bills have been introduced since the beginning of 2011 in 41 states. More than 30 states have changed voter laws since 2008, including seven that added requirements that voters show photo identification at their polling places. According to the Brennan Center for Justice at the New York University School of Law. "Sixteen states have passed restrictive voting laws that have the potential to impact the 2012 election" because they "account for 214 electoral votes, or nearly 79 percent of the total needed to win the presidency."

The Brennan Center points out that "prior to the 2006 election, no state required its voters to show government-issued photo ID at the polls in order to vote."

Republicans say limits on early voting are needed to cut the administrative costs of elections, and new ID requirements are necessary to defend polling place fraud.

Democrats say both types of rules are aimed at suppressing their vote. The Obama campaign was adept in 2008 at bringing first-time voters to the polls during early voting periods, and groups it targeted in 2012 – students, the elderly and the poor – are most likely not to have a government-issued photo ID.

To make matters worse, Republicans tried to repeal the public financing option for presidential campaigns in December 2011. This is the highly effective reform enacted after the the Watergate scandal. It's ironic that just as a new era of unbridled corporate and special-interest money flooded the 2012 elections, Republicans were determined to kill off the public financing option. Even as it did so, the Republican Party quietly requested and received a tidy $17.7 million in public money to pay for its presidential convention in 2012.

For decades, every major candidate opted for the subsidies and the spending limits until Congress failed to increase the federal match to account for campaign inflation. George W. Bush opted out of public money for the primary fight in his 2000 campaign, seeking a larger war chest from private donors. Barack Obama dropped it for both the primary and general elections in 2008. He vowed to fix a "broken" system – but not in 2012 as he enjoys unprecedented private financing.

General Motors, Time Warner and many other major companies have concluded that the money they were spending on political contributions is better spent elsewhere. Terry McAuliffe, a Democratic fundraiser and former party chairman who organized the single biggest fundraiser in U.S. history in the last year of the old millennium, and also helped finance President Bill Clinton's New York home, says: "There is too much money in politics." He adds: "It is a corrupting influence and we need to get rid of it." He should know – as should *We the Apathetic Maids*.

An example of this corrupting influence is the $527 million that solar energy company Solyndra received under the federal loan guarantee program before it declared bankrupcy – funds it should never have received had proper due diligence been done. It received the funds because of the lobbying efforts of Steve Spinner, an Obama fund raiser who raised more than $500,000 for the president in his 2008 campaign. Spinner helped monitor the Energy Department's issuance of $25 billion in government-backed loans to renewable energy projects like Solyndra's.

George Dubya, while supposedly resting in Crawford, Texas, in the summer of 2002 to prepare for his uncoordinated policy on how to attack Iraq and continue opening the Social Security "lockbox" wider to pay for the war and deficit, was actually fund raising. While on vacation, after the new campaign financing reform bill had passed, he attended his 49th and 50th fund raisers of 2002 and pushed his total take for the year to $110 million, prompting the *Washington Post* to editorialize that "while based in Crawford, he has raised money in 11 states. Bush is making Bill Clinton, who raised something like $50 million for his first midterm election, look like a model of restraint."

Obama and Romney in 2012 made Bush and Clinton look like amateurs.

During the 2002 midterm elections, over $900 million was spent on television advertising alone! That is more than what was spent on the 2000 presidential election. With the billions of dollars spent during the 2004,

2008 and 2012 presidential primaries and election, it is clear that unless *We the Maids* regulate the power of cash in the 21st century, what little say citizens still do have on government policy will be swept away entirely.

During Bush's tenure as governor of Texas, the state teachers' retirement fund sold several buildings without open bids, taking a $70 million loss, to a company controlled by Richard Rainwater, a prime mover behind Bush's rise to wealth. In an August 16, 1998, article in *The Houston Chronicle,* which Paul Krugman correctly suggests "should be required reading for anyone trying to understand the Bush administration," R.G. Ratcliffe summarized this and many other unusual deals thus: "A pattern emerges: When a Bush is in power, Bush's business associates benefit." How can career politicians bite the hand that feeds their political campaigns? They can't. That is why it is up to *We the Maids* to sweep in the necessary changes.

Economic theorist Adam Smith warned that a nation built "for the sole purpose of raising up a people of customers" would not be in the interest of shopkeepers but merely "a nation whose government is influenced by shopkeepers." A self-serving government of career politicians at the service of self-serving corporations and their management at the expense of *We the Apathetic People,* taxpayers, shareholders and employees.

The U.S. Supreme Court has long recognized that campaign contributions represent not only property but "free speech". They are part of the process designed to influence government. Edward Kangas, former chairman of Deloitte Touche Tohmatsu, said that the out-of-control drive by politicians for campaign donations has become "a shakedown, bordering on extortion, and even protection money."

Warren Buffet, the chairman of Berkshire Hathaway, says: "Only individuals vote – and then just once per election. Let only individuals contribute – with sensible limits per election. Otherwise, we are well on our way to ensuring that a government of the moneyed, by the moneyed, and for the moneyed shall not perish from the earth."

Nothing has really changed in America's sullied monied politics since the days of Mark Twain's 19th century or Will Rogers early 20th century. Twain's The Gilded Age and early 21st-century America are indistinguishable. Twain's education in the costs of "persuading" the politicians of his day hasn't really changed. The only difference today is the astronomically higher cost.

### The Beneficiaries

The two-party system that used to be dominated by *We the People* has declined and became irrelevant because of our apathy. The vacuum was quickly and quietly filled by political action committees created by corporations and trade associations. Political action committees that raise and contribute hundreds of millions of dollars for presidential races, Senate races and congressional campaigns. The consultants, media planners, campaign managers of all these races make millions in the process.

Criminal inquiries and harsh publicity have rained legal, financial and personal ruin on many of the people who raised the money for Bill Clinton's re-election. Yet, many of those in charge of spending the money reaped a bonanza – with several earning profits in the neighborhood of $1 million or more while avoiding criminal prosecution. This practice was carried over into the 21st century when Howard Dean's campaign manager, lobbyist Joe Trippi, made sure a firm in which he was a partner made some $700,000 in commissions for the millions of dollars of television advertising placed by the Dean campaign. Bush and Obama advisors did even better.

The American campaign finance system could not work better if it had been deliberately designed to ensure government of the rich, by the rich, and for the rich. In a misguided 1976 decision, *Buckley v. Valeo,* the Supreme Court held that Congress could not limit spending by rich Americans promoting their own candidacies. This decision was to the equalization of voting power what *Dred Scott* was to abolitionism. In the *Yale Law Review,* Jamin Raskin and John Boniface have argued that political candidates in the United States must win a "wealth primary." Candidates without enormous amounts of money, either from their own fortunes or from rich backers and special interest groups, cannot hope to win primaries – much less general elections. Indeed, the Buckley decision is one reason why more than half of the members of the Senate today are millionaires. The bias toward the rich embodied in American campaign finance practices makes quite a joke of America's democratic ideal that anyone can become president.

President Dwight D. Eisenhower said, "Politics ought to be the part-time profession of every citizen who would protect the rights and privileges of free people and who would preserve what is good and fruitful in our national heritage."

Isn't it time *We the Maids* reaffirm America's national heritage of democratic ideals that the Founding Fathers preached, practiced and advocated?

It has gotten so out of control that congressional Democrats filed a lawsuit accusing Representative Tom DeLay, the House majority whip, of engaging in extortion, racketeering and money laundering in his aggressive fund-raising for Republican candidates and causes. Post 9/11 fund raising for the congressional elections in 2002 broke all previous records. Vice President Dick Cheney raised $1 million at one dinner from 35 couples. This was after the new campaign finance reform law was passed and deliberately legislated to go into effect on November 6, one day after the 2002 midterm congressional elections so America's elected leadership could raise more money instead of governing. New York Mayor Rudy Giuliani helped House Republicans raise $5 million for the midterm elections headlining a "Salute to America's Heroes."

Alison Mitchell of *The New York Times* accurately summed up the winners of the so-called campaign finance reform legislation. "Thus far, the one clear winner in all this is George W. Bush. In 2000, Mr. Bush raised so much in $1,000 chunks that he spurned federal matching funds in the primary, allowing him to ignore spending limits. And if he signs the new bill into law, Mr. Bush should be able to raise at least twice as much in 2004. Individual donors will be able to give $2,000 to a federal candidate instead of $1,000. And if Mr. Bush's popularity ratings stay high, some Republicans predict he will be able to opt out of the public finance system altogether." No wonder Bush signed the bill quietly without any fanfare.

How about the first New York City mayoral race of the 21st century? The primary was put off because of 9/11. That did not in any way reduce the amount spent by billionaire Michael Bloomberg, who bought his way into office. He spent a record $69 million of his own money, which translates to $92.60 for each of the 744,757 votes he won. He outspent Ross Perot and Steve Forbes. The 2002 finance disclosure forms that elected officials are required to file disclosed that there are 40 millionaires in America's 100-member Senate. Is this a government of *We the People?*

### Campaign Finance Spin

The headlines heralding the passage of the "historic campaign reform victory" were just another brilliant media spin by the career politicians. The bill didn't ban soft money, it just shifted and reallocated where and how it can be contributed. The unlimited soft money banned to national parties can now go to state and local parties. In addition, individuals can now actually double the amount of their contributions from $1,000 to $2,000. Yet this has been hailed as a "reform."

The bill did not address or touch the fund raising of so-called "independent political groups" that often underwrite television advertising on particular issues, notably guns. Many election-funding experts predict that some of the soft money that went to political parties will now be rerouted to these organizations. In the 2000 presidential election, the Democratic and Republican parties raised nearly half a billion dollars in soft money, 60 per cent of which came from just 800 deep-pocketed donors. In the 2004, 2008 and 2012 presidential elections, that number jumped into the billions if not trillions as the Supreme Court essentially ruled that the sky is the limit. In fact, there are no limitations.

Let's not forget that it is soft money that is preventing the kind of desperately needed legislation *We the Maids* want swept in. Legislation for action on generic drugs, tort-reform, tobacco-control laws, new accounting rules for stock options, legalization of marijuana, national health care, and gun control. Kevin Phillips in his novel *Wealth and Democracy* reveals the destructive history and role that wealthy individuals and corporations have played in U.S. presidential politics since the founding of the nation. Phillips outlines in painstaking detail how wealth and power have worked together to perpetuate privilege – often at the expense of the national interest – and almost always at the expense of the middle and lower classes. Phillips correctly argues that America's 21st-century wealth has become a destroyer, not a builder, of the democratic process.

The Supreme Court is to be applauded for upholding the constitutionality of the McCain-Feingold Campaign Finance Law challenged by Republicans in *McConnell v. FEC*. The court did invalidate two provisions of the campaign law: the ban on campaign contributions by minors, and the requirement that parties choose between making either independent expenditures or coordinated expenditures on behalf of the candidates. The court strongly affirmed the right of the public to know who is paying for campaign advertisements, directly or through soft money, and with how much money. That all changed with *Citizens United,* which effectively busted loose the financial spigot of corporate America that has flooded the electoral process in unprecedented ways and drowned the Founding Fathers' democratic ideals – much like the floods of 2011 that inundated so many American communities and caused such catastrophic personal and financial loss to so many citizens – no different than what has happened to the political process.

In the 2000 presidential campaign, Enron gave $499,600 in contributions from individuals and $280,043 from political action committees. Those kind of contributions are still permissible under the new "campaign reform."

The new campaign finance "reform" bill plays lip service to reform. The reality is that it increases the clout of wealthy donors and the career politicians they support. It is up to *We the Maids* to sweep in true campaign finance reform if we are to ever retake control of government.

### *All About the Money*
Hong Kong has strict fund raising laws and even stricter spending limitations. Even volunteers have to comply with laws governing the amount of time and services that they can offer.

Regulations cap the amount any Hong Kong candidate can spend in an election. The amounts a candidate can spend are modest, thereby allowing anyone to run for office. Candidates running for a Geographical Constituency seat can spend from $192,000 to $320,000, depending on the size of their district. Candidates for a Functional Constituency seat can spend from $13,000 to $62,000. Again, the amount depends on the size of the district. Candidates for the Election Committee are limited to spending $20,000.

There are no limits on the amount any individual can donate to Legislative Council candidates. However, the cash or in-kind contribution received by candidates can only be used for electioneering subject to the maximum limitation on the amount a candidate can spend. Any unused contributions must be given to charitable institutions chosen by the candidates or returned to donors after the election. Isn't it time America imposed limits on how much a candidate can spend?

Money buys access to politicians, bureaucrats, lobbyists, government subsidies and business contracts all over the world. Enron was a classic example. Money buys access to all decision makers and the ability to get legislation passed to disguise corporate leaders' shortcomings or failures and enhance profitability. In turn they facilitate and generate additional money for career politicians seeking higher office. The cycle perpetuates the accumulation of mass wealth in the accounts of the few. The silent American majority can continue to be silent, or demand that the process be remade, rather than continue to be bought by the rich. *We the Apathetic People* are unknowingly and unwittingly surrendering the fundamental constitutional rights that our Founding Fathers fought to enshrine for us to global corporate America.

Human nature being what it is, especially human greed, people don't give money to politicians for nothing. It's money for something and the votes and chicks are free! Public financing of elections is an alternative option for America to consider in the New World Order of the 21$^{st}$ century. Public financing removes that influence of donors and creates a level playing field for all Americans who want to seek public office.

How deep does the American political system have to sink into the Florida swamps before *We the Apathetic People* utilize the periscopes available to us to reach out and grasp viable alternative solutions? *We the Maids* don't want a permanent governing class of career politicians whom we distrust.

So why don't we sweep them out? A placard at the Democratic Convention in Los Angeles in 2000 summed up many Americans' frustrations. "Two parties? Same government." Both the Democrats and Republicans have had their chance at reform and failed. It's now up to *We the Maids* to force them to sweep in comprehensive campaign finance reform. Collectively or through a third party – preferably both.

Political corruption exists wherever there are career politicians. Political contributions are a forwarded form of kickback. Just by passing a law that says it's alright to contribute to political campaigns and wine and dine politicians does not change the character of what it is. It is given to buy influence; a deposit on favors. Anyone who doubts it should look into how many people who have not contributed to political campaigns got any politician to return their phone call or to vote for or lobby for a piece of legislation.

Campaign finance reform is mandatory if the public, *We the People,* are truly going to be on a level playing field with corporate America and America's wealthy individuals and political action committees. The re-direction of soft money in the wake of the Enron collapse was an illusory small hop in the right direction. A good way to start the massive cleanup job that *We the Maids* face in the 21st century.

### *China-U.S. Influence Peddling*
Political fund raising goes on in Hong Kong for local candidates, American career politicians and Chinese officials. Most in strict compliance with applicable governing laws. Chief Executive Tung Chee-hwa's children donated funds to Senator John Kerry's 1996 presidential campaign. Former Minnesota Governor Jesse Ventura reminds us that under the current campaign finance laws, "Both parties have taken contributions from other countries, and then handed that money over to their candidates. Those laws that were put on the books to protect our electoral system from unfair advantage and inappropriate influence are easily sidestepped by going through the party system. The effect is just the same as if the laws weren't even on the books."

America and China try to influence each other's decision makers. Former

Democratic donor Johnny Chung provided information to congressional investigators about his dealings with top Chinese intelligence officials. He pleaded guilty to election law and tax violations and cooperated with the Justice Department's campaign finance investigation arising from the 1996 election.

Chung's FBI handler, James Smith, and his lawyer, Brian Sun, were also involved with Chinese double agent Katrina Leung, code-named Parlor Maid. Smith was her handler and Sun was her lawyer. Coincidence? Leung was charged with illegally funneling Chinese government money to Republican candidates in the '90s. She and her husband contributed $27,000 to Republican candidates in the 1992 through 1996 elections. The Parlor Maid was a well-known Republican fund raiser in Southern California. The Republican majority on the Senate Governmental Affairs Committee "chose to focus its investigation almost entirely on individuals who had raised or contributed money to the Democratic presidential campaign of 1996," Senator Joseph Lieberman correctly observed after Leung was arrested – and ultimately exonerated.

Leung was an FBI informant being handled by two FBI agents, Smith and William Cleveland, who also had ongoing affairs with her, while paying her $1.7 million to provide information on China's activities in America. Talk about America being screwed Chinese-style. I know first-hand.

She was also accused of taking classified information from agent Smith and giving it to the Chinese during their ongoing affair. Now, who screwed who? In the end, *We the Apathetic Maids* – the taxpayers – got screwed. The Leung-Smith case cost U.S. taxpayers $1.7 million paid out to Leung, not counting the related billable expenses, salaries to agents Smith and Cleveland, and the millions that was incurred in legal expenses to prosecute Leung. I can't help but conclude that the U.S. government is like a condom. A condom that stands up to inflation, halts production, destroys the next generation, protects a bunch of pricks, and gives us a sense of security while we're actually being screwed.

"Quite right," Arthur Hacker chuckled as the incredulous story of the taxpayer cost of the Leung-Smith affair was discussed at the FCC Main Bar in Hong Kong. "No wonder Bush has a national security advisor named Condom Squeeza Right," Hacker cracked as Americans walked away laughing in disbelief at what he had just said.

## Global Influence Peddling

America also tries to influence every election abroad that it considers vital to its interests. By the same token, many foreign governments try to influence the outcome of American elections in their favor. The only question is if it is done legally. After all, America has many campaign contribution laws that make giving money legal. Even by foreigners. Just comply with the rules laid down by the career politicians, who will take money from anyone to ensure their reelection. Why pick on the Chinese? Because they are easier to pick on than wealthy Americans who buy the elections legally since they have usurped the power of the people. Democracy in America is an *elite democracy* and not the *popular democracy* marketed overseas.

China-bashing is a fruitless self-destructive delusional denial that only ensures America's economic demise, courtesy of Washington career politicians who refuse to acknowledge their self-serving destructive practices to America's citizens.

Foreign governments buy U.S. career politicians in one of two ways. They can either contribute directly to the campaign coffers of political parties and career politicians through their various PACs, U.S. subsidiaries and employeys, or alternatively, buy U.S. bonds and treasuries, as the Saudis, Japanese and Chinese have so masterfully done. U.S. career politicians, their bureaucrats, lawyers and lobbyists turn to the Saudis, Japanese and Chinese and every other foreign government with surplus funds, to finance the U.S. government deficits so that career politicians don't have to raise taxes in America. Raising taxes is the only other viable alternative to finance deficits, other than running a balanced budget, of course, which would subject career politicians to a tough reelection campaign they would rather avoid! No wonder the foreign governments that buy U.S securities hold the U.S. government hostage.

The political clout these foreign governments exert over America's career politicians who are supposed to be representing *We the People* manifests itself in several ways. In the case of the Saudis, their royal dictatorship is left alone no matter how many terrorist organizations it supports. If anyone doubts that, look at the $200 billion the disgruntled Saudis withdrew from America when they started being criticized by the U.S. media and congressional leaders after 9/11. In the case of the Japanese, liberal legislation is adopted that allows their manufactured products, such as cars, stereos and cameras, to dominate our market. Legislation they would not even consider reciprocating to America because they have already fulfilled their reciprocal political obligation by buying U.S. securities. Is it any wonder the U.S. political spins demanding Japan and other countries open their markets to American goods are ignored? Who pays the price? *We the Apathetic Maids,* of course.

### Subversive Campaigns

Congress routinely appropriates tens of millions of dollars in covert and overt money to use in influencing politics abroad. The most recent 21st-century reminder was the failed coup in Venezuela aimed at ousting President Hugo Chavez. The U.S had channeled hundreds of thousands of dollars in grants to U.S. and Venezuelan groups opposed to Chavez, including the labor group whose protests led to his brief ouster. Bush administration officials confirmed the administration had prior contacts with several high-ranking coup supporters.

"At a time when we are trying to strengthen democratic institutions, you can't be around applauding the results of a coup without denouncing the means used to oust a democratically elected president," said Senator Christopher Dodd, who chaired the Foreign Relations Committee's Latin America sub-committee. Since the U.S. depends on Venezuela for 1.5 million barrels of oil a day, it is understandable.

The National Endowment for Democracy was created by Congress to do in the open what the CIA has done surreptitiously for decades, spend $30 million a year to support things like political parties, labor unions, dissident movements and the news media in dozens of countries, including China.

The endowment has financed unions in France, Paraguay, the Philippines and Panama. In the mid-1980s, it provided $5 million to Polish emigres to keep the Solidarity movement alive. It has underwritten moderate political parties in Portugal, Costa Rica, Bolivia and Northern Ireland.

It provided a $400,000 grant for political groups in Czechoslavakia that backed the election of Vaclav Havel as president in 1990. For the Nicaraguan election of 1990, it provided more than $3 million in "technical" assistance, some of which was used to bolster Violeta Barrios de Chamorro, the presidential candidate favored by the United States.

The endowment spent $1.6 million for political "institution building" programs in China, said Louisa Coan, the endowment's program officer for East Asia. That was in addition to millions of dollars spent on Chinese-language broadcasts by the Voice of America and cultural exchanges designed to improve the image of the United States in Asia.

Those are among the more benign American efforts to intervene in the domestic politics of nations around the globe, activities that have been revealed in declassified documents, memoirs and records of congressional hearings.

What blew everyone away and became a hot topic for several weeks in October 2011 at the FCC Main Bar was the revelation that Hong Kong media tycoon Jimmy Lai Chee-ying had since 2005 contributed more than HK$60 million to the pro-democracy parties, with HK$20 million, the largest single contribution, going to Catholic Cardinal Joseph Zen Ze-kiun.

Jimmy's response? He was being "consistent" with his well-known support of an open and free Hong Kong.

The revelations disclosed by Hong Kong media only added extra fuel to the fire already started by WikiLeaks' release of documents showing detailed connections between the U.S. Consulate in Hong Kong and government officials as well as local politicians, all naturally rebuked by Beijing for interfering in the city's constitutional affairs and development. The conspiracy between the local democratic movement's "traitorous actions" serving "U.S. puppet masters" was a continuous running thread and theme, no matter what side of the argument a participant took.

The U.S. was repeatedly accused, as it always is, of contravening the Vienna Convention on Consular Relations, which forbids diplomats from interfering in the internal affairs of host states.

In the 1950s, the CIA provided funds to support the campaign of President Camille Chamoun and selected parliamentary candidates in Lebanon; in the then British Guiana, the U.S. prevented the democratically elected Cheddi Jaggan from taking office between 1953 and 1964; in 1966, the CIA funded President Rene Barrientos of Bolivia to the tune of $600,000 in a successful attempt to influence the outcome of the general election; and in Nicaragua, as mentioned earlier, the U.S. spent millions to prevent the Sandanistas from being democratically elected.

William Blum, in his book *Rogue State,* provides a list of 23 countries in which the U.S. has "perverted elections" and interfered with the democratic process to ensure a favorable outcome: Italy 1948-70s, Lebanon 1950s, Indonesia 1955, Vietnam 1955, Guiana 1953-64, Japan 1958-70s, Nepal 1959, Laos 1960, Brazil 1962, Dominican Republic 1962, Guatemala 1963, Bolivia 1966, Chile 1964-70, Portugal 1974-75, Australia 1974-75, Jamaica 1976, Panama 1984, 1989, Nicaragua 1984, 1990, Haiti 1987-88, Bulgaria 1991-92, Russia 1996, Mongolia 1996, Bosnia 1998, and in Tibet, Hong Kong and China today.

Since the end of World War II, the United States, usually acting covertly through the CIA, has installed or toppled leaders on every continent, secretly supported political parties of close allies like Japan, formented coups, circulated false rumors, bribed political figures, spent billions of dollars swaying public opinion. Yet America takes great umbrage when other governments try to reciprocate the influence peddling that America encourages and welcomes.

"If the Chinese indeed tried to influence the election here, the United States is only getting a taste of its own medicine," said Peter Kornbluh, a researcher at the National Security Archive, an organization affiliated with George Washington University that monitors intelligence and foreign policy.

The CIA even supported the Tibetan exile movement and paid the Dalai Lama an annual subsidy of $180,000 a year in the 1960s, according to declassified intelligence documents. Must be what keeps the smile on his face.

It's the name of the game which most people choose to ignore. After all, as Jessie Unruh once said, "Money is the mother's milk of politics."

## Mutual Cooperation

China and the U.S. have to rebuild their relationship for the benefit of all mankind. FCC regular Michael Ceurvorst, a former diplomat who headed the politico-military unit in the American Embassy in Beijing, points out: "I doubt the Cox report's 'worst-case scenario' presumption is either realistic or good for anyone. To read a country's strategy, look to interests first, then to weapons development and deployment, not to what might have been downloaded from an unclassified computer." He continued, "China's only way forward is global, requiring regional peace and stability. The U.S. enjoys perhaps 50 years of infrastructural and educational progress beyond China's, to its advantage. In the long run, these countries are not competitors for world dominance, as many now grossly imply; we are functional allies in addressing national and global needs. Besides, that's where the money is."

Ezra Vogel, head of Harvard University's Asia Center and a former national security official, is right when he says "the glue is very deep" on the multitude of business and personal ties that bind China and the United States.

In Imperial times, Chinese officials expected foreigners to kowtow to the emperor, lying prostrate and knocking their foreheads on the ground nine times. U.S. Undersecretary of State Thomas Pickering, who went to Beijing to explain why NATO bombed the Chinese Embassy in Belgrade, was not authorized to bow that low. Any wonder the Chinese rejected his explanation? After Pickering left Beijing, a commentary in the *People's Daily* said, "China attaches importance to the development of Sino-U.S. ties, which is in line with the fundamental interests of the peoples of the two countries and beneficial to world peace, stability and development."

Each side, in effect, will seek good relations with the other purely for its own self interest. This is the way it must be in the New World Order of the 21st century if our children and grandchildren are to live in a peaceful and harmonious world.

### Remake Enronomics

Enron's bankruptcy filing at the dawn of the 21$^{st}$ century was at the time the largest corporate demise in U.S. history. The dawn got darker as light was shed on the corrupt Shakespearean evil scheme the Enron lawyers concocted for the actors on the Enron stage. A corporate play with a familiar theme in America today. Money, politics, lawyers, lobbyists, accountants, spin doctors, bankers and media all had supporting roles behind the "veil of secrecy" in the long-running "Evil Axis of Enron" in American politics in which the lead characters were played by career politicians in Washington, D.C. and numerous state capitals around the country.

The collapse of Enron was as bad if not worse than a terrorist assault on America. More people and families got hurt by the "white collar terrorists" in the corrupt and collusive Enron collapse than on 9/11. Granted the pain was not as searing because it was merely financial. Nevertheless, thousands of families lost their life savings.

Enron had been a Wall Street darling. It was considered one of the country's leading corporations. Analysts marveled over it. *Fortune* magazine voted it "most innovative" six years in a row. Enron, once ranked seventh on the *Fortune 500* list of corporations, slid in just weeks from Wall Street stardom to bankruptcy court, throwing thousands out of work.

A company with about $140 billion in revenue for the first nine months of 2001, more than seven times that reported by software giant Microsoft, filed for bankruptcy December 2, 2001. Enron and its employees were the largest contributors to President George W. Bush's campaigns over the years and they gave more money to politicians in the last election cycle of the 20th century than any other energy company. Since 1993, its employees and its chairman had donated nearly $2 million to Bush. It also donated more than $1 million to Washington career politicians during Election 2000. Like every corporate donor in America, Enron was paying protection money.

Let's not forget that Attorney General John Ashcroft had to recuse himself because of campaign contributions he received from Enron in his failed bid for the U.S. Senate.

The Bush administration during its first year in office in 2001 produced a report recommending that the federal government help India "maximize its domestic oil and gas production." Enron had a $2.9 billion power plant in India that was accused of excessive charges and repression of local protests.

Hong Kong's Ronnie Chan Chi-chung, chairman of Hang Lung Development, was an Enron board member representing America's global crony capitalism and continued love affair with Hong Kong. Chan was a speaker at the Fortune Global Forum 2001 in Hong Kong and had the audacity to lecture local businessmen on corporate governance and transparency and why local companies had to emulate the U.S. model if they wanted to be competitive globally. Really now?

The law firm of Vinson & Elkins, one of Houston's largest, was involved in structuring some of the creative partnerships. Enron's executive vice president and general counsel came from the firm, which resulted in Enron becoming the firm's top client. A report prepared by the firm concluded that Enron's practice of forming special-purpose partnerships to keep debt off its books was "creative and aggressive," but that "no one has reason to believe that it is inappropriate from a technical standpoint." Really?

The shredding of Enron financial information on the advice of counsel was clearly illegal. One doesn't have to be a lawyer to know that is blatant obstruction of justice.

Enronomics is a classic example of the intimate working relationship between D.C. Beltway career politician fund raising exercises, political contributions and payback – at the expense of *We the Apathetic Maids* – the citizen taxpayers without representation. Not just in Washington but in 24 states where they succeeded between 1997-2000 to deregulate energy so that new markets could open up to their aggressive energy trades. California got blacked out at the dawn of the new century because of deregulation and the negligence of the career politicians, who in their haste to accept campaign contributions from Enron neglected to look out for *We the Apathetic People* they are sworn to represent.

There was a clear correlation between campaign contributions and attendance and access to Vice President Dick Cheney's energy task force. Of the top 25 energy industry donors to the Republican Party before the November 2000 election, 18 corporations sent executives or representatives to meet with Cheney, the task force chairman, or members of the task force and its staff. The task force produced a report on May 17, 2001, that mapped a national energy policy that was favorable to the energy industry.

Is it any surprise then that Cheney refused to comply with *We the People's* General Accounting Office, the investigative arm of Congress, when it demanded he turn over his notes? Would it surprise anyone that he took advice from his accounting firm, Arthur Anderson, and shredded the evidence? The Andersen firm then folded its tent in disgrace in 2002 after it was found guilty on criminal charges related to its auditing of Enron.

### Campaign Reforms

It is time to build a wall of separation between check and state. U.S. presidential and congressional races are not the place for secret donors. If America is to get away from its criminal cowboy heritage and in fact be true to the ideals of the Founding Fathers, the super PACs and their shell games, whose sole purpose is to circumvent the $2,500 donation limits to presidential candidates, must be shut down. They get away with shoveling millions of dollars to political campaigns because they are supposedly independent from the candidates. Right! How many truly independent multi-million-dollar super PACs were there in the 2012 presidential campaign? Well, none. All were controlled or affiliated with a specific candidate, and usually run by the former chief aides of those same candidates.

As if that isn't bad enough, the U.S. tax code allows for nonprofits to accept secret donations and funnel the money to candidates. Republican strategist Karl Rove was the brains behind this bright idea ahead of the 2010 congressional elections, and GOP advocacy groups stampeded through this loophole to the tune of $135 million to help finance the party's landslide congressional win.

Is this something *We the Maids* want to perpetuate? The reality is that so-called free speech is not only expensive, it's very expensive and getting more so each election, and goes to the highest bidder! Doesn't take much to figure out who they are.

It's no different that what has been happening within college football and athletic organizations. Whatever it takes to get those dollars coming in and the victims of abuses be damned. Penn State reminded the world in November 2011 that lobbying is not limited to political capitals like Washington and Beijing, but wherever there is a lot of money and donors willing to part with it in exchange for who knows what?

Lobbying has not only become a new industry, but a destructive one that the Founding Fathers failed to mention or envision. They would probably vote unanimously to ban lobbyists from having access to elected officials for the sole and specific purpose of financially and economically benefiting their high-flying clients at the expense of the majority of citizens of the Republic.

Curing the disease requires a correct diagnosis of its cause: the costs of political advertising. Special interests buy access and favors by donating the money needed for expensive political advertising in the media. Elaborate schemes governing the flow of money do nothing to address this problem. Instead of imposing unworkable limits on campaign financing that leave the basic system intact, we should cut the Gordian knot of campaign corruption by simply adopting public finance laws and outlaw paid political advertising on behalf of any candidate for public office. The replacement of political advertising by publicly financed ads and free informational public service notices in the electronic and print media would level the playing field of politics and kill off the parasitic industry of media consultants and spin doctors.

An outright ban on paid political advertising and the imposition of free time requirements in the media are radical measures, absolutely necessary if we are to prevent our government from continuing to be sold to the highest bidders. Britain did it. Shouldn't we follow in the footsteps of our colonial parent? After all, we did adopt their system of government. Why not adopt the restraints on campaign contributions and limitations on spending like Hong Kong did? Why allow America to be the only campaign finance delinquent among Britain's two colonial offspring in the 21st century?

Senator John McCain, a leader of the charge for campaign finance reform, bluntly says that political contributions constitute routine corruption. Not only that, it allows certain financial givers to stay entrenched at the expense of *We the Apathetic Maids*.

McCain's warning to the Republican Party that it would "slip into the mist of history" if it failed to embrace his platform of political reform applies not only to the GOP. It also applies to the Democratic Party and the entire *United States of Apathy*.

Indeed, the separation of check and state might permit us to re-create, in modern conditions, something like the American democracy of a century ago. When Illinois voters had to choose between Abraham Lincoln and Stephen A. Douglas, they were not treated to different 30-second spots — an "image" commercial for Lincoln showing a slave in chains and then cutting to a blurry, idealized log cabin, an "attack" commercial by Douglas showing quotes from Lincoln opposing the Civil War, taken out of context to make him look like a traitor. Instead, 19th-century Illinois voters could hear Lincoln and Douglas debate for several hours.

Today, television technology permits such debates without requiring candidates to travel from town to town. Our televised public debates, sponsored by nonpartisan bodies like the League of Women Voters, represent the best part of our campaign system; the paid political advertisements are the worst. The endless privately financed advertisements should go, the debates remain, be expanded and streamed into every civics and political science class in America – from grammar school through college. Town hall meetings, public forums, civics classes in all schools, and strict limitations on financial contributions to candidates for public office must be actively encouraged by *We the Apathetic People* in the 21st century.

I had lunch with Stanley Black in November 2010, just after President Obama's commission on deficit spending failed to come up with a plan. He gave me an e-mail he had received that morning that best summed up taxpayers' disgust. "Here, read this," he said. "You'll enjoy what it says."

I did. So much so that I am sharing it with you: "Alan Simpson, former Republican Senator from Wyoming, Co-Chair of Obama's deficit commission, calls senior citizens the Greediest Generation as he compared Social Security to a milk cow with 310 million teats." Here's a response in a letter from Patty Myers in Montana. I think she is a little ticked off. She also tells it like it is!

"Hey Alan, let's get a few things straight. 1. As a career politician, you have been on the public dole for FIFTY Years. 2. I have been paying Social Security taxes for 48 Years (since I was 15 years old. I am now 63.) 3. My Social Security payments, and those of millions of other Americans, were safely tucked away in an interest bearing account for decades until you political pukes decided to raid the account and give OUR money to a bunch of zero ambition losers in return for votes, thus bankrupting the system and turning Social Security into a Ponzi scheme that would have made Bernie Madoff proud. 4. Recently, just like Lucy & Charlie Brown, you and your ilk pulled the proverbial football away from millions of American seniors nearing retirement and moved the goalposts for full retirement from age 65 to age 67. NOW, you and your shill commission are proposing to move the goalposts YET AGAIN. 5. I, and millions of other Americans, have been paying into Medicare from Day One, and now you morons propose to change the rules of the game. Why? Because you idiots mismanaged other parts of the economy to such an extent that you need to steal money from Medicare to pay the bills. 6. I, and millions of other Americans, have been paying income taxes our entire lives, and now you propose to increase our taxes yet again. Why? Because you incompetent bastards spent our money so profligately that you just kept on spending even after you ran out of money. Now, you come to the American taxpayers and say you need more to pay off YOUR debt. To add insult to injury, you label us "greedy" for calling "bullshit" on your incompetence. Well Captain Bullshit, I have a few questions for YOU.

"1. How much money have you earned from the American taxpayers during your pathetic 50-year political career? 2. At what age did you retire from your pathetic political career, and how much are you receiving in annual retirement benefits from the American taxpayers? 3. How much do you pay for YOUR government provided health insurance? 4. What cuts in YOUR retirement and healthcare benefits are you proposing in your disgusting deficit reduction proposal, or, as usual, have you exempted yourself and your political cronies?

"It is you, Captain Bullshit, and your political co-conspirators called Congress who are the "greedy" ones. It is you and your fellow nutcases who have bankrupted America and stolen the American dream from millions of loyal patriotic taxpayers. And for what? Votes. That's right sir. You and yours have bankrupted America for the sole purpose of advancing your pathetic political careers. You know it, we know it, and you know that we know it.

"And you can take that to the bank, you miserable son of a bitch.

"If you like the way things are in America, delete this. If you agree with what a fellow Montana citizen Patty Myers says, PASS IT ON!!!!"

Jessie Unruh was right when he said, "Money is the mother's milk of politics." The question is, which udder should it come from? The corporate udder of wealthy American corporations and their directors, officers and employees, or the public udder? The public one is much better, fairer and minimizes favoritism and career politicians. Public financing of political campaigns should become an American reality in the 21st century. Every taxpayer should be charged up to $5 annually on their tax return for state and local campaigns and $3 for federal campaigns.

Non-taxpaying citizens could have the same amount deducted from their annual Social Security payments or social benefit payments from government or charitable organizations. Corporations should also be required to contribute to the "public finance" coffers. The amount contributed should be based on a low percentage, say 1% of company earnings.

What's wrong with public financing of political campaigns? What's wrong with having every citizen and resident contribute a set amount each year that is paid with either their taxes or other means to fund, national, state and local campaigns? It would be painless, inexpensive and would ensure accountability to the masses, *We the People,* rather than the corporate elite. That is the public udder I am referring to. We make sure all elected officials suck up to *We the People* – and not just the corporate elite!

An example of what bad money managers politicians are is the California story of the longtime treasurer to many career politicians, Kinde Durkee. She was arrested in September 2011 in a major federal fraud case that sent shock waves through the Democratic Party establishment. Durkee was accused of stealing millions of dollars from her clients, all prominent California Democrats. They included Sen. Dianne Feinstein, Rep. Loretta Sanchez, state Sen. Ted Lieu and hundreds of other career politicians. Durkee controlled more than 400 bank accounts.

She was able to survive and get away with it for so long because she represented so many career politicians.

"Politics in both parties is an old boys and old girls club, and most of the candidates ... figure if everyone else is using Durkee, she must be all right," said Dan Schnur, director of the Jesse M. Unruh Institute of Politics at USC. "If you were the only campaign thinking about hiring a person with a record, you might think twice about it, but there is safety in numbers."

*Franking*

You don't have to just look at political advertising. How about the supposed public service communications known as "franking" that Americans are supposed to get from their public officials? Well guess what? The congressmen and senators are using their franking privileges for their own personal political gain and reelection as "direct mail pieces." Naturally, at taxpayers' expense.

George Will has repeatedly addressed the franking abuses. He points out that House members did not exhaust all their energies on mailings in 1991, a typical franking year. In one two-day period in the spring of 1992, members of the House churned out 58 million pieces of franked mail. By the summer of 1992, Congress's franking excesses had cost lawmakers the support of a normally sympathetic voice, that of the newspaper *Roll Call*. That paper's patience snapped when the editors examined reports of franking in the first quarter of 1992. These reports, said a *Roll Call* editorial, "reveal that we have been naïve" and that scores of members are using the franking privilege mainly to win votes rather than for more public-spirited communications.

One awaits the great awakening when *Roll Call* recognizes that most members are using the whole government mainly to win votes. But let us stay with what has shocked *Roll Call*. In the first quarter of 1992 members spent $10.7 million, an increase of 83 percent that *Roll Call* called astounding. The difference between 1991 and 1992? The former was not an election year. *Roll Call*, slow to anger but splendid when aroused, thundered: "Members cannot be trusted with the frank under current terms." Never could. Matters only got worse as the decade ended and the 21st century dawned. What are *We the Maids* waiting for? Frank them!

### *Preferred or Proportional Representation*
The "Magnificent Seven" – The Founding Fathers – didn't design a system for the 21st century. It didn't give every American the right to vote. Only white landowners and taxpayers. Women didn't get the right to vote until early in the 20th century. African-Americans couldn't vote until after the civil rights movement of the 1960s. Today all Americans 18 and over are eligible to vote. Yet most don't. Innovations developed to expand participation such as absentee ballots have exposed the system's vulnerability to manipulation and fraud. Especially in the last presidential election of the 20th century in Florida.

The United States is one of the few democracies in the world that has non-binding straw polls and retains the archaic plurality system for electing legislators. The United States inherited the plurality system from 18th-century Britain. Australia and New Zealand have joined most other First World democracies in moving toward preferential or proportional representation; growing numbers support scrapping plurality elections in favor of proportional representation in Britain and Canada as well. Why aren't *We the Apathetic People* doing the same in America?

Under the plurality system—sometimes known as "first past the post" or "winner take all"—a representative is elected by a plurality of votes in a single district The drawbacks of this system are obvious. A candidate who gets 40 percent of the vote, as long as he gets more votes than any other candidate, can be elected—even though 60 percent of the voters voted against him. In what sense is that 60 percent majority represented by the candidate thus elected? Even worse, the plurality system encourages a two-party monopoly, because votes for third parties, witness Ralph Nader in the 2000 elections, are wasted. Finally, plurality systems reward the gerrymandering of single-member districts to give parties or, in the United States, particular racial groups, built-in advantages.

San Francisco is not only in the forefront of the sexual revolution, but the political revolution as well. It has enacted a voting method known as ranked choice. It allows voters to make three selections. They mark their favorite candidate in the first column, their second-most favorite in the second column and the third in the third column. First-choice votes are then tabulated and if there's a majority winner from just those first-choice votes, then there is a winner and the second and third columns are ignored. But if there's less than a majority, the candidate with the least number of votes is actually eliminated from the contest and not included in the counting. The second-choice candidates are then looked at and added into the pile of votes for the remaining candidates. This exercise is repeated until there is a majority winner. The voter needs to mark a different candidate in each column to fully participate in the ranked-choice method.

Such a system would have allowed Ralph Nader votes to be reassigned to Gore and Buchanan votes to Bush as they would be the most likely second choices. A more rational and appropriate system for 21st-century America?

John Stuart Mill advocated the system of the single transferable vote, a form of proportional representation.

"Over himself, over his own body and mind, the individual is sovereign," Mill reminds us!

Proportional representation is free from the defects of the "winner take all" system. Seats are allocated among the parties on the basis of the proportion they receive of the total vote.

Proportional representation encourages multiparty democracy, because it permits even small parties to elect representatives. In order to discourage tiny, extremist parties, most democracies with proportional representation now require that parties pass a minimum threshold of the total vote, usually 5%.

In the United States, proportional representation would permit us to do away with partisan and racial gerrymandering while at the same time increasing the political options as new parties formed. This would make it easier for members of minority groups – not only racial, but religious and cultural – to elect at least one member of multimember delegations, thus assuring that all active minorities are represented. Proportional representation achieves the goal of the Voting Rights Act – greater voting power for African-Americans, Asian-Americans and Hispanic-Americans – but by color-blind, non-intrusive means that benefit members of numerical minorities in general.

Good recent examples are in California, Germany, America, Switzerland and Russia. The California Supreme Court ruled in October 2011 that the new state Senate voting districts drawn up by a citizens commission should be upheld and rejected two challenges to the redistricting boundaries brought by the Republican Party seeking to undo the work of the California Citizens Redistricting Commission. California voters took the redistricting task away from the Legislature and created the citizens commission to do it every 10 years, after the census, to adjust for population changes.

In Germany, the Pirate Party won 8.9 percent of the Berlin state parliament seats in September 2011. The single-issue party – Internet freedom – made up of computer nerds and aging hippies, blew away the political pundits who considered it an unelectable fringe. Watching its elected members, one in a Captain America T-shirt and others in hooded sweatshirts in front of the imposing former Prussian state parliament building, was a refreshing change from the stuffy career politicians in their empty suits.

The state election in Berlin was full of surprising results. The pro-business Free Democrats, Chancellor Angela Merkel's coalition partners in the federal parliament, crashed and burned again, receiving less than 2 percent of the vote. That was well below the 5 percent needed to remain in the statehouse. The Green Party continued to build on its recent successes and may well become one of the governing parties in Berlin.

While online privacy and data protection may seem incredibly narrow, even irrelevant, to older voters, for young people who often spend half their waking hours online, much of it on social networking sites where they share their most intimate moments, it is anything but a small issue. The Pirates' call for complete transparency in politics resonates powerfully with a generation disillusioned by the American case for war in Iraq and galvanized by WikiLeaks' promise to put an end to secrecy.

The Pirates have promised to use online tools to give party members unprecedented power to propose policies and determine stances, in what they call "liquid democracy," a form of participation that goes beyond simply voting in elections.

The first Pirate Party was started in Sweden in 2006. I agree with its founder, Rick Falkvinge, who said while celebrating the Berlin electoral victory with his fellow pirates: "Today's cadre of politicians is missing out on asking some very relevant questions about the future."

Thanks to the interactive nature of the Internet, "you don't have to take these laws being read to you," he said. "You can stand up, stand tall and write the laws yourself."

I couldn't agree more. I am even more delighted to see Americans Elect, a well-funded "virtual third party," emerge in America. The party is a collection of Democrats, Republicans and independents who say they are fed up with the polarization that has poisoned American politics. The party, last I checked before going to press, was well on its way to collecting enough signatures to qualify in every one of the 50 American states.

A presidential election is a good place for Americans Elect to start in order to get national attention. But the party should focus more on state's rights and state elections that can redefine and restructure the federal government the way the Founding Fathers intended.

Switzerland, that stodgy conservative white Christian nation, is probably the world's most direct democracy. It takes fringiness to a whole new level because any citizen over 18 can start a political party. To get on the ballot for Parliament's lower house, all a party needs are 100 to 400 voter signatures, depending on the size of the canton. One of my favorite Swiss parties is the Anti PowerPoint Party, whose stated mission is to advocate for those souls "who, every month, are obliged to be present during boring presentations in companies, universities or at other institutions, and who had up to now no representation in politics."

Another favorite is the Auto Party, organized in 1985 to raise Swiss speed limits and hold down traffic fines.

A party I can personally relate to is Subitas, formerly known as the Men's Party, whose cause is equal rights for men. Its president, Alfredo E. Stussi, was unable to see his daughter for many years after separating from her mother.

But my all-time favorite is the Animals' Party Switzerland, launched "to give animals a voice in politics."

One party, or its philosophies, that has a very high probability of going global, either as a party or a religion, is the Church of Kopimism, whose central dogma is that file sharing is sacred. Kopimism comes from the Swedish spelling of the words "copy me."

"Our angle is not to mock religion," said Isak Gerson, a philosophy student who helped found the church in 2010 and bears the title chief missionary. "We recall that Christianity and the Gospels with their collection of little stories are examples of copying."

Human nature in its humanity and belief, believes copying is a religious right that should only be tithed and not charged for. That is a decision *We the Apathetic Maids* have to make and sweep in at home first – before it is too late.

Why shouldn't Americans, Chinese and every global citizen for that matter be able to do the same? Even the docile vodka-soaked Russians are waking up to this option and challenging Vladimir Putin and his United Russia one-party Kremlin politics.

Proportional representation could be easily adopted for city councils, county commissions and state legislatures simply by making changes in state law. Furthermore, although many people believe mistakenly that the winner-take-all plurality elections and their inevitable result, the two-party monopoly, are enshrined in the U.S. Constitution, nothing more than an act of Congress would be required to establish the election of members of the House of Representatives by proportional representation.

Article 1, Section 4 of the Constitution provides: "The Times, Places and Manner of holding Elections for Senators and Representatives shall be prescribed in each State by the Legislature thereof; *but the Congress may at any time by Law make or alter such Regulations,* except as to the Places of [choosing] Senators" (emphasis added).

### Managed Democracy

Russia's paramount leader Putin and his United Russia party are being rejected by the people who believe Putin & Company stole the 2011 election.

Putin's response? What he has done is necessary as the Western model of democracy has failed and his new "Managed Democracy" is a more practical and viable alternative. Putin is not alone in his belief that today's Western democracy model is not the best form of government. China's leaders agree.

One can argue that America's Founding Fathers did too. After all, they made it clear they were establishing a republic, not a democracy, and designed a myriad of bells and whistles to constrain the popular will of *We the People*.

After all, if the people are rational and divinely endowed with rights, and all knowledge is at their fingertips, why shouldn't they be allowed to decide on everything?

In the Athens of old, then like now, ever-increasing popular participation in politics led to the rule by demagoguery. Public fervor whipped up by Alcibiades' oratory – much like President George W. Bush's pronouncements after 9/11 – sent its fleet on that fateful mission to Syracuse, and its defeat there by Sparta started Athens' decline – just as Bush's wars in Afghanistan and Iraq have done to America today.

By any measure, it can be effectively argued that America today is a constitutional republic in name only, and an Athenian democracy in practice. Elected career politicians have no mind of their own and respond only to the whims of their financial backers and public opinion for reelection; with the abundance of information and one of the most efficient communication systems known to mankind, *We the Apathetic Maids* believe we know everything; special interests manipulate us into voting for ever lower taxes and higher government spending, even supporting self-destructive wars.

The difference between America and China and Russia is not between democracy and authoritarianism, but between two fundamentally different outlooks on political systems. America sees democracy as an end in itself, while China and Russia see any political system as a means to an end.

Eric Li, a venture capitalist in Shanghai who writes thought-provoking editorial opinions comparing U.S.-China political philosophies and systems, asks in one of his columns whether the world is ready to switch from the West's "Globilization 1.0" model, based on one set of rules for all, to the more pluralistic version championed by China.

The bottom line, it really doesn't matter which system or model one prefers. The reality is that the problems *We the Apathetic People* face are global and affect everyone, including Americans and Chinese. The question is, what are the global political and economic solutions? The answer to both questions is a global political party, carefully balancing the historical, cultural and religious differences of each country.

## No Labels

The U.S presidency and Congress are in need of fixing. No Labels is a bipartisan group of former advisers to presidents and would-be presidents who have drafted what they call a plan to make the presidency work better. Basically, unshackling the president to be more powerful and more accountable that would also fix government. Like most bipartisan groups these days, their expensive advice at taxpayers cost is ignored.

One would hope that their report would have at least prompted a debate about the dysfunction in Washington. It didn't.

What is it going to take for *We the Apathetic Maids* to start a real dialogue about what our New Order should be?

Government can and must make a positive difference in people's lives. It has in the past and must again in the future. It is up to *We the Apathetic Maids* to wake up and sweep out the career politicians stopping it from happening.

It is important to remember that nowhere in the Constitution is there any mention of a two-party system, nor are there any rules set out for nominating presidential candidates. It's hard to imagine that the Founding Fathers would think our current system is working.

The polls show that purple America is in broader agreement on most of the issues of the day than are our polarized Democratic and Republican parties and their career politicians. But we are burdened by a system that finances and favorably regulates a bullhorn controlled by a conservative minority at the expense of *We the Apathetic Majority* who have remained silent.

The time has come for the apathetic silent majority to speak up, demand change and lead the charge for change.

"We always want the best man to win an election. Unfortunately, he never runs," Will Rogers reminded us almost a century ago. Why not? Isn't it time they do?

## The Office of...

The office of the president and the officeholder have been mortally wounded, thanks to the partisan Congress and media. The president and the office have lost their stature, power and ability to effectively govern and represent the people. *We the People* should consider replacing the presidency and its historically sexually active men with an effective president or chief executive – preferably asexual. After all, the presidency is the executive branch. Select the best-qualified candidate regardless of party affiliation.

Jonathan Alter points out that "In this century alone, Warren Harding conceived an illegitimate child in a White House broom closet; Franklin Roosevelt took up with his old mistress Lucy Rutherford; John F. Kennedy frolicked with naked women in the White House swimming pool. On the honesty front, Dwight Eisenhower lied about the U-2 downing, Lyndon Johnson lied about the Gulf of Tonkin incident and Ronald Reagan lied about trading arms for hostages. It goes without saying that Richard Nixon lied repeatedly. And those are just the bald-faced ones, each arguably worse than dishonesty about sex. Bill Clinton might be the first to lie under oath, but he's also the first to be made a target under oath – to answer questions many Americans believe should not be asked."

The divisive constitutional coup d'etat that eventually saw George W. Bush limp into the White House only magnified the weakness and irrelevance of the presidency. His conduct in office confirmed it.

The presidency, notwithstanding the ideological and practical expansion of its role, regardless of who holds it, or what party they belong to, will no longer be trusted again. In our interactive cyber media dominated New World Disorder, the current and future generations of American voters learned in 1998, 2000, 2004, 2008 and 2012 not to trust what the president says or how he wins the White House. How can Americans, knowing this, get through the 21st century with the highest national office in the land not being trusted?

Presidential candidates lie through their teeth. Bush, Gore and Kerry are recent examples. They lie about each other, the issues, facts, about their past and what they will do if elected. Always have, always will. Once in office they never deliver on the promises that got them elected. So why bother subjecting ourselves to costly doubletalk, lies and deception disguised as presidential elections that only benefit political consultants and financial contributors and political cronies? A millennium example is the promises repeatedly made by Gush-Bore about maintaining a balanced budget. When Bush came to the White House, he inherited a $270 billion annual surplus. In eight years in office, he ran up a deficit of almost $5 trillion! He bushwhacked *We the Apathetic People*. What are the benefits to the silent majority of citizen-taxpayers? In any other profession or occupation, liars get punished or banned. Isn't it time to do the same with the presidency?

The low esteem with which career politicians seeking federal political office are held was best exemplified by filmmaker Michael Moore in election 2000.

"Candidates make promises and go to Washington and do nothing. We believe a potted plant could do no worse," he said while campaigning for his congressional candidate, a ficus tree!

The mudslinging and "dirty tricks" that presidential candidates and their parties practice is disgusting in this day and age. Whether it's the Willie Hortons, rats or my favorite, a flyer to Americans in Hong Kong from the 2000 Presidential Election Campaign urging Republicans and independents to vote on November 7 and Democrats to vote November 8. A day after the election! Is it any wonder absentee ballots are suspect? The fact that Republicans want to count absentee ballots from the military without postmarks is another issue.

Honest, bright, competent straight talkers like Bill Bradley, John McCain and Howard Dean can't make it in the current political system. For candidates like them to win, third parties or movements must be encouraged and the Electoral College must be eliminated or restructured. Alternatively, like the Hong Kong model, the Office of the President has to be replaced with the Office of the Chief Executive.

This scenario actually was staged in 2011 when Greece and Italy swept out career politicians who bankrupted those countries and replaced them with seasoned supposedly apolitical technocrats. These unelected technocrats were brought in to solve Greece and Italy's fiscal woes. Every country with democratically elected politicians needs technocrats to properly execute the democratically elected officials' decisions. CEOs who run the country by implementing the democratically elected bodies laws and policies.

Former President Gerald Ford lamented that the Clinton scandal and the failure to resolve it quickly with a bipartisan censure "had an adverse effect on the presidency." So did Ford's pardon of Nixon, and just about everything else.

Should America adopt a system similar to Hong Kong's? The Hong Kong Basic Law states that the second chief executive will be chosen by an Electoral Committee of 1,200 people, in turn selected by the voters of Hong Kong. The Electoral College selects a chief executive rather than president. The revised Electoral College for America proposed later in this chapter can be representative of *We the People* without wasting time and money electing a dysfunctional president. Better yet, eliminate the Electoral College and let the people elect the president directly.

If America decides that the president should be replaced by a chief executive, he can be paid like any CEO. In fact, even the president should probably be paid more to attract a broader cross section of candidates. Hong Kong offers a good model. With a population of 7 million, the chief executive earns $800,000 a year. In the United States, with a population of more than 300 million, the president earns a mere $400,000. Hong Kong pays government officials on a scale based on private industry. Some earn more than the president of the United States. The high salaries are justified to attract a competent and clean government. In Hong Kong, the colonial governor earned more than the British prime minister and the chief executive now earns more than double that of the president of the United States. What is wrong with this picture? Does it make sense in this day and age?

The U.S. presidency has been disgraced. Not just the holders of the office, but their potential successors and acting CEOs, the vice presidents. CEO Dick Cheney returned to his job as vice president with a new heart pacemaker to promote the energy strategy he put together with his cronies at Enron. Does America have to be paced by a CEO with a pacemaker? Don't *We the People* deserve better? It actually gets better. Most people have forgotten that before 9/11, the Bush administration was under intense fire and criticism from its own Republican Party, the press and the polls because the Bushies were being "arrogant, sloppy, unethical and out of touch."

"We're not unconcerned," said Mary Matalin, Cheney's chief political aide at the time. "We're not so inflexible or blind that we're like Stepford wives and husbands marching like lemmings over a cliff. What we are doing now is recalibrating."

Well, it looks to me like the lemmings went over the cliff and didn't know it.

So let's get real in the 21st century and get back to our Founding Fathers' constitutional basics. How about *We the Maids* sweeping in a Chief Executive Act or eliminate the electoral college and let the people elect the president directly? The chief executive, as proposed later, would be indirectly elected by those directly elected by the people such as electors, mayors, governors and other representative bodies, be they racial, sexual, ethnic, business, trade, professional and labor that *We the People* select. A chief executive with a Congress made up of part-time politicians, with most powers restored back to the states where they belong, and campaigns publicly financed, would give *We the People* a better chance at improving our lives. America's "beacon of hope" would finally actually be rekindled. The elimination of the electoral College is a better option.

### Rich Pardons

Article II of the Constitution gives the president broad and unreviewable power to grant "Reprieves and Pardons" for all offenses against the United States. The U.S. Supreme Court has ruled that the pardon power is "without limit." The pardons President Bill Clinton gave Marc Rich, his partner Pincus Green and cocaine dealer Carlos Vignali clearly are rich pardons bought by wealthy contributors. Pardons for money. Pardons for campaign contributions. Pardons for donations to a presidential library. Pardons for bribes. Pardons that only further disgraced the presidency. Money not only buys access but like toilet paper wipes away well-heeled criminal constipated convictions. The president's clemency power has traditionally been soiled by money. That is unless you have access because you are a family member or friend. That was brought home by Clinton's brother and brother- in-law.

Like everything else in Washington, presidential pardons are sold to the highest bidders. They are sold to political contributors, their lawyers and lobbyists. All modern presidents do it.

To impanel a grand jury to investigate the pardons was just another wasteful and vengeful Republican vendetta against Clinton, which only prolonged the bipartisan cultural political civil war into the 21$^{st}$ century. A long overdue and cost-effective solution for the new century is for *We the Maids* to sweep in new relevant amendments to the Constitution.

### *Constitutional Amendment*
The only major structural change in the Constitution in more than two centuries was that effected by the 17th Amendment, which provided for the direct election of senators, who had formerly been elected by state legislatures whose members auctioned off senatorial seats to corporations and trusts. The 17th Amendment did not alter the malapportionment built into the Senate; it merely gave small-state populations, instead of small-state legislatures, an unfair weighted vote in federal policy making.

Mark Twain, in *Banquet for a Senator,* points out that Senator William Andrews Clark of Montana "began his national political career in 1889 when he was sent to the Senate by the legislature of the newly admitted state. After a lively hearing, the Senate Committee on Elections refused to admit him, on the grounds that his seat cost him $431,000 in bribes, distributed among 35 state legislators." Twain goes on to point out that William Penn "bought the whole state of Pennsylvania from them (native Americans) and paid for it like a man – paid $40 worth of glass beads and a couple of second-hand blankets. Bought the whole state for that. Why, you can't buy its legislature for twice the money now."

That weighted vote grows heavier with each passing year. Thanks to Senate malapportionment, 16 percent of the nation can elect half the Senate – and thwart the senators representing the 84 percent of the public who live in the

25 most populous states. Does America really need the Senate in the 21st century? It is outdated, favoring the few Americans in the small states at the expense of the majority.

After the American Revolution, the desire of the Founding Fathers for good governance led to the emergence of the Constitution in 1787. The Senate was set up as a deliberate body to restrain the conflicts of democracy. Founded on the basis of the ancient Roman Senate, the U.S. Senate was also largely influenced by the British parliamentary system. Prior to the Constitution, the second Congress focused on writing the Declaration of Independence. However, in 1777, the government recommended a plan known as the Articles of Confederation, which divided power between national authority and the states and which became effective in 1781.

A central debate that arose during the formation of the Senate was how each state would be represented. James Madison initiated the Virginia Plan. It proposed a bicameral system, in which states were represented proportionately by population in both branches of Congress. This plan was countered by William Paterson's New Jersey Plan. The New Jersey Plan emphasized a bicameral system where there would be equal representation of each state. On July 16, 1787, the Great Compromise was enacted to address the controversies of the Virginia and New Jersey plans. Each state was to have equal representatives in the Senate, unlike the House of Representatives, where seats are allotted based on population.

Interestingly, before 1816, there were no permanent Senate committees; rather, there were small "select committees" created on an ad-hoc basis to fulfill specific legislative needs. The first two senators, Robert Morris and William Maclay, were elected September 30, 1788 by the Pennsylvania legislature. Maclay is particularly significant because he was the only senator who kept a diary. At the time all Senate sessions were held behind closed doors. In 1789, the Senate's first order of business was to meet jointly with the House to count the electoral ballots that officially gave George Washington his presidential victory. By 1816, the Senate decided to create permanent committees with five members each to ensure that immediate legislative proposals as well as ongoing problems receive immediate attention. Something today's Senate has forgotten.

As the Senate gained political and legislative power in directing state legislative operations, it became necessary to establish a direct popular election that allowed citizens of the states to elect their senators. By the early 20th century, the legislatures of as many as 29 states had developed referendums that allowed senatorial elections by citizens. This campaign to make senators more responsive to the people propelled the ratification of the 17th Amendment in 1913 that instituted the popular election of senators by the people.

The Senate met in secret until 1794. The initial rules were based on the belief that the role of the Senate was "special" and included advising the Executive Branch, which therefore constrained it to conducting its sessions behind closed doors. The Senate's executive sessions to consider nominations and treaties were not opened to the public until 1929. Since 1929, the Senate has held 54 sessions behind closed doors, generally for reasons involving national security.

Today a new term begins every six years for each of the two senators from all 50 states who are all elected by popular vote.

### The Senatorial Robber Barons

In establishing the Senate, the idea was to have people of high intelligence, integrity and demeanor who could defend the rights of the people of the United States as defined in the Declaration of Independence. Sadly, this criteria for qualification changed rapidly over time and senators became focused on the acquisition of personal wealth and fame at the expense of *We the Apathetic Maids*. It should come as no surprise that they supported bills and legislation that favored those who aided their acquisition of endless wealth.

The term "robber baron" dates back to the 12th century. It is used to describe ill-gotten wealth through unscrupulous exploitation of resources and people or improper government influence which is usually to the detriment of the citizens – *We the Maids*. This American tradition goes back to the early years of the 19th century with the likes of J.P. Morgan, Cornelius Vanderbilt, John D. Rockefeller, Andrew Carnegie, Philip Armour, Jay Gould and Andrew Mellon.

The irony is, most of the fortunes amassed by these cold-hearted industrialists was done so legally. It was legal because they collaborated with and had the support of government bodies and the courts – collaboration that was paid for. The beginning of legal compromise for financial gain between the Congress and robber barons started with the construction of the Union Pacific Railroad. A good example of how business was done is that of Daniel Drew and Jay Gould, who spent $1 million to bribe the New York legislature to legalize their issue of $8 million in "watered stock" on the Erie Railroad. This kind of crony political capitalism became the norm of doing business with government until the mid-20th century when Franklin Roosevelt's New Deal put an end to the robber barons' traditional way of doing business.

More recently, *The Daily Tech Summit* reports that the Commercial Felony Streaming Act passed by the Senate that will "imprison anyone who infringes content through streaming for financial gain" was paid for by the bill's supporters with $86 million in campaign contributions to senators campaigns for the six years leading up to the bill's passage. That is just the way business has always been done in the Senate. Senators sponsor legislation that is financially beneficial to their campaign benefactors. It takes money, lots of it, to sponsor legislation. Hence the system still revolves around modern billionaire robber barons.

A constitutional amendment to abolish the Senate can be made in one of two ways as prescribed in Article V of the Constitution. First, an amendment can be proposed by Congress with a two-thirds majority vote in the Senate as well as in the House or a constitutional convention can be called by two-thirds of the state legislatures. In either scenario, three-quarters of the state governments – 38 states – must then ratify the amendment for it to become part of the Constitution. Granted, it is a monumental constitutional and political undertaking.

An amendment can repeal, modify, or supersede a previous amendment. That is what happened with Prohibition. Prohibition was terminated as a result of the ratification of Amendment XXI that repealed Amendment XVIII that enacted Prohibition. That must have been one hell of a party across America. A country united in spirit.

The reality is that the U.S. Senate today is made up of frustrated people who have the illusion of power that can be taken away overnight by any one of them who changes their mind or switches party or loyalty to a political faction within the party. Political entrepreneurship has never had a more fertile field.

"You could put Buddha, Mohammed or Jesus Christ all together and let them try to run the Senate, and I'm not sure they could do any better," said former Senator Chuck Hagel of Nebraska. So why bother?

Marshall Wittman, a Hudson Institute analyst, said the divided Senate is a land of opportunity for a "resourceful senator with a national following and a great passion." Is this what America is about? A land of opportunity for wealthy career politicians?

The Bush administration filled only 11 percent of its most senior government positions in its first six months in office. The result was that the U.S. lost its seats on the U.N. human rights and drug control commissions while much of the rest of America's business was put on hold. Transition experts and Senate veterans say the appointment process has become too unwieldy to allow for a quick transition. Why? Is this any way for a government in the 21st century to be run? It happens because of the politically motivated delays the Senate creates and imposes in approving presidential appointees. The approval process has become just another partisan trade-off station for career politicians and their monied constituents seeking favors.

If the Constitution is not amended, by the middle of the 21st century a tiny, almost exclusively white minority of the U.S. population, living in the largely empty states of the continental interior, may control a majority of the seats in the Senate.

America has become "like a wife or a lover you want to throw out the window in order to rescue them," Norman Mailer pointed out.

### Unicameral System

Nebraska is the only state that has a unicameral system – a single-house governing system. The home state of Warren Buffet, like the billionaire oracle from Omaha himself, is solvent. Unlike the federal government and most of the other 49 states that are broke.

Nebraska, like all states of the union, started out with a bicameral system. It wasn't until 1934 that the unicameral legislature amendment was passed and then implemented in 1937. Senator George Norris, a New Deal Republican who served from 1913-1943, was a major proponent of the change. He argued that a bicameral system, modeled on the British Parliament, represented a system of aristocratic power whereas a unicameral system could prevent corruption and increase transparency. An additional benefit of implementing a unicameral system is that it cut government costs by decreasing career politicians from 133 to 43. Today there are just 49. Also unique to Nebraska is its nonpartisan voting system, which was an addition to the unicameral amendment.

A number of countries have instituted unicameral systems to replace bicameral arrangements. New Zealand went unicameral in 1951, abolishing the rubber-stamp upper house whose members had always been appointed rather than elected. Iceland, Sweden and Peru have gone unicameral. A unicameral system can speed up legislation, increase accountability (since only one chamber is responsible for legislation), and costs less. Maybe this is something that America and the 49 bicameral states should be taking a closer look at.

### Hereditary Democracy

America has become more like Japan, instead of the other way around, when one considers that it was America that imposed constitutional democracy on Japan after World War II. The confusion surrounding Bill Clinton's successor – the 2000 Bush-Gore mess – is similar to what happens in Japan. A biproduct of Prime Minister Keizo Obuchi's coma was the lack of a clearcut hierarchy for succession in Japan. It's up to the prime minister to appoint anyone he pleases! Even a whisper while in a coma. Japan has had more than 15 prime ministers in 20 years. Talk about a samurai geisha culture.

Almost a quarter of the seats in Japan's general elections are won by candidates who "inherit" constituencies from family members. Yuki Obuchi, 26, ran and won the seat left vacant by the death of her father, former Prime Minister Obuchi, who had won his own father's seat in 1963 when he too was 26. Prime Minister Junichiro Koizumi is the scion of a political family, following his grandfather and father into national politics.

India's dominant ruling political party, the Congress Party, has been controlled by the Gandhi-Nehru family dynasty for most of the country's recent history. The Gandhi family, which has no link to independence hero Mahatma Gandhi, stems from first post-independence Prime Minister Jawaharlal Nehru, who was succeeded by his daughter Indira Gandhi and grandson Rajiv Gandhi, whose wife Sonia took over the party after his assassination and has now passed power on to their son Rahul. Politics and its benefits is a family business, and not only in India.

Robert Vadra, the businessman husband of Priyanka Gandhi and son-in-law of India's most powerful woman, Congress Party President Sonia Gandhi, had a net worth of $100,000 when he got married but is now worth more than $100 million and the scandal surrounding his wealth cast light on a near-immutable rule of politics in India – and hereditary politics everywhere – the enrichment of relatives of those in power.

American politics, like Japanese and Indian politics, is "becoming hereditary." Sounds like the Bush, Cheney, Kennedy, Romney, Udall, Gore and Clinton families. In Japan, 122 of the 500 lower house members inherited their seats. America is heading in the same direction. Is this the direction *We the Maids* want our country to be traveling in the 21st century?

Career politicians, especially the senators in the upper house, those I affectionately refer to as the Prohibition Babies, have usurped the system while aging disgracefully. These career politicians have successfully achieved what the Constitution tried to prohibit: Americans governed by an unrepresentative group of wealthy family scions serving themselves and their financial backers.

The U.S. should be seriously debating the demise of career politicians and the senates in Washington and every state capitol. America does not need a bicameral system of government in the 21st century. Congress and state assemblies could more than adequately do the job. More efficiently, too. Many of the arguments raised in England in abolishing hereditary peers in the House of Lords apply to the U.S. Senate, and career politicians in general.

"These guys don't have any special qualifications or qualities – they might be prats, drug addicts, half-wits or deadbeats – and there's no reason for them to tell you or me what we should do," remarked Hilary Boyd, a writer whose grandfather was an earl.

Britain's effort in July 2012 to make the House of Lords more democratic failed. The legislation to cut the number of members in the House of Lords and force most of those who remain to run for election did not garner the necessary votes in parliament. Currently, no members are elected.

British hereditary peers joined the ranks of the rest of European nobility. American independence and the French revolution convinced the world that indeed all people are created equal. So why are Americans unequally represented in government at the dawn of the $21^{st}$ century?

Americans must secretly admire and respect the British landed aristocracy that has been replicated in the U.S. Senate. This latent admiration is confirmed by the popularity in the U.S. of the TV series *Downton Abbey* about the English landed aristocracy during the Edwardian era, in which all men are definitely not created equal.

America had revolted against George III and the House of Hanover, but the dynastic temptations lingered on. Federalist John Adams, America's second president, saw his eldest son, John Quincy Adams, become the sixth president. Between them stretched the Virginia dynasty – two terms of Jefferson, two terms of Madison, two terms of James Monroe – 24 years of government by friends and neighbors. That tradition has survived in America to this very day, exemplified by the Bush political dynasty.

Maybe the demise of the Daley political dynasty in Chicago is a sign of the times and the beginning of the end of hereditary politics in America.

The topic of being born into the right gene pool surfaces periodically at the FCC Main Bar in Hong Kong. Usually in the context of Hong Kong's political elite, who occupy their political offices courtesy of their wealthy well-connected fathers or through marriage.

"Politicians such as Chief Executive Tung Chee-hwa, Peter Woo Kwong-ching and James Tien Pei-chun are beneficiaries of inheritance or marriage," Philip Bowring exclaimed as the U.S. hereditary political peers were being discussed and compared to those of Britain and Hong Kong.

Chinese-born Feng Chi-shun, who graduated from Hong Kong University, studied and practiced medicine in America and became a U.S. citizen, was being complimented by a few fellow American citizens for a letter he wrote to the editor of the *South China Morning Post* lambasting the arrogance of the well-heeled politicians who had to go overseas for their studies because they could not meet the admission standards of local universities.

"I am not saying that being good in school is a prerequisite for being a great leader or, for that matter, a great human being," Feng said. "But let us remind all of them, and not just the Tien brothers, not to be so arrogant as to think they are better than the rest and say things like 'only people who have created wealth should ...' or 'no representation without taxation', or 'taxi drivers and waitresses do not care'. Without their fathers, they could conceivably be driving my taxi and waiting on my table," Feng concluded to a chorus of "Right on!" and the clinking of glasses.

America's hereditary peers should also be abolished, as it was never the intention of the Founding Fathers to create political dynasties. Whether it's a Clinton, Kennedy, Bush, Cheney, Gore, Humphrey, Roosevelt or Udall. Politics has become a family business in America – nationally and locally. George W. Bush and Al Gore are prime examples. Those families that want to make it a business should be tested by the voters rather than inheriting the title of "favorite son" because of their lineage and political connections. They sound like Saudi Arabia's House of Saud. All should take lessons from Britain's Windsors.

The Windsors certainly know how to sock it to British taxpayers. They threw a $22 million wedding for Prince William and his bride Kate in 2011, paid for by the taxpayers – but justified because more than 2 billion TV viewers around the world were swept up in the royal magic. The follow-up wedding of Zara Philips, the queen's oldest granddaughter, to England rugby star Mike Tindall, was a much lower-toned hype that nonetheless helped make 2011 an *"annus mirabilis"* for the royals. The Windsors don't even pay taxes and survived another year without doing so! Talk about the ultimate legal tax dodge.

It was a great year indeed for the royal family. They pulled off another hat-trick – not the fancy hats the royals wear – but political survival. A groundbreaking visit to the Republic of Ireland in May and a trip to Australia that ended up reviving royal fever and melting republican sentiments, not only in the U.K., but in the remaining commonwealth colonies.

Bumbling Prince Philip pulled off the ultimate heart-breaker at Christmas 2011, winning the kingdom's citizen's sympathy and support – by having a heart attack.

Queen Elizabeth's diamond jubilee in 2012 was the ultimate heart-shaped diamond in her crown and that of the royal family, reaffirming its financial and political security for the foreseeable future. In fairness, she deserves praise for having been, in the words of historian John Grigg, "a bastion of stability in an age of social and moral flux."

But the ultimate hereditary political family has got to be the cult of the Kims in North Korea. The Great Leaders Kim. Kim Il sung, the Dear Leader Kim Jong Il, and now the Great Successor Kim Jong un. This kid, all of 28, inherited the office and title because of the gene pool he was born into. He was being mentored by an uncle, 66-year-old Jang Song Thaek, a hard-drinking, accordion-playing '60s rock 'n' roller who probably recommended Kim the Younger's hip new hairdo. Jang donned the uniform of a general in the North's powerful military and was clearly pulling major strings as the Hermit Kingdom set out on the latest chapter in its odd history until he was brutally executed for being too politically and financially enterpeneurial.

The untested Brilliant Leader and most everyone else know the regime is unsustainable – as do *We the People*. It is just a question of time before the Hermit Kingdom either implodes or reunifies with the South peacefully. It is up to *We the Apathetic Maids* to make sure that if it implodes, it is a controlled implosion – one that is controlled by the five-party talks that I have recommended in earlier books. It has to be a well-managed crash landing. Kim Jong Un should study the U.K. House of Windsor model for reunification and dynastic survival. He could become Korea's George Washington and China's Deng Xiaoping all wrapped into one. It is up to China to prod him to do so with U.S. support.

Kim Jong-il's fatal heart attack is just another metaphor for how North Korea will succumb. The country has reached a dead end.

Philip Bowring, a past president of the FCC and Main Bar regular, believes "change can come only when the regime is challenged, whether from within or without. An eventual challenge from within looks the more likely, given the difficulty of popular uprisings against regimes as ruthless as this."

I believe it is a combination of pressure from both within and without that will bring about regime change.

"And change can happen, if only because enough of the beneficiaries of the system, particularly the younger ones, recognize that for their own survival, they need to be prepared to surrender some power, preferably in return for sustainable wealth," Bowring added.

A reformist group within the existing power structure might just be able to use the regime's extreme nationalism in a different and more positive way – just as Nixon and his inside circle brought an end to the Vietnam War.

As long as China can't trust U.S. containment motives, tolerating and supporting North Korea's unpredictable nuclear-powered regime is well worth the aggravation and heartburn. The young Kim's flood-ravaged and poverty-ridden country would be in even more dire straits and the Kim dynasty would collapse, and probably will anyway, were it not for China's ongoing economic support – and for good reason. Unpredictable

North Korea remains a useful buffer to the American military presence in South Korea and a convenient loose nuclear cannon. After all, a reunified Korea could let America base troops right in China's backyard. Better yet, the Kims have kept Japan off balance, focused on an unstable nuclear neighbor with scores to settle. Pyongyang's harsh anti-Japanese rhetoric has most Japanese convinced that North Korea, not China, is their No. 1 military threat.

The amount of press attributing North Korea's 2011 aggression to the leadership change from Kim Jong-il to Kim Jong-un and the ongoing rift between the military and other more conciliatory factions has few supporting facts. Granted, Un could be overthrown by older relatives or military commanders, like his '60s rebel rock 'n' roller uncle, Jang whose luck unfortunately ran out in December 2013 when he was perceived as a threat to the regime.

But that does not justify America or China's acceptance of Pyongyang's aggressive military behavior. The "smooth and stable" succession story line appears to be another example of stale U.S. State Department rehashed sound bites. Groundless Korean political theory and analysis. It's no different than the poor U.S. sound bites of former Soviet political in-fighting preceding the collapse of the Stalinist state.

The ongoing wait-and-see policy adopted by the U.S. and South Korea is also a nonstarter. How long does the world have to wait-and-see while America negotiates and sells more weapons systems to Japan and South Korea? Former Defense Secretary William Perry had the right approach when he proposed that the U.S. should deal with a real North Korea, not a North Korea based on America's wishful thinking.

The deadly military brinkmanship and nuclear show-and-tell are the last gasps of a dying regime in its death throes. Dying because it is not getting its way with either America or China. Direct talks with America, but willing to settle for six-party talks, and more aid and political support from China, America and everyone else. The lack of economic aid for a hungry people, not a succession power struggle, is the real reason for the North Korean cannon being on the loose.

America, China, South Korea, Japan and Russia must prepare themselves for the collapse of the North Korean regime and how to handle its more than 24 million undereducated, malnourished and traumatized people who will have to be absorbed by a modern South Korea and China. South Korean President Lee Myung-bak in December 2010 added to the concerns, saying: "I feel that reunification is drawing near."

The Hong Kong model of "one country, two systems" is the most practical reunification solution for the Korean peninsula. Such a model for a decade or two would keep a buffer state between the U.S. ally in South Korea and China, while still giving Beijing control to modernize the North with economic support from America, Japan, South Korea and Russia.

The U.S. and China should go ahead with five-party talks – cutting out North Korea – under the plan I proposed in my books *Custom Maid Knowledge* and *Feasting Dragon, Starving Eagle*. A plan to constructively remove the despotic Kim regime permanently – a la Haiti and Philippines style – or England's Windsors.

China used to describe its relationship with the Hermit Kingdom "as close as lips and teeth." How long will China really put up with the Kim regime biting the Chinese hand that feeds it? Only until it is worth its while to have Chinese teeth chomp on the Kim lips and make sure the "spoiled child" is not only no longer an embarrassing threat, but unable to eat at China's expense. China knows the unpredictable and embarrassing Kim regime is unsustainable and is ready to serve it up on a silver platter for the right price. Sarah Palin may yet turn out to be right with her statement that "Obviously, we've gotta stand with our North Korean allies."

America and China agree on the need and importance of a denuclearized Korean peninsula. As the two powers most responsible for maintaining peace in the region, they surely can come up with a plan for a peaceful reunification. The only problem is, they can't agree on how to go about it.

Asking China to rein in the Kim regime without reciprocating in kind on issues of interest to China, like Taiwan and removal of U.S. troops from the Korean peninsula, is a nonstarter, unless of course Chinese troops are also stationed there as part of a multinational force. But what's the point? There has to be one big tit-for-tat – a win-win for both America and China.

America's political hereditary dynasties, like China's and North Korea's, should also be put out to pasture to sit out a few elections and then see what kind of comeback, if any, they can make. They will either re-emerge like former Bulgarian King Simeon II, a relative of Britain's Queen Elizabeth II, in a democratic election in 2001 after his National Movement Simeon II won, or retire comfortably. Either way, *We the People* and they both benefit. Simeon Borisov Saxe Coburg was crowned Simeon II at the age of 6 in 1943 after the death of his popular father, Boris III. After World War II, the king was forced out of the country by the Communists following a rigged plebiscite that abolished the monarchy. Isn't it time *We the Maids* swept out America's hereditary political dynasties without rigging the elections the way they have repeatedly?

How different are the "Gush-Bore" dynasties from their Bulgarian, Chinese, Singaporean, Filipino, Japanese, Saudi counterparts or England's monarchy and hereditary peer system? The Philippines, like its colonial parent America, also has a hereditary president. Presidents who came into office at the dawn of the 21st century not by winning the popular vote at the ballot box but by legal coup d'etats. Both George W. Bush and Gloria Magapagal Arroyo are children of former presidents. Both succeeded womanizers. Both took the oath of office on January 20, 2001. One was propelled into office overnight on the shoulders of People Power II. The other was accused of stealing the office without the support of the populace. No different than Singapore's totalitarian democracy. There Lee Hsien Loong, the son of the country's first prime minister, Lee Kuan Yew, succeeded the interim prime minister Goh Chok Tong to disguise the appearance of hereditary succession. Is this the road *We the Apathetic People* want America to be taking in the new millennium? It certainly is not the road the Founding Fathers had in mind.

"The presidency has in effect become like the monarchy in England," Norman Mailer lamented at the Edinburgh International Book Festival at the dawn of the new millennium. Indeed, the relationship between Bill Clinton and Barack Obama and a Republican House is very similar to that of George III and a Whig Parliament. Why are *We the People* allowing what our Founding Fathers fought so hard to achieve to be hijacked by America's hereditary political families and their financial backers?

### Hereditary War Values

Asked what the Fourth of July and "Happy Fourth of July" meant to him in the opening year of the new century, President George W. Bush replied: "It means what these words say, for starters. The great inalienable rights of our country. We're blessed with such values in America. And I – it's – I'm a proud man to be in the nation based upon such wonderful values." America's Founding Fathers must be spinning in their graves. A hereditary, stupid illiterate imperial presidency is not what they had in mind. The Bush brothers make the Smothers brothers look serious.

A president whose wartime powers during his "War on Terror" rival Roosevelt's during World War II. A power Bush spread too thin to win. Like former world empires, its global sprawl was its flaw – its Achilles' heel. "Imperial presidency" was a term coined by Arthur Schlessinger Jr. to describe Richard Nixon's administration in 1973.

"The power President Bush is wielding today is truly breathtaking," said Tim Lynch, director of the Project on Criminal Justice at the libertarian Cato Institute. "A single individual is going to decide whether the war is expanded to Iraq. A single individual is going to decide how much privacy American citizens are going to retain."

And *We the Apathetic People* allowed a hereditary political pretender to accumulate this power and use it as it pleased.

An airport and CIA headquarters wearing the Bush name, sons as governors of Texas and Florida, and one of them succeeds his father as president, and another considering a 2016 presidential run is just too much! Sounds like Saparmurat Niyazov, the Central Asian dictator of Turkmenistan who named cities, streets, mosques, collective farms, celestial bodies and the main airport after himself.

The scariest part is that three generations of Bushes, starting with grandpa Prescott, all belong to the bizarre Skull And Bones Club at Yale. A secret society inspired by the German Brotherhood of Death that included Hitler among its members. The club operates from a windowless building, dubbed The Tomb. *The Secret Tomb,* a book by Alexandra Robbins, has made disturbing allegations about links with Nazi Germany and an unhealthy preoccupation with war.

"This is a secret society with tentacles of power that spread across America," Robbins writes. "It is a society that glorifies death and, most disturbingly, war. It doesn't surprise me that George Bush is currently worming his way into another war."

She describes The Tomb, a three-story mausoleum on Yale's campus usually closed to non-members, as a treasury of macabre memorabilia. Skeletons and skulls are hidden there, with gravestones allegedly stolen from churchyards, silverware once owned by Hitler, mementos of both World Wars and the American Civil War and even a mummy – and allegedly the skeletal remains of Geronimo. Yet more disturbing, claims Robbins, is the "outrageous anti-Semitism" of many Bonesmen. Now, I do not question the Bushes' right to assemble as they choose as guaranteed by the First Amendment to the Constitution. My only question is whether the Founding Fathers and Americans envisioned this kind of leadership? If not, why isn't it swept away by *We the Maids?*

Is this what America is all about? I think not. The Federalist Papers and debates at all the constitutional conventions unequivocally show us that our Founding Fathers wanted to create a system that deliberately shunned political heritage and dynasties. Isn't it time we revisited the issue and updated our political foundation, cornerstone and process that have created these political dynasties? After all, we have come a long way from the horse and buggy days of the constitutional convention to the information age of the 21$^{st}$ century. Isn't it time America's political process and system did as well? Isn't it time America's political gene pool is chlorinated?

On the other hand, since these political dynasties do have to stand for election at some point and since *We the Maids* are fully aware of their background, does it signify a closet yearning for monarchy among the people or some urge for the perfect shining family that cannot be found in

America's dysfunctional homes?

It is a dangerous road we are on when career politicians turn politics into a family business in the name of public service.

Socrates taught us to stand up for the truth. We must, Socrates said, question common assumptions. If they don't hold up, then we're right to stand apart from the crowd. Otherwise, what the young flamboyant Benjamin Disraeli sneered about in his novel *Coningsby* about the principles of Britain's conservative Tory Party before he became prime minister applies to America's Democratic and Republican parties. What will you conserve? The prerogatives of the crown, provided they are not exercised; the independence of the House of Lords, provided it is not asserted; the ecclesiastical estate, provided it is regulated by a commission of laymen. Everything, in short, that is established, as long as it is a phrase and not a fact. A Conservative government, in his view, like a Democratic or Republican one, in my view, was "an organized hypocrisy."

Can you imagine working for a company that has a little more than 500 employees and has the following statistics:

Nine have been accused of spousal abuse.
Seven have been arrested for fraud.
19 have been accused of writing bad checks.
117 have directly or indirectly bankrupted at least two businesses.
Three have done time for assault.
71 cannot get a credit card due to bad credit.
14 have been arrested on drug-related charges.
Eight have been arrested for shoplifting.
21 are currently defendants in lawsuits.
84 have been arrested for drunk driving in one year.

Can you guess which organization this is?

It's the 535 members of the U.S. Congress at the dawn of the 21st century. The same group of idiots who crank out hundreds of new laws each year to keep the rest of us in line.

It's time *We the Maids* took off our apathetic blinders and start to work on long overdue sweeping reforms. Otherwise, as Disraeli asked, what will be left for us to conserve? Sweep out the career politicians before it is too late and bring in part-time politicians. Firemen, teachers, police officers, a broader base of functional constituencies that represent the people.

### Political Crack Cocaine

The current system is pure and simple protectionism of unrepresentative senators, political families and career politicians. Protectionism is embedded, more accurately impaled, in the American political system. George Will accurately pinpoints how it works: "Protectionism, administered by the Commerce Department but dictated by Congress, is a form of precisely targeted government favoritism for particular firms, industries, unions and communities. It is political crack cocaine, producing quick and fierce addiction. Dealers of the drug of protectionism generate dependent clients whose gratitude is expressed in campaign contributions and votes. So protectionism is an important component of the system for protecting congressional incumbents."

Protectionism benefits only career politicians. Even when these "public servants" do the public a great disservice. A good example is the politicians and bureaucrats in 40 states who forfeited federal health care funds for poor children in the closing year of the millennium because they failed to spend it. California and Texas accounted for more than half of the unspent money – $590 million and $446 million, respectively. Together the two states have 29 percent of the nation's 11 million uninsured children.

Does this sound right? Of course not! Nevertheless, it is reality. Why did it happen? Because poor children don't vote or contribute to political campaigns. On the backs of poor children, the career politicians redistribute the funds to their subsidized financial backers. Should these kind of practices be allowed to continue in the 21st century or should they be swept out by *We the Maids?* Your call!

### Gerrymandering Filibusters

Career politicians not only sold their soul to the country's bankers, but also gerrymandered *We the Apathetic Maids* out of our popular vote in the 2012 election. The great gerrymander of 2012 came 200 years after the first use of this curious word, which comes from the salamander-shaped districts signed into law by Governor Elbridge Gerry of Massachusetts. Gerrry's party engineered its electoral coup using paper maps and ink. A matter that can easily be addressed today with the advent of inexpensive computing and free software.

Especially after the 2012 elections when we would expect more seats in Congress to go to the party that received the most votes. But that is not what happened. Democratic candidates received 1.4 million more votes for the House of Representatives, yet Republicans won control of the House by a 234 to 201 margin.

That is because through artful drawing of district boundaries, it is possible to put large number of voters on the losing side of every election. The Republican State Leadership Committee, a Washington-based political group dedicated to electing state officeholders, issued a progress report in early 2013 on Redmap, its multiyear plan to influence redistricting. The $30 million strategy consists of two steps for tilting the playing field: take over state legislatures before the decennial Census, then redraw state and congressional districts to lock in partisan advantages. The plan worked.

Gerrymandering is not hard. The core technique is to jam voters likely to favor your opponents into a few throwaway districts where the other side will win lopsided victories, a strategy known as "packing." Arrange other boundaries to win close victories, "cracking" opposition groups into many districts.

Most states are guilty of this partisan ploy. Not surprisingly, absent from the guilty list is California, because the state's voters took redistricting out of legislators' hands by creating the California Citizens Redistricting Commission – something every state in the union should do if America is to preserve majority rule and minority representation as the Founding Fathers intended.

And let's not forget that other self-serving political move that career politicians use – the filibuster – the most effective and abusive political tool to create permanent gridlock. Libertarian Senator Rand Paul of Kentucky, demonstrated its destructiveness when he decided to filibuster the nomination of CIA Director John Brennan in March 2013 over America's drone policy and talked non stop for almost 13 hours. It is a tool used primarily by Republicans. From 2006 to 2012, Republicans threatened a filibuster 385 times. That's almost double the rate of the preceding five years.

"This level of obstruction is extremely unusual," Norman Ornstein, a scholar at the conservative American Enterprise Institute, told *Newsweek*. "And the core of the problem is the GOP."

For America's democracy to work, there must be cross-party cooperation.

## *Abolish or Change the Electoral College*

The Electoral College must be abolished or changed because it discourages people from voting. A case-in-point is the letter Jerry Slocum, an independent who lives in Utah and voted for Obama in both the 2008 and 2012 elections, sent to the editors of *USA Today*. "Oh, I'll vote – I always do – but this question always nags at me: In red-state Utah, if one doesn't vote Republican why bother? The Electoral College is an anachronism that should have been scrapped long ago. Electing the president and vice president by popular vote would indeed make each person's vote count, encouraging many more people to cast ballots. A side benefit would be encouraging more third-party candidates, with new ideas, which would make our political process healthier."

Abolishing it would make every vote of every voter count equally regardless of who they are or where they live and the presidency meaningful again. If the Electoral College is to be kept, it should be changed in its entirety and be modeled on the Hong Kong Electoral College and appoint a chief executive rather than a president. The presidency, if the electoral college is to be retained, like all career politician posts, should be abolished just like hereditary peers because it has become a laughable imperial presidency. A hereditary monarchy. George Dubya acted like a monarch and for all intents and purposes the role of president was fulfilled by a dysfunctional chief executive officer – Dick Cheney. Why continue to perpetuate the myth of president and the disfunctional system that elects him or her? *Saturday Night Live* correctly portrayed Bush complaining that "Dick Cheney is a demanding boss."

The Electoral College, if it is to be retained, should also have electors elected by *We the People* to elect a Chief Executive. Since the office of the president will be eliminated, the need to elect one will be eliminated. In theory *We the People* elect the electors today. But who really knows who they are since we focus our attention on the presidential candidates and not the electors? Because electors are local people from every city and state, they are better known to the voters and more familiar with the issues of the day. Electors can and should be accountable to the public. Each state's number of electors is representative of the state's population.

Hong Kong, where an Election Committee of 1,200 members appointed by Beijing choose the territory's Beijing-approved leader, veteran pollster Dr. Robert Chung Ting-yiu, head of the University of Hong Kong's public opinion program, held a citywide vote on March 23, 2012, two days before the Election Committee made its decision – with the results announced the same day. It didn't have any legal effect or official significance, but it was a powerful indicator of what the public wanted, and probably swayed the committee members to vote accordingly – and they did.

Under the Chung plan, people used an electronic voting system, accessible from their computers or mobile devices. They were also able to use terminals at polling stations set up by Chung and his team. Many saw the plan as a referendum on choosing the chief executive. Why can't America do the same? An enforceable initiative, even a referendum on what the people – instead of Electoral College – want?

A message the Electoral College listened to and voted accordingly. Changing times – from America's founding to the 21$^{st}$ century – require changes to America's antiquated voting system. If it is to be retained. The electoral college in America should be abolished.

Pennsylvania considered changing the way the state awards its electoral votes in presidential elections for the 2012 election. A bill introduced in September 2011 would award electoral votes by congressional districts instead of the "winner take all" system. The proposed new system would guarantee both Democratic and Republican presidential candidates would win some electoral votes even if they lose the popular vote.

The measure was aimed at reducing President Obama's total electoral votes in 2012; in 2008, Obama won 55 percent of the state's popular vote and 100 percent of its 21 electoral votes. No Republican nominee had won Pennsylvania – or any of its electoral votes since 1988. Today, only Nebraska and Maine award their electoral votes by congressional district.

Electors should also be joined by "constituent electors" representing governors, mayors and other constituent interest groups that represent Americans. These would include unions, business round table, professional and trade groups, and minorities. It should be well balanced and impartial. The chief executive should be elected based on his or her credentials, ability and track record and not party affiliation. Candidates should be nominated by all parties and be given equal consideration regardless of party affiliation. Politics being what it is, we will see electors vote along party lines. That is why constituent interest groups such as business, labor, trades, professions and minorities have to be included to hopefully stack the odds in favor of the best-qualified candidate rather than any one party candidate.

### Every Vote Counts

With all the concerns that the winner of the popular vote may not win the Electoral College vote again, isn't it time American democracy updated and upgraded itself? The election to determine America's 43rd president was a wake-up call to the realization that the current election process breeds paralysis and disfunctionality. Is it American democracy for the winner of the popular vote to see their opponent take over the highest office in the land? Is it democracy for a candidate who doesn't carry their home state and Ohio to concede the highest office in the land? Ann Richards, the former governor of Texas, said about George W: "He was born on third base and thought he hit a triple." Then he tried to steal home, and succeeded. Is this anyway for the world's greatest democracy to continue in the 21$^{st}$ century?

*The Miami Herald* and *USA Today* examined the ballots that showed Bush to have beaten Gore and found them to be seriously clouded because most Florida counties could not find all the undervote ballots they reported after the November election. Why is that not surprising when you have the Florida political infrastructure run by the hereditary Bush political family, relatives and supporters? This is political hardball at its purest.

Napoleon told us that "From the sublime to the ridiculous is but a step." We have seen that step taken in America as we watched Bush being sworn in as president at the dawn of the 21st century. Do we want to continue down this road with our children? Aren't we better off taking the offramp that leads us to a modified Hong Kong electoral model customized for America and China, or alternatively abolish the electoral college?

The Founding Fathers never intended state or U.S. supreme courts, secretaries of state or state legislatures to make the decision about who should move into the White House. It is a decision *We the People* are supposed make. Why aren't we?

### Gamble For Change
*We the Apathetic People* have to take risks like Hiram Bingham, a New England WASP who risked his career and life to help Jews escape from France during World War II. Bingham was reprimanded and drummed out of the U.S. diplomatic service for violating U.S. government policy of the day. Bingham, the U.S. vice-counsul in Marseille in the early years of World War II, was posthumously given a special award for "constructive dissent" from the American Foreign Service Association in 2002.

Bingham's efforts on behalf of refugees included seeking out people at risk, sheltering them, disguising them, forging identity papers, approving their visas and smuggling them out of Vichy France, often in disguise, usually at his own expense and always in violation of U.S. policy.

Secretary of State Colin Powell said that people "owe their lives to Harry Bingham's 'visas of freedom'. [They] got out because Harry was prepared to take that risk to career to do that which he knew was right."

Bingham, like Jesus, Mohammad, Gandhi, Martin Luther King Jr., and Nelson Mandela, was prepared to take the risks necessary to achieve that which he knew was right. Shouldn't *We the Apathetic People* be doing the same in the 21$^{st}$ century?

Californians have proven repeatedly that taking risks can pay off. Their two boldest gambles were the passage of Proposition 13 limiting property tax to 1% of assessed value and recalling Governor Gray Davis and electing Arnold Schwarzenegger. Meeting Howard Jarvis, the author of Proposition 13, when he was campaigning for its passage against all odds and listening to the aged fighter fire up voters was a reminder how *We the People* can change laws and government when we have the protracted active desire. Knowing Gray Davis, and having met Arnie briefly a few times at Scratch, I still shake my head in awe whenever the topic of the California recall comes up. Two tough fighters, one a political animal, the other a Terminator, who put the people through a tough test. A test the people won. People can change anything if they want to badly enough, put their mind and soul into it as well as their time, effort and resources.

Las Vegas is not afraid to gamble for change. It elected as mayor Oscar Goodman, a mob lawyer. His populist libertarian philosophy had greater appeal than the traditional politicians representing the Democratic and Republican parties. "We are just going to go for a little ride," he told the electorate. Mayors seem to be the career politicians leading the charge for change in America.

The mayor of San Francisco made history by making the City by the Bay the first civil authority in America to officially marry gay couples in open defiance of laws banning the practice. In a letter to city officials, Mayor Gavin Newsom ordered them to grant marriage licenses to same-sex couples.

Milwaukee's former mayor John Norquist espoused a "new urbanism" – the idea that the potential of a city can be unleashed by good design and planning – and coupled it with a firm belief in free markets. He sought to put an end to monopolies, and kept on lowering taxes while maintaining the city's services as he transformed the city from a city of heavy industry and breweries to a city of art galleries, museums, theaters and homes for young professionals.

Conservative Mormon Salt Lake City is not afraid to gamble for change either. Salt Lake Mayor Rocky Anderson, who took his city on a constructive ride, is a lapsed Mormon, twice divorced. A former president of the American Civil Liberties Union board, anti-death penalty activist and a Democrat. He was marshal of the gay pride parade and is a fan of the Dalai Lama, the Kennedy brothers and artist Peter Max.

On the wall of Anderson's office hangs a quote from Dante: "The hottest places in hell are reserved for those who in time of great moral crisis maintain their neutrality."

It's time *We the Maids* go for a little ride at the dawn of the 21$^{st}$ century to sweep out the career politicians who have brought about the moral, economic and political crisis confronting us today so that we can then go about making the changes we all so desperately yearn for deep in our souls. Hong Kong, like Las Vegas and Salt Lake City, isn't and shouldn't be afraid of change. Like America, it sometimes isn't quite sure how to go about it. When that happens, *We the Apathetic People* lose while we snooze.

The electorate saw the dramatic and devastating effect that radical rebellious change can have on a political party and country when Vermont's Senator James Jefford followed in the tradition of Ethan Allen's Green Mountain Boys from the American Revolution. One man's decision to abandon the Republican Party overnight turned the Senate leadership over to Democrats who rewrote the Bush Administration's political agenda. Imagine if *We the Apathetic People* had the same change of heart and decided to bring about real change. It can and will happen. All it takes is a collective cohesive desire on the part of *We the Maids* to sweep out what we want replaced.

The last few years have seen the seeds of discontent finally sprout politicians who are not careerists from the "political class" who echo people's disenchantment with the system and promise to change it. Politicians coming to terms with their conscience. Hopefully, as we enter the New World Disorder of the 21$^{st}$ century, the few political seedlings of discontent will become lush political forests.

### *Political Turnover*

During the Jeffersonian era, congressmen came and went with what today seems remarkable rapidity. Politicians passed through Congress and then often passed on to, or back to, what we now consider, anachronistically, "lower" offices. A typical career sequence early in the 19th century would be local office, state office, U.S. House, and back to the statehouse. But as the national government grew in importance, ambition turned, like the needle of a compass, toward Congress.

"No longer was every politician eligible for and equally likely to seek every other office. The musical chairs of the early 19th century were replaced by a tacit consensus among politicians about appropriate career development," George Will astutely reminds us. The era of the career congressman was at hand.

The steady and dramatic increase in the importance of Congress as a maker of federal policy, and of federal policy as an allocator of wealth and opportunity, made congressional service more attractive to some and less to citizen part-time lawmakers. Heavier workloads and longer sessions meant longer absences. Congressman Ron Paul summed the transformation up best during his 2012 presidential campaign. "Congress is basically filled with demagogues and power mongers."

Many members of Congress are so busy fund raising that they don't even bother to show up for critical votes. Many members miss more than 10 percent of the votes.

Republican Representative Michael Forbes, who switched parties and became the first Republican to do so in 25 years because the Republican Party has been captured by extremists, put it this way: "With no Communist menace to rail against, and with an American economy that is the strongest to be sustained in our lifetime, the national Republican Party over the last 4½ years has allowed itself to become defined through the actions of extremists in the House of Representatives.

"It's become angry, narrow-minded, intolerant, uncaring, incapable of governing at all, much less from the center," he added.

"One lesson of American history is that when a majority of Americans have a strong and protracted desire for something, they get it," George Will reminds us.

During the 2002 campaign in the Czech Republic, the Czech Christian Democrats offered free alcohol to get voters to support their candidates, while the Communist Party had topless women handing out campaign literature. These are creative get-out-the-vote campaigns that get *We the Apathetic People* to get out and make hard choices for change. If we don't, the character Bob Dylan plays to save the world in *Masked and Anonymous*, set in apocalyptic times in a country where order and morality have broken down, will be seen in every neighborhood in America. And I don't mean just in movie theaters.

### *Empty Chair – Empty Mao Suits and Party*

The picture of Nobel committee chairman Thorbjoern Jagland looking down at the vacant chair meant for 2010 Nobel Peace Prize laureate Liu Xiaobo during the award ceremony, and the standing ovation the jailed activist received, were poignant symbols of the intellectually bankrupt politics of the Communist Party leaders in Beijing. The Nobel committee's guidelines say that only the winner or close relatives may collect the award. It was the first time since 1936 that no one had been present to accept the Peace Prize.

As a writer, lawyer and political activist, I can relate to, sympathise with and support Liu's poignant statement read out at the ceremony by Norwegian actress Liv Ullman after a performance of traditional Chinese music by Chinese-American violinist Lynn Chang. The statement was called "I have no enemies: my final statement," which Liu intended to be read in court by his lawyers but was prevented from doing so.

More than 40 exiled Chinese dissidents traveled to the Norwegian capital to honor Liu and protest in front of the Chinese Embassy in Oslo. It was the largest gathering of dissidents and biggest media event focusing on China's democracy movement since the June 4, 1989, Tiananmen massacre.

It's not just literary, artistic and political dissidents demanding more freedoms. Ex-Communist Party officials, including a former secretary to Mao Zedong, ex-publishers of party publications, and a one-time deputy political director of the military command in the southern metropolis of Guangzhou started circulating a letter on October 1, 2011. It was a cross between a chain letter and a petition, and was originally signed by 23 party officials, and then by more than 400. It is a letter that is not easily suppressed because of the Communist Party credentials of the signatories.

It calls for the uncensored circulation of books, newspapers, magazines and the lifting of restrictions on the Internet. It demands the dismantling of the Central Propaganda Department, the powerful body that reports directly to the Politburo and which the letter drafters refer to as an "invisible black hand."

"When our country was founded in 1949, our people cried out that they had been liberated, that they were now their own masters," the letter states.

"But even today, 61 years after the founding of our nation, after 30 years of opening and reform, we have not yet attained the freedom of speech and press to the degree enjoyed by the people of Hong Kong under the colonial rule."

The letter notes that Chinese state news media have not even reported on a recent series of remarks made by Premier Wen Jiaobao calling for political reforms. "Without the protection afforded by political reforms, the gains we have made from economic reforms will be lost," Wen said in a speech in August in Shenzhen, across from Hong Kong. Wen said political reform must take place to keep power in check, to allow people to criticize and monitor the performance of the government, to crack down on corruption and to build a fair and just society. The remarks were repeated in various interviews during a trip Wen made to New York in September 2010 coinciding with my U.S. visit.

"The people's desire and need for democracy and freedom are irresistible," Wen said in a CNN interview. Quite a U-turn for the man who in 2007 provocatively suggested that China may not be ready for democracy for another 100 years.

Wen renewed his plea for wider political and judicial reforms in April 2011 during a speech to the Malaysian parliament. He also stressed the importance of independent thinking. "The most important thing for the future development is to promote independent thinking and creativity. Our country will be invincible if all of our 1.3 billion people can think independently and be creative," he said.

Wen has to stop saying what everyone knows and push the party to start doing something to make the necessary changes everyone knows are long overdue, long over-promised and under-delivered.

As a four-day meeting of the Communist Party's 300-plus Central Committee members opened on October 15, 2010, more than 100 intellectuals released a petition calling for the body to follow through on Wen's promises of reform. China's media also clamored aboard the political reform bandwagon and started publishing and reporting the calls for political reform in the run-up to that fifth plenary session of the Central Committee.

Their words have changed China and confirmed that the pen is indeed mightier than the sword. It will be interesting to see if that is the case in China going forward. In an unusual move, the *People's Daily,* the Communist Party's newspaper, published a commentary calling for freedom of speech and tolerance of different views in April 2011. It even contained a quotation attributed to French philosopher Voltaire: "I may not agree with what you have to say, but I will defend to the death your right to say it."

The article also quoted Mao and late paramount leader Deng Xiaoping on the need for citizens to be free to criticize and supervise their government.

There are subtle political changes taking place within the Communist Party's iron-fisted rule. Premier Wen's repeated calls for Western-style political reform in 2010-2011 make him the most outspoken leader since 1989 when Hu Yaobang and Zhao Ziyang were purged for their liberal remarks, and underscores the significant changes that have taken place within the party. Wen's daring criticism on the most politically sensitive topics has raised questions about the schism – or evolution – within the party. His criticism coincided with the government's crackdown on political dissent and a tightening of the authorities' grip on the media following the widespread political upheaval in the Arab world.

Wen's explicit praise of universal values, while welcomed by the public, has earned him criticism from various factions within the ruling party. But his remarks echo increasingly louder voices within and outside the Communist Party calling for political reform, with many lower officials and academics in government think tanks joining the chorus.

One of the mainland's most high-profile dissidents, Hu Jia, was released from jail in June 2011 after serving 3½ years. Instead of staying silent like his fellow released dissidents, he expressed hope in the rise of awareness of rights and freedom among ordinary people and wanted to help push his nation toward democracy.

"When my child was born I felt that, for her sake, I had to create room for freedom, democracy and rule of law [in our country]. I can't let children of her generation suffer like us," Hu said.

Hu was arrested when his daughter was just one month old in 2007, charged with subversion for an article he wrote that was critical of the government.

"The officials are already very afraid – the more you provoke them the crueller they are," he said. "That kind of fear would bring brutal retaliation … so we have to push for reform step by step."

He said he no longer wanted to bring pain to his family or jeopardize his health, and wanted to pursue "sustainable development."

"[It's because] I want to see the historical moment of the democratization of China," said Hu, who suffers from Hepatitis B and cirrhosis.

"You might think I'm an optimist," Hu added, "but I believe the moment of truth and reconciliation will come to this country, like in South Africa."

I agree that it will, not only in China, but in America.

Hu is surrounded by official security guards wherever he or his wife go. "This is what I had expected – out of a small prison into a big prison," he said.

He now wants to push for the rule of law rather than just tackle individual cases where people's rights have been abused.

"We have to get down to the root cause," he said.

He added: "If the charge of 'inciting subversion of sovereignty' is never scrapped, police will carry on arresting government critics.

"I told them the charge 'inciting subversion' is an infringement of people's freedom of speech... . I told them we must have this law abolished and we cannot allow it to be a sword of Damocles forever dangling over everyone's head," he said, his voice rising.

Mao's legacy is increasingly being debated and challenged in China and within the party itself. Especially the Cultural Revolution, an orgy of political violence that killed perhaps 2 million people. Many argue that the Cultural Revolution was merely a ploy to destroy Mao's many critics after the disaster of the Great Leap Forward famine, which killed some 30 million people.

Victims of Mao's 1957 Anti-Rightist Movement, former academics, lawyers, writers and intellectuals who were considered to be an ideological threat to communism and the regime, were purged. Most were sent to labor camps or banished to remote areas to work as peasants and were subjected to harsh conditions and treatment, including public criticism and torture.

In March 2007, the 50th anniversary of the Anti-Rightist Movement, 61 elders sent an open letter to the CCP's Central Committee, People's Congress and the State Council to ask for justice and compensation for the victims. Over 2,000 people signed the petition. The government has not responded and has imposed a media ban on the subject.

The new strategy is to bring Mao himself to justice by filing a class-action lawsuit at the Supreme People's Court and the International Criminal Court in the Hague for his ruthless crimes of trampling China's Constitution, contempt for life and committing murders in violation of the law and basic human rights.

Maoist revival movements in the spring of 2011, leading up to July 1, the 90th anniversary of when the Communist Party was founded in Shanghai in 1921, were launched with "red song" patriotic campaigns with martial music and performances harking back to China circa 1966. Among the musical offerings: *Without the Communist Party, There Would Be No China.*

The red-song campaign originated in Chongqing, led by the city's Communist Party boss Bo Xilai. He personally presided over a 100,000-strong rally of revolutionary songs, to which even former U.S. Secretary of State Henry Kissinger was invited. The mass singalong swept across the country.

It also swept Bo to jail and stripped him of his party titles – and exposed the corruption and weakness of China's political system and the urgent need for reform.

Bo was first dismissed from his post, stripping him of all of his titles, followed by a criminal investigation. The method is a familiar one. A corruption charge is the standard instrument used to deal with political insubordination. Two top officials were brought down the same way, former Beijing party secretary Chen Xitong, and former Shanghai party secretary Chen Liangyu. This time, it was lucky for the leadership that there was the murder of a foreigner to justify such a move.

The Bo affair is not just about massive corruption but also succession. Bo had developed a high profile with his singalongs. It was a populist, and popular, attempt by a charismatic "princeling," son of a revolutionary hero, to assert his natural right to ascend to the nine-member Politburo Standing Committee at the 18th Chinese Communist Party Congress. Among the rumors circulating in China at the time was that, once on the committee, Bo would have tried to replace the party's incoming general secretary and president agreed to by the outgoing leader, Xi Jinping.

The Bo scandal has raised questions within the Communist Party about whether it should continue to appoint top brass as municipal or provincial leaders. Bo was a Politburo member also tasked with overseeing a municipality. The Bo saga reflects a key deficiency of China's political institutions, where new leaders have advanced their political careers not only through administrative channels and their credentials, but also through nepotism and patronage.

The removal of Bo as Chongqing party chief underlines the urgency of political reform in China and the need to bring a system of checks and balances to the political system.

The party propaganda machine that kicked in to give the red-song campaign fast-paced legs only generated cynicism because of some of its far-fetched claims. Reports of children refusing to attend their parent's funeral in order to go to a red-song concert; and childless married couples becoming fertile after singing red songs are some of the extreme claims. All talk and no action. As a professor with the China University of Political Science and Law told a Phoenix TV commentator: "Yes, you are welcome to sing revolutionary songs. But you are not welcome to stage another revolution."

"You are welcome to watch the movie *The Founding of a Party*, about how the Communist Party was formed in 1921. But you're not welcome to try founding your own party."

Oh yeah? Watch me!

Better yet, watch Wang Yang, the party boss of Guangdong, who disagrees with his counterpart in Chongqiing who led the massive revolutionary red-song patriotic march across the nation. Wang called for "free thinking and mind liberation" to remove red tape and obstacles to economic development, for Guangdong to "be a vanguard of scientific development" and focus on "real happiness" for its people, themes he has reiterated in several high-profile campaigns since taking over as Guangdong party chief in 2007.

Neo-Maoists are demanding that Mao's critics be tried for treason because they refuse to even accept a newly published Communist Party history that states Mao's Great Leap Forward resulted in 10 million deaths from starvation from 1959 to 1961. Their primary aim apparently is to overturn an alleged politburo decision made in December 2010 but never publicized, to drop the use of "Mao Zedong thought" in all future party documents.

To critics, the Maoist revival has echoes of the maniacal quest for political correctness during the Cultural Revolution.

Mao's pre-eminence in China is linked to his central role in founding the People's Republic in 1949. Yet his controversial political legacy, of which the Cultural Revolution is just one example, is growing more disputed with time.

For example, why won't the Chinese government allow the truth about Mao's man-made Great Famine between 1958 and 1962 that killed more than 36 million people to be told? The toll was more than twice the number of fallen in World War I, and about six times the number of Ukrainians starved by Stalin in 1932-33 or the number of Jews murdered by Hitler in World War II.

"An honest, earnest, serious assessment of Mao based on facts is necessary," Yawei Liu, director of the Carter Center's China Program in Atlanta, said. "All this stuff indicates how central Mao is to China's political orthodoxy," Liu added. "A clear verdict and break with Mao will pave the way for real political reform to take place."

Separated from Mao, the Communist Party, for all intents and purposes, is either dead or the debate about Mao is the emergence of a Chinese-style democracy under a one-party system. Even the *People's Daily,* the party mouthpiece, offers mixed and conflicting schitzoid messages about political openness. Its commentaries and editorial opinions range from saying that the more than 78 million Communist Party members should toe the party line and be banned from making and spreading any comments contrary to official dogma, to calling for openness and urging officials to be sensitive to citizens'opinions and try to "listen to the voices of the unheard."

A document circulating online purporting to detail a proposal by top Communist Party officials to remove Mao thought from party work, documents and policies has also sharpened debate. The supposed Politburo document No. 179, dated Dec. 28, 2010, is said to have been proposed by

Xi Jinping, the man who became China's new president, and Wu Bangguo, head of the National People's Congress.

The *People's Daily* article was published amid a stepped-up crackdown on political dissent, a tightening of the authorities' grip on the media and an increasingly loud chorus for political reform within and outside the ruling hierarchy following the widespread Jasmine Revolutions in the Arab world. There are growing voices, like Wen's, within the Communist Party calling for the introduction of Western-style democracy as decades of economic progress without political reform leave the country wallowing in widespread corruption, inequalities and tense social conflict.

The unabated arrests and disappearances of human rights activists, lawyers, political activists and artists highlight the concerns Chinese party leaders have about the potential eruption of an Arab-style revolution. The arrest of political activist and artist Ai Weiwei triggered an outpouring of protest online and in the streets of Hong Kong, New York, London and other cities worldwide. In Hong Kong, giant images of Ai were projected onto landmark buildings, including police and government facilities.

An album of 28 black and white pictures was circulating on Facebook showing images with the words "Who's afraid of Ai Weiwei?"

The answer is clear. Beijing is determined to silence its critics and has succeeded in its goal of temporarily silencing Ai, one of its most vociferous critics, as well as the dozens of activists, rights lawyers, writers who have "retreated into uncharacteristic silence and seclusion" upon their release, Human Rights Watch said. Ai was just one of more than 130 activists, lawyers, bloggers and tweeters detained between February and May of 2011. "@Large: Ai Weiwei on Alcatraz" that opened in September 2014 on the island prison brought to America his message of Chinese repression.

They are silent because under Chinese law there is the concept of "deprivation of political rights." Both Ai and Hu have been deprived of their political rights, which in addition to the right to vote and stand for election, includes such basic rights as freedom of speech and the right to meet the media.

The "deprivation of political rights" at the end of a prison sentence has been part of China's justice system for decades. But now the security forces are imposing this punishment at the beginning of the criminal justice process, without going through the formality of arrest, trial and sentencing. A good way to shut people up pre-emptively, without the hassle and publicity of a trial. By being deprived of their rights, they cannot speak or meet with the media.

"Chinese people's freedoms of speech, association, assembly and religion continue to be ruthlessly suppressed, and lawless beatings, arbitrary detentions, unlawful searches, obscene tortures, coerced confessions and unfair trials prevail nationwide, despite the persistent efforts of China's many able law reformers," said Jerome A. Cohen, co-director of the U.S.-Asia Law Institute at NYU School of Law.

Cohen has spoken several times at the Foreign Correspondents Club in Hong Kong on China's human rights abuses. I've had the pleasure of discussing the subject with him not only in Hong Kong, but in a cab ride we shared from JFK airport after a flight from Hong Kong in the early '90s. When he heard I was in the television distribution business in China, he was more interested and animated talking about his granddaughter, the little girl who starred in the movie *Fatal Attraction*. I do agree with him on the rampant human rights abuses in China.

Ai Weiwei's continued detention for three months highlighted such abuses, and even violated China's Criminal Procedure law. The law requires the police to make one of three choices if, within 37 days after detaining a suspect, they do not have enough evidence to convince the prosecutor's office to approve a formal arrest. First, they can unconditionally release the suspect. Second, if the investigation is to continue, under an arrangement similar to bail in America, they can release a suspect for up to a year under a guarantee that allows him freedom in the city.

Finally, if the suspect has a local residence, they can strictly confine him to his home for up to six months. This sanction is called "residential surveillance" and is designed to allow the authorities to keep close tabs on a suspect without him or her continuing to suffer the total deprivation of personal freedom imposed by detention. Only suspects who do not have a local residence but are deemed to require "residential surveillance" can be kept at a location designated by the police.

In practice, however, the authorities frequently use "residential surveillance" as a pretext for continuing to hold someone in the detention-like custody of their designated location, even though his home is in the area, as was the case with Ai Weiwei. The authorities pretend that the suspect is under "house arrest," but don't keep him in his house – but theirs. This is in direct violation of not only the law but also the Ministry of Public Security's own interpretations of the law, which prohibit what they accurately call "disguised detention."

### A Democratic Party

The Communist Party was founded by a group of 13 idealistic and politically radical intellectuals in Shanghai, and had just 50 members nationwide. On its 90th anniversary it had more than 80 million members, most of whom have forgotten the party's founding ideals, or more likely, don't care as they have only joined the party to secure their financial well being and promote their corrupt careers.

When the party was founded, it was the champion of liberal ideals, including democracy, social justice, freedom of speech and the emancipation of women. At the time, China was reeling from foreign occupation and immersed in poverty under a corrupt and dictatorial Kuomintang government. Against this background, the 13 founders of the party, inspired by the Russian Revolution, and feeling betrayed by Western democracies after the Versailles treaty transferred German concessions in Shandong to Japan, they looked to Marxism to cure China's ills.

Chen Duxiu, one of the party co-founders, famously wrote in 1940: "All authoritarian regimes are inseperable from brutality, deception and corrupt bureaucracy."

Mao, Chen's successor, also condemned the KMT's one-party rule and spelled out his vision for a new China. "China has one big shortcoming – its lack of democracy," *the Liberation Daily* quoted Mao as telling foreign journalists in 1944. "Only with democracy can China march forward."

The Communist Party condemned the KMT government's violation of rights. The *Xinhua Daily* and *Liberation Daily* – then opposition party publications – published articles hitting out at the lack of press, publication and academic freedom, election rights, freedom of assembly and association, and the ills of one-party rule.

Retired *Xinhua* journalist Peng Di, who was 99 in 2011, was an idealistic 32-year-old in 1944, attracted to the party by its advocacy of social equality and freedom and its toleration of different voices.

"Mao wrote extensively on democracy, freedom and equality ... that's what made the party attractive," Peng said. "Most of the young people who joined the Communist Party didn't really know much about Marxism, but they yearned for democracy and equality ... so people were full of high hopes."

Mao's most influential essays – *On New Democracy* (1940) and *On Coalition Government* (1945) – declared his early aspiration for a multi-party democratic government, but when his party seized power in 1949, it reneged on many of its promises. Mao announced that the party would pursue "the people's democratic dictatorship"– a phrase incorporated into the constitution, meaning that the party and the state may use dictatorial powers against reactionary forces.

"Mao changed after the Communist Party defeated the KMT; he had a 180-degree-change," Peng said. "The party itself became a dictatorship."

Today many current and former party loyalists are demanding the party go back to its founding ideals. Sound familiar? Echoes of Americans demanding that the nation rediscover its founding ideals.

Professor Zhang Xuezhong of the East China University of Political Science and Law has written articles challenging one-party rule and Marxism. He has called for the abolition of compulsory classes and exams on Marxism that all university students are subjected to.

"I know some university students and teachers have their own religion, and when they are forced to study and to acknowledge Marxism, they won't have inner peace. With Marxism all people are forbidden to challenge it. In my lengthy letter to the minister, I said this ridiculously forced instilling of Marxism on all Chinese has downgraded their dignity, imprisoned their minds and infringed upon their freedoms of speech, spirit and religion," Zhang said.

The Party achievements on its 90th anniversary also highlighted its ideological bankruptcy. All its policies run counter to its founding principles. The only way it can survive is if it reforms. The question is how?

Democratic reform is the only answer. In a country with a fifth of the world's population, power can no longer be concentrated in the hands of a few. "Intraparty democracy" is the new party sound bite. It still falls short of democracy as it only allows party members to vote for their leaders, who in turn run the country. But it's a start.

Change, revolutionary change, is in the air everywhere, including China. 2012 will go down in history as the year that brought about revolutionary change to the leadership of the two most important countries in the world. America and China. Two diametrically different political systems that have one thing in common: *We the People*.

The Communist Party in China and the Democratic and Republican parties in the U.S. and the political systems they ran headlong into revolutionary challenges and changes starting in 2012.

One of the most outspoken critics in China demanding change is Hu Deping, the son of late reformist leader Hu Yaobang, the former Communist Party general secretary whose death in April 1989 sparked the national student-led pro-democracy movement that resulted in the army assault on Tiananmen on June 4 that year. Hu was known for his liberal views and played a key role in China's opening up in the 1980s. He was forced to resign in 1987 after arguing that political reforms should accompany China's economic opening. Deping's book, *Why China Wanted Reform – Remembering My Father Hu Yaobang,* published in 2011, recalls the late reformist leader's views and ideological shifts toward reform.

The reality is that the party is communist in name only. It is anything but communist. All one has to do is look at the people driving up to party functions in fancy cars, fancy clothes, expensive jewelry and credit cards that finance the purchases of their overseas homes.

China's response to its domestic and foreign critics? An intense new wave of scrutiny and pressure on foreign organizations and journalists by the authorities, reflecting growing fears among Chinese leaders over the influence that foreigners and Western liberal ideas wield in China. At least 60 outreach-type activities organized by the U.S. Embassy, like cultural forums, school programs and ambassadorial visits, were cancelled between February and April 2011. Some officials go so far as telling foreign diplomats that they believe the U.S. is actively fomenting revolution. It wouldn't surprise me if that were true.

Be that as it may, the fact remains that despite more than 30 years of Chinese reforms and opening up, the handling of disgraced party leaders continues to be dictated by political needs, not public accountability. The central political consideration of the elite in the Communist Party is pretty clear. They have to maintain unity, orchestrate smooth leadership transitions, and maintain policy continuity to deliver on the critical issue of economic growth. Nevertheless, its legitimacy and authority is on shaky ground without reform.

Family ties can no longer continue to pave the way for China's top leaders. Granted China's system of government is embedded in the country's Confucian culture and history – which includes corruption – but that is no longer acceptable or viable. China needs a master reform plan that is designed for maximum impact to root out corruption.

Corruption is at the root of China's demands for democratic change. It is the plague that threatens the development of a "harmonious society."

Corruption is the root cause of factory strikes, mismanaged natural disasters, confiscation of farmland for developers, high-speed train accidents and deadly mining accidents. It should come as no surprise that the Communist Party has added "social management" as a new constituency from which delegates to the Party's 18th National Party Congress in 2012 were elected, alongside those from the existing fields of economics, technology, defense, political and legal education, publicity, culture, health and sports.

Party officials got more grass-roots representatives – workers, farmers, technicians, women – to attend and participate in the 18th Congress. They wanted 32 percent of the attendees to be grass-roots representatives, up from 30 percent at the last meeting in October 2007. Still a paltry minority of *We the People*.

People are taking matters into their own hands and electing independent candidates who do not have party backing to district people's congresses, usually individuals fighting for the rights of individuals affected by illegal land grabs. Any Chinese citizen 18 years or older, except those deprived of their political rights according to law, no matter what his or her ethnic background, race, gender, occupation, religion, education, financial situation or length of residence, qualifies to vote and be elected. But the reality is that the party intimidates and makes it virtually impossible for non-party candidates to run for office.

As social unrest and violent protests rise exponentially each year throughout China, the Communist Party likewise grows more insecure. A regime that is awkward and insecure in its own political skin and uncomfortable among its own people is always in danger. Lech Walesa once said that democracy is about government having a conversation with its people. If Beijing doesn't start that conversation, its own paranoid backlash against the Nobel Peace Prize, political dissent, freedom of speech and the rule of law will end up as a backlash against the Communist Party.

Violating its own domestic laws is one thing. But violating international law while trying to be a global player is juvenile in the grown-up world of geopolitics. What was China thinking when it hosted Sudan's President Omar al-Bashir in June 2011, a man who is wanted by the International Criminal Court for genocide and war crimes and is unwelcome in most of the world?

China's lack of moral compass, its crisis of morality, political and social, horrifically exemplified by the grisly death of Wang Yue, nicknamed Yueyue, the 2-year-old hit-and-run victim who was ignored by more than 18 pedestrians, has resulted in the resurgence of religion. Taoism, China's oldest religion, which I discuss in detail in *Custom Maid Spin,* is getting government support to instill the Taoist concepts of contentment, minimizing material needs and learning to slow down in a frantic world. However, like every other issue of relevant significance within the party, there is an opposition faction questioning and challenging the conventional wisdom. The split is contentious. Sounds just like the Republicans and Democrats in Washington.

The bottom line is, what is good for the masses is not good for party members.

On the religious front, party members have to adhere to the Communist protocol. There is no room for religion because there is none. Nevertheless, the right of religious beliefs granted the masses was only on the condition that believers also supported the Communist Party and observed socialist laws, thus placing the state and party before religion. No different than America's Founding Fathers.

In practice, China suppresses religions it sees as a threat to its grip on power. And for good reason. So while it encourages some mainstream religions such as Buddhism and Taoism to fill the faith vacuum, it has also tightened its control over Catholic believers. That's because Beijing views the Catholic Church as a serious threat because it was Catholicism that played a key role in the collapse of communist Poland.

So why is anyone surprised the Chinese leadership treats religion the same way they treat their diet? What is good for party members is not good for the masses? Party members can have exclusive access to clean and healthy organic crops at a *tegong,* a secret special supply farm for the elite, while the masses eat tainted food.

Now that the Basic Law has taken root in Hong Kong, it is only a matter of time before its roots and branches spread across mainland China. They already have. Not only politically, but culturally. Tea houses in Hong Kong and the mainland are being replaced by American-style cafes serving coffee.

The Chinese tea drinkers and growers are surrendering their fields and cups to coffee. That started in 1991 when Nestle opened a joint venture factory in China to produce its signature instant coffee. From an annual yield of only 1,000 tons of coffee beans in 1988, China today produces more than 40,000 tons and is planting and percolating more.

### *Deliberative Democracy*
In a one-party or two-party system, opposition parties become irrelevant. In both America and China, the biggest obstacle people face today is moral disagreement. Neither country has an adequate way to cope with conflicts about fundamental values. So *We the People* need a deliberative democracy. A system that allows citizens and their representatives who disagree morally with each other to continue to reason together to reach mutually acceptable decisions. A deliberate democracy cannot exist when views not shared by the one or two dominant parties in America and China make different moral views impossible to express.

Deliberative democracy involves reasoning about politics, and nothing has been more controversial in political philosophy than the nature of reason in politics. Amy Gutman and Dennis Thompson in their thorough analysis of deliberative democracy in *Democracy and Disagreement* summarize the concept best: "When citizens reason reciprocally, they seek fair terms of social cooperation for their own sake; they try to find mutually acceptable ways of resolving moral disagreements. The precise content of reciprocity is difficult to determine in theory, but in general countenance is familiar enough in practice. It can be seen in the difference between acting in one's self-interest (say taking advantage of a legal loophole or a lucky break) and acting fairly (following rules in the spirit that one expects others to adopt)... . The possibility of any morally acceptable resolution depends on citizens' reasoning beyond their narrow self-interest and considering what can be justified to people who reasonably disagree with them ... . Citizens who reason reciprocally can recognize that a position is worthy of moral respect even when they think it is morally wrong.

"When a disagreement is not deliberative, citizens do not have any obligation of mutual respect toward their opponents. In deliberative disagreement, citizens should try to accommodate the moral convictions of their opponents to the greatest extent possible, without compromising their own moral convictions. We call this kind of accommodation an economy of moral disagreement, and believe that, though neglected in theory and practice, is essential to a morally robust democratic life."

Deliberation is the most appropriate way for citizens collectively to resolve their moral disagreements, not only about policies but also about the process by which policies should be adopted. Deliberation is not only a means to an end, but also a means for deciding what means are morally required to pursue our common goals. We can deliberate in politics about only what we can understand, or what we can come to understand through political interaction with our fellow citizens. Tolerance requires majorities to let minorities express their moral views in public and practice them in private. Religious and sexual toleration are the paradigms.

Mutual respect not only helps sustain a moral community in the face of conflict but also can contribute toward resolving the conflict. One way in which it can do so is simply by keeping open the possibility of a different, more accommodating solution in the future. *We the People* may legitimately decide that the need to protect basic liberty and opportunity requires some degree of secrecy. Commenting on the procedures of the Constitutional Convention, James Madison made just such an argument for secrecy: "No Constitution would ever have been adopted by the Convention if the debates had been public."

"Despite their disagreement, both Madison and Jefferson appeal to the values of deliberation. Madison points to the outcome, the Constitution, but he is also assuming that the process that produced it was better because it was secret. Members could speak candidly, change their positions, and accept compromises without constantly worrying about what the public and the press might say. Jefferson may have agreed that the secrecy improved the quality of the deliberations (though he does not say so), but he gave more weight to the value of exposing the deliberations, whatever their quality, to the wider public. Deliberation must be made part of the public fabric of political life throughout all communities and government in the 21st century."

## *The Constitution*
Let's take a brief objective look at the Constitution and its roots that are entwined in the foundation on which America was built, and how it relates to the contentious issues of today. Issues that were hotly debated during the 2012 presidential campaign.

The United States of America was founded on July 4, 1776, upon the signing of the Declaration of Independence that proclaimed freedom from British rule. The Articles of Confederation and Perpetual Union, fully adopted in 1781, was the first document that attempted to unite the 13 colonies that had broken free from Britain. The Articles of Confederation governed these new states until the Constitution took effect in 1789.

The Constitution provided a more structured government and created the executive, legislative and judicial branches of the U.S. government, which are designed to provide checks and balances for each branch. The Constitution permits the federal government to create regulations and allows for the states to legislate that which the federal government does not.

This division of power or dual sovereignty was designed to ensure checks and balances were present at the national and state levels of government. At the time, those who were in support of the Constitution and strong federal powers were known as the Federalists, while supporters of states' rights and minimal federal government were called Democrat-Republican. So what happened along the way to today?

The debate over federal power continued through the Civil War, which was fought between the North, as the United States of America, and the South, the Confederate States of America.

The Civil War involved more than a fight over slavery. It not only exemplified a struggle for power, but became a means of employing stronger powers. President Abraham Lincoln exercised tremendous presidential powers that some argue were beyond the scope allowed under the Constitution.

The next president to employ tremendous federal powers was Franklin D. Roosevelt through the New Deal. Roosevelt's programs such as the Works Progress Administration, Federal Emergency Relief Act and the Social Security Act of 1935 established a new era in the role of government. Some constitutional scholars argue that with the advent of the New Deal, the constitutional power of the national government expanded so dramatically that the doctrine of dual sovereignty virtually lost all meaning. While the New Deal was questionable in terms of constitutionality, it was eventually supported by the courts after Roosevelt proposed adding more justices to the Supreme Court.

After the New Deal, the Commerce Clause, which was designed to regulate interstate and international commerce, was strengthened by a ruling in 1942 that included intrastate commerce that has effects outside of the state. The decision paved the way for even greater federal expansion.

The 1970s also experienced an era of increased federal power. Energy in particular was heavily regulated like never before after the Organization of Petroleum Exporting Countries – OPEC – enacted an embargo against the U.S. in 1973 for aiding Israel, which created an energy crisis to the point that gasoline had to be rationed. The price and availability of gasoline was federally controlled, which led to an imbalance in supply and demand when the energy crisis occurred. To make matters worse, the government mandated that gasoline be distributed equally among states and regions, which created a surplus in rural areas and massive shortages in urban areas because of the differences in population density.

To slow the country down even more, Congress decided in 1974 to enact a national speed limit of 55 miles-per-hour to reduce gasoline consumption. It was introduced as a temporary measure to last one year, but in 1975 it was made permanent. Before 1974, states were in charge of determining their own speed limits, so to ensure compliance the federal government required that states follow and enforce the new limits in order to receive federal funding for highway projects.

Then in 1987 the Surface Transportation and Uniform Relocation Act allowed states to increase the maximum speed limit to 65 mph. The main reason was that there was no federal agency to enforce the 55-mph law. Dah!

Alternative energy and all new innovative technologies, such as the Internet, should not be allowed to ever be regulated by the feds or any central government. These advances should be left to the states and individuals to enjoy and should be available to the consumer at the best price, and when justified – free. Conversely, on the private sector side, profit margins should be reasonable.

Two of my favorite federal boondoggles that career politicians and bureaucratic bumblers heralded as creating a safer and smarter America and which I criticized at length in *Custom Maid Knowledge* are the 2001 USA Patriot Act and the No Child Left Behind Act. They strengthened the federal government's ability to intervene in our private lives as it dumbs down American children kindergarten through high school at the local and state levels. Much to my delight, some states like Vermont and Colorado opted out out of NCLB but can't escape from the Patriot Act because the feds have tightened the noose even tighter on state rights.

More states, in fact all states, should be reclaiming and retaking the state rights their citizens have under the Constitution. *We the Apathetic Maids* can sweep in this transformation. Let's not forget that the 10th Amendment states that "The powers not delegated to the United States by the Constitution, nor prohibited by it to the States, are reserved to the States respectively, or to the people."

That's us. *We the Apathetic Maids.*
The world of America's Founding Fathers, like the world of Marx, Lenin and the founders of China's Communist Party, was a lot different then than the wired-world we live in today.

"Americans have debated the Constitution since the day it was signed, but seldom have so many disagreed so fiercely about so much," wrote Richard Stengel in his exhaustive analysis of America's foundation stone in the July 4, 2011, issue of *Time*.

The Founding Fathers' spirit and intent was accurately summarized by Chief Justice John Marshall in his 1819 Supreme Court opinion in the case of *McCullough v. Maryland*. He wrote that the Constitution was "intended to endure for ages to come and consequently to be adapted to the various crises of human affairs."

The Constitution was born in crisis and interpretational conflicts are, as they always have been, at its core. It was designed to manage the onslaught of challenges it has faced. It was written in secret and in violation of the existing one, the Articles of Confederation, at a time when no one knew whether America would survive. The Constitution has never not been under threat. Benjamin Franklin was skeptical that it would work at all. Alexander Hamilton wondered whether George Washington should be king. Thomas Jefferson questioned the constitutionality of his own Louisiana Purchase.

Let's not forget that many of the constitutional precepts of federalism were adopted from the tribal practices of Native Americans, a subject I discuss at length in *Custom Maid Spin*. Which reminds me of the e-mail Vinton Rollins, a good ol' Southern boy investment banker from North Carolina, living in New York City, sent me after we discussed and debated the Founding Fathers' vision of America, China and the political morass in both at the lighting of the Rockefeller Center Christmas tree on November 29, 2011, at the office party his firm Morgan Keegan hosted.

From Vinton's e-mail: The tribal wisdom of the Dakota Indians, passed on from generation to generation, says that "when you discover that you are riding a dead horse, the best strategy is to dismount." However, in modern education and government in the United States, a whole range of far more advanced strategies are often employed, such as:

1. Buying a stronger whip.
2. Changing riders.
3. Threatening the horse with termination.
4. Appointing a committee to study the horse.
5. Arranging to visit other countries to see how others ride dead horses.
6. Lowering the standards so that dead horses can be included.
7. Reclassifying the dead horse as "living impaired."

8. Hiring outside contractors to ride the dead horse.
9. Harnessing several dead horses together to increase the speed.
10. Providing additional funding and/or training to increase the dead horse's performance.
11. Declaring that as the dead horse does not have to be fed, it is less costly, carries lower overhead and therefore contributes substantially more to the bottom line of the economy than do some other horses.
12. Doing a productivity study to see if lighter riders would improve the dead horse's performance.
13. Rewriting the expected performance requirements for all horses.
14. Promoting the dead horse to a supervisory position.

The Constitution was written in secrecy because it strengthened the federal government at the expense of the states. The states had extraordinary power under the Articles of Confederation. Most had their own currencies and navies. The truth is, the Constitution created the United States, the first such democratic union. Without it, there would be no America, a fast-running horse that became a herd. The continent would be just that. Not much different than Europe. Occupied by 48 nation states that are dying horses.

Congress was given the power to run the united country in Article I, Section 8, the longest section of the longest article of the Constitution. Let's not forget that the Founding Fathers were revolutionaries. To them, an all-powerful state was a greater threat to liberty than discord and turbulence. Jefferson, like many of the antifederalists, did think the Constitution created too much centralized power. Most of all, the framers created a weak presidency because they feared kings. They created checks and balances to neutralize any concentration of power. This often makes for disorderly government, but it does forestall any one branch from having too much influence. The framers weren't afraid of a little messiness. All the more reason we shouldn't be so sensitive or pedantic about changing the Constitution or reinterpreting it. It was written in the spirit of change and revolution.

The purpose of the Constitution was to create a government that could unite, lead and govern a new nation, a nation the framers hoped would grow in size and strength in ways they could not imagine. And it did.

America has to retrench itself and get back to the Founding Fathers' constitutional basics.

Today's nagging debt ceiling issue was addressed by the framers in Article I, Section 8: "The Congress shall have power ... to borrow money on the credit of the United States."

The Founding Fathers created a central government in part to be able to pay off the debts from the Revolutionary War. The country was broke. The idea that America can default on its debt is unconstitutional. However, it should not take on more debt than it can handle. The budget should always be balanced, ideally, with minimal or no deficit. President Bill Clinton balanced the budget before handing over the White House to George W. Bush who took national debt into the stratosphere. In 1835, for the first and only time in U.S. history, the entire national debt was paid off under Andrew Jackson, who feared that debt could "destroy the liberty of our country."

Congress has routinely raised the debt limit – 75 times since 1962. It's not a partisan issue. Section 4 of the 14th Amendment states that "The validity of the public debt of the United States ... shall not be questioned."

The key is to avoid debt in the first place. But once it is there, it has to be honored. That's what the bankers keep reminding the career politicians they elect – at the expense of *We the Apathetic Maids* who then have to clean up their mess – and pay for the privilege!

The 14th Amendment adopted in 1868 also states that "All persons born or naturalized in the United States, and subject to the jurisdiction thereof, are citizens of the United States and the state wherein they reside."

When the 14th Amendment was being drafted, the last thing the Founding Fathers thought about was illegal immigration. At the time, America needed a lot more immigrants, legal or otherwise, if it was to grow – as it has. Today, competing against China, a country of about 1.35 billion people, a fifth of the world's population, America needs a lot more immigrants and a lot faster now that China is bringing an end to its one-child policy.

In 1898, the case of Wong Kim Ark, a man born in California to non-citizen Chinese immigrants who was denied re-entry into the U.S., made its way to the Supreme Court. The court ruled that the 14th Amendment indeed made him a citizen.

The U.S. Constitution is a set of principles, not a code of laws. A codified law says you have to stop at a red light. A constitution has broad principles that are unchanging but that must accommodate each new generation and circumstance.

I agree with former Supreme Court Justice John Paul Stevens who wants to change the constitution to reflect the New World Order.

A constitution in and of itself guarantees nothing. China has a constitution, as did Bolshevik Russia, Nazi Germany, Cuba and Libya. A constitution is more than a piece of legal paper. A constitution, to be a living document, must embody passionate feelings, something that is in the hearts of people.

In the midst of World War II, the great judge Learned Hand gave a speech in New York City's Central Park that came to be known as "The Spirit of Liberty." It was a dark time, with freedom and liberty under threat in Europe. Hand noted that we are Americans by choice, not birth. That we are Americans precisely because we seek liberty and freedom – not only freedom from oppression but freedom of speech and belief and action.

"What do we mean when we say that first of all we seek liberty?" the judge asked. "I often wonder whether we do not rest our hopes too much upon constitutions, upon laws and upon courts. These are false hopes; believe me, these are false hopes. Liberty lies in the hearts of men and women; when it dies there, no constitution, no law, no court can ever do much to help it." That's a truth that tyrants and dictators in Eastern Europe and the Arab world are learning to come to grips with. The U.S. Constitution does not protect our spirit of liberty; our spirit of liberty protects the Constitution.

## Need for Change
There is a long overdue desperate need for political change on many fronts, federal and state, starting with the Republican Party if it wants to survive – and the Democratic Party if it is to continue garnering support from the growing number of independent voters and defecting Republicans. Both

parties are sitting on the precipice of a political cliff that will make the fiscal one look like an ant hill.

More than a century ago, the British conservative Marquess of Salisbury warned, "The commonest error in politics is sticking to the carcass of dead policies."

Unfortunately, the two dominant parties in America and the Communist Party in China refuse to abandon their obsolete policies to meet the challenges of the New World Order.

Some examples are in order. In Washington, the Justice Department's Voting Section is static while the rolls of at least 16 states list ineligible voters, including nonresidents, disqualified felons – and dead people. Since when can cadavers vote regardless of which party is in power overseeing the Justice Department doing nothing?

In California, as part of the redistricting process, 4 million residents won't have a state senator for two years starting in 2013, while others have two. And that is because when the legislative district maps were redrawn, some new districts overlapped old ones. Voters in only half of the 40 state Senate districts chose representatives in 2012. Some communities in the old districts were moved into new ones that will not hold elections until 2014.

The partisan self-serving redistricting system that exists in most states in America has to be done away with. The same holds true for disclosure of campaign contributions to political campaigns – especially state campaigns – something Montanans took a stand on by approving an initiative on election day 2012 to not only have contributors to state campaigns be disclosed, but that a constitutional amendment to that effect be adopted by Congress.

New York has also proposed tough rules that could require tax-exempt groups to publicly report their political budgets and donors.

The two major American political parties are becoming increasingly isolated and estranged from today's America. Each party has roughly 30 percent of registered voters, while the roughly 40 percent of registered independents keeps growing.

China's Communist Party, with less than 100 million members out of a population of a billion and a half, represents an even smaller percentage and larger number of independents.

The fundamental changes needed are what the Founding Fathers prescribed for every American regardless of their religion, sexual persuasion, color, gender – and every other freedom spelled out in the American and Chinese Constitutions. The problem is, if the three parties do so, they will start looking like each other and be saying the same thing. So what's the point?

### Third Parties

A heated dialogue has gone on since the founding of America about the merits of alternative third parties. By the early 1850s, the antislavery movement destroyed the Whig party and helped found the Republican Party. Today, people as diverse as Ralph Nader, Ross Perot, Louis Farrakan and Michael Bloomberg are examples of people forming new parties. It is just the beginning of a popular groundswell of alienation.

Political parties have become machines for allocating power rather than representing the interests of citizens. The party game has lost its representative quality. The danger of such developments is that they strengthen an already strong trend toward a new form of authoritarianism. Opposition parties in a two-party system are irrelevant today as all they seem to do is follow the oft-quoted advice given by Lord Derby in 1841, that "the duty of an opposition is to oppose everything, and propose nothing." Meanwhile, the party in power takes a no-prisoners scorched-earth approach to politics in an effort to permanently disable the opposition party. Karl Rove, George W. Bush's political Rasputin, told Nicholas Lemann of *The New Yorker* magazine: "I think we're at a point where the two major political parties have sort of exhausted their governing agendas." Both the Democratic and Republican parties have fallen into the rut of protecting historical agendas rather than creating new visions for the 21st century.

I was delighted to read that former New Mexico Governor Gary Johnson had launched a long-shot third-party bid for the White House in December 2011. Johnson announced his intention to become the nominee of the Libertarian Party, seeking to capitalize on massive voter frustration with the White House and Congress. "Never before has there been such an outcry over the two-party system in this country," Johnson told supporters.

Until his announcement, he had been running for the Republican nomination, but his polling numbers barely got off the ground and he was barred from taking part in debates between the major candidates.

With nothing but entrenched party politics to choose from, citizens naturally lose interest in boring politics as usual. They pursue their affairs and let those in power govern. Along with parties and presidents, elections have lost their charm and promise for change. Declining voter turnout of *We the Apathetic People* tells the story. The time has come for a revolt of citizens against the two party-system and the arrogance of those in power.

Not just in America and China either. At the dawn of the 21st century, far-right candidate Jean-Marie Le Pen struck a cord in France because that country, like America, has been ruled by essentially the same people regardless of their party label. The same thing happened in the Netherlands with far-right Pim Fortuyn's List party after his assassination in 2002. Fortuyn's primary criticism was that the country was run by a self-perpetuating elite. Mainstream politicians accepted his emergence as a political force and few today believe the country will be able to revert to its earlier complacency. The Dutch Reformists again reminded the post-9/11 world that if the entrenched complacent career politicians ignore the will of *We the People*, *We the Maids* will sweep them out.

That happened in Japan when outspoken political leaders Shintaro Ishihara and Toru Hashimoto, the mayors of Tokyo and Osaka, the country's two largest cities, formed a nationalist right-wing third party that helped get the traditional nationalist right-wing-leaning party that had been in power for over 50 years, until it was defeated by a democratic left-leaning party in 2009, back in power and gave the country a prime minister who is a war-atrocity-denier. He denies that the Rape of Nanking happened or that Japan enslaved women across Asia to be "comfort women" in military-run whorehouses to service the conquering Japanese armed forces.

On a more positive note, a new centrist third party in Israel surprised political experts and pundits in that country's January 2013 election by its surprisingly big win that made it the kingmaker of the new Israeli government. One that will veer back to the center from its rightist policies and become more representative of secular Israelis than the minority religious ones.

Political rookie Yair Lapid, a broadcast journalist and hereditary politician, made his first foray into Israeli elections in the January 2013 election as an independent with his newly formed Yesh Atid – There is a Future – party to win 19 seats in the Knesset, the Israeli parliament, nearly overtaking Benjamin Netanyahu's Likud party, which won 20 seats.

What is fascinating about the election was that it had 34 political parties, representing all spectrum of the electoral universe, be they rich, poor, religious, hawks, doves, Jews – Ashkenazim versus Sephardim – Muslims, Christians, Arabs, vying for seats in the 120-member Knesset. The right-of-center and left-of-center parties ended up in a dead heat with each side winning 60 seats. That forces the elected politicians to collaborate in a working coalition if they want to continue in power. Gridlock brings about the downfall of governments as new elections are called because of a disgruntled coalition partner. In other words, there are always political alternatives, which ensures ongoing dialogue and compromise. Politicians are forced to listen to each other, and, like the Founding Fathers of America, know how to engage in dialogue, mindful that we are all in the same boat.

When politicians forget that they are in the same boat, whether the boat is named America, China, or any other country, political gridlock at the expense of *We the People* is unacceptable and has to be swept out by *We the Maids* to make sure none of us find ourselves suffering the same fate Belgians did for almost two years. Being without a government. It took Belgian career politicians, backed by the world's master bureaucrats, 541 days to form a coalition government in December 2011.

Lapid's "center-center" political pitch in Israel, to distinguish it from either left or right, was addressed to middle-class secular taxpayers on both the domestic and foreign policy fronts. On the home front, where voters are struggling to cope with the rising cost of living and are increasingly resentful of ultra-Orthodox families who rely on government welfare and refuse to serve in the military, or recognize the state of Israel, to the foreign front, on which Lapid says he has no illusions about a "happy marriage" with Palestinians; instead, he says, he seeks a "divorce agreement we can live with."

Iran's nuclear weapons program, which Netanyahu has described as the gravest threat facing Israel, did not play a large role in the campaign. Lapid opposes attacking Iran's nuclear program without American cooperation.

In South Africa, Mamphela Ramphele, a respected veteran of the struggle against apartheid, launched a new political party in February 2013 to compete against the governing African National Congress, calling on South Africans to "join me on a journey to build the country of our dreams."

The party is called Agang, a Sotho word meaning "build." The new party is the latest in a string of new party challengers to the dominance of the ANC, which has handily won every national election since apartheid ended in 1994 but has come under increasing scrutiny over charges of corruption and poor governance. In addition, inequality has grown in South Africa since the end of apartheid.

"The country of our dreams has unfortunately faded," Ramphele said. "The dream has faded for the many living in poverty and destitution in our increasingly unequal society. And perhaps worst of all, my generation has to confess to the young people of our country: We have failed you. We have failed to build for you an education and training system to prepare you for life in the 21st century."

Sound familiar? Doesn't that also hold true in America, China, Egypt, Greece, Italy and the rest of the world?

Bantu Holomisa, the leader of the United Democratic Movement, which he started after leaving the ANC in 1997, said that he welcomed Ramphele to politics and signaled a willingness to join forces. But efforts to blunt ANC dominance have struggled in the past. The Congress of the People, a breakaway party started in 2008 by supporters of former president Thabo Mbeki and other disgruntled ANC members, has seen its power wane.

What these third breakaway and new parties do confirm is that the Third American Revolution of the New World Order is well under way on the African continent.

In Pakistan, Tahirul Qadri, a prominent religious scholar, is demanding changes that would prevent corrupt politicians and tax cheats from seeking office. He also wants to sweep out politicians who have allowed terrorism and corruption to flourish. He has denounced the Taliban and espouses tolerance. Like Imran Khan, Qadri is becoming a significant third party political force, even though his Awami Tahreek party was only able to garner one parliament seat in the 2002 election.

One of my favorite third-party politicians is Thailand's Chuwit Kamolvisit, a Bangkok massage-parlor tycoon turned member of parliament, determined to expose the corruption he once nourished. The pimp-politician, also known as a thorn in the government's side, whistle blower and stirrer-upper in chief, saw his party win four seats in parliament in the 2011 election and articulated one of the best descriptions I have heard in years about career politicians.

"... A politician is worse than a pimp, worse than a whore. I adore the whore. The whore trades something that she owns, her body, while the politician trades the country and what belongs to the people. So I say, go ahead, call me a pimp. I am Chuwit, Super Pimp. Just don't call me a politician."

His chief of staff, Motomo, a bull terrier, was featured in most of his ads and stories. "I used my dog as a symbol of honesty, loyalty, everything you can't get from the politician," he says. I couldn't agree more. That is why my own dog Spud is my sidekick.

Fighting corruption was briber extraordinaire Chuwit's main campaign promise. He should know. For openers, he was paying senior police officers from four of Bangkok's biggest police district's 12 million baht in bribes every month. Chuwit also spoke of how he showered the officers with Rolex watches from Hong Kong and crates of fine French wine. When police dared arrest him in 2003 in a dispute over clearing commercial land he owned in Bangkok, Chuwit named names and amounts, leading to a number of police suspensions and demotions.

"Corruption in Thailand is supported by the officials, the police, the system. Nobody wants to talk. It is a big issue in this country," Chuwit said.

Sound familiar? Isn't the same thing true in America and China – and the rest of the world – as well? Isn't it time *We the Apathetic People* reverse our complacency in the 21st century before it is too late?

Singapore represents another interesting political fissure in Asia. There Prime Minister Lee Hsien Loong and his People's Action Party that dominated politics since its founding in 1965 suffered their biggest political defeat in the May 2011 elections.

Pundits and pollsters are not only repeatedly wrong about the U.S. and China political landscape, gardeners and seeds, but the political gardens everywhere because they are out of touch with reality – stuck in the 20th-century – and not the New World Order.

Voters everywhere, not just in America and China, want to legitimately buy into a system with an alternative platform that takes them back to basics and what the Founding Fathers and *We the People* thought America was really all about.

When the existing political parties don't pick up the sentiment and desires of their constituency, they run the risk of losing them to the other party. Worse yet, they might lose them to a third party!

"People within the two parties literally don't have the luxury of voting their conscience. They have to vote the way the party leaders tell them to, or they get into trouble. They know that without their party's support they're nowhere, or at least that's what they believe. The party leaders aren't making their decisions based on their consciences, either. Their platform is made up of political deals, favors, and influence. Does that sound to you like they're serving the people?" asks former Minnesota Governor Jesse Ventura. Doesn't sound like it to me. Does it to you?

Third parties are on the cutting edge of new ideas that historically are picked up by the dominant existing parties.

There is no rational representative, deliberative democratic reason that the two major American political parties don't amend their constitutions, charters or bylaws to refocus their priorities and attention on what *We the People* demand. If they don't, they should not be surprised if third parties or movements rise up to meet the people's needs.

Former Senators Olympia Snowe, Bill Bradley of New Jersey and Sam Nunn of Georgia, Representatives David Dreir and Norm Dicks and many other bright members dropped out of the Senate and House of Representatives and did not seek reelection because they were frustrated at their party, the political process, fund raising, and the two-party system. There is a message there. The existing political system is dysfunctional and out of touch with the people. These are smart, concerned Americans. Tune in America!

Career politicians are quitting because they can't take the polarization and partisanship that has overtaken Washington. "I do find it frustrating ... that an atmosphere of polarization and 'my way or the highway' ideologies has become pervasive in campaigns and in our governing institutions," said Snowe when she announced her retirement from the Senate.

"Everybody's got to rethink how we approach legislating and governance in the U.S. Senate," Snowe said. "We've miniaturized the process in the United States Senate," no longer allowing lawmakers to shape or change legislation and turning every vote into a take-it-or-leave-it showdown intended to embarrass the opposition. The extreme bipartisanship has bankrupted America, politically and financially.

The Tea Party activists have torn up the campaign and political rule book, especially for moderate or centrist Republicans. The intramural turmoil created by the Tea Party in the GOP reflects and magnifies the "my way or the highway" political mantra that has become pervasive in U.S. politics today.

The ultimate testimonial and endorsement of political frustrations was when lawyer-actor Senator Fred Thompson from Tennessee decided not to seek reelection because life in Washington made him "long for the sincerity and realism of Hollywood."

Campaigns today are won by political attack ads that accentuate the negative. A tactic the Tea Party has mastered. Scholars who study these things say that negative ads are often more informative – and even more accurate – than positive ads, in part because they get more scrutiny. When a candidate tells you he is fighting for America's families or working for better schools, who can prove him wrong? But if he calls his opponent a felon or – worse – a job outsourcer, he knows he'd better provide some evidence.

That's what campaigns are about. Forcing voters to adjudicate candidates' record. But that all changed in the 2012 presidential and congressional elections because so many of the political ads came from those anonymous independent committees whose commercials are less scrupulous about the facts and much more deceptive.

Richard Nixon summed up politics in America best: "If two wrongs don't make a right, try three."

That is exactly what the Republican Party and Tea Party movement are doing at the urging of their cheerleader-in-chief – talk show host Rush Limbaugh. The dogged determination with which Republicans fought to make President Obama a one-term president overlooked and ignored the fact that they were sabotaging the economy – and their party – in the process.

A brief historical review of how the conservative media movement and its talking heads have taken over the tone and direction of politics in America today is in order. The best summary of what happened to the Republican

Party is an editorial opinion Kevin Baker wrote for *The New York Times* in March 2012 titled *The Outsourced Party*.

For decades, Republicans have recruited outside groups and individuals to amplify their party's message and its influence. They have carried this off brilliantly, helping to shift the political spectrum in the U.S. significantly to the right.

When Republicans came to believe in the 1960s that they were up against a "liberal biased" media that would never give them a fair shake, they began the long march to build their own information establishment and to make it predominant.

In 1987, Mark Fowler, chairman of the Federal Communications Commission, persuaded his fellow commissioners to abolish the Fairness Doctrine. Since 1949, the commission had required television and radio stations to "devote a reasonable amount of time" to public issues and to present different viewpoints on those issues. But Fowler insisted that television was not a finite and supremely influential broadcast medium but "just another appliance – it's a toaster with pictures." He was backed by a pair of Reagan appointees on the federal bench, Robert H. Bork and Antonin Scalia, and the president himself, who vetoed a Democratic effort to codify the doctrine into law.

Right-wing radio was already prevalent on the airwaves before the Fairness Doctrine was abolished. But now it had the field virtually to itself. Conservatives gained a direct outreach to the public, free of any intercession by the "elites" Newt Gingrich is still denouncing. Right-leaning media networks like Fox and Clear Channel Communications became major media conglomerates – with no obligation to broadcast any conflicting views.

The biggest media coup of all for the Republican Party, though, was the advent of nakedly partisan Fox News, created by Roger Ailes, a leading Republican media adviser. Ailes thereby managed to throw the weight of Rupert Murdoch's worldwide media empire behind the party. Conservative politicians and advocates saw both their ideas amplified and their wallets fattened by a dizzying array of Murdoch television shows, books and newspapers.

But it wasn't just the daily media where the Republican Party proved ingenious in outsourcing its rhetoric and shifting the national dialogue. In 1971, Lewis F. Powell Jr., a Republican corporate lawyer soon to be appointed to the Supreme Court by Richard M. Nixon, summoned the business community to the cause with his famous memorandum, "Attack on American Free Enterprise System." Powell wanted business to fight back against what he saw as the many enemies of free enterprise, and his call to arms inspired the founding of the Heritage Foundation, the Cato Institute, the Manhattan Institute and other think tanks. Wealthy right-wing individuals from Richard Mellon Scaife to the Koch brothers poured millions of dollars into the battle of ideas.

The Powell memorandum also sent a vast influx of lobbyists to Washington, increasing their numbers from, at most, a few hundred in 1971 to tens of thousands today – a great majority of them interested in "freeing" business from regulation and taxes.

"Conservative policy institutes armed the party candidates with intellectual arguments, while the conservative media barrage blasted a way through to high office for even the most lackluster Republican nominee. Yet this meant that the Republican Party was outsourcing body and soul. Both what the party believed in and the heavy lifting of campaigns was handed over to outside interests that did not necessarily share the party's wider goals," wrote Kevin Baker.

Looking at the last four Republican candidates left standing in South Carolina during the bruising presidential primary in 2012, a banker and three career politicians, I couldn't help wonder how the Republican Party is still alive and expects to survive.

Republican stalwart David Frum summed it up best in an article he wrote for *New York Magazine* in November 2011. "I've been a Republican all my adult life. I have worked on the editorial page of *The Wall Street Journal*, at *Forbes* magazine, at the Manhattan and American Enterprise Institutes, as a speechwriter in the George W. Bush administration. I believe in free markets, low taxes, reasonable regulation, and limited government. I voted for John McCain in 2008, and I have strongly criticized the major policy decisions of the Obama administration. But as I contemplate my party and my movement in 2011, I see things I simply cannot support.

"I refuse to believe that I am the only Republican who feels this way," adds Frum. "We can debate when the slide began. But what seems beyond argument is that the U.S. political system becomes more polarized and more dysfunctional every cycle, at greater and greater human cost. The next Republican president will surely find himself or herself at least as stymied by this dysfunction as President Obama, as will the people the political system supposedly serves, who must feel they have been subjected to a psychological experiment gone horribly wrong, pressing the red button in 2004 and getting a zap, pressing blue in 2008 for another zap, and now agonizing whether there is any choice that won't zap them again in 2012."

When Senator Nunn appeared on *Meet the Press,* he spoke for many about the third-party threat when he said, "I think both major parties, Democrats and Republicans in the two-party system, have served our nation well for years. But I believe we're in a new period, and I think both parties have defaulted in long-term fiscal leadership. I don't think either party is looking down the road 15 or 20 years." He is right.

Polls today reveal that some 40 percent of U.S. voters now classify themselves as independents, a record number. America is becoming a purple nation where the biggest party is no party at all.

We got third parties. The Reform Party under Perot, now heavily split, the Greens under Ralph Nader, and Americans Elect, that despite raising $35 million couldn't field a suitable candidate in the 2012 presidential election. They might not have won much, but they brought a message about what we have to do for our children and grandchildren. They do serve a valuable role. And unless we have some campaign reform and some long-term fiscal reform, we're going to have numerous full-blown third parties in the future that will dwarf the existing Democratic and Republican parties.

If the "Big Two" parties do not come to grips with their unfair distortion and continue to perpetuate it, like Taiwan's Kuomintang, the Democratic and Republican parties will be relegated to the role of perpetual opposition groups.

The Kuomintang was founded in Hawaii in 1894 by Sun Yat-sen as a revolutionary league against the Qing dynasty. Sun's followers toppled the Qing dynasty in 1911. The Republic of China was established on January 1, 1912. From running all of China back then, it got relegated to running the province of Taiwan today and now it is merely an opposition group. The same fate awaits Democrats and Republicans in the U.S. if they don't reform.

Senator John McCain gave his party fair warning when he suspended his race for the presidency. "I will never walk away from a fight for what I know is right and just for our country... . What is good for my country is good for my party. Should our party ever abandon this principle, the American people will rightly abandon us, and we will surely slip into the mists of history, deserving the allegiance of none."

Senator Bill Bradley was a little more direct when he withdrew from the 2000 presidential race. "When you do battle with entrenched power, it's very difficult. I think that's what the story of this campaign was."

Is it time for other third parties to emerge to represent the majority? The silent unrepresented deficit multi-generational burdened tax-paying majority! The current bipartisan system is so poisonous and dysfunctional, it is beyond repair and must be replaced. The Clinton impeachment process brought to light how self-centered bipartisan Democrats and Republicans are with a total disregard and disrespect for the will of *We the People*. Republicans and Democrats each hold up the nominations of judges and other presidential appointees while extorting each other. The political acrimony builds and accumulates each political term and further holds up already gridlocked legislation that is beneficial to the people. Taxes, gun control, education, health, subsidies, environment, nuclear waste and child care.

Maybe Will Rogers was right. Let's get both the Democrats and the Republicans out of politics.

"You take a Democrat and a Republican and you keep them both out of office and I bet you they will turn out to be good friends and maybe make useful citizens, and devote their time to some work instead of lectioneering all the time," he said.

Richard Nixon accurately concluded, as do most politicians when they leave Washington, that the system's current failures rest on the shoulders of both parties. Both parties are using the voters' cynicism as cover for efforts to jigger the system to fit their partisan and personal interests.

Nader best described the difference between the Democratic and Republican presidential candidates. He called them Tweedledee and Tweedledum and added, "The only difference between them is the velocity at which their knees hit the floor when the global corporations come into the room. We are dealing here with the ultimate kamikaze dive into a corrupt two-party system."

America was founded on a third-party philosophy. The Founding Fathers didn't like the existing parties or rules imposed in London's Parliament, so they started their own. Ross Perot understands this and that is why he started his own party. Are others far behind? Will the Green Party with or without Nader strike a cord in the people in years to come? To prosper in the 21st century, people need a multiparty system of true alternatives. Real political choices. One and two-party cloned look-alike political systems will vaporize like dinosaurs in the New World Order. Hong Kong's multi-party system fosters true debate, political discourse and democracy. Isn't it time America, the foundation of democracy, got back to its roots and did as well in the 21st century as it did at its creation?

In America, the institutions that are enabled by democracy can also be viewed as the very elements that reinforce and maintain individual, collective and political freedom. These institutions – American political parties – are not mentioned in the U.S. Constitution, yet seemingly maintain and ensure the freedoms embodied in the document. American history is shaped and defined by the agendas, ideologies and actions of political parties. The emergence of contemporary America can best be explained through an exploration of the history of its political parties.

Major and minor parties, splinter parties and various factions – both as independent institutions and as interacting groups – have defined American history. By analyzing the inception, growth and change of these political factions, the history of America can be best told as a history of party formation and change.

### *History of U.S. Political Parties*

The U.S. political system was not initially based on a two-party system. Disagreements within President George Washington's cabinet created a divide, and in 1796 the first election with two dominant parties was held. The Democratic-Republican Party, led by Secretary of State Thomas Jefferson, believed in a limited central government, limited commercial activity, and heavy support of agriculture. The Federalist Party, formed by Treasury Secretary Alexander Hamilton, supported a strong federal Constitution and favored a strong central government, growth of commerce and industry and the creation of a national bank. Although never affiliated with a specific party, Washington leaned toward the Federalist platform. After the War of 1812, the Federalist Party, which had stood in opposition to the war, fell apart. In 1828, the National Republican Party was formed with an agenda similar to that of the Federalists.

In 1796, the first election with two dominant parties took place. Federalist John Adams was elected president and Republican Jefferson became vice president. This split in partisanship within the Executive Branch prompted Congress to pass the 12th Amendment in 1804 to prevent the election of a president and vice president from different parties. The Federalist Party ended its presence on the political stage shortly thereafter. The 1816 election marked the last election in which the Federalists offered a candidate for election. Republican James Monroe won the 1816 election.

In the mid-1800s, a divide began to emerge within the Democratic-Republican Party. It split and two new parties were created; the Democratic Party and the National Republican Party. The Democratic Party was formed under the leadership of Andrew Jackson and supported limited national government, state rights and stood in opposition to economic aristocracy and big banks. This party eventually became the Democratic Party of today, and it is now the oldest political party in American history.

The first party convention was held in 1832. The Democratic Party initiated the convention in an effort to transfer political power back to citizens. The convention served as a means to select presidential candidates who until then were chosen by congressional caucuses. 1832 was a significant year in U.S. politics because it also marked the emergence of the first third party. A group of National Republicans who resented Jackson's membership in the Society of Freemasons formed the Anti-Mason Party.

The next political milestone, a shift in partisan nomenclature and ideology, appeared in 1834 when the National Republican Party dissolved and the Whig Party emerged. Led by Henry Clay and Daniel Webster, the Whig Party believed that Congress should have more power and wanted an increase in industry and taxes on manufactured goods, westward expansion and infrastructure development. William Henry Harrison was the first elected Whig president, running on a "log cabin" campaign in 1840 – criticizing Democrats for being too elitist and promising to return political power to the common people who lived in log cabins. Due to inter-party squabbles and disagreements, the party decided to nominate Zachary Taylor in the 1848 election because he had little political experience. Taylor won and served as the last Whig Party president.

1848 saw the emergence of another third party, the Free Soil Party. Free soilers were comprised of abolitionists who supported the Wilmot Proviso, which proposed the prohibition of slavery in any territory acquired from Mexico. Free soilers opposed slavery in general.

New party formations and combinations continued between 1852 and 1854. In 1852, the Know-Nothing Party emerged. Know-Nothings were former Democrats who objected to the wave of Catholic immigrants entering the U.S. By 1856, most of the Know-Nothing Party had joined the newly emerged Republican Party that was formed when the Whigs and Free Soilers united in 1854. The growing Republican Party elected

Abraham Lincoln in 1860, a year that represents the first of three critical U.S. elections. It was also the year that differing views on slavery created disputes within parties. In response to the tensions surrounding slavery, the Democratic Party split in two in 1860: the Southern Democrats who supported slavery and the Northern Democrats who wanted to abolish slavery.

At the end of the Civil War in 1865, the Democratic Party's two factions were reunited. At the same time, however, the Civil War Reconstruction caused the Republican Party led by Lincoln to divide into three factions: the Conservatives who believed that the Confederate states should rejoin the union – regardless of racial issues; the Radicals, who wanted the Confederate leaders to be punished by confiscating their property and protecting former slaves; and the Moderates who wished for some protection for former slaves but didn't want to cause problems with former Confederate leaders – in effect three new mini-parties. By the 1890s, both parties reorganized, forming the Democratic and Republican parties, the two major parties that dominate the American political scene today.

The Democratic Party consisted of many Catholics, immigrants and poor workers. The Republican Party was made up of many northern Protestants who supported the temperance movement and favored immigration restrictions. During the same period, in 1892, a major third party – the Populist Party – emerged, made up of small farmers, sharecroppers and tenant farmers. Populists rallied against large-scale commercial farming and supported federally regulated communication, transportation and banking systems.

After the election of 1896, Republicans gained control over the national government and remained in power for 36 years, with the exception of the two terms served by Democrat Woodrow Wilson. During the early 1900s, the Democratic Party supported farming, conservative economic and pro-labor policies. The Republicans on the other hand had strong nationalist goals rooted in expansion and development.

In 1912, former Republican Theodore Roosevelt formed another third party known as the Progressive Party or Bull Moose Party. Progressives supported women's suffrage, environmental conservation and electoral reforms, including initiative, referendum and recall. The Progressive Party was one of the most powerful third parties, receiving the second most electoral and popular votes in the 1912 election. However, it became evident that members of the Progressive Party were more closely aligned with Roosevelt himself than the party. As a result, by the 1916 election, most Progressive Party members had returned to the Republican Party, reinforcing the dominance of the American two-party system.

In 1932, the election of Democrat Franklin D. Roosevelt as president was another historical turning point, as it marked a shift in party control. FDR enacted the New Deal to lift the country out of the Great Depression with various social programs including Medicare and Social Security. The New Deal shaped the ongoing description of Democrats as socially liberal and Republicans as socially conservative. The New Deal kept the Democrats in power from 1932 until 1968, with the exception of eight years of Republican rule under Dwight Eisenhower.

By recasting the presidency as the "vital center" of American politics, the New Deal fractured the major parties at the national level, dividing them into presidential and congressional wings – thus in effect creating a "four-party system" that persisted for the remainder of the 20th century.

In the second half of the 20th century, Republicans gained control of the White House with the election of Richard Nixon in 1968, followed by Ronald Reagan in 1980, George H.W. Bush in 1988 and George W. Bush in 2000.

The notion of "responsible parties," as outlined first in the American Political Science Report in 1950, and revisited by the McGovern-Fraser Commission in 1970, further cemented the symbiotic relationship between parties and American democracy.

The two parties have distinct beliefs and policies. The Republican platform has been based on support for less government control, social conservatism, deregulation of business, decrease in funds allocated to social services, and tax cuts. The Democratic Party supports the regulation of business, civil rights, funding for social services, environmental protection, organized labor and other so-called liberal policies such as pro-choice and gay rights.

In recent times, the political scene has been dominated by this two-party system. Fiscal policies, immigration, health care, gay marriage, war, taxes, Social Security and intellectual property rights are some of the controversial topics that polarize the two parties. The George W. Bush administration ran and implemented Republican philosophies and policies through the White House for eight years until 2008, when Barack Obama was elected and Democratic policies such as health care resurfaced again.

The Republican Party still champions traditional family values, pro-military, anti-immigration, favors a free market economy and tax breaks for the rich. The Democratic Party, on the other hand, has favored policy reform for civil rights such as marriage and immigration, is anti-war and pro-working class. With rising tensions between the two parties, it is not surprising that Americans are becoming increasingly disenchanted with the bipartisan gridlock and fragmentation, resulting in the rapid emergence of third parties. Since 2000, more than 15 political parties have been founded that include the America First Party, American Heritage Party, American Independent Party, American Nazi Party, Constitution Party, Christian Falangist Party, Green Party, U.S. Marijuana Party, Independence Party, Unity Party of America, Natural Law Party, Party for Socialism and Liberation, U.S. Pirate Party, Jefferson Republic Party, Modern Whig Party, Independence Party, Objectivist Party, Reform Party, Tea Party, Americas Populist Party, Third Position Party, Conservative Party U.S.A., Veterans Party of America, We the People Party and Citizens Party of the U.S.

While many of these parties exist only in a few states, or have minimal support and backing, their existence speaks volumes about the frustration of *We the People* with the two mainstream parties.

By way of comparison, only six third parties were formed before 2000. The Anti-Masonic Party founded in 1826, Know-Nothing Party in 1840, Free-Soil Party in 1846, Populist Party in 1891, the Progressive Party, also known as the Bull Moose Party in 1912, the American Independent Party in 1968 and the Reform Party in 1995.

## Party Politics

The importance of parties in American history is twofold. First, individual parties enable the citizenry to exercise constitutional freedoms; second, competing parties allow the course of American politics to follow the will of the nation's majority. Party advocacy – and the belief in parties as a central institution in American politics – became increasingly prominent in contemporary U.S. politics as necessary foundation stones for true democracy to flourish.

Parties can be broadly defined as any aggregate combination of citizens who share similar beliefs with regard to government. Organizations, without distinction from organized interest groups or organized factions, or broad combinations of interest groups. As I pointed out earlier, the existence of parties was not written into the Constitution, yet they formed immediately upon the founding of the Republic because of the democratic freedoms granted by the Constitution. Likewise, the structure of American politics today – with two competing major parties and numerous third parties – is made possible and reinforced by the system of democracy outlined in the Constitution.

The winner take all, "first-past-the-post" system of elections in America causes parties to merge to the center, with the two major parties competing for that center, while third parties emerge and operate at the extreme ends of the spectrum. However, while current third parties are not likely to win most major elections, their importance has been more indirect – bringing together like-minded individuals winning some seats in local elections, and even making a difference in major elections by diverting votes from one of the major parties, as the Green Party has done to the Democratic Party.

In a historical context, the emergence of third parties invariably affected the creation and evolution of today's major parties in America, China and the rest of the world.

Aristotle defined a corrupt regime as one that rules for the private good rather than the public good. Jefferson similarly defined corruption as "a legislature legislating for its own interests."

A new breed of frustrated tycoon politicians who are willing and more than able to foot the massive bill to get their ideas on the public political agenda has emerged during the closing decade of the last millennium.

Michael Bloomberg, Steve Forbes and Ross Perot are the most famous and notorious of this breed of politicians in America. Tycoon-politicians are scorned by the political establishment and yet are the only ones who can afford to do something about it under the current dysfunctional system. One should not under estimate the wrath and vengeance of entrenched politicians. Hardball politics is the one game they do know how to play well. Aristotle reminds us that "man is by nature a political animal." After all, everyone has game. Especially career politicians, bureaucrats and their financial supporters. What is *We the People's* political game going to be in the 21st century?

Mayor Bloomberg exemplifies a political animal determined to become president. So much so, he switched party affiliations from Democrat to Republican to become mayor of New York and has been exploring third- party options ever since to see how he might become a viable third-party candidate for president. While doing so, he has built a media empire second only to Rupert Murdoch's. Some analysts argue it is more influential because of his ownership of *Bloomberg Television, Bloomberg Businessweek* magazine and a swarm of 350 newsletters on topics like tax, health care and labor. Bloomberg's Bureau of National Affairs churns out nuts-and-bolts information of interest to lawyers, lobbyists and lawmakers – Beltway insiders. This data can now be incorporated into his BLaw and BGov and become a one-stop-shop for lobbyists to game the system.

The Bloomberg empire owns all kinds of news outlets, including TV, radio, magazines, mobile, the Web – every medium except newspapers. "Bloomberg can be the best parts of Bill Clinton, Rupert Murdoch and Bill Gates all rolled up into one," said Kevin Sheekey, chairman of BGov.

Maybe such rich and famous men, once they make their fortunes, are merely looking for, in the words of Will Rogers, love and admiration: "What constitutes a life well spent? Love and admiration from your fellow men is all that anyone can ask."

Not only are they looking for love and admiration, but as political independent revolutionaries, they are trying to destroy and rebuild a nation. Let's keep in mind Mark Twain's admonition; "If a man be rich, he is very greatly honored, and can become a legislator, a governor, a general, a senator, no matter how ignorant an ass he is."

At a time when the state is in retreat, men with money and an inclination to act are stepping into the breach that *We the Apathetic People* have created. But who do these men really represent? Isn't it time we the frustrated apathetic people unite and take on a political system and establishment that is in dysfunctional chaos and that so far has been challenged only by frustrated tycoons who do not have a popular following? Isn't it time *We the Maids* create a functional and orderly order?

Who does Jesse "The Body" Ventura represent? He represents people who want change. Ventura beat an American hereditary political family heir, Hubert H. Humphrey III, with the battle cry "Retaliate in '98!" It worked and he was elected governor of Minnesota. Obama's "Change We Can Believe In" propelled him into the White House. How about expanding it to "Change, Retake and Remake!" or "Sweep Career Politicians Out, Sweep Change In!"? Maybe we need a catchier phrase. We definitely need a new party – make that a new movement.

Politics, like baseball, needs a change of rules to make it interesting and exciting again. Just like the 2002 World Series was a wild card series without the ever-present Yankees, the 21$^{st}$-century political series has to be without the dominant parties. When the wild cards first arrived in 1995 as part of baseball's desperate attempt to win back furious fans after the strike of '94, many self-appointed purists and pundits declared it the end of the world. Real baseball, the true meritocracy where a 162-game season provided immutably proper champions, was dead. Just like the baseball purists were wrong about change, so are the current bosses of the dominant parties.

Everywhere one looks in the world today, from America to China, the Arab world or Europe, one sees that the dominant parties of the 20th century are out of step and fashion with their people. The Democrats in America, the

Communists in China, the Christian Democrats in Germany, the Socialists in France, the Conservatives in Britain, the tyrants of the Arab world. Viable third parties are inevitable in the new millennium.

## Global Parties

Will the alternative third parties or movements of the new millennium be just national or will they go global? Interlocal communities can establish interlocal parties. The borderless society that cyberspace has created allows *We the People* anywhere to join forces and go global. Global parties with a common platform for all adherents, regardless of where they reside or vote.

The 21st century offers many opportunities for existing political parties to reform or face major challenges from other newly formed interlocal global political parties! Maybe existing parties just waited too long. The 21$^{st}$ century will see the blossoming of global third parties. It is inevitable with so many angry and frustrated people. All it takes is *We the Maids* to put our collective brooms to work.

Why should existing political parties have to be limited by national boundaries? Political parties, just like multinational corporations and labor unions, can and should become global entities. Global third parties. Not only those that arise in America, but in China, Asia, the Middle East, Europe, like the Green Party. Political ideas, passions and goals – like music, poetry, literature and the Internet – are transnational. There are no real borders. They are universal. Wherever there are people who yearn for change, they will struggle to build platforms that can bring about that change – just like the one I will propose in the following chapter.

Political consultants, campaign managers and media advisers from America can be found advising candidates in Argentina, Britain, Hong Kong, Israel, Mexico, the Philippines, Russia and South Africa. If these consultants have gone global, how long will it be before political parties, like rave parties, go global in the New World Order of the 21st century – especially now that social media makes networking so easy?

Cyberspace has eliminated national boundaries; equity and debt financial markets are global, as are politics and raves. Is it unreasonable to expect and welcome like-minded individuals and their political ideologies to converge around the globe?

The groundwork has already been laid in the closing years of the $20^{th}$ century. The Green Party, which was conceived by Goldsmith in England and born in Germany in 1979, made its way to the United States in 1984, originally focused on environmental issues, but in recent years has embraced other causes, including health care, social justice and education.

Seventy-nine Greens held elected offices in 18 U.S. states and Washington, D.C., at the end of the 20th century. They had 177 candidates run for state, local and federal offices.

"The oligarchy has made us feel powerless. The country is full of solutions for the problems. We just have to pull together," said Ralph Nader as he received the Green nomination for president in 2000.

We really shouldn't chuckle at long-shot Greens. Nader often attracted larger crowds than either Bush or Gore. Greens also formed part of Gerhard Schroeder's coalition government in Germany.

Global third parties with political platforms that appeal to people across international boundaries are a 21st-century reality. People of the world can and should unite. The Greens are the inviting hosts to the pasture of the future.

### Referendums and Recalls

To paraphrase Gao Xingjian, the last nobel laureate for literature of the last millennium: "I thought Mao was always right but in 1967 I had doubts ... . In reality we were not fighting for the party, we were just being used as puppets." Aren't all *We the Apathetic People* also being used as puppets, even in America?

Referendums and recalls are the ultimate people power expression of direct participation when elected representatives fail to listen or deliver what they promise their constituents. It has been used in America and Europe repeatedly when all else fails and ultimately is the only electoral weapon at the total discretionary disposal and control of *We the People,* as ousted California Governor Gray Davis found out. That doesn't mean that good laws or better politicians always are the result. After all, many of the ridiculous laws we live with today are the direct result of referendums. Nevertheless, when all else fails, the referendum process is a solution when career politicians fail to deliver.

This was exemplified in June 2011 in Italy where former Prime Minister Silvio Berlusconi suffered a trouncing in referendums that wiped out his flagship policy to return Italy to nuclear power and dismissed a law designed to keep him out of court by giving him legal immunity. Berlusconi was a defendant in three ongoing trials involving allegations of bribery, fraud, abuse of power and paying for sex with a 17-year-old girl.

Nearly 56 percent of registered Italian voters turned out to have their say.

"The high turnout in the referendums shows a will on the part of citizens to participate in decisions about our future that cannot be ignored," Berlusconi said after the votes were tallied.

The playboy prime minister was forced to resign a few months later.

Maybe the women of Saudi Arabia should explore the merits of introducing the initiative and referendum process to the kingdom now that they will not need a male guardian's approval to run or vote in municipal elections starting in 2015.

There are two types of referendums in America. The direct and indirect initiative. The direct initiative is a measure put directly to a vote on the next ballot after being submitted by a petition with a certain number of signatures, usually 5-10 percent of the total electorate.

The indirect initiative is a measure that is first referred to the Legislature and then put to a popular vote only if it fails to be enacted into law by the Legislature.

The process itself was first introduced in Zurich in the 1860s based on the tradition of *Landsgemeinde*, open meetings similar to what emerged from the early New England town hall meetings.

Referendums started out in Revolutionary America in those New England town hall meetings. The meetings enacted local statutes, elected local officials, set local taxes and established local appropriations by a majority vote of the town's citizens.

Thomas Jefferson proposed that the state of Virginia adopt the initiative and referendum process. Georgia and Massachusetts adopted the processes as state law.

Rapid urban growth and industrial expansion led to an increase in demand for social and political change in the late 1800s. People were dissatisfied with how government was handling issues of interest and concern to citizens and became discouraged by their lack of political power granted by the Constitution. They decided to take matters into their own hands and vote a popular issue into law, circumventing the career politicians and their resistance to do so. Isn't that something *We the People* should be doing more of to bring about the real change America so desperately needs?

The Populist and Progressive eras of the 1880s and 1890s saw the emergence of the People's Power League, the Direct Legislation League of New Jersey and the National Direct Legislation League. Early advocacy of the processes by James Sullivan and Eltweed Pomeroy in New Jersey and nationally by the influence of Samuel Gompers and the American Federation of Labor during the Industrial Revolution fanned the flames of the push for workers' rights and a say in the political process.

Farmers also took to the initiative process because of their concern over the ever-increasing cost of transportation and decrease in the cost of commodity prices.

The factors and issues that accelerated the initiative and referendum processes back then were no different than today. Immigration, racism and politics. The Northeast of the country saw a rapid increase of immigrants in the late 1800s and early 1900s, mainly Catholics from Southern and Eastern Europe. The now-outnumbered Anglo-Saxon Protestants feared erosion of their voting power to control the urban political machines. Many questioned the new immigrants' ability to read or comprehend ballot issues.

The South feared the initiative and referendum process would lead to black political power, hence no Southern state to this day has such a process in place. In the West, the victims of racism were too few in the early days of the Republic to outvote the white population. Today, most Western states have the initiative and referendum process in place.

The lagging and less industrialized Southern economy hindered the spread of the initiative and referendum. Southern politicians and their financial backers discouraged the ideals of change in the Progressive movement.

Although ballot initiatives first began in America in 1898 in South Dakota, this political tool became popular only in the opening decades of the 20th century. Twenty-four states had an initiative process at the close of the 20th century. In the 1990s, there were 312 initiatives compared with 88 in the 1960s. Controversial questions have been forced onto ballots, often with help from out-of-state businesses that recruit and pay petition circulators.

The 2003 California recall of Governor Davis was facilitated by paid out-of-state petition circulators and a celebrity running to replace him. High name recognition and celebrity status ensures successful recalls and referendums. Recalls bring out a higher turnout of voters. In the California recall, the turnout was over 60 percent. It took 32 tries since 1936 to recall a California governor. While I lived in California, Ronald Reagan and his Democratic predecessor Edmund G. Brown escaped recall attempts when not enough registered voters signed the recall petitions. In 1986, there was even an attempt to recall state Supreme Court Chief Justice Rose Elizabeth Bird and several of her liberal allies on the court.

California has a long tradition of direct democracy, found in the legacy of Governor Hiram Johnson of the Progressive Party, who introduced the initiative, referendum and recall to the state Constitution in 1911. He did so to fight off the monied interests that bought and owned politicians with their contributions, gifts and bribes. California and other progressive states introduced initiatives, referendums and recalls to give people a direct chance to override the monied interests. Ironically, today these very devices invented to fight monied political corruption are used by these very same special-interests to counter the people's will. Hundreds of laws have been passed by initiative in California – usually by special interests that cannot get it done through legislation. They have the money necessary to pay the hired petition circulators to promote the measures.

The California recall of 2003 generated countless discussions at the FCC Main Bar as non-Americans tried to understand how the California political circus was possible in this day and age.

"How can you recall someone just elected a few months earlier and have 135 clowns run to replace him by just producing a few signatures and dollars?" was a frequent question Californians David O'Rear, the chief economist for the Hong Kong General Chamber of Commerce, and I faced in the runup to the recall.

"Well, it's not a daytime soap opera with porn star Mary Carey being directed by *Hustler* magazine publisher Larry Flynt, starring actors Gary Coleman and Arnold Schwarzenegger groping her," was David's initial straight-face response to wide-eyed baffled foreigners trying to figure out what was going on in California. The California recall melodrama was not the only one being played out in America at the time.

Wisconsin state Senator Gary George, who spent almost 23 years in office, was also recalled but did not draw nearly as much attention. I was in the States during the California recall election and was flabbergasted by the public fascination in the political drama playing out there.

For Governor Davis, it was a lesson in humility. For Arnold Schwarzenegger, it was a payoff for celebrity and money. He spent more than $21 million in his campaign to replace Davis. For Californians, it was a lesson in perseverance. Davis was ousted; Arnie was elected governor, and Golden Staters reveled in people power.

Perseverance is a powerful thing on the political and personal level.

## People Power

The meaning of Silent Majority, like the definition and meaning of *We the People,* Revolutionaries, Patriots and Political Activists has changed over the centuries and will continue to do so. "Nothing so needs reforming as other people's habits," Mark Twain reminds us.

The heated dialogue of campaign reform, by people as diverse as Ross Perot and Louis Farrakhan, is being echoed by people everywhere at all economic, ethnic and racial levels. It is the beginning of a popular groundswell of disenchanted and alienated people.

The definition and meaning of the Moral Majority of yesterday has also changed. The morals have slipped back, as have the generational values, as the impeachment proceedings and bitter partisan legal and political battles in Florida's presidential swamps highlighted. Ben Franklin reminds us that "If you would not be forgotten, as soon as you are dead and rotten, either write things worth reading or do things worth writing."

*We the Maids* can write many referendums people will find worth fighting for and writing about. That's what the Republicans and Arnold Schwarzenegger did in California at the dawn of the new millennium. So what is the silent and moral majority of the 21st century going to do?

> *We hold these truths to be self-evident, that all men are*
> *created equal, that they are endowed by their Creator*
> *with certain inalienable Rights, that among these are Life,*
> *Liberty and the pursuit of Happiness. – That to secure these*
> *rights, Governments are instituted among Men, deriving*
> *their just powers from the consent of the governed.*

Thomas Jefferson's phrasing in the Declaration of Independence that created America rings just as true today. Not just in America, but in China and the entire New World Order – and not just to men.

During President Clinton's visit to Hong Kong, the debate on democracy got rather lively at the FCC Main Bar. Arthur Hacker and I started comparing "People Power" in the United States, China, Hong Kong and England. I had just remarked that the Chinese people also ultimately have the power to change their system. The Communist Party has to constructively grow like a tree. Otherwise it will die like the many trees uprooted and blown away by the strong desert winds of change that periodically blow through Beijing or the Santa Anas in Southern California. Political typhoons are more powerful than their natural sisters. New political branches only strengthen the roots and consequently the tree. "Bollocks!" Hacker exclaimed as he jumped out of his seat to articulate his opinion more expressively.

"Some democracies like Great Britain get along without having a constitution. The U.S. Constitution and the Chinese Constitution have many similarities; but the difference is how they are implemented. Article 35 of the Chinese Constitution states: 'Citizens of the People's Republic of China enjoy freedom of speech, of the press, of assembly, of association, of procession and of demonstration.' In practice they enjoy none of these freedoms. Tiananmen Square for example, or the arrest in 1994 of Hong Kong journalist Xi Yang who was sent to prison for 12 years for publishing an article in the Hong Kong newspaper *Ming Pao* about China's financial plans, which in the West would be considered about as controversial as printing the weather forecast, yet in China, Xi was accused of publishing a 'state secret'," Hacker said.

"If history has taught us anything, Arthur, James Carroll reminds us it is that 'Violence is the price of the totalitarian impulse, whether religious or political,' " I responded.

Local reporters and photo journalists started to gather around to hear Hacker expound. Some had marched to protest Xi Yang's arrest. Stuart Wolfendale had carried the FCC "Battle Flag" designed by Hacker and was quick to echo Hacker's contempt. Only he did so more gracefully even though more vocally.

"Nowadays, by contrast in the U.S. almost anything can be passed off as freedom of speech," Hacker continued when Wolfendale stopped to catch his breath. "For example there have been recent attempts by the purveyors of child pornography to use the freedom of speech clause in the First Amendment to protect them from prosecution. While most people agree that the Founding Fathers did not have child pornography in mind when they conceived the Bill of Rights in 1791, the right to question and if necessary redefine what exactly is freedom of speech is considered perfectly valid."

In 1898, Pope Leo XIII condemned the heresy of Americanism because of its democratic principles. Today, in many subtle ways, the Catholic Church and religious extremists of all ilks are paraphrasing and perpetuating Pope Leo's condemnation.

What will America be in the 21st century? "People Power" in the U.S. has completely disappeared since the '60s. The raucous and poisonous Clinton political impeachment debate and partisan 43rd presidential debates in Congress showcased just how polluted the spirit and letter of our constitutional system has become because of the lack of "People Power," which has been replaced by "Career Political Power" making the U.S. Constitution follow in the footsteps of China's Constitution. The impeachment debates resulted in the political implosion of the leadership of both parties.

"This is not a very comfortable time in our nation's history for free thinkers and free speakers. But we have to have the courage to speak our minds anyway. We can't have a democratic society without doing that," former Governor Ventura correctly reminds us. He adds, "The will of the people is still the most powerful force in America."

*We the Maids* have to again sweep in "People Power" in the 21st century if our voices are to be heard.

If *We the Maids* want to sweep in our goal in the 21st century, we have to do what 16-year-old Wayne Rooney, the youngest player ever to score in England's top professional soccer league – did. As impossible as it seems, strive for our goal and score – like the U.S. soccer team did in the 2014 World Cup.

### Fighting to Win
*We the People* have the power to win as long as we are persistent and focused in pursuit of our goals. We have to be as determined as Sir Edmund

Hillary was when in 1953 he became the first man to scale Mount Everest, the earth's highest peak. As determined as Wael Ghonim, the Egyptian youth who helped start the Egyptian uprising on Facebook.

"People who live in a country are the ones to decide their destiny because they are the ones who eventually pay the price for whatever choices they make," Wael reminds *We the Apathetic Maids*.

Quarterback John Elway is another good example and a role model of persistence and perserverence. He was sacked 516 times, an NFL record. He lost three Super Bowls. His first was in 1987, when the Denver Broncos lost to the New York Giants. His second was in 1988, when the Broncos lost to Washington. His third was in 1990, when the Bronco's lost to San Francisco.

Did Elway give up? Of course not. Not only did he return to games in which he was repeatedly knocked down, physically and otherwise, but he also became the winningest quarterback in NFL history, with a record of 148 victories, 82 losses and 1 tie, a .643 winning percentage.

"I may not always play my best," he said after his third Super Bowl, and looking for some light at the end of the tunnel, "but I always play my hardest. I'm competing all the way until the scoreboard clock reads zero-zero-zero."

No wonder he came back for a fourth time to the Super Bowl in 1998 and won it, at the tender age of 37, risking loin and limb, to scramble and dive for a crucial first down late in the 31-24 victory over the highly favored Green Bay Packers.

"You wonder if you're going to run out of years," Elway said. "But fortunately, I hung on." Then Elway came back to lead Denver to a second straight Super Bowl championship over Atlanta in 1999. His more recent successor, Tim Tebow, almost replicated Elway's feats but became a verb instead – "tebowing" – kneeling in prayer with head resting on one hand, oblivious to surroundings after victories.

Cal Ripken's work ethic that allowed him to play 2,632 consecutive baseball games, get 3,107 hits and 421 home runs, making him one of only seven players to top both the 3,000 and 400 plateaus, is another American hero who exemplifies perseverance.

America is all about perseverance, creativity and innovation.

The Perseverance Man, Michael Chang is another example of a fighting champ. A Chinese-American champion in the white sport of tennis. Although he won only one Grand Slam, he was an inspiration and will be remembered for his impact on other players as well as stretching his 5-foot-9-inch frame to the max. When young Pete Sampras became antsy about trying to put a worm on a fishing hook, Chang counseled him: "You need patience. It takes patience to crack the top 10 and patience to catch a fish. Patience, Pete, patience," according to Franz Lidz of *Sports Illustrated*, who was fishing with the tennis superstars.

Sports heroes like Elway, Ripken and Chang are great metaphors for what *We the Maids* can also do if we have the same kind of persistence and perseverance to change the political system in America in the 21st century.

*We the Maids* are no different than the numerous underdogs at Super Bowls or World Series that are repeatedly forecast to lose by the odds makers and so-called experts. The underdogs often win. I was repeatedly reminded of this as a Raiders season ticket holder when they were a Los Angeles team between their sojourns in Oakland. Watching with my son Jonas as the Raiders beat the Washington Redskins 38-9 in 1984 was a lasting reminder.

### Defying Death

The River Clyde running through Glasgow was poisoned for more than a century by the fetid byproducts of industry from the Industrial Revolution. Pollution and chemicals destroyed its fish and wildlife. Now, with heavy industry gone and Glasgow reborn as a cultural center, the Clyde is coming back to life. For the first time since the 1800s, native salmon have returned in sizable numbers, reflecting the new cleanliness of a river that once was one of the filthiest in Britain.

The return of the salmon is metaphorically symbolic of how entrenched poisonous filth – environmental and political – can be cleaned up by *We the Maids*. It just takes patience and perseverance.

Yachting's America's Cup is another millennium example of patience and perserverence. Italian-born Swiss Ernesto Bertarelli brought the America's Cup back to Europe in 2003, after it left for America after the first race run in 1851 around the Isle of Wight.

Imagine if, thousands of years ago, there had been no one crazy enough to be the first to catch and ride a horse, or to paddle out to sea astride a log. 2004 marked the 100th anniversary of the first powered flight, by the Wright Brothers. The daring of the people who performed these feats, the explorers and other assorted "crazies," are essential to the evolution of society.

The late Nelson Mandela is an example of how political change can be achieved with patience and perseverance. An activist in South Africa since his student days at Fort Hare University, Mandela opened the first black law firm in Johannesburg in 1952, along with fellow activist Oliver Tambo, and was imprisoned several times before beginning his 27-year term for treason and sabotage in 1964.

"I have fought against white domination, and I have fought against black domination," Mandela said in a famous speech from the dock during his trial, where he faced the possibility of a death sentence. "I have cherished the ideal of a democratic and free society in which all persons live together in harmony and with equal opportunities. It is an ideal which I hope to live for and to achieve. But if need be, it is an ideal for which I am prepared to die."

Many believers in human rights, democracy and equality have died for their beliefs. Sergei Yushenkov, a liberal critic of Vladimir Putin, was shot dead on a Moscow street. So was his co-chairman of the Liberal Russia party, Vladimir Golovlyov. They are just two 21st-century reminders of the countless believers prepared to die for a cause. In a letter to a newspaper in 1992, Timothy McVeigh, the Oklahoma City bomber who took down the Alfred P. Murrah Federal Building in 1995, asked: "Is civil war imminent? Do we have to shed blood to reform the current system?"

I for one don't think so. Not in America. Not in China. Not in Russia. Not in Iraq. Not in Saudi Arabia. Not in Haiti. Not anywhere. When an American president takes the oath of office he swears to "protect and defend the Constitution" of the United States. Shouldn't *We the Maids* be taking the same oath? The least we can all do is periodically reread the Constitution to remind ourselves of our rights. Our failure to do so has resulted in the slow erosion of our rights. It has also resulted in America's slow regression to the dark ages that gave the country an illegitimate president, waging illegal wars under the guise of the Patriot Act. The post-9/11 road America is on leads to the kind of police state so beautifully portrayed in the Broadway play *Urinetown*.

The exploitive lifestyle of *We the Apathetic People,* happy to have meaningless menial jobs while the idle rich, landed gentry, and corporate world buy corrupt career politicians, is no longer sustainable if humankind is to progress in the 21st century.

There is a huge difference between growing older and growing up. It is never to late to be all you can possibly be. True democracy and the rights guaranteed by the Constitution and the Bill of Rights to all Americans will see the light of day again only when *We the Maids* use our elbow grease to do the heavy political lifting needed to sweep in the reforms necessary to fulfill the dreams and vision of America's Founding Fathers.

### *Outside The Beltway*

Shouldn't *We the People,* like Mandela, Elway, Ripken and Chang, refuse to be defeated by political apathy and capitalized career politicians? We can end-run them and their bureaucrats, lawyers and lobbyists. Shouldn't we persist and persevere in building the New World Order by using all available legal political means? We need to make elections and voting as simple as possible. Why are elections held on work days? Why aren't they held on weekends or public holidays? Why are they limited to a few hours on a single day? Why aren't elections made mandatory, like they are in Australia? Why aren't eligible voters encouraged to vote with a tax benefit of some sort or other incentive?

Career politicians "prefer elections to be complicated and inconvenient, because when fewer people vote, they have a better shot at getting reelected. They count on being reelected by their loyal core of supporters. High voter turnout is bad news for incumbents," Jessie Ventura correctly points out.

"The greatest challenge we face in the next decade," the former Minnesota governor adds, "is getting citizens involved in government again. How great a light for democracy the United States can be in the coming decades depends on how successful we are at bringing the people back into government."

"If you turn away from politics, it will turn on you," Ralph Nader reminds us. Why are we allowing ourselves to succumb, to being apathetic, indentured maids when we can fight for what is rightfully ours and ultimately achieve victory? In the words of jazzman Rahsan Roland Kirk, volunteer slaves?

The political process properly structured and actively utilized and engaged by *We the Apathetic People* will not divide the country. On the contrary, it will unite it.

"Rough Rider" President Theodore Roosevelt who led the charge up San Juan Hill in Cuba, said: "Service is rendered ... by the man who ... is actually in the arena, whose face is marred by dust and sweat and blood; who strives valiantly, who erred and comes short again and again, because there is no effort without error and shortcomings; but who does actually strive to do the deeds; who knows the great enthusiasms, the great devotions; who spends himself in a worthy cause; who at the best knows in the end the triumph of high achievement and who, at the worst, if he fails, at least fails while daring greatly, so that his place shall never be with those cold and timid souls who know neither victory nor defeat."
In the words of Mexican revolutionary Emiliano Zapata, "It is better to die on your feet than to live on your knees."

The signers of the Declaration of Independence signed off with a mutual pledge: "Our lives, fortunes and sacred Honor." *We the Apathetic Maids* need the same courage and commitment to sweep out the career politicians and clean the slate of their self-serving financiers and lobbyists.

## First Amendment Guarantees

The First Amendment to the Constitution was ratified in 1791 out of fears that the new central government in the United States might enjoy too much power to interfere in the lives of individuals. Yet ironically, fear periodically short-circuits the freedoms Americans are guaranteed under the First Amendment. From Abraham Lincoln's suspension of civil liberties during the Civil War to the internment of Japanese-Americans in World War II, the McCarthyism of the 1950s to the internment of Arab-Americans after 9/11, America sometimes has lost sight of its commitment to freedom.

Fear does that.

*We the Maids* must sweep out such fears and the career politicians who dare suspend First Amendment guarantees for any reason

"No society anywhere can take its freedoms for granted. It is a truism that 'the price of freedom is eternal vigilance'," Anson Chan, Hong Kong's former chief secretary, said in her address to the Heritage Foundation in Washington. "And we must have the courage to speak up if we see any attempt to dilute these freedoms. We will not serve the best interests of our country, nor those of our children and grandchildren, if we allow them to be gradually chipped away for the sake of expedience, or a short-sighted solution to a far-reaching problem."

A 2002 survey by the First Amendment Center and American Journalism Review, conducted by the Center for Survey Research & Analysis at the University of Connecticut, concluded that the events surrounding the 2000 presidential election, combined with the terrorist attacks of 9/11, may have begun to take their toll on public support both for freedom of the press as well as for the First Amendment as a whole. *We the Maids* have to sweep out these fears if America is to grow and prosper in the 21st century.

The challenge for all Americans – today more than ever – is to truly embrace the freedoms of the First Amendment and show just how strong *We the People* really are.

### Practice What We Preach

America exports great ideas. Democracy and capitalism are in the forefront.

Why then doesn't America practice what it preaches? Why do *We the Apathetic People* perpetuate the myth of the American ideal spun by career politicians and their spin doctors and exported by gullible media? Why continue to practice hypocrisy and maintain double standards that make a mockery of American values? By way of example, look at the double standards that existed between Baghdad and Washington before America's invasion in March 2003. Washington preaches embargo while American oil companies buy up Iraqi oil through their European subsidaries. Including Halliburton, whose CEO was former Defense Secretary and Vice President Dick Cheney!

The Long March of Mao, like the first walk on the moon by Neil Armstrong, started with one small step. Both became "a giant leap for mankind" which we have to further capitalize on in the 21$^{st}$ century. George Washington said: "The basis of our political system is the right of the people to make and alter their constitutions of government. But the constitution which at any time exists, until changed by explicit and authentic act of the people, is sacredly obligatory upon it."

The U.S. Constitution was designed to be respected and changed by *We the People* as needed over time. It's up to *We the Maids* to sweep in whatever changes we believe are necessary to honor and live up to the ideals our Founding Fathers and first president mandated.

The repeated self-destructive behavior of career politicians who ignore the will of *We the People* compel us to call a new Constitutional Convention to update the Constitution to deal with the realities of the New World Order of the 21st century. The majority of career representatives should never again be allowed to attempt to overrule the will of the people expressed at the ballot box. Alan Keyes, the Republican presidential candidate, likened Americans to a frog that sits calmly in a pot while the water gets hotter. He argues that they are passively watching their freedoms evaporate. "We're past medium-rare and headed towards well-done."

He's right. America has become a land of apathetic political wusses. Elections are determined by appearances on Jay Leno's "Tonight Show," David Letterman, Jon Stewart, Regis Philbin and Oprah Winfrey. Television talk shows have replaced *We the People* as the new kingmakers in America. Is this what George Washington and our Founding Fathers had in mind? I think not.

America, to paraphrase Druse Chieftain Walid Jumblatt, is "between Hanoi and Hong Kong." Hanoi hosted representatives from 28 communist organizations in the opening year of the 21st century, including America. The U.S. Communist Party is still active and has about 20,000 members and is gaining support, particularly from America's young who are increasingly disillusioned with a system gone wrong. Isn't America better off heading to Hong Kong instead of Hanoi? Forming third parties that are representative of *We the People?*

In 1776, Samuel Adams and other New England firebrands rallied their rebellious countrymen against King George III with the stirring slogan: "No taxation without representation," which led the American colonies to declare their independence from Britain. This lofty principle on which America was founded has to be updated to meet the realities of the New World Order of the 21$^{st}$ century. The alternative is to continue to allow career politicians and their monied elite to treat us like mushrooms. Feed us misinformation and keep us in the dark.

On September 25, 2001, voters in New York City went to the polls in the primary election that had been delayed by the tragic events of 9/11. Voting became an act of defiance. It was intended to be an act of defiance by the Founders. Shouldn't *We the Maids* sweep in defiant compulsory voting in the 21$^{st}$ century?

On April 18, 1775, Paul Revere rode from Boston to Concorde to warn American militias that the British were coming. On April 18, 2001, rocker Paul Revere rode from Seattle to Washington promoting Vietnam veterans' causes. When will *We the Maids* ride to Washington to sweep out career politicians?

Why does America continue to be a law unto itself when it comes to multilateral treaties, insist on being the world's policeman and then wonder why President Vladimir Putin acts like a czarist outlaw and President Xi Jinping challenges U.S. legal assertions?

The U.S. has not ratified the Law of the Sea, the law setting up the International Criminal Court for prosecuting war crimes, rejects the Convention on the Rights of Persons with Disabilities, the Kyoto Protocol on Climate Change, the Comprehensive Nuclear-Test-Ban Treaty, the

Convention on the Rights of a Child, and the International Covenant on Economic, Social and Cultural Rights.

Any wonder Mr. Putin is flouting his treaties and international law when it comes to Georgia, Ukraine, Syria and anything else he thinks he can get away with or that President Xi's main priority is to keep the Communist Party in power and its regional neighbors and the U.S. be damned?

The more the U.S. flexes its muscle into Asia in support of Japan, the Philippines and Vietnam, the tighter a reluctant China embraces Russia. This was evident during President Obama's high-stakes April 2014 tour to Japan, Philippines and Malaysia. He gave Japan what it wanted. A U.S. assurance that America would come to Japan's defense if China tried to reclaim the Diaoyu islands. What did America get in return? Nothing. President Obama and his negotiators left Japan empty-handed after failing to strike a deal with Tokyo regarding the 12-nation Trans-Pacific Partnership trade pact initiated by the U.S. – that excludes China – why? America is saddling the wrong horse to ride in Asia. The result? China and Russia are forging closer economic and military ties.

China's response to Obama's' military pledges to Japan and the Philippines? It put on a show of solidarity with Russia. President Putin visited China, signed several hundred billion dollars worth of trade deals, and started a week long joint naval exercise in the politically sensitive East China Sea. As if that wasn't a strong enough message, China also sent a flotilla of 80 military and civilian ships to install China's first oil rig in the South China Sea near Vietnam that resulted in a naval confrontation between the two countries.

We must let go of the past and adapt to the present.

America is a rich tapestry continuously being woven from the day of its founding. Old colors fade while new ones appear, richer and brighter. Like a tapestry, people and time have a way of letting traditional beliefs fade, while holding onto the new rich and bright ones. It is up to *We the People* to reach back and take a closer look at the original principles and ideals memorialized by the Founding Fathers in the Declaration of Independence, the Constitution and the Bill of Rights.

The simple 52-word Preamble to the Constitution spells out the goal of forming a "more perfect Union," and then gets right down to business. That more perfect America in the 21$^{st}$ century requires that *We the People* reconstitute ourselves in the new millennium. A Constitutional Convention to update and fine-tune the Constitution for future generations is long overdue. Until the convention is convened, any meaningful change has to begin at the local and state levels, where initiatives and referendums give voters real power and where citizen activism can overcome the timidity and deafness of elected officials. This is a universal truth and applies to all American communities in the New World Order. As Mahatma Gandhi intoned: "You must be the change you want to see in others."

It is up to *We the Apathetic People* to stop the career politicians and their bureaucratic mismanagement who have hijacked our politics and our freedoms. If we don't, they will do to America and *We the People* what they have done to Amtrak and the Post Office. Make sure America has just enough money and resources to barely stay on track and constantly be at their mercy.

*We the Apathetic People,* taxpayers and shareholders who fail to exercise our right to vote in elections or annual proxy meetings have no right to complain if the career politicians and corporate management to whom we have deferred enrich themselves at our expense. America was designed and built as a government of the people, for the people. Not a government of the career politicians for corporate management. Until we retake these fundamental rights, *We the People* will be unable to remake America so that she can survive, thrive and continue to guide in the 21st century.

American revolutionary Tom Paine said, "We have it in our power to start the world over again." A New World Order suited for the 21st century.

*Ask not what your country can do for you, but*
*what you can do for your country.*
– John F. Kennedy

## The Promised Land Is Blind
*Grey skies are just clouds passing over.*
– Duke Ellington


### Shangri-La

Imagine an earthly paradise high in the mountains where men and women live amid spectacular scenery and never grow old. In this utopian setting, some wise monks safeguard the finest aspects of the world's culture while renouncing its violence and materialism. This is the Shangri-La that writer James Hilton conceived in 1933 in his novel *Lost Horizon*. The concept of an earthly paradise still holds wide appeal. To many, myself included, Shangri-La is what America was and can be again. That is what America represents to most of the world. That is the political ideal the Founding Fathers had in mind for the Republic.

The Aquarius New World Order can be a gentler, more harmonious and tolerant time, of earthly peace if we go with the know, flow and grow without the blow. The cornerstones of knowledge, truth, peace and acceptance are the foundation needed to build a more prosperous and just *Shangri-La* heaven on earth – the American Dream. The American ideal. Fair and equal opportunities for all. The religious myth of paradise created by political clerics has to be relegated back to its fictitious womb. *We the People* can create a simulacra heaven or hell. Here and now. Not in kingdom come. What is our judgment today? Isn't every day our judgment day?

Confucius, China's ancient philosopher, said: "At 40 I had no more doubts and at 50 I knew the will of Heaven."

*We the People* with a millennia of life behind us can better understand the power and potential of change and be more hardened in our resolve to fulfill our aspirations and ideals. To paraphrase Winston Churchill after World

War I: All it takes is a common principle of action, a plain objective that everyone can understand and work for.

The beginning of the 21ˢᵗ century offers us a chance to build a peaceful world with justice and prosperity for all. Our redemption is in our hands, power and control. There is a perfectly balanced, sweeter tasting wine from our Founding Fathers political vine that *We the People* just have to open and cherish. The emotional and physical scars, the barbed wire and thorny rose Bushes we have allowed career politicians to plant around us have to be removed by *We the Maids*. They have to be replaced by our trip wires. *We the Maids* have to wish them a nice trip as we look forward to their fall. We can sweep aside fear, career politicians and religious extremists. *We the Apathetic Maids* must no longer perpetuate our sum-zero-gain game if we are to survive and thrive in the 21ˢᵗ century. There is an achievable balance between religious extremes, politics and spirituality. They can and must be harmoniously interpreted if we are to avoid the "Japan syndrome" and build The City on the Hill – A New Jerusalem. A place where all religions can again live together peacefully. The "city of God within the city of man."

The seven astronauts who perished on the shuttle Columbia at the dawn of the 21ˢᵗ century gave their lives to explore new harmonious frontiers. Males, females, black, white and brown from America, India and Israel. People and countries that represent the fountains that sprouted the world's major religions and cultures and the right to live and practice them freely joining hands to explore how to sweep the earth toward new solutions for the 21ˢᵗcentury.

We can be our own saving grace. We can stop burning in our self-started home fires of apathy and misery and instead set the "world on fire" and remove burned-out career politicians. The biggest barriers to change and lasting resourceful solutions are self-imposed in our minds and hearts. It's up to *We the Maids* to remove them and reshape the way we think and act. Life is more than just the fortunes we get from the fortune cookies that were invented in California by coolies shanghaied to build the first transcontinental railroad. Like the coolies, *We the Apathetic People* have been shanghaied and railroaded by career politicians and their monied interests.

The railroad crossings we face after the curtain was raised on the new millennium have a green arrow pointing in the direction of Hong Kong – the bridge between America and China – where America, and the New World Order it advocates, can rebuild the Founding Fathers' ideals from the best cross-pollinated cultural, religious, political, sexual, moral and economic harmoniously blended model from the preceding millennia and discard all prejudices. There are many roads to Shangri-La. The road of anger. The road of hatred. The road of vengeance. The road of fear. Love and understanding are the main global freeways of the 21$^{st}$ century. The various main roads, side streets, pathways and alleys that lead us to these freeways are well marked and lit. The choice is ours as to which one we take. The roads of hate, fear, and anger are so self-destructive that they destroy all who dare travel them. The paths of love, knowledge, understanding and tolerance are ones that *We the People* have to get on and expand into a globalized superhighway of peaceful fulfillment and accomplishment for our children. That can be our form of redemption on judgment day. Today and everyday.

This philosophy of contentment and happiness is one of the cornerstones of all religions, but one that is rarely practiced. The one exception that comes to mind is Bhutan. The Buddhist thoughtfulness with which Bhutan is approaching the process of change is incredible – and one we can all learn from. Bhutan is asking a question we all should all be asking: How can economic modernization be combined with cultural robustness and social well being?

In Bhutan, a kingdom of 700,000 people sandwiched between China and India, the economic challenge is not growth in GDP but in GNH – gross national happiness – the idea that social welfare, personal feelings and the environment matter as much as mindless economic growth. Foreigners and the international media were first admitted in 1974, and television arrived only in 1999. Only 20,000 tourists are allowed to visit the kingdom each year. Polygamy is allowed, but rare. The insular nation has embraced democracy – slowly – after the king abdicated in 2006 to introduce parliamentary elections.

Achieving national happiness should be America and China's goal, not only for their citizens, but all citizens of Planet Earth. There is no political formula on how to maximize a nation's happiness, other than an active process of national deliberation – town hall meetings to the max. Bhutan's Prime Minister Jigme Thinley summed up individual happiness in the summer of 2010: We are each finite and fragile physical beings. How much stuff – fast foods, TV commercials, fancy cars, new gadgets and the latest fashions – can we use and consume without deranging our own psychological well being?

A growing number of economists, politicians and academics believe there is a science of happiness and are putting the theory into practice by starting a "mass movement for a happier society."

Action for Happiness was launched in London in 2010, encouraging hugging, meditation and random acts of kindness. The group had more than 4,000 members from 60 countries in 2011, and hopes to recruit millions to march forth to spread goodwill and joy around the world. Co-founder Richard Layard, a professor at the London School of Economics, said the group "doesn't have any creed or dogma. It's a secular movement grounded in science."

"Our happiness levels have been stuck for the last 60 years," he said. "Income does not make a difference. The quality of human relationships at home and in the workplace – there are a lot of ways in which those have been neglected in favor of higher incomes."

Global happiness surveys produce surprising results, putting countries such as Bangladesh and Nigeria ahead of much richer countries. The search for the reasons has spawned the growing "science of happiness" movement.

We're familiar with the expression that money can't buy happiness. But can happiness buy money? According to emerging behavioral research, the answer is yes. Inner well-being supports the right investment behavior and leads to better investment outcomes.

By articulating the life we want to live and engaging ourselves emotionally in pursuing the path, the ability to live an authentic and happy life can positively influence our finances and political behavior. In other words, "Be happy."

Wear a happy face. Smiling is often equated with just one emotion: happiness. And evidence suggests that people who smile more tend to be happier and more successful in life than those who don't. Smiling is one way people in groups build trust and cooperation. The smile is a universal language, one a global party can easily wear. I am reminded of a remark from Anne Frank's diary: "Think of all the beauty still left around you and be happy."

### Recipe for Happiness
To be happy, people have to be able to afford the necessities of life. The bountiful necessities of life must have a political recipe ensuring that necessities are inexpensive and affordable. That means government subsidies and possible price controls on certain items.

Necessities are to be differentiated from the material possessions that so many of us crave and collect because we believe we will be happier with such material objects.

Material possessions preoccupy, consume and destroy. Possessions possess you. The safe deposit boxes destroyed in the numerous bank vaults in the World Trade Center on 9/11 were left with charred collectors memories. A stark reminder of how futile going through life collecting things can be. People collect and then become distressed, disoriented and distraught when their collection is lost because of divorce, robbery, fire, an act of Mother Nature or terrorism.

I know first-hand about collecting and losing the collection. I collected in Hong Kong and America. Hong Kong after all is a shopper's paradise. Consumer heaven. I lost my collections to Mother Nature and divorce. Kept up with the Jones and Chows. Consumer extraordinaire. Right trophy wives; right addresses; right cars; right restaurants; right clubs; right clothes; right jewelery; right accessories; right briefcase; right vacations; right luggage; right class air travel; right size bank accounts; right stock portfolios; right real estate holdings; right partnerships; right boards; right friends; and countless right gorgeous conquests in every country visited.

Unfortunately, they were the wrong values. Wrong priorities. Is it worth the misery and pain one subjects oneself and their loved ones? Most collectibles left after stock markets crash wind up at estate sales or flea markets. That presumes they didn't get thrown away or pawned by the heirs!

We'd better move on in the 21st century. What is life all about? Material or personal collections? What is more important? Family and friends or material possessions? Spending time changing a system we don't like or spending it in changing rooms? The best collectible is a viable functional political system we leave our children to cherish and enjoy. One they won't throw out, pawn or sell at a flea market.

America, unlike many countries, pins its hopes for a robust economic recovery on the willingness of millions of consumers to spend substantially more.

In his book *Beyond Our Means: Why America Spends While the World Saves,* Princeton professor Sheldon Garon, who is not an economist but rather a historian with a sociological bent, says our willingness to spend is driven most prominently by our reaction to major events in our collective memory, including wars and depressions, and that it also depends on national character, which differs across countries and through time. Spending, of course, is shaped by deliberate government policies. Notably, during wartime, governments all over the world often start huge public-information campaigns to promote savings.

The U.S., however, is an exception. More than any other country, Professor Garon argues, it elevates consumer spending to a virtue, in the process minimizing saving. There is even a suggestion that it is patriotic to spend, rather than to save. For example, in a speech two weeks after 9/11, President George W. Bush urged Americans not to be cowed. "Get down to Disney World in Florida," he declared. "Take your families and enjoy life, the way we want it to be enjoyed."

Personal consumption expenditures increased sharply in October 2001, and the recession that had begun in March of that year came to an abrupt end by November.

Do collectables really make us happy? No, according to Richard A. Easterlin of the University of Southern California, who has studied the relationship between materialism and happiness. We don't get happier as our wealth increases and our possessions grow. When our closets begin to bulge, we end up moving to a larger house. The more we have, the more we need, especially if someone we know already has it. Happiness, he concludes, is not like wisdom. We don't accumulate it as we go along in life. In fact, our happiness is more or less a constant in our lives. What we start with as working adults is pretty much what we end up with at the finish line.

That is why one has to love the Rev. Billy Talen and his Church of Life After Shopping. He calls Mickey Mouse "the Antichrist" and denounces the evils of mindless consumerism. The New York-based pastor-performance artist's shows are sold out as Americans come to share the good news – many Americans, whether by necessity or choice, are opting out of the vicious cycles of getting and spending and, he suggests, finding new values and meaning in their lives.

"There's a quiet revolution happening everywhere, of people just rolling up their sleeves," said Talen. Across the country, he  says, people who've realized that corporations have failed them are "de-mediating their lives, they're meeting their neighbors, they're starting new businesses out of their garages and station wagons, farmers markets are booming."

"Changealujah!" as the Rev. Billy puts it. Dressed in a white suit, clerical collar and a dyed pompadour that would've done Elvis proud, Talen lambasted the sins of sweatshop labor outside the Disney Store in Times Square, burst into Starbucks with a megaphone to denounce the "fake bohemia" and labor practices of the coffee giant, and performed an exorcism on Wal-Mart headquarters in Bentonville, Arkansas. He has been arrested dozens of times.

The Rev. Billy leads his congregants through programs of blazing testimonials, uplifting gospel music and fervid rituals of throwing away credit cards and blurring the lines between theater, protest action and religious ceremony.

Losing everything suddenly and not having access to cash, credit cards or your own home anymore because of corrupt malicious criminal business partners or expensive divorce, in my case a package discount deal on both, is a humbling and refreshing reminder of what is really important in life. The axis of oneself. Me, I and myself rejecting the political environment I'm in!

Anger, frustration and revenge are self-corrosive energies that are better for one's well being if converted to self-reflection and self-improvement lessons on what is really important. Family and friends and the rule of law that allows me to recover what is justly mine. Without the emotional and financial support of my family and friends, I would not have been able to discover who I really am and what is really important in life – or to finish this trilogy.

While trying to come to terms with why I was in such dire straits, I actually discovered that I'd never been happier even though I'd never had less "things," because of who I was with and where in the wake of 9/11. Hong Kong allowed me to put in perspective what is important personally and politically to survive. I learned to replace the so-called important material possessions with my own spirituality, sense of self and being. Coming to terms with oneself is the most difficult challenge of all. It is the heaviest rock to push uphill. Each step gets more painful as each emotional layer of the onion-layered armor is pierced and removed. Reaching the top of the mountain emotionally drained and exhausted only makes the stroll back a delight.

Every one of us must confront our personal issues at some stage of our life. The self-protective layers of emotional armor that have to be removed is the ultimate challenge the *Maid* in all of us has to first confront and clean off and out. Family and friends are the best *Maids* to help in the heavy lifting. Once swept away, the serenity, peace of mind and acceptance of what has to be done becomes self-evident. Personally and with family, community, country and universally.

There's a lot of truth in what Robert DeNiro said in the movie *Heat*. "A guy one time told me never get attached to anything you're not prepared to walk away from in 30 seconds flat." Isn't it time *We the Maids* walk away and sweep out the career politicians and their monied constituents we have accumulated in our political wardrobe of the 20$^{th}$ century?

The fact is that we are collecting and consuming ourselves into extinction, thanks to the neglect and encouragement of career politicians, their monied contributors and spin doctors. The overuse of our natural resources to produce the consumer goods we demand is depleting everything necessary for our continued survival. Our available natural resources can be measured by the Ecological Footprint. It measures human consumption of renewable natural resources in relation to the Earth's biological capacity to regenerate them.

According to the Swiss-based World Wide Fund for Nature, which is known in North America as the World Wildlife Fund, we are not living within our means. In fact, at the end of the 20$^{th}$ century, human consumption had already "overshot the Earth's biological capacity by almost 20 percent." Meanwhile, world population continues to grow by nearly 2 percent annually.

With that in mind, collectibles are possessive and destructive. Especially the human, political and sexual kind. They create an artificial sense of worth. The seeds of materialism were sown in *We the Maids* millions of years ago. Possessions define us as a species: a life without them would barely be recognizable as human. Our closest living relatives make do without anything material. Chimps employ crude tools and build sleeping nests, but abandon them after one use. Most other animals also get by without possessions.

How did we evolve from indigent ape to hoarding human? The earliest stone tools made some 2.5 million years ago, are an obvious place to start. They were designed to do a job. They were simple and expendable, like chimpanzee tools. But as tools became more sophisticated, a sense of ownership must have started to evolve. Tools became "possessions" – items that were valued by their owner and worth fighting for. Objects became part of our sense of self – the psychology of bling.

The quality of our personal lives and the values we instill in our children will determine the quality of the geopolitical world we shall leave behind.

*Black Friday – Cyber Monday*

I left Hong Hong and arrived in America on Black Friday 2011 – the day after Thanksgiving. The mob scenes of shoppers at big box stores on television news channels in San Francisco airport where I was waiting for a connecting flight to Los Angeles were mind-boggling. A woman pepper-spraying fellow shoppers to make sure she got her super-discounted toy? People pushing and shoving as if it were their last chance for salvation? I don't get it.

One of the biggest-selling items? Guns. Black Friday 2011 was the single-day, all-time high in gun sales by 32 percent, according to the FBI, which was flooded with background checks from gun dealers.

Overall Black Friday sales hit $11.4 billion, up 6.6 percent compared to 2010, and the biggest dollar amount ever spent on the day, according to research firm Shopper Trak.

As if that is not bad enough, U.S. retail e-commerce spending rose 26 percent on Black Friday 2011 compared with the same day in 2010, according to research firm ComScore Inc., which reported $816 million in online sales for the day, up from $648 million.

In 2012, Black Friday became Black Thursday with sales beginning after Thanksgiving dinner. Shoppers had to choose between hot deals and hot apple pie. Retailers started sales as early as 8 p.m. on Thanksgiving. To entice shoppers to line up even earlier, some retailers had promotions giving the first few hundred customers free "Great Big Goody Bags" full of stocking-stuffers.

Black Friday has become America's new national holiday, one that has evolved into the country's version of Spain's Running of the Bulls. The only difference being it's people running to beat each other to the bargains, especially guns.

Black Friday is followed by Small Business Saturday and Cyber Monday, the first Monday after Thanksgiving, which traditionally marks the first big jump in online spending for the holidays. Bargain hunters spend more than $1.5 billion on retail websites annually, according to the media hype. It is now the No. 1 online spending day. The most visited online store is Amazon, followed by Walmart, Best Buy, Target and Apple. Americans have become more comfortable shopping on their laptops, smartphones and tablets. Cyber Monday is typically a hit with office workers, who use their computers at work to shop on the job. About half the day's online sales come from people at work. No wonder U.S. productivity is down.

Another cryptic reminder of why not only U.S. productivity is down, but why America is down and out on the financial services front as well, was Bank of America's decision to charge debit card users new fees, only having to cancel them after their customers rebelled and threatened to switch banks and members of Congress objected.

Banks do know how to screw their customers and it is delightfully delicious to see banks back down from their inequitable unfair practices.

In a report in early 2011, the Pew Charitable Trusts found that the 10 largest banks reserved the right to reorder debit card transactions and process the largest withdrawals first. That will drain an account more quickly and could generate multiple overdraft charges – in other words – more fees for the banks. Pew also found that banks have as many as 54 possible fees, on such things as depositing large amounts of coins, asking for staff assistance, online transfers and so on. Even the most attentive customers have a hard time figuring out what they are being charged for what service, since notice of the fees are scattered throughout disclosure documents that run an average 111 pages – which most people don't bother reading yet alone understanding.

## Minimalism

The good news at the start of the New World Order is that one of the top consumer trends for 2013, according to Ford Motor, is the rise of minimalism, a return to actual experiences rather than e-life, and a push for quantifiable happiness.

Quantifiable happiness and e-life was highlighted by Notre Dame linebacker Manti Te'o's online fake-romance. It shed a spotlight on people's feelings and emotions and how easy reality can be replaced by e-life. When asked by Katie Couric why he wouldn't want a real girlfriend to spend time with, his answer was because the fake Lennay Kukua seemed real enough. "I found a lot of peace and a lot of comfort from being able to talk to somebody who knew my faith, knew my standards and understood," Te'o said.

Comfort, acceptance, someone who understands and loves the real me. It's hard to find in real life; it's pretty easy to fake online. Because the romantic charade came to light the same week that cyclist Lance Armstrong finally came clean about doping, it was easy to regard the sporting world as a morality-free zone, where everyone's looking for an edge and Te'o was just another cheater courting the Heisman Trophy, by garnering sympathy for his dead beloved "girlfriend".

Degrees of happiness can be found online, but is it real happiness? The Manti Te'o drama has reminded us how important real happiness is and to what lengths people will go to find it. Hopefully, in the New World Order *We the Apathetic Maids* will wake up and spend more time thinking about our wasteful spending habits and important personal relationships – at home and with career politicians. I know I am.

### Rise and Shine

One person, every person can make a difference. We just have to stop wallowing in apathy and start cleaning up and sweeping out the mess created by career politicians. *We the People* can and must make a difference with a smile.

The Alliance for a New Humanity is an international network of people working for positive change in the world. Its founding members include the former president of Costa Rica, Oscar Arias Sanchez, and singer Ricky Martin. What they are trying to do is "create world peace by creating global communities of consciousness."

The Bible's Exodus story reminds us that human beings can transform themselves and their situations. It reminds us that people who embark on generational journeys are the realistic ones, because they are the ones who see all possibilities the future contains. The best things humans have done have been achieved in an Exodus frame of mind. The U.S. was settled and founded by people who adopted the Exodus mentality. That mentality has to be brought into conscious focus again to find and rebuild the Promised Land.

The American character and determination has to be consciously and actively brought back to life again to rebuild the nation. Duke Ellington's line that "Grey skies are just clouds passing over" applies to America – and China – and the world that both countries must lead through the 21st century.

Yang Fudong uses the medium of video for a meditation on the isolation felt by people in China. *Seven Intellectuals in a Bamboo Forest* shows the social, political and personal dislocation of urban intellectuals in modern China. Their conversations and activities show how they, like most people in China, have lost the ability to connect. They can't relate to the countryside or the city. They can't relate to the people they know or to strangers. It seems the modern mainland has rendered them impotent, and they have no choice but to withdraw from society and wallow in apathy.

The film is a powerful indictment of how China has divested itself of traditional values – just like America and its departure from the ideals of the Founding Fathers.

Deepak Chopra, the best-selling New Age guru, declares that "Consciousness is the only reality. Everything else is a projection of consciousness. Which means our behavior, our biology, our perception, our way of thinking, our emotions, our personal relationships, our social environment, even the forces of nature as we experience them, are a reflection or a mirror of what's happening in our consciousness."

"Once you understand consciousness," he says, "you can influence it in the direction that you want."

Consciousness is the ground of being that differentiates into space, time, energy, information and the objects of the universe. It's the only reality. It exists outside of space and time, therefore it is eternal. And the person we call "ourself" is one projection of that infinite consciousness.

Chopra defines happiness as that "which includes peace of mind, which also includes fulfilling your desires, which also includes the ability to love and have compassion; but true happiness has to be in touch with the creative source of the universe, which we all have access to."

"There's a lot of research on happiness," continues Chopra. "People have found that there's something called a brain-set point for happiness. Some people look at a situation and see a problem; other people look at the same situation and see an opportunity. Can we change that brain-set point? Yes. Through cognitive therapy and meditation."

I agree with Chopra's claims that some hard emotions have a place in changing the world.

"Anger is an outburst, sometimes the release of which causes you to feel less stressed. But cynicism doesn't have a place. Cynical mistrust is a risk factor for sudden death from premature heart disease. Hostility is anger with a need for vengeance. Anger without the need for vengeance is actually a harmless emotion when it's occasional. And politically it can be very effective, when pushing for change," Chopra says.

Isn't it time *We the Apathetic Angry Maids* bring about the changes necessary to make us happier with ourselves and our community and nation?

Matt Ridley, author of *The Rational Optimist,* writes: "Empires brought stability at the price of creating a parasitic court; monotheistic religions bought social cohesion at the expense of a parasitic priestly class; nationalism bought power at the expense of a parasitic military; socialism bought equality at the price of a parasitic bureaucracy; capitalism bought efficiency at the price of parasitic financiers."

Ridley optimistically predicts that in the 21st century, "Prosperity spreads, technology progresses, poverty declines, disease retreats, fecundity falls, happiness increases, violence atrophies, freedom grows, knowledge flourishes, the environment improves and wilderness expands."

I would agree, but only if *We the Apathetic Maids* take it upon ourselves to sweep these goals into the Promised Land.

A good place to start rebuilding is on the West Coast shores of Amerexico. Santa Monica and Venice Beach sit on the edge of the Pacific Ocean cuddling, stirring and mixing the cross-culture of two continents the currents and waves wash ashore. Many are clearly visible on the funky Venice Boardwalk. Venice, the city that sent Marco Polo to China, has its namesake on the coast in Los Angeles. The canals do not compare. The creative people fusing to challenge the establishment do. Like its renaissance namesake in Italy, L.A.'s Venice continuously shocks and challenges accepted sensibilities. Artists, musicians, tattoo artists, Native American arts and crafts and sage, alongside Chinese incense sticks. The sweet aromas blend into a smoke signal that is gently carried inland by the ocean breeze.

The numerous massage tables covered with Americans getting their stress and pain relieved by Chinese masseurs to the sound of holistic Latin tunes and the aroma of blended sage and incense is a microcosm of how harmoniously *We the People* can live together.

Impromptu percussion sessions take place a few hundred feet off the boardwalk on the beach near the crashing surf. Percussionists and drummers of all sexes, colors and creeds beat out a fused sound that is absorbed by the sweet salt air and periodic whiffs of marijuana.

The waves blend offshore the best China has to offer America and gently splash them ashore. It's up to *We the People* to pick up the constructive ideas offered. The nearby Santa Monica bike path and walkway are the American ideal. People and nature in harmony with each other. On the bikeway, all languages are spoken by people on foot, bicycles, skates, roller blades and skateboards. Well-behaved pets share the pleasure and the warm sunlight and gentle breeze, especially at sunset when the golden orb gently sinks into the ocean, destined for the viewing pleasure of others in

China and Hong Kong. Its golden bright orange and purple reflections off the clouds, dark shadows and silver lining remind me of sunsets on Lantau Island and other outer islands in Hong Kong – and the golden opportunities it offers in its silver-lined culture. Flying between the canyons of dark clouds, blue skies above and dark ocean below as the sun reflects off the wing of the plane occasionally when leaving America, I cannot help but wonder why it cannot be as beautiful everywhere.

Watching dolphins dart and dance off the California coast and pods of gray wales migrate to the warm waters of Baja California, Mexico, from a plane leaving America, is an awesome sight to behold – and a reminder of what America is.

The hundreds of seagulls populating the sandy beach between the Santa Monica Pier and Pico Boulevard are much like the wild cattle on Lantau. They ignore people, their noise and strange behavior. One is witness to Mother Nature in one of her heavenly moods. If "Americans" could transfer and transform that harmony throughout the country and our global community, we would have a world community living at peace with justice. The land of milk and honey. The Promised Land – Shangri-La!

### The Dream
On August 28, 1963, Dr. Martin Luther King Jr. delivered a pivotal moment in American history with a speech that galvanized the civil rights movement in the shadow of the Lincoln Memorial in Washington. His "I Have a Dream" speech continues to resonate around the world, galvanizing people of all colors and creeds. The speech is still relevant today to all Americans. By deleting the words Negro and citizens of color, or substituting them with American, it applies to all of *We the Apathetic People*. An example:

> "The Negro is still languishing in the corners of American society and finds himself in exile in his own land.

> So we have come here today to dramatize an apalling condition.

> In a sense we have come to our nation's capital to cash

a check. When the architects of our republic wrote the magnificent words of the Constitution and the Declaration of Independence, they were signing a promissory note to which every American was to fall heir. This note was a promise that all men would be guaranteed the inalienable rights of life, liberty and the pursuit of happiness.

It is obvious today that America has defaulted on this promissory note insofar as her citizens are concerned. Instead of honoring this sacred obligation, America has given the Negro people a bad check which has come back marked insufficient funds.

But we refuse to believe that the bank of justice is bankrupt. We refuse to believe that there are insufficient funds in the great vaults of opportunity of this nation. So we have come to cash this check – a check that will give us upon demand the riches of freedom and the security of justice."

The nine-meter-high King Memorial on the National Mall that sits between the memorials to Thomas Jefferson and Abraham Lincoln is a well-deserved tribute to a man who epitomized what determined Americans are and can do when fully committed. King is the first man, other than a president, to be so honored.

Not surprisingly, his monument, like the man himself, was controversial because it was the work a Chinese sculptor. Many felt it should have been commissioned to an African-American. They challenged the artist's qualifications because of China's "poor human rights record," which they asserted would have been "abhorred" by King. I disagree.

The Chinese people, starting with Mao Zedong, long supported King and were among African-Americans' most reliable allies in their struggle for civil rights. Mao delivered two statements supporting blacks "in their struggle against racial discrimination."

The first statement was on August 8, 1963, 20 days before the "March of Freedom" to Washington. In the statement, Mao, who admired the African-Americans' struggle against discrimination and exploitation, gave an account of their plight as second-class citizens in the United States.

Mao's second statement was delivered on April 16, 1968. In it, he expressed indignation at King's assassination. Mao reminded the world that King was an advocate of nonviolence and that the U.S. imperialists could not tolerate him and used reactionary violence to suppress him. The statements by Mao inspired millions of Chinese to demonstrate in support of "our black brothers and sisters."

In May 1968, China issued a set of commemorative stamps honoring the African-American struggle against racism.

How Mao and the Chinese reconciled their support of African-Americans and Martin Luther King at the height of the Cultural Revolution appears to be one of many Chinese conundrums. Not really. The Chinese communists believed that everyone in this world should be equal and there was no room for racism. The Chinese believed that they and all oppressed people of the world should stand together and support each other in fighting against injustice. They still do.

### The New Millennium
There is no room for prejudice in the Promised Land of the New World Order. A good place to start is coming to terms with and addressing the ongoing practices of genocide and slavery. The New World Order has to be a world without either. We have to respect life, liberty and the pursuit of happiness by all fellow human beings.

We have to learn how to let go and consciously create a human and humane world. Mark Twain said, "In the beginning of a change, the patriot is a scarce man, and brave, and hated and scorned. When his cause succeeds, the timid join him, for then it costs nothing to be a patriot."

To reach the Promised Land, we all need to become American patriots. Reform is hard. Italian political philosopher Machiavelli reminded us that reform has clear losers — entrenched interests that will be hurt — with no sure winners. Reform therefore is likely to encounter fierce resistance. For reform to succeed, reformers must tweak this Machiavellian law to suit the New World Order of the $21^{st}$ century. We have to create winners before producing losers. We the People will all win by getting active. We need to take the risk. We have to gamble for change. In the words of political commentator H.L. Mencken, "The cure for the evils of democracy is more democracy."

There should be no doubt that we reap what we sow, and sleep in the bed we make. Better the devil you know than the devil you don't doesn't necessarily apply to career politicians and entrenched political parties.

Pope John Paul II reminded us that Christians cannot welcome the third millennium without repenting of their own sins. We all can and should repent for our failures, no matter what our religion or beliefs. We became moral and political delinquents in the 20th century.

To overcome our shortcomings and heal, we as individuals and nations have to learn how to sincerely say sorry for our misdeeds. One of the most powerful gestures an individual can make toward another, a sincere apology combines two of humanity's most ennobling attributes: conscience and accountability.

"A proper apology – one that is timely, that recognizes the harm one has done to another and that doesn't attempt to excuse or explain it away – can repair a relationship that might otherwise be irreparably damaged or destroyed," says Ari Kohen, a professor of political science at the University of Nebraska, who maintains a blog chronicling the worst apologies at terribleapologies.tumblr.com.

So why, if apologies can do so much good, do we have such a hard time extending them?

"One explanation is that in such a politicized time, blame – and therefore contrition – has become partisan. We demand apologies from those with whom we disagree as a way to score political points," wrote Brendan

Tapley in an op-ed piece in the *Los Angeles Times* in December 2012. It is one of the best explanations I have come across. I highly recommend Tapley's writings on the subject.

In *The Iliad,* Homer wrote, "There is strength in the union of very sorry men." If leadership and personal integrity are still defined by pursuing what's right, wouldn't it seem only logical that both are best proved when we know, and have made amends for, what we've done wrong? When sincerely given, an apology tour may just be the trip that steers *We the Apathetic Maids* home in the New World Order.

The 21$^{st}$ century is the beginning of our new era of global understanding, cooperation and unity. The truth must be acknowledged. Our only hope for the future lies in honest local and international dialogue and cooperative action. *We the Apathetic People* must take responsibility for our frustrated geopolitical environment. We have to stop blaming politicians, parents, religions and races for our dire predicament.

### Innovative Thinking

America's flaws can be fixed. With the right rules, says Warren Buffet, our system can work again. "It's like Martin Luther King said. We aren't trying to change the heart. We're trying to restrain the heartless."

"Isn't that," he asks, "what government is all about?"

To do so, America needs to improve its human capital through education and immigration, upgrade its energy infrastructure, create a globally competitive tax system and invest in research and development. Most importantly, the country has to get back to its entrepreneurial free-wheeling and thinking ways.

The biggest crisis in America is that Americans don't think anymore. They have forgotten how because they are consumed by the Internet and all the toys they have to play with on the Net. Americans should turn off their computers and mobile devices for at least an hour a day and be forced to think and analyze to reactivate their creative innovative juices. There is no right or wrong way to think. No black or white. Just the process and the ideas that result is what has always been Americans' cutting-edge advantage.

All one has to do is look at some of America's great minds and the ideas they thought of even though they were college dropouts. Edwin Land, co-founder of Polaroid, Bill Gates, founder of Microsoft, and, of course, Mark Zuckerberg, founder of Facebook, who summed up what America needs to do best: "The next 10 years will be about all the different products and industries that can be rethought," he said.

Thinking allows us to become innovative. Alternatively, if people want to be innovative they have to think long and hard as they analyze and look for solutions. Innovation thrives only in an open environment like America, something China lacks. Innovation ultimately depends on a country's institutions. Inclusive political institutions distribute political power equally in society and constrain how that power can be exercised. They tend to nurture inclusive economic institutions, which encourage innovation and investment and provide a level playing field so that the talents of a broad cross section of society can be best deployed.

"Despite the challenges that they are facing, U.S. institutions are broadly inclusive, and thus more conductive to innovation. Despite all of the resources that China is pouring into science and technology at the moment, its political institutions are extractive and, as such, unless overhauled and revolutionized soon, they will be an impediment to innovation," wrote Daron Acemoglu and James Robinson in their book *Why Nations Fail: The Origins of Power, Prosperity and Poverty.*

The threat for the U.S. is exactly the flip side of the opportunity for China. America's inclusive institutions are in decline, and the danger that the U.S. could follow other societies in history – such as the Venetian republic in the 13th century – that have seen their inclusive institutions dismantled and their economic success undermined is a real one.

U.S. society has been undergoing profound changes since the '70s. The huge rise in economic inequality is both an important aspect of these changes and also a warning sign. The problem is that economic inequality usually comes bundled with political inequality. Those with great wealth and easy access to politicians will inevitably try to increase their political power at the expense of the rest of society. This sort of hijacking of politics is a surefire way of undermining inclusive political institutions – as it already has in the U.S.

Those with economic and political power will use it to get more tax breaks and government subsidies for their businesses, while also blocking more innovative rivals and, directly or indirectly, undermining the opportunities that the rest of society has for acquiring skills, taking risks and innovating. This is most vividly and graphically demonstrated in the U.S. by oil companies and banks.

America has been there before. The resilience of its inclusive institutions allowed it to recover then and will do so again. Things were much worse in the 19th century, both in terms of economic inequality and how totally and unscrupulously the wealthy elite, the so-called robber barons, had come to dominate politics. Yet the robber barons did not prevail.

The U.S. political system was also able to tackle the problem of Southern segregation and black disenfranchisement, which if anything looked even more insurmountable. All of this was made possible because Americans stood up and fought for political equality, and the U.S. political system was open enough to allow them to do so. The same will happen again if *We the Apathetic Maids* sweep out the old world order and sweep in the new.

Demography and geography are destiny and America has both. Its demographics and geographic placement on the shores of the Atlantic, Pacific and Gulf of Mexico – not to mention military and naval bases, port rights and the most powerful navy – will return to glory only if it realigns its international relations with the right geopolitical 21st-century relevant partners, the way Americans do domestically with their personal and political relationships.

### The Steps

A millennial 13-step program for Nirvana here and now on earth may be helpful.

The 13 steps are simple. Get involved with Family, Friends and Community, Learning, Communicating, Honestly, Patiently, Actively, without Prejudice, with Tolerance, Perseverance, Humor, Fun, Spirituality and Happiness.

Replace the three R's with 13: Rediscover, Restore, Renew, Rise, Return Revive, Reclaim, Remake, Resist, Revolution and Reunite America. Remove and Replace career politicians.

We are all children of a higher power. To fully appreciate the fruits of the universe we live in, we must share its precious few diminishing resources with each other. *We the Apathetic People* have to step up. We have to take off the tinted sunglasses we have inherited that have clouded our vision in the last millennium. We have to accept that reality is a blend of the scientific, political and spiritual world views. The New World Order has to incorporate that energy and accumulate truth and pass it on to our children. Otherwise, like the great Mayan, Sumerian and Byzantine civilizations, America will also vanish.

The Parsis, the people from Pars, or ancient Persia, fled from their homeland to India during the Middle Ages to preserve their religion amid the spread of Islam. Today they are "a race nearly finished" because they will not accept converts. At the current pace, this prosperous and highly accomplished group – members include Zubin Mehta, novelist Rohinton Mistry and the late rock star Freddie Mercury – will disappear some time in the 21$^{st}$ century. Maybe that is why Freddie Mercury lived in public denial until the bitter end. This is the Parsis conscious choice. What is ours?

The New World Order cannot afford to be blind to our history of human hypocrisy, its managed misconceptions and political, religious and bureaucratic abuses. *We the People* have to end the waste and unnecessary pain, created by career politicians, bureaucrats and religious leaders with their subsidies, taxes, welfare programs, hatred and war. Do we want to continue the dialogue of the deaf in the 21st century? Do we want to continue being blindly led by career politicians? Only with our eyes wide open and our hearts and minds being receptive can we start working together on the Long March of finding the Promised Land. Each step together enhances our collective vision.

We must keep in mind Irving Babbitt's warning: "Where there is no vision, the people perish. Where there is sham vision, they perish sooner."

What is our vision for the New World Order of the 21st century? Heaven or our current hellish nightmare?

*We the People,* regardless of our religion, have to continuously and honestly re-examine our evolutionary history if we want to continue to evolve positively and constructively.

Although we may be momentarily blinded to basic truths, we must openly and truthfully ask ourselves what is it that we as individuals and as a community can do to dust, clean up and reorganize the closets of our old world order from scratch. Forward progressive focus. Psychologically, emotionally and physically. Why continue to be blinded by fear?

### *Viagra Generation*
Viagra and Cialis have breathed a new sexually active life into seniors – the baby boomers of the '60s. These drugs have reignited the libido of the sexual revolution generation of the '60s. More than any pill ever dispensed, Viagra has played to the yearnings of American culture: eternal youth, sexual prowess and, of course, the longing for an easy fix – economic and political. No wonder it has been prescribed to more than 35 million men worldwide. Hopefully, it will reawaken and reactivate their political revolutionary zeal with the same vigor that it stirs their loins.

The prospects look promising. According to an Associated Press-LifeGoesStrong.com poll conducted in the summer of 2011, three-quarters of all baby boomers still consider themselves middle-aged or younger, and that includes most of the boomers who are 57 to 65. A quarter of boomers insist that you're not old until you're 80. Hitting 100 is becoming old news in the U.S. and many other countries.

America's population of centenarians – already the largest in the world – roughly doubled from 1991-2011 to about 72,000 and is projected to at least double again by 2020, perhaps even increase seven-fold, according to the U.S. Census Bureau.

In 2011, 77 million American boomers celebrated their 47th through 65th birthdays. A solid well-grounded wise and knowledgeable political base to bring about real revolutionary change.

### Interlocal Citizen's Action League Movement

As I concluded writing this trilogy in November 2011, at the height of the 2012 presidential debates leading up to the January Iowa and New Hampshire primaries, listening to the Occupy Wall Street and Tea Party movements voice their collective frustration with career politicians and their monied Wall Street interests, I decided to form a new global political movement – i-calm–Interlocal Citizens Action League Movement.

The platform of the new global movement I decided to become part of – is a simple manifesto to shrink the federal government and restore state rights by taking the power away from career politicians and granting it to the people, where it belongs. The movements' 13 pledges are:

1. Call for a Constitutional Convention to change or abolish the Electoral College and allow direct elections by the people.
2. Separate church from state as the Founding Fathers intended.
3. Abolish the U.S. Senate and state senates and create a unicameral system.
4. Public financing of political campaigns.
5. Flat tax on personal income and capital gains at 17 percent.
6. Abolition of the inheritance tax.
7. Term limits – president and governors limited to one six-year term – and Congress and legislatures limited to one four-year term.
8. Balance federal and state budgets.
9. Restructure and shrink the federal government by at least 33 percent within five years.
10. Restore state rights by transferring many federal functions such as education, health and welfare to the states.
11. Abolish existing international bodies such as the U.N. and IMF and establish new global bodies that reflect a new geopolitical reality.
12. Address climate change realistically and develop alternative renewable energy sources.
13. Become a global interlocal movement.

## AC Policy

The America-China Policy – the AC Policy – should be one that is based on the words of former U.S. diplomat George Kennan, who said: "This planet is never going to be ruled from any single political center, whatever its military power," and "What we ought to do at this point is to try to cut ourselves down to size in the dreams and aspirations we direct to our possibilities for world leadership."

America is not going to contain China or "shape" its rise and China is not going to be able to restrain America from playing an active regional or global role. Both countries' economic futures are bound and intertwined tightly together. Sino-American rivalry must be eliminated to avoid a new cold war. Both countries must relinquish any desire for regional or global primacy. Working together to infuse shared values into a harmonious relationship and developing a mutually balanced beneficial AC Policy that can benefit a global recovery, peace and prosperity is what both countries must do as they learn to share economic and political leadership on the regional and world stage.

America and China cannot allow a new cold war to brew as both countries flex their economic and military muscles in the Asia-Pacific Region. There is room for both to play in the Pacific pond. Bilateral cooperation between the two Pacific giants is more important than muscle flexing that unnecessarily strains relations. The Obama Doctrine to resist China's challenge to U.S. primacy in Asia by trying to restructure the region into the Trans-Pacific Strategic Economic Partnership Agreement with Australia, Brunei, Chile, Malaysia, New Zealand, Peru, Singapore and Vietnam is an obvious attempt to marginalize the APEC platform – and China.

The Obama Doctrine is a mistake and will fail. "It commits America to a strategic confrontation which will cost it dearly, which it might not win and which it could possibly avoid without sacrificing its vital interests in Asia. America should step back from the Obama Doctrine and explore the possibility of a deal with China to build a better basis for peace in the Asian Century," said Hugh White, a professor of strategic studies at the Australian National University in Canberra.

China will not accept U.S. unilateral leadership in the region. China, unlike the Soviet Union, cannot be contained. It is the most formidable strategic competitor America has ever encountered because it is the only one ever to approach the U.S. so closely in sheer economic might. China will push back and has home court advantage. The cost to America is one it cannot afford, politically, militarily or economically.

There needs to be a mutually agreed upon code of conduct and dispute-resolution process contained in the AC Policy so disputes can be avoided or resolved quickly and effectively.

The two countries must forge a pact built on mutual interests and trust.

America and China have to get back to the Founding Fathers' ideals – the foundation stones in their constitutions – on which the two great countries were built and start from scratch again.

Imagine what the world would be like if both countries were led by the same global political movement – i-calm – the Interlocal Citizens Action League Movement.

### Our Choice

There is no absolute truth. We all create our own truth. The universal truth. We are all alchemists. We have the power within us to change what we don't like about us, around us or in this world. All we have to do is listen to our heart. Climb the tree of life and eat its fruit. Truth, knowledge and wisdom. Enjoy them naturally. Without preservatives. Natural recipes without dysfunctional ingredients. *We the People* can bring about the profound political changes we yearn for. All we have to do is treat one another with mutual respect as we begin to tear down barriers and tackle our disagreements.

The wonders and natural beauty of the New World Order are simply a guarantee that there exists a world that is as perfect as we can make it. Our fear of failure is the only impediment to fulfilling our dream for a better world for our children. For them to enjoy what our Founding Fathers dreamed of. The Danish philosopher Kierkegaard warned, "Life can only be understood backwards, but it must be lived forwards."

Albert Einstein once said, "The distinction between past, present, and future is only an illusion, however persistent." Time, said Einstein, is not at all what it seems. It does not flow in only one direction, and the future exists simultaneously with the past. We have read, heard and know about the future. *The Promised Land.* At the dawn of the 21ˢᵗ century, it's time to shake off the past and seek that dream.

Isaac Newton, the other great physicist who developed the Theory of the Universe, not only said that the future already exists, but believed that it could be known in advance. It is up to *We the People.* Our guideposts must be future milestones of the American ideal, not past or present failures.

The delegates to the Federal Convention met in Philadelphia from May to September 1787 and approved the new Constitution on September 17, 1787. The deliberations and debates had been held in secret. On the day the delegates completed their handiwork, some of them gathered on the street outside Independence Hall. A woman by the name of Elizabeth Powell stopped Benjamin Franklin, the oldest delegate at age 81, and asked him, "Well, Doctor, what have we got, a republic or a monarchy?" Franklin replied, "A republic – if you can keep it." It is up to *We the Apathetic Maids* to sweep out those who dare take it away.

The Preamble to the Constitution is the clearest and most eloquent description of the general purposes of our government.

> We the people of the United States, in order to form a more perfect union, establish justice, insure domestic tranquility, provide for the common defense, promote the general welfare, and secure the blessings of liberty to ourselves and our posterity, do ordain and establish this Constitution for the United States of America.

Why continue to ignore these precious 52 words and continue to be part of the silent dull majority and waste so much dead space and precious time? For us to be at peace and harmony with ourselves, enjoy all the human, emotional, social, physical, sexual, natural, technological, political and economic opportunities before us in the New World Order, we must first be freed of our current misperceptions, fears and prejudices and get back to the constitutional foundation laid by our Founding Fathers.

We must surrender our apathy, confront the career politicians and sweep them away and replace them with our inherent authentic power. We have to resist and rise above our apathetic tendencies. We have to uplift our spirit. Overcome not only our continued apathy, but prejudices and misinformation and embrace spiritualism, mutual respect and sincere dialogue. This is a power that no campaign contribution or promise can buy, monopolize or compromise.

This was hammered home to me again during the 2014 midterm elections as Democratic and Republican candidates were gearing up for the 2016 presidential campaign in a very lethargic way when I compared the political spirit and activity to what was happening on the streets of Hong Kong where people were demanding the right of universal suffrage for the 2017 election of Hong Kong's Chief Executive.

Our evolution will be determined by our choice. We can choose to continue being apathetic in the United States of Apathy or become active citizens of these global United States of America. Do we want to continue being puppets or do we want to become the puppeteers in the 21st century?

*The Only Thing We Have to Fear Is Fear Itself.*
– President Franklin D. Roosevelt

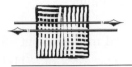

## Afterthoughts
*Full Moon Rising*
– Creedence Clearwater Revival

### *9/11 10th-Anniversary*
I've decided to end this trilogy at the same reference point I started the first volume, *Custom Maid Spin* — 9/11 and what it symbolizes and represents—in my humble view. Before doing so, I want to remind readers that I opened the trilogy with the following quote and question: *Where Were You When the World Stopped Turning?* by Alan Jackson.

The question is as indelible and as relevant today as it was back then. 9/11 was a defining day that forever changed and reshaped America and the world it once led.

The cost of change was the lives of thousands of Americans who died or were wounded that day and in the ensuing wars in Afghanistan and Iraq, alongside al Qaeda, the Taliban and other militia fighters and thousands of civilians – at a staggering cost of more than $1 trillion, according to the Pentagon. Terrorism and the terror it breeds were no longer experiences limited to distant shores.

The U.S. government was transformed by the attacks with the creation of the Homeland Security Department, the Transportation Security Administration, the National Counterterrorism Center and a raft of other centers and government panels dedicated to keeping the country safe.

Career politicians in the Beltway unscrupulously exploited the tragic occasion for their financial backers and lobbyists and their selfish greed that ensured America's political, military and economic implosion. That in turn led to the breakdown to an already dysfunctional policy and its absolute paralysis and failure. It is important that *We the Maids* make sure we take the lessons learned in the years since 9/11 and apply them to hold public officials in all parties accountable for their repeated failures.

It's no different than what they did on the financial markets front after the collapse of Bear Stearns and Lehman Brothers. The week of 9/11/11 was not only the tenth anniversary of 9/11, but the third anniversary of 9/15, the day Lehman Brothers imploded. Yet there has been less political or public will to challenge the crony capitalist corruption permeating the halls of congresses and parliaments worldwide and their bankers. Europe rock 'n' rolled from sovereign crisis-to-crisis as more and more people took to the streets from Athens to Warsaw.

America must come together again the way it did in the days after 9/11. A joining of hearts, minds, will, ingenuity, sacrifice, courage and determination to together make America strong and able to resist any assault or attack – military, economic, financial or political. The flame lit by the Founding Fathers must be rekindled and reignited.

9/11 is seared into all our minds, hearts and souls either consciously, subconsciously or unconsciously – and unfortunately many people appear to be in the third category, or is it grade? A reminder of religion and the conflicts it creates among "believers," something the Founding Fathers implored America to avoid becoming a party to because of the unnecessary and unwarranted political and economic damage, not to mention personal and emotional, and the destruction it would create for the Republic on the home front and abroad. What is the point of America's landscape being littered with so many millions of mindless bodies from the ongoing military war fronts overseas and the economic war fronts on Wall Street and every other financial and political center in the world?

I arrived in America on the 10th anniversary of 9/11, the same day I left Hong Kong. Having to go through unnecessary and wasteful delays of overpriced-incompetent-inspectors at San Francisco airport caused me to miss my connecting flight to Los Angeles. Their traditional American bureaucratic swagger buys these TSA types the time they are trying to kill to ensure they make overtime, or better yet, retirement on the government dole.

It's a chilling reminder of how America has changed since that fateful day and how its standing in the geopolitical and economic sphere was on a rapid descent and on the same crash-landing trajectory as the doomed flights that hit the Twin Towers, the Pentagon and Shanksville, Pa. – and how the country continues down a lost road to nowhere in desperation trying to rediscover the Founding Fathers' America.

The deadly armed fortress that is America was magnified by the manhunt in Northern California's redwood forests for a man who gunned down a former mayor and veteran forester, and a conservationist, with a high-powered rifle.

As if that wasn't bad enough, during my U.S. visit in February 2012, I was welcomed back with a double-barreled killing. The killing of an Immigration and Customs Enforcement agent by a fellow agent during a job performance review, and the killing of a Marine based at Camp Pendelton during his early morning "prayer walk" with his two young daughters at a local high school running track, by an Orange County deputy sheriff – and former Marine. Gung-ho America is killing its finest.

To make matters worse, the law enforcement chiefs in many American cities, like their counterparts in China, break the law while supporting their favorite political candidates running for public office. Los Angeles County Sheriff Lee Baca admitted in February 2012 that he broke state law by making a political endorsement while in uniform for an online campaign for a candidate running for district attorney.

The Northern California gunman, like the other gunmen, was a well-known local citizen who believed in an intergalactic conspiracy involving the Chinese military. That belief led to his arrest in 2009 for throwing fake bombs over the fence of the Chinese Consulate in San Francisco.

One of the unintended consequences of 9/11 was that it marked the beginning of a turnaround in Sino-U.S. ties. Before the terrorist attacks, relations between the two Pacific powers had plunged into an adversarial abyss. Events that led to that state of affairs included the U.S. bombing of the Chinese Embassy in Belgrade during the NATO air war over Yugoslavia in 1999 and escalating tensions over Taiwan issues toward the end of the 20th century. Things only got worse in April 2001 when a Chinese pilot died in a collision between a U.S. reconnaissance plane and a Chinese jet fighter over Hainan Island.

That acrimony was all but erased by cooperation between Washington and Beijing in the war on terrorism in the immediate aftermath of 9/11 when then President Jiang Zemin sent a message saying Beijing "condemned and rejected all forms of terrorist violence" and expressing his "deep sympathy and condolences" to the American people.

The Chinese even allowed the FBI to establish an office in Beijing and took part in the Container Security Initiative, a program designed to prevent terrorists from smuggling weapons to the U.S. Within the U.N., China sought to strengthen the coalition of states against terrorism, especially in supporting the early stages of the U.S. "war on terror."

That is a relationship the U.S. and China should continue to build and put aside the political grandstanding of career politicians in Washington – especially during every election year.

### *The 9/11 Flame of Life*
The reverence for life is what brought me to Ground Zero and the 9/11 Memorial a week later when I moved on to New York from California. The thought that 2,977 people died that day in New York, the Pentagon and in Pennsylvania, 2,819 of them at the World Trade Center, the remains of 1,100 of whom were never recovered – and worse, the mortuary at Dover Air Force Base in Delaware disposed of body parts of some victims by burning them and dumping the ashes in a landfill – not to mention the more than 6,000 members of the U.S. armed forces killed in the wars in Afghanistan and Iraq, was numbing. While thinking about my upcoming visit and the memories of that destructive day, I again concluded that for *We the Apathetic Maids,* especially those from the '60s and the decade-long Vietnam War we endured, the wars in Iraq and Afghanistan have persisted so long that, in a sense, they have become a way of life and lulled us into an even deeper ether of apathy.

The 10th anniversary of 9/11 came on the heels of the Afghan war's deadliest month for U.S. troops, 70 of whom died that August. Overall, the war in Afghanistan has claimed the lives of more than 2,000 American service members as this book went to print. This to support a corrupt regime surrounded by criminals fighting fanatical believers supported by the Pakistani intelligence services, their creators in the first place. Why would they stop their support now? What was America thinking, other than continuing to offer its free taxpayer financial services to the military-industrial complex.

Yet most American high school students and their desperately aspiring younger aspirants know nothing about 9/11 or the participants in that ugly drama other than they were Muslims and therefore all Muslims must be bad. A sorry commentary on America's failed, dumbed-down educational system. So much so that the Founding Fathers' vision of America and the rights enshrined in the Bill of Rights are battered and shattered beyond recognition.

Let's not forget that Saddam Hussein, Osama bin Laden and the Taliban started off as creatures of U.S. intelligence. Talk about morons and oxymorons, because of the nation's lapel flag they wear as "patriots" and the Patriot Act they make us live by.

Standing there at Ground Zero, within a week of 9/11, as I described in *Custom Maid Spin,* I shuddered at the thought of how *We the Apathetic Maids* First Amendment rights, along with our other basic constitutional rights, would be abridged and brutally violated. Unfortunately, that is exactly what happened: America's constitutional foundation took the greatest historical hit. Security became more important than freedom.

The stories of heroism on that dark day are many. The San Francisco opera *Heart of a Soldier* tells the story of Rick Rescoria, head of security for Morgan Stanley, who marched the firm's 2,700 employees in the World Trade Center's South Tower to safety and then died when he returned to look for stragglers.

And the story of Mike Hingson, who has been blind since birth and could see nothing, yet managed to escape down 1,463 steps and 78 floors of the Trade Center's North Tower, led by a fearless guide dog that brought dozens to safety with Hingson minutes before the building collapsed. Karma, luck, timing? The same question I asked in *Custom Maid Spin* when I talked about the smokers, warned that "smoking kills," who left the building to light up their cigarettes when the towers collapsed – and survived!

John Barrett, a business associate of mine was there on 9/11. He had just gotten out of the subway station when the second plane hit and found himself running for cover. He got into an argument with a man who was trying to retrieve an American Airlines life vest when he told him that it was evidence and no time to be taking souvenirs.

"Do you realize you are standing on and walking on human body parts from the first plane that may have been in that vest?" John asked the horrified man as the two of them and an unidentified female companion of the once-determined souvenir collector started screaming and running as they were enveloped by debris and choking dust.

John was looking for his twin brother Joe. He had arrived at 130 Cedar Street when someone screamed that the World Trade Center was coming down. "I ran into a nearby restaurant basement to get out of the way of the falling buildings and rubble and dust filling the street. I found my brother after the second tower fell and realized we all looked like walking zombie ghosts covered and breathing dusted body parts. The air was heavily laden with all kinds of weird tasting and smelling putrid body parts," John said.

That was after he got out of the basement he had been buried in for a couple of hours under the rubble of the Twin Towers. He found his brother, and they made their way to the Brooklyn Bridge. His brother was escorting a traumatized 21-year-old woman who had just arrived in New York City and was on her way to her new job when the planes hit.

The young woman had eight cousins and uncles serving in the New York police and fire departments. John's younger brother Richard was also serving in the police department.

"All I could think about was what may be happening to them as Joe and I looked back after crossing the bridge and all we could see was two powder puffs where the Twin Towers used to be," John muttered as he shared his 9/11 experience with me.

9/11 today defines who *We the Maids* are as a nation in more ways than we recognize. The protest by the families of victims in the New York attacks as unidentified remains were transferred to the memorial site at Ground Zero in May 2014, is a reminder of Americans inalienable Constitutional right of free speech no matter the subject.

It is time for America to step out of the shadow of 9/11 and extricate itself from the self-destructive road of financial and political misery it has taken. The resources and morale squandered on banks and wars was a critical "lost decade" in American history that led to the economic collapse of the old world order. America missed the boat on the awakening of people power in the Muslim world and the multi-polar world being created around it – at American taxpayer expense fighting the "war on terror." The political U-turn back to the Founding Fathers' ideals is long overdue.

President Bush continuing to read *My Pet Goat* to 7-and 8-year-olds for seven minutes after being visibly shocked when informed that America was under attack is probably one of the most controversial moments of his presidency. His indecisiveness, or thoughtful analysis, depending on one's point of view, was the ideal metaphor for why America is in the dire straits it is in.

To make matters worse, the only people allowed to fly the skies of America that day were Saudi officials and members of the bin Laden family out of "fear for their safety." Safety from what – prosecution for their roles in planning the attacks? This is a question the U.S. media has failed to address.

For more than a decade, questions have lingered about the possible role of the Saudi government in the attacks on 9/11.

"I am convinced that there was a direct line between at least some of the terrorists who carried out the September 11th attacks and the government of Saudi Arabia," former Senator Bob Graham of Florida said in an affidavit filed as part of a lawsuit brought against the Saudi government and dozens of institutions in the country by the families of 9/11 victims and others. Graham led a joint 2002 congressional inquiry into the attacks.

His former Senate colleague Bob Kerry of Nebraska, who served on the separate 9/11 Commission, said in a sworn affidavit of his own in the case that "significant questions remain unanswered" about the role of the Saudi institutions. "Evidence relating to the plausible involvement of possible Saudi government agents in the September 11th attacks has never been fully pursued," Kerry said.

The former senators' affidavits are part of the multibillion-dollar lawsuit that has wound its way through the federal courts since 2002. The Saudis have repeatedly tried to have the case dismissed, in part because they say American inquiries – including those in which Graham and Kerry took part – have essentially exonerated them. But Kerry and Graham said that the findings should not be seen as an exoneration and that many important questions about the Saudis' role have never been fully examined, partly because their panels simply did not have the time or resources given their wider scope. Unbelievable! America didn't have the money to investigate the role the Saudis played in 9/11 but it can afford to squander trillions of dollars on wars in Iraq and Afghanistan that further enhance the Saudi political agendas in both countries.

To make matters worse, Washington has continued to stand behind Saudi Arabia publicly, with the Justice Department joining the kingdom in trying to have the lawsuits thrown out of court on the grounds that the Saudis are protected by international immunity.

America can no longer afford to do nothing in time of crisis.

To make matters worse, knowing the U.S. is still vulnerable to terror attacks appears to justify continuing massive defense spending. In the decade since 9/11, the U.S. defense budget more than doubled from $316 billion in 2001 to $708 billion in 2011. More than $1.3 trillion has been spent on the wars in Iraq and Afghanistan, plus some $1 billion on the Libyan intervention. This as America's desperate need for those funds to generate jobs, educate and build infrastructure is ignored and the money is squandered by career politicians amid the country's decay.

The 9/11 anniversary tribute not only honors those who died, but America's evolving identity and resolve. The new Freedom Towers rising on the site of the old are a defiant statement of America's renewal.

Nothing can ever break us, "President Barack Obama reminded the world at the dedication in New York for the National September 11, Memorial Museum in May 2014.

### China & the World Beware

Why is China surprised that America has reasserted its leadership role in the world and the Asia-Pacific region under the leadership of its first "Pacific president?"

China has no one to blame but itself. It has behaved as an arrogant, hegemonist imperial superpower reminiscent of its imperial past as a regional hegemon. Traditional political pressures of the past, however, no matter how economically or militarily strong, no longer work in the 21st century. China overstepped contemporary politically correct boundaries.

China also refuses to fully acknowledge that its rise was facilitated by the U.S. Conversely, the U.S. refuses to admit that China, by plowing more than two-thirds of its mammoth foreign-currency reserves into U.S. dollar-denominated assets, has gained significant political leverage while building its military-industrial complex.

China is thus very different from previous and adversaries. America's interests are now so closely intertwined with China that a policy to isolate or confront Beijing is not feasible.

For the U.S., China's growing power actually helps validate its forward military deployments in Asia, maintain existing allies in the region and win new strategic partners. Indeed, an increasingly assertive China has proven a diplomatic boon for the U.S. in strengthening and expanding its Asian security relationships.

At the end of the 20th century and the beginning of the 21st, the U.S. was being marginalized in Asia due to several political misjudgments. I have already addressed these in my earlier books – and China's "charm offensive."

But today, America has returned and is firmly based on center stage. South Korea has beefed up its military alliance with the U.S.; Japan has backed off its efforts to persuade the U.S. to move its Marine base out of Okinawa;

Singapore has allowed the U.S. Navy to station ships there; Australia is hosting U.S. Marines and other deployments; and India, Vietnam, Indonesia and the Philippines, among others, and now Myanmar, have drawn closer to the U.S. as well.

With Xi Jinping and his fellow "princelings" – sons of China's revolutionary heroes – running the Communist Party and its Standing Committee, the case for meritocracy in China's current political system is tough to make. Something the Communist Party and those who have prospered beyond their wildest dreams from the existing system must come to terms with if they want to hold onto their gains, many ill-gotten. They must support political reforms or they will lose their assets just like their greedy self-serving ancestors did before Mao and his fellow party members came to power.

The monopoly of power in China is under threat from within the party, nation, external forces and the Internet. Something China is beginning to realize and trying to come to terms with.

China is a country that believes the world – and its citizens – should shut up and be quiet and be in awe and admiration of a government and party led by competent career politicians who have devised advanced and social policies that have transformed a poor country into the world's second-largest economy in a single generation. They have reversed five centuries of national decline, lifted hundreds of millions of people out of poverty, and offered the younger, urban generation education, personal freedom and economic opportunities that their parents and ancestors could only dream about.

The leadership is either blind, wearing rose-colored glasses, or buying denial time to the fact that a ruthless dictatorship that denies its people their basic rights, jails and tortures critics, destroys its natural environment, rewrites history, manipulates its currency and global trade rules and bullies neighboring states, really upsets not only its citizens, but the world. The corruption at almost every level of Chinese government is no longer acceptable or tolerable. The misallocation of resources to party faithful has made the wealth gap – like America's – intolerable. Actually, it makes

America look good.

The political and social immorality that prevails throughout Chinese society leads to situations like the 2-year-old child being ignored after being run over, poisoned milk, tainted food, poisoned rivers, fake goods, lack of respect for intellectual property, unsustainability of its loan-fueled investment-led growth model and dangerously defective consumer goods. Is it any wonder its consumption-led growth path has failed and people would rather save than spend?

This arrogant denial and attitude of superiority, a feeling I have experienced at several levels, is what has gotten China checkmated in the South China Sea, Myanmar, Libya and many parts of Africa and Asia.

The anti-China tide rising in the world and in America is self-inflicted because of China's aggressive pursuit of unilateral or bilateral deals and deliberately excluding America because of its temporary inattention.

China must wake up to the fact that it does not pose an existential or ideological threat to America's Founding Fathers and their ideals – something America always has to fall back on.

Just because China is America's largest creditor and is projected to surpass the U.S. as the world's largest economy in 2020 doesn't mean it can behave as a heartless banker.

"Significant downside risks" to the U.S. economy only raise fears about the prospects for global growth and result in the flight of foreign funds buying and seeking the security of the U.S. dollar. No different than what China has done. Is it any wonder some economists are predicting a tough landing for the mainland?

China's frustration at America's resilience and resurgence on the world scene was on display for all to see in August 2011, during Vice President Joe Biden's trust-building visit to China, when the Chinese Bayi Military Rockets basketball team decided to beat up Washington's Georgetown Hoyas in an on-court brawl that ended the so-called "friendly" game prematurely at Beijing's Olympic Stadium for no apparent reason – other than latent anger and frustration at America – no different than their party leaders on the international.

## The Revolution Has Started

Leaving Ladder Co. 10, the firehouse with its own memorial honoring its firefighters who perished that fateful day on its rear wall facing the World Trade Center site and the 9/11 Memorial, known as the National September 11 Memorial, I came across Zuccotti Park, boxed between Liberty Street, where I had just left the memorial, Cedar, Trinity and Broadway, where the Occupy Wall Street group of protestors had gathered a day earlier to start what would become a global clarion call for corporate and political accountability. Police had prohibited them from going to Wall Street to voice their frustrations. They had been confined to the nearby park.

I had arrived in New York City on September 18th and heard and read about the protestors objecting to corporate greed and corruption and had decided to go check them out, not realizing they were that close to Ground Zero. I had set out for Wall Street to find them when I walked right into their midst.

## Viva La Revolucion

The Occupy movement's call to revolution echoed off the placards held by protestors or lying around the park. They ranged from the symbolic "We Are the 99%," "America Wake Up," "People Over Profit," "Tax the Rich," "We Are Living Proof That Humanity Has the Right to Choose," "Tear Down This Wall Street," to – my personal favorite – "This Revolution Is for Display Purposes Only."

I listened in on a couple of workshops, music and calls to every passersby to join in as they postured for the media under the watchful eyes of the NYPD. There were times during the week when the protestors were far outnumbered by the men in blue and undercover detectives.

A few weeks later, back in Hong Kong, I was delighted to see that the Occupy movement had gone viral and similar protests had spread to major cities across America and many countries in the world. Watching them a few weeks later leave the park and head toward the Brooklyn Bridge where more than 700 were arrested, I knew I had again been witness and party to the inception of another quintessential American revolution.

### People Power

Corporate titans get multimillion-dollar golden parachutes as they exit companies they almost buried while the employees who helped them build the icons of capitalist and industrial America languish unemployed, homeless and probably living below the poverty line. So why is anyone surprised that the bright, young and unemployed student activists joined their aging forefathers from the '60s in the hope of galvanizing America and waking up *We the Apathetic Maids* to corporate and political injustice?

Watching corporate America and its presidential candidates gearing up for the 2012 campaign and preoccupied with raising more than $1 billion on each side of the Democratic and Republican presidential aisles, expecting handsome paybacks on their investment, was a good reason to get *We the Apathetic Maids* to start waking up from the dumbed and lulled-down sleep we have been subjected to.

The only time the public takes notice is when a president comes into town to raise funds for himself, his party's officials and candidates. Pedestrian and vehicular traffic is snarled and backed-up because of the security barricades and corridors – Obama's during the 2012 election campaign being the most criticized that I can recall.

### Long Overdue

Writing about the coming revolution for the past 25-plus years, I am delighted to see that 2011 was the year America's Third Revolution took to the streets of not only the U.S. – but interlocally – from Wall Street to Tunisia to China and many other countries. This acknowledgment by *Time magazine* that the Protestor is the person of the year 2011, because the protestor had the most significant effect on global society, was a heartwarming wake-up call and confirmation that *We the Apathetic Maids* have in fact awakened and are finally demanding change, something I was lamenting the lack of because people were so apathetic when Volume I of this trilogy was published in 2004.

"Leadership has come from the bottom of the pyramid, not the top," *Time* managing editor Rick Stengel said.

"For capturing and highlighting a global sense of restless promise, for up-ending governments and conventional wisdom, for combining the oldest of techniques with the newest technologies to shine a light on human dignity and, finally, for steering the planet on a more democratic though sometimes more dangerous path for the 21st-century, the Protestor is *Time's* 2011 Person of the Year."

"Is there a global tipping point for frustration?" Stengel asked on the morning talk shows as he discussed the magazine's choice.

"Everywhere, it seems, people said they'd had enough," Stengel stated. "They dissented; they demanded; they did not despair, even when the answers came back in a cloud of tear gas or a hail of bullets. They literally embodied the idea that individual action can bring collective, colossal change. And although it was understood differently in different places, the idea of democracy was present at every gathering."

Revolution is not a new phenomenon. There were food riots in the ancient world, slave rebellions in Roman times and the more than occasional revolution, peaceful or not, since the 1700s. Given how nasty, brutish and short human lives have been over the ages, it may be more of a wonder that there have been so few revolutions. And that goes to one of the points that magazine writer Kurt Andersen makes in his argument for *Time's* protestor selection.

"Massive and effective street protest was a global oxymoron until – suddenly, shockingly – starting exactly a year ago, it became the defining trope of our times. And the protestor, once again, became a maker of history," according to Andersen.

"The stakes are very different in different places. In North America and Europe, there are no dictators and dissidents don't get tortured. Any day that Tunisians, Egyptians or Syrians occupy streets and squares, they know that some of them might be beaten or shot, not just pepper-sprayed or flex-cuffed. The protestors in the Middle East and North Africa are literally dying to get political systems that roughly resemble the ones that seem intolerably undemocratic to protestors in Madrid, Athens, London and New York City."

Just as the French played a key role in the First American Revolution and the '60s protests, they did so again during the Third Revolution in 2011. If anyone has a doubt, don't forget who won the Academy Awards for best picture, actor and several other categories. A silent black-and-white non-starter French movie *The Artist*. A metaphorical reminder that just like silent movies went through a revolutionary change and have been forgotten because of the talkies – but beat the talkies in 2012 – the political spin that revolution in America is a thing of the past is itself outdated.

The question is why now? Tough economic times worldwide because of the financial meltdown that has made employment for the world's youth and middle class a dream, or is it a nightmare?

All revolutions begin with protests, but not all protests become revolutions.

For example, the Tiananmen Square protests of 1989 were crushed by Chinese troops, with the Communist Party retaining power – unlike the Soviet Communist Party, which was swept into the dustbin of history. Protests in Iran, like China, have been fruitless in forcing government change.

OWS rallies, occupations and protests took place in cities across America from New York to Los Angeles, Oakland and Seattle. The movement's roots spread across the Atlantic and Pacific to London, Frankfurt, Madrid, Rome, Sydney, Santiago, Korea, Hong Kong, Taipei and dozens of other cities across more than 80 countries. Most were peaceful, although violence broke out in New York, Oakland and Rome when protestors clashed with riot police, often instigated by the cops.

Celebrities and politicians addressed the protestors from Los Angeles to London. Julian Assange, the controversial founder of WikiLeaks, addressed the demonstrators in London in October 2011, saying the protest was "not about the destruction of law, it's about the construction of law."

A group of 100 prominent authors, including Salman Rushdie, signed an online petition declaring their support for the worldwide Occupy movement. They are supported by people from all walks of life who share the sense that our financial and political systems are no longer working for the common people. Most people's salaries have been stagnant for a generation, even as the wealth of the top 1% has skyrocketed. The global revolutionary movement reflects legitimate frustrations about the current economic inequality.

Career politicians have to acknowledge these inequalities, anxiety, anger and the fact that millions of people in America, China and around the world have lost faith in mainstream politics and are determined to change it. If they do not, they will be swept out of office by *We the Maids* in these dangerously revolutionary times.

### *Revolutionary Lesson*
A fellow writer, who actually understood what America and revolutions are all about, and whom I have quoted in my earlier books and earlier chapters in this book, is Alexis de Tocqueville, the French historian who wrote *The Old Regime and the Revolution* about the French revolution that started in 1789. Tocqueville wrote his book in 1856, six decades after the French revolution. More than 150 years later, China's communist leaders are trying to make sense of his observations.

Tocqueville analyzes the causes of the French revolution by examining social conditions under the "old regime." He wrote that when the revolution erupted, the "old regime" of Louis XVI was at its most prosperous, but that prosperity had fueled social disparity, leading to the revolution. He offered an explanation as to why prosperity did not prevent a major revolution but, on the contrary, fomented one – a point China's new leadership is taking to heart as it tries to re-instill Maoist-type party discipline and loyalty.

Although China is the second-largest economy in the world, with its people enjoying unprecedented wealth, polarization has also reached an all-time high. Its Gini coefficient, which measures income disparities, is 0.61 – way above the internationally recognized danger threshold of 0.4. On the scale, 0 means perfect equality and 1 maximum inequality.

Tocqueville also believed that not all the revolution's legacies were positive, even though it overthrew the old regime and took France into a new era of equality and democracy. After overthrowing the autocratic monarchy by violent means, social ills reappeared after undergoing a temporary makeover. It looks and sounds familiar in Egypt, Tunisia, Libya and even Syria.

China's leaders are afraid that a revolution – the price to pay for modernization – is looming in the world's last major communist-ruled nation.

The factors that contributed to the French revolution and the waves of revolution that are ricocheting through North Africa and the Middle East can be seen in today's China. These include widespread discontent caused by despotism, corruption, social inequality, social injustice, unemployment and inflation, along with the rise of the middle class. Public protests in China, officially described as "mass incidents," now exceed more than 100,000 a year. What Tocqueville saw in France two centuries ago has an almost exact replica in today's China – a fact that China's new leadership is trying to address.

Revolutions do not generally occur during a time of poverty. They take place when economic development has brought about acute polarization. At such times, conflict between social classes is easily incited, with those at the bottom of society turning their anger into the flames of war.

Another of Tocqueville's conclusions was that a regime with centralized power actually intensified tensions between social classes. The French political system had placed executive, legislative and judicial powers under centralized authority before the old regime was toppled.

Today's China, with its system of one-party rule, is seen by some as the modern-day equivalent. Many academics say the party's monopoly on power is the chief reason behind China's widening wealth gap, rampant corruption and abuse of power by officials – all major sources of public dissatisfaction with the government.

But the most discomforting of Tocqueville's conclusions for China's leaders is that the "most dangerous moment for a bad government is when it begins to reform."

"It is almost never when a state of things is the most detestable that it is smashed, but when it beginning to improve, it permits men to breathe, to reflect, to communicate their thoughts with each other, and to gauge by what they already have the extent of their rights and their grievances. The weight, although less heavy, seems then all the more unbearable," Tocqueville wrote.

This advice that reform could be just as dangerous as the status quo, if not more so, presents the Communist leadership with a dilemma wrapped in a conundrum, otherwise known as a cluster fuck, given the party's long-held belief that as long as it could bring prosperity to the people it could maintain its hold on power.

That political conundrum has also been summed up in a famous statement by the late Kuomintang leader Chiang Kai-shek when he responded to his reformist son Chiang Ching-kuo's request that he overhaul the then-corrupt ruling party during the civil war. "If we reform the Kuomintang, the party will perish; if we don't, the state will perish," the father replied.

The reality today is that China is not alone on the long and winding revolutionary road. America and its Tea Party and Occupy Wall Street movements ignited the revolutionary fires that were smoldering across the country for the same reasons people in China, Russia, India and the rest of our interlocal world are resentful and angry. Even though millions have been lifted out of poverty and a sizeable global middle class created as a result, inequality in many of its dimensions appears to have worsened rather than eased. A dramatic concentration of incomes and wealth is on display in every part of the globe – from America to China – and across the rest of the revolutionary world.

From mega financial institutions to energy conglomerates, from real estate developers to telecom giants, the world's biggest corporations raked in $36 trillion in revenues in 2011 and over $2.6 trillion in net profits, according to the Global 2000 list compiled by *Forbes* magazine. These companies had accumulated assets of $149 trillion – 2.1 times global GDP – and collectively employed 83 million people. The sales and assets of these mega firms amounted to 1.5 and 6.4 times respectively of the total GDP of developing countries.

It is even more startling that the "We are the 99 percent" movements are not based on some radical, fringe notions but are supported by damning evidence that first appeared in the UK's *New Scientist* magazine in October 2011. It quotes a fascinating study by a trio of complex systems theorists at the Swiss Federal Institute of Technology in Zurich, which studied 43,000 transnational corporations. It combines the "mathematics long used to model natural systems with comprehensive corporate data to map ownership among the world's TNC's."

The results: A core of 1,318 companies with interlocking relationships has a grip on the global economy. Through their shareholding, this core appeared to collectively own a majority of the world's large blue chip and manufacturing firms – representing around 80 percent of global revenues.

Further analysis of the ownership structures of these companies led to perhaps the most astonishing fact: That a "super entity" of 147 tightly knit companies with a completely interlocked ownership structure controlled 40 percent of the total wealth in the entire network. Most of these entities are financial institutions.

In terms of individual wealth, there are approximately 1,300 billionaires in the world. Of these, the top 10 alone had a cumulative net worth of just short of $400 billion at the end of 2011 – larger than the combined GDP of 71 percent of the world's poorest countries.

Another even more gripping statistic relating to individual wealth comes from the UK-based Tax Justice Network – that a staggering $21 trillion has been stashed in tax havens around the world by just 92,000 people. As Warren Buffet observed regarding the global economy and the proliferation of wealth in the recent past: "The tide lifted all the yachts" – instead of all the boats.

No surprise therefore that the 1% yacht owners homes, garages, cars and white picket fences in affluent Silicon Valley enclave of Atherton have been spray-painted with hate-filled messages. Class warfare has arrived at the homes of CEOs making in 2014, 257 times the average workers salary, up from 181 times in 2009, while the 99% demand and protest for a higher minimum wage.

As a wealth of bounty and opportunity is bestowed on a mere handful, hunger, malnutrition, vulnerability to disease, displacement, loss of income, and the pernicious effects of climate change are the lot of an ever-larger expanding crowd of *We the Apathetic Maids* who are waking up – the ideal recipe for the Third American Revolution.

The revolution has already started in the Founding Fathers' backyard. The 2012 election saw New Hampshire elect an all female delegation to Congress – the first state ever to do so.

### Palestinian Power
My New York visit to commemorate the 10th anniversary of 9/11 coincided with the Palestinian statehood bid that week at the U.N. to become its 194th member. The Palestinians submitted an application to the Security Council, setting the stage for one of the most dramatic annual gatherings of world leaders in New York in years – and a collision course with the U.S. that sought an 11th-hour compromise to avoid a confrontation at the U.N.

The application needed to win approval from nine of the 15 members of the Security Council, including the U.S. and the four other veto-wielding permanent members. America opposed the bid, saying that statehood can come about only through direct negotiations with Israel. Talks between the two sides had been moribund for more than a year.

I decided to go to the U.N. to witness what would surely be an outdoor kaleidoscope of protests from all corners of the earth. Not just regarding the question of Palestinian statehood, but human rights abuses worldwide, Iran and China being at the top of the list. I was not disappointed.

Access to the U.N. was blocked by city sanitation trucks full of sand parked at all major arteries leading to the U.N. Along with other curious onlookers, I was shepherded to the Dag Hammarskjold Park at the corner of Second Avenue and 49th Street, where all protestors assembled to express their points of view. The Iranians put on the loudest and liveliest theatrical display. Palestinians, Tibetans and various indigenous peoples all contributed their vocal slogans to the choir of protest that emanated from the park.

The various signs and placards displayed by the protestors caught my attention, especially those held by Hasidic Jews dressed in their black garb. "Judaism Rejects Zionism and the State of Israel," and "All Palestine Under Palestinian Rule" being the most eye-catching. Jewish extreme fundamentalists refuse to recognize the existence of Israel until the Messiah arrives.

The Jewish protestors were confirmation of why church and state must be separated as the Founding Fathers mandated, I thought to myself. Here are people supported by the state to pursue their religious studies, they don't work, don't serve in the Israeli military and refuse to accept an Israel that finances and supports them and their religious studies as a state. Talk about tolerant democracies – America and Israel – in the midst of all the cries for freedom and democracy emanating from people from all corners of the earth that week.

The demonstrators changed daily, depending on who was speaking at the U.N. that day. The one constant was the Hasidim denouncing and rejecting Israel.

### Land of Milk and Money

My next stop after New York that late September was Israel to coincide with the Jewish New Year. I decided to go and take a closer look at the peaceful demonstrations there. I had been following with interest the protest movement started by two Israeli women a few weeks earlier demanding lower food prices, affordable housing, education and day-care centers for working parents that turned into a national movement of more that half a million people taking to the streets and camping out on Rothschild Boulevard in an exclusive upper-class Tel Aviv neighborhood to make sure they got the attention of the 1 percenters.

The contrast with occupiers in New York's Zuccotti Park was staggering. Couches, chairs and sofas on carpets under tarpaulins and tents in a clean well-kept camp that stretched for several city blocks. The movement not only got the government's attention – it got it to act. Israel appointed a committee on socioeconomic change headed up by Professor Manuel Tratjenberg. The committee's final report was released during my visit – and what an eye-opener it was.

The scathing and critical report on the government for not fairly distributing Israel's economic growth and wealth to all of its citizens, although warmly accepted by the prime minister and government, was criticized by the movement for not going far enough. The report highlighted the fact that despite the many security threats facing Israel, the social security of its citizens was as important as its military might.

"The government must set social goals alongside its traditional macroeconomic goals, including quantitative goals to increase employment and equality and reduce poverty.... Economic growth is not everything. It does not include important aspects of the quality of life, such as the level of inequality, health, the environment and more. We must expand the way we measure the economy's performance," the report recommended.

The committee proposed a number of important reforms, the cost and timing of which was questioned. It recommended marketing 200,000 housing units over five years. Its recommendations to implement a compulsory education law from the age of 3, a longer school day and building of more day-care centers, was also expected to take five years because of fiscal restraints. Among the committee's main recommendations were providing free education from the age of 3, rather than 5, making significant cuts to the defense budget and raising taxes on the wealthy as well as corporate taxes.

The panel also called for housing reforms to make home ownership more accessible, stricter enforcement of labor laws, lower gas prices and the expansion of antitrust regulations.

"We were entrusted with a task that looked totally impossible," Trajtenberg told reporters at a news conference he convened on September 26, 2011. "A committee cannot bring about change, but it can lay strong foundations from which a more just society can grow for the benefit of all its citizens," he said.

Isn't that what America, China and the rest of the world should be striving for?

Even before Prof. Trajtenberg's news conference had ended in Jerusalem,

Daphni Leef and her fellow social protest leaders watching in a Tel Aviv office were signaling to the many reporters present that the committee's proposals were insufficient. No surprise there, as the summer's tent protest movement had made it clear when the Trajtenberg committee was established that the panel's authority was too limited to bring any significant change in socioeconomic priorities, and Leef had even called on Trajtenberg to resign.

As if that wasn't bad enough, the defense establishment added fuel to the fire by expressing its anger at the committee's plan to finance its recommendations largely by cutting the defense budget. A senior defense official accused the treasury of "exploiting the social protest to achieve its own ideological goals, which have nothing at all to do with changing priorities. These are goals that the treasury was talking about long before the social protest or the Trajtenberg committee."

Sound familiar?

An editorial comment by Gideon Levy on the Trajtenberg report, titled *Good morning hangover* in the *Haaretz* newspaper that day, caught my attention. "Trajtenberg waxed lyrical. But it is doubtful there will be anything left for the history books. If the summer ends with this autumnal committee, if Stav Shaffir and Daphni Leef make do with this bunch of dry bones that was thrown at them yesterday, we have had one summer of transient, forgettable happiness.

"So if the quiet that prevailed in the past few weeks endures, it's the end of the summer. If on Saturday night we don't meet in the streets again, everything was for nothing.

"There is only one lesson to be learned from last night's conference: The protest ended too soon... .

"Good morning hangover."

### The Messiah's Antichrist
Lubavitcher Rebbe King Messiah, the Rebbe who viewed himself as

the Messiah, was quoted by Israeli Prime Minister Benjamin Netanyahu reverently in a speech at the United Nations on the question of Palestinian statehood. The Lubavitcher Rebbe inculcated his followers with the doctrine of "your people are the land's only nation." In the land of his messianic rule, there is no room for Arabs.

"Relying on the Lubavitcher Rebbe and his teachings in a speech that was ostensibly in favor of a Palestinian state is like relying on a racist who fervently supports slavery in a speech that is ostensibly in favor of abolition," wrote Sefi Rachlevsky in an editorial in *Haaretz* in September 2011.

The Rebbe's pronouncements are no different than the Antichrist concerns in American politics. Apocalyptic fears in America helped fuel the anti-statist movements of the 1930s and clearly influenced the 2012 presidential election in America.

The world in 2011 and 2012 resembled the world of the 1930s in many respects. International turmoil and a prolonged economic downturn have fueled distrust of government, as has the rise of new activism represented in the explosive growth of the Tea Party and Occupy Wall Street.

In the 2008 presidential campaign, Senator John McCain, the Republican nominee, presciently tapped into evangelicals' apocalyptic fears by producing an ad, "The One," that sarcastically heralded Barack Obama as a messiah. McCain was onto something. Not since Roosevelt has America had a president of such charisma and global popularity as Obama, who so perfectly fits the evangelicals' Antichrist mold.

The 2012 presidential campaign was no different. The leadership vacuum on the evangelical right was something Republicans Michele Bachmann, Rick Perry, Rick Santorum, Newt Gingrich and even Ron Paul exploited.

### Going Country

I have always been an outlaw. That's why after I arrived in California and explored the West I continued going west and went outlaw for more than 25 years in the Wild West of China – Asia and the developing world. That is what led to my self-imposed exile from America. I wanted to better understand the American empire from the perspective of other older civilizations and failed empires.

The Founding Fathers were outlaws, as is every American. That includes illegal immigrants – the ultimate outlaws. As a global multicultural cowboy who has ridden down many roads and dead-end streets on many types of horses, the real McCoys, those made of iron, steel, on trails, rails, oceans or the sky, I can testify that humanity is self-destructing – make that imploding – with outdated political, economic and religious laws that are irrelevant and passe in today's Internet interlocal-wired-world communities. This was self-evident, maybe even a self-evident prophecy, in America during the brutal gut-wrenching Republican 2012 primary – especially after the killing of Trayvon Martin in Florida in March of that year that rekindled the ugly underbelly issue of racism in America.

During my spring 2012 visit to America, I decided to take a daytime flight instead of my usual red-eye from California to New York that allows me, like the rest of America – to sleep. Gazing out the window was a pleasant reminder of not only the vastness and open big country America is, but how much room there is on its barren plains for change, not only political, but for the millions of talented and hard-working people it could so easily absorb from all over the world.

The undulating pure white cotton candy clouds were overshadowed by a bright blue sky and the ever-elusive horizon, which periodically opened up to reveal deep valleys and beautiful mountain ranges with cloud-piercing peaks. The varied shades of pink plains that followed the snow-capped mountains of the Sierras and Rockies, with their sky-piercing pinnacles, were a reminder of the melting disappearing glaciers that were re-creating themselves in their own vapors in the clouds. There is more to clouds than computing. Listening to Brad Paisley's *Life's Railway to Heaven* here on earth as I watched other smaller private iron birds fly by in the distance, I couldn't help wonder if they were carrying career politicians or their fat-cat contributors – or both.

It is time elected officials live by the same laws and regulations as all citizens – no exceptions. The alternative is that America will just become another failed empire.

### Failed Empires
Ancient empires and their symbols, from the Parthenon of Athens and the pyramids of Egypt, to the Great Wall of China, the epic monuments of the ancient world not only remind us of the builders' greatness, but the forces that toppled such vigor and genius – the powers and pitfalls of career politicians, scheming religious leaders, jealous aristocrats and merchants and military disasters on which the lives of millions depended. The one thing they all have in common is the fact that they failed to stave off their own demise.

I hope this book, along with the first two volumes of this trilogy, can contribute to the forces that will stop America from continuing to stumble blindly down the same imperial highway to ruin.

The only way to do that is if the class warfare between the rich and their well-financed career politicians and lobbyists reach a fair and equitable political truce with their employed and unemployed employees and the unions that helped them line their pockets and bank accounts, without either side bringing along their respective career politicians or lobbyists. The best and fastest way to do that is to truly get down to the principles laid out in the Constitution by the Founding Fathers – not just the Supreme Court. The alternative is a global political and economic Armaggedon as predicted by the Sumerians and Mayans.

The people and personal experiences discussed in this book, as in all my books, are real. In the interest of fluidity and easier reading, some events and conversations have been transposed and condensed into one. The observations are honest, notwithstanding the occasional heated, controversial debates and name calling they may generate. God knows, I've been called every imaginable name in many more languages than I can remember.

Many great politicians, philosophers, historians, political scientists and writers whose ideas I endorse and echo, and even disagree with, are incorporated or referenced and all are acknowledged in the chapter notes and bibliographies of all the earlier books, as they have been here. I encourage those who want to stop running on empty, who want to explore or learn more, to carefully read the chapter notes and relevant bibliography.

### *Full Moon Rising*

The weekend of August 5, 2011 – the anniversary of the atomic bombing of Hiroshima – and the week that followed was a phenomenal week to watch the full moon rise in Hong Kong over the dragon's back as America, China, Europe, the Middle East and North Africa erupted in political protests and riots demanding real change – which they got – as America got downgraded from AAA to AA+, the financial and stock markets collapsed, and the continuing Great Recession was acknowledged, but now labeled a double dip and spun as new.

The moon rose nightly until it became a clear bright round reddish pumpkin. It was a week of the sun throwing bursts of highly charged particles into space in a phenomenon known as coronal mass ejections, or CMEs.

In fact, three large CMEs prompted U.S. government scientists to warn of solar storms that can cause power blackouts and the aurora borealis, or northern lights, caused by disturbances in the Earth's atmosphere, were spotted as far south as New England and Colorado, NASA said. "Earth's magnetic field is still reverberating from a CME strike on August 5 that sparked one of the strongest geomagnetic storms in years," the website SpaceWeather said.

Some academics claim such geomagnetic storms can affect humans, altering moods and leading people into negative behavior by affecting their biochemistry. Some studies have found evidence that hospital admissions for depression rise during the geomagnetic storms and that incidents of suicide increase. A 2003 study by the Federal Reserve Bank of Atlanta found that such storms could affect even the stock market, as traders are more likely to make pessimistic choices.

"Unusually high levels of geomagnetic activity have a negative, statistically and economically significant effect on the following week's stock returns for all U.S. stock market indices," the authors found in their report.

Bathed in moonlight at the end of a scorcher of a humid day with a nice cool Hong Kong breeze tempering the night heat, I watched a helicopter in the distance descend at the Clearwater beach and listened to its muffled blades chopping through the misty clouds. The noise stirred a nearby family of crickets that decided to chirp in rhythm with the chopper as a moving pair of red and white flashing lights of an ascending jet leaving town evaporated in the even higher misty clouds. The serene silence of the night was finally restored, a momentary reminder of how fast life, our surroundings, the environment and politics can change.

A star-laden clear blue bright moonlit night with white cotton candy puffs of clear white 3D clouds reflecting the flames of the burning stock and financial markets, together with the cities and towns across England, the Middle East and China, all sparked by a hot August summer awash with CMEs.

Pulling together the events of the week was mind-boggling. Especially when it came to Sino-American relations. Here was China, America's lead creditor, criticizing America for its wasteful military spending as it continued to buy U.S. Treasuries – even as the dollar continued its nosedive. China being the holder of the largest hoard of dollars was certainly a domestic concern, both in America and China. This as Gary Locke, America's new ambassador to China, arrived and held his first news conference at his residence.

As a child of Chinese immigrants to the U.S., Locke is the first Chinese-American to serve as ambassador in the land of his ancestors.

The new moon rising also brought new hope to the China-U.S. relationship.

"My wife and our children are very excited to be moving here to build a new friendship between the people of the U.S. and China, and to continue to expand our two countries' growing cooperation and collaboration on key bilateral and international issues," Locke said.

"The most important is to promote stronger and better understanding between the people of the U.S. and China at all levels."

2011 ended with a lunar eclipse on December 10th. At six hours, it was the longest eclipse since 2000, and the second eclipse of the year. During an eclipse, the earth is between the sun and moon so sunlight cannot reach the moon directly. Much like the relationship between the citizens of China and America, who are repeatedly antagonized against each other by their career politicians.

On the West Coast of America, the eclipse began before 5 a.m., just as Americans were waking up and Chinese sky watchers were going to bed. Hopefully, 2012 will be the year that citizens of both countries and the world wake up to the benefits the others have to offer.

### Geocatching
The American geocache – or GPS-enabled treasure hunt craze – began in 2000 when decent GPS technology became more accessible to the masses. In 2011 it had more than 1.5 million caches hidden all over the world – in cities and remote areas, in trees and in buildings, even one on the International Space Station and another so far below the ocean surface that its seekers need scuba gear.

The first cachers were a few computer geeks in the Pacific Northwest, hiding things in nature, logging the coordinates, and challenging one another to find them.

Los Angeles and San Francisco have evolved into major hubs for the hobby. There were more than 100,000 geocachers in California and 18,000 within 50 miles of Los Angeles alone, according to Eric Schudiske, PR manager for Groundspeak, the Seattle-based company that runs Geocatching.com.

At the cache site there is usually a logbook to sign, and sometimes trinkets that can be swapped, but caches rarely have value beyond the thrill of the find, which you can tally on your geocatching.com profile page.

Maybe we can geocatch America's overseas forces and bring them back home. They are a valuable prize. Better yet, geocatch career politicians and send them home.

### Broken Iraq, Afghan and Iran Promises

Democrats ran on a platform of bringing the troops home from Iraq in the 2006 election and in a much quieter way, in the 2008 election, they promised they would not precipitously withdraw. Democrats took both the House of Representatives and Senate in 2006 for the first time since 1994 and the Republicans lost the White House in 2008. But instead of coming home, troop levels increased in 2007 and have remained high – like America's unemployment – in 2009 and 2010, propelling the Republicans and their Tea Party locomotive to take over the House.

The political excuse for troop escalation, instead of the promised de-escalation and precipitous withdrawal, is to buy time to train and build the Iraqi army and allow Iraqis to make up their minds about their future. Iraqis, like Americans, have made up their minds – and like Americans – want American troops back in America. More than two-thirds of Iraqis say the U.S.-led invasion was wrong, while a majority also consider attacks on U.S. forces as justified.

The situation is the same in Afghanistan, where locals in uniform have taken to gunning down their NATO allies.

To make matters even more insulting, the Iraqis have ordered more than $100 million in military equipment from China because deliveries of the equipment from the U.S. are slow and unreliable.

Isn't the partition of Iraq long overdue so that all U.S. military personnel can return home instead of making the U.S. military presence there another long-term commitment like Korea?

Meanwhile, America, without any confirmed or verifiable information on Iran's nuclear program, threatened to attack and destroy Iran's nuclear facilities – just like it contemplated doing against China when it developed nuclear weapons in the '60s. America is better off offering Iran the same deal it offered North Korea and refashioning a comprehensive strategic relationship with Tehran. History teaches us that unilateral military action alone does not work. Striking at the root cause of the problem as well as its harmful effects is the prescription *We the Maids* have to sweep in – first and foremost at home for the welfare and care of our children – and then abroad.

Speaking of Korea, where thousands of U.S. troops are stationed, the South Korean government also lied about its promise not to pay the Taliban any ransom for the release of 21 Christian volunteers who were held hostage for nearly six weeks in 2007. The Taliban claim they were paid $10 million by Korea, which "was a God-sent opportunity" to multiply their stockpile of weapons and explosives to wage war against America. Up north, Kim Jong Il also lied about his arsenal of hundreds of short-range mobile ballistic missiles.

It seems career politicians and the governments they lead are programmed to lie no matter what their political system is – democratic or dictatorship.

### North Korea & Myanmar
Petulant North Korea not only upset South Korea, Japan and America with its rocket launch on 12.12.12 and nuclear test of early 2013 – but its major patron China. The successful launch of the rocket and nuclear explosion consolidated and cemented the legitimacy of Kim Jong-un at home and established his successor role as an independent punker. He succeeded in putting a satellite into orbit, a feat that long eluded his father and remains a challenge even for rival South Korea.

North Korea's nuclear brinkmanship is testing China's newly installed party general Xi Jinping. Should China continue supplying North Korea with the food and fuel it desperately needs to survive or should it call Kim's geopolitical bluff? Should Beijing put Kim on notice that China no longer needs North Korea as a buffer state between its border and U.S. ally South Korea, especially now that the U.S. is demanding China tame its belligerent benefactor if America and China are to build a closer working relationship? Besides, what good is a buffer run by an insolent and disobedient punk?

China and the Asia Pacific region will benefit from a united Korea, one that can easily be glued together again and united if my "five party" formula advocated in earlier books is adopted. The alternative? Kim's nuclear brinkmanship and Dennis Rodman's basketball diplomacy?

China did join other members of the United Nations Security Council in condemning North Korea's launch of the rocket as a "clear violation" of U.N. resolutions. This modest step surprised and enraged Pyongyang and set the stage for the nuclear test meant as a warning to China that North Korea will not play the traditional role of a vassal state.

China could easily respond and make it clear that, much as it prefers North Korea to survive and prosper, it can afford to let North Korea implode. After all, the Chinese leadership already sees that sustaining this erratic and unpredictable regime that readily disregards Chinese national interests is more a liability than an asset for Beijing.

A South Korea-led unification of the peninsula is no threat to China. China already enjoys a smoother relationship with the South than with the North. Korean reunification would take at least two decades, during which the U.S., Japan and Russia would need to inject a huge amount of money. Rebuilding and reincorporating North Korea would preoccupy Korea and Japan for a generation. This hardly affects Chinese interests adversely as it continues its own advance to become the world's largest economy.

If this process unfolds under the auspices of China and the U.S., the U.S. motivation for keeping its own military forces in South Korea would dissipate. A nuclear-armed united Korea should work to China's advantage as it would reduce the likelihood of U.S. troops remaining in Korea.

Now that Kim Jong-il is dead, it is time to bring North Korea in from the cold and build mutual trust between the two Koreas, China and the U.S.

North and South Korea have for too long been engaged in the dangerous game of deterrence, showing force and the willingness to use it. But Pyongyang has been more adept at walking the tightrope between confrontation and compromise. America has to be realistic about what it will take for the North to give up its nuclear ambitions. A lot more than just food aid. The Kim dynasty and its military establishment need to receive genuine and convincing personal and national security guarantees.

North Korea has a per capita income of $1,800, one of the lowest in the world, because of the Kims' mismanagement of the economy. Kim Jong-un could emerge as the real unifying hero of the Korean people by initiating re-unification talks, adopting economic reform policies on the Chinese model and opening nuclear disarmament talks.

It's important to keep in mind a few key political, economic and military facts. Punk, hip hairdo late-20-something Kim is a paper tiger Brilliant Leader. A four-star general with no military experience. Does anyone really think the North's rough-and-tough military establishment, which has sworn allegiance to the Kim dynasty in exchange for economic and financial perks, will take any lip or orders from a leader they disagree with?

The one point is that "The North Korean leadership is united," said Andrei Lankov of Seoul's Kookmin University – a Russian academic who once lived in Pyongyang. "They understand that they should hang together in order not to be hanged separately."

Based on historical record, no modern authoritarian ruler has ever managed to pass power to his grandchildren. While succession from the first-generation dictator to his sons is fairly common, no succession from the second to the third generation has ever taken place in non-monarchical autocracies.

In all cases, the second-generation rulers, typically more corrupt and less competent than their fathers, were overthrown before they had a chance to hand power over to their sons. Kim Jong-il, although fitting the second-generation corruption mold to a tee, managed to hand power to his son who knows he is killing time before he is sterilized or terminated politically.

Kim the younger is ill-prepared for the job and lacks his father's establishment power base, hard-headed attitude to governing and lack of concern for his starving citizenry. Nevertheless, he is lucky because Washington, Beijing, Seoul and Tokyo want to see a smooth transition to stable power in order to resolve the impasse of issues that could lead to a peaceful and prosperous reunification.

I was in South Korea in October 2011, while its President Lee Myung-bak, a member of President Obama's best political world leaders good buds club, was in Washington to celebrate the U.S. Congress' ratification of the Korea-U.S. Free Trade Agreement during summit talks with Obama. Meanwhile, in South Korea, the political parties could not agree on the terms and conditions of the FTA, some calling for protective measures.

The geopolitical reality is that reunification will take place. The only remaining questions are when and how – and how to best go about it.

The military issues, disarmament, reduction of U.S. troop levels in South Korea, or the addition of Chinese troops in the North to work with the U.S. forces to ensure a smooth reunification and then both withdraw under mutually agreed terms and time-lines are questions that the relevant parties must come to terms with as soon as possible.

Myanmar, runner-up to North Korea as Asia's worst regime, and its democratizing military junta, is a good model for Kim's generals to study and emulate. So is Turkey's.

Surely, even the smart North Korean generals, like their counterparts in America, China, Turkey and Myanmar, see the hand-wringing-and-writing on the wall. Their regime's unsustainability – military, economic and political – can only be crystallized to them by China, with strong American support.

Kim Jong-un's radical hairdo is a metaphor that reflects his radical new way of thinking. Surely, watching Myanmar push back against China by halting construction on the Chinese-led Myitsone dam project, Myanmar's largest hydopower project, release of pro-democracy leader Aung San Suu Kyi, herself the daughter of a military general, and not just any general, but the founding revolutionary leader who lead the country's independence war against Britain – its George Washington – and allowing her to run for office and win again, abolishing censorship, revamping labor laws, holding talks with ethnic rebels, securing a ceasefire with the Karen National Union, releasing political prisoners and embracing the U.S. as a geopolitical partner and accepting its democratic ideals, must make young Kim and Uncle Jong wonder why, or is it why not? What better way for the Kim dynasty and its military supporters to survive?

Surely Suu Kyi's words are ringing in Kim's musical ears. In echoes of her writings on democracy when she was under house arrest, Suu Kyi elaborated on what she called the "revolution of the spirit."

"I mean a revolution that will help our people to overcome fear, to overcome poverty, to overcome indifference," she said, "and to take the fate of their country into their own hands."

Watching client states leaders like Libya's Gaddaffi and Syria's Assad go the way of Russia and other Eastern European communist dictatorships, while exhausting China's patronage, can only lead to one conclusion. Change or die!

But then again, Kim may think to adopt Yemen's Ali Abdullah Salch's bargaining strategy for his exit deal. Safe passage to New York on a private jet, the keys to a "huge treasure chest," and a guarantee of immunity – all "solemnly" decreed by parliament. Opposition protestors are unlikely to see Saleh brought to justice for his crimes, but who knows. Anything is possible today. Look what happened to Assad.

Kim can survive and preserve the family dynastic goals by marching his generals down the economic path that China has strongly suggested and Myanmar's generals have adopted.

While there is no turning back for Myanmar, there is a huge swath of U-turn ground available for Kim and North Korea.

Turning back is not an option for Myanmar.

"We are on the right track to democracy," President Thein Sein said in an interview with *The Washington Post* published in January 2012, his first with Western media. "Because we are on the right track, we can only move forward, and we don't have any intention to draw back."

A typically dark piece of political humor that made the rounds of Yangoon's tea shops after democratic icon Suu Kyi was released from house arrest and allowed to run for a parliament seat suggested that all the generals had to do to finally neutralize her aura was to make her electricity minister after her election to parliament. The rolling blackouts and power surges that affect the former capital daily would see her reputation destroyed within six months.

In the eyes of many supporters, a place in Myanmar's 440-seat lower house of parliament would be the vital springboard for Suu Kyi to eventually lead the country. "President Thein Sein and his government have clearly decided they'd rather have her inside their tent than out," says one Western diplomat.

Nobel Peace Prize laureate Suu Kyi is loved and respected by her fellow citizens, not just because her father was the rebellious military officer who led the country to independence and became its first president, but because of her willingness to be held in house arrest for more than 15 years rather than compromise her principles of democracy. Thousands of people line the roads wherever she goes just to catch a glimpse of her as they cheer and wave and hand her red roses and jasmine flowers.

Myanmar also ended years media censorship in August 2012 as part of its reform policies.

Myanmar's reforms appear genuine. Notwithstanding the fact that the military has ruled directly and indirectly throughout most of Burma's independent history since 1948, under the so-called "democratically elected government" of Thein Sein, that control continues through a number of constitutional provisions. These constitutional controls are supplemented by a pervasive government party that swept 80 percent of the legislative seats and is military-dominated.

After half a century of strong-fisted military rule, the army organized elections in late 2010, and officially handed power to a civilian in March 2011. But critics say the new government is a proxy for continued military rule and that little has changed.

The motto over the gate of the Myanmar Military Academy sums up the attitude of the Tatmadaw, or armed forces: "The Triumphant Elites of the Future."

Sounds a lot like Turkey's constitution and political framework instituted by Kemal Attaturk when he came to power after World War I. Myanmar, like Turkey, will eventually become a full-fledged democracy with a military neutralized in domestic political affairs – but very effective with foreign adversaries.

Washington rushed to boldly and publicy embrace the new Myanmar and its democratic reforms. While the U.S. aggressively stomped into China's "sphere of influence," China did the same to the U.S. in Saudi Arabia and its oil-rich Gulf neighbors that America has dominated.

Premier Wen Jiabao signed economic and trade agreements worth $16 billion with Saudi Arabia and the United Arab Emirates during his bonanza visit to the Middle East in January 2012. The visit by a Chinese premier to Saudi Arabia was the first in 21 years. Wen's visit to the UAE and Qatar were the first ever by a Chinese premier.

It should therefore come as no surprise to *We the Apathetic Maids* that career politicians in Washington, who are even more apathetic than us, are constantly caught off guard by foreign events and are blind-sided by their self-serving domestic and foreign policies that only benefit their financial backers – oil companies, financial institutions, pharmaceuticals, the military-industrial complex and their lobbyists.

### Libya, Syria – and Turkey's Future Role
Libya is a good example for North Korea's new Brilliant Leader to study closely. A one-term military dictator's term and life cut short as his hierarchical sons fought and fled for their lives because suppressed anger and bitterness among citizens – and being deprived of the most fundamental

human necessities – will inevitably explode into irresistable protests demanding changes that in many cases cause the ruling one-term dictators to flee, get imprisoned or be executed. Saddam Hussein, Gaddafi, Hosni Mubarak and Ben-Ali being prime examples.

Citizens expressing their right to speak freely and openly without fear of political repression by the ruling party. Libyans sending their long-term tyrant to an unexpectedly early unmarked grave without any foreign troops on the ground. Libyans themselves – pardon the pun – calling the shots.

What a better way to fight a war. None of the truckloads of $100 bills and costly Iraqi-style "reconstruction" teams that drained the U.S. Treasury while the battle with insurgents was costing thousands of American lives there, and now in Afghanistan.

How much nicer and cost effective it is to run a government with the ill-gotten billions of dollars of a deposed ruler rather than American taxpayers' money.

Libyan cities, while in political and military chaos, have running water and electricity, something that still hasn't completely returned to Baghdad and other Iraqi cities.

The U.S. ineptitude in responding to the brutal, bloody Syrian regime's putdown of protests baffles me. The excuses given are that a collapse of Syria could lead to an external explosion that would affect Iran, Lebanon, Jordan, Israel and even Iraq, foreign policy experts say, particularly if it dissolves into an Iraq-style civil war. That is because, unlike Libya, Syria is of strategic importance, sitting at the center of ethnic, religious and regional rivalries that give it the potential to become a whirlpool that draws in powers, great and small, in the region and beyond.

"Syria is almost the only country where the so-called Arab Spring could change the geostrategic concept of the region," said Oliver Roy, a French historian of the Middle East. He offered as a counterexample Egypt and Tunisia, where new leaders seemed to be keeping similar alliances and geopolitical positions, "But in Syria," Roy said, "if the regime is toppled, we have a totally new landscape."

And so what? It's a new landscape that is long overdue. One the U.S. should actively and openly and proudly support from the get-go. For decades Syria has been the linchpin of the old world order that allowed the Russians and Iranians to extend their influence in the region. The Russians have a naval base there and supply the Assad regime and its terrorist proxies with arms while Iran uses Syria as the gateway to supply arms and support to Hezbollah in Lebanon and Hamas in Palestine. So what am I missing?

Shiite Iran and Sunni Saudi Arabia getting into a regional conflict that has been brewing for centuries? It's long overdue and better now than before Iran becomes a nuclear nation. America can and should stay out of such a conflict and not compromise its democratic principles out of concern for the Saudis. America's moral principles must always override its strategic interests dictated by oil.

What is wrong with Russia and Iran losing their influence in the region? Why perpetuate a potential military conflict with a cold war adversary of the last century? Russia has been the arms supplier of choice to the Assad regime and its terrorist puppets in the region. The fall of the Assad regime would be a major defeat for Russia and Iran. A new Syrian government would be a greater blow to Iranian influence than any sanctions the West has mustered and could also revive democratic protests and an Iranian cleansing.

This inconvenient truth was obvious for all to see when Iran tried to put its own "Islamic" stamp on the Arab cleansing in February 2012 when it flew more than a thousand young activists to Tehran for a conference on "the Islamic awakening" – its effort to rebrand the regional revolutions after the Iranian revolution of 1979. Iran had invited revolutionaries from Egypt, Tunisia, Libya, Bahrain and Yemen, but not from Syria because Iran routinely dismisses the Syrian protesters as foreign agents despite their being Muslims fighting a secular dictatorship.

The guests in Tehran ended the charade as soon as the conference began by asking why Syrian protestors were not invited and began chanting the slogan of the Syrian protestors, "God, Freedom and Syria!"

Secretary of State Hillary Clinton has called any comparison of Syria to Libya a "false analogy." B.S. is my response. All the fore-mentioned countries can handle the fallout. Those that can't will only go America's way, as what America's Founding Fathers have to offer is what inspires protest and revolutionary movements interlocally.

America's alibis for not helping helpless Syrian citizens and intervening are inexcusable. Not to provide arms to the Syrian opposition because they could end up in the wrong hands and would "militarize" the conflict is utter hogwash. What would the outcome have been had France and others not come to the support of America during our revolution?

For America to stand by as Syria blocked Red Cross convoys from delivering aid to devasted rebel enclaves in Homs while Syrian security forces conducted house-to-house searches and summary executions and graphic videos showed hundreds of protestors fleeing in panic at the rocket explosions which sent body parts flying is unbelievable and criminal.

The silence of the Obama administration on Syria reveals the general retreat of American power in the Middle East and the re-emergence of Turkey and France. America should have taken the lead to topple the Assad regime.

"The tortured dissertations on the uniqueness of Syria's strategic landscape are in fact proofs for why we must thwart the Iran-Syria-Hezbollah nexus. Topple the Syrian dictatorship and the access of Iran to the Mediterranean is severed, leaving the brigands of Hamas and Hezbollah scrambling for a new way. The democracies would demonstrate that regimes of plunder and cruelty, perpetrators of terror, have been cut down to size," wrote Fouad Ajami, a senior fellow at Stanford University's Hoover Institution.

America's indifference is inexcusable. America is and must be the provider of order in the Middle East. It cannot retreat from the region just because it is ending its failed mission in Iraq.

Let's not forget it was the Assad regime that helped the jihadists in their campaign against America in Iraq. It provided sanctuary and transit for jihadists who crossed into Iraq to do battle against the Americans and the Shiites; it even released its own Islamist prisoners and dispatched them to Iraq with the promise of pardon.

Plainly, the Syrian tyranny's writ has expired. Assad has implicated his own Alawite community in a war to defend his family's reign. The ambiguity that allowed the Assad tyranny to conceal its minority, schismatic identity, to hide behind a co-opted Sunni religious class, was torn asunder. Calls for a jihad, a holy war, against a godless lot have been made in Sunni religious circles everywhere – even in America.

When America finally did wake up to the need to intervene in Syria, it went about it the wrong way – via the U.N. where it was obvious its resolution calling on President Bashar al-Assad to step aside would be vetoed by Russia and China and only inflame the conflict, which it did. The U.N. veto became a "license to kill" for Assad and the best reason yet the U.N. should be restructured or buried as obsolete, as I discussed in an entire chapter in *Custom Maid Knowledge*.

The defeated resolution would have "fully" supported the Arab League plan for "a Syrian-led political transition to a democratic, plural political system" – the last thing China and Russia want to see. So why didn't America follow it's NATO strategy the way it did with Libya?

Why is anyone surprised that Russia and China, two countries scared to death of regime change, would vote against a resolution calling for one? That is precisely why the U.N. infrastructure, like America, China – and Russia for that matter – have to change.

Russian Foreign Minister Sergey V. Lavrov, who met with Assad after the U.N. veto, argued that Russia's efforts were far more productive and balanced than the combined Western and Arab plan that was the object of the joint veto. Lavrov stressed that Russia would seek to inaugurate open negotiations between the Syrian government and the opposition. Right. Why doesn't Russia start by doing the same at home and lead by example instead of more self-serving regime rhetoric that reminds us of the non-starters the USSR embarked on and failed – and will fail again? How out of touch is Russia, not only with its foreign policy, but with domestic policy and politics?

The cold war mindset of sustaining of dictatorships, whether in Syria or Russia, is over. The same holds true for China.

China's veto of the U.N. resolution sent a clear message to America. China is angry at America's active re-engagement politically and militarily in the Asia-Pacific region and the hard lesson it learned by abstaining on the Libya resolution that provided a green light for unrestricted military and covert operations that eventually led to regime change in Libya. Beijing feels that in international affairs, America has remained stronger than China in terms of monopolizing the language and conceptual framework, something China is determined to change. To do so, Beijing has become more assertive in expressing itself, even though such assertiveness does not always yield positive results, as in the case of the South China Sea. The Chinese feel they must fully utilize the U.N. and other international organizations to gain more experience in great-power diplomacy. China feels its veto action at the Security Council thus heralds its coming of age as a leading player in great-power politics.

A Syrian opposition delegation visited Beijing two days after China vetoed the U.N. resolution. "China is willing to maintain contacts and communication with relevant Syrian opposition groups, is willing to push and encourage talks and make great efforts to ameliorate the situation," said Foreign Ministry spokesman Liu Weimin. "The Syrian government should earnestly fulfill its promises, urgently begin an inclusive reform process that has wide participation, and resolve disputes and conflicts via talks and consultations," he added.

Well, it tried to, by holding a referendum on a new constitution at the end of February 2012, an offer of reform that critics dismissed as too little too late and Western leaders labeled a sham. Syrian forces continued to kill hundreds of civilians on the bloody Sunday the referendum was held, and the absence of outside observers also raised questions about the legitimacy of the vote.

The referendum was rushed to a vote in an apparent attempt to counter the rising domestic violence and provide cover for Russia and China, who have objected to any outside intervention, saying that government reform efforts must be given a chance. The Syrian government announced that nearly 90 percent of voters had approved the new Constitution. Russia and China called it a step toward reform while Western leaders called it a farce.

In Syria, referendums traditionally produce the results sought by the government, so the huge plurality in favor of the Constitution was no surprise.

Beijing's move is similar to the one it took in Libya in 2011 before the fall of Muammar Gaddafi. After months of criticizing foreign intervention and ignoring the rebels, China began meeting anti-Gaddafi leaders, but was still the last major nation to recognize the opposition.

What was China thinking when it cast its veto? It makes no geopolitical sense if China really wants to become a global-power-player. Self-preservation of the Communist Party regime? That makes short-term sense but is not in China's interest long term. Was it responding to pressure from Iran, where it buys about 20 percent of its oil, to support Iran's ally Assad? That makes even less sense.

Beijing lost on every front with its vote, especially in its longstanding effort to win hearts and minds in the Middle East and Africa. Arab League Chief Nabil Elarby said that China "has lost diplomatic credit in the Arab world" following the vote. Leaders of several Middle East countries that are major oil exporters to China have also expressed dismay. Libyans pelted the Chinese Embassy in Tripoli with stones to show their displeasure with Beijing's ongoing resistance to the Arab cleansing.

One might have thought someone in Beijing would have learned the lesson of Libya, where they failed to gain the goodwill of the new government by refusing to cut their links with the Gaddafi regime. Potential contracts in oil and infrastructure worth billions of dollars have now gone to the

Europeans and Americans. Unlike Russia, China does not have close military or economic ties with Syria's Assad regime to worry about. In the face of overwhelming international condemnation of Syria, Beijing could have upheld its principle of "nonintervention in the internal affairs of other countries" simply by abstaining, allowing the resolution to proceed without Beijing's support.

This willingness to act in a way so far counter to what would appear to be in China's normal interest is an important signal. Beijing is sending a message about its evolving attitude toward the U.S. The veto is Beijing's way of thumbing its nose at Washington, which it believes is masterminding a series of "color revolutions" to undermine nondemocratic regimes around the world. Anti-American sentiments seem to have surged within the Chinese party establishment, particularly after President Obama's recent "pivot to Asia" policy.

"This is interpreted – not entirely wrongly – by Beijing as an exacerbation of what China calls Washington's 'anti-China containment policy'," wrote Willy Lam, an adjunct professor of history at the Chinese University of Hong Kong in a poignant editorial opinion in *The Wall Street Journal*, echoing my thoughts on the subject.

If the responsibility to protect civilians is a legitimate new part of international law, why would it apply to Libya and not to Syria? Why shouldn't America, China and the world intervene in a one-sided Syrian slaughter of innocents seeking their freedom from a repressive murderous regime? Why should America with so much lethal power provide only "nonlethal" aid for so long?

Hugo Grotius (1583-1645) was among the founders of international law. He wrote that when a state undertakes mass killings of its own citizens, it is not only the right but also the duty of surrounding nations to intercede. Since President Bill Clinton called on NATO in 1995 to bomb Bosnia and Herzegovina, ending war crimes that are still being prosecuted, and President Obama organized a coalition for military intervention in Libya, international law has developed in line with the proposition advanced by Grotius – and Syria justified intervention from the get-go – not more than a year later.

Assad is a war criminal for his relentless and tragic crackdown and should be referred to the International Criminal Court.

The leadership of the Free Syrian Army is based in Turkey and thousands of refugees from Syria have fled to Turkey. Turkey has imposed sanctions against Syria and has become the Muslim model of democracy for the region. Turkey clearly wants to carve out and re-establish a sphere of influence in the Middle East. It has been less than a century since the British released the Arabs from the dominion of the Ottoman Empire.

France, like Turkey, has taken a pro-active role and has demanded that the EU freeze the assets of the Syrian Central Bank. While America and China sit on the sidelines, it is France and Turkey that are vying for lucrative business ties and the chance to mold a new generation of leaders in the lands they once controlled. This rivalry is nothing new. Since Napoleon invaded Egypt in 1798, France and Turkey have competed for dominance in the Middle East. As the Ottoman Empire gradually collapsed, France acquired Algeria, Tunisia and, temporarily, Egypt. The French took one final bite from the dying empire by securing control over Lebanon and Syria after World War I.

This rivalry is one reason France has objected to Turkey's bid for European Union membership. It is also the reason that the French Senate periodically introduces legislation to criminalize the denial of the Armenian genocide by the Ottoman Turks that continuously sours relations between the two countries.

Turkey looked to France as a political model after the collapse of the Ottoman Empire. When modern Turkey's Founding Father Mustafa Kemal Attaturk founded the Republic in 1923, he championed the French model of hard secularism, which stipulates freedom from religion in government, politics and education. Since 2002, Attaturk's French-inspired model has collapsed and a softer form of secularism has been promoted that allows for more religious expression in government, politics and education. This has made the Turkish model appealing to Arab countries. The Arab cleansing is providing Turkey with an unprecedented opportunity to spread its influence in newly free Arab societies.

Turkey today is striving to become the dominant power in the region – something I predicted would happen in *Custom Maid Knowledge* when I encouraged Europe to embrace Turkey as a member of the EU. France's strong opposition to Turkey's membership and its efforts to create a European-Mediterranean Union, which Nicolas Sarkozy conceived in 2008 as a way to place France at the helm of the Mediterranean world, has only encouraged Turkey to become more active in cultivating ties with former Ottoman lands that were ignored for much of the 20th century. Of the 33 new Turkish diplomatic missions opened in the first decade of the 21st century, 18 are in Muslim and African countries.

If Turkey wants to become a true beacon of democracy in the Middle East, its new constitution must provide broader individual rights for the country's citizens, especially the Kurds. It must also fulfill Foreign Minister Ahmet Davutoglu's vision of a "no problems" foreign policy. This means moving past the 2010 flotilla incident and rebuilding strong ties with Israel and forging a political working relationship with the Greek Cypriots in Southern Cyprus. Turkish Cypriots control the North of the divided island. The conflict there has lasted since the early '70s. The Turkish Cypriots want a loose federation while the Greek Cypriots want a strong central government.

The recent discovery of natural gas off the south coast of Cyprus is a major opportunity. Turkey must rise above the fray by proposing unification of the island in exchange of an agreement to share gas revenues. Such a deal, coupled with improved Turkish-Israeli ties, could facilitate cooperation in extracting even larger gas deposits off Israel's coast. Turkey is the most logical destination for a pipeline from there to foreign markets.

The subject of Turkish-Israeli relations was a topic I discussed with both Israelis and Turkish Cypriots in September 2011 when I visited Israel and Cyprus.

"Turkey and Israel need each other and are natural allies in a region of

Arabs," said Taskin Agaoglu, a Turkish Cypriot builder I was having a Turkish coffee with at a seaside hotel in Famagusta as we discussed the future of the strained Turkey-Israel relationship and the future of Iran.

The nearby Eastern Mediterranean University in Famagusta had students from Turkey, Israel and Iran, as well as many other countries in the Middle East and Africa. Taskin shared some of the promiscuous sexual exploits of the students that had become legendary local lore in response to my question of how the students got along with each other – especially the Iranian female students. But back to politics.

"You're right," I responded. "Turkey and Israel are the only two democratic non-Arab countries on the Asia continent on the Eastern Mediterranean surrounded by Arabs and Iran who are run by repressive dictatorships. That can only change with Turkey and Israel re-aligning themselves to address and deal with the new geopolitical realities of the Middle East."

The Arab cleansing and active supportive role Turkey played, especially in Egypt, was a painful blow to many Israelis. In 1949 Turkey was the first Muslim-majority country to recognize Israel as a Jewish state, and in 1979, Egypt was the first Arab country to sign a peace treaty with Israel.

Taskin and I agreed that the biggest threat to both Israel and Turkey is a nuclear-armed Iran. The single biggest danger in the Middle East today "is not the risk of a six-day Israeli war against Iran. It is the risk that Western wishful nonthinking allows the mullahs of Tehran to get their hands on nuclear weapons. Because I am in no doubt that they would take full advantage of such a lethal lever. We would have acquiesced in the creation of an empire of extortion," British historian Niall Ferguson wrote in February 2012 in *Newsweek*.

Taskin's wife was expecting their first child and the evil of war and what our families had experienced in Cyprus figured in what became a painful and almost tearful discussion.

That conversation with Taskin echoed several I had in Israel and Turkey. I never cease to be amazed how well informed the average person on the street in Israel, Turkey and Cyprus is when compared to Americans or Chinese. Cafe societies in the Middle East, where people meet to discuss issues of the day over a cup of coffee or puffing on a hooka, are so much better informed that they actually enable themselves to elect better qualified political representatives. In America and China, people in coffee shops seem to be absorbed with themselves and their mobile devices and don't talk to each other or discuss pressing political and economic matters. It is not unusual to see a couple, or a few people, sitting together all texting or e-mailing and not talking to each other. How sad.

Tradition in Middle Eastern cultures is respected and passed on from generation to generation, something America has lost and China is losing. Respect for elders, families, friends and acquaintances, discussing and debating political, economic and religious issues of the day – something that is sorely lacking in America and China.

Turkey will continue to rise as a regional power only if it sets a genuine corruption-free example as a liberal democracy and builds strong ties with all its neighbors.

We must give credit to the revolutionaries in Tunisia, Egypt, Libya and Syria. First they get rid of the corrupt self-serving political establishment and then take on the military establishment that served the political one. They are to be applauded for sweeping out the old political models and sweeping in the new. The Arab cleansing needs to be emulated both in America and China.

The military-industrial complex puppeteers of the political puppet parties in Washington and Beijing have to be swept out by *We the Maids*. If Arabs are prepared to die for democracy and Burmese generals reluctantly acknowledge that their days are numbered unless they democratize and initiate change, shouldn't *We the Apathetic Maids* be doing the same in America and China?

## Africa
The changes taking place in Africa are also worth noting. The evolution from subsistence to commercial agriculture has phenomenal implications for the continent. Seven in 10 Africans live off the land. Commercializing agriculture – increasing the scale and profitability of farming – would spur

meaningful participation in an economy, often for the first time, by 700 million people. Moving from subsistence farming to more competitive, organized agriculture could spell the end of chronic poverty on the continent. Studies by the International Food Policy Research Institute and the World Bank suggest that every 1 percent rise in agricultural income per capita reduces the number of people in extreme poverty by 0.6 percent to 1.8 percent.

While aid agencies warn that high food prices fall hardest on the poor, high prices only sharpen the opportunity for Africa's farmers – if they can manage to hold onto enough of the profits.

The world has had agricultural revolutions before, and their effects can be profound. The domestication of plants and animals more than 13,000 years ago was a prerequisite for civilization. In 16th-century Britain, enclosure, mechanization, crop rotation and selective breeding produced the surplus and the spare workforce that drove the Industrial Revolution. India's Green Revolution, which introduced irrigation, fertilizer, pesticide and high-yield seeds in the late 1960s and the 1970s, ended widespread famine in that country and turned it into a rice exporter.
Now it's Africa's turn.

### Russia and France

Change and revolution is not limited to the developing world, but is simmering in Russia] and its former Soviet states. Russia is a country that many argue is also still developing – economically and politically. The aspirations Mikhail S. Gorbachev had for Russia are still an elusive dream.

Democratic reform and capitalism did not replace communism. Kleptocracy did. Vladimir V. Putin and his loyal financial and political supporters being the biggest beneficiaries. The kleptocrats hoped to keep their political puppet in power by having him reappoint himself, as he did, when he shoved his interim placeholder President Dmitri Medvedev aside in his attempt to stay in power until 2024. Is it any wonder Russians took to the streets to protest the rigged election and Putin's unabashed refusal to cede power? The Ukrainians also took to the streets to let Putin know they wanted to join the European Union and how angry they were with his unilateral and illegal annexation of Crimea.

I went to watch a Washington Capitals hockey game during my spring 2012 visit to the U.S. Hearing Capital fans in their red team shirts yell "Let's go Reds!" as they cheered on number 8, Russian Alexander Ovechkin, arguably the best player in the league, I couldn't help think about the '60s slogan "Better Dead Than Red!"

America and its capital sure have come a long way.

Kind of ironic that the only credible opposition to Putin's United Russia Party is the Communist Party – the party the people are turning to to voice their peaceful democratic anger and opposition to Putin's iron-fisted refusal to give up power and abide by the people's democratic aspirations, honestly expressed at the ballot box – until corrupted like every thing else. The Communist Party has again become the popular party of the people who are the 99 percenters fighting Putin's 1 percenters. There are better alternatives, not only for the Russians, but for the French, who in September 2011 overwhelmingly voted for leftist and socialist candidates and handed them the French Senate for the first time since the Fifth Republic was founded in 1958.

The left, led by the Socialists, won 177 seats in the 348-seat upper house of Parliament, compared to the right's 171; President Nicolas Sarkozy's UMP Party held just 124 seats. When Sarkozy took office in 2007, the right held 203 seats in the Senate.

And it's not just Russia and France that are starting to lean to the left, but many countries in the former Eastern Europe and between, including Germany, Holland, Hungary and Romania. The world is leaning left, after the right turn world that political leaders took at the start of the new millennium that crashed and crushed the global economy.

### Reunification

I have shared quite a few thoughts and opinions in my books about the cross-strait relationship between mainland China and Taiwan – and the new role America should take on – and realized I hadn't been to Taiwan in years. So I decided to spend a few days there around Hanukkah and Christmas 2011.

My friend Steve Chicorel, who is Jewish, married to a Taiwanese, invited Pauline – who is a Protestant – and I, to come spend the holidays with him and his family and share the meaning of the holidays with his young children Philip and Anabel.

Hanukkah and Christmas coincided in December 2011. Pauline regaled the children with the story of Jesus and Christmas and I did the same about Hanukkah. The Hebrew word Hanukkah means "dedication." In the second century BC, during the time of the Second Temple, the Syrian-Greek regime of Antiochus sought to pull Jews away from Judaism, with the hopes of assimilating them into Greek culture. Antiochus outlawed Jewish observance, including circumcision, Shabbat and Torah study with the death penalty.

When the Greeks challenged the Jews to sacrifice a pig to a Greek god, a few took to the hills of Judea in open revolt against this threat to Jewish life. Led by Matitiyahu, and later his son Judah the Maccabee, this small band of pious Jews fought a guerrilla war against the well-armed Syrian-Greek army and after three years miraculously defeated them. When the Jewish fighters entered Jerusalem, they found the Holy Temple in shambles and desecrated with idols. The Macabees cleansed the Temple and rededicated it on the 25th of Kislev, the day Hanukkah, the Festival of Lights, begins.

The first thing the Jews did when they recaptured the Holy Temple was light the golden menorah. They only had enough oil to last for one day, and new oil would take seven days to prepare. But a miracle happened. Instead of burning for one day, the menorah stayed lit for eight days.

Hanukkah has some significant characteristics with the number eight. The world was created in seven days. There are seven notes in the musical scale, seven days of the week. Therefore the number seven represents the physical world that we can touch, smell and feel. The number eight, on the other hand, transcends the natural world. That is why the miraculous days of Hanukkah are eight. Though eight emanates from beyond our senses, your soul can still reach out and be touched by its force.

The miracle of the oil lasting for eight days was a reminder that Jewish life is hewn from the Rock of Transcendence. Hence the Hanukkah celebration lasts for eight days and the menorah has eight candles that are lit by an extra helper candle – one candle a day. The menorah should be lit in a window facing the public thoroughfare which fulfills the mitzvah of "publicizing the miracle."

Giving children Hanukkah gelt – money or candy – for eight days in addition to the Christmas day presents, is a joyous time of year. Sharing the occasion with Philip and Anabel in Taiwan was no exception. They are typical of today's kids. They would rather have new bikes, iPods and iPhones instead of Hanukkah gelt.

What had to be explained to them is that one of the most important contributions of Judaism to the world is the idea of being unsatisfied. Israel President Shimon Peres said it best during his visit to Los Angeles in March 2012. "Jews are never satisfied. Jews without a land, without resources, have come so far because when you're not satisfied, you dream on."

Peres paid homage to the idea when talking to a Hollywood crowd about Hollywood's Jewish origins. "I know among the founders of Hollywood there were many Jewish people," he said. "Because they didn't have a land, they had to have a dream."

It was also an interesting time to go because Taiwan, like America and China, elected a new president and government in 2012. In Taiwan's case, a few months earlier on January 14, 2012. Being a political junkie, I thoroughly relish being a witness to any election, especially a close one like that of Taiwan's that impacts on geopolitical relations and has ramifications for America and China.

The decisions of Taiwan's 13 million voters who exercised their electoral franchise greatly affected its Asia-Pacific neighbors and America. Taiwan has long been a diplomatic battleground between Beijing and Washington. The cross-straits situation has often been contentious, making the island a major roadblock to the betterment of China-U.S. relations.

Sitting on my balcony in the Silks Place Hotel in Taroko National Park at dusk overlooking the famous Gorge, the marble-walled jewel in the park's crown – topped by a pagoda with red lights and a nearby pyramid-shaped rock with the symbol of Buddha's heart – the same symbol adopted by the Nazis, watching the flickering fireflies and fluttering swallows – another metaphor for what will happen to Taiwan, I wondered? As I admired the beauty of Mother Nature, I couldn't help comparing the Gorge to the beauty of America's Grand Canyon and China's Guilin mountains.

I reflected on the day's tour of the park and thought about the hundreds, if not thousands, of mainland Chinese tourists I had encountered in the park and in the Palace Museum, Taipei 101 Shopping Mall, Sun Yat Sen Memorial and Chiang Kai Shek memorials earlier in the week. They were everywhere.

There was only one conclusion I could reach. Taiwan was being wrapped in China's economic embrace – one it cannot resist or avoid – and conversely, neither can the motherland.

Now that Hong Kong and Macau have opened trade and cultural offices in Taipei in 2011, and Taiwan has done the same in Hong Kong and Macau in early 2012, it is clear that Hong Kong and Macau have become gateways for Taiwanese firms eying the mainland – and conversely, mainland firms sizing up their Taiwan bite-size investment – now that Taiwan is relaxing mainland investment criteria.

Mainland banks are now allowed to own minority stakes in Taiwanese lenders and financial firms for the first time in more than 60 years. Taiwanese banks have branches and liaison offices on the mainland and mainland banks are setting up satellite offices in Taiwan.

Taiwan also opened a pavilion dedicated to Taiwan fruits, vegetables and marine products in a popular Shanghai shopping mall – the same day I was mulling Taiwan's reunification with mainland China.

Tsai Ing-wen, the Democratic Progressive Party presidential candidate, had said that day in the hotly contested election at a campaign stop in Kinmen Island, the site of heavy artillery exchanges in the '50s between Taiwan and mainland China, that if elected she would promote bilateral relations to advance and not regress, echoing incumbent KMT President Ma Ying-jeou, clearly distancing herself from her party's former President Chen Shui-bien who shunned reunification and wanted independence for Taiwan.

That did not help her, even though it was a battle to the wire. Ma and the KMT maintained a narrow edge and won. Ma's engagement approach brought a clear shift in cross-strait relations. Since 2008, the sides had signed 16 agreements, including direct cross-strait flights, the opening of the island to mainland tourists, joint efforts to fight cross-strait crimes and assure food safety, as well as numerous other economic and cultural exchanges. Most notable was the signing of the Economic Cooperation Framework Agreement in 2010 that brought dramatic benefits to the island's economy due to a series of preferential tariffs and treatments.

After his victory, Ma said his Beijing-friendly policies had resonated with voters. "They gave us support for our policy to put aside differences with the mainland, to search for peace and turn it into business opportunities," he said.

More than 200,000 mainland-based Taiwanese businesspeople flocked back to vote, joined by more than 20,000 based in Hong Kong. Not surprisingly, most of the returnees were Ma supporters spurred by polls that had showed him in a close race. A record number of more than 74 percent of registered voters turned out. Taiwanese voters broke out of their apathy – something American and mainland Chinese citizens can take a cue from.

The vote was the fifth presidential contest since Taiwan emerged from single-party rule in 1996.

How ironic, I thought to myself, that while China and Taiwan are working hard at reunifying the Chinese way, America is still pushing arms sales to Taiwan. A front-page story in *The China Post* that day – December 27 – detailed the test flight of Taiwan's two newly acquired U.S.–made E-2K early- warning aircraft that were part of a U.S. arms deal criticized by China.

A front-page story in the *Taipei Times* the following day reported on

Taiwan's Air Force upgrading its "Skyguard" short-range air defense system that will be completed in 2012. The program includes the acquisition of high-tech explosive projectiles intended to destroy incoming aircraft, guided missiles and other targets that China may send its way.

Taiwan and China have been in a formal state of war since 1949, when the Nationalists lost the Chinese civil war and fled the mainland, moving their Republic of China government to Taipei.

To make matters worse for politicians on both sides of the straits, America sent more high-level officials in the preceding three months leading up to the election than in the previous three years in its concerted effort to ensure the status quo. Was this a politically strategic decision as some political commentators say, based on criticism Obama received from Congress for the U.S.'s lax policy toward Taiwan, or was it siding with Ma's candidacy? Many commentators believe it was the latter, especially when it was announced that the U.S. had nominated Taiwan for its Visa Waiver Program. Top U.S. officials rarely visit Taiwan in order to avoid triggering an adverse reaction from Beijing, something that didn't happen this time. That is because China did not disagree with the strategy and U.S. goal at a time of political transition for both major powers.

Beijing also dangled more trade and economic carrots ahead of the elections and warned the pro-independence opposition that closer ties would be at risk if it did not change its stance and put Taiwan's voters on notice that it, like America, wanted to maintain the status quo and continue the rapprochement process. The challenge now is how to secure the peace and reunification.

Ma's election victory belongs to the Chinese on both sides as it underscores the fact that after six decades of separation, people need healing; they need to be back together economically, culturally, socially – and politically. Their areas of togetherness need to keep expanding as each side finds its missing half to form a new, complete whole.

The outcome of Taiwan's leadership election has not only reassured many countries of the region's future security, but also spread the experience of elections to millions of Chinese on the mainland.

That prospect is not that far away. The millions of mainland Chinese tourists and businesspeople visiting Hong Kong and Taiwan are the best emissaries for the benefits of an open democratic political system.

Mainland media and Internet users flooded cyberspace with positive comments about the benefits of democracy in the run-up to Taiwan's presidential election. Mainlanders could follow the campaign, including watching the debates between the candidates. Some bloggers expressed admiration for the fact that Taiwan's people are able to vote for their leaders and stirred hopes among Chinese for democracy. "I am 24. Can I cast my ballot for my country's leaders before I die?" one asked.

Another said: "I dreamed of getting Taiwan back when I was young. But now I want the mainland to be 'returned' to Taiwan."

"Don't talk about unification. Taiwan people have a good life and they have their elections. I have not even cast a ballot once."

One blogger provoked a strong response when a picture was uploaded showing Ma along with a phrase saying that holders of Republic of China passports can gain visa-free entry access to 124 countries. "This kind of election advertisement will definitely hit the nerves of mainland citizens," came one reply. "Can I immigrate to Taiwan?"

"On the other side of the sea, Taiwan erected a mirror. And on this side of the sea, we saw ourselves in the future," read one well-forwarded comment by Xu Wei, a wine expert.

After his re-election, Ma did something that resonated on the mainland and triggered more blogs urging mainland officials to do the same. He disclosed his personal wealth and holdings – something no mainland official has done to date.

Ma also brought the "two territories" closer together by describing cross-strait relations as "one country, two territories."

Ma made a direct appeal in January 2013 to Xi Jinping to work with him to further expand cross-strait ties. In his New Year's address, Ma called on Xi by name as he reaffirmed his commitment to strengthen all aspects of the relationship between Beijing and Taipei and bolster their landmark 2010

Economic Cooperation Framework Agreement and – they are.

It is rare for a Taiwanese president to address a mainland leader as "mister" with his full name in a public pronouncement. Ma's predecessors always used the term "Beijing authorities" or "Beijing leadership."

The prospects for closer political ties is very good as Xi spent 17 years in Fujian, just across the strait from Taiwan, and therefore has a better understanding of Ma's political obstacles than other Beijing leaders.

More than 4.5 million mainlanders have visited the island since Taipei started allowing travel in July 2008, adding billions of dollars to the Taiwanese economy.

The mainland has become Taiwan's top trading partner, accounting for some 40 percent of its exports in 2011 compared with 15 percent for the U.S. Trade between the two Chinas totaled $100 billion in 2011. Nevertheless, Taiwan rejected Chinese President Xi Jinping's 2014 suggestion that the island adopt the Hong Kong "one country two systems" model of reunification. With what's taking place in Hong Kong the rejection is understandable. The growing economic ties and proposed 2014 free-trade agreement sparked student protests in Taiwan. Students occupied Taiwan's legislative chamber for a week in March 2014 and were joined by Hong Kong supporters.

Taipei wasted no time in joining Beijing in condemning Japan's nationalization of the Diaoyus and was quick to claim sovereignty over the island chain for Taiwan. Ma was also the first to propose cooperation between all concerned parties to formulate an agreement to ensure regional peace.

What mainlanders continue to hear and see in Hong Kong and Taiwan can only lead to progressive democracy on the mainland – with Chinese characteristics.The foundation stones for democracy in Greater China have been laid in Taiwan and Hong Kong.

When will America, China and Taiwan learn that their relationship can be as beautiful as the marble walls of the Gorge, the Grand Canyon and Guilin? Hopefully, sooner rather than later. That is because of the "One China" policy both sides agreed to and embraced in the "1992 Consensus." It will be a democratic China modeled after Taiwan and Hong Kong.

## The Three Principles of the People

Sun Yat-sen, the father of modern China, is recognized and honored as such in Beijing and Taipei. The three pillars of the late Chinese leader's political philosophy – *Minzu,* nationalism, *Minquan,* democracy, and *Minsheng,* people's livelihood, are so ingrained in the Chinese soul that streets in every major city on the Chinese mainland and Taiwan are named after him and his three principal philosophies. There are 187 Sun Yat-sen roads in mainland cities and many more streets, parks, museums and public places named in his memory. They are geographic proof that the communist leadership has recognized the impact of Sun and his revolution on modern Chinese history. The same holds true in Taiwan. As well as roads, there are monuments, schools, parks and other structures in the 390-odd townships, counties and cities in Taiwan named after Sun, who was educated in Hong Kong and the U.S.

These names were given shortly after the 1911 revolution overthrew the Qing dynasty and established the first republic – bringing more than 2,000 years of almost unbroken imperial history to an abrupt end – and they have survived under communist rule even after the Kuomintang, founded by Sun Yat-sen, fled to Taiwan at the end of the civil war in 1949.

While Beijing focused on nationalism, Taipei pushed for democracy, and it now boasts the most mature democracy of any Chinese society.

Despite their bitter ideological differences and a rivalry stretching back more than 90 years, both the ruling Communist Party on the mainland and Taiwan's KMT regard the revolution as a hugely important milestone on China's road to modernization. The three principles were the core of Sun's political philosophy in his efforts to make China a free, prosperous and powerful nation.

It was a legacy claimed wholesale as the basis for the ideology of the KMT under Chiang Kai-shek and one also tacitly accepted by the early communists, including Mao Zedong and all the party's leaders since. Calling Sun a "great patriot" and "a great pioneer of the Chinese democratic revolution," communist leaders have sought to depict themselves as loyal successors to the revolution he initiated.

Today, both parties largely agree on the meaning of nationalism but differ sharply on the meaning of democracy and people's livelihood. The KMT sees them in Western social democratic terms, while the Communist Party interprets them from a Marxist perspective, but that is quietly evaporating as the economy, protest movements and the political mood are embracing the Western models.

On the 100th anniversary of Sun's October 1911 revolution that ended the nation's long imperial history, China's Hu Jintao called for Taiwan and the Chinese mainland to to reunite. "Achieving reunification through peaceful means is what most suits Chinese people's fundamental interests, including Taiwan compatriots," he said.

Sun wanted a unified nation and an end to foreign colonialism and rule by warlords – something the Communist Party can claim to have fulfilled with the founding of the People's Republic in 1949. China is now a world power and no longer subject to bullying by the West. The party has become the bully and tolerates no political dissent.

As for the people's livelihood, social inequality on the mainland – like in America – has never been greater in more than a century.

### *Linsanity*

It is the inequality of the haves and have-nots at home – China and Taiwan included – that gets people to come to America for a better life for themselves and their children. Basketball phenom Jeremy Lin and his parents are among millions of such examples. His parents Shirley and Gie-Ming were born in Taiwan and came to the States as students; his great grandparents had migrated to Taiwan from Fujian, China, in 1707.

In Taiwan, Gie-Ming battled a language barrier in elementary school because his family spoke Minnanese, a dialect from Fujian province that is different from the Mandarin Chinese spoken in Taiwan. In Virginia in 1977 when he arrived to study at Old Dominion University, he struggled with English. In addition to earning his master's degree in engineering at Old Dominion, Gie-Ming also met his future wife, Wu Xinxin – who changed her name to Shirley Wu after arriving in Virginia. She was studying computer science, and after finishing their studies at ODU, the couple went together to Lafayette, Ind., to pursue additional degrees at Purdue University.

For the first four years of Jeremy's life, his parents worked continually – Gie-Ming as an electronics engineer and Shirley as an engineer for airports, specializing in ticket dispensers. Gie-Ming's mother spent 11 months a year in the U.S. to help raise the children.

In 1993, the family moved to Silicon Valley and paid $370,000 for a 1,700-square-foot house, putting down roots in the place where Jeremy developed into a basketball star – Palo Alto. For Shirley and Gie-Ming, like many Americans today, money became tighter as their family grew. Not long after they bought their home, their debts forced Gie-Ming to file for bankruptcy in 1995.

Jeremy, who was born in California, was on the Palo Alto High School team that went to the state championships. No scholarships were offered, so he went to Harvard. He was picked up and discarded by the Golden State Warriors and Houston Rockets. He landed at the end of the bench with the Knicks. His big break came in February 2012. He was inserted in the lineup and, suddenly he became a play-making sensation, thrust into fame and fortune.

A 6-3, 200-pound Asian-American basketball player in a league dominated by African-Americans who is defying stereotypes and disproving all the scouts and coaches who thought he'd never make it in the NBA, Lin is a metaphor for how America missed China's emergence as a geopolitical superstar.

Lin seemingly came from nowhere to lead the NBA's previously uninspired New York Knicks to seven straight wins as their point guard. He can split a double team and distribute the ball in a way that makes his teammates better, not unlike, metaphorically speaking, immigrants in other fields. That is what makes Team America a winner.

Lin represents many metaphors. His rapid rise from basketball obscurity to global stardom mirrors the same virtues that propelled Taiwan from agricultural backwater to high-tech powerhouse. Those virtues embody hard work, devotion to family and modesty.

At a time when U.S.-China relations remain prickly, Lin and basketball are a binding and bonding common denominator proudly proclaimed and embraced by both.

Secretary of Education Arne Duncan, who played basketball at Harvard, has developed a relationship with Lin and worked out with him on the court. "Everyone who thinks this is an overnight success fundamentally gets this wrong," Duncan said in an interview with *USA Today*. "Jeremy has been very good for a long time and just never quite had the opportunity."

Incredibly, the Knicks let the wildly popular Lin go in free-agency, and he took the court for the Houston Rockets in the 2012-2013 season. I'm delighted he is now with the L.A. Lakers.

I can relate to both Jeremy and his dad. First as a struggling immigrant student and then as an undiscovered or unread author.

"You know, your books are great and so informative and well written," said Dave Weiner, a book salesman I met and befriended in New York at Book Expo America in 2005. "You just need a lucky break. Your timing could not be worse. The publishing industry as we know it is dying. Major changes are taking place as the book world goes digital. Be patient. You're good."

Life is about playing out each hand we are dealt – be it by Mother Nature, family, community, country, religion, sex, or any and all of the foregoing combinations. We have to adapt and not only do what it takes to survive, but insure the survival and well being of our children and the world they are left to live in, no matter what career path they choose.

### Noble Nobel

Alfred Nobel made his fortune from war by selling his patented mercury fulminate detonator – a crucial component in the development of high explosives – that was used with dynamite and nitroglycerin. Nobel established munitions factories in Hamburg, Stockholm, New York and California. He held more than 350 patents, and by his death in December 1896, he was one of the world's wealthiest men. Nevertheless, he became a man of peace and, like Sun Yat-sen, wanted a better world for his people.

Nobel recognized the futility and stupidity of war when he established five awards for accomplishments in chemistry, literature, medicine or physiology, physics and peace. The Peace Prize named in his honor has generated the most controversy in recent years.

"I'm out standing in my field," said Graeme Scott, a Kiwi living in Christchurch, after the 2010 earthquake there, when I asked him who in his opinion was "outstanding in their field for the Nobel awards."

"Good one, Graeme," I laughed. "It took me a couple seconds there to figure it out. Those Isla single malts are making you creative."

Graeme is a single-malt scotch connoisseur and member of various single malt clubs around the world. As a jumbo jet pilot for Air New Zealand who needs to gas up around the world, the whiskey memberships come in handy and are put to good use.

Nobel put to good use the wealth he accumulated from war economies, realizing that our future depends on peace, harmony, science and knowledge – not war, nor an economy dependent on war and oil – the very industries that gave him his immense wealth.

Hopefully, America and China can become activists for peace, just like Alfred Nobel.

Nobel's Swedish Scandinavian Viking fighting heritage, which I can relate to, being a Viking Swede descendant myself, evolved and matured among a people and culture that can afford to advocate peace because it is not dependent on a war economy, nor any other country for its economic well-being. In his will, Nobel assigned the Norwegian Parliament to hand out the Peace Prize – to objectively do what is best for humanity. Norway's sovereign fund is the world's largest shareholder of public companies, so it doesn't give a damn what America or China thinks about who it honors with the Nobel Peace Prize because it is not dependent on either economically or politically.

That is what true revolutionaries – countries or people – say and do.

### Revolutionaries

An iconic figure who symbolized revolutionary change in the '60s – and still does today – is Che Guevara. He is revered by many around the world, as his romantic image of a dashing outlaw with flowing locks and soldier's beret on T-shirts, mugs, magazines, billboards and even bikinis around the world remind us.

Although his calls for armed insurrection and class warfare now seem outdated to a new wired generation that has found a peaceful path to change and democracy, Che is still widely admired. He may no longer inspire admirers to insurrection, but he remains a potent anti-establishment symbol for some born long after he was fomenting revolution from Cuba to the Congo.

"In the 1960s and 1970s, people rightly took up arms to change a system, a model, in search of justice and equality," Bolivian President Evo Morales told reporters in 2007 when asked about Che's legacy. "But these are different times.... After 40 years, Che is still a symbol of liberation, of sovereignty, dignity and, above all, justice and equality."

A more relevant revolutionary renaissance man for today is author, playwright and former president of the Czech Republic Vaclav Havel, who died at age 75 in December 2011. His most memorable play was Velvet Revolution. Havel's career as a literary figure, intellectual and political dissident confronted the tyranny of the former communist regime, and he oversaw the country's peaceful transition to democracy and a free market economy.

He started to write in the 1950s, but his immersion into Prague's artistic underground really began when he became a stagehand for the Theater on the Balustrade in 1960, amid a Moscow-inspired thaw that later blossomed into the Prague Spring. What struck Havel most about the 1968 Soviet invasion was the futility of military power when confronted by unarmed civilians.

"The world's greatest shortage is not of oil, clean water, or food, but of moral leadership. With a commitment to truth – scientific, ethical and personal – a society can overcome the many crises of poverty, disease, hunger and instabilty that confront us. Yet power abhors truth and battles it relentlessly. So let us pause to express gratitude to former Czech President Vaclav Havel for enabling a generation to gain the chance to live in truth," wrote Jeffrey Sachs, a professor of economics and director of the Earth Institute at Columbia University.

Havel held to his essential paradoxical beliefs: the need to speak the truth, and to beware the power of words. For Havel, a once-banned writer, truth and words were the only weapons he allowed himself.

He paid the price both in harassment, arrest and the "non-person category" he gained in opposition, especially after the thwarted expectations of the Prague Spring in 1968. His role as a dissident spanned the darkest decades of the old communist regime. In 1977, he and his fellow dissidents supported the "Charter 77" human rights manifesto, which emerged as a political template from Central Europe to China today.

When the web of lies collapsed in Czechoslavakia in November 1989, hundreds of thousands of Czechs and Slovaks poured into the streets to proclaim their freedom – and to sweep the banished and jailed playwright into Prague Castle as Czechoslovakia's newly elected president.

Havel was a tireless and unapologetic campaigner for human rights. The Czech Republic to this day is a proud and vocal sponsor of human rights movements around the globe.

Havel's death came at a time of massive demonstrations in Russia to protest alleged ballot fraud; violence in Egypt as democratic activists battled the deeply entrenched military; an uprising in rural China against corrupt local officials, and police in body armor violently dismantling the Occupy protest camps in the U.S. Power and truth remain locked in combat around the world.

The revolutionary titans of dissent who like Havel advocated truth over force include, but are not limited to, Mahatma Gandhi, Martin Luther King Jr., and Mikhail Gorbachev.

I hope Havel was able to see reports from Wukan, China, before he died. In that fishing village, the "power of the powerless" that he promoted as a means to undermine totalitarian rule was demonstrated anew, and with such enormous dignity and discipline that it has galvanized China.

Wukan's furious residents evicted the government and entrenched party officials who had held office for decades. They were angered by a local land dispute and became a symbol of rural defiance against land grabs and corruption that blight villages across China. The local Communist Party then selected the protest leader to be the village's new party secretary – and gave the villagers a taste of democracy by allowing them to vote to seat an independent election committee to oversee upcoming elections, including the one for village committee.

Xue Jianwan, daughter of protest organizer Xue Jinbo, 42, who died in police custody – sparking further protests – visited his memorial in the village square before the voting. "This is something my father would have hoped for," she said, bursting into tears. "We just want to do our best to fulfill his final wishes."

"For 40 years we've never had a proper election," said villager Chen Junchao, clutching a white ballot registration slip stamped with an official red ink government seal.

"I've never seen these papers before. I was crying when I saw this," Chen said.

Political activists and leaders are not the only revolutionaries. Every one of us, *We the Apathetic Maids,* are capable of change, like Jim Henry of Mystic, Connecticut. His father pulled him out of third grade so he could help support his family. He never learned to read, hiding his illiteracy from others for the better part of a century. Then in his mid-90s, after retiring as a lobsterman, he set out to continue his education. He took reading lessons and practiced writing. Not only is he reading and writing now, but he published a book in November 2011 at age 98 called *In a Fisherman's Language*.

"I'm so happy, I catch myself crying," he says. "It's the difference between night and day for me. It's like I'm born again."

Isn't this a feeling more of *We the Apathetic Maids* should have? People are never to old to learn or change – even political systems and models.

### *Kamikaze Partner*

Change also applies to political alliances and partnerships, especially America's relationship with Japan – a scandalous country when it comes to political whitewashing and the degree to which career politicians will go to deceive their citizens and the world. This is a subject I have touched upon in my previous books and in the introduction to this one. The Japanese corrupt political industrial syndrome is exemplified by two scandalous reports released at the end of 2011, which again make me question why America continuously chooses to partner with a kamikaze government that can only take down America, the way it tried to do at Pearl Harbor.

The scandals, corruption and government coverups that are systemic and endemic in Japan were highlighted when a powerful and independent panel of specialists, appointed by Japan's parliament, challenged the government's account of the Fukushima Daiichi nuclear power plant meltdown, including how much the March 2011 earthquake may have damaged the plant's reactors even before the tsunami. The bipartisan Fukushima Nuclear Accident Independent Investigation Commission investigated the nuclear calamity, which has displaced more than 100,000 people and rendered thousands of hectares of land unusable for decades. The panel was spurred by public criticism that the government has been more interested in protecting vested industry interests than in discovering how three reactors were allowed to melt down and release huge amounts of radiation.

Amazingly, each new independent report about the failures that led up to the nuclear disaster and its fallout criticize the government for new unknown shortcomings. One panel investigating the disaster said that the former prime minister and his aides caused confusion at the height of the crises by heavily interfering in the damaged nuclear plant's operation.

The Japanese government compounded the problems at the very outset by assigning a team to set reactor safety standards that was funded by the utility companies and atomic-industry manufacturers, a fact that should have raised serious questions about the experts' neutrality – but did not.

To make matters worse, the U.S. shared detailed radiation measurements with Japan in the early days of the disaster that the Japanese government did not make public or use in conducting evacuations and as a result actually ordered people to flee into the path of the radioactive plume. Others stayed for more than a month in areas with dangerous radiation, because they lay beyond the arbitrary government-imposed 12-mile evacuation zone. The government apologized for the blunder 15 months after the blowout.

The U.S. sent aircraft to measure radiation levels in the vicinity of the tsunami-stricken nuclear power plant in the immediate aftermath of the disaster. The U.S. Energy Department then used the data, collected from over 40 hours of flight time over Fukushima, to compile a detailed map that showed an area of high radiation extending northwest from the plant. Measurements "show an area of greater radiation extending northwest from the accident," materials accompanying the maps warned. "This area may be of interest to public safety officials and responders."

The bureaucratic excuses for not getting the information to the right officials on time is blamed on Japan's tradition of bureaucratic constipation.

The failure is seen by critics in Japan as one more example of the government's early attempts to play down the severity of the accident by withholding damaging information. Government officials also withheld forecasts from a computer system that calculated the spread of radiation because they believed that the estimates were incomplete and inaccurate.

Yet Prime Minister Shinzo Abe insisted in 2014, that Japan continue building nuclear power plants, even though most Japanese, including two former prime ministers, Morihiro Hosokawa and Junichiro Koizumi, were opposed.

The corruption in the private sector of Japan Inc. was highlighted in the multi-billion-dollar scandal involving questionable transactions at Olympus Corp., possibly involving criminal gangs. That resulted in a "catalog of calamitous errors and exceptionally poor judgment ... which has resulted in the destruction of shareholder value of US$1.3 billion," according to its ousted former president, Michael Woodford.

An independent audit concluded that it could not rule out improper conduct and listed "other potential offenses to consider, including false accounting, financial assistance and breaches of director's duties by the board."

It brings to light the severe failings of Japanese businesses, that were papered over during the 1980s boom-years.

The Olympus scandal exposes the all-too-cozy nature of Japanese business that was subject to so much praise in the 1980s. Japanese corporations are dominated by insiders, and companies are often run for the benefit of these insiders rather than shareholder interests – even if these insiders are criminals.

The Olympus scandal brought the murky triangle of yakuza gangsters, companies and politicians back into focus. Is it any wonder Japan's alleged efficient police force is actually arrogant, complacent and incompetent?

Japan Inc. and its bureaucratic career politicians ignore public sentiment and continue kicking their conspiratorial cans of corrupt practices down Japan's streets hoping they will get lost. Japanese maids are long overdue to sweep their streets clean.

U.S. media and career Washington politicians repeatedly criticize China and its *yuan* policy while seemingly ignoring Japan and its yen policy. The Bank of Japan repeatedly meddles in the foreign-exchange market manipulating the yen, weakening it against the dollar to increase exports.

In a semiannual report in December 2011 on foreign exchange, the U.S. Treasury made it clear the U.S. didn't back Japan's unilateral interventions in August and October. "The United States did not support" the two large-scale interventions, the report said, adding that Japan should instead "take fundamental and thoroughgoing steps to increase the dynamism of the domestic economy."

Japan is now a dirty word in economics, a synonym for never-ending malaise and decay. The only good thing Japan has to offer America is lessons on how to avoid economic quicksand. One of Japan's biggest problems is its refusal to admit that its economic system has failed. As Kazuo Hirai put it when he took over as CEO of SONY in February 2012, "... Holy shit now what?"

Tokyo's bureaucrats and career politicians have hoped that a bit more cash or fiscal spending would finally return Japan to the good old days. The reason this never succeeded is that the government hasn't admitted, let alone addressed, the country's serious structural obstacles to growth. Excessive regulation has stymied entrepreneurship and competition, and policymakers have never done enough to encourage Japanese consumers – perennial savers – to spend. All Japan has ended up with is a dangerous level of national debt – more than 200 percent of GDP – even higher than Greece's – and it will only get worse as the population ages, imposing new strains on health and social welfare budgets.

Japan's inherent cultural, bureaucratic and government shortcomings were highlighted in the fall of 2012, when in September of that year it was disclosed by horrified scientists that Japan has no disaster plan in place if Mount Fuji were to erupt after an earthquake, a likely scenario in a country that had experienced nearly 12,000 earthquakes since the magnitude-9 tremor that led to the March 11, 2011 nuclear plant disaster and the release of the damning report. In December 2012, hundreds of concrete ceiling slabs in an expressway tunnel collapsed onto moving vehicles below, killing nine people.

A volcano that erupted on Mount Ontake without warning in September 2014, killed hikers enjoying the autumn foliage.

The grounding of all Boeing 787 Dreamliners in January 2013 because of defective lithium batteries made by a Japanese company highlighted the suspicion that Boeing awards major contracts to Japanese companies regardless of their qualifications, because the country's airlines buy Boeing planes almost exclusively. Japan's market for commercial aircraft is dominated by Boeing to a degree unrivaled by any other country.

The head of the U.S.'s transport safety agency was right in fiercely criticizing the process that approved the new defective Japanese-made batteries that started fires on the 787s.

Japan is a nation on suicide watch. The country continues to unravel economically, politically and demographically. The government forecast in January 2012 that Japan's population, already declining, would fall from 128 million in 2012 to 87 million by the year 2060. That is an unprecedented decline for any modern country. By 2060, more than 40 percent of all Japanese people will be over 65, a expensive burden that no country has had to deal with.

Spending on social benefits has surged by more than 60 percent in the 15 years since 1997. Add to this reality the fact that Japan's youth has retreated to virtual sexual reality and are not interested in the real thing and procreation, and there is only one conclusion one can reach – a dying nation staring into the abyss.

Polls of 16 to 19-year-olds show that 36 percent of Japanese men and 59 percent of women are either uninterested or averse to sex. They prefer to develop relationships with virtual partners.

Japan is rapidly falling back as an economic power. According to a report by the 21st Century Public Policy Institute, the research institute of Nippon Keidanren, the country's most powerful business organization, in the very best-case scenario Japan's gross domestic product in 2050 will be only one-sixth of China's and one-third of India's, as the country struggles to stay ahead of Brazil as the world's fourth-biggest economy. If Japan does not take remedial measures, it will drop to ninth place in the world behind France and barely ahead of Indonesia.

The one possible saving grace that, according to 21st CPPI, would help rescue Japan from coming economic oblivion would be greater participation of women in the economy. Japan rates a lowly 94th among 134 countries in the World Economic Forum's ranking for women in the economy. But women still have difficulty moving up in a male-dominated society.

Shinzo Abe is the fifth Japanese prime minister to vist Washington in the four years since President Barack Obama took office in 2009. He, like his predecessors, promised stronger economic and security ties between the two allies on his February 2913 visit while Japan goes down the nationalistic and revisionist path that not only infuriates China and other Asian countries that suffered at the hands of the Japanese during World War II – but should infuriate America which was attacked by Japan, especially now that Japan has decided to reinterpret Article 9 of it's pacifist constitution to allow its military to go on the offensive again.

How can America continue to embrace a right-wing militaristic Japan when its leaders still won't acknowledge their country's wartime atrocities and continue in the 21st century to honor wartime criminals at the Yasukuni Shrine in Tokyo and want to amend their Constitution to go on the offensive again?

So why does America continue to tighten its embrace of Japan? Why does Washington persist in infuriating China over the disputed Diaoyu Islands – which Japan calls the Senkaku Islands – by saying the islands fall within the U.S.-Japan mutual defense treaty?

The most important lesson from Japan is the perils of procrastination. America, like Japan, is now just kicking the can down the road on both the domestic and foreign fronts.

What America needs is quick and smarter restructuring of mortgages to repair the housing market and extensive job retraining for the unemployed – and restructured foreign policies. What Japan teaches us is the importance of political will. Without it, America might turn Japanese.

To make sure America doesn't become Japanese, Americans – and the Japanese for that matter – have to wake up from their lethargic risk-averse slumber and become entrepreneurial risk takers, movers and shakers.

### Conspiracies

Political conspiracies are not limited to Japan. America's political and military history is a well-endowed web of conspiracies. So much so that many people wonder if 9/11 was a U.S. conspiracy to give America an excuse to invade Afghanistan to fight al Qaeda and Iraq to remove Saddam Hussein. Others alleged 9/11 was to cover the laundering of over $200 billion in bonds from the secretive CIA Black Eagle Trust Fund due 9/12. The Reuters news service report on the massive volume of electronic financial transactions conducted from inside the WTC just before the towers collapsed that did not need to be reported because of an SEC regulation only ever implemented on 9/11 was spiked. The investigation results of the story are being kept secret.

On September 25, New Zealand SAS intelligence officer Major Louisa Parkinson produced an internal report entitled "Afghanistan's Operational Environment: a summarised overview." It was a matter-of-fact summary of crucial flaws in the U.S. approach that could only lead to one conclusion – conspiracy. As Parkinson noted: "Osama bin Laden's organization al Qaeda is not limited to the confines of Afghanistan. The bulk of his organization, particularly the logistics and intelligence infrastructure, is in Pakistan and Saudi Arabia, with elements scattered around the Islamic world, Europe, and the United States itself. Financial support for bin Laden comes from collections in regional mosques as well as larger donations from private donors in the United Arab Emirates and Saudi Arabia."

So why was the U.S. invading Afghanistan but not Pakistan, Saudi Arabia or the Gulf states? What about Roman Polanski v. UBS, or is it U.S. v. Switzerland all about? The Black Eagle Trust Fund?

Was JFK's assassination another conspiracy to keep America in Vietnam, as many claim? Were Lincoln, Malcolm X, Kennedys and King assassinations conspiracies? How about General George Patton? The number of historical events that have dimmed America's shining beacon-lit path and led it to economic ruination are laced with deep conspiratorial theories so voluminous that library sections are dedicated to the subject.

The history of conspiracies is nothing new or limited to America. This is best exemplified in the movie *Anonymous,* which depicts Shakespeare as a barely literate actor providing a front for a brilliant nobleman, Edward de Vere, the Earl of Oxford, the secret author of the plays. The crux of the dispute is whether an otherwise obscure William Shakespeare of Stratford-upon-Avon, with a grammar-school education, could have crafted works with the breadth and depth of *Hamlet, Romeo and Juliet* and *Macbeth,* some of the most brilliant works ever written in the English language.

Most Shakespeare scholars don't take the Oxfordian theory seriously, but plenty of other smart people have over the decades, including Mark Twain, Sigmund Freud and Supreme Court Justice Antonin Scalia.

The questions and the issues they raise are legitimate. How did a guy with a fourth-grade or maybe sixth-grade education in a rural village learn fluent French, courtly French, Italian, Greek and Latin? Where did he learn legal terms and military terms and use them metaphorically?

Shakespeare's contribution to the English language is exemplified by the number of phrases he gave us, which *We the Apathetic Maids* don't know or realize. From "In my heart of hearts," from *Hamlet,* "What's done is done," from *Macbeth,* "Eaten me out of house and home" from *Henry IV,* "Dead as a doornail," from *Henry VI,* "Come full circle," from *Tempest,* and one of my favorites, "Foregone conclusion," from *Othello.*

I have walked past the Othello Tower in the Old City of Famagusta, Cyprus, on hundreds if not thousands of occasions, first as a child growing up in a nearby neighborhood. I usually walked by after a good swim and fishing expedition – to get a better-priced soft drink on the way home after the beach, and then as a tour guide working with my mother, explaining the history of the tower and Shakespeare's writing about it. I have often wondered how someone who never left his local town and tavern could have a clue about the rest of the world – especially Othello and his tower in Cyprus.

The Obama conspiracy theories raised by Republicans in the 2012 presidential election defied objective reality. When unemployment numbers made the administration look good, they were obviously "cooked." When poll numbers put Obama ahead, they were skewed. His birth certificates are forgeries – and my favorite, he is the secret love child of a Communist Party activist.

Legitimate conspiracy questions are: Is the Diaoyu Islands dispute and the Japan-Korea island dispute the result of America's anger at the three countries signing a treaty to replace the dollar with their currencies in international transactions between China, Japan and South Korea, as some conspiracy theorists claim? Was former IMF chief Dominique Strauss-Kahn set up in his alleged maid rape case, not by Sarkozy, but by America because of his dogged determination to add the euro and *yuan* in international transactions, or even replace the dollar, as some claim? And how about Sarkosy being indicted in July 2014?

Did George W. Bush lead the 9/11 conspiracy as many gun advocates claim? Is that a good enough reason for Americans to load up on semi-automatic weapons to defend themselves against the impending "tyranny" of government as these gun advocates claim? And how about Sarkozy being indicted in July 2014?

Do the Illuminati run the world and is the Bush family a member?

Is Apple the "ringmaster" of a conspiracy to raise prices of e-books?

What about Zecharia Sitchin's revelatory series *The Earth Chronicles* that discusses in detail how life on earth was started by aliens from another planet? The story of the gods, the Anunnaki, "Those who from heaven to Earth came," as the Sumerians called them, begins with their coming to earth from Nibiru, one of the planets in Orion's Belt, to search for gold and other minerals.

Sitchin puts the theory of man's origins into a whole new perspective. He is one of the top scholars in the field of ancient languages and offers his vision of the extraterrestrial origins of *Homo sapiens* on earth. His main premise is that all ancient documents are written on the basis of observations and facts and should not be taken symbolically.

Sitchin confirms that civilization originated in Mesopotamia and explains why from its start it was highly developed, that it blossomed virtually out of nothing and created incredible works, which are not capable of being performed or duplicated to date. Sitchin quotes many ancient documents, including the Bible and Epic of Gilgamesh, which he can read in Akkadian and Babylonian, and offers an objective and more sensible translation of these scripts. He explains in detail the discrepancies of single/plural God in Genesis and shows how the extraterrestrial wisdom spread.

Sitchin postulates that life on earth was formed and developed more than 450,000 years ago because of its unique mineral resources needed by planet

Nibiru, Marduk in Babylonian. The first settlements were established in Mesopotamia because of its vast deposits of the fuels needed for space travel. Man was created by genetic manipulation in the image of the extraterrestrials – a mixture of hominid genes with their own in order to increase the human IQ level – to do the mining work for them.

These aliens, according to Sitchin, built the pyramids, Stonehenge, the Western Wall and the Nazca Lines in Peru that look like wide runways for spacecraft. *In The End of Days, Armageddon* and *Prophesies of The Return*, Sitchin, who did his homework, concludes that the aliens fought a nuclear war in the Sinai desert in 2100 B.C., built space stations in Lebanon, Africa, India and Peru. He offers biblical proof from Sumerian tablets at various museums around the world, Dead Sea scrolls and biblical prophesies from both the old and new testaments of the Bible – as well as numerous scientific studies – to support his conclusions.

Are the asteroids and meteors hitting and hurling past earth since February 2013 sent by aliens to wake up *We the Apathetic Maids* – or is that just another conspiracy?

Where did we come from? Are we here alone? Are there UFOs and transformers or are such discussions just another conspiracy?

When Russian scientists reached an enormous ancient Antarctic freshwater lake in February 2012, after spending a decade drilling through more than three kilometers of solid ice, in the coldest spot on the earth's coldest continent, the need and concern was to prevent even the slightest contamination of the lake because its environment is comparable to conditions on the moons of Jupiter, which are among the candidates for extraterrestrial life in our solar system.

Lake Vostok, named after the Russian research station above it, is the largest of more than 280 lakes under the thick ice that covers most of the Antarctic continent, and the first to have a drill bit break through to liquid water from the ice that has kept it sealed off from light and air for 15 million to 34 million years. The water stays liquid because of the pressure and the warmth of the earth below it. If life exists in Vostok, it could well exist on Europa, one of the moons of Jupiter, which has subsurface icy water.

Is it any wonder Bob Dylan, who has drawn on a variety of sources in creating his music and has previously raised questions of attribution in his work, is again stirring debate – this time over an exhibition of his paintings? Since his exhibition opened in the Gagosian Gallery in Manhattan in September 2011, fans and so-called Dynalolonoligsts have raised questions about whether some paintings are based on the singer's experiences and observations, or on photos that are widely available and were not taken by Dylan. Another conspiracy?

A great political conspiracy thriller is the 2012 TV series *Last Resort*. After the captain of a U.S. nuclear submarine receives a mysterious order to launch nuclear weapons against Pakistan during a constitutional crisis in Washington, he asks for more formal confirmation – and is attacked by his own Navy instead. Trying to figure out the conspiracy and how the captain and his crew can prove they are heroes rather than traitors is quite a challenge for any conspiracy buff.

Military and energy establishment conspiracy theories – and practices – are among those that *We the Apathetic Maids* not only have to tune in to, but sweep out.

### Climate Change
And how about the conspiracy theories that surround and abound in the climate change debate – and the energy industry-driven sound bites and spins – that have led many people to believe there is no climate change and that the unseasonal climate changes and extremes we are experiencing are just part of the "normal" weather cycle?

Earthquakes on America's East Coast in August 2011 had office workers milling in the streets of Washington, D.C. and New York, waiting nervously for aftershocks. No different than their watch over the shaky economy.

There is a strong possibility that the rise of quakes in the U.S. is linked to fracking – hydraulic fracturing – which involves pumping water and chemicals under pressure into underground rock formations to extract natural gas and oil. The waste water generated by fracking and other extraction processes may contribute to instability of geological faults, causing earthquakes. It's only logical.

The number of earthquakes in the central U.S. rose spectacularly near where oil and gas fracking has ocurred. The average number of earthquakes of magnitude 3 or greater in the U.S. mid-continent, including the states of Arkansas, Colorado, Oklahoma, New Mexico and Texas, increased in 2011 to six times the 20th-century average, scientists at the U.S. Geological Survey said.

In 2009 there were 50 earthquakes of magnitude 3 or greater in the U.S., 2010 had 87 and 2011 had 134.

"We don't know why, but we doubt that it is a natural process, because in nature, the only time you see such a big increase is during an aftershock sequence, with a series of quakes, or in a volcanic setting where you often get swarms of earthquakes due to magnetic activity," said Arthur McGarr of the geologic survey's Earthquake Science Center in California.

Earthquakes, economic and earth-rattling, are shaking us as the number of hurricanes that pummel America's East Coast rises and as typhoons do the same in China.

Is what America and China are experiencing on the weather front not only the beginning of the end of the environment as we know it, our way of life economically and politically because of climate change? Look at Australia, the canary in our global coal mine, where Mother Nature over the course of a few weeks in 2011 struck with record heatwaves, a crippling drought, bush fires, floods that swamped an area the size of France and Germany combined, even a plague of locusts.

In a study published online in the summer of 2012 by the journal *Science,* Harvard University scientists reported that some storms send water vapor miles into the stratosphere – which is normally drier than a desert – and showed how such events could rapidly set off ozone-destroying reactions with chemicals that remain in the atmosphere from CFCs, refrigerant gases that are now banned.

The study showed how strong summer thunderstorms that pump water high into the upper atmosphere pose a threat to the protective ozone layer, drawing one of the first links between climate change and ozone loss over populated areas.

Ozone helps shield people, animals and crops from damaging ultraviolet rays from the sun. Much of the concern about the ozone layer has focused on Antarctica, where a seasonal hole, or thinning, has been seen for more than two decades, and the Arctic, where a hole was observed in 2011. But those regions have almost no population.

A thinning of the ozone layer over the U.S. and other populated areas during summers could mean an increase in ultraviolet exposure for millions of people and a rise in the incidence of skin cancer.

2011 was a year of devastation, wreckage and warnings about the dangers of climate change. And the worst is yet to come!

And it started in the winter of 2011. A big chill blanketed Europe in arctic conditions, with temperatures plunging as low as minus 22 degrees Fahrenheit – a 100-year record. Rome was paralyzed after the heaviest snowfall in 27 years. Airports were shut, flights and trains delayed, highways gridlocked and more than 300 people were killed by the cold snap across Europe. Deaths were reported in Poland, Romania, Bosnia and Herzegovina, Latvia, Lithuania, Estonia, Bulgaria, the Czech Republic, Italy, Slovakia, France, Austria and Greece. Ukraine suffered the heaviest toll.

In Brussels, the iconic "pissing boy" statue was switched off for fear that the extreme cold would damage his mechanical parts.

Frigid temperatures even edged into North Africa, dropping below freezing in Algiers. In Peru's Andes, 1,600 years of ice melted in 25 years.

Tornadoes and strong winds killed and injured people and ripped roofs off buildings and crushed towns across America's Midwest and South in late February 2012.

The frigid winter of 2011-12 was followed by the firestorm fires of summer.

Colorado's Waldo Canyon fire was a perfect firestorm – exactly what climate models are predicting for arid Western landscapes from California to the Rocky Mountains.

Wildfires in the U.S. charred more than 7 million acres in 2011, more than any year since accurate records began in early 1960s. That's an area larger than the state of Maryland.

The world's biggest and oldest trees are dying at an alarming rate at the dawn of the New World Order. Research by universities in Australia and the U.S. published in *Science* in December 2012 warned that ecosystems worldwide were in danger of losing forever the largest organisms on the planet, the giant 100-300 year-old trees that harbor and sustain countless birds and other wildlife.

The study showed that trees were not only dying en masse in forest fires, but were also perishing at 10 times the normal rate in non-fire years. It said it appeared to boil down to a combination of rapid climate change causing drought and high temperatures as well as rampant logging and agricultural land clearing.

Meanwhile, the Arctic sea ice has shrunk to its smallest surface area since record-keeping began, taking the world into "unchartered territory" as climate change intensifies, U.S. scientists warned. Scientists use Arctic sea ice extent as a gauge of the overall climate. Whereas most of the ice previously stayed frozen through several summers, much of it now melts and freezes each season.

"Twenty years from now in August, you might be able to take a ship right across the Arctic Ocean," once blocked year-round by ice, said Julienne Stroeve, a scientist at the National Snow and Ice Data Center in Colorado. Models predict "ice-free conditions" before 2050, she said, but the decline appears to be happening faster than predicted.

Hurricane Sandy was the wake-up call America needed. It even got President Obama to acknowledge that climate change is an issue that must be addressed.

The reality is that the Arctic Ocean will probably be ice-free by 2030. As the polar ice melts away into the seas, the effects for much of the planet could be catastrophic. Another worry is the Greenland ice shelf, which is also melting at an unprecedented rate.

Sea levels around the world will rise between six and seven meters, wiping out cities like New York, London and Shanghai. The addition of so much cold fresh water into the seas would also change ocean currents and weather patterns in ways we can't even imagine. At the same time, rising temperatures in the northern hemisphere now risk melting much of the Siberian permafrost, which, like Greenland, will release vast clouds of trapped methane, accelerating the speed of climate change even more. This risks starting a chain reaction, which we could do nothing to stop.

When predictions were made a few years ago, scientists said it would all be more or less OK if we limited the rise in average global temperatures to two degrees Celcius. We have missed that target.

"Without change, we are now heading for a four-degree rise, which will take the earth's average temperature back to levels seen 40 million years ago. This will cause the Antarctic to melt too, with sea levels rising 60-70 meters. The droughts and floods we would experience along the way would make the planet virtually uninhabitable," says Graeme Maxton, a fellow of the Club of Rome.

The biggest threat to our existence is not the lack of economic growth or terrorists – it is climate change. It is something I encounter frequently when I travel across the U.S., especially in winter. The thousands of travel advisories and flights canceled is a nightmare for frequent fliers like myself.

I was delighted to read that one global warming skeptic, prominent physicist Richard Muller, who was on the payroll of the energy companies, had come clean and in from the cold, reluctantly admitting after two years of trying to find out if mainstream climate scientists were wrong that they were right and that temperatures really are rising. Muller's study was partially funded by a foundation connected to global warming deniers. He pursued long-held skeptic theories in analysing the data. He was spurred to action because of

"Climategate," a British scandal involving hacked e-mails of scientists.

Yet he found that the land is 1 degree Celsius warmer than it was in the 1950s. Those numbers from Muller, who works at the University of California Berkeley and Lawrence Berkeley National Lab, match those from the National Oceanic and Atmospheric Administration and NASA. He said he went even further back, studying readings from Founding Fathers Benjamin Franklin and Thomas Jefferson.

What got everyone's attention and raised a lot of eyebrows was the fact that one-quarter of the $600,000 to do the research came from the Charles Koch Foundation, whose founder is a major funder of not only the Tea Party movement, but of skeptic groups. The Koch brothers, Charles and David, run a large private company involved in oil and other related industries.

An overwhelming majority of climate scientists agree that the problem is very real and that climate change is man-made from the burning of fossil fuels such as coal and oil. "Greenhouse gases could have a disastrous impact on the world," Muller concludes.

Shawn Lawrence Otto, author of the book *Fool Me Twice* that castigates science skeptics, said Muller should expect to be harshly treated by global warming deniers. "Now he is considered a traitor. For the skeptic community, this isn't about data or facts. It's about team sports. He's been traded to the Indians. He's playing for the wrong team now."

Who isn't?

So what is America doing about it? Raising gasoline prices. The price of gas hit $4 a gallon in February 2012 on Presidents Day weekend with predictions it would hit $5 by the end of the year. This when "the U.S. is the closest it has been in almost 20 years to achieving energy self-sufficiency ... . Domestic oil output is the highest in eight years. The U.S. is producing so much natural gas that, where the government warned four years ago of a critical need to boost imports, it now may approve an export terminal," according to a *Bloomberg News* report in February 2012.

This transformation could make America the world's top energy producer by 2020, raise more tax revenue, free us from worrying about the Middle East, and, if we're smart, build "a bridge to a much cleaner energy future.... Higher environmental standards may cost more, but only incrementally, if at all, and they'll make the industry and the environment safer," Thomas L. Friedman extolled in his February 26, 2012 column, in the *New York Times*.

The ultimate metaphor for what should happen to career politicians if they ignore the warning signs is what happened to Hong Kong's career politicians who moved into their new government quarters on Hong Kong's famous waterfront at the end of 2011 – the killer Legionnaires' disease.

Is it any wonder China is open to binding carbon emission cuts? Why isn't America? Why is America continuing to perpetuate its Hollywood spin on climate change and the military?

### Hollywood Firing Line

The 1986 post-Vietnam hit movie *Top Gun* proved a major force in resuscitating the military's image and became the template for the U.S. military's conspiratorial alliance with Tinseltown. Demands for cuts in the military budget, and the Army reporting record suicide rates among soldiers in Iraq and Afghanistan and among GIs returning from those wars, a subject I discussed and said would become an epidemic in *Custom Maid War,* only further encourage the desperate conspiratorial relationship.

*Hurt Locker* director Kathryn Bigelow, won an oscar for her election-year movie chronicling the operation that killed Osama bin Laden. It's a double whammy for the military and its commander in chief – President Barack Obama.

A page from Hollywood mavin Ronald Reagan. Not only did enlistment spike when *Top Gun* was released and the Navy set up recruitment tables at theaters playing the movie, but polls soon showed rising confidence in the military. With Reagan wrapping military adventurism in the flag and the armed forces scoring low-risk but high-profile victories in Libya and Grenada, America fell in love with *Maverick* and *Iceman* and other silver screen super-pilots screaming about "the need for speed."

Although *Top Gun* wasn't the first movie to exchange creative input for Pentagon resources – make that taxpayer resources – its success set the bargain as a standard for other film-makers. By the time of the 1991 Persian Gulf War, Phil Strub, the Pentagon's liaison to the movie industry, told the *Hollywood Reporter* that he'd seen a 70 percent increase in the number of requests from film-makers for assistance – effectively changing the way Hollywood works.

Mace Neufeld, producer of the 1990 film *The Hunt for Red October*, told *Variety* that studios in the post-*Top Gun* era instituted an unstated rule, telling screenwriters and directors to get military cooperation "or forget about making the picture." *Time* reported in 1986 that "without such billion-dollar props, producers [have to] spend an inordinate amount of time and money searching for substitutes."

Emboldened, military officials became increasingly blunt about how they deploy the carrot of subsidized hardware and the stick of denied access. Strub described the approval process to *Variety* in 1994: "The main criteria we use is how could the proposed production benefit the military ... could it help in recruiting [and] is it in sync with present policy?"

The result is an entertainment culture rigged to produce blockbusters glorifying the military.

ISIS videos do a better recruitment job and threaten the defense cuts of more than $500 billion. ISIS also got democratic and republican career politicians to agree on one thing - War and demonstrating the F-22 fighter jet capabilities - a jet like the military agenda that was supposed to be cancelled. In the words of Grahm Nash, *Military Madness*.

### Capitalism

More should be done on the production of blockbusters about capitalism than militarism. In this era of late-stage capitalism, the next generation won't be as lucky as their baby boomer parents have been. The problem of inequality is likely to get worse. When people can't climb up the ladder, it's bad for the economy, the country and the world.

The Western model of capitalism has crash-landed. The eurozone crisis highlighted how even the combined economic power of 17 European countries can be brushed aside by bankers who dictate economic policy by keeping any money they make if successful, but fall back on governments to bail them out if unsuccessful, as was the case with Greece, Italy, Portugal and Spain – a model America has emulated.

Having been a director of a national bank, and a lawyer who represented and knows many directors who ripped off the banking system, I agree wholeheartedly with Warren Buffett, who believes that corporate governance should get tougher on directors. "They should forfeit five years' pay if their firms have to be bailed out; CEOs and their spouses should be on the hook for their net worth," is what Buffet would do. So would I.

We don't want to crush America's animal capitalistic spirit or completely control market volatility by dictating every iota of the rules of capitalism. What we must do is make sure governments of *We the People,* with transparent policies, accountability and legitimacy, govern policy and not the obscure funds and the anonymous people who run them and who control our destiny today.

Policy paralysis and the "new normal" gridlock in Washington is no longer acceptable or tolerable. The lingering economic pain is bankrupting America. Washington, like the rest of the country, has to get back to a system of meritocracy and true capitalism and away from crony capitalism that controls policy making for the primary benefit of plutocrats if the country is to become great again.

Where Buffett, whom I admire and respect, and I part company is whether Americans will take to the streets en masse to protest the ever-increasing inequality between the 99 percenters and the wealthy 1 percent.

"I just don't think this is a country that has the tinder for social instability," Buffett said. "I mean, the classic test of that was actually the 2000 election. If you think about it, half the people in America felt that they were screwed, and the next day, they all went to work."

Political apathy of Americans is something we do agree on. But I believe that economic disparity will see that apathy boil and stir the public's blood into action – much like the steam engine did for the Industrial Revolution. The Tea Party and Occupy Wall Street movements are the advance revolutionary reconnaissance scouts prodding for the weaknesses in the current American model of capitalism and democracy. A new capitalist revolution is in the making between rich and poor. Inequality has stalled economic mobility. Income inequality is a threat to America and the very middle class that made the country great. The flaws of America's capitalist model have been exposed by the financial crisis, but they can and must be fixed – by Americans.

Elizabeth Warren, who won the Massachusetts Senate seat in 2012, rebuts the myth of class warfare best by reframing the discussion in terms of a "social contract" between the rich and the rest of society: "There is nobody in this country who got rich on his own. Nobody. You build a factory out there, good for you. But I want to be clear: you moved your goods to market on the roads the rest of us paid for. You hired workers the rest of us paid to educate. You were safe in your factory because of the police forces and fire forces that the rest of us paid for. You didn't have to worry that marauding bands would come and seize everything at your factory and hire someone to protect against this, because of the work the rest of us did. Now look, you built a factory and it turned into something terrific or a great idea. God bless. Keep a big hunk of it. But part of the underlying social contract is you take a hunk of that and pay forward for the next kid who comes along."

That is the corporate Contract With America: societal symbiosis. We create a society in which smart, hard-working people can be safe and prosper, and they in turn reinvest a fair share of that prosperity back into society for posterity, Charles M. Blow wrote in an op-ed piece in *The New York Times*.

Will Rogers, the popular humorist during the Depression years, put it in comfortable agrarian terms: "All the feed is going into one manger and the stock on the other side of the stall ain't getting a thing. We got it, but we don't know how to split it up."

Front running, high-frequency stock trading is a 21st-century example of Will Rogers' feed being in one manger. The high-frequency trader deploys massive computer capacity and complex algorithms to get inside information to buy and sell individual stocks multiple times in a fraction of a second, all in search of micro-profits with each trade. Today, high-frequency trading, rather than traditional investing to raise capital in pursuit of enterprise profit and economic growth, makes up the majority of all trades on Wall Street.

Dark pools, trading venues where investors are granted a greater degree of anonymity than in public markets must also be shut down.

High-frequency trading and dark pools have triggered flash market crashes. In August 2012, Knight Capital Group nearly collapsed after malfunctions in its computers sent the shares of 148 companies on wild rides.

Stock markets have to return to their core business – raising capital for business at a reasonable profit – not profit at any cost solely by trading.

America's national wealth didn't come from stock market traders or career politicians. It came from capitalists. People like Andrew Carnegie and more recently Sam Walton, Bill Gates and others like them who are the ultimate wealth creators.

Steve Forbes in his book *Freedom Manifesto: Why Free Markets Are Moral and Big Government Isn't* correctly points out that capitalism is all about voluntary, free-will transactions that foster entrepreneurship and ultimately create national wealth and power.

A recent example that caught my attention is live baby eels, known as elvers, that are caught off the coast of Maine and South Carolina during a 10-week season and sold for thousands of dollars per kilogram to Chinese fish farms where they are raised for several years. These farms need a constant supply of juveniles from the wild because eels do not reproduce in captivity.

In the Silicon Valley, Chinese venture capitalists have partnered with U.S. counterparts to launch tech start-ups to enter the Chinese market with cash infusions and business-incubation services. That Sino-American capitalism should be a model for U.S.-Sino global political leadership.

Karl Marx said the worst kind of capitalism is a monopolistic capitalism, and Lenin said the worst kind of monopolistic capitalism is state monopolistic capitalism. I agree with *New York Times* columnist Friedman, who says America, like China, is practicing both.

Now that companies have gone interlocal and are running America and the world through their network of political puppets who are afraid of taking bold people initiatives – other than those that benefit their corporate benefactors – is it any wonder that *We the Apathetic Maids,* especially middle-class Americans who are jobless and homeless – are damned?

The Justice Department finally in February 2013 sued Standard & Poor's for issuing glowing reviews and high ratings on troubled mortgage securities whose subsequent failure helped cause the worst financial crisis since the Great Depression.

The government contends that S&P deliberately inflated the ratings on complex mortgage securities by placing too much trust in its computer models. S&P routinely relied on historical projections that failed in an environment where home prices were falling fast.

The complaint asserts that S&P staff chose not to update computer programs because these changes would have led to harsher ratings, and a potential loss of business.

The government and S&P have tangled before. The rating agency in August 2011 issued a historic downgrade of U.S. creditworthiness and threatened to lower it even further. Payback time?

The federal action does not involve any criminal allegations. Critics have complained that the government has yet to send any senior bankers or Wall Street executives to jail for potential illegal behavior that led to the crisis. The government's response? Bankers are "too big to jail."

Several state attorneys are also investigating and getting ready to sue the major ratings agencies – and hopefully bankers personally and criminally.

The financial crisis could never have happened without the credit-ratings agencies issuing stellar ratings on toxic mortgage securities that inflated the bubble until it popped.

The bankers and politicians who blew up the world economy are the ones preaching and dictating on how it should be fixed – at *We the Maids* expense. Why not theirs? Why should they not pay for the mess they created? Why have *We the Apathetic Maids* not swept out this old world order and swept in a new order?

For capitalism to work again, we need economies that are truly competitive and entrepreneurial. Only then will the engine of growth and prosperity drive employment and economic recovery.

Restructuring and managing capitalism in America today is long overdue.

The original model is quite simple and provides the most fair opportunity and reward for hard work, support for those who cannot help themselves and the pursuit of happiness for as many people as possible. Traditional capitalism should be adhered to again.

Traditional capitalism: You have two cows. You sell one and buy a bull and reproduce and sell the calves.

Socialism: You have two cows. The government takes one and gives it to your neighbor.

Communism: You have two cows. You give them to the government, and the government then gives you some milk.

Fascism: You have two cows. You give them to the government, and the government then sells you some milk.

Nazism: You have two cows. The government shoots you and takes the cows.

Bureaucracy: You have two cows. You give them to the government, which shoots one and milks the other, then pours the milk down the drain.

Modern American Capitalism: You have two cows. You sell three of them on paper to your publicly listed company, using letters of credit opened by your brother-in-law at the bank, then execute a debt/equity swap with an associated general offer so that you get all four cows back, with a tax deduction for keeping five cows. The milk rights of six cows are transferred via a Panamanian intermediary to a Cayman Islands company secretly owned by the majority shareholder, who sells the rights to all seven cows' milk back to the listed company. The annual report says that the company owns eight cows, with an option on one more. Meanwhile, you kill two cows to collect insurance and get a tax write-off.

### Credit Binge

Fund manager Richard Duncan published a book in 2003 called *The Dollar Crisis*. In it he argued that the economic boom in the U.S. was in reality a credit fueled bubble that would burst when the property market ran out of steam. He warned that the result would be a slump in the U.S. dollar and global recession. He was right-on. Duncan came out with a new book in 2012 titled *The New Depression* and subtitled *The breakdown of the paper money economy*.

Duncan trawls back through history to argue that for 40 years, ever since the U.S. government severed the link between the dollar and gold, the world has pursued a new economic growth model based on ever-expanding supplies of credit. Gold as a monetary anchor had many problems, but its great virtue was that it prevented governments from printing money at will. With that anchor cut loose, the U.S. embarked on a credit creation binge that Duncan says blurred, and even eliminated, the distinction between money and credit. Between 1968 and 2007, the amount of credit in the U.S. economy shot up from $1 trillion to $50 trillion. Duncan argues that this explosion created a new growth paradigm – not capitalism, which was based on savings, investment and profit, but "creditism," which relied on credit-fueled consumption.

But in the mid-1980s, things started to go wrong. The credit expansion continued hitting double-digit rates in real terms, but GDP growth struggled to top 4 percent. In a nutshell, the U.S. was getting less bang for its buck. Part of the problem was that America began to run a sizable trade deficit. As

Duncan says: "U.S. credit growth was creating economic growth, just not in the U.S. – but in Japan, Korea and later on in China."

The boom continued in the 1990s, propelled largely by Fannie Mae and Freddie Mac, which took on some $7 trillion in mortgage debt in just eight years, pushing total U.S. credit up to 360 percent of GDP. Eventually, the party had to stop. In 2007 households reached the limit of the debts they could service. The property market collapsed, credit creation stopped and the economy sank into recession.

The only thing preventing the U.S. economy from sinking into an outright depression on the scale of the 1930s is Washington's massive deficit spending, paid for by money created by the Federal Reserve. Politics aside, Duncan reckons the government will be able to keep things more or less afloat for five years. But on its current trajectory, in 10 years, the U.S. will resemble Greece, he warns.

What does this mean for China? China has done well over the past two decades by investing in manufacturing goods for export to developed countries. Now that the rich world's demand has hit the buffers, there is no way China can hope to consume all that it produces. Beijing's short-term solution has been to ramp up China's own domestic credit growth to fund yet more investment. That has maintained rapid growth rates, but it has fueled asset price inflation and exacerbated overcapacity. In short, Beijing's policy response is unsustainable.

"The whole China model is over," says Duncan. "With no one to buy the stuff it is making, China has got to stop growing."

As I said in *Feasting Dragon, Starving Eagle,* it's "food for thought." I believe Duncan will be wrong this time if the U.S. and China can learn to work together as I propose. Otherwise, Duncan will be proven right again.

### *Closer to Home and Country*
The U.S. recession has resulted in the nation's population growing at its slowest rate since the Great Depression – after decades of robust increases. Births and immigration numbers are dramatically down, a sure sign of

economic decline. Today's youth, for the most part, are afraid to venture too far away from their desktop computers. Meantime 25-40-year-olds are moving back home with their parents in staggering numbers. For much of America's history, a booming population symbolized economic vitality and growing global influence. That vitality and character have to be restored.

Americans have to put all their games and other pertinent personal information onto their mobile devices and hit the road and take it to wherever it leads to jobs, innovation and entrepreneurship. The spirit of the uninhibited cowboy in the Wild West has to be re-created in the contemporary setting that is America – starting with NASA's Curiosity robot landing on Mars in August 2012 and Neal Mueller, Scott Mortensen, Paul Ridley and Collin West, the four Americans who set off in a rowboat in July 2012 across the Arctic Ocean, nonstop and without support, to highlight changes in the environment. Americans can and must continue inventing the future. To successfully do that we have to look at the successful models of the past, Bell Labs being a prime example of an American incubator of creativity. A book I highly recommend is *The Idea Factory: Bell Labs and the Great Age of American Innovation* by John Gertner.

I was reminded how innovative America can be on October 12, 2012, after I landed at Los Angeles International Airport and was being driven to the car rental agency in its shuttle bus. The driver decided to take a detour and play tour guide as she took us to the intersection of Sepulveda and Manchester boulevards to see the massive space shuttle Endeavour that towered over the parking lot and surrounding gawkers. Spectators were walking from all directions from wherever they parked their cars. Trying to get from the car rental agency to a lunch meeting in Marina del Rey was hellish. Traffic was redirected through residential neighborhoods on streets that seemed to have a stop sign at every intersection.

Taking a long-hard close-up look of the Endeavour at the starting point of its long and tortuous trip through Los Angeles was a stark reminder of how great and innovative America can be.

The sexual revolution of the 1960s spawned the creative generation that seeded the Silicon Valleys across America – and the New World capitalists.

A prime example is the Oracle from Omaha, Warren Buffett. His wife set him up with his mistress, whom he later married, something Americans don't like to talk about or acknowledge.

Americans have to get back to their roots and be true Americans again in the mold of the nation's Founding Fathers. To paraphrase Richard McGregor, the *Financial Times* Washington bureau chief in 2011, America has to get over its bitter religious and political divisions. The country is spending too much time and money struggling with deep and bitter divisions and the political and economic systems have been configured to reflect rather than overcome them. That has to change.

People have to start taking responsibility for their actions. Watching the news clips and listening to the audio clips of the Italian coast guard ordering Francesco Schettino, the captain of the grounded cruise ship Costa Concordia that ran aground off the Island of Giglio in January 2012, back to his ship after he abandoned it with hundreds of passengers still aboard, was another timely metaphor of our times. Like J. Bruce Ismay, chairman of the White Star that owned the Titanic, who survived after boarding one of the few lifeboats, was criticized for not going down with the ship.

Shouldn't the captains of banking and industry also have to go down with their bankrupt sinking companies and be required to pay their fair share instead of being bailed out by taxpayers while they keep their ill-gotten gains? Why should Richard Fuld, the chairman and CEO of Lehman Brothers, walk away with $480 million as he sinks Lehman? All captains must pay for their shortcomings and failures, regardless of the type of ship they run.

### Proud to Be an American
Whenever I am in Los Angeles, I try to make it to Saturday morning breakfast at Nate 'n' Al's Delicatessen in Beverly Hills. It is a breakfast get-together that Stanley Black started decades ago with a group of concerned community political activists and developers to address, discuss and sometimes debate issues of the day. On Saturday July 7, 2012, Larry Field, one of the longtime breakfast-clutch diners, shared his Fourth of July celebration experience.

"I went to El Cajon for a special holiday celebration at Cysuan, an Indian reservation with a casino that put on a great patriotic evening with Lee Greenwood, the country-western singer. Let me tell you, when he did his hit song *Proud to Be an American,* everyone was on their feet singing along. I had goose pimples," Larry said. "I was proud to be an American as was everyone else in the audience. It was unbelievable."

"Of course, I can imagine," said Charles Dizengoff, a long-time breakfast regular, as soon as Larry finished and all of us who had been mesmerized by his American holiday experience started talking again, sharing our Fourth of July stories. "Who here isn't proud to be an American?" Dizzen, as Charles is known, asked. "If anyone is not proud to be an American they should leave. Not just this table, but America."

It was unanimous. Everyone was a proud American.

My Fourth of July started out by watching the HBO special *1776* about how the Founding Fathers came up with the Declaration of Independence and the Constitution. It was a nice historical musical refresher course I needed before I headed to Marina del Rey that midafternoon to join Brian Wald and his guests on his five-star converted Catalina ferry for a holiday celebration on the water with all the trimmings, including one of California's greatest firework shows right there in the marina.

It was unbelievable. Coming from Hong Kong and China where phenomenal firework displays are the norm, I was blown away. Brian had navigated his boat to less than 100 feet from the barges launching the fireworks and it felt like we were right in – part of – the fireworks show itself.

"The Chinese don't have to bomb us. They know we'll do it to ourselves with their fireworks," said Brian as I complimented him on maneuvering us in front of the hundreds of boats crowded in the marina for the fireworks show. It was a sight to behold. The thousands of bobbing lights on the boats behind us and the fireworks in front and above. It was awesome.

"Welcome to the future, America," I said as I raised my glass of wine and toasted Brian and thanked him for his gracious hospitality.

Former Secretary of State Condoleeza Rice echoed the Founding Fathers' dream in her speech at the 2012 Republican Convention in Tampa, Florida. America is exceptional because it was united by an idea rather than by race or religion – "that it doesn't matter where you come from but where you are going."

Where are *We the Apathetic Maids* going and where are we taking America?

### America the Beautiful

The beauty, joy and hope that is America is expressed in many ways and places across the nation year round. One event in particular, the Christmas tree-lighting at New York's Rockefeller Center, which attracts thousands of tourists, not only from all over America, but the world, is "an iconic event" in the words of Scott Kirton, 35, who came from England to see the 75-year-old 74-foot Norway spruce adorned with 30,000 lights be lit on November 30, 2011.

I was there to watch the ceremony from the 29th floor of Rockefeller Center as a guest of investment banking firm Morgan Keegan. Mingling with investment bankers, lawyers and their corporate clients, discussing the dire straights America is in, as I sipped delightful French wines and ate delicious food, knowing America, China and the world were on the verge of imploding financially because of the lack of the necessary financial nutrients, was a wake-up call for how resilient America is, no matter how down and out it may be. Looking out the window at the scurrying masses below, I decided to go and join them to experience their heartfelt uplifting mood and outlook.

It turned out to be a nightmare. President Obama had decided to come to town to attend three fundraisers, one not too far from the lighting ceremony. It made New York City's normal gridlock look good. The gridlock the president created was enough to make Congress envious.

"Every time Obama comes to New York, it's a nightmare," said Tom Hall, 52, who was trying to get home to the Upper West Side from Midtown. "It probably wasn't a good idea to have both of these events the same night."

What a metaphor, I thought. That is what America is all about. Organized political chaos that somehow finds its beacon of hope and its entrepreneurial spirit gets rekindled and refocused by *We the People,* that re-energizes the Republic and the world, something that is long overdue and has to start again with the known knowns and unknown unknowns, domestically and with China as its global partner.

Before I headed to New York that late November in 2011, I celebrated Thanksgiving at home in Hong Kong. And what a Thanksgiving it was. Pauline and I decided to host a holiday dinner for three other couples, who like us, one of the partners in each couple was an American. Ana and Mark Sharp, Bruce and Mari Noel Grill, Caroline Gary and Rod, the Americans being the first name in each coupling. Ana and Mark are the parents of Nicola and Samantha, both born in Hong Kong.

Starting with the Americans, I asked each person to tell the gathered guests what Thanksgiving meant to them. I asked Nicky and Sam to listen carefully and then give their answer. It was their first Thanksgiving.

Bottom line, the consensus of the adults – American and significant other – was family and shopping. Tradition, history, Harvest Festival were parallels brought up by everyone in terms of meaning. What started out as a few minutes presentation by each guest as to what Thanksgiving meant to them turned into a 20-minute question and rebuttal session by the rest of the guests as we periodically toasted the Pilgrims and their bountiful and peaceful harvest.

Thanksgiving is an immigrant's holiday, and since all Americans are either immigrants or descendants of immigrants, the concept of everyone celebrating their cultural family traditions and eating and being thankful as immigrants, is based on the legend that the settlers of the Plymouth colony, in desperate gratitude to God for their first good harvest, gave thanks to the Lord and the natives. The previous winter, they had lost nearly half their number to starvation, illness and attacks. A succesful harvest, along with the peaceful participation of the Wampanoag Indians in the feast, meant that from that point on the Pilgrims might endure.

But history tells us that the Plymouth settlers, when sure of a good harvest – and good defenses – repaid their native hosts with mistrust, disease and war. It's hard to survive, even harder to stop behaving like a survivor. One of the great human virtues is gratitude.

Jews are encouraged to make a least 100 blessings of gratitude a day. The very first words Jews say every morning are, "I give thanks before you, eternal King, for having restored to me my soul."

Most Jews believe in the idea of gratitude because it is woven into the name Jews. Jews are descended from Judah. Of the 12 children who came from Jacob, 10 of the tribes of Israel were lost, scattered to unknown destinations and no longer identifiable by their heritage. Those remaining, other than the priests and Levites, stem either from the large tribe of Judah or the much smaller tribe of Benjamin. The majority of survivors of historic diminution by assimilation or persecution are from Judah, hence they are called Jews.

But what is it about the tribe of Judah that helped it survive above the others? According to Rabbi Benjamin Blech, "A number of Jewish commentators believe the secret of Judah's blessings are implicit in the Hebrew meaning of his name. When Leah, his mother, gave birth to him she said, 'This time I will give thanksgiving unto the Lord; therefore she called his name Judah' (Genesis 29:35) – from the Hebrew hodah, giving thanks."

"I don't understand Thanksgiving because it seems there is a lot of thanks but not a lot of giving," Nicky and Sam responded to my question of what Thanksgiving means to them after they had heard what it meant to all the adults. From the mouths of babes.

Thanksgiving is followed by Black Friday, the mother of all shopping sprees when people shop for Christmas presents to give to loved ones. America – make that *We the Apathetic Maids* worldwide – are going to hell in a shopping basket. I agree with professor Robert Reich, the former U.S. secretary of Labor under President Bill Clinton, who wrote: "Consumers and investors are doing increasingly well but job insecurity is on the rise, inequality is widening, communities are becoming less stable and climate change is worsening. None of this is sustainable over the long term, but no one has yet figured out a way to get capitalism back into balance. Blame global finance and worldwide corporations all you want. But save some of the blame for the insatiable consumers and investors inhabiting almost every one of us who are entirely complicit."

So how do *We the People* survive these difficult and troubled times? Starting with the knowns: We know things can only get worse and continue to deteriorate unless we get a grip on ourselves. The word of the year for 2011, chosen by the American Dialect Society, was "occupy," though some radical spirits recommended "a\*\*holocracy," which they defined as rule by multi-millionaires – the types that hang out at the World Economic Forum in Davos.

The main message of the forum's Global Risks 2012 report, based on a survey of 469 experts from industry, government, academia and civil society who examine 50 global risks, is that economic turmoil, financial stringency and social upheaval could not only roll back the gains the world has made from globalization, but could lead to a "dystopian future for much of humanity."

The report explains that "dystopia, the opposite of a utopia, describes a place where life is full of hardship and devoid of hope." The risks are not single, but come from the "constellation of fiscal, demographic and societal risks. ... The interplay among these risks could result in a world where a large youth population contends with chronic high levels of unemployment, while concurrently, the largest population of retirees in history becomes dependent upon already indebted governments."

It gets worse: "Both young and old could face an income gap, as well as a skills gap so wide as to threaten social and political stability." This could jeopardize the social contract between states and citizens and then, "in the absence of viable alternatives, this could precipitate a downward spiral of the global economy, fuelled by protectionism, nationalism and populism."

But that is only one set of risks. Another comes under the headline, "How safe are our safeguards?" The report judges that "the constellation of risks arising from emerging technologies, financial interdependence, resource depletion and climate change exposes the weak and brittle nature of existing safeguards – the policies, norms, regulations or institutions which serve as a protective system. Our safeguards may no longer be fit to manage vital resources and ensure orderly markets and public safety."

That means revisiting and rewriting some of the rules that have put in place safety nets that benefit only the rich and bankers. I agree with the uber-capitalist Warren Buffett who says it is wrong for America to repeatedly bail out its billionaires, a culture of selfishness and a loss of opportunities. "We can rise to any challenge, but not if people feel we're in a plutocracy," he says. "We have to get serious about shared sacrifice."

We agree that CEOs of publicly bailed-out institutions should be on the hook for everything they own if their institutions go bust.

It's time the U.S. heeded not only Buffett's advice, but that of its diplomats.

### Trust Deficit

The "trust deficit" that hampered relations between Beijing and Washington before Xi Jinping made his Valentine Day visit to Washington in February 2012 unfortunately still lingers. Xi's U.S. tour came at a politically challenging time in U.S.-China relations, with the White House sending stern messages on currency and trade policies, and Republican presidential candidates claiming Obama wasn't doing enough to keep America's economy competitive with China's. The good news is that Xi showed America that he is a down to earth open and confident self-assured leader comfortable with America and its democratic open ways.

The fact that he suffered personally during the Cultural Revolution, the reformist communist sympathies of his father, his evident pragmatism, that he has a sister in Canada, a brother in Hong Kong and a daughter at Harvard, all suggest someone who might push forward essential reforms at home and a closer bilateral working partnership with the U.S.

His image is helped among ordinary Chinese by his wife, the superstar

People's Liberation Army singer Peng Liyuan, who is possibly more famous than her husband.

"The trust deficit sums up a very clear fact: that is, the level of mutual trust between China and the United States is lagging behind what is required for the further expansion of our bilateral relationship," said Chinese Vice Foreign Minister Cui Tiankai on the eve of Xi's visit to the U.S. in a speech commemorating the 40th anniversary of the Shanghai Communique signed during U.S. President Richard Nixon's ground-breaking visit to China.

The trust deficit was there for all to see at the Munich Security Conference in February 2012. Zhang Zhijun, China's vice minister of foreign affairs, waffled on about how "the people of Asia" had chosen a different path from the West and how the West should simply leave China to go its own way. And by the way, there was no problem at all in the South China Sea, where everyone enjoys free navigation.

Sitting next to Zhang was, U.S. Sen. John McCain who launched into a ballistic attack. It is a matter of concern, he said, when a Vietnamese ship has its cables cut by a Chinese vessel. The Vietnamese remember 2,000 years of Chinese domination. People are immolating themselves in Tibet. The Arab Spring represents universal aspirations and "the Arab Spring is coming to China," he said.

Australia's Foreign Minister Kevin Rudd summed it up best. China will have the world's largest economy by 2020. For the first time in 200 years, the world's largest economy will be a non-democracy; for the first time in 500 years, it will be a non-Western country. Moreover, according to what Rudd called "credible" analysis, China's total military expenditure is likely to exceed that of the U.S. by 2025. In a region filled with every kind of strategic challenge, including the divided Korean peninsula, and the standoff between nuclear-armed India and Pakistan, U.S. hegemony can no longer be relied on to keep the peace.

To craft a new Pax Pacifica – is therefore the great strategic challenge of our time. Implicitly rejecting the positions taken by both McCain and Zhang, Rudd said, "We need to shape global values together."

It's a concept I put forth when I applied for the Greatest Job on Earth in Australia and proposed it be used to bring China and America together in Australia and try and bring about peace, prosperity and environmental solutions to ensure the survival of mankind through the 21st century.

President Nixon's week-long visit to China in 1972 concluded with the publication of the Shanghai Communique that established the principles for normalizing U.S.-China relations. The visit represented one of the most dramatic and transforming diplomatic initiatives of the 20th century. Full normalization of Sino-American relations was completed by former U.S. President Jimmy Carter and China's Deng Xiaoping in late 1978.

The times have changed dramatically. In President Nixon's time the relatively new technology of television could be used to change public opinion from the top down. Today, the Internet and social networking media give people the ability to exert political influence from the bottom up.

Both countries today must confront the primary source of economic tension – the shared concern with "jobs, jobs, jobs."

"In the Cold War era, the shared strategic concern with the Soviet threat helped pull the two countries together. Today the common concern with jobs tends to pull the countries apart, although the reality is that globalization has created enormous numbers of jobs in both countries," wrote Richard H. Solomon, the president of the United States Institute of Peace in an editorial opinion in the *China Daily*.

The Sino-U.S. relationship can create more jobs in both countries and reduce, if not eliminate, unemployment. Americans can be put to work on farms and infrastructure projects to get food from farms to storage and port facilities to export to China to feed the masses there. Chinese can participate at both ends of the food chain by investing and providing the labor force to educate farmers there on America's agricultural technologies and distribution systems to get the food to China's hungry masses.

China became the top market for U.S. farm goods in 2011, purchasing $29 billion in U.S. agricultural exports, according to the U.S. Department of Agriculture.

Then Vice President Xi Jinping told his counterpart Joe Biden during his visit that the two countries should work to strengthen their relationship because they are "in the same boat."

Nixon called his visit to China in 1972 "the week that changed the world."

That was not an exaggeration. Xi's visit to America in 2012 could prove to be the week that solidified the Sino-U.S. partnership and solidified the AC Policy I proposed earlier by casting its principles in stone – make that engraving them on the bow of the boat – as a stone might sink it.

Xi's five-day trip to the U.S. was met with considerable pomp – he was greeted with a 19-gun salute at the Pentagon – and his arrival at the Port of Los Angeles where he wrapped up his trip was no different. A long row of Chinese flags had been lined up alongside a sleek, green China Shipping freighter.

"I look forward to conducting extensive and in-depth discussions with the U.S. side on bilateral issues and other major issues to consolidate the consensus," Xi said. "We hope we can convey a positive message that China and the U.S. will stick to the principle of showing mutual support to people in the same boat and strengthen cooperation."

Xi's first major assignment in the U.S. was a dinner meeting on February 13 in Washington with seven former senior government officials who have contributed to fostering bilateral relations. They included former U.S. Secretaries of State Henry Kissinger and Madeleine Albright, former national security advisers Brent Scowcroft and Zbigniew Brzezinski and former Treasury Secretary Henry Paulson, all of whom are powerful opinion leaders in the U.S.

On Valentine's Day, Xi was closeted in discussions with top officials of the Obama administration, including the president, vice president, secretaries of state and defense. In his discussions with Obama, Xi expressed the hope that his visit would deepen mutual understanding and friendship between the two countries.

"It is only appropriate that China and the U.S. exclude various forms of obstacles and persist on being friends and partners," Xi told Obama.

Xi said that China is looking forward to improving trust, consolidating consensus, deepening cooperation and managing disputes with the U.S. He promised to continue dialogue and cooperation instead of resorting to protectionism in trade disputes.

"A cooperative U.S.-China relationship is in the interests of the world," said Obama.

After a full day of meeting top administration officials, Xi went to Capitol Hill on the morning of February 15 to meet congressional leaders, including Senate Majority Leader Harry Reid and Minority Leader Mitch McConnell as well as House Speaker John Boehner and Majority Leader Eric Cantor.

Xi focused on enhancing old relationships and forging new ones – *Guanxi*. Back to America's heartland on the farms in Muscatine, Iowa, where he visited 27 years earlier as the director of a feed cooperative from Hebei province on an agricultural research trip. Iowa is America's leading soybean producer and a big supplier of the beans to China. He pushed for more agricultural cooperation with Iowa and America.

"Coming here is like coming home," Xi told the group. "You can't even imagine what a deep impression I had from my visit 27 years ago to Muscatine, because they were the first group of Americans that I came in contact with. My impression of the country came from you. For me, you are America."

America should get back to its agrarian roots and look at expanding farming and employing more Americans displaced from their jobs and homes in urban centers. According to the USDA, the value of U.S. farm exports to China supported more than 160,000 American jobs last year across a variety of business sectors. Farm goods represent one rare area where the U.S. is running a large trade surplus with China.

Muscatine's moment in the spotlight was not to be squandered. It was the sort of rural wisdom that Mark Twain – a local hero who lived briefly there on the banks of the Mississippi River and wrote for *The Muscatine Journal* in the 1850s – might well have praised or parodied: When opportunity knocks, shake it by the labels until the coins fall out.

Xi made clear that China wants a deeper relationship with the U.S. and even welcomed its engagement in the Asia-Pacific region, as long as it respects China's interests and concerns. "A prosperous and stable China will not be a threat to any country," Xi said. "It will only be a positive force for world peace and development."

Xi said that the two nations must respect each other's "core interests" while working to build trust and cooperation on a variety of issues, including trade policies and diplomacy with North Korea and Iran. Xi's use of the term "core interests" was intended to emphasize the existence of a line that the U.S. and other countries not cross in discussions with China. In particular, "core interests" has come to mean territorial sovereignty, and Xi stressed that the U.S. should oppose those advocating independence for Taiwan and Tibet.

To drive home the point that the U.S. isn't doing enough to respect such "core interests," Xi borrowed a line from George Washington that "actions, not words, are the true criterion of the attachment of friends."

Xi, who in November 2012 succeeded. President Hu Jintao, had to appear willing to stand up for the interests of China while being able to build a relationship with the U.S. Any sign of weakness could have given ammunition to his political opponents.

Coverage of Xi's visit in the Chinese media was relatively subdued – reflecting a desire not to upstage President Hu, or to play up any contrast between them.

The so-called Fifth Generation of officials, led by Xi, moved up in what was the biggest political turnover in the history of the People's Republic of China. During the 18th Party Congress in the autumn of 2012, more than 60 percent of personnel within the 370-member Central Committee changed. This leadership change also means key players in the nation's economic, financial, foreign policy, public security and military establishment are newcomers.

Such a massive transition is rare in China. It's happened only three times since 1949. The first during the 1960s ended in purges, widespread persecution of intellectuals and the anarchy of the Cultural Revolution. The second in the late 1980s unraveled when top leaders disagreed over whether to use force to disperse the protesters in Tiananmen Square. The most recent previous shift, when party head Hu Jintao succeeded Jiang Zemin in 2002, was an impressive and stable transfer of power. That was the only succession plan that went according to script.

In the run-up to the 2012 transition, the party was composed of two increasingly competitive coalitions, referred to as "populists" and "elitists." The populists, led by President Hu Jintao, relied on a powerful nationwide network of cadres in the Communist Youth League; their policies aimed to ameliorate the growing gap between China's have and have-nots, which is most pronounced in China's impoverished western regions. Elitists are known for their free-market economic views and favoring coastal export industries. They include many "princelings" like Xi who are offspring of former high-level cadres.

The unusual nature of this rivalry was evident in the way Xi became heir apparent during the 17th Party Congress in 2007. To ensure continued political dominance by the populists, Hu had handpicked a different heir, Li Keqiang. But the elitist camp objected to Li, hoping to find a compromise candidate with greater neutrality. The choice was determined by a secret intraparty poll among grassroots and senior cadres and it turned out that Xi won. Xi essentially won a popularity contest. Li Keqiang wound up being tipped to become premier in the shuffle.

After Washington and Iowa, Xi swept into Los Angeles for a brief but action-packed visit before heading off to Europe. Los Angeles Mayor Antonio Villaraigosa and California Gov. Jerry Brown welcomed Xi and drove him to the Port of Los Angeles on the last leg of his visit.

The port has invested $245 million in recent years to nearly double the size of the China Shipping terminal, which Xi called "a good foundation for the further development of U.S. trade and economic cooperation."

Xi did not mention the trade deficit between the two countries. Instead he praised the environmentally friendly measures in place at China Shipping.

In 2004, the company became the first shipping line to plug its vessels into electric power sources while docked, rather than burn fossil fuel.

The Port of Los Angeles is the nation's busiest. Nearly 60 percent of the imports moving through the port come from China. Chinese imports have helped Americans improve their standard of living and created more than 3 million new jobs in the U.S. from 2001 to 2010, Xi said.

U.S.-China trade is expected to top $500 billion soon, and the countries have moved from "mutual estrangement to a close exchange with increasingly intertwined interests," he said.

China has been America's fastest-growing export market, according to Kenneth Lieberthal, director of the John L. Thornton China Center at the Brookings Institution.

The timing of Xi's visit, in the midst of a U.S. presidential election and the impending change in leadership in China, not to mention upcoming elections in Hong Kong, South Korea, Russia and possibly Japan, in addition to the regime change in North Korea, meant that major breakthroughs in U.S.-China relations were not likely in 2012. Never before had so many key countries in the region faced possible leadership changes during the same 12 months.

I was delighted to see Xi attend a Lakers game during his stop in L.A. He was the first Chinese leader to attend an NBA game, which was significant in light of the ugly brawl at the U.S.-China basketball game in Beijing during Vice President Biden's visit in 2011. Xi's appearance at the Staples Center was a symbolic nod to the iconic moment when Deng Xiaoping, the leader who re-established diplomatic ties with the U.S. and launched China's economic reforms, donned a cowboy hat during a Texas rodeo in 1979.

As a Californian, I was delighted to hear Xi say that "Los Angeles and California are at the forefront of Sino-U.S. exchanges."
"In 1980, my father Xi Zhongxun, while governor of Guangdong province, visited Los Angeles and was presented with a key to the city as a token of friendship. The following year, Guangzhou and Los Angeles became sister cities. This was a memorable moment in my father's tenure."

He said Los Angeles had a memorable role in Sino-U.S. ties as China's first Olympic athlete, Liu Changchun, participated in the Olympic Games in L.A. in 1932. Then in 1984, China sent its first delegation to the Olympics in the city after gaining membership to the International Olympic Committee.

Xi received an unusual gift on his 2012 visit to the U.S. – an album of photographs taken during his father's visit to America in 1980. The photos show his father, former Vice Premier Xi Zhongxun, leading a delegation of provincial leaders on a tour of New York, Washington, Iowa, Colorado, California and Hawaii, according to the National Committee on United States-China Relations, which organized the trip and presented the album.

Xi's father was best known as the architect of China's successful and quasi-capitalist "special economic zones" launched in the era of Deng Xiaoping's market-based economic reforms.

What a contrast Xi Jinping's visit was to that of Hu Jintao, who made a grand U.S. state visit a year earlier. What a difference a year can make in Sino-U.S. relations. Hopefully there will be more positive changes in the years to come. That is what the citizens of both America and China want, according to two surveys commissioned at the end of 2011 by *China Daily* with Gallup in Washington and Horizon Research Group in Beijing.

The China Daily-Gallup survey covered 2,007 members of the general public and 250 opinion leaders in the U.S. Seven in 10 U.S. respondents said strong relations between the U.S. and China are "somewhat" or "very" important. Opinion leaders were even more emphatic, as 85 percent said strong relations between the two countries are important.

Similar results were found in the *China Daily*-Horizon survey, which polled residents from Beijing, Shanghai, Guangzhou, Wuhan, Chengdu, Shenyang and Xi'an, most of which host U.S diplomatic offices. More than 90 percent of the Chinese public, regardless of their location, have believed for many years that the Sino-U.S. relationship is important, according to the survey.

Xi is a leader America can work with. Before embarking on his U.S. visit, Xi remarked that "our commitment to the development of the Sino-U.S. cooperative partnership should never waiver in the face of passing developments."

"By no means can we let relations again suffer major interference," he said. Perfect! I couldn't say it any better.

Xi has set the right tone for future U.S.-Sino relations. A long overdue conciliatory tone the world's two most powerful countries need to adhere to as they forge ahead through the turbulent sea of their rocky relationship.

Xi's visit to America came just a week before the 40th anniversary of President Richard Nixon's historic 1972 visit to China. On February 21, 1972, the day of Nixon's arrival in Beijing, the U.S. president said: "There is no reason for us to be enemies. ... This is the day for our two peoples to rise to the heights of greatness which can build a new and better world."

Recalling Nixon's visit in a ceremony in Beijing, Xi pledged China's unwavering "commitment to developing the Sino-U.S. cooperative partnership."

After Nixon, Mao and Deng, Xi is firmly taking China's political and military reins, hoping to lead it through the revolutionary changes that will be forced upon him and the party to be put in place by the "Chinanet" generation in the New World Order. He knows it's a tall order on a rocky road of reform, but one that China must implement for the country to be accepted as a world leader alongside America. That will indeed be revolutionary.

There is no reason for the two equally confident civilizations to be enemies. As the spirit of 1972 echoes, new generations of American and Chinese leaders ought to demonstrate the same wisdom and courage that Nixon displayed so that the two countries can continue working together to build a New World Order for the next 40 years and beyond.

Referring to China, Secretary of State Hillary Clinton said in March 2012 that Washington is "now trying to find an answer to the ancient question of what happens when an established power and a rising power meet."

The much-needed answer is detailed in this *Custom Maid* trilogy for America's Third Revolution and was echoed by Le Yucheng, China's assistant foreign minister, at an economic forum in Beijing in April 2012. "Like it or not ... I believe our two countries have the responsibility, ability and wisdom to forge a new type of relationship between major countries, marked by sound interaction and win-win cooperation."

"In this networked world of myriad challenges, win-win cooperation is not a choice but the choice," Le said, stressing that this is precisely the "new answer" Washington is seeking in its attempts to reconcile with China's rise.

With slow job growth at home and worries of a hard landing by the Chinese economy in an already hard-hit global economy, analysts, myself included, are questioning and challenging whether Washington is able or capable of continuing to improve the state of the world economy alone. While some observers believe the rising powers pose a challenge to, and may ultimately help end Western supremacy, Le said that the "zero-sum game" mentality must change in an increasingly interconnected world.

"Emerging countries are not troublemakers. Their rise is not a challenge, much less a threat, but an important contribution and rare opportunity for the world," he said.

Both countries met the challenge in May 2012, when Hillary Clinton and Treasury Secretary Timothy Geithner went to Beijing for the annual Strategic and Economic Dialogue.

The dramatic escape from house arrest by blind activist Chen Guangcheng, who took shelter in the U.S. Embassy a few days before the U.S. secretaries arrived, threatened to derail the extraordinarily complex talks, but instead confirmed the new solid and mature foundation of U.S.-Sino relations and the constructive dialogue both countries are pursuing. The terms of Chen's repatriation from the embassy to Chinese officials were worked out, as were several long overdue economic and political "breakthroughs."

The success of the political and economic meetings in Beijing was further nourished and built upon the next day with the departure of Defense Minister Laing Guanglie to the U.S. for meetings with his counterpart Defense Secretary Leon Panetta in Washington. It was the first visit of a Chinese defense minister to D.C. in nine years. "Under the current complicated international situation, China and the United States share vast common interests and their relations have great development potential," Liang said upon his arrival in San Francisco.

"The United States and China are powers in the Pacific and our goal is to establish a constructive relationship for the future," Panetta said. "It is essential for our two nations to communicate effectively on a range of very challenging issues."

Liang reminded Americans of the history of U.S.-Sino military cooperation by visiting the families of the Flying Tigers, the American air squadron that flew on the side of the Chinese against the Japanese during World War II.

### Xi's China Pivot

Xi Jinping's unexplained two-week absence from public view in early September 2012, and cancellation of meetings with visiting U.S. Secretary of State Clinton, Singapore Prime Minister Lee Hsien Loong and Danish Prime Minister Helle Thorning-Schmidt, triggered a frenzy of rumors. Was he nursing a bad back after pulling a muscle in a pick-up football game or a swim? Was he convalescing after narrowly escaping a revenge assassination attempt by supporters of ousted Communist Party boss Bo Xilai? Was he in a car accident? Or just really busy getting ready to lead China ahead of his promotion?

Rumors about Xi were churned more by Russian President Putin's cryptic remarks at the start of the Asia-Pacific Economic Forum summit meeting he was hosting, when he said that the start had to be delayed because China's Hu Jintao had to attend to an important but unspecified domestic issue.

I was in Shanghai on September 13 and in Beijing on September 14 and 15. The question of Xi's whereabouts and reason for his disappearance from public view dominated my discussions with friends and business associates. The answer was much simpler. Now that China is a linchpin of the global economy and a force in international diplomacy, its leaders are acting accordingly, refusing to kowtow to the U.S. or anyone else – especially if they are seen to be supporting Japan in the explosive Sino-Japanese territorial dispute over the Diaoyu island chain.

America and Singapore are seen to be supporting Japan. Thus it was Xi's subtle way of letting the visiting dignitaries know that he and China were starting their own political pivot ahead of Xis taking over the leadership of China.

The Danish prime minister just happened to be at the wrong place at the wrong time – or was she taking on the redirected aggression of China toward Denmark's Scandinavian neighbor Norway and its Nobel Prizes?

When the U.S. led a 25,000-troop, 22-nation maritime exercise in Hawaii in the summer of 2012 that included Singapore, a Japanese naval commander served as second in command. It was the highest rank ever given a Japanese officer in the four decades since the drill was launched, and a signal of how Tokyo has steadily expanded its military clout as the U.S. relies more on Japan as its leading regional ally to counter China's rise.

China wasn't invited. Thankfully, it was invited to the 2014 U.S.-led Rim of the Pacific military exercise as a result of the Xi-Obama Sunnylands Summit.

"We don't have any enemy – officially speaking, that is," Japanese Rear Adm. Fumiyuki Kitagawa said when asked about the focus of the 2012 five-week military campaign. He then laughed out loud.

The reality is that China's growth of its military prowess is viewed with fear and suspicion by the U.S. That, combined with fiscal restraints in America, is forcing the Pentagon to seek bigger contributions from its key regional allies. Japan has the third-largest navy in the Asia-Pacific region after the U.S. and China.

To make matters worse – after the military exercise – Japan decided to buy three of the 19 offshore Diaoyu islands from their Japanese owners and nationalize the chain. China does not recognize the Japanese ownership.

China claims the Diaoyu Islands have been its sovereign territory since ancient times – since the Ming Dynasty (1368-1644) to be exact. Their surrounding waters have been traditional fishing grounds for thousands of Chinese fishermen for centuries.

After World War II, under the terms of the Cairo Declaration signed in 1943 and the Potsdam Proclamation of 1945, the Chinese government resumed its sovereignty over the Diaoyu Islands that had been occupied by Japan since the end of the Sino-Japanese War of 1894-95.

In 1951, the U.S. and Japan signed what China considers an illegal treaty, whereby the islands were "entrusted" to the U.S. China, not having been a party to the agreement, never recognized what it considers an illegal transfer of its sovereign territory.

During the Cold War, America decided in 1971 to hand over the administration of Okinawa, which was under its trusteeship, and the Diaoyu Islands to Japan. China protested vehemently to the transfer, as did Taiwan, both claiming the islands were their sovereign territory and that the U.S. had no right to transfer the islands to Japan. The U.S. agreed to extend the U.S.-Japan security treaty to cover the Diaoyu Islands should China decide to attack and retake the islands. In other words, the U.S., in its efforts to contain China, created the current Diaoyu Islands dispute.

When China and Japan reestablished diplomatic relations and signed the Treaty of Peace and Friendship in 1978, they agreed to settle all their disputes by peaceful means. Japan's nationalization of the islands is seen by China as a provocation to initiate a clash between the two countries.

"History does repeat itself," said Nelson Wong, a friend and business associate during dinner on September 13 in Shanghai when I asked him how he thought the island dispute would be resolved and whether the issue had anything to do with Xi's unexplained absence from public view. "China has never been an advocate of war. But at the same time, it can't ignore what Japan is doing and allow Japan, a proven advocate of war, to repeat its past aggressions with China, America and Russia.

"Japan is a natural historical enemy that has humiliated China, something Chinese leaders today cannot forget or allow to be repeated. What Japan has done, nationalizing the Diaoyu Islands, has not only infuriated the Chinese people, but has given China's incoming leaders both a political and economic reason to seriously consider a military solution once and for all with Japan. Whether they do remains to be seen. But it is definitely an option.

"Japan has a history of aggressive behavior, something China and its leaders cannot allow to happen again without China responding, not only politically and economically, but possibly militarily, to once and for all put Japan in its long overdue place. Something America has failed to do. Hopefully, if America and China are to be the dominant leaders of the world in the 21st century, America will agree with China's point of view and discard Japan as its Pacific ally and cornerstone. After all, America and China were allies in World War II and together defeated Japan. Why not do so again?"

China's initial response to Japan's nationalization of the islands was to announce its territorial coordinates – base points and baselines – for waters off the islands and its intention to patrol those waters.

Xi knows that finding a solution to the territorial dispute is his first major challenge as China's leader. Failing to find a satisfactory solution will result in him being labeled the leader of a "traitor government,' with his right to lead China revoked by the people.

Japan's seizure of the islands resulted in a nationalistic public outcry, not just in China, but in Chinese communities around the world – and especially in Hong Kong and. The furor showcased how highly explosive an political issue the islands are.

Hong Kong Diaoyu activists sailed to the islands in August 2012 and planted a Chinese flag on one of them. They were arrested by the Japanese coast guard and taken to Japan before being sent back home. The activists promptly filed a lawsuit in Beijing against Japan for their illegal "capture" and false imprisonment in Japan.

For over a century, political, economic and military supremacy over the Asia-Pacific region has been the preoccupation of Japan and the U.S. In the absence of a serious challenger, the two have gone through major military conflicts to establish their dominant position. Japan's defeat in the World War II ended its claim to a preeminent position in the region, leaving the U.S. as the unrivaled power.

China no longer accepts America's role as the sole power in the region and is prepared to flex its economic and military muscles to make its point.

During my visit to Bejing on September 14th, I asked Albert Louie, a Beijing- based business associate, the same question I had asked Nelson the day before. "I believe Xi is chairing a military commission meeting to plan how to deal with Japan's aggression by nationalizing the Diaoyu Islands. China has to develop a very careful and well thought out plan on how to respond. This is a very sensitive time because of the upcoming 18th National Congress, Bo Xilai scandal and change in leadership. Xi Jinping wants to make sure the Diaoyu issue is handled smartly and sends a strong message to Japan and America that what Japan has done is unacceptable.

"Frankly, he could even be exploring all military options available to China after he becomes the country's leader."

Nelson and Albert's hunches made sense. Especially when the next day a healthy, smiling Xi, showing no signs of any physical ailments, resurfaced in a very public way and violent anti-Japanese protests gripped the nation. The thousands of protestors who converged on the Japanese Embassy, department stores and businesses in Beijing and over 50 cities across China, many hurling rocks, eggs and bottles, confirmed that China had a carefully choreographed plan on how to deal with Japan.

Trying to get to the airport to catch my flight back to Hong Kong was a challenge because I was staying at a hotel near the diplomatic compound.

China's anti-Japan protests cost Japan hundreds of millions of dollars. The cost includes the vandalism of buildings and other physical damage, as well as the indirect effects such as reduced sales. The figure does not include the effect of a consumer boycott on Japanese goods that badly hit auto and electronic makers. Japanese airlines had thousands of seat cancellations.

China is the single largest purchaser of Japanese goods. In 2011, it accounted for 20.6 percent of Japan's total exports, nearly three times the figure from a decade earlier. By the end of 2010, the number of Japanese enterprises in China had reached 22,307, with total registered capital of more than $94 billion.

The last thing Japan needs is an economic war or trade war with China, let alone a real hot-war over the disputed islands. Japan is already crippled with government debt of more than 240 percent of gross domestic product, higher than Greece's, and an overvalued yen driving companies offshore and hollowing out industry is bad enough. Tensions with China, Japan's biggest trade and investment partner, have merely added a damaging downward twist to the economic spiral.

Japan's former Prime Minister Yoshihiko Noda admitted he miscalculated Beijing's reaction to his government's purchase of the Diaoyu Islands.

China cannot and will not make any concessions to Japan when it comes to the disputed islands.

Beijing appeared to tread a fine line between sending a strong message to Tokyo while not allowing social unrest that might destabilize the upcoming domestic political transition.

Xi, did use a tougher tone and language than the current leaders on the Diaoyu dispute and made it clear that China would stand firm on the issue of sovereignty. Since taking the top party post, Xi has visited several PLA bases to shore up military support and repeatedly demanded "battle readiness" from the military and sent ships and aircraft to assert China's claims over the islands.

Frankly, I was surprised that Xi didn't cancel his meeting with U.S. Defense Secretary Leon Panetta, who came to China a few days later from Japan, where he announced the sale of of an additional missile defense shield, seen by China as an additional step at containment.

### *Diaoyu Flashpoint*
In his first published speech setting out his foreign policy views in January 2013, Xi said, "No foreign country should ever nurse hopes that we will bargain over our core national interests." "Nor should they nurse hopes that we will swallow the bitter fruit of harm to our country's sovereignty, security and development interests."

Xi will press territorial claims more determinedly than his predecessors. He has already told Chinese military forces to focus on training for possible conflict.

As tensions rose between China and Japan, China's giant sovereign-wealth fund warned Japan about deliberately devaluing the yen and starting a potential currency war, while in the city of Nanjing more than 10,000 mourners gathered to remember the 300,000 civilians and soldiers who died in the six-week Nanking massacre by the Japanese in December 1937.

Meanwhile, new Prime Minister Shinzo Abe immediately repeated Japan's undisputed territorial claim to the Diaoyus and repeated that he may map out a new statement appropriate for the 21st century about the country's historical perspective on World War II, effectively reviewing a 1995 statement apologizing for Japan's wartime actions.

Japan's plan to issue a "future-oriented" statement to supercede the 1995 statement indicated that Abe was paving the way for him and other Japanese leaders to resume visits to the Yasukuni Shrine and for his country to exercise the right to collective self-defense. The shrine honors Japan's war dead, including war criminals.

Abe appears determined to force through constitutional changes that will allow Japan to become an offensive military force, and not merely a self-defense force. A nationalist Japan with Abe leading the charge harks back to militaristic Japan pre-World War II and imperialist Japan during the war.

Giving up the disputed islands would be tantamount to caving in to Chinese threats. It would be unacceptable to most Japanese and probably also to Japan's protector, the U.S.

The aggressive stand each country is taking means that the issue is unlikely to be resolved peacefully in the foreseeable future – and may well become the flashpoint of a Sino-Japanese war in the 21st century.

### *Military Accident in the Making*
Tokyo claims that Chinese frigates targeted a Japanese military helicopter and destroyer with fire-control radar in January 2013. China has increased its maritime surveillance of the disputed islands, and continues to do so – as does Japan. Both sides scramble fighter jets that fly through the disputed airspace over the islands. Tokyo is considering authorizing the country's Air Self-Defense Force jets to fire warning shots when Chinese planes enter air space claimed by Japan.

A military accident could easily result from miscalculation or mis-communication and a conflict between the two Asian military powers would unfortunately break out. Behind the combative rhetoric, both Beijing and Tokyo understand very well that war would be the worst imaginable outcome, economically for both, and politically for the loser. Yet the rhythm of war beats on now that president Obama confirmed in April 2014 that the U.S. shall come to Japan's defense if China tries to retake the Diaoyus and Japan has reinterpreted its constitution to allow it to deploy its armed forces offensively.

### *Military Preparations*
The U.S. approved plans to send a squadron of F-22 fighter jets, America's most advanced warplane, to Japan. The U.S. and Japan are reviewing their defense cooperation rules to give Japan a greater role in regional security as both countries are concerned that Japan's island disputes with China and South Korea could degenerate into conflict.

The U.S. Senate's backing in November 2012 for Japan's administration of the disputed East China Sea islands only escalated tensions between Beijing and Tokyo – and its American protector. It reaffirms the U.S. commitment to Japan under the Treaty of Mutual Cooperation and Security and warns that an armed attack against either party "in the territories under the administration of Japan" would be met in accordance with its provisions.

How smart a move is that? China has branded the U.S.-Japan security treaty "a product of the cold war" and warned America that the Sino-Japanese row is none of Washington's business.

Meanwhile, thousands of Japanese rallied against the American deployment of Osprey military aircraft on Okinawa amid escalating anti-U.S. military sentiment following recent alleged rapes of local women by American servicemen.

U.S. and Japanese armed forces meanwhile conduct joint military exercises, developing strategies for taking back islands occupied by enemy troops.

The Chinese air force is not sitting idly by. It is training for aerial combat with a "third force," while conducting live fire by missile-carrying aircraft in the East China and South China seas. PLA troops are beefing up their combat readiness to be prepared for war by subjecting the army to rigorous training on an actual combat basis.

China and the U.S. are each other's second-largest trading partners. Their bilateral trade volume reached $446.7 billion in 2011 with U.S. exports to China exceeding $100 billion. By comparison, the U.S.-Japan trade in 2011 was worth only $194.6 billion, and U.S. exports to Japan just $65.7 billion. So why is the U.S. again supporting and siding with Japan while trying to contain China?

To make matters worse for the U.S., Japan is also in a territorial dispute over an island with South Korea, complicating the picture even more for the U.S.

### New World Order – From Scratch
*We the Maids* must sweep out career politicians and their stale moribund ideas and get back to America's Founding Fathers, ideals from scratch. A

good time to start is now – the end of one Mayan calender cycle of the old world order and start the New World Order in the Year of the Dragon – with i-calm.

December 21, 2012, marks the end of an era – the old world order – and the start of the New World Order.

The Mayan long calendar count begins in 3,114 BC and is divided into roughly 394-year periods called called *baktun*. Mayans held that the number 13 is sacred and the 13th *baktun* – which takes the form 13.0.0.0.0. – ends on December 21, the winter solstice 2012. The date signifies the end of a five-millennia cycle in the ancient Mayan calendar, not the end of the world. Many ancient Mayan monuments discuss events far into the future.

The Sumerians reached the same conclusion about 2012 and the future on the same date on the other side of the globe in the deserts of Israel.

Scratch was a popular bar and grill my then-wife Gail and I created on Main Street in Santa Monica in 1984. Every thing served was "made from scratch," with a different menu each week during its three-year existence. Many of the ideas articulated in this book were also created from scratch at Scratch as a result of late-night, or more accurately, early-morning loaded discussions with "glassmates." It was a popular watering hole that attracted politicians, celebrities, has-beens, movie stars, musicians, titans of industry, drug dealers, wanabees, neer-do-wells, movers and shakers, users, losers, financiers, real estate developers and real salts of the earth from far and wide.

Scratch also metaphorically symbolizes the numerous creative watering holes where I have "gassed up" globally and exchanged many both sober and incoherent frustrations and ideas over the  last 30-plus years with employed and unemployed career politicians, journalists, professors, students, workers, farmers and people from all walks of life.

Issues of the day have always been a constant source of discussion with family, friends, business associates, clients and strangers.

The people, conversations and concerns are real, universal and represent personal encounters with individuals of all ethnic, racial, religious and sexual orientations.

My memory and recollections of incidents and conversations is, thankfully, still intact. The conclusion I have reached during my travels, is that a global revolutionary movement is riding a rising tide of interlocal frustration over economic injustice and inequality. From Tea Party activists to Occupiers, and every style of Arab cleansing that individually and collectively inspired revolutionary movements in Europe and Asia – and continues to sprout across the world today – remind us of the growing economic divide and unfairness between rich and poor, people and nations, which continues to feed and build a growing global cause and calling for a new political world order. One that reaches out across state lines and national boundaries and adopts a simple well-defined constitution and 13-step program to embrace and unite citizens from all countries – in the promised land.

A global movement- a moving political party that advocates political and economic fairness – i-calm, an organization I have established in the U.S. and Hong Kong. I welcome all *Maids*, everywhere, who believe it is time to sweep out career politicians of the Old World Order and sweep in a New World Order with the neglected ideals of Americas' Founding Fathers, to join me. A formal invitation and movement registry can be found on page 1057.

Many people have written about peace, justice and prosperity. Writers, politicians, philosophers and prophets have preached and advocated better understanding, cooperation and justice among *We the People*. Many of the ideas I have proposed have been put forth by others, at different times, in different ways, mediums and places. My hope is that this book will serve as a helpful condensed version of the relevant history, and religious, political and economic ideals necessary to improve our world in the New World Order.

*There is Hope Ahead.*
– Billy Ray Cyrus

## Postscript

*Who controls the past controls the future; who controls the present controls the past.*

– George Orwell, 1984

### Revolutionary Changes

The Third American Revolution of the New World Order was well under way when I returned to the States from Scotland in January 2013. Sequestration, sex, same-sex marriage, immigration, the future of the country's two major political parties and gun control debates were blowing the republic apart. The 113th Congress (2013-2014) was the laziest-least productive ever. Thankfully, more states had legalized the medical and recreational use of marijuana, which helped *We the People* mellow out and manage our rage at political and religious dysfunctional opponents on these and other pressing gridlocked domestic economic, fiscal and foreign policy issues.

Sequestration became a dirty word and the federal spending cutbacks that went into effect March 1, 2013, were the fault of Democrats, according to Republicans – who, of course, the Democrats blame as the real culprits – as does the American public, according to the polls.

Speaking of polls, with John Boehner's House speakership on the line and Senate Republican leader Mitch McConnell of Kentucky, who faces re-election in 2014 in a state with a strong Tea Party faction, why is anyone surprised that while Congress sleeps, American children are gunned down and war veterans are dying because they are denied the care they deserve?

Investors on March 1 shrugged off the onset of the cuts, sending the Dow Jones Industrial Average up 35.17 points to 14,089, its third-highest close of all time. The blue-chip index rose 0.6 percent for the week, its second consecutive weekly advance. The Dow went on to reach new heights a week later when it hit its second highest close ever, just 37 points away from a new record – more than double its level during the dark days of

March 2009.

Meanwhile, back in China, stocks plunged on Beijing's plan to impose a 20 percent capital gains tax on home sales profits. As if that wasn't bad enough, the government also announced that it would make it more difficult for people to buy a second home.

The ripple-impact on the entire Chinese economy was instant. The fear was that demand for steel, cement, household appliances and many other mainstays of China's manufacturing-dependent economy would plunge.

The irony is that to combat the Great Recession, the Fed bought trillions of dollars of mortgage bonds and U.S. Treasuries to juice the housing market and the economy in general and now has to scale back the bond-buying spree and get ready to unwind some of the Fed's massive portfolio which tops $3 trillion – about the same amount China holds in U.S. Treasuries.

Should the portfolio of either the Fed or China grow to $4 trillion or more, *We the Apathetic Maids* will be staring at a much uglier world.

"Of course, the immediate future is uncertain," Warren Buffet wrote in his annual letter to shareholders released March 1st. "America has faced the unknown since 1776.... . American business will do fine over time."

Congressional leaders were never close to an agreement to block or replace the $85 billion in cuts and Wall Street knew for weeks, but investors preferred the sequester to tax increases and had already factored in the financial costs.

The fact is, the cuts are a good beginning of what America needs to do to balance its budget. Unfortunately, many of the cuts, such as education, are wrong and unnecessary, but had to be part of the "across the board" cuts for everyone – except for the career politicians, of course.

Cutting a mere $85 billion from the 2013 budget of $3.6 trillion – a reduction of 2.3 percent, amounts to two cents on the dollar. Much bigger cuts must be made to balance the budget.

The sequestration will cause federal spending over 10 years to drop from $46 trillion all the way down to $44.8 trillion! Is this any way to cut the deficit and balance a budget? Of course not. Especially when it is the poor who are disproportionately hard hit.

The way for career politicians to cut the deficit is to cut overspending, not pass an across-the-board meat-cleaver law that tries to pressure Congress to act, costs 700,000 jobs in 2013 and shaves at least a half percentage point from economic growth.

The showdown over the debt row has left the discretionary programs to bear the brunt of deficit reduction measures. Those domestic and military programs are so named because Congress has discretion to set spending levels annually in appropriations bills; entitlement benefits, in contrast, grow automatically unless changed by law.

Lobbyists went into high gear to blunt the pain on their special-interest clients, even before the sequestration went into effect and turned their attention to the next budget deadline – the need to pass a bill extending routine government funding after a stop-gap bill that expired March 27, 2013. Without an extension, a partial government shutdown would occur.

The can has been kicked too far down the road and is starting to run out of space at *We the Apathetic Maids'* expense. Meanwhile, career politicians do what is necessary to ensure their financial backers continue to fill their political campaign coffers that they use as they please – Congressman Jesse Jackson Jr., who admitted spending $750,000 on personal luxuries in February 2013 and is facing jail time – being an extreme example.

So now career politicians are focused on fixing and cleaning up the mess they created in the first place, instead of working on jobs, the economy, education, immigration and other pressing domestic and foreign policy issues.

Sex and the military became a public epidemic and moved down the ranks from former General David Petraeus to Army Brigadier General Jeffrey A. Sinclair, who was charged with two counts of forcible sodomy for allegedly compelling a married female captain to perform oral sex and pressing female officers to send him nude photos, to forcible rape and sexual abuse charges in the different branches of the military and military academies that go unpunished in the world of military justice.

Kinky sex was not limited to the military. Harvard, America's oldest university, formally recognized Harvard College Munch, a year-old campus group promoting alternative sex.

Not to be outdone, Washington and its career politicians came through with the biggest political-sex story of the New World Order in February 2013. Former Senator Pete Dominici of New Mexico admitted that even as he was blasting President Clinton for having an affair with an intern, Dominici himself was having an affair with Michelle Laxalt, the daughter of Senator Paul Laxalt of Nevada – and had a son who was raised by Michelle in secret because Pete already had a wife and eight children.

Career politicians know how to screw us in more ways than one. With the budget cuts and sequestration kicking in on March 1, 2013, what do the politicians do in late February? They go on a break and continue to blame each other for their failure to reach an agreement.

Gays, lesbians and same-sex couples are finally getting the legal recognition long overdue due them, not only in the military, but many states and the federal government. The Boy Scouts' reluctant acceptance to end the membership ban on gays reflects revolutionary America on the sexual frontier.

Immigration and how to legally recognize illegal immigrants became a top legislative priority and was pushed to the forefront by President Obama and a bipartisan group of senators and members of Congress.

Immigration and why it is an economically driven two-way street was a subject former Mexican President Vicente Fox elucidated during a breakfast I had with him on January 27, 2013, at Canter's, a Jewish delicatessen in Los Angeles. His grandfather had immigrated to Mexico from America, for the same economic reasons many Mexicans have come to America – and gone back to Mexico – to provide a better life for their families.

Immigration is not just an American issue. It is a global issue that has to be addressed urgently. The U.S. clearly has a leadership opportunity to promote immigration reform and free-flow of immigrants beyond our borders.

"With the right set of immigration and visa reforms, we can help usher in a new era of American opportunity and economic vitality while giving the global economy a boost," wrote Muhtar Kent, chairman and CEO of the Coca-Cola Company in a *USA Today* op-ed piece.

Legalizing illegal immigrants and making them pay a hefty fine, which the government can finance and deduct from their paychecks if necessary – plus taxes – and forcing employers to cooperate and turn in illegals who decide not to register and become legal taxpayers is a natural global solution.

An immigration fix that is long overdue is the recognition due Philippine vets and Hmong soldiers who fought alongside American troops in World War II and the Vietnam War. I have met some of these unsung heroes in the Philippines and America and understand their pain and anger. It is time for America to deliver on its broken promises to these American patriots.

On the subject of war, John Brennan, President Obama's head of the CIA, brought increased scrutiny to the use of armed drones to kill al-Qaeda leaders around the world – including Americans – a key part of the administration's counterterrorism strategy. Brennan helped manage the drone program as Obama's top counterterrorism adviser.

Drone strikes are a better alternative than boots on the ground, even if the target happens to be an American citizen who is an al-Qaeda leader and an "imminent threat" targeting America or its citizens. U.S. citizenship doesn't create a legal force field around Americans who treasonably join the enemy. During the Civil War, every Confederate soldier remained a U.S. citizen.

It's ironic that leading right-wing pro-gun politicians challenging President Obama's efforts to control the guns that kill thousands of Americans at home are questioning the president's right to kill American terrorists who want to kill Americans. Definitely something wrong with that picture.

Even more ironic are the pro-lifers opposed to *Roe v. Wade* who are fighting controls on guns that kill and maim so many Americans.

Gun violence in America was highlighted during my U.S. visit by the case of Jimmy Lee Dykes in Alabama, who killed a school bus driver and held a 5-year-old boy hostage in a bunker until Dykes was killed by FBI sharpshooters and the boy was released unharmed; the murderous rogue trigger-happy disgruntled revenge-seeking former Los Angeles police officer Christopher Dorner, who killed the daughter of a former LAPD captain, the woman's fiance and two police officers; seven Los Angeles County sheriff's deputies fired for belonging to a secret clique who celebrated shootings and branded its members with matching tattoos; and the cold-blooded murder of Chris Kyle, America's untouchable most-decorated military sniper, who was killed at a Texas shooting range by an ex-Marine he was counseling while a New York City police officer was on trial accused of plotting to kidnap, kill and cannibalize women.

Doomsday preppers, whom I discuss in *Feasting Dragon, Starving Eagle,* took center stage on many talk shows with their displays of underground shelters and armories to make sure they are not one of the more than 30,000 people killed each year by guns in the U.S. – more than one million since 1960.

I can relate to and support guns for hunting. I wished I had a gun when I went hunting in Cyprus as a child. I had to settle for a homemade catapult because a gun would have had me branded a terrorist or worse, subject to being shot by a policeman or British soldier.

I was saddened to read that the songbirds I hunted as a child, a Cypriot delicacy for centuries, which today are illegal to kill because they are an endangered species – a condition the European Union imposed in 2004 on Cyprus as a condition for EU membership – are again being hunted because Cyprus is bankrupt and Cypriots are back in the centuries-old trade risking fines and even jail time.

Cyprus has been kept afloat by a $3.5 billion loan from Russia and, like

Greece, Spain, Portugal and other European countries, is in desperate need of a financial bailout. An opportune time for Europe's leaders to tell the Greek Cypriots that financial aid requires a reunification settlement with the Turkish Cypriots on the diplomatic front, something that is doable now that Nicos Anastasiades won a presidential runoff in February 2013.

Watching and listening to career politicians in Washington take the U.S. over the fiscal cliff with sequestration and down the road that Cyprus, Greece and other European Union countries have been traveling, starting with the U.S. Postal Service, is heartbreaking. I made a point of going to different post offices at least twice a week in Los Angeles to see how a government monopoly can lose roughly $25 million a day and how bad things really are – and to support the post office by using its express service and other courier services instead of going to UPS or FedEx. It's definitely cheaper, but the service leaves a lot to be desired. I was amazed to find that sometimes that they were out of stamps, cutting services and hearing employees complaining loudly that they have "never seen it so bad." Is this anyway to run a government business?

The Postal Service, is not supported by tax dollars and has to cover its own operational costs like a private sector company, because it is unable to do anything without congressional approval. In other words, career politicians are trying to run a business the way they run the government. Career politicians have to come to grips with the fact that they will have to run the post office and the rest of the federal and state governments prudently and will need to reinvent the post office and all branches of government for the digital age.

The Postal Service, like the rest of the federal government, has to come to grips with the fact that it has maxed out its credit with *We the Apathetic Maids*.

A big part of the problem is a 2006 law requiring the Postal Service to pay about $5.5 billion a year into a health-benefit fund for retirees. No other government agency faces such a requirement.

Thankfully, libraries appear to be avoiding the fate of the post office in our digital age by adapting. The "Library Services in the Digital Age," a report released in January 2013 by the Pew Research Center's Internet & America Life Project, assures us that, even in the digital age, libraries serve a variety of functions, with nearly 60 percent of respondents having had some kind of interaction with a library in the previous 12 months, and 91 percent saying that "public libraries are important to their communities." Libraries do indeed play a vital role in our communities.

I am delighted to see that more people are reading, not just the skinny dumbed-down anorexic 200 pagers or less, but the robust 600 pages plus of history, current events like mine and many great authors out there, even fiction writers whose stories are often based on fact.

Meantime, the federal government should not only debate the cessation of the enforcement of laws banning medical and recreational use of marijuana – but cease and desist from having anything to do with the $50 billion taxable industry – and delegate the issue back to the states where it belongs and allow Americans to mellow out the way the Founding Fathers did.

A mellow America is a financially constructive America and a much healthier country than a drunk and belligerent gun-toting America – especially if the virtual currency bitcoin continues to surge.

Bitcoin is the Napster of money: It's maintained by a globally distributed peer-to-peer network running on open source software – and appreciating in value – in an abstract sense, perfect money. We definitely need to smoke this idea out! Digital currencies make it cheaper and easier to finance transactions and move money.

Reading that blues legend Muddy Waters' home in Chicago, where he lived for about 20 years with his wife, was going to be demolished because city inspectors deemed it to be in a "dangerous" condition, was heartbreaking. Muddy's music is America's music – and what made America great. The free enterprise spirit without bureaucratic interference.

The Harlem Shake, driven by the Internet and not bureaucrats, reaffirmed America's global cultural dominance – and has shaken up the leadership in

China – and the Muslim leadership in Tunisia, Egypt and Iran.

The Muddy Waters home demolition story is just another metaphor for America's self-destructive decline – highlighted by Detroit – the home of Motown and the American automobile industry – which filed for bankruptcy.

Career politicians cannot run governments or elections. The flaws of the American election system are deep and widespread, extending beyond isolated voting issues in a few locations and flaring up in states rich and poor, according to a major new study released by the Pew Charitable Trusts in February 2013. Lost votes, problem ballots, long lines, provisional ballots, absentee ballots, inconsistencies in rejection rates resulting in the disenfranchisement of millions of eligible voters. Is this any way to run the lighthouse of the beacon of democracy?

How come counties such as Virginia's Loudoun, Ohio's Lucas and Colorado's Larimer play a bigger role than California or New York? There is something definitely wrong with this picture.

The Third American Revolution was well under way in China when I returned to Hong Kong from America on February 9, 2013, to celebrate Chinese New Year.

People are angry and vocal about the record-breaking pollution, tainted food, quality of life, Japan, North Korea and America. America for its military buildup in Asia and support of Japan in the Diaoyu Island dispute. Many welcomed the confirmation of Senator John Kerry as secretary of state and his call for "fresh thinking" and broadening America's relationship with China. Many hope to immigrate to America to enjoy its freedoms, which they are denied in China.

Reformers are trying to get China to live up to its Constitution, a document that guarantees full powers for a representative legislature, the right to ownership of private property, and freedoms of speech, press and assembly. Though the Constitution was ratified in 1982 by the National People's Congress, it has languished ever since.

Xi Jinping is determined to keep the Communist Party in power and intact and not allow it to suffer the fate of its Soviet counterpart. Xi's remarks on the lessons of the Soviet Union, as well as warnings in the state news media, betray a fear that China's strains could overwhelm the party, especially if vows of change founder because of political sclerosis and opposition by privileged interest groups. It is a well founded fear. The supporters of disgraced Bo Xilai set up a new political party in direct challenge to the ruling Communist Party's defacto ban on new political groups. The Zhi Xiao Party, meaning "The Constitution is the supreme authority" party, was formed in November 2013.

Judicial independence, a traditional pillar of the rule of law in Hong Kong, was publicly questioned and challenged by politicians, the legal fraternity and the dean of the Hong Kong University law school when the government decided to have the Court of Final Appeal refer the right of abode issue to Beijing instead of making the decision itself.

In Hong Kong, thousands marched in politically charged rallies demanding the "cheating" chief executive resign for lying during the election about the illegal rooms he added to his home – and that the rule of law be restored and universal suffrage be adopted to elect the chief executive in 2017.

The protest movements in Hong Kong reflect the depth and despair that people everywhere share about their political establishments. They mirror the disillusionment expressed at the ballot boxes and on the streets in Greece, Spain, Egypt and Tunisia – the birthplace of Arab cleansing.

Italy's anti-establishment crusade, the Five Star Movement founded by comedian Beppe Grillo, brought the Third American Revolution to Italy's February 2013 election. Grillo and his movement were the biggest winners in the election. They won a quarter of all ballots cast. So the future of Italy – and the eurozone – hinges on the movement.

Two months before the election, Grillo had become Italy's leading protest politician when he held a rally in Bologna known as V-day, where the V stood for *vaffancula* – an Italian obsenity. A screen on the piazza displayed the names of 24 convicted criminals who were then serving in parliament.

*"Vaffancula!"* the crowd roared.

Grillo wants to sweep out Italy's old career politicians, "those who have destroyed the country." Shouldn't America, China and the rest of the world be doing the same?

"We are a response to government 'parasitism', corruption, a system of political diarrhea," said Grillo. He referred to Silvio Berlusconi, the center-right leader and former prime minister as the "psycho dwarf." Mario Monti, the technocrat centrist and acting prime minister, is "Rigor Montis." After the election, he accused Pier Luigi Bersani, the center-left leader, of being a "political stalker" and a "dead man talking."

Grillo's biggest edge has been exploiting the Internet and social media. When he started a political blog in 2005, people logged in by the millions to engage in debate. His movement has surged and crossed over to Austria where Team Stronach, founded by the Austrian-Canadian auto-parts magnate Frank Stronach, won state parliament seats in early 2013 in Carinthia and Lower Austria, as it built momentum for the fall's national elections.

The same happened in India where one year old Aam Aadmi Party, meaning "Common Man's" party, challenged India's establishment by taking on the two biggest parties in the state election in Delhi in 2013 – and winning. A broom is the party symbol.

Back in America, Facebook CEO Mark Zuckerberg and other Silicon Valley leaders have launched Fwd.us, a political group aimed at changing immigration policy, boosting education and encouraging investment in scientific research.

The Third American Revolution is spreading and becoming firmly rooted globally, and for good reason. Corrupt autocratic leaders are no longer acceptable in the New World Order.

The Obama administration launched its first-term foreign policy with the president making his historic speech at Cairo University. Some experts cite that speech as the spark that ignited the Arab cleansing. Former Secretary of State Hillary Clinton headed to Beijing and other Asian capitals on her first foreign overseas trip in 2009, putting the world on notice that America was interested in developing a closer relationship with China – and did – at the expense of Europe and the Middle East, the leaders of which complained they were being ignored and neglected by America.

President Obama decided to refocus America's attention on Europe and the Middle East in his second term, sending Secretary of State John Kerry to nine capitals in both regions immediately after Kerry took office in February 2013, as the president headed to Israel in March 2013 in hopes of restarting the Middle East peace process, instituting economic reforms in Egypt, and saving the eurozone.

With China and Japan staring each other down their gun scopes over the Diaoyu Islands, isn't that where America should be focusing its attention to avert a potentially devastating war?

Hopefully, Kerry can bring back lessons from Europe on how America can shrink government and be more favorable to business. That's right, America can learn from Europe how to shrink government and ease poverty and inequality. Historians, sociologists and political scientists have all uncovered evidence that points to a surprisingly large government presence in the U.S. throughout the 20th century and even earlier, in some cases surpassing what is found in Western Europe today.

European countries do have larger public welfare states, and this brings down their poverty and inequality rates. But European corporations receive a gift in return: a political economy biased against consumption and geared toward production.

Beginning after World War II, Germany, France and several other countries aimed to restrain private consumption and channel profits toward export industries in a bid to reconstruct their war-devastated economies. Loose regulation was part of this business-friendly strategy. These supply-side incentives for producers were implemented at the expense of demand-side measures that would benefit consumers.

The U.S., on the other hand, developed a consumer economy based on government-subsidized mortgage credit. Increasing consumption was a Depression-era response to a problem that puzzled observers at the time. On the one hand, unemployment and hunger were everywhere. On the other, the government was actively engaging in crop destruction to raise prices – like the great pig slaughter of 1933, in which millions of piglets and pregnant sows were destroyed so that hog prices would go up. In the words of Huey P. Long, the populist governor and senator of Louisiana: "Why is it? Why? Too much to eat and more people hungry than during the drought years; too much to wear and more people naked; too many houses and more people homeless than ever before. Why? This is a land of super-abundance and super-plenty. Then why is it also a land of starvation and nakedness and homelessness?"

The answer to Long's question is that a restricted money supply was constraining the economy – just as it is today. But at the time, career politicians thought the problem was that wealth was concentrated in so few hands that consumers did not have purchasing power to buy the goods that lay rotting in the fields. Increasing consumer purchasing power became the paradigm that drove economic policy during the New Deal and for decades after. A central element of this was encouraging citizens to take on large debts – credit and consumerism.

Where Europeans focused on restraining consumption, Americans saw consumption as the machine that drives growth – and we still do. It is time *We the Maids* sweep out consumption strategies and sweep more savings strategies into the economy.

I was reminded of savings strategies, metaphorically speaking, on February 1, 2013 – the centennial celebration of Grand Central Terminal in New York City. I happened to be there, as I am whenever I am in the city and commute from Old Greenwich into the city, this time to also see the architectural masterpiece and a New York City icon through 100 years of American history – saved, restored and adapted to serve the 21st century and beyond. And what a grand celebration it was. The West Point Brass & Percussion concert and presentation of colors by West Point's Cadet Color Guard set the tone for the day-long celebration.

Revolutions aren't easy. Bringing about economic change is hard. Bringing about democratic change is even more difficult, as witnessed in Egypt. But with time and determination, revolutionary changes can be made. I was reminded of this political reality when I went in January 2013 to see the off-Broadway musical *Fiorello!* – about New York's beloved reform-minded Mayor Fiorello H. LaGuardia, who, like Jacqueline Kennedy who led the charge to save Grand Central Terminal – saved the New York Opera House from the wrecker's ball that today is named New York City Center, where the play was staged. LaGuardia also took on Tammany Hall and won.

Grand Central Terminal and New York City Center are metaphorical reminders of America's ability to survive and flourish – notwithstanding its adversaries' determination to tear it down.

*Politics and Poker* is a catchy *Fiorello!* song and dance beautifully performed with a clear message: Political change, especially revolutionary change, is like a high-stakes poker game. It is a game that *We the Maids,* like LaGuardia, against all odds, can and must win.

## Invitation

Dear Fellow Citizen,

Now that you have read this book, you are cordially invited to become an active citizen. If you are not already registered to vote, please register as soon as it is personally convenient.

Your participation in the political process is essential if *We the Maids* are to sweep out the career politicians and recapture our government. *We the People* have the authentic power and ability to bring about revolutionary changes – a New World Order.

You are also invited to share your opinions and desires about any of the ideas articulated in this book. Your thoughts can be sent to me personally at *peter@i-calm.org*. I look forward to hearing them Should you have any questions regarding how to most constructively participate in the political process, please do not hesitate to ask me. *We the People* are America's "spiritual partners." Soulmates who collectively are empowered to change any political system. I hope you agree.

Warmest Regards,

*Get on Board or Continue Being Politically Ignored*

www.i-calm.org

*In the Morning.*

– Norah Jones

## Acknowledged Resources & Support

*Polls are for dancing and skiing.*
– Sarah Palin, former governor of Alaska

Key resources I rely on and want to acknowledge, as I have done in my earlier works, are the people who helped me put this book together, as well as other authors and their books. These are authors who, in addition to those specifically mentioned in the book or listed in the bibliography, helped me focus on issues that they personally experienced or painstakingly researched that was a great time saver for me. They include Will Bunch, *The Backlash,* which details the growth of the tea party movement and how the snake oil salesman Glenn Beck repeatedly reinvented and repackaged himself; James P. Owen, *Cowboy Ethics, What Wall Street Can Learn from the Code of the West,* a timely reminder of what the true American frontier spirit, ethics and values that made America great are and if utilized again today can make America great again; Erin McHugh's *COFFEE TEA or KOOL AID: Which Party Politics Are You Swallowing?* – a quick, humorous book that is perfect for a quick read before a snooze on the red eye across America. Also, *The Quotable Founding Fathers: A Treasury of 2,500 Wise and Witty Quotations From the Men and Women Who Created America,* superbly edited by F. Melton JR., It is an essential one-book-source of the Founding Fathers' most memorable quotes.

More contemporary and relevant political manifestos and observations for our troubled times are *You Can't Be President: The Outrageous Barriers to Democracy in America,* by John R. MacArthur, publisher of Harper's Magazine; Ron Paul's *The Revolution;* Jesse Ventura's *Don't Start the Revolution Without Me!;* Naomi Wolf's *Give Me Liberty, A Handbook for American Revolutionaries;* Greg Palast's *The Best Democracy Money Can Buy;* David North's *The Crisis of American Democracy;* Bill Moyers' *Moyers on Democracy;* Robert Kagan's *The Return of History and the End of Dreams,* and the political executive summary crib book *Red State, Blue*

*State, Rich State, Poor State, Why Americans Vote the Way They Do,* by Andrew Gelman, David Park, Boris Shor, Joseph Bafumi and Jeronimo Cortina. I highly recommend these insightful works.

Writing a political manifesto for a new interlocal political party that is rich in history, yet socially contemporary and relevant today, is a challenge that can be met only with honest input, criticism, challenges and constructive advice from researchers, friends, family and, of course, a politically knowledgeable and savvy editor.

To my children Alexandra, Jonas and Austen, and my grandchildren Lily, Jonas and Macie, thank you for everything, from your innocent gurgles to loud complaints and criticisms that, individually and collectively, triggered some politically fertile thoughts and ideas for the New World Order.

To my former wife Gail in Los Angeles, thank you for always telling it like it is and doing things right – most times, anyway. To my ex-wife Tiffany in Shanghai, thank you for clarifying the meaning of Shanghaied and why China – like you – must change in the New World Order.

To my partner Pauline, thanks for putting up with me and my ways and the papers and books strewn everywhere. Without your love and support, this trilogy would have taken a lot longer to see the light of day and contribute to the New World Order.

To my friends everywhere, thank you for your love, friendship, respect and tolerance for different points of view. May the constructive discussions – including the never-ending differences – continue ad infinitum in the New World Order!

To Jim Houston, my editor, let's keep sharing those beers and margaritas as we fine-tune the New World Order!

**Chapter Notes**

Extensive chapter notes are available for your intellectual stimulation at
http://www.custommaidbooks.com

*The law and how it is enforced always has and always will be the most powerful and lethal weapon.*

– Peter G. de Krassel

## Revolution Underway – A Tactical Alert

*Posterity! You will never know how much it cost the present generation to preserve your freedom! I hope you will make good use of it.*

— John Adams (Second U.S. President)

### *Exodus*

Proofreading the book galleys in Los Angeles in the summer of 2013, I couldn't believe the revolutionary transformational changes taking place across the globe since I did my last two postscripts. I was gobsmacked when I realized I would have to again delay publication of this book to add this tactical alert.

*We the Maids* took to the old well-trodden revolutionary streets of America to demand more long overdue changes. The racial divide, although narrowed substantially since the '60s, is still alive and well and needs to be totally healed during the Third Revolution. Witness the cries of outrage and protest when the not-guilty verdict was announced in the Florida slaying of black teenager Trayvon Martin, the killing of Michael Brown in Ferguson, Missouri in August 2014 and the unreasonable handcuffing of Daniele Watts in Los Angeles shortly thereafter. And then there was the Supreme Court decision to rein in the Voting Rights Act ending the requirement that Southern states get federal approval to change election laws – which they are actively trying to do to limit African-Americans' ability to vote and the NBA's' tarnished sterling silver, over Clippers basketball team owner Donald Sterling's' racist comments that resulted in a lawsuit with the NBA and its Commissioner Ronald Silver, over the forced sale of the team.

*We the Maids,* like the government – no matter which government – now know, much to our chagrin, that all pertinent confidential information and secrets, personal, business, military and governmental are accessible and in the public domain and can be mined by any interested party. Big brother and his minions of contract relatives have triggered a long overdue discussion on the Founding Fathers' constitutional concern of unreasonable search and seizure. Thank you, Edward Snowden.

*We the Maids* got the Supreme Court to recognize same-sex marriages and grant all couples, regardless of their sexual orientation, the same benefits and rights as traditional couples to the pursuit of life, liberty and of happiness.

*We the Maids* got the Justice Department to issue new "shield law" guidelines representing a historic step toward restraining the reach of government and affirming the rights of a free press.

*We the Maids* are now actively calling for the abolition of the IRS because of its abusive and illegal misconduct of wasting millions of taxpayer dollars and flagging politically "progressive" and Tea Party affiliated groups for special scrutiny.

*We the Maids* in July 2013 witnessed the most monstrous farm subsidy bill ever passed benefiting corporate America and wealthy individuals at the expense of millions of Americans in desperate need of nutritional aid, mainly in the form of food stamps – because of career politicians' belief that corporate America is too-big-to-fail and the poor be damned.

Coming amid continuing congressional gridlock, sequestration, debt-ceiling brinkmanship and nagging budget deficits, the farm bill may well be the tipping point that propels America and the world into the next global financial crisis and sends our interlocal wired world into the streets. It's already happening in Greater China, Asia, Europe, Latin America, the Middle East and a few cities in America.

*We the Maids* of Hong Kong, Taiwan and mainland China have formed a loose-knit New World Order protest movement questioning and challenging government policies.

*We the Maids of China* lawyers, writers, students, workers and farmers -- are objecting to Beijing's harassment and arrest of lawyers, writers, political activists, and ordinary citizens protesting official corruption, confiscation of property and the government's collective amnesia of the Tiananmen massacre.

*We the Maids* of Taiwan took to the streets of the capital and occupied Taiwan's parliament over a cross-strait trade agreement that threatened the island's jobs and independence.

*We the Maids* took to the streets of Hong Kong again on July 1, 2013, 2014 and September-October 2014, in a self initiated movement demanding direct elections and removal of the Chinese territory's chief executive, a prospect that alarms Beijing, local career politicians and their apparatchiks.

Hong Kong, because of its unique historical fusion of Eastern and Western political thought and systems, is the epicenter of the New World Order and the bridge that connects and melds the best of American and Chinese political movements and philosophies, a topic my next book *Custom Maid Political System* will address.

*We the Maids* of India swept out the Ghandhi elite hereditary political family – and the Indian National Congress party they dominated – and swept in Narendra Modi, a man of humble origin who promised to eradicate bureaucracy and corruption.

*We the Maids* in America and China can do the same to our hereditary political families.

*We the Maids* in Pakistan, led by Muhammad Tahir-ul Qadri, have mounted a declared revolution against Prime Minister Nawaz Sharif's government.

*We the Maids* of Thailand have been fighting on the streets of Bangkok to sweep out the royalist establishment.

*We the Maids* of Cambodia have taken to the streets of Phnom Penh to protest the closure of the city's Freedom Park and a crackdown on garment industry strikers.

*We the Maids* of Bosnia, Britain, France, Greece, Italy and Spain have taken to the streets of Europe to protest unemployment, austerity programs, corruption, political inertia and the European Union.

*We the Maids* of the Ukraine not only swept out a corrupt dictator, but our women's biathlon team won a gold medal even though one of our teammates left in protest over Russia's invasion of Crimea.

*We the Maids,* like the *Maids* of Ukraine, have to sweep out the Vladimir Putin model of dictatorship and every country that adopts it, as well as every politician who advocates Putinism.

*We the Maids* of Brazil took to the streets protesting World Cup spending as the country kicked off the soccer tournament and Eduardo Campos, the former governor of the northeastern state of Pernambuco, offered Brazilians a third way to the long-running two-party hegemony. Was Campos death another conspiracy?

*We the Maids* of Brazil, Russia, India, China and South Africa launched the New Development bank – nicknamed the BRICS Development Bank – in the Brazilian city of Fortaleza in July 2014, with a blockbuster capital contribution of $100 billion, as an alternative to the U.S.-dominated World Bank and the International Monetary Fund.

*We the Maids* of Venezuela took to the streets to protest the country's high crime rate, food shortages, struggling economy and to demand that pro-government vigilante groups be disarmed.

*We the Maids* of Egypt returned to the streets to bring about another revolutionary change of government, spitting in the eye of religious extremists. It is the same wake-up call sounded by America's Founding Fathers. Egyptians, Americans and all progressive-thinking people must separate church and state and rein in military adventurism if humankind is to regain its footing.

*We the Maids* of Tunisia and Turkey took to the streets to sweep out secular career politicians and corruption and demand access to social media and restoration of judicial independence.

*We the Maids* of Iraq have again taken up weapons to restore the country's natural borders of Kurdistan, Sunnistan and Shiitestan, a political solution I advocated that America implement in *Custom Maid Knowledge*.

"Amid the sectarian bloodbaths, the Bush administration is in denial that there is a 'civil war' in Iraq and rejects the idea that the only peaceful democratic solution and honorable U.S. legacy is to divide Iraq into three separate independent countries. Not federal states held together in any manner shape or form... . Truly independent sovereign states that fulfill America's moral responsibility to the Iraqis who want a better Iraq – partition. Mission accomplished," I wrote and lectured back in 2007.

In *Custom Maid Spin,* written in 2003 as America was getting ready to invade Iraq, I voiced my concern that it would be Americans and not Iraqis who would be "shocked and awed."

What has happened in Iraq and Syria with the establishment of the Islamic State of Iraq and Syria caliphate should come as no surprise. It was inevitable in the wake of America's failed Iraq-Syria military and foreign policy. In *Custom Maid War,* written in 2005, I warned that America would face the same fate in Afghanistan.

*We the Maids* in Iran pushed back at the mullahs' strict rules governing social interaction. Men and women danced together on rooftops and in alleyways, the women without Islamic covering, to Pharrell Williams song *Happy* and filmed the video *Happy in Tehran* on an iPhone and uploaded it on to YouTube and attracted about 160,000 hits.

*We the Maids* of New York City elected Bill de Blassio, a progressive Democrat, who promised and now promotes social change. Tackling income inequality, constitutional rights by ending the racially discriminatory stop-and-frisk police practice, initiating an early and good education curriculum for all to ensure a future smart dynamic economy and prosperity.

*We the Maids* are finally acknowledging that global warming is real. The Atlanta snow-driven 24-48 hour gridlock of January 28, 2014, being the latest reminder of not only climate change, but unapologetic bureaucratic incompetence. Unseasonable tornadoes, thunderstorms, snow and hail storms, heat waves, droughts, earthquakes, wildfires and floods are causing food shortages and trillions of dollars in damage around the globe, and people are demanding change.

*We the Maids* of Las Vegas, who are tired of demanding change, were witness to one of our happily married couples, who had long spoken of antigovernment revolution, fatally shoot two police officers and a third man who tried to stop them, as they shouted antigovernment slogans before killing themselves.

### A New Beginning
Lady Liberty, America's enduring symbol of liberty and resilience, reopened on July 4, 2013. It had been closed after Superstorm Sandy walloped the island, trashing nearly everything but the iconic statute itself. The hurricane hit on October 29, 2012, one day after the 126th anniversary of the statute's dedication.

America, unlike almost all other countries, welcomes everyone regardless of their religion, color or country of origin and embraces them as full members of society. The 7,800 new American citizens naturalized on

July 4, 2013, were a reminder of the thousands, make that millions worldwide who dream of becoming Americans and the long overdue need to reform immigration laws.

I was delighted to read that three of the world's richest men, Bill Gates, Warren Buffet and Sheldon Adelson have castigated the U.S. Congress, particularly the Republican-led House, over its failure to revamp immigration laws.

Immigration to the U.S. is as old as the nation's foundation. America is an immigrant nation. Formed from 13 American colonies of Great Britain, America has derived most of its culture and population from immigrants. The 1790 Act limited American naturalization to "free white persons" who came from Europe and British Canada. At the same time, hundreds of thousands African slaves worked the burgeoning American economy, the same capitalist economy that has attracted successive waves of immigrants from everywhere to this very day.

Immigration policy has always been about cultural erosion rather than what it should be – national economic growth.

The ceaseless stream of child migrant-refugees fleeing the violence of drug gangs and cartels in Central America brings home the urgency.

As an immigrant who came to America in 1964 as part of the British invasion, I am delighted to see that the critics of the Beatles music and American tour of the same year have been proven wrong 50 years later – something the opponents of immigration reform should keep in mind – especially after the Sochi 2014 Olympics that showcased U.S. resident NHL players compete for Canada, Finland, Russia, Sweden, Switzerland and Slovenia, their countries of birth.

### Game of the Goalies

The Los Angeles Kings and New York Rangers goalies in the 2014 Stanley Cup final were a timely metaphor of the Democratic and Republican career politicians in Washington who won't let each other score a political victory. Walking home on Venice Beach under a full moon after watching the final game between the Kings and Rangers at Hinanos, a local bar packed with Kings fans, the political metaphor of the game came into full focus. *We the Maids,* like the Kings and their fans who endured nearly two full overtime agonizing periods before winning the Stanley Cup, cannot give up hope.

Like the Kings, whose Stanley Cup run appeared over at the start, *We the Maids* have to draw on the same unshakable resolve – a resolve America is built on that will enable it to re-emerge politically and economically a winner again. America, like the Kings and San Antonio Spurs, can rally its political willpower. *We the Maids* have to sweep out "Party-over-policy" politics. Gridlock and permanent partisan conflict is an unacceptable form of government.

The Spurs NBA win over the Miami Heat is another timely 2014 metaphor. A team of "old geezers" written off by the pundits. A team built with a long-term strategy in mind rather than the Miami approach of buying young talent for a quick fix. History has proven that long-term carefully thought out strategies and game plans prevail over ill-thought short-term plans.

Americas' Founding Fathers wrote the best long-term political plan in the political arena today – based on hope and vision for a better tomorrow. America also has the best economic team and, like the Spurs and Kings, can win back its global political and economic status.

Watching the July 4, 2013 Independence Day fireworks celebrations with neighbors from an upper-floor landing at our Marina del Rey apartment building was a delight.

"America is alive and well!" I cried out over the din to my neighbor Ivo Knotek, a Czech revolutionary immigrant.

"Yes!" Ivo proclaimed defiantly. "America is back! It is time America leads the world revolution again!"

We clinked glasses and toasted "To America."

For those *Maids* who haven't heard, Washington state passed laws legalizing gay marriage and marijuana. The fact that gay marriage and weed were legalized on the same day makes perfect biblical sense. Leviticus 20:13 says, "If a man lies with another man they should be stoned." We just hadn't interpreted it correctly until now.

The same holds true for Washington D.C., where the Founding Fathers revolutionary Constitution must be correctly interpreted. It is time *We the Maids* again sweep in the American principles the founders bequeathed us.

# Bibliography

Extensive chapter notes are available for your intellectual stimulation at
http://www.custommaidbooks.com

*The only way you make something totally new is*
*to break the mold of what was old.*
– Vice President Joe Biden

# Index

"Peter de Krassel aptly and cogently provides a blueprint for the kind of watershed change that must occur within the American domestic and geopolitical arena. More importantly, his tome strategically pinpoints those political, cultural, educational, and historical factors that are key to understanding 'how' and 'why', this change will occur."

Brandon Royal, award-winning educational writer and author *The Little Blue Reasoning Book*.

*We Won't Be Fooled Again* and *My Generation*
– The Who